ELEVENTH EDITION

BUSINESS ETHICS

Ethical Decision Making and Cases

O.C. Ferrell
Belmont University

John Fraedrich
Southern Illinois University—Carbondale

Linda Ferrell
Belmont University

CENGAGE
Learning®

Australia • Brazil • Japan • Korea • Mexico • Singapore • Spain • United Kingdom • United States

CENGAGE
Learning®

Business Ethics: Ethical Decision Making & Cases, 11e
O.C. Ferrell, John Fraedrich and Linda Ferrell

Vice President, General Manager, Social Science & Qualitative Business: Erin Joyner

Product Director: Jason Fremder

Product Manager: Mike Roche

Content Developer: Zach Fleischer

Product Assistant: Brian Pierce

Marketing Director: Kristen Hurd

Marketing Manager: Emily Horowitz

Marketing Coordinator: Christopher Walz

Art and Cover Direction, Production Management, and Composition: Cenveo Publisher Services

Intellectual Property

   Analyst: Diane Garrity

   Project Manager: Sarah Shainwald

Manufacturing Planner: Ron Montgomery

Cover Image(s): © Kenneth Keifer / Shutterstock.com

Library of Congress Control Number: 2015955985

ISBN 13: 978-1-305-50084-6

Cengage Learning
20 Channel Center Street
Boston, MA 02210
USA

Cengage Learning is a leading provider of customized learning solutions with employees residing in nearly 40 different countries and sales in more than 125 countries around the world. Find your local representative at **www.cengage.com.**

Cengage Learning products are represented in Canada by Nelson Education, Ltd.

To learn more about Cengage Learning Solutions, visit **www.cengage.com.**

Purchase any of our products at your local college store or at our preferred online store **www.cengagebrain.com.**

Printed in Canada
Print Number: 01   Print Year: 2015

To James Collins Ferrell and
George Collins Ferrell.

—O.C. Ferrell

To Emma, Matthew,
Hyrum, and Ammon.

—John Fraedrich

To Brett Nafziger.

—Linda Ferrell

BRIEF CONTENTS

CONTENTS

PART 5: CASES 380

PREFACE

This is the Eleventh Edition of *Business Ethics: Ethical Decision Making* and Cases. Our text has become the most widely used business ethics book, with approximately one out of three business ethics courses in schools of business using our text. We were the first major business ethics textbook to use a managerial framework that integrates ethics into strategic decisions. Today in corporate America, ethics and compliance has become a major functional area that structures responsible managerial decision making. Now that ethics has been linked to financial performance, there is growing recognition that business ethics courses are as important as other functional areas such as marketing, accounting, finance, and management.

Our approach is to help students understand and participate in effective ethical decision making in organizations. We approach business ethics from an applied perspective, focusing on conceptual frameworks, risks, issues, and dilemmas that will be faced in the real world of business. We prepare students for the challenges they will face in understanding how organizational ethical decision making works. We describe how ethical decisions in an organization involve collaboration in groups, teams, and discussions with peers. Many decisions fall into gray areas where the right decision may not be clear and requires the use of organizational resources and the advice of others. Students will face many ethical challenges in their careers, and our approach helps them to understand risks and be prepared to address ethical dilemmas. One approach to business ethics education is to include only a theoretical foundation related to ethical reasoning. Our method is to provide a balanced approach that includes the concepts of ethical reasoning as well as the organizational environment that influences ethical decision making.

The Eleventh Edition includes the most comprehensive changes we have made in any revision. Each chapter has been revised based on the latest research and knowledge available. Throughout the book, up-to-date examples are used to make foundational concepts come to life. There are 4 new cases, and the other 16 cases have been revised with all major changes occurring through the middle of 2015. The most significant change is the inclusion of social entrepreneurship in Chapter 4. Social entrepreneurship is a growing trend as organizations and individuals realize they can use entrepreneurial principles to effect social change. One of our cases, Belle Meade, strongly demonstrates how a nonprofit is able to use the same type of entrepreneurial activities found in business. It develops and sells wine to create sustainability for its organization, making it the nation's first nonprofit winery.

Using a managerial framework, we explain how ethics can be integrated into strategic business decisions. This framework provides an *overview of the concepts, processes, mandatory, core,* and *voluntary business practices* associated with successful business ethics programs. Some approaches to business ethics are excellent as exercises in intellectual reasoning, but they cannot deal with the many actual issues and considerations that people in business organizations face. Our approach supports ethical reasoning and the value of individuals being able to face ethical challenges and voice their concerns about appropriate behavior. Employees in organizations are ultimately in charge of their own behavior and need to be skillful in making decisions in gray areas where the appropriate conduct is not always obvious.

We have been diligent in this revision to provide the most relevant examples of how the lack of business ethics has challenged our economic viability and entangled countries and companies around the world. This book remains the market leader because it *addresses the complex environment of ethical decision making in organizations and pragmatic, actual business concerns.* Every individual has unique personal principles and values, and every organization has its own set of values, rules, and organizational ethical culture. Business ethics must consider the organizational culture and interdependent relationships between the individual and other significant persons involved in organizational decision making. Without effective guidance, a businessperson cannot make ethical decisions while facing a short-term orientation, feeling organizational pressure to perform well and seeing rewards based on outcomes in a challenging competitive environment.

By focusing on individual issues and organizational environments, this book gives students the opportunity to see roles and responsibilities they will face in business. The past decade has reinforced the value of understanding the role of business ethics in the effective management of an organization. Widespread misconduct reported in the mass media every day demonstrates that businesses, governments, nonprofits, and institutions of higher learning need to address business ethics.

Our primary goal has always been to enhance the awareness and the ethical decision-making skills that students will need to make business ethics decisions that contribute to responsible business conduct. By focusing on these concerns and issues of today's challenging business environment, we demonstrate that the study of business ethics is imperative to the long-term well-being of not only businesses, but also our economic system.

PHILOSOPHY OF THIS TEXT

The purpose of this book is to help students improve their ability to make ethical decisions in business by providing them with a framework that they can use to identify, analyze, and resolve ethical issues in business decision making. Individual values and ethics are important in this process. By studying business ethics, students begin to understand how to cope with conflicts between their personal values and those of the organization.

Many ethical decisions in business are close calls. It often takes years of experience in a particular industry to know what is acceptable. We do not, in this book, provide ethical answers but instead attempt to prepare students to make informed ethical decisions. First, we do not moralize by indicating what to do in a specific situation. Second, although we provide an overview of moral philosophies and decision-making processes, we do not prescribe any one philosophy or process as best or most ethical. Third, by itself, this book will not make students more ethical nor will it tell them how to judge the ethical behavior of others. Rather, its goal is to help students understand and use their current values and convictions in making business decisions and to encourage everyone to think about the effects of their decisions on business and society.

Many people believe that business ethics cannot be taught. Although we do not claim to teach ethics, we suggest that by studying business ethics a person can improve ethical decision making by identifying ethical issues and recognizing the approaches available to resolve them. An organization's reward system can reinforce appropriate behavior and help shape attitudes and beliefs about important issues. For example, the success of some campaigns to end racial or gender discrimination in the workplace provides evidence that attitudes and behavior can be changed with new information, awareness, and shared values.

CONTENT AND ORGANIZATION

In writing *Business Ethics*, Eleventh Edition, we strived to be as informative, complete, accessible, and up-to-date as possible. Instead of focusing on one area of ethics, such as moral philosophy or social responsibility, we provide balanced coverage of all areas relevant to the current development and practice of ethical decision making. In short, we have tried to keep pace with new developments and current thinking in teaching and practices.

The first half of the text consists of 12 chapters, which provide a framework to identify, analyze, and understand how businesspeople make ethical decisions and deal with ethical issues. Several enhancements have been made to chapter content for this edition. Some of the most important are listed in the next paragraphs.

Part 1, "An Overview of Business Ethics," includes two chapters that help provide a broader context for the study of business ethics. Chapter 1, "The Importance of Business Ethics," has been revised with many new examples and survey results to describe issues and concerns important to business ethics. Chapter 2, "Stakeholder Relationships, Social Responsibility, and Corporate Governance," has been significantly reorganized and updated with new examples and issues.

Part 2, "Ethical Issues and the Institutionalization of Business Ethics," consists of two chapters that provide the background that students need to identify ethical issues and understand how society, through the legal system, has attempted to hold organizations responsible for managing these issues. Chapter 3, "Emerging Business Ethics Issues," has been reorganized and updated and provides expanded coverage of business ethics issues. Chapter 4, "The Institutionalization of Business Ethics" examines key elements of core or best practices in corporate America today along with legislation and regulation requirements that support business ethics initiatives. The chapter is divided into three main areas: voluntary, mandated, and core boundaries.

Part 3, "The Decision-Making Process" consists of three chapters, which provide a framework to identify, analyze, and understand how businesspeople make ethical decisions and deal with ethical issues. Chapter 5, "Ethical Decision Making," has been revised and updated to reflect current research and understanding of ethical decision making and contains a section on normative considerations in ethical decision making. Chapter 6, "Individual Factors: Moral Philosophies and Values," has been updated and revised to explore the role of moral philosophies and moral development as individual factors in the ethical decision-making process. Chapter 7, "Organizational Factors: The Role of Ethical Culture and Relationships," considers organizational influences on business decisions, such as role relationships, differential association, and other organizational pressures, as well as whistle-blowing.

Part 4, "Implementing Business Ethics in a Global Economy," looks at specific measures that companies can take to build an effective ethics program as well as how these programs may be affected by global issues, leadership, and sustainability issues. Chapter 8, "Developing an Effective Ethics Program," has been refined and updated with corporate best practices for developing effective ethics programs. Chapter 9, "Managing and Controlling Ethics Programs," offers a framework for auditing ethics initiatives as well as the importance of doing so. Such audits can help companies pinpoint problem areas, measure their progress in improving conduct, and even provide a "debriefing" opportunity after a crisis. Chapter 10, "Globalization of Ethical Decision Making" has been updated to reflect the complex and dynamic events that occur in global business. This chapter will help students understand the major issues involved in making decisions in a global environment. Chapter 11 focuses on ethical leadership. Reviewers indicated that they wanted more information provided on the importance of leadership to an ethical culture, and this chapter answers these requests. Finally, Chapter 12 is a chapter on sustainability. It examines the ethical and social responsibility dimensions of sustainability.

Part 5 consists of 20 cases in the texts that bring reality into the learning process. Four of these cases are new to the eleventh edition, and the remaining 14 have been revised and updated. In addition, four shorter cases are available on the Instructor's Companion website:

- Toyota: Challenges in Maintaining Integrity
- The Container Store: An Employee-centric Retailer
- The Ethics Program at Eaton Corporation
- Barrett-Jackson Auction Company: Family, Fairness, and Philanthropy

The companies and situations portrayed in these cases are real; names and other facts are not disguised; and all cases include developments up to the middle of 2015. By reading and analyzing these cases, students can gain insight into ethical decisions and the realities of making decisions in complex situations.

TEXT FEATURES

Many tools are available in this text to help both students and instructors in the quest to improve students' ability to make ethical business decisions.

- Each chapter opens with an outline and a list of learning objectives.
- Immediately following is "An Ethical Dilemma" that should provoke discussion about ethical issues related to the chapter. The short vignette describes a hypothetical incident involving an ethical conflict. Questions at the end of the "Ethical Dilemma" section focus discussion on how the dilemma could be resolved. All new ethical dilemmas have been provided for this edition.
- Each chapter has a contemporary real-world debate issue. Many of these debate issues have been updated to reflect current ethical issues in business. These debate issues have been found to stimulate thoughtful discussion relating to content issues in the chapter. Topics of the debate issues include the truthfulness of health claims, the universal health care debate, the contribution of ethical conduct to financial performance, legislation concerning whistle-blowing, and the impact of carbon emission restrictions.

- At the end of each chapter are a chapter summary and an important terms' list, both of which are handy tools for review. Also included at the end of each chapter is a "Resolving Ethical Business Challenges" section. The vignette describes a realistic drama that helps students experience the process of ethical decision making. The "Resolving Ethical Business Challenges" minicases presented in this text are hypothetical; any resemblance to real persons, companies, or situations is coincidental. Keep in mind that there are no right or wrong solutions to the minicases.

The ethical dilemmas and real-life situations provide an opportunity for students to use concepts in the chapter to resolve ethical issues.

Each chapter concludes with a series of questions that allow students to test their EQ (Ethics Quotient).

- Cases. In Part 5, following each real-world case are questions to guide students in recognizing and resolving ethical issues. For some cases, students can conduct additional research to determine recent developments because many ethical issues in companies take years to resolve.

EFFECTIVE TOOLS FOR TEACHING AND LEARNING

Instructor's Resource Website. You can find the following teaching tools on the password-protected instructor site.

- **Instructor's Resource Manual.** The *Instructor's Resource Manual* contains a wealth of information. Teaching notes for every chapter include a brief chapter summary, detailed lecture outline, and notes for using the "Ethical Dilemma" and "Resolving Ethical Business Challenges" sections. Detailed case notes point out the key issues involved and offer suggested answers to the questions. A separate section provides guidelines for using case analysis in teaching business ethics. Detailed notes are provided to guide the instructor in analyzing or grading the cases. Simulation role-play cases, as well as implementation suggestions, are included.

- **Role-Play Cases.** The eleventh edition provides six behavioral simulation role-play cases developed for use in the business ethics course. The role-play cases and implementation methods can be found in the *Instructor's Resource Manual* and on the website. Role-play cases may be used as a culminating experience to help students integrate concepts covered in the text. Alternatively, the cases may be used as an ongoing exercise to provide students with extensive opportunities for interacting and making ethical decisions.

Role-play cases simulate a complex, realistic, and timely business ethics situation. Students form teams and make decisions based on an assigned role. The role-play case complements and enhances traditional approaches to business learning experiences because it (1) gives students the opportunity to practice making decisions that have business ethics consequences; (2) recreates the power, pressures, and information that affect decision making at various levels of management; (3) provides students with a team-based experience that enriches their skills and understanding of group processes and dynamics; and (4) uses a feedback period to allow for the exploration of complex and controversial issues in business ethics decision making. The role-play cases can be used with classes of any size.

- **Cengage Learning Testing Powered by Cognero.** This is a flexible, online system that allows you to author, edit, and manage test bank content from multiple Cengage Learning solutions; create multiple test versions in an instant; and deliver tests from your LMS, your classroom or wherever you want.

B-Reality Simulation: This online simulation helps to reinforce basic business ethics concepts, increases textbook comprehension, and helps the user better understand that business decisions usually have an ethics, moral, and/or legal component. The simulation makes no judgments; rather, it takes what is imputed by the user, and at the end of each year it explains whether the user acted ethically, unethically, legally/illegally, and why. At the end of four decades of decisions, a report is generated giving a list of the user's morals, income, promotions, and how the company defined which decisions were ethical or unethical and which were legal or illegal. Users better understand all angles of the reality of their business decisions before they confront them in the workplace.

Additional Teaching Resources. The University of New Mexico (UNM) Daniels Fund Ethics Initiative is part of a four-state initiative to develop teaching resources to support principle-based ethics education. Their publicly accessible website contains original cases, debate issues, videos, interviews, and PowerPoint modules on select business ethics topics, as well as other resources such as articles on business ethics education. It is possible to access this website at http://danielsethics.mgt.unm.edu.

Students also have the ability to receive ethical leadership certification from the National Association of State Boards of Accountancy (NASBA) Center for Public Trust. This program is comprised of six modules of online content (delivered through Brainshark, containing videos, graphics, and a voice over). At the end of each of the six modules, students will take an online examination through NASBA. When students complete all six modules successfully, they will receive NASBA Center for the Public Trust Ethical Leadership Certification. As business ethics increases in importance, such certification can give your students an edge in the workplace. For more information, visit https://www.thecpt.org/ethical-leadership-certification-program/.

ACKNOWLEDGMENTS

A number of individuals provided reviews and suggestions that helped to improve this text. We sincerely appreciate their time and effort.

Donald Acker
Brown Mackie College

Donna Allen
Northwest Nazarene University

Suzanne Allen
Philanthropy Ohio

Carolyn Ashe
University of Houston—Downtown

Laura Barelman
Wayne State College

Russell Bedard
Eastern Nazarene College

B. Barbara Boerner
Brevard College

Serena Breneman
University of Arkansas at Pine Bluff

Lance Brown
Miami Dade College

Judie Bucholz
Guilford College

Greg Buntz
Conflict Resolution Center of Iowa, LLC

Hoa Burrows
Miami Dade College

Robert Chandler
University of Central Florida

April Chatham-Carpenter
University of Northern Iowa

Leslie Connell
University of Central Florida

Peggy Cunningham
Dalhousie University

Carla Dando
Idaho State University

James E. Donovan
Detroit College of Business

Douglas Dow
University of Texas at Dallas

A. Charles Drubel
Muskingum College

Philip F. Esler
University of Gloucestershire

Joseph M. Foster
Indiana Vocational Technical College—Evansville

Lynda Fuller
Wilmington University

Terry Gable
Truman State University

Robert Giacalone
University of Richmond

Suresh Gopalan
Winston-Salem University

Karen Gore
Ivy Technical College

Mark Hammer
Northwest Nazarene University

Charles E. Harris, Jr.
Texas A&M University

Kenneth A. Heischmidt
Southeast Missouri State University

Neil Herndon
South China University of Technology

Walter Hill
Green River Community College

Jack Hires
Valparaiso University

David Jacobs
Morgan State University

R. J. Johansen
Montana State University—Bozeman

Jeff Johnson
Athens State University

Eduard Kimman
Vrije Universiteit

Janet Knight
Purdue North Central

Anita Leffel
University of Texas at San Antonio

Barbara Limbach
Chadron State College

Victor Lipe
Trident Tech

Nick Lockard
Texas Lutheran College

Terry Loe
Kennesaw State University

Nick Maddox
Stetson University

Isabelle Maignan
Dutchwaters B.V.

Phylis Mansfield
Pennsylvania State University—Erie

Robert Markus
Babson College

Therese Maskulka
Kutztown University

Randy McLeod
Harding University

Francy Milner
University of Colorado

Ali Mir
William Paterson University

Debi P. Mishra
Binghamton University, State University of New York

Patrick E. Murphy
University of Notre Dame

Lester Myers
Georgetown University

Catherine Neal
Northern Kentucky University

Cynthia Nicola
Carlow College

Carol Nielsen
Bemidji State University

Sharon Palmitier
Grand Rapids Community College

Lee Richardson
University of Baltimore

James Salvucci
Curry College

William M. Sannwald
San Diego State University

Ruth Schaa
Black River Technical College

Zachary Shank
Central New Mexico Community College

Cynthia A. M. Simerly
Lakeland Community College

Karen Smith
Columbia Southern University

Filiz Tabak
Towson University

Debbie Thorne
Texas State University—San Marcos

Wanda V. Turner
Ferris State College

Gina Vega
Salem State College

William C. Ward
Mid-Continent University

David Wasieleski
Duquesne University

Jim Weber
Duquesne University

Ed Weiss
National-Louis University

Joseph W. Weiss
Bentley University

Jan Zahrly
University of North Dakota

We wish to acknowledge the many people who assisted us in writing this book. We are deeply grateful to Jennifer Sawayda for her work in organizing and managing the revision process. Finally, we express appreciation to the administration and to colleagues at the University of New Mexico, Belmont University, and Southern Illinois University at Carbondale for their support.

We invite your comments, questions, or criticisms. We want to do our best to provide teaching materials that enhance the study of business ethics. Your suggestions will be sincerely appreciated.

– O. C. Ferrell
– John Fraedrich
– Linda Ferrell

CHAPTER 1

THE IMPORTANCE OF BUSINESS ETHICS

AN ETHICAL DILEMMA*

Sophie just completed a sales training course with one of the firm's most productive sales representatives, Emma. At the end of the first week, Sophie and Emma sat in a motel room filling out their expense vouchers for the week. Sophie casually remarked to Emma that the training course stressed the importance of accurately filling out expense vouchers.

Emma replied, "I'm glad you brought that up, Sophie. The company expense vouchers don't list the categories we need. I tried many times to explain to the accountants that there are more expenses than they have boxes for. The biggest complaint we, the salespeople, have is that there is no place to enter expenses for tipping waitresses, waiters, cab drivers, bell hops, airport baggage handlers, and the like. Even the government assumes tipping and taxes them as if they were getting an 18 percent tip. That's how service people actually survive on the lousy pay they get from their bosses. I tell you, it is embarrassing not to tip. One time I was at the airport and the skycap took my bags from me so I didn't have the hassle of checking them. He did all the paper work and after he was through, I said thank you. He looked at me in disbelief because he knew I was in sales. It took me a week to get that bag back."

"After that incident I went to the accounting department, and every week for five months I told them they needed to change the forms. I showed them the approximate amount the average salesperson pays in tips per week. Some of them were shocked at the amount. But would they change it or at least talk to the supervisor? No! So I went directly to him, and do you know what he said to me?"

"No, what?" asked Sophie.

"He told me that this is the way it has always been done, and it would stay that way. He also told me if I tried to go above him on this, I'd be looking for another job. I can't chance that now, especially in this economy. Then he had the nerve to tell me that salespeople are paid too much, and that's why we could eat the added expenses. We're the only ones who actually generate revenue and he tells me that I'm overpaid!"

"So what did you do?" inquired Sophie.

"I do what my supervisor told me years ago. I pad my account each week. For me, I tip 20 percent, so I make sure I write down when I tip and add that to my overall expense report."

"But that goes against company policy. Besides, how do you do it?" asked Sophie.

"It's easy. Every cab driver will give you blank receipts for cab fares. I usually put the added expenses there. We all do it," said Emma. "As long as everyone cooperates, the Vice President of Sales doesn't question the expense vouchers. I imagine she even did it when she was a lowly salesperson."

"What if people don't go along with this arrangement?" asked Sophie.

"In the past, we have had some who reported it like corporate wants us to. I remember there was a person who didn't report the same amounts as the co-worker traveling with her. Several months went by and the accountants came in, and she and all the salespeople that traveled together were investigated. After several months the one who ratted out the others was fired or quit, I can't remember. I do know she never worked in our industry again. Things like that get around. It's a small world for good salespeople, and everyone knows everyone."

"What happened to the other salespeople who were investigated?" Sophie asked.

"There were a lot of memos and even a 30-minute video as to the proper way to record expenses. All of them had conversations with the vice president, but no one was fired."

"No one was fired even though it went against policy?" Sophie asked Emma.

"At the time, my conversation with the VP went basically this way. She told me that corporate was not going to change the forms, and she acknowledged it was not fair or equitable to the salespeople. She hated the head accountant because he didn't want to accept the reality of a salesperson's life in the field. That was it. I left the office and as I walked past the Troll's office—that's what we call the head accountant—he just smiled at me."

This was Sophie's first real job out of school and Emma was her mentor. What should Sophie report on her expense report?

QUESTIONS | EXERCISES

1. Identify the issues Sophie has to resolve.
2. Discuss the alternatives for Sophie.
3. What should Sophie do if company policy appears to conflict with the firm's corporate culture?

*This case is strictly hypothetical; any resemblance to real persons, companies, or situations is coincidental.

The ability to anticipate and deal with business ethics issues and dilemmas has become a significant priority in the twenty-first century. In recent years, a number of well-publicized scandals resulted in public outrage about deception, fraud, and distrust in business and a subsequent demand for improved business ethics, greater corporate responsibility, and laws to protect the financially innocent. The publicity and debate surrounding highly publicized legal and ethical lapses at well-known firms highlight the need for businesses to integrate ethics and responsibility into all business decisions. On the other hand, the majority of ethical businesses with no or few ethical lapses are rarely recognized in the mass media for their conduct, mainly because good companies doing business the right way do not generate media interest.

Highly visible business ethics issues influence the public's attitudes toward business and destroy trust. Ethically charged decisions are a part of everyday life for those who work in organizations at all levels. Business ethics is not just an isolated personal issue; codes, rules, and informal communications for responsible conduct are embedded in an organization's operations. This means ethical or unethical conduct is the province of everyone who works in an organizational environment, from the lowest level employee to the CEO.

Making good ethical decisions are just as important to business success as mastering management, marketing, finance, and accounting. While education and training emphasize functional areas of business, business ethics is often viewed as easy to master, something that happens with little effort. The exact opposite is the case. Decisions with an ethical component are an everyday occurrence requiring people to identify issues and make quick decisions. Ethical behavior requires understanding and identifying issues, areas of risk, and approaches to making choices in an organizational environment. On the other hand, people can act unethically simply by failing to identify a situation that has an ethical issue. Ethical blindness results from individuals who fail to sense the nature and complexity of their decisions.[1] Some approaches to business ethics look only at the philosophical backgrounds of individuals and the social consequences of decisions. This approach fails to address the complex organizational environment of businesses and pragmatic business concerns. By contrast, our approach is managerial and incorporates real-world decisions that impact the organization and stakeholders. Our book will help you better understand how business ethics is practiced in the business world.

It is important to learn how to make decisions in the internal environment of an organization to achieve personal and organizational goals. But business does not exist in a vacuum. As stated, decisions in business have implications for investors, employees, customers, suppliers, and society. Ethical decisions must take these stakeholders into account, for unethical conduct can negatively affect people, companies, industries, and society as a whole. Our approach focuses on the practical consequences of decisions and on positive outcomes that have the potential to contribute to individuals, business, and society at large. The field of business ethics deals with questions about whether specific conduct and business practices are acceptable. For example, should a salesperson omit facts about a product's poor safety record in a sales presentation to a client? Should accountants report inaccuracies they discover in an audit of a client, knowing the auditing company will probably be fired by the client for doing so? Should an automobile tire manufacturer intentionally conceal safety concerns to avoid a massive and costly tire recall? Regardless of their legality, others will certainly judge the actions in such situations as right or wrong, ethical or unethical. By its very nature, the field of business ethics is controversial, and there is no universally accepted approach for resolving its dilemmas.

All organizations have to deal with misconduct. Even prestigious colleges such as Harvard and Dartmouth are not exempt. Students at Dartmouth were disciplined for cheating on their attendance and participation in an undergraduate ethics course. Because the course used hand clickers registered to each student as a sign of attendance and participation, students who wanted to cut class would give their hand clickers to other classmates.[2] Two administrators at the University of North Carolina at Chapel Hill oversaw courses where the students—often athletes—did not have to show up. The courses included lectures that never met spanning back to the 1990s.[3]

Before we get started, it is important to state our approach to business ethics. First, we do not moralize by stating what is right or wrong in a specific situation, although we offer background on normative guidelines for appropriate conduct. Second, although we provide an overview of group and individual decision-making processes, we do not prescribe one approach or process as the best or most ethical. However, we provide many examples of successful ethical decision making. Third, by itself, this book will not make you more ethical, nor will it give you equations on how to judge the ethical behavior of others. Rather, its goal is to help you understand, use, and improve your current values and convictions when making business decisions so you think about the effects of those decisions on business and society. Our approach will help you understand what businesses are doing to improve their ethical conduct. To this end, we aim to help you learn to recognize and resolve ethical issues within business organizations. As a manager, you will be responsible for your decisions and the conduct of the employees you supervise. For this reason, we provide a chapter on ethical leadership. The framework we developed focuses on how organizational decisions are made and on ways companies can improve their ethical conduct. This process is more complex than many think. People who believe they know how to make the "right" decision usually come away with more uncertainty about their own decision skills after learning about the complexity of ethical decision making. This is a normal occurrence, and our approach will help you evaluate your own values as well as those of others. It also helps you to understand the nature of business ethics and incentives found in the workplace that change the way you make decisions in business versus at home.

In this chapter, we first develop a definition of business ethics and discuss why it has become an important topic in business education. We also discuss why studying business ethics can be beneficial. Next, we examine the evolution of business ethics in North America. Then we explore the performance benefits of ethical decision making for businesses. Finally, we provide a brief overview of the framework we use for examining business ethics in this text.

BUSINESS ETHICS DEFINED

To understand business ethics, you must first recognize that most people do not have specific definitions they use to define ethics-related issues. The terms morals, principles, values, and ethics are often used interchangeably, and you will find this is true in companies as well. Consequently, there is much confusion regarding this topic. To help you understand these differences, we discuss these terms.

For our purposes, **morals** refer to a person's personal philosophies about what is right or wrong. The important point is that when one speaks of morals, it is personal or singular. Morals, your philosophies or sets of values of right and wrong, relate to you and you alone.

You may use your personal moral convictions in making ethical decisions in any context. **Business ethics** comprises organizational principles, values, and norms that may originate from individuals, organizational statements, or from the legal system that primarily guide individual and group behavior in business. **Principles** are specific and pervasive boundaries for behavior that should not be violated. Principles often become the basis for rules. Some examples of principles could include human rights, freedom of speech, and the fundamentals of justice. **Values** are enduring beliefs and ideals that are socially enforced. Several desirable or ethical values for business today are teamwork, trust, and integrity. Such values are often based on organizational or industry best practices. Investors, employees, customers, interest groups, the legal system, and the community often determine whether a specific action or standard is ethical or unethical. Although these groups influence the determination of what is ethical or unethical for business, they also can be at odds with one another. Even though this is the reality of business and such groups may not necessarily be right, their judgments influence society's acceptance or rejection of business practices.

Ethics is defined as behavior or decisions made within a group's values. In our case we are discussing decisions made in business by groups of people that represent the business organization. Because the Supreme Court defined companies as having limited individual rights,[4] it is logical such groups have an identity that includes core values. This is known as being part of a corporate culture. Within this culture there are rules and regulations both written and unwritten that determine what decisions employees consider right or wrong as it relates to the firm. Such evaluations are judgments by the organization and are defined as its ethics (or in this case their business ethics). One difference between an ordinary decision and an ethical one lies in "the point where the accepted rules no longer serve, and the decision maker is faced with the responsibility for weighing values and reaching a judgment in a situation which is not quite the same as any he or she has faced before."[5] Another difference relates to the amount of emphasis decision makers place on their own values and accepted practices within their company. Consequently, values and judgments play a critical role when we make ethical decisions.

Building on these definitions, we begin to develop a concept of business ethics. Most people agree that businesses should hire individuals with sound moral principles. However, some special aspects must be considered when applying ethics to business. First, to survive and contribute to society, businesses must earn a profit. There is no conflict or trade-offs between profits and business ethics. For instance, Google, Texas Instruments, and Starbucks are highly profitable companies that have earned a reputation for ethical conduct.[6] Second, to be successful businesses must address the needs and desires of stakeholders. The good news is the world's most ethical companies often have superior stock performance.[7] To address these unique aspects of the business world, society has developed rules—both legal and implicit—to guide businesses in their efforts to earn profits in ways that help individuals or society and contribute to social and economic well-being.

WHY STUDY BUSINESS ETHICS?

A Crisis in Business Ethics

Business ethics has become a major concern in business today. The Ethics Resource Center conducts the National Business Ethics Survey (NBES) of more than 6,000 U.S. employees

FIGURE 1–1 Global Trust in Industry Sectors

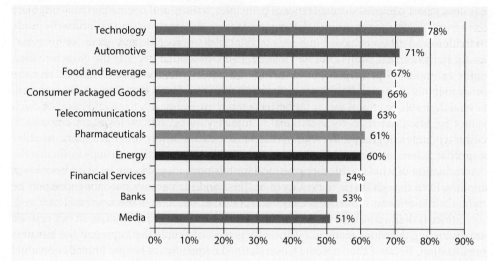

Source: Edelman, *2015 Edelman Trust Barometer*, http://www.edelman.com/insights/intellectual-property/2015-edelman-trust-barometer/trust-and-innovation-edelman-trust-barometer/global-results/ (accessed January 30, 2015).

to gather reliable data on key ethics and compliance outcomes and to help identify and better understand the ethics issues that are important to employees. The NBES found that 41 percent of employees reported observing at least one type of misconduct. Approximately 63 percent reported the misconduct to management, an increase from previous years.[8] Business ethics decisions and activities have come under greater scrutiny by many different stakeholders, including consumers, employees, investors, government regulators, and special interest groups. For instance, regulators carefully examined risk controls at JP Morgan Chase to investigate whether there were weaknesses in its system that allowed the firm to incur billions of dollars in losses through high-risk trading activities. Regulators are placing financial institutions under greater scrutiny and holding them increasingly accountable. There has been a long conflict between U.S. regulators and Swiss banks regarding whether these banks were being used to evade U.S. taxes. Credit Suisse pled guilty to helping Americans evade their taxes and was forced to pay a $2.6 billion fine.[9] Figure 1–1 shows the percentage of global respondents who say they trust a variety of businesses in various industries. Financial institutions and banks have some of the lowest ratings, indicating that the financial sector has not been able to restore its reputation since the most recent recession. There is no doubt negative publicity associated with major misconduct lowered the public's trust in certain business sectors.[10] Decreased trust leads to a reduction in customer satisfaction and customer loyalty, which in turn can negatively impact the firm or industry.[11]

Specific Issues

There are a number of ethical issues that must be addressed to prevent misconduct. Misuse of company resources, abusive behavior, harassment, accounting fraud, conflicts of interest, defective products, bribery, product knockoffs, and employee theft are all problems cited as potential risk areas. Chinese e-commerce giant Alibaba, which trades on the

New York Stock Exchange, was reprimanded by Chinese government authorities for ignoring the sales of knockoff products through Taobao, its biggest e-commerce platform. They also accused Alibaba employees of engaging in anticompetitive behavior such as bullying merchants to stay away from rival sites. As China attempts to secure a more solid reputation in the business world, its government recognizes that it must take steps to eliminate organizational misconduct.[12] Other ethical issues relate to recognizing the interests of various stakeholders. For instance, residents of Swansboro, North Carolina attempted to adopt an ordinance to prevent Walmart from opening a superstore in the area. The fear is that smaller independent stores cannot compete when big-box retailers come to town.[13] Although large companies like Walmart have significant power, pressures from the community still limit what they can do.

General ethics plays an important role in the public sector as well. In government, several politicians and high-ranking officials have experienced significant negative publicity, and some resigned in disgrace over ethical indiscretions. Former New Orleans mayor Ray Nagin was sentenced to 10 years in prison for misconduct during his tenure as mayor, including bribery, money laundering, and conspiracy.[14] Such political scandals demonstrate that political ethical behavior must be proactively practiced at all levels of public service.

Every organization has the potential for unethical behavior. For instance, the U.S. Defense Secretary ordered a renewed focus on military ethics after cheating scandals occurred in different branches of the military. Air force officers at the Malmstrom Air Force Base in Montana were suspended after it was discovered that there had been widespread cheating on monthly proficiency tests on operating warheads. Similarly, the U.S. Navy was criticized when sailors were found to have cheated on qualification exams for becoming nuclear reactor instructors. The Defense Secretary is concerned that the issue might be systemic, requiring an ethics overhaul in the military.[15]

Even sports ethics can be subject to lapses. The National Football League was heavily criticized for initially giving Baltimore Ravens player Ray Rice a two-game suspension after videos surfaced of him abusing his girlfriend. The scandal caused outrage among consumers who felt the NFL did not take domestic abuse incidents seriously. The NFL apologized and changed its policies on domestic abuse.[16] This incident along with other sports scandals has led to calls for greater accountability among sports players and coaches.

Whether they are made in the realm of business, politics, science, or sports, most decisions are judged either right or wrong, ethical or unethical. Regardless of what an individual believes about a particular action, if society judges it to be unethical or wrong, new legislation usually follows. Whether correct or not, that judgment directly affects a company's ability to achieve its business goals. You should be aware that the public is more tolerant of questionable consumer practices than of similar business practices. Double standards are at least partly due to differences in wealth and the success between businesses and consumers. The more successful a company, the more the public is critical when misconduct occurs.[17] For this reason alone, it is important to understand business ethics and recognize ethical issues.

The Reasons for Studying Business Ethics

Studying business ethics is valuable for several reasons. Business ethics is more than an extension of an individual's own personal ethics. Many people believe if a company hires good people with strong ethical values, then it will be a "good citizen" organization. But as we show throughout this text, an individual's personal moral values are only one factor in the ethical decision-making process. True, moral values can be applied to a variety of situations in life, and some people do not distinguish everyday ethical issues from business ones. Our concern, however, is with the application of principles, values, and standards in the business context. Many important issues are not related to a business context, although they remain complex moral dilemmas in a person's own life. For example, although abortion and human cloning are moral issues, they are not an issue in most business organizations.

Professionals in any field, including business, must deal with individuals' personal moral dilemmas because such dilemmas affect everyone's ability to function on the job. Normally, a business does not dictate a person's morals. Such policies would be illegal. Only when a person's morals influence his or her performance on the job does it involve a dimension within business ethics.

Just being a good person and having sound personal values may not be sufficient to handle the ethical issues that arise in a business organization. Although truthfulness, honesty, fairness, and openness are often assumed to be self-evident and accepted, business-strategy decisions involve complex and detailed discussions. For example, there is considerable debate over what constitutes antitrust, deceptive advertising, and violations of the Foreign Corrupt Practices Act. A high level of personal moral development may not prevent an individual from violating the law in a complicated organizational context where even experienced lawyers debate the exact meaning of the law. For instance, the National Labor Relations Board ruled that employees have the right to use company email systems to discuss working conditions and unionization as long as it is not on company time. Employer groups claim that employees have plenty of options for discussing these topics and maintain that it will be hard to ensure employees are not using company computer servers for these purposes during work hours. The right of employees versus employers is a controversial topic that will continue to need clarification from the courts.[18]

Some approaches to business ethics assume ethics training is for people whose personal moral development is unacceptable, but that is not the case. Because organizations are culturally diverse and personal morals must be respected, ensuring collective agreement on organizational ethics (that is, codes reasonably capable of preventing misconduct) is as vital as any other effort an organization's management may undertake.

Many people with limited business experience suddenly find themselves making decisions about product quality, advertising, pricing, sales techniques, hiring practices, and pollution control. The morals they learned from family, religion, and school may not provide specific guidelines for these complex business decisions. In other words, a person's experiences and decisions at home, in school, and in the community may be quite different from his or her experiences and decisions at work. Many business ethics decisions are close calls. In addition, managerial responsibility and ethical leadership for the conduct of others requires knowledge of ethics and compliance processes and systems. Years of experience in a particular industry may be required to know what is acceptable. For example, when are advertising claims more exaggeration than truth? When does such exaggeration become unethical? Pet food manufacturer Blue Buffalo's claims that its food contains no byproducts and is superior to competitors' did not set well with Purina. Purina filed a lawsuit against Blue Buffalo claiming that an independent test detected byproducts in Blue Buffalo's pet food. Blue Buffalo denied the allegations. While misleading advertising violates the law, puffery—or an exaggerated claim that customers should not take seriously—is considered acceptable. In this case, Blue Buffalo's claims are clearly not puffery, which is why Purina challenged the company through a lawsuit.[19]

Studying business ethics will help you begin to identify ethical issues when they arise and recognize the approaches available for resolving them. You will learn more about the ethical decision-making process and about ways to promote ethical behavior within your organization. By studying business ethics, you may also begin to understand how to cope with conflicts between your own personal values and those of the organization in which you work. As stated earlier, if after reading this book you feel a little more unsettled about potential decisions in business, your decisions will be more ethical and you will have knowledge within this area.

THE DEVELOPMENT OF BUSINESS ETHICS

The study of business ethics in North America has evolved through five distinct stages—(1) before 1960, (2) the 1960s, (3) the 1970s, (4) the 1980s, and (5) the 1990s—and continues to evolve in the twenty-first century (see Table 1–1).

Before 1960: Ethics in Business

Prior to 1960, the United States endured several agonizing phases of questioning the concept of capitalism. In the 1920s, the progressive movement attempted to provide citizens with a "living wage," defined as income sufficient for education, recreation, health, and retirement. Businesses were asked to check unwarranted price increases and any other practices that would hurt a family's living wage. In the 1930s came the New Deal that specifically blamed business for the country's economic woes. Business was asked to work more closely with the government to raise family income. By the 1950s, the New Deal evolved into President Harry S. Truman's Fair Deal, a program that defined such matters as civil rights and environmental responsibility as ethical issues that businesses had to address.

Until 1960, ethical issues related to business were often discussed within the domain of theology or philosophy or in the realm of legal and competitive relationships. Religious leaders raised questions about fair wages, labor practices, and the morality of capitalism. For example, Catholic social ethics, expressed in a series of papal encyclicals, included concern for morality in business, workers' rights, and living wages; for humanistic values rather than materialistic ones; and for improving the conditions of the poor. The Protestant work ethic encouraged individuals to be frugal, work hard, and attain success in the capitalistic system. Such religious traditions provided a foundation for the future field of business ethics.

The first book on business ethics was published in 1937 by Frank Chapman Sharp and Philip G. Fox. The authors separated their book into four sections: fair service, fair treatment of competitors, fair price, and moral progress in the business world. This early textbook discusses ethical ideas based largely upon economic theories and moral philosophies. However, the section's titles indicate the authors also take different stakeholders into account. Most notably, competitors and customers are the main stakeholders emphasized, but the text also identifies stockholders, employees, business partners such as suppliers, and government agencies.[20] Although the theory of stakeholder orientation would not evolve for many more years, this earliest business ethics textbook demonstrates the necessity of the ethical treatment of different stakeholders.

TABLE 1-1 Timeline of Ethical and Socially Responsible Concerns

1960s	1970s	1980s	1990s	2000s
Environmental issues	Employee militancy	Bribes and illegal contracting practices	Sweatshops and unsafe working conditions in third-world countries	Cybercrime
Civil rights issues	Human rights issues	Influence peddling	Rising corporate liability for personal damages (for example, cigarette companies)	Financial misconduct
Increased employee-employer tension	Covering up rather than correcting issues	Deceptive advertising	Financial mismanagement and fraud	Global issues, Chinese product safety
Changing work ethic	Disadvantaged consumers	Financial fraud (for example, savings and loan scandal)	Organizational ethical misconduct	Sustainability
Rising drug use	Transparency issues			Intellectual property theft

Source: Adapted from "Business Ethics Timeline," Ethics Resource Center, http://www.ethics.org/resource/business-ethics-timeline (accessed June 13, 2013).

The 1960s: The Rise of Social Issues in Business

During the 1960s American society witnessed the development of an anti-business trend because many critics attacked the vested interests that controlled the economic and political aspects of society—the so-called military–industrial complex. The 1960s saw the decay of inner cities and the growth of ecological problems such as pollution and the disposal of toxic and nuclear wastes. This period also witnessed the rise of consumerism—activities undertaken by independent individuals, groups, and organizations to protect their rights as consumers. In 1962 President John F. Kennedy delivered a "Special Message on Protecting the Consumer Interest" that outlined four basic consumer rights: the right to safety, the right to be informed, the right to choose, and the right to be heard. These came to be known as the **Consumers' Bill of Rights**.

The modern consumer movement is generally considered to have begun in 1965 with the publication of Ralph Nader's *Unsafe at Any Speed* that criticized the auto industry as a whole, and General Motors Corporation (GM) in particular, for putting profit and style ahead of lives and safety. GM's Corvair was the main target of Nader's criticism. His consumer protection organization, popularly known as Nader's Raiders, fought successfully for legislation requiring automobile makers to equip cars with safety belts, padded dashboards, stronger door latches, head restraints, shatterproof windshields, and collapsible steering columns. Consumer activists also helped secure passage of consumer protection laws such as the Wholesome Meat Act of 1967, the Radiation Control for Health and Safety Act of 1968, the Clean Water Act of 1972, and the Toxic Substance Act of 1976.[21]

After Kennedy came President Lyndon B. Johnson and the "Great Society," a series of programs that extended national capitalism and told the business community the U.S. government's responsibility was to provide all citizens with some degree of economic stability, equality, and social justice. Activities that could destabilize the economy or discriminate against any class of citizens began to be viewed as politically unethical and unlawful.

The 1970s: Business Ethics as an Emerging Field

Business ethics began to develop as a field of study in the 1970s. Theologians and philosophers laid the groundwork by suggesting certain moral principles could be applied to business activities. Using this foundation, business professors began to teach and write about **corporate social responsibility**, an organization's obligation to maximize its positive impact on stakeholders and minimize its negative impact. Philosophers increased their involvement, applying ethical theory and philosophical analysis to structure the discipline of business ethics. Companies became more concerned with their public image, and as social demands grew, many businesses realized they needed to address ethical issues more directly. The Nixon administration's Watergate scandal focused public interest on the importance of ethics in government. Conferences were held to discuss the social responsibilities and ethical issues of business. Centers dealing with issues of business ethics were established. Interdisciplinary meetings brought together business professors, theologians, philosophers, and businesspeople. President Jimmy Carter attempted to focus on personal and administrative efforts to uphold ethical principles in government. The Foreign Corrupt Practices Act was passed during his administration, making it illegal for U.S. businesses to bribe government officials of other countries. Today this law is the highest priority of the U.S. Department of Justice.

By the end of the 1970s, a number of major ethical issues had emerged, including bribery, deceptive advertising, price collusion, product safety, and ecology. *Business ethics* became a common expression. Academic researchers sought to identify ethical issues and describe how businesspeople might choose to act in particular situations. However, only limited efforts were made to describe how the ethical decision-making process worked and to identify the many variables that influence this process in organizations.

The 1980s: Consolidation

In the 1980s, business academics and practitioners acknowledged business ethics as a field of study, and a growing and varied group of institutions with diverse interests promoted it. Centers for business ethics provided publications, courses, conferences, and seminars. R. Edward Freeman was among the first scholars to pioneer the concept of stakeholders as a foundational theory for business ethics decisions. Freeman defined stakeholders as "any group or individual who can affect or is affected by the achievement of the organization's objectives."[22] Freeman's defense of stakeholder theory had a major impact on strategic management and corporations' views of their responsibilities. Business ethics were also a prominent concern within leading companies such as General Electric, Hershey Foods, General Motors, IBM, Caterpillar, and S. C. Johnson & Son, Inc. Many of these firms established ethics and social policy committees to address ethical issues.

In the 1980s, the **Defense Industry Initiative on Business Ethics and Conduct** (DII) was developed to guide corporate support for ethical conduct. In 1986 eighteen defense contractors drafted principles for guiding business ethics and conduct.[23] The organization has since grown to nearly fifty members. This effort established a method for discussing best practices and working tactics to link organizational practice and policy to successful ethical compliance. The DII includes six principles. First, the DII supports codes of conduct and their widespread distribution. These codes of conduct must be understandable and cover their more substantive areas in detail. Second, member companies are expected to provide ethics training for their employees as well as continuous support between training periods. Third, defense contractors must create an open atmosphere in which employees feel comfortable reporting violations without fear of retribution. Fourth, companies need to perform extensive internal audits and develop effective internal reporting and voluntary disclosure plans. Fifth, the DII insists that member companies preserve the integrity of the defense industry. And sixth, member companies must adopt a philosophy of public accountability.[24]

The 1980s ushered in the Reagan–Bush era, with the accompanying belief that self-regulation, rather than regulation by government, was in the public's interest. Many tariffs and trade barriers were lifted and businesses merged and divested within an increasingly global atmosphere. Thus, while business schools were offering courses in business ethics, the rules of business were changing at a phenomenal rate because of less regulation. Corporations that once were nationally based began operating internationally and found themselves mired in value structures where accepted rules of business behavior no longer applied.

The 1990s: Institutionalization of Business Ethics

The administration of President Bill Clinton continued to support self-regulation and free trade. However, it also took unprecedented government action to deal with health-related social issues such as teenage smoking. Its proposals included restricting cigarette advertising, banning cigarette vending machine sales, and ending the use of cigarette logos in connection with sports events.[25] Clinton also appointed Arthur Levitt as chairman of the Securities and Exchange Commission in 1993. Levitt unsuccessfully pushed for many reforms that, if passed, could have prevented the accounting scandals exemplified by Enron and WorldCom in the early twenty-first century.[26]

Federal Sentencing Guidelines for Organizations (FSGO), approved by Congress in November 1991, set the tone for organizational ethical compliance programs in the 1990s. The guidelines, which were based on the six principles of the DII,[27] broke new ground by codifying into law incentives to reward organizations for taking action to prevent misconduct, such as developing effective internal legal and ethical compliance programs.[28] Provisions in the guidelines mitigate penalties for businesses striving to root out misconduct and establish high ethical and legal standards.[29] On the other hand, under FSGO, if a company lacks an effective ethical compliance program and its employees violate the law, it can incur severe penalties. The guidelines focus on firms taking action to prevent and detect business misconduct in cooperation with government regulation. At the heart of the FSGO is the carrot-and-stick approach—that is, by taking preventive action against misconduct, a company may avoid onerous penalties should a violation occur. A mechanical approach using legalistic logic will not suffice to avert serious penalties. The company must develop corporate values, enforce its own code of ethics, and strive to prevent misconduct. The law develops new amendments almost every year. We will provide more detail on the FSGO's role in business ethics programs in Chapters 4 and 8.

The Twenty-First Century of Business Ethics

Although business ethics appeared to become more institutionalized in the 1990s, new evidence emerged in the early 2000s that not all business executives and managers had fully embraced the public's desire for high ethical standards. After George W. Bush became President in 2001, highly publicized corporate misconduct at Enron, WorldCom, Halliburton, and the accounting firm Arthur Andersen caused the government and the public to look for new ways to encourage ethical behavior.[30] Accounting scandals, especially falsifying financial reports, became part of the culture of many companies. Firms outside the United States, such as Royal Ahold in the Netherlands and Parmalat in Italy, became major examples of global accounting fraud. Although the Bush administration tried to minimize government regulation, there appeared to be no alternative to developing more regulatory oversight of business.

Such abuses increased public and political demands to improve ethical standards in business. To address the loss of confidence in financial reporting and corporate ethics, in 2002 Congress passed the **Sarbanes–Oxley Act**, the most far-reaching change in organizational control and accounting regulations since the Securities and Exchange Act of 1934. The new law made securities fraud a criminal offense and stiffened penalties for corporate fraud. It also created an accounting oversight board that requires corporations to establish codes of ethics for financial reporting and to develop greater transparency in financial reports to investors and other interested parties. Additionally, the law requires top executives to sign off on their firms' financial reports, and risk fines and long prison sentences if they misrepresent their companies' financial positions. The legislation further requires company executives to disclose stock sales immediately and prohibits companies from giving loans to top managers.[31]

Amendments to the FSGO require that a business's governing authority be well informed about its ethics program with respect to content, implementation, and effectiveness. This places the responsibility squarely on the shoulders of the firm's leadership, usually the board of directors. The board is required to provide resources to oversee the discovery of risks and to design, implement, and modify approaches to deal with those risks.

The Sarbanes–Oxley Act and the FSGO institutionalized the need to discover and address ethical and legal risk. Top management and the board of directors of a corporation are accountable for discovering risk associated with ethical conduct. Such specific industries as the public sector, energy and chemicals, health care, insurance, and retail have to discover the unique risks associated with their operations and develop ethics programs to prevent ethical misconduct before it creates a crisis. Most firms are developing formal and informal mechanisms that affect interactive communication and transparency about issues associated with the risk of misconduct. Business leaders should consider the greatest danger to their organizations lies in *not* discovering any serious misconduct or illegal activities that may be lurking. Unfortunately, most managers do not view the risk of an ethical disaster as being as important as the risk associated with fires, natural disasters, or technology failure. In fact, ethical disasters can be significantly more damaging to a company's reputation than risks managed through insurance and other methods. The great investor Warren Buffett stated it is impossible to eradicate all wrongdoing in a large organization and one can only hope the misconduct is small and is caught in time. Buffett's fears were realized in 2008 when the financial system almost collapsed because of pervasive, systemic use of instruments such as credit default swaps, risky debt such as subprime lending, and corruption in major corporations.

In 2009 Barack Obama became president in the middle of a great recession caused by a meltdown in the global financial industry. Many firms, such as AIG, Lehman Brothers, Merrill Lynch, and Countrywide Financial, engaged in ethical misconduct in developing and selling high-risk financial products. President Obama led the passage of legislation to provide a stimulus for recovery. His legislation to improve health care and provide more protection for consumers focused on social concerns. Congress passed legislation regarding credit card accountability, improper payments related to federal agencies, fraud and waste, and food safety. The **Dodd–Frank Wall Street Reform and Consumer Protection Act** addressed some of the issues related to the financial crisis and recession. The Dodd–Frank Act was the most sweeping financial legislation since the Sarbanes–Oxley Act and possibly since laws put into effect during the Great Depression. It was designed to make the financial services industry more ethical and responsible. This complex law required regulators to create hundreds of rules to promote financial stability, improve accountability and transparency, and protect consumers from abusive financial practices.

The basic assumptions of capitalism have been questioned as countries around the world work to stabilize markets and question those who manage the finances of individual corporations and nonprofits. The financial crisis caused many people to question government institutions that provide oversight and regulation. As societies work to create change for the better, they must address issues related to law, ethics, and the required level of compliance necessary for government and business to serve the public interest. Not since the Great Depression and President Franklin Delano Roosevelt has the United States seen such widespread government intervention and regulation—something most deem necessary, but is nevertheless worrisome to free market capitalists.

Future ethical issues revolve around the acquisition and sales of information. Cloud computing has begun a new paradigm. Businesses must no longer develop strategies based on past practices; they begin with petabytes of information and look for relationships and correlations to discover the new rules of business. Big data deal with massive data files obtained from structured and unstructured databases.[32] What once was thought of as intrusive is now accepted and promoted. Only recently have people begun to ask whether the information collected by business is acceptable. Companies are becoming more sophisticated in understanding their customers by the use of predictive analytic technologies. Such technologies as well as advances in consumer behavior research have reduced the consumer's probability to choose independently. Businesses now know how to better manipulate at an elemental level.

Is it acceptable for a business to review your Facebook or other social networking services? When shopping, does the fact that Q codes and microchips give your information to businesses regarding where you are, what you are looking at, and what you have done in the last day (via cell phone tower triangulation) bother you? Should your non-professional life be subject to the ethics of the corporation when you are not at work? Finally, are you a citizen first and then an employee or an employee first and then a citizen? These are some of the business ethics issues in your future.

DEVELOPING AN ORGANIZATIONAL AND GLOBAL ETHICAL CULTURE

Compliance and ethics initiatives in organizations are designed to establish appropriate conduct and core values. A national survey of corporate legal officers found that 96 percent said ethics and compliance are important in preventing illegal conduct. The ethical component of a corporate culture relates to the values, beliefs, and established and enforced patterns of conduct employees use to identify and respond to ethical issues. In our book the term **ethical culture** is acceptable behavior as defined by the company and industry. Ethical culture is the component of corporate culture that captures the values and norms an organization defines and is compared to by its industry as appropriate conduct. The goal of an ethical culture is to minimize the need for enforced compliance of rules and maximize the use of principles that contribute to ethical reasoning in difficult or new situations.

Ethical culture is positively related to workplace confrontation over ethics issues, reports to management of observed misconduct, and the presence of ethics hotlines.[33] To develop better ethical corporate cultures, many businesses communicate core values to their employees by creating ethics programs and appointing ethics officers to oversee them. An ethical culture creates shared values and support for ethical decisions and is driven by the ethical leadership of top management.

On the other hand, corrupt organizational cultures support unethical behavior. These cultures have been identified as creating negative values and norms such as "the ends justify the means." In these cultures, ethical employees may be punished for failure to engage in unethical activities.[34] Regulators want firms to focus on their culture to avoid excessive risk taking and unethical behavior. There is a fundamental belief that an ethical culture will lead to good behavior.[35]

Globally, businesses are working closely together to establish standards of acceptable behavior. We are already seeing collaborative efforts by a range of organizations to establish goals and mandate minimum levels of ethical behavior, from the European Union, the North American Free Trade Agreement (NAFTA), the Southern Common Market (MERCOSUR), and the World Trade Organization (WTO) to, more recently, the Council on Economic Priorities' Social Accountability 8000 (SA 8000), the Ethical Trading Initiative, the U.S. Apparel Industry Partnership, and ISO 19600. ISO 19600 is a global compliance management standard that addresses risks, legal requirements, and stakeholder needs. Companies that choose to abide by ISO 19600 can use these standards to improve their approaches to compliance management, which can reassure stakeholders of their commitment toward ethics and compliance.[36] Some companies refuse to do business with organizations that do not support and abide by these standards. Many companies demonstrate their commitment toward acceptable conduct by adopting globally recognized principles emphasizing human rights and social responsibility. For instance, in 2000 the United Nations launched the Global Compact, a set of ten principles concerning human rights, labor, the environment, and anti-corruption. The purpose of the Global Compact is to create openness and alignment among business, government, society, labor, and the United Nations. Companies that adopt this code agree to integrate the ten principles into their business practices, publish their progress toward these objectives on an annual basis, and partner with others to advance broader objectives of the UN.[37] These ten principles are covered in more detail in Chapter 10.

THE BENEFITS OF BUSINESS ETHICS

The field of business ethics continues to change rapidly as more firms recognize the benefits of improving ethical conduct and the link between business ethics and financial performance. Both research and examples from the business world demonstrate that building an ethical reputation among employees, customers, and the general public pays off. Figure 1–2 provides an overview of the relationship between business ethics and organizational performance. Although we believe there are many practical benefits to being ethical, many businesspeople make decisions because they believe a particular course of action is simply the right thing to do as responsible members of society. NiSource, a distributor of natural gas, electricity, and water in the Midwest and Northeast United States, has earned a place in *Ethisphere's* "World's Most Ethical Companies" for three consecutive years.

FIGURE 1–2 The Role of Organizational Ethics in Performance

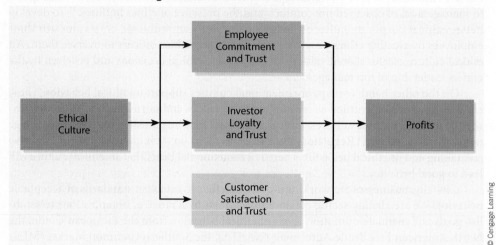

NiSource has adopted a strong code of business conduct that stresses how employees are all responsible for ethical conduct in the company. NiSource has four values—fairness, honesty, integrity, and trust—that it puts into action in what it calls the NiSource Way. It makes sure that every organization in its portfolio of businesses abides by these values, which has placed it among the Fortune 500.[38] Among the rewards for being more ethical and socially responsible in business are increased efficiency in daily operations, greater employee commitment, increased investor willingness to entrust funds, improved customer trust and satisfaction, and better financial performance. The reputation of a company has a major effect on its relationships with employees, investors, customers, and many other parties.

Ethics Contributes to Employee Commitment

Employee commitment comes from workers who believe their future is tied to that of the organization and from a willingness to make personal sacrifices for the organization.[39] The more a company is dedicated to taking care of its employees, the more likely the employees will take care of the organization. Issues that foster the development of an ethical culture for employees include the absence of abusive behavior, a safe work environment, competitive salaries, and the fulfillment of all contractual obligations toward employees. An ethics and compliance program can support values and appropriate conduct. Social programs improving the ethical culture range from work–family programs to stock ownership plans to community service. Home Depot associates, for example, participate in disaster-relief efforts after hurricanes and tornadoes, rebuilding roofs, repairing water damage, planting trees, and clearing roads in their communities. Because employees spend a considerable number of their waking hours at work, a commitment by an organization to goodwill and respect for its employees usually increases the employees' loyalty to the organization and their support of its objectives. The consulting and engineering firm Burns & McDonnell has been nominated as one of *Fortune Magazine's* "Best Companies to Work For" because of the way it values its employees. The company is completely employee-owned with what many consider to be the best company stock ownership plan in the United States.

It also offers workers a variety of unique benefits, including onsite health and fitness centers and charging stations for electric vehicles.[40]

Employees' perceptions that their firm has an ethical culture lead to performance-enhancing outcomes within the organization.[41] A corporate culture that integrates strong ethical values and positive business practices has been found to increase group creativity and job satisfaction and decrease turnover.[42] For the sake of both productivity and teamwork, it is essential employees both within and among departments throughout an organization share a common vision of trust. The influence of higher levels of trust is greatest on relationships within departments or work groups, but trust is a significant factor in relationships among departments as well. Programs that create a trustworthy work environment make individuals more willing to rely and act on the decisions of their coworkers. In such a work environment, employees can reasonably expect to be treated with full respect and consideration by their coworkers and superiors. Trusting relationships between upper management and managers and their subordinates contribute to greater decision-making efficiencies. One survey found that when employees see values such as honesty, respect, and trust applied frequently in the workplace, they feel less pressure to compromise ethical standards, observe less misconduct, are more satisfied with their organizations overall, and feel more valued as employees.[43]

The ethical culture of a company matters to employees. According to a report on employee loyalty and work practices, companies viewed as highly ethical by their employees were six times more likely to keep their workers.[44] Also, employees who view their company as having a strong community involvement feel more loyal to their employers and positive about themselves.

Ethics Contributes to Investor Loyalty

Ethical conduct results in shareholder loyalty and contributes to success that supports even broader social causes and concerns. Investors today are increasingly concerned about the ethics and social responsibility that creates the reputation of companies in which they invest, and various socially responsible mutual funds and asset management firms help investors purchase stock in ethical companies. Investors also recognize that an ethical culture provides a foundation for efficiency, productivity, and profits. Investors know, too, that negative publicity, lawsuits, and fines can lower stock prices, diminish customer loyalty, and threaten a company's long-term viability. Many companies accused of misconduct experienced dramatic declines in the value of their stock when concerned investors divested. Warren Buffett and his company Berkshire Hathaway command significant respect from investors because of their track record of financial returns and the integrity of their organizations. Buffett says, "I want employees to ask themselves whether they are willing to have any contemplated act appear the next day on the front page of their local paper—to be read by their spouses, children and friends—with the reporting done by an informed and critical reporter."

The demand for socially responsible investing is increasing. It is estimated that socially responsible investments in the United States have funds valued at more than $6 trillion. Social investing is becoming increasingly important to millennials born between 1980 and 2000, who view socially responsible behavior as more of a requirement than an option for companies.[45] Investors look at the bottom line for profits or the potential for increased stock prices or dividends, but they also look for any potential flaws in the company's performance, conduct, and financial reports. Therefore, gaining investors' trust and confidence is vital to sustaining the financial stability of the firm.

DEBATE ISSUE
TAKE A STAND

Does Being Ethical Result in Better Performance?

While research suggests ethical businesses have better performance, there is also an alternate view. Many businesspeople think ethics and social responsibility require resources that do not contribute to profits, and time spent in ethics training could be better used for other business activities. One viewpoint is that when companies push the edge, pay minor fines for misconduct, or are not caught in wrongdoing, they may end up being more profitable than companies with a strong ethical culture. Many financial companies became extremely profitable when taking high-risk opportunities with limited transparency about the nature of the complex products they sold. To gain competitive advantage, a firm needs to be able to reach markets and make sales. If a firm is too ethical, it might lose competitive advantages. On the other hand, *Ethisphere*'s World's Most Ethical Companies index indicates ethical companies have better financial performance.

1. Ethical businesses are the most profitable.
2. The most ethical businesses are not the most profitable.

Ethics Contributes to Customer Satisfaction

It is generally accepted that customer satisfaction is one of the most important factors in a successful business strategy. Although a company continues to develop and adapt products to keep pace with customers' changing desires and preferences, it must also develop long-term relationships with its customers and stakeholders. As mentioned earlier, high levels of perceived corporate misconduct decreases customer trust.[46] On the other hand, companies viewed as socially responsible increase customer trust and satisfaction. Southwest Airlines has a reputation for its customer service and friendliness. When Southwest Airlines experienced problems with on-time performance due to operational changes, the company's senior vice president of communications sent letters to the company's most loyal customers explaining the situation and assuring them the airline was committed toward maintaining their loyalty. As a result of its strong customer focus, the company has been profitable for the past 40 years when most airlines have struggled.[47]

For most businesses, both repeat purchases and an enduring relationship of mutual respect and cooperation with customers are essential for success. By focusing on customer satisfaction, a company continually deepens the customer's dependence on the company, and as the customer's confidence grows, the firm gains a better understanding of how to serve the customer so the relationship may endure. Successful businesses provide an opportunity for customer feedback that engages the customer in cooperative problem solving. As is often pointed out, a happy customer will come back, but disgruntled customers will tell others about their dissatisfaction with a company and discourage friends from dealing with it.

Trust is essential to a good long-term relationship between a business and consumers. The perceived ethicality of a firm is positively related to brand trust, emotional identification with the brand, and brand loyalty.[48] A Nielsen survey revealed 55 percent of global consumer respondents stated they would pay more for products from companies that give back to society in a socially responsible and sustainable manner.[49] As social responsibility becomes more important for companies, corporate social responsibility may be viewed as a sign of good management and may, according to one study, indicate good financial performance. However, another study indicates the reverse may be true, and companies who have good financial performance are able to spend more money on social responsibility.[50] As a highly successful company, Adobe invests heavily in community development and sustainability. It invests 1 percent of its pretax profits in the Adobe Foundation, which partners with teams of employees to use the funds to improve local communities. The company donates software to more than 15,000 nonprofits. It has also made significant strides in energy conservation, waste reduction, and green building, earning the company a spot on *Newsweek's* list of the world's greenest companies.[51]

When an organization has a strong ethical environment, it usually focuses on the core value of placing customers' interests first. However, putting customers first does not mean the interests of employees, investors, and local communities should be ignored. An ethical culture that focuses on customers incorporates the interests of all employees, suppliers, and other interested parties in decisions and actions. Employees working in an ethical environment support and contribute to the process of understanding customers' demands and concerns.

Ethics Contributes to Profits

A company cannot nurture and develop an ethical culture unless it has achieved adequate financial performance in terms of profits. Businesses with greater resources—regardless of their staff size—have the means to be ethical and practice social responsibility while serving their customers, valuing their employees, and contributing to society. Ethical conduct toward customers builds a strong competitive position shown to positively affect business performance and product innovation.[52] Some dimensions of ethical culture have been found to create innovativeness that is directly related to performance. Intuit adopted a strong customer focus with a goal to make software that customers could easily use. Strong customer initiatives help Intuit receive the feedback needed to release innovative products customers desire, including its flagship product TurboTax. As a result of its customer focus, Intuit has become a leading company in the personal and small business software industry.[53] Despite this example of a positive company, it seems like every day business newspapers and magazines offer new examples of the consequences of business misconduct. It is worth noting, however, that most of these companies learned from their mistakes and recovered after they implemented programs to improve ethical and legal conduct.

Ample evidence shows being ethical pays off with better performance. Even the cost of equity and financing for firms that are socially responsible is less than for firms that do not engage stakeholders.[54] Investors see more risk in firms without an ethical culture. As indicated earlier, companies perceived by their employees as having a high degree of honesty and integrity have a much higher average total return to shareholders than do companies perceived as having a low degree of honesty and integrity.[55] The World's Most Ethical Companies index was developed through methodology designed by a committee of leading attorneys, professors, and organization leaders. The companies in this index performed as well as—and often better than—companies on the Standard & Poor's 500 index over 5- and 10-year periods.[56] These results provide strong evidence that corporate concern for ethical conduct is becoming a part of strategic planning toward obtaining the outcome of higher profitability. Rather than being just a function of compliance, ethics is becoming an integral part of management's efforts to achieve competitive advantage.

OUR FRAMEWORK FOR STUDYING BUSINESS ETHICS

We developed a framework for this text to help you understand how people make ethical decisions and deal with ethical issues. Table 1–2 summarizes each element in the framework and describes where each topic is discussed in this book.

In Part One, we provide an overview of business ethics. This chapter defines the term *business ethics* and explores the development and importance of this critical business area. In Chapter 2, we explore the role of various stakeholder groups in social responsibility and corporate governance.

Part Two focuses on ethical issues and the institutionalization of business ethics. In Chapter 3, we examine business issues that lead to ethical decision making in organizations. In Chapter 4, we look at the institutionalization of business ethics, including both mandatory and voluntary societal concerns.

TABLE 1–2 Our Framework for Studying Business Ethics

Chapter	Highlights
1. The Importance of Business Ethics	• Definitions
	• Reasons for studying business ethics
	• History
	• Benefits of business ethics
2. Stakeholder Relationships, Social Responsibility, and Corporate Governance	• Stakeholder relationships
	• Stakeholder influences in social responsibility
	• Corporate governance
3. Emerging Business Ethics Issues	• Recognizing an ethical issue
	• Honesty, fairness, and integrity
	• Ethical issues and dilemmas in business: abusive and disruptive behavior, lying, conflicts of interest, bribery, corporate intelligence, discrimination, sexual harassment, environmental issues, fraud, insider trading, intellectual property rights, and privacy
	• Determining an ethical issue in business
4. The Institutionalization of Business Ethics	• Mandatory requirements
	• Voluntary requirements
	• Core practices
	• Federal Sentencing Guidelines for Organizations
	• Sarbanes–Oxley Act
5. Ethical Decision Making	• Ethical issue intensity
	• Individual factors in decision making
	• Organizational factors in decision making
	• Opportunity in decision making
	• Business ethics evaluations and intentions
	• Normative considerations in ethical decision making
	• Role of institutions in normative decision making
	• Importance of principles and core values to ethical decision making

6. Individual Factors: Moral Philosophies and Values	• Moral philosophies, including teleological development philosophies and cognitive moral deontological, relativist, virtue ethics, and justice philosophies
	• Stages of cognitive moral development
7. Organizational Factors: The Role of Ethical Culture and Relationships	• Corporate culture
	• Interpersonal relationships
	• Whistle-blowing
	• Opportunity and conflict
8. Developing an Effective Ethics Program	• Ethics programs
	• Codes of ethics
	• Program responsibility
	• Communication of ethical standards
	• Systems to monitor and enforce ethical standards
	• Continuous improvement of ethics programs
9. Implementing and Auditing Ethics Programs	• Implementation programs
	• Ethics audits
10. Business Ethics in a Global Economy	• Global culture and cultural relations
	• Economic foundations of business ethics
	• Multinational corporations
	• Global cooperation
	• Global ethics issues
11. Ethical Leadership	• Requirements for ethical leadership
	• Managing ethical conflicts
	• Ethical leadership communication
	• Leader-follower relationships
12. Sustainability: Ethical and Social Responsibility Dimensions	• Sustainability and ethical decision making
	• Global environmental issues
	• Business response to sustainability issues
	• Strategic implementation of environmental responsibility

© Cengage Learning

In Part Three, we delineate the ethical decision-making process and then look at both individual factors and organizational factors that influence decisions. Chapter 5 describes the ethical decision-making process from an organizational perspective. Chapter 6 explores individual factors that may influence ethical decisions in business, including moral philosophies and cognitive moral development. Chapter 7 focuses on organizational dimensions including corporate culture, relationships, and conflicts.

In Part Four, we explore systems and processes associated with implementing business ethics into global strategic planning. Chapter 8 discusses the development of an effective ethics program. In Chapter 9, we examine issues related to implementing and auditing ethics programs. Chapter 10 considers ethical issues in a global context. Chapter 11 examines ethical leadership and its importance in creating an ethical corporate culture. Finally, Chapter 12 discusses the ethical and social responsibility considerations of sustainability.

We hope that this framework helps you develop a balanced understanding of the various perspectives and alternatives available to you when making ethical business decisions. Regardless of your own personal values, the more you know about how individuals make decisions, the better prepared you will be to cope with difficult ethical decisions. Such knowledge will help you improve and control the ethical decision-making environment in which you work.

It is your job to make the final decision in business situations that affect you. Sometimes that decision may be ethical; sometimes it may be unethical. It is always easy to look back with hindsight and know what you should have done in a particular situation. At the time, however, the choices might not have seemed so clear. To give you practice making ethical decisions, Part Five of this book contains a number of cases. In addition, each chapter begins with a vignette, "An Ethical Dilemma," and ends with a mini-case, "Resolving Ethical Business Challenges," that involves ethical problems. We hope these give you a better sense of the challenges of making ethical decisions in the business world.

SUMMARY

This chapter provided an overview of the field of business ethics and introduced the framework for the discussion of this subject. Business ethics comprises organizational principles, values, and norms that may originate from individuals, organizational statements, or from the legal system that primarily guide individual and group behavior in business. Investors, employees, customers, special interest groups, the legal system, and the community often determine whether a specific action is right or wrong, ethical or unethical.

Studying business ethics is important for many reasons. Recent incidents of unethical activity in business underscore the widespread need for a better understanding of the factors that contribute to ethical and unethical decisions. Individuals' personal moral philosophies and decision-making experience may not be sufficient to guide them in the business world. Studying business ethics helps you begin to identify ethical issues and recognize the approaches available to resolve them.

The study of business ethics evolved through five distinct stages. Before 1960 business ethics issues were discussed primarily from a religious perspective. The 1960s saw the emergence of many social issues involving business and the concept of social conscience as well as a rise in consumerism, which culminated with Kennedy's *Consumers' Bill of Rights*. Business ethics began to develop as an independent field of study in the 1970s, with academics and practitioners exploring ethical issues and attempting to understand how individuals and organizations make ethical decisions. These experts began to teach and write about the idea of corporate social responsibility, an organization's obligation to maximize its positive impact on stakeholders and minimize its negative impact. In the 1980s, centers of business ethics provided publications, courses, conferences, and seminars, and many companies established ethics committees and social policy committees. The Defense Industry Initiative on Business Ethics and Conduct was developed to guide corporate support for ethical conduct; its principles had a major impact on corporate ethics.

However, less government regulation and an increase in businesses with international operations raised new ethical issues. In the 1990s, government continued to support self-regulation. The FSGO sets the tone for organizational ethics programs by providing incentives for companies to take action to prevent organizational misconduct. The twenty-first century ushered in a new set of ethics scandals, suggesting many companies had not embraced the public's desire for higher ethical standards. The Sarbanes–Oxley Act stiffened penalties for corporate fraud and established an accounting oversight board. The Dodd–Frank Wall Street Reform and Consumer Protection Act was later passed to reform the financial system. The current trend is away from legally based ethical initiatives in organizations and toward cultural initiatives that make ethics a part of core organizational values. The ethical component of a corporate culture relates to the values, beliefs, and established and enforced patterns of conduct employees use to identify and respond to ethical issues. The term *ethical culture* describes the component of corporate culture that captures the rules and principles an organization defines as appropriate conduct. Ethical culture can be viewed as the character of the decision-making process employees use to determine whether their responses to ethical issues are right or wrong.

Research and anecdotes demonstrate building an ethical reputation among employees, customers, and the general public provides benefits that include increased efficiency in daily operations, greater employee commitment, increased investor willingness to entrust funds, improved customer trust and satisfaction, and better financial performance. The reputation of a company has a major effect on its relationships with employees, investors, customers, and many other parties, and thus has the potential to affect its bottom line.

Finally, this text introduces a framework for studying business ethics. Each chapter addresses some aspect of business ethics and decision making within a business context. The major concerns are ethical issues in business, stakeholder relationships, social responsibility and corporate governance, emerging business ethics issues, the institutionalization of business ethics, understanding the ethical decision-making process, moral philosophies and cognitive moral development, corporate culture, organizational relationships and conflicts, developing an effective ethics program, implementing and auditing the ethics program, global business ethics, ethical leadership, and sustainability.

IMPORTANT TERMS FOR REVIEW

morals 4

business ethics 5

principles 5

values 5

Consumers' Bill of Rights 10

Corporate social responsibility 11

Defense Industry Initiative on Business Ethics and Conduct 11

Federal Sentencing Guidelines for Organizations 12

Sarbanes–Oxley Act 13

Dodd–Frank Wall Street Reform and Consumer Protection Act 13

ethical culture 14

RESOLVING ETHICAL BUSINESS CHALLENGES*

Lael was just hired by Best East Motels into their manager training program and was excited about the potential benefits after her graduation from Florida State University. Working part-time and going to school full-time was the norm for her, but the Best East job replaced her two part-time jobs. With this new job, she would be the one to assign work times. Her luck continued when she met her mentor Nikhil, who was the son of the owner. Best East Motels was a franchise motel chain in the United States. Owners bought into the chain with a $500,000 franchise fee and paid for the construction of the motel. In return for the fee, Best East gave each owner a comprehensive package of marketing, management, accounting, and financial materials to boost motel success rates to over 90 percent. In addition, Best East assisted each owner with groups of people that trained staff for every new job, from housekeeping to accounting. The new-hire training course for each type of employee was developed and based on the best practices within the industry. This particular motel had been in business for 10 years and was seen as successful.

As Lael went through the manager training program, everything she heard was great. It sounded like Best East was a career path she would want to pursue long-term. Six months into her job, however, Lael started to hear strange rumors. For example, on the night shift she found there was heavy employee turnover and most were females. Lael began to investigate by scheduling herself onto several night shifts. One night, as she chatted with one of the front desk employees, she discovered the girl planned on quitting. She was seventeen and worked at this Best East motel for a year. "Why are you leaving?" asked Lael.

Her reply startled Lael. "I don't want trouble, just my last paycheck, a good letter of recommendation, and that's it."

As Lael pressed her for more information, the 17-year-old opened up. She spoke about Nikhil talking suggestively about her to other employees and how he made suggestive physical gestures when she was around. She told Lael about other female employees treated similarly, and this always occurred during night shifts when Nikhil was on duty.

Digging a little deeper, Lael spoke to several former employees. Most were fairly young female employees. They told her essentially the same thing. For example,

Nikhil would routinely make suggestive comments to female employees. In one incident under Nikhil's watch, some male employees flirted with female employees, including undocumented workers. Nikhil reportedly sat there with a smile. They also told her Nikhil allowed customers at the motel to offer their room keys to female employees.

After a few weeks, Lael heard the same story from younger female employees and even some of the maids. Their responses to these situations were similar. They ranged from "Nikhil told me if I was older he would ask me out" to "I don't want to make a big deal out of this because it might appear I'm a tattle tale." Another common excuse for not reporting was that Nikhil assured them this was part of the motel business and was normal. Most employees were afraid to report on the boss's son and put their jobs on the line.

Lael reviewed the section of the franchise employee handbook. It clearly stated sexual harassment of any kind would not be tolerated and should be reported immediately to the proper manager. Lael could tell from the manual the allegations against Nikhil constituted sexual harassment. While the Best East Franchise Corporation had no ethics hotline, Lael thought this could be a legal issue.

She knew putting pressure on the female employees to report the behavior of the boss's son was problematic. Lael also felt that going to Nikhil personally about these allegations may not be a wise move. If the behavior was reported to the owner, it would become an official allegation and impact the motel's reputation and image in the community, and she would be responsible for it. The things these women were saying had not personally happened to her yet.

QUESTIONS | EXERCISES

1. Why should Lael get involved in reporting if she has not experienced any of the allegations the other employees are making?
2. What are some of the characteristics of Best East's ethical culture that would create the current dilemma for Lael?
3. What should Lael do to resolve her concerns?

*This case is strictly hypothetical; any resemblance to real persons, companies, or situations is coincidental.

> > > CHECK YOUR EQ

Check your EQ, or Ethics Quotient, by completing the following. Assess your performance to evaluate your overall understanding of the chapter material.

1. Business ethics focuses mostly on personal ethical issues.   Yes   **No**

2. Business ethics deals with right or wrong behavior within a particular organization.   **Yes**   No

3. An ethical culture is based upon the norms and values of the company.   **Yes**   No

4. Business ethics contributes to investor loyalty.   **Yes**   No

5. The trend is away from cultural or ethically based initiatives to legal initiatives in organizations.   Yes   **No**

6. Investments in business ethics do not support the bottom line.   Yes   **No**

ANSWERS 1. **No.** Business ethics focuses on organizational concerns (legal and ethical—employees, customers, suppliers, society). 2. **Yes.** That stems from the basic definition. 3. **Yes.** Norms and values help create an organizational culture and are key in supporting or not supporting ethical conduct. 4. **Yes.** Many studies have shown that trust and ethical conduct contribute to investor loyalty. 5. **No.** Many businesses are communicating their core values to their employees by creating ethics programs and appointing ethics officers to oversee them. 6. **No.** Ethics initiatives create consumer, employee, and shareholder loyalty and positive behavior that contribute to the bottom line.

ENDNOTES

1. Guido Palazzo, Franciska Krings, and Ulrich Hoffrage, "Ethical Blindness," *Journal of Business Ethics* 109, 3 (2012): 323–338.

2. Matt Rocheleau, "64 Dartmouth College students face discipline over cheating," The *Boston Globe*, January 8, 2015, http://www.bostonglobe.com/metro/2015/01/08/dartmouth/GN8oLJcgKj7R1nOoPNiLdL/story.html (accessed January 27, 2015).

3. Sharon Terlep, "North Carolina Academic Fraud Went on for Years amid Lax Oversight, Report Finds," *The Wall Street Journal*, October 22, 2014, http://www.wsj.com/articles/report-details-academic-scandal-at-north-carolina-1413997202 (accessed January 27, 2015).

4. United v. Federal Election Commission, 558 U.S. 310 (2010), http://www.supremecourt.gov/opinions/09pdf/08-205.pdf (accessed July 27, 2015).

5. Wroe Alderson, *Dynamic Marketing Behavior* (Homewood, IL: Irwin, 1965), 320.

6. Ethisphere Institute, "2014 World's Most Ethical Companies,"*Ethisphere*, http://ethisphere.com/worlds-most-ethical/wme-honorees/ (accessed January 29, 2015).

7. Jacquelyn Smith, "The World's Most Ethical Companies," *Forbes*, March 6, 2013, http://www.forbes.com/sites/jacquelynsmith/2013/03/06/the-worlds-most-ethical-companies-in-2013/ (accessed February 5, 2015).

8. Ethics Resource Center, *National Business Ethics Survey of the U.S. Workforce* (Arlington, VA: Ethics Resource Center, 2014), 10–13.

9. Dan Fitzpatrick and Robin Sidel, "New J.P. Morgan Jam," *The Wall Street Journal*, November 16, 2012, C1–C2; Robert W. Wood, "Credit Suisse: Guilty, $2.6 Billion Fine, But Avoids Death in U.S.—UBS Was Luckier," *Forbes*, May 19, 2014, http://www.forbes.com/sites/robertwood/2014/05/19/credit-suisse-guilty-2-5-billion-fine-but-avoids-death-in-u-s-ubs-was-luckier/ (accessed January 28, 2015).

10. Edelman, 2015 *Edelman Trust Barometer*, http://www.edelman.com/insights/intellectual-property/2015-edelman-trust-barometer/trust-and-innovation-edelman-trust-barometer/global-results/ (accessed January 30, 2015).

11. Leonidas C. Leonidou, Olga Kvasova, Constantinos N. Leonidou, and Simo Chari, "Business Unethicality as an Impediment to Consumer Trust: The Moderating Role of Demographic and Cultural Characteristics," *Journal of Business Ethics* 112, 3 (2013): 397–415.

12. Carlos Tejada, "China, Alibaba Clash Publicly Over Fake Goods," *The Wall Street Journal*, January 28, 2015, http://www.wsj.com/articles/chinas-saic-criticizes-alibaba-over-fake-goods-1422425378 (accessed January 28, 2015).

13. Carmen Nobel, "Banning Big-Box Stores Can Hurt Local Retailers," *Forbes*, July 7, 2014, http://www.forbes.com/sites/hbsworkingknowledge/2014/07/07/banning-big-box-stores-can-hurt-local-retailers/ (accessed January 28, 2015).

14. Associated Press, "Ex-New Orleans Mayor Ray Nagin reports to federal prison to begin 10-year sentence," *Fox News*, September 8, 2014, http://www.foxnews.com/politics/2014/09/08/ex-new-orleans-mayor-ray-nagin-reports-to-federal-prison-to-begin-10-year/ (accessed January 28, 2015).

15. Associated Press, "Hagel orders renewed focus on military ethics amid Air Force, Navy cheating scandals," *Fox News*, February 5, 2014, http://www.foxnews.com/us/2014/02/05/hagel-orders-renewed-focus-on-military-ethics-amid-air-force-navy-cheating/ (accessed January 28, 2015); Helene Cooper, "Cheating Accusations among Officers Overseeing Nuclear Arms," *The New York Times*, January 15, 2014, http://www.nytimes.com/2014/01/16/us/politics/air-force-suspends-34-at-nuclear-sites-over-test-cheating.html?_r=0 (accessed January 28, 2015); Associated Press, "Navy kicks out 34 for cheating on nuclear training tests," *CBS News*, August 20, 2014, http://www.cbsnews.com/news/navy-kicks-out-34-for-cheating-on-nuclear-training-tests/ (accessed January 28, 2015).

16. "Roger Goodell: We Didn't See Full Ray Rice Video," *CBS* September 10, 2014, http://www.wsj.com/articles/u-k-plans-to-outlaw-branding-on-cigarette-packs-1421947530 (accessed January 28, 2015).

17. Tim De Bock, Iris Vermeir, and Patrick Van Kenhove, "'What's the Harm in Being Unethical? These Strangers are Rich Anyway!' Exploring Underlying Factors of Double Standards," *Journal of Business Ethics* 112, 2 (2013): 225–240.

18. Daniel Fisher, "Twin NLRB Rulings Are a Big Christmas Present for Labor," *Forbes*, December 12, 2014, http://www.forbes.com/sites/danielfisher/2014/12/12/nlrb-rulings-are-a-big-christmas-present-for-labor/ (accessed January 28, 2015).

19. Paul M. Barrett, "First World Dog Problems," *Bloomberg Businessweek*, July 24, 2014, pp. 52–56.

20. Frank Chapman Sharp and Philip G. Fox, *Business Ethics* (New York, NY: D. Appleton-Century Company Incorporated, 1937).

21. Archie B. Carroll and Ann K. Buchholtz, *Business and Society: Ethics and Stakeholder Management* (Cincinnati, OH: South-Western, 2006), 452–455.

22. R. Edward Freeman, *Strategic Management: A Stakeholder Approach* (Boston, MA: Pitman, 1984).

23. Alan R. Yuspeh, "Development of Corporate Compliance Programs: Lessons Learned from the DII Experience," in *Corporate Crime in America: Strengthening the "Good Citizenship" Corporation* (Washington, DC: U.S. Sentencing Commission, 1995), 71–79.

24. Eleanor Hill, "Coordinating Enforcement Under the Department of Defense Voluntary Disclosure Program," in *Corporate Crime in America: Strengthening the "Good Citizenship" Corporation* (Washington, DC: U.S. Sentencing Commission, 1995), 287–294.

25. "Huffing and Puffing in Washington: Can Clinton's Plan Curb Teen Smoking?" *Consumer Reports* 60 (1995): 637.

26. Arthur Levitt with Paula Dwyer, Take on the Street (New York: Pantheon Books, 2002).

27. Hill, "Coordinating Enforcement."

28. Richard P. Conaboy, "Corporate Crime in America: Strengthening the Good Citizen Corporation," in *Corporate Crime in America: Strengthening the "Good Citizenship" Corporation* (Washington, DC: U.S. Sentencing Commission, 1995), 1–2.

29. United States Code Service (Lawyers' Edition), 18 U.S.C.S. Appendix, Sentencing Guidelines for the United States

Courts (Rochester, NY: Lawyers Cooperative Publishing, 1995), sec. 8A.1.

30. "Enron on Trial," *CNN/Money*, http://money.cnn. com/news/specials/corruption/ (accessed February 3, 2015); "SEC Formalizes Investigation into Halliburton Accounting," *The Wall Street Journal online*, December 20, 2002, http://www.wsj.com/articles/ SB1040396377531531753 (accessed February 3, 2015); Jake Ulick, "WorldCom CEO Slaps Arthur Andersen," CNN, July 8, 2002, http://edition.cnn.com/2002/ BUSINESS/asia/07/08/us.worldcom.index.html?related (accessed February 3, 2015).

31. "Corporate Reform Bill OK'd," *CNN*, July 26, 2002, http:// money.cnn.com/2002/07/26/news/corporate_congress/ (accessed February 3, 2015).

32. William Pride and O.C. Ferrell, *Marketing*, 16e (Mason, OH: South-Western Cengage Learning), p. 147.

33. Muel Kaptein, "From Inaction to External Whistleblowering: The Influence of the Ethical Culture of Organizations on Employee Responses to Observed Wrongdoing," *Journal of Business Ethics* 98, 3 (2011): 513–530.

34. Jamie-Lee Campbell and Anja S. Göritz, "Culture Corrupts! A Qualitative Study of Organizational Culture in Corrupt Organizations," *Journal of Business Ethics* 120, 3 (2014), 291-311.

35. Emily Glazer and Christina Rexrode, "As Regulators Focus on Culture, Wall Street Struggles to Define It," *The Wall Street Journal*, February 2, 2015, A1, A8.

36. PPT presentation presented at 2014 ECOA conference in Atlanta, presented by Martin Tolar, GRC Institute, entitled "The First ISO Standard in E&C: What You Need to Know," Presented October 2, 2014; Dick Hortensius, "What Is the General Idea Behind the Proposed ISO 19600?" *Ethics Intelligence*, April 2014, http://www.ethic-intelligence.com/experts/4636-general-idea-behind-iso-19600/ (accessed October 14, 2014).

37. United Nations, "Global Compact: Corporate Citizenship in the World Economy," http://www.unglobalcompact. org/docs/news_events/8.1/GC_brochure_FINAL.pdf (accessed February 15, 2011).

38. Information taken from "NiSource and Columbia Gas of Kentucky Maintain a Values-Based Ethics Program," *UNM Daniels Fund Ethics Initiative*, http://danielsethics. mgt.unm.edu/pdf/columbia-gas.pdf (accessed January 28, 2015).

39. Bernard J. Jaworski and Ajay K. Kohli, "Market Orientation: Antecedents and Consequences," *Journal of Marketing* 57, 3 (1993): 53–70.

40. "Best Companies to Work For 2014: Burns & McDonnell," *Fortune*, http://fortune.com/best-companies/burns-mcdonnell-14/ (accessed January 28, 2015).

41. Terry W. Loe, "The Role of Ethical Culture in Developing Trust, Market Orientation and Commitment to Quality" (PhD diss., University of Memphis, 1996).

42. Sean Valentine, Lynn Godkin, Gary M. Fleischman, and Rolan Kidwell, "Corporate Ethical Values, Group Creativity, Job Satisfaction and Turnover Intention: The Impact of Work Context on Work Response," *Journal of Business Ethics* 98, 3 (2011): 353–572.

43. Ethics Resource Center, 2000 National Business Ethics Survey, 5.

44. John Galvin, "The New Business Ethics," SmartBusinessMag.com, June 2000, 99.

45. Tom Petruno, "Beyond profits: Millennials embrace investing for social good," *Los Angeles Times*, December 7, 2014, http://www.latimes.com/business/la-fi-socially-conscious-investing-20141207-story.html#page=1 (accessed January 28, 2015).

46. Leonidas C. Leonidou, Olga Kvasova, Constantinos N. Leonidou, and Simo Chari, "Business Unethicality as an Impediment to Consumer Trust: The Moderating Role of Demographic and Cultural Characteristics," *Journal of Business Ethics* 112, 3 (2013): 397–415.

47. "World's Most Admired Companies 2014: Southwest Airlines," *Fortune*, http://fortune.com/worlds-most-admired-companies-9/ (accessed January 28, 2015); Lewis Lazare, "Southwest Airlines sends a letter of love and astounding admissions to its frequent travelers," *Chicago Business Journal*, October 15, 2014, http://www.bizjournals.com/chicago/ news/2014/10/15/southwest-airlines-sends-a-letter-of-love-and.html?page=all (accessed January 28, 2015).

48. Jatinder J. Singh, Oriol Iglesias, and Joan Manel Batista-Foguet, "Does Having an Ethical Brand Matter? The Influence of Consumer Perceived Ethicality on Trust, Affect and Loyalty," *Journal of Business Ethics* 111, 4 (2012): 541–549.

49. Nielsen, "Doing Well by Doing Good," *Nielsen Wire*, June 17, 2014, http://www.nielsen.com/us/en/insights/ reports/2014/doing-well-by-doing-good.html (accessed January 29, 2015).

50. Marjorie Kelly, "Holy Grail Found. Absolute, Definitive Proof that Responsible Companies Perform Better Financially," *Business Ethics*, Winter 2004.

51. Adobe Systems, "Adobe Corporate Responsibility," 2015, http://www.adobe.com/corporate-responsibility.html (accessed January 29, 2015).

52. O. C. Ferrell, Isabelle Maignan, and Terry W. Loe, "The Relationship between Corporate Citizenship and Competitive Advantage," in *Rights, Relationships, and Responsibilities*, ed. O. C. Ferrell, Lou Pelton, and Sheb L. True (Kennesaw, GA: Kennesaw State University, 2003).

53. Jeanne Liedtka and Andrew King, "Use 'design thinking' to reach customers," *Washington Post*, May 4, 2014, http://www.washingtonpost.com/business/ capitalbusiness/use-design-thinking-to-reach-customers/2014/05/02/6e7a99c0-d05c-11e3-937f-d3026234b51c_story.html (accessed January 29, 2015).

54. Isabelle Girerd-Potin, Sonia Jimenez-Garcés, and Pascal Louvet, "Which Dimensions of Social Responsibility Concern Financial Investors?" *Journal of Business Ethics* 121, 4 (2014), 559–576.

55. Galvin, "The New Business Ethics."

56. Ethisphere Institute, "2015 World's Most Ethical Companies® Recognition Program Opens September 15," *Ethisphere*, August 27, 2014, http://ethisphere.com/2015-worlds-most-ethical-companies-recognition-program-opens-september-15/ (accessed January 29, 2015).

CHAPTER 2

STAKEHOLDER RELATIONSHIPS, SOCIAL RESPONSIBILITY, AND CORPORATE GOVERNANCE

CHAPTER OBJECTIVES

- Identify stakeholders' roles in business ethics
- Define social responsibility
- Examine the relationship between stakeholder orientation and social responsibility
- Delineate a stakeholder orientation in creating corporate social responsibility
- Explore the role of corporate governance in structuring ethics and social responsibility in business
- List the steps involved in implementing a stakeholder perspective in social responsibility and business ethics

CHAPTER OUTLINE

AN ETHICAL DILEMMA*

After Megan Jones finished her BS degree in Management at The University of Rhode Island, she landed a great job with the "app" developing company Global App Creations (GAC). In her six months of training in Human Resources (HR) she faced challenges, but enjoyed working with people and solving their problems.

On Monday morning Megan's boss, Debbie, placed a 20-inch-thick personnel folder on her desk. "Megan, I want you to review these files and by Friday start the process of finding possible ethics violations. Some employees know this is coming, while others don't have a clue. It's your job to write them up for ethics violations and suggest whether you think some of them should go to legal as well. I will add my write-up to each one so you won't be the only one making the decisions. For now, I'll make the primary decisions, but sooner or later you'll be in charge of these tasks. If you have any questions, just stop by and we can talk."

That afternoon Megan began going through the files. Some were straightforward involving theft of office supplies, inappropriate remarks, and tardiness. GAC's code was straightforward on such matters. Yet other events appeared confusing. One salesperson was getting an official reprimand for using a company car for personal activities. This didn't make sense because all the salespeople drove company cars they took home after work. According to the file, the person visited a hospital ten miles away every evening for the past month. Megan realized every GAC car was equipped with a GPS device. While she didn't think it was illegal for companies to install tracking devices on items they owned, she heard having information about health or religion could become the basis of a lawsuit if the person's employment was terminated.

The most shocking file Megan reviewed was that of another employee being fired for sharing confidential information with a competitor. The file contained reports on computer activity, cell phone usage, GPS tracking, and included audio and video of personal conversations, dinners, and hotel rooms. On Tuesday Megan went to Jeremy, who worked for the company for several years, and asked him if he knew of employee tracking at the company.

Jeremy responded, "Well, I have heard rumors that managers want to keep track of employees and monitor whether they share confidential information with competitors. I've also heard they monitor where each

employee goes through the GPS located in the company car."

Megan felt uneasy. "Jeremy, is what they are doing legal? Can they track and monitor our every move and conversation?"

Jeremy shrugged. "As far as I know it's legal, but I've never looked into the actual laws. I don't know why a company should track my personal time outside the office. But what are we supposed to do about it? We all need a job, and each one comes with a price."

On Thursday Megan met with Debbie and expressed her concerns about the information GAC collects through the employee tracking activities. After she finished, Debbie responded. "Don't be so naïve, Megan. You know as well as I do what employees do outside of work could legally hurt the company. It's also necessary to make sure employees aren't sharing confidential information with rivals. This is a competitive industry."

"But what about this employee using the company car to visit his daughter in the hospital? It was outside work hours and I heard his daughter is sick. What about an individual's right to privacy concerning medical records?"

Debbie brushed her concerns aside. "We don't have access to anybody's medical records. We got this from the GPS device in the company-owned car issued to him. We can't make exceptions for these types of things. Our reputation for ethics is excellent."

Then Debbie said, "I hope you haven't spoken to anyone about these cases because that violates confidentiality. Your job is to review the files and suggest appropriate action. All files and communications about the files are confidential."

QUESTIONS | EXERCISES

1. If tracking employees through technology is not illegal, why should Megan be concerned if she is not involved in any misconduct?
2. At this point, what are Megan's alternatives to resolve her current dilemma about her involvement and knowledge about GAC's tracking of employees?
3. Who should have a stake or an interest in how GAC tracks and monitors its employees?

*This case is strictly hypothetical; any resemblance to real persons, companies, or situations is coincidental.

Business ethics issues, conflicts, and successes revolve around relationships. Building effective relationships is considered one of the most important areas of business today. Many companies consider business ethics a team sport where each member performs and supports others. A business exists because of relationships between employees, customers, shareholders or investors, suppliers, managers, and the community who develop strategies to attain success. In addition, an organization usually has a governing authority, often called a board of directors that provides oversight and direction to assure the organization stays focused on its objectives in an ethical, legal, and socially responsible manner. When unethical acts are discovered in organizations, in most instances cooperation or complicity facilitated the acceptance and perpetuation of the unethical conduct.[1] Few decisions are made by one individual. Therefore, relationships are associated with organizational success and also organizational misconduct.

A stakeholder framework identifies the internal stakeholders (employees, boards of directors, and managers), and the external stakeholders (customers, special interest groups, regulators, and others) who agree, collaborate, and engage in confrontations on ethical issues. Most ethical issues exist because of conflicts in values and belief patterns about right and wrong among and within stakeholder groups. This framework allows an organization to identify, monitor, and respond to the needs, values, and expectations of different stakeholder groups.

The formal system of accountability and control of ethical and socially responsible behavior is corporate governance. In theory, the board of directors provides oversight for all decisions and use of resources. Ethical issues relate to the role of the board of directors, relationships with shareholders, internal control, risk management, and executive compensation. Ethical leadership is associated with appropriate corporate governance.

In this chapter, we first focus on the concept of stakeholders and examine how a stakeholder framework helps us understand organizational ethics. Then we identify stakeholders and the importance of a stakeholder orientation. Using the stakeholder framework, we explore the concept and dimensions of social responsibility. Next, we examine corporate governance as a dimension of social responsibility and ethical decision making to provide an understanding of the importance of stakeholder oversight. Finally, we provide the steps for implementing a stakeholder perspective on social responsibility and ethical decisions in business.

STAKEHOLDERS DEFINE ETHICAL ISSUES IN BUSINESS

In a business context, customers, shareholders, employees, suppliers, government agencies, communities, and many others who have a "stake" or claim in some aspect of a company's products, operations, markets, industry, and outcomes are known as **stakeholders**. Businesses engage and influence these groups, but these groups also have the ability to engage and influence businesses; thus, the relationship between companies and their stakeholders is a two-way street.[2] Sometimes activities and negative press generated by special interest groups force a company to change its practices. For example, consumer groups have put pressure on government and business for more stringent rules regulating e-cigarette advertising on television. In a two-year period, adolescent exposure to e-cigarette television advertising rose 256 percent. Groups such as the Campaign for Tobacco-Free Kids point out the need for greater regulation to reduce exposure. E-cigarette manufacturers claim they are acting to limit when and where they advertise on television so minors are not targeted.[3] This provides an example of how consumer groups in the community can engage businesses through regulators and firms.

There are three approaches to stakeholder theory: normative, descriptive, and instrumental approaches.[4] The normative approach identifies ethical guidelines that dictate how firms should treat stakeholders. Normative stakeholder theory affirms that stakeholders have legitimacy and a right to engage organizations. Principles and values provide direction for normative decisions. The descriptive approach focuses on the actual behavior of the firm and usually addresses how decisions and strategies are made for stakeholder relationships. The instrumental approach to stakeholder theory describes what happens if firms behave in a particular way.[5] This approach is useful because it examines relationships involved in the management of stakeholders including the processes, structures, and practices that implement stakeholder relationships within an organization. The survival and performance of any organization is a function of its ability to create value for all primary stakeholders and its attempt to do this by not favoring one group over the others.[6]

Many firms experience conflicts with key stakeholders and consequently damage their reputations and shareholder confidence. While many threats to reputations stem from uncontrollable events such as economic conditions, ethical misconduct is more difficult to overcome than poor financial performance. Stakeholders most directly affected by negative events experience a corresponding shift in their perceptions of a firm's reputation. On the other hand, firms sometimes receive negative publicity for misconduct that destroys trust and tarnishes their reputations, making it more difficult to retain existing customers and attract new ones.[7] To maintain the trust and confidence of its stakeholders, CEOs and other top managers are expected to act in a transparent and responsible manner. Executives who are involved in misconduct create negative perceptions of their companies. Dov Charney, founder and former CEO of American Apparel, was fired for allegedly misusing funds and violating sexual harassment policies.[8] Providing untruthful or deceptive information to stakeholders is, if not illegal, certainly unethical, and can result in a loss of trust.

Ethical misconduct and decisions that damage stakeholders generally impact the company's reputation in terms of both investor and consumer confidence. As investor perceptions and decisions begin to take their toll, shareholder value drops, exposing the company to consumer scrutiny that can increase the damage. According to a recent Edelman Trust Survey, three industries in terms of the lowest level of trust were the media, banks, and financial services; the most trusted industries were technology, consumer electronics, and automotive.[9] Reputation is a factor in consumers' perceptions of product attributes and corporate image and can lead to consumer willingness to purchase goods and services at profitable prices. Perceived wrongdoing or questionable behavior may lead to boycotts and aggressive campaigns to dampen sales and earnings. A petition placed on the website Change.org demanding that Old Navy stop charging more for plus-sized women's clothing garnered more than 16,000 signatures. Consumers became angry when they learned that plus-sized clothing for women was more expensive than smaller sizes and plus-sized men's clothing. They felt that it was discriminatory to charge more for plus-sized women's clothing than plus-sized men's clothing since they both use more fabric. Old Navy defended its practice by claiming that plus-sized women's clothing costs more due to curve-enhancing and other features that men's clothing does not have. Even if its claims are legitimate, the perceived discrepancy caused a public relations snafu for Old Navy.[10] This example illustrates how stakeholders can be subject to the risks and costs resulting from business decisions that are not regulated. The more democratic involvement of various stakeholders is one solution to resolve legitimacy deficits.[11]

New reforms intended to improve corporate accountability and transparency suggest that stakeholders, including regulatory agencies, local communities, attorneys, and public accounting firms play a major role in fostering responsible decision making.[12] Stakeholders apply their values and standards to diverse issues, including working conditions, consumer rights, environmental conservation, product safety, and proper information disclosure that may or may not directly affect an individual stakeholder's own welfare. We can assess the level of social responsibility an organization bears by scrutinizing its effects on the issues of concern to its stakeholders.[13]

Stakeholders provide resources critical to a firm's long-term success. These resources may be tangible and intangible. Shareholders, for example, supply capital; suppliers offer material resources or intangible knowledge; employees and managers grant expertise, leadership, and commitment; customers generate revenue and provide loyalty with word-of-mouth promotion; local communities provide infrastructure; and the media transmits positive corporate images. In a spirit of reciprocity, stakeholders should be fair, loyal, and treat the corporation in a responsible way.[14] When individual stakeholders share expectations about desirable business conduct, they may choose to establish or join formal communities dedicated to defining and advocating these values and expectations. Stakeholders' abilities to withdraw these needed resources gives them power over businesses.[15] For instance, in the United Kingdom, the government announced plans to outlaw branding on cigarette packaging. Although cigarette companies have threatened legal action, successful passage of the law would significantly change how cigarette manufacturers do business in the U.K.[16]

Identifying Stakeholders

We can identify two types of stakeholders. **Primary stakeholders** are those whose continued association and resources are absolutely necessary for a firm's survival. These include employees, customers, and shareholders, as well as the governments and communities that provide necessary infrastructure. Figure 2–1 indicates that strong ethical corporate cultures are on the rise. Ethical corporate cultures are important because they are linked to positive relationships with stakeholders. By the same token, concern for stakeholders' needs and expectations is necessary to avoid ethical conflicts.

Secondary stakeholders do not typically engage directly in transactions with a company and are therefore not essential to its survival. These include the media, trade associations, and special interest groups like the American Association of Retired People (AARP), a special interest group working to support retirees' rights such as health care benefits. Both primary and secondary stakeholders embrace specific values and standards that dictate acceptable and unacceptable corporate behaviors. It is important for managers to recognize that while primary groups may present more day-to-day concerns, secondary groups cannot be ignored or given less consideration in the ethical decision-making process because they have legitimacy.[17] Sometimes a secondary stakeholder can have as much—if not more—power to influence outcomes than a primary stakeholder. Table 2–1 shows a select list of issues important to various stakeholder groups and identifies how corporations impact these issues.

Figure 2–2 offers a conceptualization of the relationship between businesses and stakeholders. In this **stakeholder interaction model**, there are reciprocal relationships between the firm and a host of stakeholders. In addition to the fundamental input of investors, employees, and suppliers, this approach recognizes other stakeholders and explicitly acknowledges that dialogue exists between a firm's internal and external environments. Corporate social responsibility actions that put employees at the center of activities gain the support of both external and internal stakeholders.[18]

Primary Stakeholder

Second. Stakeholder

FIGURE 2–1 Two in Three Companies Now Have Positive Ethics Cultures

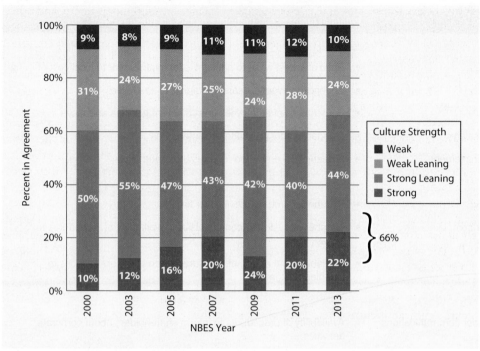

Note: Due to rounding, some numbers do not equal 100 percent.

Source: Ethics Resource Center, *National Business Ethics Survey of the U.S. Workforce* (Arlington, VI: Ethics Resource Center, 2014), p. 17.

A Stakeholder Orientation

The degree to which a firm understands and addresses stakeholder demands can be referred to as a **stakeholder orientation**. A stakeholder orientation involves "activities and processes within a system of social institutions that facilitate and maintain value through exchange relationships with multiple stakeholders."[19] This orientation comprises three sets of activities: (1) the organization-wide generation of data about stakeholder groups and assessment of the firm's effects on these groups; (2) the distribution of this information throughout the firm; and (3) the responsiveness of the organization as a whole to this information.[20]

Generating data about stakeholders begins with identifying the stakeholders relevant to the firm. Relevant stakeholder groups should be analyzed on the basis of the power each enjoys, as well as by the ties between them and the company. Next, the firm should identify the concerns about the business's that are relevant to each stakeholder group. This information is derived from formal research, including surveys, focus groups, Internet searches, and press reviews. For example, Shell has an online discussion forum that invites website visitors to express their opinions on the implications of the company's activities. Employees and managers also generate this information informally as they carry out their daily activities. For example, purchasing managers know about suppliers' demands, public relations executives are tuned into the media, legal counselors are aware of the regulatory environment, financial executives connect to investors, sales representatives are in touch with customers, and human resources advisers communicate directly with employees.

TABLE 2-1 Examples of Stakeholder Issues and Associated Measures of Corporate Impacts

Stakeholder Groups and Issues	Potential Indicators of Corporate Impact on These Issues
Employees	
1. Compensation and benefits	• Ratio of lowest wage to national legal minimum or to local cost of living
2. Training and development	• Changes in average years of training of employees
3. Employee diversity	• Percentages of employees from different genders and races
4. Occupational health and safety	• Standard injury rates and absentee rates
5. Communications with management	• Availability of open-door policies or ombudsmen
Customers	
1. Product safety and quality	• Number of product recalls over time
2. Management of customer complaints	• Number of customer complaints and availability of procedures to answer them
3. Services to disabled customers	• Availability and nature of measures taken to ensure services to disabled customers
Investors	
1. Transparency of shareholder communications	• Availability of procedures to inform shareholders about corporate activities
2. Shareholder rights	• Frequency and type of litigation involving violations of shareholder rights
Suppliers	
1. Encouraging suppliers in developing countries	• Prices offered to suppliers in developed countries in comparison to countries' other suppliers
2. Encouraging minority suppliers	• Percentage of minority suppliers
Community	
1. Public health and safety protection	• Availability of emergency response plan
2. Conservation of energy and materials	• Data on reduction of waste produced and comparison to industry
3. Donations and support of local organizations	• Annual employee time spent in community service
Environmental Groups	
1. Minimizing the use of energy	• Amount of electricity purchased; percentage of "green" electricity
2. Minimizing emissions and waste	• Type, amount, and designation of waste generated
3. Minimizing adverse environmental effects of goods and services	• Percentage of product weight reclaimed after use

© Cengage Learning

Finally, companies should evaluate their impact on the issues of importance to the various stakeholders they identify.[21] While shareholders desire strong profitability and growth, societal stakeholders have needs extending beyond these two requirements.[22]

FIGURE 2–2 **Interactions between a Company and Its Primary and Secondary Stakeholders**

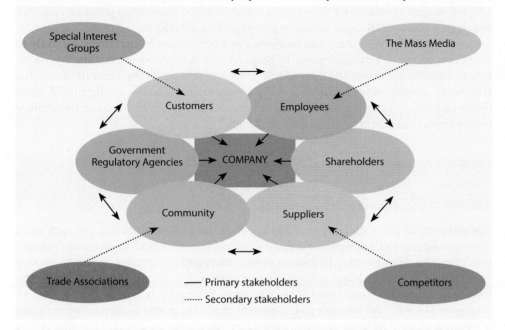

Source: Adapted from Isabelle Maignan, O. C. Ferrell, and Linda Ferrell, "A Stakeholder Model for Implementing Social Responsibility in Marketing."
European Journal of Marketing 39 (2005): 956–977.

Given the variety of employees involved in the generation of information about stakeholders, it is essential the information gathered be circulated throughout the firm. The firm must facilitate the communication of information about the nature of relevant stakeholder communities, concerns, and impact of the firm on these issues to all members of the organization. The dissemination of stakeholder intelligence can be formally organized through newsletters and internal information forums.[23] Companies should use these activities to communicate the company's code of conduct to employees. Such communication informs employees about appropriate and inappropriate conduct within the organization. Research suggests employees in organizations with ethical codes of conduct are less accepting of potential misconduct toward stakeholders.[24] Ethical codes are of little use if they are not effectively communicated throughout the firm.

A stakeholder orientation is not complete without including activities that address stakeholder issues. For example, manufacturers in some countries have been under attack for product quality issues and safety violations. Nonprofit groups attacked Apple for alleged abuse by one of its suppliers. According to the groups, workers at a Chinese factory run by Taiwan-based Catcher Technology Co. handled toxic chemicals without protective gear. The factory was also accused of dumping toxic chemicals into a sewer that leads into a river. As the most powerful member of the supply chain, Apple is expected to promote safety and workers' rights throughout its distribution network.[25]

The responsiveness of an organization as a whole to stakeholder intelligence consists of the initiatives the firm adopts to ensure it abides by or exceeds stakeholder expectations and has a positive impact on stakeholder issues. Such activities are likely specific to a particular stakeholder group (for example, family friendly work schedules) or to a particular stakeholder issue (such as pollution reduction programs). These responsive processes typically involve participation of the concerned stakeholder groups. Nestlé, for example, adopted tougher standards for their suppliers that included eliminating gestation crates for female pigs after animal rights advocacy groups pushed for reform.[26]

A stakeholder orientation can be viewed as a continuum in that firms are likely to adopt the concept to varying degrees. To gauge a firm's stakeholder orientation, it is necessary to evaluate the extent the firm adopts behaviors that typify the generation and dissemination of stakeholder intelligence and the responsiveness to this intelligence. A given organization may generate and disseminate more intelligence about some stakeholder communities than others and respond accordingly.[27]

SOCIAL RESPONSIBILITY AND BUSINESS ETHICS

The terms *ethics* and *social responsibility* are often used interchangeably, but each has a distinct meaning. In Chapter 1, we defined *social responsibility* as an organization's obligation to maximize its positive impact on stakeholders and minimize its negative impact. For example, Starbucks began selling reusable cups and installing recycling areas at the front of its company-owned stores.[28] The Container Store pays its average retail worker an average of $48,000.[29] SC Johnson gives 5 percent of pre-tax profits to corporate giving and is investing in wind turbines to power some of its manufacturing plants.[30] Conversely, one study found that a firm's sales margin will be damaged by the unethical treatment of stakeholders.[31] Many other businesses have tried to determine what relationships, obligations, and duties are appropriate between their organizations and various stakeholders. Social responsibility can be viewed as a contract with society, whereas business ethics involves carefully thought-out rules or heuristics of business conduct that guide decision making.

There are four levels of social responsibility—economic, legal, ethical, and philanthropic (see Figure 2–3).[32] At the most basic level, companies have a responsibility to be profitable at an acceptable level to meet the objectives of shareholders and create value. Of course, businesses are expected to obey all relevant laws and regulations. For example, the European Union passed a law giving EU Internet users the "right to be forgotten." This means that

FIGURE 2–3 Steps of Social Responsibility

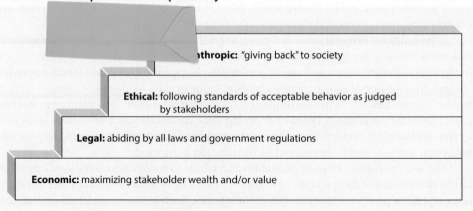

Source: Adapted from Archie B. Carroll, "The Pyramid of Corporate Social Responsibility: Toward the Moral Management of Organizational Stakeholders," *Business Horizons* (July–August 1991): 42, Fig. 3.

consumers have the right to request Google to delete content they no longer want recorded from search results. Individual countries in the European Union have the freedom to enforce this ruling as they see fit. An EU panel believes this ruling should apply to all countries, not just those limited to the European Union. A worldwide enforcement of this law would require Google to make extensive changes to how it manages customer information.[33]

Business ethics, as previously defined, comprises principles and values that meet the expectations of stakeholders. Philanthropic responsibility refers to activities that are not required of businesses but that contribute to human welfare or goodwill. Ethics, then, is one dimension of social responsibility. Ethical decisions by individuals and groups drive appropriate decisions and are interrelated with all of the levels of social responsibility. For example, the economic level can have ethical consequences when making managerial decisions.

The term **corporate citizenship** is often used to express the extent to which businesses strategically meet the economic, legal, ethical, and philanthropic responsibilities placed on them by various stakeholders.[34] Corporate citizenship has four interrelated dimensions: strong sustained economic performance, rigorous compliance, ethical actions beyond what the law requires, and voluntary contributions that advance the reputation and stakeholder commitment of the organization. A firm's commitment to corporate citizenship indicates a strategic focus on fulfilling the social responsibilities its stakeholders expect. Corporate citizenship involves acting on the firm's commitment to corporate citizenship philosophy and measuring the extent to which it follows through by actually implementing citizenship initiatives. Table 2–2 lists some of the world's most ethical companies, all of which have demonstrated their commitment to stakeholders. As Chapter 1 demonstrated, many of these companies have superior financial performance compared to the indexes of other publicly traded firms.

Reputation is one of an organization's greatest intangible assets with tangible value. The value of a positive reputation is difficult to quantify, but it is important. A single negative

TABLE 2–2 A Selection of the World's Most Ethical Companies

3M Company	Allstate Insurance Company
Xerox	Cisco
Dell	Colgate-Palmolive
Deere & Co.	Microsoft Corporation
Google	Henry Schein, Inc.
General Electric	Johnson Controls
The Hershey Company	Weyerhaeuser Company
International Paper Company	Visa Inc.
Aflac	Marriott
Petco	Hitachi Data Systems
Kellogg Company	Levi Strauss & Co.
Starbucks	UPS
Thomson Reuters	Waste Management

Source: Ethisphere Institute, "2015 World's Most Ethical Companies," *Ethisphere*, http://ethisphere.com/worlds-most-ethical/wme-honorees/ (accessed July 17, 2015).

incident can influence perceptions of a corporation's image and reputation instantly and for years afterward. Corporate reputation, image, and brands are more important than ever and are among the most critical aspects of sustaining relationships with constituents including investors, customers, employees, media, and regulators. Although an organization does not control its reputation in a direct sense, its actions, choices, behaviors, and consequences influence stakeholders' perceptions of it. For instance, employees are likely to perceive their firm's corporate social responsibility initiatives as authentic if the program appears to fit with the company's true identity and if they take a leadership role in these initiatives. Employees who feel their firms' corporate social responsibility programs are authentic are more likely to identify and connect with the organization.[35] Even lower-level, frontline, and service contact employees identify and move with an organization if they perceive that management and the firm's customers support social responsibility programs. This means social responsibility initiatives can create observable changes in employee behavior.[36]

ISSUES IN SOCIAL RESPONSIBILITY

Social responsibility rests on a stakeholder orientation. The realities of global warming, obesity, consumer protection, and other issues are causing companies to look at a broader, more inclusive stakeholder orientation. In other words, a broader view of social responsibility looks beyond pragmatic and firm-centric interests and considers the long-term welfare of society. Each stakeholder is given due consideration. There needs to be a movement away from self-serving "co-optation" and a narrow focus on profit maximization.[37] In fact, there is strong evidence that an overemphasis on profit maximization is counter-productive. Long-term relationships with stakeholders develop trust, loyalty, and the performance necessary to maintain profitability. Issues generally associated with social responsibility can be separated into four general categories: social issues, consumer protection, sustainability, and corporate governance.

Social issues are associated with the common good. The common good is the idea that because people live in a community, social rules should benefit the community. This supports the premise that all people have the right to try and obtain the basic necessities of life.[38] In other words, social issues deal with concerns affecting large segments of society and the welfare of the entire society. In terms of social responsibility, managers address social issues by examining the different groups to which they have an obligation. Managers failing to meet these social obligations can create criticism and negative publicity for their organizations.

Social issues may encompass events such as jobs lost through outsourcing, health issues, gun rights, and poverty. While these issues may be indirectly related to business, there is a need to reflect on them in developing strategies in certain cases. Issues that directly relate to business include obesity, smoking, and exploiting vulnerable or impoverished populations, as well as a number of other issues. For example, marketers are increasingly targeting food advertising to children through Internet websites. One study found approximately 85 percent of food brands have websites with content targeted toward children.[39] With the childhood obesity epidemic increasing, marketers of foods perceived to be unhealthy are being pressured to change their strategies to account for this growing concern. In addition, some economic issues have ramifications to society such as antitrust, employee well-being, insider trading, and other issues that diminish competition and consumer choice.

A major social issue gaining prominence involves loss of privacy for marketing purposes. Many consumers are shocked when they realize marketers are using cookies and other mechanisms to track their online activity. Internet privacy may soon become a consumer protection issue because the government is considering passing legislation limiting the types of tracking companies can perform over the Internet without users' permission. On the other hand, companies that develop signals on their websites reassuring consumers their information will be kept private are more likely to establish trust with consumers, which could help to build mutually beneficial online relationships.[40]

The second major issue is consumer protection, which often occurs in the form of laws passed to protect consumers from unfair and deceptive business practices. Issues involving consumer protection usually have an immediate impact on the consumer after a purchase. Major areas of concern include advertising, disclosure, financial practices, and product safety. Because consumers are less knowledgeable about certain products or business practices, it is the responsibility of companies to take precautions to prevent consumers from being harmed by their products. For instance, businesses marketing products that could potentially be harmful have the responsibility to put warning labels on their products. The Federal Trade Commission and the Consumer Financial Protection Bureau are intent on enforcing consumer protection laws and pursuing violations.

Deceptive advertising has been a hot topic in the consumer protection area. For instance, covert marketing occurs when companies use promotional tools to make consumers believe the promotion is coming from an independent third party rather than from the company.[41] Often companies are forced to disclose to consumers if they are paying another entity to promote their products. However, as with many business ethics issues, some advertising practices skirt the line between ethical and questionable behavior. For instance, some believe promotions embedded into television programs without informing consumers are a type of covert marketing that warrants greater consumer protection.[42] Native advertising has become another issue. Native advertising blends digital advertisements or company promotions with content on the website where it is featured. The promotion has the look and feel of the content. Critics claim that native advertising might confuse consumers if they cannot tell the difference between an advertisement and legitimate content.[43] Companies must be knowledgeable about consumer protection laws and recognize whether their practices could be construed as deceptive or unfair.

The third major issue is sustainability. We define sustainability as the potential for the long-term well-being of the natural environment, including all biological entities, as well as the mutually beneficial interactions among nature and individuals, organizations, and business strategies. With major environmental challenges such as global warming and the passage of new environmental legislation, businesses can no longer afford to ignore the natural environment as a stakeholder. Companies with an effective environmental management system certified by ISO 14001—an international environmental management standard—tend to have improved financial performance in the long run.[44] Even industries traditionally considered high in pollution, such as the oil and gas industry, are investing in sustainable practices like alternative energy. Because sustainability is a major ethical issue, we cover this topic in more detail in Chapter 12.

Corporate governance is the fourth major issue of corporate social responsibility. **Corporate governance** involves the development of formal systems of accountability, oversight, and control. Strong corporate governance mechanisms remove the opportunity for employees to make unethical decisions. Research has shown that corporate governance has a positive relationship with social responsibility. For instance, one study revealed a positive correlation with corporate governance and corporate social responsibility engagement.[45] Additionally, firms with strong corporate governance mechanisms that prompt them to disclose their social responsibility initiatives can establish legitimacy and trust among their stakeholders.[46] We discuss corporate governance in more detail later in this chapter.

SOCIAL RESPONSIBILITY AND THE IMPORTANCE OF A STAKEHOLDER ORIENTATION

DEBATE ISSUE
TAKE A STAND

Is It Acceptable to Promote a Socially Irresponsible but Legal Product to Stakeholders?

When you think of cheating, you may think of irresponsible behavior in the classroom. But Noel Biderman created a company called Avid Life Media (based in Toronto) that is dedicated to another form of cheating.

Avid Life Media is owner of several different love-connection brands, including Cougar Life and its most controversial brand, Ashley Madison. With the motto "Life is Short. Have an Affair," the website has had more than 31 million users over its lifetime. The company encourages married men and women to spend less than a minute to register on the largest website to openly promote infidelity. The company employs hundreds of programmers, designers, and marketers and has conducted a private placement for investors. While many stakeholders would say the purpose of the website is wrong, there is nothing illegal about this business. But the fact that the website helps people engage in cheating on their spouses—including providing an e-mail address to which one's spouse would never have access—has many people concerned. They consider facilitating secrecy for socially questionable conduct to be wrong. In response to these concerns, the site was hacked and a threat was made to reveal the real names of the members of Ashley Madison if the site was not shut down.[52]

1. There is nothing wrong in providing a legal service many people desire, and those that hack the site to close it down should be punished.

2. From a stakeholder perspective, it is wrong to provide socially irresponsible services, and those who hacked the site to have it shut down were providing a public service.

Many business people and scholars question the role of ethics and social responsibility in business. Legal and economic responsibilities are generally accepted as the most important determinants of performance. "If this is well done," say classical economic theorists, "profits are maximized more or less continuously and firms carry out their major responsibilities to society."[47] Some economists believe if companies address economic and legal issues they satisfy the demands of society, and trying to anticipate and meet additional needs would be almost impossible. Milton Friedman has been quoted as saying "the basic mission of business [is] … to produce goods and services at a profit, and in doing this, business [is] making its maximum contribution to society and, in fact, being socially responsible."[48] Even with the business ethics scandals of the twenty-first century, Friedman suggests that although those individuals guilty of wrongdoing should be held accountable, the market is a better deterrent to wrongdoing than new laws and regulations.[49] Thus, Friedman would diminish the role of stakeholders such as the government and employees in requiring businesses to demonstrate responsible and ethical behavior. Friedman's capitalism is a far cry from Adam Smith, one of the founders of capitalism. Smith developed the concept of the invisible hand and explored the role of self-interest in economic systems; however, he went on to explain that the "common good is associated with six psychological motives and that each individual has to produce for the common good, with values such as Propriety, Prudence, Reason, Sentiment and promoting the happiness of mankind."[50] These values correlate with the needs and concerns of stakeholders. Smith established normative expectations for motives and behaviors in his theories about the invisible hand. For instance, he distinguished justice as consisting of perfect or inalienable rights, such as the right to property, from beneficence, consisting of imperfect rights that *should* be performed but cannot be forced. A stakeholder orientation perspective would advocate managers take into account both the perfect and imperfect rights of stakeholders. Yet when tradeoffs are necessary, justice should be given priority over beneficence.[51]

Evidence suggests caring about the well-being of stakeholders leads to increased profits. One study found when firms were placed on a socially responsible index, stakeholders reacted positively.[53] Other studies also associate

TABLE 2–3 CR's Best Corporate Citizens

1. Microsoft Corporation

2. Hasbro

3. Johnson & Johnson

4. Xerox Corp.

5. Sigma-Aldrich Corp.

6. Bristol-Myers Squibb

7. Intel Corp.

8. Campbell Soup Co.

9. Ecolab, Inc.

10. Lockheed Martin Corp.

Source: *CR's 100 Best Corporate Citizens 2015,* http://www.thecro.com/files/100%20Best%20List%202015.pdf (accessed July 17, 2015).

a stakeholder orientation with increased profits.[54] Therefore, although the purpose of a stakeholder orientation is to maximize positive outcomes that meet stakeholder needs,[55] the support stakeholders have for companies they perceive to be socially responsible also serve to enhance the firms' profitability. Table 2–3 lists *CR Magazine*'s best companies in terms of corporate citizenship and social responsibility. Many of these firms are highly profitable, succeeding both ethically and financially.

CORPORATE GOVERNANCE PROVIDES FORMALIZED RESPONSIBILITY TO STAKEHOLDERS

Most businesses, and often many subjects taught in business schools, operate under the assumption that the purpose of business is to maximize profits for shareholders—an assumption manifest, for example, in the 1919 decision of the Michigan Supreme Court. In *Dodge v. Ford Motor Co.*[56] the court ruled that a business exists for the profit of shareholders, and the board of directors should focus on that objective. In contrast, the stakeholder model places the board of directors in the position of balancing the interests and conflicts of a company's various constituencies. External control of the corporation resides not only with government regulators but also with key stakeholders including employees, consumers, and communities, which exert pressure for responsible conduct. In fact, social responsibility activities have a positive impact on consumer identification with and attitude toward the brand.[57] Mandates for stakeholder interests have been institutionalized in legislation that provides incentives for responsible conduct. Shareholders have been pushing for more power in the boardroom, as many feel their interests have not been well represented in the resolution of issues such as executive compensation.

Today, the failure to balance stakeholder interests can result in a failure to maximize shareholders' wealth. As a result, investors often examine executive actions that could involve a conflict of interest with great scrutiny. When Alibaba CEO Jack Ma invested in another company on Alibaba's behalf, shareholders and corporate-governance experts were wary because it appeared Mr. Ma could easily go from investing to benefit the company to investing to benefit himself with little recourse available to shareholders.[58] Most firms are moving toward a more balanced stakeholder model as they see that this approach sustains the relationships necessary for long-term success.

Both directors and officers of corporations are fiduciaries for the shareholders. Fiduciaries are persons placed in positions of trust that act on behalf of the best interests of the organization. They have what is called a duty of care, or a *duty of diligence,* to make informed and prudent decisions.[59] Directors have a duty to avoid ethical misconduct and provide leadership in decisions to prevent ethical misconduct in the organization.

Directors are not generally held responsible for negative outcomes if they have been informed and diligent in their decision making. Board members have an obligation to request information, conduct research, use accountants and attorneys, and obtain the services of ethical compliance consultants to ensure the corporations in which they have an interest are run in an ethical manner. The National Association of Corporate Directors, a board of directors' trade group, has helped formulate a guide for boards to help them do a better job of governing corporate America.[60]

Directors share a *duty of loyalty,* which means all their decisions should be in the best interests of the corporation and its stakeholders. Conflicts of interest exist when a director uses the position to obtain personal gain, usually at the expense of the organization. For example, before the passage of the Sarbanes–Oxley Act in 2002, directors could give themselves and their officers interest-free loans. Scandals at Tyco, Kmart, and WorldCom are all associated with officers receiving personal loans that damaged the corporation.

Officer compensation packages present a challenge for directors, especially those on the board who are not independent. Directors have an opportunity to vote for others' compensation in return for their own increased compensation. Following the global financial crisis, many top executives at failed firms received multimillion dollar bonuses in spite of the fact their companies required huge government bailouts simply to stay afloat. This has led to a greater amount of shareholder activism regarding the issue of executive pay. Directors now find shareholders want to vote on executive officers' compensation, and although their votes are not binding in the United States, investor pressure has increased the shareholder role in deciding executive compensation. For instance, shareholders of Staples Inc. rejected an executive pay program because of dissatisfaction with executive compensation. They also requested an independent chairman of the board.[61]

Directors' knowledge about the investments, business ventures, and stock market information of a company creates issues that could violate their duty of loyalty. Insider trading of a firm's stock has specific rules, and violations should result in serious punishment. The obligations of directors and officers for legal and ethical responsibility interface and fit together based on their fiduciary relationships. Ethical values should guide decisions and buffer the possibility of illegal conduct. With increased pressure on directors to provide oversight for organizational ethics, there is a trend toward directors receiving training to increase their competency in ethics programs development, as well as other areas. As issues increase, more pressure is placed on the board's audit committee to address anything related to risk. While their primary role has been financial reporting, today boards are responsible for issues such as whistleblower claims, cybersecurity, and bribery.[62]Automated systems to monitor and measure the occurrence of ethical issues within organizations are increasingly used in this oversight process.

TABLE 2–4 Corporate Governance Topics

| Shareholder rights |
| Board composition |
| Financial oversight |
| Risk management |
| Board engagement and communication |
| Link between executive compensation and performance |
| CEO and executive succession |
| Board oversight of company talent development |
| Ethics and compliance programs |

Source: Cydney Posner, "NACD releases 'Critical Issues for Board Focus in 2015'," PubCo @ Cooley, November 13, 2014, http://cooleypubco.com/2014/11/13/nacd-releases-critical-issues-for-board-focus-in-2015/ (accessed February 3, 2015).

Accountability is an important part of corporate governance. *Accountability* refers to how closely workplace decisions align with a firm's stated strategic direction and its compliance with ethical and legal considerations. *Oversight* provides a system of checks and balances that limit employees' and managers' opportunities to deviate from policies and strategies aimed at preventing unethical and illegal activities. *Control* is the process of auditing and improving organizational decisions and actions. Table 2–4 lists examples of major corporate governance issues.

A clear delineation of accountability helps employees, customers, investors, government regulators, and other stakeholders understand why and how the organization identifies and achieves its goals. Corporate governance establishes fundamental systems and processes for preventing and detecting misconduct, for investigating and disciplining, and for recovery and continuous improvement. Effective corporate governance creates a compliance and ethics culture so employees feel integrity is at the core of competitiveness.[63] Even if a company adopts a consensus approach for decision making, there should be oversight and authority for delegating tasks, making difficult and sometimes controversial decisions, balancing power throughout the firm, and maintaining ethical compliance. Governance also provides mechanisms for identifying risks and planning for recovery when mistakes or problems occur.

The development of a stakeholder orientation should interface with the corporation's governance structure. Corporate governance also helps establish the integrity of all relationships. A governance system without checks and balances creates opportunities for top managers to indulge self-interest before those of important stakeholders. For example, while many people lost their investments during the recent financial crisis some CEOs actually made a profit from it. Some directors tweaked performance targets in order to make goals easier to achieve so they could receive more bonus money. Bonuses have become a contentious issue since they are the part of an executive's pay most tied to performance. Many people ask why executives receive bonuses as their companies fail; the fact is most executive bonuses are tied to targets other than stock prices.[64] Concerns about the need for greater corporate governance are not limited to the United States. Reforms in governance structures and issues are occurring all over the world.[65] Table 2–5 outlines some of the changes we have seen in corporate governance.

TABLE 2-5 Changes in Corporate Governance

51% of directors say their company has split the CEO and Chair functions

Public company directors spend an average of 219 hours on their responsibilities

51% of directors say their boards have adopted a mandatory retirement age

41% of directors are involved in overseeing the company's monitoring of social media for adverse publicity

One-third of directors say their boards have interacted with an activist in the past year

24% of all new S&P 500 directors in the last two years have been women

Issues that boards want to focus on: strategic planning, IT risks, succession planning, and IT strategy

Important characteristics in directors: strong expertise in financial, industry, operational, and risk management areas

The three major reasons for not replacing an underperforming director: leadership discomfort in addressing the issue, no individual director assessments, and board assessment processes not effective

73% of directors believe it is appropriate to discuss executive compensation with shareholders

Source: PricewaterhouseCoopers LLP, *Trends shaping governance and the board of the future: PwC's 2014 Annual Corporate Directors Survey*, http://www.pwc.com/us/en/corporate-governance/annual-corporate-directors-survey/assets/annual-corporate-directors-survey-full-report-pwc.pdf (accessed February 3, 2015).

Corporate governance normally involves strategic decisions and actions by boards of directors, business owners, top executives, and other managers with high levels of authority and accountability. In the past these people have been relatively free from scrutiny, but changes in technology such as social media, consumer activism, as well as recent ethical scandals have brought new attention to communication and transparency. Corporate managers engage in dialogue with shareholder activists when the firm is large, responsive to stakeholders, the CEO is the board chair, and there are few large institutional investors that control significant shares of stock.[66]

Views of Corporate Governance

To better understand the role of corporate governance in business today, we must consider how it relates to fundamental beliefs about the purpose of business. Some organizations take the view that as long as they are maximizing shareholder wealth and profitability, they are fulfilling their core responsibilities. Other firms, however, believe that a business is an important member, even a citizen, of society, and therefore must assume broad responsibilities that include complying with social norms and expectations. From these assumptions, we can derive two major approaches to corporate governance: the shareholder model and the stakeholder model.[67]

The **shareholder model of corporate governance** is founded in classic economic precepts, inclu___ ___ ___ ___ealth for investors and owners. For publicly traded firms ___ ___ ___ developing and improving the formal system for main___ ___ ___ ___ty between top management and the firm's shareholders.[68] Thus, a shareholder orientation should drive a firm's decisions toward serving the best interests of investors. Underlying these decisions is a classic agency problem, in which ownership (investors) and control (managers) are separate. Managers act as agents for investors, whose primary goal is increasing the value of the stock they own. However, investors and managers are distinct parties with unique insights, goals, and values with respect to the business. Managers, for example, may have motivations beyond stockholder value, such as market share, personal compensation, or attachment to particular products and projects. Because of these potential differences, corporate governance mechanisms are needed to align investor and management interests. The shareholder model has been criticized for its singular purpose and focus because there are other ways of "investing" in a business. Suppliers, creditors, customers, employees, business partners, the community, and others also invest their resources into the success of the firm.[69]

The **stakeholder model of corporate governance** adopts a broader view of the purpose of busines   v has a responsibility for economic success and viability t   lso answer to other stakeholders, including employee   rs, communities, and the special interest groups with which it interacts. Because of limited resources, companies must determine which of their stakeholders are primary. Once the primary groups are identified, managers must implement the appropriate corporate governance mechanisms to promote the development of long-term relationships.[70] This approach entails creating governance systems that consider stakeholder welfare in tandem with corporate needs and interests. Patagonia, Yahoo!, and Google all use the stakeholder model of corporate governance to direct their business activities.

Although these two approaches represent the ends of a continuum, the reality is the shareholder model is a more restrictive precursor to the stakeholder orientation. Many businesses evolved into the stakeholder model as a result of government initiatives, consumer activism, industry activity, and other external forces.

The Role of Boards of Directors

For public corporations, boards of directors hold the ultimate responsibility for their firms' success or failure, as well as the ethics of their actions. This governing authority is held responsible by amendments to the Federal Sentencing Guidelines for Organizations (FSGO) for creating an ethical culture that provides leadership, values, and compliance. The members of a company's board of directors assume legal responsibility for the firm's resources and decisions, and they appoint its top executive officers. Board members have a fiduciary duty, meaning they have assumed a position of trust and confidence that entails certain responsibilities, including acting in the best interests of those they serve. Thus, board membership is not intended as a vehicle for personal financial gain; rather, it provides the intangible benefit of ensuring the success of both the organization and the people involved in the fiduciary arrangement. The role and expectations of boards of directors assumed greater significance in the last 15 years after accounting scandals, and the global financial crisis motivated many stakeholders to demand greater accountability from boards.[71]

Despite this new emphasis on accountability for board members, many continue to believe current directors do not face serious consequences for corporate misconduct. Although directors may be sued by shareholders, the SEC does not usually pursue corporate directors for misconduct unless it can be proved they acted in bad faith. The traditional approach to directorship assumed board members managed the corporation's business, but research and practical observation show that boards of directors rarely, if ever, perform the management function.[72] Boards meet only a few times a year, which precludes them from managing directly. In addition, the complexity of modern organizations mandates full attention on a daily basis to manage effectively. Therefore, boards of directors primarily concern themselves with monitoring the decisions made by executives on behalf of the company. This function includes choosing top executives, assessing their performance, helping to set strategic direction, and ensuring oversight, control, and accountability mechanisms are in place. Thus, board members assume ultimate authority for their organization's effectiveness and subsequent performance.

Again, perhaps one of the most challenging ethical issues boards of directors must deal with is compensation. When considering executive pay raises, directors may put their own self-interest above the interests of shareholders.[73] Another issue is the compensation the directors themselves receive. Trends show that director compensation is rising. Total mean compensation for directors at *Fortune* 500 companies is approximately $240,000.[74] Proponents argue that high compensation for part-time work is necessary because directors have a difficult job and good pay is needed to attract top-quality talent. On the other hand, critics believe this level of compensation causes a conflict of interest for directors. Some speculate compensation over $200,000 makes directors more complacent; they become less concerned with "rocking the boat" and more concerned with maintaining their high-paying positions.[75] Clearly, the debate over director accountability continues to rage.

Greater Demands for Accountability and Transparency

Just as improved ethical decision making requires more of employees and executives, boards of directors are also experiencing a greater demand for accountability and transparency. In the past, board members were often retired company executives or friends of current executives, but the trend today is toward "outside directors" who have little vested interest in the firm before assuming the director role. Inside directors are corporate officers, consultants, major shareholders, and others who benefit directly from the success of the organization. Directors today are increasingly chosen for their expertise, competence, and ability to bring diverse perspectives to strategic discussions. Outside directors are also thought to bring independence to the monitoring function because they are not bound by past allegiances, friendships, a current role in the company, or some other issue that creates a conflict of interest.

Many of the corporate scandals uncovered in recent years might not have occurred if the companies' boards of directors were better qualified, knowledgeable, and less biased. Diversity of board members, especially in age and gender, has been associated with improved social performance.[76] Shareholder involvement in changing the makeup of boards has always run into difficulties. Most boards are not true democracies, and many shareholders have minimal impact on decision making because they are so dispersed. The concept of board members being linked to more than one company is known as an **interlocking directorate**. The practice is not considered illegal unless it involv   petitor.[77] A survey by *USA Today* found that corporate boards have consid   More than 1,000 corporate board members sit on four or more boards, and   00 boards of directors in the United States, more than 22,000 of their members a   to boards of more than one company. In some cases, it seems individuals earned placement on multiple boards of directors because they gained a reputation for going along with top management and never asking questions. Such a trend fosters a corporate culture that limits outside oversight of top managers' decisions.

Although labor and public pension fund activities waged hundreds of proxy battles in recent years, they rarely had much effect on the target companies. Now shareholder activists attack the process by which directors themselves are elected. Resolutions at hundreds of companies require candidates for director to gain a majority of votes before they can join the board. It is hoped this practice makes boards of directors more attentive and accountable.[78]

Executive Compensation

One of the biggest issues corporate boards of directors face is **executive compensation**. In fact, most boards spend more time deciding how much to compensate top executives than they do ensuring the integrity of the company's financial reporting systems.[79] How executives are compensated for their leadership, organizational service, and performance has become a controversial topic. Coca-Cola revised its executive compensation plan after shareholders, including Warren Buffett, heavily criticized the plan as being "excessive." As a result, Coca-Cola reduced the number of shares that executives would receive for their yearly performance.[80]

Many people believe no executive is worth millions of dollars in annual salary and stock options, even if he or she brings great financial return to investors. Their concerns often center on the relationship between the highest-paid executives and median employee wages in the company. If this ratio is perceived as too large, critics believe employees are not being compensated fairly or high executive salaries represent an improper use of company resources. According to the AFL-CIO, the average CEO compensation of an S&P 500 index company is nearly $11.7 million, approximately 331 times higher than the average worker's pay. Executive bonuses can reach into the millions of dollars.[81]

Many stakeholders support high levels of executive compensation only when directly linked to strong company performance. Although the issue of executive compensation has gained much attention, some business owners long recognized its potential ill effects. In the early twentieth century, for example, JP Morgan implemented a policy limiting the pay of top managers in the businesses he owned to no more than 20 times the pay of any other employee.[82] The ethics issue relates to executives taking advantage of their positions of power and influencing the board of directors to provide excessive compensation.

On the other hand, because executives assume so much risk on behalf of the company, it can be argued that they deserve the rewards that follow from strong company performance. In addition, many executives' personal and professional lives meld to the extent they are on call 24 hours a day. Because not everyone has the skill, experience, and desire to take on the pressure and responsibility of the executive lifestyle, market forces dictate a high level of compensation. When the pool of qualified individuals is limited, many corporate board members feel offering large compensation packages is the only way to attract and retain top executives, thus ensuring their firms maintain strong leadership. In an era when top executives are increasingly willing to "jump ship" for other firms offering higher pay, potentially lucrative stock options, bonuses, and other benefits, such thinking is not without merit.[83] But research has shown a correlation between the highest paid CEOs and lower company performance, which may cast doubt on the belief that large compensation packages positively impact corporate performance.[84]

Executive compensation is a difficult but important issue for boards of directors and other stakeholders to consider because it receives much attention in the media, sparks shareholder concern, and is hotly debated in discussions of corporate governance. One area board members must consider is the extent executive compensation is linked to company performance. Plans basing compensation on the achievement of performance goals, including profits and revenues, are intended to align interests of owners with those of management. Amid rising complaints about excessive executive compensation, an increasing number of corporate boards impose performance targets on the stock and stock options they include in their CEOs' pay packages. Some boards also reduce executive compensation or oust the CEO for corporate losses or misconduct. For example, McDonald's forced its CEO to resign after declining customer traffic and a supplier disaster in China lowered the company's reputation and decreased sales.[85]

The SEC proposed companies disclose how they compensate lower-ranking employees as well as top executives. This proposal was part of a review of executive pay policies that addressed the belief that many financial corporations have historically provided incentives that encouraged employees to take excessive risks.[86] Another issue is whether performance-linked compensation encourages executives to focus on short-term performance at the expense of long-term growth.[87] Shareholders today, however, may be growing more concerned about transparency and its impact on short-term performance and executive compensation. One study determined companies that divulge more details about their corporate governance practices generate higher shareholder returns than less transparent companies.[88]

IMPLEMENTING A STAKEHOLDER PERSPECTIVE

An organization that develops effective corporate governance and understands the importance of business ethics and social responsibility in achieving success should also develop processes for managing these important concerns. Although there are different approaches to this issue, we provide basic steps found effective in utilizing the stakeholder framework to manage responsibility and business ethics. The steps include (1) assessing the corporate culture, (2) identifying stakeholder groups, (3) identifying stakeholder issues, (4) assessing organizational commitment to social responsibility, (5) identifying resources and determining urgency, and (6) gaining stakeholder feedback. These steps include getting feedback from relevant stakeholders in formulating organizational strategy and implementation.

Step 1: Assessing the Corporate Culture

To enhance organizational fit, a social responsibility program must align with the corporate culture of the organization. The purpose of this first step is to identify the organizational mission, values, norms, and behavior likely to have implications for social responsibility. Relevant existing values and norms are those that specify the stakeholder groups to engage and stakeholder issues deemed most important by the organization. Often, relevant organizational values and norms can be found in corporate documents such as the mission statement, annual reports, sales brochures, and codes of ethics. For example, REI states its mission is to "inspire, educate and outfit for a lifetime of outdoor adventure and stewardship." REI fulfills its mission by offering high-quality outdoor products, investing in green energy, and providing outdoor classes in areas such as rock climbing, cycling, and camping.[89]

Step 2: Identifying Stakeholder Groups

In managing this stage, it is important to recognize stakeholder needs, wants, and desires. Many important issues gain visibility because key constituencies such as consumer groups, regulators, or the media express an interest. When agreement, collaboration, or even confrontations exist, there is a need for a decision-making process such as a model of collaboration to overcome adversarial approaches to problem solving. For example, regulatory stakeholders have been found to have a negative influence on both innovation and performance.[90] Managers can identify relevant stakeholders who may be affected by or may influence performance and social responsibility.

Stakeholders have a level of power over a business because they are in the position to withhold organizational resources to some extent. Stakeholders have the most power when their own survival is not affected by the success of the organization and when they have access to vital organizational resources. For example, most consumers of shoes do not need to buy Nike shoes. Therefore, if they decide to boycott Nike, they endure only minor inconveniences. Nevertheless, consumer loyalty to Nike is vital to the continued success of the sports apparel giant. A proper assessment of the power held by a given stakeholder includes an evaluation of the extent to which that stakeholder collaborates with others to pressure the firm. This creates a need to prioritize the stakeholders that are most important to engage.

Step 3: Identifying Stakeholder Issues

Together, steps 1 and 2 lead to the identification of the stakeholders who are both the most powerful and legitimate. The level of stakeholders' power and legitimacy determines the degree of urgency in addressing their needs. Step 3, then, consists of understanding the main issues of concern to these stakeholders. Conditions for collaboration exist when problems are so complex that multiple stakeholders are required to resolve the issue, and adversarial approaches to problem solving are clearly inadequate.

The weight given to ethical issues may vary by society. For example, obesity in Mexico has become a major problem, with rates of diabetes and other health problems skyrocketing. The Mexican government imposed a tax on sodas to decrease consumption of sugary drinks.[91] Companies such as CVS are taking advantage of a growing concern for health care in the United States by repositioning itself as a health care company rather than a pharmacy. To show its commitment CVS has forgone $2 billion in sales by eliminating cigarettes from its stores. The ability of CVS to identify an issue important to Americans demonstrates the company's willingness to adopt a stakeholder orientation.

Step 4: Assessing Organizational Commitment to Stakeholders and Social Responsibility

Steps 1 through 3 are geared toward generating information about social responsibility among a variety of influences in and around an organization. Step 4 brings these three stages together to arrive at an understanding of social responsibility that specifically matches the organization of interest. This general definition will then be used to evaluate current practices and to select concrete social responsibility initiatives. Firms such as Starbucks selected activities that address stakeholder concerns. Starbucks formalized its initiatives in official documents such as annual reports, web pages, and company brochures. Starbucks is concerned with the environment and integrates policies and programs throughout all aspects of its operations to minimize its environmental impact. The company also has many community-building programs that help it to be a good neighbor and contribute positively to the communities where its partners and customers live, work, and play.[92] It has been found that social responsibility disclosures in company annual reports are directly related to the quality of corporate governance.[93] Therefore, transparency in reporting social responsibility commitment is important for top company officers and the board of directors.

Step 5: Identifying Resources and Determining Urgency

The prioritization of stakeholders and issues and the assessment of past performance lead to the allocation of resources. Two main criteria can be considered: the level of financial and organizational investments required by different actions, and the urgency when prioritizing social responsibility challenges. When the challenge under consideration is viewed as significant and stakeholder pressures on the issue can be expected, the challenge is considered urgent. For example, the Federal Trade Commission filed a lawsuit against AT&T over its "unlimited" data plans. Although the plans were marketed as unlimited, AT&T slowed down data speeds for some of the customers with the plan. The FTC considered this to be misleading advertising.[94] The government has supported the passage of regulation that allows the Federal Communications Commission to regulate the Internet and ensure net neutrality. Net neutrality means that service providers are required to provide equal access to all content without blocking or prioritizing some websites over others. This would prevent companies such as AT&T from slowing down data speeds, but the AT&T CEO claims it introduces a number of burdens such as taxation that would need to be worked out, as well as extensive litigation.[95] Internet privacy is also a major concern for the FTC. Snapchat reached a settlement with the agency on accusations that the app was not totally secure and photos could be saved despite the company's claims to the contrary.[96]

Step 6: Gaining Stakeholder Feedback

Stakeholder feedback is generated through a variety of means. First, stakeholders' general assessment of a firm and its practices can be obtained through satisfaction or reputation surveys. Second, to gauge stakeholders' perceptions of a firm's contributions to specific issues, stakeholder-generated media such as blogs, websites, podcasts, and newsletters can be assessed. Many firms use media tracking services to identify and classify content related to the company. Third, more formal research may be conducted using focus groups, observation, and surveys. Many watchdog groups use the web to inform consumers and publicize their messages. For example, Consumer Watchdog, a California-based group that keeps an eye on everything from education to the oil industry, filed a lawsuit against health insurer Aetna claiming discrimination against patients with HIV. The group claims that under a new policy, Aetna began requiring patients with HIV to obtain their medications solely from their mail-order pharmacy without having a chance to opt out. Aetna claims its move is consistent with industry standards and that members could opt out of the policy.[97] This illustrates the impact of secondary stakeholders as a special interest group.

CONTRIBUTIONS OF A STAKEHOLDER PERSPECTIVE

While we provide a framework for implementing a stakeholder perspective, balancing stakeholder interests requires information and good judgment. When businesses attempt to provide what consumers want, broader societal interests can create conflicts.

Consider, for example, that many of the metals in consumer electronics products come from countries such as the Democratic Republic of the Congo riddled by warfare and human rights violations. The Securities and Exchange Commission passed a law requiring companies to report on the due diligence of their supply chains regarding these metals to determine whether the money could have been used to fund armed groups. It was estimated that initial compliance with the new regulation would be $4 billion. These costs associated with due diligence as well as sourcing minerals from other areas could result in higher prices for consumers.[98] This is another example of how regulation can limit financial performance and innovation, as reported earlier in the chapter. Consumers desire electronics such as iPads to be affordably priced. However, without regulation consumer desires for affordable prices could lead companies to purchase minerals from conflict areas. In other words, what is most advantageous for consumers is not beneficial to the people living in the conflict region. It is clear that balancing stakeholder interests can be a challenging process.

This chapter provides a good overview of the issues, conflicts, and opportunities of understanding more about stakeholder relationships. The stakeholder framework recognizes issues, identifies stakeholders, and examines the role of boards of directors and managers in promoting ethics and social responsibility. A stakeholder perspective creates a more ethical and reputable organization.

SUMMARY

Business ethics, issues, and conflicts revolve around relationships. Customers, investors and shareholders, employees, suppliers, government agencies, communities, and many others who have a stake or claim in an aspect of a company's products, operations, markets, industry, and outcomes are known as stakeholders. Stakeholders are influenced by and have the ability to affect businesses. Stakeholders provide both tangible and intangible resources that are critical to a firm's long-term success, and their relative ability to withdraw these resources gives them power. Stakeholders define significant ethical issues in business.

Primary stakeholders are those whose continued association is absolutely necessary for a firm's survival. Secondary stakeholders do not typically engage in transactions with a company and are not essential to its survival. The stakeholder interaction model suggests there are reciprocal relationships between a firm and a host of stakeholders. The degree to which a firm understands and addresses stakeholder demands is expressed as a stakeholder orientation and includes three sets of activities: (1) the generation of data about its stakeholder groups and the assessment of the firm's effects on these groups, (2) the distribution of this information throughout the company, and (3) the responsiveness of every level of the business to this intelligence. A stakeholder orientation can be viewed as a continuum in that firms are likely to adopt the concept to varying degrees.

Although the terms *ethics* and *social responsibility* are often used interchangeably, they have distinct meanings. Social responsibility in business refers to an organization's obligation to maximize its positive impact and minimize its negative impact on society. There are four levels of social responsibility—economic, legal, ethical, and philanthropic—and they can be viewed as a pyramid. The term *corporate citizenship* is used to communicate the extent businesses strategically meet the economic, legal, ethical, and philanthropic responsibilities placed on them by their stakeholders.

From a social responsibility perspective, business ethics embodies standards, norms, and expectations that reflect the concerns of major stakeholders including consumers, employees, shareholders, suppliers, competitors, and the community. Only if firms include ethical concerns in foundational values and incorporate ethics into business strategies can social responsibility as a value be embedded in daily decision making.

Issues in social responsibility include social issues, consumer protection issues, sustainability, and corporate governance. Social issues are associated with the common good and include such issues as childhood obesity and Internet privacy. Consumer protection often occurs in the form of laws passed to protect consumers from unfair and deceptive business practices. Sustainability is the potential for the long-term well-being of the natural environment, including all biological entities, as well as the mutually beneficial interactions among nature and individuals, organizations, and business strategies. Corporate governance involves the development of formal systems of accountability, oversight, and control.

Most businesses operate under the assumption that the main purpose of business is to maximize profits for shareholders. The stakeholder model places the board of directors in the position of balancing the interests and conflicts of various constituencies. Both directors and officers of corporations are fiduciaries for the shareholders. Directors have a duty to avoid ethical misconduct and provide leadership in decisions to prevent ethical misconduct in their organizations. To remove the opportunity for employees to make unethical decisions, most companies develop formal systems of accountability, oversight, and control known as corporate governance. Accountability refers to how closely workplace decisions are aligned with a firm's stated strategic direction and its compliance with ethical and legal considerations. Oversight provides a system of checks and balances that limit employees' and managers' opportunities to deviate from policies and strategies intended to prevent unethical and illegal activities. Control is the process of auditing and improving organizational decisions and actions.

There are two perceptions of corporate governance that can be viewed as a continuum. The shareholder model is founded in classic economic precepts, including the maximization of wealth for investors and owners. The stakeholder model adopts a broader view of the purpose of business that includes satisfying the concerns of other stakeholders, from employees, suppliers, and government regulators to communities and special interest groups.

Two major elements of corporate governance that relate to ethical decision making are the role of the board of directors and executive compensation. The members of a public corporation's board of directors assume legal responsibility for the firm's resources and decisions. Important issues related to boards of directors include accountability, transparency, and independence. Boards of directors are also responsible for appointing top executive officers and determining their compensation. Concerns about executive pay center on the often-disproportionate relationship between executive pay and median employee wages in the company.

An organization that develops effective corporate governance and understands the importance of business ethics and social responsibility in achieving success should develop a process for managing these important concerns. Although there are different approaches, steps have been identified that have been found effective in utilizing the stakeholder framework to manage responsibility and business ethics. These steps are (1) assessing the corporate culture, (2) identifying stakeholder groups, (3) identifying stakeholder issues, (4) assessing organizational commitment to social responsibility, (5) identifying resources and determining urgency, and (6) gaining stakeholder feedback.

IMPORTANT TERMS FOR REVIEW

RESOLVING ETHICAL BUSINESS CHALLENGES*

Demarco just graduated from Texas University and had been snatched up by Xeon Natural Resources Incorporated, one of the top natural resource extraction companies in the world. Because he was Brazilian, bilingual, and spoke several specific Brazilian dialects, his stationing in Brazil was a no-brainer. Xeon was deeply involved with a project within the Brazilian rain forests in mining an extremely valuable element called niobium. Niobium is a rare earth element essential for micro alloying steel as well as other products such as jet engines, rocket subassemblies, superconducting magnets, and super alloys. Brazil accounts for 92 percent of all niobium mined, and Xeon Natural mines much of the element in Brazil. Xeon discovered a large niobium deposit, and estimates the corporation could make an additional $5 billion in profits over the next two decades.

Demarco soon discovered he was one of several employees assigned to explain to the indigenous population that Xeon wanted to extract the niobium from the lands given to the tribes by the Brazilian government. The land was, by decree, compensation for native minorities. Having spent several months with various tribes, Demarco learned they were communities that had not been altered by western culture. It was obvious to Demarco if Xeon began strip mining the area, thousands of "outsiders" would be brought in and would impact the cultural heritage of the indigenous populations.

Demarco discussed this with his boss, Barbara. "Yes, I understand all you are saying, and I agree this will change their lives as well as their children and grandchildren's lives," Barbara said. "But think of it this way, their standard of living will be greatly enhanced. Schools will be built, hospitals will be available, and there will be more employment opportunities."

Demarco responded, "While the tribal leaders want a better life for their people, I feel they are being steamrolled into accepting something they don't understand. I've talked to some of the tribal leaders, and I am positive they have no idea of the impact this will have on their culture. We have many stakeholders involved in this decision, including Xeon's employees, the tribes, the Brazilian government, and even communities beyond the tribal lands. I think we need to reevaluate the impact on all of these stakeholders before proceeding."

Barbara sighed. "I think you make some good points, and I am concerned about these different stakeholders. But you should understand we already have buy-in from the key decision makers, and our business depends upon being able to mine niobium. We've got to continue this project."

Demarco returned to the camp. The other specialists questioned him about Barbara's reaction. As he spoke, some of the specialists became concerned about their jobs. A few admitted they heard the local and national media were raising awareness about the negative impact mining this mineral could have on the indigenous populations.

A few days later, Demarco heard that some of the tribal leaders had new concerns about the project and were organizing meetings to obtain feedback from members. Demarco approached one of the mining specialists that studied the potential impact of strip mining the land. The specialist said that while he understood stakeholder interests, he felt the extraction methods Xeon used were environmentally friendly. While creating a temporary disruption in the ecosystem of the rainforest, Xeon's strip mining methods provided an opportunity for restoration. In fact, strip mining that was done in the United States before there were any regulations provides a good example of how the forest can recover and grow back to its original condition.

Demarco knew despite the potential benefits, there would still likely be opposition from the tribal community. Additionally, no method of strip mining is entirely environmentally friendly. Demarco realized even with restoration, the lives of the indigenous tribes would be forever altered.

Demarco was to meet with tribal elders the next day to discuss their concerns. He understood that whatever the decision, it would negatively impact some stakeholders. On the one hand, the tribal members might compromise their traditional way of life and the environment would be harmed if the strip mining project began. On the other hand, Xeon's future and the future of its employees depended upon being able to mine the niobium. It could also benefit the tribes economically. He was not sure what he should tell the tribal leaders.

QUESTIONS | EXERCISES

1. How should Demarco approach this issue when he meets with the tribal leaders?
2. What should be the priorities in balancing the various stakeholder interests?
3. Can the CEO and board of directors of Xeon continue operations and maintain a stakeholder orientation?

*This case is strictly hypothetical; any resemblance to real persons, companies, or situations is coincidental.

> > > CHECK YOUR EQ

Check your EQ, or Ethics Quotient, by completing the following. Assess your performance to evaluate your overall understanding of the chapter material.

1. Social responsibility in business refers to maximizing the visibility of social involvement. Yes <u>No</u>

2. Stakeholders provide resources that are more or less critical to a firm's long-term success. <u>Yes</u> No

3. Three primary stakeholders are customers, special interest groups, and the media. Yes <u>No</u>

4. The most significant influence on ethical behavior in an organization is the opportunity to engage in unethical behavior. Yes <u>No</u>

5. The stakeholder perspective is useful in managing social responsibility and business ethics. <u>Yes</u> No

ANSWERS **1. No.** Social responsibility refers to an organization's obligation to maximize its positive impact on society and minimize its negative impact. **2. Yes.** These resources are both tangible and intangible. **3. No.** Although customers are primary stakeholders, special interest groups and the media are usually considered secondary stakeholders. **4. No.** Other influences such as corporate culture have more impact on ethical decisions within an organization. **5. Yes.** The six steps to implement this approach were provided in this chapter.

ENDNOTES

1. Vikas Anand, Blake E. Ashforth, and Mahendra Joshi, "Business as Usual: The Acceptance and Perpetuation of Corruption in Organizations," *Academy of Management Executive* 18, 2 (2004): 39–53.

2. Debbie Thorne, O. C. Ferrell, and Linda Ferrell, *Business and Society* (Boston: Houghton Mifflin, 2003), 64–65.

3. Michelle Healy, "Youth exposure to e-cigarette TV ads increase," *USA Today,* June 2, 2014, 3A.

4. T. Donaldson and L.E. Preston, "The stakeholder theory of the corporation: concepts, evidence, and implications," *Academy of Management Review* 20, 1 (1995): 65–91.

5. T.M. Jones, "Instrumental stakeholder theory: A synthesis of ethics and economics," *Academy of Management Review* 20, 2 (1995): 404–437.

6. Max B. E. Clarkson, "A stakeholder framework for analyzing and evaluating corporate social performance," *Academy of Management Review* 20, 1 (1995): 92–117.

7. Lynn Brewer, Robert Chandler, and O. C. Ferrell, *Managing Risks for Corporate Integrity: How to Survive an Ethical Misconduct Disaster* (Mason, OH: Texere/Thomson, 2006), 11.

8. Tom Huddleston, "American Apparel fires Dov Charney, names new CEO," *Fortune,* December 16, 2014, http://fortune.com/2014/12/16/american-apparel-paula-schneider/ (accessed January 30, 2015).

9. Edelman, *Edelman Trust Barometer 2015 Annual Global Study,* http://www.edelman.com/insights/intellectual-property/2015-edelman-trust-barometer/ (accessed February 3, 2015).

10. Hunter Stuart, "Old Navy Under Fire For Charging Plus-Sized Women More Than Plus-Sized Men," *The Huffington Post,* November 11, 2014, http://www.huffingtonpost.com/2014/11/11/old-navy-plus-size-_n_6140478.html (accessed February 3, 2015).

11. Anselm Schneider and Andreas Georg Scherer, "Corporate Governance in a Risk Society," *The Journal of Business Ethics* 126, 2 (2015): 309–323.

12. Adapted from Isabelle Maignan, O. C. Ferrell, and Linda Ferrell, "A Stakeholder Model for Implementing Social Responsibility in Marketing," *European Journal of Marketing* 39, 9/10 (2005): 956–977.

13. Ibid.

14. Yves Fassin, "Stakeholder Management, Reciprocity and Shareholder Responsibility," *Journal of Business Ethics* 109, 1 (2012): 83–96.

15. Ibid.

16. Peter Evans, "U.K. Plans to Outlaw Branding on Cigarette Packs," *The Wall Street Journal,* January 22, 2015, http://www.wsj.com/articles/u-k-plans-to-outlaw-branding-on-cigarette-packs-1421947530 (accessed January 28, 2015).

17. Thorne, Ferrell, and Ferrell, *Business and Society.*

18. Sharon C. Bolton, Rebecca Chung-hee Kim, and Kevin D. O'Gorman, "Corporate Social Responsibility as a Dynamic Internal Organizational Process: A Case Study," *Journal of Business Ethics* 101, 1 (2011): 61–74.

19. G. Tomas M. Hult, Jeannette A. Mena, O.C. Ferrell, and Linda Ferrell, "Stakeholder marketing: a definition and conceptual framework," *AMS Review* 1, 1 (2011): 44–65.

20. Isabelle Maignan and O. C. Ferrell, "Corporate Social Responsibility: Toward a Marketing Conceptualization," *Journal of the Academy of Marketing Science* 32, 1 (2004): 3–19.

21. Ibid.

22. Wenlong Yuan, Yongjian Bao, and Alain Verbeke, "Integrating CSR Initiatives in Business: An Organizing Framework," *Journal of Business Ethics* 101, 1 (2011): 75–92.

23. Ibid.

24. Joseph A. McKinney, Tisha L. Emerson, and Mitchell J. Neubert, "The Effects of Ethical Codes on Ethical Perceptions of Actions toward Stakeholders," *Journal of Business Ethics* 97, 4 (2010): 505–516.

25. Newley Purnell, Eva Dou, and Daisuke Wakabayashi, "Apple Supplier in China Target of Safety Report," *The Wall Street Journal,* September 5, 2014, B4.

26. Jacob Bunge and Kelsey Gee, "The Business Side of Animal Rights," *The Wall Street Journal,* January 27, 2015, http://www.wsj.com/articles/animal-rights-advocates-get-proxy-advisory-firms-onboard-1422303269?mod=WSJ_hpp_MIDDLENexttoWhatsNewsThird (accessed January 28, 2015).

27. Maignan and Ferrell, "Corporate Social Responsibility."

28. Starbucks, "Environment," http://www.starbucks.com/responsibility/environment (accessed February 3, 2015).

29. Rachel Feintzeig, "Container Store Bets on $50,000 Retail Worker," *The Wall Street Journal,* October 15, 2014, B6.

30. PR Newswire, "SC Johnson Named as a 2011 Corporate Social Responsibility Company by Shanghai Pudong Government," February 22, 2012, http://www.prnewswire.com/news-releases/sc-johnson-named-as-a-2011-corporate-social-responsibility-company-by-shanghai-pudong-government-140024703.html (accessed February 14, 2013); SC Johnson, "Wind Energy to Power Windex®," June 21, 2012, http://www.scjohnson.com/en/press-room/press-releases/06-21-2012/Wind-Energy-to-Power-Windex%C2%AE.aspx (accessed February 14, 2013).

31. Les Coleman, "Losses from Failure of Stakeholder Sensitive Processes: Financial Consequences for Large U.S. Companies from Breakdowns in Product, Environmental, and Accounting Standards," *Journal of Business Ethics* 98 (2011): 247–258.

32. Archie B. Carroll, "The Pyramid of Corporate Social Responsibility: Toward the Moral Management of Organizational Stakeholders," *Business Horizons* 34, 4 (1991): 42.

33. Mark Scott, "Right to Be Forgotten Should Apply Worldwide, E.U. Panel Says," *The New York Times,* November 26, 2014, http://www.nytimes.com/2014/11/27/technology/right-to-be-forgotten-should-be-extended-beyond-europe-eu-panel-says.html?_r=0 (accessed January 29, 2015).

34. Isabelle Maignan, O. C. Ferrell, and G. Tomas M. Hult, "Corporate Citizenship: Cultural Antecedents and Business Benefits," *Journal of the Academy of Marketing Science* 27, 4 (1999): 457.

35. Lindsay McShane and Peggy Cunningham, "To Thine Own Self Be True? Employees' Judgments of the Authenticity of Their Organization's Corporate Social Responsibility Program," *Journal of Business Ethics* 108, 1 (2012): 81–100.

36. Daniel Korschun, C.B. Bhattacharya, and Scott D. Swain, "Corporate Social Responsibility, Customer Orientation, and the Job Performance of Frontline Employees," *Journal of Marketing* 78, 3 (2014): 20–37.

37. Gene R. Laczniak and Patrick E. Murphy, "Stakeholder Theory and Marketing: Moving from a Firm-Centric to a Societal Perspective," *Journal of Public Policy & Marketing* 31, 2 (2012): 284–292.

38. Patrick Murphy, Gene R. Laczniak, and Andrea Prothero, *Ethics in Marketing: International Cases and Perspectives* (London: Routledg, 2012), p. 38.

39. E. Moore and V.J. Rideout, "The Online Marketing of Food to Children: Is It Just Fun and Games?" *Journal of Public Policy & Marketing* 26, 2 (2007): 202–207.

40. Z. Tange, Y. Hu, and M.D. Smith, "Gaining Trust through Online Privacy Protection: Self-Regulation, Mandatory Standards, or *Caveat Emptor*," *Journal of Management Information Systems* 24, 4 (2008): 153–173.

41. R.D. Petty and J.C. Andrews, "Covert Marketing Unmasked: A Legal and Regulatory Guide for Practices that Mask Marketing Messages," *Journal of Public Policy & Marketing* 27, 1 (2008): 7–18.

42. R. M. Cain, "Embedded Advertising on Television: Disclosure, deception, and free speech rights," *Journal of Public Policy & Marketing* 30, 2 (2011): 226–238.

43. Jennifer Zarzosa, "Native Advertising as a Way to Break through the Clutter," Daniels Fund Ethics Initiative at the University of New Mexico, 2013, http://danielsethics.mgt.unm.edu/pdf/native-advertising-debate.pdf (accessed February 13, 2015).

44. Pieter de Jong, Anthony Paulraj, and Constantin Blome, "The Financial Impact of ISO 14001 Certification: Top-Line, Bottom-Line, or Both?" *Journal of Business Ethics* 119, 1 (2014): 131–149.

45. H. Jo and M.A. Harjoto, "The Causal Effect of Corporate Governance on Corporate Social Responsibility," *Journal of Business Ethics* 106, 1 (2012): 53–72.

46. Arifur Khan, Mohammed Badrul Muttakin, and Javed Siddiqui, "Corporate Governance and Corporate Social Responsibility Disclosures: Evidence from an Emerging Economy," *Journal of Business Ethics* 114, 2 (2013): 207–223.

47. G. A. Steiner and J. F. Steiner, *Business, Government, and Society* (New York: Random House, 1988).

48. Milton Friedman, "Social Responsibility of Business Is to Increase Its Profits," *The New York Times Magazine*, September 13, 1970, 122–126.

49. "Business Leaders, Politicians and Academics Dub Corporate Irresponsibility 'An Attack on America from Within,'" *Business Wire*, November 7, 2002, via America Online.

50. Adam Smith, *The Theory of Moral Sentiments*, Vol. 2. (New York: Prometheus, 2000).

51. Jill A. Brown and William R. Forster, "CSR and Stakeholder Theory: A Tale of Adam Smith," *Journal of Business Ethics* 112 (2013): 301–312.

52. Sheelah Kolhatkar, "Cheating, Incorporated," *Bloomberg Businessweek*, February 14–February 20, 2011, 60–66; "Brands," *Avid Life Media*, http://www.avidlifemedia.com/ (accessed February 21, 2011); Adam Tanner, "Profiting From Cheating," *Forbes,* February 9, 2015, 46-48; Danny Yadron, "Hackers Target Users of Infidelity Website Ashley Madison," *The Wall Street Journal,* July 20, 2015, http://www.wsj.com/articles/affair-website-ashley-madison-hacked-1437402152 (accessed July 24, 2015).

53. Iain Clacher and Jens Hagendorff, "Do Announcements about Corporate Social Responsibility Create or Destroy Shareholder Wealth? Evidence from the UK," *Journal of Business Ethics* 106, 3 (2012): 253–266.

54. Isabelle Maignan, Tracy L. Gonzalez-Padron, G. Tomas M. Hult, and O.C. Ferrell, "Stakeholder orientation: development and testing of a framework for socially responsible marketing," *Journal of Strategic Marketing* 19, 4 (2011): 313–338.

55. Isabelle Maignan, Tracy L. Gonzalez-Padron, G. Tomas M. Hult, and O.C. Ferrell, "Stakeholder Orientation: Development and Testing of a Framework for Socially Responsible Marketing."

56. *Dodge v. Ford Motor Co.*, 204 Mich.459, 179 N.W. 668, 3 A.L.R. 413 (1919).

57. Yuan-Shuh Lii and Monle Lee, "Doing Right Leads to Doing Well: When the Type of CSR and Reputation Interact to Affect Consumer Evaluations of the Firm," *Journal of Business Ethics* 105, 1 (2012): 69–81.

58. Juro Osawa, "Alibaba Founder's Deals Raise Flags," *The Wall Street Journal*, July 8, 2014, B1.

59. Alfred Marcus and Sheryl Kaiser, *Managing beyond Compliance: The Ethical and Legal Dimensions of Corporate Responsibility* (Garfield Heights, OH: North Coast Publishers, 2006), 79.

60. Joann S. Lublin, "Corporate Directors' Group Gives Repair Plan to Boards," *The Wall Street Journal*, March 24, 2009, http://online.wsj.com/article/SB123784649341118187.html (accessed February 3, 2015).

61. Nicholas Turner, "Staples Shareholders Vote Against Executive-Compensation Plan," *Bloomberg,* June 2, 2014, http://www.bloomberg.com/news/articles/2014-06-03/staples-shareholders-vote-against-executive-compensation-plan (accessed February 3, 2015).

62. Michael Rapoport and Joann S. Lublin, "The Board's Fire Department," *The Wall Street Journal*, February 3, 2015, B7.

63. Ben W. Heineman, Jr., "Are You a Good Corporate Citizen?," *The Wall Street Journal*, June 28, 2005, B2.

64. Phred Dvorak, "Poor Year Doesn't Stop CEO Bonuses," *The Wall Street Journal*, March 18, 2009, http://online.wsj.com/article/SB123698866439126029.html (accessed April 14, 2011).

65. Darryl Reed, "Corporate Governance Reforms in Developing Countries," *Journal of Business Ethics* 37, 3 (2002): 223–247.

66. Kathleen Rehbein, Jeanne M. Logsdon, and Harry J. Van Buren III, "Corporate Responses to Shareholder Activists: Considering the Dialogue Alternative," *Journal of Business Ethics* 112, 1 (2013): 137–154.

67. Maria Maher and Thomas Anderson, *Corporate Governance: Effects on Firm Performance and Economic Growth* (Paris: Organization for Economic Co-operation and Development, 1999).

68. Demb and F. F. Neubauer, *The Corporate Board: Confronting the Paradoxes* (Oxford: Oxford University Press, 1992).

69. Maher and Anderson, *Corporate Governance.*

70. Organization for Economic Co-operation and Development, *The OECD Principles of Corporate Governance* (Paris: Organization for Economic Co-operation and Development, 1999).

71. Louis Lavelle, "The Best and Worst Boards," *BusinessWeek*, October 7, 2002, 104–114.

72. Melvin A. Eisenberg, "Corporate Governance: The Board of Directors and Internal Control," *Cardozo Law Review* 19 (1997): 237.

73. S. Trevis Certo, Catherine Dalton, Dan Dalton, and Richard Lester, "Boards of Directors' Self-Interest: Expanding for Pay in Corporate Acquisitions?," *Journal of Business Ethics* 77, 2 (2008): 219–230.

74. Business Wire, "Compensation for U.S. Corporate Directors Increased 6%, Towers Watson 2014 Analysis Finds," *Yahoo! Finance,* September 24, 2014, http://finance.yahoo.com/news/compensation-u-corporate-directors-increased-130500227.html (accessed February 3, 2015).

75. Gary Strauss, "$228, 000 for a part-time job? Apparently, that's not enough," *USA Today*, March 4–6, 2011, 1A.

76. Taïeb Hafsi and Gokhan Turgut, "Boardroom Diversity and its Effect on Social Performance: Conceptualization and Empirical Evidence," *Journal of Business Ethics* 112, 3 (2013): 463–479.

77. Business Dictionary, http://www.businessdictionary.com/definition/interlocking-directorate.html (accessed February 3, 2015).

78. Amy Borrus, "Should Directors Be Nervous?" *BusinessWeek*, March 6, 2006 http://www.bloomberg.com/bw/stories/2006-03-05/should-directors-be-nervous (accessed February 3, 2015).

79. John A. Byrne with Louis Lavelle, Nanette Byrnes, Marcia Vickers, and Amy Borrus, "How to Fix Corporate Governance," *BusinessWeek*, May 6, 2002, 69–78.

80. CNN Money, "Coke cuts exec pay after Buffett criticism," *CNN Money,* October 1, 2014, http://money.cnn.com/2014/10/01/news/companies/coca-cola-compensation/ (accessed February 13, 2015).

81. Brandon Rees, "S&P 500 CEO Pay Is Now 331 Times Average Worker's Pay from AFL-CIO Investment Trust," International Brotherhood of Electrical Workers, 2014, http://www.local3.com/?q=node/7598 (accessed February 3, 2015); Kathryn Dill, "Report: CEOs Earn 331 Times As Much As Average Workers, 774 Times As Much As Minimum Wage Earners," *Forbes,* April 15, 2014, http://www.forbes.com/sites/kathryndill/2014/04/15/report-ceos-earn-331-times-as-much-as-average-workers-774-times-as-much-as-minimum-wage-earners/ (accessed February 13, 2015).

82. Sarah Anderson, John Cavanagh, Ralph Estes, Chuck Collins, and Chris Hartman, *A Decade of Executive Excess: The 1990s Sixth Annual Executive.* Boston: United for a Fair Economy, 1999, online, June 30, 2006, http://www.faireconomy.org/press_room/1999/a_decade_of_executive_excess_the_1990s (accessed February 3, 2015).

83. Louis Lavelle, "CEO Pay, The More Things Change…," *BusinessWeek*, October 16, 2000, 106–108.

84. Susan Adams, "The Highest-Paid CEOs Are The Worst Performers, New Study Says," *Forbes,* June 16, 2014, http://www.forbes.com/sites/susanadams/2014/06/16/the-highest-paid-ceos-are-the-worst-performers-new-study-says/ (accessed February 3, 2015).

85. Associated Press, "McDonald's faces many problems after ousting its longtime CEO," *Fox News,* January 29, 2015, http://www.foxnews.com/leisure/2015/01/29/mcdonald-ceo-steps-down-amid-falling-sales/ (accessed February 3, 2015).

86. Kara Scanell, "SEC Ready to Require More Pay Disclosures," *The Wall Street Journal*, June 3, 2009, http://online.wsj.com/article/SB124397831899078781.html (accessed April 14, 2011).

87. Gary Strauss, "America's Corporate Meltdown," *USA Today,* June 27, 2002, 1A, 2A.

88. Li-Chiu Chi, "Do transparency and performance predict firm performance? Evidence from the Taiwan Market," *Expert Systems with Applications* 36, 8 (2009), 11198–11203.

89. REI, "REI's 2009 Stewardship Report Highlights Environmental Sustainability, Community Connections and Workplace Engagement," September 8, 2010, http://www.rei.com/about-rei/newsroom/2010/10stewardship.html (accessed February 14, 2013); REI, "REI Outdoor School Classes and Outings," http://www.rei.com/outdoorschool.html (accessed February 14, 2013).

90. Economist staff, "The Criminalisation of American Business, *The Economist*, August 30–September 5, 2014, pp. 21–24; Tracy L. Gonzalez-Padron, G. Tomas M. Hult, and O.C. Ferrell, "Stakeholder Marketing Relationships to Social Responsibility and Firm Performance," *Research in Marketing*, Forthcoming.

91. Amy Guthrie, "Survey Shows Mexicans Drinking Less Soda After Tax," *The Wall Street Journal,* October 13, 2014, http://www.wsj.com/articles/survey-shows-mexicans-drinking-less-soda-after-tax-1413226009 (accessed January 29, 2015).

92. "Being a Responsible Company," http://www.starbucks.com/aboutus/csr.asp (accessed April 14, 2011).

93. MuiChing Carina Chan, John Watson, and David Woodliff, "Corporate Governance Quality and CSR Disclosures," *Journal of Business Ethics* 125, 1 (2014): 59–73.

94. Timothy Stenovec, "AT&T Sued For Reducing Speed Of 'Unlimited' Data Plans," http://www.huffingtonpost.com/2014/10/28/att-slowing-speeds-data-throttling-ftc_n_6062360.html (accessed February 3, 2015).

95. Matthew J. Belvedere, "AT&T CEO warns FCC and Obama over net neutrality," *CNBC,* February 13, 2015, http://www.cnbc.com/id/102424165 (accessed February 13, 2015).

96. "Snapchat settles FTC charges for lying about privacy," *CNN Money,* May 8, 2014, http://money.cnn.com/2014/05/08/technology/security/snapchat-ftc/ (accessed February 3, 2015).

97. Katie Thomas, "Group Sues Aetna, Claiming Discrimination Against H.I.V. Patients," *The New York Times,* December 22, 2014, http://www.nytimes.com/2014/12/23/business/group-sues-aetna-claiming-discrimination-against-hiv-patients.html (accessed February 3, 2015).

98. Dune Lawrence, "A Month Before Deadline, Firms Play for Time on Conflict-Mineral Reporting," *Bloomberg,* April 29, 2014, http://www.bloomberg.com/bw/articles/2014-04-29/secs-conflict-mineral-rules-are-in-limbo-a-month-before-deadline (accessed February 3, 2015); Business & Human Rights Resource Centre, "Conflict minerals disclosure reports (June 2014)," http://business-humanrights.org/en/conflict-peace/conflict-minerals/conflict-minerals-disclosure-reports-jun-2014 (accessed February 3, 2015).

CHAPTER 3

EMERGING BUSINESS ETHICS ISSUES

CHAPTER OBJECTIVES

- Define ethical issues in the context of organizational ethics

- Examine ethical issues as they relate to the basic values of honesty, fairness, and integrity

- Delineate misuse of company resources, abusive and intimidating behavior, lying, conflicts of interest, bribery, corporate intelligence, discrimination, sexual harassment, fraud, financial misconduct, insider trading, intellectual property rights, and privacy as business ethics issues

- Examine the challenge of determining an ethical issue in business

CHAPTER OUTLINE

AN ETHICAL DILEMMA*

Jayla just landed an internship with Acme Incorporated in the Payroll Department. She was excited because these internships usually turned into a full-time job after graduation. Jayla was hired by Deon, the head of the Payroll Department. He told her about their policies and stressed the need for maintaining strict confidentiality regarding employee salaries and pay scales. "Several years ago we had an intern who violated the confidentiality policy and was given a negative internship summary," explained Deon.

"I understand, sir," Jayla responded.

Jayla was determined to learn as much as she could about the job. She made sure she was always on time, followed all of the policies and procedures, and got along well with her co-workers. She started to feel like she fit in at Acme and dreamed of the day when she worked there permanently. However, one day while studying the books, Jayla began to notice abnormalities in one salesperson's salary. Greg, one of the senior sales representatives, made three times as much as the next highest earning salesperson in the company. Jayla assumed he must be a spectacular salesperson and worked efficiently. She often overheard Mia, the General Manager, and Deon praise Greg for his sales numbers. She also noticed the three of them would often go to lunch together.

One morning, Deon handed a stack of client folders to Jayla. He explained, "These are the clients for the salespeople for the week. They will come to you when they need more work, and they are only to take the files on top of the pile. You are in charge of making sure the salespeople don't pick and choose the files. This is how we keep things fair among the sales force."

"I will make sure the files are distributed fairly," Jayla promised. She was excited to be trusted with this responsibility, and she made sure she did her best. Mary, one of the salespeople, came by to get files for the week. They made small talk as Mary looked into her files. She looked disappointed.

"You didn't get any good clients?" Jayla asked.

"Nope, not a one," replied Mary, "which is just my luck!" She threw down the files in exasperation. Jayla was concerned and asked, "What's the matter?"

"I'm sorry," she replied, "It's just that my sales have been slipping, and my pay checks are much smaller than they used to be. If my pay decreases much further, I may lose my health benefits. My daughter is asthmatic, and she has been in and out of the hospital over the last few months." Jayla looked at Mary sympathetically and tried her best to console her.

The next week, before the salespeople started coming into the office to pick from the pile, Jayla had some documents for Deon to sign. When she arrived at his office, the door was slightly open. She peeked in and saw Deon and Greg going through the stack of clients. Jayla watched as Greg rifled through the pile and picked out files.

"Thanks, Deon. These are the top clients for the week," Greg said.

"No problem, Greg," Deon responded "Anything for my favorite brother-in-law. Just keep up the good work."

Jayla stood there, mouth open. She turned to walk back toward her desk. She could not believe what she just saw. The boss was giving Deon all the good clients, while the rest of the salespeople had no choice in which they were assigned. Jayla knew this favoritism was a serious conflict of interest. Then she thought of Mary and her situation.

"What am I supposed to do?" Jayla wondered. "If I say something to Deon, he will give me a bad evaluation. If I say anything to Mia, I may get fired. And I definitely can't say anything to the other salespeople. There would be a riot." Saddened, she sat at her desk and wondered what to do.

QUESTIONS | EXERCISES

1. Discuss how this conflict of interest situation affects other salespeople, the organizational culture, and other stakeholders.
2. Describe the decision that Jayla must make. What are the potential ramifications of her choices?
3. Are there legal ramifications to this kind of behavior? If so, what are the potential consequences?

*This case is strictly hypothetical; any resemblance to real persons, companies, or situations is coincidental.

Stakeholder concerns determine in large part whether specific business actions or decisions are perceived as right or wrong, which drives what the organization defines as ethical or unethical. In the case of the government, community, and society, what was merely an ethical issue can become a legal debate and eventually law. Ethical conflicts in which damages occur can turn into litigation. Additionally, stakeholders often raise issues when they exert pressure on businesses to make decisions that serve their particular agendas. For example, pilots from private-jet company NetJets—owned by Berkshire Hathaway—picketed outside a hotel where Berkshire Hathaway CEO Warren Buffett was attending to protest their dissatisfaction with management. Although Berkshire Hathaway is well-known for its high-paid managers and ethical culture, NetJets employees felt that management had unfairly cut costs in the form of incentives and health benefits. This shows that even well-respected companies experience conflicts with stakeholders that they must address.[1]

People make ethical decisions only after they recognize a particular issue or situation has an ethical component; therefore, a first step toward understanding business ethics is to develop *ethical issue awareness*. Ethical issues typically arise because of conflicts among individuals' morals and the core values and culture of the organizations where they work. Institutions in society provide foundational principles and values that influence both individuals and organizations. The business environment presents many potential ethical conflicts. Organizational objectives can clash with its employees' attempts to fulfill their own personal goals. Similarly, consumers' need for safe, quality, and competitively priced products may create a demand for consumer regulation. For instance, the Food and Drug Administration considered regulation on the use of pure caffeine powder after two people died from using the substance.[2]

In this chapter, we consider some of the ethical issues emerging in business today, including how they arise from the demands of specific stakeholder groups. In the first half of the chapter, we explain certain universal concepts that pervade business ethics, such as integrity, honesty, and fairness. The second half of the chapter explores a number of emerging ethical issues, including misuse of company time and resources, abusive and intimidating behavior, lying, conflicts of interest, bribery, corporate intelligence, discrimination, sexual harassment, fraud, financial misconduct, insider trading, intellectual property rights, and employee privacy. We also examine the challenge of determining decisions that have an ethical component for the firm to consider. Because of the rise of the multinational corporation—as well as increased vertical systems competition—there are certain practices and products that become ethical and legal issues. It is important you understand that what was once a legal activity can become an ethical issue, resulting in well-known practices becoming unethical or illegal.

RECOGNIZING AN ETHICAL ISSUE (ETHICAL AWARENESS)

Although we have described a number of relationships and situations that may generate ethical issues, in practice it can be difficult to recognize them. Failure to acknowledge or be aware of ethical issues is a great danger in any organization. Some issues are difficult to recognize because they are gray areas that are hard to navigate. For example, when does a small gift become a bribe? Employees may engage in questionable behaviors because they are trying to achieve firm objectives related to sales or earnings. Our personal or moral issues are easier to define and control. The complexity of the work environment, however, makes it harder to become aware of, define, and reduce ethical issues.

Business decisions, like personal decisions, may involve a dilemma. In a dilemma all of the alternatives have negative consequences, so the less harmful choice is made. An ethical issue is simply a situation involving a group, a problem, or even an opportunity that requires thought, discussion, or investigation before a decision can be made. Because the business world is dynamic, new ethical issues emerge all the time. Table 3–1 defines specific ethical issues identified by employees in the National Business Ethics Survey (NBES). Misuse of company time, abusive behavior, and lying to employees are personal in nature, but are committed in the belief that the action is furthering organizational goals. Falsifying time or expenses, safety violations, and abuse of company resources are issues that directly relate to an ethical conflict that could damage the firm. The table compares the percentage of employees who observed specific types of misconduct over the past two National Business Ethics Surveys.

Employees could engage in more than one form of misconduct; therefore, each type of misconduct represents the percentage of employees who witnessed that particular act. Although it is impossible to list every conceivable ethical issue, any type of manipulation or deceit—or even just the absence of transparency in decision making—can create harm to others. For example, *collusion* is a secret agreement between two or more parties for a fraudulent, illegal, or deceitful purpose. "Deceitful purpose" is the relevant phrase in regard to business ethics, as it suggests trickery, misrepresentation, or a strategy designed to lead others to believe something less than the whole truth. Collusion violates the general business value of honesty. Next, we examine three foundational values that are used to identify ethical issues.

TABLE 3–1 Specific Types of Observed Misconduct

Behavior	2013 (%)	2011 (%)
Abusive behavior	18	21
Lying to employees	17	20
Conflicts of interest	12	15
Violating company Internet use policies	12	16
Discrimination	12	15
Health or safety violations	10	13
Lying to outside stakeholders	10	12
Retaliation against someone who reported misconduct	10	
Falsifying time reports or hours worked	10	12
Stealing/theft	9	12
Employee benefit violations	9	12
Delivery of substandard products	9	10

Source: Ethics Resource Center, National Business Ethics Survey of the U.S. Workforce (Arlington, VA: Ethics Resource Center, 2014), p. 41.

FOUNDATIONAL VALUES FOR IDENTIFYING ETHICAL ISSUES

Integrity, honesty, and fairness are widely used values for evaluating activities that could become ethical issues. Ethical issues can emerge from almost any decision made in an organization. Understanding these foundational values can help identify and develop discussions and a constructive dialogue on appropriate conduct. It is just as important to emphasize appropriate conduct associated with these values as it is to discover inappropriate conduct.

Integrity

Integrity is one of the most important and oft-cited elements of virtue, and refers to being whole, sound, and in an unimpaired condition. Integrity is a global value that relates to all activities, not just business issues. Integrity relates to product quality, open communication, transparency, and relationships. Therefore, it is a foundational value for managers to build an ethical internal organizational culture. In an organization, integrity means uncompromising adherence to a set or group of values. It is connected to acting ethically; in other words, there are substantive or normative constraints on what it means to act with integrity. An organization's integrity usually rests on its enduring values and unwillingness to deviate from standards of behavior as defined by the firm and industry.

At a minimum, businesses are expected to follow laws and regulations. In addition, organizations should not knowingly harm customers, clients, employees, or even other competitors through deception, misrepresentation, or coercion. Although they often act in their own economic self-interest, business relations should be grounded in integrity. Failure to live up to this expectation or abide by laws and standards destroys trust and makes it difficult, if not impossible, to continue business exchanges.[3] Integrity complements honesty, which becomes the glue that holds business relationships together to make everything else more effective and efficient.

Honesty

Honesty refers to truthfulness or trustworthiness. To be honest is to tell the truth to the best of your knowledge without hiding anything. Confucius defined an honest person as *junzi*, or one who has the virtue *ren*. *Ren* can be loosely defined as one who has humanity. *Yi* is another honesty component and is related to what we should do according to our relationships with others. Another Confucian concept, *li*, relates to honesty but refers to the virtue of good manners or respect. Finally, *zhi* represents whether a person knows what to say and what to do as it relates to honesty. The Confucian version of Kant's Golden Rule is to treat your inferiors as you would want your superiors to treat you. As a result, virtues such as familial honor and reputation for honesty become paramount.

Issues related to honesty also arise because business is sometimes regarded as a game governed by its own rules rather than those of society as a whole. Author Eric Beversluis suggests honesty is a problem because people often reason along these lines:

1. Business relationships are a subset of human relationships governed by their own rules that in a market society involve competition, profit maximization, and personal advancement within the organization.

2. Business can therefore be considered a game people play, comparable in certain respects to competitive sports such as basketball or boxing.

3. Ordinary ethics rules and morality do not hold in games like basketball or boxing. (What if a basketball player did unto others as he would have them do unto him? What if a boxer decided it was wrong to try to injure another person?)

4. Logically, then, if business is a game like basketball or boxing, ordinary ethical rules do not apply.[4]

This type of reasoning leads many to conclude that anything is acceptable in business. Indeed, several books have compared business to warfare—for example, *The Guerrilla Marketing Handbook* and *Sun Tsu: The Art of War for Managers.* The common theme is that surprise attacks, guerrilla warfare, and other warlike tactics are necessary to win the battle for consumer dollars. New England Patriots coach Bill Belichick uses lessons from *The Art of War* to help shape his coaching philosophy. Believing that games can be won before players even take to the field, Belichick believes attention to detail and the ability to use an opponent's weaknesses against him is crucial to success.[5] Although this business-as-war mentality can help a company remain competitive, it could also foster the idea that honesty is unnecessary in business. For instance, accusations that the New England Patriots used slightly deflated footballs during a game to gain an advantage could be construed as a dishonest way to win. The National Football League attempted to suspend Patriots quarterback Tom Brady for the first four games of the season, fined the Patriots $1 million, and took away two draft picks.[6]

Many argue that because people are not economically self-sufficient, they cannot withdraw from the relationships of business. Therefore, business must not only make clear what rules apply but also develop rules appropriate to the involuntary nature of its many participants. Such rules should contain the value of honesty.

The opposite of honesty is dishonesty. *Dishonesty* can be broadly defined as a lack or absence of integrity, incomplete disclosure, and an unwillingness to tell the truth. Lying, cheating, and stealing are actions usually associated with dishonest conduct. The causes of dishonesty are complex and relate to both individual and organizational pressures. Many employees lie to help achieve performance objectives. For example, they may be asked to lie about when a customer will receive a purchase. Lying can be defined as (1) untruthful statements that result in damage or harm; (2) "white lies," which do not cause damage but instead function as excuses or a means of benefitting others; and (3) statements obviously meant to engage or entertain without malice. These definitions become important in the remainder of this chapter.

Fairness

Fairness is the quality of being just, equitable, and impartial. Fairness clearly overlaps with the concepts of justice, equity, and equality. There are three fundamental elements that motivate people to be fair: equality, reciprocity, and optimization. In business, **equality** is about the distribution of benefits and resources. This distribution could be applied to stakeholders or the greater society.

Reciprocity is an interchange of giving and receiving in social relationships. Reciprocity occurs when an action that has an effect upon another is reciprocated with an action that has an approximately equal effect. It is the return of favors approximately equal in value. For example, reciprocity implies workers be compensated with wages approximately equal to their effort. Walmart tried to display ethical reciprocity by increasing the wages it paid to its lowest level employees to $9 an hour, with plans to raise it to $10 per hour the following year. It is estimated that this wage increase will impact 500,000 Walmart workers.[7]

Optimization is the trade-off between equity (equality) and efficiency (maximum productivity). Discriminating on the basis of gender, race, or religion is generally considered unfair because these qualities have little bearing upon a person's ability to do a job. The optimal way to hire is to choose the employee who is the most talented, proficient, educated, and able. Ideas of fairness are sometimes shaped by vested interests. One or both parties in the relationship may view an action as unfair or unethical because the outcome was less beneficial than expected.

ETHICAL ISSUES AND DILEMMAS IN BUSINESS

As mentioned earlier, stakeholders and the firm define ethical issues. An **ethical issue** is a problem, situation, or opportunity that requires an individual, group, or organization to choose among several actions that must be evaluated as right or wrong, ethical or unethical. An **ethical dilemma** is a problem, situation, or opportunity that requires an individual, group, or organization to choose among several actions that have negative outcomes. There is not a right or ethical choice in a dilemma, only less unethical or illegal choices as perceived by any and all stakeholders.

A constructive next step toward identifying and resolving ethical issues is to classify the issues that are relevant to most business organizations. Table 3–2 reflects some pressing ethical issues to shareholders. Some of these issues deal with the economic conditions and/or misconduct at firms from other countries. For instance, accounting irregularities at Chinese firms caused concern for the SEC. The SEC demanded that the Chinese arms of the Big Four accounting firms—KPMG, Ernst & Young, PricewaterhouseCoopers, and Deloitte—hand over documents related to companies under investigation. The firms argued that Chinese law prevented them from handing over the documents, and the firms agreed to pay $2 million to settle the dispute.[8] In this section, we classify ethical issues in relation to misuse of company time and resources, abusive or intimidating behavior, lying, conflicts of interest, bribery, corporate intelligence, discrimination, sexual harassment, fraud, financial misconduct, insider trading, intellectual property rights, and privacy issues.

TABLE 3–2 Shareholder Issues

1. Core values
2. Shareholder participation in electing directors
3. Equitable compensation strategies
4. Ethical and legal compliance
5. Community and regulatory integrity
6. Reputation management
7. Big data and cybersecurity
8. Supply chain relationships and human rights

Source: Adapted from Jaclyn Jaeger, "Top Shareholder Issues for 2012 Proxy Season," *Compliance Week*, March 8, 2012, http://www.complianceweek.com/blogs/the-filing-cabinet/top-shareholder-issues-for-2012-proxy-season#.VOyOwnnTBVl (accessed February 24, 2015).

Misuse of Company Time and Resources

Time theft can be difficult to measure but is estimated to cost companies hundreds of billions of dollars annually. It is widely believed the average employee "steals" 4.25 hours per week with late arrivals, leaving early, long lunch breaks, inappropriate sick days, excessive socializing, and engaging in personal activities such as online shopping and watching sports while on the job.[9]

Although companies have different viewpoints and policies, the misuse of time and resources has been identified by the Ethics Resource Center as a major form of observed misconduct in organizations. One of the greatest ways that employees misuse their work time and company resources is by using the company computer for personal uses. In the latest survey, 12 percent of respondents observed others violating company Internet policies, while another 9 percent noted employees stealing from the firm. Often lax enforcement of company policies creates the impression among employees that they are entitled to certain company resources, including how they spend their time at work. Such misuse can range from unauthorized equipment usage to misuse of financial resources.

Using company computer software and Internet services for personal business is one of the most common ways employees misuse company resources. While it may not be acceptable for employees to sit in the lobby chatting with relatives or their stock brokers, these same employees go online and do the same thing, possibly unnoticed by others. Typical examples of using a computer to abuse company time include sending personal emails, shopping, downloading music, doing personal banking, surfing the Internet for information about sports or romance, or visiting social networking sites such as Facebook. It has been found that March Madness, the NCAA basketball tournament, is one of the most significant periods during which employees engage in time theft. Many firms block websites where employees can watch sports events.

Because misuse of company resources is such a widespread problem, many firms, such as Coca-Cola, have implemented policies delineating the acceptable use of such resources. Coca-Cola's policy states that some resource use for personal purposes is acceptable as long as it does not become excessive or harm work activities. Employees are expected to use their judgment to determine when personal activities might be detracting too much from work responsibilities.[10] As another example, Virgin Group adopted a new policy allowing employees to take as much vacation time as they need. Although left to the employee's discretion, CEO Richard Branson believes employees will use their judgment and not abuse the system to get out of work.[11]

Abusive or Intimidating Behavior

Abusive or intimidating behavior is another common ethical problem for employees, but what does it mean to be abusive or intimidating? These terms refer to many things—physical threats, false accusations, being annoying, profanity, insults, yelling, harshness, ignoring someone, and unreasonableness—and their meaning differs from person to person. It is important to understand that within each term there is a continuum. For example, behavior one person might define as yelling could be another's definition of normal speech. The lack of civility in our society has been a concern, and it is as common in the workplace as elsewhere. The productivity level of many organizations has been damaged by time spent unraveling problematic relationships.

Is it abusive behavior to ask an employee to complete a project rather than be with a family member or relative in a crisis situation? What does it mean to speak profanely? Is profanity only related to specific words or terms that are, in fact, common in today's business world? If you are using words acceptable to you but that others consider profanity, have you just insulted, abused, or disrespected them?

Within abusive behavior or intimidation, intent should be a consideration. If the employee tries to convey a compliment, then he or she probably simply made a mistake. What if a male manager asks a female subordinate if she has a date because she is dressed nicely? When does the way a word is said (voice inflection) become important? There is also the problem of word meanings by age and within cultures. The fact that we live in a multicultural environment and work with many different cultural groups and nationalities adds to the depth of the ethical and legal issues that may arise.

Wage theft is another way that employers create an abusive environment. Employees are increasingly claiming that companies are failing to pay them overtime for working extra hours. Federal and state regulators are investigating this uptick in wage theft allegations to see if employers are violating minimum wage and overtime laws.[12] For instance, some Subway and McDonald's franchisees have been found guilty of violating pay and hour rules. As a result, Subway franchisees were forced to reimburse employees more than $3.8 million.[13] Forcing employees to work overtime with no compensation or paying them less than what the law dictates creates a negative environment where employees often feel bullied or exploited.

Bullying is associated with a hostile workplace where someone (or a group) considered a target is threatened, harassed, belittled, verbally abused, or overly criticized. Bullying creates what is referred to as a "hostile environment," but the concept of a hostile environment is generally associated instead with sexual harassment. Regardless, bullying can cause psychological damage that may result in health-endangering consequences to the target. For example, workplace bullying is strongly associated with sleep disturbances. The more frequent the bullying, the higher the risk of sleep disturbance. Other physical symptoms include depression, fatigue, increased sick days, and stomach problems.[15] As Table 3–3 indicates, bullies can use a mix of verbal, nonverbal, and manipulative threatening expressions to damage workplace productivity. Approximately 72 percent of bullies in the workplace outrank their victims.[16] If managers do not address bullying behaviors in the organization, then what starts out as one or two bullies may begin to spread. It has been found that employees who have been bullied are more likely to find it acceptable to bully others.[17]

DEBATE ISSUE
TAKE A STAND

Is Workplace Bullying Serious Enough to Warrant Legal Action?

Workplace bullying is abusive behavior used to assert one's power over another. One survey shows that more than one-third of employees have been victims of some kind of workplace bullying behavior. In many cases, the bullies are the supervisors of the organization. Yet while some countries have laws against workplace bullying, the United States does not.

Many believe employees should be legally protected from workplace bullying because bullying is harmful to employee health. Victims of bullying suffer from symptoms including depression, anxiety, and low self-esteem. Bullying permeates the environment of the workplace, causing bystanders to feel its unpleasant effects and creating a toxic workplace. Others, however, believe anti-bullying laws would limit managers' ability to manage since they would constantly be afraid their management styles could be perceived as bullying. Also, critics of such a law argue that bullying is hard to define, making such a law difficult to enforce. Instead, they are in favor of internal ways to combat bullying, including conflict resolution, harassment awareness, and sensitivity trainings.[14]

1. Bullying in organizations can be harmful to employees and therefore warrants legal action.

2. Laws against bullying are not feasible as they are hard to define and have the potential to limit managers' ability to manage.

TABLE 3–3 Actions Associated with Bullies

1. Spreading rumors to damage others

2. Blocking others' communication in the workplace

3. Flaunting status or authority to take advantage of others

4. Discrediting others' ideas and opinions

5. Use of emails to demean others

6. Failing to communicate or return communication

7. Insults, yelling, and shouting

8. Using terminology to discriminate by gender, race, or age

9. Using eye or body language to hurt others or their reputations

10. Taking credit for others' work or ideas

Source: Based on Cathi McMahan, "Are You a Bully?" *Inside Seven,* California Department of Transportation Newsletter, June 1999, 6.

There is currently no U.S. law prohibiting workplace bullying. However, twenty-seven states have introduced the Healthy Workplace Bill to consider ways to combat bullying.[18] Workplace bullying is illegal in many other countries. Some suggest employers take the following steps to minimize workplace bullying:

• Create policies that place reprimand letters and/or dismissal for such behavior.

• Emphasize mutual respect in the employee handbook.

• Encourage employees who feel bullied to report the conduct via hotlines or other means.

In addition to the three items mentioned, firms are now helping employees understand what bullying is by the use of the following questions:

• Is your supervisor requiring impossible things from you without training?

• Does your supervisor always state that your completed work is never good enough?

• Are meetings to be attended called without your knowledge?

• Have others told you to stop working, talking, or socializing with them?

• Does someone never leave you alone to do your job without interference?

• Do people feel justified screaming or yelling at you in front of others, and are you punished if you scream back?

• Do human resources officials tell you that your harassment is legal and you must work it out between yourselves?

• Do many people verify that your torment is real, but do nothing about it?[19]

Bullying also occurs between companies that are in intense competition. Even respected companies such as eBay have been accused of monopolistic bullying. The Justice Department accused eBay of having a secret agreement with Intuit to avoid hiring workers from each other's companies. The Justice Department believes this agreement served to limit competition and hinder employment opportunities. eBay settled for $3.75 million.[20] In many cases, the alleged misconduct can have not only monetary and legal implications but can also threaten reputation, investor confidence, and customer loyalty.

Lying

Earlier in this chapter, we discussed the definitions of **lying** and how lying relates to distorting the truth. We mentioned three types of lies, one of which is joking without malice. The other two can become troublesome for businesses: lying by commission and lying by omission. *Commission lying* is creating a perception or belief by words that intentionally deceive the receiver of the message—for example, lying about being at work, expense reports, or carrying out work assignments. Commission lying also entails intentionally creating "noise" within the communication that knowingly confuses or deceives the receiver. *Noise* can be defined as technical explanations the communicator knows the receiver does not understand. It can be the intentional use of communication forms that make it difficult for the receiver to actually hear the true message. Using legal terms or terms relating to unfamiliar processes and systems to explain what was done in a work situation facilitate this type of lie.

Lying by commission can involve complex forms, procedures, contracts, words that are spelled the same but have different meanings, or refuting the truth with a false statement. Forms of commission lying include puffery in advertising. For example, saying a product is "homemade" when it is made in a factory is lying. "Made from scratch" in cooking technically means that all ingredients within the product were distinct and separate and were not combined prior to the beginning of the production process. Many food and cleaning supply labels use the word "natural" to imply that its ingredients are healthier, organic, or nongenetically modified. In reality, the word "natural" is not regulated and does not have to mean any of these things.

Omission lying is intentionally not informing others of any differences, problems, safety warnings, or negative issues relating to the product or company that significantly affect awareness, intention, or behavior. A classic example of omission lying was in the tobacco manufacturers' decades-long refusal to allow negative research about the effects of tobacco to appear on cigarettes and cigars. When lying damages others, it can be the focus of a lawsuit. For example, prosecutors and civil lawsuits often reduce misconduct to lying about a fact, such as financial performance, that has the potential to damage others. A class-action lawsuit was filed against Ticketmaster for charging what customers thought were order processing and UPS delivery fees that actually turned out to be profit centers for the firm.[21] Manipulating financial reports to inflate earnings is also a form of omission lying that can result in fraud.

The point at which a lie becomes unethical in business is based on the *context* of the statement and its *intent* to distort the truth. A lie becomes illegal if it is determined by the courts to have damaged others. Some businesspeople may believe one must lie a little or that the occasional lie is sanctioned by the organization. The question you need to ask is whether lies are distorting openness and transparency and other values associated with ethical behavior.

Conflicts of Interest

A **conflict of interest** exists when an individual must choose whether to advance his or her own interests, those of the organization, or those of some other group. The three major bond rating agencies—Moody's, Standard & Poor's, and Fitch Ratings—analyze financial deals and assign letters (such as AAA, B, CC) to represent the quality of bonds and other investments. Prior to the financial meltdown, these rating agencies had significant conflicts of interest. The agencies earned as much as three times more for grading complex products than for corporate bonds. They also competed with each other for rating jobs, which contributed to lower rating standards. Additionally, the companies who wanted the ratings were the ones paying the agencies. Because the rating agencies were highly competitive, investment firms and banks would "shop" the different agencies for the best rating. Conflicts of interest were inevitable.

To avoid conflicts of interest, employees must be able to separate their private interests from their business dealings. Organizations must also avoid potential conflicts of interest when providing products. The U.S. General Accounting Office found conflicts of interest when the government awarded bids on defense contracts. Conflicts of interest usually relate to hiring friends, relatives, or retired military officers to enhance the probability of getting a contract.[22]

Bribery

Bribery is the practice of offering something (often money) in order to gain an illicit advantage from someone in authority. Gifts, entertainment, and travel can also be used as bribes. The key issue regarding whether or not something is considered bribery is whether it is used to gain an advantage in a relationship. Bribery can be defined as an unlawful act, but it can also be a business ethics issue in that an industry or even national culture may include such payments as standard practice. Related to the ethics of bribery is the concept of active corruption or **active bribery**, meaning the person who promises or gives the bribe commits the offense. Passive bribery is an offense committed by the official who receives the bribe. It is not an offense, however, if the advantage was permitted or required by the written law or regulation of the foreign public official's country, including case law.

Small **facilitation payments** made to obtain or retain business or other improper advantages do not constitute bribery for U.S. companies in some situations. Such payments are often made to officials to perform their functions, such as issuing licenses or permits. Outside of these facilitation payments are illegal.[23] Ralph Lauren Corp. employees gave Argentine customs officials dresses, perfume, and cash to accelerate the passage of merchandise into the country. Over $580,000 was paid. This amount was not considered to be facilitation payments—they were considered to be bribes. When discovered, Ralph Lauren reported the bribery and cooperated with an investigation. As a result of their cooperativeness, they were not prosecuted under the Foreign Corrupt Practices Act. However, they agreed to pay $1.6 million to resolve the investigation.[24]

In most developed countries, it is generally recognized that employees should not accept bribes, personal payments, gifts, or special favors from people who hope to influence the outcome of a decision. However, bribery is an accepted way of doing business in other countries, which creates challenging situations for global businesses. Bribes have been associated with the downfall of many managers, legislators, and government officials. It is also not limited to rogue employees—approximately 53 percent of the bribery cases reported involve bribes that had been authorized by managers.[25]

When a government official accepts a bribe, it is usually from a business that seeks some advantage, perhaps to obtain business or the opportunity to avoid regulation. Giving bribes to legislators or public officials is both a legal and a business ethics issue. Federal as well as state anti-bribery laws exist. It is a legal issue in the United States under the U.S. Foreign Corrupt Practices Act (FCPA) to bribe a foreign official. This act maintains it is illegal for individuals, firms, or third parties doing business in American markets to "make payments to foreign government officials to assist in obtaining or retaining business."[26] Companies have paid billions of dollars in fines to the Department of Justice for bribery violations. The law does not apply only to American firms, but to all firms transacting business with operations in the United States. This could also mean firms do not necessarily have to commit the bribery in the United States to be held accountable. For instance, Alcoa paid $384 million to settle allegations that it had paid bribes to a Bahraini state-controlled smelter.[27]

Corporate Intelligence

Many issues related to corporate intelligence have surfaced in the last few years. Defined broadly, **corporate intelligence** (CI) is the collection and analysis of information on markets, te   petitors, as well as on socioeconomic and external politica   pes of intelligence models: a passive monitoring system   upport, and support dedicated to top-management strategy.

CI involves an in-depth discovery of information from corporate records, court documents, regulatory filings, and press releases, as well as any other background information about a company or its executives. Corporate intelligence can be a legitimate inquiry into meaningful information used in staying competitive. For instance, it is legal for a software company to monitor its competitor's online activities such as blogs and Facebook posts. If the company learns from monitoring its competitor's public postings it is likely planning to launch a new product, the company could use this intelligence to release the product first and beat the competition. Such an activity is acceptable.

CI has its own set of procedures. For example, can you tell which of the following are acceptable strategies and practices in CI?

1. Develop an effective network of informants. Encourage staff members to gather competitive information as they interact with people outside the company.

2. Have every salesperson talk to those customers who are believed to have talked to competitors.

3. When interviewing job applicants from competitors, have Human Resources ask about critical information, including social network accounts.

4. Have purchasers talk to suppliers to attempt to discover who is demanding what and when it is needed.

5. Interview every employee about his or her knowledge or expertise and leverage it for outside information about other firms within the industry.

6. When you interview consultants, ask them to share examples of their work.

7. Use press releases announcing new hires as an indicator of what type of talent companies are hiring.

8. Use web services to track all the changes anyone makes on a company's website, thus giving you an indication of which areas a competitor is thinking about and where it might be headed.

9. Use a proxy or other firm to act as a client for the competitor so as to ask about a company's pricing structure, how fast they ship, turnaround time, and number of employees. Ask for references and call those people as well.

TABLE 3–4 Ways to Steal Corporate Trade Secrets

Method of Corporate Espionage	Definition	Examples
Hacking	Breaking into a computer network to steal information	**System hacking**: Assumes the attacker already has access to a low-level, privileged-user account
		Remote hacking: Involves attempting to remotely penetrate a system across the Internet
		Physical hacking: Requires the hacker to enter a facility physically and find a vacant unsecured workstation with an employee's login and password
Social engineering	Tricking individuals into revealing their passwords or other valuable corporate information	**Shoulder surfing**: Someone simply looks over an employee's shoulder while he or she types a password
		Password guessing: When an employee is able to guess a person's password after finding out personal information about him or her
Dumpster diving	Digging through trash to find trade secrets	An employee obtains several organizational charts from a rival business by digging through that organization's trash
Whacking	Using wireless hacking to break into a network	An intruder uses a radio to tap into a wireless network to access unencrypted data
Phone eavesdropping	Using a digital recording device to monitor and record a fax line	A person records a message from a fax line and recreates an exact copy of the message by playing back the recording

All of these scenarios are legal and frequently used by corporate intelligence departments and firms.

However, corporate intelligence, like other areas in business, can be abused if due diligence is not taken to maintain legal and ethical methods of discovery. Computers, local-area networks (LANs), and the Internet have made the theft of trade secrets very easy. Proprietary information like secret formulas, manufacturing schematics, merger or acquisition plans, and marketing strategies all have tremendous value.[28] Theft of corporate trade secrets has been on the rise among technology companies such as Samsung. Corporate espionage is estimated to cost the world economy $445 billion each year—about 1 percent of global income.[29] If discovered, corporate espionage can lead to heavy fines and prison sentences. A lack of security and proper training allows a person to use a variety of techniques to gain access to a company's vital information. Some techniques for accessing valuable corporate information are included in Table 3–4.

Discrimination

Although a person's racial and sexual prejudices belong to the domain of individual ethics, racial and sexual discrimination in the workplace create ethical issues within the business world. **Discrimination** on the basis of race, color, religion, sex, marital status, sexual orientation, public assistance status, disability, age, national origin, or veteran status is illegal in the United States. Additionally, discrimination on the basis of political opinions or affiliation with a union is defined as harassment. Discrimination remains a significant ethical issue in business despite decades of legislation attempting to outlaw it.

A company in the United States can be sued if it (1) refuses to hire an individual, (2) maintains a system of employment that unreasonably excludes an individual from employment, (3) discharges an individual, or (4) discriminates against an individual with respect to hiring, employment terms, promotion, or privileges of employment as they relate to the definition of discrimination. Nearly 89,000 charges of discrimination were filed with the **Equal Employment Opportunity Commission** (EEOC) in 2014.[30]

Race, gender, and age discrimination are major sources of ethical and legal debate in the workplace. Once dominated by European American men, the U.S. workforce today includes significantly more women, African Americans, Hispanics, and other minorities, as well as disabled and older workers. These groups traditionally faced discrimination and higher unemployment rates and been denied opportunities to assume leadership roles in corporate America. For example, only five Fortune 500 companies are led by African American CEOs.[31]

Another form of discrimination involves discriminating against individuals on the basis of age. The **Age Discrimination in Employment Act** specifically outlaws hiring practices that discriminate against people 40 years of age or older, as well as those that require employees to retire before the age of 70. The act prohibits employers with 20 or more employees from making employment decisions, including decisions regarding the termination of employment, on the basis of age or as a result of policies requiring retirement after the age of 40. Despite this legislation, charges of age discrimination persist in the workplace. Age discrimination accounts for approximately 23 percent of the complaints filed with the EEOC.[32] Given the fact that nearly one-third of the nation's workers are 55 years old or over, many companies need to change their approach toward older workers.[33]

To help build workforces that reflect their customer base, many companies have initiated **affirmative action programs**, which involve efforts to recruit, hire, train, and promote qualified individuals from groups that have traditionally been discriminated against on the basis of race, gender, or other characteristics. Such initiatives may be imposed by federal law on an employer that contracts or subcontracts for business with the federal government, as part of a settlement agreement with a state or federal agency, or by court order.[34] For example, McCormick & Schmick's Seafood Corporation paid a settlement of $1.3 million to settle a lawsuit that it discriminated against African American workers. It also adopted recruitment procedures to attract African American job applicants.[35] However, many companies voluntarily implement affirmative action plans in order to build a more diverse workforce. Although many people believe affirmative action requires the use of quotas to govern employment decisions, it is important to note two decades of Supreme Court rulings made it clear that affirmative action does not permit or require quotas, reverse discrimination, or favorable treatment of unqualified women or minorities. To ensure affirmative action programs are fair, the Supreme Court established standards to guide their implementation: (1) There must be a strong reason for developing an affirmative action program; (2) affirmative action programs must apply only to qualified candidates; and (3) affirmative action programs must be limited and temporary and therefore cannot include "rigid and inflexible quotas."[36]

Discrimination can also be an ethical issue in business when companies use race or other personal factors to discriminate against specific groups of customers.

Many companies have been accused of using race, disabilities, gender, or age to deny service or to charge higher prices to certain ethnic groups. Employees have also been terminated or denied jobs due to discrimination. Upper Chesapeake Health System paid $180,000 to settle an EEOC lawsuit alleging that it failed to provide reasonable accommodations and rehire a worker due to her disability, despite the worker's positive performance reviews.[37]

Sexual Harassment

Sexual harassment is a form of sex discrimination that violates Title VII of the Civil Rights Act of 1964. Title VII applies to employers with 15 or more employees, including state and local governments. **Sexual harassment** can be defined as any repeated, unwanted behavior of a sexual nature perpetrated upon one individual by another. It may be verbal, visual, written, or physical and can occur between people of different genders or those of the same gender. Displaying sexually explicit materials "may create a hostile work environment or constitute harassment, even though the private possession, reading, and consensual sharing of such materials is protected under the Constitution."[38] Nearly 30 percent of the charges filed with the EEOC involve sexual harassment or pregnancy discrimination.[39]

To establish sexual harassment, an employee must understand the definition of a **hostile work environment**, for which three criteria must be met: the conduct was unwelcome; [it was severe,] pervasive, and regarded by the claimant as so hostile or offensive [as to alter the] conditions of employment; and the conduct was such that a reasonable [person woul]d it hostile or offensive. To assert a hostile work environment, an [employee need not pr]ove it seriously affected his or her psychological well-being or that it caused an injury; the decisive issue is whether the conduct interfered with the claimant's work performance.[40]

Sexual harassment includes unwanted sexual approaches (including touching, feeling, or groping) and/or repeated unpleasant, degrading, or sexist remarks directed toward an employee with the implied suggestion that the target's employment status, promotion, or favorable treatment depend on a positive response and/or cooperation. It can be regarded as a private nuisance, unfair labor practice, or, in some states, a civil wrong (tort) that may be the basis for a lawsuit against the individual who made the advances and against the employer who did not take steps to halt the harassment. The law is primarily concerned with the impact of the behavior and not its intent. An important facet of sexual harassment law is its focus on the victim's reasonable behaviors and expectations.[41] However, the definition of "reasonable" varies from state to state, as does the concept of expectations. In addition, an argument used by some in defense of what others term sexual harassment is the freedom of speech granted by the First Amendment.

A key ethical issue associated with sexual harassment is dual relationships. A **dual relationship** is defined as a personal, loving, and/or sexual relationship with someone with whom you share professional responsibilities. Dual relationships where the relationship could potentially cause a direct or indirect conflict of interest or a risk of impairment to professional judgment can be an ethical or even legal issue.[42] Another important factor in these cases is intent. If the sexual advances in any form are considered mutual, then consent is created. The problem is unless the employee or employer gets something in writing before the romantic action begins, consent can always be questioned, and when it comes to sexual harassment, the alleged perpetrator must prove mutual consent. When relationships end, the potential for ethical conflicts increases.

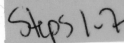

To avoid sexual misconduct or harassment charges a company should take at least the following steps:

1. *Establish a statement of policy* naming someone in the company as ultimately responsible for preventing harassment at the company.

2. *Establish a definition of sexual harassment* that includes unwelcome advances, requests for sexual favors, and any other verbal, visual, or physical conduct of a sexual nature; that provides examples of each; and reminds employees the list of examples is not all-inclusive.

3. *Establish a nonretaliation policy* that protects complainants and witnesses.

4. *Establish specific procedures for prevention* of such practices at early stages. However, if a company puts these procedures in writing, they are expected by law to train employees in accordance with them, measure their effects, and ensure the policies are enforced.

5. *Establish, enforce, and encourage* victims of sexual harassment to report the behavior to authorized individuals.

6. *Establish a reporting procedure.*

7. *Make sure the company has timely reporting requirements to the proper authorities.* Usually, there is a time limitation (ranging from six months to a year) to file a complaint for a formal administrative sexual charge. However, the failure to meet a shorter complaint period (for example, 60 to 90 days) so a rapid response and remediation may occur and to help ensure a harassment-free environment could be a company's defense against charges it was negligent.

Once these steps have been taken, a training program should identify and describe forms of sexual harassment and give examples, outline grievance procedures, explain how to use the procedures and discuss the importance of them, discuss the penalty for violation, and train employees about the essential need for a workplace free from harassment, offensive conduct, or intimidation. A corporation's training program should cover how to spot sexual harassment; how to investigate complaints, including proper documentation; what to do about observed sexual harassment, even when no complaint has been filed; how to keep the work environment as professional and non-hostile as possible; how to teach employees about the professional and legal consequences of sexual harassment; and how to train management to understand follow-up procedures on incidents.

Fraud

When individuals engage in intentional deceptive practices to advance their own interests over those of the organization or some other group, they are committing fraud. In general, **fraud** is any purposeful communication that deceives, manipulates, or conceals facts in order to harm others. Fraud can be a crime and convictions may result in fines, imprisonment, or both. Global fraud costs organizations more than $3.7 trillion a year; the average company loses about 5 percent of annual revenues to fraud.[43] For instance, one 71-year-old former business owner was found guilty of making false statements on his inventory reports so he could obtain credit for his business—a type of misconduct known as loan-application fraud.[44] Figure 3–1 indicates some of the major ways fraud is detected. Note the majority of fraud detection occurs due to tips, thereby making reporting an important way of preventing and detecting wide-scale fraud. In recent years, accounting fraud has become a major ethical issue, but as we will see, fraud can also relate to marketing and consumer issues as well.

FIGURE 3–1 Initial Detection of Occupational Frauds

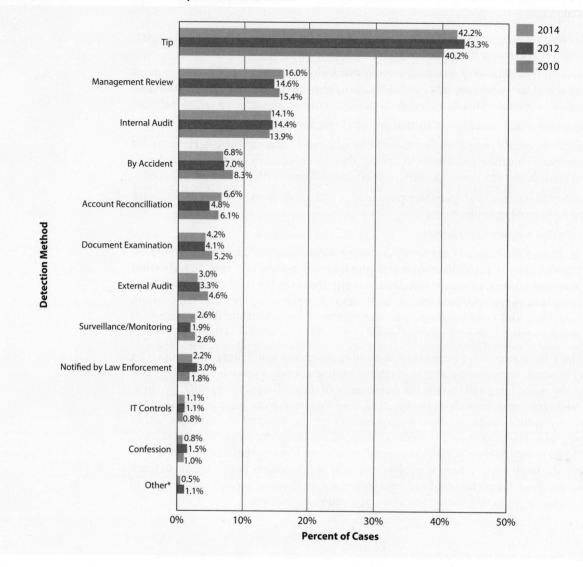

*The category *other* was not included in the 2010 report.

Source: Association of Certified Fraud Examiners, *Report to the Nations on Occupational Fraud and Abuse: 2014 Global Fraud Study,* p. 19

    Accounting fraud usually involves a corporation's financial reports, in which companies provide important information on which investors and others base decisions involving millions of dollars. If the documents contain inaccurate information, intentional or not, lawsuits and criminal penalties may result. Diamond Foods paid $5 million to settle SEC charges that former executives had knowingly misled investors by manipulating walnut costs. This manipulation caused the financials to appear better than they were in reality.[45] Research has shown that chief financial officers are more likely to manipulate accounting statements because of pressure from the CEO than from personal gain.[46] Three factors, known as the fraud triangle, seem to predict why people commit fraud: pressure, opportunity, and rationalization.

The field of accounting has changed dramatically over the last decade. Ethical issues for accountants today include time, reduced fees, client requests to alter opinions concerning financial conditions or lower tax payments, and increased competition. Other issues accountants face daily involve compliance with complex rules and regulations, data overload, contingent fees, and commissions. An accountant's life is filled with rules and data that must be interpreted correctly, and because of these pressures and the ethical predicaments they spawn, problems within the accounting industry are on the rise. As an example of a possible ethical issue, accountants are permitted to charge performance-based fees rather than hourly rates, a rule change that encouraged some large accounting firms to promote tax-avoidance strategies for high-income individuals because the firms can charge 10 to 40 percent of the amount of taxes saved.[47]

As a result, accountants must abide by a strict code of ethics that defines their responsibilities to their clients and to the public interest. The code also discusses the concepts of integrity, objectivity, independence, and due care. Despite the standards the code provides, the accounting industry has been the source of numerous fraud investigations in recent years. Congress passed the Sarbanes–Oxley Act in 2002 to address many of the issues that create conflicts of interest for accounting firms auditing public corporations. The law generally prohibits accounting firms from providing both auditing and consulting services to the same firm. Additionally, the law specifies corporate boards of directors must include outside directors with financial knowledge on the company's audit committee.

One of the results of Sarbanes–Oxley was the establishment of the Public Company Accounting Oversight Board (PCAOB). This nonprofit organization oversees the audits of public companies. The intent of the PCAOB is to protect investors and ensure that the public is receiving accurate audit reports.[48] The PCAOB therefore has the authority to audit public accounting firms; investigate accounting firms for compliance; establish disciplinary proceedings for noncompliance; establish ethics, auditing, quality control, and other standards for auditing public companies; and enforce compliance with Sarbanes–Oxley.[49] We discuss the PCAOB more in the next chapter.

Marketing fraud—the process of dishonestly creating, distributing, promoting, and pricing products—is another business area that generates potential ethical issues. False or misleading marketing communications destroys customers' trust in a company. Lying, a major ethical issue involving communication, is a potentially significant problem. In both external and internal communications, it causes ethical predicaments because it destroys trust. T-Mobile paid $90 million to settle charges that it had billed customers millions of dollars for unwanted text messages such as horoscopes.[50] Misleading marketing can also cost consumers hard-earned money.

False or deceptive advertising is a key issue in marketing communications. One set of laws common to many countries concerns deceptive advertising—that is, advertisements not clearly labeled as advertisements. In the United States, Section 5 of the Federal Trade Commission (FTC) Act addresses deceptive advertising. Abuses in advertising range from exaggerated claims and concealed facts to outright lying, although improper categorization of advertising claims is the critical point. Courts place false or misleading advertisements into three categories: puffery, implied falsity, and literal falsity.

Puffery can be defined as exaggerated advertising, blustering, and boasting upon which no reasonable buyer would rely upon and is not actionable under the *Lanham Act*. For example, the National Advertising Division ruled that Tropicana's promotional claims to be the "world's best fruit and vegetable juice" is an example of puffery rather than misleading advertising.[51] However, the lines between puffery and deceptive advertising can be murky. The Federal Trade Commission settled with four weight-loss companies for deceptive advertising after determining that their weight-loss claims were unsubstantiated and that the companies made it appear easy to lose weight when in fact it is not.[52]

Implied falsity means the message has a tendency to mislead, confuse, or deceive the public. Advertising claims that use implied falsity are those that are literally true but imply another message that is false. In most cases, accusations of implied falsity can be proved only through time-consuming and expensive consumer surveys, the results of which are often inconclusive. An example of implied falsity might be a company's claim that its product has twice as much of an ingredient in its product, implying that it works twice as well, when in reality the extra quantity of the ingredient has no effect over performance.

The characterization of an advertising claim as **literally false** can be divided into two subcategories: *tests prove* (*establishment claims*), when the advertisement cites a study or test that establishes the claim; and *bald assertions* (*nonestablishment claims*), when the advertisement makes a claim that cannot be substantiated, as when a commercial states a certain product is superior to any other on the market. Kellogg paid $5 million to settle false advertising claims that its Rice Krispies cereal helped children's immune systems. A class-action lawsuit was later filed against Kellogg for marketing its Kashi as "All Natural" or "Nothing Artificial" when it contained some synthetic and artificial ingredients. Kellogg paid $5 million to settle the suit and agreed to no longer use this labeling.[53]

Another form of advertising abuse involves making ambiguous statements—when the words are so weak or general that the viewer, reader, or listener must infer the advertiser's intended message. These "weasel words" are inherently vague and enable the advertiser to deny any intent to deceive. The verb *help* is a good example (as in expressions such as "helps prevent," "helps fight," "helps make you feel").[54] Consumers may view such advertisements as unethical because they fail to communicate all the information needed to make a good purchasing decision or because they deceive the consumer outright.

Labeling issues are even murkier. For example, Kroger agreed to remove the term "raised in a humane environment" from its packages of Simple Truth chicken when it was discovered that the chickens, supplied by Perdue Farms, were raised in traditional factory farm environments.[55] Additionally, marketers of chia seeds are focused on making accurate claims about the nutritional characteristics of chia seeds on their labeling but are careful not to make claims about their impact on health. Despite their nutritional benefits, the body only processes a small amount of the nutrients. This makes it more complex to tie actual health benefits to consumption of chia seeds.[56]

Advertising and direct sales communication can also mislead consumers by concealing the facts within the message. For instance, a salesperson anxious to sell a medical insurance policy might list a large number of illnesses covered by the policy but fail to mention it does not include some commonly covered illnesses. Indeed, the fastest-growing area of fraudulent activity is in direct marketing, which uses the telephone and digital media to communicate information to customers, who then purchase products via mail, telephone, or the Internet. For instance, CEO Shawn Hogan of Digital Point Solutions was arrested and charged with defrauding eBay of $28 million in online marketing fees. Hogan was hired to place eBay links and advertisements on different websites to generate traffic for eBay, receiving a cut of sales generated from his marketing efforts. However, Hogan had distributed thousands of tracking codes, or cookies, among unknowing users so that if the user later made a sale on eBay, Hogan would get a cut of the sale without actually promoting the site.[57]

Consumer Fraud

Consumer fraud occurs when consumers attempt to deceive businesses for their own gain. Shoplifting comprises 37.4 percent of retail shrinkage (losses incurred from employee theft, shoplifting, administrative errors, and supplier fraud) in the United States.[58] Consumers engage in many other forms of fraud against businesses, including price tag switching, item switching, lying to obtain age-related and other discounts, and taking advantage of generous return policies by returning used items, especially clothing that has been worn (with the price tags still attached). Table 3–5 describes some common types of consumer fraud. Such behavior by consumers affects retail stores as well as other consumers who, for example, may unwittingly purchase new clothing that has actually been worn. Fraudulent merchandise returns are estimated to cost about $10.9 billion a year.[59]

Consumer fraud involves intentional deception to derive an unfair economic advantage by an individual or group over an organization. Examples of fraudulent activities include shoplifting, collusion or duplicity, and guile. *Collusion* typically involves an employee who assists the consumer in fraud. For example, a cashier may not ring up all merchandise or may give an unwarranted discount. *Duplicity* may involve a consumer staging an accident in a grocery store and then seeking damages against the store for its lack of attention to safety. A consumer may purchase, wear, and then return an item of clothing for a full refund. In other situations, a consumer may ask for a refund by claiming a defect. *Guile* is associated with a person who is crafty or understands right/wrong behavior but uses tricks to obtain an unfair advantage. The advantage is unfair because the person has the intent to go against the right behavior or result. Although some of these acts warrant legal prosecution, they can be difficult to prove, and many companies are reluctant to accuse patrons of a crime when there is no way to verify wrongdoing. Businesses that operate with the philosophy "the customer is always right" have found some consumers take advantage of this promise and have therefore modified return policies to curb unfair use.

TABLE 3–5 Types of Consumer Fraud

Type of fraud	Definition	Example
Friendly fraud	Making a big purchase with a credit card and then filing a fraud claim with the credit card company.	After receiving her large shipment in the mail, Melanie filed a claim with her credit card company claiming it was never shipped.
Price arbitrage	Substituting differently priced but similar items for a higher return.	Daniel placed a 1-terabyte hard drive into the box for a 20-terabyte drive and returned it for a full refund.
Return fraud	Replacing an item with something different and returning it for a full refund.	Joe filled a PlayStation box with rocks, resealed it, and received a full refund when the store clerk failed to check the merchandise.
Wardrobing	Wearing an expensive item once for an event and then returning it for a full refund.	Jessica wore an expensive dress to a dinner party and then returned it for a full refund.
Returning stolen goods	Receiving a full refund on goods that had been stolen.	Samantha stole some clothing and then returned it to the retailer for a refund.

Source: Rich Johnson, "How Do Customers Take Advantage of Retailers," *Site Jabber,* September 24, 2010, http://www.sitejabber.com/blog/2010/09/24/how-do-customers-take-advantage-of-retailers/ (accessed February 20, 2015).

Financial Misconduct

The failure to understand and manage ethical risks played a significant role in the financial crisis. The difference between bad business decisions and business misconduct can be hard to determine, and there is a thin line between the ethics of using only financial incentives to gauge performance and the use of holistic measures that include ethics, transparency, and responsibility to stakeholders. From CEOs to traders and brokers, all-too-tempting lucrative financial incentives existed for performance in the financial industry.

The most recent global recession was caused in part by a failure of the financial industry to take appropriate responsibility for its decision to utilize risky and complex financial instruments. Loopholes in regulations and the failures of regulators were exploited. Corporate cultures were built on rewards for taking risks rather than rewards for creating value for stakeholders. Ethical decisions were based more on what was legal rather than what was the right thing to do. Unfortunately, most stakeholders, including the public, regulators, and the mass media, do not always understand the nature of the financial risks taken on by banks and other institutions to generate profits. The intangible nature of financial products makes it difficult to understand complex financial transactions. Problems in the subprime mortgage markets sounded the alarm for the most recent recession.

Ethics issues emerged early in subprime lending, with loan officers receiving commissions on securing loans from borrowers with no consequences if the borrower defaulted on the loan. "Liar loans" were soon developed to create more sales and higher personal compensation for lenders. Lenders encouraged subprime borrowers to provide false information on their loan applications in order to qualify for and secure the loans. Some appraisers provided inflated home values in order to increase loan amounts. In other instances consumers were asked to falsify their incomes to make the loans more attractive to the lending institutions. The opportunity for misconduct was widespread. Top managers and CEOs were complacent about the wrongdoing as long as profits were good. Congress and President Clinton encouraged Fannie Mae and Freddie Mac to support home ownership among low-income people by giving out home mortgages. Throughout the early 2000s, in an economy with rapidly increasing home values, the culture of unethical behavior was not apparent to most people. When home values started to decline and individuals were "upside down" on their loans (owing more than the equity of the home), the failures and unethical behavior of lending and borrowing institutions became obvious.

The top executives or CEOs are ultimately responsible for the repercussions of their employees' decisions. This is why many leaders step down after a misconduct disaster at a firm. For example, the executive chairman and mortgage mogul William Erbey of Ocwen Financial Corp. stepped down due to alleged misconduct of the company. According to allegations, Ocwen mishandled foreclosures, engaged in conflicts of interest, and abused borrowers who were delinquent in paying back their loans. As a leader, Erbey was expected to exert oversight over the company and its employees to ensure appropriate conduct. [60] Risk management in the financial industry continues to be a key concern. A rise in subprime automobile loans and the bundling of these loans into securities has caused concern among some stakeholders.[61] Subprime loans were a major contributor to the last financial crisis, leading some to believe that the finance industry has not learned its lesson from the past.

This past widespread financial misconduct led to a call for financial reform. The Dodd–Frank Wall Street Reform and Consumer Protection Act was passed in 2010 to increase accountability and transparency in the financial industry and protect consumers from deceptive financial practices. The act established a Consumer Financial Protection

Bureau (CFPB) to protect consumers from unsafe financial products. The CFPB was provided with supervisory power over the credit market. Its responsibility includes making financial products easier to understand, curtailing unfair lending and credit card practices, and ensuring the safety of financial products before their launch into the market. The Dodd–Frank Wall Street Reform and Consumer Protection Act also gives federal regulators more power over large companies and financial institutions to prevent them from engaging in risky practices, or becoming "too big to fail." The act also holds CEOs responsible for the behavior of their companies. Large financial firms must retain at least half of top executives' bonuses for at least three years. The goal is to tie compensation to the outcomes of the executives' decisions over time.[62] We will discuss the Dodd–Frank Act and the Consumer Financial Protection Bureau in detail in Chapter 4.

Insider Trading

An insider is any officer, director, or owner of 10 percent or more of a class of a company's securities. There are two types of **insider trading**: illegal and legal. *Illegal insider trading* is the buying or selling of stoc   ʳmation that is not yet public. This act, that puts insiders i   ʾn be committed by anyone who has access to nonpubli   ɣ, friends, and employees. In addition, someone caught "ⁱᵖᵖⁱⁿᵍ ᵃⁿ ᵒᵘᵗˢⁱᵈᵉʳ ᵂⁱᵗʰ ⁿᵒⁿpublic information can also be found liable. To determine if an insider gave a tip illegally the SEC uses the *Dirks test,* that states if a tipster breaches his or her trust with the company and understands that this was a breach, he or she is liable for insider trading.

Legal insider trading involves legally buying and selling stock in an insider's own company, but not all the time. Insiders are required to report their insider transactions within two business days of the date the transaction occurred. For example, if an insider sold 10,000 shares on Monday, June 12, he or she would have to report the sale to the SEC by Wednesday, June 14. To deter insider trading, insiders are prevented from buying and selling their company stock within a six-month period, thereby encouraging insiders to buy stock only when they feel the company will perform well over the long term.

Insider trading is often done in a secretive manner by an individual who seeks to take advantage of an opportunity to make quick gains in the market. The Justice Department has cracked down on insider trading in recent years, including recording phone calls of suspected insider traders to gather evidence. Galleon Group founder Raj Rajaratnam and former Goldman Sachs director Rajat Gupta were both sentenced after secretly videotaped phone conversations appeared to implicate them in an insider trading scheme. An ex-trader at SAC Capital received a nine-year jail sentence for insider trading, and the company paid $1.2 billion in penalties.[63] Surveys revealed people who get involved in this type of activity often feel superior to others and are blind to the possibility of being discovered or facing consequences.[64] However, a decision by a federal appeals court might make insider trading convictions more difficult. The court determined that a conviction must depend on whether the person received a tangible benefit from using nonpublic information.[65]

Intellectual Property Rights

Intellectual property rights involve the legal protection of intellectual property such as music, books, and movies. Laws such as the Copyright Act of 1976, the Digital Millennium Copyright Act, and the Digital Theft Deterrence and Copyright Damages Improvement Act of 1999 were designed to protect the creators of intellectual property. However, with the advance of technology, ethical issues still abound for websites. For example, until it was sued for copyright infringement and subsequently changed its business model, Napster. com allowed individuals to download copyrighted music for personal use without providing compensation to the artists.

A decision by the Federal Copyright Office (FCO) helped lay the groundwork for intellectual property rules in a digital world. The FCO decided to make it illegal for web users to hack through barriers that copyright holders erect around material released online, allowing only two exceptions. The first exception was for software that blocks users from finding obscene or controversial material on the web, and the second was for people who want to bypass malfunctioning security features of software or other copyrighted goods they have purchased. This decision reflects the fact that copyright owners are typically being favored in digital copyright issues.[66]

However, digital copyrights continue to be a controversial issue in the United States and across the world, and existing laws are often difficult to enforce. Approximately 22 percent of all Internet traffic involves copyrighted material, including illegally downloaded or uploaded music, movies, and television shows.[67] As China grew into an economic powerhouse, the market for pirated goods of all types, from DVDs to pharmaceuticals and even cars, became a multibillion dollar industry.[68] Traditionally, China's government proved weak in protecting intellectual property, and the underground market for such pirated goods—which are sold all over the world—has grown at a rapid pace. Downloaders of illegal content are less concerned with the law than non-downloaders and are more likely to engage in other forms of illegal conduct such as shoplifting.[69]

While intellectual property rights' infringement always poses a threat to companies that risk losing profits and reputation, it can also threaten the health and well-being of consumers. For example, illegally produced medications, when consumed by unknowing consumers, can cause sickness and even death. Research on software piracy has shown that high levels of economic well-being and an advanced technology sector are effective deterrents to software piracy.[70] However, as the number of patents filed in China increase, so are intellectual property lawsuits. China is convening special intellectual property courts to handle cases of alleged violations involving software piracy and patent and copyright infringement. It seems intellectual property theft is becoming a more important issue in China as China tries to boost its business image in the international community.[71]

Privacy Issues

Consumer advocates continue to warn consumers about new threats to their privacy, especially within the health care and Internet industries. As the number of people using the Internet increases, the areas of concern related to its use increase as well. Some **privacy issues** that must be addressed by businesses include the monitoring of employees' use of available technology and consumer privacy. Current research suggests that even when businesses use price discounts or personalized services in exchange for information, consumers remain suspicious. However, certain consumers are still willing to provide personal information despite the potential risks.[72]

A challenge for companies today is meeting their business needs while protecting employees' desire for privacy. There are few legal protections of an employee's right to privacy, which allows businesses a great deal of flexibility in establishing policies regarding employee privacy while using company equipment on company property. For example, the Electronic Communications Privacy Act of 1986 prohibits the interception of electronic communication and access to stored electronic communications. However, exemptions are made for the "normal course of employment," and it is generally agreed that employers have to right to monitor company email. Additionally, employee consent also removes protection.[73] From computer monitoring and telephone taping to video surveillance and GPS satellite tracking, employers are using technology to manage their productivity and protect their resources. The ability to gather and use data about employee behavior creates an ethical issue related to trust and responsibility.

Electronic monitoring allows a company to determine whether productivity is being reduced because employees spend too much time on personal activities. Having this information enables the company to take steps to remedy the situation. Many employers have policies that govern personal phone and Internet use on company time. Additionally, some companies track everything from phone calls and Internet history to keystrokes and the time employees spend at their desks.[74] One study found that 48 percent of professionals have sent personal emails from their work email account.[75] This can be frustrating for employers if they believe employees are spending too much time on personal matters or using their work emails to send inappropriate messages. However, employers must also exert caution. As mentioned in Chapter 1, the National Labor Relations Board has ruled that employees can use their employer's email system for union organizing and communications about wages.[76] Instituting practices that show respect for employee privacy but do not abdicate the employer's responsibility helps create a climate of trust that promotes opportunities for resolving employee–employer disputes without lawsuits. On the other hand, if personal data is gathered that includes medical or religious information, it can result in litigation.

There are two dimensions to consumer privacy: consumer awareness of information collection and a growing lack of consumer control over how companies use the personal information they collect. For example, many are not aware that Google, Inc., reserves the right to track every time you click on a link from one of its searches.[77] Online purchases and even random web surfing can be tracked without a consumer's knowledge. In the European Union, websites that use cookies, or small bits of information stored on a user's computer that can collect personal information, must first ask users for consent.[78]

Personal information about consumers is valuable not only to businesses but also criminals. It is estimated an identity is stolen once every two seconds.[79] Personal information is stolen and sold online. Although some of this information comes from sources such as social networking profiles, poorly protected corporate files are another major source. U.S. organizations report hundreds of security breaches annually.[80]

Companies are working to find ways to improve consumers' trust in their websites. For example, an increasing number of websites display an online seal from the Better Business Bureau, available only to sites that subscribe to certain standards. A similar seal is available through TRUSTe, a nonprofit global initiative that certifies those websites adhering to its principles. (Visit http://e-businessethics.com for more on Internet privacy.)

THE CHALLENGE OF DETERMINING AN ETHICAL ISSUE IN BUSINESS

Most ethical issues concerning a business will become visible through stakeholder concerns about an event, activity, or the results of a business decision. The mass media, special interest groups, and individuals, through the use of blogs, podcasts, and other individual-generated media, often generate discussion about the ethical nature of a decision. Another way to determine if a specific behavior or situation has an ethical component is to ask other individuals in the business how they feel about it and whether they view it as ethically challenging. Trade associations and business self-regulatory groups such as the Better Business Bureau often provide direction for companies in defining ethical issues. Finally, it is important to determine whether the organization adopted specific policies on the activity. An activity approved by most members of an organization, if it is also customary in the industry, is probably ethical. An issue, activity, or situation that can withstand open discussion between many stakeholders, both inside and outside the organization, probably does not pose ethical problems.

However, over time, problems can become ethical issues as a result of changing societal values. For example, today big data and marketing analytics are becoming new ethical issues as they can reduce employees and consumers to quantitative measurements. Many employers are beginning to use digital dashboards to treat employees like any other organizational asset, using measurements and predictability to determine deviations from the norm so that managers can know which issues need to be addressed. While this has profound implications for understanding employee behavior and how it impacts firm success, some critics believe it is unacceptable to replace humans with a computer in personnel decisions. Some also point out that human behavior can be complex and there could be patterns that cannot be accounted for using a digital dashboard.[81] Assessing employee integrity and ability to make ethical decisions is an area that is hard to quantify. Additionally, cybersecurity is a major concern today. Hacker attacks against Sony, Target, Home Depot, and JP Morgan highlight the responsibility businesses have to protect consumer and employee personal information by deploying resources to prevent these attacks.

Once stakeholders trigger ethical issue awareness and individuals openly discuss it and ask for guidance and the opinions of others, one enters the ethical decision-making process, which we examine in Chapter 5.

SUMMARY

Stakeholders' concerns largely determine whether business actions and decisions are perceived as ethical or unethical. When government, communities, and society become involved, what was merely an ethical issue can quickly become a legal one. Shareholders can unwittingly complicate the ethical conduct of business by demanding managers make decisions to boost short-term earnings, thus maintaining or increasing the value of their stock.

A first step toward understanding business ethics is to develop ethical issue awareness, that is, to learn to identify which stakeholder issues contain an ethical component. Characteristics of the job, the corporate or local culture, and the society in which one does business can all create ethical issues. Recognizing an ethical issue is essential to understanding business ethics and therefore to create an effective ethics and compliance program that minimizes unethical behavior. Businesspeople must understand the universal moral constants of honesty, fairness, and integrity. Without embracing these concepts, running a business becomes difficult.

Fairness is the quality of being just, equitable, and impartial, and overlaps with concepts of *justice, equity,* and *equality.* The three fundamental elements that motivate people to be fair are equality, reciprocity, and optimization. Equality relates to how wealth is distributed between employees within a company, country, or globally; reciprocity relates to the return of favors approximately equal in value; and integrity refers to a person's character and is made up of two basic parts, a formal relation one has to oneself and a person's set of terminal, or enduring, values from which he or she does not deviate.

An ethical issue is a problem, situation, or opportunity that requires an individual, group, or organization to choose among several actions that must be evaluated as right or wrong, ethical or unethical. By contrast, an ethical dilemma has no right or ethical solution.

The misuse of company time and resources—especially computer resources—has become a major ethical issue. Abusive or intimidating behavior includes physical threats, false accusations, being annoying, profanity, insults, yelling, harshness, ignoring someone, and unreasonableness. Bribery is the practice of offering something (usually money) in order to gain an illicit advantage. A conflict of interest occurs when individuals must choose whether to advance their own interests, those of the organization, or some other group. Corporate intelligence is the collection and analysis of information on markets, technologies, customers, and competitors, as well as on socioeconomic and external political trends. The tools of corporate intelligence are many. Corporate intelligence can be a legitimate business activity but becomes unethical if deception is used to steal another firm's trade secrets.

Another ethical/legal issue is discrimination, which is illegal in the United States when it occurs on the basis of race, color, religion, sex, marital status, sexual orientation, public-assistance status, disability, age, national origin, or veteran status. Additionally, discrimination on the basis of political opinions or affiliation with a union is defined as harassment. Sexual harassment is a form of sex discrimination. To build workforces that reflect their customer base, many companies initiated affirmative action programs. In general, fraud is any purposeful communication that deceives, manipulates, or conceals facts in order to create a false impression. There are several types of fraud: accounting, marketing, and consumer.

An insider is any officer, director, or owner of 10 percent or more of a class of a company's securities. There are two types of insider trading: legal and illegal. Intellectual property rights involve the legal protection of intellectual property such as music, books, and movies. Consumer advocates continue to warn consumers about new threats to their privacy.

IMPORTANT TERMS FOR REVIEW

integrity 63	bribery 70
honesty 63	active bribery 70
fairness 64	passive bribery 70
equality 64	facilitation payment 70
reciprocity 64	corporate intelligence 71
optimization 65	hacking 72
ethical issue 65	system hacking 72
ethical dilemma 65	remote hacking 72
abusive or intimidating behavior 66	physical hacking 72
lying 69	social engineering 72
conflict of interest 69	shoulder surfing 72

RESOLVING ETHICAL BUSINESS CHALLENGES*

Daniel just graduated from Michigan University and landed a job as a copywriter at Young, Olsen, Lindle, and Olson (YOLO) Advertising assigned to one of the subsidiary accounts of Delicious Uber Bacon Ingredients Extraordinaire Corporation. This conglomerate was primarily a food processing manufacturer beginning 100 years ago with pork in the Midwest. Overall corporate sales of beef, chicken, pork, and seafood were more than $750 million each year. YOLO considered many advertising options and opted for a celebrity spokesperson. That meant Daniel would work with Gloria Kunies as the celebrity endorser. Ms. Kunies is a well-known, well-loved, young, and vibrant actress with a large younger following.

Chloe, President of YOLO, asked Daniel to step into her office. "Daniel, this new account is a good start for you. We usually don't let our new copywriters handle accounts by themselves, but you have proven to be a capable employee. Your job on this account is to write copy for the commercials using Ms. Kunies's product testimonials. The copy needs to be crafted as a testimonial, targeting the market of 17- to 30-year-olds. Ms. Kunies already signed an affidavit as to being a bona fide user of the product. The scripts should feature her testifying to the quality, value, and tastiness of the bacon. I want you to meet her tomorrow so you can start the writing process and understand her personality in order to script the messages. Spend the rest of the day immersing yourself in her biography and researching her on the Internet." As Daniel left Chloe's office he remembered a Facebook post about Ms. Kunies being a vegetarian.

The next day at their meeting, Daniel asked her if she had actually tasted the bacon. Ms. Kunies replied, "Why yes, technically and legally I have tried Uber. In fact, I've been a huge fan since I was a kid. Bacon is my favorite food. I've done several testimonials in the past and know the American Advertising Federation (AAF) rules. I know as long as my comments are based on verifiable personal use, the message cannot be challenged as deceptive. In fact, Uber bacon has been a favorite of mine since I was young. It wasn't until a month ago I became a vegetarian. Eating all that bacon for decades really did a number on my cholesterol."

"So, you feel comfortable about endorsing Uber even though you don't eat it now?" asked Daniel.

"No question about it. As far as bacon goes, Uber is second to none in taste. If people are going to eat bacon, why not eat the best? Even if it is a heart attack waiting to happen," Ms. Kunies joked.

The next day Chloe asked Daniel how it went. He explained their conversation and expressed concern over the fact Ms. Kunies is currently a vegetarian, and she attributed her high cholesterol to Uber bacon. Daniel felt relief when he saw the concern in Chloe's face, but soon realized her concern was about Ms. Kunies pulling out of the advertisement. Daniel reassured Chloe that Ms. Kunies still wanted to promote the product, but it seemed like a contradiction to have a vegetarian promoting bacon. Chloe responded by saying as long as Ms. Kunies had eaten the bacon at some point in her life and thinks it is a good product, it makes no difference as to whether she currently eats the bacon. She continued, "Sometimes in advertising, you have to add a spin to the message you are communicating so it fits with the product you are selling. Not only are you selling a product, but more importantly, you are selling an experience, a feeling, an idea that appeals to consumers."

As Daniel walked home that evening, he wondered how he was going to write this advertisement. He did not want to begin his career in a dishonest manner, but he also wanted to produce work that pleased his boss. He tried to think of creative ways to mask the contradiction of the advertisement. Maybe with humor? He asked himself if this approach would still feel dishonest. The next morning Daniel was going to meet with both Ms. Kunies and Chloe about what he had written thus far.

QUESTIONS | EXERCISES

1. Describe the ethical issues that Daniel is encountering.
2. Does this situation in any way violate the concepts of fairness, honesty, and integrity?
3. If the advertisement does not violate any laws, then why should Daniel be concerned? What are the possible consequences of the advertisement?

*This case is strictly hypothetical; any resemblance to real persons, companies, or situations is coincidental.

> > > CHECK YOUR EQ

Check your EQ, or Ethics Quotient, by completing the following. Assess your performance to evaluate your overall understanding of the chapter material.

1. Business can be considered a game people play, like basketball or boxing.   **Yes**   **No**

2. Key ethical issues in an organization relate to fraud, discrimination, honesty and fairness, conflicts of interest, and privacy.   **Yes**   **No**

3. Only 10 percent of employees observe abusive behavior in the workplace.   **Yes**   **No**

4. Fraud occurs when a false impression exists, which conceals facts.   **Yes**   **No**

5. Time theft is a major type of misconduct.   **Yes**   **No**

ANSWERS **1. No.** People are not economically self-sufficient and cannot withdraw from the game of business. **2. Yes.** Fraud, discrimination, honesty and fairness, conflicts of interest, and privacy are some key ethical issues that businesses face. **3. No.** According to Table 3–1, 18 percent of employees observe abusive behavior in the workplace. **4. No.** Fraud must be purposeful rather than accidental, and exists when deception and manipulation of facts are concealed to create a false impression that causes harm. **5. Yes.** It is estimated the average employee steals approximately 4.25 hours per week.

ENDNOTES

1. Anupreeta Das, "NetJets Unrest Puts Warren Buffett in a Rare Pinch," *The Wall Street Journal*, January 5, 2015, http://www.wsj.com/articles/netjets-unrest-puts-warren-buffett-in-a-rare-pinch-1420485740 (accessed February 10, 2015).

2. Tennille Tracy, "FDA Flags Danger of Caffeine Powder," *The Wall Street Journal*, December 17, 2014, A8.

3. Vernon R. Loucks, Jr., "A CEO Looks at Ethics," *Business Horizons* 30, 2 (1987): 4.

4. Eric H. Beversluis, "Is There No Such Thing as Business Ethics?" *Journal of Business Ethics* 6, 2 (1987): 81–88. Reprinted with permission of Kluwer Academic Publishers, Dordrecht, Holland.

5. Kevin Clark, "Bill Belichick's Army of History Buffs," *The Wall Street Journal*, January 29, 2015, http://www.wsj.com/articles/belichicks-army-of-history-buffs-1422556828 (accessed February 10, 2015); "Super Bowl: Bill Belichick and Tom Brady head for fourth win," BBC, February 1, 2015, http://www.bbc.com/sport/0/american-football/31056519 (accessed February 10, 2015); Damon Hack, "For Patriots' Coach, War Is Decided Before Game," *The New York Times*, February 3, 2005, http://www.nytimes.com/2005/02/03/sports/football/03belichick.html?fta=y (accessed February 10, 2015).

6. Mike Downey, "Deflate-gate: Will the air go out of a phony scandal?" *CNN*, January 23, 2015, http://www.cnn.com/2015/01/19/opinion/downey-football-deflate-investigation/ (accessed February 10, 2015); Associated Press, "NFL suspends Patriots' QB Tom Brady 4 games for deflated footballs," *Fox News*, May 11, 2015, http://www.foxnews.com/sports/2015/05/11/nfl-suspends-patriot-qb-tom-brady-4-games-for-deflated-footballs/ (accessed July 27, 2015).

7. Steven Greenhouse, "Workers and critics greet Walmart pay raise but say much remains to be done," *The Guardian*, February 23, 2015, http://www.theguardian.com/business/2015/feb/23/workers-activists-walmart-pay-raise (accessed February 24, 2015).

8. Michael Rapoport, "SEC, Big Four Accounting Firms in China Settle Dispute," *The Wall Street Journal*, February 6, 2015, http://www.wsj.com/articles/sec-big-four-accounting-firms-in-china-settle-dispute-1423237083 (accessed February 10, 2015).

9. William Atkinson, "Stealing time," *BNet*, November 2006, http://cf.rims.org/MGTemplate.cfm?Section=MagArchive&NavMenuID=304&template=/Magazine/DisplayMagazines.cfm&Archive=1&IssueID=283&AID=3224&Volume=53&ShowArticle=1 (accessed February 10, 2015).

10. Coca-Cola Company, *Code of Business Conduct: Acting Around the Globe*, p. 13.

11. "Branson: Take as much vacation as you want!" *CNN Money*, September 24, 2015, http://money.cnn.com/2014/09/24/news/virgin-vacation-branson/ (accessed February 24, 2015).

12. Steven Greenhouse, "More Workers Are Claiming 'Wage Theft'," *The New York Times*, August 31, 2014, http://www.nytimes.com/2014/09/01/business/more-workers-are-claiming-wage-theft.html?_r=0 (accessed February 24, 2015).

13. "Subway leads fast food industry in underpaying workers," *CNN Money*, May 1, 2014, http://money.cnn.com/2014/05/01/news/economy/subway-labor-violations/ (accessed February 24, 2015).

14. Adam Piore, "Kick Me or Don't," *Bloomberg Businessweek*, November 26–December 2, 2012 93–95; Melissa Korn, "Bullying is a Buzzkill for Colleagues, Too," *The Wall Street Journal*, July 18, 2012, http://blogs.wsj.com/atwork/2012/07/18/bullying-is-a-buzzkill-for-colleagues-too/ (accessed February 10, 2015); Canadian Centre for Occupational Health and Safety, "Bullying in the Workplace," http://www.ccohs.ca/oshanswers/psychosocial/bullying.html (accessed February 10, 2014); Anita Bruzzese, Gannett, "On the Job: How to Battle Bullying at Work," *USA Today*, December 9, 2012, http://www.usatoday.com/story/money/columnist/bruzzese/2012/12/05/on-the-job-bully-workplace/1749697/ (accessed February 10, 2015); Anita Bruzzese, "Workplace Becomes New Schoolyard for Bullies, USA Today, August 24, 2011, http://usatoday30.usatoday.com/money/jobcenter/workplace/bruzzese/2011-08-24-bully-bosses-overtake-workplace_n.htm (accessed February 10, 2015); Emily Kimber, "Dealing with Workplace Bullies," *Canadian Living*, http://www.canadianliving.com/life/work/dealing_with_workplace_bullies.php (accessed February 10, 2015); Suzanne Lucas, "Why Workplace Bullying Should Be Legal," *Money Watch*, March 23, 2011, http://www.cbsnews.com/8301-505125_162-44941976/why-workplace-bullying-should-be-legal/ (accessed February 10, 2015).

15. I. Niedhammer, S. David, S. Degioanni, A. Drummond, and P. Philip, "Workplace bullying and sleep disturbances: Findings from a large-scale cross-sectional survey in the French working population," *Sleep* 32, 9 (2009): 1211–1219.

16. Carolyn Kinsey Goman, "Is Your Boss a Bully?" *Forbes*, April 6, 2014, http://www.forbes.com/sites/carolkinseygoman/2014/04/06/is-your-boss-a-bully/ (accessed January 15, 2015).

17. M. Claybourn, "Relationships between Moral Disengagement, Work Characteristics and Workplace Harassment," *Journal of Business Ethics* 100, 2 (2011): 283–301.

18. "Healthy Workplace Bill," http://www.healthyworkplacebill.org/index.php (accessed February 10, 2015).

19. Barbara Safani, "Bullying at Work a Growing Trend," *AOL Jobs*, January 24, 2011, http://jobs.aol.com/articles/2011/01/24/bullying-at-work-a-growing-trend/ (accessed February 10, 2015).

20. David Streitfeld, "EBay Settles No-Poaching Antitrust Case," *The New York Times*, May 1, 2014, http://www.nytimes.com/2014/05/02/technology/ebay-settles-antitrust-case-over-no-poaching-deal.html (accessed February 10, 2015).

21. Hannah Karp, "Ticketmaster Agrees to Tentative Settlement," *The Wall Street Journal*, June 2, 2014, http://www.nytimes.com/2014/05/02/technology/ebay-settles-antitrust-case-over-no-poaching-deal.html (accessed February 10, 2015).

22. "GAO Document B-295402," Lockheed Martin Corporation, February 18, 2005, http://www.gao.gov/decisions/bidpro/295402.htm (accessed February 10, 2015).

23. Samuel Rubenfeld, "The Morning Risk Report: Bribery Act Review Considers Facilitation Payment Exception," *The Wall Street Journal*, May 31, 2013, http://blogs.wsj.com/riskandcompliance/2013/05/31/the-morning-risk-report-bribery-act-review-considers-facilitation-payment-exception/ (accessed February 10, 2015).

24. Chad Bray, "Ralph Lauren Corp. Settles Bribe Probe," *The Wall Street Journal*, April 22, 2013, http://online.wsj.com/article/SB10001424127887324235304578438704093187288.html?mod=googlenews_wsj (accessed February 10, 2015).

25. The Economist staff, "Graft Work," *The Economist*, December 6, 2014, p. 73.

26. United States Department of Justice, "Foreign Corrupt Practices Act Anti-bribery Provisions," http://acfcs.org/wp-content/uploads/2012/05/FCPA-DoJ-Laypersons-Guide.pdf (accessed February 10, 2015).

27. Reuters, "Alcoa to Pay $384 Million to Settle Bribery Charges," *The New York Times,* January 9, 2014, http://www.nytimes.com/2014/01/10/business/alcoa-to-pay-384-million-to-settle-bribery-charges.html (accessed February 10, 2015).

28. Ira Winkler, *Corporate Espionage: What Is It, Why It's Happening in Your Company, What You Must Do about It* (New York: Prima, 1997).

29. Ellen Nakashima and Andrea Peterson, "Report: Cybercrime and espionage costs $445 billion annually," *The Washington Post*, June 9, 2014, http://www.washingtonpost.com/world/national-security/report-cybercrime-and-espionage-costs-445-billion-annually/2014/06/08/8995291c-ecce-11e3-9f5c-9075d5508f0a_story.html (accessed February 10, 2015).

30. U.S. Equal Employment Opportunity Commission, "Charge Statistics: FY 1997 Through FY 2014," http://eeoc.gov/eeoc/statistics/enforcement/charges.cfm (accessed February 10, 2015).

31. "African-American Chairman & CEO's of Fortune 500 Companies," *Black Profiles: Entrepreneurs + Executives,* January 29, 2015, http://www.blackentrepreneurprofile.com/fortune-500-ceos/ (accessed February 10, 2015).

32. Jena McGregor, "In an improving economy, is age discrimination getting better or worse?" *The Washington Post,* July 25, 2014, http://www.washingtonpost.com/blogs/on-leadership/wp/2014/07/25/in-an-improving-economy-is-age-discrimination-getting-better-or-worse/ (accessed February 10, 2015).

33. "AARP Best Employers for Workers over 50: About the Program," *AARP* June 2013, http://www.aarp.org/work/employee-benefits/info-09-2009/about_the_best_employers_program.html (accessed February 10, 2015).

34. CivilRights.org, "Affirmative Action?" *The Leadership Conference*, 2015, http://www.civilrights.org/resources/civilrights101/affirmaction.html (accessed February 10, 2015).

35. U.S. Equal Employment Opportunity Commission, "McCormick & Schmick's to Pay $1.3 Million and Provide Significant Injunctive Relief to Resolve EEOC Class Race Discrimination Suit," September 12, 2014, http://www.eeoc.gov/eeoc/newsroom/release/9-12-14a.cfm (accessed February 10, 2015).

36. Debbie M. Thorne, O. C. Ferrell, and Linda Ferrell, *Business and Society: A Strategic Approach to Social Responsibility and Ethics*, 4th ed. (Mason, OH: South-Western Cengage Learning, 2011), 182.

37. U.S. Equal Employment Opportunity Commission, "Upper Chesapeake Health System to Pay $180,000 to Settle EEOC Disability Discrimination Lawsuit," April 15, 2014, http://www.eeoc.gov/eeoc/newsroom/release/4-15-14a.cfm (accessed February 10, 2015).

38. Paula N. Rubin, "Civil Rights and Criminal Justice: Primer on Sexual Harassment Series: NIJ Research in Action," October 1995, https://www.ncjrs.gov/txtfiles/harass.txt (accessed February 10, 2015).

39. U.S. Equal Employment Opportunity Commission, "EEOC Releases Fiscal Year 2014 Enforcement and Litigation Data," February 4, 2015, http://www.eeoc.gov/eeoc/newsroom/release/2-4-15.cfm (accessed February 10, 2015).

40. *Zabkowicz v. West Bend Co.*, 589 F. Supp. 780, 784, 35 EPD Par.34, 766 (E.D. Wis.1984).

41. Iddo Landau, "The Law and Sexual Harassment," *Business Ethics Quarterly* 15, 2 (2005): 531–536.

42. R.A. Lindsay, "Enhancements and Justice: Problems in Determining the Requirements of Justice in a Genetically Transformed Society," *Kennedy Institute Ethics Journal* 15, 1 (2005): 3–38.

43. Association of Certified Fraud Examiners, *Report to the Nations on Occupational Fraud and Abuse: 2014 Global Fraud Study* (Austin, TX: Association of Certified Fraud Examiners, 2014), 8.

44. AP, "Former Missouri business owner admits defrauding bank," *St-Louis Post Dispatch,* February 18, 2015, http://www.stltoday.com/news/state-and-regional/missouri/former-missouri-business-owner-admits-defrauding-bank/article_ce632d7e-ad2e-5096-a6e8-7756724d4101.html (accessed February 24, 2015).

45. Sarah N. Lynch, "Diamond Foods to pay $5 million to settle SEC fraud case," *Reuters*, January 9, 2014, http://www.reuters.com/article/2014/01/09/us-diamond-sec-accountingfraud-idUSBREA0813020140109 (accessed February 10, 2015).

46. Mei Feng, Weili Ge, Shuqing Luo, and Terry Shevlin, "Why do CFOs become involved in material accounting manipulations?" *Journal of Accounting and Economics* 51, 1–2 (2011): 21–36.

47. Cassell Bryan-Low, "Accounting Firms Face Backlash over the Tax Shelters They Sold," *The Wall Street Journal* online, February 7, 2003, http://online.wsj.com/article/SB1044568358985594893.html?mod=googlewsj (accessed February 10, 2015).

48. Public Company Accounting Oversight Board, "About the PCAOB," http://pcaobus.org/About/Pages/default.aspx (accessed February 24, 2015).

49. Securities and Exchange Commission, "Public Company Accounting Oversight Board (PCAOB)," http://www.sec.gov/answers/pcaob.htm (accessed February 24, 2015).

50. Edward Wyatt, "T-Mobile to Pay $90 Million to Settle Claims of Wrongful Phone Charges," *The New York Times,* December 19, 2014, http://www.nytimes.com/2014/12/20/technology/t-mobile-to-pay-90-million-to-settle-claims-of-wrongful-phone-charges.html (accessed February 10, 2015).

51. ASRC, "NAD Determines Tropicana Ad Is Puffery Following Campbell Challenge," July 30, 2013, http://www.asrcreviews.org/2013/07/nad-determines-tropicana-

ad-is-puffery-following-campbell-challenge/ (accessed February 24, 2015).

52. Alison Young, "FTC moves on products to control weight," *USA Today*, January 8, 2014, 1B.

53. Associated Press, "Suit Prompts Kellogg's to Drop 'Natural' Labels on Kashi Products," *NBC News,* May 8, 2014, http://www.nbcnews.com/business/consumer/ suit-prompts-kelloggs-drop-natural-labels-kashi-products-n100391 (accessed February 24, 2015); "The Too-Good-to-Be-True Product Hall of Fame," *Time,* October 6, 2011, http://business.time.com/2011/10/11/14-products-with-notoriously-misleading-advertising-claims/slide/kelloggs-rice-krispies-cereals/ (accessed February 24, 2015); Federal Trade Commission, "FTC Investigation of Ad Claims that Rice Krispies Benefits Children's Immunity Leads to Stronger Order Against Kellogg," June 3, 2010, http://www.ftc.gov/news-events/ press-releases/2010/06/ftc-investigation-ad-claims-rice-krispies-benefits-childrens (accessed February 24, 2015).

54. Archie B. Carroll, *Business and Society: Ethics and Stakeholder Management* (Cincinnati, OH: South-Western, 1989), 228–230.

55. Lynn Terry, "Kroger removing 'humanely raised' on chicken labels in settlement following Perdue deal," *Oregon Live,* October 15, 2014, http://www.oregonlive. com/health/index.ssf/2014/10/kroger_removing_ humanely_raise.html (accessed February 10, 2015).

56. Molly Soat, "Chia," *Marketing News,* January 2015, https://www.ama.org/publications/MarketingNews/ Pages/chia.aspx (accessed January 28, 2015); Norlaily Mohd Ali, Swee Keong Yeap, Wan Yong Ho, and Boon Kee Beh, Sheau Wei Tan, and Soon Guan Tan, "The Promising Future of Chia, *Salvia Hispanic L.,*" *Journal of Biomedicine and Biotechnology,* November 21, 2012, doi: 1155/2012/171956, http://www.ncbi.nlm.nih.gov/pmc/ articles/PMC3518271/ (accessed January 28, 2015).

57. Jim Edwards, "How eBay Worked with the FBI to Put Its Top Affiliate Marketers in Prison," *Business Insider,* May 3, 2013, http://www.businessinsider.com/ebay-the-fbi-shawn-hogan-and-brian-dunning-2013-4 (accessed February 24, 2015).

58. Checkpoint Systems, Inc., "Global Retail Theft Barometer Study Finds Shrink Cost Retailers $128 Billion Worldwide, Averaging 1.29 Percent of Sales," November 6, 2014, http://us.checkpointsystems.com/news-events/ news-item/grtb-2014/ (accessed February 10, 2015).

59. Kathy Grannis, "Retailers Estimate Holiday Return Fraud Will Cost Them $3.8 Billion, According to NRF Survey," National Retail Federation, December 19, 2014, https:// nrf.com/media/press-releases/retailers-estimate-holiday-return-fraud-will-cost-them-38-billion-according-nrf (accessed February 10, 2015).

60. Antoine Gara, "Bill Erbey of Embattled Mortgage Giant Ocwen Loses Over $300M In Hours, No Longer Billionaire," *Forbes,* December 22, 2014, http://www.forbes.com/sites/ antoinegara/2014/12/22/bill-erbey-of-embattled-mortgage-giant-ocwen-loses-over-300m-in-hours-no-longer-billionaire/ (accessed February 10, 2015); James Sterngold and Alan Zibel, "Ocwen Head to Resign in New York Settlement," *The Wall Street Journal,* December 22, 2014, http://www.wsj.com/articles/ocwen-head-to-resign-in-new-york-settlement-1419224476 (accessed February 10, 2015).

61. Jody Shenn, "Subprime Auto-Loan Bonds Called Small Part of Loan Growth," *Bloomberg,* February 9, 2015, http://www.bloomberg.com/news/articles/2015-02-10/

subprime-auto-loan-bonds-called-small-part-of-lending-expansion (accessed February 10, 2015).

62. Jennifer Liberto and David Ellis, "Wall Street reform: What's in the bill," *CNNMoney.com,* June 30, 2010, http:// money.cnn.com/2010/06/25/news/economy/whats_in_ the_reform_bill/index.htm (accessed February 10, 2015).

63. Matthew Goldstein, "Martoma, SAC Capital Ex-Trader, Gets 9 Years in Prison," *The New York Times,* September 8, 2014, http://dealbook.nytimes.com/2014/09/08/hours-before-sentencing-u-s-judge-says-cohen-trades-should-count-against-martoma/ (accessed January 15, 2015).

64. Jason Zweig, "Insider Trading: Why We Can't Help Ourselves," *The Wall Street Journal,* April 2, 2011, http:// online.wsj.com/article/SB1000142405274870453020457 6236922024758718.html (accessed February 10, 2015).

65. Christopher M. Matthews, "Ruling Puts Dent In Insider Probes," *The Wall Street Journal,* December 11, 2014, A1.

66. Anna Wilde Mathews, "Copyrights on Web Content Are Backed," *The Wall Street Journal,* October 27, 2000, B10.

67. Rightscorp Inc., "Recent Study Cites 374% More File Sharing Activity on ISPs Not Participating in Rightscorp's Digital Loss Prevention Service," *Nasdaq Global Newswire,* March 10, 2014, http://globenewswire. com/news-release/2014/03/10/616971/10071896/en/ Recent-Study-Cites-374-More-File-Sharing-Activity-on-ISPs-Not-Participating-in-Rightscorp-s-Digital-Loss-Prevention-Service.html (accessed February 10, 2015).

68. Roger Bate, "China's Bad Medicine," *The Wall Street Journal,* May 5, 2009, http://online.wsj.com/article/ SB124146383501884323.html (accessed February 10, 2015); "Chinese Intellectual Property Violations," *Idea Buyer,* http://www.ideabuyer.com/news/chinese-intellectual-property-violations/ (accessed February 10, 2015).

69. Kirsten Robertson, Lisa McNeill, James Green, and Claire Roberts, "Illegal Downloading, Ethical Concern, and Illegal Behavior," *Journal of Business Ethics* 108, 2 (2012): 215–227.

70. Deli Yang, Mahmut Sonmez, Derek Bosworth, and Gerald Fryzell, "Global Software Piracy: Searching for Further Explanations," *Journal of Business Ethics* 87, 2 (2008): 269–283.

71. Bloomberg News, "China Opens Intellectual Property Courts to Improve Image," *Bloomberg,* November 3, 2014, http://www.bloomberg.com/news/articles/2014-11-03/ china-opens-intellectual-property-courts-to-improve-image (accessed February 10, 2015).

72. Nora J. Rifon, Robert LaRose, and Sejung Marina Choi, "Your Privacy Is Sealed: Effects of Web Privacy Seals on Trust and Personal Disclosures," *Journal of Consumer Affairs* 39, 2 (2002): 339–362.

73. "Office of General Counsel," *The Catholic University of America,* February 21, 2013, http://counsel.cua.edu/ fedlaw/ecpa.cfm (accessed February 11, 2015); "Electronic Communications Privacy Act of 1986 (ECPA), 18 U.S.C.§ 2510–2522," *Justice Information Sharing,* July 30, 2013, https://it.ojp.gov/default.aspx?area=privacy&page=1285 (accessed February 11, 2015).

74. American Management Association, "2005 Electronic Monitoring and Surveillance Survey: Many Companies Monitoring, Recording, Videotaping— and Firing—Employees," *American Management Association,* May 18, 2005, via http://www.cbia.com/ cbianews/2005/07/200507_CompaniesMonitoring.htm (accessed February 10, 2015).

75. Javier Soltero, "When Personal Identity & Work Email Collide," Acompli, March 14, 2014, https://www.acompli.com/personal-identity-work-email-collide/ (accessed February 10, 2015).

76. Melanie Trottman, "NL'ORB Rules to Give Workers Right to Use Employer Email for Union Organizing," *The Wall Street Journal*, December 11, 2014, http://www.wsj.com/articles/nlrb-rules-to-give-workers-right-to-use-employer-email-for-union-organizing-1418313255 (accessed February 10, 2015).

77. Mitch Wagner, "Google's Pixie Dust," *InformationWeek*, no 1061 (2005): 98.

78. Samuel Gibbs, "Europe's next privacy war is with websites silently tracking users," *The Guardian*, November 28, 2014, http://www.theguardian.com/technology/2014/nov/28/europe-privacy-war-websites-silently-tracking-users (accessed February 10, 2015).

79. "Identity fraud hits new victim every two seconds," *CNN Money*, February 6, 2014, http://money.cnn.com/2014/02/06/pf/identity-fraud/ (accessed February 10, 2015).

80. Ben Worthen, "Hackers Aren't Only Threat to Privacy," *The Wall Street Journal*, June 22, 2010, http://online.wsj.com/article/SB10001424052748704122904575314703487356896.html (accessed February 10, 2015).

81. Steven Pearlstein, "People analytics: 'Moneyball' for human resources," *The Washington Post*, August 1, 2014, http://www.washingtonpost.com/business/people-analytics-moneyball-for-human-resources/2014/08/01/3a8fb6ac-1749-11e4-9e3b-7f2f110c6265_story.html (accessed February 24, 2015); Christopher Mims, "In 'People Analytics,' You're Not Human, You're a Data Point," *The Wall Street Journal*, February 16, 2015, http://www.wsj.com/articles/in-people-analytics-youre-not-a-human-youre-a-data-point-1424133771 (accessed February 24, 2015).

CHAPTER 4

THE INSTITUTIONALIZATION OF BUSINESS ETHICS

AN ETHICAL DILEMMA*

One year out of the Pennsylvania university system, Randy was hired by Meeker, a medical warehouse that provides pharmaceutical products to various hospitals and clinics within a three-state area. Meeker was the dominant company in the market. Equipped with his BS degree, Randy was eager to learn, get ahead, and begin his career. As a new employee, he was required to go through extensive training to learn about hospital and clinic regulations, laws, various system procedures, and software applications. The two-month training included descriptions of the usual type of emergencies experienced in clinics and hospitals and what the needs were concerning equipment and supplies. He learned how to use various products and equipment and to train others in these areas. Part of his training was working in all areas of the medical warehouse.

One day Randy's supervisor, Cheryl, brought him into her office to discuss his next assignment. She explained to him that several of the hospitals they serve were about to begin their annual inventory counts. When these inventory counts occur, a representative from Meeker must go into the hospitals and replace all expired supplies and equipment with new ones.

"One of the problems we've been having is the expiration dates on the products we supply are shorter than those of our competitors," Cheryl explained. "To keep our clients loyal, we offer a credit to our clients when we take back the expired products. Unfortunately, that's caused us to lose profits."

Cheryl paused for a moment, then continued. "We can't keep losing profits like this, so I've developed an idea for cutting costs and increasing our competitive advantage."

Cheryl handed several sheets of sticky labels to Randy. He looked them over and found they were exact replicas of the labels on their medical products for over-the-counter medications. The expiration dates on these labels were three months from the current date. Randy looked at Cheryl for more of an explanation.

Cheryl turned to Randy and told him to replace the old labels with the new ones and leave the inventory in the hospitals. Randy began to get uncomfortable.

"But Cheryl, couldn't this be dangerous if the hospital uses expired products?"

Cheryl shook her head. "You don't have to worry. Our competitors offer similar products with a longer expiration date, and there's really no harm in using these products after their expiration date. They are just a little less potent, but not more harmful in any way."

Randy took the labels and headed to the hospitals. As he drove, he went over the instructions in his head. Something about this made him feel uneasy, but he also understood there was no harm in changing the labels. In fact, there were times he remembered taking expired over-the-counter medication himself and it didn't hurt him in any way. Additionally, he would only be extending the date by three months, which is not a long time for medications.

On the other hand, he recalled a moment from his training when he was cautioned about expired medical products. Thinking back, Randy only recalled being cautioned against using expired prescription medications, not anything about over-the-counter medications. Randy also wondered if he would be questioned by the hospital administration staff when he asked for their signature on the inventory paperwork. He knew they would find it odd if there were no credits to their account for expired medications. How would he explain the "new policy" to them without being dishonest?

QUESTIONS | EXERCISES

1. How should Randy deal with the dilemma he is facing?
2. What are the implications of comparing Meeker's practices with those of its competitors?
3. What kind of responsibility does Randy have to the different stakeholders involved in this situation? Does his responsibility to Meeker differ from his responsibility to the hospitals?

*This case is strictly hypothetical; any resemblance to real persons, companies, or situations is coincidental.

To understand the institutionalization of business ethics, it is important to understand the differences between voluntary and legally mandated organizational practices. In addition, there are core practices, sometimes called "best practices," that responsible firms embrace and implement. The effective organizational practice of business ethics requires all three dimensions (legal, voluntary, and core practices) to be integrated into ethics and compliance programs. This integration can create an ethical culture that effectively manages the risks of misconduct. Institutionalization relates to legal and societal forces that provide both rewards and punishment to organizations based on stakeholder evaluations of specific conduct. Institutionalization of business behavior relates to established laws, corporate culture, and industry best practices in establishing an ethical reputation. This means deviations from expected conduct are often considered ethical issues and are therefore a concern to stakeholders. Various institutions provide requirements, structure, and societal expectations that reward and sanction ethical decision making. For example, institutions such as federal regulatory agencies establish rules and procedures for legal conduct and even suggest core or best practices for industries.

In this chapter, we examine the boundaries of ethical conduct and focus on voluntary and core practices and mandated requirements for legal compliance—three important areas in developing an ethical culture. In particular, we concentrate on compliance in specific areas related to competition, consumers, and safety. We consider the requirements of the Sarbanes–Oxley legislation, its implementation by the SEC, and how its implementation has affected companies. We also examine the Dodd–Frank legislation and its rules affecting the finance industry. We provide an overview of the FSGO, along with recommendations and incentives for developing ethical corporate cultures. The FSGO, the Sarbanes–Oxley Act and Dodd–Frank legislation, and industry trade associations support core or best practices. Finally, we examine voluntary responsibilities and review cause-related marketing, strategic philanthropy, and social entrepreneurship in managing stakeholder relationships.

MANAGING ETHICAL RISK THROUGH MANDATED AND VOLUNTARY PROGRAMS

Table 4–1 provides an overview of the three dimensions of institutionalization. **Voluntary practices** include the beliefs, values, and voluntary contractual obligations of a business. ˉ level of commitment to voluntary activities to benefit both ˉers. Google works hard to give its employees a positive ˉenefits package. In addition to being a famously great place to work, Google offices offer such amenities as swimming pools, gyms, volleyball courts, ping-pong tables, and dance classes. The company even allows employees to bring their dogs to work.[1]

Most firms engage in **philanthropy**—giving back to communities and causes. There is strong evidence to suggest that voluntary corporate social responsibility practices provide benefits to stakeholders and increases performance.[2] In addition, research has demonstrated that when both ethical and legal responsibilities are respected through core practices, economic performance benefits.[3]

TABLE 4–1 Voluntary Boundary, Core Practices, and Mandated Boundaries of Ethical Decisions

Voluntary boundary	A management-initiated boundary of conduct (beliefs, values, voluntary policies, and voluntary contractual obligations)
Core practice	A highly appropriate and common practice that helps ensure compliance with legal requirements, industry self-regulation, and societal expectations
Mandated boundary	An externally imposed boundary of conduct (laws, rules, regulations, and other requirements)

Source: Based on the "Open Compliance Ethics Group (OCEG) Foundation Guidelines," v1.0, Steering Committee Update, December 2005, Phoenix, AZ.

© Cengage Learning 2015

Core practices are documented best practices, often encouraged by legal and regulatory forces as well as industry trade associations. The **Better Business Bureau** (BBB) is a leading self-regulatory body that provides directions for managing customer disputes and reviews advertising cases. For instance, the National Advertising Division (NAD), an investigatory division of the BBB's National Advertising Review Council, recommended that Virtua Joint Replacement Institute discontinue its claims that their "quad sparing" knee replacement technique would result in shorter hospital stays. The division did not find substantial evidence to back the claim.[4] Although Virtua is not legally mandated to follow the decision, advertising perceived to be misleading could attract the attention of regulatory authorities if not corrected.

Core practices are appropriate and common practices that have industry acceptance and meet societal expectations. Although these practices are not enforced, there are consequences for ignoring them that lead to misconduct. For example, the FSGO suggest the governing authority (board of directors) be responsible for and assess an organization's ethical and compliance activities. No reporting or investigation is required by government regulatory bodies, but there are incentives for the firms that effectively implement this recommendation. For example, if misconduct occurs, firms may have opportunities to avoid serious punishment if they operated in a proactive, responsible manner. On the other hand, if the board has made no effort to oversee ethics and compliance, its failure could increase and compound the level of punishment the company suffers. In this way, in institutionalizing core practices the government provides organizations with the opportunity to structure their own approaches and only takes action if violations occur. **Mandated boundaries** are externally imposed boundaries of conduct, such as laws, rules, regulations, and other requirements. Antitrust and consumer protection laws create boundaries that must be respected by companies.

Organizations need to maintain an ethical culture and manage stakeholder expectations for appropriate conduct. They achieve these ends through corporate governance, compliance, risk management, and voluntary activities. The development of these drivers of an ethical culture has been institutionally supported by government initiatives and the demands of stakeholders. The compliance element represents areas that must conform to existing legal and regulatory requirements. Established laws and regulatory decisions leave limited flexibility to organizations in adhering to these standards. For example, regulators have a positive impact on the quality of financial reporting. As top managers have been required to increase transparency and complete disclosures, tone at the top has improved.[5] Corporate governance (as discussed in Chapter 2) is structured by a governing authority that provides oversight as well as checks and balances to ensure that the organization meets its goals and objectives for ethical performance. Risk management analyzes the probability

FIGURE 4–1 **Elements of an Ethical Culture**

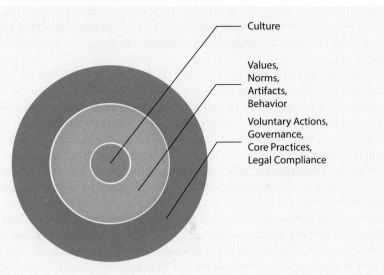

Culture

Values,
Norms,
Artifacts,
Behavior

Voluntary Actions,
Governance,
Core Practices,
Legal Compliance

© Cengage Learning

or chance that misconduct could occur based on the nature of the business and its exposure to risky events. Voluntary activities often represent the values and responsibilities that firms accept in contributing to stakeholder needs and expectations.

Figure 4–1 depicts the key elements of an organizational culture. These elements include values, norms, artifacts, and behavior. An ethical culture creates an environment to structure behavior that is evaluated by stakeholders. As mentioned in previous chapters, values are broad and viewed as long-term enduring beliefs such as integrity, trust, openness, diversity, and individual respect and responsibility. Norms dictate and clarify desirable behaviors through principles, rules, policies, and procedures. For example, norms provide guiding principles for anti-bribery issues, sustainability, and conflicts of interest. Artifacts are visible, tangible external symbols of values and norms. Websites, codes of ethics, rituals, language, and physical settings are artifacts. These three elements have different impacts on behaviors. Organizational decisions on such issues as governance, codes of ethics, ethics training, and legal compliance are shaped by the ethical culture.

MANDATED REQUIREMENTS FOR LEGAL COMPLIANCE

Laws and regulations are established by governments to set minimum standards for responsible behavior—society's codification of what is right and wrong. Laws regulating business conduct are passed because some stakeholders believe business cannot be trusted to do what is right in certain areas, such as consumer safety and environmental protection. Because public policy is dynamic and often changes in response to business abuses and consumer demands for safety and equality, many laws have been passed to resolve specific problems and issues. But the opinions of society, as expressed in legislation, can change over time, and different courts and state legislatures may take diverging views. For example, the thrust of most business legislation can be summed up as follows: Any practice is permitted that does not substantially lessen or reduce competition or harm consumers or society. Courts differ, however, in their interpretations of what constitutes a "substantial" reduction of competition. Laws can help businesspeople determine what society believes at a certain time, but what is legally wrong today may be perceived as acceptable tomorrow, and vice versa.

Instructions to employees to "just obey the law" are meaningless without experience and effective training in dealing with specific legal risk areas. One area that illustrates the complexity of the law is patents. Large technology companies aggressively defend their patents in order to maintain their strategic advantages. Lawsuits among direct competitors in hardware and software have shifted to the mobile industry as technology companies fight to come out on top. For example, Silicon Valley technology firm Nvidia sued Samsung and Qualcomm for infringing on their patent for graphic chips.[6] Patent issues have become so important that some firms, such as IBM and Qualcomm, have created their own patent licensing businesses.[7]

Laws are categorized as either civil or criminal. **Civil law** defines the rights and duties of individuals and organizations (including businesses). **Criminal law** not only prohibits specific actions—such as fraud, theft, or securities trading violations—but also imposes fines or imprisonment as punishment for breaking the law. The primary difference between criminal and civil law is the state or nation enforces criminal laws, whereas individuals (generally, in court) enforce civil laws. Criminal and civil laws are derived from four sources: the U.S. Constitution (constitutional law), precedents established by judges (common law), federal and state laws or statutes (statutory law), and federal and state administrative agencies (administrative law). Federal administrative agencies established by Congress control and influence business by enforcing laws and regulations to encourage competition and to protect consumers, workers, and the environment. The Consumer Financial Protection Bureau was established after the latest financial crisis, which resulted in many consumers losing their homes. State and local laws and regulatory agencies also exist to achieve these objectives.

The primary method of resolving conflicts and serious business ethics disputes is through lawsuits, or when one individual or organization uses civil laws to take another individual or organization to court. However, businesses often want to avoid lawsuits if possible because of the high costs involved. For instance, DuPont and Monsanto resolved a lawsuit involving antitrust and patent claims with a licensing agreement. DuPont agreed to license technology for genetically modified seeds from Monsanto for $1.75 billion.[8] To avoid lawsuits and maintain the standards necessary to reduce risk and create an ethical culture, both legal and organizational standards must be enforced. When violations of organizational standards occur, the National Business Ethics Survey (NBES) notes many employees do not feel their company has a strong ethics program. On the other hand, effective ethics programs reduce misconduct. Figure 4–2 demonstrates how well-implemented ethics programs decrease ethical risks within an organization. It is therefore important for a company to have a functioning ethics program in place long before an ethical disaster strikes.

The role of laws is not so much to distinguish what is ethical or unethical as to determine the appropriateness of specific activities or situations. In other words, laws establish the basic ground rules for responsible business activities. Most of the laws and regulations that govern business activities fall into one of five groups: (1) regulation of competition, (2) protection of consumers, (3) promotion of equity and safety, (4) protection of the natural environment, and (5) incentives to encourage organizational compliance programs to deter misconduct that we will examine later.

Laws Regulating Competition

The issues surrounding the impact of competition on businesses' social responsibility arise from the rivalry among businesses for customers and profits. When businesses compete unfairly, legal and social responsibility issues can result. Intense competition sometimes makes managers feel their company's survival is threatened. In these situations, managers may begin to see unacceptable alternatives as acceptable, and they begin engaging in questionable practices to ensure the survival of their organizations. Both Intel and Microsoft have been hit with fines amounting to billions of dollars for alleged antitrust activity in Europe. The European Union is famous for being tough on companies suspected of antitrust activities. Google has been forced to change its practices in Europe because of claims that it is unfairly dominating the search engine market, and some are even calling for the company to break up its search engine business from its other activities within the European Union. Being aware of antitrust laws is important for all large corporations around the world.

Size frequently gives some companies an advantage over others. Large firms can often generate economies of scale (for example, by forcing their suppliers to lower their prices) that allow them to put smaller firms out of business. Consequently, small companies and even whole communities may resist the efforts of firms like Walmart, Home Depot, and Whole Foods to open stores in their vicinity. These firms' sheer size enables them to operate at such low costs that small, local firms often cannot compete. Some companies' competitive strategies may focus on weakening or destroying a competitor that harms competition and ultimately reduces consumer choice. Many countries have laws restricting such anticompetitive behavior. For instance, China is cracking down on price collusion, which occurs when businesses get together and inflate prices above what they would be if each business priced its products independently. The government fined Japanese auto parts makers $201 million for manipulating prices.[9] Other examples of anticompetitive strategies include sustained price cuts, discriminatory pricing, and bribery. While the U.S. Justice Department aggressively enforces the Foreign Corrupt Practices Act prohibiting bribery of foreign government officials, the U.K. has even more sweeping anti-bribery laws.

FIGURE 4–2 **Misconduct Declines as Ethical Culture Improves**

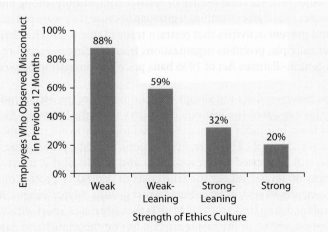

Source: Ethics Resource Center, *National Business Ethics Survey of the U.S. Workforce* (Arlington, VA: Ethics Resource Center, 2014), p. 18.

These laws apply to all companies doing business in Britain and prohibit bribes to foreign officials and private businesspeople. Other nations, including China, are taking a tougher stance on bribery and are prosecuting companies caught in the act.[10] Brazil passed an anti-corruption law to comply with the Organisation for Economic Cooperation's anti-bribery convention.[11]

The primary objective of U.S. antitrust laws is to distinguish competitive strategies that enhance consumer welfare from those that reduce it. The difficulty of this task lies in determining whether the intent of a company's pricing policy is to weaken or even destroy a competitor.[12] A U.S. district judge had to undergo this process before ruling against American Express in an antitrust lawsuit. The lawsuit claimed the company used anticompetitive tactics to force merchants to drive customers away from other types of payment, including rival credit cards. The behavior was deemed to be anticompetitive because it unfairly restricted trade.[13]

Intense competition also leads companies to resort to corporate espionage. Corporate espionage is the act of illegally taking information from a corporation through computer hacking, theft, intimidation, sorting through trash, and impersonation of organizational members. Together, corporate espionage and cybercrimes cost global businesses approximately $445 billion annually.[14] Unauthorized information collected includes patents in development, intellectual property, pricing strategies, customer information, unique manufacturing and technological operations, marketing plans, research and development, and future plans for market and customer expansion.[15] Chesapeake Energy accused former CEO and founder Aubrey McClendon of trade secret theft. According to accusations, when McClendon left the company, he took maps and prospect data from the firm that he used to start new companies. McClendon argued that the company had promised him this type of information as part of his exit agreement.[16] Determining an accurate amount for corporate espionage losses is difficult because most companies do not report such losses for fear the publicity will harm their stock price or encourage further break-ins. Espionage may be carried out by outsiders or employees—executives, programmers, network or computer auditors, engineers, or janitors who have legitimate reasons to access facilities, data, computers, or networks. They may use a variety of techniques for obtaining valuable information, such as dumpster diving, whacking, and hacking, as mentioned in Chapter 3.

Laws have been passed to prevent the establishment of monopolies, inequitable pricing practices, and other practices that reduce or restrict competition among businesses. These laws are sometimes called **procompetitive legislation** because they were enacted to encourage competition and prevent _____ ade (Table 4–2). The Sherman Antitrust Act of 1890, for exam_____ from holding monopolies in their industry, and the Robinson_____ rice discrimination between retailers and wholesalers.

In U.S. law, however, there are always exceptions. Under the McCarran–Ferguson Act of 1944, Congress exempted the insurance industry from the Sherman Antitrust Act and other antitrust laws. Insurance companies joined together to set insurance premiums at specific industry-wide levels. However, even actions that take place under this legal "permission" could still be viewed as irresponsible and unethical if it neutralizes competition and if prices no longer reflect the true costs of insurance protection. What is legal is not always considered ethical by some interest groups. Major League Baseball has an antitrust exemption dating back to 1922. MLB is the only major sport with such a sweeping antitrust exemption, although the major effect it has on the game these days is that sports teams cannot relocate without MLB's permission.[17]

TABLE 4–2 Laws Regulating Competition

Sherman Antitrust Act, 1890	Prohibits monopolies
Clayton Act, 1914	Prohibits price discrimination, exclusive dealing, and other efforts to restrict competition
Federal Trade Commission Act, 1914	Created the Federal Trade Commission (FTC) to help enforce antitrust laws
Robinson–Patman Act, 1936	Bans price discrimination between retailers and wholesalers
Wheeler–Lea Act, 1938	Prohibits unfair and deceptive acts regardless of whether competition is injured
Lanham Act, 1946	Protects and regulates brand names, brand marks, trade names, and trademarks
Celler–Kefauver Act, 1950	Prohibits one corporation from controlling another where the effect is to lessen competition
Consumer Goods Pricing Act, 1975	Prohibits price maintenance agreements among manufacturers and resellers in interstate commerce
FTC Improvement Act, 1975	Gives the FTC more power to prohibit unfair industry practices
Antitrust Improvements Act, 1976	Strengthens earlier antitrust laws; gives Justice Department more investigative authority
Foreign Corrupt Practices Act, 1977	Makes it illegal to pay foreign government officials to facilitate business or to use third parties such as agents and consultants to provide bribes to such officials
Trademark Counterfeiting Act, 1980	Provides penalties for individuals dealing in counterfeit goods
Trademark Law Revision Act, 1988	Amends the Lanham Act to allow brands not yet introduced to be protected through patent and trademark registration
Federal Trademark Dilution Act, 1995	Gives trademark owners the right to protect trademarks and requires them to relinquish those that match or parallel existing trademarks
Digital Millennium Copyright Act, 1998	Refines copyright laws to protect digital versions of copyrighted materials, including music and movies
Controlling the Assault of Non-Solicited Pornography and Marketing Act (CAN-SPAM), 2003	Bans fraudulent or deceptive unsolicited commercial email and requires senders to provide information on how recipients can opt out of receiving additional messages
Fraud Enforcement and Recovery Act, 2009	Strengthens provisions to improve the criminal enforcement of fraud laws, including mortgage fraud, securities fraud, financial institutions' fraud, commodities fraud, and fraud related to the federal assistance and relief program

© Cengage Learning

Laws Protecting Consumers

Laws that protect consumers require businesses to provide accurate information about their goods and services and follow safety standards (Table 4–3). The first **consumer protection law** was passed in 1906, partly in response to a novel by Upton Sinclair. *The Jungle* describes, among other things, the atrocities and unsanitary conditions of the meatpacking industry in turn-of-the-century Chicago. The outraged public response to this book and other exposés of the industry resulted in the passage of the Pure Food and Drug Act. Similarly, Ralph Nader had a tremendous impact on consumer protection laws with his book *Unsafe at Any Speed*. His critique and attack on General Motors' Corvair had far-reaching effects on cars and other consumer products. Other consumer protection laws emerged from similar processes.

TABLE 4–3 Laws Protecting Consumers

Pure Food and Drug Act, 1906	Prohibits adulteration and mislabeling of foods and drugs sold in interstate commerce
Federal Hazardous Substances Labeling Act, 1960	Controls the labeling of hazardous substances for household use
Truth in Lending Act, 1968	Requires full disclosure of credit terms to purchasers
Consumer Product Safety Act, 1972	Created the Consumer Product Safety Commission to establish safety standards and regulations for consumer products
Fair Credit Billing Act, 1974	Requires accurate, up-to-date consumer credit records
Consumer Goods Pricing Act, 1975	Prohibits price maintenance agreements
Consumer Leasing Act, 1976	Requires accurate disclosure of leasing terms to consumers
Fair Debt Collection Practices Act, 1978	Defines permissible debt collection practices
Toy Safety Act, 1984	Gives the government the power to recall dangerous toys quickly
Nutritional Labeling and Education Act, 1990	Prohibits exaggerated health claims and requires all processed foods to have labels showing nutritional information
Telephone Consumer Protection Act, 1991	Establishes procedures for avoiding unwanted telephone solicitations
Children's Online Privacy Protection Act, 1998	Requires the FTC to formulate rules for collecting online information from children under age 13
Do Not Call Implementation Act, 2003	Directs the FCC and the FTC to coordinate so that their rules are consistent regarding telemarketing call practices including the Do Not Call Registry and other lists, as well as call abandonment
Credit Card Accountability Responsibility and Disclosure Act, 2009	Implemented strict rules on credit card companies regarding topics such as issuing credit to youth, terms disclosure, interest rates, and fees
Dodd–Frank Wall Street Reform and Consumer Protection Act (2010)	Promotes financial reform to increase accountability and transparency in the financial industry, protects consumers from deceptive financial practices, and establishes the Bureau of Consumer Financial Protection

Large groups of people with specific vulnerabilities have been granted special levels of legal protection relative to the general population. For example, children and the elderly have received proportionately greater attention than other groups. American society responded to research and documentation showing young consumers and senior citizens encounter difficulties in the acquisition, consumption, and disposition of products. Special legal protection provided to vulnerable consumers is considered to be in the public interest.[19] For example, the Children's Online Privacy Protection Act (COPPA) requires commercial Internet sites to carry privacy policy statements, obtain parental consent before soliciting information from children under the age of 13, and provide an opportunity to remove any information provided by children using such sites. Those who believe COPPA does not go far enough argue that children aged 13 and older should not be treated as adults on the web. In a study of children ages 10 to 17, nearly half indicated they would give their name, address, and other demographic information in exchange for a gift worth $100 or more. Internet safety among children is another major topic of concern. Research shows filtering and age verification are not effective in making the Internet safer, and businesses, regulators, and parents are trying to decipher how to better protect children from dangers ranging from online predators to pornography.[20] Mobile technology also called for updates in the law. The FTC adopted changes to COPPA to account for mobile phone applications. Many standard mobile marketing practices, such as collecting location information and photos, are now considered to be personal information when applied to children under the age of 13.[21]

Seniors are another highly vulnerable demographic. New laws took aim at financial scams directed at seniors, such as free lunch seminars. The state of Arkansas took the lead on this issue, conducting police sweeps of suspected scams, increasing fines, and amending laws to impose increased penalties for those who prey on the elderly. Older people are the most vulnerable group for financial scams because they rely on their savings for retirement security.[22] The role of the FTC's Bureau of Consumer Protection is to protect consumers against unfair, deceptive, or fraudulent practices. The bureau, which enforces a variety of consumer protection laws, is divided into five divisions. The Division of Enforcement monitors compliance with and investigates violations of laws, including unfulfilled holiday delivery promises by online shopping sites, employment opportunities fraud, scholarship scams, misleading advertising for health care products, high-tech and telemarketing fraud, data security, and financial practices.

DEBATE ISSUE
TAKE A STAND

The FTC versus POM Wonderful

The Federal Trade Commission sued POM Wonderful, maker of pomegranate juice products, for misleading advertising. Specifically, the FTC found that POM's claims that pomegranate juice can help lower the risk of heart disease, erectile dysfunction, and prostate cancer were unsubstantiated and based on faulty evidence. The FTC further ordered that POM could not make health claims about its products without evidence from two human clinical trials. This is the FTC's attempt to adopt the more stringent standards used by the Food and Drug Administration (FDA) to approve drugs.

POM claimed that the FTC's verdict infringed upon its First Amendment right to free speech. The case was taken to the U.S. Court of Appeals for the D.C. Circuit. They upheld the FTC's claims that POM had engaged in deceptive advertising, which is not protected under the First Amendment. However, they also determined that the FTC had overstepped its bounds in requiring two human clinical trials. They felt that one trial is sufficient to communicate health benefits to consumers. Two trials, on the other hand, would place a burden on companies and might result in consumers not receiving positive information about a product that could improve their health. Additionally, a major difference between pomegranate juice and many pharmaceuticals is that pomegranate juice does not cause harm. It is widely recognized for its anti-inflammatory and antioxidant properties. Studies have demonstrated that it stabilizes blood flow and lowers blood pressure that can relate to heart health. Therefore, it could be argued that two human clinical trials are not necessary.[18]

1. The Federal Trade Commission's ruling on two clinical trials is necessary to determine causality and ensure that consumers are receiving the most accurate information.

2. The Federal Trade Commission's ruling on clinical trials oversteps its authority because documentation suggests that POM has health benefits and poses no danger to consumers.

The FDA regulates food safety, human drugs, tobacco, dietary supplements, vaccines, veterinary drugs, medical devices, cosmetics, products that give off radiation, and biological products. The FDA has the power to authorize the marketing of these products as well as to ban those deemed unsafe for the public.[23] For example, the FDA warned surgeons against using high-power morcellators, a type of power tool used to remove uterine growths, after strong evidence suggested that these tools could spread undetected cancer.[24]

Laws Promoting Equity and Safety

Laws promoting equity in the workplace were passed during the 1960s and 1970s to protect the rights of minorities, women, older persons, and persons with disabilities; other legislation sought to protect the safety of all workers (Table 4–4). Of these laws, probably the most important to business is Title VII of the Civil Rights Act, originally passed in 1964 and amended several times since. Title VII specifically prohibits discrimination in employment on the basis of race, sex, religion, color, or national origin. The Civil Rights Act also created the Equal Employment Opportunity Commission (EEOC) to enforce the provisions of Title VII. Among other things, the EEOC assists businesses in designing affirmative action programs. These programs aim to increase job opportunities for women and minorities by analyzing the present pool of employees, identifying areas where women and minorities are underrepresented, and establishing specific hiring and promotion goals, along with target dates for meeting those goals.

Other legislation addresses more specific employment practices. The Equal Pay Act of 1963 mandates that women and men who do equal work must receive equal pay. Wage differences are allowed only if they can be attributed to seniority, performance, or qualifications. The Americans with Disabilities Act of 1990 prohibits discrimination against people with disabilities. Despite these laws, inequities in the workplace still exist. Women earn an average of 78 cents for every dollar men earn. The disparity in wages is higher for African American women (68 cents for every dollar a white man earns) and Hispanic women (60 cents for every dollar).[25]

Congress passed laws that seek to improve safety in the workplace. By far the most significant of these is the Occupational Safety and Health Act of 1970 that mandates employers provide safe and healthy working conditions for all workers. The **Occupational Safety and Health Administration** (OSHA) enforces the act and makes regular surprise inspections to ensure businesses maintain safe working environments.

Even with the passage and enforcement of safety laws, many employees still work in unhealthy or dangerous environments. Safety experts suspect that companies underreport industrial accidents to avoid state and federal inspection and regulation. The current emphasis on increased productivity has been cited as the main reason for the growing number of such accidents. Competitive pressures are also believed to lie behind the increases in manufacturing injuries. Greater turnover in organizations due to downsizing means employees may have more responsibilities and less experience in their current positions, thus increasing the potential for accidents. Overworked employees are often cited as a primary factor in careless accidents, both in the United States and in other countries. For instance, cruise ship lawyers cite overworked employees as one of the major causes for the increase in cruise ship accidents. They state because cruise ship employees are no longer subject to the U.S. court system—but are directed to foreign arbitration when they have problems—they have experienced a deterioration in working conditions that have led to additional accidents.[26]

TABLE 4–4 U.S. Laws Promoting Equity and Safety

Equal Pay Act of 1963	Prohibits discrimination in pay on the basis of sex
Equal Pay Act of 1963 (amended)	Prohibits sex-based discrimination in the rate of pay to men and women doing the same or similar jobs
Title VII of the Civil Rights Act of 1964 (amended in 1972)	Prohibits discrimination in employment on the basis of race, color, sex, religion, or national origin
Age Discrimination in Employment Act, 1967	Prohibits discrimination in employment against persons between the ages of 40 and 70
Occupational Safety and Health Act, 1970	Designed to ensure healthful and safe working conditions for all employees
Title IX of Education Amendments of 1972	Prohibits discrimination based on sex in education programs or activities that receive federal financial assistance
Vocational Rehabilitation Act, 1973	Prohibits discrimination in employment because of physical or mental handicaps
Vietnam Era Veterans Readjustment Act, 1974	Prohibits discrimination against disabled veterans and Vietnam War veterans
Pension Reform Act, 1974	Designed to prevent abuses in employee retirement, profit-sharing, thrift, and savings plans
Equal Credit Opportunity Act, 1974	Prohibits discrimination in credit on the basis of sex or marital status
Age Discrimination Act, 1975	Prohibits discrimination on the basis of age in federally assisted programs
Pregnancy Discrimination Act, 1978	Prohibits discrimination on the basis of pregnancy, childbirth, or related medical conditions
Immigration Reform and Control Act, 1986	Prohibits employers from knowingly hiring a person who is an unauthorized alien
Americans with Disabilities Act, 1990	Prohibits discrimination against people with disabilities and requires that they be given the same opportunities as people without disabilities
Civil Rights Act, 1991	Provides monetary damages in cases of intentional employment discrimination

© Cengage Learning

THE SARBANES–OXLEY (SOX) ACT

In 2002, largely in response to widespread corporate accounting scandals, Congress passed the Sarbanes–Oxley Act to establish a system of federal oversight of corporate accounting practices. In addition to making fraudulent financial reporting a criminal offense and strengthening penalties for corporate fraud, the law requires corporations to establish codes of ethics for financial reporting and develop greater transparency in financial reporting to their investors and other stakeholders.

Supported by both Republicans and Democrats, the Sarbanes–Oxley Act was enacted to restore stakeholder confidence after accounting fraud at Enron, WorldCom, and hundreds of other companies resulted in investors and employees losing much of their savings. During the resulting investigations, the public learned hundreds of corporations failed to report their financial results accurately. Many stakeholders believed accounting firms, lawyers, top executives, and boards of directors developed a culture of deception to ensure investor approval and gain a competitive advantage. As a result of public outrage over the accounting scandals, the Sarbanes–Oxley Act garnered nearly unanimous support not only in Congress but also from government regulatory agencies, the president, and the general public. When President George W. Bush signed the Sarbanes–Oxley Act into law, he emphasized the need for new standards of ethical behavior in business, particularly among the top managers and boards of directors responsible for overseeing business decisions and activities.

At the heart of the Sarbanes–Oxley Act (SOX) is the **Public Company Accounting Oversight Board** that monitors accounting firms auditing public corporations and establish auditors in accounting firms. The law gave the board investi ver auditors and securities analysts who issue reports about alth. The law attempts to eliminate conflicts of interest by promoting accounting firms from providing both auditing and consulting services to the same client companies without special permission from the client firm's audit committee; it also places limits on the length of time lead auditors can serve a particular client. The Sarbanes–Oxley Act requires corporations to take greater responsibility for their decisions and to provide leadership based on ethical principles. Additionally, the law modifies the attorney–client relationship to require lawyers to report wrongdoing to top managers and/or the board of directors. It also provides protection for "whistle-blowing" employees who report illegal activity to authorities. This "whistle-blower" protection was strengthened with the passage of the Dodd–Frank Act several years later.

On the other hand, SOX raised a number of concerns. The complex law imposed additional requirements and costs on executives. Additionally, the new act caused many firms to restate their financial reports to avoid penalties. Big public companies spent thousands of hours and millions of dollars annually to make sure someone looked over the shoulder of key accounting personnel at every step of every business process, according to Financial Executives International. Perhaps the biggest complaint is in spite of Sarbanes–Oxley, financial executives discovered new loopholes that allowed them to engage in the misconduct that contributed to the global financial crisis.

A major change to Sarbanes-Oxley occurred with a new law in 2012. During 2012, the administration passed the Jumpstart Our Business Startups (JOBS) Act in an effort to jumpstart the economy. This act exempts what is termed as "emerging growth companies" from having to observe the auditor attestation requirements from Sarbanes–Oxley 404(b). The exemption can last a maximum of two to five years. The purpose of the law is to allow startups to easily attract funding and investors. One of the biggest provisions of this law is that qualified firms can raise funds in private and small public offerings without registering with the Securities and Exchange Commission, thus saving them money. In order to qualify, firms must have annual gross revenues of less than $1 billion. Since the bill's passage, researchers believe the JOB Act has led to an additional 21 IPOs filed annually.[27] The JOBS Act is one way the government tries to lessen the burden of Sarbanes–Oxley on newer, smaller businesses and encourage entrepreneurship.

Public Company Accounting Oversight Board

SOX aims to promote transparency, reduce conflicts of interest, and increase accountability. For instance, one provision called for the establishment of a board to oversee the audit of public companies in order to protect the interests of investors and further the public interest in the preparation of informative, accurate, and independent audit reports for companies. The Public Company Accounting Oversight Board faced several challenges throughout the years, including a lawsuit claiming the board was unconstitutional. The lawsuit passed to the Supreme Court, which ruled in favor of the board. The board must also overcome obstacles with foreign auditing firms. Although Sarbanes–Oxley requires registration from all auditors listed on the U.S. public market including foreign auditors, several countries, such as the European Union and China, do not allow inspections of their auditing firms.[28]

Auditor and Analyst Independence

The Sarbanes–Oxley Act seeks to eliminate conflicts of interest among auditors, security analysts, brokers, dealers, and the public companies they serve in order to ensure enhanced financial disclosures of public companies' true conditions. To accomplish auditor independence, Section 201 prohibits registered public accounting firms from providing both non-audit and audit services to a public company. National securities exchanges and registered securities associations have adopted similar conflict-of-interest rules for security analysts, brokers, and dealers who recommend equities in research reports. Such independence enables the Sarbanes–Oxley Act to ensure compliance with the requirement for more detailed financial disclosures representing public companies' true condition. For example, registered public accounting firms are now required to identify all material correcting adjustments to reflect accurate financial statements. Also, all material off-balance-sheet transactions and other relationships with unconsolidated entities that affect current or future financial conditions of a public company must be disclosed in each annual and quarterly financial report. In addition, public companies must report "on a rapid and current basis" material changes in their financial condition or operations.

Whistle-Blower Protection

Employees of public companies and accounting firms are accountable to report unethical behavior. The Sarbanes–Oxley Act intends to motivate employees through whistle-blower protection that prohibits the employer from taking certain actions against employees who lawfully disclose private employer information to parties in a judicial proceeding involving a fraud claim, among others. Whistle-blowers are granted a remedy of special damages and attorneys' fees. Unfortunately, this law did not protect certain whistle-blowers from being penalized prior to the financial crisis. Whistle-blowers at Lehman Brothers, Madoff Securities, and Stanford Financial Group (that also operated a Ponzi scheme) warned auditors and government officials of misconduct at the companies. Some whistle-blowers were fired or, after losing lawsuits filed against the offending company, were forced to pay large sums in back pay and attorney's fees.[29] These cases prompted a provision for stronger whistle-blower protection in the Dodd–Frank Act, discussed in the next section.

Cost of Compliance

The national cost of compliance of the Sarbanes–Oxley Act can be extensive and includes internal costs, external costs, and auditor fees. For example, Section 404 requires companies to document both the results of financial transactions and the processes they used to generate them. A company may have thousands of processes that have never been written down. Writing down the processes is time consuming and costly.[30] Also, because the cost of compliance is so high for many small companies, some publicly traded companies even considered delisting themselves from the U.S. Stock Exchange.

However, studies show although compliance costs were high shortly after Sarbanes–Oxley was passed, they have declined over the years. Companies have reported their compliance costs decreased 50 percent from the level when the laws were put into effect. One reason why the costs may be decreasing is that companies have more experience with Sarbanes–Oxley and therefore require less time to complete the process.[31] Audit standards were also revised in 2007, saving companies an estimated 25 percent or more annually.[32]

DODD–FRANK WALL STREET REFORM AND CONSUMER PROTECTION ACT

In 2010 President Obama signed into law the Dodd–Frank Wall Street Reform and Consumer Protection Act. It was heralded as "a sweeping overhaul of the financial regulatory system … on a scale not seen since the reforms that followed the Great Depression."[33] The new law seeks to improve financial regulation, increase oversight of the industry, and prevent the types of risk-taking, deceptive practices, and lack of oversight that led to the 2008–2009 financial crisis.[34] The Act contains 16 provisions that include increasing the accountability and transparency of financial institutions, creating a bureau to educate consumers in financial literacy and protect them from deceptive financial practices, implementing additional incentives for whistle-blowers, increasing oversight of the financial industry, and regulating the use of complex derivatives.

Response to the law was split along party lines, with vocal opponents as well as proponents. Critics have several concerns, including claims the rules on derivatives are too burdensome, the belief such wide-scale changes will create chaos in the regulatory system, and the fear the government will gain too much power.[35] Other companies support the law in general but oppose certain provisions.[36] The following sections describe some of the most notable provisions of the Dodd–Frank Act.

Financial Agencies Created by the Dodd–Frank Act

One provision of the Dodd–Frank Act instituted the creation of two new financial agencies, the Office of Financial Research and the Financial Stability Oversight Council (FSOC). The Office of Financial Research is charged with improving the quality of financial data available to government officials and creating a better system of analysis for the financial industry.[37] FSOC is responsible for maintaining the stability of the financial system in the United States through monitoring the market, identifying threats, promoting market discipline among the public, and responding to major risks that threaten stability.[38] FSOC has the authority to limit or closely supervise financial risks, create stricter standards for banking and nonbanking financial institutions, and disband financial institutions that present a serious risk to market stability.[39] The addition of these two new agencies is intended not only to improve information collecting and oversight, but to close the types of loopholes that allowed financial industries to engage in risky and deceptive conduct prior to the financial crisis.

Consumer Financial Protection Bureau

Another agency the Dodd–Frank Act created was the **Consumer Financial Protection Bureau** (CFPB), an independent agency within the Federal Reserve System that "regulate[s] the offering and provision of consumer financial products or services under the Federal consumer financial laws."[40] One of the problems leading up to the 2008–2009 financial crisis was that average investors often did not understand the complex financial products they purchased. The CFPB aims to protect consumers from this problem in the future. The government granted the agency supervisory power over credit markets as well as the authority to monitor lenders and ensure they are in compliance with the law.[41] The CFPB also has the responsibility to curtail unfair lending and credit card practices, enforce consumer financial laws, and check the safety of financial products before their launch into the market.[42]

The CFPB is not without its critics. Several financial firms and legislators believe the bureau has too much power. Additionally, financial institutions are concerned the bureau's powers could lead to strict sanctions or burdensome regulations.[43] Goldman Sachs, for instance, limited its profitable practice of investing in its own private-equity funds to comply with the Volcker rule, part of the Dodd-Frank Act restricting financial institutions from using their own money to make large bets.[44] To protect against misconduct at all levels, the CFPB has oversight powers for institutions often accused of questionable dealings, such as payday lenders and debt collectors.[45] The goal of the CFPB is to create a more equitable and transparent financial environment for consumers. For instance, the CFPB is developing federal regulations to place limits on payday lenders. Lenders, on the other hand, claim that too many restrictions would make it too expensive for them to loan to high-risk customers.[46]

Whistle-Blower Bounty Program

It is clear the whistle-blower provisions implemented in Sarbanes–Oxley were not enough to prevent the massive misconduct occurring at business institutions before the financial crisis. To encourage more employees to come forward when they witness misconduct, the Dodd–Frank law instituted a whistle-blower bounty program. Whistle-blowers who report financial fraud to the Securities and Exchange Commission and Commodities Exchange Commission are eligible to receive 10 to 30 percent of fines and settlements if their reports result in convictions of more than $1 million in penalties.[47]

While this will encourage more people to step forward, there are some challenges that need to be considered for the program to be a success. For instance, the SEC will certainly be flooded with tips, some of which will come from people who just want the money. Still, the SEC is optimistic that half the tips it receives will result in payouts, suggesting the number of credible whistle-blower complaints will increase dramatically.[48] One of the biggest payouts has gone to four whistle-blowers that helped the government secure a conviction against Bank of America for improper mortgage practices during the last financial crisis. The $16.65 billion penalty against the bank resulted in a payout of $170 million for the whistle-blowers involved.[49]

LAWS THAT ENCOURAGE ETHICAL CONDUCT

Violations of the law usually begin when businesspeople stretch the limits of ethical standards, as defined by company or industry codes of conduct, and then choose to engage in schemes that either knowingly or unwittingly violate the law. In recent years, new laws and regulations have been passed to discourage such decisions—and to foster programs designed to improve business ethics and social responsibility (Table 4–5). The most important of these are the Federal Sentencing Guidelines for Organizations (FSGO), the Sarbanes–Oxley Act, and the Dodd–Frank Act. One of the goals of these acts is requiring employees to report observed misconduct. The development of reporting systems has advanced, with most companies having some method for employees to report observed misconduct. However, a sizable percentage of employees still do not report misconduct. Figure 4–3 shows the percentage of workers who report misconduct when they observe it in the workplace.

TABLE 4–5 Institutionalization of Ethics through the U.S. Sentencing Guidelines for Organizations

1991	*Law:* U.S. Sentencing Guidelines for Organizations created for federal prosecutions of organizations. These guidelines provide for just punishment, adequate deterrence, and incentives for organizations to prevent, detect, and report misconduct. Organizations need to have an effective ethics and compliance program to receive incentives in the case of misconduct.
2004	*Amendments:* The definition of an effective ethics program now includes the development of an ethical organizational culture. Executives and board members must assume the responsibility of identifying areas of risk, providing ethics training, creating reporting mechanisms, and designating an individual to oversee ethics programs.
2007–2008	*Additional definition of a compliance and ethics program:* Firms should focus on due diligence to detect and prevent misconduct and promote an organizational culture that encourages ethical conduct. More details are provided, encouraging the assessment of risk and outlining appropriate steps in designing, implementing, and modifying ethics programs and training that will include all employees, top management, and the board or governing authority. These modifications continue to reinforce the importance of an ethical culture in preventing misconduct.
2010	*Amendments for reporting to the board:* Chief compliance officers are directed to make their reports to their firm's board rather than to the general counsel. Companies are encouraged to create hotlines, perform self-audit programs, and adopt controls to detect misconduct internally. More specific language has been added to the word *prompt* in regards to what it means to promptly report misconduct. The amendment also extends operational responsibility to all personnel within a company's ethics and compliance program.
2014	The Commission investigated how the sentencing guidelines could be used by regulatory and law enforcement agencies to recommend effective ethics and compliance programs. The Commission assessed its efforts to encourage corporations, nonprofits, government agencies, and other organizations to form institutional cultures that discourage misconduct.

Source: "U.S. Sentencing Guidelines Changes Become Effective November 1," FCPA Compliance and Ethics Blog, November 2, 2010, http://tfoxlaw. wordpress.com/2010/11/02/us-sentencing-guidelines-changes-become-effective-november-1/ (accessed February 25, 2015); United States Sentencing Commission, *Amendments to the Sentencing Guidelines*, April 30, 2012, http://www.ussc.gov/Legal/Amendments/Reader-Friendly/20120430_RF_ Amendments.pdf (accessed February 25, 2015); Paula Desio, Deputy General Counsel, *An Overview of the Organizational Guidelines*, http://www.ussc.gov/ sites/default/files/pdf/training/organizational-guidelines/ORGOVERVIEW.pdf (accessed February 25, 2015).

FIGURE 4-3 **Percent of Employees Who Report Observed Misconduct**

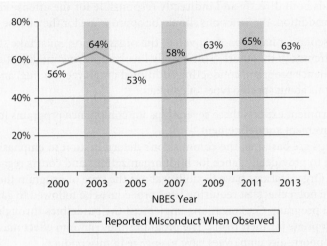

Source: Ethics Resource Center, *National Business Ethics Survey of the U.S. Workforce* (Arlington, VA: Ethics Resource Center, 2014), p. 26.

FEDERAL SENTENCING GUIDELINES FOR ORGANIZATIONS

As mentioned in Chapter 1, Congress passed the FSGO in 1991 to create an incentive for organizations to develop and implement programs designed to foster ethical and legal compliance. These guidelines, developed by the U.S. Sentencing Commission, apply to all felonies and class A misdemeanors committed by employees in association with their work. As an incentive, organizations that demonstrated due diligence in developing effective compliance programs to discourage unethical and illegal conduct may be subject to reduced organizational penalties if an employee commits a crime.[50] Overall, the government philosophy is that legal violations can be prevented through organizational values and a commitment to ethical conduct.

The commission delineated seven steps companies must implement to demonstrate due diligence:

1. A firm must develop and disseminate a code of conduct that communicates required standards and identifies key risk areas for the organization.

2. High-ranking personnel in the organization who are known to abide by the legal and ethical standards of the industry (such as an ethics officer, vice president of human resources, general counsel, and so forth) must have oversight over the program.

3. No one with a known propensity to engage in misconduct should be put in a position of authority.

4. A communications system for disseminating standards and procedures (ethics training) must also be put into place.

5. Organizational communications should include a way for employees to report misconduct without fearing retaliation, such as an anonymous toll-free hotline or an ombudsman. Monitoring and auditing systems designed to detect misconduct are also required.

6. If misconduct is detected, the firm must take appropriate and fair disciplinary action. Individuals both directly and indirectly responsible for the offense should be disciplined. In addition, the sanctions should be appropriate for the offense.

7. After misconduct has been discovered, the organization must take steps to prevent similar offenses in the future. This usually involves making modifications to the ethical compliance program, conducting additional employee training, and issuing communications about specific types of conduct.

The government expects these seven steps for compliance programs to undergo continuous improvement and refinement.[51]

These steps are based on the commission's determination to emphasize compliance programs and to provide guidance for both organizations and courts regarding program effectiveness. Organizations have flexibility about the type of program they develop; the seven steps are not a checklist requiring legal procedures be followed to gain certification of an effective program. Organizations implement the guidelines through effective core practices appropriate for their firms. The programs they put into effect must be capable of reducing the opportunity employees have to engage in misconduct.

A 2004 amendment to the FSGO requires a business's governing authority to be well informed about its ethics program with respect to content, implementation, and effectiveness. This places the responsibility squarely on the shoulders of the firm's leadership, usually the board of directors. The board must ensure there is a high-ranking manager accountable for the day-to-day operational oversight of the ethics program; provide for adequate authority, resources, and access to the board or an appropriate subcommittee of the board; and ensure there are confidential mechanisms available so the organization's employees and agents may report or seek guidance about potential or actual misconduct without fear of retaliation. Finally, the board is required to oversee the discovery of risks and to design, implement, and modify approaches to deal with those risks. Figure 4–4 demonstrates the growth in ethics programs over time. If board members do not understand the nature, purpose, and methods available to implement an ethics program, the firm is at risk of inadequate oversight and ethical misconduct that may escalate into a scandal.[52]

A 2005 Supreme Court decision held that the federal sentencing guidelines were not mandatory but should serve only as recommendations for judges to use in their decisions. Some legal and business experts believe this decision might weaken the implementation of the FSGO, but most federal sentences remained in the same range as before the Supreme Court decision. The guidelines remain an important consideration in developing an effective ethics and compliance program.[53]

The 2007–2008 amendments to the FSGO extend the required ethics training to members of the board or governing authority, high-level personnel, employees, and the organizations' agents. This change applies not only oversight but mandatory training to all levels of the organization. Merely distributing a code of ethics does not meet the training requirements. The 2007 and 2008 amendments now require most governmental contractors to provide ethics and compliance training.

As new FSGO amendments are implemented, more explicit responsibility is being placed on organizations to improve and expand ethics and compliance provisions to include all employees and board members, as demonstrated in four amendments to the guidelines implemented in 2010. The first amendment concerned chief compliance officers who report misconduct to the general counsel. The guidelines recommend simplifying the complexity of reporting relationships by having the chief compliance officer make reports directly to the board or to a board committee. Companies are also encouraged to extend their internal ethical controls through hotlines, self-auditing programs, and other mechanisms so misconduct can be detected internally rather than externally. In the third amendment, the FSGO added more specific language of the word *prompt* to help employees recognize what it means to report an ethical violation promptly. Finally, the FSGO amended the extent of operational responsibility to apply to all personnel within a company's ethics and compliance program.[54]

The 2010 amendment also made it possible for companies to have their penalties for misconduct reduced if their ethics programs met four conditions. First, the organization itself must have discovered the misconduct before it was discovered externally. Second, the violation should be promptly reported to regulators (the expanded definition of the word "prompt" helps to clarify this condition). Third, nobody with operational responsibility can be involved in the misconduct. Finally, the compliance officer must have direct access to the governing authority to report the misconduct.[55]

In 2014 the Federal Sentencing Commission focused their attention on the sharing of best practices among regulatory and law enforcement agencies. Agencies such as the Department of Justice's Antitrust Division are developing compliance programs based on aspects of the FSGO's seven steps for effective ethics programs. The Commission encourages the development of such programs and also supports the sharing of best practices among industry associations. In addition to studying the progress of these developments, the Commission also assesses the efforts of nonprofit organizations, for-profit companies, government agencies, and other organizations in formulating effective institutional cultures that prevent unethical conduct.[56]

In 1999 the Holder memo (Deputy Attorney General Eric Holder's 1999 memo to U.S. attorneys) provided guidance to prosecutors and judges in cases where corporations or their managers were prosecuted. Prosecutors were encouraged to be aware of all incentive programs established by respective divisions and regulatory agencies, including the Federal Sentencing Guidelines.[57] As a follow-up in the Department of Justice, the Thompson Memo (Deputy Attorney General Larry Thompson's 2003 memo to U.S. Attorneys) advanced general principles to consider in cases involving corporate wrongdoing. This memo makes it clear ethics and compliance programs are important to detecting the types of misconduct most likely to occur in a particular corporation's line of business. Additionally, the prosecutor generally has wide latitude in determining when, whom, and whether to prosecute violations of federal law. U.S. attorneys are directed that charging for even minor misconduct may be appropriate when the wrongdoing was perpetuated by a large number of employees in a particular role or was condoned by upper management. Without an effective program to identify an isolated rogue employee involved in misconduct, a firm may suffer serious consequences

FIGURE 4–4 Ethical Culture Perceptions of Employees

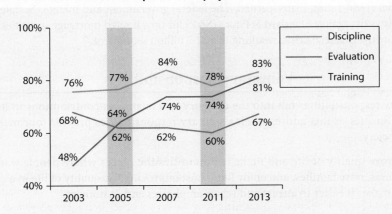

in terms of regulatory issues, enforcement, and sentencing.[58] Therefore, there is general agreement both in law and administrative policy that an effective ethics and compliance program is necessary to prevent misconduct and reduce the legal consequences if it does occur.

CORE OR BEST PRACTICES

The focus of core or best practices is on integrity in developing structurally sound organizational practices and integrity for financial and nonfinancial performance measures, rather than on an individual's morals. Although the Sarbanes–Oxley Act and the Dodd–Frank Act provide standards for financial performance, most ethical issues relate to nonfinancials such as marketing, human resource management, and customer relations. Abusive behavior, lying, and conflict of interest are still three significant issues.

The majority of executives and board members want to measure nonfinancial performance, but no standards currently exist. The Open Compliance Ethics Group (OCEG) (oceg.org) developed benchmarking studies that are available to organizations wanting to conduct self-assessments to determine the elements of their ethics programs. Developing organizational systems and processes is a requirement of the regulatory environment, but organizations are given considerable freedom in developing these programs. Core practices exist and can be identified in every industry. Trade associations' self-regulatory groups and research studies often provide insights into the expected best core practices. An important priority is for each firm to assess its legal and ethical risk areas, and then develop structures to prevent, detect, and quickly correct any misconduct.

Use of gatekeepers is an important part of core practices. Trust allows businesses to depend upon one another as they make transactions or exchange value. Ethics creates the foundational trust between two parties in a transaction. Many people must trust and be trusted to make business work properly. Sometimes these parties are referred to as *gatekeepers*. Gatekeepers include accountants, who are essential to certifying the accuracy of financial information, as well as lawyers, financial rating agencies, and even financial reporting services. These groups are critical in providing information allowing stakeholders to gain an understanding of the financial position of an organization. Most of these gatekeepers operate with professional codes of ethics and face legal consequences, or even disbarment, if they fail to operate within agreed-upon principles of conduct. Therefore, there is a strong need for gatekeepers to uphold ethical standards and remain independent through using standard methods and procedures that can be audited by other gatekeepers, the regulatory system, and investors. Conversely, the failure of gatekeepers to adequately account for risks can result in serious consequences, as financial credit-rating firms learned. The federal government and many U.S. states filed a string of lawsuits against Standard & Poor's (S&P) for how it rated mortgage securities prior to 2008 before the financial crisis, resulting in a $1.5 billion settlement.[59]

Voluntary Responsibilities

Voluntary responsibilities fall into the category of a business's contributions to its stakeholders. Businesses that address their voluntary responsibilities provide four major benefits to society:

1. Improve quality of life and make communities the places where people want to do business, raise families, and enjoy life. Thus, improving the quality of life in a community makes it easier to attract and retain employees and customers.

2. Reduce government involvement by providing assistance to stakeholders.

3. Develop employee leadership skills. Many firms, for example, use campaigns by the United Way and other community service organizations as leadership- and skill-building exercises for their employees.

4. Create an ethical culture and values that act as a buffer to organizational misconduct.[60]

The most common way businesses demonstrate their voluntary responsibilities is through donations to local and national charitable organizations. For example, Wells Fargo & Co. contributes around $275.5 million annually to nonprofit organizations and communities, and employees volunteer approximately 1.7 million hours to their local communities. The company also purchases green energy and has a website devoted to financial education.[61] Indeed, many companies are concerned about the quality of education in the United States after realizing the current pool of prospective employees lacks many basic work skills. Recognizing today's students are tomorrow's employees and customers, firms such as Kroger, Campbell Soup Co., American Express, Apple, Xerox, and Coca-Cola donate money, equipment, and employee time to improve schools in their communities and throughout the nation.

The Walmart Foundation, the charitable giving branch of Walmart Inc., donated $1.3 billion to charities and communities across the globe and is one of the largest corporate cash contributors in the nation. The money supports a variety of causes such as child development, education, the environment, and disaster relief. Walmart officials believe the company makes the greatest impact on communities by supporting issues and causes important to its customers and associates in their own neighborhoods. By supporting communities at the local level, Walmart encourages customer loyalty and goodwill.[62]

Cause-Related Marketing

The first attempts by organizations to coordinate organizational goals with philanthropic giving emerged with cause-related marketing in the early 1980s. **Cause-related marketing** ties an organization's product(s) directly to a social concern through a marketing program. More than 80 percent of customers claim they view firms more positively when they support issues which they care about. Many marketing directors feel that cause-related marketing will increase in the near future.[63]

With cause-related marketing, a percentage of a product's sales is donated to a cause that appeals to the target market. Target, for example, launched a back-to-school initiative called Buy One Give One. During the campaign, the company donated school supplies to children in need every time a customer purchased Target's brand of school supplies. The initiative not only helped children, it also encouraged purchases of Target's Up & Up brand.[64]

Cause-related marketing also affects buying patterns. For such a campaign to be successful, consumers must sympathize with the cause, the brand and cause must be perceived as a good fit, and consumers should be able to transfer their feelings about the cause to their brand perceptions and purchase intentions. When consumers identify with a cause, this identification leads to more positive evaluations of the campaign.[65] This finding lends support to the idea that cause-related marketing can bolster a firm's reputation.

Cause-related marketing has its weaknesses too. For instance, consumers may perceive a company's cause-related campaign as merely a publicity stunt, especially if they cannot understand the link between the campaign and the company's business practices. Also, cause-related campaigns are often of short duration, so consumers may not adequately associate the business with a particular cause. Strategic philanthropy is more holistic, as it ties the company's philanthropic giving to its overall strategy and objectives.

Strategic Philanthropy

Strategic philanthropy is the synergistic and mutually beneficial use of an organization's core ~~es~~ to deal with key stakeholders so as to bring about organiza~~s~~. It uses the profit motive, but argues that philanthropy must ~~ositive~~ impact. For example, Goldman Sachs's 10,000 Woman initiative was created to provide 10,000 women from 43 countries with education, networking, and mentoring so that women could increase their revenue and business opportunities. Goldman Sachs partnered with more than 30 schools worldwide to implement its initiative. About 82 percent of women who graduated from the program saw their revenue increase within 30 months.[66]

Companies that utilize strategic philanthropy recognize that companies do not operate independently of society, and that improved social conditions could lead to improved economic benefits. For instance, Cisco's Network Academy has 9,000 different academies that teach individuals the skills needed to build and design computer networks. By increasing the skill sets of students in areas pertaining directly to the firm, Cisco not only makes a social difference but also introduces a pool of qualified candidates into the workforce. Additionally, strategic philanthropy can help organizations stand out from similar firms to give it a competitive advantage.[67] Finally, a strategic approach to philanthropy tends to create a better image for the company, increase customer loyalty, and enhance customer relationships.[68]

To be successful a strategic philanthropy program should pertain to the mission and operations of the company. It must also have strong support from top managers. Home Depot's strategic philanthropy program, for instance, involves partnering with organizations to build affordable housing and provide aid for disaster recovery—a clear fit with its business strategy as a home improvement retailer. Home Depot has contributed $43 million in cash grants and $37 million in product donations to nonprofits for repairing, remodeling, and maintaining affordable housing.[69] These organizations demonstrate how companies successfully incorporate voluntary responsibilities into their business strategies.

Social Entrepreneurship

Social entrepreneurship occurs when an entrepreneur founds an organization with the purpose of creating social value. Social entrepreneurs desire to find a solution to a social problem rather than to simply earn profits.[70] These types of organizations, also called *social enterprises*, can be for-profit, nonprofit, government-based, or hybrids. For instance, Toms was founded as a for-profit business with a nonprofit component. Founder Blake Mycoskie founded the organization with the social mission to provide one pair of shoes to children in need for each pair of shoes sold. His one-to-one model worked so well that he later expanded into eyewear (for each pair of sunglasses sold, a person in need would receive necessary eye care) as well as coffee (for each bag of coffee sold, the company would donate 140 liters of clean water to those in need).[71]

The concept of social entrepreneurship was popularized with the founding of micro-lending organization Grameen Bank in Bangladesh. Founder Muhammad Yunus wanted to help alleviate poverty in Bangladesh by offering individuals the chance to become entrepreneurs through small loans. Many times would-be entrepreneurs in these countries cannot afford to take out loans due to the high interest rates associated with them. Grameen Bank provided loans in groups of five, with each borrower guaranteeing the other borrowers' debt.[72] At interest rates of 16 percent, Grameen Bank charged much less than traditional bank rates. Due to social pressure, repayment has been high, with 95 percent of borrowers paying back their loans.[73] Yunus's social enterprise has had such an impact on the Bangladesh economic environment that he was awarded the Nobel Peace Prize. The success of his social enterprise paved the way for other entrepreneurs to start their own social enterprises.

Many social entrepreneurs choose to organize their enterprises as nonprofits. The mission of nonprofits is to perform some type of public service, and all profits are reinvested into the organization.[74] The major difference between a social enterprise and a nonprofit is the use of entrepreneurial principles and business-led strategies to create social change.[75] Even though its mission is social rather than economic, social enterprises use business-like strategies as well as organizational structures, norms, values, and innovation to reach its social objectives.[76] A good example of a social enterprise organized as a nonprofit is Belle Meade Plantation's wine-making venture. Belle Meade Plantation, located in Nashville, Tennessee, is a historic site carefully preserved so that individuals can tour the property and learn about Tennessee's past. When the managers realized that tour revenue would not be enough to maintain the property, they decided to open a wine-making organization on the premises. The grapes are grown on the plantation, and wine tastings have been incorporated into plantation tours. Proceeds from wine sales are reinvested back into the maintenance of the property. Despite its nonprofit structure, Belle Meade uses entrepreneurial and marketing practices to sell a legitimate product to support its social goals.[77]

Clear differences exist between strategic philanthropy and social entrepreneurship. Although both stress philanthropy and social change, companies engaged in strategic philanthropy will often outsource their philanthropic programs and/or partner with other organizations. While strategic philanthropy is strongly integrated into a business's operations, the organization is not necessarily organized around a philanthropic purpose. Social enterprises, on the other hand, directly implement their programs and are organized around achieving social objectives.[78] Both types of organization are important in supporting the growth of social responsibility among businesses.

THE IMPORTANCE OF INSTITUTIONALIZATION IN BUSINESS ETHICS

Institutionalization involves embedding values, norms, and artifacts in organizations, industries, and society. In the United States and many other countries, institutionalization involves legislation often finalized through Supreme Court decisions. This chapter provides an overview of legal as well as cultural institutions that work both outside and inside the organizational environment to support and control ethical decision making in organizations.

As discussed in Chapter 2, those in charge of corporate governance should be especially mindful of the institutions, including mandated requirements for legal compliance as well as core practices and voluntary actions that support ethics and social responsibility. While voluntary conduct, including philanthropic activities, is not required to run a business, the failure to understand highly appropriate and common practices, referred to as core practices, provides the opportunity for unethical conduct.

It is important to recognize the institutionalization of business ethics has advanced rapidly over the last 20 years as stakeholders recognized the need to improve business ethics. The government stepped in when scandals and misconduct damaged consumers, investors, and other key constituents important for businesses. More recently, gatekeepers such as lawyers, financial rating agencies, and financial reporting services have been questioned because some of their decisions contributed to major scandals. Legislation and amendments related to the Federal Sentencing Guidelines for Organizations, the Sarbanes–Oxley Act, and the Dodd–Frank Act attempted to develop and enforce ethical practices that support trust in business.

SUMMARY

To understand the institutionalization of business ethics, it is important to understand the voluntary and legally mandated dimensions of organizational practices. Core practices are documented best practices, often encouraged by legal and regulatory forces as well as by industry trade associations. The effective organizational practice of business ethics requires three dimensions to be integrated into an ethics and compliance program. This integration creates an ethical culture that effectively manages the risks of misconduct. Institutionalization in business ethics relates to established laws, customs, and the expectations of organizational ethics programs considered a requirement in establishing reputation. Institutions reward and sanction ethical decision making by providing structure and reinforcing societal expectations. In this way, society as a whole institutionalizes core practices and provides organizations with the opportunity to take their own approach, only taking action if there are violations.

Laws and regulations established by governments set minimum standards for responsible behavior—society's codification of what is right and wrong. Civil and criminal laws regulating business conduct are passed because society—including consumers, interest groups, competitors, and legislators—believes business must comply with society's standards. Such laws regulate competition, protect consumers, promote safety and equity in the workplace, and provide incentives for preventing misconduct.

In 2002, largely in response to widespread corporate accounting scandals, Congress passed the Sarbanes–Oxley Act to establish a system of federal oversight of corporate accounting practices. In addition to making fraudulent financial reporting a criminal offense and strengthening penalties for corporate fraud, the law requires corporations to establish codes of ethics for financial reporting and develop greater transparency in financial reporting to investors and other stakeholders. The Sarbanes–Oxley Act requires corporations to take greater responsibility for their decisions and provide leadership based on ethical principles. For instance, the law requires top managers to certify their firms' financial reports are complete and accurate, making CEOs and CFOs personally accountable for the credibility and accuracy of their companies' financial statements. The Act establishes an oversight board to oversee the audit of public companies.

The oversight board aims to protect the interests of investors and further the public interest in the preparation of informative, accurate, and independent audit reports for companies.

In 2010, largely in response to the widespread misconduct leading to the global recession, the Dodd–Frank Wall Street Reform and Consumer Protection Act was passed. The purpose of the Dodd–Frank Act is to prevent future misconduct in the financial sector, protect consumers from complex financial instruments, oversee market stability, and create transparency in the financial sector. The Act created two financial agencies, the Financial Stability Oversight Council and the Office of Financial Research. It also created the Consumer Financial Protection Bureau to regulate the industry and ensure consumers are protected against overly complex and/or deceptive financial practices. Whistle-blower protection was extended to include a whistle-blower bounty program whereby whistle-blowers who report corporate misconduct to the SEC may receive 10 to 30 percent of settlement money if their reports result in a conviction of more than $1 million in penalties.

Congress passed the FSGO in 1991 to create an incentive for organizations to develop and implement programs designed to foster ethical and legal compliance. These guidelines, developed by the U.S. Sentencing Commission, apply to all felonies and class A misdemeanors committed by employees in association with their work. As an incentive, organizations that have demonstrated due diligence in developing effective compliance programs that discourage unethical and illegal conduct may be subject to reduced organizational penalties if an employee commits a crime. Overall, the government philosophy is that legal violations can be prevented through organizational values and a commitment to ethical conduct. A 2004 amendment to the FSGO requires a business's governing authority be well-informed about its ethics program with respect to content, implementation, and effectiveness. This places the responsibility squarely on the shoulders of the firm's leadership, usually the board of directors. The board must ensure there is a high-ranking manager accountable for the day-to-day operational oversight of the ethics program. The board must provide adequate authority, resources, and access to the board or an appropriate subcommittee of the board. The board must also ensure there are confidential mechanisms available so the organization's employees and agents report or seek guidance about potential or actual misconduct without fear of retaliation. A 2010 amendment to the FSGO directs chief compliance officers to make their reports to the board rather than to the general counsel.

The FSGO and the Sarbanes–Oxley Act provide incentives for developing core practices that ensure ethical and legal compliance. Core practices move the emphasis from a focus on the individual's moral capability to a focus on developing structurally sound organizational core practices and integrity for both financial and nonfinancial performance.

Voluntary responsibilities touch on businesses' social responsibility insofar as they contribute to the local community and society as a whole. Voluntary responsibilities provide four major benefits to society: improving the quality of life, reducing government involvement by providing assistance to stakeholders, developing staff leadership skills, and building staff morale. Companies contribute significant amounts of money to education, the arts, environmental causes, and the disadvantaged by supporting local and national charitable organizations. Cause-related marketing ties an organization's product(s) directly to a social concern through a marketing program. Strategic philanthropy involves linking core business competencies to societal and community needs. Social entrepreneurship occurs when an entrepreneur founds an organization with the purpose of creating social value.

IMPORTANT TERMS FOR REVIEW

voluntary practices 95

Philanthropy 95

core practices 96

Better Business Bureau 96

mandated boundaries 96

civil law 98

criminal law 98

procompetitive legislation 100

consumer protection law 101

Occupational Safety and Health Administration 104

Public Company Accounting Oversight Board 106

Consumer Financial Protection Bureau 109

cause-related marketing 115

strategic philanthropy 116

social entrepreneurship 116

RESOLVING ETHICAL BUSINESS CHALLENGES*

Like most students at Arizona University, Ahmed was a student and spent 20 hours each week working at the university library. He liked the library because it was quiet and he could study some of the time. One interesting aspect of the library was the access to incredible databases, some of which were only for the professors. As a student worker he was privy to all the database codes, and soon discovered large amounts of materials for almost every class on campus.

Bill, one of Ahmed's fellow library student workers, was constantly talking about doing weird stunts and antics to put on YouTube. He was a nice person to be around but sometimes he was a little overbearing. One evening when Ahmed started work, Bill was talking about the many ways to download pirated music, movies, and books from the library's system. "It is very easy and untraceable. I just route my requests to a professor's IP address, then send it to several other faculty IP addresses so it is difficult to trace. I then go to one of the library computers, log in as someone else, put in a CD or Blu-Ray DVD, and burn what I want. The people's computers I route through get a message that someone logged into their account, but the IT guys just tell them it's no big deal and it happens all the time. IT never really looks into it because of the many systems and IP addresses on campus. Do you want me to get you any movies or CDs?" Ahmed politely refused, knowing full well this could get a person expelled from the university.

Several months passed and Bill became more popular. Every day someone stopped by the library desk where he worked and talked to Bill. The person walked to one of the library's computers, stuck in a disk, and several minutes later was gone. Ahmed looked at Bill and shook his head. Bill responded with a smile. One day, Ahmed found an envelope with his name on it when he went to his usual desk. When he opened it, there was $500 with a note saying, "Enjoy." He started to ask people about the money, but then saw Bill smiling. At that moment, Ahmed knew the money was from Bill. He tried to give it back, but Bill refused to take it or admit he had given it to Ahmed in the first place.

Ahmed became increasingly uncomfortable with Bill's behavior. He knew what Bill did was wrong and possibly illegal. He didn't want to be involved with it in any way, but he also didn't want to become a snitch. Now he was receiving money for his involvement. Ahmed felt the situation was escalating and he should say something to his supervisor before something really bad happened, but he didn't want to be the one to get Bill in trouble. Ahmed knew Bill could be expelled for something like this, which could potentially damage his entire future. Then again, Ahmed had his own future to worry about. Could he be expelled just for knowing what kind of activities Bill was involved in? What should he do with the money Bill gave him? What might happen if he doesn't blow the whistle?

QUESTIONS | EXERCISES

1. Describe the stakeholders involved in this ethical dilemma. What stake do they have in the situation?
2. Are Bill's actions an ethical issue, a legal issue, or both? Explain your reasoning.
3. What are some of the risks Ahmed faces if he becomes a whistle-blower? What are the risks if he remains silent?

*This case is strictly hypothetical; any resemblance to real persons, companies, or situations is coincidental.

> > > CHECK YOUR EQ

Check your EQ, or Ethics Quotient, by completing the following. Assess your performance to evaluate your overall understanding of the chapter material.

1. Voluntary practices include documented best practices.   **Yes**   <u>**No**</u>

2. The primary method for resolving business ethics disputes is through the criminal court system.   **Yes**   <u>**No**</u>

3. The FSGO provides an incentive for organizations to conscientiously develop and implement ethics programs.   <u>**Yes**</u>   **No**

4. The Sarbanes–Oxley Act encourages CEOs and CFOs to report their financial statements accurately.   **Yes**   <u>**No**</u>

5. Strategic philanthropy represents a new direction in corporate giving that maximizes the benefit to societal or community needs and relates to business objectives.   <u>**Yes**</u>   **No**

ANSWERS **1. No.** Core practices are documented best practices. **2. No.** Civil litigation is the primary way in which business ethics disputes are resolved. **3. Yes.** Well-designed ethics and compliance programs can minimize legal liability when organizational misconduct is detected. **4. No.** The Sarbanes–Oxley Act *requires* CEOs and CFOs to accurately report their financial statements to a federal oversight committee; they must sign the document and are held personally liable for any inaccuracies. **5. Yes.** Strategic philanthropy helps both society and the organization.

ENDNOTES

1. Google, "Corporate Information: Our Culture," http://www.google.com/corporate/culture.html (accessed February 25, 2015).

2. Isabelle Maignan, Tracy L. Gonzalez-Padron, G. Tomas M. Hult, and O.C. Ferrell, "Stakeholder orientation: development and testing of a framework for socially responsible marketing," *Journal of Strategic Marketing* 19, 4 (2011): 313–338.

3. Paul K. Shum and Sharon L. Yam, "Ethics and Law: Guiding the Invisible Hand to Correct Corporate Social Responsibility Externalities," *Journal of Business Ethics* 98, 4 (2011): 549–571.

4. Kim Mulford, "BBB disputes Virtua's knee replacement advertising claim," *Courier-Post,* September 2, 2014, http://www.courierpostonline.com/story/life/wellness/2014/09/03/bbb-disputes-virtua-advertising-claim/15018877/ (accessed February 25, 2015).

5. Bradley Lail, Jason MacGregor, Martin Stuebs, and Timothy Thomasson, "The Influence of Regulatory Approach on Tone at the Top," *Journal of Business Ethics* 126, 1 (2015): 25–37.

6. Don Clark, "Nvidia Sues Samsung and Qualcomm Alleging Patent Infringement," *The Wall Street Journal,* September 4, 2014, http://www.wsj.com/articles/nvidia-sues-samsung-and-qualcomm-alleging-patent-infringement-1409864408 (accessed February 16, 2015).

7. Don Clark and Shayndi Raice, "Tech Firms Intensify Clashes over Patents," *The Wall Street Journal*, October 4, 2010, B3.

8. Carey Gillam, "Monsanto, DuPont strike $1.75 billion licensing deal, ends lawsuits," *Reuters*, March 26, 2013, http://www.reuters.com/article/2013/03/26/us-monsanto-dupont-gmo-idUSBRE92P0IK20130326 (accessed February 16, 2015); Reuters, "DuPont, Monsanto settle patent lawsuits over technology," December 23, 2014, http://www.reuters.com/article/2014/12/23/us-monsanto-e-i-du-pont-de-settlement-idUSKBN0K11PA20141223 (accessed February 16, 2015).

9. Aaron Back, "China Acts to Prevent Collusion on Prices," *The Wall Street Journal*, January 5, 2011, http://online.wsj.com/article/SB10001424052748704723104576061160620783364.html (accessed February 18, 2015); Matthew Miller and Yoko Kubota, "China fines Japanese auto parts makers record $201 million for price-fixing," Reuters, August 20, 2014, http://www.reuters.com/article/2014/08/20/us-china-autos-idUSKBN0GK08R20140820 (accessed February 18, 2015).

10. Dionne Searcey, "U.K. Laws on Bribes Has Firms In a Sweat," *The Wall Street Journal*, December 28, 2010, B1.

11. Economist staff, "Hard to reach," The Economist, January 29, 2014, http://www.economist.com/blogs/schumpeter/2014/01/brazil-s-new-anti-corruption-law (accessed February 18, 2015).

12. Gregory T. Gundlach, "Price Predation: Legal Limits and Antitrust Considerations," *Journal of Public Policy & Marketing* 14, 2 (1995): 278.

13. Maggie McGrath, "Antitrust Lawsuit Loss Puts Amex among the Dow's Worst Performers," *Forbes,* February 19, 2015, http://www.forbes.com/sites/maggiemcgrath/2015/02/19/antitrust-lawsuit-loss-puts-amex-among-the-dows-worst-performers/ (accessed February 25, 2015).

14. Ellen Nakashima and Andrea Peterson, "Report: Cybercrime and espionage costs $445 billion annually," *The Washington Post,* June 9, 2014, http://www.washingtonpost.com/world/national-security/report-cybercrime-and-espionage-costs-445-billion-annually/2014/06/08/8995291c-ecce-11e3-9f5c-9075d5508f0a_story.html (accessed February 18, 2015).

15. "10 Ways to Combat Corporate Espionage," *Data Destruction News,* http://www.imakenews.com/accushred/e_article001225805.cfm?x=bdtNVCP,bbGvRs5c,w (accessed February 25, 2015).

16. Ed Crooks, "Chesapeake accuses McClendon of stealing secrets," *Financial Times,* February 17, 2015, http://www.ft.com/cms/s/0/08c38302-b6c6-11e4-95dc-00144feab7de.html#axzz3S7qcp8eb (accessed February 18, 2015).

17. "Baseball's Antitrust Exemption: Q&A," *ESPN,* December 5, 2001, http://sports.espn.go.com/espn/print?id=1290707&type=story (accessed February 18, 2015).

18. Diane Bartz, "POM Wonderful loses bid to tout health benefits in drink ads," *Reuters,* January 30, 2015, http://www.reuters.com/article/2015/01/30/us-pomwonderful-ftc-idUSKBN0L31TL20150130 (accessed February 13, 2015); "D.C. Circuit: FTC's Two RCT Requirement Violates the First Amendment," Emord & Associates, PC, February 2, 2015, http://emord.com/blawg/d-c-circuit-ftcs-two-rct-requirement-violates-the-first-amendment/ (accessed February 13, 2015); Federal Trade Commission, "FTC Commissioners Uphold Trial Judge Decision that POM Wonderful, LLC; Stewart and Lynda Resnick; Others Deceptively Advertised Pomegranate Products by Making Unsupported Health Claims," January 16, 2013, http://www.ftc.gov/news-events/press-releases/2013/01/ftc-commissioners-uphold-trial-judge-decision-pom-wonderful-llc (accessed February 13, 2015); Brent Kendall, "Appeals Court Likely to Uphold FTC Ruling on Juice Maker Pom," *The Wall Street Journal,* May 2, 2014, http://www.wsj.com/articles/SB10001424052702303678404579538123825242670 (accessed February 13, 2015); Brent Kendall, "Pom's Ads Misled Consumers, Court Says," *The Wall Street Journal,* January 31-February 1, 2015, B3; POM website, http://www.pomwonderful.com/ (accessed February 16, 2015); Rich Samp, "The D.C. Circuit's POM Wonderful Decision: Not So Wonderful For FTC's Randomized Clinical Trial Push," *Fortune,* February 4, 2015, http://www.forbes.com/sites/wlf/2015/02/04/the-d-c-circuits-pom-wonderful-decision-not-so-wonderful-for-ftcs-randomized-clinical-trial-push/ (accessed February 13, 2015).

19. Julia Angwin, "How to Keep Kids Safe Online," *The Wall Street Journal,* January 22, 2009, http://online.wsj.com/article/SB123238632055894993.html (accessed February 19, 2015).

20. Anton Troianovski, "Developers Brace for New Rules on Kids' Apps," *The Wall Street Journal*, April 5, 2013, B1.

21. Jennifer Levitz, "Laws Take on Financial Scams against Seniors," *The Wall Street Journal*, May 19, 2009, http://

online.wsj.com/article/SB124269210323932723.html (accessed February 19, 2015).

22. Gerald Albaum and Robert A. Peterson, "Multilevel (Network) Marketing: An Objective View," *The Marketing Review* 11, 4 (2011): 347–361; Daniel B. Ravicher, "Might Other Companies Be Liable If Herbalife Is a Pyramid Scheme?" *Seeking Alpha*, February 5, 2013, http://seekingalpha.com/article/1157581-might-other-companies-be-liable-if-herbalife-is-a-pyramid (accessed February 19, 2015); Karen E. Klein. "A Charm Offensive by Direct Sellers," *Bloomberg Businessweek*, June 25–July 1, 2012, 52–54; Duane Stanford, "Bill Ackman's Crusade Against Herbalife," *Bloomberg Businessweek*, January 14–20, 2012, 40; Gerald Albaum, "Multi-level Marketing and Pyramid Scheme: Myth versus Reality," *AMS Quarterly 9*, 2 (November 2008): 10; Herbalife, "Herbalife announces Results of Study on Distributors and End Users in the U.S., June 11, 2013, http://ir.herbalife.com/releasedetail.cfm?ReleaseID=770738 (accessed February 19, 2015).

23. "What We Do," *U.S. Food and Drug Administration*, http://www.fda.gov/AboutFDA/WhatWeDo/default.htm (accessed February 19, 2015).

24. Joseph Walker and Jon Kamp, "FDA's Cancer Warning: Bad News for Surgical Robots," *The Wall Street Journal*, April 23, 2014, http://blogs.wsj.com/corporate-intelligence/2014/04/23/fdas-cancer-warning-bad-news-for-surgical-robots/ (accessed February 18, 2015).

25. National Committee on Pay Equity, "Wage gap narrows slightly but statistically unchanged," April 14, 2015, http://www.pay-equity.org/ (accessed February 18, 2015).

26. Business Wire, "Cruise Lawyers to Senator Rockefeller: Overworked Cruise Employees Denied," *Bloomberg*, April 11, 2013, http://www.bloomberg.com/article/2013-04-11/amJSvA8pDWGk.html (accessed February 18, 2015).

27. Edward Teach, "On the IPO On-Ramp," *CFO*, September 15, 2014, http://ww2.cfo.com/capital-markets/2014/09/ipo-ramp/ (accessed February 18, 2015).

28. Floyd Norris and Adam Liptak, "Justices Uphold Sarbanes-Oxley Act," *The New York Times*, June 28, 2010, http://www.nytimes.com/2010/06/29/business/29accounting.html?pagewanted=1&_r=1 (accessed February 19, 2015).

29. Tim Elfrink, "The Rise and Fall of the Stanford Financial Group," *Houston Press*, April 9, 2009, http://www.houstonpress.com/content/printVersion/1173931/ (accessed February 19, 2015); Shira Ovide, "Lehman Brothers Whistle-blower Matthew Lee Again in Spotlight," *The Wall Street Journal*, December 21, 2010, http://blogs.wsj.com/deals/2010/12/21/lehman-brothers-whistleblower-matthew-lee-again-in-spotlight/ / (accessed February 19, 2015).

30. Tricia Bisoux, "The Sarbanes–Oxley Effect," *BizEd*, July/August 2005, 24–29.

31. Protiviti, 2010 *Sarbanes-Oxley Compliance Survey*, http://www.protiviti.com/en-US/Documents/Surveys/2010-SOX-Compliance-Survey-Protiviti.pdf (accessed February 19, 2015).

32. Julia Hanna, "The Costs and Benefits of Sarbanes-Oxley," *Forbes*, March 10, 2014, http://www.forbes.com/sites/hbsworkingknowledge/2014/03/10/the-costs-and-benefits-of-sarbanes-oxley/ (accessed February 18, 2015).

33. President Barack Obama, "Remarks by the President on 21st Century Financial Regulatory Reform," The White House, June 17, 2009, http://www.whitehouse.gov/the_press_office/Remarks-of-the-President-on-Regulatory-Reform/ (accessed February 19, 2015).

34. Ibid.

35. Joshua Gallu, "Dodd-Frank May Cost $6.5 Billion and 5,000 Workers," *Bloomberg*, February 14, 2011, http://www.bloomberg.com/news/2011-02-14/dodd-frank-s-implementation-calls-for-6-5-billion-5-000-staff-in-budget.html (accessed February 19, 2015); Binyamin Appelbaum and Brady Dennis, "Dodd's overhaul goes well beyond other plans," *The Washington Post*, November 11, 2009, http://www.washingtonpost.com/wp-dyn/content/article/2009/11/09/AR2009110901935.html?hp id=topnews&sid=ST2009111003729 (accessed February 19, 2015).

36. Steve Mufson and Tom Hamburger, "Jamie Dimon himself called to urge support for the derivatives rule in the spending bill," *The Washington Post*, December 11, 2014, http://www.washingtonpost.com/blogs/wonkblog/wp/2014/12/11/the-item-that-is-blowing-up-the-budget-deal/ (accessed February 18, 2015).

37. "Office of Financial Research," *U.S. Department of Treasury*, http://financialresearch.gov/ (accessed February 19, 2015).

38. "Initiatives: Financial Stability Oversight Council," *U.S. Department of Treasury*, http://www.treasury.gov/initiatives/Pages/FSOC-index.aspx (accessed February 19, 2015).

39. "Financial Stability Oversight Council Created Under the Dodd-Frank Wall Street Reform and Consumer Protection Act: Frequently Asked Questions," October 2010, http://www.treasury.gov/initiatives/wsr/Documents/FAQs%20-%20Financial%20Stability%20Oversight%20Council%20-%20October%202010%20FINAL%20v2.pdf (accessed February 19, 2015).

40. "Subtitle A—Bureau of Consumer Financial Protection," *One Hundred Eleventh Congress of the United States of America*, 589.

41. "Wall Street Reform: Bureau of Consumer Financial Protection (CFPB)," U.S. Treasury, http://www.treasury.gov/initiatives/Pages/cfpb.aspx (accessed February 19, 2015).

42. "Wall Street Reform: Bureau of Consumer Financial Protection (CFPB)," *U.S. Treasury*, http://www.treasury.gov/initiatives/Pages/cfpb.aspx (accessed February 19, 2015); Sudeep Reddy, "Elizabeth Warren's Early Words on a Consumer Financial Protection Bureau," *The Wall Street Journal*, September 17, 2010, http://blogs.wsj.com/economics/2010/09/17/elizabeth-warrens-early-words-on-a-consumer-financial-protection-bureau/ (accessed February 19, 2015); Jennifer Liberto & David Ellis, "Wall Street reform: What's in the bill," *CNN*, June 30, 2010); http://money.cnn.com/2010/06/25/news/economy/whats_in_the_reform_bill/index.htm (accessed February 19, 2015).

43. Jean Eaglesham, "Warning Shot on Financial Protection," *The Wall Street Journal*, February 9, 2011, http://online.wsj.com/article/SB10001424052748703507804576130370862263258.html?mod=googlenews_wsj (accessed February 19, 2015).

44. Liz Rappaport, Liz Moyer, and Anupreeta Das, "Goldman Sets Funds for 'Volcker'," *The Wall Street Journal*, February 8, 2013, C1–C2.

45. Jean Eaglesham, "Warning Shot on Financial Protection."

46. Jessica Silver-Greenberg, "Consumer Protection Agency Seeks Limits on Payday Lenders," *The New York Times*, February 8, 2015, http://dealbook.nytimes.com/2015/02/08/consumer-protection-agency-seeks-limits-on-payday-lenders/?_r=0 (accessed February 18, 2015).

47. Jean Eaglesham and Ashby Jones, "Whistle-blower Bounties Pose Challenges," *The Wall Street Journal*, December 13, 2010, C1, C3.

48. Ibid.

49. Christina Rexrode and Timothy W. Martin, "Whistleblowers Score Big," The Wall Street Journal, December 20-21, 2014, B1–B2.

50. Win Swenson, "The Organizational Guidelines' 'Carrot and Stick' Philosophy, and Their Focus on 'Effective' Compliance," in Corporate Crime in America: Strengthening the "Good Citizenship"-Corporation (Washington, DC: U.S. Sentencing Commission, 1995), 17–26.

51. United States Code Service (Lawyers' Edition), 18 U.S.C.S. Appendix, Sentencing Guidelines for the United States Courts (Rochester, NY: Lawyers Cooperative Publishing, 1995), sec. 8A.1.

52. O. C Ferrell and Linda Ferrell, "Current Developments in Managing Organizational Ethics and Compliance Initiatives," University of Wyoming, white paper, Bill Daniels Business Ethics Initiative 2006.

53. Open Compliance Ethics Group 2005 Benchmarking Study Key Findings, http://www.oceg.org/view/Benchmarking2005 (accessed June 12, 2009).

54. "US Sentences Guidelines Changes Become Effective November 1," *FCPA Compliance and Ethics Blog*, November 2, 2010, http://tfoxlaw.wordpress.com/2010/11/02/us-sentencing-guidelines-changes-become-effective-november-1/ (accessed February 19, 2015).

55. USSG §8C2.5(3); Ethics Resource Center, *The Federal Sentencing Guidelines for Organizations at Twenty Years* (Arlington, VA: Ethics Resource Center, 2012), pp. 27–28, from http://www.ethics.org/files/u5/fsgo-report2012.pdf (accessed February 11, 2015).

56. Paula Desio, Deputy General Counsel, *An Overview of the Organizational Guidelines,* http://www.ussc.gov/sites/default/files/pdf/training/organizational-guidelines/ORGOVERVIEW.pdf (accessed February 25, 2015).

57. Deputy Attorney General Eric Holder to All Component Heads and United States Attorneys, Washington, D.C., June 16, 1999, http://www.justice.gov/criminal/fraud/documents/reports/1999/charging-corps.PDF (accessed February 25, 2015).

58. Ferrell and Ferrell, "Current Developments in Managing Organizational Ethics and Compliance Initiatives."

59. Aruna Viswanatha and Karen Freifeld, "S&P reaches $1.5 billion deal with U.S., states over crisis-era ratings," *Reuters*, February 3, 2015, http://www.reuters.com/article/2015/02/03/us-s-p-settlement-idUSKBN0L71C120150203 (accessed February 18, 2015).

60. Ingrid MurroBotero, "Charitable Giving Has 4 Big Benefits," *Business Journal of Phoenix*, online, January 1, 1999, www.bizjournals.com/phoenix/stories/1999/01/04/smallb3.html (accessed February 19, 2015).

61. Wells Fargo, *Wells Fargo & Company Corporate Social Responsibility Report 2013*, https://www08.wellsfargomedia.com/downloads/pdf/about/csr/reports/2013-social-responsibility-report.pdf (accessed February 18, 2015).

62. Walmart, "Community Giving," http://foundation.walmart.com/(accessed February 18, 2015).

63. Steve Hoeffler and Kevin Lane Keller, "Building Brand Equity through Corporate Societal Marketing," *Journal of Public Policy & Marketing* 21, 1 (Spring 2002): 78–89; Sue Adkins and Nina Kowalska, "Consumers Put 'Causes' on the Shopping List," *M2 PressWire*, November 17, 1997; Matt Carmichael, "Stat of the Day: 83% Want Brands to Support Causes," *Ad Age*, January 18, 2012, http://adage.com/article/adagestat/stat-day-83-brands-support/232141/ (accessed February 25, 2015).

64. Kaitlyn Krasselt, "Target's giving back for Back to School," *USA Today*, July 11, 2014, 4B.

65. Joëlle Vanhamme, Adam Lindgreen, Jon Reast, and Nathalie van Popering, "To Do Well by Doing Good: Improving Corporate Image Through Cause-Related Marketing," *Journal of Business Ethics* 109, 3 (2012): 259–274.

66. Goldman Sachs, "10,000 Women: About the Program," http://www.goldmansachs.com/citizenship/10000women/about-the-program/index.html (accessed February 18, 2015).

67. Michael E. Porter and Mark R. Kramer, "The Competitive Advantage of Corporate Philanthropy," *Harvard Business Review,* December 2002, https://hbr.org/2002/12/the-competitive-advantage-of-corporate-philanthropy (accessed February 18, 2015); Cisco, "Cisco Networking Academy," http://www.cisco.com/web/learning/netacad/index.html (accessed February 18, 2015).

68. Jessica Stannard and Tamara Backer, "How Employee Volunteers Multiply Your Community Impact PART 2," *OnPhilanthropy.com*, December 29, 2005, http://cwop.convio.net/site/News2?page=NewsArticle&id=5470 (accessed February 25, 2015).

69. The Home Depot Foundation, "By the Numbers," http://www.homedepotfoundation.org/page/by-the-numbers (accessed February 18, 2015).

70. Samer Abu-Saifan, "Social Entrepreneurship: Definition and Boundaries," *Technology Innovation Management Review*, February 2012, pp. 22–27.

71. Scott Gerber, "Blake Mycoskie," *Inc.*, December 2014/January 2015, p. 144.

72. Anand Giridharadas and Keith Bradsher, "Microloan Pioneer and His Bank Won Nobel Peace Prize," *The New York Times*, October 13, 2006, http://www.nytimes.com/2006/10/13/business/14nobelcnd.html?_r=0&adxnnl=1&pagewanted=1&adxnnlx=1406646197-P8A97M3K4GYHoZx4UHWYWA (accessed February 25, 2015); Grameen Bank, "History," http://www.grameen-info.org/index.php?option=com_content&task=view&id=449&Itemid=514 (accessed February 25, 2015).

73. Ibid.; Grameen Bank, "Credit Delivery System," http://www.grameen-info.org/index.php?option=com_content&task=view&id=24&Itemid=169 (accessed February 25, 2015).

74. "Nonprofit Corporation," *Entrepreneur*, http://www.entrepreneur.com/encyclopedia/nonprofit-corporation (accessed February 25, 2015).

75. H. Haugh, "Social Enterprise: Beyond Economic Outcomes and Individual Returns," in *Social Entrepreneurship*, ed. J. Mair, J. Robinson, and K. Hockerts (Basingstoke, UK: Palgrave Macmillan, 2006).

76. Raymond Dart, "The Legitimacy of Social Enterprise," *Nonprofit Management & Leadership* 14, 4 (Summer 2004): 411–424.

77. Developed by Robert P. Lambert and Joe Alexander, "Belle Meade Plantation: The First Nonprofit Winery Engages in Social Entrepreneurship," published in O.C. Ferrell, Debbie Thorne, and Linda Ferrell, *Marketing and Society,* 5th ed. (Chicago, IL: Chicago Business Press, 2015).

78. Sean Stannard-Stockton, "The Effective Strategic Philanthropist," *Tactical Philanthropy,* March 16, 2011, http://www.tacticalphilanthropy.com/2011/03/the-effective-strategic-philanthropist/ (accessed February 25, 2015); Sean Stannard-Stockton, "The Social Entrepreneur," *Tactical Philanthropy,* March 15, 2011, http://www.tacticalphilanthropy.com/2011/03/the-effective-social-entrepreneur/ (accessed February 25, 2015).

CHAPTER 5

ETHICAL DECISION MAKING

CHAPTER OBJECTIVES

- Provide a comprehensive model for ethical decision making in business
- Examine issue intensity as an important element in the ethical decision-making process
- Introduce individual factors that influence business ethical decision making
- Introduce organizational factors that influence business ethical decision making
- Explore the role of opportunity in ethical decision making in business
- Understand normative considerations in ethical decision making
- Recognize the role of institutions in normative decision making
- Examine the importance of principles and core values to ethical decision making

CHAPTER OUTLINE

AN ETHICAL DILEMMA*

Steven, a junior at Northeast State, just started working part-time at a local fast food restaurant chain. Although not his dream job, it paid for tuition and books, and the restaurant gave him the flexible schedule he needed for school. After a few months, Steven found he got along well with all of his coworkers, but it was apparent they did not respect the company or the management. The employees made fun of their bosses and treated the work area like a playground. In some respects, Steven thought it was a fun environment to work in, especially after hours when management was gone for the day. They played their music loudly, laughed, and talked with one another during the down times instead of cleaning up their work areas like they were supposed to. Despite the fact there were ethical policies telling employees how they were expected to act in the workplace, these policies never seemed to be enforced.

One day, while working with his coworker Julie on the food assembly table, Steven saw Julie accidentally drop a meat patty on the floor. Without so much as a flinch, she bent down, picked up the patty, stuck it back on the bun, and wrapped it up. It happened so fast that Steven wasn't even sure he had seen right—especially since Julie had done it so casually. Steven watched in dismay as another worker took the hamburger out to the customer.

Over the next few weeks, Steven saw others, including the shift supervisor, do the same thing with burgers and other products. Once, an entire cheeseburger hit the greasy floor, was picked up, and was taken to the customer. This time the customer complained the burger tasted funny and sent it back. Steven noticed other unsanitary practices such as employees not washing their hands between handling meat and vegetables and not washing utensils between uses. Obviously, such practices were against company policies and, if reported, the supervisors in charge could get in trouble and the restaurant would face investigations from the health department. However, there was ample opportunity for things like this to occur. There was no one watching them, and the shift supervisor also engaged in these activities. Steven felt it was the company's responsibility to hire good people, so they were to blame if these things happened.

One day, Steven approached Julie and asked, "Why do so many people here serve food that has fallen on the floor to customers?"

Julie thought about it briefly as though she had never considered it before and replied, "I guess it's because it would take too much time to get another beef patty out of the freezer, cook it, and serve it to the customer. This is a fast food restaurant, after all, and I'm not interested in hearing customers complain about the time it takes for them to get their food. Besides, the restaurants with the fastest service get a bonus from corporate headquarters. Last year the supervisors rewarded us with some extra money for doing our jobs so quickly."

Steven was somewhat taken aback by the honest reply and asked, "Wouldn't you be disgusted if you were served dirty food at a restaurant?"

This time Julie's response was quick. She said, "What I don't know won't hurt me." She walked off.

Several weeks went by and the same practices continued. Steven became more and more concerned about the consequences that could happen in an environment so laid back and unconcerned about safety and health. It seemed like the more time that passed, the worse everyone's attitude became.

One day, at the beginning of his shift, Steven noticed the walk-in freezer had been left open. As he went to shut the door, he discovered a smell of rotten meat. It almost made him vomit. "How could this happen?" he wondered. He threw away the rotten meat without asking anyone because he was afraid of what the answer might be.

After Steven threw out the spoiled meat, he began to wonder how the culture of the restaurant got to the point of supporting such practices. He realized the seemingly minor unsanitary practices allowed major issues to arise that could possibly hurt someone. Steven felt he should say or do something, but to whom? He sat down and pondered what he should do.

QUESTIONS | EXERCISES

1. Describe the nature of the organizational culture in the restaurant. What kind of opportunities are there for unethical behavior to occur? Are there any opportunities for ethical behavior?
2. What are some of the incentives employees might have to engage in this type of behavior?
3. If the organizational culture of the restaurant does not change, what are some likely outcomes and consequences?

*This case is strictly hypothetical; any resemblance to real persons, companies, or situations is coincidental.

To improve ethical decision making in business, you must first understand how individuals make organizational decisions. Too often it is assumed people in organizations define ethical decisions in exactly the same way they would at home, in their families, or in their personal lives. Within the context of an organizational work group, however, few individuals have the freedom to personally decide ethical issues independent of the organization and its stakeholders.

This chapter summarizes our current knowledge of ethical decision making in business and provides a model so you may better visualize the ethical decision making process. Although it is impossible to describe exactly how any one individual or work group might make ethical decisions, we can offer generalizations about average or typical behavior patterns within organizations. These generalizations are based on many studies and at least six ethical decision models that have been widely accepted by academics and practitioners.[1] Based on this research, we present a model for understanding ethical decision making in the context of business organizations. The model integrates concepts from philosophy, psychology, sociology, and organizational behavior. This framework should be helpful in understanding how organizations decide and develop ethical programs. Additionally, we describe some normative considerations that prescribe how organizational decision making should approach ethical issues. Principles and values are used by organizations as a foundation for establishing core values to provide enduring beliefs about appropriate conduct. Therefore, we provide both a descriptive understanding of how ethical decisions are made as well as the normative framework to determine how decisions ought to be made.

A FRAMEWORK FOR ETHICAL DECISION MAKING IN BUSINESS

As Figure 5–1 shows, our model of the ethical decision-making process in business includes ethical issue intensity, individual factors, and organizational factors such as corporate culture and opportunity. All these interrelated factors influence the evaluations of and intentions behind the decisions that produce ethical or unethical behavior. This model does not describe how to make ethical decisions, but it does help you to understand the factors and processes related to ethical decision making.

Ethical Issue Intensity

The first step in ethical decision making is to recognize that an ethical issue exists, requiring an individual or work group to choose among several actions that various stakeholders will ultimately evaluate as right or wrong. **Ethical awareness** is the ability to perceive whether a situation or decision has an ethical dimension. Costly problems can be avoided if employees are able to first recognize whether a situation has an ethical component. However, ethical awareness can be difficult in an environment when employees work in their own areas of expertise with the same types of people. It is easier to overlook certain issues requiring an ethical decision, particularly if the decision becomes a routine part of the job. This makes it important for organizations to train employees how to recognize the potential ethical ramifications of their decisions. Familiarizing employees with company values and training them to recognize common ethical scenarios can help them develop ethical awareness.

FIGURE 5-1 **Framework for Understanding Ethical Decision Marking in Business**

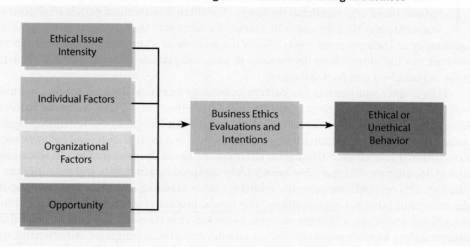

The intensity of an ethical issue relates to its perceived importance to the decision maker.[2] **Ethical issue intensity** can be defined as the relevance or importance of an event or decision in the eyes of the individual, work group, and/or organization. It is personal and temporal in character to accommodate values, beliefs, needs, perceptions, the special characteristics of the situation, and the personal pressures prevailing at a particular place and time.[3] Senior employees and those with administrative authority contribute significantly to ethical issue intensity because they typically dictate an organization's stance on ethical issues. Potential ethical issues are identified as risk areas, and employees are trained to recognize these issues. For example, sexual harassment, conflict of interest, bribery, and time theft are all ethical issues that have been identified as risk areas. Additionally, insider trading is considered a serious ethical issue by the government because the intent is to take advantage of information not available to the public. Therefore, it is an ethical issue of high intensity for regulators and government officials. This often puts them at odds with financial companies such as hedge funds. A survey of hedge fund companies revealed 35 percent of respondents feel pressured to break the rules.[4] Because of their greater ability to gather financial information from the market—some of which might not be public information—hedge funds and other financial institutions have often come under increased scrutiny by the federal government.

Under current law, managers can be held liable for the unethical and illegal actions of subordinates. In the United States, the Federal Sentencing Guidelines for Organizations (FSGO) contain a liability formula judges use as a guideline regarding illegal activities of corporations. For example, many of the Enron employees and managers aware of the firm's use of off-the-balance-sheet partnerships—that turned out to be the major cause of the energy firm's collapse—were advised these partnerships were legal, so they were not perceived as an ethical issue. Although such partnerships were legal at that time, the way Enron officials designed them and the methods they used to provide collateral (that is, Enron stock) created a scheme that brought about the collapse of the company.[5] Thus, ethical issue intensity involves individuals' cognitive state of concern about an issue, or whether they have knowledge that an issue is unethical, that in turn indicates their involvement in making choices. The identification of ethical issues often requires the understanding of complex business relationships.

Ethical issue intensity reflects the ethical sensitivity of the individual and/or work group facing the ethical decision-making process. Research suggests that individuals are subject to six "spheres of influence" when confronted with ethical choices—the workplace, family, religion, legal system, community, and profession—and the level of importance of each of these influences varies depending on how important the decision maker perceives the issue to be.[6] Additionally, individuals' moral intensity increases their perceptiveness of potential ethical problems for the firm, which in turn reduces their intention to act unethically.[7] **Moral intensity** relates to individuals' perceptions of social pressure and the harm they believe their decisions will have on others.[8] All other factors in Figure 5–1, including individual factors, organizational factors, and intentions, determine why different individuals perceive ethical issues differently. Unless individuals in an organization share common concerns about ethical issues, the stage is set for ethical conflict. The perception of ethical issue intensity can be influenced by management's use of rewards and punishments, corporate policies, and corporate values to sensitize employees. In other words, managers can affect the degree to which employees perceive the importance of an ethical issue through positive and/or negative incentives.[9]

For some employees, business ethical issues may not reach critical awareness if managers fail to identify and educate them about specific problem areas. One study found that more than a third of the unethical situations that lower and middle-level managers face come from internal pressures and ambiguity surrounding internal organizational rules. Many employees fail to anticipate these issues before they arise.[10] This lack of preparedness makes it difficult for employees to respond appropriately when they encounter an ethics issue. One field recognized as having insufficient ethics training is science. An Iowa State University scientist resigned and was charged with four felony counts of making false statements after falsifying lab results for AIDS research.[11] Although this type of scandal is a rare occurrence in the scientific profession, a panel of experts found young scientists tend to lack knowledge about ethical frameworks to navigate ethical gray areas. Many are therefore unprepared when faced with an ethical issue.[12] Organizations that consist of employees with diverse values and backgrounds must train workers in the way the firm wants specific ethical issues handled. Identifying the ethical issues and risks employees might encounter is a significant step toward developing their ability to make ethical decisions. Many ethical issues are identified by industry groups or through general information available to a firm. Flagging certain issues as high in ethical importance could trigger increases in employees' ethical issue intensity. The perceived importance of an ethical issue has a strong influence on both employees' ethical judgment and their behavioral intention. In other words, the more likely individuals perceive an ethical issue as important, the less likely they are to engage in questionable or unethical behavior.[13] Therefore, ethical issue intensity should be considered a key factor in the ethical decision-making process.

Individual Factors

When people need to resolve issues in their daily lives, they often base their decisions on their own values and principles of right or wrong. They generally learn these values and principles through the socialization process with family members, social groups, religion, and in their formal education. Good personal values have been found to decrease unethical practices and increase positive work behavior. The moral philosophies of individuals, discussed in detail in Chapter 6, provide principles, values, and rules people use to decide what is moral or immoral from a personal perspective. Values of individuals can be derived from moral philosophies that are applied to daily decisions. However, these values can be subjective and vary a great deal across different cultures. For example, some individuals might place greater importance on keeping their promises and commitments than others would. Values applied to business can also be used in negative rationalizations, such as "Everyone does it," or "We have to do what it takes to get the business."[14] Research demonstrates that individuals with certain personalities will violate basic core values, causing a work group to suffer a performance loss of 30 to 40 percent compared to groups with no "bad apples."[15] The actions of specific individuals in scandal-plagued financial companies such as JP Morgan often raise questions about those individuals' personal character and integrity. They appear to operate in their own self-interest or in total disregard for the law and the interests of society.

Although an individual's intention to engage in ethical behavior relates to individual values, organizational and social forces also play a vital role. An individual's attitudes as well as social norms help create behavioral intentions that shape his or her decision-making process. While an individual may intend to do the right thing, organizational or social forces can alter this intent. For example, an individual may intend to report the misconduct of a coworker, but when faced with the social or financial consequences of doing so, may decide to remain complacent. In this case, social forces overcome a person's individual values when it comes to taking appropriate action.[16] At the same time, individual values strongly influence how people assume ethical responsibilities in the work environment. In turn, individual decisions can be heavily dependent on company policy and the corporate culture.

The way the public perceives business ethics generally varies according to the profession in question. Financial institutions, car salespersons, advertising practitioners, stockbrokers, and real estate brokers are often perceived as having the lowest ethics. Research regarding individual factors that affect ethical awareness, judgment, intent, and behavior include gender, education, work experience, nationality, age, and locus of control.

Extensive research regarding the link between **gender** and ethical decision making shows that in many aspects there are no differences between men and women. However, when differences are found, women are generally more ethical than men.[17] By "more ethical," we mean women seem to be more sensitive to ethical scenarios and less tolerant of unethical actions. One study found that women and men had different foundations for making ethical decisions: women rely on relationships; men rely on justice or equity.[18] In another study on gender and intentions for fraudulent financial reporting, females reported higher intentions to report than male participants.[19] As more and more women work in managerial positions, these findings may become increasingly significant.

Education is also a significant factor in the ethical decision-making process. The important thing to remember about education is that it does not reflect experience. Work experience is defined as the number of years in a specific job, occupation, and/or industry. Generally, the more education or work experience people have, the better they are at making ethical decisions. The type of education someone receives has little or no effect on ethics. For example, it doesn't matter if you are a business student or a liberal arts student—you are similar in terms of ethical decision making. Current research, however, shows students are less ethical than businesspeople, which is likely because businesspeople have been exposed to more ethically challenging situations than students.[20] Additionally, those well-versed in business ethics knowledge, including regulatory officials and ethics researchers, are likely to take more time and raise more concerns going through the ethical decision-making process than novices such as graduate students.[21] This implies that those more familiarized with the ethical decision-making process due to education or experience are likely to spend more time examining and selecting different alternatives to an ethics issue.

Nationality is the legal relationship between a person and the country in which he or she is born. In the twenty-first century, nationality is redefined by regional economic integration such as the European Union (EU). When European students are asked their nationality, they are less likely to state where they were born than where they currently live. The same thing is happening in the United States, as people born in Florida living in New York might consider themselves to be New Yorkers. Research about nationality and ethics appears to be significant in how it affects ethical decision making; however, just how nationality affects ethics is somewhat hard to interpret.[22] Because of cultural differences, it is impossible to state that ethical decision making in an organizational context will differ significantly among individuals of different nationalities. The reality of today is that multinational companies look for businesspeople that make good decisions regardless of nationality. Perhaps in 20 years, nationality will no longer be an issue because the multinational individual's culture will replace national status as the most significant factor in ethical decision making.

Age is another individual factor within business ethics. Several decades ago, we believed age was positively correlated with ethical decision making. In other words, the older you are, the more ethical you are. However, recent research suggests there is probably a more complex relationship between ethics and age.[23] We believe older employees with more experience have greater knowledge to deal with complex industry-specific ethical issues. Younger managers are far more influenced by organizational culture than older managers.[24]

Locus of control relates to individual differences in relation to a generalized belief about how you are affected by internal versus external events or reinforcements. In other words, the concept relates to how people view themselves in relation to power. Those who believe in **external control** (externals) see themselves as going with the flow because that is all they can do. They believe the events in their lives are due to uncontrollable forces. They consider what they want to achieve depends on luck, chance, and powerful people in their company. In addition, they believe the probability of being able to control their lives by their own actions and efforts is low. Conversely, those who believe in **internal control** (internals) believe they control the events in their lives by their own effort and skill, viewing themselves as masters of their destinies and trusting in their capacity to influence their environment.

Current research suggests we still cannot be sure how significant locus of control is in terms of ethical decision making. One study that found a relationship between locus of control and ethical decision making concluded that internals were positively correlated whereas externals were negatively correlated with ethical decisions.[25] In other words, those who believe they formed their own destiny were more ethical than those who believed their fate was in the hands of others. Classifying someone as being entirely an internal or entirely an external is probably impossible. In reality, most people have experienced situations where they were influenced by others—particularly authority figures—to engage in questionable actions, as well as other situations where they adhered to what they knew was the correct choice. This does not necessarily mean that externals are unethical or internals are ethical individuals.

Organizational Factors

Although people can and do make individual ethical choices in business situations, no one operates in a vacuum. Indeed, research has established that in the workplace, the organization's values often have greater influence on decisions than a person's own values.[26]

DEBATE ISSUE
TAKE A STAND

Conflicts over Privacy in the Workplace

There is tension between companies and their employees over privacy in the workplace. Some companies track employees via company-issued GPS-enabled smartphones and monitor employees' behavior through social networking sites such as Facebook and Twitter. Currently, there are no laws preventing companies from monitoring and tracking employees. Companies believe not monitoring these platforms leaves them vulnerable to misconduct. For instance, the Internet increased the number of distractions in the workplace, and some employees may spend up to 30 percent of their time at work using social media sites for non-work purposes.

On the other hand, employees argue they have a right to their privacy. They see tracking as a clear sign that their employers do not trust them. Another major argument is that employers with access to employee social media sites or smartphones might be able to monitor employee activity outside the workplace. Where is the line drawn on ensuring employees are working appropriately versus their rights to privacy?

1. Companies should have the right to track employees through company smartphones and monitor their personal Facebook and Twitter accounts.

2. Employees should be able to maintain their personal privacy and not be tracked through their company smartphones or their Facebook and Twitter accounts.

Ethical choices in business are most often made jointly, in work groups and committees, or in conversations and discussions with coworkers. Employees approach ethical issues on the basis of what they learned not only from their own backgrounds, but also from others in the organization. The outcome of this learning process depends on the strength of personal values, the opportunities to behave unethically, and the exposure to others who behave ethically or unethically. An alignment between a person's own values and the values of the organization help create positive work attitudes and organizational outcomes. Research has further demonstrated that congruence in personal and organizational values is related to commitment, satisfaction, motivation, ethics, work stress, and anxiety.[27] Although people outside the organization such as family members and friends also influence decision makers, the organization develops a personality that helps determine what is and is not ethical. Just as a family guides an individual, specific industries give behavioral cues to firms. Within the family develops what is called a culture, and so too in an organization.

Corporate culture can be defined as a set of values, norms, and artifacts, including ways of solving problems that members (employees) of an organization share. As time passes, stakeholders come to view the company or organization as a living organism with a mind and will of its own. The Walt Disney Co., for example, requires all new employees to take a course in the traditions and history of Disneyland and Walt Disney, including the ethical dimensions of the company. The corporate culture at American Express stresses that employees help customers out of difficult situations whenever possible. This attitude is reinforced through numerous company legends of employees who have gone above and beyond the call of duty to help customers. This strong tradition of customer loyalty might encourage an American Express employee to take unorthodox steps to help a customer who encounters a problem while traveling overseas. Employees learn they can take some risks in helping customers. Such strong traditions and values have become a driving force in many companies, including Starbucks, IBM, Procter & Gamble, Southwest Airlines, and Hershey Foods.

One way organizations can determine the ethicalness and authenticity of their corporate cultures is having organizations go back to their mission statement or goals and objectives. These goals and objectives are often developed by various stakeholders, such as investors, employees, customers, and suppliers. Comparing the firm's activities with its mission statement, goals, and objectives helps the organization understand whether it is staying true to its values. Additionally, most industries have trade associations that disperse guidelines developed over time from others in the industry. These rules help guide the decision-making process as well. The interaction between the company's internal rules and regulations and industry guidelines form the basis of whether a business is making ethical or unethical decisions. It also gives an organization an idea of how an ethical or unethical culture may look.

An important component of corporate or organizational culture is the company's ethical conduct. Corporate culture involves values and norms that prescribe a wide range of behavior for organizational members, while **ethical culture** reflects the integrity of decisions made and is a function of many factors, including corporate policies, top management's leadership on ethical issues, the influence of coworkers, and the opportunity for unethical behavior. Communication is also important in the creation of an effective ethical culture. There is a positive correlation between effective communication and empowerment and the development of an organizational ethical culture.[28] Within the organization as a whole, subcultures can develop in individual departments or work groups, but these are influenced by the strength of the firm's overall ethical culture, as well as the function of the department and the stakeholders it serves.[29] For instance, salespeople are heavily influenced by the subculture of the sales department and face many ethical issues that are not necessarily common to other departments.[30] Additionally, because salespeople tend to operate largely outside of the organization, they may not be as socialized to other employees and the organization's ethical culture.[31]

Corporate culture and ethical culture are closely associated with the idea that significant others within the organization help determine ethical decisions within that organization. Research indicates the ethical values embodied in an organization's culture are positively correlated to employees' commitment to the firm and their sense that they fit into the company. These findings suggest companies should develop and promote their values to enhance employees' experiences in the workplace.[32] The more employees perceive an organization's culture to be ethical, the less likely they are to make unethical decisions.

Those who have influence in a work group, including peers, managers, coworkers, and subordinates, are referred to as **significant others**. They help workers on a daily basis with unfamiliar tasks and provide advice and information in both formal and informal ways. Coworkers, for instance, can offer help in the comments they make in discussions over lunch or when the boss is away. Likewise, a manager may provide directives about certain types of activities employees perform on the job. Indeed, an employee's supervisor can play a central role in helping employees develop and fit in socially in the workplace.[33] Numerous studies conducted over the years confirm that significant others within an organization may have more impact on a worker's decisions on a daily basis than any other factor.[34]

Obedience to authority is another aspect of the influence significant others can exercise. Obedience to authority helps explain why many employees resolve business ethics issues by simply following the directives of a superior. In organizations that emphasize respect for superiors, employees may feel they are expected to carry out orders by a supervisor even if those orders are contrary to the employees' sense of right and wrong. Rewards and punishments that managers control influence ethical decisions. If firms place all rewards around financial performance, then how objectives are achieved can become a secondary concern. This situation occurred in major banks prior to the financial crisis. If the employee's decision is judged to be unethical, he or she is likely to say, "I was only carrying out orders," or "My boss told me to do it this way." In addition, research shows the type of industry and size of the organization were found to be relevant factors, with larger companies at greater risk for unethical activities.[35]

Opportunity

Opportunity describes the conditions in an organization that limit or permit ethical or unethical behavior. Opportunity results from conditions that either provide rewards, whether internal or external, or fail to erect barriers against unethical behavior. Examples of internal rewards include feelings of goodness and personal worth generated by performing altruistic or ethical acts. External rewards refer to what an individual expects to receive from others in the social environment in terms of overt social approval, status, and esteem.

An example of a condition that fails to erect barriers against unethical behavior is a company policy that does not punish employees who accept large gifts from clients. The absence of punishment essentially provides an opportunity for unethical behavior because it allows individuals to engage in such behavior without fear of consequences. The prospect of a reward for unethical behavior can also create an opportunity for questionable decisions. For example, a salesperson given public recognition and a large bonus for making a valuable sale obtained through unethical tactics will probably be motivated to use such tactics again, even if such behavior goes against the salesperson's personal value system. If employees observe others at the workplace abusing drugs or alcohol and nobody reports or responds to this conduct, then the opportunity exists for others to engage in these activities.[36]

Opportunity relates to individuals' **immediate job context**—where they work, whom they work with, and the nature of the work. The immediate job context includes the motivational "carrots and sticks" superiors use to influence employee behavior. Pay raises, bonuses, and public recognition act as carrots, or positive reinforcements, whereas demotions, firings, reprimands, and pay penalties act as sticks, or negative reinforcements. One survey reports more than two-thirds of employees steal from their workplaces, and most do so repeatedly.[37] As Table 5–1 shows, many office supplies, particularly smaller ones, tend to "disappear" from the workplace. Small supplies such as Post-It notes, copier paper, staples, and pens appear to be the more commonly pilfered items, but some office theft sometimes reaches more serious proportions. For instance, a Charles Schwab & Co. broker used the company's order system to order office supplies and equipment and then sold them to other people. It is alleged he stole $1 million worth of office equipment from the firm.[38] The retail industry is particularly hard hit—total losses from employee theft are often greater than shoplifting at retail chains.[39] If there is no enforced policy against this practice, one concern is employees will not learn where to draw the line and get into the habit of taking more expensive items for personal use.

The opportunities that employees have for unethical behavior in an organization can be eliminated through formal codes, policies, and rules adequately enforced by management. For instance, the International Federation of Accountants, a global organization that consists of 175 member organizations and associates, periodically updates its ethics standards to cover new risk areas. It updated its conflict of interest policies as well as actions taken against member organizations that violate the code of ethics.[40] Financial companies—such as banks, savings and loan associations, and securities companies—developed elaborate sets of rules and procedures to avoid creating opportunities for individual employees to manipulate or take advantage of their trusted positions. In banks, one such rule requires most employees to take a vacation and stay out of the bank a certain number of days every year so they cannot be physically present to cover up embezzlement or other diversions of funds. This rule prevents the opportunity for inappropriate conduct.

TABLE 5-1 Most Common Office Supplies Stolen by Employees

1 Pens, pencils, and highlighters

2 Paper products

3 Paper or binder clips

4 Staplers

5 Scissors

6 Tape dispensers

7 Printer ink

8 Binders

Source: "The most stolen office supplies" *Boston.com*, http://www.boston.com/business/gallery/stolenofficesupplies/ (accessed February 19, 2015).

Despite the existence of rules, misconduct can still occur without proper oversight. JP Morgan covers conflicts of interest in its code of conduct, but lapses in oversight resulted in investigations with company officials ignoring corporate policies. Regulators showed concern over whether JP Morgan might have been driving clients toward its own investment products over outside offerings.[41] A later investigation tried to determine whether the firm hired an unqualified employee because he was the son of China's commerce minister. The commerce minister allegedly promised to help the bank in its operations in China.[42] Such a violation would not only be a conflict of interest but could also qualify as a type of bribery violating the Foreign Corrupt Practices Act. To avoid these types of situations, companies must adopt checks and balances that create transparency.

Opportunity also comes from knowledge. A major type of misconduct observed among employees in the workplace is lying to employees, customers, vendors, or the public or withholding needed information from them.[43] A person with expertise or information about the competition has the opportunity to exploit this knowledge. Individuals can be a source of information because they are familiar with the organization. Individuals employed by one organization for many years become "gatekeepers" of its culture and often have the opportunity to make decisions related to unwritten traditions and rules. They socialize newer employees to abide by the rules and norms of the company's internal and external ways of doing business, as well as understanding when the opportunity exists to cross the line. They function as mentors or supervise managers in training. Like drill sergeants in the army, these trainers mold the new recruits into what the company wants. Their training can contribute to either ethical or unethical conduct.

The opportunity for unethical behavior cannot be eliminated without aggressive enforcement of codes and rules. A national jewelry store chain president explained to us how he dealt with a jewelry buyer in one of his stores who took a bribe from a supplier. There was an explicit company policy against taking incentive payments to deal with a specific supplier. When the president of the firm learned about the accepted bribe, he immediately traveled to the office of the buyer in question and terminated his employment. He then traveled to the supplier (manufacturer) selling jewelry to his stores and terminated his relationship with the firm. The message was clear: Taking a bribe is unacceptable for the store's buyers, and salespeople from supplying companies could cost their firm significant sales by offering bribes. This type of policy enforcement illustrates how the opportunity to commit unethical acts can be eliminated or at least significantly reduced.

As defined previously, stakeholders are those directly and indirectly involved with a company and can include investors, customers, employees, channel members, communities, and special interest groups. Each stakeholder has goals and objectives that somewhat align with other stakeholders and the company. It is the diverging of goals that causes friction between and within stakeholders and the corporation. Most stakeholders understand firms must generate revenues and profit to exist, but not all. Special interest groups or communities may actively seek the destruction of the corporation because of perceived or actual harm to themselves or those things held important to them. The employee is also affected by such stakeholders, usually in an indirect way. Depending upon the perceived threat level to the firm, employees may act independently or in groups to perpetrate unethical or illegal behaviors. For example, one author knew of a newspaper firm that had been losing circulation to one of its competitors, and the loss was putting people at the firm out of work. The projection was if the newspaper could not turn subscriptions around they would be closed within a year. As a result of the announcement employees started pulling up newspaper receptacles and damaging the competition's automatic newspaper dispensers. Both activities were illegal, yet the employees felt justified because they believed they were helping the company survive.

Business Ethics Intentions, Behavior, and Evaluations

Ethical business issues and dilemmas involve problem-solving situations where the rules governing decisions are often vague or in conflict. The results of the decision are often uncertain; it is not always immediately clear whether the decision was ethical. There are no magic formulas, nor is there computer software that ethical business issues or dilemmas can be plugged into to get a solution. Even if they mean well, most businesspeople make ethical mistakes. Therefore, there is no substitute for critical thinking and the ability to take responsibility for our own decisions.

Individuals' intentions and the final decision regarding what action they take are the last steps in the ethical decision-making process. The work environment culture has been found to impact recognition and judgment.[44] When intentions and behavior are inconsistent with their ethical judgment, people may feel guilty. For example, when an advertising account executive is asked by her client to create an advertisement she perceives as misleading, she has two alternatives: to comply or refuse. If she refuses, she stands to lose business from that client and possibly her job. Other factors—such as pressure from the client, the need to keep her job to pay her debts and living expenses, and the possibility of a raise if she develops the advertisement successfully—may influence her resolution of this ethical dilemma. Because of these factors, she may decide to act unethically and develop the advertisement even though she believes it to be inaccurate. In this example her actions are inconsistent with her ethical judgment, meaning she will probably feel guilty about her decision.

Guilt or uneasiness is the first sign an unethical decision may have occurred. The next step is changing the behavior to reduce such feelings. This change can reflect a person's values shifting to fit the decision or the person changing his or her decision type the next time a similar situation occurs. You can eliminate some of the problematic situational factors by resigning your position. For those who begin the value shift, the following are the usual justifications that reduce and finally eliminate guilt:

1.   I need the paycheck and can't afford to quit right now.

2.   Those around me are doing it, so why shouldn't I? They believe it's okay.

3. If I don't do this, I might not be able to get a good reference from my boss or company when I leave.

4. This is not such a big deal, given the potential benefits.

5. Business is business with a different set of rules.

6. If not me, someone else would do it and get rewarded.

The road to success depends on how the businessperson defines *success*. The success concept drives intentions and behavior in business either implicitly or explicitly. Money, security, family, power, wealth, and personal or group gratification are all types of success measures people use. The list described is not comprehensive, and in the next chapter, you will understand more about how success can be defined. Another concept that affects behavior is the probability of rewards and punishments, an issue explained further in Chapter 6.

USING THE ETHICAL DECISION-MAKING MODEL TO IMPROVE ETHICAL DECISIONS

The ethical decision-making model presented cannot tell you if a business decision is ethical or unethical. It bears repeating that it is impossible to tell you what is right or wrong; instead, we attempt to prepare you to make informed ethical decisions. Although this chapter does not moralize by telling you what to do in a specific situation, it does provide an overview of typical decision-making processes and factors that influence ethical decisions. The model is not a guide for how to make decisions, but is intended to provide you with insights and knowledge about typical ethical decision-making processes in business organizations.

Business ethics scholars developing descriptive models have focused on regularities in decision making and the various phenomena that interact in a dynamic environment to produce predictable behavioral patterns. Furthermore, it is unlikely an organization's ethical problems will be solved strictly by having a thorough knowledge about how ethical decisions are made. By its very nature, business ethics involves value judgments and collective agreement about acceptable patterns of behavior. In the next section, we discuss normative concepts that describe appropriate ethical conduct.

We propose gaining an understanding of the factors that make up ethical decision making in business will sensitize you concerning whether the business problem is an ethical issue or dilemma. It will help you know what the degree of ethical intensity may be for you and others, as well as how individual factors such as gender, moral philosophy, education level, and religion within you and others affect the process. We hope you remember the organizational factors that impact the ethics of business decisions and what to look for in a firm's code of ethics, culture, opportunity, and the significance of other employees and how they sway some people's intentions and behaviors. You now know non-business factors such as friends, family, and the economic reality of an employee's situation can lead to unethical business decisions. Finally, we hope you remember that the type of industry, the competition, and stakeholders are all factors that can push some employees into making unethical decisions. In later chapters we delve deeper into different aspects of the ethical decision-making process so ultimately you can make better, more informed decisions and help your company do the right things for the right reasons.

One important conclusion that should be taken into account is that ethical decision making within an organization does not rely strictly on the personal values and morals of individuals. Knowledge of moral philosophies or values must be balanced with business knowledge and an understanding of the complexities of the dilemma requiring a decision. For example, a manager who embraces honesty, fairness, and equity must understand the diverse risks associated with a complex financial instrument such as options or derivatives. Business competence must exist, along with personal accountability, in ethical decisions. Organizations take on a culture of their own, with managers and coworkers exerting a significant influence on ethical decisions. While formal codes, rules, and compliance are essential in organizations, an organization built on informal relationships is more likely to develop a high level of integrity within an organization's culture.[45]

NORMATIVE CONSIDERATIONS IN ETHICAL DECISION MAKING

In the first part of the chapter, we described how ethical decision making occurs in an organization. This descriptive approach provides an understanding of the role of individuals in an organizational context for making ethical business decisions. Understanding what influences the ethical decision-making process is important in sensitizing you to the intensity of issues and dilemmas as well as the management of ethics in an organization.

However, understanding how ethical decisions are made is different from determining what should guide decisions. A normative approach to business ethics examines what ought to occur in business ethical decision making. The word "normative" is equivalent to an ideal standard. Therefore, when we discuss **normative approaches**, we are talking about how organizational decision makers *should* approach an issue. This is different from a descriptive approach that examines *how* organizational decision makers approach ethical decision making. A normative approach in business ethics revolves around the standards of behavior within the firm as well as within the industry. These normative rules and standards are based on individual moral values as well as the collective values of the organization. The normative approach for business ethics is concerned with general ethical values implemented into business. Concepts like fairness and justice are highly important in a normative structure. Strong normative structures in organizations are positively related to ethical decision making. Normative considerations also tend to deal with moral philosophies such as utilitarianism and deontology that we will explore in more detail in the next chapter.

Most organizations develop a set of core values to provide enduring beliefs about appropriate conduct. Core values are central to an organization and provide directions for action. For most firms, the selection of core values relates directly to stakeholder management of relationships. These values include an understanding of the descriptive approaches we covered in the first part of this chapter. It also includes instrumental elements that justify the adoption of core values. An instrumental concern focuses on positive outcomes, including firm profitability and benefits to society. Normative business dimensions are rooted in social, political, and economic institutions as well as the recognition of stakeholder claims.

By incorporating stakeholder objectives into corporate core values, companies begin to view stakeholders as significant. Each stakeholder has goals and objectives that somewhat align with other stakeholders and the company. The diverging of goals causes friction between and within stakeholders and the corporation. Ethical obligations are established for both internal stakeholders such as employees as well as external stakeholders such as the community.[46] For instance, Camden Property Trust organizes its activities around its core values of fun, team players, results-oriented, customer-focused, lead by example, work smart, act with integrity, people driven, and always do the right thing. The company relies heavily on these core values and uses them significantly in the hiring process to ensure the people they hire are the right fit for the firm.[47] Ethical decisions are often embedded in many organizational decisions—both managerial and societal—so it is necessary to recognize the importance of core values in providing ideals for appropriate conduct.

Institutions as the Foundation for Normative Values

Institutions are important in establishing a foundation for normative values. According to institutional theory, organizations operate according to taken-for-granted institutional norms and rules. For instance, government, religion, and education are institutions that influence the creation of values, norms, and conventions that both organizations and individuals should adhere.[48] Indeed, many researchers argue that normative values largely originate from family, friends, and more institutional affiliations such as religion and government.[49] In other words, organizations face certain normative pressures from different institutions to act a certain way. These pressures can take place internally (inside the organization itself) and/or externally (from the government or other institutions).[50] For our purposes, we sort institutions into three categories: political, economic, and social.

Consider for a moment how political institutions influence the development of values. If you live in country with a democratic form of government, you likely consider freedom of speech and the right to own property as important ideals. Organizations must comply with these types of institutional norms and belief systems in order to succeed—to do otherwise would result in the failure of the organization.[51] Companies such as IBM should recognize that using bribery to gain a competitive advantage is inappropriate according to U.S. and U.K. bribery laws. Political influences can also take place within the organization. An ethical organization has policies and rules in place to determine appropriate behavior. This is often the compliance component of the firm's organizational culture. Failure to abide by these rules results in disciplinary action. For instance, engineering and construction company Fluor Corporation's code of conduct states that it is every employee's duty to report unsafe conduct in the workplace. Those who fail to report can be subject to disciplinary procedures.[52]

Normative business ethics takes into account the political realities outside the legal realm in the form of industry standards. Different types of industries have different standards and policies which either increase or decrease the ethicality and legality of their decisions. Legal issues such as price fixing, antitrust issues, and consumer protection are important in maintaining a fair and equitable marketplace. Antitrust regulators tend to scrutinize mergers and acquisitions between large firms to make sure these companies do not gain so much power they place competitors at a major disadvantage. Price-fixing is illegal because it often creates unfair prices for buyers. Bridgestone Corporation pled guilty to charges of price-fixing on parts it sold to automakers. The company agreed to a $425 million criminal fine.[53] Because of their impact on the economy, these issues must be major considerations for businesses when making ethical decisions.

Competition is also important to economic institutions and ethical decision making. The nature of competition can be shaped by the economic system as it helps determine how a particular country or society distributes its resources in the production of products. Basic economic systems such as communism, socialism, and capitalism influence the nature of competition. Competition affects how a company operates as well as the risks employees take for the good of the firm. The amount of competition in an industry can be determined and described according to the following: (1) barriers to entry into the industry, (2) available substitutes for the products produced by the industry rivals, (3) the power of the industry rivals over their customers, and (4) the power of the industry rivals' suppliers over the industry rivals. An example of a highly competitive industry is smartphone manufacturing, whereas the vacuum cleaning manufacturing industry is competitively low. High levels of competition create a higher probability that firms cut corners because margins are usually low. Competitors aggressively seek differential advantages from others so as to increase market share, profitability, and growth. When taken to extremes, unethical and illegal activities can become normal. An investigation into HSBC's Swiss banking subsidiary, for instance, showed that the bank had helped their clients avoid taxes. While the misconduct might have started out small, at the time of discovery it had become a systematic part of the Swiss bank's activities.[54]

Social institutions impact a firm's normative values as well. They include religion, education, and individuals such as the family unit. There are laws meant to ensure an organization acts fairly, but there is no law saying people should do to others as they would prefer to have done to them. Yet many cultures adopted this rule that has been institutionalized into businesses with standards on competing fairly, being transparent with consumers, and treating employees with respect. These social institutions help individuals form their personal values and the moral philosophies they bring into the workplace. From an organizational context, societal trends influence which values to adopt as well as when to adapt decisions to take into account new concerns. For instance, because of the changing sociocultural concerns over obesity, Walmart decided to support an initiative to sell healthier foods.

While we might not consider stakeholders to be institutions, it should now be clear that many stakeholders actually act as institutions in terms of values. Stakeholders closely align with institutions. The regulatory system aligns with political institutions, competition relates to economic institutions, and personal values and norms derive from social institutions. There is therefore a clear link between institutional theory and the stakeholder orientation of management.

As we reiterated, an organization uses rules dictated by its institutional environment to measure the appropriateness of its behavior.[55] Organizations facing the same environmental norms or rules (for example, those in the same industry) become isomorphic, or institutionalized.[56] Although organizations in a particular industry might differ, most share certain values that characterize the industry. Additionally, institutional factors often overlap in ethical decision making. For example, Toyota invested heavily in fuel-cell technology with the release of its Mirai hydrogen fuel-cell. We could characterize this decision as having political, economic, and social considerations. Politically, new laws are requiring automobile companies to increase the fuel efficiency of their vehicles. As the first automaker to mass produce a car line powered entirely by hydrogen fuel-cell technology, Toyota differentiates its product from rivals, many of whom are focusing on hybrid or electric car technology.[57] Toyota's investment in greater fuel efficiency results from society's increasing demands for more sustainable vehicles.

While industry shared values promote organizational effectiveness when linked to goals, it can also hinder effectiveness if more efficient means of organization and structure are avoided in exchange for stability.[58] There is a risk that organizations might sacrifice new ideas or methodologies in order to be more acceptable.[59] This can limit innovativeness and productivity. On the other hand, it is important that an organization does not stray so far from industry norms and values that it creates stakeholder concerns. A company known for selling environmentally friendly apparel would not likely succeed in selling a new clothing line made of animal fur. From both a social and managerial standpoint, knowing which institutional norms to comply with and when it would be more beneficial to explore new norms and values is important for organizations to consider.

How does this fit with ethical theory? Institutions directly impact a firm's norms, values, and behavior as well as "the long-run survival of the organization."[60] When Galleon Group's founder Raj Rajaratnam and other employees were found guilty of insider trading, the firm floundered. In this case, the government was the major institution involved. By violating the law, the organization did not have the ability to bounce back from this type of misconduct. The firm did not have normative values in place to dictate appropriate (and in this case legal) behavior.

Conversely, when values from political, economic, and social institutions are embedded into the organizational culture to provide incentives for appropriate behavior, firms tend to act more socially responsible.[61] If incentives such as organizational rewards align with the organization's normative values and society's cultural institutions, employees—and therefore the organization as a whole—are more likely to act in a socially responsible manner. Stakeholders can translate normative demands for ethical behavior into economic incentives through reciprocal relationships.[62] These reciprocal behaviors can explain why there can be sanctions to provide a mechanism for ethical normative behavior. Many organizations provide employees with a certain amount of time off to volunteer in their communities. This incentive matches the normative institutional value of giving back to the community. If incentives do not align with institutional normative values or if they contradict these values, then misconduct is likely. While Enron and Countrywide Financial outwardly supported ethical conduct, in reality the company culture rewarded those who took risks even if they violated normative values.

Implementing Principles and Core Values in Ethical Decision Making

Political, economic, and social institutions help organizations determine principles and values for appropriate conduct. Principles and values are important normative considerations in ethical decision making. We learned from Chapter 1 that principles are specific and pervasive boundaries for behavior that should not be violated. Principles are important in preventing organizations from "bending the rules." Values are enduring beliefs and ideals that are socially enforced. Together, principles and values set an ideal standard for the organization. Figure 5–2 demonstrates some of the similarities and differences between principles and values.

John Rawls was one of the most influential philosophers in his research on how principles support the concept of justice.[63] Rawls believed justice principles were beliefs that everyone could accept—a key element in our own definition of principles. According to our definition, principles are beliefs that are universal in nature. For instance, most cultures agree that honesty and fairness are essential to a well-functioning society, although there may be differences on how to implement this principle in daily living.

In his experiments, Rawls used what he called the *veil of ignorance*, a thought experiment that examined how individuals would formulate principles if they did not know what their future position in society would be. A person might emerge from the veil of ignorance as a rich person or as a beggar. While individuals might formulate different values based on their position in society, Rawls believed that because principles were universally accepted both the rich person and the beggar would agree upon them. Thus, using the veil of ignorance, Rawls identified principles that were not biased by one's social position.[64]

Rawls's work led him to develop two main principles of justice: the liberty principle and the difference principle. The liberty principle, also known as the equality principle, states that each person has basic rights that are compatible to the basic liberties of others. This is similar to the U.S. Constitution's statement that everyone has certain inalienable rights such as life, liberty, and the pursuit of happiness. The difference principle states that economic and social equalities (or inequalities) should be arranged to provide the most benefit to the least-advantaged members of society. This means the most ethical course of action is one that increases the benefits of those that are the least well-off. Actions that harm disadvantaged members of society should be avoided.[65] It is important to note that the difference principle does not advocate for the complete elimination of inequalities in society, but that the most ethical decision seeks to benefit and not harm disadvantaged populations. In the corporate world, organizations operating according to the difference principle would not take actions that could create economic and social harm to the least advantaged members of society. For example, a firm might avoid accepting business from a foreign country with a record of human rights abuses because the country supports the exploitation of disadvantaged groups.[66] Both of Rawls's justice principles relate to political, economic, and social institutions.

While organizations might agree that they should behave honestly, transparently, and responsibly toward stakeholders, they might differ on how to implement these principles. Companies take basic principles and translate them into core values. Core values provide the abstract ideals that are distinct from individual values and daily operational procedures. Value practices evolve and are translated into normative definitions of ethical or unethical. Value practices become the end results and are distinct from organizational practices driven by technical or efficiency considerations.[67]

Individual and organizational values can differ significantly[68] because of ethical diversity among individuals. To join an organization, members need to accept that some values are superior and deal with the organizational need to develop collective agreement. This results in possible tensions that must be worked out between individual and organizational values.[69]

FIGURE 5–2 Principles and Values

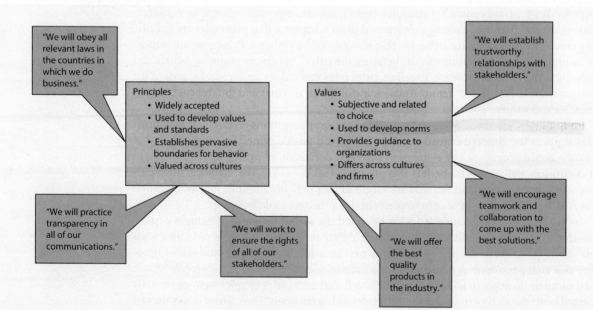

TABLE 5–2 Core Values of Marriott

1. Put People First

2. Pursue Excellence

3. Embrace Change

4. Act with Integrity

5. Serve Our World

Source: Marriott, "Core Values & Heritage," http://www.marriott.com/
culture-and-values/core-values.mi (accessed February 19, 2015).

Instead of individuals just accepting core values from top management, there needs to be group discussions, negotiations, and adjustments to determine how core values are implemented.[70]

Remember that leaders, stakeholders, and the organizational culture impact the development of core values. Core values might include operating in a sustainable manner, collaboration and teamwork, and avoiding bribery. Unlike principles, values are shaped by company-specific, industry-specific, country-specific, and global-specific factors.[71] Firms from countries that stress individualism encourage the ability to work independently, whereas firms from more collectivist nations place more value on teamwork. Additionally, core values differ depending upon the industry. For example, although safety is a core value of many firms, it is more likely to be emphasized as a core value in a factory environment than in an office environment.

A firm's core values provide a blueprint into the firm's purpose as well as how it views ethical decision making and prioritizes stakeholders. Table 5–2 provides an example of the core values of Marriot International. How Marriot organized its core values provides a snapshot of what the firm considers important. For instance, its first value, to put people first, provides guidance for all of the firm's stakeholder relationships. From its other core values you can determine that Marriot strives to deliver excellent customer service and operate with the highest forms of integrity. All five of Marriott's values reinforce its vision "to be the #1 hospitality company in the world."[72] Organizational core values such as these are essential to ethical decision making in organizations. Organizations that have ethics programs based on a values orientation are found to make a greater contribution than those based simply on compliance, or obeying laws and regulations.[73]

UNDERSTANDING ETHICAL DECISION MAKING

Our organizational ethical decision-making framework demonstrates the many factors that influence ethical decisions. Ethical issue intensity, individual factors, organizational factors, and opportunity result in business ethics evaluations and decisions. An organizational ethical culture is shaped by effective leadership. Without top level support for ethical behavior, the opportunity for employees to engage in their own personal approaches to ethical decision making will evolve. An ethical corporate culture needs shared values along with proper oversight to monitor the complex ethical decisions being made by employees. It requires the establishment of a strong ethics program to educate and develop compliance policies. Consider the ethics program at construction and engineering company Bechtel Corporation. Top managers at Bechtel show strong support for ethical conduct, with the chief ethics officer and vice chairman speaking at events such as the Ethics and Compliance Officer Association meeting to share best industry practices. Every year the company holds an ethics awareness workshop for its employees and supports organizations such as Transparency International and Business Ethics Leadership Alliance.[74]

On the other hand, some companies with a strong reputation for ethical conduct sometimes fail to maintain their ethical culture. Target has been a frequent honoree on *Ethisphere's* World's Most Ethical companies list, but Target's failure to act upon warnings that its system was being hacked resulted in a major scandal that seriously damaged its reputation. Hackers stole more than 40 million credit and debit cards from Target's customers as well as personal information from an additional 70 million customers. This occurred despite warnings from its security firm that suspected hacking activities were being detected. The debacle cost the Target CEO his job, and both banks and customers filed lawsuits against the company.[75] To continue maintaining credibility among stakeholders, Target must learn from its mistakes and return to the values in its code of ethics that made it a role model for ethical conduct.

Normative dimensions are also important to ethical decision making. Normative perspectives set forth ideal goals to which organizations should aspire. Normative considerations also provide the foundation needed to develop organizational principles and values, the building blocks of a firm's ethical culture. Without this foundation, companies will not be able to develop an ethical culture or have the basis to make ethical decisions. The Ford Pinto case is an interesting example of how normative considerations can be easily ignored. Ford recognized that its Pintos had a design flaw that made it easier for explosions to occur in accidents. However, it refused to initiate a recall. This led to needless deaths. It is interesting to note that in one class discussing the Ford Pinto case students tended to point out the monetary and reputational impact of Ford's actions, but only later did a student state that Ford should not have knowingly sold a dangerous car that could harm people.[76] Normative frameworks are largely influenced by political, economic, and social institutions. However, a normative perspective also recognizes the existence of universal ethical behaviors, such as honesty and justice. Total, a French oil and gas company, lists human rights, integrity, and safety among its main principles.[77]

Finally, the more you know about ethical decision making in business, the more likely you will make good decisions. There are many challenges in organizations beyond the control of any one individual. On the other hand, as you move to higher levels of the organization, there is the opportunity for ethical leadership to become a role model for good ethics. The descriptive framework of ethical decision making in this chapter provides many insights into the relationships that contribute to an ethical culture.

SUMMARY

The key components of the ethical decision-making framework include ethical awareness, ethical issue intensity, individual factors, organizational factors, and opportunity. These factors are interrelated and influence business ethics evaluations and intentions that result in ethical or unethical behavior.

The first step in ethical decision making is to recognize that an ethical issue requires an individual or work group to choose among several actions that will ultimately be evaluated as ethical or unethical by various stakeholders. Ethical issue intensity is the perceived relevance or importance of an ethical issue to an individual or work group. It reflects the ethical sensitivity of the individual or work group that triggers the ethical decision-making process. Other factors in our ethical decision-making framework influence this sensitivity, and therefore different individuals often perceive ethical issues differently.

Individual factors such as gender, education, nationality, age, and locus of control affect the ethical decision-making process, with some factors being more important than others. Organizational factors such as an organization's values often have greater influence on an individual's decisions than that person's own values. In addition, decisions in business are most often made jointly, in work groups and committees, or in conversations and discussions with coworkers. Corporate cultures and structures operate through the ability of individual relationships among the organization's members to influence those members' ethical decisions. A corporate culture is a set of values, beliefs, goals, norms, and ways of solving problems that members (employees) of an organization share. Corporate culture involves norms that prescribe a wide range of behavior for the organization's members. The ethical culture of an organization indicates whether it has an ethical conscience. Significant others—including peers, managers, coworkers, and subordinates—who influence the work group have more daily impact on an employee's decisions than any other factor in the decision-making framework. Obedience to authority may explain why many business ethics issues are resolved simply by following the directives of a superior.

Ethical opportunity results from conditions that provide rewards, whether internal or external, or limit barriers to ethical or unethical behavior. Included in opportunity is a person's immediate job context that includes the motivational techniques superiors use to influence employee behavior. The opportunity employees have for unethical behavior in an organization can be eliminated through formal codes, policies, and rules that are adequately enforced by management.

The ethical decision-making framework is not a guide for making decisions. It is intended to provide insights and knowledge about typical ethical decision-making processes in business organizations. Ethical decision making within organizations does not rely strictly on the personal values and morals of employees. Organizations have cultures of their own that when combined with corporate governance mechanisms may significantly influence business ethics.

Normative approaches describe how organizational decision makers *should* approach an ethical issue. Institutional theory is an important normative concept that states that organizations operate according to taken-for-granted institutional norms and rules. Political, economic, and social institutions help organizations determine principles and values for appropriate conduct. Principles are important in preventing organizations from "bending the rules." Philosopher John Rawls contributed important work on principles, particularly principles of justice. Core values are enduring beliefs about appropriate conduct and provide guidance for the ethical direction of the firm.

IMPORTANT TERMS FOR REVIEW

ethical awareness 129	internal control 133
ethical issue intensity 130	corporate culture 134
moral intensity 131	ethical culture 135
gender 132	significant other 135
education 132	obedience to authority 135
nationality 133	opportunity 136
age 133	immediate job context 136
locus of control 133	normative approach 140
external control 133	

RESOLVING ETHICAL BUSINESS CHALLENGES*

CrudeOil, a subsidiary of a major energy multinational that manufactures oil drilling parts around the world, experienced a lag in sales. The board of directors brought in a new manager to revamp the company. They recommended Jim Stone as the new manager because he had an impeccable reputation for achieving results, and top managers in the industry liked him because of his west Texas demeanor. After 18 months, Jim was successful in increasing the company's sales and profits. He began his tenure as manager by laying off several salespeople who had not performed according to his high standards. This made those who stayed with the company uneasy and they responded in different ways. Some tried to get on Jim's good side, while others focused on achieving their sales goals and avoiding any type of interaction with him.

The problem was Jim's managing style was harsh and unpredictable. For example, when a mistake was made, he blamed salespeople he disliked even if it was not their fault. On one occasion, Marjorie, one of the newest salespeople, brought in an unusually big sale. Rather than giving her positive feedback, Jim acted like it was a normal occurrence. What was ironic was the company's most important value was to treat everyone with respect. It was considered so significant it was printed on a banner and hung at the front of the office for all to see. When Jim lost his temper, it often happened while he stood in front of all the employees underneath the banner.

His personality really came out when he got angry. At several meetings he would randomly pick out salespeople and engage in intimidating behaviors such as staring at them for long periods of time, discounting their ideas, or simply ignoring them. Jim treated all of the employees with intimidating behavior, even the ones he claimed to like. Every so often Jim picked out an employee and make snide comments over the course of several days. He made no excuses about it.

One day, when one of the employees finally broached Jim about the matter, Jim announced to the entire office, "I pick out the employees who are underperforming. I am the boss, and I need to make sure you people make as many sales as possible." He paused and looked at the expressions on the employees' faces. He then continued, "Actually, you should make more sales than that!" Jim turned toward his office, laughing as he shut the door. The employee who spoke up was given the subsidiary's lesser sales accounts.

Madison, who hired in as a salesperson a few months before Jim took control of the company, was continuously in Jim's crosshairs. He told her even though she made her sales quota, it was not satisfactory. Furthermore, he took credit for her performance at meetings. When her numbers exceeded the quota, he spread rumors suggesting she wasn't meeting her goals because of problems in her personal life.

One day Peter, another salesperson, approached Madison and asked her how she was doing. Madison looked at him confusedly, and responded, "I'm as fine as anyone else here. Why?"

Peter answered, "Jim told me you had been in the hospital lately and you might be suffering from a serious illness." Madison was taken aback. "Peter, Jim is just saying that because my sales numbers were low this last quarter. Believe me, I am fine." Madison sat there infuriated that Jim would be spreading rumors about her.

Madison knew initiating a conversation with Jim would not be the way to resolve this issue. She felt she would be fired if she confronted him about his behavior or demoted like the other employee. She tried talking to others Jim had bullied, but many feared for their jobs and preferred to remain silent. She also considered speaking with the board of directors, but she did not know any one of them well and she knew they had a good relationship with Jim. Some kind of action had to take place because Madison could not work in an environment like that much longer. Besides, other employees' tolerance would wear out soon and the company as a whole could suffer lasting consequences. As Madison walked toward the front door at the end of the day, she avoided looking at the banner featuring CrudeOil's most important value.

QUESTIONS | EXERCISES

1. Describe the organizational culture at CrudeOil. How does it contribute to the current situation?
2. How is CrudeOil violating its core value of treating others with respect? What are some ways it could reincorporate this core value into its organizational culture?
3. If Madison cannot report her problems to her immediate supervisor, what are some other ways she can handle the situation?

*This case is strictly hypothetical; any resemblance to real persons, companies, or situations is coincidental.

> > > CHECK YOUR EQ

Check your EQ, or Ethics Quotient, by completing the following. Assess your performance to evaluate your overall understanding of the chapter material.

1. The first step in ethical decision making is to understand the individual factors that influence the process.   Yes   No

2. "Opportunity" describes the conditions within an organization that limit or permit ethical or unethical behavior.   Yes   No

3. Core values are enduring beliefs about appropriate conduct.   Yes   No

4. The most significant influence on ethical behavior in an organization is the opportunity to engage in (un)ethical behavior.   Yes   No

5. Obedience to authority relates to the influence of corporate culture.   Yes   No

ANSWERS **1. No.** The first step is to become more aware that an ethical issue exists and to consider its relevance to the individual or work group. **2. Yes.** Opportunity results from conditions that provide rewards or fail to erect barriers against unethical behavior. **3. Yes.** Core values are enduring beliefs about appropriate conduct. **4. No.** Significant others have more impact on ethical decisions within an organization. **5. No.** Obedience to authority relates to the influence of significant others and supervisors.

ENDNOTES

1. Thomas M. Jones, "Ethical Decision Making by Individuals in Organizations: An Issue-Contingent Model," *Academy of Management Review* 16, 2 (February 1991): 366–395; O. C. Ferrell and Larry G. Gresham, "A Contingency Framework for Understanding Ethical Decision Making in Marketing," *Journal of Marketing* 49, 3 (Summer 1985): 87–96; O. C. Ferrell, Larry G. Gresham, and John Fraedrich, "A Synthesis of Ethical Decision Models for Marketing," *Journal of Macromarketing* 9, 2 (Fall 1989): 55–64; Shelby D. Hunt and Scott Vitell, "A General Theory of Marketing Ethics," *Journal of Macromarketing* 6, 2 (Spring 1986): 5–16; William A. Kahn, "Toward an Agenda for Business Ethics Research," *Academy of Management Review* 15, 2 (April 1990): 311–328; Linda K. Trevino, "Ethical Decision Making in Organizations: A Person-Situation Interactionist Model," *Academy of Management Review* 11, 3 (March 1986): 601–617.

2. Jones, "Ethical Decision Making," 367–372.

3. Donald P. Robin, R. Eric Reidenbach, and P. J. Forrest, "The Perceived Importance of an Ethical Issue as an Influence on the Ethical Decision Making of Ad Managers," *Journal of Business Research* 35, 1 (January 1996): 17.

4. Andrew Tangel, "Many at hedge funds still feel pressure to break rules, survey finds," *Los Angeles Times*, April 4, 2013, http://www.latimes.com/business/money/la-fi-mo-wall-street-insider-trading-survey-20130404,0,7610072.story (accessed February 26, 2015).

5. Jack Beatty, "The Enron Ponzi Scheme," *The Atlantic Monthly*, March 13, 2002, http://www.theatlantic.com/magazine/archive/2002/03/the-enron-ponzi-scheme/303156/ (accessed February 26, 2015).

6. Roselie McDevitt and Joan Van Hise, "Influences in Ethical Dilemmas of Increasing Intensity," *Journal of Business Ethics* 40, 3 (October 2002): 261–274.

7. Anusorn Singhapakdi, Scott J. Vitell, and George R. Franke, "Antecedents, Consequences, and Mediating Effects of Perceived Moral Intensity and Personal Moral Philosophies," *Journal of the Academy of Marketing Science* 27, 1 (Winter 1999): 19.

8. Ibid.

9. Ibid.

10. Kathy Lund Dean, Jeri Mullins Beggs, and Timothy P. Keane, "Mid-level Managers, Organizational Context, and (Un)ethical Encounters," *Journal of Business Ethics* 97, 1 (2010): 51–69.

11. Grant Rodgers, "Scientist faces fraud charges," *USA Today*, June 25, 2014, 4A.

12. Beryl Benderly, "Inadequate Ethics Training Leaves Young Scientists Unprepared for "Ethical Emergencies," *Science Careers Blog*, July 14, 2012, http://blogs.sciencemag.org/sciencecareers/2012/07/difficult-ethic.html (accessed February 26, 2015).

13. Singhapakdi, Vitell, and Franke, 17.

14. Damodar Suar and Rooplekha Khuntia, "Influence of Personal Values and Value Congruence on Unethical Practices and Work Behavior," *Journal of Business Ethics* 97, 3 (2010): 443–460.

15. "Lead the Way," *Spirit*, February 2011, 41.

16. B. Elango, Karen Paul, Sumit K. Kundu, and Shishir K. Paudel, "Organizational Ethics, Individual Ethics, and Ethical Intentions in International Decision-Making," *Journal of Business Ethics* 97, 4 (2010): 543–561.

17. T. W. Loe, L. Ferrell, and P. Mansfield, "A Review of Empirical Studies Assessing Ethical Decision Making in Business," *Journal of Business Ethics* 25, 3 (2000): 185–204.

18. C. Gilligan, "In a Different Voice: Women's Conceptions of Self and Morality," *Harvard Educational Review* 47, 4 (1977): 481–517.

19. Steven Kaplan, Kurt Pany, Janet Samuels, and Jian Zhang, "An Examination of the Association between Gender and Reporting Intentions for Fraudulent Financial Reporting," *Journal of Business Ethics* 87, 1 (June 2009): 15–30.

20. Michael J. O'Fallon and Kenneth D. Butterfield, "A Review of the Empirical Ethical Decision-Making Literature: 1996–2003," *Journal of Business Ethics* 59, 4 (July 2005): 375–413; P. M. J. Christie, J. I. G. Kwon, P. A. Stoeberl, and R. Baumhart, "A Cross-Cultural Comparison of Ethical Attitudes of Business Managers: India, Korea and the United States," *Journal of Business Ethics* 46, 3 (September 2003): 263–287; G. Fleischman and S. Valentine, "Professionals' Tax Liability and Ethical Evaluations in an Equitable Relief Innocent Spouse Case," *Journal of Business Ethics* 42, 1 (January 2003): 27–44; A. Singhapakdi, K. Karande, C. P. Rao, and S. J. Vitell, "How Important Are Ethics and Social Responsibility? A Multinational Study of Marketing Professionals," *European Journal of Marketing* 35, 1/2 (2001): 133–152.

21. Thomas Van Valey, David Hartmann, Wayne Fuqua, Andrew Evans, Amy Day Ing, Amanda Meyer, Karolina Staros, and Chris Walmsley, "The Process of Ethical Decision-Making: Experts vs. Novices," *Journal of Business Ethics* 13, 1 (2015): 45–60.

22. Robert W. Armstrong, "The Relationship between Culture and Perception of Ethical Problems in International Marketing," *Journal of Business Ethics* 15, 11 (November 1996): 1199–1208; J. Cherry, M. Lee, and C. S. Chien, "A Cross-Cultural Application of a Theoretical Model of Business Ethics: Bridging the Gap between Theory and Data," *Journal of Business Ethics* 44, 4 (June 2003): 359–376; B. Kracher, A. Chatterjee, and A. R. Lundquist, "Factors Related to the Cognitive Moral Development of Business Students and Business Professionals in India and the United States: Nationality, Education, Sex and Gender," *Journal of Business Ethics* 35, 4 (February 2002): 255–268.

23. J. M. Larkin, "The Ability of Internal Auditors to Identify Ethical Dilemmas," *Journal of Business Ethics* 23 (February 2000): 401–409; D. Peterson, A. Rhoads, and B. C. Vaught, "Ethical Beliefs of Business Professionals: A Study of Gender, Age and External Factors," *Journal of Business Ethics* 31, 3 (June 2001): 225–232; M. A. Razzaque and T. P. Hwee, "Ethics and Purchasing Dilemma: A Singaporean View," *Journal of Business Ethics* 35, 4 (February 2002): 307–326.

24. B. Elango, Karen Paul, Sumit K. Kundu, Shishir K. Paudel, "Organizational Ethics, Individual Ethics, and Ethical Intentions in International Decision-Making," *Journal of Business Ethics* 97, 4 (2010): 543–561.

25. J. Cherry and J. Fraedrich, "An Empirical Investigation of Locus of Control and the Structure of Moral Reasoning: Examining the Ethical Decision-Making Processes of Sales Managers," *Journal of Personal Selling and Sales*

Management 20, 3 (Summer 2000): 173–188; M. C. Reiss and K. Mitra, "The Effects of Individual Difference Factors on the Acceptability of Ethical and Unethical Workplace Behaviors," *Journal of Business Ethics* 17, 14 (October 1998): 1581–1593.

26. O. C. Ferrell and Linda Ferrell, "Role of Ethical Leadership in Organizational Performance," *Journal of Management Systems* 13 (2001): 64–78.

27. Barry Z. Posner, "Another Look at the Impact of Personal and Organizational Values Congruency," *Journal of Business Ethics* 97, 4 (2010): 535–541.

28. K. Praveen Parboteeah, Hsien Chun Chen, Ying-Tzu Lin, I-Heng Chen, Amber Y-P Lee, and Anyi Chung, "Establishing Organizational Ethical Climates: How Do Managerial Practices Work?" *Journal of Business Ethics* 97, 4 (2010), 599–611.

29. James Weber and Julie E. Seger, "Influences upon Organizational Ethical Subclimates: A Replication Study of a Single Firm at Two Points in Time," *Journal of Business Ethics* 41, 1–2 (November 2002): 69–84.

30. K.R. Evans, R.G. McFarland, B. Dietz, and F. Jaramillo "Advancing sales performance research: A focus on five underresearched topic areas," *Journal of Personal Selling and Sales Management* 32, 1 (2012): 89–106.

31. Alan J. Dubinsky, R.D. Howell, Thomas N. Ingram, and D.N. Bellenge, "Salesforce Socialization," *Journal of Marketing* 50, 4 (1986): 192–207.

32. Sean Valentine, Lynn Godkin, and Margaret Lucero, "Ethical Context, Organizational Commitment, and Person-Organization Fit," *Journal of Business Ethics* 41, 4 (December 2002): 349–360.

33. Bruce H. Drake, Mark Meckler, and Debra Stephens, "Transitional Ethics: Responsibilities of Supervisors for Supporting Employee Development," *Journal of Business Ethics* 38, n1–2 (June 2002): 141–155.

34. Ferrell and Gresham, "A Contingency Framework," 87–96.

35. R. C. Ford and W. D. Richardson, "Ethical Decision Making: A Review of the Empirical Literature," *Journal of Business Ethics* 13, 3 (March 1994): 205–221; Loe, Ferrell, and Mansfield, "A Review of Empirical Studies."

36. National Business Ethics Survey, *How Employees Perceive Ethics at Work* (Washington, DC: Ethics Resource Center, 2000), 30.

37. "Top Office Supplies That Are Stolen & The Average Value of Contents In A Woman's Purse," *KMLE*, May 16, 2012, http://kmle1079.cbslocal.com/2012/05/16/top-office-supplies-that-are-stolen/ (accessed March 9, 2015).

38. Mason Braswell, "Ex-Schwab broker barred for alleged theft of $1 million in office supplies," *Investment News*, November 19, 2014, http://www.investmentnews.com/article/20141119/FREE/141119887/ex-schwab-broker-barred-for-alleged-theft-of-1-million-in-office (accessed February 26, 2015).

39. National Retail Federation, "Retail Theft Decreased in 2011, According to Preliminary National Retail Security Survey Findings," June 22, 2012, http://www.nrf.com/modules.php?name=News&op=viewlive&sp_id=1389 (accessed April 12, 2013).

40. International Federation of Accountants, *International Ethics Standards Board for Accountants™—Handbook of the Code of Ethics for Professional Accountants*, 2013 ed, http://www.ifac.org/sites/default/files/publications/files/2013-IESBA-Handbook.pdf (accessed February 26, 2015); International Federation of Accountants, "Membership," November 7, 2014, http://www.ifac.org/about-ifac/membership (accessed February 26, 2015).

41. Julie Steinberg and Emily Glazer, "J.P. Morgan Questioned for Conflicts of Interest," *The Wall Street Journal*, July 27, 2014, http://www.wsj.com/articles/j-p-morgan-examined-for-conflicts-of-interest-1406504236 (accessed February 26, 2015).

42. Ned Levin, Emily Glazer, and Christopher M. Matthews, "Emails Track J.P. Morgan Hire in China," *The Wall Street Journal*, February 7–8, 2015, A1, A8.

43. National Business Ethics Survey, 30.

44. David Hollingworth and Sean Valentine, "The Moderating Effect of Perceived Organizational Ethical Context on Employees' Ethical Issue Recognition and Ethical Judgments," *Journal of Business Ethics*, 2014, doi: 10.1007/s10551-014-2088-9.

45. Peter Verhezen, "Giving Voice in a Culture of Silence: From a Culture of Compliance to a Culture of Integrity," *Journal of Business Ethics* 96, 2 (2010): 187–206.

46. Gene R. Laczniak and Patrick E. Murphy, "Stakeholder Theory and Marketing: Moving from a Firm-Centric to a Societal Perspective," *Journal of Public Policy & Marketing* 31, 2 (2012): 284–292.

47. "Camden Values," Camden website, http://camdenliving.com/about-camden/meet-camden/camden-values/index.htm (accessed February 10, 2015); Christopher Tkaczyk, "Pass Go, Collect Dough," *Fortune*, June 16, 2014, p. 28.

48. R.L. Jepperson, "Institutions, institutional effects, and institutionalism," In Walter W. Powell and Paul J. DiMaggio (eds.), *The New Institutionalism in Organizational Analysis* (Chicago, IL: University of Chicago Press, 1991).

49. Patrick E. Murphy, Gene R. Laczniak, G. R., and Andrea Prothero, *Ethics in Marketing: International Cases and Perspectives* (New York, NY: Routledge, 2012).

50. Lynn G. Zucker, "The Role of Institutionalization in Cultural Persistence," *American Sociological Review* 42, 5 (October 1977): 726–743.

51. Paul J. DiMaggio and Walter W. Powell, "The Iron Cage Revisited: Institutionalized Isomorphism and Collective Rationality in Organizational Fields," *American Sociological Review* 48, 2 (April 1983): 147–60; John W. Meyer and Brian Rowan, "Institutionalized Organization: Formal Structure as Myth and Ceremony," *American Journal of Sociology* 83, 2 (September 1977): 340–363.

52. Fluor Corporation, *The Code of Business Conduct and Ethics*, October 2014.

53. Jaclyn Trop, "Bridgestone Admits Guilt in U.S. Price-Fixing Case," *The New York Times*, February 13, 2014, http://www.nytimes.com/2014/02/14/business/bridgestone-admits-guilt-in-us-price-fixing-case.html?_r=0 (accessed February 26, 2015).

54. Patrick Wintour, "HSBC scandal caused horrible damage to reputation, says chairman," *The Guardian*, February 25, 2015, http://www.theguardian.com/business/2015/feb/25/hsbc-scandal-horrible-damage-reputation-chairman (accessed February 26, 2015); Margot Patrick and Max Colchester, "Chairman Says HSBC Reputation Damaged by Swiss Unit Allegations," *The Wall Street Journal*, February 25, 2015, http://www.wsj.com/articles/chairman-says-hsbc-reputation-damaged-by-swiss-bank-charges-1424888628 (accessed February 26, 2015).

55. Walter W. Powell and Paul J. DiMaggio (eds.), *The New Institutionalism in Organizational Analysis* (Chicago, IL: University of Chicago Press, 1991).

56. Tina M. Dacin, "Isomorphism in Context: The Power and Prescription of Institutional Norms," *Academy of Management Journal* 40, 1 (February 1997): 46–81.

57. Sebastian Anthony, "Batteries are so passé: Toyota unveils its fuel cell car production line," *Ars Technica*, http://arstechnica.com/cars/2015/02/batteries-are-so-passe-toyota-*unveils*-its-fuel-cell-car-production-line/ (accessed February 26, 2015); Doug Newcomb, *Forbes*, "Toyota's 'Future' Rides On Mirai Hydrogen Vehicle and Its Free Fuel-Cell Patents," *Forbes*, February 25, 2015, http://www.forbes.com/sites/dougnewcomb/2015/02/25/toyotas-future-rides-on-mirai-hydrogen-vehicle-and-its-free-fuel-cell-patents/ (accessed February 26, 2015).

58. Lynn G. Zucker, "The Role of Institutionalization in Cultural Persistence," *American Sociological Review* 42, 5 (October 1977): 726–743.

59. John W. Meyer and Brian Rowan, "Institutionalized Organization: Formal Structure as Myth and Ceremony," *American Journal of Sociology* 83, 2 (September 1977): 340–363.

60. Jay M. Handelman and Stephen J. Arnold, "The Rule of Marketing Actions with a Social Dimension," *Journal of Marketing* 63, 3 (1999): 33–48.

61. John L. Campbell, "Why Would Corporations Behave in Socially Responsible Ways? An Institutional Theory of Corporate Social Responsibility," *Academy of Management Review* 32, 3 (2007): 946–967; J. Galaskiewicz, "Making corporate actors accountable: Institution-building in Minneapolis-St. Paul," In W. W. Powell & P. J. DiMaggio (eds.), *The New Institutionalism in Organizational Analysis*, 293–310 (Chicago, IL: University of Chicago Press, 1991).

62. Tobias Hahn, "Reciprocal Stakeholder Behavior: A Motive-Based Approach to the Implementation of Normative Stakeholder Demands," *Business & Society* 54, 1 (2015): 9–51.

63. Bart Victor and Carroll Underwood Stephens, "Business Ethics: A Synthesis of Normative Philosophy and Empirical Social Science," *Business Ethics Quarterly* 4, 2 (1994): 145–155.

64. John Rawls, *A Theory of Justice*, (Cambridge, MA: Harvard University Press, 1971).

65. Ibid.

66. Patrick E. Murphy, Gene R. Laczniak, G. R., and Andrea Prothero, *Ethics in Marketing: International Cases and Perspectives* (New York, NY: Routledge, 2012).

67. Joel Gehman, Linda K. Treviño, and Raghu Garud, "Values Work: A Process Study of the Emergence and Performance of Organizational Values Practices," *Academy of Management Journal* 56, 1 (2013): 84–112.

68. Shalom H. Schwartz, "Cultural value differences: Some implications for work," *Applied Psychology: An International Review* 48, 1 (1999): 23–47.

69. M. Callon, P. Lascoumes, and Y. Barthe, *Acting in an Uncertain World: An Essay on Technical Democracy* (Cambridge, MA: MIT Press, 2009).

70. Joel Gehman, Linda K. Treviño, and Raghu Garud, "Values Work: A Process Study of the Emergence and Performance of Organizational Values Practices," *Academy of Management Journal* 56, 1 (2013): 84–112.

71. Bert Scholtens and Lammertjan Dam, "Cultural Values and International Differences in Business Ethics," *Journal of Business Ethics* 75, 3 (2007): 273–284.

72. Marriott, *2011 Annual Report*, http://investor.shareholder.com/mar/marriottAR11/index.html (accessed March 9, 2015).

73. Gary R. Weaver and Linda K. Trevino, "Compliance and Values Oriented Ethics Programs: Influences on Employees' Attitudes and Behavior," *Business Ethics Quarterly* 9, 2 (1999): 315–335.

74. Bechtel Corporation, "Bechtel's approach to ethics training," YouTube, January 24, 2013, http://www.youtube.com/watch?v=EG9qWOloLR0 (accessed March 9, 2015); Bechtel Corporation, "Ethics," http://www.bechtel.com/ethics.html (accessed March 9, 2015); Bechtel Corporation, "Bechtel's Chief Ethics and Compliance Officer Shares Best Practices at European Ethics Conference," January 24, 2013, http://www.bechtel.com/2013-01-24.html (accessed April 12, 2013); Bechtel, "Ethics & Compliance," 2015, http://www.bechtel.com/about-us/ethics-compliance/ (accessed February 26, 2015).

75. UNM Daniels Fund Ethics Imitative, "Target: Putting Customers First?" http://danielsethics.mgt.unm.edu/pdf/target.pdf (accessed February 26, 2015); Susan Adams, "The World's Most Ethical Companies 2014," *Forbes*, March 20, 2014, http://www.forbes.com/sites/susanadams/2014/03/20/the-worlds-most-ethical-companies/ (accessed February 26, 2015);

76. Mark. D. Promislo and Robert A. Giacalone, "Sick about Unethical Business," *BizEd*, January/February 2013, 20–26.

77. Total, "Code of Conduct," http://www.total.com/sites/default/files/atoms/files/code_poster_va.pdf (accessed March 9, 2015).

CHAPTER 6

INDIVIDUAL FACTORS: MORAL PHILOSOPHIES AND VALUES

CHAPTER OBJECTIVES

- Understand how moral philosophies and values influence individual and group ethical decision making in business

- Compare and contrast the teleological, deontological, virtue, and justice perspectives of moral philosophy

- Discuss the impact of philosophies on business ethics

- Recognize the stages of cognitive moral development and its shortcomings

- Introduce white-collar crime as it relates to moral philosophies, values, and corporate culture

CHAPTER OUTLINE

AN ETHICAL DILEMMA*

Connor graduated from Southern Arizona University with a B.S. in operations and logistics after he came back from his tour in the army. His work in the army prepared him well as a manager in operations and logistics, and it showed when he was hired at AlumaArc, a manufacturing facility that produced various tank parts for the U.S. Army. Connor's coworkers and fellow managers at his company respected him for the proficiency he showed in his work. Within 18 months he became the key person in the logistics department, and a few months after that Connor became one of 20 managers in charge of the third shift. Above him were two Assistant General Managers (AGMs) and the General Manager. The plant employed 2,000 general workers and several hundred specialists.

Recently, the U.S. Army asked AlumaArc to step up production. This meant adding another shift with existing personnel and a number of incentives for increased productivity. At first, Connor was happy with the new business AlumaArc was getting. However, as he began examining the amount of output required to meet the army's expectations, he grew concerned. Even with overtime, the plant would still find it difficult to meet output goals running at maximum capacity. He also noticed many of the workers appeared worn out.

Because the plant had heavy equipment that required workers to take several safety precautions, it was standard procedure for workers to fill out a checklist marking off the different safety requirements before they began operating the machinery. One day Connor noticed the checklist for his shift hadn't been filled out. He asked Joe, one of the employees, about why it hadn't been done.

"Oh, we've been so busy lately trying to meet our production quota that George told us we could just skip it," Joe explained. George was one of the AGMs.

"But these checklists are used to make sure you're operating everything safely," Connor responded.

Joe looked grim. "Well, if we filled them out, we'd just be lying anyway." He informed Conner that to save time, the workers were encouraged to bypass standard safety procedures. Additionally, Connor was horrified to realize many of the workers were not taking their required breaks in order to get rewarded for increasing their output.

Later that day, Connor confronted George. "George, these incentives are encouraging careless and unsafe behaviors. Employees are skipping safety procedures and breaks to get the work done. It's only a matter of time before someone gets seriously hurt."

George looked firmly at Connor. "I realize there are potential risks, but we can't afford to hire additional workers right now. If we can just meet this output, it'll increase our business 10-fold. We'll be able to hire new workers and pay our current employees more."

Connor was stunned. "But these are people we are putting at risk!"

George sighed. "Connor, each worker has a choice whether or not they take advantage of these incentives. They are not being forced to do anything they don't want to do. Besides, these are not my rules. The GM put these incentives in place. It's really out of my control. Just think about it...we're doing it for the greater good of our company and our employees."

Connor replied, "But if they refuse, they are probably afraid they'll lose their jobs. And even if they do feel the risks are worth it, isn't it our job to make sure they have safe work conditions?"

Although George continued to reassure him, Connor left George's office determined to enforce all safety protocols and force his employees to take their required breaks. He figured if top management would not consider the well-being of the employees, he would do what he could to protect those who fell under his authority.

Later that week, George came up to Connor and said, "I'm sorry to tell you this, but your shift is not meeting the required output levels. We need to meet these deadlines quickly and accurately, and your shift has always been our fastest. Without you we're never going to get the work done on time. That means we'll have to start laying off employees who aren't performing up to expectations." Connor recognized George's veiled threat but refused to compromise his workers' safety. Meanwhile, he began hearing stories of employees getting injured on other shifts.

Connor decided to talk to Wendy Smith, the General Manager. He knew she probably was not pleased with him, but he felt it necessary to try to persuade her about the dangers of what the company was doing. Connor wondered how he should approach Wendy. If he was not careful, she could fire him. He did not want to be disrespectful, but he also didn't want to be a part of a company that knowingly put their employees in harm's way.

QUESTIONS | EXERCISES

1. Describe Conner's moral dilemma.
2. In AlumaArc's reasoning, the benefits of increasing production outweigh the risks of potential injuries. How could this approach potentially backfire?
3. How should Connor approach this issue?

*This case is strictly hypothetical; any resemblance to real persons, companies, or situations is coincidental.

Most discussions of business ethics address the moral philosophies of the individual in ethical decision making, and the model we provided in Chapter 5 identifies individual moral perspectives as a central component of ethical decision making. In this chapter, we provide a detailed description and analysis of how individuals' backgrounds and philosophies influence their decisions. People often use their individual moral philosophies to justify decisions or explain their actions. To understand how people make ethical decisions, it is useful to have a grasp of the major types of moral philosophies. In this chapter, we discuss the stages of cognitive development as they relate to these moral philosophies. We also explain why cognitive moral development theory may not explain as much as we thought. Additionally, we examine white-collar crime as it relates to personal morals and philosophies.

MORAL PHILOSOPHY DEFINED

When people talk about philosophy, they usually refer to the general system of values by which they live. **Moral philosophy**, on the other hand, refers to the specific principles or values people use to decide what is right and wrong. It is important to understand the distinction between moral philosophies and business ethics. Moral philosophies are person-specific, while business ethics is based on decisions made by groups or when carrying out tasks to meet business objectives. A moral philosophy is a person's principles and values. In the context of business, ethics refers to what the group, firm, or organization defines as right or wrong actions that pertain to its business operations and the objective of profits, earnings per share, or some other financial measure of success. For example, a production manager may be guided by a general philosophy of management that emphasizes encouraging workers to get to know as much as possible about the product they are manufacturing. However, the manager's moral philosophy comes into play when he must make decisions such as whether to notify employees in advance of upcoming layoffs. Although workers prefer advance warning, issuing that warning could jeopardize the quality and quantity of production. Such decisions require a person to evaluate the "rightness," or morality of choices in terms of his or her own principles and values.

Moral philosophies are guidelines for "determining how conflicts in human interests are to be settled and for optimizing mutual benefit of people living together in groups."[1] These philosophies direct people as they formulate business strategies and resolve specific ethical issues. However, there is no single moral philosophy everyone accepts. Moral philosophies are often used to defend a particular type of economic system and individuals' behavior within these systems.

Adam Smith is considered the father of free-market capitalism. He was a professor of logic and moral philosophy and wrote the treatise "The Theory of Moral Sentiments" (1759) and the book *Inquiry into the Nature and Causes of the Wealth of Nations* (1776). Smith believed business was and should be guided by the morals of good people. But in the eighteenth century, Smith could not imagine the complexity of modern markets, the size of multinationals, or the fact that four or five companies could gain control of the vast majority of the resources of the world. His ideas did not envision the full force of democracy, or the immense wealth and power some firms could wield within countries.

Under capitalism, some managers view profit as the ultimate goal of an enterprise and may not be concerned about the impact of their firms' decisions on society. The economist Milton Friedman supports this viewpoint, contending the market will reward or punish companies for unethical conduct without the need for government regulation.[2]

The emergence of this Friedman-type capitalism as the dominant and most widely accepted economic system created market-driven societies around the world. Even China's communist government adapted national capitalism and free enterprise to help it become a leading economic power.

The United States exported the idea that the invisible hand of free-market capitalism can solve the troubles of mankind and guide societies toward greater happiness and prosperity as a result of the increased availability of products. Marketing helps consumers understand, compare, and obtain these products, thereby increasing the efficiency and effectiveness of the exchange. However, free markets will not solve all problems. For example, excessive consumption has negative effects on the environment and can be psychologically, spiritually, and physically unhealthy.[3] More is not necessarily best in every situation.

Economic systems not only allocate resources and products within a society but also influence, and are influenced by, the actions and beliefs of individuals (morals) and of society (laws) as a whole. The success of an economic system depends on both its philosophical framework and on the individuals within the system who maintain moral philosophies that bring people together in a cooperative, efficient, and productive marketplace. There is a long Western tradition going back to Aristotle of questioning whether a market economy and individual moral behavior are compatible. Individuals in today's society exist within a framework of social, political, and economic institutions.

People facing ethical issues often base their decisions on their own values and principles of right or wrong, most of which they learned through the socialization process with the help of family members, social groups, religions, and formal education. Individual factors that influence decision making include personal moral philosophies. Ethical dilemmas arise in problem-solving situations when the rules governing decision making are vague or in conflict. In real-life situations, there is no substitute for an individual's own critical thinking and ability to accept responsibility for his or her decisions.

Moral philosophies are ideal moral perspectives that provide individuals with abstract principles for guiding their social existence. For example, a person's decision to recycle waste or to purchase or sell recycled or recyclable products is influenced by moral philosophies and individual attitudes toward recycling.[4] It is often difficult to implement an individual moral philosophy within the complex environment of a business organization. On the other hand, our economic system depends on individuals coming together and sharing philosophies to create the values, trust, and expectations that allow the system to work. Most employees within a business organization do not think about the particular moral philosophy they are using when confronted with an ethical issue.

Many theories associated with moral philosophies refer to a value orientation and concepts such as economics, idealism, and relativism. The concept of the **economic value orientation** is associated with values quantified by monetary means; according to this theory, if an act produces more economic value for its effort, then it should be accepted as ethical. **Idealism**, on the other hand, is a moral philosophy that places special value on ideas and ideals as products of the mind. The term refers to the efforts required to account for all objects in nature and experience and to assign to them a higher order of existence. Studies uncovered a positive correlation between idealistic thinking and ethical decision making. **Realism** is the view that an external world exists independent of our perceptions. Realists assume humankind is not naturally benevolent and kind, but instead inherently self-centered and competitive. According to realists, each person is ultimately guided by his or her own self-interest. Research shows a negative correlation between realistic thinking and ethical decision making. The belief that all actions are ultimately self-motivated seems to lead to a tendency toward unethical decision making.

MORAL PHILOSOPHIES

There are many moral philosophies, but because a detailed study of all of them is beyond the scope of this book, we will limit our discussion to those that are most applicable to the study of business ethics. Our approach focuses on the most basic concepts needed to help you understand the ethical decision-making process in business. We do not prescribe the use of any particular moral philosophy, for there is no one correct way to resolve ethical issues in business.

To help you understand how the moral philosophies discussed in this chapter may be applied in decision making, we use a hypothetical situation as an illustration. Suppose that Sam Colt, a sales representative, is preparing a sales presentation for his firm, Midwest Hardware, which manufactures nuts and bolts. Sam hopes to obtain a large sale from a construction firm that is building a bridge across the Mississippi River near St. Louis, Missouri. The bolts manufactured by Midwest Hardware have a 3 percent defect rate, which, although acceptable in the industry, makes them unsuitable for use in certain types of projects, such as those that may be subject to sudden, severe stress. The new bridge will be located near the New Madrid Fault line, the source of the United States' greatest earthquake in 1811. The epicenter of that earthquake, which caused extensive damage and altered the flow of the Mississippi, is less than 200 miles from the new bridge site. Earthquake experts believe there is a 50 percent chance that an earthquake with a magnitude greater than 7 will occur somewhere along the New Madrid Fault by the year 2030. Bridge construction in the area is not regulated by earthquake codes, however. If Sam wins the sale, he will earn a commission of $25,000 on top of his regular salary. But if he tells the contractor about the defect rate, Midwest may lose the sale to a competitor that markets bolts with a lower defect rate. Sam's ethical issue is whether to point out to the bridge contractor that, in the event of an earthquake, some Midwest bolts could fail, possibly resulting in the collapse of the bridge.

We will come back to this illustration as we discuss particular moral philosophies, asking how Sam Colt might use each philosophy to resolve his ethical issue. We don't judge the quality of Sam's decision, and we do not advocate any one moral philosophy; in fact, this illustration and Sam's decision rationales are necessarily simplistic as well as hypothetical. In reality, the decision maker would probably have many more factors to consider in making his or her choice and thus might reach a different decision. With that note of caution, we introduce the concept of goodness and several types of moral philosophy: teleology, deontology, the relativist perspective, virtue ethics, and justice (see Table 6–1).

Instrumental and Intrinsic Goodness

To appreciate moral philosophy, you must understand the different perspectives on the notion of goodness. Is there a clear and unwavering line between "good" and "bad"? What is the relationship between the ends and the means in generating "good" and "bad" outcomes? Is there some way to determine if the ends can be identified independently as good or bad? Because the answers can be complex and confusing, we have simplified the discussion. Aristotle, for example, argued that happiness is an intrinsically good end and that its goodness is natural and universal, without relativity. On the other hand, the philosopher Immanuel Kant argued that goodwill, seriously applied toward accomplishment, is the only thing good in itself.

TABLE 6–1 A Comparison of the Philosophies Used in Business Decisions

Teleology	Stipulates acts are morally right or acceptable if they produce some desired result, such as realization of self-interest or utility
Egoism	Defines right or acceptable actions as those that maximize a particular person's self-interest as defined by the individual
Utilitarianism	Defines right or acceptable actions as those that maximize total utility, or the greatest good for the greatest number of people
Deontology	Focuses on the preservation of individual rights and on the intentions associated with a particular behavior rather than on its consequences
Relativist	Evaluates ethicalness subjectively on the basis of individual and group experiences
Virtue ethics	Assumes what is moral in a given situation is not only what conventional morality requires but also what the mature person with a "good" moral character deems appropriate
Justice	Evaluates ethicalness on the basis of fairness: distributive, procedural, and interactional

© Cengage Learning

Two basic concepts of goodness are monism and pluralism. **Monists** believe only one thing is intrinsically good, and pluralists believe two or more things are intrinsically good. Monists are often characterized by **hedonism**—the idea that pleasure is the ultimate good, or the best moral end involves the greatest balance of pleasure over pain. Hedonism defines right or acceptable behavior as that which maximizes personal pleasure. Moral philosophers describe those who believe more pleasure is better as **quantitative hedonists** and those who believe it is possible to get too much of a good thing (such as pleasure) as **qualitative hedonists**.

Pluralists, often referred to as non-hedonists, take the opposite position that no *one* thing is intrinsically good. For example, a pluralist might view beauty, aesthetic experience, knowledge, and personal affection as ultimate goods. Plato argued that the good life is a mixture of (1) moderation and fitness, (2) proportion and beauty, (3) intelligence and wisdom, (4) sciences and arts, and (5) pure pleasures of the soul.

Although all pluralists are non-hedonists, all monists are not necessarily hedonists. An individual can believe in a single intrinsic good other than pleasure; Machiavelli and Nietzsche held power to be the sole good, for example, and Kant's belief in the single virtue of goodwill classifies him as a monistic non-hedonist.

A more modern view is expressed in the instrumentalist position. Sometimes called pragmatists, **instrumentalists** reject the ideas that (1) ends can be separated from the means that produce them and (2) ends, purposes, or outcomes are intrinsically good in and of themselves. The philosopher John Dewey argued that the difference between ends and means is merely a matter of the individual's perspective; thus, almost any action can be an end or a mean. Dewey gives the example that people eat to be able to work, and they work to be able to eat. From a practical standpoint, an end is only a remote mean, and the means are but a series of acts viewed from an earlier stage. From this conclusion it follows there is no such thing as a single, universal end.

A discussion of moral value often revolves around the nature of goodness, but theories of moral obligation change the question to "What makes an action right or obligatory?" **Goodness theories** typically focus on the *end result* of actions and the goodness or happiness created by them. **Obligation theories** emphasize the *means* and *motives* by which actions are justified, and are divided into the categories of teleology and deontology.

Teleology

Teleology (from the Greek word for "end" or "purpose") refers to moral philosophies in which an act is considered morally right or acceptable if it produces some desired result, such as pleasure, knowledge, career growth, the realization of self-interest, utility, wealth, or even fame. Teleological philosophies assess the moral worth of a behavior by looking at its consequences, and thus moral philosophers today often refer to these theories as **consequentialism**. Two important teleological philosophies that often guide decision making in individual business decisions are egoism and utilitarianism.

Egoism defines right or acceptable behavior in terms of its consequences for the individual. Egoists believe they should make decisions that maximize their own self-interest, which is defined differently by each individual. Depending on the egoist, self-interest may be construed as physical well-being, power, pleasure, fame, a satisfying career, a good family life, wealth, or something else. In an ethical decision-making situation, an egoist will probably choose the alternative that contributes most to his or her self-interest. Many believe egoistic people and companies are inherently unethical, short-term oriented, and willing to take advantage of any opportunity for gain. Some telemarketers demonstrate egoism when they prey on elderly consumers who may be vulnerable because of loneliness or fear of losing their financial independence. Thousands of senior citizens fall victim to fraudulent telemarketers every year, in many cases losing all their savings and sometimes even their homes.

However, there also is **enlightened egoism**. Enlightened egoists take a long-range perspective and allow for the well-being of others although their own self-interest remains paramount. An example of enlightened egoism is a person helping a turtle across a highway because if it were killed the person would feel distressed.[5] Enlightened egoists may abide by professional codes of ethics, control pollution, avoid cheating on taxes, help create jobs, and support community projects not because these actions benefit others but because they help achieve some ultimate individual goal, such as advancement within their firms. An enlightened egoist might call management's attention to a coworker who is making false accounting reports, but only to safeguard the company's reputation and thus the egoist's own job security. In addition, an enlightened egoist could become a whistle-blower and report misconduct to a regulatory agency to receive a reward for exposing misconduct.

Let's return to the hypothetical case of Sam Colt, who must decide whether to warn the bridge contractor that 3 percent of Midwest Hardware's bolts are likely to be defective. If he is an egoist, he will choose the alternative that maximizes his own self-interest. If he defines his self-interest in terms of personal wealth, his personal moral philosophy may lead him to value a $25,000 commission more than a chance to reduce the risk of a bridge collapse. As a result, an egoist might well resolve this ethical dilemma by keeping quiet about the bolts' defect rate, hoping to win the sale and the $25,000 commission. He may rationalize that there is a slim chance of an earthquake, that bolts would not be a factor in a major earthquake, and even if defective bolts were a factor, no one would actually be able to prove they caused the bridge to collapse.

Like egoism, **utilitarianism** is concerned with consequences, but unlike the egoist, the utilitarian seeks the greatest good for the greatest number of people. Utilitarians believe they should make decisions that result in the greatest total *utility,* or the greatest benefit for all those affected by a decision. For instance, one might use a utilitarianism perspective to argue for companies who legally sell harmful products, such as tobacco, guns, or alcohol. It has been argued that despite their drawbacks, allowing them to be sold legally is less harmful than having them sold illegally and unregulated.[6] Such an approach influenced similar forms of legislation, such as the laws in Colorado and Washington permitting the regulated sale of recreational marijuana. Utilitarian decision making relies on a systematic comparison of the costs and benefits to all affected parties. Using such a cost–benefit analysis, a utilitarian decision maker calculates the utility of the consequences of all possible alternatives and then selects the one that results in the greatest benefit. For example, the U.S. Supreme Court ruled that supervisors are responsible for the sexual misconduct of employees, even if the employers knew nothing about the behavior, a decision that established a strict standard for harassment on the job. One of the justices wrote that the burden on the employer to prevent harassment is "one of the costs of doing business."[7] The Court decided the greatest utility to society would result from forcing businesses to prevent harassment.

In evaluating an action's consequences, utilitarians must consider all of the potential costs and benefits for all of the people affected by a decision. For example, General Motors' engineers noticed during testing that there were ignition control switch problems in some of its car models, including the Saturn Ion and Chevrolet Cobalt. Recommendations for redesigning the switch or the keys went unheeded due to cost concerns. Nearly a decade passed before recalls were implemented on these earlier models. By this time, an estimated 40 people had died in crashes thought to have been caused by ignition failures. GM recalled more than 2.5 million vehicles and the CEO had to testify before Congress as to why GM did not take action sooner when the problems were initially discovered.[8] If GM had done a utilitarian analysis and included the costs associated with massive recalls, penalties, and consumer injuries, it might have chosen to fix the problem despite the initial costs.

Utilitarians use various criteria to evaluate the morality of an action. Some utilitarian philosophers argue that general rules should be followed to decide which action is best.[9] These **rule utilitarians** determine behavior on the basis of principles or rules designed to promote the greatest utility, rather than on individual examinations of each situation they encounter. One such rule might be "Bribery is wrong." If people felt free to offer bribes whenever they might be useful, the world would become chaotic; therefore, a rule prohibiting bribery would increase utility. A rule utilitarian would not bribe an official, even to preserve workers' jobs, but instead would adhere strictly to the rule. Rule utilitarians do not automatically accept conventional moral rules, however; if they determined an alternative rule would promote greater utility, they would advocate its use instead.

Other utilitarian philosophers have argued that the rightness of each individual action must be evaluated to determine whether it produces the greatest utility for the greatest number of people.[10] These **act utilitarians** examine specific actions, rather than the general rules governing them, to assess whether they will result in the greatest utility. Rules such as "Bribery is wrong" serve only as general guidelines for act utilitarians. They would likely agree that bribery is generally wrong, not because there is anything inherently wrong with bribery, but because the total amount of utility decreases when one person's interests are placed ahead of those of society. In a particular case, however, an act utilitarian might argue that bribery is acceptable. For example, sales managers might believe their firm will not win a construction contract unless a local government official gets a bribe, and if the firm does not obtain the contract, it will have to lay off 100 workers. The manager might therefore argue that bribery is justified because saving 100 jobs creates more utility than obeying a law. For example, Goodyear Tire & Rubber paid $16 million to settle charges of bribery. According to the SEC, two African subsidiaries of the firm paid more than

$3.2 million to gain tire sales in Kenya and Angola. These bribes were recorded as legitimate business expenses.[11] These Goodyear subsidiaries may have decided winning the contracts generated the most utility for the company.

Now suppose that Sam Colt, the bolt salesperson, is a utilitarian. Before making his decision, he would conduct a cost–benefit analysis to assess which alternative would create the greatest utility. On the one hand, building the bridge would improve roadways and allow more people to cross the Mississippi River to reach jobs in St. Louis. The project would create hundreds of jobs, enhance the local economy, and unite communities on both sides of the river. Additionally, it would increase the revenues of Midwest Hardware, allowing the firm to invest more in research to lower the defect rate of the bolts it produces in the future. On the other hand, a bridge collapse could kill or injure as many as 100 people. But the bolts have only a 3 percent defect rate, there is only a 50 percent probability of an earthquake *somewhere* along the fault line, and there might be only a few cars on the bridge at the time of a disaster.

After analyzing the costs and benefits of the situation, Sam might rationalize that building the bridge with his company's bolts would create more utility (jobs, unity, economic growth, and company growth) than telling the bridge contractor the bolts might fail in an earthquake. If so, a utilitarian would probably not alert the bridge contractor to the defect rate of the bolts.

Deontology

Deontology (from the Greek word for "ethics") refers to moral philosophies that focus on the rights of individuals and the intentions associated with a particular behavior rather than its consequences. Fundamental to deontological theory is the idea that equal respect must be given to all persons. Unlike utilitarians, deontologists argue that there are some things we should *not* do, even to maximize utility. For example, deontologists would consider it wrong to kill an innocent person or commit a serious injustice against someone, no matter how much greater social utility might result from doing so, because such an action would infringe on individual rights. The utilitarian, however, might consider an action resulting in a person's death acceptable if that action leads to some greater benefit. Deontological philosophies regard certain behaviors as inherently right, and the determination of this rightness focuses on the individual actor, not on society. Therefore these perspectives are sometimes referred to as **nonconsequentialism**, a system of ethics based on *respect for persons.*

Contemporary deontology has been greatly influenced by the German philosopher Immanuel Kant, who developed the so-called **categorical imperative**: "Act as if the maxim of thy action were to become by thy will a universal law of nature."[12] Simply put, if you feel comfortable allowing everyone in the world to see you commit an act and if your rationale for acting in a particular manner is suitable to become a universal principle guiding behavior, then committing that act is ethical. People who borrow money and promise to return it with no intention of keeping that promise cannot "universalize" their act. If everyone borrowed money without the intention of returning it, no one would take such promises seriously, and all lending would cease.[13] The rationale for the action would not be a suitable universal principle, and the act could not be considered ethical.

The term *nature* is crucial for deontologists. In general, deontologists regard the nature of moral principles as permanent and stable, and they believe compliance with these principles define ethicalness. Deontologists believe individuals have certain absolute rights, including freedom of conscience, freedom of consent, freedom of privacy, freedom of speech, and due process.[14]

To decide if a behavior is ethical, deontologists look for conformity to moral principles. For example, if a manufacturing worker becomes ill or dies as a result of conditions in the workplace, a deontologist might argue that the company must modify its production processes to correct the condition, no matter what the cost—even if it means bankrupting the company and thus causing all workers to lose their jobs. In contrast, a utilitarian would analyze all the costs and benefits of modifying production processes and make a decision on that basis. This example is greatly oversimplified, of course, but it helps to clarify the difference between teleology and deontology. In short, teleological philosophies consider the *ends* associated with an action, whereas deontological philosophies consider the *means*.

Returning again to our bolt salesperson, let's consider a deontological Sam Colt. He would probably feel obligated to tell the bridge contractor about the defect rate because of the potential loss of life that might result from an earthquake-caused bridge collapse. Even though constructing the bridge would benefit residents and earn Sam a substantial commission, the failure of the bolts during an earthquake would infringe on the rights of any person crossing the bridge at the time of the collapse. Thus, the deontological Sam would likely inform the bridge contractor about the defect rate and point out the earthquake risk, even though he would probably lose the sale as a result.

As with utilitarians, deontologists may be divided into those who focus on moral rules and those who focus on the nature of the acts themselves. **Rule deontologists** believe conformity to general moral principles based on logic determines ethicalness. Examples include Kant's categorical imperative and the Golden Rule of the Judeo-Christian tradition: "Do unto others as you would have them do unto you." Such rules, or principles, guiding ethical behavior override the imperatives that emerge from a specific context. One could argue that Jeffery Wigand—who exposed the underside of the tobacco industry when he blew the whistle on his employer, Brown & Williamson Tobacco—was such a rule deontologist. Although it cost him financially and socially, Wigand testified to Congress about the realities of marketing cigarettes and their effects on society.[15]

Rule deontology is determined by the relationship between the basic rights of the individual and a set of rules governing conduct. For example, a video store owner accused of distributing obscene materials could argue from a rule deontological perspective that the basic right to freedom of speech overrides the indecent or pornographic aspects of his business. Indeed, the free-speech argument has held up in many U.S. courts. Kant and rule deontologists would support a process of discovery to identify the moral issues relevant to a firm's mission and objectives. Then they would follow a process of justifying that mission or those objectives based on rules.[16] An example of a rule deontologist might be Tony Hsieh, CEO of Zappos. When one of Zappos' websites called 6pm.com malfunctioned—causing all items to be priced at $49.95 for six hours—Zappos honored all the orders made during this time period. The company lost approximately $1.6 million from the technical glitch but valued its relationships with customers as more important.[17] This fits with Zappos' philosophy of delivering "WOW through service."

Act deontologists, in contrast, hold that actions are the proper basis to judge morality or ethicalness. Act deontology requires a person use equity, fairness, and impartiality when making and enforcing decisions.[18] For act deontologists, past experiences are more important than rules; rules serve only as guidelines in the decision-making process. In effect, act deontologists suggest people simply *know* that certain acts are right or wrong, regardless of their consequences. In addition, act deontologists consider the unique characteristics of a particular act or moment in time as taking precedence over any rule. For example, many people view data collection by Internet sites as a violation of personal privacy; regardless of any website's stated rules or policies, many Internet users want to be left alone unless they provide permission to be tracked while online. Privacy has become such an issue that the government is considering regulation to protect online users.[19] Research suggests that rule and act deontological principles play a larger role in a person's decision than teleological philosophies.[20]

As we have seen, ethical issues can be evaluated from many different perspectives. Each type of philosophy discussed here provides a clear basis for deciding whether a particular action was right or wrong. Adherents of different personal moral philosophies may disagree in their evaluations of a given action, yet all are behaving ethically *according to their own standards*. The relativist perspective may be helpful in understanding how people make such decisions in practice.

Relativist Perspective

From the **relativist perspective**, definitions of ethical behavior are derived subjectively from the experiences of individuals and groups. Relativists use themselves or the people around them as their basis for defining ethical standards, and the various forms of relativism include descriptive, meta-ethical, and normative.[21] **Descriptive relativism** relates to observations of other cultures. Different cultures exhibit different norms, customs, and values, but these observations say nothing about the higher questions of ethical justification. At this point meta-ethical relativism comes into play. **Meta-ethical relativism** proposes that people naturally see situations from their own perspectives, and there is no objective way of resolving ethical disputes between different value systems and individuals. Simply put, one culture's moral philosophy cannot logically be preferred to another's because no meaningful basis for comparison exists. Because ethical rules are embedded in a specific culture, the values and behaviors of people in one culture do not generally influence the behaviors of people in another culture.[22] Finally, at the individual level of reasoning, we have **normative relativism**. Normative relativists assume one person's opinion is as good as another's.[23]

Basic relativism acknowledges that we live in a world in which people have many different views and bases from which to justify decisions as right or wrong. The relativist looks to the interacting groups and tries to determine probable solutions based on group consensus. When formulating business strategies and plans, for example, a relativist would try to anticipate the conflicts that might arise between the different philosophies held by members of the organization, suppliers, customers, and the community at large.

The relativist observes the actions of members of an involved group and attempts to determine that group's consensus on a given behavior. A positive consensus signifies that the group considers the action to be ethical. However, such judgments may not remain valid forever. As circumstances evolve or the makeup of the group changes, a formerly accepted behavior may come to be viewed as wrong or unethical, or vice versa. Within the accounting profession, for example, it was traditionally considered unethical to advertise. However, advertising has now gained acceptance among accountants. This shift in ethical views may be the result of the increase in the number of accountants that led to greater competition. Moreover, the federal government investigated the restrictions accounting groups placed on their members and concluded that they inhibited free competition. Consequently, advertising is now acceptable because of the informal consensus that emerged on this issue in the accounting industry.

One problem with relativism is it emphasizes peoples' differences while ignoring their basic similarities. Similarities across different people and cultures—such as beliefs against incest, murder, and theft, or beliefs that reciprocity and respect for the elderly are good—may be hard to explain from the relativist perspective. Additionally, studies suggest relativism is negatively correlated to a person's sensitivity to ethical issues. Thus, if someone is a relativist, he or she will be less likely to detect issues with an ethical component.[24] On the other hand, managers with high relativism may show more commitment to completing a project. This indicates that relativism is associated with dedication to group values and objectives, leading to less independent ethical decision making.[25]

If Midwest Hardware salesperson Sam Colt was a relativist, he would attempt to determine consensus before deciding whether to tell his prospective customer about the bolts' defect rate. The relativist Sam Colt would look at his company's policy and at the general industry standards for disclosure. He might also informally survey his colleagues and superiors as well as consult industry trade journals and codes of ethics. Such investigations would help him determine the group consensus that should reflect a variety of moral philosophies. If he learns company policy and industry practice suggest discussing defect rates with those customers for whom faulty bolts may cause serious problems, he may infer there is a consensus on the matter. As a relativist, he probably would inform the bridge contractor that some of the bolts may fail, perhaps leading to a bridge collapse in the event of an earthquake. Conversely, if he determines that the normal practice in his company and the industry is not to inform customers about defect rates, he would probably not discuss the bolt defect rate with the bridge contractor.

Virtue Ethics

Virtue ethics argues that ethical behavior involves not only adhering to conventional moral standards but also considering what a mature person with a "good" moral character would deem appropriate in a given situation. A virtue represents an acquired disposition valued as a part of an individual's character. As individuals develop socially, they come to behave in ways they consider to be moral.[26] A person with the virtue of honesty will be disposed to tell the truth because it is considered to be the right approach in terms of human communication.

A virtue is considered praiseworthy because it is an achievement that an individual developed through practice and commitment.[27] Proponents of virtue ethics often list basic goods as virtues that are presented as positive and useful mental habits or cultivated character traits. Aristotle named loyalty, courage, wit, community, and judgment as "excellences" society requires. While listing the most important virtues is a popular theoretical task, the philosopher John Dewey cautions that virtues should not be looked at separately, and points out that examining interactions between virtues actually provides the best idea of a person's integrity of character.

The virtue ethics approach to business can be summarized as follows:

1. Good corporate ethics programs encourage individual virtue and integrity.

2. By the employee's role in the community (organization), these virtues form a good person.

3. An individual's ultimate purpose is to serve society's demands and the public good and be rewarded in his or her career.

4. The well-being of the community goes hand in hand with individual excellence.[28]

The difference between deontology, teleology, and virtue ethics is the first two are applied *deductively* to problems, whereas virtue ethics is applied *inductively*. Virtue ethics assumes societal moral rules form the foundation of virtue. Our political, social, and economic systems depend upon the presence of certain virtues among citizens in order to function successfully.[29]

Indeed, virtue ethics could be thought of as a dynamic theory of how to conduct business activities. The virtue ethicist believes a successful market economy depends upon social institutions such as family, school, church, and community where virtues can be nurtured. These virtues, including honesty, trust, tolerance, and restraint, create obligations that make cooperation possible. In a market economy based on virtues, individuals have powerful incentives to conform to prevailing standards of behavior. Some philosophers think social virtues may be eroded by the market, but virtue ethicists believe economic institutions are in balance with and support other social institutions.[30] Some of the virtues that could be seen as driving a market economy are listed in Table 6–2. Although not comprehensive, the list provides examples of the types of virtues that support the conduct of business.

The elements of virtue most important to business transactions are trust, self-control, empathy, fairness, and truthfulness. Non-virtuous characteristics include lying, cheating, fraud, and corruption. In their broadest sense, concepts of virtue appear across all cultures. The problem of virtue ethics comes in its implementation within and between cultures. If a company tacitly approves of corruption, the employee who adheres to the virtues of trust and truthfulness would consider it wrong to sell unneeded repair parts despite the organization's approval of such acts. Other employees might view this truthful employee as highly ethical; however, in order to rationalize their own behavior, they may judge his or her ethics as going beyond what

TABLE 6–2 Virtues That Support Business Transactions

Trust: The predisposition to place confidence in the behavior of others while taking the risk that the expected behavior will not be performed	Eliminates the need for and associated cost of monitoring compliance with agreements, contracts, and reciprocal agreements, as there is the expectation a promise or agreement can be relied on
Self-control: The disposition to pass up an immediate advantage or gratification; the ability to avoid exploiting a known opportunity for personal gain	Gives up short-term self-interest for long-term benefits
Empathy: The ability to share the feelings or emotions of others	Promotes civility because success in the market depends on the courteous treatment of people who have the option of going to competitors; the ability to anticipate needs and satisfy customers and employees contributes to a firm's economic success
Fairness: The disposition to deal equitably with the perceived injustices of others	Often relates to doing the right thing with respect to small matters in order to cultivate a long-term business relationship
Truthfulness: The disposition to provide the facts or correct information as known to the individual	Involves avoiding deception and contributes to trust in business relationships
Learning: The disposition to constantly acquire knowledge internal and external to the firm, whether about an industry, corporate culture, or other societies	Gaining knowledge to make better, more informed decisions
Gratitude: A sign of maturity that is the foundation of civility and decency	The recognition that people do not succeed alone
Civility: The disposition or essence of courtesy, politeness, respect, and consideration for others	Relates to the process of doing business in a culturally correct way, thus decreasing communication errors and increasing trust
Moral leadership: Strength of character, peace of mind and heart, leading to happiness in life	A trait of leaders who follow a consistent pattern of behavior based on virtues

Source: Adapted from Ian Maitland, "Virtuous Markets: The Market as School of the Virtues," *Business Ethics Quarterly* (January 1997): 97; and Gordon B. Hinckley, *Standing for Something: 10 Neglected Virtues that Will Heal Our Hearts and Homes* (New York: Three Rivers Press, 2001).

is required by the job or society. Critics of virtue ethics argue that true virtue is an unattainable goal, but to virtue ethicists, this relativistic argument is meaningless because they believe in the universality of the elements of virtue. One study found virtue ethics to be more effective than deontological and utilitarian ethical perspectives in helping to mitigate ethical risks.[31]

If bolt salesperson Sam Colt was a virtue ethicist, he would consider the elements of virtue (such as honesty and trust) and tell the prospective customer about the defect rate and his concerns regarding the building of the bridge. Sam would not resort to puffery to explain the product or its risks, and might even suggest alternative products or companies that would lower the probability of the bridge collapsing.

Justice

Justice is fair treatment and due reward in accordance with ethical or legal standards, including the disposition to deal with perceived injustices of others. The justice of a situation is based on the perceived rights of individuals and on the intentions of the people involved in a business interaction. In other words, justice relates to the issue of what individuals feel they are due based on their rights and performance in the workplace. For this reason, justice is more likely to be based on deontological moral philosophies than on teleological or utilitarian philosophies.

Three types of justice provide a framework for evaluating different situations (see Table 6–3). **Distributive justice** is based on the evaluation of the outcomes or results of a business relationship. If some employees feel they are paid less than their coworkers for the same work, they have concerns about distributive justice. Distributive justice is difficult to effect when one member of the business exchange intends to take advantage of the relationship. A boss who forces his employees to do more work so he can take more time off would be unjust because he is taking advantage of his position. Situations such as this cause an imbalance in distributive justice.

Procedural justice considers the processes and activities that produce a particular outcome. A climate that emphasizes procedural justice positively influences employees' attitudes and behaviors toward work-group cohesion. The visibility of supervisors and the work group's perceptions of its own cohesiveness are products of a climate of procedural justice.[32] When there is strong employee support for decisions, decision makers, organizations, and outcomes, procedural justice is less important to the individual. In contrast, when employees' support for decisions, decision makers, organizations, or outcomes is not very strong, then procedural justice becomes more important.[33] For example, property and casualty insurer Acuity has a corporate culture that focuses on employees. Acuity offers a number of employee incentives, including tuition reimbursement, unlimited sick days, and a strong 401(k) plan. Long-tenured employees serve on committees and participate in the company's strategic planning process. As a result of its strong employee culture, employee turnover at the firm is a mere 1 percent.[34] Thus, Acuity uses methods of procedural justice to establish positive stakeholder relationships by promoting understanding and inclusion in the decision-making process. The United Nations consumer protection guidelines adopt a highly procedural justice outlook with its concerns for safety, the right to be heard, and the right to privacy.[35] Evaluations of performance not consistently developed and applied can lead to problems with procedural justice. Employee expectations of conditions with a high degree of procedural justice can weaken perceptions of integrity and create increased job tension.[36] For instance, employees' concerns about unequal compensation relate to their perceptions that the processes of justice in their company are inconsistent.

TABLE 6–3 Types of Justice

Justice Type	Areas of Emphasis
Distributive justice: Based on the evaluation of *outcomes or results* of the business relationship	Benefits derived Equity in rewards
Procedural justice: Based on the *processes* and *activities* that produce the outcome or results	Decision-making process Level of access, openness, and participation
Interactional justice: Based on *relationships* and the *treatment* of others	Accuracy of information Truthfulness, respect, and courtesy in the process

© Cengage Learning

Interactional justice is based on the relationships between organizational members, including the way employees and management treat one another. Interactional justice is linked to fairness within member interactions. It often involves an individual's relationship with the accuracy of the information a business organization provides. Although interactional justice often refers to how managers treat their subordinates, employees can also be guilty in creating interactional justice disputes. For example, many employees admit they stay home when they are not really sick if they feel they can get away with it. Such workplace absenteeism costs businesses millions of dollars each year.

All three types of justice—distributive, procedural, and interactional—could be used to measure a single business situation and the fairness of the organization and individuals involved. One study found that distributive justice is more important in shaping the total perception of justice.[37] This may be because distributive justice relates to important considerations like pay satisfaction. In general, justice evaluations result in restitution seeking, relationship building, and evaluations of fairness in business relationships. Using the example of Sam Colt, Sam would feel obligated to tell all affected parties about the bolt defect rate and the possible consequences in order to create a fair transaction process.

APPLYING MORAL PHILOSOPHY TO ETHICAL DECISION MAKING

Individuals use different moral philosophies depending on whether they make a personal decision or a work-related decision.[38] Two things may explain this behavior. First, in the business arena, some goals and pressures for success differ from the goals and pressures in a person's life outside of work. As a result, an employee might view a specific action as good in the business sector but unacceptable outside the work environment. Some suggest business managers are morally different from other people. In a way, this is correct, in that business contains one variable that is absent from other situations: the profit motive. The various factors that make up a person's moral philosophy are weighted differently in a business (profit) situation. The comment "It's not personal, it's just business" demonstrates the conflict businesspeople can experience when their personal values do not align with utilitarian or profit-oriented decisions. The reality is if firms do not make a profit, they will fail. However, this fact should not be a justification for seeking excessive profits or executive pay, issues that are now being questioned by stakeholders.

The second reason people change moral philosophies is the corporate culture where they work. When children enter school, they learn certain rules, such as raising their hands to speak or asking permission to use the restroom. So it is with a new employee. Rules, personalities, and precedents exert pressure on the employee to conform to the firm's culture. As this process occurs, the individual's moral philosophy may change to become compatible with the work environment. Many people are acquainted with those who are respected for their goodness at home or in their communities but make unethical decisions in the workplace. Even Bernard Madoff, the perpetrator of the largest Ponzi scheme in history, had a reputation as an upstanding citizen before his fraud was uncovered.

Obviously, the concept of a moral philosophy is inexact. For that reason, moral philosophies must be assessed on a continuum rather than as static entities. Each philosophy states an ideal perspective, and most individuals shift between different moral philosophies as they experience and interpret ethical dilemmas. In other words, implementing moral philosophies from an individual perspective requires individuals to apply their own accepted value systems to real-world situations. Individuals make judgments about what they believe to be right or wrong, but in their business lives they make decisions that take into consideration how to generate the greatest benefits with the least harm. Such decisions should respect fundamental moral rights as well as perspectives on fairness, justice, and the common good, but these issues become complicated in the real world.

Problems arise when employees encounter ethical situations they cannot resolve. Sometimes gaining a better understanding of their decision rationale helps employees choose the right solutions. This results in the need for employees to exercise reasonableness. The morals of individuals help them to exercise ethical reasoning to satisfy the expectations of other stakeholders.[39] For instance, to decide whether they should offer bribes to potential customers to secure a large contract, salespeople need to understand their own personal moral philosophies as well as their firm's core values and the relevant laws. If complying with company policy or legal requirements is an important motivation to the individual, he or she is less likely to offer a bribe. On the other hand, if the salesperson's ultimate goal is a successful career and if offering a bribe seems likely to result in a promotion, then bribery might not be inconsistent with that person's moral philosophy of acceptable business behavior. Even though bribery is illegal under U.S. law, the employee may rationalize that bribery is necessary "because everyone else does it."

The virtue approach to business ethics, as discussed earlier, assumes there are certain ideals and values everyone should strive for in order to achieve the maximum welfare and happiness of society.[40] Aspects of these ideals and values are expressed through individuals' specific moral philosophies. Every day in the workplace, employees must decide what is right or wrong and act accordingly. At the same time, as members of a larger organization, employees cannot simply enforce their own personal perspectives, especially if they adhere narrowly to a single moral philosophy. Because individuals cannot control most of the decisions in their work environment, they rarely have the power (especially in entry-level and middle-management positions) to impose their own personal moral perspectives on others. In fact, although they are always responsible for their own actions, a new employee is not likely to have the freedom to make independent decisions on a variety of job responsibilities.

Sometimes a company makes questionable decisions from the perspective of individual customers' values and moral philosophies. For example, some stakeholders might consider a brewery or a distributor of sexually explicit movies unethical, based on their personal perspectives. A company's core values will determine how it makes decisions in which moral philosophies are in conflict. Most businesses have developed a mission statement, a corporate culture, and a set of core values that express how they want to relate to their stakeholders, including customers, employees, the legal system, and society. It is usually impossible to please all stakeholders at once.

COGNITIVE MORAL DEVELOPMENT AND ITS PROBLEMS

Many people believe individuals advance through stages of moral development as their knowledge and socialization progress. In this section, we examine a model that describes this cognitive moral development process. Cognitive moral processing is based on a body of literature in psychology that focuses on the study of children and their cognitive development.[41] However, cognitive moral processing is also an element in ethical decision making, and many models attempt to explain, predict, and control individuals' ethical behavior.

Psychologist Lawrence Kohlberg developed a six-stage model of cognitive development. Although not specifically designed for business contexts, this model provides an interesting perspective on the issue of moral philosophy in business. According to **Kohlberg's model of cognitive moral development (CMD)**, people make different decisions in similar ethical situations because they are in different moral development stages. The six stages identified by Kohlberg are as follows:

1. *The stage of punishment and obedience.* An individual in Kohlberg's first stage defines *right* as literal obedience to rules and authority. A person in this stage responds to rules and labels of "good" and "bad" in terms of the physical power of those who determine such rules. Right and wrong are not connected with any higher order or philosophy but rather with a person who has power. Stage 1 is usually associated with small children, but signs of stage 1 development are also evident in adult behavior. For example, some companies forbid their buyers to accept gifts from salespeople. A buyer in stage 1 might justify a refusal to accept gifts from salespeople by referring to the company's rule, or the buyer may accept the gift if he or she believes there is no chance of being caught and punished.

2. *The stage of individual instrumental purpose and exchange.* An individual in stage 2 defines *right* as what serves his or her own needs. In this stage, individuals no longer make moral decisions solely on the basis of specific rules or authority figures; they evaluate behavior on the basis of its fairness to them. For example, a sales representative in stage 2 doing business for the first time in a foreign country may be expected by custom to give customers gifts. Although gift giving may be against company policy in the United States, the salesperson may decide certain company rules designed for operating in the United States do not apply overseas. In the cultures of some foreign countries, gifts may be considered part of a person's pay. So, in this instance, not giving a gift might put the salesperson at a disadvantage. Some refer to stage 2 as the stage of reciprocity because from a practical standpoint, ethical decisions are based on an agreement of "you scratch my back and I'll scratch yours" instead of on principles of loyalty, gratitude, or justice.

3. *The stage of mutual interpersonal expectations, relationships, and conformity.* Individuals in stage 3 emphasize the interests of others rather than simply those of themselves, although ethical motivation is still derived from obedience to rules. A production manager in this stage might obey upper management's order to speed up an assembly

line if he or she believed doing so would generate more profit for the company and thus save employee jobs. These managers not only consider their own well-being in deciding to follow the order but also put themselves in upper management's and fellow employees' shoes. Thus, stage 3 differs from stage 2 in that fairness to others is one of the individual's ethical motives.

4. *The stage of social system and conscience maintenance.* Individuals in stage 4 determine what is right by considering their duty to society, not just to certain other people. Duty, respect for authority, and the maintenance of the social order become the focal points at this stage. For example, some managers consider it a duty to society to protect privacy and therefore refrain from monitoring employee conversations.

5. *The stage of prior rights, social contract, or utility.* In stage 5, individuals are concerned with upholding the basic rights, values, and legal contracts of society. Individuals in this stage feel a sense of obligation or commitment to other groups—they feel, in other words, that they are part of a social contract—and recognize that in some cases legal and moral points of view may conflict. To reduce such conflict, stage 5 individuals base their decisions on a rational calculation of overall utility. For example, the president of a firm may decide to establish an ethics program because it provides a buffer against legal problems and the firm will be perceived as a responsible contributor to society.

6. *The stage of universal ethical principles.* A person in this stage believes right is determined by universal ethical principles everyone should follow. Stage 6 individuals believe certain inalienable rights exist that are universal in nature and consequence. These rights, laws, or social agreements are valid not because of a particular society's laws or customs, but because they rest on the premise of universality. Justice and equality are examples of principles some individuals and societies deem universal in nature. A person in this stage may be more concerned with social ethical issues and therefore not rely on the business organization for ethical direction. For example, a businessperson at this stage might argue for discontinuing a product that has caused death and injury because the inalienable right to life makes killing wrong, regardless of the reason. Therefore, company profits are not a justification for the continued sale of the product.[42]

Kohlberg's six stages can be reduced to three levels of ethical concern. At the first level, a person is concerned with his or her own immediate interests and with external rewards and punishments. At the second level, an individual equates *right* with conformity to the expectations of good behavior of the larger society or some other significant reference group. Finally, at the third or "principled," level, an individual sees beyond the norms, laws, and authority of groups or individuals. Employees at this level make ethical decisions regardless of negative external pressures. However, research shows most workers' abilities to identify and resolve moral dilemmas do not reside at this third level and their motives are often a mixture of selflessness, self-interest, and selfishness.

Kohlberg suggests people continue to change their decision-making priorities after their formative years, and as a result of time, education, and experience, they may change their values and ethical behavior. In the context of business, an individual's moral development can be influenced by corporate culture, especially ethics training. Ethics training and education have been shown to improve managers' cognitive development scores.[43] Because of corporate reform, most employees in *Fortune* 1000 companies today receive some type of ethics training. Training is also a requirement of the Federal Sentencing Guidelines for Organizations.

Some experts believe experience in resolving moral conflicts accelerates an individual's progress in moral development. A manager who relies on a specific set of values or rules may eventually come across a situation when these rules do not apply. Suppose Sarah is a manager whose policy is to fire any employee whose productivity declines for four consecutive months. Sarah has an employee, George, whose productivity suffered because of depression, but George's coworkers tell Sarah George will recover and soon become a top performer again. Because of the circumstances and the perceived value of the employee, Sarah may bend the rule and keep George. Managers in the highest stages of the moral development process seem to be more democratic than autocratic, and they are more likely than those at lower stages to consider the ethical views of the other people involved in an ethical decision-making situation.

Several problems with CMD relate back to its origins. These problems have been termed the three strikes theory. For example, Kohlberg's original work of CMD came from psychologist and philosopher Jean Piaget's research with children about the nature and development of intelligence. When Kohlberg transferred Piaget's theory to adults he did not take into account the full functioning and development of the adult brain (Strike One). From a philosophical perspective CMD argues for a hierarchical or step-like progression of moral philosophies starting from the lowest and going to the highest. This contradicts basic moral philosophy because there is no hierarchy. Each moral philosophy should be equal to the others (Strike Two). Finally, research suggests that CMD has a high reliability but not validity. For example, if a person shoots at a target and the shots are all close together, you can state there is high reliability. However, if the shots are all down and to the right, and the goal was to hit the center, then you have low validity (Strike Three). As a result, it is important to be cautious when using CMD to explain why good people make bad decisions.

WHITE-COLLAR CRIME

For many people, the terms *crime* and *criminal* tend to evoke thoughts of rape, arson, armed robbery, or murder. These violent crimes are devastating, but they are no less destructive than crimes perpetrated every year by nonviolent business criminals. So-called **white-collar crime** (WCC) does more damage in monetary and emotional loss in one year than violent crimes do over several years combined.[44]

White-collar criminals tend to be highly educated people in positions of power, trust, respectability, and responsibility within a business or organization. They commit illegal acts for personal and/or organizational gains by abusing the trust and authority normally associated with their positions. The victims of WCC are often trusting consumers who believe businesses are legitimate.

At first glance, deciding what constitutes a white-collar crime seems fairly simple. According to the U.S. Department of Justice, a WCC is a "nonviolent criminal act involving deceit, concealment, subterfuge and other fraudulent activity." The corporate executive who manipulates the stock market, the tax cheat, or the doctor who falsely bills Medicaid are all obvious white-collar criminals. But a government official who accepts illegal payments is also a white-collar criminal, and guilty of official corruption. Additionally, a corporate executive who approves the illegal disposal of toxic waste is a white-collar criminal guilty of violating environmental regulations.

Online white-collar crime is a growing problem around the world. Because many companies rely on advanced technology systems, anyone with the ability to hack into a system can access the highly sensitive information necessary to commit WCC. WCCs previously originating at the top of organizations now occur at any level of a firm. Common white-collar crimes include asset misappropriation, corruption, and financial statement fraud. Often white-collar criminals commit crimes that fit into more than one category (see Figure 6–1).

FIGURE 6–1 Fraud Schemes

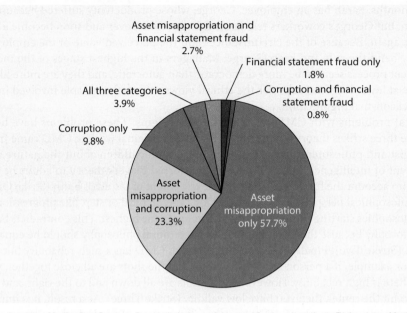

Source: Association of Certified Fraud Examiners, *Report to the Nations on Occupational Fraud and Abuse* (Austin, TX: Association of Certified Fraud Examiners, 2014), p. 15.

White-collar crime is a major problem in the financial world. For instance, eleven fraudsters got together to create a $40 million Ponzi scheme. The mastermind behind the scheme, Keith Franklin Simmons, developed what looked like a hedge fund dealing in foreign currencies. With help he recruited many individuals who had insurance experience as regional managers, who in turn recruited friends and former clients to invest with the fraudulent fund. Many investors were elderly and therefore more vulnerable. None of the money was actually invested. Keith Franklin Simmons was sentenced to 40 years in prison.[45]

Another case of white-collar crime also involves a well-known financier. Matthew Martoma, a portfolio manager for SAC Capital Advisors hedge fund firm, was sentenced to nine years in prison for insider trading—one of the longest insider trading prison sentences levied so far. Martoma was accused of gaining nonpublic insider information and trading on the information to make SAC Capital $200 million in illicit profits and $9 million in bonuses for himself.[46] While many in business feel such stiff sentences are excessive due to the permanent damage done to reputations and that these are nonviolent crimes, others argue that being robbed at gunpoint is less devastating than working and saving for a life time only to discover the sacrifices made were meaningless.

White-collar crime is increasing steadily (see Table 6–4). Consumers lose more than $1.6 billion due to fraud annually.[47] A few common white-collar offenses include antitrust violations, computer and Internet fraud, credit card fraud, bankruptcy fraud, health care fraud, tax evasion, violating environmental laws, insider trading, bribery, kickbacks, money laundering, and theft of trade secrets.

In response to the surge in white-collar crime, the U.S. government stepped up efforts to combat it. The government is concerned about the destabilizing effect WCC has on U.S. households and the economy in general. The government can charge individuals and

TABLE 6–4 U.S. Consumer Fraud Complaints

Year	Complaints Received	Amount Paid
2013	1,165,090	$1,622,784,979
2012	1,111,119	$1,412,308,747
2011	1,040,439	$1,547,435,639

Source: Federal Trade Commission, *Consumer Sentinel Network Datab Book,* February 2014, http://www.ftc.gov/system/files/documents/reports/consumer-sentinel-network-data-book-january-december-2013/sentinel-cy2013.pdf (accessed February 26, 2015).

corporations for WCC offenses. The penalties include fines, home detention, paying for the cost of prosecution, forfeitures, and prison time. However, sanctions are often reduced if the defendant takes responsibility for the crime and assists the authorities in their investigation. Many people do not feel the government is devoting enough resources to combat WCC. Others believe that no matter how many regulations and controls the government puts in place, there will always be rogue individuals who will find loopholes. It is therefore necessary for companies to implement their own controls to combat fraud and other types of white-collar crime. Capital One, for instance, employs certified fraud examiners that examine questionable activities and file Suspicious Activity Reports if it seems like fraud might be occurring. Because white-collar crime is constantly adapting, fraud examiners must be willing to share knowledge and experiences to remain current on fraud schemes likely to impact their businesses.[48]

Why do individuals commit white-collar crimes? Advocates of the organizational deviance perspective argue that a corporation is a living, breathing organism that can collectively become deviant. When companies have lives separate and distinct from biological persons, the corporate culture of the company transcends the individuals who occupy these positions. With time, patterns of activities become institutionalized within the organization, and these patterns sometimes encourage unethical behaviors.

Another common cause of WCC is the views and behaviors of an individual's acquaintances within an organization. Employees, at least in part, self-select the people with whom they associate within an organization. For companies with a high number of ethical or unethical employees, people who are undecided about their behavior (about 40 percent of businesspeople) are more likely go along with their coworkers.

Additionally, the incidence of WCCs tends to increase in the years following economic recessions. When companies downsize, the stressful business climate may anger some employees and force others to act out of desperation.

DEBATE ISSUE
TAKE A STAND

Why Do People Engage in White-Collar Crime?

White-collar crime occurs when highly trusted and educated individuals commit criminal misconduct. Two examples of white-collar criminals are Bernard Madoff, who developed one of the largest Ponzi schemes ever, and R. Allen Stanford, who developed an $8 billion certificate of deposit program promising unrealistically high interest rates. Different theories exist why individuals become white-collar criminals. Research shows 1 percent of business executives may be corporate psychopaths with a predisposition to lie, cheat, and take any other measures necessary to come out ahead. This possibility may account for the fact that many white-collar criminals become entrepreneurs, thus putting themselves in a position to control others. This theory might account for rogue individuals such as Bernard Madoff.

Many believe white-collar crime evolves when corporate cultures do not have effective oversight and control over individuals' behavior. Such toxic organizational cultures occur when unethical activities are overlooked or even encouraged. For instance, many employees engaged in liar loans at Countrywide Financial because they received rewards for bringing in additional profits. It seems unlikely they all had psychological maladies.[49]

1. White-collar criminals tend to have psychological disorders that encourage misconduct as a route to success.

2. White-collar crime occurs as a result of organizational cultures that do not effectively control organizational behavior.

TABLE 6–5 Common Justifications for White-Collar Crime

1. Denial of responsibility. (Everyone can, with varying degrees of plausibility, point the finger at someone else.)

2. Denial of injury. (White-collar criminals often never meet or interact with those who are harmed by their actions.)

3. Denial of the victim. (The offender is playing tit-for-tat and claims to be responding to a prior offense inflicted by the supposed victim.)

4. Condemnation of the condemners. (Executives dispute the legitimacy of the laws under which they are charged, or impugn the motives of the prosecutors who enforce them.)

5. Appeal to a higher authority. ("I did it for my family" remains a popular excuse.)

6. Everyone else is doing it. (Because of the highly competitive marketplace, certain pressures exist to perform that may drive people to break the law.)

7. Entitlement. (Criminals simply deny the authority of the laws they have broken.)

Source: Based on Daniel J. Curran and Claire M. Renzetti, *Theories of Crime* (Needham Heights, MA: Allyn & Bacon, 1994).

Furthermore, as businesses begin to expand and grow, fraudsters find gaps in corporate processes and exploit growth opportunities.[50]

Finally, as with criminals in the general population, there is the possibility some businesspeople may have inherently criminal personalities.[51] Corporate psychopaths, or managers who are nonviolent, selfish, and remorseless, exist in many large corporations. Corporate psychopaths may be more likely to use moral disengagement, in which they reframe the individuals or actions of a particular situation to convince themselves certain ethical standards do not apply.[52] Employees of corporate psychopaths are less likely to believe that their organization is socially responsible, the organization shows commitment to employees, or they receive recognition for their work.[53] Some organizations use personality tests to predict behavior, but such tests presuppose individual values and philosophies are constant; therefore, they seem to be ineffective in understanding the motivations of white-collar criminals.[54]

The reasons for the increases in WCC are not easy to pinpoint because many variables may cause good people to make bad decisions. Businesspeople must make a profit on revenue to exist, a fact that slants their orientation toward teleology and creates a culture in which white-collar crimes can become normalized. Table 6–5 lists top justifications given by perpetrators of white-collar crimes. The Federal Sentencing Guidelines for Organizations state that all organizations should develop effective ethics and compliance programs as well as internal controls to prevent WCC.

INDIVIDUAL FACTORS IN BUSINESS ETHICS

Of course, not everyone agrees on the roles of collective moral philosophies in ethical decision making within an organization. For example, it has been argued that intuition determines moral judgment.[55] While intuitive decisions can be triggered by emotions, there are also cognitive processes that can determine moral reasoning. Therefore, individual moral decisions are much more complex than learning about different moral philosophies.[56] Individual values are not only the main driver of ethical behavior in business. This belief can be a stumbling block in assessing ethical risk and preventing misconduct in an organizational context. The moral values learned within the family and through religion and education are certainly key factors that influence decision making, but as indicated in the models in Chapter 5, these values are only one factor. A focus mainly on personal character or moral development suggests the notion that employees can control their work environments. Although a personal moral compass is important, it is not sufficient to prevent ethical misconduct in an organizational context. According to ethics consultant David Gebler, "Most unethical behavior is not done for personal gain, it's done to meet performance goals."[57] The rewards for meeting performance goals and the corporate culture in general have been found to be the most important drivers of ethical decision making, especially for coworkers and managers.[58]

The development of strong abilities in ethical reasoning will probably lead to more ethical business decisions in the future than individualized character education for each employee.[59] Equipping employees with intellectual skills that allow them to understand and resolve the complex ethical dilemmas they encounter in complex corporate cultures will help them make the right decisions. This approach will hopefully keep employees from being negatively influenced by peer pressure and lulled by unethical managers.[60] The West Point model for character development focuses on the fact that competence and character must be developed simultaneously. This model assumes ethical reasoning has to be approached in the context of a specific profession. The military has been effective in teaching skills and developing principles and values that can be used in most of the situations a soldier encounters. In a similar manner, accountants, managers, and marketers need to develop ethical reasoning in the context of their jobs.

SUMMARY

Moral philosophy refers to the set of principles or rules people use to decide what is right or wrong. These principles or rules provide guidelines for resolving conflicts and for optimizing the mutual benefit of people living in groups. Businesspeople are guided by moral philosophies as they formulate business strategies and resolve specific ethical issues, even if they may not realize it.

Teleological, or consequentialist, philosophies stipulate that acts are morally right or acceptable if they produce some desired result such as the realization of self-interest or utility. Egoism defines right or acceptable behavior in terms of the consequences for the individual. In an ethical decision-making situation, the egoist chooses the alternative that contributes most to his or her own self-interest. Egoism can be further divided into hedonism and enlightened egoism. Utilitarianism is concerned with maximizing total utility, or providing the greatest benefit for the greatest number of people. In making ethical decisions, utilitarians often conduct cost–benefit analyses that consider the costs and benefits to all affected parties. Rule utilitarians determine behavior on the basis of rules designed to promote the greatest utility rather than by examining particular situations. Act utilitarians examine the action itself rather than the rules governing the action, to determine if it results in the greatest utility.

Deontological, or nonconsequentialist, philosophies focus on the rights of individuals and the intentions behind an individual's particular behavior rather than its consequences. In general, deontologists regard the nature of moral principles as permanent and stable and believe compliance with these principles defines ethical behavior. Deontologists believe individuals have certain absolute rights that must be respected. Rule deontologists believe conformity to general moral principles determines ethical behavior. Act deontologists hold that actions are the proper basis to judge morality or ethicalness and that rules serve only as guidelines.

According to the relativist perspective, definitions of ethical behavior derive subjectively from the experiences of individuals and groups. The relativist observes behavior within a relevant group and attempts to determine what consensus group members reach on the issue in question.

Virtue ethics states that what is moral in a given situation is not only what is required by conventional morality or current social definitions, however justified, but by what a person with a "good" moral character would deem appropriate. Those who profess virtue ethics do not believe the end justifies the means in any situation.

The concept of justice in business relates to fair treatment and due reward in accordance with ethical or legal standards. Distributive justice is based on the evaluation of the outcome or results of a business relationship. Procedural justice is based on the processes and activities that produce outcomes or results. Interactional justice is based on an evaluation of the communication process in business.

The concept of a moral philosophy is not exact; moral philosophies can only be assessed on a continuum. Individuals use different moral philosophies depending on whether they are making a personal or a workplace decision.

According to Kohlberg's model of cognitive moral development, individuals may make different decisions in similar ethical situations because they are in a different stage of moral development. In Kohlberg's model, people progress through six stages of moral development: (1) punishment and obedience; (2) individual instrumental purpose and exchange; (3) mutual interpersonal expectations, relationships, and conformity; (4) social system and conscience maintenance; (5) prior rights, social contract, or utility; and (6) universal ethical principles. Kohlberg's six stages can be further reduced to three levels of ethical concern: immediate self-interest, social expectations, and general ethical principles. Cognitive moral development may not explain as much as people once believed.

White-collar crime occurs when an educated individual who is in a position of power, trust, respectability, and responsibility commits an illegal act in relation to his or her employment, and who abuses the trust and authority normally associated with the position for personal and/or organizational gains. White-collar crime is not heavily researched because this type of behavior does not normally come to mind when people think of crime; the offender (or organization) is in a position of trust and respectability; criminology and criminal justice systems look at white-collar crime differently than average crimes; and many researchers have not moved past the definitional issues. New developments in technology seem to be increasing the opportunity to commit white-collar crime with less risk.

Individual factors such as religion, moral intensity, and a person's professional affiliations can influence an employee's decision-making process. The impacts of ethical awareness, biases, conflict, personality type, and intelligence on ethical behavior remain unclear. One thing we do know is that the interrelationships among moral philosophies, values, and business are extremely complex.

IMPORTANT TERMS FOR REVIEW

moral philosophy 155

economic value orientation 156

idealism 156

realism 156

monist 158

hedonism 158

quantitative hedonist 158

qualitative hedonist 158

pluralist 158

instrumentalist 158

goodness theory 158

obligation theory 159

teleology 159

consequentialism 159

egoism 159

enlightened egoism 159

utilitarianism 159

rule utilitarian 160

act utilitarian 160

deontology 161

nonconsequentialism 161

categorical imperative 161

rule deontologist 162

act deontologist 162

relativist perspective 163

descriptive relativism 163

meta-ethical relativism 163

normative relativism 163

virtue ethics 164

justice 166

distributive justice 166

procedural justice 166

interactional justice 167

Kohlberg's model of cognitive moral development (CMD) 169

white-collar crime 171

RESOLVING ETHICAL BUSINESS CHALLENGES*

Dr. Robert Smith owned his family practice for over 20 years. He came from a family of success. His father was a brain surgeon and his mother a well-known author. His younger brother, Saul, owned his own accounting firm for several years, but came to work with Dr. Smith after he sold it for a modest amount.

After graduating at the top of his class from Johns Hopkins University, Dr. Smith was awarded a cardio-thoracic surgery fellowship in New York. He spent a few years there and was well on his way to fulfilling his dream of becoming a heart surgeon. During this time, however, his father became ill. Dr. Smith decided to return to his hometown of Zoar, Ohio, to take care of him. Under Dr. Smith's care, his father started show-ing signs of improvement. He was glad not only for his father, but that he could go back and continue his pur-suit of becoming a heart surgeon. On the day he was set to leave, his mother became ill and died a few days later from a rare form of cancer that showed no symptoms. The devastation hit the family hard. Saul was still in col-lege, and Dr. Smith's father needed someone to be with him at all times. Dr. Smith decided to stay in Zoar to take care of his father. He opened up a family practice in the town, thus putting his dream of becoming a heart surgeon on hold indefinitely.

Over the years, Dr. Smith sometimes felt regret that he never achieved his dream, but his job as the town doctor has been fulfilling. Now Saul was working with him, helping with the business. This made things sig-nificantly easier for Dr. Smith, who haphazardly kept his own books and patient files. One day, as Saul orga-nized Dr. Smith's piles of paperwork, he noticed there were charges to Medicaid that must be a mistake. While most of the population of Zoar, Ohio, was considered low-level income and qualified for Medicaid, this was not the case for all patients. There were several elderly middle- and higher-income families who regularly vis-ited the office and usually paid with a check or cash. Saul assumed his brother's administrative office skills were poor and aimed to fix it. However, as Saul organized the paperwork and checked files, these charges to Medicaid appeared to increase, dating back at least five years.

Saul approached his brother. "Robert, are you aware you charged Medicaid for Mr. and Mrs. Bennett's visits?"

"Hmmm. Let me see the paperwork," Dr. Smith asked. Saul handed it to him. Dr. Smith glanced at the document and said, "Yes, they are over age 65, so I made a bill for Medicaid."

"But we have records they paid you with cash," Saul replied. He handed Dr. Smith an old receipt. "And there are similar instances with some of your other patients. Besides, Medicaid is for low-income patients, not the elderly. Mr. and Mrs. Bennett are clearly not low-income."

Looking a little bit flustered, Dr. Smith replied, "Saul, you know how I am with details. I'm no good at it. That's why I hired you. Thanks for catching my mistake." Dr. Smith walked back into his office and shut the door, leaving Saul standing in the hallway with a stack of files.

Saul knew what his brother gave up for their family and the good he did for the families in this small town, but he was convinced these charges were not accidental. There were too many of them and the amount of money charged exceeded $75,000.

"What happened to all that money?" Saul won-dered. He also wondered how to handle the situation. He thought to himself, "How can I report this without send-ing Robert to jail? If I don't report it and Medicaid finds out, I could go to jail and lose my accounting license. This is such a small town. If anybody finds out, we'll never live it down." At that moment, the phone rang, and Saul was the only one there to answer it.

QUESTIONS | EXERCISES

1. Describe Saul's ethical dilemma.
2. Why would Medicare fraud be a white-collar crime?
3. How should Saul approach the situation?

*This case is strictly hypothetical; any resemblance to real persons, companies, or situations is coincidental.

> > > CHECK YOUR EQ

Check your EQ, or Ethics Quotient, by completing the following. Assess your performance to evaluate your overall understanding of the chapter material.

1. Teleology defines right or acceptable behavior in terms of its consequences for the individual. — Yes / **No**

2. A relativist looks at an ethical situation and considers the individuals and groups involved. — **Yes** / No

3. A utilitarian is most concerned with bottom-line benefits. — **Yes** / No

4. Act deontology requires a person use equity, fairness, and impartiality in making decisions and evaluating actions. — **Yes** / No

5. Virtues supporting business transactions include trust, fairness, truthfulness, competitiveness, and focus. — Yes / **No**

ANSWERS **1. No.** That's egoism. **2. Yes.** Relativists look at themselves and those around them to determine ethical standards. **3. Yes.** Utilitarians look for the greatest good for the greatest number of people and use a cost–benefit approach. **4. Yes.** The rules serve only as guidelines, and past experience weighs more heavily than the rules. **5. No.** The characteristics include trust, self-control, empathy, fairness, and truthfulness—not competitiveness and focus.

ENDNOTES

1. James R. Rest, *Moral Development Advances in Research and Theory* (New York: Praeger, 1986), 1.

2. "Business Leaders, Politicians and Academics Dub Corporate Irresponsibility 'An Attack on America from Within,'" *Business Wire*, November 7, 2002, via The Free Library, http://www.thefreelibrary.com/Business+ Leaders,+Politicians+and+Academics+Dub+Corporate ...-a094631434 (accessed March 19, 2015).

3. A. C. Ahuvia, "If Money Doesn't Make Us Happy, Why Do We Act as If It Does?" *Journal of Economic Psychology* 29, 4 (2008): 491–507.

4. Abhijit Biswas, Jane W. Licata, Daryl McKee, Chris Pullig, and Christopher Daughtridge, "The Recycling Cycle: An Empirical Examination of Consumer Waste Recycling and Recycling Shopping Behaviors," *Journal of Public Policy & Marketing* 19, 1 (2000): 93; Miguel Bastons, "The Role of Virtues in the Framing of Decisions," *Journal of Business Ethics* 78, 3 (2008): 395.

5. Miquel Bastons, "The Role of Virtues in the Framing of Decisions," *Journal of Business Ethics* 78, 3 (2008): 395.

6. Margaret Lindorff, Elizabeth Prior Jonson, and Linda McGuire, "Strategic Corporate Social Responsibility in Controversial Industry Sectors: The Social Value of Harm Minimization," *Journal of Business Ethics* 110, 4 (2012): 457–467.

7. "Court Says Businesses Liable for Harassing on the Job," *Commercial Appeal*, June 27, 1998, A1; Richard Brandt, *Ethical Theory* (Englewood Cliffs, NJ: Prentice-Hall, 1959), 253–254.

8. Ryan Vlastelica, "General Motors issues three new recalls, cites ignition systems," *Reuters*, January 1, 2015, http:// www.reuters.com/article/2015/01/01/us-gm-recalls- reports-idUSKBN0KA1RZ20150101 (accessed March 5, 2015); "GM: Steps to a recall nightmare," *CNN Money*, http://money.cnn.com/infographic/pf/autos/gm-recall- timeline/ (accessed March 5, 2015).

9. J. J. C. Smart and B. Williams, *Utilitarianism: For and against* (Cambridge, UK: Cambridge University Press, 1973), 4.

10. C. E. Harris, Jr., *Applying Moral Theories* (Belmont, CA: Wadsworth, 1986), 127–128.

11. Kevin McCoy, "Goodyear agrees to $16M bribery settlement," *USA Today*, February 24, 2015, http:// www.usatoday.com/story/money/2015/02/24/ goodyear-fined-16-million/23935581/ (accessed March 5, 2015).

12. Example adapted from Harris, *Applying Moral Theories*, 128–129.

13. Gerald F. Cavanaugh, Dennis J. Moberg, and Manuel Velasquez, "The Ethics of Organizational Politics," *Academy of Management Review* 6 (1981): 363–374; U.S. Bill of Rights, http://www.law.cornell.edu/constitution/ constitution.billofrights.html (accessed March 19, 2015).

14. U.S. Bill of Rights, http://www.law.cornell.edu/ constitution/constitution.billofrights.html (accessed March 19, 2015).

15. Marie Brenner, "The Man Who Knew Too Much," *Vanity Fair*, May 1996, http://www.jeffreywigand.com/vanityfair. php (accessed March 19, 2015).

16. Norman E. Bowie and Thomas W. Dunfee, "Confronting Morality in Markets," *Journal of Business Ethics* 38, 4 (2002): 381–393.

17. Josh Smith, "Pricing error costs Zappos $1.6 Million," *Daily Finance*, May 24, 2010, http://www.dailyfinance. com/2010/05/24/pricing-error-costs-zappos-1-6-million/ (accessed March 5, 2015).

18. Immanuel Kant, "Fundamental Principles," 229.

19. Thomas E. Weber, "To Opt In or Opt Out: That Is the Question When Mulling Privacy," *The Wall Street Journal*, October 23, 2000, B1.

20. R. Bateman, J. P. Fraedrich, and R. Iyer, "The Integration and Testing of the Janus-Headed Model within Marketing," *Journal of Business Research* 56, 8 (2003): 587–596; J. B. DeConinck and W. F. Lewis, "The Influence of Deontological and Teleological Considerations and Ethical Culture on Sales Managers' Intentions to Reward or Punish Sales Force Behavior," *Journal of Business Ethics* 16, 5 (1997): 497–506; J. Kujala, "A Multidimensional Approach to Finnish Managers' Moral Decision Making," *Journal of Business Ethics* 34, 3–4 (2001): 231–254; K. C. Rallapalli, S. J. Vitell, and J. H. Barnes, "The Influence of Norms on Ethical Judgments and Intentions: An Empirical Study of Marketing Professionals," *Journal of Business Research* 43, 3 (1998): 157–168; M. Shapeero, H. C. Koh, and L. N. Killough, "Underreporting and Premature Sign-Off in Public Accounting," *Managerial Auditing Journal* 18, 6/7 (2003): 478–489.

21. William K. Frankena, *Ethics* (Englewood Cliffs, NJ: Prentice-Hall, 1963).

22. R. E. Reidenbach and D. P. Robin, "Toward the Development of a Multidimensional Scale for Improving Evaluations of Business Ethics," *Journal of Business Ethics* 9, n8 (1980): 639–653.

23. Patrick E. Murphy and Gene R. Laczniak, "Emerging Ethical Issues Facing Marketing Researchers," *Marketing Research* 4, 2 (1992): 6–11.

24. T. K. Bass and Barnett G. Brown, "Religiosity, Ethical Ideology, and Intentions to Report a Peer's Wrongdoing," *Journal of Business Ethics* 15, 11 (1996): 1161–1174; R. Z. Elias, "Determinants of Earnings Management Ethics among Accountants," *Journal of Business Ethics* 40, 1 (2002): 33–45; Y. Kim, "Ethical Standards and Ideology among Korean Public Relations Practitioners," *Journal of Business Ethics* 42, 3 (2003): 209–223; E. Sivadas, S. B. Kleiser, J. Kellaris, and R. Dahlstrom, "Moral Philosophy, Ethical Evaluations, and Sales Manager Hiring Intentions," *Journal of Personal Selling & Sales Management* 23, 1 (2003): 7–21.

25. Cheng-Li Huang and Bau-Guang Chang, "The Effects of Managers' Moral Philosophy on Project Decision under Agency Problem Conditions," *Journal of Business Ethics* 94, 4 (2010): 595–611.

26. Manuel G. Velasquez, *Business Ethics Concepts and Cases*, 5th ed. (Upper Saddle River, NJ: Prentice-Hall, 2002), 135–136.

27. Ibid.

28. Adapted from Robert C. Solomon, "Victims of Circumstances? A Defense of Virtue Ethics in Business," *Business Ethics Quarterly* 13, 1 (2003): 43–62.

29. Ian Maitland, "Virtuous Markets: The Market as School of the Virtues," *Business Ethics Quarterly* 7, 1 (January 1997): 97.

30. Ibid.

31. Subrata Chakrabarty and A. Erin Bass, "Comparing Virtue, Consequentialist, and Deontological Ethics-Based Corporate Social Responsibility: Mitigating Microfinance Risk in Institutional Voids," *Journal of Business Ethics* 126, 3 (2015): 487–512.

32. Stefanie E. Naumann and Nathan Bennett, "A Case for Procedural Justice Climate: Development and Test of a Multilevel Model," *Academy of Management Journal* 43, 5 (2000): 881–889.

33. Joel Brockner, "Making Sense of Procedural Fairness: How High Procedural Fairness Can Reduce or Heighten the Influence of Outcome Favorability," *Academy of Management Review* 27, 1 (2002): 58–76.

34. "100 Best Companies to Work For 2015," *Fortune*, http://fortune.com/best-companies/acuity-3/ (accessed March 5, 2015); Kathryn Tyler, "HR Magazine: Leveraging Long Term Tenure," *Society for Human Resource Management* 52, 5 (2007), http://www.shrm.org/publications/hrmagazine/editorialcontent/pages/0507tyler.aspx (accessed March 5, 2015).

35. Gretchen Larsen and Rob Lawson, "Consumer Rights: An Assessment of Justice," *Journal of Business Ethics* 112, 3 (2013): 515–528.

36. Martha C. Andrews, K. Michele Kacmar, and Charles Kacmar, "The Interactive Effects of Behavioral Integrity and Procedural Justice on Employee Job Tension," *Journal of Business Ethics* 126, 3 (2015): 371–379.

37. Handi Brata and Lita Juliana, "Performance-Based Reward Systems and Perceived Justice: A Case of Motorbike Dealer in Pontianak," *International Journal of Business and Society* 15, 2 (2014): 195–214.

38. John Fraedrich and O. C. Ferrell, "Cognitive Consistency of Marketing Managers in Ethical Situations," *Journal of the Academy of Marketing Science* 20, 3 (1992): 245–252.

39. Nobuyuki Fukawa and Sunil Erevelles, "Perceived Reasonableness and Morals in Service Encounters," *Journal of Business Ethics* 125, 3 (2014): 381–400.

40. Manuel Velasquez, Claire Andre, Thomas Shanks, S. J. and Michael J. Meyer, "Thinking Ethically: A Framework for Moral Decision Making," *Issues in Ethics* (Winter 1996): 2–5.

41. Lawrence Kohlberg, "Stage and Sequence: The Cognitive Developmental Approach to Socialization," in *Handbook of Socialization Theory and Research*, ed. D. A. Goslin (Chicago, IL: Rand McNally, 1969), 347–480.

42. Adapted from Kohlberg, "Stage and Sequence."

43. Clare M. Pennino, "Is Decision Style Related to Moral Development among Managers in the U.S.?" *Journal of Business Ethics* 41, 4 (2002): 337–347.

44. K. M. Au and D. S. N. Wong, "The Impact of Guanxi on the Ethical Decision-Making Process of Auditors: An Exploratory Study on Chinese CPA's in Hong Kong," *Journal of Business Ethics* 28, 1 (2000): 87–93; D. P. Robin, G. Gordon, C. Jordan, and E. Reidenback, "The Empirical Performance of Cognitive Moral Development in Predicating Behavioral Intent," *Business Ethics Quarterly* 6, 4 (1996): 493–515; M. Shapeero, H. C. Koh,

and L. N. Killough, "Underreporting and Premature Sign-Off in Public Accounting," *Managerial Auditing Journal* 18, 6 (1996): 478–489; N. Uddin and P. R. Gillett, "The Effects of Moral Reasoning and Self-Monitoring on CFO Intentions to Report Fraudulently on Financial Statements," *Journal of Business Ethics* 40, 1 (2002): 15–32.

45. Federal Bureau of Investigation, "A Ponzi Scheme Collapses," February 23, 2015, http://www.fbi.gov/news/stories/2015/february/a-ponzi-scheme-collapses/a-ponzi-scheme-collapses (accessed March 5, 2015).

46. Nathan Vardi, "Matthew Martoma Sentenced to Nine Years for Insider Trading," *Forbes*, September 8, 2014, http://www.forbes.com/sites/nathanvardi/2014/09/08/mathew-martoma-sentenced-to-nine-years-for-insider-trading/ (accessed March 5, 2015).

47. Federal Trade Commission, Consumer Sentinel Network Data Book, February 2014, https://www.ftc.gov/system/files/documents/reports/consumer-sentinel-network-data-book-january-december-2013/sentinel-cy2013.pdf (accessed March 5, 2015).

48. Association of Certified Fraud Examiners, "Keys to Success: Be Vigilant, Find a Mentor," *Anti-Fraud Resource Guide*, Fourth Quarter 2014, 5.

49. J. M. Rayburn and L. G. Rayburn, "Relationship between Machiavellianism and Type A Personality and Ethical-Orientation," *Journal of Business Ethics* 15, 11 (1996): 1209–1219.

50. Clive R. Boddy, Richard K. Ladyshewsley, and Peter Galvin, "The Influence of Corporate Psychopaths on Corporate Social Responsibility and Organizational Commitment to Employees," *Journal of Business Ethics* 97, 1 (2010): 1–19; Clive R. Boddy, Richard K. Ladyshewsley, and Peter Galvin, "The Implications of Corporate Psychopaths for Business and Society: An Initial Examination and a Call to Arms," AJBBS 1, 2 (2005): 30–40, http://www.mtpinnacle.com/pdfs/Psychopath.pdf (accessed May 3, 2011).

51. KPMG, "Fraud contagion shows no sign of abating," *Fraud Barometer*, June 2010, http://www.zurich.com/NR/rdonlyres/61135D66-3194-4362-A9D3-07AC64C40B54/0/KPMGAUFraudBarometerFindingsAustAug2010.pdf (accessed March 19, 2015).

52. Eysenck, "Personality and Crime: Where Do We Stand?" *Psychology, Crime & Law* 2, 3 (1996): 143–152; Shelley Johnson Listwan, *Personality and Criminal Behavior: Reconsidering the Individual*, University of Cincinnati, Division of Criminal Justice, 2001, http://cech.uc.edu/content/dam/cech/programs/criminaljustice/docs/phd_dissertations/2001/ShelleyJohnson.pdf (accessed March 19, 2015).

53. Gregory W. Stevens, Jacqueline K. Deuling, and Achilles A. Armenakis, "Successful Psychopaths: Are They Unethical Decision-Makers and Why?" *Journal of Business Ethics* 105, 2 (2012): 139–149.

54. "The Influence of Corporate Psychopaths on Corporate Social Responsibility and Organizational Commitment to Employees," *Journal of Business Ethics*.

55. Jonathan Haidt, "The emotional dog and its rational tail: A social intuitionist approach to moral judgment," *Psychological Review* 108, 814–834.

56. Adenekan Dedeke, "A Cognitive–Intuitionist Model of Moral Judgment," *Journal of Business Ethics* 126, 3 (2015): 371–379.

57. Quoted in Marjorie Kelly, "The Ethics Revolution," *Business Ethics* (Summer 2005): 6.

58. O. C. Ferrell and Larry G. Gresham, "A Contingency Framework for Understanding Ethical Decision Making in Marketing," *Journal of Marketing* 49, 3 (2002): 261–274.

59. Thomas I. White, "Character Development and Business Ethics Education," in *Fulfilling Our Obligation: Perspectives on Teaching Business Ethics*, ed. Sheb L. True, Linda Ferrell, and O. C. Ferrell (Kennesaw, GA: Kennesaw State University Press, 2005), 165.

60. Ibid., 165–166.

CHAPTER 7

ORGANIZATIONAL FACTORS: THE ROLE OF ETHICAL CULTURE AND RELATIONSHIPS

AN ETHICAL DILEMMA*

When Jim began working in the human resources department at KR Electronics, he was impressed with the number of advancement opportunities the job offered. His first task was to monitor reports that came in from employees through the company's ethics hotline. It was a simple job but one Jim felt would lead him to a higher position in the HR department. He spent two days learning about the company's ethical policies and values, such as the importance of integrity and confidentiality. Jim felt reassured he chose a great company in which to start a career.

KR Electronics was a competitive company, and every six months employees were evaluated for performance. While the highest performers received substantial bonuses, the lowest 15 percent were consistently fired within the year. This didn't bother Jim too much. He knew many other well-known companies had a similar system in place.

What bothered Jim was the way the supervisors treated employees who did not perform highly. Several employees approached Jim and told him of an abusive manager who often yelled at employees in front of other coworkers. Jim heard reports that the supervisor would make comments such as "I can't wait till the year is up and I can tell you to get lost. It'll be nice to actually get someone in this job with half a brain."

When Jim approached David, the human resources manager of his department, about what he heard, David shrugged off Jim's concerns. "You've got to understand, Jim," David explained. "We operate in a highly competitive field. Employees have to work quickly and efficiently in order to maintain our business. This often requires supervisors to get tough. Besides, this supervisor's unit is one of our highest performers. Apparently, whatever he's doing is working." This remark made Jim feel uncomfortable, but he did not want to argue with his boss about it.

One day Jim got a call from a woman in the company's sales department. She informed him that many of the firm's salespeople made exaggerated claims about the quality of their electronics. He also learned salespeople were making guarantees about products that were not true, such as how long the product would last.

"The salespeople are given substantial bonuses for exceeding their quotas, so many promise whatever it takes to increase their sales," the woman explained.

Although it was not required to provide a name when reporting, the person talking to Jim gave her name as Sarah Jones. She asked Jim to make sure her sales manager Rick Martin did not find out she called the hotline. Jim gave the report to his supervisor for further investigation.

Two weeks later Jim heard that Sarah Jones had been fired for poor performance. He approached David to ask him about the situation and was horrified to find out the sales manager of Sarah's division had been told about her report.

"But David, this is a violation of our confidentiality code! I promised Sarah we would keep her name anonymous when investigating this matter. What if Rick fired her out of retaliation?" Jim asked.

David looked at Jim in exasperation. "Jim, you are making too big of a deal out of this. Nobody forced Sarah to give her name to us over the hotline. And trust me, Rick's a good man. He wouldn't fire someone simply to get back at them for reporting. It seems to me that these reports don't have credibility, anyway. It's likely that Sarah made up these allegations to hide her poor performance."

Jim left David's office upset. Even if Sarah was a poor performer, he did not feel that it was right that her sales manager was told about her report when she expressly requested otherwise. As he went back to his desk, he remembered hearing that the sales manager and David were good friends and often went out together for lunch.

QUESTIONS | EXERCISES

1. How does the company's organizational culture appear to conflict with its ethical policies?
2. What are the options for Sarah if this was retaliation?
3. What should Jim do next?

*This case is strictly hypothetical; any resemblance to real persons, companies, or situations is coincidental.

Companies are much more than structures in which we work. Although they are not alive, we attribute human characteristics to them. When times are good, we say the company is "well"; when times are bad, we may try to "save" the company. Understandably, people have strong feelings about the place that provides them with income and benefits, challenges, satisfaction, self-esteem, and often lifelong friendships. In fact, excluding time spent in sleeping, almost 50 percent of our lives are spent in this second "home" with our second "family." It is important to examine how the culture and structure of these organizations influence the ethical decisions made within them.

In the ethical decision-making framework described in Chapter 5, we introduced the concept that organizational factors and interpersonal relationships influence the ethical decision-making process. We also describe the normative foundation of ethical decision making, such as organizational core values. In this chapter, we take a closer look at corporate culture and the ways a company's values and traditions can affect employees' ethical behavior. We also discuss the role of power in influencing ethical behavior within a company. Next, we describe two organizational structures and examine how they may influence ethical decisions. We discuss new organizational structures created to address the organization's corporate responsibility to employees and other stakeholders. Then we consider the impact of groups within organizations. Finally, we examine the implications of organizational relationships for ethical decision making.

DEFINING CORPORATE CULTURE

Organizational culture includes shared values, norms, and artifacts that influence employees and determine behavior, including ways of solving problems that members (employees) of an organization share. Corporate culture is "the shared beliefs top managers in a company have about how they should manage themselves and other employees, and how they should conduct their business(es)."[1] How to resolve ethical issues is part of corporate culture. Mutual of Omaha considers its corporate culture in its mission statement. Its intent is to "back our products with fair and timely service, and pursue operational excellence at every level. Above all, we will maintain the highest degree of integrity in all our interactions."[2] The company feels that its core values form the foundation for a corporate culture that helps the organization realize its vision and achieve its goals. Corporate culture is exhibited through the behavioral patterns, concepts, documents such as codes of ethics, and rituals that emerge in an organization.[3] This culture gives the members of the organization a sense of meaning and purpose and familiarizes them with the organization's internal rules of behavior.[4]

Values, beliefs, customs, rules, and ceremonies that are accepted, shared, and circulated throughout an organization represent its culture. Southwest Airlines has a strong and friendly, fun-loving organizational culture of "luv" that dates back to the days of its key founder Herb Kelleher. Kelleher embraced values of customer service and employee participation, treating his employees like family. Today, Southwest continues that legacy. Pilots willingly and enthusiastically support the "Adopt a Pilot" program. Students in classrooms around the country adopt a Southwest pilot for a four-week educational and mentoring program.[5] All organizations, not just corporations, have some sort of culture, and therefore we use the terms *organizational culture* and *corporate culture* interchangeably.

A company's history and unwritten rules are a part of its culture. For many years, IBM salespeople adhered to a series of unwritten standards for dealing with clients. The history or stories passed down from generation to generation within an organization are like the traditions perpetuated within society at large. Henry Ford, the founder of Ford Motor Co., left a legacy that emphasized the importance of the individual employee. Henry Ford pioneered the then-unheard-of high wage of $5 a day in the early years of the twentieth century. Pillsbury, founded by Charles Pillsbury and made famous by his grandson Philip, made civic and social responsibility an important part of the company's culture. Although it was acquired by General Mills in 2001, the company's traditions and history continue to impact its operations and philanthropic responsibilities.[6]

Leaders are responsible for the actions of their subordinates, and corporations should have ethical corporate cultures. For this reason, the definition and measurement of a corporate culture is important. It is defined in the Sarbanes–Oxley Act, enacted after the Enron, Tyco International, and WorldCom scandals. The characteristics of an ethical corporate culture were codified within the **Sarbanes–Oxley 404** compliance section. This section includes a requirement that management assess the effectiveness of the organization's internal controls and commission an audit of these controls by an external auditor in conjunction with the audit of its financial statements. Section 404 requires firms to adopt a set of values that forms a portion of the company's culture. The evaluation of corporate culture it mandates is meant to provide insight into the character of an organization, its ethics, and transparency.

Compliance with Sarbanes–Oxley 404 requires not merely changes in accounting but a change in corporate culture. The intent is to expose mismanagement, fraud, theft, abuse, and to sustain a corporate culture that does not allow these conditions and actions to exist. Section 406 also requires a code of ethics for top financial officers. Many consultants that filled the need of companies wanting to comply with Sarbanes–Oxley lacked understanding of what "culture" means in this case. These consultants sought to provide direction and criteria for improving an organization's ability to manage risk, not its ethics. In many firms, an ethical corporate culture is measured in the following ways:

- Management and the board demonstrate their commitment to integrity, core values, and ethics codes through their communications and actions.

- Every employee is encouraged and required to have hands-on involvement in compliance, especially internal control systems and reporting systems.

- Ethical leadership should start with the tone at the top.

- Employees are expected to receive communication through resolutions and corrective actions related to ethical issues.

- Employees have the ability to report policy exceptions anonymously to any member of the organization, including the CEO, other members of management, and the board of directors.[7]

The problem with these measurement standards is they focus more on risk, compliance, and reporting. They are not a complete measure of the aspects of a company that make up its ethical culture. Yet many assume the four aforementioned items define an ethical corporate culture. Since values, norms, and artifacts are the three major components of culture that impact behavior, all of these elements are important in measuring an ethical culture.

In the past 50 years, scholars developed at least 164 distinct definitions of culture. More recent reviews indicate the number of definitions has been increasing.[8] While these definitions of culture vary greatly, they share three common elements: (1) "culture is shared among individuals belonging to a group or society," (2) "culture is formed over a relatively long period of time," and (3) "culture is relatively stable."[9]

Different models of culture, and consequently different instruments for measuring it, focus on various levels (national, organizational, individual) and aspects (values, practices, observable artifacts and rituals, underlying implicit assumptions). Individual and organizational values are better at explaining ethical behavior than national values.[10] Geert Hofstede researched IBM's corporate culture and described it as an onion with many layers representing different levels within the corporation.[11] Today, IBM describes its culture as one of trust. The company adopted IBM Business Conduct Guidelines that describe ethics and compliance issues in-depth and provide direction for employees dealing with observed misconduct.[12] Many in business define ethics as what society considers right or wrong and develop measures that manage the risk of misconduct. Managing risk is not the same as understanding what makes up a firm's culture. We know for certain that culture has a significant effect on the ethical decision-making process of those in business. Ethical audits, ethical compliance, and risk culture surveys may be good tools, but in and of themselves they are not useful in defining organizational culture or in explaining what makes a particular organizational culture more ethical or unethical.

THE ROLE OF CORPORATE CULTURE IN ETHICAL DECISION MAKING

Corporate culture has been associated with a company's success or failure. Some cultures are so strong that to outsiders they come to represent the character of the entire organization. For example, Levi Strauss, Ben & Jerry's Homemade Ice Cream, and Hershey Foods are widely perceived as casual organizations with strong ethical cultures, whereas Lockheed Martin, Procter & Gamble, and Texas Instruments are seen as having more formal ethical cultures. The culture of an organization may be explicitly articulated or left unspoken.

Explicit statements of values, beliefs, customs, and expected behavior usually come from upper management. Memos, written codes of conduct, handbooks, manuals, forms, and ceremonies are formal expressions of an organization's culture. Many of these statements can be found on company websites, like that of U.S. Bank (Table 7–1).

Corporate culture is often expressed informally through statements, both direct and indirect, that communicate the wishes of management. In some companies, shared values are expressed by instituting informal dress codes, working late, and participating in

TABLE 7–1 U.S. Bank's Principles for Integrity

- Being a role model for ethical behaviour
- Promoting our culture of integrity
- Fostering open communication
- Recognizing behavior that exemplifies our ethical principles and values
- Responding to misconduct and reporting violations

Source: U.S. Bank, *Do the Right Thing: Code of Ethics and Business Conduct,* https://www.usbank.com/hr/docs/policies/coeHandbook.pdf (accessed March 9, 2015).

extracurricular activities. Corporate culture can be expressed through gestures, looks, labels, promotions, programs, and legends (or the lack thereof). Many catastrophic events stem from ethical deficiencies resulting in a lack of human value judgments and actions influenced by different corporate cultures. When organizational leaders involve lower-level employees in a meaningful role in shaping and maintaining an ethical culture, they are more likely to perceive the culture as strong and view it similarly to the way leaders view it.[13] Phil Knight, Nike co-founder and sports icon, created a strong and appealing organizational culture. Knight—in trying to build a collaborative culture—would seek out new employees on one of their first few days on the job to "borrow $20 for lunch." The unsuspecting new employees are astounded Knight spoke to them. Knight uses the tactic as a subtle way to let new employees know they are on his radar. Interestingly, Knight has never paid back any of the employees. Most employees know what is happening and have fun with the new employee initiation. This ritual becomes a source of camaraderie among employees, building trust and commitment and differentiating Nike's organizational culture from that of its competitors.

The "tone at the top" is a determining factor in the creation of a high-integrity organization. When leaders are perceived as trustworthy, employee trust increases; leaders are seen as ethical and as honoring a higher level of duties.[14] In a survey of global consumers (Figure 7–1), more than 6,000 consumers from 13 markets were asked what traits they believe are the most important among leaders. The most popular answer was leading by example, followed closely by open and transparent communication. It is interesting to note that leading by example was listed as more important than business savvy or the ability to make tough decisions. Attributes such as integrity are included more than any other

FIGURE 7–1 Most Important Attributes for Effective Leadership

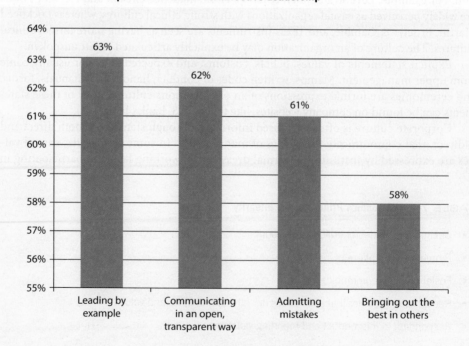

Online survey of 6,509 total respondents in 13 markets from Jan. 10-31, 2014, margin of error=+/-1.3%

Source: Ketchum Global Research & Analytics and IPSOS, 2014.

core value by organizations. A culture that emphasizes the importance of ethics and social responsibility can reduce misconduct such as earnings manipulation in the finance area.[15]

Ethical Frameworks and Evaluations of Corporate Culture

Corporate culture has been conceptualized in many ways. For example, N. K. Sethia and Mary Ann Von Glinow proposed two basic dimensions to describe an organization's culture: (1) concern for people—the organization's efforts to care for its employees' well-being, and (2) concern for performance—the organization's efforts to focus on output and employee productivity.[16] Figure 7–2 provides examples of companies that display elements of these four organizational cultures.

As Figure 7–2 shows, the four organizational cultures can be classified as apathetic, caring, exacting, and integrative. An **apathetic culture** shows minimal concern for either people or performance. In this culture, individuals focus on their own self-interest. Apathetic tendencies can occur in almost any organization. Steel companies and airlines were among the first to freeze employee pensions to keep their businesses operating. Sweeping changes in corporate America affect employee compensation and retirement plans. Simple gestures of appreciation, such as anniversary watches, rings, dinners, or birthday cards for family members, are being dropped. Many companies view long-serving employees as dead wood and do not take into account past performance. This attitude demonstrates the companies' apathetic culture.

A **caring culture** exhibits high concern for people but minimal concern for performance issues. From an ethical standpoint, the caring culture seems appealing. However, it is difficult to find nationally recognizable companies that maintain little or no concern for performance. In contrast, an **exacting culture** shows little concern for people but a high concern for performance; it focuses on the interests of the organization. United Parcel Service (UPS) has always been exacting. With over 9.4 million daily customers in over 220 countries, UPS knows exactly how many employees it needs to move 16.9 million packages and documents per day worldwide.[17] Although an exacting culture might show more concern for performance over people, a successful company cannot ignore the needs of its employees. Despite its expectations for high performance, for example, UPS offers employees a number of employee benefits, including tuition assistance and health and wellness programs.[18] Indeed, it is unlikely that any successful organization will embrace a

FIGURE 7–2 Company Examples of the Four Organizational Cultures

Ben & Jerry's—A Caring Culture
Ben & Jerry's embraces community causes, treats its employees fairly, and expends numerous resources to enhance the well-being of its customers.

Starbucks—An Integrative Culture
Starbucks always looks for ways to expand and improve performance. It also exhibits a high concern for people through community causes, sustainability, and employee health care.

Countrywide Financial—An Apathetic Culture
Countrywide seemed to show little concern for employees and customers. The company's culture appeared to encourage unethical conduct in exchange for profits.

United Parcel Systems—An Exacting Culture
Employees are held to high standards to ensure maximum performance, consistency of delivery, and efficiency.

culture that is 100 percent caring or exacting because both people and profits are necessary for long-term survival.

An **integrative culture** combines a high concern for people and performance. An organization becomes integrative when superiors recognize employees are more than interchangeable parts—employees have an ineffable quality that helps the firm meet its performance criteria. Many companies, such as the Boston Consulting Group (BCG), have such a culture. BCG is a financially successful global consulting firm with a strong reputation that specializes in business strategy. The company values employees and creates significant mentorship opportunities and extensive training that allow employees to develop rapidly. It also has what it calls "red flag reports" to signal when employees are working too many long weeks. New consultants to the company can receive $10,000 for volunteering at a nonprofit organization.[19]

Companies can classify their corporate culture and identify its specific values, norms, beliefs, and customs by conducting a cultural audit. A **cultural audit** is an assessment of an organization's values. The audit is usually conducted by outside consultants but may be performed internally as well. Communication about ethical expectations and support from top management help to identify a corporate culture that encourages ethical conduct or leads to ethical conflict.[20]

Ethics as a Component of Corporate Culture

As indicated in the framework presented in Chapter 5, ethical culture—the ethical component of corporate culture—is a significant factor in ethical decision making. If a firm's culture encourages or rewards unethical behavior, the employees may act unethically. If the culture dictates hiring people with specific, similar values and if those values are perceived as unethical by society, society will view the organization and its members as unethical. Such a pattern often occurs in certain areas of marketing. Salespeople sometimes use aggressive selling tactics to get customers to buy things based on emotional response to appeals. If a company's primary objective is to make as much profit as possible through whatever means, its culture may foster behavior that conflicts with stakeholders' ethical values. For instance, an investigation revealed that the Mexican arm of Walmart had bribed officials in Mexico to secure building permits. Although the investigation is ongoing, it appears as if high-level executives at Walmart knew or suspected that this bribery occurred. If this is the case, then it leads to questions about whether Walmart's global corporate values—including its stance against bribery—are authentic or merely window-dressing.

On the other hand, if an organization values ethical behaviors, it rewards them. It is important to handle recognition and awards for appropriate behavior in a consistent and balanced manner. All employees should be eligible for recognition. All performance at the threshold level should be acknowledged, and praise or rewards given as close to the performance as possible.[21] FedEx's Bravo Zulu Award is one example of company recognition. The award is given to employees who demonstrate exceptional performance above and beyond job expectations. Rewards for recipients can include cash bonuses, theater tickets, gift certificates, and more. By rewarding employees who go above their normal duties, FedEx provides motivation for other workers to strive for excellent work conduct.[22]

Management's sense of an organization's culture may not be in line with the values and ethical beliefs that actually guide a firm's employees. Table 7–2 provides an example of a corporate culture ethics audit. Companies interested in assessing their culture can use this tool and benchmark against previous years' results to measure organizational improvements. Ethical issues may arise because of conflicts between the cultural values perceived by management and those actually at work in the organization. For example, managers may believe their firm's organizational culture encourages respect for peers and subordinates. On the basis of the rewards or sanctions associated with various behaviors, the firm's employees may believe the company encourages competition among organizational members. A competitive orientation may result in a less ethical corporate culture. This was the case at Enron when the employees in the lowest 20 percent for performance were fired.

On the other hand, employees appreciate working in an environment designed to enhance workplace experiences through goals that encompass more than just maximizing profits.[23] Therefore, it is important for top managers to determine their organization's culture and monitor its values, traditions, and beliefs to ensure they represent the desired culture. It is also important to note that if corporate communication to improve corporate social responsibility (CSR) and ethics is reactive or focused on avoiding negative consequences, it may not make a significant contribution to creating an ethical culture. Reactive communication without commitment therefore fails to improve business ethics.[24] However, by placing high emphasis upon ethics and CSR, organizations are able to foster positive relationships with employees and enhance job satisfaction while gaining a good business image. Along with implementing CSR within the organization, the alternative benefit for some organizations is an ability to charge a premium price for their product.[25]

The rewards and punishments imposed by an organization must reflect the culture those at the top wish to create. Two business ethics experts observed, "Employees will value and use as guidelines those activities for which they will be rewarded. When a behavior that is rewarded comes into conflict with an unstated and unmonitored ethical value, usually the rewarded behavior wins out."[26] For example, if the most important and rewarded value is sales performance, then activities to achieve performance will be given top priority.

Compliance versus Values-Based Ethical Cultures

During the latter part of the twentieth century a distinction evolved between types of corporate cultures. The traditional ethics-based culture focused on compliance. The accounting professional model of rules created a **compliance culture** organized around risk. Compliance-based cultures use a legalistic approach to ethics. They use laws and regulatory rules to create codes and requirements. Codes of conduct are established with compliance as their focus, with rules and policies enforced by management. Instead of revolving around an ethical culture, the company revolves around risk management. The compliance approach is good in the short term because it helps management, stakeholders, and legal agencies ensure laws, rules, and the intent of compliance are fulfilled. A problem with the compliance approach, however, is its lack of long-term focus on values and integrity. In addition, it does not teach employees to navigate ethical gray areas.

There has been a shift from an approach focused on compliance to a values-based approach. A **values-based ethics culture** approach to ethical corporate cultures relies upon an explicit mission statement that defines the core values of the firm and how customers and employees should be treated. The board of directors as well as upper management might add to the general value statements by formulating specific value statements for its strategic business units (SBU), which can be organized by product, geography, or function within the firm's management structure. Certain areas may have rules associated with stated values, enabling employees to understand the relationship between the two. The focus of this type of corporate culture is on values such as trust, transparency, and respect to help employees identify and deal with ethical issues. It is important when using a values-based approach to explain why rules exist, what the penalties are if rules are violated, and

TABLE 7–2 Corporate Culture Ethics Audit

		Answer Yes or No to each of the following questions*
Yes	No	Has the founder or top management of the company left an ethical legacy to the organization?
Yes	No	Does the company have methods for detecting ethical concerns both within the organization and outside it?
Yes	No	Is there a shared value system and understanding of what constitutes appropriate behavior within the organization?
Yes	No	Are stories and myths embedded in daily conversations about appropriate ethical conduct?
Yes	No	Are codes of ethics or ethical policies communicated to employees?
Yes	No	Are there ethical rules or procedures in training manuals or other company publications?
Yes	No	Are penalties for ethical transgressions publicly discussed?
Yes	No	Are there rewards for good ethical decisions even if they don't always result in a profit?
Yes	No	Does the company recognize the importance of creating a culture concerned about people and their investment in the business?
Yes	No	Does the company have a value system of fair play and honesty toward customers?
Yes	No	Do employees treat each other with respect, honesty, and fairness?
Yes	No	Do employees spend their time working in a cohesive way on what is valued by the organization?
Yes	No	Are there ethically based beliefs and values about how to succeed in the company?
Yes	No	Are there heroes or stars in the organization who communicate a common understanding about which positive ethical values are important?
Yes	No	Are there day-to-day rituals or behavior patterns that create direction and prevent confusion or mixed signals on ethics matters?
Yes	No	Is the firm more focused on the long run than on the short run?
Yes	No	Are employees satisfied or happy, and is employee turnover low?
Yes	No	Do the dress, speech, and physical aspects of the work setting contribute to a sense of consistency about what is right?
Yes	No	Are emotional outbursts about role conflict and ambiguity rare?
Yes	No	Has discrimination and/or sexual harassment been eliminated?
Yes	No	Is there an absence of open hostility and severe conflict?
Yes	No	Do people act on the job in a way consistent with what they say is ethical?
Yes	No	Is the firm more externally focused on customers, the environment, and the welfare of society than on its own profits?
Yes	No	Is there open communication between superiors and subordinates about ethical dilemmas?
Yes	No	Have employees ever received advice on how to improve ethical behavior or been disciplined for committing unethical acts?

*Add up the number of "Yes" answers. The greater the number of "Yes" answers, the less likely ethical conflict is in your organization.

how employees can help improve the ethics of the company. The crux of any ethical culture is top-down integrity with shared values, norms that provide guides for behavior, and visible artifacts such as codes of ethics that provide a standard of conduct. In developing a values-based ethical culture, a compliance element is also necessary because every organization has employees who will try to take advantage if the risk of being caught is low.

Ikea represents a values-based culture, with a mission "to create a better everyday life for the many people." The company maintains a strong commitment to best business practices, ethical behavior, and environmental initiatives. Not only does Ikea sell eco-friendly products and use alternative energy to power its stores, it also supports numerous causes such as Save the Children and American Forests.[27] However, even Ikea must deal with ethical issues when they arise. For instance, Ikea withdrew its Swedish meatballs from its markets across Europe after traces of horse meat were detected.[28]

Differential Association

Differential association is the idea that people learn ethical or unethical behavior while interacting with others who are part of their role-sets or belong to other intimate personal groups.[29] The learning process is more likely to result in unethical behavior if the individual associates primarily with persons who behave unethically. Associating with others who are unethical, combined with the opportunity to act unethically, is a major influence on ethical decision making, as described in the decision-making framework in Chapter 5.[30]

Consider a company in which salespeople incur travel expenses each week. When new salespeople are hired, experienced salespeople encourage the new hires to pad their expense accounts because some expenses cannot be charged to the company. The new employee is shown how to pad the expense account and is told that failure to engage in this conduct makes others' reports look too high. In other words, the new employee is pressured to engage in misconduct.

A variety of studies support the notion that differential association influences ethical decision making, and superiors in particular have a strong influence on the ethics of their subordinates. The actions of Mark Hernandez, who worked at NASA's Michoud Assembly Facility applying insulating foam to the space shuttles' external fuel tanks, provide an example of how coworker influence can produce tragic results. Within a few weeks on the job, coworkers taught Hernandez to repair scratches in the insulation without reporting the repairs. Supervisors encouraged the workers not to complete the required paperwork on the repairs so they could meet the space shuttle program's tight production schedules. After the shuttle *Columbia* broke up on reentry, killing all seven astronauts, investigators found that a piece of foam falling off a fuel tank during liftoff had irreparably damaged the shuttle.[31]

Several research studies found that employees, especially young managers, tend to go along with their superiors' moral judgments to demonstrate loyalty. In one study, an experiment was conducted to determine how a hypothetical board of directors would respond to the marketing of one of its company's most profitable drugs that resulted in 14 to 22 unnecessary deaths a year. When the imaginary board learned that a competitor's drug was coming into the market with no side effects, more than 80 percent supported continuing to market the drug and taking legal and political action to prevent a ban. When asked their personal view on this situation, 97 percent believed that continuing to market the drug was irresponsible.[32] We have made it clear that *how* people typically make ethical decisions is not necessarily the way they *should* make these decisions. We believe you will improve your own ethical decision making once you understand potential influences of your interactions with others in your intimate work groups.

DEBATE ISSUE
TAKE A STAND

Is Government Support for External Whistle-Blowing Effective?

A number of laws have been enacted to encourage members of organizations to report misconduct. While most firms support internal reporting of misconduct through anonymous hotlines, many organizations are concerned about employees going public or reporting misconduct to the government. Whistle-blowers are protected through the Sarbanes–Oxley Act and a number of other government agencies that deal with fraud, stock trading, and corrupt practices. In 2010 the Dodd–Frank Wall Street Reform and Consumer Protection Act gave additional incentives for whistle-blowers. Whistle-blowers are encouraged to turn themselves in if they were part of a team or group that engaged in misconduct, and doing so could result in monetary rewards. Despite these incentives, whistle-blowers in general do not get good treatment and often have trouble finding employment after they report misconduct. It has also been found that companies with good internal reporting systems have fewer whistle-blowers that report externally in an attempt to obtain rewards. This could be because employees feel that their concerns will be taken seriously and misconduct will be halted before it becomes a major problem.

1. Government support through financial incentives for reporting misconduct in organizations is effective and benefits society.

2. Government support of whistle-blowing should be redirected toward stronger incentives for internal reporting of misconduct, not external whistle-blowing that could be harmful to the individual and the organization.

Whistle-Blowing

Interpersonal conflict occurs when employees think they know the right course of action in a situation, yet their work group or company promotes or requires a different, unethical decision. In such cases, employees may choose to follow their own values and refuse to participate in unethical or illegal conduct. If they conclude that they cannot discuss what they are doing or what should be done with coworkers or immediate supervisors, and if there is no method of protection for anonymous reporting, these employees may go outside the organization to publicize and correct the unethical situation. A number of laws exist to protect whistle-blowers.

Whistle-blowing means exposing an employer's wrongdoing to outsiders such as the media or government regulatory agencies. The term *whistle-blowing* is sometimes used to refer to internal reporting of misconduct to management, especially through anonymous reporting mechanisms often called hotlines. Legal protection for whistle-blowers exists to encourage reporting of misconduct. Whistle-blower laws have provisions against retaliation and are enforced by a number of government agencies. Under the Sarbanes–Oxley Act, the U.S. Department of Labor (DOL) directly protects whistle-blowers who report violations of the law and refuse to engage in any action made unlawful. The Corporate and Criminal Fraud Accountability Act (CCFA) protects employees of publicly traded firms from retaliation if they report violations of any rule or regulation to the Securities and Exchange Commission, or any provision of federal law relating to fraud against shareholders. It also requires attorneys to become internal whistle-blowers as well.

The 2010 passage of the Dodd–Frank Act proposed additional incentives for whistle-blowers. Under the new rules, whistle-blowers who provide information that aids in the recovery of over $1 million could receive 10 to 30 percent of that amount. The belief is that monetary incentives will prompt observers of corporate misconduct to come forward and report their observations. One major concern with this new provision is it may cause whistle-blowers to go externally with the information rather than internally. Because of the potential for monetary rewards, whistle-blowers might be tempted to go straight to the Securities and Exchange Commission with reports rather than reporting the misconduct to the company's internal compliance officers.[33]

The Sarbanes–Oxley Act and the Federal Sentencing Guidelines for Organizations (FSGO) institutionalized internal whistle-blowing to encourage discovery of organizational misconduct. For example, billionaire R. Allen Stanford's worst enemies were former employees turned whistle-blowers who once worked for his company Stanford Financial Group. One lawsuit alleges that an employee hired to edit the firm's corporate magazine objected and raised concerns about firm practices he believed violated federal and state laws. He was later fired. In the Stanford case, whistle-blowers provided pivotal evidence documenting corporate malfeasance at a number of companies.[34] Historically, the fortunes of external whistle-blowers have not been positive; most were labeled traitors and many lost their jobs. Even Sherron Watkins was a potential candidate for firing as the Enron investigation unfolded, with law firms assessing the implications of terminating her in light of her ethical and legal concerns about Enron.[35] The cost of inaction by regulatory institutions after a whistle-blowing claim is made can be high. Harry Markopolos attempted to alert the SEC about the Bernie Madoff "Ponzi" scheme for years. The scheme resulted in a loss to investors of about $50 billion. Listening to these whistle-blower claims might have prevented major losses to investors if addressed sooner.[36]

A study of 300 whistle-blowers by researchers at the University of Pennsylvania found that 69 percent lost their jobs or were forced to retire after exposing their companies' misdeeds.[37] For example, whistleblower Cheryl D. Eckard filed a whistleblower report claiming she had been fired after reporting quality control issues at a GlaxoSmithKline plant. Because her lawsuit resulted in a $750 million settlement with GlaxoSmithKline, Eckard was awarded $96 million.[38] Another whistle-blower who was terminated was Linda Almonte who alerted her bosses at JP Morgan Chase about a potentially fraudulent deal she was helping to close. Almonte was fired after alerting her boss and was essentially blacklisted from the banking industry.[39] This blacklisting is one reason why whistle-blower awards can be so high, since it might be impossible for a whistle-blower to find another job in the industry. If an employee provides information to the government about a company's wrongdoing under the Federal False Claims Act, the whistle-blower is known as a *qui tam relator*. Upon investigation of the matter by the U.S. Department of Justice, the whistle-blower can receive between 15 and 25 percent of the recovered funds, depending upon how instrumental his or her claims were in holding the firm accountable for its wrongdoing.[40] Although most whistle-blowers do not receive positive recognition for pointing out corporate misconduct, some turned to the courts and obtained substantial settlements. However, whistle-blowers have traditionally had a difficult time winning their cases. During the Clinton and Bush administrations, less than 5 percent of whistle blowers won settlements.[41]

To be truly effective, whistle-blowing requires that the individual have adequate knowledge of wrongdoing that could damage society. It is important to minimize risk to the whistle-blower while dealing with ethical issues.[42] Table 7–3 provides a checklist of questions an employee should ask before going to external sources. Figure 7–3 shows the increase in retaliation whistle-blowers have faced in recent years. About 21 percent of respondents to the National Business Ethics Survey indicated they experienced some form of retaliation after reporting misconduct.

TABLE 7–3 Questions to Ask before Engaging in External Whistle-Blowing

1. Have I exhausted internal anonymous reporting opportunities within the organization?

2. Have I examined company policies and codes that outline acceptable behavior and violations of standards?

3. Is this a personal issue that should be resolved through other means?

4. Can I manage the stress that may result from exposing potential wrongdoing in the organization?

5. Can I deal with the consequences of resolving an ethical or legal conflict within the organization?

© Cengage Learning

FIGURE 7-3 **Percentage of Employees Who Experience Retaliation after Reporting Misconduct**

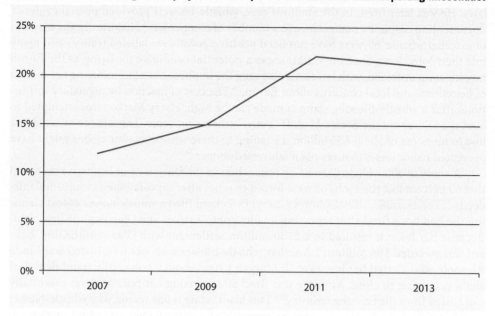

Source: Ethics Resource Center, *National Business Ethics Survey of the U.S. Workforce* (Arlington, VA: Ethics Resource Center, 2014), p. 26.

If whistle-blowers present an accurate picture of organizational misconduct, they should not fear for their jobs. Indeed, Sarbanes–Oxley and Dodd–Frank make it illegal to "discharge, demote, suspend, threaten, harass, or in any manner discriminate against" a whistle-blower and set penalties of up to 10 years in jail for executives who retaliate against whistle-blowers. The law requires publicly traded companies to implement an anonymous reporting mechanism that allows employees to question actions they believe may indicate fraud or other misconduct.[43] In addition, the FSGO provides rewards for companies that systematically detect and address unethical or illegal activities. Within the federal stimulus funds, new whistle-blower protection was supported for state and local government employees and contractors, subcontractors, and grantees. The new law provides specific protections including the right to seek investigation and review by federal Inspectors General for "adverse actions" such as termination or demotions.[44]

Most public companies are creating computer systems that encourage reporting misconduct internally, also called internal whistle-blowing. With approximately 4,500 employees, Marvin Windows (one of the world's largest custom manufacturers of wood windows and doors) wants employees to feel comfortable reporting violations of safety conditions, bad management, fraud, or theft. The system is anonymous and allows reporting in employees' native languages. This system is used to alert management to potential problems in the organization and facilitate investigations.[45] Marvin Windows is noted for its culture of integrity and won the American Business Ethics Award provided by the Foundation for Financial Service Professionals in 2014.[46]

Even before the passage of the Sarbanes–Oxley Act, an increasing number of companies set up anonymous reporting services. Through toll-free numbers, employees could report suspected violations or seek input on how to proceed when encountering ambiguous situations. These internal reporting services are perceived to be most effective when managed by an outside organization that specializes in maintaining ethics hotlines.

TABLE 7–4 How Employees Report Misconduct

Reporting Location	Percent of Reporters who (at some point) utilize This Resource*
Your supervisor	82%
Higher management	52%
Human resources	32%
Hotline/Help Line	16%
Ethics officer	15%
Someone outside your company who was not a governmental or regulatory authority	13%
Legal	11%
A govermental or regulatory authority	9%

* Responses total more than 100 percent because respondents were asked to select all that applied.

Source: Ethics Resource Center, *National Business Ethics Survey of the U.S. Workforce* (Arlington, VA: Ethics Resource Center, 2014), p. 30.

Since employees are not always accurate in detecting misconduct, most reporting does not require extensive investigations. Many reports are related to minor issues involving personal conflicts.

Table 7–4 reveals that the majority of employees report misconduct to their immediate supervisors. However, the presence of hotlines and other mechanisms helps employees who feel uncomfortable reporting to their superiors. The results of a study show that three internal actions—confrontation, reporting to management, and calling the company ethics hotline—were positively correlated to several dimensions of an ethical culture. Conversely, inaction and external whistle-blowing were negatively correlated to several dimensions of an ethical culture. External whistle-blowing generally reflects a weakness in the ethical culture.[47] The extent to which employees feel there will be no corrective action or there will be retaliation as a result of their actions is a leading factor influencing their decisions not to report observed misconduct.

LEADERS INFLUENCE CORPORATE CULTURE

Organizational leaders can shape and influence corporate culture, resulting in ethical or unethical leadership. Leaders need to be effective and ethical. An effective leader is one who does well for the stakeholders of the corporation. Effective leaders get followers to their common goals or objectives in the most effective and efficient way. Ken Lay and Jeffery Skilling were effective in transforming Enron from a small oil and gas pipeline firm into one of the largest entities in the industry. They were inspirational, imaginative, creative, and motivated their personnel to achieve goals. Because they failed to create an ethical culture, however, they were detrimental to the company in the long term. According to Alan Yuspeh, Senior Vice President and Chief Ethics and Compliance Officer of Hospital Corporation of America (HCA), ethical companies and leadership should possess "aspirations that are higher than observing the law." The CEO of HCA and its board of directors empowered Yuspeh to provide leadership and supporting values to help employees appropriately respond to difficult ethical situations.[48] Consistency is also important for successful leaders. Leaders that create congruency with other leaders and employees in the ethical culture of the organization have a significant positive effect on organizational innovativeness.[49] We discuss leadership in more detail in Chapter 11. The next section discusses how leaders use different types of power to influence corporate culture.

Power Shapes Corporate Culture

Power refers to the influence leaders and managers have over the behavior and decisions of subordinates. Individuals have power over others when their presence causes others to behave differently. Exerting power is one way to influence the ethical decision-making framework described in Chapter 5.

The status and power of leaders is directly correlated to the amount of pressure they exert on employees to get them to conform to expectations. A superior can put strong pressure on employees, even when employees' personal ethical values conflict with the superior's wishes. For example, a manager might say to a subordinate, "I want the confidential information about our competitor's sales on my desk by Monday morning, and I don't care how you get it." A subordinate who values his or her job or who does not realize the ethical questions involved may feel pressure to do something unethical to obtain the data.

There are five power bases from which one person may influence another: (1) reward power, (2) coercive power, (3) legitimate power, (4) expert power, and (5) referent power.[50] These five bases of power can be used to motivate individuals either ethically or unethically.

REWARD POWER
Reward power refers to a person's ability to influence the behavior of others by offering them something desirable. Typical rewards might be money, status, or promotion. Consider, for example, an auto salesperson that has two cars (a Toyota and a Kia) for sale. Let's assume the Toyota is rated higher in quality than the Kia but is priced the same. In the absence of any form of reward power, the salesperson logically attempts to sell the Toyota. However, if the Kia had a higher rate of commission, he would probably focus his efforts on selling the Kia. Such "carrot dangling" and incentives have been shown to be effective in getting people to change their behavior in the long run. Therefore, rewards could encourage individuals to act in their own self-interest, not necessarily in the interest of stakeholders. In the short run, reward power is not as effective as coercive power.

COERCIVE POWER
Coercive power is essentially the opposite of reward power. Instead of rewarding a person for doing something, coercive power penalizes actions or behavior. As an example, suppose a valuable client asks an industrial salesperson for a bribe and insinuates he will take his business elsewhere if his demands are not met. Although the salesperson believes bribery is unethical, her boss tells her she must keep the client happy or lose her chance for promotion. The boss imposes a negative sanction if certain actions are not performed. Many companies use a system whereby they systematically fire the lowest performing employees in their organization on an annual basis. Enron called it "rank and yank" and annually fired the lowest 20 percent. Motorola, Dow Chemical, and Microsoft use similar systems for firing employees. Coercive power relies on fear to change behavior. For this reason, it has been found to be more effective in changing behavior in the short run than in the long run. Coercion is often employed in situations where there is an extreme imbalance of power. However, people continually subjected to coercion may seek a counterbalance and align themselves with other, more powerful persons or leave the

organization. In firms using coercive power, relationships usually break down in the long run. Power is an ethical issue not only for individuals but also for work groups that establish policy for large corporations.

LEGITIMATE POWER

Legitimate power stems from the belief that a certain person has the right to exert influence and certain others have an obligation to accept it. The titles and positions of authority organizations bestow on individuals appeals to this traditional view of power. Many people readily acquiesce to those wielding legitimate power, sometimes committing acts contrary to their beliefs and values. Betty Vinson, an accountant at World-Com, objected to her supervisor's requests to produce improper accounting entries in an effort to conceal WorldCom's deteriorating financial condition. She finally gave in, however, accepting that this was the only way to save the company. She and other WorldCom accountants eventually pled guilty to conspiracy and fraud.[51]

Such loyalty to authority figures can be seen in corporations that have strong charismatic leaders and centralized structures. In business, if a superior tells an employee to increase sales "no matter what it takes" and that employee has a strong affiliation to legitimate power, the employee may try anything to fulfill that order. Dysfunctional leaders that are abusive and treat employees with contempt and disrespect can use legitimate power to pressure subordinates into unethical conduct. In these situations, employees may not voice their concerns or may use anonymous reporting systems to deal with the dysfunctional leader.[52]

EXPERT POWER

Expert power is derived from a person's knowledge (or a perception that a person possesses knowledge). Expert power usually stems from a superior's credibility with subordinates. Credibility, and thus expert power, is positively correlated to the number of years a person worked in a firm or industry, education, and honors he or she has received for performance. The perception that a person is an expert on a specific topic can also confer expert power on him or her. A relatively low-level secretary may have expert power because he or she knows specific details about how the business operates and can even make suggestions on how to inflate revenue through expense reimbursements.

Expert power may cause ethical problems when used to manipulate others or gain an unfair advantage. Physicians, lawyers, and consultants can take unfair advantage of unknowing clients, for example. Accounting firms may gain extra income by ignoring concerns about the accuracy of financial data they examine in an audit.

REFERENT POWER

Referent power may exist when one person perceives that his or her goals or objectives are similar to another's. The second person may attempt to influence the first to take actions that allows both to achieve their objectives. Because they share the same goals, the first person perceives the other's use of referent power as beneficial. For this power relationship to be effective, some sort of empathy must exist between the individuals. Identification with others helps boost the decision maker's confidence, thus increasing the referent power.

Consider the following situation: Lisa Jones, a manager in the accounting department of a manufacturing firm, is pressured to increase the rate of processing sales. She asked Michael Wong, a salesperson, to speed up the delivery of sales contracts, and, if possible, encourage advanced sales with delayed delivery. Michael protests that he does not want to push customers for future sales. Lisa makes use of referent power. She invites Michael to lunch and they discuss their work concerns, including the problem of increasing sales for accounting purposes. They agree if document processing can be done through advanced sales, both will benefit. Lisa then suggests that Michael start sending sales contracts for the *next* quarter. He agrees to give it a try and within several weeks the contracts are moving faster and sales increase for the next quarter. Lisa's job is made easier, and Michael gets his commission checks a little sooner. On the other hand, this may be the start of channel stuffing, or inflating the sales and income in the current quarter.

The five bases of power are not mutually exclusive. People typically use several power bases to effect change in others. Although power in itself is neither ethical nor unethical, its use can raise ethical issues. Sometimes a leader uses power to manipulate a situation or a person's values in a way that creates a conflict with the person's value structure. For example, a manager who forces an employee to choose between staying home with a sick child and keeping a job is using coercive power and creating a direct conflict with the employee's values. In business, titles and salary signify power, but power and wealth often breed arrogance and are easily abused.

Motivating Ethical Behavior

A leader's ability to motivate subordinates plays a key role in maintaining an ethical organization. **Motivation** is a force within the individual that focuses his or her behavior toward achieving a goal. **Job performance** is considered to be a function of ability and motivation and can be represented by the equation (job performance = ability × motivation). This equation shows that employees can be motivated to accomplish things, but resources and know-how are also needed to get a job done. To create motivation, an organization offers positive incentives that encourage employees to work toward organizational objectives. Understanding motivation is important to effective management and can relate to employees' ethical behavior. It has been found that selection and training as well as job design and employee involvement improve principled ethical cultures. On the other hand, there is a danger that compensation and performance incentives can damage the ethical climate.[53] For example, a person who aspires to higher positions in an organization may find loopholes and manipulate them to gain a financial or performance incentive. This unethical behavior is directly related to the first employee's ambition (motivation) to rise in the organization and gain personal rewards. If an organization has shared values and an ethical culture, employees should be highly engaged and motivated because of their trust in others. Motivation incentives should not create ambiguous opportunities for misconduct.

As businesspeople move into middle management and beyond, higher-order needs (social connections, esteem, and recognition) tend to become more important than lower-order needs (salary, safety, and job security). Research shows an individual's career stage, age, organization size, and geographic location affect the relative priority given to satisfying respect, self-esteem, and basic physiological needs. An individual's hierarchy of needs may influence his or her motivation and ethical behavior. After basic needs such as food, working conditions (existence needs), and survival are satisfied, relatedness needs and growth needs become important. **Relatedness needs** are satisfied by social and interpersonal relationships, and **growth needs** by creative or productive activities.[54]

From an ethics perspective, needs or goals may change as a person progresses through the ranks of the company. This shift may cause or help solve problems depending on the person's current ethical status relative to the company or society. For example, junior executives might inflate purchase or sales orders, overbill time worked on projects, or accept cash gratuities if they are worried about providing for their families' basic physical necessities. As they continue up the ladder and are able to fulfill these needs, such concerns may become less important. Consequently, these managers may go back to obeying company policy or conforming to organizational culture and be more concerned with internal recognition and achievement than their families' physical needs. Younger employees tend to rely on organizational culture for guidance, but older employees have been found to improve ethical performance.

Examining the role motivation plays in ethics offers a way to relate business ethics to the broader social context in which workers live and the moral assumptions on which society depends. Workers are individuals and will be motivated by a variety of personal interests. Although we emphasize that managers are positioned to exert pressure and force individuals' compliance on ethically related issues, we also acknowledge an individual's personal ethics and needs will significantly affect his or her ethical decisions.

Organizational Structure

An organization's structure is important to the study of business ethics because the various roles and job descriptions that comprise that structure can create opportunities for unethical behavior. The structure of organizations can be described in many ways. For simplicity's sake, we discuss two broad categories of organizational structures—centralized and decentralized. These are not mutually exclusive structures; in the real world, organizational structures exist on a continuum. Table 7–5 compares strengths and weaknesses of centralized and decentralized structures.

In a **centralized organization**, decision-making authority is concentrated in the hands of top-level managers, and little authority is delegated to lower levels. Responsibility, both internal and external, rests with top-level managers. This structure is especially suited to organizations that make high-risk decisions and have lower-level managers not highly skilled in decision making. It is also suitable for organizations when production processes

TABLE 7–5 Structural Comparison of Organizational Types Emphasis

Characteristic	Centralized	Decentralized
Hierarchy of authority	Centralized	Decentralized
Flexibility	Low	High
Adaptability	Low	High
Problem recognition	Low	High
Implementation	High	Low
Dealing with changes	Poor environmental complexity	Good
Rules and procedures	Many and formal	Few and informal
Division of labor	Clear-cut	Ambiguous
Span of control	Many employees	Few employees
Use of managerial techniques	Extensive	Minimal
Coordination and control	Formal and impersonal	Informal and personal

© Cengage Learning

are routine and efficiency is of primary importance. These organizations are usually bureaucratic, and the division of labor is typically well defined. All workers know their job and what is expected; each has a clear understanding of how to carry out assigned tasks. Centralized organizations stress formal rules, policies, and procedures backed up with elaborate control systems. Codes of ethics may specify the techniques used for decision making. General Motors, the Internal Revenue Service, and the U.S. Army are examples of centralized organizations.

Because of the top-down approach and distance between managers and decision makers, centralized organizational structures can lead to unethical acts. If formal rules and policies are unfairly executed, they lose their validity or efficacy. To some extent, rules can be deactivated even if they are formally in force.[55] If the centralized organization is bureaucratic, some employees may behave according to the letter of the law rather than the spirit. A centralized organization can have a policy about bribes that does not include wording about donating to a client's favorite charity before or after a sale. Such donations can be construed as a tacit bribe because the employee buyer could be swayed by the donation, or gift, to act in a less than favorable way or not act in the best interests of the firm.

Other ethical concerns may arise in centralized structures because they typically have little upward communication. Top-level managers may not be aware of problems and unethical activity. Some companies' use of sweatshop labor may be one manifestation of this lack of upward communication. Sweatshops produce products such as clothing by employing laborers, sometimes through forced immigrant labor, who often work 12- to 16-hour shifts for little or no pay. The UN International Labor Office says 21 million people are victims of forced labor in the form of children enslaved in sweatshops, migrant laborers working on farms and building homes, illegal immigrants subservient to their smugglers, and other forms of coercion.[56] Another ethical issue that may arise in centralized organizations is blame shifting, or scapegoating. People may try to transfer blame for their actions to others who are not responsible. The specialization and rigid division of labor in centralized organizations can also create ethical problems. Employees may not understand how their actions affect the overall organization because they work with only one piece of a much larger puzzle. This lack of connectedness can lead employees to engage in unethical behavior because they fail to understand the overall ramifications of their behavior.

In a **decentralized organization**, decision-making authority is delegated as far down the chain of command as possible. Such organizations have relatively few formal rules, and coordination and control are usually informal and personal. They focus instead on increasing the flow of information. As a result, one of the main strengths of decentralized organizations is their adaptability and early recognition of external change. With greater flexibility, managers can react quickly to changes in their ethical environment. Google is known for being decentralized and empowering its employees. A parallel weakness of decentralized organizations is the difficulty in responding quickly to changes in policy and procedures established by top management. In addition, independent profit centers within a decentralized organization may deviate from organizational objectives. Decentralized firms may have fewer internal controls and use shared values for their ethical standards. If a firm depends on abstract values without specific rules of conduct, there may be more variation in behavior. Also, it may be harder to control rogue employees engaging in misconduct. Table 7–6 gives examples of centralized versus decentralized organizations and describes their different corporate cultures.

Because of the strict formalization and implementation of ethics policies and procedures in centralized organizations, they tend to be more ethical in their practices than decentralized organizations. Centralized organizations may also exert more influence on

TABLE 7–6 Examples of Centralized and Decentralized Corporate Cultures

Company	Organizational Culture	Characterized by
Nike	Decentralized	Creativity, freedom, informality
Southwest Airlines	Decentralized	Fun, teamwork orientation, loyalty
General Motors	Centralized	Unions, adherence to task assignments, structured
Microsoft	Decentralized	Creative, investigative, fast paced
Procter & Gamble	Centralized	Experienced, dependable, a rich history and tradition of products, powerful

© Cengage Learning

their employees because they have a central core of policies and codes of ethical conduct. Decentralized organizations give employees extensive decision-making autonomy because management empowers the employees. Ambiguity in the letter versus the spirit of rules can create ethical challenges, especially for newer managers.[57] However, it is also true that decentralized organizations may avoid ethical dilemmas through the use of effective codes of conduct and ethics. If widely shared values and effective ethics programs are in place in decentralized organizations, there may be less need for excessive compliance systems. However, different units in the company may evolve with diverse value systems and approaches to ethical decision making. A high-tech defense firm like Lockheed Martin might cope with different decisions on the same ethical issue if it did not have a centralized ethics program. Boeing has become more centralized since the entrance of CEO W. James McNerney, Jr. after a corporate scandal. Before McNerney stepped in, Boeing went through several years of ethics and legal difficulties. These include the jailing of the former CFO for illegal job negotiations with Pentagon officials and abuse of attorney-client privilege to cover up internal studies showing pay inequities, and other scandals.[58]

Unethical behavior is possible in centralized or decentralized structures when specific corporate cultures permit or encourage workers to deviate from accepted standards or ignore corporate legal and ethical responsibilities. Centralized firms may have a more difficult time uprooting unethical activity than decentralized organizations as the latter has a more fluid structure in which changes may affect only a small portion of the company. Often, when a centralized firm uncovers unethical activity and it appears to be pervasive, the leadership is removed so the old unethical culture is uprooted and replaced with a more ethical one. For example, Mitsubishi Motors suggested significant management changes after it was discovered a cover-up of auto defects had gone on for more than two decades.

GROUP DIMENSIONS OF CORPORATE STRUCTURE AND CULTURE

When discussing corporate culture, we tend to focus on the organization as a whole. But corporate values, beliefs, patterns, and rules are often expressed through smaller groups within the organization. Moreover, individual groups within organizations often adopt their own rules and values.

Types of Groups

Two categories of groups affect ethical behavior in business. A **formal group** is defined as an assembly of individuals with an organized structure that is explicitly accepted by the group. An **informal group** is defined as two or more individuals with a common interest but without an explicit organizational structure.

FORMAL GROUPS Formal groups can be divided into committees, work groups, and teams.

A *committee* is a formal group of individuals assigned to a specific task. Often a single manager could not complete the task, or management may believe a committee can better represent different constituencies and improve the coordination and implementation of decisions. Committees may meet regularly to review performance, develop plans, or make decisions. Most formal committees in organizations operate on an ongoing basis, but their membership may change over time. A committee is an excellent example of a situation that coworkers and significant others within the organization can use to influence ethical decisions. Committee decisions are legitimized in part by agreement or majority rule. In this respect, minority views on issues such as ethics can be pushed aside through the majority's authority. Committees bring diverse personal moral values to the ethical decision-making process and may expand the number of alternatives considered. Also inherent in the committee structure is a lack of individual responsibility. Because of the diverse composition of the group, members may not be committed or willing to assume responsibility for the group decision. Groupthink may emerge, enabling the majority to explain ethical considerations away.

Although many organizations have financial, diversity, personnel, or social responsibility committees, only a few organizations have committees devoted exclusively to ethics. An ethics committee can raise ethical concerns, resolve ethical issues or dilemmas in the organization, and create or update the company's code of ethics. Motorola, for example, maintains a Business Ethics Compliance Committee that interprets, classifies, communicates, and enforces the company's code and ethics initiatives. An ethics committee can gather information on functional areas of the business and examine manufacturing practices, personnel policies, dealings with suppliers, financial reporting, and sales techniques to determine if the company's practices are ethical. Though much of a corporation's culture operates informally, an ethics committee is an example of a highly formalized approach for dealing with ethical issues.

Work groups are used to subdivide duties within specific functional areas of a company. For example, on an automotive assembly line, one work group might install the seats and interior design elements of the vehicle while another group installs all the dashboard instruments. This enables production supervisors to specialize in a specific area and provide expert advice to work groups.

While work groups operate within a single functional area, *teams* bring together the expertise of employees from several different areas of the organization—such as finance, marketing, and production—on a single project, like developing a new product. Many manufacturing firms, including General Motors, Westinghouse, and Procter & Gamble, use the team concept to improve participative management. Ethical conflicts may arise because team members come from different functional areas. Each member of the team has a particular role to play and probably had limited interaction with other members of the team. Conflicts often occur when members of different organizational groups interact.

However, airing viewpoints representative of all the functional areas provides more options from which to choose.

Work groups and teams provide the organizational structure for group decision making. One of the reasons individuals cannot implement their own personal ethical beliefs in organizations is that work groups collectively reach so many decisions. However, those who have legitimate power are in a position to influence ethics-related activities. The work group and team often sanction certain activities as ethical or define others as unethical.

INFORMAL GROUPS   In addition to the groups businesses formally organize and recognize—such as committees, work groups, and teams—most organizations contain a number of informal groups. These groups are usually composed of individuals, often from the same department, who have similar interests and band together for companionship or for purposes that may or may not be relevant to the goals of the organization. For example, four or five people with similar tastes in outdoor activities and music may discuss their interests while working and may meet outside work for dinner, concerts, sports events, or other activities. Other informal groups may evolve to form a union, improve working conditions or benefits, get a manager fired, or protest work practices they view as unfair. Informal groups may generate disagreement and conflict, or enhance morale and job satisfaction.

Informal groups help develop informal channels of communication, sometimes called the grapevine, that are important in every organization. Informal communication flows up, down, diagonally, and horizontally, not necessarily following the communication lines on a company's organizational chart. Information passed along the grapevine may relate to the job, the organization, an ethical issue, or it may simply be gossip and rumors. The grapevine can act as an early warning system for employees. If employees learn informally that the company may be sold or a particular action will be condemned as unethical by top management or the community, they have time to think how they will respond. Because gossip is not uncommon in an organization, the information passed along the grapevine is not always accurate, but managers who understand how the grapevine works can use it to reinforce acceptable values and beliefs.

The grapevine is an important source of information for individuals to assess ethical behavior within their organization. One way an employee can determine acceptable behavior is to ask friends and peers in informal groups about the consequences of certain actions such as lying to a customer about a product-safety issue. The corporate culture may provide employees with a general understanding of the patterns and rules that govern behavior, but informal groups make this culture come alive and provide direction for employees' daily choices. For example, if new employees learn anecdotally through the grapevine that the organization does not punish ethical violations, they may seize the next opportunity for unethical behavior if it accomplishes the organization's objectives. There is a general tendency to discipline top sales performers more leniently than poor sales performers for engaging in identical forms of unethical selling behavior. A superior sales record appears to induce more lenient forms of discipline despite organizational policies that state otherwise.[59] In this case, the grapevine has clearly communicated that the organization rewards those who break the ethical rules to achieve desirable objectives.

Group Norms

Group norms are standards of behavior groups expect of their members. Just as corporate culture establishes behavior guidelines for an organization's members, group norms help define acceptable and unacceptable behavior within a group. In particular, group norms define the limit allowed on deviations from group expectations. Norms provide explicit ethical directions. For example, there may be a behavioral expectation that personal cell phones cannot be brought into the work place. Many group norms relate directly to managerial decisions. There may be the expectation that all advertising claims are truthful. Salespersons may be required to never lie to a customer.

Most work organizations develop norms that govern group rates of production and communication with management, as well as provide a general understanding of behavior considered right or wrong, ethical or unethical, within the group. For example, group members may punish an employee who reports to a supervisor that a coworker has covered up a serious production error. Other members of the group may glare at the informant, and refuse to talk to or sit next to him or her.

Norms have the power to enforce a strong degree of conformity among group members. At the same time, norms define the different roles for various positions within the organization. A low-ranking member of a group may be expected to carry out an unpleasant task such as accepting responsibility for someone else's ethical mistake. Abusive behavior toward new or lower-ranking employees could be a norm in an informal group.

Sometimes group norms conflict with the values and rules prescribed by the organization's culture. The organization may have policies prohibiting the use of personal social networking sites during work hours and use rewards and punishments to encourage this culture. In a particular informal group, norms may accept using personal social networking sites during work hours and try to avoid management's attention. Issues of equity may arise in this situation if other groups believe they are unfairly forced to follow policies that are not enforced on the other group. These employees may complain to management or the offending group. If they believe management is not taking corrective action they, too, may begin to use social networking for personal use, thus hurting the organization's productivity. For this reason, management must carefully monitor not only the corporate culture but also the norms of all the various groups within the organization. Sanctions may be necessary to bring in line a group whose norms deviate sharply from the overall culture.

VARIATION IN EMPLOYEE CONDUCT

Although a corporation is required to take responsibility for conducting its business ethically, a substantial amount of research indicates significant differences exist in individual employees' values and philosophies and therefore in how they deal with ethical issues.[60] Because people are culturally diverse and have different values, they interpret situations differently and the ethical decisions they make on the same issue will vary.

Table 7–7 shows approximately 10 percent of employees take advantage of situations to further their own personal interests. These individuals are more likely to manipulate, cheat, or act in a self-serving manner when the benefits gained from doing so are greater than the penalties for the misconduct. Such employees may choose to take office supplies from work for personal use if the only penalty they suffer is paying for the supplies. The lower the risk of being caught, the higher the likelihood that the 10 percent most likely to take advantage of the company will be involved in unethical activities.

Another 40 percent of workers go along with the work group on most matters. These employees are most concerned about the social implications of their actions and want to fit into the organization. Although they have personal opinions, they are easily influenced by what the people around them are doing. These individuals may know using office supplies for personal use is improper, yet they view it as acceptable because their coworkers do so. These employees rationalize their actions by saying the use of office supplies is a benefit of working at their particular company and it must be acceptable because the company does not enforce a policy prohibiting the behavior. Coupled with this philosophy is the belief that no one will get into trouble for doing what everybody else is doing.

About 40 percent of a company's employees, as shown in Table 7–7, always try to follow company policies and rules. These workers not only have a strong grasp of their corporate culture's definition of acceptable behavior, but also attempt to comply with codes of ethics, ethics training, and other communications about appropriate conduct. If the company has a policy prohibiting taking office supplies from work, these employees probably will observe it. However, they are not likely to speak out about the 40 percent who choose to go along with the work group, for these employees prefer to focus on their jobs and steer clear of any organizational misconduct. If the company fails to communicate standards of appropriate behavior, members of this group will devise their own.

The final 10 percent of employees try to maintain formal ethical standards that focus on rights, duties, and rules. They embrace values that assert certain inalienable rights and actions, which they perceive to be always ethically correct. In general, members of this group believe that their values are right and superior to the values of others in the company, or even to the company's value system, when an ethical conflict arises. These individuals have a tendency to report the misconduct of others or to speak out when they view activities within the company as unethical. Consequently, members of this group will probably report colleagues who take office supplies.

The significance of this variation in the way individuals behave ethically is simply the fact that employees use different approaches when making ethical decisions. Because of the probability that a large percentage of any work group will either take advantage of a situation or at least go along with the work group, it is vital companies provide communication and control mechanisms to maintain an ethical culture. Companies that fail to monitor activities and enforce ethics policies provide a low-risk environment for those employees inclined to take advantage of situations to accomplish their personal, and sometimes unethical, objectives.

Good business practices and concern for the law require organizations to recognize this variation in employees' desires to be ethical. The percentages cited in Table 7–7 are only estimates, and the actual percentages of each type of employee may vary widely across organizations based on individuals and corporate culture. The specific percentages are less important than the fact our research has identified these variations as existing within most organizations. Organizations should focus particular attention on managers who oversee the day-to-day operations of employees within the company. They should also provide training and communication to ensure the business operates ethically, it does not become

TABLE 7–7 Variation in Employee Conduct*

10%	40%	40%	10%
Follow their own values and beliefs; believe that their values are superior to those of others in the company	Always try to follow company policies	Go along with the work group	Take advantage of situations if the penalty is less than the benefit and the risk of being caught is low

© Cengage Learning

*Estimates based on the author's research and reports from ethics and compliance officers from many industries.

the victim of fraud or theft, and employees, customers, and other stakeholders are not abused through the misconduct of people who have a pattern of unethical behavior.

As seen throughout this book, examples can be cited of employees and managers with no concern for ethical conduct but who are nonetheless hired and placed in positions of trust. Some corporations continue to support executives who ignore environmental concerns, poor working conditions, or defective products, or engage in accounting fraud. Executives who get results, meaning profits, regardless of the consequences, are often admired and lauded, especially in the business press. When their unethical or even illegal actions become public knowledge, however, they risk more than the loss of their positions.

CAN PEOPLE CONTROL THEIR ACTIONS WITHIN A CORPORATE CULTURE?

Many people find it hard to believe an organization's culture can exert so strong an influence on individuals' behavior within the organization. In our society, we want to believe individuals control their own destinies. A popular way of viewing business ethics is to see it as a reflection of the alternative moral philosophies individuals use to resolve their personal moral dilemmas. As this chapter shows, ethical decisions within organizations are often made by committees and formal and informal groups, not by individuals. Decisions related to financial reporting, advertising, product design, sales practices, and pollution-control issues are often beyond the influence of individuals alone. In addition, these decisions are frequently based on business rather than personal goals.

Most new employees in highly bureaucratic organizations have limited input into the basic operating rules and procedures for getting things done. Along with learning sales tactics and accounting procedures, employees may be taught to ignore a design flaw in a product that could be dangerous to users. Although many personal ethics issues may seem straightforward and easy to resolve, individuals entering business usually need several years of experience within a specific industry to understand how to resolve ethical close calls. Both individual and organizational ethics have an impact on an employee's ethical intention. If there is congruence between individual ethics and the organizational ethical culture, the potential for making ethical choices in organizational decision making increases. Younger managers may need more support and guidance from the organization because of their limited experience in dealing with complex issues.[61] Research also indicates congruence between individual and organizational values is greater in the private sector. On the other hand, age and organizational type aside, personal values appear to be a strong factor in decreasing unethical practices and increasing appropriate work behavior as compared to congruence in personal and organizational values.[62]

It is not our purpose to suggest you should go along with management or the group on business ethics issues. Honesty and open discussions of ethical issues are important to successful ethical decision making. We believe most companies and businesspeople try to make ethical decisions. However, because there is so much difference among individuals, ethical conflict is inevitable. If you manage and supervise others, it will be necessary to maintain ethical policies for your organization and report misconduct that occurs. Ethics is not just a personal matter.

Regardless of how a person or organization views the acceptability of a particular activity, if society judges it to be wrong or unethical, then this larger view directly affects the organization's ability to achieve its goals. Not all activities deemed unethical by society are illegal, but if public opinion decries or consumers protest against a particular activity, the result may be legislation that restricts or bans a specific business practice. For instance, concern about promoting unhealthy products to children has prompted some governments to take action.

If people believe that their personal ethics severely conflict with the ethics of the work group and those of superiors in an organization, that person's only alternative may be to leave the organization. In the highly competitive employment market of the twenty-first century, quitting a job because of an ethical conflict requires courage and, possibly, the ability to survive without a job. Obviously, there are no easy answers for resolving ethical conflicts between the organization and the individual. Our goal is not to tell you what you should do. But we do believe that the more you know about how ethical decision making occurs within organizations, the more opportunity you have to influence decisions positively and help resolve ethical conflicts more effectively.

SUMMARY

Corporate culture refers to the set of values, beliefs, goals, norms, and ways of solving problems that members (employees) of an organization share. These shared values may be formally expressed or unspoken. Corporate cultures can be classified in several ways, and a cultural audit identifies an organization's culture. If an organization's culture rewards unethical behavior, people within the company are more likely to act unethically. A company's failure to monitor or manage its culture may foster questionable behavior.

Leadership has a significant impact on the ethical decision-making process because leaders have the power to motivate others and enforce both the organization's rules and policies and their own viewpoints. A leader must not only gain the respect of his or her followers but also provide a standard of ethical conduct. Leaders exert power to influence the behaviors and decisions of subordinates. There are five power bases from which a leader may influence ethical behavior: reward power, coercive power, legitimate power, expert power, and referent power. Leaders attempt to motivate subordinates; motivation is an internal force that focuses an individual's behavior toward achieving a goal. It can be created by the incentives an organization offers employees.

The structure of an organization may create opportunities to engage in unethical behavior. In a centralized organization, decision-making authority is concentrated in the hands of top managers, and little authority is delegated to lower levels. In a decentralized organization, decision-making authority is delegated as far down the chain of command as possible. Centralized organizations tend to be more ethical than decentralized ones because they enforce more rigid controls, such as codes of ethics and corporate policies, on ethical practices. However, unethical conduct can occur in both types of structures.

In addition to the values and customs that represent the culture of an organization, individual groups within the organization often adopt their own rules and values and even create subcultures. The main types of groups are formal groups—which include committees, work groups, and teams—and informal groups. Informal groups often feed an informal channel of communication called the grapevine. Group norms are standards of behavior groups expect of their members. They help define acceptable and unacceptable behavior within a group and especially the limits on deviating from group expectations. Sometimes group norms conflict with the values and rules prescribed by the organization's culture.

Sometimes an employee's personal ethical standards conflict with what is expected of him or her as a member of an organization and its corporate culture. This is especially true given that an organization's ethical decisions are often resolved by committees, formal groups, and informal groups rather than by individuals. When such ethical conflict is severe, the individual may have to decide whether to leave the organization.

IMPORTANT TERMS FOR REVIEW

Sarbanes–Oxley 404 186	differential association 193	job performance 200
apathetic culture 189	whistle-blowing 194	relatedness needs 200
caring culture 189	*qui tam relator* 195	growth needs 200
exacting culture 189	reward power 198	centralized organization 201
integrative culture 190	coercive power 198	decentralized organization 202
cultural audit 190	legitimate power 199	
compliance culture 191	expert power 199	formal group 204
values-based ethics culture 191	referent power 199	informal group 204
	motivation 200	group norm 205

RESOLVING ETHICAL BUSINESS CHALLENGES*

Candace always tried to do the right thing, but did not know what to do in this dilemma. She knew someone would get hurt. All because of an overzealous supervisor, she thought sadly.

Two years ago Candace took a job at ABCO Corporation in its public relations division. Although new to the corporate world, Candace quickly learned the ropes of the highly bureaucratic organization and excelled at many of her projects. As a result, her bosses assigned her more lucrative responsibilities.

The only downside to the job Candace could see was many people appeared to be promoted based more upon their relationships with their superiors than their merit. While Candace knew her work was excellent, she could not help but wonder whether her friendly repertoire with her immediate supervisors had anything to do with her success so far.

A few months ago, Candace learned her division would be getting a new supervisor. Britney transferred to her division from a similar position in another subsidiary of the company because of her proven talent for organizing and improving the efficiency of operations there. A no-nonsense type of manager, Britney was experienced and determined to be successful in this assignment as well. Candace knew from Britney's reputation that her success had everything to do with hard work and a commitment to make sure everyone else was working just as hard.

On the day Britney assumed her responsibilities as the new division manager, the company held a reception for her to meet the employees. At the reception, Britney circulated throughout the room, introducing herself to people and asking each of them if they had any suggestions that would make the section a better place to work. When she approached Candace, Candace decided to let her know what was bothering her.

"I don't want to make waves or anything, but one thing I've noticed happening recently is some people seem to gain promotions and are given opportunities to work overtime based on who likes them and not on the quality of their work," Candace told her. She quickly continued. "It's not that people here don't work hard or anything. It's just that I noticed there might some favoritism going on in some of the major personnel decisions."

Britney looked concerned, but smiled at Candace. "Thank you for telling me, Candace. I assure you I will do everything in my power to make sure this problem does not continue. This kind of thing has no place in the team I'm going to lead."

The next day, Britney requested Candace meet with her. As Candace entered Britney's office for the meeting,

Britney looked her straight in the face and said, "I will not tolerate individuals in this organization who are not team players. Yesterday afternoon you led me to believe there are people in this office who are not acting in the best interests of the company, and I want to know who. These people have no place in this division."

Candace was stunned. She did not want to hurt anyone. She just wanted to express her concerns in the hopes certain practices would change.

When she did not answer right away, Britney looked at her with annoyance. "Look," she said, "I want you to tell me the names of the managers you were referring to now, and keep me informed if you see anyone hurting this company, or I've got to think maybe you're part of the problems around here."

Candace tried to explain. "I'm sorry," she said. "I didn't want to implicate anyone in particular. I just wanted to alert you to some concerns I've been having…"

Britney cut Candace off before she could continue. "Candace, you seem like a smart person. I'm trying to create an example here. There are no shortcuts in this job. You work hard, or you get out. I've got no room for slackers. Now once again, who are the managers you were talking about?"

Candace's heart raced in her chest and she felt close to tears. Britney noticed because she sighed exasperatedly. "Fine. Here's what I'll do. We'll set up another meeting tomorrow and talk then. That'll give you time to think about where your priorities lie."

Candace sat at her desk, her work forgotten. She could not believe the mess she had gotten herself into. If she told Britney what she wanted, certain managers would get disciplined or perhaps even fired. Of course, it would be her word against theirs, so Candace knew she faced the risk of being thought of as someone who was just trying to make trouble. At the very least, the managers she named would dislike her for reporting them. But if she refused Britney, she risked the ire of her new boss.

QUESTIONS | EXERCISES

1. Describe the organizational structure of ABCO Corporation.
2. Which type of leadership power is Britney using? Do you feel it is effective in this situation?
3. Does Candace have any other alternatives than the two that she is considering?

*This case is strictly hypothetical; any resemblance to real persons, companies, or situations is coincidental.

> > > CHECK YOUR EQ

Check your EQ, or Ethics Quotient, by completing the following. Assess your performance to evaluate your overall understanding of the chapter material.

1. Decentralized organizations tend to put the blame for unethical behavior on lower-level personnel.   Yes   No

2. Decentralized organizations give employees extensive decision-making autonomy.   Yes   No

3. Corporate culture provides rules that govern behavior within the organization.   Yes   No

4. An integrative culture shows high concern for performance and little concern for people.   Yes   No

5. Coercive power works in the same manner as reward power.   Yes   No

ANSWERS **1. No.** This is more likely to occur in centralized organizations. **2. Yes.** This is known as empowerment. **3. Yes.** Values, beliefs, customs, and ceremonies represent what is acceptable and unacceptable in the organization. **4. No.** This describes an exacting culture. An integrative culture combines a high concern for people with a high concern for production. **5. No.** Coercive power is the opposite of reward power. One offers rewards and the other responds with punishment to encourage appropriate behavior.

ENDNOTES

1. J. W. Lorsch, "Managing Culture: The Invisible Barrier to Strategic Change," *California Management Review* 28, 2 (1986): 95–109.

2. Mutual of Omaha, "Company Profile," http://www.mutualofomaha.com/about/mission/ (accessed March 9, 2015).

3. Richard L. Daft, *Organizational Theory and Design* (Cincinnati, OH: South-Western, 2007).

4. Stanley M. Davis, quoted in Alyse Lynn Booth, "Who Are We?" *Public Relations Journal* (July 1985), 13–18.

5. Southwest Airlines, "Welcome to Adopt-A-Pilot," https://www.southwest.com/adoptapilot/ (accessed March 9, 2015).

6. Clay Latimer, "Philip Pillsbury's Treats Turned Into Tasty Sales," *Investor's Business Daily,* August 1, 2013, A3; Funding Universe, "The Pillsbury Company History," *International Directory of Company Histories,* Vol. 62, St. James Press, 2004, http://www.fundinguniverse.com/company-histories/the-pillsbury-company-history/ (accessed November 25, 2014); Suzy Goodsell, "The powerful legacy of Pillsbury," *Taste of General Mills,* June 23, 2011, http://www.blog.generalmills.com/2011/06/the-powerful-legacy-of-pillsbury/ (accessed March 9, 2015).

7. Abstracted and adapted from "Enhancing Compliance with Sarbanes–Oxley 404," *Quantisoft,* http://www.quantisoft.com/Industries/Ethics.htm (accessed March 9, 2015).

8. Taras Vasyl, Julie Rowney, and Piers Steel, "Half a Century of Measuring Culture: Approaches, Challenges, Limitations, and Suggestions Based on the Analysis of 121 Instruments for Quantifying Culture," white paper, 2008, Haskayne School of Business, University of Calgary, http://www.ucalgary.ca/~taras/_private/Half_a_Century_of_Measuring_Culture.pdf (accessed March 9, 2015).

9. Ibid.

10. David A. Ralston, Carolyn P. Egri, Olivier Furrer, Min-Hsun Kuo, Yongjuan Li, Florian Wangenheim, and Marina Dabic, "Societal-Level Versus Individual-Level Predictions of Ethical Behavior: A 48-Society Study of Collectivism and Individualism," *Journal of Business Ethics* 122, 2 (2014): 283–306.

11. Geert Hofstede, Bram Neuijen, Denise Daval Ohayv, and Geert Sanders, "Measuring Organizational Cultures: A Qualitative and Quantitative Study across Twenty Cases," *Administrative Science Quarterly* 35, 2 (1990): 286–316.

12. "Culture of trust," *IBM,* http://www.ibm.com/ibm/responsibility/trust.shtml (accessed March 9, 2015); IBM, *Basic Conduct Guidelines,* http://www.ibm.com/investor/pdf/BCG_Feb_2011_English_CE.pdf (accessed March 9, 2015).

13. Donna D. Bobek, Amy M. Hageman, and Robin R. Radtke, "The Influence of Roles and Organizational Fit on Accounting Professionals' Perceptions of their Firms' Ethical Environment," *Journal of Business Ethics* 126, 1 (2015): 125–141.

14. Cam Caldwell, Linda A. Hayes, and Do Tien Long, "Leadership, Trustworthiness, and Ethical Stewardship," *Journal of Business Ethics* 96, 4 (2010): 497–512.

15. William E. Shafer, "Ethical Climate, Social Responsibility, and Earnings Management," *Journal of Business Ethics* 126, 1 (2015): 43–60.

16. N. K. Sethia and M. A. Von Glinow, "Arriving at Four Cultures by Managing the Reward System," in *Gaining Control of the Corporate Culture* (San Francisco, CA: Jossey-Bass, 1985), 409.

17. UPS, "UPS Facts: Worldwide," *UPS,* http://www.ups.com/content/us/en/about/facts/worldwide.html (accessed March 9, 2015).

18. UPS, "Benefits," https://ups.managehr.com/benefits.htm (accessed March 9, 2015).

19. "100 Best Companies to Work for," *Fortune,* 2013, http://archive.fortune.com/magazines/fortune/best-companies/2013/snapshots/4.html (accessed March 9, 2015).

20. *2005 National Business Ethics Survey: How Employees Perceive Ethics at Work,* 20. Copyright © 2006, Ethics Resource Center (ERC), Used with permission of the ERC, 1747 Pennsylvania Ave. NW, Suite 400, Washington, DC 2006, www.ethics.org.

21. Susan M. Heathfield, "Five Tips for Effective Employee Recognition," http://humanresources.about.com/od/rewardrecognition/a/recognition_tip.htm (accessed March 9, 2015).

22. FedEx, "About FedEx: Our People," http://about.van.fedex.com/our-people/recognition-programs/ (accessed March 9, 2015).

23. Isabelle Maignan, O. C. Ferrell, and Thomas Hult, "Corporate Citizenship, Cultural Antecedents and Business Benefit," *Journal of the Academy of Marketing Science* 27, 4 (1999): 455–469.

24. Susanne Arvidsson, "Communication of Corporate Social Responsibility: A Study of the Views of Management Teams in Large Companies," *Journal of Business Ethics* 96, 3 (2010): 339–354.

25. Kub Chieh-Peng, Yehuda Barch, and Wei-Chi Shih, "Corporate Social Responsibility and Team Performance: The Mediating Role of Team Efficacy and Team Self-Esteem," *Journal of Business Ethics* 108, 2 (2012): 167–180.

26. R. Eric Reidenbach and Donald P. Robin, *Ethics and Profits* (Englewood Cliffs, NJ: Prentice-Hall, 1989), 92.

27. IKEA, "Our Business Idea," http://www.ikea.com/ms/en_IE/about_ikea/the_ikea_way/our_business_idea/index.html (accessed March 9, 2015); "IKEA U.S. Community Support Guidelines," http://www.ikea.com/ms/en_US/img/local_store_info/centennial/DONATIONS-IKEACentennial.pdf (accessed March 9, 2015).

28. Andrew Higgins and Stephen Castle, "Ikea Recalls Meatballs after Detection of Horse Meat," *The New York Times,* February 25, 2013, http://www.nytimes.com/2013/02/26/world/europe/ikea-recalls-its-meatballs-horse-meat-is-detected.html (accessed March 23, 2015).

29. E. Sutherland and D. R. Cressey, *Principles of Criminology,* 8th ed. (Chicago, IL: Lippincott, 1970), 114.

30. O. C. Ferrell and Larry G. Gresham, "A Contingency Framework for Understanding Ethical Decision Making in Marketing," *Journal of Marketing* 49, 3 (1985): 90–91.

31. Edward Wong, "Some at Shuttle Fuel Tank Plant See Quality Control Problems," *The New York Times,* February 18, 2003, http://www.nytimes.com/2003/02/18/national/nationalspecial/18ORLE.html (accessed March 9, 2015); *Columbia Crew Survival Investigation Report,* NASA, http://www.nasa.gov/pdf/298870main_SP-2008-565.pdf (accessed March 9, 2015).

32. Deborah L. Rhode and Amanda K. Packel, "Ethics and Nonprofits," *Stanford Social Innovation Review,* Summer

200), http://www.ssireview.org/articles/entry/ethics_and_nonprofits (accessed March 9, 2015).

33. "Whistle-blower Debate Heats up," *CFO*, February 11, 2011, http://www.cfo.com/article.cfm/14554934/c_14556017 (accessed March 9, 2015).

34. Matthew Goldstein, "Ex-Employees at Heart of Stanford Financial Probe," *BusinessWeek*, February 13, 2009, http://www.businessweek.com/bwdaily/dnflash/content/feb2009/db20090213_848258.htm (accessed March 9, 2015); Michael A. Lindenberger and Murray Waas, "Allen Sanford files 299-page appeal of his 110-year sentence," *The Dallas Morning News*, October 4, 2014, http://www.dallasnews.com/business/headlines/20141004-allen-stanford-files-299-page-appeal-of-his-110-year-sentence.ece (accessed March 9, 2015).

35. Thomas S. Mulligan, "Whistle-Blower Recounts Enron Tale," *The Los Angeles Times*, March 16, 2006, via http://www.whistleblowers.org/storage/whistleblowers/documents/whistle_blower_-_la_times.pdf (accessed March 9, 2015).

36. Nielsen P Richard, "Whistle-Blowing Methods for Navigating Within and Helping Reform Regulatory Institutions," *Journal of Business Ethics* 112, 3 (2013): 385–395.

37. John W. Schoen, "Split CEO-Chairman Job, Says Panel," *NBC News*, http://www.nbcnews.com/id/3073028/t/split-ceo-chairman-job-says-panel/#.UYGd1fUmx8E (accessed March 9, 2015).

38. Gardiner Harris and Duff Wilson, "Glaxo to Pay $750 Million for Sale of Bad Products," *The New York Times*, October 26, 2010, http://www.nytimes.com/2010/10/27/business/27drug.html?pagewanted=all&_r=0 (accessed March 9, 2015).

39. Loren Berlin, "JP Morgan Chase Whistleblower: 'Essentially Suicide' To Stand Up To Bank," *Huffington Post, May, 7, 2012*, http://www.huffingtonpost.com/2012/05/07/linda-almonte-jpmorgan-chase-whistleblower_n_1478268.html (accessed March 9, 2015).

40. "Qui Tam Tips: How to File a Whistle-blower Complaint," http://www.jameshoyer.com/practice_qui_tam.html?se=Overture (accessed March 9, 2015).

41. James Sandler, "The war on whistle-blowers," *Salon*, November 1, 2007, http://www.salon.com/news/feature/2007/11/01/whistleblowers (accessed March 9, 2015).

42. Wim Vandekerckhove, and Eva E. Tsahuridu, "Risky Rescues and the Duty to Blow the Whistle," *Journal of Business Ethics* 97, 3 (2010): 365–380.

43. Paula Dwyer and Dan Carney, with Amy Borrus, Lorraine Woellert, and Christopher Palmeri, "Year of the Whistle-blower," *BusinessWeek*, December 16, 2002, 106–110.

44. Paula J. Desio, "Federal Whistle-blower Rights Increase under the Stimulus Law," *Ethics Today*, February 18, 2009, http://www.ethics.org/ethics-today/0209/policy-report3.html (accessed March 9, 2015).

45. Darren Dahl, "Learning to Love Whistle-blowers," *Inc.*, March 2006, 21–23; Andrew Martin, "Housing Slump Forces Cuts at a Company Town," *The New York Times*, September 24, 2011, http://www.nytimes.com/2011/09/25/business/economy/housing-slump-forces-cuts-at-a-small-town-company.html?pagewanted=all (accessed March 9, 2015).

46. Marvin Windows admin, "Marvin Windows and Doors Recognized as Most Ethical Large Company in the Country With 2014 American Business Ethics Award," October 23, 2014, http://www.marvin.com/news-media/blog?view=marvin-windows-and-doors-recognized-as-most-ethical-large-company-in-the-country-with-2014-american-business-ethics-award&blog=2

47. Muel Kaptein, "From Inaction to External Whistle-blowing: The Influence of the Ethical Culture of Organizations on Employee Responses to Observed Wrongdoing," *Journal of Business Ethics* 98, 3 (2011): 513–530.

48. Alan Yuspeh, "Speaking up: Letter from the Editor," *Ethisphere*, Q1, 2010, 6.

49. Elina Riivari and Anna-Maija Lämsä, "Does It Pay to Be Ethical? Examining the Relationship between Organisations' Ethical Culture and Innovativeness," *Journal of Business Ethics* 124, 1 (2014): 1–17.

50. John R. P. French and Bertram Ravin, "The Bases of Social Power," in *Group Dynamics: Research and Theory*, ed. Dorwin Cartwright (Evanston, IL: Row, Peterson, 1962), 607–623.

51. Jennifer Bayot and Roben Farzad, "Ex-WorldCom CFO Gets Five Years for Role in Accounting Fraud," *The New York Times*, August 12, 2005, http://www.nytimes.com/2005/08/12/business/12worldcom.html?pagewanted=all (accessed March 9, 2015); "Ordered to Commit Fraud, A Staffer Balked, Then Caved," *The Wall Street Journal*, June 23, 2003, http://www.wsj.com/articles/SB105631811322355600 (accessed March 9, 2015).

52. Cam Caldwell and Mayra Canuto-Carranco, "'Organizational Terrorism' and Moral Choices: Exercising Voice When the Leader Is the Problem," *Journal of Business Ethics* 97, 1 (2010): 159–171.

53. M. Guerci, Giovanni Radaelli, Elena Siletti, Stefano Cirella, and A.B. Rami Shani, "The Impact of Human Resource Management Practices and Corporate Sustainability on Organizational Ethical Cultures: An Employee Perspective," *Journal of Business Ethics* 126, 1 (2015): 325–342.

54. Clayton Alderfer, *Existence, Relatedness, and Growth* (New York, NY: Free Press, 1972), 42–44.

55. Pablo Zoghbi-Manrique-de-Lara, "Do Unfair Procedures Predict Employees' Ethical Behavior by Deactivating Formal Regulations?" *Journal of Business Ethics* 94, 3 (2010): 411–425.

56. International Labour Organization, "Ryder: We've endorsed an 'agenda that really matters,'" June 12, 2014, http://www.ilo.org/global/about-the-ilo/media-centre/press-releases/WCMS_246893/lang--en/index.htm (accessed March 9, 2015).

57. Kathy Lund Dean, Jeri Mullins Beggs, and Timothy P. Keane, "Mid-level Managers, Organizational Context, and (Un)ethical Encounters," *Journal of Business Ethics* 97, 1 (2010): 51–69.

58. Stanley Holmes, "Cleaning up Boeing," *BusinessWeek* online, March 13, 2006, http://www.businessweek.com/stories/2006-03-12/cleaning-up-boeing (accessed March 9, 2015).

59. Joseph A. Belizzi and Ronald W. Hasty, "Supervising Unethical Sales Force Behavior: How Strong Is the Tendency to Treat Top Sales Performers Leniently?" *Journal of Business Ethics* 43, 4 (2003): 337–351.

60. John Fraedrich and O. C. Ferrell, "Cognitive Consistency of Marketing Managers in Ethical Situations," *Journal of the Academy of Marketing Science* 20, 3 (1992): 243–252.

61. B. Elango, Karen Paul, Sumit K. Kundu, and Shishir K. Paudel, "Organizational Ethics, Individual Ethics, and Ethical Intentions in International Decision Making," *Journal of Business Ethics* 97, 4 (2010): 543–561.

62. Damodar Suar and Rooplekha Khuntia, "Influence of Personal Values and Value Congruence on Unethical Practices and Work Behavior," *Journal of Business Ethics* 97, 3 (2010): 443–460.

CHAPTER 8

DEVELOPING AN EFFECTIVE ETHICS PROGRAM

AN ETHICAL DILEMMA*

Even though Todd had just graduated from Indiana University, he interned with Jennings Department Store for two summers. This experience helped him get promoted to Section Manager once he graduated. Although Todd was young and most of the people he managed were older, they respected him because of his expertise and ability to form good relationships with his coworkers and customers.

Several weeks ago, Todd began to hear rumors about one of the unit managers, Zara. He checked Zara's past financial reports and verified she was one of his better managers. Her unit posted the highest sales volume and growth, received positive customer feedback, and showed excellent cost control. The unit's people also did consistently well on inspections. In fact, Zara consistently rated higher than all the other managers for the last two years. Todd wondered why she hadn't been promoted. He knew upper management went over the financials with a magnifying glass. Todd decided to investigate further.

Over the next few weeks Todd began talking informally to those that knew Zara. He heard the same story over and over again. Zara was kind, firm, great with the customers, and looked out for her employees. Zara even had a dedicated following of customers that came in to ask questions about fashion and accessories. She had a client list that followed her tweets and made her department the cash cow of the store. Even though Zara had not graduated from college, she took night classes and was about a year away from her management degree.

Next, Todd spoke to some of Zara's retail clients. The comments made him realize just how much he needed to learn about retailing. They spoke of Zara's advice on shoes, dresses, and jewelry. Some told him they routinely came in to give Zara Christmas gifts. He discovered the store was doing so well in large part because this one employee cared about her clients and workers.

Yet as he questioned more clients, Todd found something rather odd. Some of the customers told him that for small items they handed Zara cash and told her to keep the change. Todd soon discovered these sales were not rung up. Next, he checked the store's shrinkage measures or items that may have been stolen or damaged. The records indicated some shrinkage but nothing significantly "excessive."

After a few weeks of investigation Todd discovered Zara used the money or cash as unrecorded payments to her retail staff. She gave the money in the form of performance bonuses, overtime incentives, and off-hours work. He knew this was in violation of company procedures, yet he couldn't definitively prove Zara was actually taking the shrinkage money and using it to achieve the high performance that had become her trademark. It wasn't as if the employees were being over paid, compared to top management's 700:1 income disparity ratio. Most employees just scraped by, as was evident by the company's high employee turnover rates. But Zara's turnover rate had always been low.

Todd could not definitively say whether Zara was stealing. He did know there were some cash purchases that were not recorded properly. However Zara was officially getting the money, whether through theft or simply by "keeping the change" the customers gave her for purchases, he knew that because the funds were not listed as income, the extra "wages" to Zara's employees meant no payroll taxes were being withheld. This meant Jennings was at risk for a tax liability action by the IRS.

Todd thought about what to do. He looked through the company's ethics code, but found the guidelines vague. The code itself only spanned two pages and did not provide any contact information for him to ask questions. Todd murmured under his breath, "Why did I start this mess? I should have left things alone." He knew nothing at a company is secret for long and his questions would soon alert others to start asking questions. On the other hand, he knew this had gone on for quite some time. Why had nobody noticed before?

QUESTIONS | EXERCISES

1. Describe some of the weaknesses in Jennings's ethics program.
2. Discuss the alternatives for Todd.
3. How has Zara been given the opportunity to engage in misconduct?

*This case is strictly hypothetical; any resemblance to real persons, companies, or situations is coincidental.

Programs designed to foster ethical decision making in business are being embraced by most firms today. Ethics programs have to be well-designed and effective to prevent major misconduct. Enron, BP, and JP Morgan are examples of organizations with codes of ethics that experienced ethical disasters. Some business leaders believe ethics initiatives should arise naturally from a company's corporate culture and that simply hiring good employees limits unethical conduct. Moreover, business executives and board members often do not understand how organizational ethics can be systematically implemented. In business, many ethical issues are complex and require organizations to reach a consensus on appropriate action. Top executives and boards of directors must provide the leadership and a system to resolve these issues. Legislation and regulatory rules require leadership to create and implement effective ethics programs. These requirements come into play when misconduct is investigated by the government. We believe customized ethics and compliance programs assist businesses in providing guidance so employees from diverse backgrounds understand what behaviors are acceptable (and unacceptable) within the organization.

Business ethics programs have the potential to help top managers establish an ethical culture and eliminate the opportunity for unethical conduct. This chapter provides a framework for developing an ethics program consistent with research, best practices, and the decision-making process described in Chapter 5, as well as with the Federal Sentencing Guidelines for Organizations (FSGO), the Sarbanes–Oxley Act, and the Dodd–Frank Act described in Chapter 4. These legislative reforms require executives and boards of directors to assume responsibility and ensure ethical standards are properly implemented on a daily basis.

In this chapter, we first examine the corporation as a social entity, then provide an overview of why businesses need to develop organizational ethics programs. Next, we consider the factors that must be incorporated in such a program: a code of conduct, an ethics officer and the appropriate delegation of authority, an effective ethics-training program, a system for monitoring and supporting ethical compliance, and continual efforts to improve the ethics program. Finally, we consider common mistakes in designing and implementing ethics programs.

THE RESPONSIBILITY OF THE CORPORATION TO STAKEHOLDERS

Increasingly, corporations are viewed not merely as profit-making entities but also as moral agents accountable for their conduct to their stakeholders, including employees, investors, suppliers, governments, and customers. Companies are more than the sum of their parts or participants. Because corporations are chartered as citizens of a state and/or nation, they generally have the same rights and responsibilities as individuals. Through legislation and court precedents, society holds companies accountable for the conduct of their employees as well as for their decisions and the consequences of those decisions. Coverage in the news media of specific issues such as employee benefits, executive compensation, defective products, competitive practices, and financial reporting contributes to a firm's reputation as a moral agent.

As moral agents, companies are required to obey the laws and regulations that define acceptable business conduct. However, it is important to acknowledge they are not human beings who can think through moral issues. Because companies are not human, laws and regulations are necessary to provide formal structural restraints and guidance. Employees have an ethical obligation to responsibly think through complex ethical issues to contribute to the ethical conduct of the corporation as a whole.[1]

Figure 8–1 illustrates the most commonly observed forms of misconduct at Fortune 500° corporations. A key reason why people seem to engage in misconduct is they feel pressured to do "whatever it takes to meet business targets."

FIGURE 8–1 **Most Common Employee Observed Forms of Misconduct at Fortune 500© Companies**

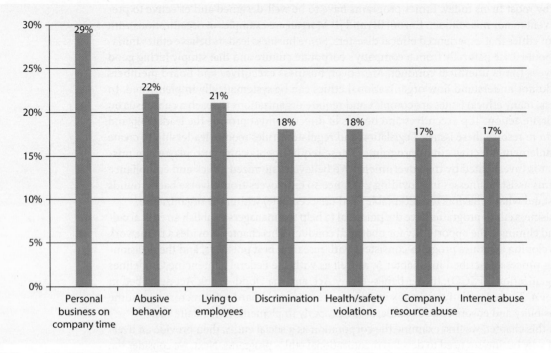

Source: Ethics Resource Center, *National Business Ethics Survey® of Fortune 500® Employees: An Investigation into the State of Ethics at America"s Most Powerful Companies* (Arlington, VA: Ethics Resource Center, 2012).

Though obviously not a person, a corporation can be considered a moral agent in society created to perform specific social functions. It is therefore responsible to society for its actions. Because corporations have characteristics of agents, responsibility for ethical behavior is assigned to them as legal entities, as well as to individuals or work groups they employ. A corporate culture without values and appropriate communication about ethics can facilitate individual misconduct. Some corporate outcomes cannot be tied to one individual or group, and misconduct can be the result of a collective pattern of decisions supported by a corporate culture. Therefore, corporations can be held accountable when they are found to be operating in a manner inconsistent with major legal requirements. Large fines and negative publicity have put many companies out of business. On the other hand, an organization that demonstrates integrity leads to increased customer trust and better business. As an example, when Granite Construction, known for its strong ethics program and guiding principles, found that it might have inadvertently overcharged customers for services, it immediately notified the customers even before it knew for sure and worked with them for years to rectify the problem. While the customers had not realized they had been overcharged, giving Granite the opportunity to allow the issue to go unnoticed, the company knew it could not ignore the issue and continue to follow the strong ethical principles that have made it a trustworthy organization.[2]

In many cases, a coherent ethical corporate culture does not evolve through independent individual and interpersonal relationships. Although ethics is often viewed as an individual matter, many believe the best way to develop an ethical corporate culture is to provide character education to existing employees or hire individuals with good character and sensitize them to ethical issues. This theory assumes ethical conduct develops through company-wide agreement and consensus. Although these assumptions are laudable and contain some truth, companies that are responsible for most of the economic activity in the world employ thousands of culturally diverse individuals who will never reach agreement on all ethical issues. Many ethical business issues are complex close calls or gray areas, and the only way to ensure consistent decisions that represent the interests of all stakeholders is to require ethical policies. This chapter provides support for the idea that implementing a centralized corporate ethics program can provide a cohesive, internally consistent set of statements and policies representing the corporation as a moral agent.

THE NEED FOR ORGANIZATIONAL ETHICS PROGRAMS

To understand why companies need to develop ethics programs, judge whether each of the following actions is unethical versus illegal.

- You want to skip work to go to a baseball game, but you need a doctor's excuse. You make up symptoms so that your insurance company pays for the doctor's visit. (unethical, illegal)

- While having a latte at a local café, you run into an acquaintance who works as a salesperson for a competing firm. You wind up chatting about future product prices. When you get back to your office, you tell your supervisor what you heard. (unethical, illegal)

- You are fired from your company, but before leaving for a position with another company, you copy a confidential list of client names and telephone numbers you compiled for your former employer. (unethical, illegal)

- You receive a loan from your parents to make the down payment on your first home, but when describing the source of the down payment on the mortgage application, you characterize it as a gift. (unethical, illegal)

- Your manager asks you to book some sales revenue from the next quarter into this quarter's sales report to help the firm reach target sales figures. You agree to do so. (unethical, illegal)

You probably labeled one or more of these five scenarios as unethical rather than illegal. The reality is all of them have the potential to be illegal. You may have chosen incorrectly because it is nearly impossible to know every detail of the highly complex laws relevant to these situations. Consider that there are 10,000 laws and regulations associated with the processing and selling of a single hamburger. Unless you are a lawyer specializing in a particular area, it is difficult to know every law associated with your job. However, you can become more sensitized to what might be unethical or, in these cases, illegal. One reason ethics programs are required in one form or another is to sensitize employees to the potential legal and ethical issues within their work environments. Studies show ethics programs can increase employees' ethical awareness, participation in ethical decision making, and ethical behavior.[3]

As previously discussed, ethics scandals in U.S. businesses have destroyed employees' trust in top management and significantly lowered the public's trust of business. Even highly respected individuals such as government officials or doctors have seen trust diminish. FDA advisory committees, for instance, have been criticized for alleged conflicts of interest when voting on new drug approval. Approximately 13 percent of members of a committee were found to have financial ties to the company whose drug was up for review. Those that have ties only to the drug maker seeking approval are 1.5 times more likely to vote for approval than committee members with no financial ties.[4] This makes it crucial to ensure proper controls are in place to detect conflict of interest, especially in areas where a decision could have significant impact on consumer well-being.

Pepsi CEO Indra Nooyi believes all businesses are challenged to restore consumer confidence and trust. She stated that rebuilding trust will "require all companies to think again about what they do to build trust, and to think again about how they make, give, and add value."[5] Understanding the factors that influence the ethical decision-making process, as discussed in Chapter 5, can help companies encourage ethical behavior and discourage undesirable conduct. Fostering ethical decision making within an organization requires terminating unethical employees and improving the firm's ethical standards. Consider the "bad apple–bad barrel" analogy. Some people are simply "bad apples" who will always do things in their self-interest regardless of their organization's goals or accepted standards of conduct.[6] For example, Raj Rajaratnam, cofounder of the hedge fund Galleon Group, allegedly used a "corrupt network" of consultants to make illegal profits. According to prosecutors, Rajaratnam and employees at Galleon Group engaged in insider trading on over 35 stocks, generating $45 million in profits. The corporate culture at Galleon Group appears to have promoted illegal behavior simply as a way of doing business.[7] Eliminating bad apples through screening techniques and enforcement of a firm's ethical standards can improve the firm's overall behavior.[8]

Organizations can also become "bad barrels," not because individuals are bad, but the pressures to succeed create opportunities that reward unethical decisions. In the case of bad barrels, firms must redesign their image and culture to conform to industry and social standards of acceptable behavior.[9] Most companies attempt to improve ethical decision making by establishing and implementing a strategic approach to improving their organizations' ethics. Companies as diverse as Texas Instruments, Starbucks, Ford Motor Co., and Whole Foods have adopted a strategic approach to organizational ethics. They continuously monitor their programs and make adjustments when problems occur.

To promote legal and ethical conduct, an organization should develop a program by establishing, communicating, and monitoring the ethical values and legal requirements that characterize its history, culture, industry, and operating environment. Without such programs, uniform standards, and policies of conduct, it is difficult for employees to determine what behaviors are acceptable within a company. As discussed in Chapters 6 and 7, in the absence of such programs and standards, employees generally make decisions based on their own observations of how their coworkers and superiors behave. A strong ethics program includes a written code of conduct; an ethics officer to oversee the program; careful delegation of authority; formal ethics training; and rigorous auditing, monitoring, enforcement, and revision of program standards. Without a strong program, problems are likely to occur. For example, despite laws protecting intellectual property in China, weak compliance programs have created piracy problems for businesses. Microsoft and other companies in the Business Software Alliance estimate almost 80 percent of software for personal computers in China is pirated material. However, top officials in China's government in charge of combating copyright violations claim this number is distorted.[10] Microsoft has also begun convincing state attorneys general to enter the debate as it is believed that software piracy can lead to significant job losses in the manufacturing industries of certain states.[11]

Although there are no universal standards that can be applied to organizational ethics programs, most companies develop codes, values, or policies to provide guidance on business conduct. The American Institute of CPAs Code of Professional Conduct and Bylaws, for instance, is nearly 400 pages and covers areas such as accounting principles, responsibilities to different stakeholders, and principles for professional conduct.[12] It would be naïve to think simply having a code of ethics solves all the ethical dilemmas a company might face.[13] Indeed, most of the companies that have experienced ethical and legal difficulties in recent years had formal ethics codes and programs. The problem is top managers have not integrated these codes, values, and standards into their firms' corporate cultures where they can provide effective guidance for daily decision making. High-status officials may be more inclined to engage in unethical organizational conduct because social isolation can create insensitivity and a lower motivation to regulate ethical decision making.[14] The tendency of managers to overlook ethical issues is called normative myopia and will be discussed further in Chapter 11. Top managers tend to focus on financial performance because their jobs and personal identities are often intimately connected to their firms' quarterly returns. A culture of short-term performance as a company's highest priority can diminish ethical decision making. On the other hand, Warren Buffett's Berkshire Hathaway corporations, such as Burlington Northern Santa Fe and GEICO, are not subject to Wall Street's quarterly returns and can focus on an unusual commitment to long-run performance and responsible conduct.[15]

If a company's leadership fails to provide the vision and support needed for ethical conduct, then an ethics program will not be effective. Ethical responsibility is not something to be delegated to lower-level employees. To satisfy the public's escalating demands for ethical decision making companies need to develop plans and structures for addressing ethical considerations. Some directions for improving ethics are mandated through regulations, but companies must be willing to put in place a system for implementing values and ethics that exceeds the minimum requirements.

AN EFFECTIVE ETHICS PROGRAM

Throughout this book, we emphasize that ethical issues are at the forefront of organizational concerns as managers and employees face increasingly complex decisions. These decisions are often made in a group environment composed of different value systems, competitive pressures, and political concerns that contribute to the opportunity for misconduct. The more misconduct occurs at a company, the less trust employees feel toward the organization—and the greater the turnover will likely be. Trust is a key component of an engaged workforce. It is important for managers to create a work environment where employees can trust organizational leaders, managers, and fellow employees.[16] When opportunities to engage in unethical conduct abound, companies are vulnerable to ethical problems and legal violations if their employees do not know how to make the right decisions.

A company must have an effective ethics program to ensure all employees understand its values and comply with the policies and codes of conduct. If the culture encourages unethical conduct, then misconduct is likely to occur even if the company has ethical guidelines in place. French bank BNP Paribas ignored red flags that its activities in sanctioned countries violated laws. Even when another banking firm reached a massive settlement with U.S. regulators for similar activities, BNP Paribas ignored internal warnings and continued to engage in processing transactions from Sudan, Cuba, and Iran. The company paid $8.7 billion to U.S. authorities for knowingly breaking trade embargos.[17]

Because we come from diverse business, educational, and family backgrounds, it cannot be assumed we know how to behave appropriately when we enter a new organization or job. The pharmaceutical company Merck requires all employees to be responsible for supporting its Code of Business Conduct that is available in 27 languages. Employees take classes in ethics to help them understand how to resolve ethical dilemmas in the workplace, as well as receiving online training to raise their awareness of ethical issues and assist them in maintaining an ethical organizational culture.[18] It would therefore appear that the creation of effective ethics programs like Merck's Code of Business Conduct acts as important deterrents to organizational misconduct. Research provides evidence that unethical behavior occurs less frequently in organizations that have a well-implemented ethics program. Within the ethics program the most important component to deter misconduct is accountability policies.[19]

An Ethics Program Can Help Avoid Legal Problems

As mentioned in Chapter 7, some corporate cultures provide opportunities for or reward unethical conduct because management is not sufficiently concerned about ethics or the company failed to comply with the minimum requirements of the Federal Sentencing Guidelines for Organizations (FSGO) (Table 8–1). Companies may face penalties and the loss of public confidence if one of their employees breaks the law. The FSGO encourages companies to assess their key risk areas and customize a compliance program to address these risks and satisfy key effectiveness criteria. An effective risk assessment involves not only examining legal issues but also environmental, health and safety, and other risk areas. Companies should prioritize and weigh these risks based on their potential impact on the organization. Firms can then use these risk assessments to change or update internal control mechanisms. It is also important to monitor and weigh the risks of third-party suppliers and/or business partners since a company can be damaged by misconduct that occurs in the supply chain.

A good example of this is SNC-Lavalin. The CEO of this leading Canadian engineering construction group was charged with fraud for allegedly approving $56 million worth of untraceable payments. Before 2013 SNC-Lavalin did not have an ethics and compliance program. In this case, concern centered on the tone from the top, so the company had to build an ethics and compliance culture from scratch. One of the first things they did was hire a top-level ethics and compliance officer. Concerned with tone at the top, the company provided managers with spreadsheets to record all the times they talked about ethics during the day and who they talked with as a form of measurement. Training was provided to third parties to assess risk and how to address it. Their new motto became "Prevent, Detect, and Act" with continuous evaluation of ethics and compliance behavior.[20]

Guidelines also hold companies responsible for the misconduct of their employees. Indeed, an Ernst & Young global survey of 2,719 executives in major corporations from 59 countries revealed that chief financial officers score higher than the average total in

TABLE 8–1 Minimum Requirements for Ethics and Compliance Programs

1. Standards and procedures, such as codes of ethics, that are reasonably capable of detecting and preventing misconduct

2. High-level personnel who are responsible for an ethics and compliance program

3. No substantial discretionary authority given to individuals with a propensity for misconduct

4. Standards and procedures communicated effectively via ethics training programs

5. Systems to monitor, audit, and report misconduct

6. Consistent enforcement of standards, codes, and punishment

7. Continuous improvement of the ethics and compliance program

Source: Based on U.S. Sentencing Commission, *Federal Sentencing Guidelines Manual*, effective November 1, 2004 (St. Paul, MN: West, 2008).

their willingness to choose from a list of questionable actions. Figure 8–2 shows the percentage of executives willing to misstate financial performance and then breaks them down by type of executive. About 6 percent claim they would be willing to misstate financial performance, with CEOs at the highest.[21] Ethics programs that provide guidelines outlining board responsibilities encourage compliance at the highest levels of the organization.

At the heart of the FSGO is a "carrot-and-stick" philosophy. Companies that act to prevent misconduct by establishing and enforcing ethical and legal compliance programs may receive a "carrot" and avoid penalties should a violation occur. The ultimate "stick" is the possibility of being fined or put on probation if convicted of a crime. Organizational probation involves using on-site consultants to observe and monitor a company's legal compliance efforts as well as to report the company's progress toward avoiding misconduct to the U.S. Sentencing Commission. Table 8–2 shows the fines the Securities and Exchange Commission has levied against well-known firms for corporate misconduct. Conversely, it is important for organizations to consider incentives for employees who do act according to ethical standards. Recently updated Foreign Corrupt Practices Act guidelines recommend incorporating incentives into the firm's corporate culture to encourage ethical behavior.[22]

FIGURE 8–2 Willingness to Misstate Financial Performance

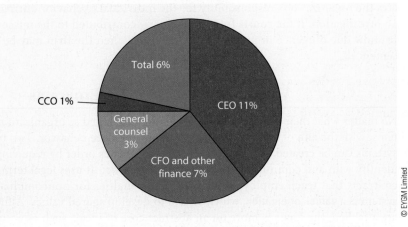

Source: Ernst & Young, *Overcoming compliance fatigue: Reinforcing the commitment to ethical growth—13th Global Fraud Survey*, 2014, p. 7

TABLE 8–2 Penalties for Corporate Misconduct

Company	Penalty	Reason
WorldCom	$750 million	Accounting fraud
Goldman Sachs	$550 million	Misleading investors
Fannie Mae	$400 million	Accounting fraud
Time Warner	$300 million	Accounting fraud
JP Morgan Securities	$296.9 million	Misleading investors
Qwest	$250 million	Accounting fraud
Bank of America	$150 million	Misleading investors
Credit Suisse Group	$196.5 million	Violating federal securities laws

Source: Matt Phillips, "SEC's Greatest Hits: Biggest Penalties. Ever." *The Wall Street Journal*, July 16, 2010, http://blogs.wsj.com/marketbeat/2010/07/16/secs-greatest-hits-some-of-the-other-biggest-penalties/ (accessed March 26, 2015); Melanie Waddell, "SEC's 16 Biggest Penalties Since Financial Crisis," *AdvisorOne*, January 24, 2013, http://www.advisorone.com/2013/01/24/secs-16-biggest-penalties-since-financial-crisis?t=risk-management&page=2 (accessed March 26, 2015); Jonathan Stempel, "Credit Suisse pays $196.5 million, admits wrongdoing in SEC settlement," *Reuters*, February 21, 2014, http://www.reuters.com/article/2014/02/21/us-creditsuisse-sec-settlement-idUSBREA1K1H620140221 (accessed August 4, 2015).

The FSGO encourages federal judges to increase fines for organizations that continually tolerate misconduct and to reduce or eliminate fines for firms with extensive compliance programs that make due diligence attempts to abide by legal and ethical standards. Until the guidelines were formulated, courts were inconsistent in holding corporations responsible for employee misconduct. There was no incentive to build effective programs to encourage employees to make ethical and legal decisions. Now companies earn credit for creating ethics programs that meet a rigorous standard. The effectiveness of a program is determined by its design and implementation. In other words, the program must deal effectively with the risks associated with a particular business and must become part of the corporate culture.

An ethics program can help a firm avoid civil liability, but the company still bears the burden of proving it has an effective program. A program developed in the absence of misconduct will be more effective than one imposed as a reaction to scandal or prosecution. A legal test of a company's ethics program may occur when an individual employee is charged with misconduct. The court system or the U.S. Sentencing Commission evaluates the organization's responsibility for the individual's behavior during the process of an investigation. If the courts find the company contributed to the misconduct or failed to show due diligence in preventing misconduct, then the firm may be convicted and sentenced.

Values versus Compliance Programs

No matter what their goals, ethics programs are developed as organizational control systems, with the aim of creating predictability in employee behavior. Two types of control systems can be created. A **compliance orientation** creates order by requiring employees to identify with and commit to specific required conduct. It uses legal terms, statutes, and contracts that teach employees the rules and penalties for noncompliance. The other system is a **values orientation**, which strives to develop shared values. Although penalties are attached, the focus is more on an abstract core of ideals such as accountability and commitment. Studies found that when personal and organizational values are compatible with one another, it tends to positively influence workplace ethics.[23]

The advantage of a values orientation is it gives employees a clearly defined basis on which to make decisions, one in which fairness, compassion, respect, and transparency are paramount. At the same time, diversity in employees' experience and personal values requires explicit communication and training on subject matter areas such as financial reporting, use of company resources, and intellectual property. Establishing compliance standards helps employees understand rules of conduct when there are identified risks. For example, rules on the recruiting and hiring of new employees will help enforce company policy and prevent legal violations. When there are new, unexpected, or ambiguous issues with no compliance requirements, values may help the employee navigate through the ethical issues at hand.

Research into compliance- and values-based approaches reveals both types of programs can interact or work toward the same end, but a values orientation has the added benefit of sparking ethical reasoning among employees. Values-based programs increase employees' awareness of ethics at work, integrity, willingness to deliver information to supervisors, use of reporting mechanisms, and perception that ethical decisions are being made. Compliance-based programs are linked to employees' awareness of ethical risks at work and a clear understanding of rules and expectations that facilitates decision making. In the final analysis, both orientations can be used to help employees and managers; however, a values-based program is the foundation of an organizational ethical culture.

CODES OF CONDUCT

The perception of business accountability has changed over the years; expectations for organizational codes of ethics have grown. Today, society expects to see employees adhere to ethical principles and standards specified through company ethics programs.[24] Most companies begin the process of establishing organizational ethics programs by developing **codes of conduct,** or formal statements that describe what an organization expects of its employees. Such statements may take three different forms: a code of ethics, a code of conduct, and a statement of values. A **code of ethics** is the most comprehensive and consists of general statements, sometimes altruistic or inspirational, that serve as principles and as the basis for rules of conduct. A code of ethics generally specifies methods for reporting violations, disciplinary action for violations, and a structure of due process. Table 8–3 describes some benefits of having a comprehensive code of ethics. A code of conduct is a written document that may contain some inspirational statements but mainly specifies acceptable and unacceptable types of behavior. A code of conduct is more akin to a regulatory set of rules and, as such, tends to elicit less debate about specific actions. Some of the key reasons that codes of ethics fail are (1) the code is not promoted and employees do not read it; (2) the code is not easily accessible; (3) the code is written too legalistically and therefore is not understandable by average employees; (4) the code is written too vaguely, providing no accurate direction; and (5) top management never refers to the code in body or spirit.[25]

The final type of ethical statement is a **statement of values** that serves the general public and also addresses distinct groups such as stakeholders. Values statements are conceived by management and are fully developed with input from all stakeholders. Despite the distinction made in this book between a code of ethics and a values statement, it is important to recognize these terms are often used interchangeably.

DEBATE ISSUE
TAKE A STAND

Examining Banking Companies' Codes of Conduct

The financial industry has been involved with significant misconduct. Much recent regulation, including the Dodd–Frank Act, is focused on protecting consumers and avoiding misconduct. Codes of conduct, sometimes referred to as codes of ethics, should provide behavioral expectations an organization maintains for its managers, employees, and agents. Section 406 of the Sarbanes–Oxley Act requires a code of ethics for financial officers. Recent research shows companies with a code of ethics for financial officers are more likely to restate their earnings voluntarily. The Ethisphere Institute developed a grade methodology for evaluating codes of conduct, using the criteria of public availability, tone from the top, readability and tone, non-retaliation and reporting, values and commitments, risk topics, comprehension aids, and presentation and style. Of the 25 companies evaluated in the banking industry, only two banks received a relatively high ranking. It is interesting that in the banking industry, 19 of the 25 companies received an F for tone at the top, indicating a lack of communication from the CEO or Chairman of the Board. This seems to suggest that misconduct tends to occur more frequently in organizations with badly written codes of conduct.[26]

1. The Ethisphere Institute's analysis of banking codes of conduct explains why widespread misconduct has been so prevalent in the financial industry.
2. Written codes of conduct are only a small part of the ethical culture of a company and cannot by themselves explain why misconduct has been so widespread in the financial industry.

Regardless of its degree of comprehensiveness, a code of ethics should reflect upper managers' desires for compliance with the values, rules, and policies that support an ethical culture. The development of a code of ethics should involve the board of directors, CEO, and executive officers who will implement the code. Legal staff should also be called on to ensure the code has correctly assessed key areas of risk and provides buffers for potential legal problems. Employee involvement enables the empowerment of all members of the organization to create shared values. Involving employees has a systematic and far-reaching impact in advancing ethical decisions.[27] A code of ethics that does not address specific high-risk activities within the scope of daily operations is inadequate for maintaining standards that prevent misconduct. Table 8–4 shows factors to consider when developing and implementing a code of ethics.

Codes of ethics may address a variety of situations, from internal operations to sales presentations and financial disclosure practices. Research found that corporate codes of ethics often contain about six core values or principles in addition to more detailed descriptions and examples of appropriate conduct.[28] The six values that have been suggested as being desirable for codes of ethics are (1) trustworthiness, (2) respect, (3) responsibility, (4) fairness, (5) caring, and (6) citizenship.[29] These values will not be effective without distribution, training, and the support of top management in making these values a part of the corporate culture. A study of 75 U.S. firms revealed that their codes of ethics were similar in content and the content was often vague.[30] This emphasizes the need for companies to develop codes that address issues common to their particular field or industry. Employees need specific examples of how these values can be implemented.

Research demonstrates that employees at organizations with effective ethical codes of conduct tend to be less tolerant of unethical behavior toward stakeholders than those at companies without ethical codes.[31] Codes of conduct will not resolve every ethical issue encountered in daily operations, but they help employees and managers deal with ethical dilemmas by prescribing or limiting specific activities. Many companies have a code of ethics, but it is not communicated effectively. A code placed on a website or in a training manual is useless if it is not reinforced each day. By communicating to employees both what is expected of them and what punishments they face if they violate the rules, codes of conduct curtail opportunities for unethical behavior and thereby improve ethical decision making. For example, the American Society for Civil Engineers' code of ethics specifies that engineers must act with zero tolerance toward bribery, fraud, and corruption in all engineering and construction projects in which they are engaged.[32] Codes of conduct do not have to be so detailed they take into account every

TABLE 8–3 Benefits of Having an Ethics Code

A Comprehensive Code of Conduct Can...

1. Guide employees in situations where the ethical course of action is not immediately obvious.

2. Help the company reinforce—and acquaint new employees with—its culture and values. A code can help create a climate of integrity and excellence.

3. Help the company communicate its expectations for its staff to suppliers, vendors, and customers.

4. Minimize subjective and inconsistent management standards.

5. Help a company remain in compliance with complex government regulations.

6. Build public trust and enhance business reputations.

7. Offer protection in preempting or defending against lawsuits.

8. Enhance morale, employee pride, loyalty, and the recruitment of outstanding employees.

9. Promote constructive social change by raising awareness of the community's needs and encouraging employees and other stakeholders to help.

10. Promote market efficiency, especially in areas where laws are weak or inefficient, by rewarding the best and most ethical producers of goods and services.

Source: Michael Josephson, "Ten Benefits of Having an Ethics Code," Josephson Institute Center for Business Ethics, December 30, 2013, http://josephsoninstitute.org/business/blog/2013/12/ten-benefits-of-having-an-ethics-code/ (accessed April 6, 2015). Originally adapted from *Good Ideas for Creating a More Ethical and Effective Workplace*.

TABLE 8–4 Developing and Implementing a Code of Ethics

1. Consider areas of risk and state the values as well as conduct necessary to comply with laws and regulations. Values are an important buffer in preventing serious misconduct.

2. Identify values that specifically address current ethical issues.

3. Consider values that link the organization to a stakeholder orientation. Attempt to find overlaps in organizational and stakeholder values.

4. Make the code understandable by providing examples that reflect values.

5. Communicate the code frequently and in language that employees can understand.

6. Revise the code every year with input from organizational members and stakeholders.

© Cengage Learning

situation, but they should provide guidelines and principles capable of helping employees achieve organizational ethical objectives and address risks in an accepted way.

Engineering and design firm Fluor has gained recognition for its leading ethics program. Nominated as one of *Ethisphere*'s World's Most Ethical Companies, Fluor is extremely focused on ethics and integrity. The company begins meetings with a focus on ethics by discussing the principles of an ethical company as well as how to react in different ethical situations. Fluor is also working with the U.S. Department of Commerce and the Asia-Pacific Economic Cooperation trade bloc to develop a code of conduct for small- and medium-sized companies in the engineering and construction industries throughout the region.[33] Ethics programs are essential in large corporations such as Fluor. However, it is not only large companies that need to develop an ethics and compliance program; small companies need to do so as well.

ETHICS OFFICERS

Organizational ethics programs must have oversight by high-ranking persons known to respect legal and ethical standards. These individuals—often referred to as **ethics officers**—are responsible for managing their organizations' ethics and legal compliance programs. They are usually responsible for (1) assessing the needs and risks an organization-wide ethics program must address, (2) developing and distributing a code of conduct or ethics, (3) conducting training programs for employees, (4) establishing and maintaining a confidential service to answer employees' questions about ethical issues, (5) making sure the company is in compliance with government regulation, (6) monitoring and auditing ethical conduct, (7) taking action on possible violations of the company's code, and (8) reviewing and updating the code. Ethics officers are also responsible for knowing thousands of pages of relevant regulations as well as communicating and reinforcing values that build an ethical corporate culture. The Ethics Resource Center reports that having a comprehensive ethics program in place, one that includes an ethics officer, helps companies reduce incidences of misconduct by as much as 75 percent.[34] Corporate wrongdoings and scandal-grabbing headlines have a profound negative impact on public trust. To ensure compliance with state and federal regulations, many corporations are now appointing chief compliance officers and ethics and business conduct professionals to develop and oversee corporate compliance programs.[35]

The Ethics & Compliance Association (ECA) has over 1,200 members who are front-line managers of ethics programs in over 30 countries.[36] Ethics officers often move into their position from other jobs in their companies. They have backgrounds in law, finance, and human resource management. Sarbanes–Oxley and the amendments to the FSGO increased the responsibility ethics officers and boards of directors have for oversight of financial reporting. Ethics officers' positions are still relatively new and somewhat ill-defined. Although tough economic times call all expenditures into question, economic uncertainty brings about the greatest need for an investment in and formalization of the ethics and compliance roles within an organization. Times of economic distress tend to generate significant organizational and individual wrongdoing.[37]

Although recommended as best practice, it is not common for ethics officers to report directly to the board of directors. Ethics officers often report directly to the chief executive officer and may have some access to the board. Ethics officers must also be prepared to address emerging risk areas. In a survey of chief financial officers, 74 percent view cyber-security as high priority but less than 20 percent felt a high amount of confidence in their ability to implement comprehensive information strategies to combat these attacks.[38] Planning, oversight, monitoring, and a review of operating procedures and outcomes by the ethics and compliance function can prevent such surprises.[39]

ETHICS TRAINING AND COMMUNICATION

A major step in developing an effective ethics program is implementing a training program and communication system to educate employees about the firm's ethical standards. The National Business Ethics Survey found that one in five workers—or 20 percent—at companies with strong ethical cultures and formal ethics programs report witnessing misconduct, compared to 88 percent in organizations with weak cultures and ethics programs.[40] A significant number of employees report they frequently find such training useful. Training can educate employees about the firm's policies and expectations, relevant laws and regulations, and general social standards. Training programs can also make employees aware of available resources, support systems, and designated personnel who can assist them with ethical and legal advice. Training can empower employees to ask tough questions and make ethical decisions. Many organizations are now incorporating ethics training into their employee and management development training efforts. The American Bar Association adopted six proposals for its Model Rules of Professional Conduct dealing with issues such as client confidentiality protection when using technology and outsourcing.[41] Governments often mandate training for officials as well. For example, employees working for the National Institutes of Health must undergo annual ethics training.[42]

As we emphasized in Chapters 5 and 7, ethical decision making is influenced by corporate culture, coworkers and supervisors, and the opportunities available to engage in unethical behavior. Ethics training can impact all three types of influence. Full awareness of a company's philosophy of management, rules, and procedures can strengthen both the corporate culture and the ethical stance of peers and supervisors. Such awareness, too, arms employees against opportunities for unethical behavior and lessens the likelihood of misconduct. Thus, the existence and enforcement of company rules and procedures limit unethical practices in the organization. If adequately and thoughtfully designed, ethics training can make employees aware of ethical issues, increase the importance of ethics training to employees, and increase employees' confidence they can make the correct decision when faced with an ethical dilemma.[43] If ethics training is to be effective, it must start with a theoretical foundation based on values, a code of ethics, procedures for airing ethical concerns, line and staff involvements, and clear executive priorities on ethics, all of which must be communicated to employees. Managers from every department must be involved in the development of an ethics training program. Training and communication initiatives should reflect the unique characteristics of an organization: its size, culture, values, management style, and employee base. To be successful, business ethics programs should educate employees about formal ethical frameworks and models for analyzing business ethics issues. Then employees can base ethical decisions on their knowledge of choices rather than on emotions.

A key component of managing an effective and efficient ethics and compliance program is a firm grasp of techniques that clearly communicate the company's values, culture, and policies for dealing with ethical issues to employees. Many feel "hands-on" training when employees are forced to confront actual or hypothetical ethical dilemmas helps them understand how their organization would like them to deal with potential problems. Lockheed Martin, for example, developed training games that include dilemmas that can be resolved in teams. Each team member offers his or her perspective, thereby helping other team members fully understand the ramifications of a decision for coworkers and the organization.

Another training device is the behavioral simulation, which gives participants a short, hypothetical ethical issue situation to review. Each participant is assigned a role within a hypothetical organization and provided with varying levels of information about the scenario. Participants must then interact to develop recommended courses of action representing short-term, mid-term, and long-term considerations. Such simulations recreate the complexities of organizational relationships as well as the realities of having to address difficult situations with incomplete information. These exercises help participants gain awareness of the ethical, legal, and social dimensions of business decision making;

develop analytical skills for resolving ethical issues; and gain exposure to the complexity of ethical decision making in organizations. Research indicates "the simulation not only instructs on the importance of ethics but on the processes for managing ethical concerns and conflict."[44]

Top executives must communicate with managers at the operations level (in production, sales, and finance, for instance) and enforce overall ethical standards within the organization. Table 8–5 lists the goals for successful ethics training. Making employees aware of the key risk areas for their occupation or profession is of major importance in any ethics training program. In addition, employees need to know whom to contact for guidance when they encounter gray areas in the organization's values, rules, policies, and training that do not provide adequate direction. On the other hand, firms that provide employees with the ability to voice their opinions but do not take their recommendations seriously can increase intra-group conflict.[45] It is therefore necessary for companies to display a strong commitment for communication and feedback mechanisms within the organization.

Although training and communication should reinforce values and provide employees with opportunities to learn about rules, they represent just one aspect of an effective ethics program. Moreover, ethics training will be ineffective if conducted solely because it is required or because it is something competing firms are doing. For instance, Enron had an ethics program in place. However, unethical executives knew they had the support of Arthur Andersen, the firm's auditing and accounting consulting partner, as well as that of law firms, investment analysts, and in some cases, government regulators. Enron's top managers therefore probably believed that efforts to hide debt in off-balance-sheet partnerships would not be exposed.

When measuring the effectiveness of an ethics program, it is important to get input from employees. Employee surveys and the incorporation of ethics measurements in performance appraisal systems are two ways to help determine the effectiveness of a firm's ethics training. If ethical performance is not a part of regular performance appraisals, employees get the message that ethics is not an important component of decision making in their company. For ethics training to make a difference, employees must understand why it is conducted, how it fits into the organization, and what their own role in implementing it is.

TABLE 8-5 Key Goals of Successful Ethics Training Programs

1. Identify key risk areas employees will face.

2. Provide experience in dealing with hypothetical or disguised ethical issues within the industry through mini-cases, online challenges, DVDs, or other experiential learning opportunities.

3. Let employees know wrongdoing will never be supported in the organization and employee evaluations will take their conduct in this area into consideration.

4. Let employees know they are individually accountable for their behavior.

5. Align employee conduct with organizational reputation and branding.

6. Provide ongoing feedback to employees about how they are handling ethical issues.

7. Allow a mechanism for employees to voice their concern that is anonymous, but provides answers to key questions (24-hour hotlines).

8. Provide a hierarchy of leadership for employees to contact when they are faced with an ethical dilemma they do not know how to resolve.

SYSTEMS TO MONITOR AND ENFORCE ETHICAL STANDARDS

An effective ethics program employs a variety of resources to monitor ethical conduct and measure the program's effectiveness. Observing employees, conducting internal audits and investigations, circulating surveys, and instituting reporting systems are ways a company can assess compliance with its ethical code and standards. An external audit and review of company activities may sometimes be helpful in developing benchmarks of compliance. (We examine the process of ethical auditing in Chapter 9.)

To determine if a person is performing his or her job adequately and ethically, observers might focus on how the employee handles an ethically charged situation. Many businesses employ role-playing exercises when they train salespeople and managers. Ethical issues can be introduced into the discussion, and the results can be videotaped so participants and their superiors can evaluate the outcome of the ethics dilemma.

Questionnaires can serve as benchmarks in an ongoing assessment of ethical performance by measuring employees' ethical perceptions of their company, their superiors, their coworkers, and themselves, as well as serving as a means of developing ratings of ethical or unethical practices within their firm and industry. Then, if unethical conduct appears to be increasing, management will have a better understanding of what types of unethical practices may be occurring and why. A change in the company's ethics training may then be necessary.

The existence of an internal system that allows employees to report misconduct is especially useful for monitoring and evaluating ethical performance. Many companies set up ethics assistance lines, also known as hotlines, to provide support and give employees the opportunity to ask questions or report concerns. The most effective ethics hotlines operate on an anonymous basis and are supported 24 hours a day, 365 days a year. Approximately 50 percent of hotline calls occur at night or on the weekends. Many times troubling ethical issues can cause people to lose sleep and occupy their thoughts during their free time.[46] Although there is always some concern employees may misreport a situation or abuse a hotline to retaliate against a coworker, hotlines have become widespread and employees do use them. An easy-to-use hotline or help desk can serve as a safety net that increases the chance of detecting and responding to unethical conduct in a timely manner. Hotlines serve as a central contact point where critical comments, dilemmas, and advice can be assigned to the person most appropriate for handling a specific case.[47] Employees often prefer to deal with ethical issues through their supervisors or managers or resolve the matter directly before using an anonymous reporting system such as a hotline.[48]

Companies are increasingly using consultants that provide professional case-management services and software. Software is becoming popular because it provides reports of employee concerns, complaints, or observations of misconduct that can be tracked and managed. Thus the company can track investigations, analysis, resolutions, and documentation of misconduct reports. This system helps prevent lawsuits and helps a company learn about and analyze ethical lapses. However, it is important for companies to choose the right software for their needs. Although only 10 to 15 percent of companies currently use some type of compliance management tool, many companies are moving toward the automated process that technology and software provide.

If a company is not making progress toward creating and maintaining an ethical culture, it needs to determine why and take corrective action, either by enforcing current standards more strictly or setting higher standards. Corrective action may involve rewarding employees who comply with company policies and standards and punishing those who do not. When employees abide by organizational standards, their efforts should be acknowledged through public recognition, bonuses, raises, or some other means. On the other hand, when employees violate organizational standards, they must be reprimanded, transferred, docked, suspended, or even fired. If a firm fails to take corrective action against unethical or illegal behavior, the inappropriate behavior is likely to continue. In the National Business Ethics survey, two major reasons for why employees do not report observed misconduct include fear of retaliation and making personal value judgments about whether it would be worthwhile to report the misconduct.[49] However, new laws and court rulings are making it more difficult for businesses to engage in retaliation. For instance, the Supreme Court ruled an employer can be sued if it retaliates against a close associate or relative of an employee who filed a discrimination claim.[50]

Consistent enforcement and necessary disciplinary action are essential to a functional ethics or compliance program. The ethics officer is usually responsible for implementing all disciplinary actions for violations of the firm's ethical standards. Many companies are including ethical compliance in employee performance evaluations. During performance evaluations, employees may be asked to sign an acknowledgment that they have read the company's current ethics guidelines. The company must also promptly investigate any known or suspected misconduct. The appropriate company official, usually the ethics officer, needs to make a recommendation to senior management on how to deal with a particular ethical infraction. In some cases, a company may be required to report substantiated misconduct to a designated government or regulatory agency so as to receive credit. Under the FSGO, such credit for having an effective compliance program can reduce fines.[51]

Efforts to deter unethical behavior are important to companies' long-term relationships with their employees, customers, and community. If the code of ethics is aggressively enforced and becomes part of the corporate culture, it can effectively improve ethical behavior within an organization. If a code is not properly enforced, however, it becomes mere window dressing and will accomplish little toward improving ethical behavior and decision making. Lack of monitoring and enforcement mechanisms results in only superficial improvements with firms enjoying the goodwill from a program without goodwill benefits.[52]

Continuous Improvement of an Ethics Program

Improving a system that encourages employees to make more ethical decisions differs little from implementing any other type of business strategy. Implementation requires designing activities to achieve organizational objectives using available resources and given existing constraints. Implementation translates a plan for action into operational terms and establishes a means by which an organization's ethical performance will be monitored, controlled, and improved. Figure 8–3 indicates the growth in global reporting among large organizations. This fact is in part due to increased resources, but also undoubtedly to increased stakeholder responsibilities and liabilities.

A firm's ability to plan and implement ethical business standards depends in part on how it structures resources and activities to achieve its ethical objectives. People's attitudes and behavior must be guided by a shared commitment to the business rather than by mere obedience to traditional managerial authority. Encouraging diversity of perspectives, disagreement, and the empowerment of people helps align the company's leadership with its employees.

FIGURE 8-3 **Growth in Global Corporate Responsibility Reporting**

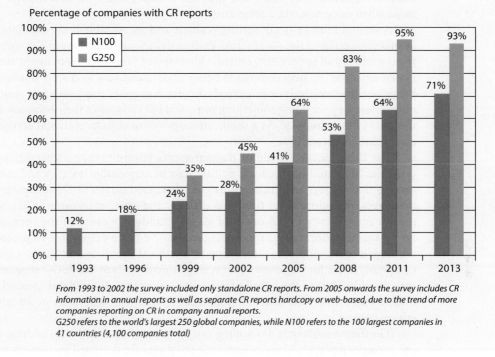

Percentage of companies with CR reports

From 1993 to 2002 the survey included only standalone CR reports. From 2005 onwards the survey includes CR information in annual reports as well as separate CR reports hardcopy or web-based, due to the trend of more companies reporting on CR in company annual reports.
G250 refers to the world's largest 250 global companies, while N100 refers to the 100 largest companies in 41 countries (4,100 companies total)

Source: KPMG International Cooperative, *The KPMG Survey of Corporate Responsibility Reporting 2013*, http://www.kpmg.com/Global/en/IssuesAndInsights/ArticlesPublications/corporate-responsibility/Documents/kpmg-survey-of-corporate-responsibility-reporting-2013.pdf (accessed March 26, 2015).

If a company determines its ethical performance has been less than satisfactory, executives may want to change how certain kinds of decisions are made. For example, a decentralized organization may need to centralize key decisions, at least for a time, so upper managers can ensure these decisions are made in an ethical manner. Centralization may reduce the opportunities lower-level managers and employees have to make unethical decisions. Executives can then focus on initiatives for improving the corporate culture and infusing more ethical values throughout the firm by rewarding positive behavior and sanctioning negative behavior. In other companies, decentralizing important decisions may be a better way to attack ethical problems so lower-level managers who are familiar with the local business environment and local culture and values can make more decisions. Whether the ethics function is centralized or decentralized, the key need is to delegate authority in such a way that the organization can achieve ethical performance.

Common Mistakes in Designing and Implementing an Ethics Program

Many business leaders recognize they need to have an ethics program, but few take the time to answer fundamental questions about the goals of such a program. As we mentioned previously, some of the most common program objectives are to deter and detect unethical behavior as well as violations of the law; to gain competitive advantages through improved relationships with customers, suppliers, and employees; and, especially for multinational corporations, to link employees through a unifying and shared corporate culture. Failure to understand and appreciate these goals is the first mistake many firms make when designing ethics programs.

A second mistake is not setting realistic and measurable program objectives. Once a consensus on objectives is reached, companies should solicit input through interviews, focus groups, and survey instruments. Finding out how employees might react in a particular situation can help companies better understand how to correct unethical or illegal behavior either reactively or proactively. Research suggests employees and senior managers often know they are doing something unethical but rationalize their behavior as being "for the good of the company." As a result, ethics program objectives should contain some elements that are measurable.[53]

The third mistake is senior management's failure to take ownership of the ethics program. Maintaining an ethical culture may be impossible if CEOs and other top officers do not support an ethical culture. As discussed earlier in this chapter, upper-level managers, including chief financial officers and chief marketing officers, may have greater insensitivity to the needs of all stakeholders because of the pressure they feel for financial performance. Top managers may be more vulnerable to pressures placed on them to push employees to engage in unethical activities and thereby become more competitive. It is for this reason that recent amendments to the FSGO suggest ethics officers should report to the board of directors rather than the general counsel. The board of directors should have ultimate responsibility and oversight to create an organizational ethical culture.

The fourth mistake is developing program materials that do not address the needs of the average employee. Many compliance programs are designed by lawyers to ensure the company is legally protected. These programs usually yield complex "legalese" few within the organization can understand. To avoid this problem, ethics programs—including codes of conduct and training materials—should include feedback from employees from across the firm, not just the legal department. Including a question-and-answer section in the program; referencing additional resources for guidance on key ethical issues; and using checklists, illustrations, and even cartoons can make program materials more user-friendly.

The fifth common mistake is transferring an "American" program to a firm's international operations. In multinational firms, executives should involve overseas personnel as early as possible in the process in order to foster an understanding of the company's values and to minimize the potential for misconduct stemming from misunderstandings. These aims can be accomplished by developing an inventory of common global management practices and processes and examining the corporation's standards of conduct in light of these international standards.

A final common mistake is designing an ethics program that is little more than a series of lectures. In such cases, participants typically recall less than 15 percent the day after the training. A more practical solution is to allow employees to practice the skills they learn through case studies or small group exercises.

A firm cannot succeed solely by taking a legalistic compliance approach to ethics. Top managers must seek to develop high ethical standards that serve as barriers to illegal conduct. Although an ethics program should help reduce the possibility of penalties and negative public reaction to misconduct, a company must want to be a good corporate citizen and recognize the importance of ethics to success in business.

SUMMARY

Ethics programs help sensitize employees to potential legal and ethical issues within their work environments. To promote ethical and legal conduct, organizations should develop ethics programs, establishing, communicating, and monitoring ethical values and legal requirements that characterize the firms' history, culture, industry, and operating environment. Without such programs and uniform standards and policies of conduct, it is difficult for employees to determine what behaviors a company deems acceptable.

A company must have an effective ethics program to ensure employees understand its values and comply with its policies and codes of conduct. An ethics program should help reduce the possibility of legally enforced penalties and negative public reaction to misconduct. The main objective of the Federal Sentencing Guidelines for Organizations is to encourage companies to assess risk and then self-monitor and aggressively work to deter unethical acts and punish unethical employees. Ethics programs are organizational control systems that create predictability in employee behavior. These control systems may have a compliance orientation, which uses legal terms, statutes, and contracts that teach employees the rules and the penalties for noncompliance, or a values orientation that consists of developing shared values.

Most companies begin the process of establishing organizational ethics programs by developing codes of conduct, or formal statements that describe what an organization expects of its employees. Codes of conduct include a company's code of ethics and/or its statement of values. A code of ethics must be developed as part of senior management's desire to ensure the company complies with values, rules, and policies that support an ethical culture. Without uniform policies and standards, employees have difficulty determining what qualifies as acceptable behavior in the company.

Having a high-level manager or committee responsible for an ethical compliance program can significantly enhance its administration and oversight. Such ethics officers are usually responsible for assessing the needs and risks to be addressed in an organization-wide ethics program, developing and distributing a code of conduct or ethics, conducting training programs for employees, establishing and maintaining a confidential service to answer questions about ethical issues, making sure the company is complying with government regulations, monitoring and auditing ethical conduct, taking action on possible violations of the company's code, and reviewing and updating the code.

Successful ethics training is important in helping employees identify ethical issues and in providing them with the means to address and resolve such issues. Training can educate employees about the firm's policies and expectations, available resources, support systems, and designated ethics personnel, as well as relevant laws and regulations and general social standards. Top executives must communicate with managers at the operations level and enforce overall ethical standards within the organization.

An effective ethics program employs a variety of resources to monitor ethical conduct and measure the program's effectiveness. Compliance with the company's ethical code and standards can be assessed by observing employees, performing internal audits and surveys, instituting reporting systems, and conducting investigations, as well as through external audits and review, as needed. Corrective action involves rewarding employees who comply with company policies and standards and punishing those who do not. Consistent enforcement and disciplinary action are necessary for a functioning ethical compliance program.

Ethical compliance can be ensured by designing activities that achieve organizational objectives using available resources and given existing constraints. A firm's ability to plan and implement ethical business standards depends in part on its ability to structure resources and activities to achieve its objectives effectively and efficiently.

In implementing ethics and compliance programs many firms make common mistakes, including failing to answer fundamental questions about the goals of such programs, not setting realistic and measurable program objectives, failing to have senior management take ownership of the ethics program, developing program materials that do not address the needs of the average employee, transferring an "American" program to a firm's international operations, and designing an ethics program that is little more than a series of lectures. Although an ethics program should help reduce the possibility of penalties and negative public reaction to misconduct, a company must want to be a good corporate citizen and recognize the importance of ethics to successful business activities.

IMPORTANT TERMS FOR REVIEW

compliance orientation 224	codes of conduct 225	statement of values 225
values orientation 224	code of ethics 225	ethics officers 228

RESOLVING ETHICAL BUSINESS CHALLENGES[*]

Mary, a recent college graduate from Stanford University, works for JSYK Incorporated, a realty company that represents clients interested in either buying or selling businesses. As a "business broker," Mary's job is to arrange sales just like a normal realtor. On the outskirts of town, a small building used for manufacturing sat idle for over a year. The realtors called it Moby Dick because no one could find a buyer for it; either the price was too high or the building did not quite match the buyer's needs. Dozens of potential buyers had come and gone. It did not help that the building was owned by Ted St. Clair, a 65-year-old miser that lived in the town all his life. The man had a reputation for hoarding every last dime. Ted made Dickens's Scrooge look saintly. While JSYK Incorporated told Ted more than once he needed to lower the price if he wanted to sell the building, Ted always refused.

One hot afternoon Reverend Smith, a retired minister, contacted JSYK and asked if he could look at the property. Because Mary was in the office it was given to her. While they inspected the building, the conversation came around to what Reverend Smith would do with the building. He had recently formed a nonprofit corporation to aid troubled youth and wanted to convert the building into a recreation center. Mary knew Reverend Smith because she formerly attended his church. She knew of his honesty and integrity as well as his decades of service.

When Mary returned to the office, the Reverend was seriously talking about the building and how it could be refitted for his purposes. As they talked, the Reverend asked about the machinery still in the building. Some of the machines at the manufacturing plant were in poor condition and required an estimated $100,000 to repair. Reverend Smith had no use for them and would need them removed.

After preliminary discussions, Mary said she would contact the owner. "Reverend, I believe the seller is asking for a $250,000 down payment on this $1,000,000 sale."

"I can't afford that much," replied the Reverend. "I've been saving donations for a number of years and I only have $150,000."

"If I may ask," asked Mary, "How are you going to pay the balance?"

"Well, I've spoken to some older church members, and they told me that if I could make the down payment, they would cover the rest."

"I'll try to work with you on this. Give me a few days and I'll call you," said Mary.

As Reverend Smith left, George, the owner and CEO of JSYK, came into the office. "What did Reverend Smith want?" asked George.

"He's actually interested in Moby Dick, and I believe it matches his needs perfectly."

"That's great!" George replied. Then he noticed Mary's face. "So what's the problem?"

"You and I both know Ted will not come down on the price." Mary quickly explained the situation, with George listening intently. After she was done, George said, "Mary, this is what you are going to do. I want you to convince Ted that repairing those machines is important to the buyer. DO NOT tell him who it is. Tell Ted the buyer wants the machines, but the repair estimate he calculated is $150,000. Tell Ted you know you can get the buyer to buy if the down payment was reduced to $150,000 and the asking price to $950,000. Finally, tell Ted he would be making an additional $50,000 for not having to do the repairs."

"I don't know about this," said Mary. "It doesn't feel honest, and besides Reverend Smith has not approved the deal, nor do I believe he would want me to lie on his behalf."

George replied, "Mary, the Reverend is going to do something good with that building. You and I both know Ted will never get more than this. We're just helping him make the best deal possible."

Mary still was not certain. Although Ted was a miser, it did not feel right to lie. Besides, she wondered what Ted would do after he found out the Reverend had no use for the machines.

QUESTIONS | EXERCISES

1. How is top management supporting a culture of ethical or unethical behavior?
2. Discuss the alternatives and duties Mary has as a representative for both the buyer and seller.
3. If realtors have a code of ethics that requires truthful and transparent information, what should Mary tell George, the owner of JSKY?

[*]This case is strictly hypothetical; any resemblance to real persons, companies, or situations is coincidental.

> > > CHECK YOUR EQ

Check your EQ, or Ethics Quotient, by completing the following. Assess your performance to evaluate your overall understanding of the chapter material.

1. A compliance program should be deemed effective if it addresses the seven minimum requirements for ethical compliance programs.   **Yes**   <u>**No**</u>

2. The accountability and responsibility for appropriate business conduct rests with top management.   <u>**Yes**</u>   **No**

3. Ethical compliance can be measured by observing employees as well as through investigating and reporting mechanisms.   <u>**Yes**</u>   **No**

4. The key goal of ethics training is to help employees identify ethical issues.   **Yes**   <u>**No**</u>

5. An ethical compliance audit is designed to determine the effectiveness of ethics initiatives.   <u>**Yes**</u>   **No**

ANSWERS **1. No.** An effective compliance program has the seven elements of a compliance program in place and goes beyond those minimum requirements to determine what will work in a particular organization. **2. Yes.** Executives in an organization determine the culture and initiatives that support ethical behavior. **3. Yes.** Sometimes external monitoring is necessary, but internal monitoring and evaluation are the norm. **4. No.** It is much more than that—it involves not only recognition but also an understanding of the values, culture, and rules in an organization as well as the impact of ethical decisions on the company. **5. Yes.** It helps in establishing the code and in making program improvements.

ENDNOTES

1. Bob Lewis, "Survival Guide: The Moral Compass—Corporations Aren't Moral Agents, Creating Interesting Dilemmas for Business Leaders," *ACCESSmyLIBRARY*, March 11, 2002, http://www.accessmylibrary.com/article-1G1-84072220/survival-guide-moral-compass.html (accessed May 6, 2013).

2. Ethisphere Institute, "The 2014 World's Most Ethical Companies," Ethisphere Magazine, Quarter 1, 2014, p. 44.

3. Itai Beeri, Rachel Dayan, Eran Vigoda-Gadot, and Simcha B. Werner, "Advancing Ethics in Public Organizations: The Impact of an Ethics Program on Employees' Perceptions and Behaviors in a Regional Council," *Journal of Business Ethics* 112 (2013): 59–78.

4. Ed Silverman, The Wall Street Journal, September 9, 2014, http://blogs.wsj.com/pharmalot/2014/09/09/not-every-conflict-of-interest-produces-the-same-vote-on-fda-panels/ (accessed March 26, 2015); Dr. Mercola, "Conflicts of Interest Rampant Among FDA Advisors, Study Shows," http://articles.mercola.com/sites/articles/archive/2014/09/24/fda-advisors-drug-approval-decisions.aspx (accessed March 26, 2015).

5. Indra Nooyi, "Business Has a Job to Do: Rebuild Trust," April 22, 2009, http://money.cnn.tv/2009/04/19/news/companies/nooyi.fortune/index.htm (accessed March 26, 2015).

6. Linda K. Trevino and Stuart Youngblood, "Bad Apples in Bad Barrels: Causal Analysis of Ethical Decision Making Behavior," *Journal of Applied Psychology* 75 (1990): 378–385.

7. Caroline Winter, David Glovin, and Jennifer Daniel, "A Guide to the Galleon Case," *Bloomberg Businessweek*, March 10, 2011, http://www.businessweek.com/magazine/content/11_12/b4220079522428.htm (accessed March 26, 2015); Ashby Jones, "Raj Opening Statements: 'Tomorrow's Trades Today' vs. 'Shoe-Leather Research,'" *The Wall Street Journal*, March 9, 2011, http://blogs.wsj.com/law/2011/03/09/raj-opening-statements-tomorrows-trades-today-vs-shoe-leather-research/?KEYWORDS=rajaratnam (accessed March 26, 2015).

8. Trevino and Youngblood, "Bad Apples in Bad Barrels."

9. Ibid.

10. Ben Blanchard, "China slams 'distorted' view of copyright piracy problem," *Reuters*, November 11, 2012, http://www.reuters.com/article/2012/11/11/us-china-congress-piracy-idUSBRE8AA04620121111 (accessed March 26, 2015).

11. James R. Hagerty and Shira Ovide, "Microsoft Pursues New Tack on Piracy," The Wall Street Journal, March 16, 2014, http://www.wsj.com/articles/SB10001424052702303287804579443442002220098 (accessed March 26, 2015).

12. American Institute of CPAs, Code of Professional Conduct and Bylaws, 2013, http://www.aicpa.org/Research/Standards/CodeofConduct/DownloadableDocuments/2013June1CodeOfProfessionalConduct.pdf (accessed March 26, 2015).

13. Constance E. Bagley, "The Ethical Leader's Decision Tree," *Harvard Business Review* (February 2003), 18–19.

14. Bella L. Galperin, Rebecca J. Bennett, and Karl Aquino, "Status Differentiation and the Protean Self: A Social-Cognitive Model of Unethical Behavior in Organizations," *Journal of Business Ethics* 98 (2011): 407–424.

15. "Warren Buffett's Berkshire Hathaway Letter to Shareholders," http://www.berkshirehathaway.com/letters/2010ltr.pdf (accessed May 6, 2013).

16. Josh Bersin, "Why Companies Fail to Engage Today's Workforce: The Overwhelmed Employee," Forbes, March 15, 2014, http://www.forbes.com/sites/joshbersin/2014/03/15/why-companies-fail-to-engage-todays-workforce-the-overwhelmed-employee/ (accessed March 26, 2015).

17. James Titcomb, "BNP Paribas ignored red flags and has paid the price," The Telegraph, July 1, 2014, http://www.telegraph.co.uk/finance/newsbysector/banksandfinance/10939453/BNP-Paribas-ignored-red-flags-and-has-paid-the-price.html (accessed March 26, 2015).

18. Merck, "About Us—Code of Conduct," http://www.merck.com/about/how-we-operate/code-of-conduct/home.html (accessed March 26, 2015).

19. Muel Kaptein, "The effectiveness of ethics programs: The role of scope, composition, and sequence," *Journal of Business Ethics*, August 2014, DOI 10.1007/s10551-014-2296-3

20. PPT presentation presented at 2014 ECOA conference in Atlanta, presented by Claire Lewis, Chief, Compliance Coordination and Corporate Compliance Officer at SNC-Lavalin, entitled "Delivering on Our Commitment to Ethics Excellence," Presented on October 1, 2014.

21. Ernst & Young, *Overcoming compliance fatigue: Reinforcing the commitment to ethical growth—13th Global Fraud Survey*, 2014 © EYGM Limited.

22. Criminal Division of the U.S. Department of Justice and the Enforcement Division of the U.S. Securities and Exchange Commission, *FCPA: A Resource Guide to the U.S. Foreign Corrupt Practices Act* (Washington, D.C.: U.S. Department of Justice and U.S. Securities & Exchange Commission, 2012).

23. Barry Z. Posner, "Another Look at the Impact of Personal and Organizational Values Congruency," *Journal of Business Ethics* 97 (2010): 535–541.

24. Frances Chua and Asheq Rahman, "Institutional Pressures and Ethical Reckoning by Business Corporations," *Journal of Business Ethics* 98 (2011): 307–329.

25. KPMG Forensic Integrity Survey 2008–2009, http://www.kpmg.com.br/publicacoes/forensic/Integrity_Survey_2008_2009.pdf (accessed May 6, 2013).

26. Christopher Sindik, "50 Banking & Insurance Industries Companies," *Ethisphere*, Q4, 15–17.

27. Ronald Paul Hill and Justine M. Rapp, "Codes of Ethical Conduct: A Bottom-Up Approach," Journal of Business Ethics 123, 4 (2014): 621–630.

28. Mark S. Schwartz, "A Code of Ethics for Corporate Code of Ethics," *Journal of Business Ethics* 41 (2002): 37.

29. Ibid.

30. Lori Holder-Webb and Jeffrey Cohen, "The Cut and Paste Society: Isomorphism in Codes of Ethics," *Journal of Business Ethics* 107 (2012): 485–509.

31. Joseph A. McKinney, Tisha L. Emerson, and Mitchell J. Neubert, "The Effects of Ethical Codes on Ethical Perceptions of Actions toward Stakeholders," *Journal of Business Ethics* 97 (2010): 505–516.

32. American Society of Civil Engineers, "Code of Ethics," http://www.asce.org/code_of_ethics/ (accessed May 6, 2013).

33. Ethisphere Institute, "The 2014 World's Most Ethical Companies," Ethisphere Magazine, Quarter 1, 2014, p. 43.

34. *National Business Ethics Survey 2007*, 39.

35. "USSC Commissioner John Steer Joins with Compliance and Ethics Executives from Leading U.S. Companies to Address Key Compliance, Business Conduct and Governance Issues," *Society for Corporate Compliance and Ethics*, PR Newswire, October 31, 2005.

36. Ethics and Compliance Association website, http://www.theecoa.org/imis15/ECOAPublic/ (accessed April 6, 2015).

37. Jim Nortz, "Compliance and Ethics Officers: A Survival Guide for the Economic Downturn," March 10, 2009, http://www.corporatecomplianceinsights.com/2010/compliance-and-ethics-officers-surviving-economic-downturn/ (accessed May 6, 2013).

38. "Cyber Risk Remains a High Priority for CFOs: Survey," The Wall Street Journal, January 5, 2015, http://deloitte.wsj.com/cfo/2015/01/05/cyber-risk-remains-a-high-priority-for-cfos-survey/ (accessed March 26, 2015).

39. Anne M. Simmons, "Want to Avoid Unpleasant Compliance Surprises? Embrace a Strong Whistle-Blowing Policy," January 8, 2009, http://ethisphere.com/want-to-avoid-unpleasant-compliance-surprises-embrace-a-strong-whistle-blowing-policy/ (accessed May 6, 2013).

40. Ethics Resource Center, National Business Ethics Survey® of the U.S. Workforce (Arlington, VA: Ethics Resource Center, 2014), p. 18.

41. "Ethics 20/20 Rule Changes Approved by ABA Delegates with Little Opposition," *Bloomberg BNA*, August 15, 2012, http://www.bna.com/ethics-2020-rule-n12884911245/ (accessed March 26, 2015).

42. National Institutes of Health, "Ethics Training," http://ethics.od.nih.gov/training.htm (accessed May 6, 2013).

43. Linda Ferrell and O. C. Ferrell, *Ethical Business* (DK Essential Managers Series, May 4, 2009): 1–72.

44. Debbie Thorne LeClair and Linda Ferrell, "Innovation in Experiential Business Ethics Training," *Journal of Business Ethics* 23 (2000), 313–322.

45. Gerdien de Vries, Karen A. Jehn, Bart W. Terwel, "When Employees Stop Talking and Start Fighting: The Detrimental Effects of Pseudo Voice in Organizations," *Journal of Business Ethics* 105 (2012), 221–230.

46. David Slovin, "The Case for Anonymous Hotlines," *Risk & Insurance*, April 15, 2007, FindArticles, http://findarticles.com/p/articles/mi_m0BJK/is_5_18/ai_n27221119/ (accessed March 15, 2011).

47. Mael Kaptein, "Guidelines for the Development of an Ethics Safety Net," *Journal of Business Ethics* 41 (2002): 217.

48. Ethics Resource Center, *Research Brief from the 2009 NBES*, 15.

49. Ethics Resource Center, National Business Ethics Survey® of the U.S. Workforce (Arlington, VA: Ethics Resource Center, 2014), p. 28.

50. Jess Bravin, "Justices Extend Protection over Workplace Retaliation," *The Wall Street Journal*, January 25, 2011, B1.

51. Curt S. Jordan, "Lessons in Organizational Compliance: A Survey of Government-Imposed Compliance Programs," *Preventive Law Reporter* (Winter 1994): 7.

52. David Berliner and Aseem Prakash, "'Bluewashing' the Firm? Voluntary Regulations, Program Design, and Member Compliance with the United Nations Global Compact," The Policy Studies Journal 43, 1 (2015): 115–138.

53. Lori T. Martens and Kristen Day, "Five Common Mistakes in Designing and Implementing a Business Ethics Program," *Business and Society Review* 104 (1999): 163–170.

CHAPTER 9

MANAGING AND CONTROLLING ETHICS PROGRAMS

AN ETHICAL DILEMMA*

Mei-li stared at the code of ethics she received when she first began to consult with Business Equipment Corporation (BEC). Right there, under the heading "Competition," it stated, "BEC strongly believes in the competitive process. While we are dedicated to selling the best products, we have a strong commitment toward competing fairly and honestly." Mei-li wondered if there was any way to do her assignment without going against this core value.

Mei-li's first consulting assignment after graduating from UCLA was to work with Kyle, an engineer at BEC. Their assignment was to help develop and produce a new copy machine. Last year BEC discovered a new technology that would enable them to manufacture a copy machine with a copy quality far superior to anything else on the market. Mei-li and Kyle are both sure they have a winning product.

"I am especially excited about this. My kids are going to be so proud," said Kyle. "I've been promised a promotion and a doubling of my salary if the new product launch is successful."

Several months went by, and one morning Kyle came in, panic stricken. "Have you read the news?" Kyle asked Mei-li. "The industry reporter says that our competitor Hiyota plans to launch a new high-quality copier machine within the next month! If the Hiyota machine is as good as this article says, I'm dead," said Kyle.

"What do we do?" asked Mei-li. Kyle thought for a while and then replied, "Mei-li, we have to do this quickly before they roll out their machine. We need to make sure ours is better. I want you to pretend to be a potential customer and call Hiyota. Tell him you'll meet at the Hilton in one of the conference rooms. When the salesperson starts up, make sure you ask about copy quality, get samples, and learn as much as possible about novel product features, pricing, advertising strategy, etc. If we can get this information this week, we can help the plant people modify our machine so that it kills Hiyota."

Mei-li replied, "Kyle, I'm not comfortable with pretending to be a buyer. What if Hiyota finds out? What about me wasting the time of this salesperson? I don't want the firm to get a reputation for this sort of thing."

Kyle replied, "This isn't a big deal. It's not illegal because we're not stealing trade secrets. If the salesperson is telling clients about the product, then it can't be illegal. Getting competitive product information takes place all the time, and it's Hiyota's responsibility to develop security procedures to prevent information from slipping out before the product hits the market. As far as the sales representative's time, you know that many of them have nonproductive sales calls. We can't afford to wait, Mei-li!"

As Mei-li left the office, she decided to ask Bob, their boss, about Kyle's proposal. As she discussed the information with Bob, he replied, "Unofficially, I'd say unless you can come up with some valid reasons to reject Kyle's plan, you should call Hiyota. Officially, I would say that BEC does not condone such practices and considers them unethical according to our code of ethics. Finally, unofficially, you need to know, Mei-li, that if Kyle doesn't pull this one out of the fire, he won't be here for very long."

"Have you ever done something like this, Bob?" asked Mei-li.

"I know this type of thing happens frequently, and I know some of the justifications for it. For example, it's common to state that the person had no choice or try to deny responsibility. Or they have a family to support, or everyone else does it. Those are the justifications I hear the most. However you want to justify it, it happens. Sometimes people get caught and sometimes they don't."

"You didn't answer my question, Bob. Have you ever done something like this?"

"Mei-li, I just answered your question." With those words, Bob excused himself and left.

That was Tuesday. Now Mei-li was sitting at her desk two days later staring at the code of conduct. She did not know what to do. It seemed like Kyle's job was on the line. She heard footsteps and looked up as Kyle approached her.

"Have you set up the appointment?" Kyle asked.

QUESTIONS | EXERCISES

1. Discuss whether Kyle's proposal would violate BEC's code of ethics.
2. Identify the organizational pressures that Mei-li is facing to call Hiyota.
3. How should Mei-li handle the situation?

*This case is strictly hypothetical; any resemblance to real persons, companies, or situations is coincidental.

Chapter 8 introduced the concept that ethics programs are a way for organizations to improve ethical decision making and conduct in business. To properly implement these programs and ensure their effectiveness, companies need to measure and evaluate their impact. Increasingly, companies are applying the principles of auditing to ascertain whether their ethics codes, policies, and corporate values are having a positive impact on the firm's ethical conduct. These audits can help companies identify risks and areas of noncompliance with laws and company policies as well as other areas that need improvement. An audit should provide a systematic and objective survey of the firm's culture and values.

We begin this chapter by examining some of the requirements of a successful ethics program. We then discuss the concept of an ethics audit as a way to execute such a program. We define the term *ethics audit* and explore its relationship to a social audit. Next, we examine the benefits and limitations of this implementation tool, especially with regard to avoiding a management crisis. We consider the challenges of measuring nonfinancial ethical performance, and review evolving standards from ISO 19600 and the Open Compliance Ethics Group. We then describe our framework for the steps of an ethics audit, including securing the commitment of directors and top managers; establishing a committee to oversee the audit; defining the scope of the audit process; reviewing the firm's mission, values, goals, and policies and defining ethical priorities; collecting and analyzing relevant information; and verifying and reporting the results. Finally, we consider the strategic importance of the ethics audit.

IMPLEMENTING AN ETHICS PROGRAM

Developing an effective business ethics program requires organizations to cope with the realities of implementing such a program. Implementation requires executing specific actions that ensure the achievement of business ethics objectives. The organization must have ways of managing, evaluating, and controlling business ethics programs. Five items in particular have a significant impact on whether an ethics program is successful: (1) the content of the company's code of ethics, (2) the frequency of communication regarding the ethical code and program, (3) the quality of communication, (4) senior management's ability to successfully incorporate ethics into the organization, and (5) local management's ability to do the same.[1]

If an organization has a culture more focused on planning than on implementation, employees may come to view unethical conduct as acceptable behavior. Without proper controls in place, lying to customers, manipulating prices, abusive behavior, and misuse of organizational resources can become a part of some employees' conduct.

Viewing a business ethics program as a part of strategic planning and management activities is critical to the success of any firm. Some companies still do not understand that ethics is a critical aspect of business strategy in action. This misunderstanding stems from a belief that the ethics of employees is primarily an individual matter, and not the responsibility of managers. The nature of ethics programs in corporate America is to determine risks, develop policies and codes of conduct, and require specific standards of conduct. However, in order to do the right thing and know when to say no or ask for assistance in gray areas, employees must have a strong sense of personal ethics.

Shared values among employees are the glue of successful management as well as of business ethics programs. When business ethics programs align and direct employees' activities toward an ethical culture, employees feel a commitment to the long-term ethical progress of the firm. Johnson Controls is a business recognized for its emphasis on ethical conduct. It has consistently earned a place in *Ethisphere*'s "World's Most Ethical Companies."[2] Johnson Controls adopted a model consisting of what it calls four spheres of ethical behavior based upon a stakeholder orientation: (1) Employees and other team members, (2) company and shareholders, (3) customers, competitors, and suppliers, and (4) public and communities. At the center of its model is integrity, symbolizing that the company must operate with integrity in each of these "spheres."[3]

Formal controls for business ethics include input controls such as proper selection of employees, effective ethics training, and strong structural systems (including communication systems). Chapter 8 discussed internal control systems whereby employees can report misconduct. Ethics assistance lines, sometimes called hotlines, provide support and give employees the opportunity to get assistance, ask questions, or report concerns. Another internal control system that can improve ethical assistance is an ethics help desk. An ethics help desk is a point of contact within an organization where employees and managers can bring their concerns and receive assistance from the most appropriate person in the firm to handle the situation. For this model to be successful, the help desk must be supportive of employees, be easily accessible, and have simple procedures for employees to follow when they express concerns.[4]

Process controls include management's commitment to the ethics program and the methods or system for ethics evaluation. These methods might involve daily coaching for managers and employee reminders regarding appropriate ethical conduct. The best way to provide leadership on ethics is to set a good example, and there are many examples of effective corporate leaders who promote ethics from the top. William Dudley, the President and CEO of the Federal Reserve Bank of New York, won recognition as a strong and ethical corporate leader. Dudley has openly expressed his commitment toward eliminating ethics "rot" from financial services companies and has called for greater accountability in the industry. Dudley exhibits good leadership qualities in his desire to change the ethical culture of the financial services industry. His actions have signified to financial firms that if they do not reduce their ethical lapses, they might have to be downsized so that their ethical risks could be more manageable.[5] A study in the banking industry found that maintaining organizational values and ethical culture requires sustained training and reinforcement.[6]

Output controls involve comparing standards with actual behavior. One of the most popular methods of evaluating ethical performance is an ethics audit. The primary purpose of an ethics audit is to identify the risks and problems in outgoing activities and plan the necessary steps to adjust, correct, or eliminate these ethical concerns. Regardless of the complexity of a firm's ethics program, an ethics audit is critical to the program's success; therefore, a major part of this chapter focuses on how such audits should be conducted. The Federal Sentencing Guidelines for Organizations' (FSGO) amendment suggests that the results of an ethics audit be reported directly to the board of directors. Such direct reporting would prevent the CEO or another top officer from covering up misconduct. In 2012 the U.S. Department of Justice and the Securities and Exchange Commission provided a guide that stressed the necessity for an ethical culture within the organization and the creation of an ethics and compliance program. These guidelines have developed into global standards embraced and revised by many governmental and private sectors.[7]

This chapter will help complete your understanding of how organizational ethics is implemented, managed, and controlled to create an effective program. Although you may never be in charge of such a program, as a manager or employee you will be part of it. The more you understand the role and function of the various parts of the program, the more effective you will be in engaging and guiding others to make ethical decisions. Business ethics in an organization is not simply a personal matter based on your individual values. You will be responsible, both ethically and legally, for engaging in ethical conduct and reporting the unethical conduct of others in your organization.

THE ETHICS AUDIT

An **ethics audit** is a systematic evaluation of an organization's ethics program and performance to determine effectiveness. A major component of the ethics program described in Chapter 8, the ethics audit includes "regular, complete, and documented measurements of compliance with the company's published policies and procedures."[8] As such, the audit provides an opportunity to measure conformity to the firm's desired ethical standards. An audit can be a precursor to setting up an ethics program, as it identifies the firm's ethical standards as well as its existing policies and risk areas. Recent legislation and FSGO amendments encourage greater ethics auditing as companies attempt to demonstrate to various stakeholders that they are abiding by the law and have established programs to improve ethical decision making. Regulation has been found to have a positive effect on financial reporting quality. Boards of directors audit committees should be mindful of all regulatory requirements to avoid misconduct.[9]

The recent addition of ISO 19600 lists global standards for compliance management systems (CMSs). Companies that adopt this standard are expected to conduct periodic audits on their CMSs to identify weaknesses and ensure the ethics program is being implemented effectively.[10] More information on ISO 19600 will be provided later in this chapter. While U.S. companies are not required to report their audits to the public, some firms, such as New Belgium Brewing, do report the results of audits in areas such as employment practices, sustainability efforts, and community outreach.

The concept of ethics auditing emerged from the movement to evaluate and report on companies' broader social responsibility initiatives, particularly with regard to sustainability. An increasing number of companies are auditing their social responsibility programs and reporting the results to document their efforts to be more responsible to various interested stakeholder groups. A **social audit** is the process of assessing and reporting on a business's performance in fulfilling the economic, legal, ethical, and philanthropic responsibilities expected of it by its stakeholders.[11] Social reports often discuss issues related to a firm's performance in the four dimensions of social responsibility as well as specific ethical issues such as employment, community economic development, volunteerism, and environmental impact.[12] In contrast, ethics audits focus more narrowly on a firm's ethical and legal conduct. However, an ethics audit can be a component of a social audit; indeed, many companies include ethical issues in their social audits. Walmart, for example, includes ethical performance in its Global Responsibility Report.[13]

Regardless of the breadth of the audit, ethics auditing is a tool companies can employ to identify and measure their ethical commitment to stakeholders. Employees, customers, investors, suppliers, community members, activists, the media, and regulators increasingly demand companies act ethical and accountable for their conduct. In response, businesses are working to incorporate accountability into their actions, from long-term planning, everyday decision making, and rethinking processes for corporate governance and financial reporting to hiring, retaining, and promoting employees and building relationships with customers. The ethics audit provides an objective method for demonstrating a company's commitment to improving strategic planning, including its compliance with legal and ethical standards and standards of social responsibility. The auditing process is important to business because it can improve a firm's performance and effectiveness, increase its attractiveness to investors, improve its relationships with stakeholders, identify potential risks, and decrease the risk of misconduct and adverse publicity that could harm its reputation.[14] As we discussed earlier, the "World's Most Ethical Companies" have often shown better financial performance than the firms in the general stock indexes.

Ethics auditing employs procedures and processes similar to those found in financial auditing to create an objective report of a company's performance. As in an accounting audit, someone with expertise from outside the organization (an external audit firm) may be chosen to conduct the ethics audit. Although the standards used in such auditing can be adapted to provide an objective foundation for ethics reporting, there are significant differences. Ethics auditing deals with the internal and broad external impact of an organization's ethical performance. Another difference is that ethics auditing is not usually directly associated with regulatory requirements. Because ethics and social audits are voluntary, there are fewer standards a company can apply with regard to reporting frequency, disclosure requirements, and remedial actions that it should take in response to results. This may change as more companies develop ethics programs in the current regulatory environment, in which regulatory agencies support requiring boards of directors to oversee corporate ethics. If boards are to track the effectiveness of ethics programs, audits will be required. In addition, nonfinancial auditing standards are developing, with data available for benchmarking and comparing a firm's nonfinancial ethical performance with its own past performance and with the performance of other firms.

BENEFITS OF ETHICS AUDITING

There are many reasons why companies should analyze, report on, and improve their ethical conduct. Assessment of an organization's ethical culture is necessary to improve ethical performance and to document in legal proceedings that a firm has an effective ethics program. Companies can use ethics audits to detect misconduct before it becomes a major problem, and audits provide evidence of a firm's attempts to identify and deal with major ethical risks. For instance, companies that prove they had corporate ethics and compliance programs and report misconduct when discovered can often receive deferred prosecution agreements (DPAs), in which the company can resolve criminal charges without having to admit guilt. Under a typical DPA, companies admit wrongdoing (but not guilt), pay a fine, cooperate with the Justice Department, and agree to meet certain terms within a certain time frame. After the compliance deadline, if the Justice Department acknowledges the company met all of the terms, the charges against the firm will be dropped.[15] This provides significant encouragement for companies to account more for their actions in a wide range of areas, including corporate governance, ethics programs, customer relationships, employee relations, environmental policies, and community involvement.

One company may want to achieve the most ethical performance possible, whereas another may use an ethics audit merely to project a good image to hide its corrupt culture. Top managers might use an ethics audit to identify ethical problems in their companies, but identification alone does not mean they will take steps to correct these lapses through punishments or sanctions.[16] Without appropriate action on the part of management, an ethics audit is mere lip service intended to enhance the firm's reputation without actually improving its ethical conduct. Other firms might conduct audits in an attempt to comply with the FSGO's requirement that the board of directors oversee the discovery of ethical risk, design and implement an ethics program, and evaluate performance. Some companies view the auditing process as tied to continuous improvement that is closely related to improved financial performance. Companies' reasons for supporting the FSGO are complex and diverse. For example, it is common for firms to conduct audits of business practices with legal ramifications such as employee safety, environmental impact, and financial reporting. Although these practices are important to a firm's ethics and social responsibility, they are also legally required and therefore constitute the minimum level of commitment. However, because stakeholders are demanding increased transparency and taking a more active role through external organizations representing their interests, government regulators are calling on companies to improve their ethical conduct and make more decisions based on principles rather than on laws alone.

Measuring the ethical work climate of an organization is one way to learn about its ethical culture. While most measurements of ethical climate are conducted by academic researchers, some firms become proactive by working with consultants to measure their ethical climate. Measures of ethical climate include collective ethical sensitivity (empathetic concern and awareness), collective character, collective judgment (focus on others and focus on self), and collective moral motivation.[17] These measures can help evaluate changes in a firm's ethical culture after the development of ethics programs.

The auditing process can highlight trends, improve organizational learning, and facilitate communication and working relationships.[18] Auditing can also help companies assess the effectiveness of their programs and policies, which often improves their operating efficiencies and reduces costs. Information from audits and reports can allow a company to ensure it achieves the greatest possible impact with available resources.[19] The process of ethics auditing also helps an organization identify potential risks and liabilities and improve its compliance with the law. Furthermore, the audit report may help document a firm's compliance with legal requirements as well as demonstrate its progress in areas where it previously failed to comply—for example, by describing the systems it is implementing to reduce the likelihood of a recurrence of misconduct.[20]

For organizations, one of the greatest benefits of the auditing process is improved relationships with stakeholders who desire greater transparency. Many stakeholders have become wary of corporate public relations campaigns. Verbal assurances by corporate management are no longer sufficient to gain stakeholders' trust. An ethics audit could have saved Countrywide Financial if liar loans and the manipulation of borrowers' financial data had been identified earlier. When companies and their employees, suppliers, and investors trust each other, the costs of monitoring and managing these relationships are lower. Companies experience less conflict with these stakeholders, resulting in a heightened capacity for innovation and collaboration. Because of these benefits shareholders and investors have welcomed the increased disclosure that comes with corporate accountability.

Table 9–1 indicates the top challenges CEOs face. Note that human capital—or developing employee knowledge, habits, and creativity including ethical conduct—is the number one challenge. Issues such as trust, sustainability, and customer relationships are among the top 10 challenges. These issues can be considered risks associated with managing and controlling ethics programs. Therefore, they represent key areas important in an ethics audit. A growing number of investors are considering *nonfinancial measures*—such

TABLE 9-1 TABLE 9–1 Top Challenges for CEOs

1.	Human capital
2.	Innovation
3.	Customer relationships
4.	Operational excellence
5.	Sustainability
6.	Corporate brand and reputation
7.	Global political/economic risk
8.	Government regulation
9.	Global/international expansion
10.	Trust in business

N = 943 total responses. Response rate varied for each challenge.
Source: The Conference Board, *CEO Challenge® 2015 Summary Report*, 2015.

as the existence of ethics programs, legal compliance, board diversity and independence, and other corporate governance issues like CEO compensation—when they analyze the quality of current and potential investments. Research suggests investors may be willing to pay higher prices for the stock of companies they deem accountable,[21] such as stock from *Fortune*'s "World's Most Admired Companies," including Apple, Boeing, Toyota, Nordstrom, Southwest Airlines, Marriott International, Procter & Gamble, Accenture, Caterpillar, IBM, UPS, and BMW, who have generally avoided major ethical disasters.[22]

However, even companies that experienced legal issues or had their ethics questioned can make a comeback and become an industry role model. One of the most famous ethical turnaround stories is Nike. When it was revealed that some of Nike's suppliers were using child labor in Asian factories, there was a public outcry against Nike and the company lost much business. In response the firm adopted a number of auditing tools to ensure factory compliance and was the first company to respond to stakeholder requests to publicly disclose the names and locations of its contracted factories. Many of Nike's reports on its factories can be accessed on the Fair Labor Association website. Nike appears to have learned the important lesson of taking stakeholder demands seriously. For instance, when Greenpeace objected to Nike and Adidas suppliers releasing toxic waste into waterways, Nike responded within a few weeks with a plan to become more transparent about chemicals being released from its contracted factories, as well as making a commitment toward eliminating toxic chemicals from its supply chain by 2020.[23]

Regular audits permit shareholders and investors to judge whether a firm is achieving the goals it established, and whether it abides by the values that it specified as important. Moreover, it permits stakeholders to influence the organization's behavior.[24] Increasingly, a broad range of stakeholder groups are seeking specific, often quantifiable, information from companies. These stakeholders expect companies to take a deeper look at the nature of their operations and to publicly disclose their progress and problems in addressing these issues. Some investors use their rights as stockholders to encourage companies to modify their plans and policies to address specific ethical issues. For instance, a group of investors filed a lawsuit against Darden Restaurants alleging that the company had changed corporate bylaws to block their ability to vote on the plan to sell its Red Lobster chain.[25]

On a broader scale, the Obama administration sought to impose limits on executive compensation of those firms seeking government financial support. The 2010 passage of the Dodd–Frank Wall Street Reform and Consumer Protection Act implemented new regulations for executive compensation. Under these new provisions, shareholders of public companies can cast advisory votes on whether they approve of the compensation awarded to top executives. While the shareholder vote is non-binding, it does place pressure on boards when determining compensation packages. Additionally, top executives must provide more disclosure on how their compensation aligns with the company's financial performance.[26]

Ethical Crisis Management and Recovery

A significant benefit of ethics auditing is that it may prevent crises resulting from ethical or legal misconduct—crises that can potentially be more devastating than natural disasters or technological disruptions. Just as companies develop crisis management plans to respond to and recover from natural disasters, they should also prepare for ethical disasters that can result in substantial legal and financial costs and disrupt routine operations, paralyze employees, reduce productivity, destroy organizational reputation, and erode stakeholder confidence. Ethical and legal crises have resulted in the demise or acquisition of a number of well-known companies including Lehman Brothers, Merrill Lynch, and Washington Mutual. Many other companies—HealthSouth, Firestone, Waste Management, Rite Aid, U.S. Foodservice, Qwest, Diamond Foods, Mitsubishi Motors, and Archer Daniels Midland, for example—have survived ethical and legal crises but paid a high price both financially and in terms of compromised reputation and diminished stakeholder trust. Lumber Liquidators experienced an ethical crisis when high levels of formaldehyde were detected in its laminate flooring made in China. There have been concerns that floors installed in thousands of houses might contain high levels of formaldehyde, convincing many to rip up their floors.[27] Bribery allegations and an internal probe at Walmart temporarily caused share prices to plummet because of fears that a scandal could harm operations and would result in a legal penalty against the firm.[28]

Organizational members engaging in questionable or illegal conduct are guilty of ethical misconduct, and these employees can threaten the overall integrity of the organization. Top leaders in particular can magnify ethical misconduct to disastrous proportions. The misconduct of Raj Rajaratnam at the Galleon Group, Andrew Fastow at Enron, Dennis Kozlowski at Tyco, and Bernie Ebbers at WorldCom caused financial disasters on both organizational and global levels.[29] An ethics audit can uncover rogue employees who violate the firm's ethical standards and policies or laws and regulations.

Ethical disasters follow recognizable phases of escalation, from ethical issue recognition and the decision to act unethically to the organization's discovery of and response to the act. Appropriate anticipation and intervention during these situations can stave off major problems. Such contingency planning assesses risks, plans for eventualities, and provides ready tools for responding to ethical crises. The process of ethical disaster-recovery planning involves assessing an organization's values, developing an ethics program, performing an ethics audit, and developing contingency plans for potential ethical disasters. The ethics audit itself provides the key to preventing ethical disasters.

TABLE 9–2 Improving Organizational Risk Management

Review the nature and scope of the risk management function.

Develop a risk and compliance plan at the beginning of major projects.

Improve performance by applying risk measures and dashboards.

Maintain a recovery plan for an ethical or compliance crisis.

Communicate risk frameworks and the effectiveness of internal and external controls.

© 2017 Cengage Learning

Formal mechanisms should be in place to discover risk as a part of evaluating compliance and the effectiveness of ethics programs. The greatest fear of most corporate leaders is discovering misconduct or illegal activity that could be reported by the mass media, used by competitors, or prosecuted by the government. Yet this process is extremely important to the long-term well-being of an organization. While risks such as earthquakes, fires, hurricanes, and other natural disasters cannot always be determined, companies can plan for ethical disasters. Unfortunately, ethical risks are often given the lowest priority. However, it is worth noting that many common risks, such as reputation, product quality, litigation, and more, have an ethical component. Indeed, ethical risks can be just as damaging as natural disaster risks because a firm that gains a reputation for being unethical will likely lose investors, customers, and employees. It can take many years for a firm to recover from a misconduct disaster.

Ernst & Young conducted an investigation into some of the ways Chief Risk Officers of global companies manage risks and used their insights to help develop a list of recommendations for managing business risk. For instance, asset managers are investing in more resources for data generation and management. Cybersecurity in particular is being recognized as not simply an IT issue but as a risk area with companywide implications.[30] By understanding new and potential legislation in different areas of the world, businesses can determine how to best meet these regulations and minimize their risks of violating the laws of a specific country. Table 9–2 lists five recommendations for improving risk management.

Measuring Nonfinancial Ethical Performance

Although much of the regulation of corporate ethics and compliance focuses on financial measures, to truly have integrity, an organization must also focus on nonfinancial areas of performance. The word **integrity** in this context implies a balanced organization that not only makes ethical financial decisions but also is ethical in the more subjective aspects of its corporate culture. The Sarbanes–Oxley Act focused on questionable accounting and the metrics that destroy shareholder value, but other models have been developed—such as Six Sigma, the Balanced Scorecard, and the triple bottom line—to capture structural and behavioral organizational ethical performance. *Six Sigma* is a methodology designed to manage process variations that cause defects, defined as unacceptable deviations from the mean or target, and to systematically work toward managing variation to eliminate those defects. The objective of Six Sigma is to deliver world-class performance, reliability, and value to the end customer. The **Balanced Scorecard** is a management system that focuses on all the elements that contribute to organizational performance and success, including financial, customer, market, and internal processes. The goal is to develop a broader perspective on performance factors and to foster a culture of learning and growth that improves all organizational communication. The **triple bottom line** provides a perspective that takes into account the social, environmental, and financial impacts of decisions made within an organization. When making an increased commitment to social responsibility, sustainability, or ethics, companies consider implementing triple bottom line reporting as a way to confirm their investments and initiatives support their organization's values and overall success. Table 9–3 provides additional detail on these three measurement tools. The purpose of a variety of measures of performance and goal achievement is to determine the quality and effectiveness of environmental, social, and ethics initiatives. Many believe that an inherent gain is realized by companies with strong ethical cultures and environmental commitments, paid in customer commitment and in avoiding the negative publicity and costs associated with wrongdoing.

The **Global Reporting Initiative** (GRI) has become a prominent framework that companies have adopted to report their social and sustainability progress.[31] The GRI advances sustainability reporting, which incorporates the triple bottom line factors of economic, social, and environmental indicators. The primary goal of the GRI is "the mainstreaming of disclosure on environmental, social, and governance performance."[32] Businesses can use the GRI to develop a more standardized method of reporting nonfinancial results in a way users of the reports can understand. Companies benefit because the GRI provides tools for improving their implementation of the triple bottom line, as well as assisting with the disclosure of their progress in this area. These tools give them the ability to compare their sustainability efforts with those of other companies and the chance to enhance their reputation in the eyes of stakeholders. Users benefit because this standardized sustainability reporting gives them a point of comparison with other companies' sustainability initiatives.[33] GRI continually revises its framework to ensure it remains relevant and encourages multiple stakeholders from global business, civil society, labor, and academic sectors to participate in the process.[34]

TABLE 9-3 Description of Measurement Tools

Measurement Systems	Description
Balanced Scorecard	Developed by Drs. Robert Kaplan and David Norton, the Balanced Scorecard incorporates nonfinancial performance indicators into the evaluation system to provide a more "balanced" view of organizational performance. The system uses four metrics—financial, internal business processes, learning and growth, and customer—to measure the overall performance of the firm.
Six Sigma	Six Sigma focuses on improving existing processes that do not meet quality specifications or that need to be improved, as well as developing new processes that meet Six Sigma standards. The goal of Six Sigma is to reduce defects in products and strive for continual improvement.
Triple Bottom Line	This approach to measuring social, financial, and environmental factors (or people, places, and planet) recognizes that business has a responsibility to positively influence a variety of stakeholders, including customers, employees, shareholders, community, and the natural environment. The challenge is how to evaluate a business's social and environmental impacts, since there are no universally standard forms of measuring these criteria.

Source: "Balanced Scorecard Basics," Balanced Scorecard Institute, http://www.balancedscorecard.org/BSCResources/AbouttheBalancedScorecard/tabid/55/Default.aspx (accessed May 14, 2013); "What is Six Sigma," iSix Sigma, http://www.isixsigma.com/index.php?option=com_k2&view=item &id=1463:what-is-six-sigma?&Itemid=155 (accessed May 14, 2013); "Triple bottom line," *The Economist*, November 17, 2009, http://www.economist.com/node/14301663?story_id=14301663 (accessed May 14, 2013).

In 2014 the International Organization for Standardization published ISO 19600 to provide international guidelines for compliance management. The International Organization for Standardization is an independent nongovernmental organization that develops voluntary standards organizations can adopt to ensure consumers that they adhere to internationally recognized standards.[35] ISO standards have become global standards and one of the most widely accepted certifications to provide assurance that various business functions and operations adhere to best practices. The adoption of a compliance standard demonstrates the increasingly global concern for ethics and compliance in business. ISO 19600 was based on an Australian compliance management standard and emphasizes a "principles'" approach to compliance management based upon commitment, implementation, monitoring and measuring, and continual improvement.[36] Principles are specific and pervasive boundaries for behavior that should not be violated. They become the foundation for rules.

Because it is a guideline, companies that adopt ISO 19600 do not receive official certification as with some other ISO standards. However, this standard is highly beneficial for global businesses as it increases their ability to adapt to the changing regulatory environment of different countries. A key part of ISO 19600 is the adoption of compliance objectives and the assignment of accountability throughout the entire organization, which has been associated with the development of an ethical culture. Under ISO 19600 all members of an organization have the responsibility to report ethical concerns or issues. The ability of employees to report is an important part of the FSGO guidelines for an effective ethics program. The CMS should be developed in the context of the organization to address the specific needs and risks of the organization.[37] Additionally, implementation of the CMS requires strong leadership and support from top management. Figure 9–1 illustrates the key clauses of ISO 19600 and how they are structured. This compliance standard is being adopted by ethics officers globally.

Figure 9–2 shows the Open Compliance Ethics Group's functions of governance, risk, and compliance framework. The Open Compliance Ethics Group (OCEG) (http://www.oceg.org) worked with more than 100 companies to create a universal framework for compliance and ethics management. The OCEG focuses on nonfinancial compliance and the more qualitative elements of internal controls. The OCEG framework deals with complex

FIGURE 9–1 **Structure of ISO 19600**

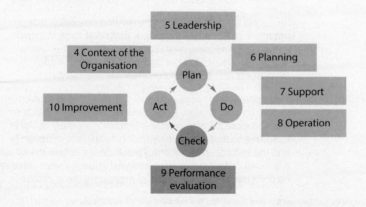

Source: Franziska Zuber, "Guidance on CMS: The new ISO 19600 standard," January 23, 2015, http://blog.kpmg.ch/guidance-on-cms-the-new-iso-19600-standard/ (accessed April 6, 2015).

issues of compliance and solutions to address the development of organizational ethics. By establishing guidelines rather than standards, OCEG provides a tool for each company to use as it sees fit, given its size, scope, structure, industry, and other factors that create individualized needs. The OCEG guidelines and benchmarking studies can be valuable to a firm conducting an ethics audit. Most significant is the opportunity to compare an organization's activities to those of other organizations. To this end, the OCEG created tools and certification procedures to help businesses, such as the *Burgundy Book* that assists in assessing the design and operating effectiveness of governance, risk management, and compliance processes.[38] Additionally, the organization awards certification to companies and individuals that demonstrate to stakeholders that they operate at the highest standards regarding governance, risk management, and compliance.[39]

FIGURE 9–2 Roles and Functions of Risk, Management, and Compliance

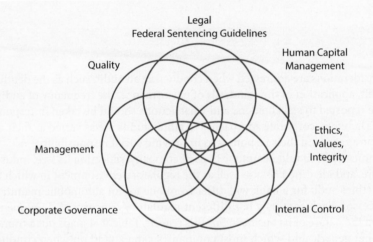

Source: The Open Compliance Ethics Group Framework Overview, http://www.oceg.org/framework.asp (accessed April 4, 2006).

Risks and Requirements in Ethics Auditing

Although ethics audits provide many benefits for individual companies and their stakeholders, they have the potential to create risks. For example, a firm may uncover a serious ethical problem it would prefer not to disclose until it has remedied the situation. It may find one or more of its stakeholders' criticisms cannot be easily addressed. Occasionally, the process of conducting an ethics audit may foster stakeholder dissatisfaction rather than stifle it. Moreover, the auditing process imposes burdens (especially with regard to recordkeeping) and costs for firms that undertake it. Auditing, although a prudent measure, provides no assurance that ethical risks and challenges can be avoided. Another challenge is in assessing risk and identifying standards of comparison. How can a company sufficiently analyze and manage its risks? What goals for improvement should it develop? Some initiatives to benchmark risk assessment and best practices have begun to emerge, but this process is in its early stages.

Many companies suspected of misconduct respond to public scrutiny of their practices by conducting an ethics audit to show their concern and respond appropriately to weaknesses in their programs. As a result of questionable conduct or legal violations, companies such as JP Morgan, Fannie Mae, Goldman Sachs, and Bank of America should conduct audits to demonstrate their visible commitment to improving decision making and business conduct.

Research suggests that generating ethics and corporate social responsibility auditing procedures can be tricky because of a lack of standardization and widely accepted measures.[40] Although ethics and social responsibility are defined and perceived differently by various stakeholders, a core of minimum standards for ethical performance is evolving. These standards represent a fundamental step in the development of minimum ethics requirements that are specific, measurable, achievable, and meaningful to a business's impact on all stakeholders. Standards help companies set measurable and achievable targets for improvement, and they form an objective foundation for reporting the firm's efforts to all direct stakeholders. Disagreements may still arise over key issues, but overall these standards should enable companies to make progress in meeting their goals. The FSGO's seven steps for effective ethical compliance, discussed in Chapters 3 and 8, as well as the Sarbanes–Oxley Act and the Dodd–Frank Act, provide standards organizations can use in ethics auditing.

THE AUDITING PROCESS

Many considerations are addressed when conducting an audit, such as the depth and width of the audit, application of the standards of performance, the frequency of audits, how the results are reported to stakeholders, and what actions should be taken in response to audit results.[41] Therefore, corporate approaches to ethics audits are as varied as their approaches to ethics programs and their responses to improving social responsibility.

An ethics audit should be unique to each company, reflecting its size, industry, corporate culture, and identified risks as well as the regulatory environment in which it operates. Thus, an ethics audit for a bank will differ from one for an automobile manufacturer or a food processor. Each company has different regulatory concerns and unique risks stemming from the nature of its business. For this reason, Table 9–4 maps out a framework that is somewhat generic and which most companies can expand on when conducting their own ethics audits. The steps in the framework can be applied to broader social audits that include specific ethical issues as well as other economic, legal, and philanthropic concerns of interest to various stakeholders. As with any new initiative, companies may choose to begin their effort with smaller, less formal audits and work up to more comprehensive

TABLE 9–4 Framework for an Ethics Audit

- Secure the commitment of top managers and board of directors

- Establish a committee to oversee the ethics audit

- Define the scope of the audit process, including subject matter areas important to the ethics audit

- Review the organization's mission, policies, goals, and objectives and define its ethical priorities

- Collect and analyze relevant information in each designated subject matter area

- Have the results verified by an independent agent

- Report the findings to the audit committee and, if approved, to managers and stakeholders

Sources: These steps are compatible with the social auditing methods prescribed by Warren Dow and Roy Crowe in *What Social Auditing Can Do for Voluntary Organizations* (Vancouver, WA: Volunteer Vancouver, July 1999), and Sandra Waddock and Neil Smith in "Corporate Responsibility Audits: Doing Well by Doing Good," *Sloan Management Review* 41 (2000): 79.

social audits. For example, a firm may choose to focus on primary stakeholders in its initial audit year and then expand to secondary groups in subsequent audits.

The framework encompasses a wide range of business responsibilities and relationships. The audit entails an individualized process and outcomes for a particular firm, since it requires a careful consideration of the unique issues that face a particular organization. For example, the auditing process at Coca-Cola must consider several specific factors. To ensure an effective internal audit, Coca-Cola's board of directors appoints an audit committee whose responsibilities include a review of the company's financial statements as well as an assessment of its risk management, internal and disclosure controls, complaints procedures, and compliance programs (including the Company's Code of Business Conduct). The committee's statement of purpose is as follows:

> The Committee will represent and assist the Board in fulfilling its oversight responsibility to the shareowners relating to the integrity of the Company's financial statements and the financial reporting process, the systems of internal accounting and financial controls, the internal audit function, the annual independent audit of the Company's financial statements, the Company's compliance with legal and regulatory requirements, and its ethics programs as established by management and the Board, including the Company's Code of Business Conduct. The Committee shall also oversee the independent auditors' qualifications and independence. The Committee will evaluate the performance of the Company's internal audit function (responsibilities, budget and staffing) and the Company's independent auditors, including a review and evaluation of the engagement partner and coordinating partner. In so doing, it is the responsibility of the Committee to act independently while maintaining free and open communication between the Committee, the independent auditors, the internal auditors, and management of the Company. The Committee is also responsible for producing an annual report for inclusion in the Company's proxy statement.[42]

Figure 9–3 provides a fictional example of how a corporate social responsibility structure might be organized within a well-known company. Notice that the 2010 amendments

FIGURE 9–3 Model Corporate Social Responsibility Structure

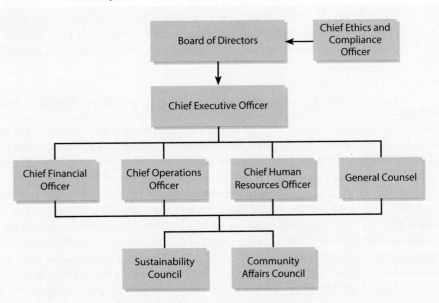

to the Federal Sentencing Guidelines for Organizations recommend that chief ethics and compliance officers report directly to the board of directors. Although this chapter presents a structure and recommendations for both general social and ethics-specific audits, there is no generic approach that will satisfy every firm's circumstances. Nevertheless, the benefits and limitations companies derive from auditing are relatively consistent.

Secure Commitment of Top Managers and Board of Directors

The first step in conducting any audit is securing the commitment of the firm's top management and, if it is a public corporation, its board of directors. Indeed, the push for an ethics audit may come directly from the board itself in response to specific stakeholder concerns or corporate governance reforms related to the Sarbanes–Oxley Act, which suggests that boards of directors provide oversight for all auditing activities. In addition, court decisions related to the FSGO hold board members responsible for the ethical and legal compliance programs of the firms they oversee. Rules and regulations associated with the Sarbanes–Oxley Act require that boards include members who are knowledgeable and qualified to oversee accounting and other types of audits to ensure these reports are accurate and include all material information. Although a board's financial audit committee will examine ethical standards throughout the organization as they relate to financial matters, it also deals with the implementation of codes of ethics for top financial officers. Many of those issues relate to corporate governance issues such as compensation, stock options, and conflicts of interest. An ethics audit can demonstrate that a firm has taken steps to prevent misconduct and is useful in cases where civil lawsuits blame the firm and its directors for the actions of a rogue employee.

Pressure for an audit can also come from top managers looking for ways to track and improve ethical performance and perhaps give their firm an advantage over competitors that face questions about their ethical conduct. Additionally, under the Sarbanes–Oxley Act, CEOs and CFOs may be criminally prosecuted if they knowingly certify misleading financial statements. They may request an ethics audit as a tool to improve the confidence in their firm's reporting processes. Some companies established a high-level ethics office in conjunction with an ethics program, and the ethics officer may campaign for an audit as a measure of the effectiveness of the firm's program. Regardless of the impetus for an audit, its success hinges on the full support of top management, particularly the CEO and the board of directors. Without this support, an audit will not improve the ethics program or the corporate culture.

Establish a Committee to Oversee the Ethics Audit

The next step in the framework is to establish a committee or team to oversee the audit process. Ideally, the board of directors' financial audit committee oversees the audit, but this does not happen in most companies. In most firms, managers or ethics officers do not always report to the board of directors when conducting social and ethics auditing. In any case, this team should include employees knowledgeable about the nature and role of ethics audits, and those people should come from various departments within the firm. The team may recruit individuals in-house or hire outside consultants to coordinate the audit and report the results directly to the board of directors. The Ethics Resource Center, a nonprofit organization engaged in supporting ethical conduct in the public and private sector, assists companies with assessments and audits.[43] As with a financial audit, an external auditor should not have conflict-of-interest relationships with top managers or board members. Based on the best practices of corporate governance, audits should be monitored by an independent board of directors' committee, as recommended by the Sarbanes–Oxley Act.

Define the Scope of the Audit Process

The ethics audit committee should establish the scope of the audit and monitor its progress to ensure it stays on track. The scope of an audit depends on the type of business, the risks it faces, and the opportunities it has to manage ethics. This step includes defining the key subject matter or risk areas important to the audit (for example, sustainability, discrimination, product liability, employee rights, privacy, fraud, financial reporting, and/or legal compliance) as well as the bases on which these areas are assessed. Assessments can be based on direct consultation, observation, surveys, or focus groups.[44] Table 9–5 lists sample subject matter areas and the audit items for each.

Review Organizational Mission, Values, Goals, and Policies and Define Ethical Priorities

Because ethics audits generally involve comparing an organization's ethical performance to its goals, values, and policies, the audit process should include a review of the mission statement and strategic objectives. A company's overall mission may incorporate ethics objectives, but these may be located in separate documents, including those that focus on social responsibility. For example, a firm's ethics statement or statement of values may offer guidance for managing transactions and human relationships that support the firm's reputation, thereby fostering the confidence of the firm's external stakeholders.[45] Franklin Energy specifies the five core values it uses in managing its business which contributes to its success: ingenuity, results orientation, frugality, integrity, and environmental stewardship.[46]

This review should include an examination of all formal documents that make explicit commitments to ethical, legal, or social responsibility, as well as less formal documents. Informal documents include marketing materials, workplace policies, ethics policies, and standards for suppliers or vendors. This review may reveal a need to create additional statements to fill the identified gaps or create a new comprehensive mission statement or ethical policy that addresses any deficiencies.[47]

It is important to examine all of the firm's policies and practices with respect to the specific areas covered by the audit. In an audit that scrutinizes discrimination issues, this review step would consider the company's goals and objectives as well as its policies related to discrimination. It would consider the means available for communicating the firm's policies and assess their effectiveness. Such an evaluation should look at whether and how managers are rewarded for meeting their goals and the systems employees have to give and receive feedback. An effective ethics audit reviews all these systems and assesses their strengths and weaknesses.[48]

Concurrent with this step in the auditing process, the firm should define its ethical priorities. Determining these priorities is a balancing act because identifying the needs and assessing the priorities of each stakeholder can be difficult. Because there are no legal requirements for ethical priorities, it is up to management's strategic planning processes to determine risks, designate appropriate standards, and outline processes of communication with stakeholders. It is important to articulate the firm's ethical priorities and values

TABLE 9-5 The Ethics Audit

		Organizational Issues*
Yes	No	1. Does the company have a code of ethics that is reasonably capable of preventing misconduct?
Yes	No	2. Does the board of directors participate in the development and evaluation of the ethics program?
Yes	No	3. Is there a person with high managerial authority responsible for the ethics program?
Yes	No	4. Are there mechanisms in place to prevent the delegation of authority to individuals with a propensity for misconduct?
Yes	No	5. Does the organization effectively communicate standards and procedures to its employees via ethics training programs?
Yes	No	6. Does the organization communicate its ethical standards to suppliers, customers, and significant others that have a relationship with the organization?
Yes	No	7. Do the company's manuals and written documents guiding operations contain messages about appropriate behavior?
Yes	No	8. Is there formal or informal communication within the organization about procedures and activities that are considered acceptable ethical behavior?
Yes	No	9. Does top management have a mechanism in place to detect ethical issues relating to employees, customers, the community, and society?
Yes	No	10. Is there a system in place for employees to report unethical behavior?
Yes	No	11. Is there consistent enforcement of standards and punishments in the organization?
Yes	No	12. Is there a committee, department, team, or group that deals with ethical issues in the organization?
Yes	No	13. Does the organization make a continuous effort to improve its ethical compliance program?
Yes	No	14. Does the firm perform an ethics audit?

		Examples of Specific Issues That Could Be Monitored in an Ethics Audit†
Yes	No	1. Are there any systems or operational procedures in place to safeguard individual employees' ethical behavior?
Yes	No	2. Is it necessary for employees to break the company's ethical rules to get the job done?
Yes	No	3. Is there an environment of deception, repression, and cover-ups concerning events that would embarrass the company?
Yes	No	4. Are there any participatory management practices that allow ethical issues to be discussed?
Yes	No	5. Are compensation systems totally dependent on performance?
Yes	No	6. Does sexual harassment occur?
Yes	No	7. Does any form of discrimination—race, sex, or age—occur in hiring, promotion, or compensation?
Yes	No	8. Are the only standards about environmental impact those that are legally required?
Yes	No	9. Do the firm's activities show any concern for the ethical value systems of the community?
Yes	No	10. Are there deceptive and misleading messages in promotion?
Yes	No	11. Are products described in misleading or negative ways or without communicating their limitations to customers?

Yes	No	12. Are the documents and copyrighted materials of other companies used in unauthorized ways?
Yes	No	13. Are expense accounts inflated?
Yes	No	14. Are customers overcharged?
Yes	No	15. Does unauthorized copying of computer software occur?

*A high number of "Yes" answers indicate ethical control mechanisms and procedures are in place within the organization.
†The number of "Yes" answers indicates the number of possible ethical issues to address.

as a set of parameters or performance indicators that can be objectively and quantitatively assessed. Because the ethics audit is a structured report with quantitative and descriptive assessments, actions should be measurable by quantitative indicators. However, it is sometimes not possible to go beyond description.[49]

At some point, a firm must demonstrate action-oriented responsiveness to ethics issues of top priority. Electricity and gas company National Grid has a long history of minimizing damage to the environment. The firm adopted the international standard for environmental management systems, ISO 14001, and the guidelines that require external auditing by a certified auditor. Additionally, National Grid has a global Corporate Responsibility Summary Report on its website.[50]

Collect and Analyze Relevant Information

The next step in the ethical audit framework is to identify the tools or methods for measuring a firm's progress to improve employees' ethical decisions and conduct. The firm should collect relevant information for each subject matter area. To understand employee issues, for example, the auditing committee should work with the firm's human resource department to gather employee survey information and other statistics and feedback. A thorough ethics audit reviews all relevant reports, including external documents sent to government agencies and others. Measuring a firm's sustainability strategy often depends upon a company's own reports and secondary data.[51] The information collected should help determine baseline levels of compliance as well as the internal and external expectations of the company. This step also identifies where the company has, or has not, met its commitments, including those dictated by its mission statement and other policy documents. The documents reviewed in this process vary from company to company based on size, type of industry, and scope of the audit.[52] At Keurig Green Mountain, the audit committee of the board of directors is responsible for providing oversight of reporting procedures and audits. Keurig Green Mountain Inc.'s code of ethics, described in Table 9–6, is an example of a framework for the principles that are the backbone of the ethics audit.[53]

Some techniques for collecting evidence might involve examining both internal and external documents, observing the data-collection process, and confirming information in the organization's accounting records. Auditors may also employ ratio analysis of relevant indicators to identify any inconsistencies or unexpected patterns. Objective measurement is the key consideration of the ethics auditor.[54]

Stakeholder involvement is another component in the successful implementation of an ethics audit since they yield significant insights. In one study examining reporting channels, employees were asked to whom they would "feel comfortable" reporting misconduct if they suspected or became aware of it. Supervisors and local managers received the most favorable responses, suggesting the need for organizations to ensure front-line managers

TABLE 9–6 Keurig Green Mountain Inc.'s Code of Ethics

- Respect the rights of others in the global community

- Maintain accurate records and report concerns

- Comply with all laws, rules, and regulatory requirements

- Avoid conflicts of interest and corruption

- Be responsible in the use, protection, and management of Keurig's assets and resources

- Understand antitrust laws and uphold fair business practices

- Share the company's story while following established guidelines on consistent communications

- Work with integrity while maintaining the confidentiality of company information

- Support the company's standards, principles, and procedures and encourage Keurig's business partners to do so as well

Source: Adapted from Keurig Green Mountain, *Keurig Green Mountain Code of Conduct* (Waterbury, VT: Keurig Green Mountain, 2014).

are equipped to respond appropriately to allegations. Personnel primarily charged with taking action in response to alleged misconduct (legal, internal audit, and board or audit committee functions) were cited among the least likely channels employees would feel comfortable using to report allegations. A company's ethical culture also determines whether those who report misconduct experience retaliation—and could determine how often employees report misconduct. Figure 9–4 shows that misconduct occurs more often in weak ethical cultures. It is essential for management to create a strong ethical culture so employees are encouraged to report observed misconduct.

Because integrating the stakeholder feedback step in the ethics audit process is so crucial, these stakeholders must be defined and interviewed during the data-collection stage. For most companies, stakeholders include employees, customers, investors, suppliers, community groups, regulators, nongovernment organizations, and the media. Both social and ethics audits typically interview and conduct focus groups with these stakeholders to gain an understanding of their perception of the company. The Canadian Space Agency (CSA) conducted an ethics audit to determine whether control activities had been implemented that effectively emphasized the importance of values and ethics in achieving organizational goals. The CSA used staff interviews and reviews of internal documentation to determine how values and ethics were communicated and integrated within the organization.[55] Some companies might also choose to survey customers and other stakeholders in order to gain a view of their ethics program from all angles. The more stakeholders auditors include in this measurement stage, the more time and resources the audit consumes. However, a larger sample of stakeholders yields a useful variety of opinions about the company. Multinational corporations must decide whether to include in the audit only the main office or all facilities around the globe.[56]

Because employees carry out business operations, understanding employee issues is vital to a successful audit. Useful indicators include staff turnover and employee satisfaction. High turnover rates could indicate poor working conditions, an unethical culture, inadequate compensation, or general employee dissatisfaction. Companies can analyze these factors to determine key areas for improvement.[57] Questionnaires that survey employees' perceptions of the ethics of their company serve as benchmarks in an ongoing assessment of ethical performance. Then, if unethical behavior increases, management will better understand what types of unethical practices may be occurring and why. Most organizations recognize employees behave in ways that lead to recognition and rewards and avoid behavior resulting in punishment. Therefore, companies can design and implement human resource policies and procedures for recruiting, hiring, promoting, compensating, and rewarding employees that encourage ethical behavior.[58]

Customers are another primary stakeholder group because their patronage and loyalty determines a company's financial success. Providing meaningful feedback is critical to creating and maintaining customer satisfaction. Through surveys and customer-initiated communication systems such as response cards, online social networks, email, and toll-free numbers, organizations can monitor and respond to customer issues and its perceived social performance. Procter & Gamble uses online social networking sites like Facebook to determine what social issues consumers are passionate about, as well as to gain insights into consumers' product needs and reactions to products.

A growing number of investors seek to include in their investment portfolios the stocks of companies that conduct ethics and social audits. Investors are more aware of the financial benefits that stem from socially responsible management systems—as well as the negative consequences of a lack of responsibility. Even allegations of potential misconduct can harm a company in the short-run. Share prices for direct selling skincare company Nu Skin plummeted after allegations arose that the company was operating a pyramid scheme in China. Nu Skin later paid $540,000 to China for misleading claims made by its distributors and for selling products approved for retail stores through direct selling. Neither of these activities constitutes a pyramid scheme. The mass media often makes pyramid scheme accusations whenever direct sellers have allegedly engaged in any misconduct. Although shares have now recovered, the immediate aftermath of the accusations caused investors to panic, and share prices dropped by 37 percent.[59]

Even the hint of wrongdoing can affect a company's relations with investors. Many investors simply do not want to invest in companies engaging in unfavorable business

FIGURE 9–4 **Misconduct Declines as Ethics Culture Improves**

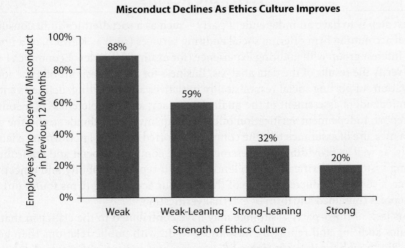

Source: Ethics Resource Center, *National Business Ethics Survey of the U.S. Workforce* (Arlington, VA: Ethics Resource Center, 2014), 18.

practices, such as the use of sweatshops or child labor. It is therefore critical that companies understand the issues of this important group of stakeholders and their expectations, both financially and socially.

Organizations can obtain feedback from stakeholders through standardized surveys, interviews, and focus groups. Companies can encourage stakeholder exchanges by inviting specific groups together for discussions. Such meetings may include an office or facility tour or a field trip by company representatives to sites in the community. Regardless of how companies collect information about stakeholders' views, the primary objective is to generate opinions about how the company is perceived and whether it is fulfilling stakeholders' expectations.[60]

Once this information is collected, the firm should compare the internal perceptions to those identified in the stakeholder assessment and summarize its findings. During this phase, the audit committee should draw some conclusions about the information obtained in the previous stages. These conclusions may include descriptive assessments of the findings, such as the costs and benefits of the company's ethics program, the strengths and weaknesses of the firm's policies and practices, the nature of feedback from stakeholders, and issues to be addressed in future audits. In some cases, it may be appropriate to see how the findings fit with standards identified earlier, both quantitatively and qualitatively.[61]

Data analysis should include an examination of other organizations in the industry and their performance in the designated subject areas. The audit committee can investigate the successes of another firm considered the best in a particular area and compare that company's performance to their own. Some common benchmarks available from corporate ethics audits are employee or customer satisfaction, community groups' perceptions, and the impact of the company's philanthropy. For example, the Ethics and Compliance Association (ECA) conducts research on legal and ethical issues in the workplace. These studies allow ECA members to compare their responses to the aggregate results obtained through the study.[62] Such comparisons can assist the audit committee to identify best practices for a particular industry or establish a baseline for minimum ethics requirements. A wide variety of standards are emerging that apply to ethics accountability. The aim of these standards is to create a tool for benchmarking and a framework for businesses to follow.

Verify the Results

The next step is to have an independent party—such as a social/ethics audit consultant, a financial accounting firm offering social auditing services (such as KPMG), or a nonprofit special interest group with auditing experience (for example, the New Economics Foundation)—verify the results of the data analysis. Business for Social Responsibility, a nonprofit organization supporting social responsibility initiatives and reporting, defined **verification** as an independent assessment of the quality, accuracy, and completeness of a company's social report. Independent verification offers a company, its stakeholders, and the general public a measure of assurance that the company reported its ethical performance fairly and honestly, as well as providing an assessment of the company's social and environmental reporting systems.[63] Verification also lends an audit report credibility and objectivity.[64] However, a survey conducted by one of the Big Four accounting firms found only a few social reports contained any form of external verification.

This lack of third-party assurance may have contributed to the criticism that social and ethics auditing and reporting have more to do with public relations than genuine change. But though the independent validation of ethics audits is not required, the number of independently verified reports is increasing.[65] Many public policy experts believe an independent, objective audit can be provided only if the auditor plays no role in the reporting process—in other words, consulting and auditing should be distinctly separate roles. The Sarbanes–Oxley Act essentially legalized this belief.

Verification of the results of an audit should involve standard procedures that control the reliability and validity of the information. As with a financial audit, auditors can apply substantive tests to detect material misstatements in the audit data and analysis. The tests commonly used in financial audits—confirmation, observation, tracing, vouching, analytical procedures, inquiry, and re-computing—can be used in ethics and social audits as well. For example, positive confirmations can be requested from the participants of a stakeholder focus group to verify that the reported results are consistent with the results the focus group believed it found. Likewise, an ethics auditor can observe a company's procedures for handling ethical disputes to verify statements made in the report. Just as a financial auditor follows supporting documents to financial statements to test their completeness, an ethics auditor or verifier examines employee complaints about an ethics issue to check whether the reporting of such complaints was complete. An auditor can also employ analytical procedures by examining plausible relationships such as the prior year's employee turnover ratio or the average turnover rate commonly reported within the industry. With the reporting firm's permission, an auditor can contact the company's legal counsel to inquire about pending litigation that may shed light on ethical and legal issues currently facing the firm.[66]

Additionally, a financial auditor may be asked to provide a letter to the company's board of directors and senior managers to highlight inconsistencies in the reporting process. The auditor may request that management reply to particular points in the letter to indicate the actions it intends to take to address problems or weaknesses. The financial auditor must report to the board of directors' financial audit committee (or equivalent) significant adjustments or difficulties encountered during the audit as well as any disagreements with management. Ethics auditors should be required to report to the board of directors' audit committee the same issues a financial auditor would report.[67]

Report the Findings

The final step in the framework is issuing the ethics audit report. This involves reporting audit findings through a formal report to the board of directors and top executives and, if approved, to external stakeholders. Although some companies prefer not to release the results of their audits to the public, more companies are choosing to make their reports available to stakeholders. The Canadian Space Agency (CSA) released the results of their audit online to show that

DEBATE ISSUE
TAKE A STAND

Which Ethics Audit Process Works Better for Smaller Companies?

ABC Specialty Marketing, Inc. is considering a formal ethics audit. The company has 200 employees, including 50 salespeople that sell promotional printing products. Recent ethical issues have raised concerns within the company, causing the board of directors to think about implementing an audit. During the meeting, one of the board members who examined the auditing process represented in Table 9–5 indicated that for a small company, this approach looked too formal. He felt the Better Business Bureau Torch Award Criteria for ethical companies was a more practical approach to auditing ethical risks and conduct. Another member pointed out that the BBB criteria were more for judging than for understanding the risk areas and ethics program implementation concerns. This led to a discussion about how to implement an ethics audit in a small company with a fairly limited ethics program. The meeting ended without a clear decision on which approach to use.

1. The Better Business Bureau Torch Award Criteria is the best method for conducting a formal ethics audit in a smaller company.

2. The auditing process represented in Table 9–5 offers a better way to understand a small company's ethical risks and conduct.

while the CSA does implement activities that promote organizational values and ethics, there is still room for improvement. Recommendations included developing a values and ethics communication plan, increasing the promotion of values and ethics within the organization, and informing staff about the process for disclosing wrongdoing.[68] Many other companies, including Johnson and Johnson, Shell, and Keurig Green Mountain, make audit reports available on their corporate websites.[69]

Based on the guidelines established by the Global Reporting Initiative, the report should spell out the purpose and scope of the audit, the methods used in the audit process (evidence gathering and evaluation), the role of the (preferably independent) auditor, auditing guidelines followed by the auditor, and any reporting guidelines followed by the company.[70] The ethics audit of the Canadian Space Agency followed these guidelines.[71] The report is more meaningful if integrated with other organizational information available, such as financial reports, employee surveys, regulatory filings, and customer feedback. The firm might want to include in the ethics audit a section on best industry practices and how it compares to other companies in its field. Such a comparison can help a firm identify its weaknesses and develop suggestions for improvement. The use of information such as the OCEG Benchmarking Study pinpoints key elements of corporate and ethics programs that help assess best practices across the industry.[72]

As mentioned earlier, ethics audits may resemble financial audits, but they take quite different forms. In a financial audit, the Statement of Auditing Standards dictates literally every word found in a financial audit report in terms of content and placement. Based on the auditor's findings, the report issued can take one of the following four forms, among other variations. An *unqualified opinion* states that the financial statements are fairly stated. A *qualified opinion* asserts that although the auditor believes the financial statements are fairly stated, an unqualified opinion is not possible either because of limitations placed on the auditor or because of minor issues involving disclosure or accounting principles. An *adverse opinion* states that the financial statements are not fairly presented. Finally, a *disclaimer of opinion* states that the auditor did not have full access to records or discovered a conflict of interest. These different opinions each have enormous consequences for companies.

THE STRATEGIC IMPORTANCE OF ETHICS AUDITING

Although the concept of auditing implies an official examination of ethical performance, many organizations audit performance informally. Any attempt to verify outcomes and compare them with standards is considered an auditing activity. Many small firms might not use the word *audit*, but they still perform auditing activities. Organizations such as the Better Business Bureau (BBB) provide awards and assessment tools to help any organization evaluate its ethical performance. Companies with fewer resources may wish to use the judging criteria from the BBB's Torch Award Criteria for Ethical Companies (Table 9–7) as benchmarks for informal self-audits. Past winners of this award included Ford Motor Company, Barney & Barney LLC, and Rockwell Automation, Inc.[73] The award criteria even provide a category for companies with less than 10 employees.

An ethics audit should be conducted regularly rather than in response to problems or questions about a firm's priorities and conduct. The ethics audit is not a control process to be used during a crisis, although it can pinpoint potential problem areas and generate

TABLE 9-7 Better Business Bureau's Torch Award Criteria for Ethical Companies

A business should demonstrate its superior commitment to exceptional standards that benefit its customers, employees, suppliers, shareholders, and surrounding communities. The business must provide supporting documentation in four areas for consideration in the Marketplace Excellence category. While examples from all four areas must be provided, the bullet points below are only suggestions and not all bullet points are required to be addressed in order for a business to compete in this category.

Management Practices Note: Owners of companies with no employees must explain how a personal commitment to exceptional standards is applied in business practices.

- Pertinent sections from an employee handbook, business manual, or training program (formal or informal) showing how the business's commitment to exceptional standards are communicated to and implemented by employees

- A vision, mission, or core values statement describing the business's commitment to exceptional standards that benefit its customers, employees, suppliers, shareholders, and surrounding communities

- Formal training and/or procedures used to address concerns an employee may have in dealing with ethical issues

- Management practices and policies that foster positive employee relations

- Employee benefits and/or workplace practices contributing to the quality of family life

- Actions taken to assess and mitigate risks, and prevent workplace injury

- Examples of sound environmental practices

- Examples of operational practices focused on security and privacy issues—on- and offline

- Illustrations of your business's commitment to standards that build trust in the marketplace (i.e., customer service program, employee relation policy or practice, vendor/supplier relationship, etc.)

Community/Investor/Stakeholder Relations

- Examples of the business's vision, mission, and/or core values statement in action— describing how the business's beliefs have been leveraged for the benefit of consumers, employees, suppliers, shareholders, and surrounding communities

- Business policies and practices that demonstrate accountability and responsibility to communities, investors, and other stakeholder audiences

- Corporate governance practices address accountability and responsibility to shareholders

- Complimentary feedback from customers, vendors, suppliers, and/or community leaders

- Actions taken by the business demonstrating service "beyond the call of duty"

- Brief case study examples of circumstances in which the business made tough decisions that had negative short-term consequences, but created long-term value and benefits

- Examples of, and results produced by, pro bono work

- Examples of the business working closely within the community and making a positive social impact—and any recognition for charitable and/or community service projects.

Communications and Marketing Practices

- Descriptions of methods the business uses to ensure all sales, promotional materials, and advertisements are truthful and accurate

- Sales training policies and/or codes of ethics used by sales personnel that ensure all transactions are made in a transparent, honest manner

- Crisis communications efforts and associated marketing actions that educated audiences, prevented negative outcomes and restored trust and confidence in the business, its products and services

- Examples of internal communications practices benefiting employees and contributing to overall business effectiveness and efficiency

Industry Reputation

- Media coverage reflecting the business's industry and community reputation as a trustworthy business

- Awards, recognition, and/or complimentary letters from within the business's industry, trade group, or community

Source: "Award Criteria," Better Business Bureau, http://www.bbb.org/council/international-torch-awards/how-to-apply/award-criteria/?id=238944 (accessed April 7, 2015).

solutions in a crisis situation. As mentioned earlier, an audit may be comprehensive and encompass all the ethics and social responsibility areas of a business, or it can be specific and focus on one or two areas. One specialized audit could be an environmental impact audit in which specific environmental issues, such as proper waste disposal, are analyzed. According to the KPMG International Survey of Corporate Responsibility Reporting, 93 percent of the 250 largest companies report on their corporate social responsibility activities.[74] Examples of other specialized audits include diversity, employee benefits, and conflicts of interest. Ethics audits can present several problems. They can be expensive and time consuming, and selecting the auditors may be difficult if objective, qualified personnel are not available. Employees sometimes fear comprehensive evaluations, especially by outsiders, and in such cases audits can be extremely disruptive.

Despite these problems, however, auditing ethical performance can generate many benefits, as you have seen throughout this chapter. The ethics audit provides an assessment of a company's overall ethical performance as compared to its core values, ethics policy, internal operating practices, management systems, and most importantly, key stakeholder expectations.[75] As such, ethics and social audit reports are useful management tools for helping companies identify and define their impacts and facilitate important improvements.[76] This assessment can be used to reallocate resources and activities as well as focus on new opportunities. The audit process can also help companies fulfill their mission statements in ways that boost profits and reduce risks.[77] More specifically, a company may seek continual improvement in its employment practices, its customer and community relations, and the ethical soundness of its general business practices.[78] An audit can pinpoint areas where improving operating practices can improve bottom-line profits and stakeholder relationships.[79]

Most managers view profitability, ethics, and social responsibility as trade-offs. This "either/or" mindset prevents them from taking a more proactive "both/and" approach.[80] But the auditing process can demonstrate the positive impact of ethical conduct and social responsibility initiatives on the firm's bottom line, convincing managers—and other primary stakeholders—of the value of adopting more ethical and socially responsible business practices.[81]

SUMMARY

Viewing a business ethics program as a part of strategic planning and management activities is critical to the success of any firm. However, for such programs to be successful, firms must put controls and systems in place to ensure they are being executed effectively. Controls include input, output, and process controls. Input controls are concerned with providing necessary tools and resources to the organization, such as good employees and effective ethics training and structural systems. Process controls include managerial commitment to an ethics program and the methods or system for the evaluation of ethics. Output controls involve comparing standards with actual behavior. One of the most popular methods of evaluating ethical performance is an ethics audit.

An ethics audit is a systematic evaluation of an organization's ethics program and/or its ethical performance. Such audits provide an opportunity to measure conformity with the firm's desired ethical standards. The concept of ethics auditing emerged from the movement toward auditing and reporting on companies' broader social responsibility initiatives. Social auditing is the process of assessing and reporting a business's performance in fulfilling the economic, legal, ethical, and philanthropic social responsibilities expected of it by its stakeholders. An ethics audit may be conducted as a component of a social audit. Auditing is a tool companies can use to identify and measure their ethical commitment to stakeholders and demonstrate their commitment to improving strategic planning, including their compliance with legal, ethical, and social responsibility standards.

The auditing process can highlight trends, improve organizational learning, and facilitate communication and working relationships. Audits help companies assess the effectiveness of their programs and policies, identify potential risks and liabilities, improve compliance with the law, and demonstrate progress in areas of previous noncompliance. One of the greatest benefits of these audits is improved relationships with stakeholders. Ethics auditing may help prevent public relations crises associated with ethical or legal misconduct. Although ethics audits provide benefits for companies and their stakeholders, they have the potential to expose risks; the process of auditing cannot guarantee a firm will not face challenges. Additionally, there are few common standards for judging disclosure and effectiveness or for making comparisons within an industry.

An ethics audit should be unique to each company based on its size, industry, corporate culture, identified risks, and the regulatory environment in which it operates. This chapter offers a framework for conducting an ethics audit that can also be used for a broader social audit.

The first step in conducting an audit is securing the commitment of the firm's top management and/or its board of directors. The push for an ethics audit may come directly from the board of directors in response to specific stakeholder concerns, corporate governance reforms, or top managers looking for ways to track and improve ethical performance. Whatever the source of the audit, its success hinges on the full support of top management.

The second step is establishing a committee or team to oversee the audit process. Ideally the board of directors' financial audit committee would oversee the ethics audit, but in most firms, managers or ethics officers conduct auditing. This committee recruits an individual from within the firm or hires an outside consultant to coordinate the audit and report the results.

The third step is establishing the scope of the audit, which depends on the type of business, the risks faced by the firm, and available opportunities to manage ethics. This step includes defining the key subject matter or risk areas important to the ethics audit.

The fourth step is a review of the firm's mission, values, goals, and policies. This step includes an examination of formal documents that make explicit commitments with regard to ethical, legal, or social responsibility issues, and informal documents including marketing materials, workplace policies, ethics policies, and standards for suppliers or vendors. During this step, the firm should define its ethical priorities and articulate them as a set of parameters or performance indicators that can be objectively and quantitatively assessed.

The fifth step is identifying the tools or methods used to measure the firm's progress, and collecting and analyzing the relevant information. Evidence-collection techniques include examining internal and external documents, observing the data-collection process (such as discussions with stakeholders), and confirming the information in the organization's accounting records. During this step, a company's stakeholders need to be defined and interviewed to understand how they perceive the company. This is accomplished through standardized surveys, interviews, and focus groups. Once information is collected, it should be analyzed and summarized. Analysis should include an examination of how other organizations in the industry are performing in the designated subject matter areas.

The sixth step is having an independent party—such as a social/ethics audit consultant, a financial accounting firm that offers social auditing services, or a nonprofit special interest group with auditing experience—verify the results of the data analysis. Verification is an independent assessment of the quality, accuracy, and completeness of a company's audit process. Such verification gives stakeholders confidence in a company's ethics audit and lends the audit report credibility and objectivity. The verification of the results of an audit should involve standard procedures that control the reliability and validity of the information.

The final step in the audit process is reporting the audit findings to the board of directors and top executives and, if approved, to external stakeholders. The report should spell out the purpose and scope of the audit, methods used in the audit process (evidence gathering and evaluation), the role of the (preferably independent) auditor, any auditing guidelines followed by the auditor, and any reporting guidelines followed by the company.

Although the concept of auditing implies an official examination of ethical performance, many organizations audit informally. Ethics audits should be conducted regularly. Although social auditing may present problems, it can also generate many benefits. Through the auditing process, a firm can demonstrate the positive impact of ethical conduct and social responsibility initiatives on its bottom line, which may convince stakeholders of the value of adopting more ethical and socially responsible business practices.

IMPORTANT TERMS FOR REVIEW

shared values 243	ethical disasters 249
formal controls 244	integrity 250
process controls 244	Balanced Scorecard 250
output controls 244	triple bottom line 250
ethics audit 245	Global Reporting Initiative 251
social audit 245	

RESOLVING ETHICAL BUSINESS CHALLENGES*

Charles worked at Butterfly Corporation for two years after graduating from the University of Texas. He liked his job but the firm was going through some rough times. Because the firm was losing money, Douglas, the CEO, set increasingly rigorous performance goals. Charles noticed a lot of employees were grumbling about these unrealistic expectations. He also heard rumors of quality control incidents and other problems.

One day Charles was called into Douglas's office. "Hello, Doug. You wanted to see me?" Charles asked.

"Yes, Charles. Come in." Doug looked grim. After Charles sat down, he began to speak. "Look, you know about the tough times we are in. We are losing money left and right. So far I've been able to keep this company afloat by drastically making cuts and speeding up production. I guess in all this cost-cutting, there have been problems that have come up. A lot of people have called the hotline to complain about ethical problems, such as employees cutting corners to make their quotas. Now I've got the board on my back."

"I'm really sorry, Doug. How can I help?" Charles asked.

"Well, the board requested we perform an ethics audit to make sure everyone is complying with company regulations. As if we don't have enough to worry about. This is only going to increase our costs. Anyway, I want you to lead the audit."

Charles was stunned. "Me? But Doug, I've only been here for two years. Shouldn't you choose a more experienced manager to lead this?"

Doug shook his head. "We need all our managers to continue doing their jobs. I don't have the time to pull one of them away from their responsibilities just because the board wants us to do an ethics audit."

Charles agreed to lead the audit process. That night he researched how to conduct an ethics audit. He promised to have a rudimentary plan outlining how the ethics audit should be conducted on Doug's desk for approval the next day. As he researched on the Internet, he became more excited. He spent hours forming objectives for the audit, determining the audit's scope, and defining what he thought should be the firm's ethical priorities. He created a plan for using focus groups of employees to see what the greatest concerns were. If time permitted, he wanted to get other stakeholders involved as well, especially their customers. Charles was interested in assessing the overall corporate culture of the firm. Because Charles knew his data analysis skills were not good, he recommended bringing in a committee of competent coworkers who had been in the organization for years and knew the system inside and out. He also developed a list of organizations Butterfly could hire to verify the results once data was collected and analyzed.

The next day, Charles turned in his report and waited while Doug read through it. When finished, he looked up at Charles and frowned.

"Charles, I can see you put a lot of work into this. However, what you have recommended is not going to suit our needs."

"What do you mean?" Charles asked.

"First off, I already told you, I don't want to remove people from their jobs to work on this. We're behind schedule as it is. Also, focus groups of employees and customer feedback? That's going to take up time and resources we can't afford to lose. You also propose hiring an independent third party? We're supposed to be cutting costs, not throwing money at some organization simply to check our results."

"So what would you like me to do then?" Charles asked.

Doug sighed. "That's why I made you the person in charge of the project. You make the decisions. Just make sure it's something that won't cost a lot of money. I want this process to go as quickly as possible so we satisfy the board and get back to work. Maybe you could survey a few employees and get it over with. Just remember to make us look good."

Doug handed back Charles's proposal. "Revise this and bring it back to me tomorrow," he said.

QUESTIONS | EXERCISES

1. What is a key component of a successful auditing process missing from this situation?
2. How would you describe the corporate culture of Butterfly?
3. What steps would you recommend Charles take?

*This case is strictly hypothetical; any resemblance to real persons, companies, or situations is coincidental.

> > > CHECK YOUR EQ

Check your EQ, or Ethics Quotient, by completing the following. Assess your performance to evaluate your overall understanding of the chapter material.

1. Ethics audits are required by the Sarbanes–Oxley Act of 2002.   Yes   No

2. In public corporations, the results of ethics audits should be reported to the board of directors.   Yes   No

3. An ethics audit helps identify risks and rogue employees.   Yes   No

4. The scope of an ethics audit depends on the type of risks and the opportunities to manage them.   Yes   No

5. Smaller companies can skip the step of verifying the results of the ethics audit.   Yes   No

ANSWERS 1. **No.** Financial audits are required, and these may address some ethical issues. 2. **Yes.** This is consistent with good corporate governance but not required. 3. **Yes.** This is the main benefit of an ethics audit. 4. **Yes.** The scope determines the risks unique to the organization. 5. **No.** Verification is necessary to maintain integrity and accuracy.

ENDNOTES

1. Muel Kaptein, "Toward Effective Codes: Testing the Relationship with Unethical Behavior," *Journal of Business Ethics* 99, 2 (2011): 233–251.

2. The Ethisphere Institute, "2015 World's Most Ethical Companies," *Ethisphere*, http://ethisphere.com/worlds-most-ethical/wme-honorees/ (accessed March 27, 2015).

3. Johnson Controls, *Ethics Policy: Integrity Every Day*, January 1, 2011, http://www.johnsoncontrols.com/content/dam/WWW/jci/corporate/our_corporate_governance/ethics_policies/ENG_EthicsPolicy.pdf (accessed March 27, 2015).

4. Muel Kaptein, "Guidelines for the Development of an Ethics Safety Net," *Journal of Business Ethics* 41, 3 (2002): 217–234.

5. Ethisphere Institute, "2014 Most Influential in Business Ethics," http://ethisphere.com/magazine/100-most-influential-in-business/ (accessed March 27, 2015); Peter Eavis, "Regulator Tells Bank to Clean Up Bad Behavior or Face Downsizing," *The New York Times*, October 20, 2014, http://dealbook.nytimes.com/2014/10/20/regulator-tells-banks-to-clean-up-bad-behavior-or-face-downsizing/?_r=0 (accessed March 27, 2015).

6. Danielle E. Warren, Joseph P. Gaspar, and Williams S. Laufer, "Is Formal Ethics Training Merely Cosmetic? A Study of Ethics Training and Ethical Organizational Culture," *Business Ethics Quarterly* 24, 1 (January 2014): 85–117.

7. Andrea Bonime-Blanc and Martin Coyne II, "A Life-Cycle Guide to Ethics and Compliance Programs," *NACD Directorship*, November/December 2014, pp. 72–75.

8. John Rosthorn, "Business Ethics Auditing—More Than a Stakeholder's Toy," *Journal of Business Ethics* 27, 1/2 (2000): 9–19.

9. Lerong He and Rong Yang, "Does Industry Regulation Matter? New Evidence on Advice Committees and Earnings Management," *Journal of Business Ethics* 123, 4 (2014): 573–589.

10. Franziska Zuber, "Guidance on CMS: The new ISO 19600 standard," *KPMG*, January 23, 2015, http://blog.kpmg.ch/guidance-on-cms-the-new-iso-19600-standard/ (accessed March 27, 2015).

11. Debbie Thorne, O. C. Ferrell, and Linda Ferrell, *Business and Society: A Strategic Approach to Corporate Citizenship*, 3rd ed. (Boston, MA: Houghton Mifflin, 2008).

12. Rosthorn, "Business Ethics Auditing."

13. *Walmart, "2014 Global Responsibility Report,"* http://corporate.walmart.com/global-responsibility/environment-sustainability/global-responsibility-report (accessed March 27, 2015).

14. "Accountability," *Business for Social Responsibility*, http://www.bsr.org/BSRResources/WhitePaperDetail.cfm?DocumentID=259 (accessed February 13, 2003).

15. Christopher M. Matthews, "The Morning Risk Report: Much Ado about DPAs," *The Wall Street Journal*, May 6, 2013, http://blogs.wsj.com/riskandcompliance/2013/05/06/the-morning-risk-report-much-ado-about-dpas-deferred-prosecution-agreements/ (accessed March 27, 2015).

16. Marcus Selart and Svein Tvedt Johansen, "Ethical Decision Making in Organizations: The Role of Leadership Stress," *Journal of Business Ethics* 99, 2 (2011): 129–143.

17. Anke Arnaud, "Conceptualizing and Measuring Ethical Work Climate," *Business & Society* 49, 2 (2010): 345–358.

18. Kevin J. Sobnosky, "The Value-Added Benefits of Environmental Auditing," *Environmental Quality Management* 9 (1999): 25–32.

19. "Accountability," Business for Social Responsibility.

20. Trey Buchholz, "Auditing Social Responsibility Reports: The Application of Financial Auditing Standards," Colorado State University, professional paper, November 28, 2000, 3.

21. "Accountability," Business for Social Responsibility.

22. *Fortune*, "Most Admired Companies 2015," 2015, http://fortune.com/worlds-most-admired-companies/ (accessed March 27, 2015).

23. Simon Birch, "How activism forced Nike to change its ethical game," *The Guardian*, July 6, 2012, http://www.guardian.co.uk/environment/green-living-blog/2012/jul/06/activism-nike (accessed March 27, 2015); "Nike commits to champion a toxic-free future," *Greenpeace*, August 17, 2011, http://www.greenpeace.org/international/en/news/features/Nike-vs-adidas/ (accessed March 27, 2015); Clare Delaney, "Nike and Puma Say No More Hazardous Chemicals (Video)," EcoExpert Blog, http://www.ecofriendlylink.com/blog/nike-and-puma-hazardous-chemical-free-video/#.UZKl0MoauSo (accessed March 27, 2015).

24. John Pearce, *Measuring Social Wealth* (London, UK: New Economics Foundation, 1996), as reported in Warren Dow and Roy Crowe, *What Social Auditing Can Do for Voluntary Organizations* (Vancouver, WA: Volunteer Vancouver, July 1999), 8.

25. "Pension funds sue Darden restaurants over shareholder rights: WSJ," *Reuters*, April 12, 2014, http://www.reuters.com/article/2014/04/13/us-darden-lawsuit-idUSBREA3B0LC20140413 (accessed April 6, 2015).

26. Colin Barr, "Obama Talks Tough on CEO Pay," February 4, 2009, http://money.cnn.com/2009/02/04/news/obama.exec.pay.fortune/index.htm (accessed March 27, 2015); "Executive Comp and Governance Provisions of Dodd–Frank Act," *Business Ethics*, July 22, 2010, http://business-ethics.com/2010/07/22/1640-executive-compensation-and-corporate-governance-provisions-of-the-dodd-frank-act/ (accessed March 27, 2015).

27. "Lumber Liquidators Linked to Health and Safety Violations," CBS News, http://www.cbsnews.com/news/lumber-liquidators-linked-to-health-and-safety-violations/ (accessed April 6, 2015).

28. Abram Brown, "Mexican Bribery Scandal Could Cost Wal-Mart $4.5 Billion; Shares Down 4.7%," *Forbes*, April 23, 2012, http://www.forbes.com/sites/abrambrown/2012/04/23/spooked-investors-sink-wal-mart-nearly-5-after-bribery-revelations-at-least-4-5b-penalty-likely/ (accessed March 27, 2015).

29. Penelope Patsuris, "The Corporate Accounting Scandal Sheet," *Forbes* online, August 26, 2002, www.forbes.com/2002/07/25/accountingtracker.html (accessed March 27, 2015).

30. Ernst & Young Global Limited, *Risk management for asset management*, 2013, http://www.ey.com/Publication/vwLUAssets/EY_Risk_Management_for_Asset_Management_Survey_2013/$FILE/EY-Risk-management-for-asset-management-survey-2013.pdf (accessed March 27, 2015).

31. David L. Levy, Halina Szejnwald Brown, and Martin de Jong, "The Contested Politics of Corporate Governance: The Case of the Global Reporting Initiative," *Business & Society* 49, 1 (March 2010): 88–115.

32. "Global Reporting Initiative (GRI)," *Ball State University*, http://cms.bsu.edu/academics/centersandinstitutes/cote/sustainability/gri (accessed March 27, 2015).

33. "FAQs: About GRI," https://www.globalreporting.org/information/FAQs/Pages/About-GRI.aspx (accessed March 27, 2015).

34. Global Reporting Initiative, "What Is GRI?" https://www.globalreporting.org/information/about-gri/what-is-GRI/Pages/default.aspx (accessed March 27, 2015).

35. International Organization for Standardization, "About Us," *ISO*, http://www.iso.org/iso/home/about.htm (accessed April 6, 2015).

36. CompliSpace, "A New Global Standard for Compiance: ISO 19600," September 15, 2014, https://complispace.wordpress.com/2014/09/15/a-new-global-standard-for-compliance-iso-19600/ (accessed April 6, 2015).

37. PPT presentation presented at 2014 ECOA conference in Atlanta, presented by Martin Tolar, GRC Institute, entitled "The First ISO Standard in E&C: What You Need to Know," Presented October 2, 2014.; Dick Hortensius, "What Is the General Idea Behind the Proposed ISO 19600?" Ethics Intelligence, April 2014, http://www.ethic-intelligence.com/experts/4636-general-idea-behind-iso-19600/ (accessed October 14, 2014).

38. "GRC Assessment Tools (Burgundy Book)," *OCEG*, http://www.oceg.org/resources/grc-assessment-tools-burgundy-book/#fullcontent (accessed March 27, 2015).

39. "Certification," *OCEG*, http://www.oceg.org/certification (accessed March 27, 2015).

40. Risako Morimoto, John Ash, and Chris Hope, "Corporate Social Responsibility Audit: From Theory to Practice," *Journal of Business Ethics* 62, 4 (2005): 315–325.

41. The methodology in this section was adapted from Thorne, Ferrell, and Ferrell, *Business and Society*.

42. The Coca-Cola Company, "Audit Committee Charter," http://www.coca-colacompany.com/investors/audit-committee-charter (accessed March 27, 2015).

43. Ethics Resource Center, "Mission and Values," http://www.ethics.org/page/erc-mission-and-values (accessed March 27, 2015).

44. "Verification," *Business for Social Responsibility*, http://www.bsr.org/BSRResources/White PaperDetail.cfm?DocumentID=440 (accessed February 13, 2003).

45. "Ethical Statement," Social Audit, *SocialAudit.org*, http://www.socialaudit.org/pages/ethical.htm (accessed March 4, 2003).

46. "Our Values," *Franklin Energy*, http://www.franklinenergy.com/about/vision-and-values/ (accessed March 27, 2015).

47. "Verification," Business for Social Responsibility.

48. "Audit and Evaluation," *Open Compliance and Ethics Group*, http://www.oceg.org/view/15839 (accessed September 3, 2009).

49. "Ethical Statement," Social Audit.

50. National Grid, *National Grid and the Environment: Environment Policy, September 2013*, http://www.nationalgridus.com/non_html/shared_env_policy.pdf (accessed March 27, 2015); National Grid, "Measuring Progress and Setting New Targets," http://www2.nationalgrid.com/responsibility/how-were-doing/ (accessed March 27, 2015).

51. Judith L. Walls, Phillip H. Phan, and Pascual Berrone, "Measuring Environmental Strategy: Construct Development, Reliability, and Validity," *Business & Society* 50, 1 (2011): 71–115.

52. "Verification," Business for Social Responsibility.

53. Keurig Green Mountain, *Keurig Green Mountain Code of Conduct* (Waterbury, VT: Keurig Green Mountain, 2014).

54. Buchholz, "Auditing Social Responsibility Reports," 15.

55. Audit and Evaluation Directorate of the Canadian Space Agency, *Audit of Values and Ethics Management Framework*, 2010, http://www.asc-csa.gc.ca/pdf/ar-0809-0103.pdf (accessed March 27, 2015).

56. "Verification," Business for Social Responsibility.

57. "Introduction to Corporate Social Responsibility," *Business for Social Responsibility*, http://www.bsr.org/BSRResources/WhitePaperDetail.cfm?Document ID=138 (accessed March 5, 2003).

58. "Introduction to Corporate Social Responsibility," Business for Social Responsibility.

59. Samantha Sharf, "Nu Skin to Resume Business in China after Pyramid Scheme Allegations," Forbes, April 21, 2014, http://www.forbes.com/sites/samanthasharf/2014/04/21/nu-skin-to-resume-business-in-china/ (accessed March 27, 2015).

60. "Accountability," Business for Social Responsibility.

61. Ibid.

62. Ethics and Compliance Officer Association, http://www.theecoa.org (accessed March 27,2015).

63. "Verification," Business for Social Responsibility.

64. Ibid.

65. Nicole Dando and Tracey Swift, "From Methods to Ideologies," *Journal of Corporate Citizenship*, December 2002, via http://www.greenleaf-publishing.com/greenleaf/journaldetail.kmod?productid=105&keycontentid=7 (accessed March 27, 2015).

66. Buchholz, "Auditing Social Responsibility Reports," 16–18.

67. Ibid., 19–20.

68. Audit and Evaluation Directorate of the Canadian Space Agency, *Audit of Values and Ethics Management Framework*, 2010, http://www.asc-csa.gc.ca/pdf/ar-0809-0103.pdf (accessed March 27, 2015).

69. "Accountability," Business for Social Responsibility.

70. Buchholz, "Auditing Social Responsibility Reports," 19–20.

71. Audit and Evaluation Directorate of the Canadian Space Agency, *Audit of Values and Ethics Management Framework*, 2010, http://www.asc-csa.gc.ca/pdf/ar-0809-0103.pdf (accessed March 27, 2015).

72. "OCEG 2005 Benchmarking Study Key Findings," *Open Compliance Ethics Group*, http://www.oceg.org/Details/18594 (accessed September 3, 2009).

73. Better Business Bureau, "Past Awards," 2015, http://www.bbb.org/council/international-torch-awards/past-awards/?id=238945 (accessed March 27, 2015).

74. KPMG, *The KPMG Survey of Corporate Responsibility Reporting 2013*, http://www.kpmg.com/Global/en/IssuesAndInsights/ArticlesPublications/corporate-responsibility/Documents/kpmg-survey-of-corporate-responsibility-reporting-2013.pdf accessed March 27, 2015).

75. KPMG, *KPMG International Survey of Corporate Responsibility Reporting 2008*, https://www.kpmg.com/EU/en/Documents/KPMG_International_survey_Corporate_responsibility_Survey_Reporting_2008.pdf (accessed March 27, 2015).

76. Buchholz, "Auditing Social Responsibility Reports," 1.

77. Sandra Waddock and Neil Smith, "Corporate Responsibility Audits: Doing Well by Doing Good," *Sloan Management Review* 41 (2000): 75–83.

78. Buchholz, "Auditing Social Responsibility Reports," 1.

79. Waddock and Smith, "Corporate Responsibility Audits."

80. J. C. Collins and J. I. Porras, *Built to Last: Successful Habits of Visionary Companies* (New York, NY: HarperCollins, 1997).

81. Waddock and Smith, "Corporate Responsibility Audits."

CHAPTER 10

GLOBALIZATION OF ETHICAL DECISION MAKING

AN ETHICAL DILEMMA*

Dun and Ready (D&R) Company is a retail firm that started out in the United Kingdom. It recently expanded into Mexico. D&R management is excited about the expansion because they anticipate a large market for their goods in Latin America. They hired Raul to negotiate contracts for getting the necessary permissions to begin building retail stores in Mexico City. Although Raul graduated from Cornell University, he spent his childhood in Mexico and knew the country well. Raul's manager, Ian Menkin, stressed to Raul the importance of getting the new locations approved as soon as possible so the company could begin building their stores.

Unfortunately, Raul ran into some difficulties receiving permissions in the required time frame. Due to unforeseen circumstances, the permissions process took longer than originally thought. When Raul explained to Ian that the building process would likely be delayed due to these problems, Ian was not pleased. "Look, Raul. We have a schedule to keep. The people here at headquarters will not take kindly to any delays."

"But what should I do, Ian?" Raul asked.

"Just do whatever it takes to get those permits approved," Ian said before hanging up the phone.

Raul called up Pedro, his main government contact that worked on approving zoning permits. Raul explained the situation, but Pedro would not budge.

"I'm sorry, Raul. But I can't make the process go any faster."

Raul, knowing his job could be on the line, begged Pedro to reconsider. Finally, Pedro agreed to meet with Raul to "talk things through."

Later that day, the two men met. Raul again presented his case. Pedro listened and finally spoke. "I understand your predicament. And although it's against policy, I believe I can help you get those permits approved. However, I'm going to need 6,000 pesos to complete the job."

Raul was uncomfortable with the idea. Again, he called up Ian in London. Raul explained the situation. "Unfortunately, this is really going to be the only way to get this process done quickly."

Ian was quiet for a little while. Then he spoke. "The money isn't that important. It amounts to less than £300. Go ahead and pay him."

"But Ian, what if anyone at the company finds out?"

Ian replied, "It's our policy to respect the different cultures in which we do business. It is one of our core values. If giving small payments is the only way to get things done quickly, then that's what we have to do."

Raul agreed and paid Pedro the money. The permits were approved, and the first store was built. The success of the store convinced the company to expand to more locations in the area. Unfortunately, Raul ran into the same problem. Management at D&R wanted their building permits to be approved in a reasonable time period. Raul explained that gaining approval could be a long process in Mexico, but D&R assumed since he had gotten approval quickly once before, he could do it again. Raul was in a bind. So whenever Pedro offered to speed up the process in exchange for a small amount of money, Raul agreed.

As a result of Raul's success, he was promoted and relocated to the United Kingdom to the corporate offices. His pay tripled since from when he had first started. Raul enjoyed London and loved his new job responsibilities. Everything seemed to be going well.

Then one day Raul got a frantic call from Ian. "We have a problem. Somehow someone figured out about the payments made to secure building permits in Mexico. They are launching an investigation."

Although Raul was nervous, he could not understand Ian's panic. "But the payments we made were not extensive. It's just the way things work in Mexico. You said everything would be fine."

Ian's voice was sharp. "You fool! It doesn't matter whether the payments were small! Any type of bribery can be prosecuted under the U.K. Bribery Act. It doesn't matter whether the bribery took place in Mexico— any company with operations in the U.K. can be held liable."

Raul swallowed. "So what do we do?" he asked.

"Listen carefully to what I'm telling you," Ian said. "I want you to find any documentation that might be incriminating and destroy it. If anyone comes asking, deny any payments. Also, contact the person you

*This case is strictly hypothetical; any resemblance to real persons, companies, or situations is coincidental.

made the payments to. Do what it takes to make sure he denies that D&R made any improper payments to him."

Raul hung up the phone. He knew if found out the company could face massive fines. Perhaps he and Ian could get into legal trouble. However, he also knew covering up the bribery would make it worse for everyone if discovered. On the other hand, Raul thought there was a good probability that the payments would not be noticed. He knew that almost all companies have to make these payments to get transactions done in different countries, and many have not been caught.

QUESTIONS | EXERCISES

1. What are the ethical issues in this situation?
2. Identify the pressures that caused the ethical issues to develop.
3. Discuss the advantages and disadvantages of each decision Raul could make.

Advances in communication, technology, and transportation have minimized the world's borders, creating a new global economy in which more and more countries are industrializing and competing internationally. These transactions across national boundaries define **global business**, a practice that brings together people from countries with different cultures, values, laws, and ethical standards. Therefore, international businesspersons must understand the values, culture, and ethical standards of their own countries and industries and also be sensitive to those of other cultures.

In this chapter, we explore the ethical complexities and challenges facing businesses that operate internationally. We help you understand how global business ethics has more complexity than domestic business ethics. The global business environment, if not understood, will destroy the trust companies need to be successful. To transition from one well-understood culture or country to the global arena requires additional knowledge. Our goal in this chapter is to help you become aware of or avoid a few of the ethical quagmires that lurk in this domain. To help you become ethically sensitive to the global environment of business ethics, we start with discussing global values and cultural dimensions used by companies to modify their business practices. Next, we examine the economic foundations of business. In addition, we help you understand there are global entities that do not necessarily conform to your country's view of the world or a particular way to do business. In this chapter we examine multinational corporations and the ethical problems they face. We then discuss the International Monetary Fund, the United Nations Global Compact, and the World Trade Organization. We conclude with an analysis of current and future ethical problems facing global businesses, including global ethical risks, bribery, antitrust activity, Internet security and privacy, human rights, health care, labor and right to work issues, compensation, and consumerism. Our goal is to help you understand how international business activities can create ethical conflicts and help you improve your ethical decision-making ability.

GLOBAL CULTURE, VALUES, AND PRACTICES

A nation's culture consists of values that are subjective, based on social and economic institutions, and used to develop norms that are socially and legally enforced. Because institutions such as government and religion affect the development of norms, conventions, and other aspects of culture, values can be specific to countries, regions, sects, or groups.

National culture is a much broader concept than organizational culture and includes everything in our surroundings made by people—both tangible items, such as artifacts, and intangible entities, such as concepts and values. Language, law, politics, technology, education, social organizations, and general values are all included within this definition. Each nation contains unique cultures and distinctive beliefs about which business activities are legal, acceptable, unethical, or illegal. Subcultures also exist within many nations, ethnic groups, and religious groups. Therefore, when transacting international business, individuals encounter values, beliefs, and ideas that may diverge from their own. When someone from another culture mentions "integrity" or "democracy," many Americans might feel confident that these are familiar concepts. However, these concepts mean different things to different people, depending on their culture. Moreover, you must keep in mind that organizational culture is different from national culture, though often organizational cultures are derived from—and influenced by—national cultures.

Most multinational corporations (MNCs) need auditors, directors, or other entities associated with corporate governance to provide independent oversight of the operations of an organization. Yet even with such a simple concept as "independent oversight," national culture can come into play. For example, in the Japanese banking system, the concept of "independent oversight" is blurred because retired Japanese bureaucrats often become auditors and directors. They are trusted simply because of their status. When those providing oversight also have relationships within and/or a vested interest in the success of the company, a truly independent relationship does not exist and could create conflicts of interest or corporate governance oversight failure.

Different national and organizational cultural values and how they affect business have intrigued management experts for years. Many have developed frameworks for classifying behavior patterns that can help businesspeople who work in different countries. One of the most well-known frameworks was proposed by Dutch management professor Geert Hofstede. Hofstede identified four cultural dimensions that can have a profound impact on the business environment: individualism/collectivism, power distance, uncertainty avoidance, and masculinity/femininity.[1] We will discuss the first three in the following paragraphs.

The **individualism/collectivism dimension** of culture refers to how self-oriented members of a culture are in their behavior. Individualist cultures place high value on individual achievement and self-interest. The United States exemplifies an individualistic culture. Collectivist cultures value working toward collective goals and group harmony. Mexico and several countries in Asia adhere to more collectivistic principles. Collectivist cultures tend to avoid public confrontations and disagreements.[2] In Thailand, for instance, negatives such as "no" tend to be avoided in business settings. By understanding this cultural dimension, you are more likely to maneuver correctly within different cultural business settings.

The **power distance dimension** refers to the power inequality between superiors and subordinates. The United States has elements of both a higher and a lower power distance culture. Over the years, the U.S. business environment adopted forms of management, such as participative management, that place supervisors and subordinates on a more equal footing. In some businesses, employees address their superiors by their first names and have the power to make decisions normally reserved for management. Arab countries score higher on the power distance dimension. Cultures with high power distance tend to be more hierarchal, and respect for (or fear of) supervisors may be so great that managerial misconduct could be hard to pinpoint.[3]

Uncertainty avoidance refers to how members of a society respond to uncertainty or ambiguity. Cultures scoring high on the uncertainty avoidance dimension, such as Great Britain, tend to avoid risk-taking. Organizations within these cultures may have more rules in place to ensure employees do not deviate from accepted standards. Cultures with low levels of uncertainty avoidance, such as Canada, believe risk-taking and innovation are important in achieving successful outcomes.[4] Businesses from either culture need to be aware of how a particular culture views uncertainty avoidance. For instance, if a businessperson from the United States gives a sales presentation to a business in Uruguay—a culture with higher uncertainty avoidance—the American businessperson might reassure the Uruguayan company by mitigating the risks involved.

As Hofstede's dimensions suggest, businesspeople traveling to other countries quickly perceive other business cultures have different modes of operation. Interestingly, research shows that consumers who score high on collectivism and uncertainty avoidance and low on masculinity and power distance tend to avoid engaging in more questionable activities than those scoring the exact opposite. This has important implications for international managers when dealing with consumers in different countries.[5]

The perception exists that American companies differ from those in other countries, and some view U.S. companies as superior to their foreign counterparts. This implied perspective of ethical superiority—"us" versus "them"—is also common in other countries. In business, the idea that "we" differ from "them" is called the **self-reference criterion** (SRC). The SRC is an unconscious reference to one's own cultural values, experiences, and knowledge. When confronted with a situation, we react on the basis of knowledge we accumulated over a lifetime, usually grounded in our culture of origin. Our reactions are based on meanings, values, and symbols that relate in a certain way to our culture but may not have the same relevance to people of other cultures. For example, while 71 percent of Americans view themselves as being honest, only 37 percent of Japanese believe Americans are honest. Figure 10–1 reveals differences in attitude in how Japanese and Americans view one another.

Transport Company Uber is an example of how the SRC might have caused potential problems as it expanded globally. Uber, which operates a mobile app-based ride-sharing service, likely anticipated that it would face some backlash in the United States as it challenged the taxi industry. However, as it expanded internationally the firm encountered laws that placed even more obstacles in its path. France and Germany banned UberPOP,

FIGURE 10–1 How Americans and Japanese View One Another

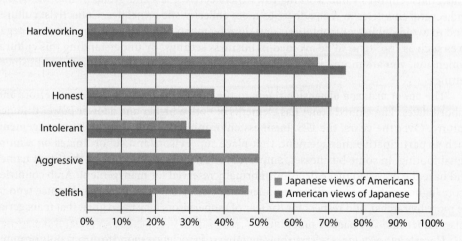

Source: 2015 Pew Research Center Survey.

one of Uber's main services that is less expensive than its licensed services. According to France and Germany, the service violates commercial passenger transportation laws as drivers operate without authorization.[6] Thailand made Uber illegal because it claims Uber vehicles are not properly registered, use drivers without proper licenses, and undercut regulated fare rates.[7] This example demonstrates how important it is for firms to understand relevant laws in the countries where they do business. In addition, some stakeholders have questioned the foundations of its business model from an ethical perspective.

One of the critical ethical business issues linked to cultural differences is the question of whose values and ethical standards take precedence during international negotiations and business transactions. When conducting business outside their home country, should businesspeople impose their own values, ethical standards, and laws on members of other cultures? Should they adapt to the values, ethical standards, and laws of the countries where they are doing business? As with many ethical issues, there are no easy answers to these questions.

"When in Rome, do as the Romans do," or "you must adapt to the cultural practices of the country where you operate" are rationalizations businesspeople sometimes offer for straying from their own ethical values when doing business abroad. By defending the payment of bribes or "greasing the wheels of business" and other questionable practices in this fashion, they are resorting to **cultural relativism**, the concept that morality varies from one culture to another and that "right" and "wrong" are defined differently.

Despite the various differences in values between countries, there are certain values broadly accepted worldwide. These **global common values** are shared across most cultures. Most laws are directly or indirectly the result of values derived from the major religions of Hinduism, Buddhism, Confucianism, Judaism, Islam, and Christianity. Although most of these religions have similar core virtues, the importance placed on these virtues may vary. For instance, predominately Hindu cultures value nonviolence, mind and sense control, and austerity[8]; traditional Chinese cultures honor respect, righteousness, and loyalty; Islamic cultures value wisdom, tolerance, self-restraint, and mercy[9]; Judaism promotes the virtues of kindness, peace, and hospitality; predominately Christian cultures cherish forgiveness, mercy, and faith[10]; and Buddhist cultures place high importance on the "four immeasurables" of equanimity, joy, loving-kindness, and generosity.[11] By understanding a different cultural values, global businesses have a better chance of forming relationships with individuals and organizations in that culture. They may also avoid conduct offensive to citizens of certain countries (for example, shaking with the left hand in Islamic nations). It is beyond our scope to explain all nuances, but there seems to be a consensus on the following desirable and undesirable common values.[12]

- Desirable common values: Integrity, family and community unity, equality, honesty, fidelity, sharing, and unselfishness
- Undesirable common values: Ignorance, pride and egoism, selfish desires, lust, greed, adultery, theft, deceit, lying, murder, hypocrisy, slander, and addiction

ECONOMIC FOUNDATIONS OF BUSINESS ETHICS

Economic and political events as well as natural disasters reflect and affect the environment for global ethical decision making. We first examine how recent economic developments influence global systems that structure the business world.

The last economic recession highlighted the fact that firms were taking extreme risks, bending rules, and engaging in unethical activity. A major part of the problem was the excessive focus on rewards and the bottom line that pervaded the global financial industry. The global financial market is a highly interconnected system that can exhibit a lack of transparency in decision making, accountability, and accounting methods. This system, combined with rampant leveraging and the widespread use of highly complex financial computer models many experts did not fully understand, resulted in a global financial meltdown.

Our financial system is complex, and this complexity provides ample opportunity to take excessive risks and manipulate various stakeholders. Many who should have known about such risks were ignorant because of risk compartmentalization. **Risk compartmentalization** occurs when profit centers within corporations are unaware of the overall consequences of their actions on the firm as a whole. As a result, no one person, company, or agency should be blamed—the problems were systemic. Before the financial meltdown, most companies remained in compliance with legal systems, while others looked for legal loopholes and unregulated means of maximizing profits and financial rewards. Many companies tried to be ethical, yet the complex nature of the global economy prevented them from seeing the impending disaster because everyone was focused on the bottom line.

Economic and social disasters and country conflicts have intensified the risks and challenges global businesses encounter. For instance, political and economic turmoil in South Africa and Nigeria has caused concern for businesses who wish to expand into these countries. The instability in certain African countries could strain business relations. On the other hand, opportunities in Kenya are increasing due to increased security and a plan to improve its power sector and infrastructure.[13] Economic stability is affected by the supply and commodity price fluctuations caused by such political events. Changes in governments result in the necessity for new social and legal processes, and also processes that support ethical and legal systems that fit into the global economy. Figure 10–2 indicates the countries that businesspeople, risk analysts, and the general public perceive as the most and least corrupt.

FIGURE 10–2 **Perceived Levels of Public Sector Corruption**

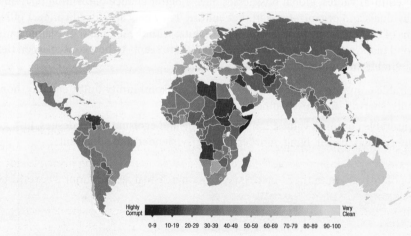

Source: Transparency International, "Corruption Perceptions Index 2014: Results," lhttps://www.transparency.org/cpi2014/results#my Anchor2 (accessed March 31, 2015).

Finally, the world is still coping with the aftereffects of the last global recession that caused public distrust of the stability of governmental institutions as well as those charged with managing the money of individuals, corporations, and countries. Some countries, such as Iceland, Zimbabwe, Hungary, Ukraine, and Serbia, declared a form of bankruptcy as a result of the recession.[14] The European Union is still struggling to recover since Portugal, Ireland, Greece, and Spain all required bailouts to stay afloat. Greece defaulted on its debt. As a lack of trust, honesty, and fairness caused major investors to question the competence of regulatory institutions, which in turn caused instability and public mistrust in the entire financial system, many questioned the foundations of capitalism and the policies needed to make it function. Today, people are discussing and even revising fundamental concepts and assumptions of capitalism. Because you will enter this new reality, we will briefly explain the global economic debate.

Economic Systems

To understand the economics of business, you must learn the fundamentals of capitalism and socialism. Economic theories or systems have a significant impact on business ethics because they determine the role of governments in business, the types of laws that regulate businesses, and the amount of freedom companies have in their activities. The main forms of capitalism and socialism are derived from the works of Adam Smith, John Maynard Keynes, and Milton Friedman.

Adam Smith was a professor of logic and moral philosophy during the late eighteenth century, as noted earlier, and he developed critical economic ideas still considered important today. Smith observed the supply and demand, contractual efficiency, and division of labor of various companies within England and wrote about what he saw. His idea of **laissez-faire**, or the "invisible hand," is critical to capitalism because it assumes the market, through its own inherent mechanisms, keeps commerce in equilibrium. Smith also believed businesses must be guided by ethical people for the market to work properly.

The second form of capitalism gained support at the beginning of the Great Depression. During the 1930s **John Maynard Keynes** argued that the state could stimulate economic growth and improve stability in the private sector through, for example, controlling interest rates, taxation, and public projects.[15] Keynes argued that government policies could be used to increase aggregate demand, thus increasing economic activity and reducing unemployment and deflation. He believed the solution was to stimulate the economy through some combination of a reduction in interest rates and government investment in infrastructure. President Franklin D. Roosevelt employed Keynesian economic theories during his time in office when he sought to pull the United States out of the Great Depression.

The third and most recent form of capitalism is associated with **Milton Friedman**, and represents a swing to the right of the U.S. political spectrum. Friedman lived through the Great Depression but rejected the Keynesian conclusion that markets sometimes need intervention to function efficiently. He believed deregulation could reach equilibrium without government intervention.[16] Friedman's ideas were the guiding principles for government policy making in the United States, and increasingly throughout the world, starting in the second half of the twentieth century.

Both Keynes and Friedman agreed that "(1) People have rational preferences among outcomes that can be identified and associated with a value; (2) Individuals maximize utility and firms maximize profits; (3) People act independently on the basis of full and relevant information."[17] Today, however, these assumptions are being questioned.

Socialism refers to economic theories advocating the creation of a society when wealth and power are shared and distributed evenly based on the amount of work expended in production. Modern socialism originated in the late nineteenth century and was a working-class political movement that criticized the effects of industrialization and private ownership. Karl Marx was one of socialism's most famous and strongest advocates. Marxism was Marx's own interpretation of socialism, and it was transformed into communism in countries such as the former Soviet Union, Cuba, and North Korea. History has shown that communism, strictly interpreted, causes economies to fail. For example, Cuba traditionally held an antagonistic view toward capitalism and private enterprise. As a result, most of the population was employed in the public sector. However, during the most recent recession, the Cuban government realized it could not support so many workers. In an attempt to save its struggling economy, the government took more steps toward privatization.[18] Trade relations between the United States and Cuba appear to be improving, and Netflix has even expanded into Cuba through the Internet.[19] Cuba is also allowing for more trade in U.S. tools, equipment, and supplies.[20] President Obama moved to reestablish diplomatic relations with the hope of improving human rights, freedom of speech, and increased opportunities for Cubans.

In the 1940s forms of **social democracy** emerged. Social democracy allows private ownership of property and also features a large government equipped to offer such services as education and health care to its citizens. Social democracies take on such problems as disease, ignorance, squalor, and idleness, and advocate governmental intervention. The Scandinavian countries of Denmark, Sweden, and Norway are examples of social democracies. Studies indicate that the populations of these small European democratic nations are some of the happiest in the world.[21]

Past economists could not imagine the multinational corporation, or that the world's energy resources would be concentrated under the control of a handful of corporations. Our world has grown increasingly bimodal in wealth distribution. **Bimodal wealth distribution** occurs when the middle class shrinks, resulting in highly concentrated wealth among the rich and increased numbers of poor people with few resources. This is not a desirable scenario and can result in political instability. Because the size and power of today's multinational corporations are immense, companies can pit one government against another for strategic advantages. You can see the same strategy by country group in trade blocs such as NAFTA (North American Free Trade Agreement), the EU (European Union), and ASEAN (Association of Southeast Asian Nations). These trade blocs give economic leverage to country groups and use the same economic principles as multinationals. To understand the future global perspective, we next discuss the difference between rational and behavioral economics.

Rational economics is based on the assumption that people are predictable and will maximize the utility of their choices relative to their needs and wants. For example, if you are hungry and have $10 to spend, rational economics suggests you will spend the money on food that satisfies your hunger needs and wants. However, people are not always rational. No one wants to go to jail. Even those who stole millions admit the reward was probably not worth the punishment. Yet this does not stop individuals from engaging in crimes to secure short-term gains. Barry Minkow, former pastor, businessman, and fraud investigator, pleaded guilty to securities fraud as a result of manipulating the stock of Lennar Corp. Minkow already served seven years in prison after being convicted in 1988 of operating a Ponzi scheme through his business.[22] He clearly did not act in a rational manner when he decided to commit another act of securities fraud.

The second assumption is that people act independently on the basis of full and relevant information. Normally, we might assume that a criminal did not have full or relevant information concerning his/her actions. However, Minkow already experienced prison time and, as a fraud investigator, likely knew the penalties he faced should he get caught. His example illustrates that some individuals will act irrationally even when they have a clear idea of the potential consequences of their actions. There are many individuals and organizations willing to take risks to achieve their objectives. This high-risk approach often results in manipulation and misconduct.

Behavioral economics assumes humans act irrationally because of genetics, emotions, learned behavior, and heuristics, or rules of thumb. Heuristics are based upon past experiences and do not always yield the most rational response. Behavioral economics assumes economic decisions are influenced by human behavior. Figure 10–3 depicts where countries may be in the process of developing economic philosophies, and helps to understand where they may want to go. China, Sweden, and the former Soviet Union are in the lower left quadrant, representing socialism as a society with behavioral economics as the vehicle to happiness. As we mentioned, each of these country's definitions of happiness is derived from social democratic goals. They are behavioral because they believe very little in laissez-faire. The dates presented are important, because they show countries can change their positions over time. In the upper right quadrant, the graphic shows how certain countries' economies define happiness and the government's role. Finally, in the upper left quadrant are the United States and (again) Sweden, representing Sweden's shift to capitalism and more laissez-faire economics, and the United States' shift to a less laissez-faire economy.

FIGURE 10–3 The Economic Capitalism Country Differential

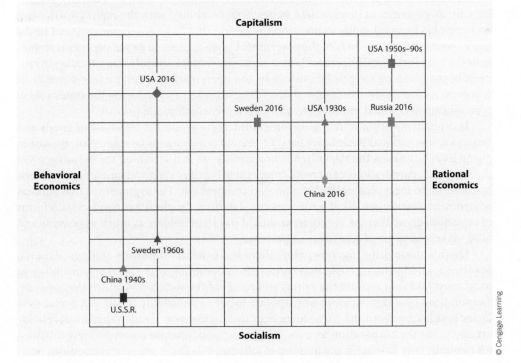

© Cengage Learning

The conflict between capitalism and socialism stems partly from the Great Depression and the Cold War. Many in the United States perceive socialism as Marxism; it is not. Outside the United States, socialism is often perceived as group-oriented as it relates to social problems. Socialism argues for the good of the community, with government helping people through manipulation of the economy. The American form of capitalism is grounded in individualism, where government is perceived as a hindrance in the pursuit of happiness.

Today, capitalism is one of the United States' many cultural exports. But while the United States practices one kind of capitalism, there are many other forms. The success of the U.S. model of capitalism during the 1990s and 2000s led many businesses and countries to champion it as the premier economic model. However, the last recession, combined with the collapse of some of the world's largest financial firms, dampened global enthusiasm for this model. It is likely that in the future, more attention will be directed toward other forms of capitalism and socialism.[23]

Sweden was one of the poorest countries in Western Europe in the 1880s. During the 1890s, it became more worker-friendly. From 1918 to 1970, Sweden's standard of living rose faster than most countries.[24] After 1970 the country changed worker policies to become more corporate friendly and continues to enjoy one of the highest standards of living in the world. It is an example of a socialist/capitalist hybrid.

India and China have introduced the free market into their systems, although their models are different. India is democratic with a lively civil society that is often empowered to stand up against the government and capitalism. States in India can adjust their economic system to accommodate more local interests. China's large communist government blurs the lines between organizations, businesses, and government to form national capitalism. These two countries represent about one-third of the world's population and are considered rising powers—yet their forms of capitalism/socialism are radically dissimilar. China's government involvement in business, combined with the rapid growth of its economy, have caused many to question the notion that large governments stand in the way of business success—in fact, the government often appears to be the premier entrepreneur.[25] China is the world's second largest economy.[26] More recently, the Chinese government began planning for private businesses and open markets to play a larger role in its economy. As the Chinese economy slows, Chinese leaders feel reducing the state's role in economic matters would improve creativity, entrepreneurship, and growth.[27]

Is capitalism with minimal government interaction and the free flow of goods and services across national boundaries best? Or should governments be more protectionist in giving local businesses the upper hand? Economists are still searching for the answer. On the one hand, corporations can create competitive barriers via government legislation or by collusion to form oligopolies for managed competition. The argument is that without government intervention, local businesses could decline. On the other hand, certain forms of capitalism argue that the corporation should pay shareholders as much as possible and other stakeholders are of secondary importance.

Despite these differing viewpoints there is a general consensus amongst experts, academics, and businesspeople that corporations operating with social responsibility in mind must take into account the norms and mores of the societies in which they operate. Corporations take varying views of corporate social responsibility (CSR).[28] A broad view includes thinking about the consequences of their actions on a wide range of stakeholders and using the corporation as a tool for public policy, while a narrow view involves, for example, only looking at the number of jobs created. These are ethical questions businesses and governments need to address as they operate on a globalized scale. There is no agreement that one form of free-market system is more ethical than others. Ethical business systems are found in capitalistic systems as well as socialistic countries. Countries, institutions, social systems, technology, and other cultural factors have a major effect on organizational ethics. To understand global ethics, we examine ethical dimensions surrounding multinational firms.

MULTINATIONAL CORPORATIONS

Multinational corporations (MNCs) are public companies that operate on a global scale without significant ties to any one nation or region. MNCs represent the highest level of international business commitment and are characterized by a global strategy focusing on opportunities throughout the world. Examples of U.S.-based multinational corporations include Nike, Monsanto, and Cisco Systems. Some of these firms have grown so large that they generate higher revenues than the gross domestic product (GDP)—the sum of all the goods and services produced in a country during one year—of some of the countries where they do business, as shown in Table 10–1.

Based on revenues versus GDP, Walmart is greater than the economies of Greece and Denmark. Because of their size and financial power, MNCs are the subject of much ethical debate, and their impact on countries where they do business is controversial. Both American and European labor unions argue it is unfair for MNCs to transfer jobs overseas where wage rates are lower. Other critics charge that multinationals use labor-saving devices that increase unemployment in countries where they manufacture. MNCs have been accused of increasing the gap between rich and poor nations and of misusing and misallocating scarce resources. Their size and financial clout enable them to control money, supplies, employment, and even the economic well-being of less-developed countries. For example, IKEA, the Swedish furniture company, dealt with the consequences of questionable labor practices that occurred over 30 years ago in Germany. The allegation is that under the Communist regime, East German political prisoners were forced to produce various parts of furniture for the company. If the inmates did not meet the given expectations of production, they were severely punished. IKEA has closely monitored its supply chain since 2000 to ensure forced labor is not a part of the production process. However, these claims from the past have shown that top management knew about the forced labor and did little to deal with the issue. Some praise IKEA for taking responsibility for the company's past actions, but others see it as a blight on the company's reputation.[29]

Critics believe the size and power of MNCs create ethical issues involving the exploitation of both natural and human resources. One question is whether MNCs should be able to pay a low price for the right to remove minerals, timber, oil, and other natural resources, and then sell products made from those resources for a much higher price. In many instances, only a fraction of the ultimate sale price of such resources comes back to benefit the country of origin. This complaint led many oil-producing countries to form the Organization of Petroleum Exporting Countries (OPEC) in the 1960s to gain control over the revenues from oil produced in those lands.

Critics also accuse MNCs of exploiting the labor markets of host countries. As noted earlier, MNCs have been accused of paying inadequate wages. Sometimes MNCs pay higher wages than local employers can afford to match; then local businesses complain the most productive and skilled workers go to work for multinationals. Measures have been taken to curtail such practices. For example, host governments levy import taxes that increase the prices MNCs charge for their products and reduce their profits. Import taxes

TABLE 10–1 A Comparison between Countries and Corporations Based on Gross Domestic Products and Revenues

Country	GDP (millions $ U.S.)	Company	Revenues (millions $ U.S.)
United States	16,720,000	Walmart	476,294
China*	9,330,000	Royal Dutch Shell	459,599
India	4,990,000	Sinopec Group	457,201
Japan	4,729,000	China National Petroleum	432,007
Germany	3,227,000	Exxon Mobile	407,666
Iran	987,100	BP	396,217
Taiwan	926,400	State Grid	333,386
Argentina	771,000	Volkswagen	261,539
Greece	267,100	Toyota Motor	256,454
Denmark	211,300	Glencore	232,694

*Because China bases its exchange rate on the fiat, purchasing power parity was used to get a better comparison of its GDP compared to other countries.

Source: Based on "Global 500 2014," *Fortune,* http://fortune.com/global500/ (accessed April 1, 2015); CIA *World Fact Book,* https://www.cia.gov/library/publications/the-world-factbook/rankorder/2001rank.html (accessed April 1, 2015).

are meant to favor local industry as supply sources for an MNC operating in the host country. If a tax raises the MNC's costs, it might lead the MNC to charge higher prices or accept lower profits, but such effects are not the fundamental goal of the law. Host governments have also imposed export taxes on MNCs to force them to share more of their profits.

The activities of MNCs also raise issues of unfair competition. Because of their diversified nature, MNCs can borrow money from local capital markets in much higher volume than smaller local firms. MNCs have also been accused of failing to carry an appropriate share of the cost of social development. They frequently apply advanced, high-productivity technologies that local companies cannot afford or implement because they lack qualified workers. The MNCs thus become more productive and can afford to pay higher wages to workers. Because of their technology, however, they require fewer employees than local firms would hire to produce the same product. Additionally, given their economies of scale, MNCs can also negotiate lower tax rates. By manipulating transfer payments among their affiliates, they pay fewer taxes. All these advantages explain why some claim MNCs compete unfairly.

Sometimes countries refuse outright to allow MNCs into their countries. For example, heavy-equipment companies from industrialized nations argue that their equipment will make it possible to complete infrastructure projects sooner, which could help boost the economies of less-developed countries. However, countries such as India believe it is better in the long run to hire laborers to do construction work since this practice provides much-needed employment and keeps currency within the local economy. Therefore, they often choose to use local laborers instead of purchasing equipment from foreign countries.

Although it is usually MNCs' unethical or illegal conduct that grabs world headlines, many MNCs strive to be good global citizens with strong ethical values. Texas Instruments (TI) adopted a three-tiered global approach to ethical integrity that asks: "(1) Are we complying with all legal requirements on a local level? (2) Are there business practices or requirements at the local level that affect how we interact with co-workers in other parts of the world? (3) Do some of our practices need to be adapted based on the local laws and customers of a specific locale? On what basis do we define the universal standards that apply to TI employees everywhere?" One of the ways Texas Instruments puts this approach into practice is specifying rules on excessive gift giving. Since what is considered to be "excessive" varies depending on country, Texas Instruments adopted an approach that forbids gift-giving "in a way that exerts undue pressure to win business or implies a quid-pro-quo [sic]."[30]

Many companies, including Coca-Cola, DuPont, Hewlett-Packard, Levi Strauss & Co., and Walmart, endorse following responsible business practices abroad. These companies support a globally based resource system called **Business for Social Responsibility** (BSR). BSR tracks emerging issues and trends, provides information on corporate leadership and best practices, conducts educational workshops and training, and assists organizations in developing practical business ethics tools. It addresses issues such as community investment, corporate social responsibility, the environment, governance, and accountability. BSR also established formal partnerships with other organizations that focus on corporate responsibility in Brazil, Israel, the United Kingdom, Chile, and Panama.[31]

Although MNCs are not inherently unethical, their size and power often seems threatening to people and businesses in less-developed countries. The ethical problems MNCs face arise from the opposing viewpoints intrinsic to multicultural situations. Differences in cultural perspectives may be as important as differences in economic interests. Because of their size and power, MNCs must take extra care to make ethical decisions that not only achieve their own objectives, but also benefit the countries where they manufacture or market their products. Even the most respected MNCs sometimes find themselves in ethical conflict and face liability as a result.

The U.S. model of the MNC is fading as developing countries such as China, India, Brazil, and South Korea form MNCs as alliances, joint ventures, and wholly owned subsidiaries.[32] The turn away from the American model does not mean less concern for ethics and social responsibility. As corporations expand internationally, ethics and social responsibility are important firm-specific capabilities that can be a resource and lend a company an advantage for growth and profit. The development of trust and corporate citizenship is a necessary capability, much like technology or marketing. A number of Chinese businesses have learned that long-term success cannot be achieved by selling products that are unsafe or of inferior quality. Ethical and responsible business conduct is a requirement for long-term success in global business. With the increasing globalization of companies has come a growing intolerance toward opportunistic business activities driven by profit and a greater acceptance for multinationals able to contribute toward economic and social improvement.[33] As a result, several global organizations have formed to support cooperation and responsible business practices.

GLOBAL COOPERATION TO SUPPORT RESPONSIBLE BUSINESS

International Monetary Fund

The **International Monetary Fund** (IMF) originated from the Bretton Woods agreement of July 1944 when a group of international leaders decided the primary responsibility for the regulation of monetary relationships among national economies should rest in an international body, the IMF. The IMF makes short-term loans to member countries with deficits and provides foreign currencies for its members. The IMF also provides information about countries that might default on their debts. Member states provide resources to fund the IMF through a system of quotas proportional to the size of their respective economies. Member states also receive IMF voting power relative to these quota contributions. Under this rule, the United States has just under one-fifth of the votes. The IMF has become the international coordinator of regulatory policy for the world.

Although the IMF's main function is to regulate monetary relationships between national economies, the organization has taken steps to promote responsible global business conduct. For instance, the IMF suggested governments adopt a "binding code of conduct across nations" to determine the conditions necessary for interceding in troubled firms, and how to share losses from financial institutions operating across multiple borders. The IMF also recommended new regulations for large firms posing the biggest "systemic risk."[34] The concept of risk and IMF bailouts took on significant importance during the last global recession. Because of a massive amount of debt, the European countries of Greece, Ireland, Portugal, and Spain required major bailout packages from the IMF. These bailouts caused a negative economic impact felt throughout the European Union.[35] The IMF also granted $17 million in aid to the Ukraine after Russia annexed the Crimea.[36]

United Nations Global Compact

The United Nations (UN) was founded in 1945 by 51 nations. Its goals are to promote worldwide peace, establish beneficial relationships between countries, and support the creation of better standards and human rights on a global scale. Today, the UN includes 193 member states from across the world. Although the United Nations is generally thought of as a peacekeeping organization, this coalition of diverse countries also focuses extensively on sustainable development, human rights and gender equality, global environmental issues, and more.[37] Another major concern for the UN is business development. Recognizing that business is "a primary driver in globalization," the UN views business as a way to increase the economic outlook of countries, create equality with fair labor practices, combat corruption, and promote environmental sustainability.[38] Conversely, unethical businesses that go global to take advantage of favorable factors such as cheap labor could have the opposite effect.

To support business as a driver for positive change, the UN created the **United Nations Global Compact**, a set of 10 principles that promote human rights, sustainability, and the eradication of corruption. Table 10–2 gives a brief description of these principles. Above all, the UN hopes the Global Compact creates a collaborative arrangement among businesses, governments, nongovernmental organizations, societies, and the United Nations to overcome challenges and advocate positive economic, social, and political change. The Global Compact is voluntary for organizations. Those that join are held accountable, and are required to annually post the organization's progress toward Global Compact goals and show commitment to UN guiding principles. Global members are expected to cooperate with the UN on social projects within developing nations where they do business. More than 12,000 entities participate in the UN Global Compact.[39]

TABLE 10–2 United Nations Global Compact

Human Rights
- Principle 1: Businesses should support and respect the protection of internationally proclaimed human rights.
- Principle 2: Make sure that they are not complicit in human rights abuses.

Labor
- Principle 3: Businesses should uphold the freedom of association and the effective recognition of the right to collective bargaining.
- Principle 4: The elimination of all forms of forced and compulsory labour.
- Principle 5: The effective abolition of child labour.
- Principle 6: The elimination of discrimination in respect of employment and occupation.

Environment
- Principle 7: Businesses should support a precautionary approach to environmental challenges.
- Principle 8: Undertake initiatives to promote greater environmental responsibility.
- Principle 9: Encourage the development and diffusion of environmentally friendly technologies.

Anticorruption
- Principle 10: Businesses should work against corruption in all its forms, including extortion and bribery.

Source: "The Ten Principles," United Nations Global Compact, http://www.unglobalcompact.org/AboutTheGC/TheTenPrinciples/index.html (accessed March 31, 2015).

While global business ethics is essential knowledge for companies, it is critical knowledge for business students. The Association to Advance Collegiate Schools of Business (AACSB) International, an organization that represents about 1,200 members, joined with groups such as the UN Global Compact to inspire a set of six principles for business schools. These principles fall under the title "Principles for Responsible Management Education."[40] The first principle encourages students to become future leaders in creating sustainable value for business, society, and the global economy. Other principles include incorporating global social responsibility into curricula; creating educational materials that cultivate responsible leaders; and encouraging dialogue among educators, students, businesses, and other stakeholders to address social responsibility and sustainability issues. The Principles for Responsible Management Education are powerfully influenced by the idea of sustainable development and corporate social responsibility.[41]

World Trade Organization

The **World Trade Organization** (WTO) was established in 1995 at the Uruguay round of negotiations of the General Agreement on Tariffs and Trade (GATT). Today, the WTO has 161 members and observer nations. On behalf of its membership, the group administers its own trade agreements, facilitates trade negotiations, settles trade disputes, and monitors the trade policies of member nations. The WTO addresses economic and social issues involving agriculture, textiles and clothing, banking, telecommunications, government purchases, industrial standards, food sanitation regulations, services, and intellectual property. It also provides legally binding ground rules for international commerce and trade policy. The organization attempts to reduce barriers to trade between and within nations and settle trade disputes. For instance, the WTO often rules on situations involving allegations of dumping.

Dumping is the practice of charging high prices for products in domestic markets while selling the same products in foreign markets at low prices, often at below cost. It places local firms at a disadvantage and is therefore illegal in many countries. The European Union filed a complaint to the WTO against Boeing, claiming that it violated international rules by receiving billions of dollars in tax breaks. According to the EU complaint, the state of Washington passed the tax breaks to keep Boeing from relocating.[42]

Not all countries agree with the WTO's particular stance on free trade. In the past, import tariffs increased on Asian plastic bags in Europe; oil in South Korea; Chinese steel pipes in the United States; and all imports in Ukraine. According to the WTO, shoes, cars, and steel are among the goods most vulnerable to protectionism, or trade restrictions among countries.[43] During global downturns, countries tend to restrict trading. However, many firms find ways to get around tariffs. If a company wants instant free trade access to the United States, for instance, it can manufacture in Israel. If the company wants free trade access for low-tech products to the EU, the company can manufacture in the African country of Senegal because of its free trade agreement with France. Companies with the right knowledge can find a number of ways to bypass tariffs, particularly as trading blocs such as the EU continue to grow.[44]

GLOBAL ETHICS ISSUES

In this section we focus on issues that have a dramatic impact on global business, including global ethical risks, bribery, antitrust activities, Internet security, and privacy. We also discuss fundamental rights such as human rights, health care, labor, and compensation, as well as the issue of consumerism. Bribery and antitrust issues are among the most targeted areas of concern for governments worldwide. Human and labor rights are some of the more commonly abused in global business environments.

Global Ethical Risks

Although globalization has many benefits, it is not without risks. Risk creates ethical issues for global companies to manage. Many of these risks require organizations conducting business globally to make ethical business decisions. Some of these risks are described below.

- Corruption continues to be one of the most visible global and economic risks. For example, executives at the Brazilian state-controlled oil firm Petrobras accepted bribes from construction officials for many years. These bribes resulted in the company losing hundreds of millions of dollars through the use of inflated contracts.[45]

- Variations in international regulation can create problems for global companies as they must adjust their business strategies to comply with different laws. Google has encountered this issue with Europe. Unlike the United States, the European Union has decided to file antitrust charges against Google regarding its Android operating system.[46]

- Supply chain issues involving human rights violations can be hard to detect in global supply chains encompassing many different nations. One report alleged that some seafood sold in the United States originated from slave labor on ships sailing close to Thailand and Indonesia. President Obama has mandated that government contractors need to ensure their supply chains are free of forced labor.[47]

Corporations worldwide have become more global in their compliance actions. Table 10–3 represents a compilation of important compliance issues of global companies based in the United States and the European Union. Global competition laws, anti-bribery requirements, ethics and values, and export controls are considered more relevant by the EU than confidentiality, records management, and labor and employment laws. These differences give us clues as to the types of laws governments will formulate in the future.

Bribery

Bribery is a difficult topic because its acceptance and legal definition vary from country to country. While bribery between businesses is illegal in countries such as the United States, it is an accepted way of doing business in other countries. It is not unusual for managers in BRIC countries (Brazil, Russia, India, and China) to offer favors in order to attain business goals. Because these "favors" are of minimal value and are not considered to be bribery within these countries, their use is generally considered to be ethical in these cultures.[48] Today, most developed countries recognize that bribery is not a responsible or fair way of conducting business because of the potential to damage consumers and competition. However, companies must determine what constitutes a bribe. In Japan it is considered courteous to present a small gift before doing business. Are such gifts bribes or merely acts of gratitude? Without clear guidelines, the topic of bribery remains ambiguous enough

TABLE 10–3 Global Business Ethics and Legal Issues

U.S. Ranking	European Ranking	Important Issues
1	1	Code of Conduct
2	5	U.S. Antitrust
3	3	Mutual Respect
4	7	U.S. Foreign Corrupt Practices Act (FCPA)
5	4	Conflicts of Interest and Gifts
6	9	Proper Use of Computers
7		Insider Trading
8	6	Financial Integrity
9		Confidentiality
10		Records Management
11		Labor and Employment Law
12	8	Intellectual Property
	2	Global Competition Law
	10	Global Anti-bribery Requirements
	11	Ethics and Values
	12	Export Controls

Source: Based on Integrity Interactive Corporation, "Top Compliance Concerns of Global Companies," http://www.i2c.com (accessed April 1, 2015).

for misconduct to occur. For this reason, both the United States and the United Kingdom passed regulations defining bribery and set legal precedents for businesses that encounter these situations.

U.S. FOREIGN CORRUPT PRACTICES ACT
The U.S. Foreign Corrupt Practices Act (FCPA) prohibits American companies from making payments to foreign officials for the purpose of obtaining or retaining business. In 1988 Congress became concerned that American companies operated at a disadvantage compared to foreign companies whose governments allowed bribes. In 1998 the United States and 33 other countries signed an agreement intended to combat the practice of bribing foreign public officials in international business transactions, with an exception for payments made to facilitate or expedite routine governmental actions (known as facilitation or "grease" payments). Prosecution of bribery has increased, with the U.S. Justice Department making violations of the FCPA a top priority.

Bribery has become a problem for some major corporations. Walmart is under investigation for alleged bribes in Mexico. Sometimes bribery does not involve money directly but may include other favors. JP Morgan is being investigated for hiring the son of a Chinese commerce minister. Despite what seemed to be low qualifications, executives allegedly hired the son to appease the father, who agreed to help the company in any way that he could in China.[49] In these two cases top managers allegedly knew about the bribery. Although sometimes bribery is done with the full compliance of top management, larger companies with multiple branches, global operations, and many employees have a harder time detecting such misconduct. The FCPA was modified recently and now provides a "best practices" guide for companies and guidelines used by the U.S. Department of Justice and the Securities and Exchange Commission to assess compliance. The guidelines can be helpful to ensure companies comply with the FCPA. These guidelines are outlined in Table 10–4.

Violations of the act can result in individual fines of $100,000 and jail time. Penalties for companies can reach into the millions.[50] Some FCPA violations are easier to detect than others. Some of the riskiest practices include payment for airline tickets, hotel and meal expenses of traveling foreign officials, the wiring of payments to accounts in offshore tax havens, and the hiring of agents recommended by government officials to perform "consulting" services.[51] Current enforcement agencies are targeting these third-party bribery payments.

U.K. BRIBERY ACT
Many nations, including China and European nations, are taking a tougher stance against bribery. The United Kingdom instituted perhaps the most sweeping anti-bribery legislation to date.[52] The U.K.'s Bribery Act will likely cause companies doing business in the United Kingdom to dramatically change their compliance reports. While the act overlaps with the U.S. Foreign Corrupt Practices Act, it takes further steps to curb bribery. Under the law British residents and businesses, as well as foreign companies with operations in the United Kingdom, can be held liable for bribery, no matter where the offense is committed or who in the company commits the act, even if the bribe itself has no connection with the United Kingdom. Unlike the FCPA, companies are not required to have explicit knowledge of a bribe to be held criminally liable.[53] Additionally, the law classifies bribes between private businesspeople as illegal. Initially, the law did not make provisions allowing for "grease payments" to speed up services that otherwise would be delayed, although this part of the law is being reconsidered. The law also requires corporations to determine if their subsidiaries or joint-venture partners are involved in bribery at any level.[54] Finally, the act increased the maximum jail time for bribery from 7 to 10 years.[55]

TABLE 10–4 FCPA "Best Practices" for Compliance Guidelines

The development of clear policies against FCPA violations

Support by senior management for the company's compliance policy

The development of standards and policies relating to the acceptance of gifts, hospitality, entertainment, expenses, customer travel, political contributions, charitable donations and sponsorships, facilitation payments, solicitation, and extortion

The development of compliance procedures that include risk assessment and internal controls

Annual reviews of compliance procedures and updates when needed

The development of appropriate financial and accounting procedures

The implementation of policies to properly communicate procedures to directors, officers, employees, and other appropriate stakeholders

The establishment of a system that provides legal guidance to appropriate stakeholders

Disciplinary procedures for violations of anticorruption rules

The exercise of due diligence to ensure compliance with anticorruption policies

The inclusion of anticorruption provisions in agreements and contracts with suppliers, agents, and other partners

Periodic reviews of codes and procedures to ensure they measure up to FCPA regulations

Prompt reporting of violations to the SEC

Source: Based on "U.S. Securities and Exchange Commission and Department of Justice Clarify 'Best Practices' for FCPA Compliance," *Mayer Brown,* January 11, 2011.

Such encompassing provisions against bribery created concern for businesses that operate in the United Kingdom. Some fear something as simple as taking a client out to dinner will be considered a bribe under U.K. law. However, U.K. officials and legal experts state that acts of hospitality will not be considered illegal. Additionally, businesses can protect themselves from heavy penalties by instituting an effective compliance program that management supports. Managers should set the correct tone at the top along with implementing proper reporting procedures, periodic reviews of the company's code of conduct and compliance programs, risk assessments, and other policies discussed in this book and outlined in the U.S. Federal Sentencing Guidelines.[56] Legal experts question if the Serious Fraud Office (SFO) in the United Kingdom will choose to prosecute cases that deal with small "grease" payments or prosecute cases that occur outside the United Kingdom.[57] Officially, the SFO states that acts of hospitality and promotional expenditures are a normal part of doing business and will not be considered as bribes. However, companies have often disguised bribery in the form of hospitality "gifts" and legitimate business expenditures.[58] The former director of the SFO set forth criteria that can be used to determine whether top-level bribery has occurred: (1) cases that undermine confidence in the U.K. Financial PLC and/or the City of London; (2) cases that compromise a fair playing field; (3) cases of serious bribery and corruption; and (4) cases that have a strong public interest dimension.[59]

Antitrust Activity

Fair competition is viewed favorably in many countries, with the belief that competition yields the best products at the best prices. This basic concept of capitalism has begun to change, however. During the nineteenth and early twentieth centuries, U.S. corporations began using what today would be considered anticompetitive practices, creating high barriers of entry for competitors in an attempt to dominate markets. These practices led to higher prices and fewer options for consumers. In 1890 the United States passed the Sherman Antitrust Act to prevent such anticompetitive behavior. Other countries have similar laws. Issues of competition become more complicated when companies do business in countries with differing laws. For instance, the EU has stricter antitrust laws than does the United States, making it harder for some MNCs to compete in Europe. EU antitrust probes have been launched against Google, Microsoft, and IBM, among other companies.

Because large MNCs create economies of scale and barriers to entry, they tend to reduce overall competition and can put smaller companies out of business. If these firms remain unregulated, they could engage in a vertical systems approach to become monopolies. A **vertical system** is created when a channel member (manufacturer, wholesaler, distributor, or retailer) has control of the entire business system, via ownership or contract, or through its purchasing ability. Vertical systems create inertia, causing channel members to stay with their various retailers and distributors even though competitors may have better products and prices. Sometimes MNCs use their size to coerce other companies to do business exclusively with them. The EU investigated Google because it believed the Internet company was manipulating search results to favor its own offerings. If true, this could violate their antitrust laws.[60] The EU has even considered breaking up Google's different businesses in Europe so that it does not have such a strong hold over different areas. On the other hand, some U.S. regulators and consumers believe the EU might be targeting Google because it is so much more successful than their own Web firms.

Internet Security and Privacy

Today's computer hackers can use tools like the Internet and computer viruses to commit corporate espionage, launch cyber attacks against government infrastructures, and steal confidential information.[61] Until recently, Internet security has not been a significant part of business ethics. However, serious Internet crimes have brought this issue to the public's attention. Computer hackers became particularly problematic in the United States and China. Not only are attacks directed toward businesses and their trade secrets, but more alarmingly, they are directed at the country's power grid systems, financial systems, and military information systems. The United States admits to cyber hacking as a form of national security, as does China. However, the United States is increasing pressure on China to acknowledge that hackers from its country are stealing secrets from its companies. In one allegation, the United States accused five Chinese military officials of cyberespionage. U.S. government officials have warned that they may take retaliatory measures if the actions continue.[62]

Hacking, Trojan horses (devices that look desirable but steal information once installed), and worms are not necessarily illegal in some countries. However, the global community has begun to classify such practices as unethical, arguing they should become illegal. Although companies develop software to track down viruses and malware and keep them from infecting computers, hackers constantly create new ways to bypass these systems. Many companies use questionable Internet practices that may not be illegal but could be construed as unethical. For instance, many websites install cookies, or small identifying strings of text, onto users' computers. This allows the website to identify the user's computer when he or she revisits the site. These companies use cookies as a way to tailor their offerings to specific users. For example, Amazon.com uses cookies to make product recommendations to users. Despite the consumer convenience and competitive advantages of cookies, being able to identify users without their consent or direct knowledge creates an ethical issue: privacy.

While some Internet privacy violations, such as breaking into users' accounts and stealing their financial information, are clearly unethical, many other situations present more challenging ethical issues. For instance, mobile advertising networks face privacy issues for the way they display advertisements to mobile application users. Businesses hire ad networks to post their advertisements on Internet pages and mobile applications. The businesses buy a certain amount of space on the mobile or website page and do not always know how the ad networks display their ads. The ad networks started using tracking methods within the mobile devices to determine the user's location and preferences in order to display ads relevant to each individual. Apple, after discovering their methods, has prohibited ad networks from using personal information for advertising. The ad networks claim people are identified by a random set of numbers that cannot be traced back to anyone's personal identity, but others claim this information is stored in specific profiles that could eventually be traced to personal identifying characteristics. There is no current legislation on this issue, but the Federal Trade Commission is investigating the matter to determine if it is a violation of consumer privacy.[63]

Another ethical dilemma regarding privacy is the use of personal information by companies. Facebook, the most popular social networking site worldwide, has been criticized for lax privacy policies and making member information too public. Privacy has become such a concern that governments have begun considering new legislation to regulate information collection on the Internet. The United States government is debating whether to regulate the Internet to limit the types of information websites track.[64] The European Union has passed laws such as the right to be forgotten and has proposed recommendations for furthering EU consumers' right to privacy. The EU Data Protection Directive also sets forth principles to protect the privacy of EU citizens. According to these principles, those whose data is being collected must be informed, the data must be protected, and the subjects should be given access to their personal data to check for inaccuracies.[65]

In countries such as Saudi Arabia and China, Internet privacy is not just a corporate issue. Governments take an active role in censoring citizens' use of the Internet. Although Facebook and Twitter are popular in Iran, government censorship has dissuaded many foreign firms from developing Iranian versions of their websites. YouTube is banned in the country. This has paved the way for Iranian technology firms to gain an edge. Café Bazaar, an Iranian site similar to Google Play in the West, currently faces little competition from foreign firms.[66] The Chinese government routinely uses an Internet-filtering system called the "Great Firewall" to censor Internet sites. It often does not tell its citizens when materials are censored. Instead, the filtering looks like a technical glitch. Networks such as YouTube and Facebook are blocked completely. The Chinese government has made recent changes to the filtering system that makes it harder to circumvent and access forbidden sites.[67] This censorship makes it difficult for foreign businesses such as Google, which adheres to a "Don't Be Evil" policy, to justify doing business with China. Many of Google's services are blocked in China.[68] These scenarios demonstrate the types of ethical issues companies encounter when conducting business globally.

Human Rights

The meaning of the term **human rights** is codified in a UN document, and is defined as an inherent dignity with equal and inalienable rights and the foundation of freedom, justice, and peace in the world. The concept of human rights is not new in business. It was established decades ago, but few companies took it into consideration until recently. Table 10–5 presents three articles from the UN Human Rights Declaration. Their implementation in the world of business has serious ethical ramifications. Article 18 concerns freedom of religion. From a Western perspective this is straightforward. However, how should firms respond to employees from countries where it is acceptable to have multiple wives? Should they all be granted health insurance? In response to such challenges, Ford Motor Co. started the Ford Interfaith Network to educate employees about different religions and foster respect for the beliefs of its diverse employees across the world.[69]

On the other hand, research on FTSE 100 firms demonstrates that while many large corporations have basic human rights policies listed in their documents, including nondiscrimination and the right to join unions, other rights in the UN Human Rights Declaration such as right to privacy, right to work, and equal pay are mentioned far less.[70] Child labor has become a big issue. There have been many movements against child labor, and special-interest groups are proactively boycotting and labeling products found to have used child labor.[71] Samsung cut ties with a Chinese supplier due to allegations that the supplier had employed seven children under the age of 16.[72]

Health Care

Another ethical issue gaining in importance is health care. Globally, a billion people lack access to health care systems, and about 7.5 million children under the age of five die from malnutrition and preventable diseases each year.[73] As a result, global concern about the priorities of pharmaceutical companies is on the rise. This ethical dilemma involves profits versus health care. Those who believe pharmaceutical companies are inherently unethical suggest the quest for profits led these companies to research drugs aimed at markets that can afford luxuries, such as cures for baldness or impotence, rather than focusing on cures for widespread deadly diseases like malaria, HIV, and AIDS.

Patents are another challenging issue. Since patents give pharmaceutical companies exclusive rights to their products for a certain period, the companies can charge higher prices—prices those in emerging economies cannot often afford. This has led to disputes not only between health care activists and pharmaceutical companies but also between countries. For instance, Brazil and South Africa are considering reform that would make pharmaceuticals cheaper, while Eli Lilly filed a lawsuit against Canada claiming that the country's compliance in letting rivals sell copies of its medicines violates the North American Free Trade Agreement.[74] Pharmaceutical companies such as Eli Lilly argue that

TABLE 10–5 Selected Articles from the UN Human Rights Declaration

Article 18. Freedom of thought, conscience, and religion … either alone or in community … in public or private …
Article 23. The right to work … to just and favorable conditions of work and to protection against unemployment … equal pay for equal work … ensuring for himself and his family an existence worthy of human dignity … right to form and to join trade unions …
Article 25. Right to a standard of living adequate for the health and well-being … Motherhood and childhood are entitled to special care and assistance.

Source: United Nations, "The Universal Declaration of Human Rights," https://www.un.org/en/documents/udhr/ (accessed April 1, 2015).

high prices are needed to recoup the costs of creating the drugs, and without profits their companies would not be able to function. Another argument is that since other firms are allowed to patent their products, pharmaceutical companies should be allowed the same privileges. Yet when the issue is one of life or death, businesses must find ways to balance profitability with human need.

A related issue affecting both developing and developed countries is the affordability of health care. Rising health care costs continue to pose a critical challenge, particularly in the United States. Studies have revealed that the United States spends more per capita on health care than other industrialized countries—but without better results for the investment. Prices of health care products and procedures can vary greatly within the country.[75] When health care becomes too costly, businesses tend to either drop health care packages offered to employees or downgrade to less expensive—and less inclusive—packages. For instance, some unions, companies, and insurers have begun dropping mental health care plans due to a law that states mental health care, if offered, must be as "robust" as the rest of the medical benefits. Rather than offer the more costly mental health benefits, some companies are choosing to drop them entirely.[76]

Global health care fraud is a serious ethics issue, costing businesses and governments millions and depriving individuals of funds needed for critical care. One estimate places the losses from global health care fraud and error at $487 billion annually.[77] Fraud includes providing less medicine in packages for the same price, filing false Medicare claims, and providing kickbacks for referrals, and fraud can be committed by individuals, companies, doctors, and pharmacists. A doctor, pharmacist, and marketer were convicted of health care fraud in the form of false billing and the diversion of drugs. The pharmacist bribed doctors to prescribe expensive prescriptions bought from his pharmacies. Prescriptions were also billed to Medicare and Medicaid that were never dispensed to the patients but were instead sold on the street.[78]

The fundamental issue leading some businesses into ethical and legal trouble around the world is the question of whether health care is a right or a privilege. Many people in the United States see health care as a privilege, not a right; thus, it is the responsibility of individuals to provide for themselves. People in other countries, such as Germany, consider it a right. German employees have been guaranteed access to high-quality, comprehensive health care since 1883.[79] Many countries believe health care is important because it increases productivity; therefore, governments should provide it. As health care costs continue to increase, the burden for providing it falls on companies, countries, employees, or all three.

DEBATE ISSUE
TAKE A STAND

Is Health Care a Right or a Privilege?

The Universal Declaration of Human Rights, adopted by the United Nations in 1948, proclaims "everyone has the right to a standard of living adequate for the health and well-being of oneself and one's family, including food, clothing, housing, and medical care." Hard work and healthy living does not assure being healthy. With the high costs of health care, many consumers cannot afford health insurance. The U.S. government is following other industrialized nations in adopting universal health care.

Critics argue it is the individual's responsibility, not the government's, to ensure personal health. Many health problems, such as obesity and diabetes, can often be prevented by individuals choosing to live healthier lifestyles. Another concern involves the cost of health care. Critics believe universal health insurance will increase costs because more people will depend upon the government for health care. This in turn might cause costs to be passed onto consumers and prompt the government to limit certain types of care. Guaranteeing health care for all may lead people to make riskier decisions because they know if they get hurt, they are guaranteed health care coverage.

1. Because health care protects life, it is a fundamental right and should therefore be ensured by the federal government.

2. Health care is a privilege and should not be provided by the government because of the high costs involved.

Labor and Right to Work

Another global issue businesses encounter is labor. Today, many people live and work in a country other than their homeland. In the European Union, workers can carry benefits across countries within the EU without any reductions or changes. Many workers therefore ask the question, "Am I a multinational employee first and then a citizen of a country, or am I a citizen first and an employee second?" Because businesses must make a profit, there are increasing occasions when nationality is no longer a deciding factor. In business, we are becoming global citizens. As a result, firms need to understand that certain employee issues, once country-specific, have become global.

One example of a global labor issue involves gender pay inequality. This debate has spread throughout the globe, in both developing and industrialized countries. On average women in the European Union earn 16 percent less than their male counterparts.[80] Despite these disparities, equal pay is recognized as a fundamental right by the UN Human Rights Declaration, and gender pay inequality is illegal in many countries. Businesses, particularly multinationals, must consider this issue carefully. Failure to do so could lead to lawsuits or reputational damages. Walmart spent years fighting a class-action lawsuit from hundreds of female employees claiming they were discriminated against in pay and promotions. Companies working to eliminate gender pay inequalities within their organizations will be acting ethically and protecting themselves legally as well.

In addition to equal pay, Article 23 of the UN Human Rights Declaration discusses the right to work and join trade unions. Within the European Union, trade unions are accepted, but in many other countries, including North Korea, Cuba, and Iran, trade unionists risk imprisonment.[81] European companies with employees in these countries face many ethically charged decisions. Trade unions are an issue in the United States, too. McDonald's and Walmart have discouraged attempts to unionize in the United States, but they acquiesced to their workers in China and allowed them to unionize. Both companies have unions in all of their Chinese facilities, yet they continue to fight against unions in their home countries.[82]

Article 25 of the UN Human Rights Declaration mentions a standard of living and special rights related to pregnancy. The United States lags behind other industrialized nations in its treatment of pregnant women and new mothers. While other countries allow female employees a specific amount of paid maternity leave, the United States guarantees only 12 weeks of unpaid leave.[83] Some countries have argued for allowing men to take off the same amount of leave (either paid or unpaid). This debate never takes place in Sweden because Swedish parents get 480 paid days off that can be split between parents at 100 percent pay.[84]

Compensation

The last global recession set off a spark prompting employees worldwide to question their compensation relative to those of others. Employees, particularly those in places without strong employee protections, began questioning why high-level executives get so many benefits while their incomes have stayed the same or fallen. These questions highlight two wage issues having a profound effect on business: the living wage and executive compensation.

A LIVING WAGE   A living wage refers to the minimum wage workers require to meet basic needs. Many countries have passed minimum wage laws to provide employees with a living wage (whether the "minimum wage" is actually enough to meet a worker's basic needs is highly debatable). These laws vary from country to country. While the United States has a federal minimum wage law of $7.25 per hour, Australia's minimum wage is $16.87 per hour, while the United Kingdom's minimum wage equals $9.64 per hour for workers of 21 years or older.[85] Regions within these countries may adopt higher regional minimum wage laws to account for higher costs of living. The issue of a living wage is a controversial topic for MNCs. Because laws of industrialized countries dictate employers must pay a minimum wage, some MNCs choose to outsource their labor to other countries where no minimum wage exists. While not necessarily unethical in and of itself, this practice becomes a significant ethical dilemma when the public perceives the organization as paying foreign laborers unfair wages. The problem multinationals face is finding a solution that balances the interests of the company as a whole with those of its employees and other interested stakeholders. Nike continues to be criticized for the wages paid to factory workers in other countries. While Nike claims it pays workers in these countries higher than the mandated minimum wage laws of the country, critics point out the amount is not suitable to cover living expenses of workers or their families. Nike contends that a "fair" wage is hard to determine when dealing with other countries, a statement with which many multinationals would likely agree.[86] However, the concept of a living wage is a challenge companies must acknowledge if they hope to successfully do business in the global environment.

EXECUTIVE COMPENSATION   The issue of executive pay came to the forefront during the last global recession. In the United States the government felt it necessary to bail out firms that would go bankrupt otherwise. However, when companies that received taxpayer money such as American International Group and Merrill Lynch subsequently paid their executives millions in compensation, the public was outraged. These types of incidents led to a global demand for better alignment between managerial performance and compensation.

The Swiss government, after bailing out several organizations, recently passed a referendum called "say-on-pay" that requires a yearly shareholder vote determining executive pay.[87] This kind of mentality on executive pay, often called "shareholder activism," is spreading to American companies as well.[88] Meanwhile, the Chinese government ruled the disparity between the country's executives and its workers was too great. It therefore cut the salaries of top executives at state-owned banks and insurers.[89] The gap between executive and worker compensation will likely remain a major business ethics issue until stakeholders are satisfied that executives earn their compensation.

Consumerism

Consumerism is the belief that the interests of consumers, rather than those of producers, should dictate the economic structure of a society. It refers to the theory that consumption of goods at an ever-increasing rate is economically desirable, and equates personal happiness with the purchase and consumption of material possessions. However, over the past 50 years consumption placed significant strains on the environment. Many scientists argue that human factors (such as the increase in fossil fuel emissions from industrialization and development and deforestation) have caused global warming. Many countries contend that consumer choices are moral choices, that choosing a high rate of consumption affects vulnerable groups such as the poor, and the world will be less habitable if people refuse to change their behaviors.[90]

As nations increase their wealth, consumers increase their quality of living with luxury items and technological innovations that improve the comfort, convenience, and efficiency of their lives. Such consumption beyond basic needs is not necessarily a bad thing; however, as more people engage in this type of behavior, waste and pollution increase. Some important issues must be addressed in relation to consumerism. For example:

- What are the impacts of production on the environment, society, and individuals?
- What are the impacts of certain forms of consumption on the environment, society, and individuals?
- Who influences consumption, and how and why are goods and services produced?
- What goods are necessities, and what are luxuries?
- How much of what we consume is influenced by corporations rather than by our needs?
- What is the impact on poorer nations of the consumption patterns of wealthier nations?[91]

China's rise to dominance in manufacturing and world trade caused it to outpace the United States as a consumer. It now exceeds the United States in consumption of basic goods such as grain, meat, coal, and steel. China also surpassed the United States in greenhouse gas emissions. Some fear China's newfound consumerism will drive up global prices for goods, as well as speed up global warming, even as other nations take measures to stop it. Chinese consumers are pushing for more cars, appliances, and technology like never before. With 1.3 billion consumers, this causes a major strain on the environment. China has taken some steps to curb its negative environmental impact, such as becoming the largest investor in wind turbines in the world. Although most of China's energy needs are still produced by fossil fuels that cause its carbon dioxide emissions to increase, renewable energy is also growing.[92]

India, with its 1.1 billion people, is following China and the West on the consumerist path. India has the world's fastest-growing information technology market, creating skilled, high-wage jobs for software engineers, business process experts, and call-center workers. The country is well-situated to weather global recessions because much of the country's demand for goods is domestic. India has the second-largest domestic market for goods in the world.[93] While this demand has fueled growth, it has also led to an enormous increase in greenhouse gas emissions. India suffers from some of the worst air quality in the world.[94]

The ethics of these consumerism issues are many. Large emerging economies are the profit-making centers of the future. Most in business understand it is in the best interests of the firm that consumer needs and desires are never completely or permanently fulfilled, so consumers can repeat the consumption process and buy more products. For example, **made-to-break**, or *planned obsolescence*, products are better for business since they keep consumers returning to buy more. It also is profitable to make products part of a continuously changing fashion market. Thus, items still in good condition and that last for many years are deemed in need of constant replacement to keep up with fashion trends. In this way, steady profits are assured—as well as waste. It is estimated that 1 percent of the global population has 50 percent of the wealth.[95]

One ethical question being asked by more people and countries is, "Does consumerism lead to happiness?" Consumer detractors are gaining ground globally, and the United States is their example of non-sustainable consumption. They note that the richest countries consume 10 times more natural resources than the world's poorest countries.[96] The United States also wastes up to 40 percent of the food it produces.[97]

These consumption statistics point to a different lifestyle for the future, and global business will drive it. The moral conflict between countries, especially between the United States and the developing world, will increase, with corresponding ethical challenges for business. The future may be one filled with international violence, to which business must respond, or it may be characterized by a lifestyle that global business creates and markets to avoid civil and global war. It is up to you and others to decide.

THE IMPORTANCE OF ETHICAL DECISION MAKING IN GLOBAL BUSINESS

Ethical decision making is essential if a company is to operate successfully within a global business context. Without a clear understanding of the complexities of global ethics, companies will face a variety of legal and political snares that could result in disaster. It is important to realize that many of the same issues we discussed in this chapter can be applied to domestic markets as well. Internet security, for instance, can be just as much of an ethical issue domestically as it is in companies operating internationally. As such, businesses should incorporate both global and domestic ethical issues into their risk management strategies.

For companies looking to expand globally, the multitude of ethical issues to consider seems daunting. Many companies choose to adopt global business codes of ethics to provide guidelines for their international operations. To this end, several organizations created ethics and social responsibility frameworks businesses can adopt in formulating their own global ethics codes. The International Organization for Standardization has developed ISO 19600 (ethical compliance systems), ISO 14000 (sustainability), and ISO 26000 (social responsibility), among other guidelines, to address issues such as ethics, sustainability, and social responsibility. Another set of global principles were developed by Reverend Leon Sullivan as a way to rise above the discrimination and struggles in post-apartheid South Africa. Reverend Sullivan worked with the UN Secretary General to revise the principles to meet global needs. Since then, both large and small companies have agreed to abide by the Global Sullivan Principles that encourage social responsibility throughout the world. The Global Sullivan Principles, the UN Global Compact, the UN Human Rights Declaration, as well as others promote foundational principles of conduct for global businesses. Table 10–6 provides a synthesis of typical foundational statements.

For multinational corporations, risk management and global ethics are so integral to the stability of their overseas operations they have created special officers or committees to oversee global compliance issues. Walmart created a global ethics office to communicate company values and encourage ethical decision making throughout its global stores.[98] General Motors' Board Audit Committee created the Global Ethics and Compliance Department after revisions were implemented to the U.S. Federal Sentencing Guidelines. GM not only wanted to comply with these guidelines, it also wanted to create a centralized system of compliance that would be used at all GM locations worldwide.[99]

The successful implementation of a global ethics program requires more than just a global ethics committee. It also requires extensive training for employees. As this chapter demonstrated, various differences exist between cultures and businesses from different countries. Employees of global companies should be trained to understand and respect these differences, particularly those employees directly involved in global operations.

TABLE 10–6 Global Principles for Ethical Business Conduct

Global principles are integrity statements about foundational beliefs that should remain constant as businesses operate globally. These principles address issues such as accountability, transparency, trust, natural environment, safety, treatment of employees, human rights, importance of property rights, and adhering to all legal requirements. The principles are designed to focus on areas that may present challenges to the ethical conduct of global business.

1. **Require accountability and transparency in all relationships.** Accountability requires accurate reporting to stakeholders, and transparency requires openness and truthfulness in all transactions and operations.

2. **Comply with the spirit and intent of all laws.** Laws, standards, and regulations must be respected in all countries as well as global conventions and agreements developed among nations.

3. **Build trust in all stakeholder relationships through a commitment to ethical conduct.** Trust is required to build the foundation for high integrity relationships. This requires organizational members to avoid major international risks such as bribery and conflicts of interest. Laws supporting this principle include the U.S. Foreign Corrupt Practices Act, the U.K. Bribery Act, OECD Convention, and UN Convention against Corruption.

4. **Be mindful and responsible in relating to communities where there are operations.** The communities where businesses operate should be supported and improved as much as possible to benefit employees, suppliers, customers, and the community overall.

5. **Engage in sustainable practices to protect the natural environment.** This requires the protection of the long-term well-being of the natural environment including all biological entities as well as the interaction among nature, individuals, organizations, and business strategies.

6. **Provide equal opportunity, safety, and fair compensation for employees.** Employees should be treated fairly, not exploited or taken advantage of, especially in developing countries. Laws supporting this principle include equal opportunity legislation throughout the world.

7. **Provide safe products and create value for customers.** Product safety is a global issue as various governments and legal systems sometimes provide opportunities for firms to cut corners on safety. All products should provide their represented value and performance.

8. **Respect human rights as defined in the UN Global Compact.** Human rights are a major concern of the UN Global Compact and most other respected principles statements of international business.

9. **Support the economic viability of all stakeholders.** Economic viability supports all participants in business operations. Concerns such as fair trade and payment of a living wage are embedded in this principle.

10. **Respect the property of others.** Respect for property and those who own it is a broad concept that is an ethical foundation for the operation of economic systems. Property includes physical assets as well as the protection of intellectual property.

Source: O.C. Ferrell and Linda Ferrell, Anderson School of Management, University of New Mexico, Copyright © 2016.

Ford Motor Co. has an online global ethics training program for employees available in 13 languages. The company also offers hotlines for employees in 24 countries and trains its Office of the General Counsel how to handle global complaints.[100] Codes of global ethical conduct, global ethics training, and global channels for employees to communicate misconduct are important mechanisms in creating a culture of globalized ethical decision making.

A global firm cannot succeed simply by applying its domestic ethical programs to other global environments. Businesses are increasingly encountering social and environmental concerns that society expects them to take responsibility for as public issues.[101] Although ethical issues such as honesty and integrity are common to most countries, differences in laws, political systems, and cultures require a more targeted approach to ethical decision making. Global ethics is not a "one size fits all" concept. With that said, it is important for companies to act with integrity even if they are doing business in a country with lax laws on certain ethical subjects. Those companies who incorporate globalized ethical decision making throughout their international operations not only enhance their reputations, but also demonstrate a respect for their employees and cultures—as well as avoid the costly litigation that often accompanies misconduct.

SUMMARY

In this chapter we tried to sensitize you to the important topic of ethical decision making in an international context. We began by looking at values and culture. A country's values are influenced by ethnic groups, social organizations, and other cultural aspects. Hofstede identified four cultural dimensions that can have a profound impact on the business environment: individualism/collectivism, power distance, uncertainty avoidance, and masculinity/femininity. The self-reference criterion is the unconscious reference to one's own cultural values, experiences, and knowledge and is a common stumbling block for organizations. Another approach organizations tend to take is that of cultural relativism, or the idea that morality varies from one culture to another and business practices are defined as right or wrong differently.

Risk compartmentalization is an important ethical issue and occurs when various profit centers within corporations become unaware of the overall consequences of their actions on the firm as a whole. The last financial meltdown was in part the result of risk compartmentalization. Understanding rational economics and systems is an important foundation for understanding business ethics. Rational economics assumes people make decisions rationally based upon utility, value, profit maximization, and relevant information. Capitalism bases its models on these assumptions. Behavioral economics, by contrast, argues that humans may not act in a rational way as a result of genetics, learned behavior, emotions, framing, and heuristics, or rules of thumb. Social democracy, a form of socialism, allows private ownership of property and features a large government equipped to offer services such as education and health care to its citizens. Sweden, Denmark, and Finland are social democracies.

Multinational corporations are public companies that operate on a global scale without significant ties to any one nation or region. MNCs contributed to the growth of global economies but are by no means immune to criticism. The International Monetary Fund makes short-term loans to member countries that have deficits and provides foreign currencies for its members. The UN Global Compact is a set of 10 principles that promote human rights, sustainability, and the eradication of corruption, while the World Trade Organization administers its own trade agreements, facilitates trade negotiations, settles trade disputes, and monitors the trade policies of member nations.

There are several critical ethics issues of which global businesses should be aware. Global risks create ethical issues for global companies to manage. Bribery is a major ethical issue, prompting legislation such as the U.S. Foreign Corrupt Practices Act and the U.K. Bribery Act. Antitrust activities are illegal in most industrialized countries and are pursued even more ardently in the European Union than in the United States. Internet security is an ethical issue, and hacking and privacy violations are on the rise. The United Nations codified human rights as a function of inherent human dignity and includes equal and inalienable rights such as the foundation of freedom, justice, and peace in the world. Health care and labor issues are important ethical issues but tend to vary by country. Wage issues such as a living wage and executive compensation are controversial topics that affect a variety of global stakeholders. Consumerism is the belief that the interests of consumers should dictate the economic structure of a society, rather than the interests of producers; it refers to the theory that an increasing consumption of goods is economically desirable, and equates personal happiness with the purchase and consumption of material possessions.

IMPORTANT TERMS FOR REVIEW

global business 276

national culture 277

individualism/collective dimension 277

power distance dimension 277

self-reference criterion 278

cultural relativism 279

risk compartmentalization 280

global common values 279

Adam Smith 281

laissez-faire 281

John Maynard Keynes 281

Milton Friedman 281

Socialism 282

social democracy 282

bimodal wealth distribution 282

rational economics 282

behavioral economics 283

multinational corporations 285

Business for Social Responsibility 287

International Monetary Fund 287

United Nations Global Compact 288

World Trade Organization 289

Dumping 290

vertical system 294

human rights 295

consumerism 299

made-to-break 300

RESOLVING ETHICAL BUSINESS CHALLENGES*

After graduating from college and working a few years at a small technology firm, Preet scored a high-level job in the logistics department at Amex Corporation. Amex sells high-quality electronic products that are extremely popular among technical savvy young adults. Part of Preet's job involves working with a team to oversee Amex's contractors in China. Amex contracts with factories across Asia to build components for the company's electronics. Preet's team was to ensure the shipments were as orderly as possible. Preet's team had innovative people, and they performed so well the company began giving them more responsibility, including solving major challenges that arose within the factories.

One day Preet was to visit the factory in the Shandong province of China. Shipments were falling behind schedule, and there seemed to be more accidents occurring there. Preet was to observe the factory and meet with management to determine where the problems occurred. Preet looked forward to her first trip to China and to actually visit a factory to learn more about the manufacturing process.

When Preet arrived at the airport, the managers of the factory greeted her and showed her around. When she got to the factory, all of the employees were hard at work. One group of workers cleaned the components using special chemicals. Preet noticed they did not wear protective face masks, even though she knew the chemicals could be harmful if inhaled. When Preet asked about this, she was told that face masks were recommended but not required because the chances of getting sick from the chemicals were low.

As Preet spent time at the factory, she noticed more things wrong. She discovered employees, on average, worked at least 12 hours per day, sometimes with no breaks. She knew company policy mandated an eight-hour work day. Sometimes employees would put in as much as 18-hour shifts. Preet spoke with one of the employees who told her on condition of anonymity that they were denied sick leave. Any perceived idleness on the employee's part resulted in reduced pay. He also informed her there had been several suicides at the plant from overworked employees. When Preet asked the supervisor why the factory did not hire more workers, he replied they did not have the money.

When Preet returned to the United States, she wrote a list of recommendations for improving the factory. Later that month, her team met with the company's top managers in the logistics department. They expressed concern about Preet's findings but offered no recommendations for how to fix them. Afterward, Preet complained to members of her team.

"Of course they aren't going to do anything," said Jim, who had been working in the logistics department for 12 years. "Why should they? As long as the company gets their shipments, they aren't going to disrupt the process by requiring major changes."

Dawn, who had only been working for six months, chimed in. "But Jim, they have to do something. From what Preet said, the workers have terrible working conditions."

Jim sighed. "Dawn, you haven't been in this business long enough to see how things work. The factory in Shandong really isn't that bad compared to many other factories in China. It's not unusual for factory workers to work longer hours. Besides, you might think the employees there don't make much for the amount that they work, but it's a lot better than what people get in other factories. For better pay people are willing to work in less than ideal conditions."

Preet spoke up. "Just because that's normal in the culture doesn't necessarily make it right. Many of these problems could be avoided if the factory ensured their workers wore appropriate safety gear and hired more employees."

"The factory probably can't hire more workers," Jim said. "Where are they going to get the money?"

"Well, maybe Amex should begin paying them more," Dawn replied. "That would translate into higher wages and the ability to hire more staff."

"You've got to be kidding!" Jim said. "The whole reason why Amex is there in the first place is because labor costs are so cheap. Besides, being able to keep costs low is the only way to price our products reasonably. Consumers want low-priced products."

"But consumers also care about how workers are treated, don't they?" Preet asked.

"They might show some concern," Jim replied. "But if it's between higher-priced products or better working conditions, I guarantee consumers will choose the latter."

QUESTIONS | EXERCISES

1. Discuss some of the choices of the firm and the advantages and disadvantages of each.
2. Describe how Jim takes a cultural relativism approach to the problem.
3. Since Amex does not own the Chinese factory, are they still accountable for the working conditions of its suppliers? Why or why not?

*This case is strictly hypothetical; any resemblance to real persons, companies, or situations is coincidental.

> > > CHECK YOUR EQ

Check your EQ, or Ethics Quotient, by completing the following. Assess your performance to evaluate your overall understanding of the chapter material.

1. Most countries have a strong orientation toward ethical and legal compliance.   **Yes**   **No**

2. The self-reference criterion is an unconscious reference to one's own cultural values, experience, and knowledge.   **Yes**   **No**

3. One of the critical ethical business issues linked to cultural differences is the question of whose values and ethical standards take precedence during international negotiations and business transactions.   **Yes**   **No**

4. Multinational corporations have identifiable home countries but operate globally.   **Yes**   **No**

5. Certain facilitating payments are acceptable under the Foreign Corrupt Practices Act.   **Yes**   **No**

ANSWERS 1. **No** That's an ethnocentric perspective; in other countries laws may be viewed more situationally. 2. **Yes.** We react based on what we have experienced over our lifetimes. 3. **Yes.** Ethical standards and values differ from culture to culture, and this can be a critical point in effective business negotiations. Some people believe in cultural relativism, which means that the standards of the host country hold sway. However, many MNCs are legally bound to adhere to the standards of the host country. 4. **No** Multinational corporations have no significant ties to any nation or region. 5. **Yes.** A violation of the FCPA occurs when the payments are excessive or are used to persuade the recipients to perform other than normal duties.

ENDNOTES

1. Philip R. Cateora, Mary C. Gilly, and John L. Graham, *International Marketing*, 15th ed. (New York, NY: McGraw-Hill Irwin, 2011), 109–110.

2. Linda K. Treviño and Katherine A. Nelson, *Managing Business Ethics*, 3rd ed. (Hoboken, NJ: John Wiley & Sons, Inc., 2004), 319.

3. Cateora, Gilly, and Graham, *International Marketing*, 110–111.

4. Ibid.

5. Zaid Swaidan, "Culture and Consumer Ethics," *Journal of Business Ethics* 108, 2 (2012): 201–213.

6. Sam Schechner and Inti Landauro, "France Blocks Uber Yet Again," *The Wall Street Journal,* December 15, 2014, B4; Reuters and Fortune editors, "German court places nationwide ban on UberPOP," *Fortune*, March 18, 2015, http://fortune.com/2015/03/18/german-court-ban-uber/ (accessed April 14, 2015).

7. "Uber declared illegal in Thailand," November 28, 2014, http://www.bangkokpost.com/news/general/445978/uber-declared-illegal-in-thailand-drivers-face-heavy-fines (accessed March 31, 2015).

8. The Heart of Hinduism website, http://hinduism.iskcon.org/ (accessed April 1, 2015).

9. Mecca Centric Dawa Group, "Islamic virtues from the Quran," *Muslim Internet Directory*, http://www.2muslims.com/directory/Detailed/224066.shtml (accessed April 1, 2015).

10. Gordon B. Hinckley, *Standing for Something: Ten Neglected Virtues That Will Heal Our Hearts and Homes*, 1st ed. (New York, NY: Times Books, 2000).

11. "Unit Six: The Four Immeasurables," Buddhist Studies," http://www.buddhanet.net/e-learning/buddhism/bs-s15.htm (accessed April 1, 2015).

12. John (Jack) Ruhe and Monle Lee, "Teaching Ethics in International Business Courses: The Impacts of Religions," *Journal of Teaching in International Business* 19, 4 (2008): 362–388; Andrew Wilson, editor, *World Scripture: A Comparative Anthology of Sacred Texts*, A project of the international religious foundation (New York, NY: Paragon House, 1995).

13. Ian Bremmer, "The New World of Business," *Fortune*, January 2015, 86–92.

14. Economist staff, "What happens when a country goes bust?" *The Economist*, November 24, 2014, http://www.economist.com/blogs/economist-explains/2014/11/economist-explains-20 (accessed April 1, 2015).

15. Alan S. Blinder, *Keynesian Economics*, Library of Economics and Liberty, http://www.econlib.org/library/Enc/KeynesianEconomics.html (accessed April 1, 2015).

16. Robert L. Formaini, "Milton Friedman—Economist as Public Intellectual," *Economic Insights* 7, no. 2 (Dallas, TX: Federal Reserve Bank of Dallas, 2002).

17. E. Roy Wientraub, "Neoclassical Economics," *Library of Economics and Liberty*, http://www.econlib.org/library/Enc1/NeoclassicalEconomics.html (accessed April 1, 2015).

18. Jose De Cordoba and Nicholas Casey, "Cuba Unveils Huge Layoffs in Tilt toward Free Market," *The Wall Street Journal*, September 14, 2010, A1, A15.

19. Emma S. Hinchliffe, "On Obama's cue, Netflix launches in Cuba," *USA Today*, February 10, 2015, 1A.

20. Alan Gomez, "New Cuba Rules Come with Big Surprise," *USA Today*, January 19, 2015, 1B-2B.

21. David G. Blanchflower and Andrew J. Oswald, "International Happiness: A New View on the Measure of Performance," *The Academy of Management Perspectives* 25, no. 1 (February 2011): 6–22.

22. Robbie Whelan, "Barry Minkow Charged in Fraud against Lennar," *The Wall Street Journal*, March 25, 2011, http://online.wsj.com/article/SB10001424052748704438104576219662795056534.html (accessed April 1, 2015).

23. Richard Whitely, "U.S. Capitalism: A Tarnished Model?" *The Academy of Management Perspectives 23, 2* (May 2009): 11–22.

24. Thayer Watkins, "The Economy and the Economic History of Sweden," *San Jose State University Department of Economics*, http://www.sjsu.edu/faculty/watkins/sweden.htm (accessed April 1, 2015).

25. Tarun Khanna, "Learning from Economic Experiments in China and India," *The Academy of Management Perspectives* 23, 2 (May 2009): 36–43.

26. Andrew Monahan, "China Overtakes Japan as World's No. 2 Economy," *The Wall Street Journal*, February 14, 2011, http://online.wsj.com/article/SB1000142405274870336190457614283274143940 2.html (accessed April 1, 2015).

27. David Barboza and Chris Buckley, "China Plan Cuts the State's Role in the Economy," *The New York Times*, May 25, 2013, A1.

28. Timothy M. Devinney, "Is the Socially Responsible Corporation a Myth? The Good, the Bad, and the Ugly of Corporate Social Responsibility," *The Academy of Management Perspectives* 23, 2 (May 2009): 44–56.

29. James Angelos, "IKEA Rues Using Prison Labor," *The Wall Street Journal*, November 19, 2012, B7; Kate Connolly, "Ikea Says Sorry to East German Political Prisoners Forced to Make its Furniture," *The Guardian*, http://www.guardian.co.uk/business/2012/nov/16/ikea-regrets-forced-labour-germany (accessed April 1, 2015).

30. "Ethics in Texas Instruments," http://training.itcilo.it/actrav_cdrom1/english/global/code/texas.htm (accessed April 1, 2015).

31. Business for Social Responsibility, http://www.bsr.org (accessed April 1, 2015).

32. Mauro F. Guillén and Esteban García-Canal, "The American Model of the Multinational Firm and the "New" Multinationals From Emerging Economies," *The Academy of Management Perspectives 23, 2* (May 2009): 23–25.

33. Roland Bardy, Stephen Drew, and Tumenta F. Kennedy, "Foreign Investment and Ethics: How to Contribute to Social Responsibility by Doing Business in Less-Developed Countries," *Journal of Business Ethics* 106, 3 (2012), 267–282.

34. "Global Roundup," *International Business Ethics Review* 8, no. 1 (Spring/Summer 2005), 17.

35. Abigail Moses, "Greek Contagion Concern Spurs European Sovereign Default Risk to Record," *Bloomberg*, April 26, 2010, http://www.bloomberg.com/news/2010-04-26/greek-contagion-concern-spurs-european-sovereign-default-risk-to-record.html (accessed April 1, 2015); James G. Neuger and Joe Brennan, "Ireland Weighs Aid as EU Spars over Debt-Crisis Remedy," *Bloomberg*, http://www.bloomberg.com/news/2010-11-16/ireland-

discusses-financial-bailout-as-eu-struggles-to-defuse-debt-crisis.html (accessed April 1, 2015).

36. Geoff Colvin, "Lagarde: We're Turning the Corner," *Fortune*, June 2, 2014, pp. 123–126.

37. "About the UN," *UN*, http://www.un.org/en/aboutun/index.shtml (accessed April 1, 2015).

38. "Overview of the UN Global Compact," *United Nations Global Compact*, http://www.unglobalcompact.org/AboutTheGC/index.html (accessed April 1, 2015).

39. Ibid.

40. "About AACSB," *AACSB International*, http://www.aacsb.edu/about/ (accessed March 31, 2015); Principles for Responsible Management Education home page, 2015, http://www.unprme.org/ (accessed March 31, 2015); AACSB International, "Frequently Asked Questions," http://www.aacsb.edu/en/faq/#152394ca0dfa4fa78edc308436973f76 (accessed March 31, 2015).

41. "Six Principles," *PRME*, http://www.unprme.org/about-prme/the-six-principles.php (accessed March 31, 2015).

42. Matthew Dalton, "EU Steps Up Boeing Trade Battle," The Wall Street Journal, December 22, 2014.

43. John W. Miller, "WTO Details Rising Protectionism, Pushes Countries to Reverse Course," *The Wall Street Journal*, March 26, 2009, http://online.wsj.com/article/SB123808014186248481.html (accessed April 1, 2015).

44. "Global Village Investment Club," *Articles Factory*, http://www.articlesfactory.com/articles/finance/the-global-village-investment-club.html (accessed April 1, 2015).

45. Will Connors and Luciana Magalhaes, "How Brazil's 'Nine Horsemen' Cracked a Bribery Scandal," *The Wall Street Journal*, April 6, 2015, http://www.wsj.com/articles/how-brazils-nine-horsemen-cracked-petrobras-bribery-scandal-1428334221 (accessed April 14, 2015).

46. Tom Fairless, Rolfe Winkler, and Alistair Barr, "EU Files Formal Antitrust Charge Against Google," *The Wall Street Journal*, April 15, 2015, http://www.wsj.com/articles/eu-files-formal-charges-against-google-1429092584 (accessed April 16, 2015).

47. Ben DiPietro, "Supply Chain Slavery Comes Into Focus for Companies," *The Wall Street Journal*, March 30, 2015, http://blogs.wsj.com/riskandcompliance/2015/03/30/supply-chain-slavery-comes-into-focus-for-companies/ (accessed April 14, 2015).

48. Daniel J. McCarthy, Sheila M. Puffer, Denise R. Dunlap, and Alfred M. Jaeger, "A Stakeholder Approach to the Ethicality of BRIC-firm Managers' Use of Favors," *Journal of Business Ethics* 109, 1 (2012): 27–38.

49. Ned Levin, Emily Glazer, and Christopher M. Matthews, "Emails Track J.P. Morgan Hire in China," *The Wall Street Journal*, February 7-8, 2015, A1, A8.

50. "Foreign Corrupt Practices Act's Antibribery Provisions," *The 'Lectric Law Library*, Excerpted from U.S. Commerce Dept., May 10, 1994, http://www.lectlaw.com/files/bur21.htm (accessed April 1, 2015).

51. "Global Fact Gathering," James Mintz Group, June 2009, http://mintzgroup.com/wp-content/uploads/2012/05/GFG-Issue41.pdf (accessed April 1, 2015).

52. Dionne Searcey, "U.K. Law on Bribes Has Firms in a Sweat," *The Wall Street Journal*, December 28, 2010, B1.

53. Julius Melnitzer, "U.K. enacts 'far-reaching' antibribery act," *Law Times*, February 13. 2011, http://www.lawtimesnews.com/201102148245/Headline-News/UK-enacts-far-reaching-anti-bribery-act (accessed April 1, 2015).

54. Searcey, "U.K. Law on Bribes Has Firms in a Sweat"; Melnitzer, "U.K. enacts 'far-reaching' anti-bribery act."

55. Searcey, "U.K. Law on Bribes Has Firms in a Sweat."

56. Melnitzer, "U.K. enacts 'far-reaching' anti-bribery act."

57. Michael Volkov, "The U.K. Antibribery Act: Let's Cool Down the Hysteria," http://www.fcpablog.com/blog/2011/1/18/the-uk-anti-bribery-act-lets-cool-down-the-hysteria.html (accessed April 1, 2015).

58. SFO, "Business expenditure," October 9, 2012, http://www.sfo.gov.uk/bribery-corruption/the-bribery-act/business-expenditure.aspx (accessed April 1, 2015).

59. David Green Speech, "6th Annual European Forum on Anti-Corruption on 26 June 2012," *SFO*, June 26, 2012, http://www.sfo.gov.uk/about-us/our-views/director%27s-speeches/speeches-2012/6th-annual-european-forum-on-anti-corruption-on-26-june-2012.aspx (accessed April 1, 2015).

60. Tom Fairless, "Google Must Improve Search Settlement or Face Charges, EU's Alumunia Says," *The Wall Street Journal*, September 23, 2014, http://www.wsj.com/articles/google-must-improve-search-settlement-or-face-charges-eus-almunia-says-1411462097 (accessed April 1, 2015).

61. Jack T. Ciesielski, "Cyber security: An afterthought for corporate America?" *Fortune*, March 10, 2015, http://fortune.com/2015/03/10/cyber-security-an-afterthought-for-corporate-america/ (accessed April 1, 2015).

62. Siobhan Gorman, Devlin Barrett, and James T. Areddy, "U.S. to Rev Up Hacking Fight," *The Wall Street Journal*, May 24-25, 2014, A1–A2.

63. Joel Schectman and Jessica E. Vascellaro, "Ad Networks Get Around iPhone Privacy Rules," *The Wall Street Journal*, June 5, 2012, B4.

64. Jon Swartz, "Facebook changes its status in Washington," *USA Today*, January 13, 2011, 1B–2B.

65. "EU Data Protection Directive (Directive 95/46/EC)," SearchSecurity.co.UK, http://searchsecurity.techtarget.co.uk/definition/EU-Data-Protection-Directive (accessed March 31, 2015).

66. Benoît Faucon and Rory Jones, "What It's Like Doing Business in Iran," *The Wall Street Journal*, February 26, 2015, B1–B2.

67. Eva Dou, "China's Great Firewall Gets Taller," The Wall Street Journal, January 30, 2015, http://www.wsj.com/articles/chinas-great-firewall-gets-taller-1422607143 (accessed April 1, 2015); Paul Wiseman, "Cracking the 'Great Firewall' of China's Web censorship," *ABC*, 2015, http://abcnews.go.com/Technology/story?id=4707107 (accessed April 1, 2015).

68. Jane Onyanga-Omara, "Google's Gmail service blocked in China," *USA Today*, December 29, 2014, http://www.usatoday.com/story/tech/2014/12/29/gmail-blocked-china/20996633/ (accessed April 1, 2015).

69. Megan Whalen, "Ford Interfaith Network Joins for National Day of Prayer," *@FordOnline*, May 7, 2013, http://www.at.ford.com/news/TeamContent/Pages/GFTCFord-Interfaith-Network-Joins-for-National-Day-of-Prayer.aspx (accessed April 1, 2015).

70. Lutz Preuss and Donna Brown, "Business Policies on Human Rights: An Analysis of Their Content and Prevalence Among FTSE 100 Firms," *Journal of Business Ethics* 109, 3 (2012): 289–299.

71. Jérôme Ballet, Augendra Bhukuth, and Aurélie Carimentrand, "Child Labor and Responsible Consumers: From Boycotts to Social Labels, Illustrated by the Indian

Hand-Knotted Carpet Industry," *Business & Society* 53, 1 (2014): 71–104.

72. Se Young Lee, "Samsung halts business with supplier in China on child labor concern," *Reuters*, July 14, 2014, http://www.reuters.com/article/2014/07/14/us-samsung-elec-child-labour-china-idUSKBN0FJ05Y20140714 (accessed April 14, 2015).

73. Anup Shah, "Health Issues," *Global Issues*, September 27, 2014, http://www.globalissues.org/issue/587/health-issues (accessed April 1, 2015).

74. Economist staff, "Hard pills to swallow," *Economist*, January 4, 2015, http://www.economist.com/news/international/21592655-drug-firms-have-new-medicines-and-patients-are-desperate-them-arguments-over (accessed April 1, 2015).

75. Katherine Hobson, "Two Surveys Spotlight Health Care Cost Variations," *The Wall Street Journal*, November 22, 2010, http://blogs.wsj.com/health/2010/11/22/two-surveys-spotlight-health-care-cost-variations/ (accessed April 1, 2015).

76. "Law Prompts Some Health Care Plans to Drop Mental-Health Benefits," *The Wall Street Journal*, December 23, 2010, http://online.wsj.com/article/SB10001424052748703395904576025410628499574.html (accessed April 1, 2015).

77. PR Newswire, "The Financial Cost of Healthcare Fraud 2014," March 25, 2015, http://www.prnewswire.com/news-releases/the-financial-cost-of-healthcare-fraud-2014-252162971.html (accessed April 1, 2015).

78. United States Department of Justice, "Jury Convicts Doctor, Pharmacist, Marketer in Health Care Fraud Scheme," *The United States Attorney's Office Eastern District of Michigan*, March 7, 2014, http://www.justice.gov/usao-edmi/pr/jury-convicts-doctor-pharmacist-marketer-health-care-fraud-scheme (accessed April 1, 2015).

79. "Germany: Development of the Health Care System," Country Database, http://www.country-data.com/cgi-bin/query/r-4924.html (accessed April 1, 2015).

80. European Commission, *Tackling the gender pay gap in the European Union* (Luxembourg: Publications Office of the European Union, 2014). doi:10.2838/42323.

81. "Survey of violations of Trade Union Rights," *ITUC*, http://survey.ituc-csi.org/+-Whole-World-+.html (accessed April 1, 2015).

82. David Barboza, "McDonald's in China Agrees to Unions," *The New York Times*, April 10, 2007, http://query.nytimes.com/gst/fullpage.html?res=9D00E6DC153FF933A25757C0A9619C8B63&n=Top/Reference/Times%20Topics/Subjects/F/Fringe%20Benefits (accessed April 1, 2015); Ylan Q. Mui, "Wal-Mart works with unions abroad, but not at home," *The Washington Post*, June 7, 2011, http://www.washingtonpost.com/business/economy/wal-mart-works-with-unions-abroad-but-not-at-home/2011/06/07/AG0nOPLH_story.html (accessed April 1, 2015).

83. Claire Suddath, "Can the U.S. Ever Fix Its Messed-Up Maternity Leave System?" *Bloomberg*, January 27, 2015, http://www.bloomberg.com/news/features/2015-01-28/maternity-leave-u-s-policies-still-fail-workers/ (accessed April 1, 2015).

84. Economist staff, "Why Swedish men take so much paternity leave," *The Economist*, July 22, 2014, http://www.economist.com/blogs/economist-explains/2014/07/economist-explains-15 (accessed April 1, 2015).

85. "Wages," United States Department of Labor, http://www.dol.gov/dol/topic/wages/minimumwage.htm (accessed April 1, 2015); "The National Minimum Wage Rates," Directgov, http://www.direct.gov.uk/en/Employment/Employees/TheNationalMinimumWage/DG_10027201 (accessed April 1, 2015); Rachel Pannett, "Australia Weighs Whether Its Minimum Wage Is Too High," *The Wall Street Journal*, January 25, 2015, http://www.wsj.com/articles/australia-debates-whether-its-minimum-wage-is-too-high-1422210360 (accessed April 1, 2015).

86. "Corporate Social Responsibility: Companies in the News—Nike," Mallenbaker.net, http://www.mallenbaker.net/csr/CSRfiles/nike.html (accessed April 1, 2015).

87. Andrew Peaple, "Swiss Shareholders Get More Say on Pay," *The Wall Street Journal*, March 4, 2013, http://www.wsj.com/articles/SB100014241278873245394045783400526797931408 (accessed April 1, 2015).

88. John Revill, "Swiss Expected to Vote on More Pay Limits," *The Wall Street Journal*, March 21, 2013, B6.

89. "China bosses told to cut salaries," *BBC News*, April 09, 2009, http://news.bbc.co.uk/2/hi/7993377.stm (accessed April 1, 2015).

90. Anup Shah, "Consumption and Consumerism," *Global Issues*, September 3, 2008, http://www.globalissues.org/issue/235/consumption-and-consumerism (accessed April 1, 2015).

91. Ibid.

92. Brian Kench, "China Is Losing Some of Its Appetite for Coal," *Bloomberg Businessweek*, December 29, 2014, 16–17

93. Subhash Agrawal, "India's Premature Exuberance," *The Wall Street Journal*, June 16, 2009, http://online.wsj.com/article/SB124513568534118169.html (accessed April 1, 2015).

94. Natalie Obiko Pearson and Rakteem Katakey, "India's Diesel Cars Are Proving Lethal," *Bloomberg Businessweek*, March 10–16, 2014, pp. 18–20.

95. Kim Hjelmgaard, "By 2016 1% Will Have 50% Total Global Wealth," *USA Today*, January 20, 2015, 1B.

96. "Overconsumption: Our use of the world's natural resources," academia.edu, http://www.academia.edu/223160/Overconsumption_Our_use_of_the_world_s_natural_resources (accessed April 1, 2015).

97. Ira Sager, "Living in the United States of Food Waste," *Bloomberg*, January 10, 2013, http://www.bloomberg.com/bw/articles/2013-01-10/living-in-the-united-states-of-food-waste (accessed April 1, 2015).

98. "Walmart Global Ethics Office," Walmart Corporate, https://walmartethics.com/Landing.aspx (accessed April 1, 2015).

99. "As GM Struggles, Its Ethics and Compliance Office Moves On," *Ethikos and Corporate Conduct Quarterly*, September/October 2008, http://www.ethikospublication.com/html/generalmotors.html (accessed April 1, 2015).

100. Mary Swanton, "Combating Corruption: GCs Aim to Establish Global Ethics Codes," *InsideCounsel*, January 1, 2011, http://www.insidecounsel.com/Issues/2011/January/Pages/Combating-Corruption-GCs-Aim-to-Establish-Global-Ethics-Codes.aspx?page=3 (accessed April 1, 2015).

101. Andreas Georg Scherer, Guido Palazzo, and Dirk Matten, "The Business Firm as a Political Actor: A New Theory of the Firm for a Globalized World," *Business & Society* 53, 2 (2014): 143–156.

CHAPTER 11

ETHICAL LEADERSHIP

CHAPTER OBJECTIVES

- Define ethical leadership
- Examine requirements for ethical leadership
- Realize the benefits that come from effective ethical leadership
- Understand how ethical leadership impacts organizational culture
- Learn about the different styles of conflict management
- Understand how employees can be empowered to take on responsibilities in ethical leadership
- Examine leader–follower relationships
- Learn about leadership styles and how they influence ethical leadership
- Use the RADAR model to determine how ethical leaders handle misconduct situations

CHAPTER OUTLINE

Defining Ethical Leadership

Requirements for Ethical Leadership

Benefits of Ethical Leadership

Ethical Leadership and Organizational Culture

Managing Ethical Business Conflicts

    Conflict Management Styles

Ethical Leaders Empower Employees

Ethical Leadership Communication

    Ethical Leadership Communication Skills

Leader–Follower Relationships

    Ethics Programs and Communication
    Power Differences and
    Workplace Politics
    Feedback

Leadership Styles and Ethical Decisions

The RADAR Model

AN ETHICAL DILEMMA*

Stacy, a recently hired employee of a growing local CPA firm called Dewey, Cheatume, and Howe, just passed all four parts of the CPA exam. The University of Virginia prepped her well for her new job, and the partners had high expectations for Stacy because she scored near the top of her graduating class. As a result, Stacy was fast tracked and performed at an advanced level on some jobs. This was due, in part, to her excellent skill set but also because of heavy firm turnover at the senior level.

Because of the long hours and her inexperience, Stacy started to make simple errors such as not meeting time budgets. She began working off the clock because she did not want management to know she had a hard time handling the workload. After a few months, she casually mentioned the extra hours to a coworker, who told her working off the clock is considered unethical and the company has strict policies against it. Stacy was embarrassed but also upset that the company never made this known to her—particularly since she knew her immediate supervisor knew full well what she was doing. Stacy stopped working off the clock and began to work more quickly to get things done in the expected time frame.

A few weeks ago, Stacy learned her recent work on a tax return had to be redone; Stacy mistakenly charged the wrong client for the return. Doug, one of the partners, publicly reprimanded her by saying, "Next time it's coming out of your pay check." Later that same week, as Stacy helped interview a candidate for one of the open accounting positions, she accidentally chipped the glass table in the conference room. When Doug heard about it, he said, "I hope your personal insurance covers the table. You'll need to speak to the secretary and get this replaced."

Over the following months, the firm continued having more resignations. It became so problematic that the Senior Board requested a psychologist interview all staff members. When Stacy was interviewed, she described the poor treatment of employees and unreasonable expectations. Apparently, other employees had the same complaint. The resulting report from the consultant pointed toward numerous management problems at the company. Shortly thereafter, the partners responded in a way the staff did not expect: they took the report personally. As a result, rumors began to surface that the firm was going to go up for sale. Still, the interviews for staff positions continued. One Monday morning a memo surfaced stating that all staff doing interviews for new hires were to "present the firm in a positive and favorable manner." Stacy was one of those staff members doing the interviews.

Stacy did not know how to portray the firm in a positive manner when she was so miserable. She particularly disliked Doug. It seemed to Stacy that Doug made it his mission to torment her by criticizing her every move. He hovered around her desk and made comments about making sure not to mess up again.

After getting advice from one of her coworkers, Stacy decided to approach Doug about his behavior. He did not take it well.

"Look, if you think I'm being too hard on you, then maybe you should just leave," Doug responded. "It's obvious you are not cut out for this business." Doug continued to berate Stacy for her "shoddy" work until she was close to tears.

"If you want to make it in this business, honey, you got to realize when to pick your fights. Me, I'm not in the habit of losing." Doug walked off in a huff.

The next day Stacy was to interview someone for a lower-level accounting position. As she walked down the hallway, Doug approached her.

"I hear you're going to be interviewing a new candidate today. Just remember, make this company look good. No whining about your bad work experience."

Stacy contained her anger when she entered the room and sat down in front of the candidate. She did her best to act professional and stifle her emotions. The real dilemma came when the candidate asked about the firm's culture and how Stacy personally liked working there. She swallowed. She did not know how to sugarcoat her answer without making it an outright lie.

QUESTIONS | EXERCISES

1. Describe the deficiencies in ethical leadership at Stacy's firm.
2. What type of conflict management style does Doug have? Are there more constructive ways for him to handle conflicts with employees?
3. Describe the alternatives Stacy has answering the candidate's question and the advantages and disadvantages of each.

*This case is strictly hypothetical; any resemblance to real persons, companies, or situations is coincidental.

Leadership is a basic requirement for developing an ethical corporate culture and reinforcing ethical decision making among employees. For this reason, we devote an entire chapter to the leadership qualities that support ethical conduct in business. While it is important to have a CEO and board of directors committed to ethical decision making, it is equally important all employees understand their roles in becoming ethical leaders. There are many examples of ethical leadership failures, resulting in ethical and legal crises that damage firms. The former CEO of Diamond Foods led the company on a massive acquisition spree using debt to finance the purchases. In order to make its financial statements look better, the company used improper accounting methods to artificially inflate earnings. As a result of this misconduct, Diamond's reputation suffered and both the company and the CEO were forced to pay penalties to the Securities and Exchange Commission for the fraud.[1] On the other hand, companies such as IBM, Procter & Gamble, and Zappos may have minor ethical transgressions; however, their leadership keeps them on the right course in responding appropriately and recovering from ethical issues. Many companies founded by ethical leaders such as Milton Hershey, founder of Hershey Foods, experienced few ethical crises over the years.

This chapter demonstrates the importance of leadership in creating an ethical culture. We first provide a definition of ethical leadership and explore its relationship to ethical decision making. Next, requirements of ethical leadership are provided, followed by how ethical leadership benefits the company. The relationship between ethical leadership and organizational culture is examined, as well as ways ethical leaders can manage conflict. Managing conflict appropriately identifies potential issues and reinforces a firm's ethical climate. An important part of leadership is the implementation of employee-centered leadership. Employee-centered leadership recognizes that while not everyone will be a manager, every employee can and should practice leadership skills to support ethical decision making. An essential component of employee-centered leadership is communication. Without communication all attempts at maintaining an ethical culture fail. We describe common ethical leadership styles proven effective in building an ethical corporate culture. Finally, we conclude with a model to address ethical issues and misconduct disasters. Leaders can use this model to guide the firm's ethical culture, detect ethical risk areas before they become problematic, and develop methods of recovery if an unethical decision or disaster occurs.

It should be obvious that ethical companies are not 100 percent misconduct free. There will always be employees or managers that push the boundaries of acceptable conduct as well as situations not anticipated in ethics, compliance, or risk assessment programs. Recall the 10-40-40-10 rule in employee conduct; people are motivated by different values, resulting in ethical diversity. Additionally, ethics programs can always be improved, making it important to periodically audit the program to uncover weaknesses. Similarly, ethical leaders have weaknesses and are not free from mistakes, or lapses and blind spots, in oversight. What separates them from unethical leaders is how they respond to ethical issues, interact with stakeholders, and learn from their mistakes. All managers and most employees will witness misconduct at some point in their careers. What is important is how they respond to it.

DEFINING ETHICAL LEADERSHIP

Leadership is the ability or authority to guide and direct others toward a goal. Most people agree that effective leadership is essential for any organization. Ethical decisions are one dimension of leadership. Successful companies develop based upon the leadership and creative abilities of their founders. Without the leadership capabilities of entrepreneurs such as Steve Jobs of Apple, Bill Gates of Microsoft, Sam Walton of Walmart, and Mark Zuckerberg of Facebook, the most successful companies today would be greatly diminished, or nonexistent. However, a strong founder is only one part of a company's success. Strong ethical leadership must be demonstrated through successors, other managers, and employees to continue the firm's success. The ethical leadership skills of Tim Cook of Apple, Steve Balmer of Microsoft, and Sheryl Sandberg, COO of Facebook, are as important as problem solving, planning, delegation, internal communications, and meeting management for the continued success of the company.

Ethical leadership creates an ethical culture. If top managers fail to express desired ethical behaviors and goals, a corporate culture evolves on its own to reflect the values and norms of the company. Consider the fate of one highly profitable and successful accounting company. The founder of the company was known for his integrity—so much so that he refused to make an improper accounting entry for a major client despite the consequences. That man was Arthur E. Andersen, who went on to found Arthur Andersen, one of the top five accounting firms in the United States.[2] Yet despite the ethical integrity of its founder, Arthur Andersen strayed from its original values. Successive leaders stressed business over integrity, leading the firm to inaccurately audit companies later found guilty of accounting misconduct, most notably Enron. Arthur Andersen, which started out with such strong ethical leadership, was destroyed. Thus, it is not enough to have strong ethical leaders and corporate values initially—an ethical corporate culture must be maintained through effective leadership at all times during the firm's existence. Table 11–1 provides a snapshot of leaders admired for their ethical conduct.

Leadership has a significant impact on ethical decision making because leaders have the power to motivate others and enforce the organization's norms, policies, and viewpoints. Ethical leaders ensure these goals are met in an ethical manner. Leaders are central to influencing an organization's corporate culture and ethical posture. Ethical leadership is not simply allowing employees to follow their own moral codes. It is about helping to implement and reinforce shared ethical values to promote an ethical culture, as well as assume responsibility to model ethical conduct for employees.[3] Ethical leadership has a positive relationship with the organizational citizenship of employees and a negative relationship with deviance, or misconduct. In other words, ethical business leaders are more likely to have employees that follow their example and less likely to have deviants that create trouble in the company.[4]

Although we often think of CEOs and other managers as the most important leaders in an organization, the corporate governance reforms discussed in Chapter 4 make it clear a firm's board of directors is also an important leadership component. Indeed, directors have a legal obligation to manage companies "for the best interests of the corporation." To determine what is in the best interest of the firm, directors must consider the effects a decision has not only on shareholders and employees but other important stakeholders as well.[5] Ethical leadership is not limited to management or board members. Therefore, it is important to realize that although ethical leadership is often discussed in terms of corporate directors and top executives, even lower-level employees exhibit ethical leadership traits. All responsible employees must engage in ethical decision making and exhibit ethical leadership characteristics.

Many CEOs articulate the firm's core values but fail to exhibit ethical leadership. Unfortunately, some CEOs and other managers intentionally deceive stakeholders. In the presence of competing stakeholder expectations, CEOs may "muddle through," depending

TABLE 11-1 Leaders Admired for Ethical Conduct

Leaders	Company	Ethical Leadership Activities
Warren Buffett	Berkshire Hathaway	• Promotes ethical conduct as a necessity of business • Shares responsibility and decision making with managers of various companies
Howard Schultz	Starbucks	• Offers health care to part-time workers • Launched the Starbucks College Achievement Plan offering paid college tuition to Arizona State University
Larry Merlo	CVS	• Discontinued the sale of tobacco products because it doesn't fit with their mission of a health care firm • Committed to public health over short-term losses
Elon Musk	Tesla	• Embracing a sustainable business model to combat climate change • Concerned with the responsible use of technology
Kip Tindell	The Container Store	• Creates a corporate culture in which employees feel appreciated and motivated to perform beyond expectations • Employees are provided with better pay and more training than competing retailers

Source: Ethisphere Institute, "100 Most Influential in Business," Online MBA, *Ethisphere*, http://ethisphere.com/magazine/100-most-influential-in-business/ (accessed April 2, 2015); Davey Alba, "Elon Musk Donates $10M to Keep AI from Turning Evil," *Wired*, January 15, 2015, http://www.wired.com/2015/01/elon-musk-ai-safety/ (accessed April 2, 2015).

on the degree of consensus among managers and their reactions to stakeholder demands.[6] Managers that muddle through are not consistent to core values. However, other CEOs are genuine in their commitment to stakeholder engagement and balance interests as well as prioritize initiatives. For ethical leadership to exist, CEOs must go beyond initiatives such as sponsorships and other activities seen as simply good public relations.[7] They need to support an ethical culture that provides leadership for incorporating ethics into daily decisions.

Despite the importance of core values to an ethical organizational culture, there is a risk for managers to experience **normative myopia**, which occurs when managers overlook or stifle the importance of core values in their business decisions. This tendency is thought to occur for three reasons: (1) the belief that normative values do not apply to managerial decisions, (2) the belief that facts and values can be separated in decision making, and (3) the belief that normative values are outside the realm of business.[8] This can lead to ethical blindness, or the propensity to rationalize an unethical action or turn a blind eye to it.[9] For example, the unethical tactics of a top salesperson may be overlooked if that salesperson is a significant contributor to revenue targets. This can culminate in the corporation neglecting or negating its responsibilities to its stakeholders.[10] Top managerial support for core values is therefore crucial to the acceptance and implementation of core values within the organization.

In the long run, if stakeholders are unsatisfied with a company's leader, he or she will not retain that position. A leader must have followers' respect and also provide a standard of conduct. For example, CEO of Tesla and SpaceX Elon Musk is known for his strong work ethic. He does not ask his employees to work hard without putting in long work hours himself. Musk sets an example of hard work and persistence for his employees to follow.[11] On the other hand, failure to demonstrate effective leadership qualities at the top creates the perception that managers either do not care about the company's ethics program or they feel they are above ethics and compliance requirements.

REQUIREMENTS FOR ETHICAL LEADERSHIP

While ethical leaders need good character and competence, they also require skills to lead and guide others. Ethical leadership skills develop through years of training, experience, and learning other best practices of leadership. In pinpointing what makes someone a "good" leader, experts remain divided; leadership qualities differ for each situation. However, a number of requirements have been identified. For instance, ethical leaders must model organizational values, place what is best for the organization over their own interests, train and develop employees throughout their careers, establish reporting mechanisms, understand employee values and perceptions, and recognize the limits of organizational rules and values.[12] These characteristics can be developed through proper training. Most importantly, ethical leaders should not turn a blind eye to observed misconduct.

Ethical leaders never operate in a silo of decision making. They seek to encourage the development of other leaders within the organization. The strength of ethical leaders involves recognizing their own weaknesses and relying on others to help them. Ethical leaders encourage employees to reach their full potential and emphasize their role as important co-creators of value.[13] Holistic reasoning allows leaders to relate decisions to the functions and activities that impact the entire organization. They also try to develop policies and procedures that provide incentives to those who train new leaders.[14] Developing leaders should be a cyclical, or never-ending, process in the organization.

We have researched many books on leadership and have discovered that a good example within business ethics is Archie Carroll's "7 Habits of Highly Moral Leaders" based on Stephen Covey's *The 7 Habits of Highly Effective People.*[15] We adapted Carroll's "7 Habits of Highly Moral Leaders"[16] to create "Seven Habits of Strong Ethical Leaders" (Table 11–2). In particular, we believe ethical leadership is based on holistic thinking that embraces the complex and challenging issues companies face on a daily basis. Ethical leaders need knowledge and experience to make the right decisions. Strong ethical leaders have the knowledge, wisdom, and courage to pull the pertinent information together so the best or most ethical decisions are made. This is no easy task because of various stakeholders and the subsequent conflicts in objectives. This means ethical leaders must stick to their principles and, if necessary, leave the organization if its corporate governance system is so flawed that it is impossible to make the right choice.

TABLE 11–2 Seven Habits of Strong Ethical Leaders

1. Ethical leaders have strong personal character.

2. Ethical leaders have a passion to do right.

3. Ethical leaders are proactive.

4. Ethical leaders consider all stakeholders' interests.

5. Ethical leaders are role models for the organization's values.

6. Ethical leaders are transparent and actively involved in decision making.

7. Ethical leaders take a holistic view of the firm's ethical culture.

© Cengage Learning

Finally, strong ethical leaders are those passionate about the organization and act in the organization's best interests.[17] They develop a vision and ethical habits to lead their organization. We discuss some of these habits in more detail in the following paragraphs.

Many corporate founders—including Sam Walton, Bill Gates, Milton Hershey, Michael Dell, Steve Jobs, and Ben Cohen and Jerry Greenfield—left their ethical stamp on their companies. Their conduct set the tone, making them role models for desired conduct in the early growth of their respective corporations. For instance, Milton Hershey's legacy endures, and Hershey Foods continues to be a role model for an ethical corporate culture. In the case of Sam Walton, Walmart employees shared many stories about Sam Walton's concern for ethical conduct. Honesty was an important value to him, and when employees hid excess inventory on the top of a store roof to keep him from seeing it, the employees were fired. Walmart embarked on a course of rapid growth after Walton's death and became involved in numerous conflicts with various stakeholder groups, especially employees, regulators, competitors, and communities. Despite the ethical foundation left by Sam Walton, Walmart, like most large corporations, deals with hundreds of reported ethical lapses every month.[18] As mentioned earlier, ethical leaders must maintain and build upon an ethical firm's culture to maintain the stamp of the original founders through successive generations.

There is general agreement that ethical leadership is highly unlikely without a strong personal character. The question is how to teach or develop a moral person in a corporate environment. Thomas I. White, a leading authority on character development, believes the focus should be developing "ethical reasoning" rather than being a "moral person." According to White, the ability to resolve the complex ethical dilemmas encountered in a corporate culture requires intellectual skills.[19] For example, the CEO of Airbus recognized the need to have a review performed of the company's anti-corruption program. The review helped Airbus identify areas for program improvement. The CEO clearly recognized the importance of an ethical culture and strongly supported the actions of the ethics and compliance officer.[20] A fundamental problem in traditional character development is that specific values and virtues are used to teach a belief or philosophy. This approach becomes muddled in a business environment where cultural diversity, privacy, and the profit motive must be respected. On the other hand, teaching individuals who want to do the right thing regarding corporate values and ethical codes, and equipping these individuals with the intellectual skills to address the complexities of business decisions with ethical/unethical results, is the correct approach.

Ethical leaders do not wait for ethical problems to arise. They anticipate, plan, and act proactively to avoid potential crises.[21] One way to be proactive is to take a leadership role in developing effective programs that provide employees with guidance and support for making more ethical choices, even in the face of considerable pressure to do otherwise. Ethical leaders who are proactive understand social needs and apply or develop the best practices of ethical leadership that exist in their industry. The Chairman of NuStar, operator of oil pipelines and liquid storage terminals, takes a proactive stance toward safety, philanthropy, job security, and employee benefits. As a result, employees identify with him and follow his standards of ethical and safe behavior at their jobs.[22] Such strong leadership is crucial in maintaining impressive ethical credentials over the long term.

Additionally, ethical leaders must model the organization's values. If leaders do not actively serve as role models for the organization's core values, then those values become nothing more than lip service. According to behavioral scientist Brent Smith, as role models, leaders are the primary influence on individual ethical behavior. For example, when CEOs use narrative language that is resolute, complex, and not engaging, it is positively

TABLE 11-3 Whole Foods's Core Values

- Sell the highest quality natural and organic products available

- Satisfy, delight and nourish our customers

- Support team member happiness and excellence

- Create wealth through profits and growth

- Serve and support our local and global communities

- Practice and advance environmental stewardship

- Create ongoing win-win partnerships with our suppliers

- Promote the health of our stakeholders through healthy eating education

Source: "Our Core Values," Whole Foods Markets, http://www.wholefoodsmarket.com/mission-values/core-values (accessed February 19, 2015).

associated with aggressive financial reporting.[23] Language is the way top managers enact leadership. Leaders whose language and actions are contrary to the firm's values send a signal that the values are trivial or irrelevant.[24] Consider Whole Foods, the world's largest organic and natural grocer. Since its 1980 conception in Austin, Texas, Whole Foods demonstrated a commitment to social responsibility and strong core values (see Table 11–3). In addition to providing consumers with fresh, healthy foods, Whole Foods leaders care for their employees by creating a transparent and friendly work environment. The company encourages a sense of teamwork by imposing a salary cap for top executives. It also supports growers and the environment through sourcing from sustainable growers and supporting efforts such as recycling and reducing energy. At each store, Whole Foods holds community-giving days in which it donates 5 percent of profits to local communities. Many people are drawn to Whole Foods because of its high-quality standards, educational initiatives, and close supplier relationships.[25]

BENEFITS OF ETHICAL LEADERSHIP

Ethical leadership creates many benefits for an organization. Most importantly, ethical leadership has a direct impact on the corporate culture of the firm. For instance, ethical leaders communicate and monitor an organization's values, ensuring that employees are familiar with the company's purpose and beliefs.[26] They also provide cultural motivations for ethical behavior, such as reward systems for ethical conduct and decision making. This reinforcement is positively correlated with ethical employee behavior patterns.[27] Thus, ethical leadership encourages employees to act in an ethical manner in their day-to-day work environment. It is a well-known fact that a firm is only as good as its employees, so instilling employees with a strong sense of integrity is crucial to creating an ethical organization.

Ethical leadership can also lead to higher employee satisfaction and employee commitment.[28] Research shows that employees like to work for ethical companies and are less likely to leave ethical organizations.[29] These factors translate into significant cost savings for the firm and serve to increase employee productivity. At The Container Store, for instance, employees are given first priority. They receive 263 hours of training, higher pay than comparable retailers, and are treated to special appreciation events such as We

Love Our Employees Day. The purpose of this employee-centered corporate culture is to increase employee productivity and the quality of customer service. As a result, The Container Store's turnover rate is 10 percent (compared to 100 percent for other retailers in the industry) and customer loyalty is high (many employees originated as loyal customers of the company).[30]

While ethical leadership can create competitive advantages through employee satisfaction and productivity, it also creates strong relationships with external stakeholders. For instance, customers are willing to pay higher prices for products from ethical companies.[31] As consumer trust for businesses increases, they develop loyalty and gain a competitive advantage over other firms.

Ethical leadership is a foundational requirement for impacting the long-term market valuation of the firm. There is a positive association between the ethical commitment of employees and a firm's valuation on the stock market.[32] A firm's reputation for corporate social responsibility also impacts investor decisions. Corporate social responsibility is negatively related to ethical risks in the long-term, and investors view risk as a factor when determining whether to invest in the firm.[33] The ethical reputation of the company can therefore assure them about the short and long-term sustainability of the company. Finally, as demonstrated in Chapter 4, the Federal Sentencing Guidelines for Organizations mandates that public firms have ethics programs in place to detect organizational misconduct. Those companies that demonstrate they have strong ethics programs are more likely to see their fines reduced if misconduct occurs.[34] Through the creation of favorable relationships with employees, customers, investors, and regulators, ethical leaders create significant competitive advantages and value for their companies.

ETHICAL LEADERSHIP AND ORGANIZATIONAL CULTURE

Organizational culture emerges whether or not there is effective leadership. The ethical dimension is dependent on how the company's leaders influence the culture. In organizations where leaders are tolerant or indifferent toward misconduct, a culture will likely develop in which employees cut corners and/or take excessive risks to advance their careers. On the other hand, ethical leaders recognize that organizational culture will directly impact employee conduct and make a greater effort to promote a culture of ethics and compliance. Leaders help set the tone for such a culture through shared values, attitudes, and ethical practices. For example, Dan Price, the CEO of Gravity Payments, wanted to raise the salaries of the lowest paid workers at his firm to a minimum of $70,000. In order to afford to raise salaries, Price lowered his own $1 million salary down to $70,000 to match his workers. By demonstrating his own willingness to make concessions, Price has set the tone for a caring corporate culture that values employee contributions.[35]

Ethical leaders generally adopt one of two approaches to leadership: a compliance-based approach or an integrity-based approach. These approaches are similar to the compliance orientation and values orientation discussed in Chapter 8. Leaders that adopt a compliance-based approach emphasize obedience to rules and regulations and set processes in place to ensure compliance. Such an approach deters illegal conduct and stresses a culture of avoidance. Corporate annual reports may give clues as to the type of approach a company chooses to adopt. If those in charge of ethics are called compliance officers or risk managers, then it is highly likely the firm is more compliance-based. Also, if those in charge of the ethics and compliance program are mostly accountants and legal professionals, the firm tends to be more compliance-based. Some see this as achieving the bare minimum to avoid getting in trouble with the law.

An integrity-based approach views ethics as an opportunity to implement core values. Leaders who adopt an integrity-based approach take responsibility for the firm's ethical culture and hold employees accountable for practicing ethical behaviors and core practices.[36] Integrity-based approaches usually have chief officers, human resource managers, and board member committees involved with the ethics and compliance program. This type of approach not only empowers employees but helps them integrate ethical values and principles established by the firm. Finally, it helps the firm understand where questionable practices are occurring and where possible new ethical issues are arising. Remember, business is not static; it is dynamic. While it might seem that an integrity-based approach is preferable, many ethical leaders use a combination of the two approaches. Without compliance to laws and basic rules and regulations the company and industry have set, an organization will not survive in the long-term.

Another way to classify leader types includes the following categories: the unethical leader, the apathetic leader, and the ethical leader. Each of these types influences the development of an organizational culture, whether positive or negative. While we use this classification typology, the reality is that each leader type falls on a continuum or line and not a box. We use this classification to analyze the most desirable type of leader.

The unethical leader is usually egocentric and often does whatever it takes to achieve personal and organizational objectives. This leader looks at laws as minimum guidelines and searches for loopholes. If the laws go against the company, then the leader attempts to find a way to bypass the law. Unethical leaders perceive ethics codes, compliance regulations, and industry standards as optional. The justification used for breaking laws or rules is usually that doing so serves a greater good and the risk of getting caught is low. An example of an unethical leader is A. Alfred Taubman. After acquiring the legendary auction house Sotheby's, Taubman conspired with rival Christie's to raise commission fees without regard for the future of the company or for stakeholders. He was later convicted of price fixing, spent a year in prison, and paid a $7.5 million fine.[37] He was willing to face the risks and paid for his misconduct.

Another type of unethical leader is known as a psychopathic leader, or corporate psychopath. We discussed this briefly in Chapter 6. Research suggests that 1 percent of the population could qualify as a corporate psychopath. These leaders are characterized as having superficial charm, no conscience, grandiose self-worth, little or no empathy, and enjoyment in flouting the rules. Companies with such leaders usually experience increases in the following problems: heightened level of conflict, lower employee commitment, higher organizational constraints, heavier workloads, poor levels of training, lower job satisfaction, and an increase in employee absenteeism. Research suggests these leaders are disproportionately at higher levels within an organization, possibly because their tendencies are to be in a position of control.[38]

Apathetic leaders are not necessarily unethical, but they care little for ethics within the company.[39] They often view ethics as relative and optional in a business context. Apathetic leaders often display no passion for the firm or the mission of the organization.[40] Employees do not see the sacrifices in them that other managers or leaders display.[41] One possible example of this leader type might be Tony Hayward, former BP CEO. As the oil spill in the Gulf of Mexico leaked over 172 million gallons of oil into the ocean, Mr. Hayward attended a yacht race and allegedly directed employees to downplay the disaster to keep stock prices afloat.

At the same time he complained, "I'd like my life back."[42] He later resigned, and BP pled guilty to 11 counts of manslaughter and agreed to pay a fine of $18.7 billion.

Ethical leaders include ethics at every operational level and stage of the decision-making process.[43] There will always be ethical lapses in any organization, but ethical leaders address issues as soon as they appear. Oftentimes ethical leaders try to create participative organizational cultures to which employees are encouraged to provide input. Ethical leaders view such employee collaboration as an important resource. In this type of organizational culture, employees are seen as major co-contributors of value.[44] Leaders must therefore establish strong systems of communication, including language that informs employees of company activities and encourages them to report concerns to company leaders.[45] To ensure employees are on the same page, ethical leaders must also communicate the company's guiding values and principles and display competence and credibility in ethical decision making. Above all, ethical leaders must model the ethical values they promote.[46] Hence, ethical leadership is a requirement for building a culture where ethical decisions occur daily.

MANAGING ETHICAL BUSINESS CONFLICTS

Ethical business conflicts occur when there are two or more positions on a decision that conflicts with organizational goals. Sometimes ethical conflicts emerge because employees feel uncomfortable about their own or their coworkers' decisions. One benefit of ethical conflict is it helps pinpoint ethical issues. Ethical decision making does not occur unless an ethical issue is identified and needs to be resolved. For example, suppose the board of directors of a major company discovered that the CEO embellished his résumé. The company had gone through a succession of CEOs and must make the choice whether to fire another one. Even if the CEO is fired, the company receives a blow to its reputation for not vetting its CEO candidates appropriately. The board has an ethical conflict it must resolve. This situation occurred at Yahoo!, and a former CEO was pressured to resign. While leaders cannot totally avoid ethical conflict, they can maintain an ethical corporate culture through appropriate conflict management.

Before describing ethical conflict management styles, note that ethical conflict issues will not be brought to management's attention without effective mechanisms for transparent communication. It is common for companies to have some means for employees to express concerns or give suggestions, such as hotlines, feedback forms, or suggestion boxes. Indeed, these mechanisms for communication establish a participative organizational culture. However, failure to act on employee concerns or suggestions can do more harm than good. Employees who believe that their concerns are ignored feel deceived and are likely to experience more group conflict.[47] Instead, leaders must take an authentic, proactive approach to communication. This not only involves listening to employee input but attempts to identify ethical issues before they lead to conflict.[48] Bringing ethical issues into the open may lead to ethical conflict, but it enables ethical leaders to manage that conflict and bring it closer to resolution.

Employees themselves should be trained to handle conflict situations. Training employees to recognize and resolve conflict can prevent employees from being the victims of questionable conduct such as bullying.[49] Employees may choose to approach a conflict situation in one of five ways: ignore the issue, confront the other person, report the conflict to management, use a hotline, or engage in external whistle-blowing. Employees who feel their leaders are ethical and willing to listen to their concerns are more likely to approach the other person or report the conflict internally.[50]

Conflict Management Styles

There are many instances in the workplace when a leader must step in to resolve an ethical conflict. How a leader approaches conflict situations determines which strategy he or she adopts when resolving conflicts. We categorize conflict management into five styles: competing, avoiding, accommodating, collaborating, and compromising. These styles are based on two dimensions: assertiveness and cooperativeness. Assertiveness is acting in one's own best interests, while cooperativeness means working toward the best interests of the other person.[51] Figure 11–1 provides a visual representation of these five conflict management styles based on levels of assertiveness and cooperativeness. In developing conflict management styles to resolve ethical issues, a leader may need to adjust the style to fit a particular ethical dilemma.

In the upper left quadrant is a competing conflict style of management. Leaders having a competing conflict management style are highly assertive and not very cooperative. Competing leaders believe in winning at any cost and measure success by how much the other side loses.[52] Cofounder and Chairman of Dish Network Charlie Ergen has a confrontational management style, and many former employees detail how he yelled and berated them when they did something wrong.[53] These leaders are usually not considered to be ethical because their conflict style makes them abusive and less likely to consider the concerns of employees and other stakeholders. Managers with this style are likely to be more power-oriented and even narcissistic. While leaders should exhibit competing characteristics in certain situations, firms must be careful they do not hire leaders willing to win so much that ethical values and the company's well-being are ignored. However, high assertiveness is not always a problem. For instance, leaders enforce compliance with rules when compromise is impossible. Ethical leaders should never cooperate in misconduct or in behavior that goes against the firm's ethical principles and values. In fact, studies have shown that when business leaders "cheat" by lying to customers, evading taxes, outsourcing to companies that hire underage employees, etc., their misbehavior makes employees less productive, more likely to leave the organization, and more likely to cheat the company themselves.[54]

In the lower left quadrant is an avoiding style of conflict management. Leaders with this approach are not effective because they avoid conflict at any costs—even if it leads to misconduct. They are uncooperative and non-assertive. Even if they are aware of misconduct, they have no desire to manage it. Chairman Ken Lay and CEO Jeff Skilling of Enron appeared to adopt this style. They were aggressive in terms of managing the operations of the business, but they were ethically passive as Enron became increasingly complacent toward misconduct. Leaders who adopt this style automatically assume that conflict is always undesirable. However, conflict provides the organization with the ability to explore new points of view and consider the most ethical choice from a variety of options.[55] Ethical conflict also alerts leaders to ethical issues within the company that they might not have noticed otherwise. The avoiding leader has commonly been associated with ethical crises that have destroyed the reputations of organizations. Enron collapsed because of its ethical complacency and the adoption of an avoiding style toward ethical conflict.

FIGURE 11-1 **Conflict Management Styles**

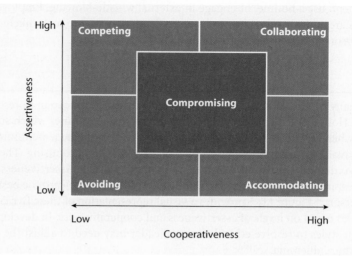

Source: Adapted from Kenneth W. Thomas and Ralph H. Kilmann (March 2, 2010). *Thomas-Kilmann Conflict Mode Instrument: Profile and Interpretive Report.* © CPP, Inc.

In the lower right quadrant is the accommodating style of conflict management. Leaders who adopt this style are highly cooperative but non-assertive. Individuals with this approach to conflict give in to the other side even if it means sacrificing their own interests and values.[56] When a leader accommodates those engaging in misconduct, the result can be an ethical disaster. For instance, a sales manager who knows her salespeople engage in bribery and kickbacks to sell products but allows the misconduct to continue because of their high performance has an accommodating style of conflict management. An accommodating style makes it increasingly hard to compete in a business environment. Because it is necessary to remain competitive in order to survive, businesses must be assertive to keep an edge over the competition. Although you might not consider an accommodating leader unethical, sacrificing the company's principles and values to accommodate the other side is a serious breach of an ethical leader's responsibility.

In the middle is a compromising style of conflict management. Leaders who adopt this management style are in between the assertiveness and cooperativeness dimensions. They believe the best approach to resolving conflicts is for each side to give something up in order to gain something of value.[57] Compromising leaders are still able to receive part of what they want, and that makes it different from an accommodating style of conflict management. On the other hand, they allow the other side a partial victory that prevents them from assuming a competing style of conflict management. This management style is useful in resolving ethical dilemmas when all solutions have disadvantages. Compromising chooses a solution that is the most beneficial to all participants. While there are advantages to compromising in a conflict situation, leaders who overly use this style may find that their rivals will expect them to compromise even when doing so would harm the firm. Also, the parties involved likely experience less commitment since each gave something up.[58] However, an ethical culture is built on participants sharing, compromising, and in some cases, accommodating on issues once they become aware of the consequences.

In the upper right quadrant is the collaborating style of conflict management. The collaborating style is the most advantageous. Leaders who adopt a collaborating style to conflict management are cooperative and assertive. Rather than immediately compromising, collaborative leaders collaborate with others to find a creative way to obtain a beneficial solution.

Collaborative leaders desire to meet the needs of stakeholders. However, they also strongly adhere to organizational values and principles. Collaboration requires both parties to concentrate on the conflict at hand. Leaders with collaborative styles are flexible because they can be both assertive and cooperative, depending upon the situation. They are careful to make sure they do not abuse their power and consider the needs of their rivals in the conflict.[59] Because a collaborative style of conflict management is most in sync with ethical leadership, it is the role of the ethical leader to foster, model, and facilitate a collaborative conflict style. A collaborative style works particularly well in gray areas requiring the need to listen, learn, and share in coming up with the best solution.

While we have separated conflict management into five styles, in reality effective leaders can use different styles depending upon the situation. For instance, while a collaborative style might normally be the most ethical means of managing conflict, it would be ethically questionable to collaborate with an employee caught committing serious misconduct, such as fraud or embezzlement. Compromise may be the best solution when two parties reach an impasse. Companies might choose to avoid an issue if pursuing action would take up too much time and resources.[60]

Ethical leaders should also have the ability to identify the conflict management styles of others. Understanding how other stakeholders manage conflicts can help ethical leaders determine whether their own style should be adapted. This is the heart of ethical leadership. Observing and understanding others' styles of conflict management is important in making the best decision.[61] For instance, if you assume the other person will always be accommodating, you might choose to adopt a competing approach in the next conflict. If both sides to a conflict have competing styles of conflict management, then an outside mediator may be required to assist. This form of organizational learning is important and can lead toward a solution that is most beneficial to both parties. An effective leader must therefore have enough knowledge and emotional intelligence to determine the style of others involved in an ethical conflict.

Additionally, an ethical leader must know which style of conflict management to apply to a particular issue. An ethical leader is not someone who always avoids risks or continuously seeks to beat his or her opponent. Rather, an ethical leader engages in ethical decision making to determine when to be assertive, when to compromise, and when to accommodate or avoid. However, an ethical leader should never attempt to compromise an organization's ethical values. The organization's ethical values can be used as a benchmark to determine the right course of action for conflict resolution. While ethical conflict management is not an easy process, knowledge of the firm's ethical principles, values, and culture helps leaders determine the appropriate course of action.

ETHICAL LEADERS EMPOWER EMPLOYEES

Ethical leaders within an organization cannot make every ethical decision by themselves. In fact, many of the day-to-day decisions will not be made by management, but by employees. Employees constantly face organizational pressures and opportunities in the workplace to engage in ethical conduct or misconduct. Because employee decisions have wide ranging repercussions on an organization, ethical leaders must empower employees to make ethical decisions and take responsibility for their conduct. Employees at all levels of the organization should have an opportunity to develop and employ ethical leadership skills.

Employee empowerment is an essential component of a values-based organizational culture. A values-based culture encourages employees to express concerns, bring up ethical issues, and take a proactive approach toward resolving conflicts. Easy access to ethical codes and policies assists employees when making ethical decisions. Creating an open communication culture where discussion of ethics topics is commonplace encourages employees to come forward with concerns.[62] Periodic feedback between leaders and followers can bring ethical issues into the light and allow the firm to identify and work toward resolving these issues before they become major problems.

Organizations are increasingly realizing the advantages of empowering employees to become ethical leaders. For instance, W.L. Gore & Associates expects employees to manage themselves. Without a formal hierarchy, W.L. Gore employees receive recognition from their fellow coworkers and are allowed to choose their own job titles. This has not only created a supportive and empowered work environment for employees, it also has led employees to brainstorm and create innovative new products.[63] However, there is still disagreement between company leaders and employees regarding how this process is implemented. For instance, in one study managers were eight times more likely than employees to believe their firms' corporate cultures were based upon values. Employees, on the other hand, were much more likely to view their companies' corporate cultures as more command-and-control based, in that organizational leaders make all the decisions.[64] Organizational leaders may therefore misjudge their firms' corporate cultures. For this reason, it is important organizational leaders solicit constant feedback from employees and encourage their input.

Ethical leadership training for both managers and employees is helpful. Training for employees should include ethical decision making, teamwork, and conflict resolution skills. Managers should be trained on how to create a participative organizational culture that encourages employees to engage in ethical decision making.[65]

Employee empowerment is important in creating employee-centered ethical leadership. Managers still have many ethical responsibilities that employees do not have. For instance, they are responsible for making the final decision and for overseeing the firm's corporate culture to ensure ethics and compliance. Yet employees can contribute to the firm's ethical culture by reporting questionable activities, providing suggestions to improve the firm's culture, and modeling the firm's values to new employees. Non-leader employee group members making decisions on behalf of the group result in lower levels of unethical conduct. However, the leader can weaken this through his or her influence.[66] A firm's ethical culture relies not simply on documents such as a code of ethics, but on how formal leaders and employees embody the principles of integrity that the organization values.

ETHICAL LEADERSHIP COMMUNICATION

The way an ethical leader communicates to employees has just as much impact on the firm's ethical culture. A narcissistic leader, for instance, is highly controlling and does not tolerate any criticism of his or her leadership decisions. Consider other leaders who tell employees they do not care how they get a task done as long as they do it. This type of communication signals to employees that they need to get their work done at any cost. Ethical leaders, on the other hand, communicate with employees regularly regarding expectations and progress toward company goals. Table 11–4 describes some of the ways leaders can use communication to improve their leadership skills.

TABLE 11–4 Communication for Becoming a Better Leader

1. Have the tough conversations that you have been meaning to have, including telling people what they need (and not necessarily want) to hear.

2. Stop talking and listen more.

3. Pick up the phone or walk down the hall to actually talk with someone rather than relying on more impersonal emails.

4. Communicate bad news in the same way, with the same zest, as good news.

5. Share performance feedback with others regularly so that others know how they can improve.

6. Be purposeful and thoughtful in how you communicate.

7. Ask for feedback so you can improve your skills.

8. Work on your blind spots in your leadership abilities.

Source: Adapted from David K. Grossman, "13 Ways to Become a Better Leader," *The Public Relations Strategist*, Winter 2012, pp. 12–13.

Transparency and *reporting* are two major dimensions of ethical communication. Ethical leaders create transparency by developing a culture where ethics is frequently discussed. Openness and leader accessibility are important in addressing and resolving ethical issues. Reporting is a two-way process in which the communicator communicates with superiors and subordinates. While it is common practice to report to superiors, it is less common to feel a responsibility to report to one's subordinates. Yet ethical leaders hold themselves accountable for reporting to their employees, because they recognize that employees have an important stake in the ethical success of the organization.

Reporting can be a formal or informal process. Formal reporting happens in environments such as meetings and conferences. Formal processes of reporting also include anonymous reporting systems. Informal reporting occurs when leaders interact among employees, keeping them informed about company decisions, policies, and ethical expectations.[67] Ethical issues are often identified through these types of casual conversations, especially as employees are often more aware of questionable conduct in the workplace. An ethical leader should engage in both formal and informal systems of reporting to create an open communication culture where employees feel comfortable stepping forward with concerns or suggestions.

Ethical leadership is not possible without effective communication. How a leader communicates provides employees with a clear idea of company roles and expectations. For instance, communication about ethics topics demonstrates that the leader cares enough about the ethical culture and employee participation to communicate goals and values among employees. Secondly, it increases employee morale. Employees are made aware that their contributions and ability to make ethical decisions are important to the firm. Next, it shows employees they can bring up issues without fears of retaliation. Finally, ethical communication creates leader–follower relationships that can lead to mutually beneficial relationships between the firm and employees. Leaders who want to encourage ethical organizational conduct must make ethical communication skills a major consideration.

Ethical Leadership Communication Skills

Much like ethical leadership skills, ethical communication skills do not come easily. While some might be better communicators than others, these communication skills take practice. A well-intentioned leader might not be a good communicator, and each individual communicates differently. However, with proper training an individual can learn how to effectively and ethically communicate with other stakeholders. Organizational communication is separated into four categories: interpersonal communication, small group communication, nonverbal communication, and listening. Figure 11–2 lists the four categories of communication.

Interpersonal communication is the most well-known form of communication and occurs when two or more people interact with one another.[68] Interpersonal communication provides an intimate opportunity for the ethical leader to receive or dispense information. It also provides an opportunity to coach employees when potential ethical issues arise. How to communicate effectively can be a difficult skill to master. An ethical method of communicating treats the other person with respect—even when leaders are forced to discipline employees. Respectful interpersonal communication does not involve placating the other person and never involves condoning misconduct. However, appreciating the dignity of another person even during disciplinary procedures is an important way to maintain ethical interpersonal communication. Ideally, civil interpersonal communication in these situations leads to positive behavioral changes.

It is often difficult to communicate to a superior. Differences in power status and fears that their concerns will be rebuffed make employees more hesitant to approach organizational leaders.[69] An ethical leader must work to reassure employees by balancing the interests of all relevant stakeholders.[70] While power distance cannot be completely eliminated between a superior and subordinate—and in many cases should not be—substituting respect and openness for judgmental language makes employees feel comfortable enough to speak up about their concerns.[71]

Like everything else, communication has gray areas. Lying to employees or consumers would generally be considered wrong. However, some find small white lies that do not damage stakeholders permissible. Sometimes communication takes on more serious dimensions. For instance, is discussing the nonpublic financial situation of your firm with a friend to use in his trades merely doing him a favor, or does your communication constitute insider trading? Former CEO of McKinsey Company Rajat Gupta told his hedge fund friend Raj Rajaratnam nonpublic financial information about Goldman Sachs. He was a board member, and did not know his personal conversation was monitored by the government. While Gupta might publicly argue this information was merely a simple business discussion with an old friend, the government saw it as insider trading. Top managers have

FIGURE 11–2 **Four Categories of Communication**

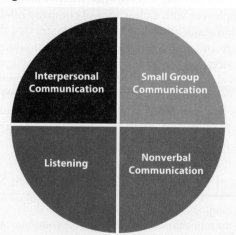

many situations where they must consider the ethical implications of their communication and look toward the interests of all relevant stakeholders.

Collaboration and assessing the issue are good approaches to ethical interpersonal communication. Interacting with employees and maintaining strong relationships is essential to communicating the firm's values and positively influencing its ethical culture. Leaders who make an effort to maintain ethical interpersonal communication can create employee empowerment while also exercising their responsibility in carrying out organizational ethics.

Small group communication is growing in organizations. As such, this type of communication becomes increasingly important to ethical decision making.[72] Today many of an organization's ethical decisions are made in teams, and these decisions impact the ethical success of the firm. Ethical decision making in small groups is beneficial because it allows a number of individuals to collaborate and spread out responsibilities. It also empowers employees to engage in greater decision-making responsibilities.

There are advantages and disadvantages to small group communication. Small groups can increase collaboration and generate a variety of different perspectives and opinions on a particular issue. However, engaging in repetitive or routine decision making can cause small groups to overlook certain ethical issues. It is difficult to anticipate all the repercussions of the group's ethical decisions. Groupthink and group polarization are common negative side effects. *Groupthink* occurs when one or more group members feel pressured to conform to the group's decision even if they personally disagree. *Group polarization* refers to the fact that a group is more likely to move toward a more extreme position than the group members might have done individually.[73] As a result, groups have been known to make riskier decisions than an average individual member from the group would have made.

Group decision making can, however, yield ethical outcomes. The diversity of opinions and discussions can result in better solutions than what would occur individually. If members are encouraged to speak up and create checks and balances in the team, then they are better able to hold other group members accountable. To ensure all group members are empowered to contribute, everyone should be familiar with the firm's ethical values and principles, trained in ethical communication techniques and how to listen to other member's input, attempt to understand the other person's point of view, show a willingness to seek common ground, explore different options, and commit to finding the most ethical solution.[74] Additionally, the ethical leader should make sure anonymous mechanisms are in place so team members can seek support if necessary. Table 11–5 provides a seven-step process for eliminating groupthink in small groups.

TABLE 11–5 Ways to Avoid Groupthink in Small-Group Decision Making

1. Emphasize to each team member that he or she is a "critical evaluator" with the responsibility to express opinions and objections freely

2. Eliminate leadership biases by refusing to express an opinion when assigning tasks to a group

3. Set up a number of independent groups to work on the same issue

4. Encourage each team member to express the group's ideas with someone he or she can trust from outside the group

5. Express the need to examine all alternatives

6. Invite outside experts into group meetings, and allow members to interact with these experts

7. Assign one person to be "Devil's advocate"

Source: Irving L. Janis, *Victims of Groupthink: A Psychological Study of Foreign-Policy Decisions and Fiascos* (Boston, MS: Houghton-Mifflin, 1972).

So far we have only covered spoken communication. However, non-spoken communication is just as important to ethical leadership. *Nonverbal communication* is communication expressed through actions, body language, expressions, or other forms of communication not written or oral. Nonverbal communication provides major clues about an individual's emotional state.[75] It includes gestures, facial expressions, proximity, time, dress, and paralanguage. Paralanguage is the way we talk, such as volume, inflection, tone, and rhythm.[76] Paralanguage provides important indicators of the person's emotional status. For instance, we can tell whether another person is angry based on loudness and inflection of voice, as well as other nonverbal cues such as frowning and redness of face. These nonverbal indicators can tell us what a person really feels even if the person's language indicates otherwise.

Often a person's nonverbal cues are deemed more reliable than what he or she states verbally. This is because unlike speaking, nonverbal communication is often subconscious. It is hard for people to control what they are communicating nonverbally. Nonverbal communication is also helpful in clarifying language that might be ambiguous or confusing. Leaders should pay close attention to the nonverbal behaviors of employees. Additionally, they should show respect to others in the organization both verbally through language and nonverbal behaviors. Those who take the time to learn how to interact with those they work with can make great strides in communicating in a way that employees understand.

Listening involves paying attention to both verbal and nonverbal behavior.[77] Listening is just as important as speaking. If one of the parties to a dialogue does not listen, communication becomes ineffective. From an ethical perspective, leaders with poor listening skills or who fail to listen to concerns often overlook ethical issues. Listening is also important to employee morale. Employees cite the failure to take their concerns seriously as one of the top complaints in the workplace.[78] Failing to listen limits leaders' decision-making capacity because they cannot get the information they need to make ethical decisions. Because employee reporting is one of the primary ways leaders discover ethical concerns, failing to listen to employee reports causes them to miss key information.

On the other hand, ethical leaders developing good listening skills tend to establish credibility and trustworthiness with employees.[79] Leaders who encourage employees to provide input and assure them their concerns are taken seriously support an open communication culture. Companies with strong communication methods identify strengths and weaknesses within the firm. Additionally, leaders who spend time listening to their employees encourage employees to reciprocate in kind, further promoting the adoption and acceptance of ethical principles and values.

LEADER–FOLLOWER RELATIONSHIPS

Communication is essential for reducing leader isolation and creating leader–follower congruence. **Leader–follower congruence** occurs when leaders and followers share the same vision, ethical expectations, and objectives for the company. Although each individual has his or her own personal goals and personalities, it is important for a company to get leaders and followers to adopt shared values and work toward goals for the organization. If followers feel disconnected from the leader, they will not likely be committed toward promoting the firm's vision and goals.

The *leader–exchange theory* claims that leaders form unique relationships with followers through social interactions. Therefore, a leader who is socially isolated from employees will have a tenuous relationship because employees are left to make their own decisions. On the other hand, micromanaging employees makes them feel stifled and believe leaders do not trust them. Micromanaged employees often have lower morale, productivity, and greater willingness to leave the company.[81] Conversely, leaders that have positive and respectful relationships with employees can increase job satisfaction and commitment to the firm.[82]

Because organizational leaders often occupy a managerial position, their job responsibilities are likely to differ from lower-level employees. This creates a greater tendency for the leader to be isolated. To decrease this social isolation, it is important for ethical leaders to frequently communicate and interact with employees. Communication that incorporates respect, listening, and feedback can create mutually beneficial relationships. Leaders must take a proactive stance toward the communication of ethical values, expectations, and concerns. This is particularly important because ethical issues and questionable behavior are difficult for many employees to discuss.[83] An ethical leader must therefore use communication to reassure employees that their concerns will be taken seriously.

Ethics Programs and Communication

Perhaps one of the most observable ways of communicating ethical values to employees is through codes of ethics and training in how to make ethical decisions. Codes of ethics provide important guidelines for employees on how to act in different situations. Although it is impossible for any code to discuss every potential ethical issue an employee may face, effective codes should familiarize employees with the firm's values, make them aware of some of the more common ethical and legal issues they will likely face, and reinforce the firm's ethical corporate culture. For a code to be truly effective, it should be accessible and supported by every level of the company. Ethical training is another important way values are communicated. While codes provide employees with basic ethical guidelines, training allows employees to practice these guidelines. Effective ethical training programs teach employees how to apply the firm's values to some of the organization's most common ethical risk areas.

Interpersonal communication that is both formal and informal is also important between leaders and followers. Leader–follower communication connects followers with those in the company who are most familiar with the firm's ethical values. One survey found that 46 percent of employees polled cited lack of transparent communication from company leaders as a reason for wanting to leave the company.[84] Bringing awareness to ethical topics in the workplace not only makes employees feel comfortable discussing them, but also demonstrates a commitment toward ethical conduct on the part of organizational leaders.

DEBATE ISSUE
TAKE A STAND

Should the CFO Be the Key Leader to Deal with Ethical Risks?

In many public companies the chief financial officer (CFO) is the leader in assessing risks. Many ethical risks relate to the financial area. The Sarbanes–Oxley Act requires the CFO to abide by a code of ethics. The top concerns of CFOs are the ability to maintain margins, costs (especially health care), and forecasts of results, as well as working capital management. Therefore, some firms put the CFO as the key leader in managing risks.

However, CFOs may not define ethical risks the right way. For instance, they tend to focus on insurance coverage, regulatory compliance, and operational risks. Another viewpoint is based on a consulting firm's findings that more shareholder value is lost through strategic and ethical risks. Therefore, ethical leadership should be companywide rather than left to one person. The entire senior leadership team should self-assess their divisions of the business and report their top risks. According to this argument, risk management becomes a part of the organizational culture, and ethics is woven through all key decisions.[80]

1. To prevent financial misconduct and operational risks, the CFO should be the key leader.

2. Companywide ethical risk management is the best approach to manage financial and operational risks.

Southern Co. develops videos and brings in speakers to emphasize the importance of ethics in the workplace. One of its initiatives involved developing a video series for new front-line managers to explain what is expected of them as they assume their new jobs.[85]

Power Differences and Workplace Politics

While there will likely be power differences between managers and employees within the organization, it is important that ethical leaders attempt to reduce these differences when ethical communication is involved. Some leaders occupying positions of authority within the organization might have the tendency to view information from employees as unimportant.[86] Such a perspective is detrimental to the health of the company. Employees who feel their concerns are not taken seriously are less likely to bring them up—and more likely to ignore observed misconduct in the workplace. Employees who feel intimidated by the power differences might try to avoid communication with the organizational leader.

Ethical leaders can mitigate power differences through frequent communication with workers. They should move among employees and listen to their feedback and concerns. The point of this interaction is to create more beneficial relationships with employees and also reduce perceived power differences between these groups.

Workplace politics can be another detriment to communication in the workplace. Organizational politics is often perceived as trying to achieve one's own ends even if it means harming others in the organization. Gossip, manipulation, playing favorites, and taking credit for another's work are all examples commonly associated with workplace politics. In a highly politicized environment, employees are encouraged to compete rather than collaborate in order to win the leader's favor.[87] This leads to lower morale, higher turnover, and negative behaviors by employees who feel they are treated unfairly.[88] Ethical leaders should try to avoid having such a workplace environment.

On the other hand, there is a difference between having a high degree of office politics and having good political skills. Ethical leaders should avoid the former but adopt the latter. Political skills can be used to promote organizational goals and help rather than hinder other employees. Ethical leaders with good political skills are able to navigate difficult situations, reduce uncertainty, and advocate for positive change.[89] An ethical leader leads employees through challenges while avoiding office politics by distributing rewards fairly and communicating the firm's corporate values. Effective ethical leadership and employees' emotional reactions and attributions have a direct influence on lowering employee misconduct.[90]

Feedback

Most companies recognize the need for organizational leaders to provide feedback to employees. Feedback can occur through informal methods like a simple conversation or through more formal systems such as employee performance evaluations. Ethical leaders understand the importance of both positive and negative feedback for employees. Negative feedback, while sometimes difficult to convey, is important to inform employees of weaknesses and provide constructive ways for improving them. However, it is important for leaders to recognize that positive feedback is just as necessary as negative feedback. Leaders who only provide negative feedback may create the perception that the organization is characterized by weaknesses, which in turn can lower employee morale. It also does not allow employees to identify and improve upon their strengths. Reinforcing the positive behavior and ethical decisions of employees is important for both the development of an ethical culture and the overall success of the firm.

While most companies understand the need for leader-to-follower feedback, not as many recognize the need for organizational leaders to get feedback from their employees. It is important to remember that while leaders might implement an ethics program, employees will be responsible for applying the company's principles and values into their daily decisions. Additionally, because they often observe conduct that leaders do not see, developing feedback mechanisms for employees is crucial for identifying ethical issues. Third party or external reporting channels increase the intentions of lower-level employees to report misconduct.[91] Finally, it is helpful to incorporate feedback and reports of misconduct when measuring the effectiveness of the company's ethics program.

Employee feedback can be generated in many different ways, including interviews, anonymous surveys, ethics audits, and websites. Encouraging employees to provide feedback is important in making employees feel involved in developing the firm's corporate culture. U.K. utility company Centrica solicits feedback through annual employee engagement surveys. These surveys help Centrica identify areas in which employees are highly satisfied as well as areas that require improvement.[92] Feedback remains one of the most vital means of testing the effectiveness of a firm's ethical culture and decision-making abilities.

LEADERSHIP STYLES AND ETHICAL DECISIONS

Leadership styles influence many aspects of organizational behavior, including employees' acceptance of and adherence to organizational norms and values. Styles that focus on building strong organizational values among employees contribute to shared standards of conduct. They also influence the organization's transmission and monitoring of values, norms, and codes of ethics.[93] In short, the leadership style of an organization influences how its employees act. The challenge for leaders is in gaining the trust and commitment of organizational members, which is essential if organizational leaders are to steer their companies toward success. Those leaders recognized as trustworthy are more likely to be perceived as ethical stewards.[94] Studying a firm's leadership styles and attitudes also helps to pinpoint where future ethical issues may arise. Even for actions that may be against the law, employees often look to their organizational leaders to determine how to respond.

Ethical leadership by a CEO requires an understanding of his or her firm's vision and values, as well as of the challenges of responsibility and the risks involved in achieving organizational objectives. Lapses in ethical leadership can occur in people who possess strong ethical character, especially if they view the organization's ethical culture as being outside the realm of decision making that exists in the home, family, and community. This phenomenon has been observed in countless cases of so-called good community citizens engaging in unethical business activities. Rajat Gupta, for instance, who was convicted of insider trading, was well-respected and donated money to a number of good causes.

There is no one leadership style or an absolute list of attributes, values, or skills needed to be an effective leader. However, three elemental ingredients for leadership include character, stewardship, and experience.[95] Strong ethical leaders must have the right kind of moral integrity or character. Such integrity must be transparent; in other words, they must "do in private as if it were always public." Stewardship involves managing the responsibilities and duties of being a leader. A leader must assume his or her responsibilities to lead effectively. Such a person must be concerned with shareholders as well as the lowest-paid employees.

Even with extensive experience, no leader can always be right or judged ethical by stakeholders in every case. The acknowledgment of this fact may be perceived as a weakness, but in reality it supports integrity and increases the debate exchange of views on ethics and openness.

The most effective ethical leaders possess the ability to manage themselves and their relationships with others effectively, a skill known as **emotional intelligence**. Emotionally intelligent leaders are skilled in self-awareness, self-control, and relationship building. They are outward directed and have a vision about achieving "something greater than themselves."[96] Warren Buffett is an example of an emotionally intelligent leader able to align employees behind a common vision and provide them with the motivation to make decisions and contribute. Emotional intelligence has many positive effects on corporate culture. Because emotionally intelligent leaders exhibit self-control and self-awareness, they handle stressful situations better. Additionally, employees tend to view leaders with high emotional intelligence as effective leaders because of their ability to motivate and make employees feel like an important part of the organization.[97] Because of the increased importance of emotional intelligence to productivity and leadership, many employers view emotional intelligence as more important than IQ when recruiting new employees.[98]

Six leadership styles that are based on emotional intelligence have been identified by Daniel Goleman.[99]

1. The coercive leader demands instantaneous obedience and focuses on achievement, initiative, and self-control. Although this style can be very effective during times of crisis or during a turnaround, it otherwise creates a negative climate for organizational performance.

2. The authoritative leader—considered to be one of the most effective styles—inspires employees to follow a vision, facilitates change, and creates a strongly positive performance climate.

3. The affiliative leader values people, their emotions, and their needs and relies on friendship and trust to promote flexibility, innovation, and risk taking.

4. The democratic leader relies on participation and teamwork to reach collaborative decisions. This style focuses on communication and creates a positive climate for achieving results.

5. The pacesetting leader can create a negative climate because of the high standards that he or she sets. This style works best for attaining quick results from highly motivated individuals who value achievement and take the initiative.

6. The coaching leader builds a positive climate by developing skills to foster long-term success, delegating responsibility, and skillfully issuing challenging assignments.

Richard Boyatzis and Annie McKee adapted Goleman's work on emotional intelligence to describe what they call a resonant leader. Resonant leaders demonstrate mindfulness of themselves and their own emotions, a belief that goals can be met, and a caring attitude toward others within the organization. These abilities create resonance within the organization, enabling employees to work toward common goals.[100] Resonant leaders create an ethical corporate culture as well as leader–follower congruence.

The most successful leaders do not rely on one style, but alter their techniques based on the characteristics of the situation. Different styles are effective in developing an ethical culture depending on the leader's assessment of risks and the desire to achieve a positive climate for organizational performance. Additionally, many emotional intelligence characteristics can be taught. Starbucks, for instance, has their new employees go through a training program called the "Latte Method" where employees learn to recognize negative emotions from their customers and respond appropriately.[101]

Another way to consider leadership styles is to classify them as transactional or transformational. **Transactional leaders** attempt to create employee satisfaction through negotiating, or "bartering," for desired behaviors or levels of performance. **Transformational leaders** strive to raise employees' level of commitment and foster trust and motivation.[102] Both transformational and transactional leaders can positively influence the corporate culture.

Transformational leaders communicate a sense of mission, stimulate new ways of thinking, and enhance as well as generate new learning experiences. These leaders consider employee needs and aspirations in conjunction with organizational needs. They also build commitment and respect for values that promote effective responses to ethical issues. Thus, transformational leaders strive to promote activities and behavior through a shared vision and common learning experience. As a result, they have a stronger influence on coworker support for ethical decisions and for building an ethical culture than transactional leaders. Transformational ethical leadership is best suited for organizations that have higher levels of ethical commitment among employees and strong stakeholder support for an ethical culture. A number of industry trade associations—including the American Institute of Certified Public Accountants, Defense Industry Initiative on Business Ethics and Conduct, Ethics and Compliance Association, and Mortgage Bankers Association of America—are helping companies provide transformational leadership.[103]

In contrast, transactional leaders focus on ensuring required conduct and procedures are implemented. Their negotiations to achieve desired outcomes result in a dynamic relationship with subordinates where reactions, conflict, and crisis influence the relationship more than ethical concerns. Transactional leaders produce employees who achieve a negotiated level of performance, including compliance with ethical and legal standards. As long as employees and leaders both find this exchange mutually rewarding, the relationship is likely to be successful. However, transactional leadership is best suited for rapidly changing situations, including those that require responses to ethical problems or issues. For example, when Eric Pillmore took over as senior vice president of corporate governance at Tyco after a major scandal involving CEO Dennis Kozlowski, the company needed transitional leadership. To turn the company around, many ethics and corporate governance decisions needed to be made quickly. Pillmore helped install a new ethics program that changed leadership policies and allowed him direct communications with the board of directors in order to implement the leadership transition.[104] Research indicates that companies characterized by transformational leadership are more likely to be involved in corporate social responsibility (CSR) activities. No link was found between transactional leadership and CSR activities.[105]

Finally, another leadership style gaining attention recently is known as authentic leadership. **Authentic leaders** are passionate about the company, live out corporate values daily in their behavior in the workplace, and form long-term relationships with employees and other stakeholders. Kim Jordan, CEO of craft brewery New Belgium Brewing (NBB), is an authentic leader who constantly strives to live NBB's mission to "operate a profitable company which makes our love and talent manifest."[106] As a role model for other employees, Jordan aligned them toward a common vision of providing high-quality products and adopting a stakeholder orientation.

Authentic leaders do not mimic other leaders, but they do learn by observing them.[107] Authentic leaders display principle-centered power, because they are able to effectively handle difficult situations and display a strong commitment to their organizations.[108] Notice the similarity between principle-centered power and the self-control exhibited by emotionally intelligent leaders. Finally, authentic leaders demonstrate core values and integrate these values into the operation of the firm. Authentic leadership should be a goal for any leader who wants to create a strong ethical company.

THE RADAR MODEL

We mentioned earlier that ethical leaders must be proactive and cannot just wait for problems to arrive. They must interact with employees and have systems in place to recognize or detect ethical issues before they arise. The best way of handling misconduct is to avoid it completely. However, even the best organizations suffer from ethical risks. For instance, Warren Buffett, considered to be one of the most ethical and highly respected CEOs, faced an ethical issue after one of his managers was accused of engaging in questionable stock trades based on confidential information inside the organization. Buffett accepted the manager's resignation. When ethical misconduct or issues arise, the leader should have plans in place to answer stakeholder concerns and recover from misconduct. We adopted the acronym RADAR to describe an ethical leader's duty to *recognize* ethical issues, *avoid* misconduct whenever possible, *discover* ethical risk areas, *answer* stakeholder concerns when an ethical issue comes to light, and *recover* from a misconduct disaster by improving upon weaknesses in the ethics program (see Figure 11-3).

FIGURE 11-3 The RADAR Model

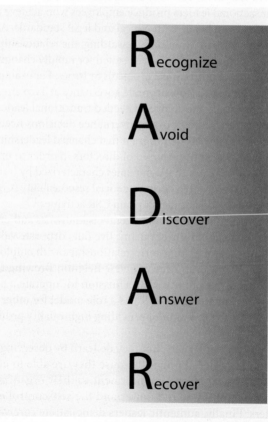

The first step to prevent misconduct is recognizing the firm's ethical risk areas. Ethical leaders must determine what issues the firm is most likely to face so controls can be implemented to limit the opportunity for misconduct. A good way to create recognition is to teach employees about common types of ethical issues through ethical training programs. It is important that all employees recognize their responsibility to identify ethical issues before they become major problems. Additionally, part of the recognition process should include plans for how to address ethical issues once identified and whether disciplinary action is warranted. For instance, the CEO of sports catering company Centerplate was fired after a video surfaced of him engaging in animal abuse. After recognizing it as an ethical issue, the board of directors replaced him.[109] Recognizing and identifying ethical issues helps leaders develop internal controls to limit certain types of conduct and/or have plans in place to handle misconduct should it occur.

After identifying ethical risk areas, ethical leaders should develop policies and procedures for detecting and avoiding misconduct. This process is an important part of risk management. While companies might adopt risk management plans to deal with economic, marketing, technology, and environmental risks, they are less likely to consider ethical risks as a major area of concern. However, as seen throughout this text, some of the biggest dangers to a company are internal to the organization. For this reason, ethical leaders should engage in ethics continuity planning. Ethics continuity planning involves the identification of risk areas and the development of a response plan to deal with major issues. By imagining worst case scenarios, leaders brainstorm with others in the firm on the best way to avoid them. Ethics continuity planning also considers the ethical goals the firm wishes to accomplish.[110] Nike, for instance, developed supplier codes of conduct as well as auditing tools to monitor whether their suppliers adhere to the firm's ethical expectations. Nike's actions seek to avoid misconduct disasters in the supply chain and also provide directions for the firm to take if suppliers are found in violation of corporate policies.

Discovery involves proactively uncovering ethical risk areas that could lead to misconduct. Many managers are reluctant to engage in this process because they fear doing so will uncover questionable conduct that could put the firm in an unfavorable light. However, ignoring risk areas makes it much harder to resolve ethical issues when they do occur. Instead, ethical leaders engage in an assessment process to evaluate the firm's ethical weaknesses so the firm can address them. Ethics audits are a good assessment tool to discover ethical issues. While discovery is often thought of as the responsibility of management, it is important that all employees have the ability to discover ethical issues before they snowball into a misconduct disaster. Table 11–6 describes some questions ethical leaders should ask in assessing the firm's ethics program and corporate culture.

The last two steps of the process occur when a firm is faced with an ethical conflict or dilemma. It is not a question of *if* a firm is faced with an ethical dilemma, but *when*. Answering involves responding to the discovery of an ethical dilemma through communication both internally and externally. When an ethical issue is detected, a leader should communicate with employees so everyone is aware of the issue, its importance, and the necessity for resolving it. Codes of ethics, ethics training, and hotlines are just a few of the ways leaders and employees communicate internally.[111] Externally, leaders should also answer stakeholder concerns and reassure them that actions will be taken to resolve the issue. Remaining silent can be one of the biggest public relations blunders a firm makes after a disaster. The National Football League's (NFL) initial disciplinary action taken against Ray Rice of the Baltimore Ravens after domestic abuse footage surfaced led to outrage among consumers. They believed that the NFL's response was hardly a reaction that fit the seriousness of domestic abuse.

TABLE 11–6 Questions to Ask for Discovery and Assessment Processes

- *Does the company have a written code of conduct?*

- *Have individuals from high-level positions in the organization been assigned overall responsibility to oversee compliance with standards and procedures?*

- *What are the processes or other means by which ethics are integrated into any or all manufacturing, marketing, distribution, electronic commerce, and general corporate strategy decisions?*

- *Is there a review process whereby legal, ethical, and business practice considerations are presented, reviewed, or otherwise considered by the board of directors?*

- *What steps has the company taken to communicate its standards, procedures, and policies to all employees through training programs or publications that describe company expectations?*

- *Has the organization taken reasonable steps to achieve compliance by utilizing, monitoring, and auditing systems designed to detect misconduct and by providing a reporting system whereby employees can report without fear of retribution?*

- *Is adherence to, and implementation of, the code of ethics one of the standards by which the corporate culture can be linked directly to performance measures?*

- *Has the organization used due care not to delegate substantial responsibility to individuals that it knows do not have the ability to implement organization-wide risk-reduction processes?*

- *Have the standards been sufficiently enforced through appropriate methods, such as discipline of employees who violated ethical policies?*

Source: Based on Lynn Brewer, Robert Chandler, and O.C. Ferrell (2006). *Managing Risks for Corporate Integrity* (Mason, OH: Thomson), 76–84.

Recovery occurs when a firm begins to rebuild its reputation. From an ethical standpoint, leaders should use this period to fix any weaknesses in the ethics program and develop improved ways of detecting misconduct. Recovery involves a four-step process: (1) take corrective action; (2) compensate stakeholders harmed by the misconduct; (3) express regret for the misconduct; and (4) reinforce the firm's reputation with positive messages.[112] By improving the company's internal controls and addressing areas of ethical weakness, firms can sometimes emerge from a disaster stronger than they were before.[113] For instance, a major fraud disaster at Hospital Corporation of America provided the impetus for the development of a strong ethics and compliance program that in turn helped restore the firm's reputation as an ethical company.

SUMMARY

Leadership is the ability or authority to guide and direct others toward a goal. Ethical decisions should be one dimension of leadership. Ethical leadership has a significant impact on ethical decision making because leaders have the power to motivate others and enforce the organization's norms and policies.

Ethical leadership skills are developed through years of training, experience, and learning from other best practices of leadership. Ethical leadership involves modeling organizational values, placing what is best for the organization over the leader's own interests, training and developing employees throughout their careers, establishing reporting mechanisms, understanding employee values and perceptions, and recognizing the limits of organizational rules and values. Ethical leaders have strong personal characters, a passion to do what is right, are proactive, consider all stakeholders' interests, are role models for the organization's values, are transparent and actively involved in decision making, and take a holistic view of the firm's ethical culture.

There are many benefits to ethical leadership. Ethical leadership encourages employees to act in an ethical manner in their daily work environment. Ethical leadership can also lead to higher employee satisfaction and employee commitment. Customers are often willing to pay higher prices for products from ethical companies. Ethical leadership can also impact the long-term market valuation of the firm. Finally, companies that demonstrate they have strong ethics programs are more likely to see their fines reduced if misconduct should occur.

Ethical leaders generally adopt one of two approaches to leadership: a compliance-based approach or an integrity-based approach. A compliance approach is more focused upon risks, while an integrity approach views ethics more as an opportunity. Leaders can be classified as unethical leaders, apathetic leaders, and ethical leaders. The unethical leader is usually egocentric and will often do whatever it takes to achieve personal and organizational objectives. A small proportion may even be classified as psychopathic, in which they have no conscience and little or no empathy toward others. This type of leader does not try to learn about best practices for ethics and compliance. Apathetic leaders are not necessarily unethical, but they care little for ethics within the company. Ethical leaders include ethics at every operational level and stage of the decision-making process.

Ethical leaders are skilled at conflict management. Ethical business conflicts occur when there are two or more positions on a decision that conflicts with organizational goals. Sometimes ethical conflicts emerge because employees feel uncomfortable about their own or their coworkers' decisions. There are five types of conflict management styles: competitive, avoiding, accommodating, compromising, and collaborating. However, an ethical leader should be able to adapt his or her style depending on the situation. Additionally, ethical leaders are often skilled at recognizing the conflict management styles of others and adapting their styles accordingly.

While we tend to focus on top managers when discussing ethical leadership, ethical leadership is not limited to managers or supervisors. Employee empowerment is an essential component of a values-based organizational culture. Employees can contribute to the firm's ethical culture by reporting questionable activities, providing suggestions to improve the firm's culture, and modeling the firm's values to new employees. A firm's ethical culture relies not simply on documents such as a code of ethics, but on how employees embody the principles of integrity the organization values.

Communication is an important part of ethical leadership. Four types of communication include interpersonal communication, small group communication, nonverbal communication, and listening. Communication is essential for reducing leader isolation and creating leader–follower congruence. Leader–follower congruence occurs when leaders and followers share the same vision, ethical expectations, and objectives for the company. An important way of communicating ethical values to employees is through codes of ethics and training on how to make ethical decisions. Minimizing power differences and workplace politics and encouraging feedback from employees are also ways to create leader–follower congruence to support an ethical organizational culture.

As teams become increasingly important, particularly in organizations requiring complex problem solving, knowing how to manage teams has taken on a significant role for organizational leaders. Ethical leaders can increase the effectiveness of teams by supporting the team's ability to make decisions, initiating the structure of the team, and assigning tasks if needed. Team members should be trained in effective team building skills to help them arrive at more ethical decisions while avoiding common pitfalls such as groupthink.

Leadership styles influence many aspects of organizational behavior, including employees' acceptance of and adherence to organizational values. The most effective ethical leaders possess the ability to manage themselves and their relationships with others effectively, a skill known as emotional intelligence. Resonant leaders are emotionally intelligent leaders who demonstrate mindfulness of themselves and their own emotions, a belief that goals can be met, and a caring attitude toward others within the organization. Transactional leaders attempt to create employee satisfaction through negotiating, or "bartering," for desired behaviors or levels of performance. Transformational leaders strive to raise employees' level of commitment and to foster trust and motivation. Another leadership style gaining attention is authentic leadership. Authentic leaders are passionate about the company, live out corporate values daily in their behavior in the workplace, and form long-term relationships with employees.

The RADAR model stands for Recognize, Avoid, Discover, Answer, and Recover. An ethical leader can use this model to identify ethical risk areas, respond to ethical issues, and, if necessary, help the organization recover from ethical mishaps. First, an ethical leader must be able to identify or recognize issues having an ethical component. Next, the leader should seek to avoid having the ethical risk areas turn into ethical disasters by putting systems and controls in place to limit the opportunity for misconduct. Discovery involves proactively uncovering ethical risk areas that could lead to misconduct. Ethical audits are a good discovery tool. When an ethical issue or a misconduct disaster occurs, answering involves responding to the discovery of an ethical dilemma through communication both internally and externally. Finally, recovery involves fixing any weaknesses in the ethics program and developing improved ways of detecting misconduct.

IMPORTANT TERMS FOR REVIEW

Leadership 312

normative myopia 314

ethical business conflicts 320

leader–follower congruence 328

emotional intelligence 332

transactional leader 333

transformational leader 333

authentic leader 333

RESOLVING ETHICAL BUSINESS CHALLENGES*

David Hannigan had come far since he started working at a subsidiary of Emper Corp., a manufacturer of automobile parts. He began as a line manager after graduating from UCLA four years ago. His skills at maintaining efficiency, his leadership, and his repartee with the factory workers soon gained the attention of management. Even the lowest factory workers seemed to respect David for his caring attitude and his ability to empathize with employees. While he made it clear he expected hard work, David had the ability to make every member of the factory floor feel like their contributions mattered. He shot up through the ranks and was recently promoted to Director of Personnel of this subsidiary when the previous director retired. In the entire history of the firm, nobody had moved through the ranks so quickly. David even received a letter of congratulations from the CEO of Emper Corp. after his promotion was announced. David was confident that within a few more years, he would be able to secure a high-level job at the corporate headquarters in Chicago.

A few months into his new position, David had lunch with a few key personnel from the company. One of them included Vice President Stanley Martin. Stan began the lunch meeting by praising all of them for their success. Later into his talk, he said, "You all know Emper Corp. wants to increase revenues and give big bonuses to as many employees as possible, but we need to become more efficient. That said, corporate decided the amount of automation in some of our factories, namely this one, needs to be increased."

Jane Newton from the accounting department replied, "But the cost and accounting analyses we sent to headquarters showed it wouldn't be profitable to make changes like that in this particular plant. Why did they pick this one?"

"Apparently," replied Stan, "Top management wants to test robots and all the high-tech gadgets at one factory to see if they increase product quality and pay for themselves. They think that in the long run, stockholders will benefit from automation. Anyway, the decision has been made, and it's our job to make it work. We're going to have to sell the work force and the community on the decision."

David knew what this meant. He replied, "That won't be easy. Hundreds of people are going to lose their jobs, and we are the largest source of employment for this town."

Stan's reply was pleasant, yet forceful. "Some of the factory people will be able to stay on if they get additional training. We can convince the workers and the people in town that the decision was necessary, if we can show them accounting and cost information to justify the decision. If they see good, sound reasoning for the action, they'll be less likely to resist and cause trouble. We all need to maintain productivity and efficiency until the new equipment is here. I want the accountants to work on a cost summary we can release to the employees and the town newspaper that shows why automation is a good idea."

Jane spoke up once more. "But Stan, I already told you. The net present value and other analyses I did earlier show this plant would benefit from staying the way it is."

Stan countered, "Jane, when you were working on the analyses, you said yourself that the benefits of automation are hard to identify and assign numbers to. You had to make several assumptions in order to do those analyses. If you change some of your assumptions, you can make the numbers look better. Try a longer useful life for the new equipment, or change some of the projected cost information. As soon as you have the new numbers, bring them to me to look at."

He stood up and addressed each member at the table and said, "Remember, if you can pull this off, your yearly bonuses will triple your annual salaries." Stan walked out of the room.

David felt uncomfortable about the situation. He could not understand why one of the company's top leaders would advocate for such a massive change when the numbers clearly stated that automating the factory would cause more harm than good. He remembered hearing a rumor that Stan was under serious consideration as a candidate for a prestigious position at corporate headquarters. He wondered if Stan was trying to gain favor with those at corporate. Then again, this was mere speculation on his part. What David really worried about was what he was going to tell the employees.

QUESTIONS | EXERCISES

1. Compare and contrast the leadership characteristics of Stan and David.
2. Discuss whether David has any alternatives other than implementing Stan's orders.
3. Even if the automation is successful at increasing productivity, what might be some other consequences of Stan's decision that could negatively impact the firm?

*This case is strictly hypothetical; any resemblance to real persons, companies, or situations is coincidental.

> > > CHECK YOUR EQ

Check your EQ, or Ethics Quotient, by completing the following. Assess your performance to evaluate your overall understanding of the chapter material.

1. Ethical leadership is solely the concern of top management.   **Yes**   <u>**No**</u>

2. Ethical conflicts occur when there are two or more positions on a decision that conflict with organizational goals.   <u>**Yes**</u>   **No**

3. The four types of communication are interpersonal, small group, nonverbal, and listening.   <u>**Yes**</u>   **No**

4. Transactional leadership strives to raise employees' level of commitment and to foster trust and motivation.   **Yes**   <u>**No**</u>

5. Discovery in the RADAR model involves proactively trying to uncover ethical risk areas that could lead to misconduct.   <u>**Yes**</u>   **No**

ANSWERS 1. **No.** While we often discuss ethical leadership in the context of top managers, all employees should be encouraged to practice ethical leadership. 2. **Yes.** Ethical conflicts occur when there are two or more positions on a decision that conflict with organizational goals. 3. **Yes.** The four types of communication an ethical leader should master are interpersonal communication, small group communication, nonverbal communication, and listening. 4. **No.** Transformational leadership strives to raise employees' level of commitment and to foster trust and motivation. Transactional leaders attempt to create employee satisfaction through negotiating, or "bartering," for desired behaviors or levels of performance. 5. **Yes.** Discovery involves proactively trying to uncover ethical risk areas that could lead to misconduct. Ethics audits are a good tool to use in the discovery process.

ENDNOTES

1. Tess Stynes and Paul Ziobro, "Diamond Foods to Pay $5 Million to Settle SEC Fraud Charges," *The Wall Street Journal*, January 9, 2014, http://www.wsj.com/articles/SB10001424052702303848104579310690154877108 (accessed April 2, 2015).

2. Chris Golis, "Emotional Intelligence: Did Meyers-Brigg Destroy Arthur Andersen?" *CBS*, April 16, 2011, http://www.cbsnews.com/8301-505125_162-31147296/emotional-intelligence-did-myers-briggs-destroy-arthur-andersen/ (accessed April 2, 2015).

3. R. Edward Freeman & Lisa Stewart, "Developing Ethical Leadership," *Business Roundtable Institute for Corporate Ethics*, 2006, www.corporate-ethics.org.

4. James B. Avey, Michael E. Palanski, and Fred O. Walumbwa, "When Leadership Goes Unnoticed: The Moderating Role of Follower Self-Esteem on the Relationship between Ethical Leadership and Follower Behavior," *Journal of Business Ethics* 98, 4 (2011): 573–582.

5. Constance E. Bagley, "The Ethical Leader's Decision Tree," *Harvard Business Review*, January–February 2003, 18.

6. Donal Crilly, Morten T. Hansen, and Maurizio Zollo, "Faking It or Muddling through? Understanding Decoupling in Response to Stakeholder Pressures," *Academy of Management Journal* 55, 6 (2012): 1429–1448.

7. Patrick E. Murphy, Magdalena Öberseder, and Gene R. Laczniak, "Corporate Societal Responsibility in Marketing: Normatively Broadening the Concept," *AMS Review* 3, 2 (2013): 86–102.

8. Marc Orlitzky, Diane L. Swanson, Laura-Kate Quartermaine, "Normative Myopia, Executives' Personality, and Preference for Pay Dispersion: Toward Implications for Corporate Social Performance," *Business & Society* 45, 2 (2006): 149–177; Diane L. Swanson, "Toward an integrative strategy of business and society: A research strategy for corporate social performance," *Academy of Management Review* 24, 3 (1999): 506–521.

9. Max H. Bazerman and Ann E. Tenbrunsel, *Blind Spots* (Princeton, NJ: Princeton University Press, 2011).

10. Marc Orlitzky, Diane L. Swanson, Laura-Kate Quartermaine, "Normative Myopia, Executives' Personality, and Preference for Pay Dispersion: Toward Implications for Corporate Social Performance," *Business & Society* 45, 2 (2006): 149–177; Diane L. Swanson, "Toward an integrative strategy of business and society: A research strategy for corporate social performance," *Academy of Management Review* 24, 3 (1999): 506–521.

11. "16 Billion Reasons Why You Should Follow Elon Musk," *The Wall Street Flaneur*, August 28, 2013, http://wallstreetflaneur.com/16-billion-reasons-you-should-follow-elon-musk/#axzz3WBNvV7sK (accessed April 2, 2015).

12. R. Edward Freeman and Lisa Stewart, "Developing Ethical Leadership. *Business Roundtable Institute for Corporate Ethics*, 2006, www.corporate-ethics.org.

13. J.M. Burns, *Leadership* (New York, NY: Harper & Row, 1985).

14. John P. Kotter, "What Leaders Really Do," *Harvard Business Review*, December 2001, http://fs.ncaa.org/Docs/DIII/What%20Leaders%20Really%20Do.pdf (accessed April 2, 2015).

15. Stephen R. Covey, *The 7 Habits of Highly Effective People* (New York, NY: Simon & Schuster, 1989).

16. Archie B. Carroll, "Ethical Leadership: From Moral Managers to Moral Leaders," in *Rights, Relationships and Responsibilities*, Vol. 1, ed. O. C. Ferrell, Sheb True, and Lou Pelton (Kennesaw, GA: Kennesaw State University, 2003), 7–17.

17. Jim Collins, "Leadership Lessons," *Leadership Excellence* 29, 2 (February 2012): 10.

18. Andy Serwer, "Walmart: Bruised in Bentonville," *Fortune* online, April 4, 2005, http://money.cnn.com/magazines/fortune/fortune_archive/2005/04/18/8257005/index.htm (accessed April 2, 2015).

19. Thomas I. White, "Character Development and Business Ethics Education," in *Rights, Relationships and Responsibilities*, Vol. 1, ed. O. C. Ferrell, Sheb True, and Lou Pelton (Kennesaw, GA: Kennesaw State University, 2003), 137–166.

20. Pedro Montoya, "How AIRBUS Group Strengthens Its Anti-Corruption Program through Certification," *Ethic Intelligence*, 2015, http://www.ethic-intelligence.com/experts/5321-airbus-strengthens-anti-corruption-program-certification/ (accessed April 2, 2015).

21. Carroll, "Ethical Leadership," 11.

22. Time Warner Inc., "100 Best Companies to Work For: NuStar Energy," *Fortune*, 2015, http://fortune.com/best-companies/nustar-energy-18/ (accessed April 2, 2015).

23. Lorenzo Patelli and Matteo Pedrini, "Is Tone at the Top Associated with Financial Reporting Aggressiveness?" *Journal of Business Ethics* 126, 1 (2015): 3–19.

24. Michael W. Grojean, Christian Resick, Marcus Dickson, and Brent Smith, "Leaders, Values and Organizational Climate: Examining Leadership Strategies for Establishing an Organizational Climate Regarding Ethics," *Journal of Business Ethics* 55, 3 (2004): 223–241.

25. Whole Foods, "Our Core Values," http://www.wholefoodsmarket.com/company/corevalues.php (accessed April 2, 2015).

26. Daniel J. Brass, Kenneth D Butterfield, and Bruce C. Skaggs, "Relationship and Unethical Behavior: A Social Science Perspective," *Academy of Management Review* 23, 1 (January 1998): 14–31.

27. Linda Klebe Trevino, Gary R. Weaver, David G. Gibson, and Barbara Lay Toffler, "Managing Ethics and Legal Compliance: What Works and What Hurts," *California Management Review* 41, 2 (1999): 131–151; Michael E. Brown and Linda K. Trevino, "Ethical Leadership: A review and future directions," *The Leadership Quarterly* 17, 6 (December 2006): 595–616.

28. Mitchell J. Neubert, Dawn S. Carlson, K. Michele Kacmar, James A. Roberts, and Lawrence B. Chonko, "The Virtuous Influence of Ethical Leadership Behavior: Evidence from the Field," *Journal of Business Ethics* 90, 2 (2009): 157–170.

29. Sean Valentine, Lynn Godkin, Gary M. Fleischman, Roland E. Kidwell, and Karen Page, "Corporate Ethical Values, Group Creativity, Job Satisfaction and Turnover Intention: The Impact of Work Context on Work Response," *Journal of Business Ethics* 98, 3 (2011): 353–372.

30. Fortune, "100 Best Companies to Work For 2009," *CNNMoney*, http://money.cnn.com/magazines/fortune/bestcompanies/2009/snapshots/32.html (accessed April 2, 2015); "The Container Store: An Employee-Centric Retailer," UNM Daniels Fund Business Ethics Initiative, http://danielsethics.mgt.unm.edu/pdf/Container%20Store%20Case.pdf (accessed April 2, 2015); The Container Store," Employee-First Culture," *What We Stand for Blog*, http://standfor.containerstore.com/putting-our-employees-first/ (accessed April 2, 2015).

31. Remi Trudel and June Cotte, "Does It Pay to Be Good?" *MIT Sloan Management Review* 50, 2 (2009): 60–68.

32. Tae Hee Choi and Jinchul Jung, "Ethical Commitment, Financial Performance, and Valuation: An Empirical Investigation of Korean Companies," *Journal of Business Ethics* 81, 2 (2008): 447–463.

33. Jin-Woo Kim, "Assessing the long-term financial performance of ethical companies," *Journal of Targeting, Measurement and Analysis for Marketing* 18, 3/4 (2010): 199–208.

34. Win Swenson, "The Organizational Guidelines' 'Carrot and Stick' Philosophy, and Their Focus on 'Effective' Compliance," In *Corporate Crime in America: Strengthening the "Good Citizenship" Corporation*, 17–26, 1995, Washington, D.C.: U.S. Sentencing Commission.

35. Alexander C. Kaufman, "CEO Slashes $1 Million Salary to Give Lowest-Paid Workers a Raise," *The Huffington Post*, April 15, 2015, http://www.huffingtonpost.com/2015/04/14/gravity-payments-raise_n_7061676.html (accessed April 20, 2015).

36. Lynn Sharp Paine, "Managing for Organizational Integrity," *Harvard Business Review* (1994): 105–117.

37. "Ex-Chairman of Sotheby's Gets Jail Time," *The New York Times*, April 23, 2002, http://www.nytimes.com/2002/04/23/nyregion/ex-chairman-of-sotheby-s-gets-jail-time.html (accessed April 2, 2015).

38. Clive R. Boddy, *Corporate Psychopaths: Organizational Destroyers* (Basingstroke, UK: Palgrave Macmillan, 2011), 23–25: William D. Cohan, "Did Psychopaths Take Over Wall Street Asylum," *Bloomberg*, January 2, 2012, http://www.bloomberg.com/news/2012-01-03/did-psychopaths-take-over-wall-street-asylum-commentary-by-william-cohan.html (accessed April 2, 2015).

39. Adapted from Archie B. Carroll (2003), "Ethical Leadership: From Moral Manager to Moral Leader," In O.C. Ferrell, Sheb L. True, and Lou E. Pelton, *Rights, Relationships, & Responsibilities, Vol. 1* (Kennesaw, GA: Kennesaw State University), 7–17.

40. Kenneth R. Williams, "An Assessment of Moral and Character Education in Initial Entry Training (IET)," *Journal of Military Ethics*, 1 (2010): 41–56.

41. Jim Kouzes and Barry Posner, "Five Best Practices," *Leadership Excellence*, 7 (2009): 3–4.

42. The Associated Press, "Former BP CEO Hayward makes brief appearance at oil spill trial," *CBC News*, February 27, 2013, http://www.cbc.ca/news/business/story/2013/02/27/bp-gulf-spill-trial.html (accessed April 2, 2015).

43. Adapted from Archie B. Carroll (2003), "Ethical Leadership: From Moral Manager to Moral Leader," In O.C. Ferrell, Sheb L. True, and Lou E. Pelton, *Rights, Relationships, & Responsibilities, Vol. 1* (Kennesaw, GA: Kennesaw State University), 7–17.

44. R. Edward Freeman and Lisa Stewart, "Developing Ethical Leadership," *Business Roundtable Institute for Corporate Ethics*, 2006, www.corporate-ethics.org.

45. Quantisoft. "Enhancing Compliance with Sarbanes–Oxley 404," http://www.quantisoft.com/Industries/Ethics.htm (accessed April 2, 2015).

46. Lynn Sharp Paine, "Managing for Organizational Integrity," *Harvard Business Review* (1994): 105–117.

47. Gerdien de Vries, Karen A. Jehn, and Bart W. Terwel, "When Employees Stop Talking and Start Fighting: The Detrimental Effects of Pseudo Voice in Organizations," *Journal of Business Ethics* 105, 2 (2012): 221–230.

48. Susanne Arvidsson, "Communication of Corporate Social Responsibility: A Study of the Views of Management Teams in Large Companies," *Journal of Business Ethics* 96, 3 (2010): 339–354.

49. Al-Karim Samnani, "The Early Stages of Workplace Bullying and How It Becomes Prolonged: The Role of Culture in Predicting Target Responses," *Journal of Business Ethics* 113, 1 (2012): 119–132.

50. Muel Kaptein, "From Inaction to External Whistleblowing: The Influence of the Ethical Culture of Organizations on Employee Responses to Observed Wrongdoing," *Journal of Business Ethics* 98, 3 (2011): 513–530.

51. Kenneth W. Thomas and Ralph H. Kilmann (March 2, 2010). *Thomas-Kilmann Conflict Mode Instrument: Profile and Interpretative Report*. © CPP, Inc.

52. Ibid.

53. Caleb Hannan, "Dish Network, the Meanest Company in America," *Bloomberg Business*, January 2, 2013, http://www.bloomberg.com/bw/articles/2013-01-02/dish-network-the-meanest-company-in-america#p1 (accessed April 2, 2015).

54. Geoffrey James, "When Leaders Cheat, Companies Lose," *Inc.*, February 10, 2014, http://www.inc.com/geoffrey-james/when-leaders-cheat-companies-lose.html (accessed April 2, 2015).

55. Deborah Harrington-Mackin, *Team Building Tool Kit: Tips, Tactics, and Rules for Effective Workplace Teams* (Nashville, TN: New Direction Management Services, Inc., 1994), 21.

56. Kenneth W. Thomas and Ralph H. Kilmann, *Thomas-Kilmann Conflict Mode Instrument: Profile and Interpretative Report*, March 2, 2010. © CPP, Inc.

57. MindToolsTM, "Conflict Resolution," http://www.mindtools.com/pages/article/newLDR_81.htm (accessed April 2, 2015).

58. Joseph P. Folger, Marshall Scott Poole, and Randall K. Stutman, *Working through Conflict: Strategies for Relationships, Groups, and Organizations*, 6th ed. (Upper Saddle River, NJ: Pearson Education Inc., 2009).

59. Ibid.

60. Kenneth W. Thomas and Ralph H. Kilmann, *Thomas-Kilmann Conflict Mode Instrument: Profile and Interpretative Report*, March 2, 2010. © CPP, Inc.

61. Joseph P. Folger, Marshall Scott Poole, and Randall K. Stutman, *Working through Conflict: Strategies for Relationships, Groups, and Organizations*, 6th ed. (Upper Saddle River, NJ: Pearson Education Inc., 2009).

62. N. Leila Trapp, "Staff Attitudes to Talking Openly about Ethical Dilemmas: The Role of Business Ethics Conceptions and Trust," *Journal of Business Ethics* 103, 4 (2011): 543–552.

63. Time Inc., "100 Best Companies to Work for: W.L. Gore & Associates," *Fortune*, 2015, http://fortune.com/best-companies/w-l-gore-associates-17/ (accessed April 2, 2015).

64. "The view from the top, and bottom," *The Economist*, September 24, 2011, http://www.economist.com/node/21530171 (accessed April 2, 2015).

65. C.L. Pearce and C.C. Manz, *The New Silver Bullets of Leadership*: The Importance of Self- and Shared Leadership in Knowledge Work," *Organizational Dynamics* 34, 2 (2005): 130–140.

66. Crystal L. Hoyt and Terry L. Price, "Ethical Decision Making and Leadership: Merging Social Role and Self-Construal Perspectives," *Journal of Business Ethics* 126, 4 (2015): 531–539.

67. Gary T. Hunt, *Communication Skills in the Organization* (Upper Saddle River, NJ: Prentice-Hall, February 1989).

68. Ibid.

69. Robert Gatewood, Robert Taylor, and O.C. Ferrell, *Management* (Homewood, IL: Richard D. Irwin, Inc., 1995).

70. Sally Planalp and Julie Fitness, "Interpersonal Communication Ethics," In George Cheney, Steve May, and Debashish Munshi, *The Handbook of Communication Ethics* (New York, NY: Taylor and Francis, 2011), 135–147.

71. Jack R. Gibb, "Defensive Communication," *Journal of Communication* 11, 3 (September 1961): 141–148.

72. Gary T. Hunt, *Communication Skills in the Organization* (Upper Saddle River, NJ: Prentice-Hall, 1989).

73. Cass R. Sunstein, "The Law of Group Polarization," John M. Olin Law & Economics Working Paper 91(1999) (2D Series), http://www.law.uchicago.edu/files/files/91.CRS_.Polarization.pdf (accessed April 2, 2015).

74. Mary Ellen Guffey, Kathleen Rhodes, and Patricia Rogen, *Business Communication: Process and Product* (Toronto, Canada: Nelson Education Ltd., 2010).

75. Robert Gatewood, Robert Taylor, and O.C. Ferrell, *Management* (Homewood, IL: Richard D. Irwin, Inc., 1995), 530.

76. Cynthia Burgraff Torppa, *Nonverbal Communication: Teaching Your Child the Skills of Social Success*, 2009, http://ohioline.osu.edu/flm03/FS10.pdf (accessed April 2, 2015).

77. Gary T. Hunt, *Communication Skills in the Organization* (Upper Saddle River, NJ: Prentice-Hall, 1989).

78. Susan M. Heathfield, "Top Ten Employee Complaints," About.com, http://humanresources.about.com/od/retention/a/emplo_complaint.htm (accessed April 2, 2015).

79. Ibid.

80. SK Collins and KS Collins, "Micromanagement—A costly management style," *Radiology Management* 24, 6 (2002): 32–35.

81. G. Yukl, "Managerial Leadership: A Review of Theory and Research," *Journal of Management* 15, 2 (June 1989): 251–289.

82. Ryan S. Bisel, Katherine M. Kelley, Nicole A. Ploeger, and Jake Messersmith, "Workers' Moral Mum Effect: On Facework and Unethical Behavior in the Workplace," *Communication Studies* 62, 2 (2011): 153–170.

83. Kate O'Sullivan, "Business Outlook Survey: Proceeding with Caution," *CFO*, January/February 2012, 37–42; Alix Stuart, "How to Direct a Risk Team," *CFO*, April 2012, 46–53.

84. PR Newswire, "Trust and Ethics in the Workplace Have Been Battered by the Recession, Deloitte's 2010 Ethics & Workplace Survey Finds," July 26, 2010, http://www.prnewswire.com/news-releases/trust-and-ethics-in-the-workplace-have-been-battered-by-the-recession-deloittes-2010-ethics--workplace-survey-finds-99228989.html (accessed April 2, 2015).

85. Dori Meinert, "Creating an Ethical Workplace," *Society for Human Resource Management* 59, 4 (April 1, 2014), http://www.shrm.org/publications/hrmagazine/editorialcontent/2014/0414/pages/0414-ethical-workplace-culture.aspx (accessed April 2, 2015).

86. Robert Gatewood, Robert Taylor, and O.C. Ferrell, *Management* (Homewood, IL: Richard D. Irwin, Inc., 1995).

87. K. Michele Kacmar, Martha C. Andrews, Kenneth J. Harris, and Bennett J. Tepper, "Ethical Leadership and Subordinate Outcomes: The Mediating Role of Organizational Politics and the Moderating Role of Political Skill," *Journal of Business Ethics* 15, 1 (2013): 33–44.

88. C. Chang, C.C. Rosen, and P.E. Levy, "The relationship between perceptions of organizational politics and employee attitudes, strain, and behavior: A meta-analytic examination," *Academy of Management Journal* 52, 4 (2009): 779–801; K. Michele Kacmar, Martha C. Andrews, Kenneth J. Harris, and Bennett J. Tepper, "Ethical Leadership and Subordinate Outcomes: The Mediating Role of Organizational Politics and the Moderating Role of Political Skill," *Journal of Business Ethics* 115, 1 (2013): 33–44.

89. J. Pfeffer, "Understanding power in organizations," *California Management Review* 34 (1992): 29–35; K. Michele Kacmar, Martha C. Andrews, Kenneth J. Harris, and Bennett J. Tepper, "Ethical Leadership and Subordinate Outcomes: The Mediating Role of Organizational Politics and the Moderating Role of Political Skill," *Journal of Business Ethics* 115, 1 (2013): 33–44.

90. Ozgur Demirtas, "Ethical Leadership Influence at Organizations: Evidence from the Field," *Journal of Business Ethics* 126, 2 (2015): 273–284.

91. Jingyu Gao, Robert Greenberg, and Bernard Wong-On-Wing, "Whistleblowing Intentions of Lower-Level Employees: The Effect of Reporting Channel, Bystanders, and Wrongdoer Power Status," *Journal of Business Ethics* 126, 1 (2015): 85–99.

92. Centrica "Our Stories," March 26, 2015, http://www.centrica.com/index.asp?pageid=1130&blogid=1045 (accessed April 2, 2015).

93. Daniel J. Brass, Kenneth D. Butterfield, and Bruce C. Skaggs, "Relationship and Unethical Behavior: A Social Science Perspective," *Academy of Management Review* 23, 1 (January 1998): 14–31.

94. Cam Caldwell, Linda A. Hayes, and Do Tien Long, "Leadership, Trustworthiness, and Ethical Stewardship," *Journal of Business Ethics* 96, 4 (2010): 497–512.

95. Al Gini and Ronald M. Green, "Three Critical Characteristics of Leadership: Character, Stewardship, Experience," *Business & Society Review* 119, 4 (2014): 435–446.

96. Jim Collins, "Be Great Now." *Inc.*, June 2012, 72–73.

97. Robert Kerr, John Garvin, Norma Heaton, and Emily Boyle, "Emotional intelligence and leadership effectiveness," *Leadership & Organizational Development Journal* 27, 4 (2006): 265–279.

98. "Seventy-One Percent of Employers Say They Value Emotional Intelligence over IQ, According to CareerBuilder Survey," *CareerBuilder*, August 18, 2011, http://www.careerbuilder.com/share/aboutus/pressreleasesdetail.aspx?id=pr652&sd=8/18/2011&ed=8/18/2099 (accessed April 2, 2015).

99. Lynn Brewer, Robert Chandler, and O.C. Ferrell, *Managing Risks for Corporate Integrity: How to Survive an Ethical Misconduct Disaster* (Mason, OH: Thomson, 2006).

100. Richard Boyatzis and Annie McKee, *Resonant Leadership: Renewing Yourself and Connecting with Others through Mindfulness, Hope and Compassion* (Boston, MA: Harvard Business Review Press, 2005); Bruce Rosenstein, "Resonant leader is one in tune with himself, others," *USA Today*, November 27, 2005, http://usatoday30.usatoday.com/money/books/reviews/2005-11-27-resonant-book-usat_x.htm (accessed April 2, 2015).

101. Peter Ubel, "Do Starbucks Employees Have More Emotional Intelligence than Your Physician?" *Forbes*, November 2, 2012, http://www.forbes.com/sites/peterubel/2012/11/02/do-starbucks-employees-have-more-emotional-intelligence-than-your-physician/ (accessed April 2, 2015).

102. J. M. Burns, *Leadership* (New York, NY: Harper & Row, 1985).

103. Royston Greenwood, Roy Suddaby, and C. R. Hinings, "Theorizing Change: The Role of Professional Associations in the Transformation of Institutionalized Fields," *Academy of Management Journal* 45, 1 (January 2002): 58–80.

104. Eric Pillmore, "How Tyco International Remade Its Corporate Governance," speech at Wharton Business School, September 2006.

105. Shuili Du, Valérie Swaen, Adam Lindgreen, and Sankar Sen, "The Roles of Leadership Styles in Corporate Social Responsibility," *Journal of Business Ethics* 114, 1 (2013): 155–169.

106. New Belgium Brewing, "Our Company," http://www.newbelgium.com/Brewery/company.aspx (accessed April 2, 2015).

107. Bill George, Peter Sims, Andrew M. McLean, and Diana Mayer, "Discovering Your Authentic Leadership," *Harvard Business Review*, February 2007, http://hbr.org/2007/02/discovering-your-authentic-leadership/ar/1 (accessed April 2, 2015).

108. Stephen R. Covey, *Principle-Centered Leadership* (New York, NY: Franklin Covey Co., 1991), 102–105.

109. Hilary Hanson, "Desmond Hague, Puppy-Kicking CEO, Ousted from Job," *The Huffington Post*, September 2, 2014, http://www.huffingtonpost.com/2014/09/02/desmond-hague-fired-centerplate-puppy-kicking_n_5754316.html (accessed April 2, 2015).

110. Lynn Brewer, Robert Chandler, and O.C. Ferrell, *Managing Risks for Corporate Integrity: How to Survive an Ethical Misconduct Disaster* (Mason, OH: Thomson, 2006).

111. O.C. Ferrell, John Fraedrich, Linda Ferrell, *Business Ethics: Ethical Decision Making and Cases*, 9th ed. (Mason, OH: South-Western Cengage Learning, 2013).

112. Robert C. Chandler, J.D. Wallace, and D.P. Ferguson, "Corporate Reconciliation with Critical Stakeholders through Communication: An Empirical Assessment of Efficacy, Ethicality, and Utilization Likelihood of Benoit's Image Restoration Strategies in Crisis Management Situational Contingencies," July 2002, unpublished manuscript presented at the International Communication Association, Seoul, Republic of Korea.

113. Open Compliance and Ethics Group, *GRC 360°: Perspectives on Governance, Risk, Compliance & Culture*, Fall 2005, 13.

CHAPTER 12

SUSTAINABILITY: ETHICAL AND SOCIAL RESPONSIBILITY DIMENSIONS

AN ETHICAL DILEMMA*

Jared worked for Darwin Chemical Company (DCC) for four years. DCC is a multinational corporation with subsidiaries in eight countries. About six months ago Jared was offered a job as a plant manager for its Chinese subsidiary.

"We don't usually offer this opportunity to someone who has only been with the company for a few years," said Jonathan, Jared's supervisor. "But in the short time you've been with the firm, we feel you've shown a lot of management potential. We also see from your résumé you spent a semester abroad in China as part of your MBA program. We believe this makes you a better fit than other candidates since you are more familiar with the culture." Jared saw this promotion as a stepping stone to a much higher position within the company. He agreed to the promotion and arrived in China a few months later.

Jared found the transition in dealing with another culture challenging, but rewarding. He especially appreciated his assistant manager Bojing, who helped him learn the ropes and communicate with the employees. DCC gave Jared free rein in running the plant. Its main measure of performance is the bottom line, and employees are well aware of this fact.

A few weeks ago Jared noticed something odd about the plant's waste disposal procedures of one of its more popular chemicals. Developing this particular chemical involves a complex process, and every liter of water used results in half a liter of chemical waste. Company procedures stated this waste had to be disposed of safely. The problem was the paperwork employees were required to submit and file with corporate detailing how they performed the procedure was missing. In fact, Jared could not find any records of any paperwork ever being filed.

Jared approached Bojing about the issue. "The paperwork is more of a formality," Bojing replied. "Nobody seems to follow up on it."

"That's beside the point," Jared said. "We need to have these systems in place to make sure we are disposing of waste properly."

After more questions, Bojing finally confessed that while they usually tried to dispose of the waste properly, in a time crunch the entire process took too long. This resulted in employees sometimes dumping the waste in the local river.

Jared was shocked. The local river was not large, and many of the rural villagers in the area used it for drinking water. "But this is a toxic chemical! How long has this been going on?"

"Several years now," Bojing stated. "However, the previous plant manager told us not to worry. He said when mixed with water the chemical byproduct loses its potency. You would need to consume a lot for it to be harmful."

Jared immediately took action. He ordered a halt to the operations to investigate the matter further. He called the employees of the plant together and stated that from then on they would be following all procedures for disposing of waste properly. He also reported the situation to his supervisor Jonathan back home and told him about the previous plant manager's knowledge and noncompliance with proper waste disposal.

When Jared called Jonathan, he detailed all of the changes he made and was planning to make. Jonathan congratulated him on detecting and immediately putting a stop to the improper disposal practices. Then Jared started to discuss how the company should report the situation to the Chinese authorities and discuss cleanup methods.

Jonathan was quiet for a while. "Look, Jared, you must understand that in China, water pollution and improper disposal of waste is more accepted than it is here. I'm not sure we should be worried about cleaning up the river, particularly as other companies in the area likely use the river to get rid of waste. We are not the only factory around there, after all."

"But Jonathan, people who use the river for drinking water might get sick," Jared replied.

"I don't know, Jared. A cleanup would cost millions of dollars, and we'd probably be cleaning up the mess of other factories in the area. Additionally, we would probably be given heavy fines since we're a foreign company. Besides, you said yourself people would have to consume a lot of this chemical waste before they got sick."

Jared hung up the phone, more confused than ever. He thought perhaps Jonathan was right. Maybe he was overreacting. However, later that day some reports he requested showed up. The reports stated that local fishing in the area had decreased dramatically in the past few years, and some of the fishes were deformed or sickly. Jared was worried the chemicals could be impacting the fish population in the river. If this was the case, what kind of an impact might it have on the rural villagers using the river as drinking water and eating the fish?

QUESTIONS | EXERCISES

1. Describe the ethical dilemma Jared faces.
2. How does Jonathan rationalize his reasons for not reporting the pollution?
3. How might the water pollution impact different stakeholders?

*This case is strictly hypothetical; any resemblance to real persons, companies, or situations is coincidental.

Environmental sustainability has become mainstream for businesses. Many consumers are willing to buy sustainable products, especially when there is no increase in price, while other consumers are willing to pay more for such products. The reality is we live in a world with limited resources being used up by more than seven billion people. These global environmental issues have numerous consequences for business. The collective participation of employees in making sustainable decisions can result in business success and at the same time contribute to finding positive solutions to questions about the use of natural resources and the well-being of society.

Our focus is how business ethics can be integrated into strategic business decisions. In most firms guiding principles, values, and norms create an ethical culture that shapes decisions. Artifacts of ethical decision making reflecting the ethical culture include statements and strategic plans such as policies about sustainability initiatives. While most decisions can have ethical implications, organizations must be mindful that inaction concerning the natural environment creates a host of ethical issues. Using non-renewable natural resources can inflict damage on consumers, communities, and society at large. The BP *Deepwater Horizon* oil spill, the second largest oil spill in the world, destroyed not only marine life but also put the livelihoods of fisherman and other industries relying on the Gulf of Mexico on hold, resulting in massive losses for the regions bordering the Gulf. Sustainability issues need to be evaluated by relevant stakeholders, and organizations are expected to make accurate and truthful disclosures.

Our purpose is to outline key issues and risks in making business decisions that impact the natural environment. This is not a chapter on the scientific evaluation of environmental ethical decisions. Identifying issues and risks provides opportunities for responsible individual and organizational responses to promote sustainability. We examine the concept of sustainability and the concerns of various stakeholders about our future. Next, we look at some of the major issues that relate to sustainability. We then examine some of the major environmental agencies and legislation that impact business sustainability practices. We look at businesses' responses to sustainability issues, including green marketing and greenwashing. Finally, we link sustainability to a stakeholder orientation that addresses the ethical and financial concerns of organizations. Firms that adopt a stakeholder orientation in their sustainability initiatives need to conduct stakeholder assessments and environmental audits to ensure they meet stakeholder needs while not overlooking financial performance.

DEFINING SUSTAINABILITY

Sustainability from a strategic business perspective is the potential for the long-term well-being of the natural environment, including all biological entities, as well as mutually beneficial interactions among nature and individuals, organizations, and business strategies. Sustainability includes the assessment and improvement of business strategies, economic sectors, work practices, technologies, and lifestyles while maintaining the natural environment. **Sustainable development** has become a top concern for many businesses as it involves meeting the needs of the present without compromising the ability of future generations to meet their own needs. Before going any further, you should note that "sustainability" can have different definitions, particularly in different cultures. In Europe, for example, sustainability includes both environmental and economic connotations. In the United States, sustainability is associated more with environmental concerns. The Brundtland Report developed by the United Nations World Commission on Environment and Development views sustainable development in terms of environmental, economic, and social well-being for both current and future generations.[1] These different definitions make it complex for businesses to determine what to evaluate when investigating ways to increase the sustainable impact of their organizations. For the purposes of this chapter, we reiterate our earlier definition of sustainability with an emphasis on the natural environment.

HOW SUSTAINABILITY RELATES TO ETHICAL DECISION MAKING AND SOCIAL RESPONSIBILITY

Sustainability falls into the social responsibility domain of maximizing positive and minimizing negative impacts on stakeholders. As a result, sustainability issues fit into our stakeholder model addressed in Chapter 2. Because most stakeholders have concerns about some aspects of the natural environment, organizations should respond to those issues in their strategies, policies, and operations. Decisions in this area relate to assessing risks, monitoring legal compliance, and avoiding misconduct within the environment.

A corporate culture that includes a sustainability agenda or a corporate social responsibility (CSR) report can create long-term favorable stakeholder responses.[2] In addition, corporate social responsibility performance can increase employees' company identification and commitment.[3] Values are an important part of an ethical culture and support an organization's sustainability agenda.[4] Research indicates employees' exposure to sustainability activities increases the ability to implement sustainability programs as well as economic benefits.[5] Many firms use sustainable business practices to demonstrate their social commitment through such activities as sponsoring cleanup events, recycling, modifying manufacturing processes to reduce waste and pollution, using more alternative energy sources, and generally reevaluating the effects of their products on the natural environment. Table 12–1 provides a list of some of the world's most sustainable companies. Some companies are even becoming involved politically. For example, Exxon Mobil's CEO Rex Tillerson encouraged the U.S. Congress to enact a tax on greenhouse gas emissions and views climate change

TABLE 12–1 World's Most Sustainable Companies

Company	Industry	Country
Biogen Idec	Health care	United States
Allergan	Pharmaceuticals	United States
Adidas	Textiles, apparel, luxury goods	United States
Keppel Land	Real estate management and development	Singapore
Kesko	Food and staples retailing	Finland
BMW	Automobiles	Germany
Reckitt Benckiser	Household products	United States
Centrica	Multi-utilities	United Kingdom
Schneider Electric	Electrical equipment	France
Danske	Banks	Denmark

Source: Kathryn Dill, "The World's Most Sustainable Companies 2015," *Forbes*, January 21, 2015, http://www.forbes.com/sites/kathryndill/2015/01/21/the-worlds-most-sustainable-companies-2015/ (accessed February 3, 2015).

as a risk management problem for the firm.[6] Companies that do not recognize the potential impact of green programs on future profits and corporate reputation may pay later.

Sustainability, social responsibility, and ethics should not be used interchangeably. Some take the approach that if an organization is sustainable then it is also ethical. However, an organization cannot ignore basic principles, values, and legal obligations to society. For instance, Walmart made a name for itself in sustainability with its attempt to sell more organic food, develop more environmentally friendly supply chain practices, and invest in other green alternatives. Yet allegations it used bribery to conduct business in Mexico demonstrates that although it has made great strides in sustainability, it has experienced lapses in other areas of ethical decision making. Because ethical decisions relate to specific conduct and relationships in the decision-making process, it becomes clear that sustainability is only one aspect of ethical decision making.

Additionally, social responsibility is a much broader area than sustainability. Examples of social responsibility topics relating to various stakeholders include consumer protection, corporate governance, employee well-being, and more. All of these social responsibility areas have an ethical decision-making dimension. Figure 12–1 describes how ethical decisions impact sustainability as a component of CSR.

The concept of CSR—and by relation sustainability—has become a major initiative because of stakeholder expectations. Common questions asked of companies might include how they use energy resources, how they control for pollution, whether they recycle, and how pure their food products might be. This prompted organizations like Best Buy to release corporate social responsibility reports to answer these questions. In the United States such reports are optional, whereas in the European Union they are mandatory for publicly held corporations.

There are four reasons social responsibility became such an issue for organizations. First, *socially responsible activities such as sustainable business practices can create competitive advantages.* Consumers' buying behavior, the interaction of stakeholders with representatives of the organization, advertising practices, and participation in social media can help a firm stay on top of market knowledge and create beneficial relationships with stakeholders. Second, *both positive and negative information about products and organizations became more available.* Therefore, consumers and other stakeholders gained power and can influence the economic success of the company.[7] Third, *organizations can use their products and brand identity to create social value, quality, and consumer loyalty.* Finally, in this interconnected society, *companies use their sustainable and socially responsible decisions to differentiate their firms and promote their products.* Patagonia, for instance, uses organic cotton in its apparel. As a result of these reasons, social responsibility is becoming part of the budget, and sustainability is becoming a tool for ethical decision making and financial performance.[8] By responding to multiple stakeholders, the firm taps into valuable resources and provides a means to forge enduring relationships of strategic importance.[9]

FIGURE 12–1 **Ethical Decisions Affect Sustainability as a Component of Social Responsibility**

Examples of Social Responsibility Concerns

| Ethical Issue Awareness | → | Social Issues
Employee Well-Being
Legal Responsibilities
Sustainability
Philanthropy
Consumer Protection
Corporate Governance | → | Decisions |

Stakeholder Evaluations

GLOBAL ENVIRONMENTAL ISSUES

The protection of air, water, land, biodiversity, and renewable natural resources emerged as a major issue in the twentieth century in the face of increasing evidence that mankind was putting pressure on the long-term sustainability of these resources. As the environmental movement sounded the alarm over these issues, governments responded with environmental protection laws during the 1970s. In recent years, companies are increasingly incorporating these issues into their overall business strategies. Most of these issues are the focus of concerned citizens as well as government and corporate efforts. Some nonprofit organizations have stepped forward to provide leadership in gaining the cooperation of diverse groups in responsible business activities. For example, the Coalition for Environmentally Responsible Economies (CERES), a union of businesses, consumer groups, environmentalists, and other stakeholders, established a set of goals for environmental performance. By being proactive in addressing these issues, companies can reduce their environmental impact and generate a reputation as an eco-responsible company.

In the following sections, we examine some of the most significant environmental issues facing business and society today, including air pollution, acid rain, global warming, water pollution and water quantity, land pollution, waste management, deforestation, urban sprawl, biodiversity, and genetically modified foods.

Atmospheric

Among the most far-reaching and controversial environmental issues are those that relate to the air we breathe. These include air pollution, acid rain, and global warming.

AIR POLLUTION   As emerging economies become more industrialized, air pollution is an increasingly serious issue. Air pollution typically arises from three different sources: stationary sources such as factories and power plants; mobile sources such as cars, trucks, planes, and trains; and natural sources such as windblown dust and volcanic eruptions.[10] These sources discharge gases, as well as particulates, that can be carried long distances by surface winds or linger when air stagnation occurs. Air pollution can cause markedly shorter life spans, along with chronic respiratory problems (for example, asthma, bronchitis, and allergies) in humans and animals. The most susceptible people are children, seniors, and endurance athletes. Some of the toxic chemicals associated with air pollution contribute to birth defects, cancer, and brain, nerve, and respiratory system damage. Air pollution harms plants, animals, and bodies of water. Ozone creates a haze that reduces visibility and interferes with traveling.[11]

Recently, another air pollution concern emerged with the increased use of hydraulic fracturing, or fracking. Fracking occurs when water, chemicals, and sand are pumped into a well at high pressure. This process fractures the rock layers deep in the ground, allowing natural gas to be extracted. Because the United States has a great amount of shale, fracking can increase the country's energy independence. Combustion of natural gas is more carbon efficient—it releases about half the particulates and gaseous emissions of oil and coal.[12] However, critics are concerned because companies do not have to publicly list the chemicals used in fracking operations. For this reason, the Environmental Protection Agency is considering rules that would require companies to disclose the chemicals pumped into the ground.[13]

ACID RAIN   In addition to the health risks posed by air pollution, when nitrous oxides and sulfur dioxides are emitted from manufacturing facilities, the compounds are exposed to air and rain and form new compounds, resulting in what is commonly called acid rain. This phenomenon contributes to the deaths of many valuable forests and lakes in North America and Europe. Acid rain corrodes paint and deteriorates stone, leaving automobiles, buildings, and cultural resources such as architecture and outside art vulnerable.[14] Cleaning up emissions from factories and cars is one way to reduce acid rain. Acid rain legislation in the United States appears effective. Research shows sulfates in rain (a major contributor to acid rain) in the northeastern United States have decreased 40 percent.[15]

GLOBAL WARMING   When carbon dioxide and other gases collect in Earth's atmosphere, they trap the sun's heat like a greenhouse and prevent Earth's surface from cooling. Without this process, the planet becomes too cold to sustain life. However, during the twentieth century, the burning of fossil fuels—gasoline, natural gas, oil, and coal—accelerated dramatically, increasing the concentration of "greenhouse" gases (carbon dioxide, methane, nitrogen oxides, and fluorinated gases) in Earth's atmosphere. At the same time, chlorofluorocarbons—from refrigerants, coolants, and aerosol cans—are believed to be the cause of a giant hole in the Earth's atmospheric ozone layer. The ozone layer filters out the sun's harmful ultraviolet light. To further complicate things, while the United States and China give off the most greenhouse gases, developing nations like India are going to make up an increasing percentage of overall emissions. Emerging economies are also more likely to use coal, which is the dirtiest of all fossil fuels and the most expensive to control. Because controlling the levels of pollutants is costly, businesses have to decide whether to take action and spend resources to control these gases or take a wait-and-see approach.

Global warming remains a hotly debated issue, especially among scientists, politicians, environmental groups, and industries. Scientific proof of global warming can be difficult as the test tube for global warming is the Earth and its atmosphere. The Earth goes through natural heating and cooling cycles. However, many scientists believe that concentrations of greenhouse gases in the atmosphere accelerate global warming. Greenhouse gas accumulations increased dramatically in the past century, with 2014 being the hottest year on record to date.[16] The accumulation of five gases increased average temperatures by over 1° Fahrenheit over the last century. This is sufficient to increase the rate of polar ice sheet melting. For the first time in thousands of years, ships are able to cross through areas of the North Pole previously covered with ice. Climate change also affects weather. For instance, climate change is blamed for making northern countries more prone to flooding and southern countries more drought-ridden. As the polar icecaps melt, scientists fear rising sea levels will flood many coastal areas and submerge low-lying island nations. The Arctic is warming twice as fast as the rest of the planet, resulting in increased melting and habitat loss for Arctic animals such as the polar bear. However, the melting Arctic also provides the ability for ships once blocked by ice to travel more efficiently. Geologists believe the arctic region holds huge oil and gas reserves. For this reason, countries bordering the Arctic are eager to use these new passages for oil and gas exploration.[17]

One attempt at addressing global warming is the **Kyoto Protocol** created in 1997. This protocol is an international treaty meant to curb global greenhouse gas emissions by having countries voluntarily reduce national outputs. The United States did not ratify the treaty and therefore is not bound to it. Since 1997 the Kyoto Protocol has been highly unpopular among polluting multinational corporations. Signing the treaty required slashing their level of greenhouse gas emissions by 6 percent of their 1990 levels. U.S. leaders

DEBATE ISSUE
TAKE A STAND

The Impact of Carbon Restrictions

To combat global warming the Obama administration is using the wide-scale reach of the Clean Air Act to push through regulations placing limits on air pollution. This extends the power of the Environmental Protection Agency to regulate sources of greenhouse gases. One major goal is to obtain a 30 percent reduction in emissions from coal-powered plants by 2030.

The new regulations could have major benefits for the nation. The average age of U.S. coal plants is 42 years, making them less efficient than newer coal plants. Power plants also account for 38 percent of the nation's carbon emissions. Stricter regulation of power plants could reduce carbon emissions and hinder global warming.

On the other hand, many utilities see the regulations as too burdensome and believe they will result in lost jobs. States such as Arkansas would also be affected due to their reliance on coal-powered plants. This has led the EPA to reconsider the timetable and provide more flexibility to states in implementing these changes.[24]

1. Carbon emissions regulations will benefit both the nation and the environment in the long-run.

2. Carbon emissions regulations will be detrimental to the nation because it will cause many to lose their jobs.

feared compliance would jeopardize U.S. businesses and the economy.[18] The treaty went into effect in 2005, and by 2006 the number of signatory nations topped 150.

In 2010 most of the world's nations agreed to a package of climate initiatives called the **Cancun Package**. The agreement called for industrialized countries to cut greenhouse gas emissions and create a $100 billion a year green fund by 2020 to help poorer countries. The goal was to limit global warming to less than 3.6° Fahrenheit above pre-industrial levels. The United States, China, Japan, and India did not agree to a binding climate treaty but did discuss emissions reductions.[19] Two years later another attempt was made to develop a universal, legally binding international agreement to cut greenhouse gas emissions. Called the Doha Gateway Agreement, it is an amendment to the Kyoto Protocol. The agreement calls for both developed and developing countries to reduce greenhouse gas emissions. The commitment period for this global agreement will last until 2020.[20]

Coal is another area of contention among different countries. Burning coal contributes to air pollution by releasing large amounts of gaseous and particulate emissions into the atmosphere. Some countries are combating coal usage by implementing cap-and-trade programs. A cap-and-trade program sets carbon emissions limits (caps) for businesses, countries, or individuals. Companies are given a certain amount of carbon they are allowed to emit, and to legally emit anything beyond the limit requires a company to purchase carbon credits from another company that does not pollute as much. The EU, which has been at the forefront of emissions reductions, mandated and implemented a cap-and-trade program on carbon emissions, known as the European Union Emission Trading Scheme. Today the European Union accounts for 11 percent of greenhouse gas emissions, significantly lower than the United States (16 percent) and China (29 percent).[21] Efforts to create a cap-and-trade program in the United States have met with much criticism, but most states in the United States have a form of cap-and-trade. Additionally, the Supreme Court ruled that the administration can impose new regulations on coal-fired power plants to cut emissions 30 percent below 2005 levels by 2030.[22] Unfortunately, coal burning is also the main source of electricity in many countries. In Poland 90 percent of electricity is generated using coal.[23] Coal is less expensive compared to renewable energy, representing a major dilemma between the well-being of the environment and humanity.

Water

Water is emerging as the most important and contested resource of the twenty-first century. Nothing is more important to human survival, yet fresh water is being polluted and consumed at an unprecedented rate. More than 780 million people lack access to improved or uncontaminated water sources; over 2.5 billion people live without basic sanitation; and only half of rural populations have access to improved sanitation facilities, versus 80 percent of those living in urban areas.[25] In order to remain viable, all businesses must think about water conservation, purification, and allocation.

WATER POLLUTION   Water pollution is one of the biggest contributors to illnesses in developing countries. Chemicals found in commonly used fertilizers and pesticides can drain into water supplies with each rainfall. Mercury, a common chemical found in batteries and some household products, is another concern as it contaminates oceans and therefore human food supplies. Even in the United States, which has one of the safest drinking water supplies in the world, pollution remains a problem. Two officials from Freedom Industries were found guilty of water pollution after a chemical leak polluted the water supply for 300,000 West Virginia residents.[26] Pollutants come from a wide variety of sources in today's industrialized world, and many of them have unknown side effects on people and wildlife. Water pollution associated with fracking is also a major issue. Chemicals and methane have been released into water sources from fracking operations.[27] The waste stream causes pollution in aquifers and can increase the number of earthquakes in the area. Ohio has had earthquakes thought to be a result of fracking activities. These concerns led France to abolish hydraulic fracturing.[28] Table 12–2 lists common causes of global water pollution.

For some corporations the sustainability of water has become a major consideration. For example, Unilever is developing products that require 50 percent less water associated with consumer usage.[29] Levi's manufactured 100,000 women's jeans using 100 percent recycled water.[30] Even energy companies are investigating new ways to reduce water usage. Alberta-based energy services firm GasFrac developed a fracking method that does not use water. General Electric and Halliburton are investigating similar technologies to reduce the environmental impact of fracking operations.[31]

TABLE 12–2 Facts about Water Pollution

1. In developing countries as much as 80 percent of illnesses are linked to poor water and sanitation conditions.

2. Agriculture is the biggest water user and accounts for 70 percent of global water withdrawals.

3. Everyday, 2 million tons of untreated sewage, industrial and agricultural waste are put into some water source.

4. Nearly one out of every five deaths of children under the age of five is due to a water-related disease.

5. About 60 percent of the world's 227 biggest rivers have interrupted stream flows because of dams or other infrastructure.

6. More than half of the world's primary schools do not have access to water or sanitation facilities.

7. Nitrate is the most common chemical contaminant in groundwater aquifers, and nitrate levels have risen 36 percent in global waterways since 1990.

8. For every $1 invested in clean water, there is an economic return of between $3 and $34.

Sources: The Water Project, "Facts about Water: Statistics of the Water Crisis," August 12, 2014, http://thewaterproject.org/water_stats (accessed March 9, 2015); Pacific Institute, "World Water Quality Facts and Statistics," *World Water Day 2010*, March 22, 2010, http://www.pacinst.org/wp-content/uploads/sites/21/2013/02/water_quality_facts_and_stats3.pdf (accessed March 9, 2015).

While environmental groups in the United States criticize U.S. water policy, special interests make it even more difficult to regulate water pollution in other parts of the world. Tougher regulations are needed globally to address pollution from activities such as the dumping of waste into the ocean, large animal-feeding operations, logging sites, public roads, parking lots, oil spills, and industrial waste created by production operations.

WATER QUANTITY   In addition to concerns about the quality of water, some parts of the globe are increasingly worried about its quantity. Water use has increased dramatically in the last two decades, creating serious consequences for the global water supply and for business. For instance, many rivers and streams are drying up, and droughts are diminishing farmers' ability to grow crops.[32] It is estimated that by 2030, almost half of the world's population will live in areas with major water stress.

Proactive companies are facing this reality and coming forward with solutions. For instance, Starbucks installed a manually operated pump faucet to replace regular turn-on fixtures in their stores, estimated to save approximately 100 gallons of water per store each day. Volkswagen set a target to reduce its water consumption by 25 percent by 2018. To reach its goal, the company studied its water usage to gain a broader understanding of its corporate impact to target water reduction activities more effectively.

Land

Land sustainability issues include everything from pollution and waste to loss of biodiversity and genetically modified food. These ethical issues are decreasing the use of viable land for human and animal habitation. Because businesses generate waste, contribute to urban sprawl, and often require the use of hard-to-restore natural resources, they have an ethical responsibility to minimize their harmful impact on the land.

LAND POLLUTION   Land pollution results from the dumping of residential and industrial wastes, strip mining, and poor forest conservation. Such pollution causes health problems in humans, jeopardizes wildlife habitats, causes erosion, alters watercourses (leading to flooding), and can eventually poison groundwater supplies. China is at the epicenter of a debate over pollution. Chinese officials revealed that soil pollution is a serious problem, perhaps more so than air and water pollution. Much of the soil contamination in China comes from arsenic, a byproduct from mining operations.[33] However, mining also creates many jobs for the Chinese economy. While soil pollution may not be as much of a problem in other countries, balancing the needs of stakeholders, including consumers, businesses, the environment, and society at large, is an important ethical consideration. In order to reduce pollution around the planet, all businesses must become aware of and accept responsibility for the problem of pollution.

Trying to pinpoint who is responsible for environmental degradation is not always easy, especially when it involves different countries. The exact cost of damages is also easily disputed. Royal Dutch Shell acknowledged that its Trans Niger Pipeline had experienced two spills that contaminated water supplies and harmed fisherman in a community within the Niger Delta, but it disputed the cost of damages. When talks broke down, a legal battle ensued between the company and the community. Royal Dutch Shell eventually reached an out-of-court settlement for $80 million, one of the largest environmental payouts in Nigeria.[34]

WASTE MANAGEMENT   One of the biggest factors in land pollution is the dumping of waste into landfills. American consumers are by far the world's biggest wasters. The nation has up to 40,000 abandoned landfills that are often left untreated and are filled with plastics and other materials that can take 1,000 years to degrade. The United Arab Emirates and Bangladesh have all banned plastic grocery bags, and Ireland and Washington D.C. charge grocery-goers for plastic bags.[35] Some stores such as Whole Foods banned plastic bags voluntarily, and other companies offer incentives for consumers to use more recyclable materials such as canvas grocery bags. This is particularly important in Asia, where studies have found that plastic waste from countries such as China and Indonesia are washing out to sea.[36]

Electronic waste is becoming a big problem since it can release harmful toxins into the air and water. Increasingly, electronics firms are pressured to take back used electronics for recycling. Large chains such as Best Buy now offer e-cycling to keep this waste out of landfills. 3M voluntarily stopped making Scotchguard, a successful product for 40 years with $300 million in sales, after tests showed it did not decompose in the environment.[37] Other organizations like Terracycle organized a business around turning trash into sellable products. Many stakeholders believe companies that produce the goods should be responsible for their proper disposal and recycling. Companies, on the other hand, argue this practice would be too expensive and argue for greater responsibility on the part of individuals. Perhaps a more suitable solution would be to balance environmental responsibility between companies, governments, and individuals.

One solid-waste problem is the result of rapid innovations in computer hardware, which render machines obsolete after just 18 months. Today, hundreds of millions of computers have reached obsolescence and tens of millions are expected to end up in landfills. Cell phones are another problem, with billions destined for landfills. Computers and cell phones contain such toxic substances as lead, mercury, and polyvinyl chloride, which leach into the soil and contaminate groundwater when disposed of improperly. The Environmental Protection Agency (EPA) hosts its own electronics recycling program, stores like Staples and Best Buy offer limited recycling programs, and companies like Dell and Samsung are all seeking to extend the availability of recycling for their products.[38] Laws are also changing how consumers discard their old electronics. Many states, including Minnesota, Connecticut, North Carolina, and New Jersey, banned e-waste from landfills. Instead, it must be recycled properly.[39]

DEFORESTATION   The world's forests are being destroyed at a rate of 46,000 to 58,000 square miles annually.[40] The reasons for this wide-scale destruction are varied. Because of the boom in biofuels, Southeast Asia and the Pacific regions cut down trees to make room for palm oil plantations. Brazil cuts down the Amazon rain forests for farming or raising sugarcane. On a more optimistic note, Brazil has begun to transform itself into an environmental leader. Deforestation rates in recent years have gone down 70 percent. The Brazilian government credits improved oversight and police monitoring for the reduction in deforestation.[41]

A competitive global economy drives the need for money in economically challenged tropical countries. In the short term, logging and converting forestlands to other uses seems the profitable thing to do. However, the profits from deforestation for farmers are usually short-lived since rainforest soil is of poor quality. This prompts low-income farmers to destroy more forest to eke out a living. Unless this cycle of poverty is stopped, the destruction of forests is likely to continue.

Companies are adopting designations like one granted by the Forest Stewardship Council (FSC), a nonprofit organization comprised of loggers, environmentalists, and sociologists. The FSC seeks to coordinate forest management around the world and develop a uniform set of standards. Being FSC-certified helps companies indicate to consumers and stakeholders they are committed to preserving forest resources, they are socially responsible, and they take a long-term view of environmental management. Home Depot sells more FSC-certified wood products than any other retailer in the United States.[42]

URBAN SPRAWL   Urban sprawl began in the United States with the post–World War II building boom. This boom transformed the nation from primarily low-density communities designed to accommodate one-car households, bicyclists, and pedestrians to large-scale suburban developments at the edges of established towns and cities. Downtowns and inner cities deteriorated as shopping malls, office parks, corporate campuses, and residential developments sprang up on what was once forest, prairie, or farmland. As the places where people live, work, and shop grew further apart, people began spending more time in automobiles driving greater distances. Urban sprawl consumed wildlife habitat, wetlands, and farmland, but has also contributed to land, water, and especially air pollution. Lack of urban planning means these places grow without reason. In an age of erratic gas prices, traffic congestion, and obesity, it becomes increasingly expensive in terms of dollars and health to live in sprawling cities. Walmart as well as other big-box stores have been accused of contributing to urban sprawl.

Some urban areas fight to limit sprawl. Portland, Oregon, for example, established an Urban Growth Boundary to restrict growth and preserve open space and rural land around the city. Adding to the appeal of returning to cities is a movement to increase urban parks. Rather than allowing loggers to profit from forests, more cities are buying forested land to convert to park space. Stemming sprawl preserves natural spaces outside the city. People also realize that living near their place of employment is more convenient, cheaper, and better for their health. Although limiting urban sprawl creates disadvantages for car and oil companies, many businesses can benefit from urban renewal movements that reduce sprawl.

BIODIVERSITY   Deforestation, pollution, development, and urban sprawl put increasing pressure on wildlife, plants, and their habitats. Many plants and animals became extinct, and thousands more are threatened. The Yangtze River Dolphin is a recent extinction, and thousands more animals, including the Florida panther, tigers, frog species, and most lemurs, face the same fate. It is estimated that two major species go extinct per 10 percent of forest loss, a process that accelerates as forest loss increases.[43]

Experts fear overutilization of natural resources will cause catastrophic imbalances in the environment. Because each biological species plays a unique role in its ecosystem and is part of a complex chain of events, the loss of any of them may threaten the entire ecosystem. Pollinators, for example, play a significant role in the growth of fruits and vegetables by spreading pollen from plant to plant. Increasing development and widespread use of pesticides reduced the populations of bees, insects, and bats needed to help plants reproduce. Without these species, the world's food supply would be seriously jeopardized. People and businesses must use resources more carefully in order to maintain a livable world for many generations to come.

GENETICALLY MODIFIED ORGANISMS   Depending on whom you ask, genetically modified foods are going to save impoverished areas from starvation and revolutionize agriculture, or destroy biodiversity and make us all sick. **Genetically modified (GM) organisms** are created through manipulating plant and animal DNA to produce a desired effect like resistance to pests and viruses, drought resistance, or high crop yield. This process generally involves transferring genes from one organism to another in a way that would never occur naturally, in order to create a new life form with unique traits. Companies like Monsanto and DuPont develop genetically modified corn, soybeans, potatoes, canola oil seeds, and cotton plants they claim are more weed and insecticide resistant and provide higher yields. Many people fear these unnatural genes will have negative effects on nature, somewhat like how invader species of plants and animals can wipe out native ones. People are also afraid that GM food will have negative effects on humans. Also, because GM seeds are patented, farmers cannot keep any of the seed themselves but must purchase seeds each year from companies such as Monsanto.

Despite the controversy, interest in GM products remains high. In countries where malnutrition is a problem, the idea of higher yields is appealing. It can also make food last longer. The first genetically modified apple approved for growth in the United States contains genes that make the fruit resist browning when cut open, which could be highly beneficial to restaurants and grocery stores.[44] A recent study has implied that GM crops have had a beneficial impact on farming.[45]

However, the long-term impact of this genetic tinkering is not known, although the Food and Drug Administration deemed GM food safe to consume. Today, as much as 75 percent of all processed food contains GM ingredients—and the United States does not require these products to be labeled with the exception of Vermont. This causes many consumers to turn toward organic foods, creating a market opportunity for organic and all-natural grocery chains like Whole Foods. Other parts of the world boycott products made from GM crops. For instance, it is illegal to grow GM crops in Thailand. In addition, studies show that certain GM crops are losing their effectiveness as insects become increasingly resistant. In fact, U.S. regulators have begun to consider limits for planting some genetically modified corn because of heightened insect resistance.[46]

As with GM plants, the problem with the genetic engineering of animals or animal products is that the long-run effects are unknown. Large numbers of genetically altered animals could upset the balance in relationships among various species with undetermined effects, such as the ability to reproduce or fight diseases and pests. Additionally, if genetically modified plant seeds are carried by wind or pollinators to areas with native plants, it is possible genetic contamination could take place among native plants, thus reducing biological diversity. Further research is needed to address public concerns about the safety and long-term environmental effects of these technologies.

ENVIRONMENTAL LEGISLATION

Until the 1970s, environmental concerns were of little importance to many organizations. However, with the first Earth Day, increasing stakeholder awareness of environmental concerns and the creation of the Environmental Protection Agency brought sustainability to the forefront. As the world's resources become increasingly depleted, the costs to business and consumers simultaneously increase.[47] As such, it is no longer acceptable for businesses to continue their day-to-day business operations without concern for how their activities impact the environment. Laws such as the Clean Air Act and the Environmental Protection Act are meant to protect the environment by limiting activities that create damage or harm to the planet. Organizations found to be in violation of these laws can receive severe penalties. However, while some companies adopt sustainability initiatives simply to avoid getting in trouble with the law, more companies are recognizing that all of their activities either directly or indirectly affect the planet—and thereby the lives and well-being of its inhabitants.[48] For these companies, sustainability is not merely a legal issue but a significant ethical issue that must be addressed. Recognizing the finiteness of the world's resources and the changing preferences of consumers, many firms are adapting their marketing activities and operational areas toward a more sustainable framework.[49]

The United States, like most other nations, passed numerous laws and established regulatory agencies to address environmental issues. Most of these efforts focused on the activities of businesses, government agencies, and other organizations that use natural resources in providing goods and services.

Environmental Protection Agency (EPA)

The most influential regulatory agency that deals with environmental issues and enforces environmental legislation in the United States is the **Environmental Protection Agency**. The EPA was created in 1970 to coordinate environmental agencies involved in conducting environmental research, providing assistance in fighting pollution, and enforcing the nation's environmental laws. Establishing the EPA was the culmination of a decade of growing protests over the deterioration of environmental quality. This movement reached a significant climax with the publication of Rachel Carson's *Silent Spring,* an attack on the indiscriminate use of pesticides, which rallied scientists, activists, and citizens from around the country to crusade to protect the environment from abuses of the time. President Nixon responded with the establishment of the EPA. The agency is charged with ensuring the following:

- Protecting Americans from significant health and environmental risks.

- Managing environmental risks based on empirical information.

- Ensuring the fairness and effectiveness of laws protecting human health and the environment.

- Ensuring environmental protection is an integral consideration in U.S. policies.

- Making available access to accurate information that allows participation in managing health and environmental risks.

- Making sure environmental legislation contributes to diverse, sustainable, and economically productive communities and ecosystems.[50]

To fulfill its mission, the EPA established five strategic goals to define its planning, budgeting, analysis, and accountability processes (see Table 12–3). These goals reflect public priorities in the form of statutes and regulations designed to achieve clean air and water, proper waste management, and other important concerns.[51]

The EPA can file civil charges against companies that violate the law. For instance, the EPA instituted a penalty of $12.5 million and community service payments of $12.2 million against Tonawanda Coke Corporation, the largest fine in an air pollution case to date. Allegations included releasing gas containing benzene into the air, operating without a required pollution-control tool, and disposing hazardous waste without a permit.[52]

Environmental Regulations

A significant number of laws have been promulgated to address both general and specific environmental issues, including public health, threatened species, toxic substances, clean

TABLE 12–3 Goals of the Environmental Protection Agency

Goal	Long-Term Outcome
1	Reduce air pollution
2	Improve access to clean and safe water
3	Promote materials management, waste management, and clean sites
4	Enhance joint preparedness for environmental response
5	Enhance compliance assurance and environmental stewardship

Source: Environmental Protection Agency, "Goals and Objectives," http://www2.epa.gov/border2020/goals-and-objectives (accessed March 9, 2015).

air and water, and natural resources. For instance, leaded gasoline was phased out during the 1990s because catalytic converters, used to reduce pollution caused by automobile emissions and required by law on most vehicles, do not work properly with leaded gasoline. In addition, lead exposure harms people, particularly children. Increased Corporate Average Fuel Economy (or CAFE) standards are forcing the automobile industry to determine methods to increase gas mileage. For instance, automobiles must get 35.5 miles per gallon (mpg) by 2016 and 54.5 mpg by 2025.[53] This has led car makers to look for alternative ways of building their cars to get better gas mileage, such as replacing steel with lighter aluminum.[54] Strategies include increased production and sales of hybrid vehicles, as well as improving electric cars and hydrogen fuel-cell technology. Table 12–4 summarizes significant laws related to environmental protection.

TABLE 12–4 Laws Protecting the Environment

Clean Air Act, 1970	Established air quality standards; requires approved state plans for implementation of the standards
National Environmental Policy Act, 1970	Established broad policy goals for all federal agencies; created the Council on Environmental Quality as a monitoring agency
Coastal Zone Management Act, 1972	Provides financial resources to the states to protect coastal zones from overpopulation
Federal Water Pollution Control Act, 1972	Designed to prevent, reduce, or eliminate water pollution
Noise Pollution Control Act, 1972	Designed to control the noise emission of certain manufactured items
Federal Insecticide, Fungicide, and Rodenticide Act, 1972	Provides federal control of pesticide distribution, sale, and use
Endangered Species Act, 1973	Provides a program for the conservation of threatened and endangered plants and animals and the habitats in which they are found
Safe Drinking Water Act, 1974	Established to protect the quality of drinking water in the United States; focuses on all waters actually or potentially designed for drinking use, whether from above ground or underground sources; establishes safe standards of purity and requires all owners or operators of public water systems to comply with primary (health-related) standards
Energy Policy and Conservation Act, 1975	Requires auto dealers to have "gas mileage guides" in their showrooms

© Cengage Learning

Toxic Substances Control Act, 1976	Requires testing and restricts use of certain chemical substances to protect human health and the environment
Resource Conservation and Recovery Act, 1976	Gives the EPA authority to control hazardous waste from the "cradle to grave"; includes the generation, transportation, treatment, storage, and disposal of hazardous waste, as well as a framework for the management of nonhazardous waste
Comprehensive Environmental Response, Compensation, and Liability Act, 1980	Created a tax on chemical and petroleum industries and provides broad federal authority to respond directly to releases or threatened releases of hazardous substances that may endanger public health or the environment
Emergency Planning and Community Right-to-Know Act, 1986	The national legislation on community safety, designed to help local communities protect public health, safety, and the environment from chemical hazards
Oil Pollution Act, 1990	Streamlined and strengthened the EPA's ability to prevent and respond to catastrophic oil spills; a trust fund financed by a tax on oil is available to clean up spills when the responsible party is incapable of doing so or unwilling to do so
Pollution Prevention Act, 1990	Focuses industry, government, and public attention on reducing the amount of pollution through cost-effective changes in production, operation, and raw materials use
Food Quality Protection Act, 1996	Amended the Federal Insecticide, Fungicide, and Rodenticide Act and the Federal Food Drug and Cosmetic Act; the requirements include a new safety standard—reasonable certainty of no harm—that must be applied to all pesticides used on foods
Energy Policy Act, 2005	Addresses the way energy is produced in the United States in terms of energy efficiency, renewable energy, oil and gas, coal, Tribal energy, nuclear matters and security, vehicles and motor fuels, hydrogen, electricity, energy tax incentives, hydropower and geothermal energy, and climate change technology
Energy Independence and Security Act, 2007	Established a plan for moving the United States toward a more sustainable future, with steps that include the phasing out of the incandescent light bulb

CLEAN AIR ACT   The Clean Air Act (CAA) is a comprehensive federal law that regulates atmospheric emissions from a variety of sources.[55] The law established national air quality standards as well as standards for significant new pollution sources emitting hazardous substances. These maximum pollutant standards, called National Ambient Air Quality Standards (NAAQS), were federally mandated to protect public health and the environment. Individual states were directed to develop state implementation plans (SIPs) to meet the NAAQS by restricting emissions of criteria pollutants from stationary sources (industries) within the state.

Under the Clean Air Act, states are responsible for the quality of their air and cannot negatively impact the air quality in bordering states. The EPA continues to develop stricter standards to address this issue. This has important implications for businesses and their relationships with consumers, particularly those in industries that have a greater tendency to contribute to air pollution. Violators of the Clean Air Act incur significant penalties, as Hyundai and Kia found out when they paid $100 million for misstating the fuel-economy capabilities of 1.2 million vehicles.[56]

ENDANGERED SPECIES ACT   The Endangered Species Act established a program to protect threatened and endangered species as well as the habitats in which they live.[57] An endangered species is one in danger of extinction, whereas a threatened species is one that may become endangered without protection. The U.S. Fish and Wildlife Service of the Department of the Interior maintains the list of endangered and threatened species, which currently includes more than 2,000 endangered and threatened species, including the bald eagle, American bison, and Ozark big-eared bat.[58] The Endangered Species Act prohibits any action that results in the harm or death of a listed species or that adversely affects endangered species habitat. It also makes the import, export, interstate, and foreign commerce of listed species illegal. Protected species may include birds, insects, fish, reptiles, mammals, crustaceans, flowers, grasses, cacti, and trees.

The Endangered Species Act is highly controversial. In some cases, threatened or endangered species deemed a nuisance by ranchers and farmers have been harmed or killed by landowners seeking to avoid the hassle or expense of compliance. For instance, both the Gray wolf and the Red wolf are endangered in the United States, and livestock owners would like to eliminate them. Concerns about the restrictions and costs associated with the law are not entirely unfounded. There have been cases where consumers bought land only to be told they could not use it because it was home to an endangered species. This becomes a business ethics issue when the Endangered Species Act impacts firms.

TOXIC SUBSTANCES CONTROL ACT   Congress passed the Toxic Substances Control Act (TSCA) to empower the EPA with the ability to track the 75,000 industrial chemicals currently produced or imported into the United States. The agency repeatedly screens these chemicals and requires reporting or testing of those that pose an environmental or human health hazard. It can also ban the manufacture and import of chemicals that pose an unreasonable risk. The EPA tracks thousands of new chemicals developed each year with either unknown or dangerous characteristics. The agency can control these chemicals as necessary to protect human health and the environment.[59] For instance, the Environmental Protection Agency considered using the Toxic Substances Control Act to decide upon new rules for bisphenol A (BPA), a toxic chemical found in some plastics. Not only is this chemical deemed to have a negative impact on the environment, but it can also be harmful for humans who consume it. BPA has been used in plastic baby bottles as well as food packaging.[60]

CLEAN WATER ACT   In 1977, Congress amended the Federal Water Pollution Control Act of 1972 as the Clean Water Act (CWA). This law granted the EPA the authority to establish effluent standards on an industry basis and continued the earlier law's requirements to set water quality limits for all contaminants in surface waters. The Clean Water Act makes it illegal for anyone to discharge any pollutant from a point source directly into navigable waters without a permit.[61] This rule also requires industrial companies to draft plans to prevent storm water run-off. BP faced up to a $13.7 billion fine for violating the Clean Water Act after the *Deepwater Horizon* accident spilt 3.19 million barrels of crude oil into the Gulf.[62] It was fined $5.5 billion.

POLLUTION PREVENTION ACT   The Pollution Prevention Act focuses on reducing pollution through cost-effective changes in production, operation, and raw materials use. Practices include recycling, source reduction, sustainable agriculture, and other practices that increase efficiency in the use of energy, water, or other natural resources and protect resources through conservation.[63]

One common method for reducing pollution has been designing buildings to be more environmentally friendly. Although buildings are rarely considered major pollution sources, 40 percent of total U.S. energy consumption comes from residential and commercial constructions.[64] Two competitive certification groups—LEED and Green Globes—authorize schools, houses, and commercial buildings as "green." **Leadership in Energy & Environmental Design (LEED)** is a certification program that recognizes sustainable building practices and strategies. It has fewer ties to business interests and is the most popular green certification program worldwide. Table 12–5 provides global facts on LEED certification projects. Green Globes is led by a former timber company executive and received much of its seed money from timber and wood products companies. Already two states, Maryland and Arkansas, have adopted Green Globes as an alternative to LEED, giving officials an alternative for government-funded construction. The Clinton Presidential Library in Little Rock as well as 7 World Trade Center, the first tower rebuilt near Ground Zero in New York, were certified by Green Globes.[65]

FOOD QUALITY PROTECTION ACT   In 1996, the Food Quality Protection Act amended the Federal Insecticide, Fungicide, and Rodenticide Act and the Federal Food, Drug, and Cosmetic Act to fundamentally change the way the EPA regulates pesticides. The law included a new safety standard—reasonable certainty of no harm—that must be applied to all pesticides used on foods.[66] The legislation establishes a consistent, science-based regulatory environment and mandates a single health-based standard for all pesticides in all foods. The law also provides special protections for infants and children, expedites approval of safer pesticides, provides incentives for the development and maintenance of effective crop protection tools for farmers, and requires periodic reevaluation of pesticide registrations and tolerances to ensure they are up-to-date and based on good science.

ENERGY POLICY ACT   Signed into law in 2005, the Energy Policy Act's focus is on promoting alternative forms of energy in the desire to lessen U.S. dependence on foreign oil. The bill gives tax breaks and loan guarantees to alternative energy companies like nuclear

TABLE 12–5 Facts about LEED Certification

1. More than 3.6 billion square feet of building space is LEED certified.
2. LEED is referenced in project specifications for 71 percent of projects valued at $50 million and over.
3. 675.9 million square feet of real estate became LEED certified in 2014.
4. LEED certification is a top sustainable goal for private and public organizations.
5. There are 69,000 LEED building projects in 150 countries and territories.
6. 44 percent of all square footage pursuing LEED certification is outside the United States.
7. LEED projects are estimated to divert 80 million tons of waste from landfills.
8. The top 10 countries in LEED certification projects outside of the United States include Canada, China, India, South Korea, Taiwan, Germany, Brazil, Singapore, United Arab Emirates, and Finland.

Sources: Selina Holmes, "Top 10 Countries for LEED," *U.S. Green Building Council,* May 5, 2014, http://www.usgbc.org/articles/top-10-countries-leed (accessed March 10, 2015); U.S. Green Building Council, *U.S. Green Building Council,* February 23, 2015, http://www.usgbc.org/articles/green-building-facts (accessed March 10, 2015).

power plants, solar, and wind energy and requires utilities to comply with federal reliability standards for the electricity grid. Additionally, the bill provided temporary tax benefits to consumers who purchased hybrid gasoline-electric cars and took other energy-saving measures. Tax credits were given for plug-in electric drive conversion kits.[67] In addition, the bill extended daylight savings time by one month to save energy.[68]

ALTERNATIVE ENERGY SOURCES

Alternative energy sources already have a major impact on many stakeholders. In some cases, they significantly decreased the carbon footprint of communities, cities, and even countries. Figure 12–2 provides a sustainability map of the world's different countries based on actual consumers' sustainability behaviors. Businesses such as New Belgium Brewing incorporated alternative energy sources into their operations, decreasing their carbon emissions as well as their energy costs. The following section will describe some of the more popular forms of alternative energy sources being explored.

Wind Power

Wind power holds great promise for the United States and has already taken off in many countries. For instance, one-fifth of Denmark's electricity needs are supplied by wind farms.[69] Because the United States is home to the Great Plains—one of the greatest sources

FIGURE 12–2 Sustainability Index Based on Consumer Choice

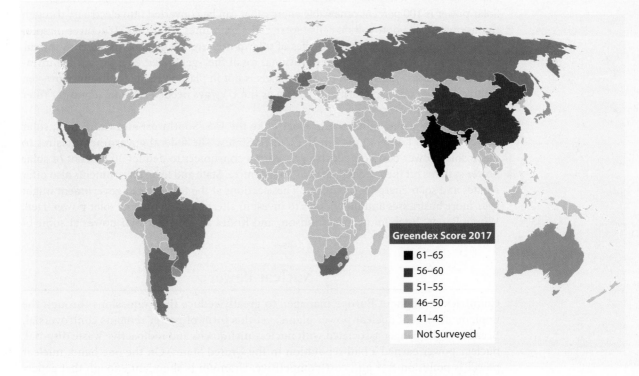

Greendex Score 2017

- 61–65
- 56–60
- 51–55
- 46–50
- 41–45
- Not Surveyed

Source: "Greendex," National Geographic, 2014, http://environment.*nationalgeographic*.com/environment/greendex/ (accessed February 19, 2015).

of wind energy in the world—experts believe wind energy could meet as much as 20 percent of the nation's energy needs. However, restructuring the nation's power grids to efficiently transmit wind-generated power will take huge investments. Widespread adoption of wind power is slowed by the high cost of the turbines as well as limitations on an outdated national power grid. Despite these roadblocks, many people believe the United States will be a wind power hot spot in the future. Wind power also offers opportunities for businesses, even those for whom alternative energy might otherwise be perceived as a threat. BP, for example, invested in several wind farms in North America and in other parts of the globe.

Geothermal Power

Geothermal power has significant advantages and disadvantages that either advance or limit its adoption. On the one hand, geothermal energy provides a constant source of heat. It is subsequently a more dependable energy source than some other forms of alternative energy. Geothermal plants also emit fewer carbon emissions than coal powered plants. On the other hand, geothermal energy is expensive, and geothermal drilling sites are not readily available everywhere. However, in spite of these initial costs, those who use geothermal energy reported a savings in overall energy costs. Due to its reliability, geothermal power could be a good substitute for natural gas in powering buildings and homes. Some IKEA stores as well as Lipscomb University and Belmont University in Nashville, Tennessee, use geothermal power to meet their energy needs.

Solar Power

Solar power is 100 percent renewable energy that can be converted into electricity through the use of either photovoltaic cells (solar cells) on homes and other structures or solar power plants. The major disadvantages of solar power are the technology remains expensive and inefficient compared to traditional fossil fuel–generated energy, and the infrastructure for mass production of solar panels is not in place in many locations. However, cloudy days are not necessarily a problem as the UV rays needed to generate power filter through clouds.

Given the strong sunshine in places like the U.S. Southwest and California, solar power gained a lot of support in the United States. The federal government desires to make solar power cost competitive and allows consumers to deduct 30 percent of solar power systems off their federal taxes as an incentive. State and local governments also offer rebates and solar energy tax credits.[70] These actions at the top levels of government might spur more businesses and individuals to invest in alternative energy like solar power. Dell, Whole Foods, Intel, Johnson & Johnson, and Kohl's already use solar power at some of their locations.[71]

Nuclear Power

Countries throughout Europe managed to greatly reduce their emissions through the implementation of nuclear power plants, yet this form of power remains controversial. Because of the danger associated with nuclear meltdowns and radioactive waste disposal, nuclear power earned a bad reputation in the United States. On the one hand, nuclear power is pollution-free and cost-competitive. Uranium is abundant enough that generating even 60 times more energy than what is produced today would not be a problem.

Nuclear energy is France's main source of power and reduced the country's nitrogen oxide and other emissions by 70 percent.[72] With careful oversight, nuclear energy could change the world's dependence on oil.

On the other hand, critics are concerned with the safety of nuclear power plants and the disposal of waste. Since production of nuclear power gives off radiation, the safety of workers and the transport of nuclear waste is a prime concern. The Chernobyl nuclear disaster in the Ukraine, which resulted in deaths, sicknesses, and birth defects, made this a viable concern. The crisis that occurred in Japan after nuclear reactors were damaged in the 2011 earthquake and tsunami further decreased support for nuclear energy.

Biofuels

Perhaps the most controversial form of alternative energy after nuclear power is ethanol. Critics argue manufacturing ethanol takes a lot of energy and is not much more sustainable than oil. Carmakers said the models they currently manufacture are not calibrated to handle greater amounts of ethanol. Because ethanol in the United States is made from corn, opponents believe it decreases the world's food supply and increases food prices. One study showed expanding ethanol production in the United States cost net corn importing countries an additional $11.6 billion in prices for corn. With 870 million people who go hungry worldwide, higher prices for a common food staple could become a problem.[73] This prompted some companies to begin looking at alternatives to corn ethanol.

However, ethanol has taken off in countries like Brazil, leading to legal mandates to incorporate biofuels as a substitute for fossil fuels. In 1976, for example, the Brazilian government made it a requirement to blend gasoline with ethanol. As a result, Brazil currently is the largest exporter of bioethanol. Biofuel production in countries like the Philippines has been criticized because it has contributed to rapid deforestation of ecologically sensitive areas—companies in a rush to create profits from the popularity of biofuels installed plantations on former jungle land, for example.

To solve these problems and take advantage of the benefits of ethanol, scientists are researching alternative sources for this fuel. Algae and nonedible plants such as grasses are currently being explored. Since grass and algae are not food sources and do not require the destruction of trees, ethanol proponents are excited to see whether these alternatives will be adopted.

Hydropower

Throughout history people used water as a power source and means of transportation. From the water-powered mills of centuries past to modern hydroelectric dams, water is a powerful renewable energy source. Although in the United States, hydroelectric power provides only 7 percent of total output, hydroelectric provides 19 percent of total electricity production worldwide, making it the largest form of renewable energy.[74] The Three Gorges Dam in China resulted in reducing greenhouse gases for the country, although there are other environmental issues associated with the dam.[75]

As with all other forms of energy production, hydropower has benefits and downsides. One of the major downsides is the destruction of wildlife and human habitats when valleys are flooded using dams. Hydroelectricity also disrupts the lifecycles of aquatic life. However, hydroelectric power decreases greenhouse gas emissions and air pollution. To be a suitable and sustainable alternative to fossil fuels, hydroelectric facilities should be built to minimize negative environmental impacts.

BUSINESS RESPONSE TO SUSTAINABILITY ISSUES

Many businesses responded to sustainability by adopting a triple-bottom line approach. This approach takes into consideration social and environmental performance variables in addition to economic performance. Many firms are learning that being environmentally friendly and sustainable has numerous benefits—including increased goodwill from stakeholders and money savings from being more efficient and less wasteful. Several companies have a vice president of environmental affairs, like Staples, Disney, and Hyatt Hotels & Resorts. This position is designed to help firms achieve their business goals in an environmentally responsible manner. Businesses like Walmart and IBM developed environmental scorecards for their suppliers.[76] Corporate efforts to respond to environmental issues focus on green marketing, recycling, emissions reductions, and socially responsible buying.

Yet despite the importance of the environment, companies are in business to make a profit. Economic performance is still a necessary bottom line. Studies suggest improving a company's environmental performance can in fact increase revenues and reduce costs. Figure 12–3 suggests mechanisms through which this can occur.

As shown in the figure, better environmental performance can increase revenue in three ways: through better access to certain markets, differentiation of products, and the sale of pollution-control technology. A firm's innovation in sustainability can be based on applying existing knowledge and technology or creating a completely new approach. Improving a firm's reputation for environmental stewardship helps companies capture a growing market niche. Large companies like Walmart are requiring their suppliers to be more environmentally friendly, and improving a supply chain's environmental performance may be key to attracting more business from the retail industry. "Greening" a company's supply chain is particularly important because it is an often overlooked part of improving a company's sustainability. In one study, 42 percent of responding companies stated they do not include supply chain members when considering their environmental footprint.[77] This suggests companies tend to focus more on their own efforts as a distinct unit rather than on the entire supply chain.[78] Recognizing the interconnectedness of firms regarding sustainability could be a major step in improving corporate environmental impact.

Going green may help firms differentiate their products from competitors. Whole Foods, a natural foods retailer, made being environmentally friendly part of its image from the start. Method built an entire business around green cleaning products. Finally, going green opened up a new industry referred to as the eco-industry, where some firms actually discovered pollution-control technology and are now able to sell this technology to other firms.

Better environmental performance can reduce costs by improving risk management and stakeholder relationships, reducing the amount of materials and energy used, and reducing capital and labor costs. Improved environmental standards should prevent major environmental disasters in the future. For those disasters that cannot be avoided, the firm can at least show it applied due diligence with its environmental performance, which may reduce the company's culpability in the public's eye. Companies can decrease the costs of compliance with governmental regulations and reduce fines if they become more energy efficient.

Today's greener firms may find they have better access to capital. Banks often have environmental experts evaluate the environmental performance of potential borrowers to determine whether to grant bank loans. Banks recognize poor environmental management as an increased liability. Finally, labor surveys show that workers care about the environmental impact of the firms for whom they work. Clearly, company environmental performance is ceasing to be just an environmental matter; it also influences the bottom line.

FIGURE 12–3 **Positive Links between Environmental and Economic Performance**

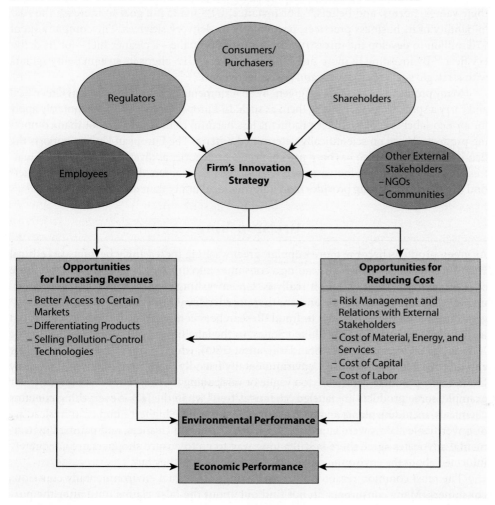

Source: Stefan Ambec and Paul Lanoie, "Does It Pay to Be Green? A Systematic Overview," *The Academy of Management Perspectives* 22, 4 (2008): 47.

Green Marketing

Green marketing is a strategy involving stakeholder assessment to create meaningful long-term relationships with customers, while maintaining, supporting, and enhancing the natural environment. Two of the largest craft brewers are known for their commitment to sustainability. Sierra Nevada gets 20 percent of its energy from solar power and 40 percent from hydrogen fuel cells.[79] New Belgium Brewing gets 100 percent of its energy from wind power, its facilities use natural lighting, and it provides its employees with bikes so they can travel to work and reduce fossil fuel usage. Some real estate developers are attempting to integrate environmental concerns into new communities to protect the land. As environmental mandates on emissions and waste become stricter, real estate developers can cut costs and increase compliance by using green technology and materials as much as possible. When organizations create partnership with consumers on green initiatives, these consumers tend to positively support green products.[80]

Firms that want to become leaders in sustainability should embed sustainability into their values, norms, and beliefs.[81] For instance, UPS made it a goal to increase the sustainability of its business practices, particularly its delivery services. The company spent $70 million to develop the infrastructure for using propane—a cleaner fuel—for its delivery fleet.[82] By investing in more fuel-efficient delivery, UPS aligns its sustainability agenda with strategic goals of efficiency and cost-effectiveness.

Many products are certified as "green" by environmental organizations such as Green Seal and carry a special logo identifying them as such. In Europe, companies can voluntarily apply for an Eco-label to indicate their product is less harmful to the environment than competing products, based on scientifically determined criteria. The European Union supports the Eco-label program, which has been used in product categories as diverse as refrigerators, mattresses, vacuum cleaners, footwear, and televisions.[83] Consumers that desire green products find that green advertising provides more informational utility than do other consumers.[84]

Greenwashing

As green products become more popular, greenwashing increasingly becomes an ethical issue. **Greenwashing** involves misleading a consumer into thinking a good or service is more environmentally friendly than it really is. Greenwashing ranges from making environmental claims required by law and are therefore irrelevant (CFC-free) to puffery (exaggerating environmental claims) to fraud. Researchers compared claims on products sold in 10 countries, including the United States, to the labeling guidelines established by the International Organization for Standardization (ISO), which prohibits vague, misleading and unverifiable claims such as "environmentally friendly" and "nonpolluting." The study found many products' claims are too vague or misleading to meet the ISO standards.[85] For example, some products are labeled "chemical-free," when the fact is everything contains chemicals, including plants and animals. Products with the highest number of misleading or unverifiable claims were laundry detergents, household cleaners, and paints. Environmental advocates agree there is still a long way to go to ensure shoppers are adequately informed about the environmental impact of the products they buy.[86]

The most common reason for greenwashing is to attract environmentally conscious consumers. Many consumers do not find out about the false claims until after the purchase.[87] Therefore, greenwashing may increase sales in the short-term. However, while greenwashing might make a company appear sustainable, this strategy can seriously backfire when consumers find out they are being deceived. Greenwashing is negatively related to financial performance; therefore, companies that engage in greenwashing can expect to receive criticism and decreased sales in the long-run.[88] On the other hand, because the term "green" and "sustainability" can be hard to define, some greenwashing might not be intentional. Is a product green if one component is environmentally friendly, even if the other components are not? Often stakeholders look at the product itself but may not consider the sustainability practices throughout the rest of the supply chain. To reduce this ambiguity, the Federal Trade Commission released green guidelines to help marketers determine the truthfulness of "green" claims.[89]

Another challenge with greenwashing is determining if companies are actually engaging in deception. Consumers often perceive certain practices as being more sustainable or healthier even when marketers never make claims to support this assumption. For instance, it has long been an assumption that locally grown food is more eco-friendly. New research suggests local food may not be much more environmentally friendly than non-local.[90] Using certain colors on products can lead consumers to believe the products are sustainable.

Consumers associate the color brown with recycled materials, leading firms like Dunkin' Donuts to use brown recycled napkins in their stores.[91] While these may be good cues for consumers to pinpoint more "eco-friendly" items, it also leads to the possibility that marketers could use consumer perceptions to market products without actually changing their content. If consumers already have a low-performance brand attitude toward a product, green advertising will create a negative effect compared to general corporate advertising or no advertising.[92] In addition, greenwashing has been found to destroy consumer trust and create consumer confusion and perceived risk associated with green products.[93]

Although environmentalists and businesses are often at odds, there is growing agreement between them that companies should work to protect and preserve sustainability by implementing a number of goals. First, companies should strive to eliminate waste. Because pollution and waste stems from inefficiency, the issue should not be what to do with waste, but how to make things more efficiently so no waste is produced. Second, companies should rethink the concept of a product. Products are classified as consumables, that are eaten or biodegradable; durable goods, such as cars, televisions, computers, and refrigerators; and unsalables, including undesirable byproducts such as radioactive materials, heavy metals, and toxins. The design of durable goods should use a closed loop system of manufacture and use, and a return to the manufacturing process that allows products and resources to be disassembled and recycled while minimizing the disposal of unsalables. Third, the price of products should reflect their true costs, including the costs of replenishing natural resources used or damaged during the production process. Finally, businesses should seek ways to make their commitment to the environment profitable.[94]

STRATEGIC IMPLEMENTATION OF ENVIRONMENTAL RESPONSIBILITY

Businesses have responded to the opportunities and threats created by environmental issues with varying levels of commitment. Some companies, like New Belgium Brewing, consider sustainability a core component of the business. Other companies engage in greenwashing and do not actively seek to be more sustainable. As Figure 12-4 indicates, a low-commitment business attempts to avoid dealing with environmental issues and hopes nothing bad happens or no one ever finds out about an environmental accident or abuse. Such firms may try to protect themselves against lawsuits. Other firms are proactive in anticipating risks and environmental issues. Such firms develop strategic management programs that view the environment as an opportunity for advancing organizational interests. These companies respond to stakeholder interests, assess risks, and develop a comprehensive environmental strategy.

Recycling Initiatives

Many organizations engage in **recycling**. Recycling is the reprocessing of materials, especially steel, aluminum, paper, glass, rubber, and some plastics, for reuse. In fact, recycling is one of the country's greatest sustainability success stories. Paper consists of one-third of the recyclables in the United States.[95] More than 50 percent of all products sold in stores are packed in recycled paperboard.

Paper is not the only material that is recyclable, however. Gills, the largest onion processor in the country, uses onion waste to make 600 kilowatts of electricity and cattle feed.[96]

FIGURE 12–4 **Strategic Approaches to Environmental Issues**

Low Commitment	Medium Commitment	High Commitment
Deals only with existing problems	Attempts to comply with environmental laws	Has strategic programs to address environmental issues
Makes only limited plans for anticipated problems	Deals with issues that could cause public relations problems	Views environment as an opportunity to advance the business strategy
Fails to consider stakeholder environmental issues	Views environmental issues from a tactical, not a strategic, perspective	Consults with stakeholders about their environmental concerns
Operates without concern for long-term environmental impact	Views environment as more of a threat than an opportunity	Conducts an environmental audit to assess performance and adopts international standards

In India a chemist found a way to turn the country's massive amounts of plastic litter into a material that can be used to construct roads.[97] Additionally, several organizations are part of a group called WasteWise that aims to reduce municipal solid waste and industrial waste.[98] Groups like this help companies save money through reducing waste, receive positive publicity, and track how they reduce waste over time.

Companies and local and regional governments are finding ways to recycle water to avoid discharging chemicals into rivers and streams and preserve diminishing water supplies. Companies such as Coca-Cola took steps to reduce water use. These types of concerns and efforts led to the formation of the Beverage Industry Environmental Roundtable, developed by 18 companies in 2006 to investigate water conservation, energy use, and other issues that impact the industry. Since its creation, companies partnered with environmental groups and cities to enhance water conservation and bring water to consumers living in low-income countries.

Stakeholder Assessment

Stakeholder assessment is an important part of a high-commitment approach to environmental issues. This process requires acknowledging and actively monitoring the environmental concerns of all legitimate stakeholders. Thus, a company must have a process in place for identifying and prioritizing the many claims and stakes on its business and for dealing with trade-offs related to the impact on different stakeholders. Although no company satisfies every claim, all risk-related claims should be evaluated before a firm takes action or ignores a particular issue. To make accurate assumptions about stakeholder interests, managers need to conduct research, assess risks, and communicate with stakeholders about their respective concerns.

However, not all stakeholders are equal. There are specific regulations and legal requirements that govern some aspects of stakeholder relationships, such as air and water quality. A business cannot knowingly harm the water quality of other stakeholders in order to generate a profit. Additionally, some special-interest groups take extreme positions that, if adopted, would undermine the economic base of many other stakeholders (for example, fishing rights, logging, and hunting). Regardless of the final decision a company makes with regard to particular environmental issues, information should be communicated consistently across all stakeholders. This is especially important when a company faces a crisis or negative publicity about a decision. Another aspect of strong relationships with stakeholders is the willingness to acknowledge and openly address potential conflicts. Some degree of negotiation and conciliation is necessary to align a company's decisions and strategies with stakeholder interests.

Risk Analysis

The next step in a high-commitment response to environmental concerns is assessing risk. Through industry and government research, an organization can usually identify environmental issues that relate to manufacturing, marketing, and consumption and use patterns associated with its products. Through risk analysis, it is possible to assess the environmental risks associated with business decisions. The real difficulty is measuring the costs and benefits of environmental decisions, especially in the eyes of interested stakeholders. Research studies often conflict, adding to the confusion and controversy over sustainability.

Debate surrounding environmental issues force corporate decision makers to weigh evidence and take some risks in final decisions. The important point for high-commitment organizations is to continue to evaluate the latest information and maintain communication with all stakeholders. For example, if the millions of sport utility vehicles (SUVs) on U.S. roads today were replaced with fuel-efficient electric-powered cars and trucks, there would be a tremendous reduction of greenhouse gas emissions. However, the cooperation and commitment needed to gain the support of government, manufacturers, consumers, and other stakeholders to accomplish this would be almost impossible to achieve. Although SUVs may harm the environment, many of their owners have prioritized other concerns, such as protection in case of an accident. A compromise might be to increase the use of mass transit to limit the use of those SUVs. Urban sprawl makes this an unattractive option. Additionally, it is important that companies remain competitive. An eco-friendly company will not be able to survive for long if it cannot compete against rivals in price or product differentiation.

This issue illustrates that many environmental decisions involve trade-offs for various stakeholders' risks. Through risk management, it is possible to quantify the trade-offs to determine whether to accept or reject environmentally related activities and programs. Usually, the key decision is between the amount of investment required to reduce the risk of damage and the amount of risk acceptable in stakeholder relationships. A company should assess these relationships on an ongoing basis. Both formal and informal methods are used to get feedback from stakeholders. For example, the employees of a firm can use formal methods such as exit interviews, an open-door policy, and toll-free telephone hot lines. Conversations between employees could provide informal feedback. But it is ultimately the responsibility of the organization's management to make the best decision possible after processing all available research and information. Then, if it is later discovered a mistake was made, change is still possible through open disclosure and thoughtful reasoning. Finally, a high-commitment organization will incorporate new information and insights into the strategic planning process.

The Strategic Environmental Audit

Organizations highly committed to environmental responsibility may conduct an audit of their efforts and report the results to all interested stakeholders. Table 12–6 provides a starting point for examining environmental sensitivity. Such organizations may use globally accepted standards, such as ISO 14000, as benchmarks in a strategic environmental audit. The International Organization for Standardization developed ISO 14000 as a comprehensive set of environmental standards that encourage a cleaner, safer, and healthier world. Currently, there is considerable variation among the environmental laws and regulations of nations and regions, making it difficult for high-commitment organizations to find acceptable solutions on a global scale. The goal of the ISO 14000 standard is to promote a common approach to environmental management and help companies attain and measure improvements in environmental performance. Companies that choose to abide by the ISO standards must review their environmental management systems periodically and identify all aspects of their operations that could impact the environment.[99] Other performance benchmarks available for use in environmental audits come from nonprofit organizations such as CERES, which has also developed standards for reporting information about environmental performance to interested stakeholders.

As this chapter demonstrated, social responsibility entails responding to stakeholder concerns about the environment, and many firms are finding creative ways to address environmental challenges. Measuring corporate environmental performance is challenging and requires evaluating many dimensions of a firm's operations.[100] Although many of the companies mentioned in this chapter chose to implement strategic environmental initiatives to capitalize on opportunities and achieve greater efficiency and cost savings, most also believe responding to stakeholders' concerns about environmental issues will improve relationships with stakeholders and make the world a better place.

TABLE 12–6 Strategic Sustainability Audit

Yes	No	Checklist
O	O	Does the organization show a high commitment to a strategic environmental policy?
O	O	Do employees know the environmental compliance policies of the organization?
O	O	Do suppliers and customers recognize the organization's stand on environmental issues?
O	O	Are managers familiar with the environmental strategies of other organizations in the industry?
O	O	Has the organization compared its environmental initiatives with those of other firms?
O	O	Is the company aware of the best practices in environmental management regardless of industry?
O	O	Has the organization developed measurable performance standards for environmental compliance?
O	O	Does the firm reconcile the need for consistent responsible values with the needs of various stakeholders?
O	O	Do the organization's philanthropic efforts consider environmental issues?
O	O	Does the organization comply with all laws and regulations that relate to environmental impact?

SUMMARY

Sustainability from a strategic business perspective is the potential for the long-term well-being of the natural environment, including all biological entities, as well as the mutually beneficial interactions among nature and individuals, organizations, and business strategies. Sustainable development involves meeting the needs of the present without compromising the ability of future generations to meet their own needs. Sustainability includes the assessment and improvement of business strategies, economic sectors, work practices, technologies, and lifestyles while maintaining the natural environment. Sustainability falls into the social responsibility domain of maximizing positive and minimizing negative impacts on stakeholders.

The protection of air, water, land, biodiversity, and renewable natural resources emerged as a major issue in the twentieth century in the face of increasing evidence that mankind was putting pressure on the long-term sustainability of these resources. Global sustainability topics include atmospheric issues, including air pollution, acid rain, and global warming; water issues, including water pollution and water depletion; and land issues, including land pollution, waste management, deforestation, urban sprawl, biodiversity, and genetically modified organisms. By being proactive in addressing these issues, companies can reduce their environmental impact and generate a reputation as an eco-responsible company.

The most influential regulatory agency that deals with environmental issues and enforces environmental legislation in the United States is the Environmental Protection Agency (EPA). The EPA was created in 1970 to coordinate environmental agencies involved in conducting environmental research, providing assistance in reducing pollution, and enforcing the nation's environmental laws. A significant number of laws were promulgated to address both general and specific environmental issues, including public health, threatened species, toxic substances, clean air and water, and natural resources. Some of the most important environmental laws include the Clean Air Act, the Endangered Species Act, the Toxic Substances Control Act, the Clean Water Act, the Pollution Prevention Act, the Food Quality Protection Act, and the Energy Policy Act. LEED is a certification program that recognizes sustainable building practices and strategies. Alternative energy sources also have a major impact on many stakeholders. Some of the major alternative forms of energy include wind, geothermal, solar, nuclear, biofuels, and hydropower.

Better environmental performance can increase revenue in three ways: through better access to certain markets, differentiation of products, and the sale of pollution-control technology. Good environmental performance also reduces costs by improving risk management and stakeholder relationships, reducing the amount of materials and energy used, and reducing capital and labor costs.

Green marketing is a strategic process involving stakeholder assessment to create meaningful long-term relationships with customers while maintaining, supporting, and enhancing the natural environment. However, some companies desire to obtain the benefits of green marketing without the investment. Greenwashing involves misleading a consumer into thinking a good or service is more environmentally friendly than it really is. While it might seem to be helpful to a firm, companies discovered engaging in greenwashing may suffer reputational damage.

Businesses have responded to the opportunities and threats created by environmental issues with varying levels of commitment. Those firms proactive in anticipating risks and environmental issues develop strategic management programs that view the environment as an opportunity for advancing organizational interests. Many organizations engage in recycling, the reprocessing of materials, especially steel, aluminum, paper, glass, rubber, and some plastics, for reuse. Additionally, stakeholder assessment, risk analysis, and the strategic environmental audit are important parts of a high-commitment approach to environmental issues. Stakeholder assessment is a process that acknowledges and actively monitors the environmental concerns of all legitimate stakeholders. Through risk analysis, it is possible to assess the environmental risks associated with business decisions. Organizations highly committed to environmental responsibility may conduct an audit of their efforts using standards such as ISO 14000 and report the results to all interested stakeholders.

IMPORTANT TERMS FOR REVIEW

Sustainability 347

Sustainable development 347

Kyoto protocol 351

Cancun Package 352

Genetically modified (GM) organisms 356

Environmental Protection Agency (EPA) 358

Leadership in Energy & Environmental Design (LEED) 362

Green marketing 367

Greenwashing 368

Recycling 369

RESOLVING ETHICAL BUSINESS CHALLENGES*

After graduating from Ohio State, Keisha got a job in the marketing and public relations department at a small soda company called Smith's Sodas. Smith's Sodas specializes in high-quality fruit-flavored soft drinks with unique flavors such as pomegranate, raspberry, blueberry, and coconut. The company had great plans for the future. In 10 years Smith's Sodas wanted to become a competitor to its larger rivals, Pepsi and Coca-Cola. The company sold sodas with lower calories than its rivals and offered them in a variety of flavors. However, the product was only half the battle. The rest was up to the marketing department to promote the sodas as being superior to the competition.

Recently, Keisha was called into her supervisor's office and assigned a new project. She would take the lead in a marketing initiative that promoted a new feature meant to appeal to the eco-conscious consumer: biodegradable packaging. One of the company's suppliers came up with a soda bottle made with a new biodegradable plastic manufactured with plant materials. Keisha was told the supplier struggled to develop this plastic for years and Smith's Sodas was staking much of its credibility on developing an image as an environmentally friendly organization.

Keisha immediately began learning about the plastic and writing up press releases to send to local news stations. She put in long hours working on a marketing campaign touting the product's sustainability and how much better it is for the environment. She stressed the fact that the plastic should be composted rather than simply thrown in the trash to biodegrade properly.

A few days ago Keisha received a call from a local reporter. "I've heard all of the hype concerning these biodegradable bottles your company is using. I wanted to test just how biodegradable this plastic really is. I contacted scientists at the local university to test its biodegradability. They tested the bottle under 10 different conditions with different types of soil. Only four out of the ten tests resulted in the plastic degrading to any major extent."

When Keisha hung up the phone, she decided to investigate whether the reporter's claims were accurate. After two days of phone calls, she finally contacted someone who had been involved in the actual development of the plastic.

"Yes, it's true the plastic only degrades under certain conditions," he informed her. "But that's still better than a lot of other plastics."

Keisha approached her manager, Louis, to discuss the issue. Louis did not understand Keisha's concern. "I don't see what the problem is, Keisha, other than the fact that this reporter is trying to cause trouble. As long as the plastic biodegrades under certain natural conditions, then we are fine."

"Yes, but Louis, our claims made it seem the bottles degrade fairly easily, when in reality people must compost them. Even then they only degrade under certain conditions. Isn't this a type of greenwashing?"

Louis frowned at the mention of *greenwashing*. "Keisha, the term biodegradable is vague. We have a supplier, and it is not our responsibility to prove the packaging is biodegradable. We are not being deceitful, and it is up to the consumer to know how to dispose of the package so it degrades properly. We can't control what happens to the product after the consumer buys it. Many may simply toss it into the garbage."

"What happens if the reporter publishes her findings?" Keisha asked.

Louis looked adamant. "We are not lying when we say the plastic is biodegradable. Besides, most companies have to rely on supplier claims. I don't see any reason why we need to change our marketing claims."

QUESTIONS | EXERCISES

1. Are Smith's Sodas's marketing claims accurate and truthful?
2. Discuss the justifications Louis uses to argue for the truthfulness of the company's marketing claims.
3. Assume there is a news story questioning the sustainability of Smith's Sodas packaging. How should Keisha respond?

*This case is strictly hypothetical; any resemblance to real persons, companies, or situations is coincidental.

> > > CHECK YOUR EQ

Check your EQ, or Ethics Quotient, by completing the following. Assess your performance to evaluate your overall understanding of the chapter material.

1. Sustainability is the potential for the long-term well-being of the natural environment, including all biological entities, as well as the mutually beneficial interactions among nature and individuals, organizations, and business strategies.   Yes   No

2. The Environmental Protection Agency (EPA) deals with environmental issues and enforces environmental legislation in the United States.   Yes   No

3. Ethanol, fracking, and hydropower are all forms of alternative energy.   Yes   No

4. Greenwashing is a strategic process involving stakeholder assessment to create meaningful long-term relationships with customers, while maintaining, supporting, and enhancing the natural environment.   Yes   No

5. Stakeholder assessment is an important part of a high-commitment approach to environmental issues.   Yes   No

ANSWERS 1. **Yes.** Sustainability is the potential for the long-term well-being of the natural environment, including all biological entities, as well as the mutually beneficial interactions among nature and individuals, organizations, and business strategies. 2. **Yes.** The Environmental Protection Agency deals with environmental issues and enforces environmental legislation in the United States. 3. **No.** Fracking is not a form of alternative energy. 4. **No.** Green marketing is a strategic process involving stakeholder assessment to create meaningful long-term relationships with customers, while maintaining, supporting, and enhancing the natural environment. 5. **Yes.** Stakeholder assessment is an important part of a high-commitment approach to environmental issues.

ENDNOTES

1. International Institute for Sustainable Development, "What is Sustainable Development?" https://www.iisd.org/sd/#one (accessed March 10, 2015).

2. Sean Valentine, Lynn Godkin, Gary M. Fleischman, and Roland Kidwell, "Corporate Ethical Values, Group Creativity, Job Satisfaction and Turnover Intention: The Impact of Work Context on Work Response," *Journal of Business Ethics* 98, 3 (2011): 353–372.

3. Hae-Ryong Kim, Moonkyu Lee, Hyoung-Tark Lee, and Na-Min Kim, "Corporate Social Responsibility and Employee-Company Identification," *Journal of Business Ethics* 95, 4 (2010): 557–569.

4. Liviu Florea, Yu Ha Cheung, and Neil C. Herndon, "For All Good Reasons: Role of Values in Organizational Sustainability," *Journal of Business Ethics* 114, 3 (2013): 393–408.

5. Marcus Wagner, "'Green Human Resource Benefits: Do They Matter as Determinants of Environmental Management System Implementation?" *Journal of Business Ethics* 114, 3 (2013): 443–456.

6. Russell Gold and Ian Talley, "Exxon CEO Advocates Emissions Tax," *The Wall Street Journal*, January 9, 2009, http://online.wsj.com/article/SB123146091530566335.html (accessed March 10, 2015); John Funk, "Exxon's Rex Tillerson sees climate change as risk management problem," *Cleveland.com*, June 14, 2013, http://www.cleveland.com/business/index.ssf/2013/06/exxons_rex_tillerson_see_clima.html (accessed March 10, 2015).

7. Patrick E. Murphy, Magdalena Öberseder, and Gene R. Laczniak, "Corporate Societal Responsibility in Marketing: Normatively Broadening the Concept," *AMS Review* 3, 2 (2013): 86–102.

8. Ibid.

9. Alain Verbeke and Vincent Tung, "The Future of Stakeholder Management Theory: A Temporal Perspective," *Journal of Business Ethics* 112, 3: 529–543.

10. "Air Quality," Office of Air Quality Planning and Standards, *Environmental Protection Agency*, www.epa.gov/oar/oaqps/cleanair.html (accessed April 1, 2015).

11. "The Plain English Guide to the Clean Air Act," Office of Air Quality Planning and Standards, *Environmental Protection Agency*, http://www.epa.gov/air/caa/peg/ (accessed April 1, 2015).

12. Bryan Walsh, "The Gas Dilemma," *Time*, April 11, 2011, pp. 40–48; Jim Efstathiou Jr. and Kim Chipman, "The Great Shale Gas Rush," *Bloomberg BusinessWeek*, March 7–13, 2011, pp. 25–28.

13. Alicia Mundy, "EPA Weighs Fracking Disclosure Rule," *The Wall Street Journal*, May 10–11, 2014, A2.

14. "The Effects of Acid Rain," *Environmental Protection Agency*, http://www.epa.gov/acidrain/effects/index.html (accessed April 1, 2015).

15. Bill Chameides, "U.S. Acid Rain Regulations: Did They Work?" *The Huffington Post*, May 10, 2012, http://www.huffingtonpost.com/bill-chameides/us-acid-rain-regulations_b_1507392.html (accessed April 1, 2015).

16. Mark Kinver, "2014 warmest year on record, say US researchers," *BBC*, January 16, 2015, http://www.bbc.com/news/science-environment-30852588 (accessed April 1, 2015).

17. Economist Staff, "The melting north," Special Report, *The Economist*, June 16, 2012.

18. Mark Alpert, "Protections for the Earth's Climate," *Scientific American* 293 (December 2005): 55.

19. Cassandra Sweet, Casandra (2010), "Nations Approve Cancun Climate Package," *The Wall Street Journal*, December 11, 2010, http://online.wsj.com/article/SB10001424052748703518604576012922254366218.html? KEY WORDS=global+warming+initiatives (accessed March 10, 2015); UNFCCC The Cancun Agreements, "Financial, technology and capacity-building support," http://cancun.unfccc.int/financial-technology-and-capacity-building-support/new-long-term-funding-arrangements/ (accessed March 10, 2015).

20. Fiona Harvey, "Doha climate gateway: the reaction," *The Guardian*, December 10, 2012, http://www.guardian.co.uk/environment/2012/dec/10/doha-climate-gateway-reaction (accessed April 1, 2015); "Conference leaders hail Doha Gateway agreement," Doha 2012*Qatar Is Booming*, December 8, 2012, http://qatarisbooming.com/article/conference-leaders-hail-gateway-after-agreement (accessed April 1, 2015); "The Doha Climate Gateway," United Nations Framework Convention on Climate Change, 2014, http://unfccc.int/key_steps/doha_climate_gateway/items/7389.php (accessed March 9, 2015); United Nations, "UN and Climate Change," http://www.un.org/climatechange/towards-a-climate-agreement/ (accessed March 10, 2015).

21. Economist staff, "The Environmental Union," *The Economist*, November 1, 2014, 53.

22. Richard Wolf, "Greenhouse Gas Rules Survive Court," *USA Today*, June 24, 2014, 3B.

23. Economist staff, "The Environmental Union," *The Economist*, November 1, 2014, 53.

24. Coral Davenport, "Obama Builds Environmental Legacy with 1970 Law," *The New York Times*, November 26, 2014, http://www.nytimes.com/2014/11/27/us/without-passing-a-single-law-obama-crafts-bold-enviornmental-policy.html (accessed March 10, 2015); Sarah D. Wire, "Arkansas joining states challenging EPA on emissions," *Arkansas Online*, March 10, 2015, http://www.arkansasonline.com/news/2015/mar/10/arkansas-joining-states-challenging-epa/ (accessed March 10, 2015); Richard Wolf, "Supreme Court limits greenhouse gas emissions," *USA Today*, June 23, 2014, http://www.usatoday.com/story/news/nation/2014/06/23/supreme-court-greenhouse-gas/8567453/ (accessed March 10, 2015); Juliet Eilperin and Steven Mufson, "Everything you need to know about the EPA's proposed rule on coal plants," *The Washington Post*, June 2, 2014, http://www.washingtonpost.com/national/health-science/epa-will-propose-a-rule-to-cut-emissions-from-existing-coal-plants-by-up-to-30-percent/2014/06/02/f37f0a10-e81d-11e3-afc6-a1dd9407abcf_story.html (accessed March 10, 2015); Mark Drajem, "EPA Considers Delaying Carbon Deadline After Utilities Object," *Bloomberg*, February 17, 2015, http://www.bloomberg.com/news/articles/2015-02-17/epa-considers-revised-timing-for-complying-with-power-plant-rule (accessed March 10, 2015).

25. UNICEF and World Health Organization, *Progress on Drinking Water and Sanitation 2012 Update*, 2012, http://www.unicef.org/media/files/JMPreport2012.pdf (accessed April 1, 2015).

26. Patrick Fitzgerald, "Two to Plead Guilty in Water Case," *The Wall Street Journal*, February 13, 2015, A3.

27. Bryan Walsh, "The Gas Dilemma," *Time,* April 11, 2011, 40–48; Jim Efstathiou Jr. and Kim Chipman, "The Great Shale Gas Rush," *Bloomberg Business Week*, March 7–13, 2011, 25–28.

28. Tara Patel, "The French Say No to 'Le Fracking,'" *Bloomberg Business Week*, April 4–10, 2011, 60–62.

29. Carbon Disclosure Project: Collective responses to rising water challenges: CDP Global Water Report 2012 by Deloitte. Available upon written request to Paul Simpson, CEO.

30. Reza Hosseini, http://www.levistrauss.com/unzipped-blog/2014/02/recycling-water-to-make-your-jeans-infographic/ (accessed March 10, 2015).

31. Patrick J. Kiger, "Green Fracking? 5 Technologies for Cleaner Shale Energy," *National Geographic,* March 21, 2014, http://news.nationalgeographic.com/news/energy/2014/03/140319-5-technologies-for-greener-fracking/ (accessed March 10, 2015).

32. Brian Dumaine, "What Is Water Worth?" *Fortune*, May 19, 2014, 94–100.

33. Jonathan Watts, "The clean-up begins on China dirty secret—soil pollution," *The Guardian*, June 12, 2012, http://www.guardian.co.uk/environment/2012/jun/12/china-soil-pollution-bonn-challenge (accessed April 1, 2015).

34. Margaret Coker and Benoît Faucon, "Shell to Pay for Oil Spills in Nigeria," *The Wall Street Journal*, January 8, 2015, A12.

35. Baldev Chauhan, "Indian state outlaws plastic bags," *BBC News,* August 7, 2003, http://news.bbc.co.uk/2/hi/south_asia/3132387.stm (accessed April 1, 2015); Beth Slovic, "Portland adopts ban on plastic bags that takes effect Oct. 15," July 21, 2011, *The Oregonian*, http://www.oregonlive.com/portland/index.ssf/2011/07/portland_adopts_ban_on_plastic.html (accessed April 1, 2015); "Should Cities Ban Plastic Bags?" *The Wall Street Journal*, October 8, 2012, http://online.wsj.com/article/SB100008 72396390444165804578006832478712400.html (accessed April 1, 2015).

36. Robert Lee Hotz, "Asia Leads World in Dumping Plastic in Seas," *The Wall Street Journal*, February 13, 2015, A10.

37. Michael Arndt, Wendy Zellner, and Peter Coy, "Too Much Corporate Power," *Business Week*, September 11, 2000, 149.

38. "Electronics Recycling Is Making Gains, Says EPA," *PC World*, January 8, 2009, http://www.pcworld.com/businesscenter/article/156721/article.html?tk=nl_bnxnws (accessed April 1, 2015).

39. Wendy Koch, "More states ban disposal of electronics in landfills," *USA Today*, December 18, 2011, http://usatoday30.usatoday.com/tech/news/story/2011-12-18/electronics-recycling/52055158/1 (accessed March 9, 2015).

40. World Wildlife Fund, "Threats—Deforestation," 2015, https://www.worldwildlife.org/threats/deforestation (accessed March 10, 2015).

41. Economist staff, "Cutting down on cutting down," *The Economist*, June 7, 2014, 83.

42. Home Depot, "Frequently Asked Questions," https://corporate.homedepot.com/CorporateResponsibility/Environment/WoodPurchasing/Pages/FAQs.aspx (accessed March 10, 2015).

43. University of Cambridge, "Amazon deforestation 'threshold' causes species loss to accelerate," *ScienceDaily,* March 4, 2015, http://www.sciencedaily.com/releases/2015/03/150304104224.htm (accessed March 10, 2015).

44. Tennille Tracy, "Gene-Altered Apple Approved," *The Wall Street Journal*, February 14–15, 2015, A3.

45. Economist staff, "Field research," *The Economist*, November 8, 2014, 82.

46. Jacob Bunge, "EPA Urges Limits on GMO Corn; Bug Adapts," *The Wall Street Journal*, March 6, 2015, B1.

47. Patrick Penfield, "Sustainability within the Supply Chain," March 2008, *e-Journal USA*, US Department of State.

48. Victoria L. Crittenden, William F. Crittenden, Linda K. Ferrell, O.C. Ferrell, and Christopher Pinney, "Market-oriented sustainability: a conceptual framework and propositions," *Journal of the Academy of Marketing Science* 39, 1 (2011): 71–85.

49. Philip Kotler, "Reinventing Marketing to Manage the Environmental Imperative," *Journal of Marketing* 75, 4 (2012): 132–135.

50. Environmental Protection Agency, "About EPA," http://www2.epa.gov/aboutepa (accessed April 1, 2015).

51. Ibid.

52. United States Environmental Protection Agency, "2014 Major Criminal Cases," http://www2.epa.gov/enforcement/2014-major-criminal-cases (accessed March 10, 2015).

53. James R. Healey, "The Big Squeeze Has Begun," *USA Today*, August 29, 2012, 1B–2B.

54. John W. Miller, "Preparing for a Shift to Aluminum," *The Wall Street Journal*, January 8, 2015, B5.

55. "The Plain English Guide to the Clean Air Act," http://www.epa.gov/air/caa/peg/ (accessed April 1, 2015).

56. Chris Woodyard, "Hyundai, Kia Pay $100M," *USA Today*, November 4, 2014, 1B.

57. "Summary of the Endangered Species Act," Environmental Protection Agency, http://www2.epa.gov/laws-regulations/summary-endangered-species-act (accessed April 1, 2015).

58. U.S. Fish & Wildlife Service, "Summary of Listed Species Listed Populations and Recovery Plans as of Thu, 28 Feb. 2013," *U.S. Fish and Wildlife Services Species Report*, http://ecos.fws.gov/tess_public/TESSBoxscore (accessed February 28, 2013).

59. "Summary of the Toxic Substances Control Act," Environmental Protection Agency, http://www2.epa.gov/laws-regulations/summary-toxic-substances-control-act (accessed April 1, 2015).

60. Environmental Protection Agency, "Bisphenol A (BPA) Action Plan Summary," 2012, http://www.epa.gov/opptintr/existingchemicals/pubs/actionplans/bpa.html (accessed April 1, 2015); Laura Blue, "Are Plastic Baby Bottles Harmful?" *Time*, February 8, 2008, http://www.time.com/time/health/article/0,8599,1711398,00.html (accessed April 1, 2015).

61. "Summary of the Clean Water Act," *Environmental Protection Agency*, http://www2.epa.gov/laws-regulations/summary-clean-water-act (accessed April 1, 2015).

62. Daniel Gilbert, "BP Faces Up to $13.7 Billion in Fines in Deepwater Gulf Spill Case," *The Wall Street Journal*, January 15, 2015, http://www.wsj.com/articles/bp-faces-up-to-13-7-billion-in-fines-in-deepwater-gulf-spill-case-1421361155

63. "Summary of the Pollution Prevention Act," Environmental Protection Agency, http://www2.epa.gov/laws-regulations/summary-pollution-prevention-act (accessed April 1, 2015).

64. U.S. Energy Information Administration, "Frequently Asked Questions," June 18, 2014, http://www.eia.gov/tools/faqs/faq.cfm?id=86&t=1 (accessed March 10, 2015).

65. Alex Frangos, "Timber Backs a New 'Green' Standard," *The Wall Street Journal*, March 29, 2006, B6.

66. "Food Quality Protection Act (FQPA)," Environmental Protection Agency, http://www.epa.gov/agriculture/lqpa.html (accessed April 1, 2015).

67. Nicolas Loris and David W. Kreutzer, "Economic Realities of the Electric Car," *The Heritage Foundation*, January 24, 2011, http://www.heritage.org/research/reports/2011/01/economic-realities-of-the-electric-car (accessed April 1, 2015).

68. Associated Press, "Bush signs $12.3 billion energy bill into law," *MSNBC*, August 8, 2005, http://www.msnbc.msn.com/id/8870039 (accessed April 1, 2015).

69. Bertrand d'Armagnac, "Danish wind farms show sustainable attitude toward renewable energy," *guardian.co.uk*, August 10, 2010, http://www.guardian.co.uk/world/2010/aug/10/denmark-renewable-wind-farm-energy (accessed April 1, 2015).

70. SolarCity, "Solar energy tax credits and rebates," http://www.solarcity.com/residential/solar-energy-tax-credits-rebates (accessed March 10, 2015).

71. Nate Lew, "The Top Five Fortune 500 Companies Using Solar Power," SolarEnergy.net, May 13, 2010, http://www.solarenergy.net/News/2010051301-the-top-five-fortune-500-companies-using-solar-power.aspx (accessed April 1, 2015).

72. Ami Cholia, "Top Ten Green Countries," *The Huffington Post*, August 21, 2009, http://www.huffingtonpost.com/2009/07/21/top-10-green-countries-ph_n_241867.html?slidenumber=7 (accessed April 1, 2015).

73. Louise Lucas, "Enough to go round but millions still starve," *Financial Times*, November 21, 2012, 1–2.

74. "Hydroelectric power water use," *USGS*, http://ga.water.usgs.gov/edu/wuhy.html (accessed April 1, 2015).

75. Chen Jialu, "Three Gorges Dam champions clean energy program," *China Daily*, February 23, 2010, http://www.chinadaily.com.cn/cndy/2010-02/23/content_9486733.htm (accessed April 1, 2015).

76. Stefan Ambec and Paul Lanoie, "Does It Pay to Be Green? A Systematic Overview," *The Academy of Management Perspectives* 22, 4 (2008): 45–62.

77. Environmental Leader, "Study reveals companies lack supply chain sustainability," 2009, http://www.environmentalleader.com/2009/07/18/study-reveals-companies-lack-supply-chain-sustainability/ (accessed April 1, 2015).

78. Bill Schneiderman, "Supply chain and sustainability—will this marriage last?" *Supply Demand Executive*, March 23, 2009, http://www.sdcexec.com/article/10269461/supply-chain-and-sustainability-will-this-marriage-last (accessed April 1, 2015).

79. Sierra Nevada, "Sustainability: Energy," http://www.sierranevada.com/brewery/about-us/sustainability#/energy (accessed March 10, 2015).

80. Simona Romani, Silvia Grappi, and Richard P. Bagozzi, "Corporate Socially Responsible Initiatives and Their Effects on Consumption of Green Products," published online November 26, 2014, doi: 10.1007/s10551-014-2485-0.

81. Victoria L. Crittenden, William F. Crittenden, Linda K. Ferrell, O.C. Ferrell, and Christopher C. Pinney, *Journal of the Academy of Marketing Science* 39, 1 (2011): 71–85.

82. Michael Calia, "UPS to Run Part of Fleet on Propane," *The Wall Street Journal*, March 6, 2014, B10.

83. "The Eco-label Catalogue," http://ec.europa.eu/ecat/ (accessed April 1, 2015).

84. Jörg Matthes and Anke Wonneberger, "The Skeptical Green Consumer Revisited: Testing the Relationship between Green Consumerism and Skepticism toward Advertising," *Journal of Advertising* 43, 2 (2014): 115–127.

85. "The Seven Sins of Greenwashing," Terra Choice, http://sinsofgreenwashing.org/ (accessed April 1, 2015).

86. "Eco-Friendly Product Claims Often Misleading," *NPR*, November 30, 2007, http://www.npr.org/templates/story/story.php?storyId=16754919 (accessed April 1, 2015).

87. Timothy N. Carson and Lata Gangadharan, "Environmental Labeling and Incomplete Consumer Information in Laboratory Markets," *Journal of Environmental Economics and Management* 43, 1 (2002): 113–134.

88. Kent Walker and Fang Wan, "The Harm of Symbolic Actions and Green-Washing: Corporate Actions and Communications on Environmental Performance and Their Financial Implications," *Journal of Business Ethics* 109, 2 (2012), 227–242.

89. Amy Westervelt, "FTC Finalizes Green Guides," *Forbes*, October 1, 2012, http://www.forbes.com/sites/amywestervelt/2012/10/01/ftc-finalizes-green-guides-puts-greenwashers-on-notice/ (accessed April 1, 2015).

90. Wendy Koch, "Local food may be trendy, but is it really more eco-friendly?" *USA Today*, August 9, 2012, 7B.

91. Sarah Nassauer, "To Scream Green, Dyeing Paper a Light Brown," *The Wall Street Journal*, January 25, 2012, D3.

92. Gergely Nyilasy, Harsha Gangadharbatla, and Angela Paladino, "Perceived Greenwashing: The Interactive Effects of Green Advertising and Corporate Environmental Performance on Consumer Reactions," *Journal of Business Ethics* 125, 4 (2014): 693–707.

93. Yu-Shan Chen and Ching-Hsun Chang, "Greenwash and Green Trust," The Mediation Effects of Green Consumer Confusion and Green Perceived Risk," *Journal of Business Ethics* 114, 3 (2013): 489–500.

94. Paul Hawken and William McDonough, "Seven Steps to Doing Good Business," *Inc.*, November 1993, 79–90.

95. Environmental Protection Agency, "Frequent Questions," http://www.epa.gov/osw/conserve/materials/paper/faqs.htm (accessed April 1, 2015).

96. Gills, "Waste to Energy," http://www.gillsonions.com/?q=waste-to-energy (accessed March 9, 2015).

97. Akash Kapur, "It's a Future Highway," *Bloomberg Businessweek*, July 10, 2014, 54–57.

98. "About WasteWise," http://www.epa.gov/smm/wastewise/about.htm (accessed March 10, 2015).

99. "Environmental Management Systems/ISO 14001: Frequently Asked Questions," *United States Environmental Protection Agency*, http://www.epa.gov/OWM/iso14001/isofaq.htm (accessed April 1, 2015).

100. C. Trumpp, J. Endrikat, C. Zopf, and E. Guenther, "Definition, Conceptualization, and Measurement of Corporate Environmental Performance: A Critical Examination of a Multidimensional Construct," *Journal of Business Ethics* 126, 2 (2015): 185–204.

Cases

CASE 1

Monsanto Attempts to Balance Stakeholder Interests*

INTRODUCTION

When you think of Monsanto, the phrase *genetically modified* likely comes to mind. The Monsanto Company is the world's largest seed company, with sales of over $15.9 billion. It specializes in biotechnology, or the genetic manipulation of organisms. Monsanto scientists have spent the last few decades modifying crops—often by inserting new genes or adapting existing genes within plant seeds—to meet certain aims, such as higher crop yields or insect resistance. Monsanto develops genetically-engineered seeds of plants that can survive weeks of drought, ward off weeds, and kill invasive insects. Monsanto's genetically modified (GM) seeds have increased the quantity and availability of crops, helping farmers worldwide increase food production and revenues.

Today, 90 percent of the world's GM seeds are sold by Monsanto or companies that use Monsanto genes. Monsanto also holds a 70 to 100 percent market share on certain crops. Yet Monsanto has met its share of criticism from sources as diverse as governments, farmers, activists, and advocacy groups. Monsanto supporters say the company creates solutions to world hunger by generating higher crop yields and hardier plants. Critics accuse the multinational giant of attempting to take over the world's food supply and destroying biodiversity. Since biotechnology is relatively new, critics also express concerns about the possibility of negative health and environmental effects from biotech food. A Harris Poll shows that Monsanto is considered to be the fourth most hated company in the United States. However, these criticisms have not kept Monsanto from becoming one of the world's most successful businesses.

This analysis first looks at the history of Monsanto as it progressed from a chemical company to an organization focused on biotechnology. It then examines Monsanto's current focus on developing GM seeds, including stakeholder concerns regarding the safety and environmental effects of these seeds. Next, we discuss key ethical concerns, including organizational misconduct and patent issues. We also look at Monsanto's corporate responsibility initiatives. We conclude by examining the challenges and opportunities that Monsanto may face in the future.

*This case was prepared by Jennifer Sawayda and Danielle Jolley for and under the direction of O. C. Ferrell and Linda Ferrell © 2015. It was prepared for classroom discussion rather than to illustrate either effective or ineffective handling of an administrative, ethical, or legal decision by management. All sources used for this case were obtained through publicly available material.

HISTORY: FROM CHEMICALS TO FOOD

Monsanto was founded by John F. Queeny in 1901 in St. Louis, Missouri. He named the company after his wife, Olga Monsanto Queeny. The company's first product was the artificial sweetener saccharine, which it sold to Coca-Cola. Monsanto also sold Coca-Cola caffeine extract and vanillin, an artificial vanilla flavoring. At the start of World War I, company leaders realized the growth opportunities in the industrial chemicals industry and renamed the company The Monsanto Chemical Company. The company began specializing in plastics, its own agricultural chemicals, and synthetic rubbers.

Due to its expanding product lines, the company's name was changed back to the Monsanto Company in 1964. By this time, Monsanto was producing such diverse products as petroleum, fibers, and packaging. A few years later, Monsanto created its first Roundup herbicide, a successful product that propelled the company even more into the spotlight.

However, during the 1970s Monsanto encountered a major legal obstacle. The company had produced a chemical known as Agent Orange, which was used during the Vietnam War to quickly deforest the thick Vietnamese jungles. Agent Orange contained dioxin, a chemical that caused a legal nightmare for Monsanto. Dioxin was found to be extremely carcinogenic, and in 1979 a lawsuit was filed against Monsanto on behalf of hundreds of veterans who claimed they were harmed by the chemical. Monsanto and several other manufacturers agreed to settle for $180 million, but the repercussions of dioxin continued to plague the company for decades.

In 1981 Monsanto leaders determined that biotechnology would be the company's new strategic focus. In 1986 Monsanto successfully spliced bacterium DNA into a seed. The bacterium was lethal to certain types of insects that feed on corn, potatoes, and cotton. The quest for biotechnology was on, and in 1994 Monsanto introduced the first biotechnology product to win regulatory approval. Soon the company was selling soybean, cotton, and canola seeds engineered to be tolerant to Monsanto's Roundup Ready herbicide. Many other herbicides killed good plants as well as the bad ones. Roundup Ready seeds allowed farmers to use the herbicide to eliminate weeds while sparing the crop.

In 1997 Monsanto spun off its chemical business as Solutia, and in 2000 the company entered into a merger and changed its name to the Pharmacia Corporation. Two years later, a new Monsanto, focused entirely on agriculture, broke off from Pharmacia, and the companies became two legally separate entities. The company before 2000 is often referred to as "old Monsanto," while today's company is known as "new Monsanto."

The emergence of new Monsanto was tainted by disturbing news about the company's conduct. For nearly 40 years the Monsanto Company had released toxic waste into a creek in the Alabama town of Anniston. The company had also disposed of polychlorinated biphenyls (PCBs), a highly toxic chemical, in open-pit landfills in the area. The results were catastrophic. Fish from the creek were deformed, and the population had elevated PCB levels that astounded environmental health experts. A paper trail showed that Monsanto leaders had known about the pollution since the 1960s but had not stopped the dumping. Once the cover-up was discovered, thousands of plaintiffs from the city filed a lawsuit against the company. In 2003 Monsanto and Solutia agreed to pay a settlement of $700 million to more than 20,000 Anniston residents.

When current CEO Hugh Grant took over in 2003, scandals and stakeholder uncertainty over Monsanto's GM products had tarnished the company's reputation. The price of Monsanto's stock had fallen by almost 50 percent, down to $8 a share. The company had lost $1.7 billion the previous year. Grant knew the company was fragile and decided to shift its strategic focus. Through a strong strategic focus on GM foods, the company has recovered and is now prospering.

In spite of their controversial nature, GM foods have become popular in developed and developing countries. Monsanto became so successful with its GM seeds it acquired Seminis, Inc., a leader in the fruit and vegetable seed industry. The acquisition transformed Monsanto into a global leader in the seed industry. Today, Monsanto employs approximately 22,000 people worldwide. It is recognized as one of the 100 best corporate citizens by *Corporate Responsibility Magazine*.

MONSANTO'S EMPHASIS ON BIOTECHNOLOGY

While the original Monsanto made a name for itself through the manufacturing of chemicals, the new Monsanto took quite a different turn. It changed its emphasis from chemicals to food. Today's Monsanto owes its $15.9 billion in sales to biotechnology, specifically to its sales of GM plant seeds. These seeds have revolutionized the agriculture industry. Not content with resting on its laurels, Monsanto continues to use its $1.5 billion research budget to investigate new methods of farming at its 1.5-million-square-foot complex in Missouri.

Throughout history, weeds, insects, and drought have been the bane of the farmer's existence. In the twentieth century, synthetic chemical herbicides and pesticides were invented to ward off pests. Yet applying these chemicals to an entire crop was both costly and time consuming. Then Monsanto scientists, through their work in biotechnology, were able to implant seeds with genes that make the plants themselves kill bugs. They also created seeds containing the herbicide Roundup, an herbicide that kills weeds but spares the crops. Since then Monsanto has used technology to create many innovative products, such as drought-tolerant seeds for dry areas like Africa.

The company utilizes its technological prowess to gain the support of stakeholders. For example, Monsanto has a laboratory in St. Louis that gives tours to farmers. One of the technologies the company shows farmers is a machine known as the corn chipper, which picks up seeds and removes genetic material from them. That material is analyzed to see how well the seed will grow if planted. The "best" seeds are the ones Monsanto sells for planting. Monsanto is extending its reach into the computing industry as well. The company offers software and hardware that use big data to yield important information to help farmers in the field. It even provides recommendations on when and where to plant. Monsanto also arranges tours for its critics to help them understand the process of GM crops and their implications. Impressing farmers with its technology is one way Monsanto attracts potential customers.

However, GM crops are not without critics. Opponents believe influencing the gene pools of the plants we eat could result in negative health consequences. Others worry about the health effects on beneficial insects and plants, fearing that pollinating GM plants could affect nearby insects and non-GM plants. CEO Hugh Grant decided to curtail the tide of criticism by focusing biotechnology on products not directly placed on the dinner plate but on seeds that produce goods like animal feed and corn syrup. In this way, Grant reduced some of the opposition. The company invests largely in four crops: corn, cotton, soybeans, and canola. Monsanto owes much of its revenue to its work on GM seeds, and today more than half of U.S. crops, including most soybeans and 90 percent of corn, are genetically modified.

Farmers who purchase GM seeds can grow more crops on less land and with less left to chance. GM crops have saved farmers billions by preventing loss and increasing crop yields. For example, in 1970 the average corn harvest yielded approximately 70 bushels an acre. With the introduction of biotech crops, the average corn harvest increased to roughly 150 bushels an acre. Monsanto predicts even higher yields in the future, possibly up to 300 bushels an acre by 2030. According to Monsanto CEO Hugh Grant, this increase in productivity will increase crop yields without taking up more land, helping to meet the world's growing agricultural needs.

Monsanto's GM seeds have not been accepted everywhere. Attempts to introduce them into Europe met with consumer backlash. The European Union banned most Monsanto crops except for one variety of corn. Consumers have gone so far as to destroy fields of GM crops and arrange sit-ins. Greenpeace has fought Monsanto for years, especially in the company's efforts to promote GM crops in developing countries. Even China placed bans on certain GM corn imports, although it has since relaxed the ban and appears to be encouraging more acceptance of GM crops among its citizens. This animosity toward Monsanto's products is generated by two main concerns: the safety of GM food and the environmental effects of genetic modification.

Concerns about the Safety of GM Food

Of great concern to many stakeholders are the moral and safety implications of GM food. Many skeptics see biotech crops as unnatural, with the Monsanto scientist essentially "playing God" by controlling what goes into the seed. Because GM crops are relatively new, critics maintain that the health implications of biotech food may not be known for years to come. They also contend that effective standards have not been created to determine the safety of biotech crops. Some geneticists believe the splicing of these genes into seeds could create small changes that might negatively impact the health of humans and animals that eat them. Also, even though the Food and Drug Administration (FDA) has declared biotech crops safe, critics say they have not been around long enough to gauge their long-term effects.

One concern is toxicity, particularly considering that many Monsanto seeds are equipped with a gene to allow them to produce their own Roundup herbicide. Could ingesting this herbicide, even in small amounts, cause detrimental effects on consumers? Some stakeholders say yes, and point to statistics on glyphosate, Roundup's chief ingredient, for support. According to an ecology center fact sheet, glyphosate exposure is the third most commonly reported illness among California agriculture workers, and glyphosate residues can last for a year. Yet the Environmental Protection Agency (EPA) lists glyphosate as having low skin and oral toxicity, and a study from the New York Medical College states that Roundup does not create a health risk for humans.

In March 2013 over 250,000 people signed a petition in response to President Barack Obama's signing of H.R. 933 into law. The new law, called the Agricultural Appropriations Bill of 2013, contains a provision that protects GM organisms and genetically engineered seeds from litigation concerning their health risks. In other words, courts cannot bar the sale of GM food even if future health risks are revealed. Critics of the provision claim the provision was slipped in at the last moment and that many members of Congress were not aware of it. For consumers, questions pertaining to the health risks associated with GM crops have gone unanswered and are the primary reason the petition was started. Many people have called this bill the "Monsanto Protection Act" and believe it will help protect the survival of biotech corporations. Critics also say that the continuing resolution spending bill will no longer allow the court system to protect consumers, which could create a further disconnect between consumers and producers.

Despite consumer concerns, the FDA and the American Association for the Advancement of Science have proclaimed that GM food is safe to consume. The European Commission examined more than 130 studies and concluded that GM food does not appear to be riskier than crops grown by conventional methods. As a result of its research, the FDA has determined that Americans do not need to know when they are consuming GM products. Therefore, this information is not placed on labels in most states, although other countries, notably those in the European Union, do require GM food products to state this fact in their labeling. Some states in the United States have also entered the fight to have GM food labeled. For instance, a new law in Vermont was passed that now makes it mandatory for GM food to be labeled. Organizations who would be negatively impacted by the law have sued Vermont, claiming that the law creates burdensome costs for companies without any provable advantages to the consumer. Hawaii also tried to curb types of GM crops and require labeling, but a federal judge overturned the law.

Concerns about Environmental Effects of Monsanto Products

Some studies have supported the premise that Roundup herbicide, used in conjunction with the GM seeds called "Roundup Ready," can be harmful to birds, insects, and particularly amphibians. Such studies revealed that small concentrations of Roundup may be deadly to tadpoles. Other studies suggest that Roundup might have a detrimental effect on human cells, especially embryonic, umbilical, and placental cells. Monsanto has countered these claims by questioning the methodology used in the studies. The EPA maintains glyphosate is not dangerous at recommended doses. On the other hand, the World Health Organization (WHO) ruled that glyphosate probably does have the potential to cause cancer in humans. The finding caused Monsanto shares to drop 2 percent. Monsanto has challenged this assertion and wants to meet with WHO officials to discuss the findings.

As honeybees have begun to die off, critics are blaming companies like Monsanto and Bayer. They believe the companies' pesticides are killing off the good insects as well as the bad ones. While there is no definitive evidence that the honeybees are dying off due to pesticide use, opposition against Monsanto is rising as the honeybee population continues to decline. One of the projects in which Monsanto has invested is working with the Defense Advanced Research Projects Agency (DARPA) in developing mechanical bee-like drones that can be used to pollinate crops. Nicknamed Robobees, these drones could help with pollinating crops, which could lead to an increase in food crops. Opponents, on the other hand, claim Monsanto is killing the bees and will obtain even more power by gaining control of their mechanical substitutes.

Another concern with GM seeds in general is the threat of environmental contamination. Bees, other insects, and wind can carry a crop's seeds to other areas, sometimes to fields containing non-GM crops. These seeds and pollens might then mix with the farmer's crops. Organic farmers have complained that GM seeds from nearby farms have "contaminated" their crops. This environmental contamination could pose a serious threat. Some scientists fear that GM seeds spread to native plants may cause those plants to adopt the GM trait, thus creating new genetic variations of those plants that could negatively influence (through genetic advantages) the surrounding ecosystem. A major dispute has arisen between vegetable farmers and Monsanto for just this reason. Monsanto and its competitor Dow Chemical are developing seeds to be resistant to stronger herbicides because plants are starting to become resistant to Roundup. However, these stronger herbicides have been known to drift to other farms after a farmer sprays his or her crops. While the special interest group Save Our Crops successfully convinced Dow to reformulate its herbicide to decrease the likelihood of drift, Monsanto maintains its resistant seeds will be able to coexist with other crops without a contamination problem.

Another controversy involves the discovery of a field in Oregon filled with an experimental form of Monsanto's GM wheat. The wheat was not approved by the United States Department of Agriculture. The discovery of this wheat raised concern over whether it could have contaminated U.S. wheat supplies. As a result, Japan temporarily instituted a ban on U.S. wheat. Initial investigations revealed that the wheat had been stored in a Colorado facility but were unable to provide an explanation for how it showed up in an Oregon field. Monsanto denied involvement and stated that it suspected someone had covertly obtained the GM wheat and planted it. The company also claims that this incident was an isolated occurrence. The altered wheat is not believed to have caused any damage, and Japan lifted the ban. However, some farmers filed lawsuits against Monsanto seeking class-action status.

Monsanto has taken action in addressing environmental and health concerns. The company maintains that the environmental impact of everything it creates has been studied by the EPA and approved. Monsanto officials claim that glyphosate in Roundup rarely ends up in ground water, and when it does contaminate ground water, it is soluble and will not have much effect on aquatic species. The firm has stated that it will not file lawsuits against farmers if GM crops accidentally mix with organic. Monsanto has also partnered with Conservation International in an effort to conserve biodiversity. Stakeholders are left to make their own decisions regarding GM crops.

Resistance to Pesticides and Herbicides

Another environmental problem that has emerged is weed and insect resistance to the herbicides and pesticides in Monsanto crops. On the one hand, it is estimated that GM crops have prevented the use of £965 million (approximately $1.5 billion) of pesticide use. On the other hand, critics fear that continual use of the chemicals could result in "super weeds" and "super bugs," much like the overuse of antibiotics in humans has resulted in drug-resistant bacteria. The company's Roundup line, in particular, has come under attack. GM seeds labeled Roundup Ready are engineered to withstand large doses of the herbicide Roundup. Because Roundup is used more frequently, weeds have started to develop a resistance to this popular herbicide. Significant numbers of Roundup resistant weeds have been found in the United States and Australia.

To combat "super bugs," the government requires farmers using Monsanto's GM products to create "refuges," in which they plant 20 percent of their fields with a non-GM crop. The theory is that this allows nonresistant bugs to mate with those that are resistant, preventing a new race of super bugs. To prevent resistance to the Roundup herbicide, farmers are required to vary herbicide use and practice crop rotations. However, since Roundup is so easy to use, particularly in conjunction with Roundup Ready seeds, some farmers do not take the time to institute these preventative measures. When they do rotate their crops, some will rotate one Roundup Ready crop with another. As a result, agricultural pests such as rootworm are becoming resistant to genes in GM crops intended to kill them. This resistance is causing some farmers to turn toward more traditional herbicides and pesticides. For the first time, regulators in the United States are encouraging limits on certain kinds of GM corn to prevent the spread of resistant bugs. The EPA acknowledges that farmers and seed companies have not done enough to curb resistance. It is recommending that 35 percent of fields be planted with another crop other than biotech corn. Resistance is of particular concern in Latin America, Africa, and Asia, where farmers may not be as informed of the risks of herbicide and pesticide overuse.

DEALING WITH ORGANIZATIONAL ETHICAL ISSUES

In addition to concerns over the safety of GM seeds and environmental issues, Monsanto has dealt with concerns about organizational conduct. Organizations face significant risks from strategies and employees striving for high performance standards. Such pressure sometimes encourages employees to engage in illegal or unethical conduct. All firms have these concerns. In the case of Monsanto, patents and other legal issues have resulted in legal, ethical, and reputational consequences.

Patent Issues

As bioengineered creations of the Monsanto Company, Monsanto's seeds are protected under patent law. Under the terms of the patent, farmers using Monsanto seeds are not allowed to harvest seeds from the plants for use in upcoming seasons. Instead, they must purchase new Monsanto seeds each season. By issuing new seeds each year, Monsanto ensures it secures a profit as well as maintains control over its property. This patent protection has become a controversial subject among farmers and has led to numerous litigation battles for Monsanto.

Throughout agricultural history, farmers have collected and saved seeds from previous harvests to plant the following year's crops. Critics argue that requiring farmers to suddenly purchase new seeds year after year puts an undue financial burden on them and gives Monsanto too much power. However, the law protects Monsanto's right to have exclusive control over its creations, and farmers must abide by these laws. When they are found guilty of using Monsanto seeds from previous seasons, either deliberately or out of ignorance, they are often fined.

Since it is fairly easy for farmers to violate the patent, Monsanto has found it necessary to employ investigators from law firms to investigate suspected violations. The resulting investigations are a source of contention between Monsanto and accused farmers. According to Monsanto, investigators deal with farmers in a respectful manner. They approach the farmers suspected of patent infringement and ask them questions. The company claims that investigators practice transparency with the farmers and tell them why they are there and who they represent. If after the initial interview is completed and suspicions still exist, the investigators may pull the farmer's records. They may bring in a sampling team, with the farmer's permission, to test the farmer's fields. If found guilty the farmer must often pay Monsanto. However, some farmers tell a different story about Monsanto and its seed investigators. They claim that Monsanto investigators have used unethical practices to get them to cooperate. They call the investigators the "seed police" and say they behave like a "Gestapo" or "mafia."

In 2007 Monsanto sued Vernon Bowman, an Indiana farmer who Monsanto claims used second-generation Monsanto seeds to plant soybeans. Monsanto claimed its patent protection reaches past first-generation seeds and Mr. Bowman infringed upon its patent. In 2009 the court ruled in favor of Monsanto and ordered Bowman to pay $84,000 in damages. Mr. Bowman did not accept defeat, and in 2013 brought his case before the Supreme Court. The Supreme Court ruled in favor of Monsanto, representing a great victory for biotechnology companies.

Monsanto does not limit its investigations to farmers. It filed a lawsuit against DuPont, the world's second-largest seed maker, for combining DuPont technology with Roundup Ready. Monsanto won that lawsuit, but was countersued by DuPont for anticompetitive practices. These accusations of anticompetitive practices garnered the attention of federal antitrust lawyers. With increased pressure coming from different areas, Monsanto agreed to allow patents to expire on its seeds starting in 2014. This will allow other companies to create less expensive versions of Monsanto seeds. However, Monsanto announced it would continue to strictly enforce patents for new versions of its products, such as Roundup Ready 2 soybeans.

Legal Issues

Many major companies have government and legal forces to deal with, and Monsanto is no exception. The government has begun to examine Monsanto's practices more closely. In 1980 the Supreme Court allowed living organisms to be patented for the first time, giving Monsanto the ability to patent its seeds. Despite this victory, Monsanto came to the attention of the American Antitrust Institute for alleged anticompetitive activities. The institute suggested that Monsanto hinders competition, exerting too much power over the transgenic seed industry and limiting seed innovation. When Monsanto acquired DeKalb and Delta Land and Pine, it had to obtain the approval of antitrust authorities, and gained that approval after agreeing to certain concessions. As a result of complaints, the Department of Justice (DOJ) began a civil investigation into Monsanto's practices. Although the DOJ eventually dropped the antitrust probe, concerns over Monsanto's power continue. Monsanto must be careful to ensure that its activities cannot be seen as anticompetitive.

In early 2013 Monsanto settled with local residents in Nitro, West Virginia, after claims of health problems became persistent in a now-closed Agent Orange plant. The company agreed to spend up to $93 million on medical testing and local cleanup of as many as 4,500 homes. It also agreed to establish a medical monitoring program and will make additional money available to continue the program's operation for 30 years.

The most talked about litigation involving Monsanto is its constant battle with competitor DuPont. In the past, DuPont has filed multiple lawsuits against Monsanto. One lawsuit claimed Monsanto used its power and licenses to block DuPont products. In March 2013, the battle for dominance between these two companies was settled. A patent-licensing deal was reached and DuPont agreed to pay Monsanto at least $1.75 billion over the next 10 years. This payment enables DuPont to have rights and access to technology for genetically engineered soybeans that resist herbicides. DuPont will also obtain rights to combine patented genes from Monsanto with other genes to develop multiple crop traits. On the opposing side, Monsanto is given access to DuPont patents for corn defoliation and crop-disease resistance techniques. This settlement will hopefully create positive results for farmers and enable the development of technologies that will aid in higher crop yields for years to come.

CORPORATE RESPONSIBILITY AT MONSANTO

Despite criticisms levied against Monsanto, a study has provided evidence that GM crops have greatly benefited farming. The study estimated that farmers who adopted GM crops have seen their profits increase to 69 percent higher than those who did not. Today, the public generally expects multinational corporations to advance the interests and well-being of the people in the countries where they do business. Monsanto has given millions of dollars in programs to improve communities in developing countries. In fact, *Corporate Responsibility Magazine* ranked Monsanto number 38 on its 100 Best Corporate Citizens list.

Monsanto created a Code of Business Conduct to provide guidance on the firm's ethical expectations and is concerned with maintaining integrity among its many different stakeholders. In 2003 the company adopted an additional Code of Conduct for its chief executives and financial officers and a Human Rights Policy in 2006 to ensure the rights of Monsanto employees and those in its supply chain. The company's Business Conduct Office is responsible for investigating cases of alleged misconduct as well as maintaining the company's anonymous hotline.

As part of Monsanto's culture, the company wrote a pledge informing stakeholders about what it sees as its ethical commitments. According to Monsanto, the pledge "helps us to convert our values into actions, and to make clear who we are and what we champion." Table 1 provides the values Monsanto pledges to uphold, including integrity, dialogue, transparency, sharing, benefits, respect, acting as owners to achieve results, and creating a great place to work.

As an agricultural company, Monsanto must address the grim reality that the world's population is increasing fast, and the amount of land and water available for agriculture is decreasing. Some experts believe our planet must produce more food in the next 50 years to feed the world's population than what has grown in the past 10,000 years, requiring us to double our food output. As a multinational corporation dedicated to agriculture, Monsanto is expected to address these problems. The company developed a three-tiered commitment policy: (1) produce more yield in crops, (2) conserve more resources, and (3) improve the lives of farmers. The company hopes to achieve these goals through initiatives in sustainable agriculture.

Sustainable Agriculture

Monsanto's CEO Hugh Grant has said, "Agriculture intersects the toughest challenges we all face on the planet. Together, we must meet the needs for increased food, fiber, and energy while protecting the environment. In short, the world needs to produce more and conserve smarter." Monsanto is quick to point out that its biotech products added more than 100 million tons to worldwide agricultural production in a 10-year period, and the company estimates that this has increased farmers' incomes by $33.8 billion. Monsanto also created partnerships between nonprofit organizations across the world to enrich the lives of farmers in developing countries. The company's goal is to double its core crop

TABLE 1: The Monsanto Pledge

Integrity

Integrity is the foundation for all that we do. Integrity includes honesty, decency, consistency, and courage. Building on those values, we are committed to:

Dialogue

We will listen carefully to diverse points of view and engage in thoughtful dialogue. We will broaden our understanding of issues in order to better address the needs and concerns of society and each other.

Transparency

We will ensure that information is available, accessible, and understandable.

Sharing

We will share knowledge and technology to advance scientific understanding, to improve agriculture and the environment, to improve crops, and to help farmers in developing countries.

Benefits

We will use sound and innovative science and thoughtful and effective stewardship to deliver high-quality products that are beneficial to our customers and to the environment.

Respect

We will respect the religious, cultural, and ethical concerns of people throughout the world. The safety of our employees, the communities where we operate, our customers, consumers, and the environment will be our highest priorities.

Act as owners to achieve results

We will create clarity of direction, roles, and accountability; build strong relationships with our customers and external partners; make wise decisions; steward our company resources; and take responsibility for achieving agreed-upon results.

Create a great place to work

We will ensure diversity of people and thought; foster innovation, creativity, and learning; practice inclusive teamwork; and reward and recognize our people.

Source: Monsanto Corporation, *Monsanto Code of Business Conduct,* http://www.monsanto.com/SiteCollectionDocuments/Code-of-Business-Conduct-PDFs/code_of_conduct_english.pdf (accessed April 20, 2015).

yields by 2030. Monsanto intends to achieve this goal through new product innovations such as drought-tolerant seeds and better technology. Two regions Monsanto is now focusing on are India and Africa.

The need for better agriculture is apparent in India, where the population is estimated to hit 1.3 billion by 2017. Biotech crops have helped improve the size of yields in India, and Monsanto has estimated that Indian cotton farmers using biotech crops earn approximately $176 more in revenues per acre than their non-biotech contemporaries. Monsanto launched Project SHARE, a sustainable yield initiative created in conjunction with the nonprofit Indian Society of Agribusiness, to improve the lives of 10,000 cotton farmers in 1,050 villages.

In Africa Monsanto partnered with organizations, scientists, and philanthropists to develop and introduce drought-tolerant and virus-resistant seeds for African farmers. For instance, the Monsanto Fund is working with scientists to develop cassava plants that are resistant to two common types of viruses. The cassava is an important food product for many African communities. As CEO Hugh Grant writes, "This initiative isn't simply altruistic; we see it as a unique business proposition that rewards farmers and shareowners." But not all view Monsanto's presence in Africa as an outreach in corporate responsibility.

Some see it as another way for Monsanto to improve its bottom line. Opponents see the company as trying to take control of African agriculture and destroy African agricultural practices that have lasted for thousands of years.

Charitable Giving

In 1964 the Monsanto Company established the Monsanto Fund. This fund contributes to educational opportunities and the needs of communities across the world. One recipient of the Monsanto Fund is Nanmeng Village in China. The company is helping to train farmers in the area about ways to improve agricultural methods and infrastructure development. The Monsanto Company also committed $10 million to provide fellowship opportunities for Ph.D. students seeking to get their degree in rice or wheat plant breeding.

Another program implemented by the company is the Matching Gifts Program. This program matches employee contributions to charitable and educational organizations, dollar-for-dollar, by the Monsanto Fund. The program matches a maximum of $5,000 per employee every year and includes organizations supporting the environment, arts and culture, and disaster relief, among many others.

In the first decade of the twenty-first century, Monsanto supported youth programs and donated nearly $1.5 million in scholarships to students wanting to pursue agriculture-related degrees. The company supports 4-H programs and the program Farm Safety 4 Just Kids, a program that teaches rural children about safety while working on farms. Monsanto also partnered with the organization Agriculture Future of America (AFA), providing more than $100,000 in scholarships to youth in eight states who want to pursue agricultural careers.

CONCLUSION

Monsanto faces challenges that it must address, including lingering concerns over the safety and the environmental impact of its products. The company needs to enforce its code of conduct effectively to avoid organizational misconduct. Monsanto also faces increased competition from other companies. The seed company Pioneer Hi-Bred International, Inc. uses pricing strategies and seed sampling to attract price-conscious customers. Chinese companies are formidable rivals for Monsanto since their weed killers began eating into some of Monsanto's Roundup profits. As a result, Monsanto announced plans to restructure the Roundup area of the business.

Yet despite the onslaught of criticism from Monsanto detractors and the challenge of increased competition from other companies, Monsanto has numerous opportunities to thrive in the future. The company is currently working on new innovations that could increase its competitive edge as well as benefit farmers worldwide. Monsanto has teamed up with a Danish biotechnology firm to develop microscopic organisms that could be used to aid plant growth and ward off pests. These microorganisms could be a possible alternative to GM seeds. The company is also taking advantage of big data and its potential uses for farming. Monsanto's inroads into the computing industry are likely to grow in the coming years.

Although Monsanto has made ethical errors in the past, it is trying to portray itself as a socially responsible company dedicated to improving agriculture. As noted, the company still has problems. The predictions from Monsanto critics about biotech food have not yet come true, but that has not eradicated the fears among stakeholders. Non-GM food products are becoming more popular, despite their increased costs. Sales of non-GM food grew 28 percent in one year to about $3 billion in sales. Faced with the increasing popularity of organic food and staunch criticism from opponents, Monsanto needs to continue working with stakeholders to promote its technological innovations and eliminate fears concerning its industry.

QUESTIONS FOR DISCUSSION

1. Does Monsanto maintain an ethical culture that effectively responds to various stakeholders?
2. Compare the benefits of growing GM seeds for crops with the potential negative consequences of using them.
3. How should Monsanto manage the potential harm to plant and animal life from using products such as Roundup?

SOURCES

Akane Otani, "America's Most Loved and Most Hated Companies," *Bloomberg*, February 5, 2015, http://www.bloomberg.com/news/articles/2015-02-05/america-s-most-loved-and-most-hated-companies (accessed April 20, 2015); Annie Gasparro, "GMO Fight Ripples Down Food Chain," *The Wall Street Journal*, August 8, 2014, A1; Associated Press, "Another Wheat Lawsuit," *The Kansas City Star*, July 8, 2013, http://www.kansascity.com/2013/07/08/4334882/another-wheat-lawsuit-filed-against.html (accessed April 20, 2015); Brian Hindo, "Monsanto: Winning the Ground War," *BusinessWeek*, December 5, 2007, 35–41; Carey Gillam, "UPDATE 1-Monsanto Unapproved GMO Wheat Stored in Colorado through '11," *Reuters*, June 28, 2013, http://www.reuters.com/article/2013/06/28/monsanto-wheat-idUSL2N0F40QR20130628 (accessed April 20, 2015); "China GMO Corn Approval Seen Spurring Recovery in U.S. Imports," *Bloomberg*, December 18, 2014, http://www.bloomberg.com/news/articles/2014-12-18/china-gmo-corn-approval-seen-spurring-recovery-in-u-s-imports (accessed April 20, 2015); Claire Oxborrow, Becky Price, and Peter Riley, "Breaking Free," *Ecologist* 38, no. 9 (November 2008): 35–36; Connor Adam Sheets, "Farmers and Food Safety Advocates Lead Monsanto Backlash," *Salon*, March 27, 2013, http://www.salon.com/2013/03/27/farmers_and_food_safety_advocates_lead_monsanto_backlash_partner/ (accessed April 20, 2015); "CR's 100 Best Corporate Citizens 2014," *CR Magazine*, March/April 2014, 1–7; Crystal Gammon and Environmental Health News, "Weed-Whacking Herbicide Proves Deadly to Human Cells," *Scientific American*, June 23, 2009, http://www.scientificamerican.com/article.cfm?id=weed-whacking-herbicide-p&page=3 (accessed April 20, 2015); David Alire Garcia and Adriana Barrera, "Mexico Postpones Approval of Large-scale GM Corn Fields," *Reuters*, November 22, 2012, http://www.reuters.com/article/2012/11/23/us-mexico-corn-idUSBRE8AM00O20121123 (accessed April 20, 2015); Dennis K. Berman, Gina Chon, and Scott Kilman, "Monsanto Pushes Deeper Into China," *The Wall Street Journal*, July 11, 2011, B1–B2; Donald L. Barlett and James B. Steele, "Monsanto's Harvest of Fear," *Vanity Fair*, May 5, 2008, http://www.vanityfair.com/politics/features/2008/05/monsanto200805 (accessed April 20, 2015); Drake Bennett, "What Are They Doing at Monsanto?" *Bloomberg Businessweek*, July 3, 2014, 52–59; "DuPont and Monsanto Agree to End Lawsuits," *Bloomberg*, March, 26, 2013, http://www.bloomberg.com/news/2013-03-26/dupont-monsanto-agree-to-end-lawsuits.html (accessed April 20, 2015); Economist staff, "Field research," *The Economist*, November 8, 2014, 82; E. Freeman, "Seed Police?" *Monsanto*, November 10, 2008, http://www.monsanto.com/newsviews/Pages/Seed-Police-Part-4.aspx (accessed April 20, 2015); Ellen Gibson, "Monsanto," *BusinessWeek*, December 22, 2008, 51; Elizabeth Weise, "Monsanto in Dispute with Veggie Farmers," *USA Today*, March 18, 2014, 7B; "Even Small

Doses of Popular Weed Killer Fatal to Frogs, Scientist Finds," *ScienceDaily,* August 5, 2005, http://www.
sciencedaily.com/releases/2005/08/050804053212.htm (accessed April 20, 2015); Georgina Gustin, "Justice
Department Ends Monsanto Antitrust Probe," *St. Louis Post-Dispatch*, November 19, 2012, http://www.stltoday.
com/business/local/justice-department-ends-monsanto-antitrust-probe/article_667ceab6-e568-57c8-a110-
3d99efc31c4c.html (accessed April 20, 2015); "GMOs under a Microscope," Science and Technology in Congress,
October 1999, http://www.aaas.org/spp/cstc/pne/pubs/stc/bulletin/articles/10-99/GMOs.htm (accessed March 25,
2009); G. M. Williams, R. Kroes, and I. C. Monro, "Safety Evaluation and Risk Assessment of the Herbicide
Roundup and Its Active Ingredient, Glyphosate, for Humans," *NCBI*, April 2000, http://www.ncbi.nlm.nih.gov/
pubmed/10854122 (accessed April 20, 2015); Ian Berry, "Monsanto's Seeds Sow a Profit," *The Wall Street Journal,*
January 7, 2011, B3; Ian Berry, "Pesticides Make a Comeback," *The Wall Street Journal, May 21, 2013,* http://online.
wsj.com/article/SB10001424127887323463704578496923254944066.html (accessed April 20, 2015); Ian Berry, "The
Future of Patent Law Rest in a Farmer's Hands," *Wall Street Journal,* February 15, 2013, B1; "India's Green Counter-
Revolution," *The Wall Street,* February 13, 2010, http://online.wsj.com/article/SB10001424052748704140104575058
383515565108.html (accessed April 20, 2015); Jack Kaskey, "Monsanto Says Rogue Wheat in Oregon May Be
Sabotage," *Bloomberg,* June 5, 2013, http://www.bloomberg.com/news/2013-06-05/monsanto-says-rogue-wheat-
didn-t-contaminate-oregon-seed.html (accessed April 20, 2015); Jack Kaskey, "Monsanto Sets a Soybean Free,"
Bloomberg Businessweek, February 1–8, 2010, 19; Jack Kaskey, "Monsanto 'Warrior' Grant Fights Antitrust
Accusations, Critics," *Bloomberg Businessweek,* March 4, 2010, http://www.bloomberg.com/apps/news?pid=newsa
rchive&sid=axVdNmPtSgts (accessed April 20, 2015); Jacob Bunge, "EPA Urges Limits on GMO Corn; Bug
Adapts," *The Wall Street Journal*, March 6, 2015, B1; Jacob Bunge, "GMOs, under Assault, Have a New Defender,"
The Wall Street Journal, September 4, 20914, B1–B2; Jacob Bunge, "Judge Overturns GMO Crop Curbs in Hawaii,"
Wall Street Journal, August 26, 2014, B1; Jacob Bunge, "Monsanto Slams Weed-Killer Finding," *The Wall Street
Journal,* March 24, 2015, B2; Jacob Bunge, "Monsanto Strikes Deal to Develop Plant Microbes," *The Wall Street
Journal,* December 11, 2013, B4; Jacob Bunge, "U.S. Corn Exports to China Dry Up over GMO Concerns," *The
Wall Street Journal,* April 11, 2014, B1; Jean Guerrero, "Altered Corn Advances Slowly in Mexico," *The Wall Street
Journal,* December 9, 2010, B8; John W. Miller, "Monsanto Loses Case in Europe over Seeds," *The Wall Street
Journal,* July 7, 2010, B1; Jutia Group, "Monsanto Mania: The Seed of Profits," *iStockAnalyst,* http://www.
istockanalyst.com/article/viewarticle.aspx?articleid=1235584&zoneid=Home (accessed April 20, 2015); Lindsey
Boerma, "Critics Slam Obama for protecting Monsanto," *CBS NEWS,* March 28, 2013, http://www.cbsnews.
com/8301-250_162-57576835/critics-slam-obama-for-protecting-monsanto/ (accessed April 20, 2015); Margie
Kelly, "Top 7 Genetically Modified Crops," *The Huffington Post,* October 30, 2012, http://www.huffingtonpost.
com/margie-kelly/genetically-modified-food_b_2039455.html (accessed April 20, 2015); Mark Memmot,
"Supreme Court Rules for Monsanto in Case against Farmer," *NPR*, May 13, 2013, http://www.npr.org/blogs/
thetwo-way/2013/05/13/183603368/supreme-court-rules-for-monsanto-in-case-against-farmer (accessed April 20,
2015); Mark Peters and Kris Maher, "Monsanto Settles Lawsuits," *Wall Street Journal,* February 25–26, 2012,
B3; Matt Ridley, "The Perils of Always Ignoring the Bright Side," *The Wall Street Journal,* http://online.wsj.com/
article/SB10000872396390444004704578030340322277954.html (accessed April 20, 2015); Michael Grunwald,
"Monsanto Hid Decades of Pollution," *The Washington Post,* January 1, 2002, A1; Michael Pollan, "Playing God in
the Garden," *The New York Times Magazine,* October 25, 1998, http://www.michaelpollan.com/article.php?id=73
(accessed April 20, 2015); Monsanto Company, "Backgrounder: Glyphosate and Environmental Fate Studies,"
http://www.monsanto.com/glyphosate/documents/glyphosate-and-environmental-fate-studies.pdf (accessed
April 20, 2015); Monsanto Company, "Code of Ethics for Chief Executives and Senior Financial Officers,"
February 19, 2003, http://www.monsanto.com/whoweare/Pages/code-of-ethics.aspx (accessed April 20,
2015); "Monsanto Company—Company Profile, Information, Business Description, History, Background
Information on Monsanto Company," http://www.referenceforbusiness.com/history2/92/Monsanto-Company.
html (accessed April 20, 2015); Monsanto Company, "Corporate Profile," http://www.monsanto.com/investors/
Pages/corporate-profile.aspx (accessed April 20, 2015); Monsanto Company, "Do GM Crops Increase Yields?"
http://www.monsanto.com/newsviews/Pages/do-gm-crops-increase-yield.aspx (accessed April 20,
2015); Monsanto Company, "Financial Highlights," http://www.monsanto.com/investors/pages/financial-

highlights.aspx (accessed April 20, 2015); Monsanto Company, "India Cotton Success," http://www.monsanto.com/improvingagriculture/pages/celebrating-bollgard-cotton-india.aspx (accessed April 20, 2015); Monsanto Company, "Is Bt or GMO Cotton the Reason for Indian Farmer Suicides," http://www.monsanto.com/newsviews/pages/india-farmer-suicides.aspx (accessed April 20, 2015); Monsanto Company, "Monsanto Code of Business Conduct," http://www.monsanto.com/SiteCollectionDocuments/Code-of-Business-Conduct-PDFs/code_of_conduct_english.pdf (accessed April 20, 2015); Monsanto Company, "Virus Resistant Cassava for Africa (VIRCA)," http://www.monsanto.com/improvingagriculture/pages/virus-resistant-cassava-for-africa.aspx (accessed April 20, 2015); Monsanto Company, "What Is Monsanto Doing To Help?" http://www.monsanto.com/improvingagriculture/Pages/what-is-monsanto-doing-to-help.aspx (accessed April 20, 2015); Monsanto Company, "Youth and Education," http://www.monsanto.com/whoweare/Pages/youth-and-education.aspx (accessed August 15, 2014); Nancy Remsen, "Lawsuit Challenges Vermont's GMO Labeling Law," *USA Today*, June 12, 2014, http://www.usatoday.com/story/news/nation/2014/06/12/lawsuit-challenges-vermonts-gmo-labeling-law/10402301/ (accessed April 20, 2015); Nina Easton, "Why the March on Genetically Modified Food Hurts the Hungry," *Fortune*, June 10, 2013, 64; Reverend Billy, "The Promised Land of the Robobee, Monsanto and DARPA," *The Huffington Post*, August 3, 2014, http://www.huffingtonpost.com/reverend-billy/the-promised-land-of-the-_b_5441190.html (accessed April 20, 2015); Scott Kilman, "Monsanto's Net Profit Declines by 45%," *The Wall Street Journal,* July 1, 2010, B7; Seralini Gilles-Eric, Emilie Clair, Robin Mesnage, Steeve Gress, Nicolas Defarage, Manuela Malatesta, Didier Hennequin, and Joel Spiroux de Vendomois, "Long Term Toxicity of a Roundup Herbicide and a Roundup-tolerante Genetically Modified Maize," *Food and Chemical Toxicology* 57 (March 2013): 476–483; "$700 Million Settlement in Alabama PCB Lawsuit," *The New York Times,* August 21, 2001, http://www.nytimes.com/2003/08/21/business/700-million-settlement-in-alabama-pcb-lawsuit.html (accessed April 20, 2015); The Monsanto Fund website, http://www.monsantofund.org/ (accessed April 20, 2015). "The Parable of the Sower," *The Economist,* November 21, 2009, 71–73; World Health Organization, "Food Security," http://www.who.int/trade/glossary/story028/en/ (accessed April 20, 2015).

CASE 2

Starbucks Mission: Social Responsibility and Brand Strength[*]

Howard Schultz joined Starbucks in 1982 as director of retail operations and marketing. Returning from a trip to Milan, Italy, with its 1,500 coffee bars, Schultz recognized an opportunity to develop a similar retail coffee bar culture in Seattle.

In 1985 the company tested the first downtown Seattle coffeehouse, served the first Starbucks café latté, and introduced its Christmas Blend. Since then, Starbucks expanded across the United States and around the world, now operating over 21,000 stores in 65 countries. Historically, Starbucks grew at a rate of about three stores a day, although the company cut back on expansion in recent years. The company serves 70 million customers per week and has revenues of approximately $16.4 billion a year. It is the largest coffeehouse company in the world.

Starbucks locates its retail stores in high-traffic, high-visibility locations. The stores are designed to provide an inviting coffee bar environment that is an important part of the Starbucks product and experience. It was the intention of Howard Schulz to make Starbucks into "the third place" for consumers to frequent, after home and work. Because the company is flexible regarding size and format, it locates stores in or near a variety of settings, including office buildings, bookstores, and university campuses. It can situate retail stores in select rural and off-highway locations to serve a broader array of customers outside major metropolitan markets and further expand brand awareness.

In addition to selling products through retail outlets, Starbucks sells coffee and tea products and licenses its trademark through other channels and partners. For instance, its Frappuccino coffee drinks, Starbucks Doubleshot espresso drinks, super-premium ice creams, and VIA coffees can be purchased in grocery stores and through retailers like Walmart and Target. Starbucks partnered with Courtesy Products to create single-cup Starbucks packets marketed toward hotel rooms. Starbucks also partnered with Green Mountain Coffee Roasters to introduce Starbucks-branded coffee and tea pods to the market. These pods target consumers who own Keurig single-cup brewing machines. Although the two businesses would normally be rivals, this partnership is beneficial for both Green Mountain and Starbucks. Since Green Mountain owns Keurig's single-serve machines, the partnership enables Starbucks to access this technology to market a new product. Green Mountain benefits because the partnership generates new users of Keurig single-cup brewing machines attracted to the Starbucks name.

This partnership between Green Mountain and Starbucks did not stop Starbucks from launching its own line of single-serve machines. In 2012 Starbucks introduced its Verismo

---

[*]This case was prepared by Michelle Urban and Jennifer Sawayda for and under the direction of O.C. Ferrell and Linda Ferrell © 2015. It was prepared for classroom discussion rather than to illustrate either effective or ineffective handling of an administrative, ethical, or legal decision by management. All sources used for this case were obtained through publicly available material and the Starbucks website.

580 Brewer that allows consumers to brew a cup of Starbucks coffee in their own homes (later versions include the Verismo 583 and 600). The coffee has the strong, bold flavor of a cup purchased in any Starbucks retail location. Starbucks offers a limited assortment of coffees to emphasize quality rather than quantity. Not to be outdone, Green Mountain released another type of single-serve coffee brewer called the Rivo. Unlike the Verismo that uses powdered milk pods, the Rivo uses fresh milk. The race to conquer the single-serve coffee market is intensifying between the two companies.

A common criticism of Starbucks is the company's strategy for location and expansion. Its "clustering" strategy, placing a Starbucks literally on every corner in some cases, forced many smaller coffee shops out of business. This strategy dominated for most of the 1990s and 2000s and Starbucks became the butt of jokes. Many people began to wonder whether two Starbucks directly across the street from each other were really needed. The last recession brought a change in policy, however. Starbucks pulled back on expansion, closed hundreds of stores around the United States, and focused more on international markets. Now Starbucks is beginning to focus on U.S. expansion once more.

At the end of 2014, Starbucks opened a 15,000 square foot Starbucks Reserve Roastery and Tasting Room in Seattle, a place where coffee is roasted, bagged, sold, and shipped internationally. Equipped with a Coffee Library and Coffee Experience Bar, the roastery is intended to redefine the coffee retail experience for customers. The roastery sells 28 to 30 different coffees and gets 1,000 to 2,000 customers daily. CEO Howard Schultz believes the roastery has the potential to redefine the Starbucks retail experience.

NEW PRODUCT OFFERINGS

Starbucks introduced a number of new products over the years to remain competitive. In 2008 Starbucks decided to return to its essentials with the introduction of its Pike Place Blend that the company hoped would return Starbucks to its roots of distinctive, expertly blended coffee. In order to get the flavor perfect, Starbucks enlisted the input of 1,000 customers over 1,500 hours. To kick off the new choice, Starbucks held the largest nationwide coffee tasting in history. To make the brew even more appealing, Starbucks joined forces with Conservation International to ensure the beans were sustainably harvested. Also, after feedback revealed many of its customers desired a lighter blend, Starbucks introduced Blonde Roast blend in 2011. In 2015 the company commercialized the Flat White based on a latte drink popular in Australia. Unlike previous new offerings, the company did not perform limited-market testing but instead introduced it nationwide in an attempt to remain competitive with rivals.

Starbucks executives believe the experience customers have in the stores should be consistent. Therefore, Starbucks began to refocus on the customer experience as one of the key competitive advantages of the Starbucks brand. To enhance the European coffee shop experience for which Starbucks is known, shops are replacing their old espresso machines with new, high-tech ones. To keep the drink-making operation running efficiently and accurately, Starbucks mandated baristas to make no more than two drinks at the same time. It is also introducing more lines of single-origin coffees to appeal to coffee enthusiasts interested in where their coffee comes from.

Additionally, Starbucks fosters brand loyalty by increasing repeat business. One of the ways it accomplishes this is through the Starbucks Card, a reloadable card introduced in 2001. For the tech-savvy visitor, Starbucks introduced the Starbucks Reward mobile app. With the app customers are able to order or pre-order their coffee, and merely scan their phone for payment. Today the company has 12 million active users of its Starbucks Reward mobile app—the third most popular digital payment app in the country. It is estimated that Starbucks processes five million mobile payments a week. Howard Schultz believes the future is digital and is placing more emphasis on digital marketing strategies.

STARBUCKS CULTURE

In 1990 the Starbucks senior executive team created a mission statement that specified the guiding principles for the company. They hoped the principles included in the mission statement would assist partners in determining the appropriateness of later decisions and actions. After drafting the mission statement, the executive team asked all partners of Starbucks to review and comment on the document. Based on their feedback, the final statement put "people first and profits last." In fact, the number one guiding principle in the company's mission statement is to create a great and respectable work environment for its employees.

Starbucks has done three things to keep the mission and guiding principles alive over the decades. First, it distributes the mission statement and comment cards for feedback during orientation to all new partners. Second, Starbucks continually relates decisions back to the guiding principle or principles it supports. These principles focus on coffee, partners, customers, stores, neighborhoods, and shareholders. And finally, the company formed a "Mission Review" system so partners can comment on a decision or action relative to its consistency with one of the six principles. These guiding principles and values have become the cornerstone of a strong ethical culture of predominately young and educated workers.

Starbucks founder and CEO Howard Schultz has long been a public advocate for increased awareness of ethics in business. In a 2007 speech at Notre Dame, he spoke to students about the importance of balancing "profitability and social consciousness." Schultz is a true believer that ethical companies do better in the long run, something that has been confirmed by research. Schultz maintains that, while it can be difficult to do the right thing at all times, in the long term it is better for a company to take short-term losses than lose sight of its core values.

The care the company shows its employees is a large part of what sets it apart. Starbucks offers all employees who work more than 20 hours per week a comprehensive benefits package that includes stock options as well as medical, dental, and vision benefits. In another effort to benefit employees, Starbucks partnered with Arizona State University (ASU) to offer tuition assistance to those who want to earn a degree from the university's online program. In 2015 it was voted as one of the most ethical companies on *Ethisphere*'s annual list for the ninth consecutive year.

Another key part of the Starbucks image involves its commitment to ethics and sustainability. To address concerns related to these issues, Starbucks launched the Shared Planet website. Shared Planet has three main goals: to achieve ethical sourcing, environmental stewardship, and greater community involvement. The website is a means of keeping customers current on initiatives within the company. It describes how well Starbucks fares on achieving its social responsibility goals, and it provides a means for customers to learn things like the nutrition data of Starbucks offerings and other concerns related to its products.

Starbucks actively partners with nonprofits around the globe. Starbucks is one of the largest buyers of Fair Trade Certified as well as certified organic coffee. Another organization Starbucks partnered with is the Foodservice Packaging Institute/Paper Recovery Alliance.

The partnership addresses the issue of responsible foodservice packaging in terms of its use, recovery, and processing. Starbucks has also invested over $70 million in programs for farmers around the world.

Conservation International joined with Starbucks in 1998 to promote sustainable agricultural practices, namely shade-grown coffee, and help prevent deforestation in endangered regions around the globe. The results of the partnership proved to be positive for both the environment and farmers. For example, in Chiapas, Mexico, shade-grown coffee acreage (that reduces the need to cut down trees for coffee plantations) increased well over 220 percent, while farmers receive a price premium above the market price. Starbucks and Oprah, two of the biggest global brands, joined forces to create Oprah's Chai Tea in 2014. A specially created blend from the stores of Teavana, these branded products contribute to youth education programs. All profits made from this tea go toward this cause.

Starbucks works with many other organizations as well, including the African Wildlife Foundation and Business for Social Responsibility. The company's efforts at transparency, the treatment of its workers, and its dozens of philanthropic commitments demonstrate how genuine Starbucks is in its mission to be an ethical and socially responsible company.

CORPORATE SOCIAL MISSION

Although Starbucks supported responsible business practices virtually since its inception, as the company has grown, so has the importance of defending its image. At the end of 1999, Starbucks created a Corporate Social Responsibility department, now known as the Global Responsibility Department. Global Responsibility releases an annual report in order for shareholders to keep track of its performance and can be accessed through the Shared Planet website. Starbucks is concerned about the environment, its employees, suppliers, customers, and communities. Howard Schultz has commented that achieving social change to improve society is an important part of the company's core identity.

Environment

In 1992, long before it became trendy to be "green," Starbucks developed an environmental mission statement to clearly articulate the company's environmental priorities and goals. This initiative created the Environmental Starbucks Coffee Company Affairs team, the purpose of which was to develop environmentally responsible policies and minimize the company's "footprint." As part of this effort, Starbucks began using environmental purchasing guidelines to reduce waste through recycling, conserving energy, and educating partners through the company's "Green Team" initiatives. Concerned stakeholders can now track the company's progress through its website that clearly outlines its environmental goals and how Starbucks fares in living up to those goals. Starbucks also began offering a $1 plastic cup for purchase that is good for a recommended 30 uses. This is part of an attempt by Starbucks to make all cups reusable or recyclable by 2015.

Employees

Growing up poor with a father whose life was nearly ruined by an unsympathetic employer who did not offer health benefits, Howard Schultz always considered the creation of a good work environment a top priority. He believes companies should value their workers. When forming Starbucks, he decided to build a company that provided opportunities his father did not have. The result is one of the best health care programs in the coffee shop industry. Schultz's key to maintaining a strong business is developing a shared vision among employees as well as an environment to which they can actively contribute. Understanding how vital employees are, Schultz is the first to admit his company centers on personal interactions: "We are not in the coffee business serving people, but in the people business serving coffee." Starbucks is known for its diversity, and 40 percent of its baristas are ethnic minorities.

However, being a great employer does take its toll on the company. In 2008 Starbucks closed 10 percent of stores in order to continue to provide employees with health insurance. This decision, based on its guiding principle of "people first, profits last," shows how much the company values its employees. Employees have an opportunity to join Starbuck's stock-sharing program called Bean Stock. They have generated $1 billion in financial gains through stock options. In 2015 Starbucks gave employees a raise and increased starting pay rates across the country.

Starbucks is committed toward the well-being of its employees—both physically and intellectually. As a way to improve employee health, Starbucks established a program for employees called "Thrive Wellness" that offers various resources aimed at assisting employees in incorporating wellness into their lives. The program offers resources such as smoking cessation, weight loss, and exercise. Starbucks also estimates that 70 percent of employees are either currently in college or desire to earn a degree. The aforementioned partnership with ASU provides this opportunity as students can choose from 40 programs online or in person. More than 2,000 employees applied to the program when it was initially launched. The rising cost of education is an important issue that CEO Howard Schultz wants to help alleviate.

Suppliers

Even though it is one of the largest coffee brands in the world, Starbucks maintains a good reputation for social responsibility and business ethics throughout the international community of coffee growers. It builds positive relationships with small coffee suppliers while also working with governments and nonprofits wherever it operates. Starbucks practices conservation as well as Starbucks Coffee and Farmer Equity Practices (C.A.F.E.), a set of socially responsible coffee-buying guidelines that ensure preferential buying status for participants that receive high scores in best practices. Starbucks pays coffee farmers premium prices to help them make profits and support their families. More than 95 percent of total coffee purchases are C.A.F.E. verified, and the company is on track to have 100 percent of its coffee purchases verified in 2015.

The company is also involved in social development programs, investing in programs to build schools and health clinics, as well as other projects that benefit coffee-growing communities. Starbucks collaborates directly with some of its growers through Farmer Support Centers, located in Costa Rica, Rwanda, Tanzania, South America, and China. Farmer Support Centers provide technical support and training to ensure high-quality coffee into the future. It is a major purchaser of Fair Trade Certified, shade-grown, and certified organic beans that further support environmental and economic efforts. In 2013 Starbucks bought its first coffee farm, located in Costa Rica and employing about 70 people. The purchase was one step toward the company's goal of increasing its ethically sourced coffee to 100 percent by 2015.

Customers

Strengthening its brand and customer satisfaction is more important than ever as Starbucks seeks to regroup after the latest recession forced the company to rethink its strategy. Starbucks refocused the brand by upgrading its coffee-brewing machines, introducing new food and drink items for health- and budget-conscious consumers, and refocusing on its core product. Recognizing the concern over the obesity epidemic, Starbucks ensures that its grab-and-go lunch items are under 500 calories and is involved in two sodium reduction programs: the National Salt Reduction Initiative in New York and the U.K. Food Standards Agency Salt Campaign. The company focuses more on the quality of the coffee, the atmosphere of the coffee shops, and the overall Starbucks experience, rather than continuing its rapid expansion of stores and products. Enhancing the customer experience in its stores became a high priority. As a way to encourage people to relax and spend time there, Starbucks offers free wireless Internet access in all its U.S. stores. They have also partnered with Duracell Powermat to install over 100,000 wireless phone chargers in Starbucks and Teavana locations across the United States.

Communities

Starbucks coffee shops have long sought to become the "instant gathering spot" wherever they locate, a "place that draws people together." The company established community stores, which not only serve as a meeting place for community programs and trainings but also as a source of funding to solve issues specific to the local community. There are currently five such locations (including one in Thailand), and Starbucks aims to establish a total of 50 by 2018. The company has partnered with the Schultz Family Foundation (founded by Howard Schultz) to provide training to 700 disadvantaged young people in retail and customer service. Schultz even used the advance and ongoing royalties from his book, *Pour Your Heart into It,* to create the Starbucks Foundation that provides opportunity grants to nonprofit literacy groups, sponsors young writers' programs, and partners with Jumpstart, an organization helping children prepare developmentally for school. The company announced its intention to hire 10,000 veterans by 2018.

Although Starbucks is known for putting its corporate muscle behind social issues—including unemployment—not all of its social activities have been perceived positively. After the Ferguson, Missouri shooting of a young African American man by a white police officer and the resulting protests, Starbucks created the campaign "Race Together" to encourage discussions of race relations among customers. For one week during the campaign, baristas were encouraged to write "Race Together" on customer cups. It also published "Race Together" newspaper supplements in the hope of taking this discussion national. Despite Schultz's intention to encourage discussion of a serious topic, many consumers reacted negatively to the campaign. Outrage over Twitter was so intense that the senior vice president of global communications at Starbucks temporarily deleted his Twitter account. Because the issue of race is such an emotionally charged issue and can be difficult to discuss even with family and friends, some marketing experts believe Starbucks took on too much with its campaign. Critics also claimed that they did not want to be reminded of this serious topic on their morning cups of coffee, and some believed the campaign was more of a public-relations stunt. Even in the face of backlash, Schultz and Starbucks continue to support the company's involvement in discussing serious issues that affect the communities in which it does business.

BRAND EVOLUTION

Although Starbucks achieved massive success in the last four decades, the company realizes it must modify its brand to appeal to changing consumer tastes. All established companies, no matter how successful, must learn to adapt their products and image to appeal to the shifting demands of their target markets. Starbucks is no exception. The company is associated with premium coffee beverages, an association that served it well over the years. However, as competition in specialty coffee drinks increases, Starbucks recognized the need to expand its brand in the eyes of consumers.

One way it is doing this is through adopting more products. In addition to coffee, Starbucks stores sell coffee accessories, teas, muffins, CDs, water, grab-and-go products, Starbuck Petites, upscale food items, hand-crafted sodas called Fizzios, as well as wine and beer in select locations. Food sales make up 20 percent of company revenue. The rise in coffee prices has created an opportunity for expansion into consumer packaged goods that will protect Starbucks against the risks of relying solely on coffee. In order to remain competitive, Starbucks made a series of acquisitions to increase the value of its brand, including Bay Bread (a small artisan bakery), La Boulange (a bakery brand), Evolution Fresh (a juice brand), and Teavana (a tea brand). This allowed Starbucks to offer high quality breakfast sandwiches as well as Paninis and wraps for lunch.

To symbolize this shift into the consumer packaged goods business, Starbucks gave its logo a new look. Previously, the company's circular logo featured a mermaid with the words "Starbucks Coffee" encircling it. In 2011 Starbucks removed the words and enlarged the mermaid to signal to consumers Starbucks is more than just the average coffee retailer.

SUCCESS AND CHALLENGES

For decades Starbucks revolutionized our leisure time. Starbucks is the most prominent brand of high-end coffee in the world but also one of the defining brands of our time. In most large cities, it is impossible to walk more than a few blocks without seeing the familiar mermaid logo.

In the past few decades, Starbucks achieved amazing levels of growth, creating financial success for shareholders. The company's reputation is built on product quality, stakeholder concern, and a balanced approach to all of its business activities. Of course, Starbucks does receive criticism for putting other coffee shops out of business and creating a uniform retail culture in many cities. Yet the company excels in its relationships with its employees and is a role model for the fast-food industry in employee benefits. In addition, in an age of shifts in supply chain power, Starbucks is as concerned about its suppliers and meeting their needs as it is about any other primary stakeholder.

In spite of its efforts to support sustainability and maintain high ethical standards, Starbucks garnered harsh criticism in the past on issues such as a lack of fair trade coffee, hormone-added milk, and Howard Schultz's alleged financial links to the Israeli government. In an attempt to counter these criticisms, in 2002 Starbucks began offering Fair Trade Certified coffee, a menu item that was quickly made permanent. Approximately 95 percent of coffee in the United States is ethically sourced currently.

Starting in late 2008, Starbucks had something new to worry about. A global recession caused the market to bottom out for expensive coffee drinks. The company responded by slowing its global growth plans after years of expanding at a nonstop pace and instead refocused on strengthening its brand, satisfying customers, and building consumer loyalty. After Starbucks stock started to plummet, Howard Schultz returned as CEO to return the company to its former glory.

Schultz was successful, and Starbucks rebounded from the effects of the recession. The company is once again looking toward possibilities in international markets. This represents both new opportunities and challenges. When attempting to break into the U.K. market, for instance, Starbucks met with serious resistance. Realizing the homogenization of its stores did not work as well in the United Kingdom, Starbucks began to remodel its stores so they took on a more local feel. At the end of 2012, Starbucks came under public scrutiny for allegedly not paying taxes for the last 14 of the 15 years it was established in the United Kingdom. A protest group called UK Uncut began "sitting in" at the stores, encouraging coffee drinkers to buy their coffee elsewhere. Starbucks claims it did not pay taxes because it did not make a profit. However, the company said it would stop using certain accounting techniques that showed their profits overseas. Starbucks also agreed to pay 20 million pounds over the next two years, whether or not it makes a profit.

Starbucks is rapidly expanding in China, and the country is set to become the company's second largest market behind the United States. Starbucks effectively overcame obstacles in tapping into the Chinese market and adapted its strategy to attract Chinese consumers. After the 2007 closure of the retail operation in the Forbidden City, resulting from cultural concerns of the presence of a Western staple in a sacred area, Starbucks became more sensitive to the specific needs and nuances of the country. Through educating Chinese consumers on coffee (because the beverage is not largely consumed there), they are now drinking as much coffee as Americans.

Another challenge Starbucks must address is despite the company's emphasis on sustainability, billions of disposable Starbucks cups are thrown into landfills each year. Although Starbucks has taken initiatives to make the cups more eco-friendly, such as changing from polyethylene No. 1 to the more eco-friendly polypropylene No. 5, the cup represents a serious waste problem for Starbucks. Starbucks encourages consumers to bring in reusables (such as the Starbucks tumblers it sells) for a 10-cent rebate, yet these account for less than 2 percent of drinks served. The company hopes to achieve less cup waste with its new $1 reusable cup. It remains to be seen whether Starbucks will achieve its goal of total recyclability in the short term.

CONCLUSION

Despite the setbacks it experienced during the recession, the future looks bright for Starbucks. In 2015 the company underwent a 2-for-1 stock split as its way of addressing record highs in the company's stock history. It is estimated that Starbucks may double its food revenues within the next five years if its present growth continues.

The company continues to expand globally into markets such as Bangalore, India; San Jose, Costa Rica; Oslo, Norway; and Ho Chi Minh City, Vietnam. Schultz is hopeful that the new roastery in Seattle will continue to spread the Starbucks name and the distribution of its coffee globally. The challenges the company experienced and will continue to experience in the future have convinced the firm to focus on its strengths and embrace the opportunity to emphasize community involvement, outreach work, and its overall image and offerings. The company must continue to apply the balanced stakeholder orientation that is so crucial to its success.

QUESTIONS FOR DISCUSSION

1. Why do you think Starbucks has been so concerned with social responsibility in its overall corporate strategy?
2. Is Starbucks unique in being able to provide a high level of benefits to its employees?
3. Do you think Starbucks has grown rapidly because of its ethical and socially responsible activities or because it provides products and an environment customers want?

SOURCES

Chris Barth, "Green Mountain Hopes to Beat Starbucks in the U.S. with One Simple Ingredient," *Forbes*, November 9, 2012, http://www.forbes.com/sites/chrisbarth/2012/11/09/green-mountain-hopes-to-beat-starbucks-in-the-u-s-with-one-simple-ingredient/ (accessed April 23, 2015); Susan Berfield, "Starbucks' Food Fight," *Businessweek*, June 12, 2012, http://www.businessweek.com/articles/2012-06-12/starbucks-food-fight (accessed April 23, 2015); Christine Birkner, "Taking Care of Their Own," *Marketing News*, February 2015, 45–49. Ilan Brat, "Starbucks Lines Up Delivery Options," *The Wall Street Journal*, March 19, 2015, B2; Laurie Burkitt, "Starbuck Menu Expands in China," *The Wall Street Journal*, March 9, 2011, B7; Peter Campbell, "Starbucks caves in to pressure and promises to hand the taxman £20m after public outcry," *dailymail.co.uk*, December 6, 2012, http://www.dailymail.co.uk/news/article-2244100/Starbucks-caves-pressure-promises-pay-20m-corporation-tax-2-years.html (accessed April 23, 2015); CC, "Starbucks Brings Imported Coffee to a Land of Exported Coffee," *Fast Company*, May 2012, 30; Geoff Colvin, "Questions for Starbucks' Chief Bean Counter," *Fortune*, December 9, 2013, 78–82; "Coffee Deal Has Stocks Soaring," *USA Today*, March 11, 2011, 5B; "Coffee and Farmer Equity (C.A.F.E.) Practices," *Conservation International*, 2013, http://www.conservation.org/campaigns/starbucks/Pages/CAFE_Practices_Results.aspx (accessed April 23, 2015); Eartheasy.com, "Shade Grown Coffee," http://www.eartheasy.com/eat_shadegrown_coffee.htm (accessed April 23, 2015); Eatocracy editors, "Starbucks Introduces $1 Reusable Cup to Cut Down on Waste," *Eatocracy*, January 3, 2013, http://eatocracy.cnn.com/2013/01/03/starbucks-introduces-1-reusable-cup-to-cut-down-on-waste/ (accessed April 23, 2015); Roxanne Escobales and Tracy McVeigh, "Starbucks hit by UK Uncut Protests as Tax Row Boils Over," *guardian.co.uk*, December 8, 2012, http://www.guardian.co.uk/business/2012/dec/08/starbucks-uk-stores-protests-tax (accessed April 23, 2015); Ethisphere Institute, "World's Most Ethical Companies—Honorees," *Ethisphere*, 2015, http://ethisphere.com/worlds-most-ethical/wme-honorees/ (accessed April 23, 2015); Rana Foroohar, "Starbucks for America," *Time*, February 16, 2015, 18–23; Bobbie Gossage, "Howard Schultz, on Getting a Second Shot," *Inc.*, April 2011, 52–54; Haley Geffen, "Starbucks: Howard Schultz on the Coffee Chain's Expansion under His Leadership," *Bloomberg Businessweek*, December 8–14, 2014, 32; Jason Groves and Peter Campbell, "Starbucks Set to Cave in and Pay More Tax after Threats of Boycott at its 'immoral' Financial Dealings," *dailymail.co.uk*, December 3, 2012, http://www.dailymail.co.uk/news/article-2242596/Starbucks-pay-tax-public-outcry-financial-dealings.html (accessed April 23, 2015); Bruce Horovitz, "For Starbucks, a split and a jolt," *USA Today*, March 19, 2015, 2B; Bruce Horovitz, "Handcrafted Sodas to Bubble Up At Starbucks," *USA Today*, June 23, 2014, 4B; Bruce Horovitz, "Starbucks Aims beyond Lattes to Extend Brand to Films, Music and Books," *USA Today*, May 19, 2006, A1, A2; Bruce Horovitz, "Starbucks Brews Wireless Charging," *USA Today*, June 12, 2014, 2B; Bruce Horovitz, "Starbucks Remakes Its Future," *USA Today*, October 18, 2010, 1B–2B; Bruce Horovitz, "Starbucks Sales Pass BK, Wendy's," *USA Today*, April 27, 2011, 1A; Bruce Horovitz, "Starbucks Serving Alcohol At More Sites," *USA Today*, March 21, 2014, 3B; Bruce Horovitz, "Starbucks Shells Out Bread for Bakery," *USA Today*, June 5, 2012, 1B; Bruce Horovitz, "Starbucks taps into tasting room fad," *USA Today*, December 5, 2014, 1B–2B; Bruce Horovitz and Howard Schultz, "Starbucks Hits 40 Feeling Perky," *USA Today*, March 7, 2011, 1B, 3B; John Jannarone, "Green Mountain Eclipses Starbucks," *The Wall Street Journal*, March 9, 2011, C14; John Jannarone, "Grounds for Concern at Starbucks," *The Wall Street Journal*, May 3, 2011, C10; Julie Jargon, "At

Starbucks, Baristas Told No More than Two Drinks," *The Wall Street Journal,* October 13, 2010, http://online.wsj. com/article/SB10001424052748704164004575548403514060736.html (accessed April 23, 2015); Julie Jargon, "Coffee Talk: Starbucks Chief on Prices, McDonald's Rivalry," *The Wall Street Journal,* March 7, 2011, B6; Julie Jargon, "Starbucks Brews Plan Catering to Aficionados," *The Wall Street Journal,* September 11, 2014, B7; Julie Jargon, "Starbucks CEO to Focus on Digital," *The Wall Street Journal,* January 30, 2014, B6; Julie Jargon, "Starbucks Logo Loses 'Coffee,' Expands Mermaid as Firm Moves to Build Packaged-Goods Business," *The Wall Street Journal,* January 6, 2011, B4; Julie Jargon, "Starbucks in Pod Pact," *The Wall Street Journal,* March 11, 2011, B4; Julie Jargon and Douglas Belkin, "Starbucks to Subsidize Online Degrees," *The Wall Street Journal,* June 16, 2014, B3; Sarah Jones, "Starbucks Shows That Healthcare Isn't a Job Killer by Adding 1,500 Cafes," *PoliticusUSA,* December 6, 2012, http://www.politicususa.com/healthcare-providing-starbucks-expanding-1500-cafes.html (accessed April 23, 2015); David Kesmodel and Ilan Brat, "Why Starbucks Takes on Social Issues," *The Wall Street Journal,* March 24, 2015, B3; Beth Kowitt, "Coffee Shop, Contained," *Fortune,* May 20, 2013, 24; Katie Lobosco, "Oprah Chai Tea Comes to Starbucks," *CNN Money,* March 19, 2014, http://money.cnn.com/2014/03/19/news/ companies/oprah-starubucks-tea/ (accessed April 23, 2015); Laura Lorenzetti, "Where Innovation Is Always Brewing," *Fortune,* November 17, 2014, 24; Kate McClelland, "Starbucks Founder Speaks on Ethics," *Notre Dame Observer,* March 30, 2007, http://ndsmcobserver.com/2007/03/starbucks-founder-speaks-on-ethics/ (accessed April 23, 2015); Adam Minter, "Why Starbucks Won't Recycle Your Cup," *Bloomberg View,* April 7, 2014, http:// www.bloombergview.com/articles/2014-04-07/why-starbucks-won-t-recycle-your-cup (accessed April 23, 2015); *MSNBC.com,* "Health Care Takes Its Toll on Starbucks," September 14, 2005, http://www.msnbc.msn.com/ id/9344634/ (accessed April 23, 2015); Reuters, "Starbucks to Open First Outlet in Vietnam in Early February," *Economic Times,* January 3, 2013, http://www.reuters.com/article/2013/01/03/starbucks-vietnam-idUSL4N0A815420130103 (accessed April 23, 2015); Mariko Sanchanta, "Starbucks Plans Big Expansion in China," *The Wall Street Journal,* April 14, 2010, B10; David Schorn, "Howard Schultz: The Star of Starbucks," *60 Minutes,* http://www.cbsnews.com/stories/2006/04/21/60minutes/main1532246.shtml (accessed April 23, 2015); E. J. Schultz, "How VIA Steamed up the Instant Coffee Category," *Advertising Age,* January 24, 2011, http:// adage.com/article?article_id=148403 (accessed April 23, 2015); SCS Global Services. "Starbucks C.A.F.E. Practices," http://www.scsglobalservices.com/starbucks-cafe-practices (accessed April 23, 2015); Starbucks, *2014 Annual Meeting of Shareholders,* 2014, https://news.starbucks.com/2014annualmeeting (accessed April 23, 2015); Starbucks, "2008 Annual Report," http://media.corporate-ir.net/media_files/irol/99/99518/AR2008.pdf (accessed April 23, 2015); "Starbucks: A Farm of Its Own," *Bloomberg Businessweek,* March 25–31, 2013, 23; Starbucks, "Community Stores," http://www.starbucks.com/responsibility/community/community-stores (accessed April 23, 2015); "Starbucks Corp.," *Market Watch,* August 7, 2014, http://www.marketwatch.com/ investing/stock/sbux/financials (accessed April 23, 2015); Starbucks Corporation, "Goals & Progress: Farmer Support," 2015, http://www.starbucks.com/responsibility/global-report/ethical-sourcing/farmer-support (accessed April 23, 2015); "Starbucks Corporation (SBUX)," *YAHOO! Finance,* http://finance.yahoo.com/q/is?s=S BUX+Income+Statement&annual (accessed April 23, 2015); Starbucks, "Farming Communities," http://www. starbucks.com/responsibility/community/farmer-support (accessed April 23, 2015); Starbucks, "Food," http:// www.starbucks.com/menu/food (accessed August 8, 2014); Starbucks, "Goals & Progress: Cup Recycling," http:// www.starbucks.com/responsibility/global-report/environmental-stewardship/cup-recycling (accessed April 23, 2015); Starbucks, "Investing in Farmers," http://www.starbucks.com/responsibility/community/farmer-support/ farmer-loan-programs (accessed April 23, 2015); Starbucks, "Recycling & Reducing Waste," http://www.starbucks. com/responsibility/environment/recycling (accessed April 23, 2015); Starbucks, "Starbucks Company Profile," September 2013, http://news.starbucks.com/uploads/documents/AboutUs-CompanyProfile-Q3-2013-9.18.13. pdf (accessed April 23, 2015); "Starbucks to Enter China's Tea Drinks Market," *China Retail News,* March 11, 2010, www.chinaretailnews.com/2010/03/11/3423-starbucks-to-enter-chinas-tea-drinks-market (accessed April 23, 2015); "Starbucks Unveils Minimalist New Logo," *USA Today,* January 6, 2011, 11B; Starbucks, "Nutrition," http://www.starbucks.com/responsibility/wellness (accessed April 23, 2015); "Statistics and Facts on Starbucks," *Statista,* October 2013, http://www.statista.com/topics/1246/starbucks/ (accessed April 23, 2015); Charlie Rose, "Charlie Rose Talks to Howard Schultz," *Bloomberg Businessweek,* April 7–13, 2014, 32; Trefis Team, "Starbucks'

Profits Surge Despite Sales Slowing Down," *Forbes*, January 30, 2014, http://www.forbes.com/sites/greatspeculations/2014/01/30/starbucks-profits-surge-despite-sales-slowing-down/ (accessed April 23, 2015); David Teather, "Starbucks Legend Delivers Recovery by Thinking Smaller," *The Guardian,* January 21, 2010, www.guardian.co.uk/business/2010/jan/21/starbucks-howard-schultz (accessed April 23, 2015); Rachel Tepper, "Starbucks: Square Mobile Payment System Now Live at 7,000 Locations," *The Huffington Post*, November 9, 2012, http://www.huffingtonpost.com/2012/11/09/starbucks-square-mobile-payment_n_2101791.html (accessed April 23, 2015); Jorge Velasquez, "Starbucks Debuts $1 Reusable Cup," *KRCA*, January 3, 2013, http://www.kcra.com/news/Starbucks-debuts-1-reusable-cup/-/11797728/17994788/-/5dbclr/-/index.html (accessed April 23, 2015); Daisuke Wakabayashi, "Starbucks Drops Square App as Mobile-Payments Battle Intensifies," *The Wall Street Journal*, December 22, 2014, http://blogs.wsj.com/digits/2014/12/22/starbucks-drops-square-app-as-mobile-payments-battle-intensifies/ (accessed April 23, 2015); Nicole Wakelin, "The New Starbucks Verismo Single-Serve Home Coffee Brewer," *Wired*, November 18, 2012, http://archive.wired.com/geekmom/2012/11/starbucks-verismo/ (accessed April 23, 2015); Jonathan Watts, "Starbucks Faces Eviction from the Forbidden City," *www.guardian.co.uk*, January 18, 2007, http://www.guardian.co.uk/world/2007/jan/18/china.jonathanwatts (accessed April 23, 2015); Dan Welch, "Fairtrade Beans Do Not Mean a Cup of Coffee Is Entirely Ethical," *guardian.co.uk*, February 28, 2011, http://www.guardian.co.uk/environment/green-living-blog/2011/feb/28/coffee-chains-ethical (accessed April 23, 2015); Venessa Wong, "Starbucks Serves up 'Flat Whites,' Tries to Prove It Can Still Be Different," *Bloomberg Businessweek*, January 6, 2015, http://www.bloomberg.com/news/articles/2015-01-06/starbucks-serves-up-flat-whites-tries-to-prove-it-can-still-be-different (accessed April 23, 2015).

CASE 3

Walmart Manages Ethics and Compliance Challenges*

Walmart Stores, Inc., is an icon of American business. With net sales of nearly $500 billion and more than 2 million employees, the world's largest retailer and one of its largest public corporations must carefully manage many stakeholder relationships. Its stated mission is to help people save money and live better. Despite past controversies, Walmart has attempted to restore its image with an emphasis on diversity, charitable giving, support for nutrition, and sustainability. The company, along with its Walmart Foundation, has donated $1.3 billion in cash and in-kind contributions. Walmart often tops the list of U.S. donors to charities. However, more recent issues such as bribery accusations in Mexico have created significant ethics and compliance challenges that Walmart is addressing in its quest to become a socially responsible retailer.

This analysis begins by briefly examining the growth of Walmart. Next, it discusses the company's various relationships with stakeholders, including competitors, suppliers, and employees. The ethical issues concerning these stakeholders include accusations of discrimination, leadership misconduct, bribery, and unsafe working conditions. We discuss how Walmart has dealt with these concerns, as well as some of its recent endeavors in sustainability and social responsibility. The analysis concludes by examining what Walmart is currently doing to increase its competitive advantage and repair its reputation.

HISTORY: THE GROWTH OF WALMART

The story of Walmart begins in 1962, when founder Sam Walton opened the first Walmart Discount Store in Rogers, Arkansas. Although its growth was initially slow, over the next 40 years the company expanded from a small chain to more than 8,000 facilities in 27 countries. The company now serves more than 200 million customers weekly. Much of Walmart's success can be attributed to its founder. A shrewd businessman, Walton believed in customer satisfaction and hard work. He convinced many of his associates to abide by the "10-foot rule," whereby employees pledged that whenever a customer came within 10 feet of them, they would look the customer in the eye, greet him or her, and ask if he or she needed help with anything. Walton's famous mantra, known as the "sundown rule," was: "Why put off until tomorrow what you can do today?" Due to this staunch work ethic and dedication to customer care, Walmart claimed early on that a formal ethics program was unnecessary because the company had Mr. Walton's ethics to follow.

*This case was prepared by O.C. Ferrell, Jennifer Sawayda, Michelle Urban, and Isaac Emmanuel. Jennifer Jackson made significant contributions to previous editions of this case. It was prepared for classroom discussion rather than to illustrate either effective or ineffective handling of an administrative, ethical, or legal decision by management. All sources used for this case were obtained through publicly available material and the Walmart website © 2015.

In 2002 Walmart officially became the largest grocery chain, topping the Fortune 500 list for that year. *Fortune* magazine named Walmart the "most admired company in America" in 2003 and 2004. Although it has slipped since then, it remains within the top 50. In 2015 *Fortune* ranked Walmart the 38th most admired company in the world.

Effects on Competitive Stakeholders

Possibly the greatest complaint against Walmart is it puts other companies out of business. With its low prices, Walmart makes it harder for local stores to compete. Walmart is often accused of being responsible for the downward pressure on wages and benefits in towns where the company locates. Some businesses have filed lawsuits against Walmart, claiming the company uses unfair predatory pricing to put competing stores out of business. Walmart countered by defending its pricing, asserting that it is competing fairly and its purpose is to provide quality, low-cost products to the average consumer. Yet although Walmart has saved consumers millions of dollars and is a popular shopping spot for many, there is no denying that many competing stores go out of business once Walmart comes to town.

In order to compete against the retail giant, other stores must reduce wages. Studies show that overall payroll wages, including Walmart wages, decline by 5 percent after Walmart enters a new market. As a result, some activist groups and citizens have refused to allow Walmart to take up residence in their areas. This in turn brings up another social responsibility issue: What methods of protest may stakeholders reasonably use, and how should Walmart respond to such actions? While it is acceptable for stakeholder activists to protest the building of a Walmart store in their area, other actions may be questionable, especially when the government gets involved. When Walmart announced plans to open stores in Washington D.C., for instance, a chairman of the D.C. City Council introduced a law that required non-unionized retail companies with over $1 billion in total sales and stores that occupy more than 75,000 square feet to pay their employees a minimum of $12.50 per hour—in contrast to the city's minimum wage of $8.25 an hour. The terms of the law made it essentially apply only to Walmart and a few other large chains such as Home Depot and Costco. While supporters of the law argued that it is difficult to live on a wage of $8.25 an hour, critics stated that the proposal gave employees at large retailers an unjustified benefit over those working comparable jobs at small retailers. Perhaps the most scathing criticism was that Walmart and other big-box retailers were being unfairly targeted by a governmental entity. Walmart also responded directly, threatening to cancel its expansion into D.C. if the law passed and emphasizing the economic and development benefits the city would lose out on. The D.C. City Council eventually passed the law, but it was vetoed by the city mayor, and there are now several Walmart stores in D.C. As with most issues, determining the most socially responsible decision that benefits the most stakeholders is a complex issue not easily resolved.

Relationships with Supplier Stakeholders

Walmart achieves its "everyday low prices" (EDLPs) by streamlining the company. Well known for operational excellence in its ability to handle, move, and track merchandise, Walmart expects its suppliers to continually improve their systems as well. Walmart typically works with suppliers to reduce packaging and shipping costs, which lowers prices for consumers. Since 2009, the company has worked with The Sustainability Consortium, an association of businesses that helps its members achieve sustainability goals, to develop a measurement and reporting system known as the Walmart Sustainability Index (discussed in further detail later in this case). Among its many goals, Walmart desires to use the Sustainability Index to increase the sustainability of its products and create a more efficient, sustainable supply chain.

In 2008 Walmart introduced its "Global Responsible Sourcing Initiative," a list providing details of the policies and requirements included in new supplier agreements. In 2012 then-CEO Mike Duke expanded upon these initiatives to set improved goals for increasing the sustainability of the company's supply chain. He highlighted four main sustainability goals: (1) by 2017, purchase 70 percent of merchandise sold in U.S. Walmart stores and Sam's Clubs from global suppliers that use the Sustainability Index to assess and share information about their products; (2) use the Sustainability Index as a model for U.S. private brands; (3) apply new evaluative criteria for key sourcing merchants to encourage sustainability to become a more important consideration in buyers' daily jobs; and (4) donate $2 million to fund The Sustainability Consortium.[1] If fully achieved, these goals will increase the sustainability of Walmart suppliers significantly. Company leaders stated Walmart was moving into "phase three" of its sustainability plan, which will involve "reshap[ing] entire systems" toward achieving sustainability goals. Further details have not yet been revealed.

Some critics of Walmart's approach note that pressure to achieve its standards will shift more of the cost burden onto suppliers. When a supplier does not meet Walmart's demands, the company may cease to carry that supplier's product or, often, will be able to find another willing supplier of the product at the desired price.

Walmart's power over its suppliers stems from its size and the volume of products it requires. Many companies depend on Walmart for much of their business. This type of relationship allows Walmart to significantly influence terms with its vendors. For example, Walmart generally refuses to sign long-term supply contracts, giving it the power to easily and quickly change suppliers at its discretion. Despite this, suppliers will invest significantly into long-term strategic and business commitments to meet Walmart demands, even without any guarantee that Walmart will continue to buy from them. There are corresponding benefits to being a Walmart supplier; by having to become more efficient and streamlined for Walmart, companies develop competitive advantages and are able to serve their other customers better as well. Numerous companies believe supplying Walmart has been the best thing that has ever happened to their businesses. However, many others find the amount of power Walmart wields to be disconcerting.

The constant drive by Walmart for lower prices can negatively affect suppliers. Many have been forced to move production from the United States to less expensive locations in Asia. In fact, Walmart is considered to have been one of the major driving forces behind the "offshoring" trend of the past several decades. Companies such as Master Lock, Fruit of the Loom, and Levi's, as well as many other Walmart suppliers, moved production overseas at the expense of U.S. jobs. Some experts now estimate as much as 80 percent of Walmart's global suppliers are stationed in China. The challenges and ethical issues associated with managing a vast network of overseas suppliers will be discussed later in this case.

This offshoring trend was not founder Sam Walton's original intention. In the 1980s, after learning his stores were putting other American companies out of business, Walton

[1]Walmart, "Walmart Announces New Commitments to Drive Sustainability Deeper into the Company's Global Supply Chain," October 25, 2012, http://news.walmart.com/news-archive/2012/10/25/walmart-announces-new-commitments-to-drive-sustainability-deeper-into-the-companys-global-supply-chain (accessed May 15, 2015).

started his "Buy American" campaign. More recently, Walmart launched a "Made in America" initiative, pledging to increase the amount of U.S.-made goods it buys by $50 billion over the next 10 years and developing agreements with many suppliers to move their production back to the states. Critics argue Walmart is merely putting a public relations spin on the fact that rising wages in Asian countries and other international economic changes have actually made local production more cost-efficient than outsourcing for many industries. They also point out that $50 billion is a veritable "drop in the bucket" considering Walmart's size. Still, the symbolic effect of Walmart throwing its considerable influence behind "Made in America" is likely to spur many suppliers to freshly consider or speed up plans to bring production back to the United States.

Ethical Issues Involving Employee Stakeholders

EMPLOYEE BENEFITS   Much of the Walmart controversy over the years has focused on the way the company treats its employees, or "associates" as Walmart refers to them. Although Walmart is the largest retail employer in the world, it has been roundly criticized for paying low wages and offering minimal benefits. Walmart has been accused of failing to provide health insurance for more than 60 percent of its employees. In a memo sent to the board of directors by Susan Chambers, Walmart's executive vice president for benefits, she suggested Walmart could slow the rise of benefits costs by hiring "healthier, more productive employees," as well as more part-time workers (who are less likely to be eligible for health care benefits). After this bad publicity, between 2000 and 2005 Walmart's stock decreased 27 percent.

As a result of the deluge of bad press, Walmart took action to improve relations with its employee stakeholders. In 2006 Walmart raised pay tied to performance in about one-third of its stores. The company also improved its health benefits package by offering lower deductibles and implementing a generic prescription plan estimated to save employees $25 million. Walmart estimates over 75 percent of its employees have insurance (though not always through Walmart). Walmart is quick to point out that the company's health care benefits are competitive in the retail industry.

Despite these improvements, a Walmart policy eliminated health care coverage for new hires working less than 30 hours a week. Walmart also stated that it reserves the right to cut health care coverage of workers whose work week falls below 30 hours. Some analysts claim that Walmart might be attempting to shift the burden of health care coverage onto the federal government, as some employees make so little that they qualify for Medicaid under the new Affordable Care Act. It is important to note that Walmart is not alone in this practice; many firms are moving more of their workforces to part time, and cutting benefits to part-time workers, to avoid having to pay health care costs. However, as such a large employer, Walmart's actions are expected to have more of a ripple effect on the economy.

Another criticism levied against Walmart is that it decreased its workforce at the same time it expanded. In the United States, Walmart decreased its workforce by 1.4 percent while increasing its number of retail stores by 13 percent. Employee dissatisfaction often translates to customer dissatisfaction. With fewer employees it is harder to provide quality customer service. This led some customers to complain of longer lines and fewer items on shelves. In the 2014 American Customer Satisfaction Index, Walmart tied for lowest among discount stores and department stores. Walmart claims the dissatisfaction expressed by some customers is not reflective of the shopping experience of customers as a whole.

Walmart announced it was raising its employee minimum wage rate across the United States to $9 an hour in 2015 and $10 an hour in 2016. The company says this is part of a new employee-oriented initiative that will also include better training and shift scheduling. The wage hike will apply to at least 500,000 employees and is expected to have a noticeable effect on both the industry and the economy as a whole. Whether it is enough to improve Walmart's reputation as an employer and regain the company some goodwill with dissatisfied employees and advocacy groups remains to be seen—some analysts believe the wage increase may be simply a profit-maximizing response to the realities of a changing labor market (necessary to continue hiring and retaining good employees) rather than an employee-oriented or socially responsible decision. Walmart's competitors are also watching closely; considering Walmart's dominance and influence in the sector, other retailers may have to follow suit to remain competitive. Home Depot, T.J. Maxx, Marshalls, and several other companies also announced raises to their lowest-paid workers.

WALMART'S STANCE ON UNIONS   Some critics believe Walmart workers' benefits could improve if they unionized. Unions have been discouraged since Walmart's foundation; Sam Walton believed they were a divisive force and might render the company uncompetitive. Walmart maintains that it is not against unions in general, but it sees no need for unions to come between workers and managers. The company says it supports an "open-door policy" in which associates can bring problems to managers without resorting to third parties. Walmart associates have at times voted against unions in the past.

Although the company's official position is that it is not opposed to unions, Walmart often seems to fight against them. Critics claim that when the word "union" surfaces at a Walmart location, the top dogs in Bentonville are called in. In 2000 seven of ten Walmart butchers in Jacksonville, Texas, voted to join the United Food Workers Union. Walmart responded by announcing it would only sell precut meat in its supercenters, getting rid of its meat-cutting departments entirely. In 2004 employees at a Canada Walmart location voted to unionize; six months later, Walmart closed the store. In 2014 two internal Walmart PowerPoint presentations were leaked that provided reasons for why unions would negatively impact associates and directing managers to call the "Labor Relations Hotline" if they spot "warning signs" of union activity. Although Walmart offers justifications for actions such as this, many see the company as aggressively working to prevent unionization in its stores, and the U.S. National Labor Relations Board (NLRB) has cited Walmart on multiple occasions for violating labor laws.

However, Walmart's stance against unions has not always held up to the practical realities of doing business in some foreign countries. In China, for example, Walmart found it necessary to accept a union in order to grow. Only one union is legally permitted to operate in China: The All-China Federation of Trade Unions (ACFTU), which is run by the ruling Communist Party. The Chinese government promotes the ACFTU (although the union has been criticized as pro-business and not necessarily looking out for the best interests of workers) and especially seeks to have foreign companies unionized. When poor working conditions and low wages generated social unrest, the government attempted to craft a new set of labor laws providing employees greater protection and giving the ACFTU more power. In 2004 the Chinese Labor Federation pushed Walmart to allow employees to unionize. Walmart initially resisted, and although it eventually complied, critics claimed the company then began making unionization progressively more difficult in practice for its Chinese workers. Despite this, within a span of just two weeks in 2006, the ACFTU was able to establish union branches at five separate China Walmart locations.

Walmart reacted by stating it would not renew the contracts of unionized workers. However, the pressure mounted, and later that year Walmart signed a memorandum with the ACFTU allowing unions in stores. Some analysts believe Walmart fought so hard against unionization in China, despite the clear unlikelihood of prevailing against the Chinese government itself, because it feared workers in other countries would use the precedent to redouble their own unionization demands. Since then, Walmart has permitted or negotiated with unions in several other countries as well, including Brazil, Chile, Mexico, Argentina, the United Kingdom, and South Africa.

WORKPLACE CONDITIONS AND DISCRIMINATION   Despite accusations of low employee benefits and a strong stance against unions, Walmart remains the largest nongovernment employer in the United States, Mexico, and Canada. It provides jobs to millions of people and has been a mainstay of *Fortune*'s "Most Admired Companies" list since the start of the twenty-first century. However, in December 2005, Walmart was ordered to pay $172 million to more than 100,000 California employees in a class-action lawsuit claiming that Walmart routinely denied meal breaks. The California employees also alleged they were denied rest breaks and Walmart managers deliberately altered time cards to prevent overtime. Similar accusations began to pop up in other states as well. Walmart denied the allegations and filed an appeal in 2007. In 2008 Walmart agreed to pay up to $640 million to settle 63 such lawsuits. This is only one example of the many lawsuits filed against Walmart; in 2005, it was estimated that the company was sued at least 5,000 times per year.

Walmart has also been accused by its employees of discrimination. Although women account for more than two-thirds of all Walmart employees, they make up less than 10 percent of store management. Walmart insists it trains and promotes women fairly, but in 2001 an internal study showed the company paid female store managers less than males in the same positions. In 2004 a federal judge in San Francisco granted class-action status to a sex-discrimination lawsuit against Walmart involving 1.6 million current and former female Walmart employees—the largest gender discrimination class action lawsuit in U.S. history. The plaintiffs claimed Walmart discriminated against them in regard to promotions, pay, training, and job assignments. Walmart fought the class-action suit, claiming there was no such pattern of discrimination and promotions and other employment decisions were made on an individual basis by the managers of each store. Thus, the company as a whole could not be held liable for any discrimination that might exist. Walmart took the case all the way to the Supreme Court. The Court declined to rule on the merits of the case itself but instead determined that the women in the lawsuit did not have enough in common to qualify for class-action status and would have to re-file as smaller qualifying class-action groups or individually. Although many of the original plaintiffs are now attempting to do so, they have found limited success; even narrower class-action attempts, such as a suit on behalf of 150,000 female employees in the company's "California region," have been dismissed as still too broad to qualify, and many civil rights lawyers will not take on individual employment discrimination cases because the likely payout will be too small even to cover the legal fees. Even if some of the women do end up successful in their claims, the impact on the company will be far less than if the nationwide class-action lawsuit had been allowed to proceed.

In 2010 dissatisfied Walmart employees started the Organization United for Respect at Walmart, or OUR Walmart. Although not a labor union, OUR Walmart receives much of its funding from the United Food and Commercial Workers International Union (UFCW), which has been trying to unionize U.S. Walmart employees for years. Eventually realizing it needed a different approach, UFCW backed the idea of a non-union advocacy group and hired a market research company to develop OUR Walmart's brand message and activism strategy. OUR Walmart claims support from at least 5,000 members, all current or former associates, who desire to change working conditions at the company. Their demands include lowering the number of hours needed for part-time workers to qualify for benefits, removing caps on the wages of some long-term workers, and ending the practice of using work-scheduling systems to decrease hours for employees so they will not qualify for benefits. In 2011 100 OUR Walmart members traveled to Walmart's headquarters and presented a 12-point declaration of their demands to the company's senior vice president for global labor relations. Since then, OUR Walmart has arranged a variety of protests and pickets. They have especially targeted the busy holiday season, organizing demonstrations and walkouts at many Walmart stores on every Black Friday since 2012.

Walmart's position is that OUR Walmart is a small, fringe movement that does not represent the views of the average associate, most of which are satisfied with their jobs. The company has repeatedly complained to the National Labor Relations Board, claiming, among other things, that OUR Walmart used illegal methods and that it is actually a union in disguise. Walmart has also accused the UFCW of anti-labor practices and filed at least one lawsuit against the UFCW and others who protested around its stores for illegal trespassing and disrupting customers. Walmart may have made a tactical error by choosing to acknowledge OUR Walmart as a threat. The number of OUR Walmart members is very small compared to the number of U.S. Walmart employees as a whole, and not as many Walmart employees have participated in protests as anticipated. Although Walmart claims this demonstrates that the movement is not as popular as it tries to appear, the company may have unintentionally granted it legitimacy and a large amount of free publicity by responding so directly and forcefully. OUR Walmart has claimed credit for Walmart's recent minimum wage hike to $10 starting in 2016, labeling it a "victory" and calling for further support to reach their eventual goal of a $15 minimum wage for all U.S. Walmart associates.

Ethical Leadership Issues

Aside from Sam Walton, other distinguished people have been associated with Walmart. One of them is Hillary Clinton, who served on Walmart's board for six years before her husband assumed the presidency. However, the company has not been immune from scandal at the top. In March 2005 board vice chair Thomas Coughlin was forced to resign because he stole as much as $500,000 from Walmart in the form of bogus expenses, reimbursements, and the unauthorized use of gift cards. Coughlin, a protégé and hunting buddy of Sam Walton, was a legend at Walmart. He often spent time on the road with Walton expanding the Sam's Club aspect of the business. At one time, he was the second highest-ranking Walmart executive and a candidate for CEO.

In January 2006, Coughlin agreed to plead guilty to federal wire-fraud and tax-evasion charges. Although he took home millions of dollars in authorized compensation, Coughlin secretly used Walmart funds to pay for a range of personal expenses including hunting vacations, a $2,590 dog enclosure at his home, and a pair of handmade alligator boots. Coughlin's deceit was discovered when he asked a subordinate to approve $2,000 in expense payments without receipts. Walmart rescinded Coughlin's retirement agreement, worth more than $10 million. For his crimes, he was sentenced to 27 months of home confinement, $440,000 in fines, and 1,500 hours of community service.

Despite this setback, confidence in Walmart's governance generally rose under the leadership of Lee Scott, who was CEO from 2000 to 2009. However, it suffered another serious blow in 2012 when a bribery scandal in Walmart's Mexico branch was uncovered that directly implicated much of the company's top management (the scandal is explored in detail later in this case). That same year, a significant percentage of Walmart's non-family shareholders voted against the reelection of then-CEO Mike Duke to the board. They also voted against the reelection of other board members, including former CEO Lee Scott and board chairman Robson Walton—Sam Walton's eldest son. While these board members still received enough support to be reelected, the votes signaled serious investor disappointment and lack of confidence in the leadership for not preventing the misconduct. Since the scandal, Walmart has invested heavily in demonstrating a renewed commitment toward ensuring the company adheres to ethics and compliance standards.

Bribery Scandal

The biggest blow to Walmart's reputation in recent years has been the uncovering of a large-scale bribery scandal within its Mexican arm, Walmex. Walmex executives allegedly paid millions in bribes to obtain licensing and zoning permits for store locations. The Mexican approval process for zoning licenses often takes longer than in the United States; therefore, paying bribes to speed up the process is advantageous for Walmart but places competing retailers who do not offer bribes at a disadvantage. Walmex apparently even used bribes to have zoning maps changed or certain areas re-zoned in order to build stores in more ideal locations, as well as to overcome environmental or other concerns. The Walmex executives covered their tracks with fraudulent reporting methods.

In recent years, bribery has become a hot button issue for the U.S. government, which has levied its largest fines and penalties ever against firms found guilty of bribery. It is not unusual for large firms with operations in many countries to face bribery allegations at some point considering the size of their operations and the diversity of cultures they do business with. However, Walmart's bribery scandal in Mexico was exacerbated by two major considerations. First, the evidence indicated that the top executives at Walmart, not just Walmex, knew about the bribery and turned a blind eye to it. Second, it gave weight to concerns that bribery by Walmart in foreign countries was widespread and accepted in the company's culture.

Walmart first reported to the U.S. Justice Department that it was launching an internal investigation of suspected bribery at its Mexico stores in December 2011. However, that report to the U.S. Justice Department was not submitted until after Walmart learned *The New York Times* was conducting an independent investigation. *The New York Times*'s final report revealed that top leaders at Walmart had been alerted to the possibility of bribery as early as 2005. That year, Walmart received an email warning of the bribery from a former Walmex executive who claimed he had been involved. The email included cold, hard facts, such as names, dates, bribery amounts, and other information. Walmart sent investigators to Mexico City, who corroborated much of the informant's allegations and discovered evidence that approximately $24 million in bribes had been paid to public officials to get necessary building permits. Walmex's top executives, including the subsidiary's CEO and general counsel, were implicated in the scheme. However, when the investigators reported their preliminary findings to Walmart's top executives, including then-CEO Lee Scott, the executives were reluctant to report the bribery because they knew it would be a serious blow to the firm's reputation, which was already suffering due to other issues. The prospect of revealing the scandal was especially bitter because Walmart had been drawing media and investor attention for its explosive growth in Mexico as a shining success story.

Admitting that this growth had been significantly fueled by bribery would look very bad for the company.

Instead, the investigation was turned over to the Walmex general counsel, even though the preliminary report found he had approved of and been involved in the scheme. This move was against the advice of one of Walmart's top lawyers, who recommended an independent third-party investigator and later resigned in protest. The Walmex general counsel's final report found no evidence of bribery or wrongdoing by Walmex executives. The investigation was closed without anyone being disciplined, and no one external to the company was notified until after the *New York Times* began its investigation.

If the top leaders at Walmart did indeed know of the bribery and covered it up, it is a serious ethical and legal violation. The executives that may have had knowledge of the scandal include then-CEO Lee Scott and the CEO after him, Mike Duke, who at the time was in charge of Walmart International. Under the U.S. Foreign Corrupt Practices Act (FCPA), it is illegal to bribe foreign officials, and all those with knowledge of such a crime are potentially implicated. Walmart could face billions in fines, and its executives could lose their jobs or face prison time if it is found they helped cover up knowledge of the bribery. Indeed, many of those that occupied high-level positions when the scandal was unearthed have quietly retired or stepped down since it became public.

The scandal's impact on Walmart was significant. Shortly after the *New York Times*'s investigation was published, the stock lost $1 billion in value, and shareholders began filing lawsuits against the company and its executives. Additionally, Walmart has had to pay for its own internal probe, not to mention hire a number of lawyers to represent itself and its top management as well as advisors and consultants to help restructure its internal ethics and compliance systems—all of which have already cost it over $612 million. Costs are expected to continue rising as Walmart's internal probe continues. To date investigations by the SEC and the Justice Department are also still ongoing and may end in official charges.

Walmart's internal probe revealed the likelihood of bribery going on in other countries as well. The company therefore expanded the investigation to include its operations in China, India, and Brazil. For example, at its Indian branch, Walmart suspended some key executives believed to have engaged in bribery. This investigation halted Walmart's expansion in the country. Indian authorities began investigating Walmart and its joint venture partner at the time, Bharti Enterprises, to determine if they attempted to circumvent Indian laws on foreign investment. Foreign retailers like Walmart are allowed to partner with local businesses and open stores in the country so long as they do not own a majority stake in the venture (less than 51 percent ownership). It is alleged that Walmart offered Bharti an interest-free, $100 million loan that would later enable it to gain a majority stake in the company. Both companies deny they tried to violate foreign investment rules and have since broken off their partnership. Such accusations not only have serious consequences for Walmart but also for other foreign retailers in India. Many Indian political officials are against allowing foreign retailers to open stores in the country at all. This alleged misconduct has added fuel for their opposition. Hence, the operation of other foreign retailers may be threatened. This situation demonstrates how the misconduct of one or two companies can impact entire industries.

In the wake of the Mexico scandal, many Walmart shareholders demanded, among other things, disciplinary action and compensation cuts against those involved. Shareholders are also demanding that the leaders of Walmart continue to improve transparency and compliance standards. As part of its compliance overhaul, Walmart announced it would begin tying some executive compensation to compliance efforts.

Safety Issues

Using overseas suppliers has also caused trouble for Walmart. Many of its suppliers, both inside the United States and in other countries, employ subcontractors to manufacture certain products. This makes the supply chain complex, and retailers like Walmart are forced to exert more oversight to ensure its suppliers meet compliance standards. Citing safety concerns or telling a supplier not to work with a certain subcontractor is not enough without enforcement. Walmart learned this the hard way after a Bangladeshi factory fire killed 112 workers.

The factory, Tazreen Fashions Ltd., had several assembly lines devoted to Walmart apparel because at least one of Walmart's suppliers used the factory to subcontract work for Walmart. However, Walmart claims the supplier was unauthorized to do so as Walmart had removed Tazreen Fashions from its list of approved factories months before the incident. Walmart subsequently terminated its relationship with that supplier. Previous inspections at Tazreen showed many fire dangers, including blocked stairwells and a lack of firefighting equipment. The fire burned down the building and killed 112 employees, some of whom jumped to their deaths.

Many were outraged that Walmart did not do a better job of ensuring the safety of factory workers that produce merchandise for it. While Walmart does have auditing and approval mechanisms for subcontracted facilities, third parties usually perform the audits. Suppliers often pay for the inspection processes as well. This limits the amount of information that actually gets to the parent company. Critics have also accused Walmart of advocating against equipping factories with better fire protection due to the costs involved. Walmart claims it takes fire dangers and worker safety seriously.

Walmart has also faced criticism on its home front. Workers at warehouses in the United States that do business with Walmart have complained about harsh working conditions and violations of labor laws. Safety violations are also a common complaint. For example, in 2012 a group of delivery packing workers at a warehouse in Mira Loma, California, went on strike and walked for six days to Los Angeles to draw attention to allegedly miserable and unsafe working conditions and to deliver a petition to the Los Angeles Walmart office. The situation is complex because such warehouse workers are hired and employed by staffing agencies or third-party contractors, making it harder for Walmart to assess working conditions. Walmart has argued that these third-party contractors are responsible for working conditions. Yet as the firm hiring the contractors, Walmart has the responsibility and generally the power to ensure their contractors and subcontractors obey proper labor laws.

The Bangladeshi fire and ongoing worker complaints have increased the pressure on Walmart to improve its oversight and auditing mechanisms. Previously, Walmart employed a three-strike policy for suppliers and subcontractors who violated its ethical standards. However, after the Bangladeshi fire Walmart changed its policy to adopt a zero-tolerance approach. Whereas before, suppliers that violated sourcing policies had three chances to rectify problems, now Walmart exerts the right to terminate relationships with suppliers immediately after discovering a violation. Walmart also requires all suppliers to have an independent agency assess the electrical and building safety conditions of their factories. To address domestic complaints, Walmart applies the same monitoring system to U.S. suppliers. Walmart furthermore stated it has begun making unannounced visits to U.S. third-party operated warehouses by independent auditors to check whether they adhere to the firm's ethical standards. Walmart hopes these stricter measures improve compliance by its suppliers as well as reiterate the company's commitment to ethical sourcing practices.

Yet these measures have failed to appease some critics, who believe that Walmart cannot truly be held accountable until the results of its factory audits are made public.

The controversy of worker safety in Bangladesh intensified after yet another factory collapsed in 2013, killing 1,127 workers. The tragedy caused Walmart and other retailers to consider new safety plans. A group of European retailers, worker safety groups, and labor unions came together to develop and sign a five-year legally binding workplace safety agreement that improved worker safety in Bangladesh by requiring retailers to pay suppliers more so factories could afford to make safety improvements, as well as through the development of a standardized worker complaint and risk reporting process. Walmart declined to sign the agreement, however, and instead devised its own safety plan. Its plan primarily involved hiring an independent auditor to inspect all of the more than 200 Bangladeshi factories that produced goods for Walmart and publishing the results publicly, including which factories failed the audit and were no longer allowed to produce for Walmart, as well as requiring factories that did not fail but still had some unsafe conditions to improve safety standards. Critics argue that Walmart's independent plan is insufficient and much less ambitious than the workplace safety agreement it declined to join.

RESPONDING TO STAKEHOLDER CONCERNS

Walmart has suffered significantly from these recent scandals. Studies reveal that between 2011 and 2012, consumer interest, customer loyalty, and other factors important to a brand's value diminished 50 percent for Walmart's brand among college-educated adults. The brand's recent decline in value is also due to stagnant company growth, caused by a variety of problems such as increased competition from online retailers like Amazon.com and the simple fact that Walmart has saturated many markets at this point. Walmart's brand has continued to lose value, although it remains by far the most valuable retail brand in the world.

As has been discussed, being a large multinational corporation brings many global risks, including bribery and supplier issues. In response to the allegations of bribery, Walmart quietly replaced many top-level executives in both Mexico and the United States and is conducting an investigation into the allegations. In addition, former CEO Mike Duke assured the public that the company is reevaluating its global compliance program with assistance from top auditing and law firms.

At a pep rally held in May of 2012, Mike Duke emphasized integrity in operations and employee behavior at all levels and rewarded 11 employees for "leading with integrity." In highlighting the actions of these select employees, he reiterated the firm's ethics hotline and open-door policy. He assured employees and other stakeholders that the company is cooperating with the U.S. Department of Justice in order to get to the bottom of the bribery allegations. Mike Duke acknowledged that there were ethical issues in some Walmart stores and stated that he planned to slow expansion so the company could focus on improving these issues.

As a form of damage control, Walmart ran an advertising campaign to frame the company as an "American success story." Additionally, after market research revealed Walmart's brand image had lost traction among college-educated adults, Walmart developed a multimillion dollar advertising campaign called "The Real Walmart." The advertisements featured customers, truck drivers, and employees sharing their happy experiences with the company.

Walmart particularly wanted to target opinion leaders who could then convince others of the company's value and positive brand image. The ads were first released during the Kentucky Derby and were also featured on Sunday news shows. This advertising campaign was similar to those released by other companies attempting to restore their image, such as Toyota during its recall crisis and BP after the *Deepwater Horizon* disaster.

Sustainability Leadership

Among Walmart's long-term sustainability goals are its intentions to be supplied entirely by renewable energy, create no waste, and sell products that sustain people and the environment. In order to achieve these ambitious goals, Walmart has built relationships with influential people in supplier companies, government, NGOs, and academia. Together they have organized Walmart's environmental goals into 14 Sustainable Value Networks (SVN), from "Global Greenhouse Gas Strategy" to "Packaging" to "Forest & Paper," which allow them to efficiently integrate, implement, and evaluate their sustainability efforts. This approach has served them well. By 2012 Walmart had 115 onsite rooftop solar installations in seven countries providing 71 million annual kilowatt hours of electricity. They had completed 26 fuel cell installations in the United States, providing 65 million kilowatt hours of annual electricity, and were also testing micro-wind and solar water heating projects in various locations. Walmart's company value of everyday low costs translates to its renewable energy endeavors through the signing of long-term contracts with renewable energy providers. These contracts finance utility-scale projects in renewable resources, allowing these options to be offered at lower cost not only to Walmart but also to other clients of these providers.

Walmart has well over 335 renewable energy projects in operation or under development, including micro-wind installations in parking lots and biodiesel generator sets. Their solar installations provided 105 megawatts of solar capacity, the most of any company in the world by far and greater than the total solar capacity of any of at least 35 U.S. states. Due to these endeavors, Walmart can boast that fully 25 percent of its global energy consumption now comes from renewable sources, and it has pledged to double its solar installation numbers by 2020. In addition, nearly 350 Mexico stores have reduced emissions by 137,000 tons annually through wind power, and all 14 of its stores in Northern Ireland are powered by wind energy. The Environmental Protection Agency's Green Power Partnership Program ranks Walmart as the third largest purchaser of green power among its U.S. retail competitors and ninth largest purchaser in the Fortune 500. It is the largest onsite green power generator in the United Sates.

To reduce energy consumption, Walmart facilities conserve energy in two major ways. For instance, Walmart efficiently manages heating and cooling energy consumption by centrally controlling the temperature of Walmart stores worldwide from its Bentonville headquarters. The company is also opening new stores and retrofitting existing ones with high-efficiency LED and low-mercury fluorescent lighting and is in the process of replacing open freezers with secondary loop refrigeration systems. These improvements will help the company meet its goal of reducing greenhouse gas emissions by 20 million metric tons globally by the end of 2015. Walmart is furthermore attempting to reduce fossil fuel use and sell more "green" products. The company has doubled its fuel efficiency for its 6,000 trucks that cross the United States. Since 2007, Walmart has been able to deliver more products while reducing mileage by 300 million. This improved shipping has decreased carbon emissions by at least 41,000 tons.

The retailer has also begun selling more products made from sustainable or recycled materials and has taken efforts to reduce packaging. For example, the firm is selling pre-school toys made from wood that is Forest Stewardship Council-certified. Walmart also started a program to sell more local produce (defined as produce grown and sold in the same state). According to the company, 11 percent of its U.S. produce is now sourced locally. Walmart is also investing in medium- and smaller-sized farms, particularly in emerging economies.

In line with its zero waste goals, Walmart Mexico (Walmex) has been successful in converting 1.2 million pounds of used cooking oil into biodiesel, soap, and supplements for cattle feed as well as composting over 1,900 metric tons of organic waste. Walmart has also been testing recycling methods, which it aims to incorporate into all of its stores. Walmart's recycling efforts have allowed the company to reduce its global plastic bag waste by over 38 percent since 2007. The company has been able to keep 80 percent of its U.S. operational waste out of landfills.

One of the most unique and well-regarded of Walmart's sustainability efforts is its Sustainability Index, which it developed with the help of a nonprofit coalition known as The Sustainability Consortium. The Sustainability Index is essentially an attempt to rate and categorize all of Walmart's products and suppliers on a variety of sustainability-related issues. Between 2009 and 2012, Walmart worked with researchers to develop the basic categories and determine what information would be required for the Index to work. Then, starting in 2012, it began sending out requests for this information to its suppliers. For example, suppliers of products that contain wheat, such as cakes, cookies, and bread, were asked to provide detailed information about the sourcing of that wheat, from fertilizer use tracking to soil fertility monitoring to biodiversity management. Computer and jewelry suppliers were asked about the mining practices used to extract their materials; toy makers about the chemicals used in their manufacturing processes; and so on. Walmart uses this information to rank its suppliers from best to worst on the Sustainability Index, and then gives that information to those in charge of making Walmart purchasing decisions to use in determining which suppliers to buy from. Presumably, the end result is that more sustainable products end up on Walmart shelves, and suppliers are incentivized to improve their practices to better compete with others on the Index.

The initiative is exciting because Walmart's industry power is so great that a successful implementation could truly drive change throughout entire supplier industries and chains. As actual implementation of the Index is still in progress, details on its workings and effectiveness are still scarce, but industry onlookers and sustainability advocates are watching closely to see what effect it will have on Walmart and its supplier network.

Although Walmart's environmental overhaul is a step in the right direction, some are skeptical as to whether it can accomplish its goals. Many claim that Walmart's apparent sustainability gains are overstated, lacking in critical information, or downright misleading; in other words, "greenwashing" advertising rather than actual change. Some suppliers are worried about the Sustainability Index, including the amount of increased time and expense it will take to provide the required information and the business implications of products that receive higher "sustainability" rankings being given preferential treatment. Also, the concept of "being green" is subjective, since not everyone agrees on how it is defined or whether one environmentally friendly practice is necessarily more beneficial than another. Despite these obstacles, Walmart seems to have achieved some substantial successes in this area through its dedication to its goals and the strength of its partnerships.

WHAT IS WALMART DOING TO IMPROVE ETHICS AND SOCIAL RESPONSIBILITY?

Walmart is working to improve its ethical reputation along with its reputation for social responsibility and corporate governance. In 2004 Walmart formed its Global Ethics Office and released a revised Global Statement of Ethics. The intent of the Global Ethics Office is to spread an ethical corporate culture among its global stakeholders. The Global Ethics Office provides guidance on ethical decision making based on the Global Statement of Ethics and an ethics helpline. The helpline is an anonymous and confidential way for associates to contact the company regarding ethical issues. Additionally, Walmart has an Ethical Standards Team to monitor the compliance of supplier factories with the company's "Standards for Suppliers" and local laws. Walmart claims that in a period of several months the firm interviewed 1,000 market personnel in various countries, dedicated $35 million to new processes and procedures, and developed ethical training sessions for more than 19,000 associates.

In response to the bribery scandal, Walmart has completely overhauled its global compliance program. In 2014 it released its first Global Compliance Program Report detailing the changes it has made. The report categorized the changes into three broad areas: people, policies and processes, and systems. The changes include a completely new corporate division that combines ethics, compliance, investigations, and legal matters into a unified organization all reporting to an Executive Vice President of Global Governance. The company has also hired "Subject Matter Leaders" and "Subject Matter Experts" to provide expertise and advice in 14 areas of concern, such as anti-corruption and responsible sourcing. Other highlights are a multi-year compliance training plan, improvements to reporting and collaboration communications channels, establishment of multiple compliance and ethics committees, and a commitment to being completely bribery-free, regardless of the culture Walmart is operating in. Analysts have stated that, at least on paper, Walmart's initiatives are extremely thorough and innovative and deserve close watch to see how they work in practice. Walmart will continue to release Global Compliance Program Reports annually to further detail its accomplishments and the compliance and governance steps it continues to take.

Walmart has contributed significantly to disaster management projects and economic empowerment for women. The company donated over $1.5 million in aid for the victims of Hurricane Sandy, including money, food, and goods. In 2001 Walmart established The Associates in Critical Need Trust, which provides grants to associates who have experienced unexpected emergencies such as natural disasters or death of a spouse; the trust has given over $100 million in grants so far. In terms of increasing opportunities for women, Walmart made a commitment in partnering with 150 factories and 60,000 women to teach women valuable skills to help them escape poverty. It has also collaborated with the Women's Business Enterprise National Council to add a unique "Women Owned" logo to products from women-owned businesses so customers can easily identify and support them if desired.

The company has recently embarked on a health initiative to address the growing problem of obesity in America. Walmart U.S. President Bill Simon met with First Lady Michelle Obama to discuss the issue. Walmart announced it would lower the prices of its fruits and vegetables and reduce the amounts of fats, sugars, and salts in the foods it sells. Specifically, the company formulated goals that included cutting sodium by 25 percent and sugars by 10 percent in food under its Great Value brand over a five-year period.

By putting its weight behind solving the obesity epidemic, the world's largest retailer might be able to create significant change toward healthier eating habits.

Walmart Today

Walmart remains the preferred shopping destination for many consumers, particularly after the financial meltdown of 2008–2009. Although Walmart prospered during the recession while other retailers suffered, the company's sales in many of its established markets have begun to stagnate or even decline. Walmart itself acknowledged that it strayed from Sam Walton's original vision of everyday low prices in order to court higher-income customers. Several initiatives, such as Walmart's adoption of organic food and trendy clothes, did not achieve much success with discount shoppers. Walmart also underwent a renovation effort that cut certain products, such as fishing tackle, from its stores. These actions alienated Walmart's original customer base. Households earning less than $70,000 annually defected to discounters like Dollar Tree and Family Dollar. Analysts believe Walmart's mistake was trying to be everything to everyone, along with copying its more "chic" rivals like Target. Because of these blunders, in addition to external pressures such as market saturation and strong competition from other retail giants, Walmart's sales in many markets are experiencing a slump. As a result, Walmart is returning to Sam Walton's original vision and its "everyday low prices" mantra. The company launched a campaign, "It's Back," to signal the return of the merchandise it removed, and Walmart executives are encouraging store managers to compare prices with competitors to ensure Walmart offers the lowest prices. Walmart is also investing significantly into e-commerce as an untapped area of growth in the hopes of competing more directly with Amazon and other e-commerce retailers that have drawn away some of its customer base.

Although Walmart's stagnating domestic sales were counterbalanced for a period by continuing steady growth in international markets, even its growth in many foreign markets has slowed. The company continues to look for new opportunities to expand internationally to make up for lower growth in its established markets. This strategy requires Walmart to continually adapt to different social, cultural, regulatory, economic, and political factors. Walmart is known for its ability to adapt quickly to different environments, but even this large-scale retailer has experienced trouble. For instance, it was forced to withdraw completely from Germany and South Korea after failing to interest the local populations, and still has just a small number of wholesale-only stores in India, one of the world's largest markets, after failing to find a way to navigate the country's complex regulatory environment for foreign retailers to sell directly to the public. Walmart's Brazil branch has also failed to achieve profitability after over two decades in the country, which some attribute to the retailer's everyday low pricing strategy simply being incompatible with the Brazilian shopper culture of always checking multiple retailers for sales. The more Walmart expands internationally, the more the company must decide what concessions it is willing to make to enter certain markets.

Despite the difficulties of operating globally, Walmart has achieved a number of successes. After years of struggling in the Japanese market, for example, Walmart began turning a profit in 2008 through its acquisition of Japanese retailer Seiyu Ltd. It has also recently turned its attention again to India, expressing a new commitment to expanding its operations in the market, and is continually focused on further developing its presence in China, with plans to open 115 new stores in the country by 2017. Though the company will likely experience several bumps in the road, many of its international markets appear to offer strong growth potential.

The Future of Walmart

Walmart can be viewed through two very different lenses. Some think the company represents all that is wrong with America, while others love it. In response to criticism, and in an attempt to initiate goodwill with consumers, the company has continued to improve stakeholder relationships and make efforts to demonstrate it is an ethically responsible company. Although it has faced controversy regarding competition, suppliers, employees, and global corruption, among other things, it has also demonstrated concern for sustainability initiatives and social responsibility. Its goals of decreasing its waste and carbon emissions and its new Sustainability Index extend to all facets of its operations, including suppliers. These efforts demonstrate Walmart's desire (whether through genuine concern for the environment or for its own bottom-line profits) to become a more sustainable company.

Similarly, Walmart's creation of a sophisticated global ethics and compliance program shows it has come a long way since its beginning, when formal ethics programs were deemed unnecessary. However, without strong monitoring systems and a commitment from top management to enforce the company's ethics policies such efforts will prove fruitless. Overseas bribery scandals and employee discontent have tarnished Walmart's reputation. As a result, the company is working to improve internal control mechanisms and supplier auditing. Both critics and supporters of Walmart alike are waiting to see whether Walmart's efforts will position the company as a large retailer truly dedicated to social responsibility.

QUESTIONS FOR DISCUSSION

1. Assess how Walmart is managing ethics and social responsibility as one of the largest corporations in the world.
2. Evaluate various ethical issues Walmart has faced and how the company responded to stakeholders.
3. What are Walmart's contributions to improving the well-being of consumers and the economic sustainability of society?

SOURCES

$15 & Full Time website, http://15atwalmart.org/ (accessed May 18, 2015); James Arkin, "D.C. Council panel hears testimony on 'living wage' bill targeting large retailers," *The Washington Post*, March 20, 2013, http://articles. washingtonpost.com/2013-03-20/local/37864098_1_minimum-wage-retailers-outlets (accessed May 15, 2015); Associated Press, "Former Wal-Mart executive is resentenced, avoids prison," *Los Angeles Times*, February 2, 2008, http://articles.latimes.com/2008/feb/02/business/fi-coughlin2 (accessed May 15, 2015); Vikas Bajaj, "India Unit of Wal-Mart Suspends Employees," *The New York Times*, November 23, 2012, http://www.nytimes. com/2012/11/24/business/global/wal-marts-india-venture-suspends-executives-as-part-of-bribery-inquiry. html?_r=0 (accessed May 15, 2015); James Bandler, "Former No. 2 at Wal-Mart Set to Plead Guilty," *The Wall Street Journal*, January 7, 2006, A1; James Bandler and Ann Zimmerman, "A Wal-Mart Legend's Trail of Deceit," *The Wall Street Journal*, April 8, 2005, A10; Shelly Banjo, "Wal-Mart Ads Tout 'American Success Story'," *The Wall Street Journal*, May 3, 2013, http://online.wsj.com/article/SB10001424127887324582004578460973584445016. html (accessed May 15, 2015); Shelly Banjo, "Wal-Mart Cheer: I-n-t-e-g-r-i-t-y," *The Wall Street Journal*, May 31, 2012, B3; Shelly Banjo, "Wal-Mart to Monitor Warehouses," *The Wall Street Journal*, December 28, 2012, B4; Shelly Banjo, "Wal-Mart Toughens Supplier Policies," *The Wall Street Journal*, February 22, 2013, B1, B7;

Shelly Banjo, "Wal-Mart Will Tie Executive Pay to Compliance Overhaul," *The Wall Street Journal*, April 23, 2013, B8; Shelly Banjo and Ann Zimmerman, "Protestors Wage Campaign against Wal-Mart," *The Wall Street Journal*, November 23, 2012, http://online.wsj.com/article/SB10001424127887323713104578136992890118444.html (accessed May 15, 2015); Shelly Banjo, Ann Zimmerman, and Suzanne Kapner, "Wal-Mart Crafts Own Bangladesh Safety Plan," *The Wall Street Journal*, May 15, 2013, B1–B2; Michael Barbaro, "Image Effort by Wal-Mart Takes a Turn," *The New York Times*, May 12, 2006, C1, C4; David Barstow, "Vast Mexico Bribery Case Hushed Up by Wal-Mart after Top-Level Struggle," *The New York Times*, April 21, 2012, http://www.nytimes.com/2012/04/22/business/at-wal-mart-in-mexico-a-bribe-inquiry-silenced.html?pagewanted=all (accessed May 15, 2015); Noelle Barton DeFazio and Caroline Preston, "Wal-Mart tops list of charitable cash contributors, AT&T No. 2," *USA Today*, August 9, 2010, http://usatoday30.usatoday.com/money/companies/2010-08-08-corporate-philanthropy-interactive-graphic_n.htm (accessed May 18, 2015); Susan Berfield, "Walmart vs. Union-Backed OUR Walmart," *Bloomberg Businessweek*, December 13, 2012, http://www.bloomberg.com/bw/articles/2012-12-13/walmart-vs-dot-union-backed-our-walmart#p1 (accessed May 18, 2015); Susan Berfield, "Walmart vs. Walmart," *Bloomberg Businessweek*, December 13, 2012, 53–60.; Ira Boudway, "Labor Disputes, the Walmart Way," *Bloomberg Businessweek*, December 13, 202, http://www.businessweek.com/articles/2012-12-13/labor-disputes-the-walmart-way (accessed May 15, 2015); Abram Brown, "Mexican Bribery Scandal Could Cost Wal-Mart $4.5 Billion Shares Down 4.7%," *Forbes*, http://www.forbes.com/sites/abrambrown/2012/04/23/spooked-investors-sink-wal-mart-nearly-5-after-bribery-revelations-at-least-4-5b-penalty-likely/ (accessed May 18, 2015); Abram Brown, "Wal-Mart Bribery Probe Expands Past Mexico To Brazil, China, And India," *Forbes*, November 15, 2012, http://www.forbes.com/sites/abrambrown/2012/11/15/probe-into-wal-mart-bribery-past-mexico-to-brazil-china-and-india/ (accessed May 15, 2015); Chris Burritt, "Wal-Mart Overseas Expansion to Accelerate, CEO Says (Update5)," *Bloomberg Businessweek*, June 2, 2010, http://www.businessweek.com/news/2010-06-02/wal-mart-overseas-expansion-to-accelerate-ceo-says-update5-.html (accessed February 8, 2011); Miguel Bustillo, "Wal-Mart Faces Risk in Mexican Bribe Probe," *The Wall Street Journal*, April 23, 2012, http://online.wsj.com/article/SB10001424052702303978104577360283629622556.html (accessed May 15, 2015); Miguel Bustillo, "Wal-Mart Pledges to Promote Healthier Foods," *The Wall Street Journal*, January 20, 2011, http://online.wsj.com/article/SB10001424052748704881304576093872178374258.html (accessed May 15, 2015); Miguel Bustillo, "Wal-Mart to Assign New 'Green Ratings,'" *The Wall Street Journal*, July 16, 2009, http://online.wsj.com/article/SB124766892562645475.html (accessed May 15, 2015); Miguel Bustillo, "Wal-Mart Merchandise Goes Back to Basics," *The Wall Street Journal*, April 11, 2011, B3; Miguel Bustillo, "Wal-Mart Tries to Recapture Mr. Sam's Winning Formula," *The Wall Street Journal*, February 22, 2011, A1, A11; Miguel Bustillo, "With Sales Flabby, Wal-Mart Turns to Its Core," *The Wall Street Journal*, March 21, 2011, B1, B8; Stephanie Clifford, "More Dissent Is Expected over a Wal-Mart Scandal," *The New York Times*, June 6, 2013, http://www.nytimes.com/2013/06/07/business/more-dissent-is-in-store-over-wal-mart-scandal.html?pagewanted=all&_r=1& (accessed May 15, 2015); Stephanie Clifford, "Wal-Mart to Buy More Local Produce," *The New York Times*, October 14, 2010, http://www.nytimes.com/2010/10/15/business/15walmart.html (accessed May 15, 2015); Andrew Clark, "Wal-Mart, the U.S. retailer, taking over the world by stealth," guardian.co.uk, January 12, 2010, http://www.guardian.co.uk/business/2010/jan/12/walmart-companies-to-shape-the-decade (accessed May 15, 2015); Lauren Coleman-Lochner, "Independent Look at Wal-Mart Shows Both Good and Bad: With Savings and Jobs Come Falling Wages and Rising Medicaid Costs," *The San Antonio Express-News*, November 5, 2005, 4D; Bryce Covert, "Walmart Penalized for Closing Store Just after It Unionized," *Think Progress*, June 30, 2014, http://thinkprogress.org/economy/2014/06/30/3454511/walmart-canada-union/ (accessed May 18, 2015); Lydia DePillis "Wal-Mart's threatening to pull out of D.C. if it has to *Washington Post*, July 10, 2013, http://www.washingtonpost.com/blogs/wonkblog/wp/2013/07/10/wal-marts-threatening-to-pull-out-of-d-c-if-it-has-to-pay-a-higher-minimum-wage-so-what/ (accessed May 18, 2015); Renee Dudley, "Customers Flee Wal-Mart Empty Shelves for Target, Costco," *Bloomberg*, March 26, 2013, http://www.bloomberg.com/news/2013-03-26/customers-flee-wal-mart-empty-shelves-for-target-costco.html (accessed May 15, 2015); Renee Dudley, "Wal-Mart Releases Names of Bangladesh Factories Inspected," *Bloomberg*, November 18, 2013, http://www.bloomberg.com/news/articles/2013-11-18/wal-mart-releases-names-of-bangladesh-factories-inspected (accessed

May 18, 2015); Renee Dudley, "Wal-Mart won't sign Bangladesh building safety agreement," *Washington Post*, May 14, 2013, http://www.washingtonpost.com/business/economy/wal-mart-to-conduct-safety-inspections-at-all-279-bangladesh-supplier-factories/2013/05/14/c90598e2-bce7-11e2-97d4-a479289a31f9_story.html (accessed May 18, 2015); Renee Dudley, Christiana Sciaudone, and Jessica Brice, "Why Wal-Mart Hasn't Conquered Brazil," May 8, 2014, http://www.bloomberg.com/bw/articles/2014-05-08/why-wal-mart-hasnt-conquered-brazil (accessed May 18, 2015); Bruce Einhorn, "Wal-Mart Tries Again in India," *Bloomberg*, October 23, 2014, http://www.bloomberg.com/bw/articles/2014-10-23/wal-mart-struggles-to-crack-retail-market-in-india (accessed May 18, 2015); Lauren Etter, "Gauging the Wal-Mart Effect," *The Wall Street Journal*, December 3–4, 2005, A9; Charles Fishman, "5 Surprises at the New Big City Walmart in Washington, D.C." *Fast Company*, http://www.fastcompany.com/3023007/5-surprises-at-the-new-big-city-walmart-in-washington-dc (accessed May 18, 2015); Charles Fishman, "The Wal-Mart You Don't Know: Why Low Prices Have a High Cost," *Fast Company*, December 2003, 68–80; Mei Fong and Ann Zimmerman, "China's Union Push Leaves Wal-Mart with Hard Choice," *The Wall Street Journal*, May 13–14, 2006, A1, A6; Fortune, "Most Admired 2015," http://fortune.com/worlds-most-admired-companies/wal-mart-stores-38/ (accessed May 18, 2015); Emily Jane Fox, "Wal-Mart Toughens Regulations after Bangladesh Fire," *CNNMoney*, January 22, 2013, http://money.cnn.com/2013/01/22/news/companies/walmart-supplier-regulations/index.html (accessed May 15, 2015); Global Insight, "Global Insight Releases New Study on the Impact of Wal-Mart on the U.S. Economy," http://www.globalinsight.com/MultiClientStudy/MultiClientStudyDetail2438.htm (accessed January 23, 2005); Steven Greenhouse, "Documents Indicate Wal-Mart Blocked Safety Push," *The New York Times*, December 5, 2012, http://www.nytimes.com/2012/12/06/world/asia/3-walmart-suppliers-made-goods-in-bangladeshi-factory-where-112-died-in-fire.html (accessed May 15, 2015); Steven Greenhouse and Stephanie Clifford, "Wal-Mart steps up efforts to suppress strike," *The New York Times*, November 20, 2012, 15; Marc Gunther, "The Gunther Report: Game on: Why Walmart is ranking suppliers on sustainability," *GreenBiz*, April 15, 2013, http://www.greenbiz.com/blog/2013/04/15/game-why-walmart-ranking-suppliers-sustainability (accessed May 18, 2015); Elizabeth A. Harris, "After Bribery Scandal, High-Level Departures at Walmart," *New York Times*, June 4, 2014, http://www.nytimes.com/2014/06/05/business/after-walmart-bribery-scandals-a-pattern-of-quiet-departures.html?_r=2 (accessed May 18, 2015); Ben W. Heineman, Jr., "Who's Responsible for the Walmart Mexico Scandal?" *Harvard Business Review*, May 15, 2015, https://hbr.org/2014/05/whos-responsible-for-the-walmart-mexico-scandal/ (accessed May 18, 2015); Alice Hines, "Walmart's New Health Policy Shifts Burden to Medicaid, Obamacare," *The Huffington Post*, December 1, 2012, http://www.huffingtonpost.com/2012/12/01/walmart-health-care-policy-medicaid-obamacare_n_2220152.html (accessed May 15, 2015); Dave Jamieson, "Feds Charge Walmart with Breaking Labor Law in Black Friday Strikes," *The Huffington Post*, January 25, 2014, http://www.huffingtonpost.com/2014/01/15/walmart-complaint_n_4604069.html (accessed May 18, 2015); John Jannarone, "Wal-Mart's Tough Work Experience," *The Wall Street Journal*, February 23, 2011, C 14; Marcus Kabel, "Wal-Mart at War: Retailer Faces Bruised Image, Makes Fixes," *Marketing News*, January 15, 2006, 25; Matt Krantz, "Walmart's wages get CEOs' attention," *USA Today*, March 2, 20115, 2B; Andy Kroll, "Walmart Workers Get Organized—Just Don't Say the U-Word," *Mother Jones*, March/April 2013, http://www.motherjones.com/politics/2013/02/our-walmart-black-friday-union (accessed May 18, 2015); Kabir Kumar, "Walmart Associates Show Compassion in Times of Crisis," September 22, 2014, http://blog.walmart.com/walmart-associates-show-compassion-in-times-of-crisis (accessed May 18, 2015); Walter Loeb, "How Walmart Plans to Bring Manufacturing Back to the United States," *Forbes*, November 12, 2013, http://www.forbes.com/sites/walterloeb/2013/11/12/walmart-taking-steps-to-bring-manufacturing-back-to-the-united-states/ (accessed May 18, 2015); Walter Loeb, "Walmart: What Happened In India?" *Forbes*, October 16, 2013, http://www.forbes.com/sites/walterloeb/2013/10/16/walmart-what-happened-in-india/ (accessed May 18, 2015); Hadley Malcolm, "Scraping by at Walmart," *USA Today*, June 7, 2012, http://usatoday30.usatoday.com/MONEY/usaedition/2012-06-08-Walmart-workers-strugglenew--_CV_U.htm (accessed May 15, 2015); Sagar Malviya, "Anti-Bribery Saga in India: Walmart puts new outlets in freezer," *The Economic Times*, March 13, 2013, http://articles.economictimes.indiatimes.com/2013-03-13/news/37683765_1_bharti-walmart-new-stores-new-outlets (accessed May 15, 2015); Nina Martin, "The Impact and Echoes of the Wal-Mart Discrimination Case," *ProPublica*, http://www.propublica.org/article/the-impact-and-echoes-of-the-wal-mart-discrimination-case (accessed

May 18, 2015); Jessica Mason Pieklo, "Why It's So Hard to Sue Wal-Mart for Gender Discrimination," *RH Reality Check*, August 7, 2013, http://rhrealitycheck.org/article/2013/08/07/will-corporations-like-wal-mart-ever-be-liable-for-discriminatory-employment-practices/ (accessed May 18, 2015); Daniel McGinn, "Wal-Mart Hits the Wall," *Newsweek*, November 14, 2005, 44–46; Kathleen Miles, "Walmart Warehouse Workers Rally in Downtown LA Ends 6-Day Pilgrimage (PHOTOS)," *Huffington Post*, September 18, 2012, http://www.huffingtonpost.com/2012/09/18/walmart-warehouse-workers-rally-la-pilgrimage_n_1893843.html (accessed May 18, 2015); *Newser*, "Wal-Mart Will Pay \$640M to Settle Wage Lawsuits," December 23, 2008, http://www.newser.com/story/46142/wal-mart-will-pay-640m-to-settle-wage-lawsuits.html?utm_source=ssp&utm_medium=cpc&utm_campaign=story (accessed May 15, 2015); Janet Novack, "Walmart Wins Again as Washington D.C. Mayor Vetoes \$12.50 Minimum Wage," *Forbes*, September 12, 2013, http://www.forbes.com/sites/janetnovack/2013/09/12/walmart-wins-again-as-washington-d-c-mayor-vetoes-12-50-minimum-wage/ (accessed May 18, 2015); Occupy Solidarity Network, "Walmart Organizes against Workers," January 14, 2014, http://occupywallst.org/article/point-of-public-information/ (accessed May 18, 2015); Karen Olsson, "Up against Wal-Mart," *Mother Jones*, March/April 2003, http://www.motherjones.com/politics/2003/03/against-wal-mart (accessed May 15, 2015); OUR Walmart, http://forrespect.org/ (accessed May 18, 2015); Erica L. Plambeck and Lyn Denend, "Case Study: The Greening of Wal-Mart," *Stanford Social Innovation*, Spring 2008, 52–59.PR Newswire, "Interbrand Releases the 2014 Best Retail Brands Report," April 8, 2014, http://www.prnewswire.com/news-releases/interbrand-releases-the-2014-best-retail-brands-report-254348521.html (accessed May 18, 2015); Alan Pyke, "Here's Walmart's Internal Guide to Fighting Unions and Monitoring Workers," *Think Progress*, January 16, 2014, http://thinkprogress.org/economy/2014/01/16/3171251/walmart-leaked-powerpoint-unions/ (accessed May 18, 2015); Steve Quinn, "Wal-Mart Green with Energy," *The Fort Collins Coloradoan*, July 24, 2005, E1–E2; Reuters, "Walmart Threatened Workers for Trying to Organize, Judge Rules," *The Huffington Post*, December 10, 2014, http://www.huffingtonpost.com/2014/12/11/walmart-threatened-workers_n_6305972.html (accessed May 18, 2015); Kate Rockwood, "Will Wal-Mart's 'Sustainability Index' Actually Work?" *Fast Company*, February 1, 2010, http://www.fastcompany.com/magazine/142/attention-walmart-shoppers-clean-up-in-aisle-nine.html (accessed May 15, 2015); Mariko Sanchanta, "Wal-Mart Bargain Shops for Japanese Stores to Buy," *The Wall Street Journal*, November 14, 2010, http://online.wsj.com/article/SB10001424052748704327704575613861567263350.html (accessed May 15, 2015); Michael Scher, "Walmart is now the world's living laboratory for compliance," *The FCPA Blog*, http://www.fcpablog.com/blog/2014/5/21/walmart-is-now-the-worlds-living-laboratory-for-compliance.html# (accessed May 18, 2015); "Small Farmers Aren't Cashing In with Wal-Mart," February 4, 2013, http://www.npr.org/sections/thesalt/2013/02/04/171051906/can-small-farms-benefit-from-wal-mart-s-push-into-local-foods (accessed May 18, 2015); Kyle Smith, "You Won't Believe the Stupidity of the Latest Attack on Walmart," *Forbes*, March 21, 2013, http://www.forbes.com/sites/kylesmith/2013/03/21/you-wont-believe-the-stupidity-of-the-latest-attack-on-walmart/ (accessed May 15, 2015); Kim Souza, "Wal-Mart eyes 'phase three' of its sustainability plan, critics want more," *The City Wire*, February 24, 2015, http://www.thecitywire.com/node/36580#.VVoHWo5Vikr (accessed May 18, 2015); Alisha Staggs, "An up-close assessment of Walmart's sustainability index," *GreenBiz*, May 17, 2013, http://www.greenbiz.com/blog/2013/05/17/up-close-assessment-walmarts-sustainability-index (accessed May 18, 2015); Greg Stohr, "Wal-Mart vs. a Million Angry Women," *Bloomberg Businessweek*, November 22–28, 2010, 39–40; Rick Ungar, "Walmart Pays Workers Poorly and Sinks while Costco Pays Workers Well and Sails—Proof that You Get What You Pay For," *Forbes*, April 17, 2013, http://www.forbes.com/sites/rickungar/2013/04/17/walmart-pays-workers-poorly-and-sinks-while-costco-pays-workers-well-and-sails-proof-that-you-get-what-you-pay-for/ (accessed May 15, 2015); United States Security and Exchange Commission, "Wal-Mart Stores, Inc.," January 31, 2008, http://msnmoney.brand.edgar-online.com/EFX_dll/EDGARpro.dll?FetchFilingHTML1?ID=5835838&SessionID=5RgcWZDBP11rCl9 (accessed May 15, 2015); Tom Van Riper, "Wal-Mart Stands Up to Wave of Lawsuits," *Forbes*, November 10, 2005, http://www.forbes.com/2005/11/09/wal-mart-lawsuits-cx_tvr_1109walmart.html (accessed May 18, 2015); "The Wal-Mart Bribery Scandal: Three Years Later," Create.org, April 21, 2015, https://create.org/news/the-wal-mart-bribery-scandal-three-years-later/ (accessed May 18, 2015); "Wal-Mart Class Website," http://www.walmartclass.com/public_home.html (accessed May 18, 2015); Walmart, "Community Giving," http://foundation.walmart.com/ (accessed May 15, 2015); "Wal-Mart Concedes China Can Make Unions," *China Daily*, November 23, 2004, http://www.chinadaily.com.cn/english/doc/2004-11/23/content_394129.htm (accessed May 15, 2015); Walmart, "Disaster Relief," http://news.walmart.com/disaster-response (accessed May 15, 2015); Walmart, "Environmental Sustainability," http://walmartstores.com/Sustainability/7785.aspx (accessed May 15, 2015); Walmart, "Frequently Asked Questions," http://corporate.walmart.com/frequently-asked-questions (accessed May 15, 2015); Walmart, "Global Compliance Program Report on Fiscal Year 2014," http://corporate.walmart.com/global-responsibility/global-compliance-program-report-on-fiscal-year-2014 (accessed May 18, 2015); Wal-Mart, "Global Ethics Office," https://www.walmartethics.com/ (accessed May 15, 2015); "Walmart Launches 'Women Owned' Logo In-store & Online," March 11, 2015, http://news.walmart.com/news-archive/2015/03/11/walmart-launches-women-owned-logo-in-store-online (accessed May 18, 2015); Walmart, "Renewable Energy," http://corporate.walmart.com/global-responsibility/environment-sustainability/waste (accessed May 18, 2015); Walmart, "Sustainability Index," http://corporate.walmart.com/global-responsibility/environment-sustainability/sustainability-index (accessed May 15, 2015); "Walmart to open 115 stores in China," *BBC News*, April 29, 2015, http://www.bbc.com/news/business-32509077 (accessed May 18, 2015); Walmart, "Truck Fleet," http://corporate.walmart.com/global-responsibility/environment-sustainability/truck-fleet (accessed May 18, 2015); Walmart, "Waste," http://corporate.walmart.com/global-responsibility/environment-sustainability/waste (accessed May 18, 2015); Walmart, "Walmart Announces New Commitments to Drive Sustainability Deeper into the Company's Global Supply Chain," October 25, 2012, http://news.walmart.com/news-archive/2012/10/25/walmart-announces-new-commitments-to-drive-sustainability-deeper-into-the-companys-global-supply-chain (accessed May 15, 2015); Walmart, "Walmart Statement in Response to December 17 New York Times Article about Allegations of Corruption in Mexico," http://news.walmart.com/news-archive/2012/12/17/walmart-statement-in-response-to-new-york-times-article-about-allegations-of-corruption-in-mexico (accessed May 15, 2015); Walmart, "Walmart reports Q4 underlying EPS of $1.60, Fiscal 2014 underlying EPS of $5.11," February 20, 2014, http://news.walmart.com/news-archive/investors/2014/02/20/walmart-reports-q4-underlying1-eps-of-160-fiscal-2014-underlying1-eps-of-511 (accessed May 18, 2015); Wal-Mart Watch, "Event Highlights the Wal-Mart Health Care Crisis: New Study Declares Wal-Mart in Critical Condition," Making Change at Walmart, November 16, 2005, http://makingchangeatwalmart.org/2005/11/16/the-wal-mart-health-care-crisis-new-study-declares-wal-mart-in-critical-condition/ (accessed May 15, 2015); Wal-Mart Watch, "Is Wal-Mart Really a 'Green' Company?" http://walmartwatch.com/img/blog/environmental_fact_sheet.pdf (accessed May 15, 2015); "Walmart's Mexican morass," *The Economist*, April 28, 2012, 71; "Wal-Mart's Raise Could Be a Turning Point for the Whole Economy," *The Huffington Post*, February 19, 2015, http://www.huffingtonpost.com/2015/02/19/raises-for-everyone-thanks-walmart_n_6714936.html (accessed May 18, 2015); Esther Wang, "As Wal-Mart Swallows China's Economy, Workers Fight Back," *The American Prospect*, April 23, 2013, http://prospect.org/article/wal-mart-swallows-chinas-economy-workers-fight-back (accessed May 18, 2015); Rick Wartzman, "Wal-Mart, Starbucks, Aetna's pay hikes. Why now?" *Fortune*, March 4, 2015, http://fortune.com/2015/03/04/walmart-pay-hikes-why-now/ (accessed May 18, 2015); Jack and Suzy Welch, "Whistleblowers: Why You Should Heed Their Warnings," *Fortune*, June 11, 2012, 86; Stuart Weinberg and Phred Dvorak, "Wal-Mart's New Hot Spot: Canada," *The Wall Street Journal*, January 27, 2010, B3; Jordan Weissman, "Walmart Is Killing the Rest of Corporate America in Solar Power Adoption," *Slate*, October 21, 2014, http://www.slate.com/blogs/moneybox/2014/10/21/walmart_green_energy_it_can_produce_more_solar_power_than_35_states.html (accessed May 18, 2015; Jessica Wohl, "'No' votes jump against Wal-Mart CEO, directors," *Reuters*, June 4, 2012, http://www.reuters.com/article/2012/06/04/us-walmart-vote-idUSBRE8530IR20120604 (accessed May 15, 2015); Jessica Wohl, "Walmart Sues Grocery Workers Union, Others Who Have Protested at Florida Stores," *The Huffington Post*, March 25, 2013, http://www.huffingtonpost.com/2013/03/25/walmart-sues-protesters-florida-stores_n_2950992.html (accessed May 15, 2015); Jessica Wohl and James B. Kelleher, "Insight Wal-Mart 'Made to America' drive follows suppliers' lead," *Reuters*, September 25, 2013, http://www.reuters.com/article/2013/09/25/us-walmart-manufacturing-insight-idUSBRE98O04Q20130925 (accessed May 18, 2015); Syed Zain Al-Mahmood, Tripti Lahiri, and Dana Mattioli, "Fire Warnings Went Unheard," *The Wall Street Journal*, December 11, 2012, B1, B9; Ann Zimmerman, "Federal Officials Asked to Probe Wal-Mart Firing," *The Wall Street Journal*, April 28, 2005, http://www.wsj.com/articles/SB111462458171818501 (accessed May 15, 2015).

CASE 4

Sustainability Challenges in the Gas and Oil Industry*

Despite the many controversies surrounding the economic and environmental effects of drilling for oil and gas, there is no denying the world's dependence on these commodities. It is estimated that total global demand for natural gas will reach over 4 trillion cubic meters by 2017. Global crude oil demand is already at 90 million barrels per day. While petroleum products are most often associated with machines or factories, they are also used to produce commercial products including plastic, pesticides, fertilizers, and even certain pharmaceuticals.

Unfortunately, the world's dependence on oil and gas has created significant challenges. The demand for oil depletes the world's oil reserves at an alarming rate; while there appears to be little agreement on when the world's oil reserves will be completely depleted, fears that demand is quickly outstripping supply have increased the drive toward investigating alternative energy sources. Additionally, the oil and gas industry has many risks. Safety is a large concern, and major accidents have caused the gas and oil industry to be heavily criticized.

However, one of the greatest concerns of the oil and gas industry is the environmental risks associated with it. Drilling operations are accused of contributing to water pollution and the release of air contaminants into the atmosphere. These greenhouse gases in turn contribute to the warming of the Earth's atmosphere, leading to greater risks of polar ice cap melting, flooding, and other environmental damages. Yet what attracts the most attention are when oil and gas companies experience major disasters leading to massive environmental damage—namely, oil spills. Because many of the world's oil reserves are located beneath the ocean—requiring petroleum companies to use drilling rigs to extract the oil from beneath the surface of the ocean floor—any leak has the potential to create serious harm in a quick amount of time. Petroleum companies must guard against these industry-specific risks.

As a result of these risks, the oil and gas industry adopted safety procedures and processes meant to reduce their environmental impact and prevent these disasters from occurring. However, ethical lapses on the part of these companies have led to major environmental mishaps. The first oil spill that gained widespread attention in the United States was the *Exxon Valdez* spill, important not only for its environmental impact but also for increasing the liability and responsibility oil companies have for cleanup and restoration. Despite the lessons learned from the *Exxon Valdez* spill, two decades later an accident on the *Deepwater Horizon* oil rig managed by BP led to the worst oil spill in U.S. history to date.

*This case was prepared by Jennifer Sawayda and Julian Mathias for and under the direction of O. C. Ferrell and Linda Ferrell. The case was prepared for classroom discussion rather than to illustrate either effective or ineffective handling of an administrative, ethical, or legal decision by management. All sources used for this case were obtained through publicly available material © 2015.

Both disasters took place as a result of the companies ignoring ethical risk areas and, in some cases, taking risks that directly led to the disasters.

This analysis highlights the environmental risks of the oil industry by examining specific cases that have impacted stakeholder views on the industry's responsibility for sustainability. We begin by examining the *Exxon Valdez* oil spill and the negligence that caused the disaster. Next, we describe some of the risks and causes of the BP *Deepwater Horizon* oil spill in 2010. However, our analysis would not be complete without considering the sustainability concerns of an emerging industry quickly gaining traction within the United States: hydraulic fracturing, or fracking, for shale gas. We conclude by emphasizing how oil and gas companies need to improve their safeguards to protect against environmental catastrophes. Ethical leadership and ethical responsibility at all management levels are needed to manage the risks of the industry.

THE WRECK OF THE *EXXON VALDEZ*

On March 24, 1989, the *Exxon Valdez* was under the command of Third Mate Gregory Cousins, who was not licensed to pilot the vessel through the waters of Prince William Sound. The ship's captain, Joseph Hazelwood, slept below deck. In an effort to dodge floating ice in the sound, Cousins performed what officials later described as an unusual series of right turns. The ship ran aground on Bligh Reef, spilling much of its cargo through the ruptured hull. According to the transcripts of radio conversations between Captain Hazelwood and the Coast Guard immediately after the accident, the captain tried for an hour to rock the tanker free from the reef. The Coast Guard claims that Hazelwood ignored their warnings that rocking the ship might make the oil spill much worse. The spill spread rapidly during the next few days, killing thousands of sea birds, sea otters, and other wildlife; covering the coastline with oil; and closing the fishing season in the sound for several years.

The Prince William Sound area was home to abundant wildlife. More than 200 species of birds had been reported there, including one-fifth of the world's trumpeter swans. The fishing industry derived annual sales of $100 million from the sound's abundant fish species, as well as crabs and shrimp. The world's largest concentration of killer whales and about one-fourth of the total U.S. sea otter population inhabited the sound at the time of the wreck. Later tests revealed Captain Hazelwood had a blood-alcohol content of 0.061, although it is a violation of Coast Guard regulations for a person operating a ship to have a blood-alcohol level in excess of 0.04. Exxon officials later admitted they knew the captain went through an alcohol detoxification program, yet they still gave him command of the *Exxon Valdez*, Exxon's largest tanker.

Response to the Disaster

From the onset the situation went from bad to worse. Alyeska Pipeline Service Co., one of the companies that operated the Trans-Alaska pipeline and the shipping terminal in Valdez, Alaska, was supposed to arrive shortly after the disaster to help contain the spill. After being notified of the accident, Alyeska Pipeline Service sent an observation tug to the scene and began to assemble its oil-spill containment equipment, much of which was in disarray. It loaded containment boom and lightering equipment (emergency pumps to suction oil from the *Exxon Valdez* onto other vessels) onto a damaged barge. The Coast Guard decided the barge was too slow and the need for the lightering equipment more urgent, so Alyeska crews reloaded the lightering equipment onto a tugboat, losing still more time.

The first Alyeska containment equipment did not arrive at the scene until hours after the disaster; the rest of the equipment came the next morning. Neither Alyeska nor Exxon had enough containment booms and chemical dispersants to fight the spill. They were not ready to test the effectiveness of the dispersants until 18 hours after the spill, and they conducted the test by tossing buckets of chemicals out the door of a helicopter. The helicopter's rotor dispersed the chemicals, and they missed their target. Moreover, the skimmer boats used to scoop oil out of the sea kept breaking down. The skimmers filled up rapidly and had to be emptied into nearby barges, taking them out of action for long periods of time. Cleanup efforts were further hampered by communication breakdowns between coordinators on shore and crews at the scene because of technical problems and limited range. In addition, although a fleet of private fishing boats stood by ready to assist with the containment and cleanup, Exxon and Alyeska failed to mobilize them. Because of inclement weather and other problems, by the end of the week the oil slick had spread to cover 2,600 miles of coastline and sea.

Some of the problems could have resulted from cutting safety corners. For instance, Alyeska convinced the Coast Guard that certain additional safety features were not needed on tankers. Its contingency plan underestimated the time needed for containing the spill, and it also lacked equipment needed to contain the spill. Overall, Alyeska gave the impression that it was unprepared for a major disaster.

Exxon received blame as well. For instance, it saved $22 million by not building the *Exxon Valdez* with a second hull. At the time of the spill, Chairman Lawrence Rawl did not comment on the spill for nearly six days, and then he did so from New York. Although Rawl personally apologized for the spill, crisis-management experts say it is important for the chief executive to be present at the site of an emergency. Perhaps most damaging was Exxon's insistence that it would stop all cleanup operations on September 15, 1989, regardless of how much shoreline remained to be cleaned. In a memorandum released in July 1989, the September deadline was said to be "not negotiable." After much public and government protest, however, the company's president promised Exxon would return in the spring of 1990 if the Coast Guard determined further cleanup was warranted. Exxon returned that spring and for the next four years for further cleanup efforts.

The Aftermath

During the period of the oil spill, Exxon spent more than $2.2 billion for cleanup and reimbursements to the federal, state, and local governments. The company faced numerous lawsuits, including a lawsuit from the state of Alaska for mismanaging the response to the oil spill. In a civil settlement with the state of Alaska and the federal government, Exxon agreed to make 10 annual payments totaling $900 million for injuries to natural resources and services and the restoration and replacement of natural resources. In addition, $5 billion was awarded in punitive damages, to be divided evenly among the 14,000 commercial fishermen, natives, business owners, landowners, and native corporations that were part of the class-action suit. By 2009 that amount was reduced to $507 million. In a criminal plea agreement, Exxon was fined $150 million, of which $125 million was remitted in recognition of its cooperation in cleaning up the spill and paying private claims. In addition, Exxon agreed to pay restitution of $50 million to the United States and $50 million to the state of Alaska.

Exxon, now called ExxonMobil, insists the area has completely recovered. However, a study by the National Marine Fisheries Service found that toxins leaching from *Exxon Valdez* oil remaining on the beaches continued to harm sea life more than two decades after the disaster. Most of the oil is now subsurface and hardened into a semi-solid layer underwater, which poses less of a threat to plants and animals than liquid oil. Twenty acres of Prince William Sound shoreline are still contaminated, and there are several "pits" of oil and sludge in the area.

The one positive from the *Exxon Valdez* disaster is the industry has better response time to oil spills. However, has the oil industry learned from the mistakes of the *Exxon Valdez*? The 2010 *Deepwater Horizon* oil spill in the Gulf of Mexico suggests oil and gas companies still engage in risky behavior to increase profits.

DEEPWATER HORIZON OIL SPILL

For some years BP tried to change its image. After a series of major scandals, including a Texas refinery explosion that killed 15 employees, the firm expressed a renewed commitment to make safety and sustainability top priorities. For instance, the company changed its name to BP and then tried to rebrand itself as Beyond Petroleum. This rebranding signaled to stakeholders that it was focused on sustainability and the need to move beyond nonrenewable energy sources. It adopted an extensive code of conduct and invested heavily in alternative energy sources. BP was the first oil company to acknowledge global warming. But when a company tries to reposition itself as socially responsible and sustainable, it has an obligation to live up to its promises. BP's failures to do so became tragically clear when the *Deepwater Horizon* oil rig, operated under the oversight of BP, exploded in the Gulf of Mexico.

BP had subcontracted an oil rig from Transocean, Ltd. to tap into a new, highly profitable oil reservoir in the Gulf of Mexico. On April 20, 2010, an explosion rocked the rig, killing 11 employees. The burning rig sank two days later. A damaged oil well was leaking thousands of gallons of crude oil into the Gulf of Mexico, quickly creating an environmental catastrophe.

BP immediately started drilling other holes in the hopes they would relieve pressure on the damaged well, but these and other efforts proved unsuccessful. Soon as much as 2.5 million gallons of oil was pouring into the Gulf of Mexico daily. Oil washed up on the coasts of Louisiana, Texas, Alabama, Mississippi, and Florida, wreaking havoc on the livelihoods of fishermen and others dependent on the Gulf for income.

While the ocean rig had safety systems in place, these systems were not as safe as they could have been. For instance, the rig did not have a remote-control shut-off switch that could have been used as a last resort in a major spill (such a switch was not required by law). Investigations revealed BP's contingency plan in case of disaster was inadequate and contained many inaccuracies. One of the wildlife experts listed as an emergency responder had been dead since 2005. The contingency plan also estimated that should a spill occur, the company could recover about 500,000 barrels of oil per day. In reality, it took BP months to contain the leak, at a spill rate much less than that listed in the contingency plan. The inaccuracies in BP's contingency plan highlight how unprepared the company was for a disaster like the *Deepwater Horizon* spill.

What Caused the Explosion?

The explosion was likely caused by a number of events. Investigations suggest that actions on BP's part made the well more vulnerable. One investigation implies BP cut short procedures and quality testing of the pipe—tests meant to detect gas in the well. Some experts hypothesize that one of the final steps in installing the pipe, which involved cementing the steel pipe in place, could have been the catalyst for the explosion. The cement was not able to hold back the surging oil and gas that led to the explosion. In addition, BP decided to use a less costly well design that some Congressional investigators deemed "risky." Installation of this design is easier and costs are lower. However, it provides a better path for gas to rise outside the pipe. Although BP did not break any laws by using such a design, it ignored safer alternatives that might have prevented, or at least hindered, the accident.

Another reason why the spill became such a wide-scale disaster is likely due to a faulty blowout preventer. Instead of sealing the pipe completely, the blowout preventer blades stuck in the pipe, leaving enough space for oil to leak out. BP filed lawsuits against the manufacturer of the blowout preventer, Cameron International Corp. There is also some speculation that BP engineers ignored warning signs from safety tests conducted on the rig hours before the explosion. Two BP engineers who conducted negative pressure tests on the drilling rig recorded results they found to be confusing. However, after talking with others on the rig, one of the engineers gave the go-ahead. At the time there were no federal rules that clarified the test procedures.

Repercussions of the Disaster

The BP oil spill has had wide-ranging repercussions for BP and the entire industry. An immediate consequence of the disaster was the resignation of BP CEO Tony Hayward. Despite an impressive track record, Hayward became the face of the worst oil spill in U.S. history. Additionally, the firm spent or will spend $36.5 billion on cleanup costs. BP was fined the largest environmental fine to date at $18.7 billion. It was fined $5.5 billion under the Clean Water Act.

Drilling contractors and oil service companies also suffered from the spill because of plummeting stock values. The Obama administration issued a six-month moratorium on deepwater and oil gas drilling in the Gulf of Mexico, which shut down 33 deepwater rigs. With one-third of America's oil coming from the Gulf, this is an essential area for many oil and gas companies.

The Aftermath

It took nearly three months to contain the oil leaking into the Gulf. In the interim, thousands of marine animals died in the oily waters, oil turned beaches black, and hundreds of people depending on the Gulf of Mexico lost part or all of their income. By the time the leak was sealed in August 2010, more than 640 miles of shoreline across several states were "tarred" with oil. The Gulf had suffered a massive loss of wildlife and was left with a tremendous amount of oil lurking beneath the water's surface. Scientists are finding evidence that oil has settled across several thousand square miles of seafloor, posing a potential threat to coral reefs and other marine life.

In an attempt to compensate stakeholders that depend on the Gulf, BP set aside $20 billion in an escrow fund, and a government-appointed administrator is overseeing the claims. Another issue that concerns the public is safety. Many worry about the safety of consuming seafood along the Gulf coast. It is largely unknown whether the oil and chemicals will have long-term effects on the quality of seafood. This situation demonstrates that it is often not enough for global companies involved in an ethical crisis to pay only for immediate costs like compensation; often they must pay for testing, additional safeguards, and environmental degradation in both the short and long term.

Such efforts are already underway. After the ousting of CEO Tony Hayward, Bob Dudley took over operations. While BP originally downplayed the disaster, Dudley freely admitted the incident was a "catastrophe" and the company was committed to the cleanup. BP hired former Federal Emergency Management Agency chief James Lee Witt and his public safety and crisis management consulting firm to help manage the incident and establish plans for long-term recovery. BP also created a safety organization given authority to stop operations whenever danger is detected.

Fracking: More Beneficial or Harmful to the Environment?

Hydraulic fracturing, or fracking, occurs when water, sand, or chemicals are pumped into shale rock to force natural gas to rise to the surface. Fracking has been around for approximately 60 years. However, only recently has this type of drilling attracted wide-scale media attention. One reason is the recent discovery of large shale gas reserves in the United States. Some scientists estimate that these reserves will last for more than 100 years. New hydraulic fracking techniques make it possible to drill for this gas, which increased 45 percent in a one-year period. This has created an energy boom that could lead the United States to energy independence. It also created more jobs in areas where wells are located, such as Pennsylvania and North Dakota. The Marcellus shale range in Pennsylvania is believed to have gas equivalent to 86 billion barrels of oil.

In addition to the economic benefits of fracking, proponents claim fracking results in greater sustainability than other traditional energy sources. Natural gas releases half the carbon emissions of oil and coal. Supporters claim natural gas is cleaner than coal because it releases less sulfur dioxide, nitrogen oxide, and mercury into the atmosphere. The benefits convinced supporters that fracking represents a revolutionary opportunity to reduce emissions and import natural gas to other countries. While fracking uses chemicals, it is estimated that fracking chemicals only consist of 0.5 percent of drilling fluid.

However, fracking carries significant risks as well. Fracking has been accused of releasing chemicals and methane into water near the drilling sites. It also releases fast-moving gases such as methane into the atmosphere. There have even been accusations that fracking causes small seismic shifts in the area. Fracking requires large amounts of water, from two to five million gallons per well. This means that while drilling fluid might only contain 0.5 percent of chemicals, the millions of gallons used per well results in a significant amount of chemicals used. While some of these chemicals are harmless, others, including benzene, diesel, and hydrochloric acid, have carcinogenic properties. Critics also claim that hydraulic fracking is exempt from certain federal regulations that normally apply to drilling activities.

Proponents of fracking are quick to point out that proper procedures can greatly reduce the environmental risk. Ensuring the well-shafts are properly sealed can act as a strong deterrent against water contamination. This requires wells to be properly cemented. Fracking companies can attempt to reduce the amount of water used by recycling or reusing the water. The Environmental Protection Agency (EPA) also determined that methane contaminating ground water might not be as serious as it appears. In one study of a town with high methane levels in its drinking water, the EPA found that the methane did not come from the fracking operations in the area.

However, the environmental risks of fracking are not to be taken lightly. New York, Vermont, and some cities in Colorado have banned fracking activities, as well as certain countries and regions such as France, Bulgaria, Germany, and Scotland. Additionally, individuals have complained of environmental damage as a result of drilling activities.

For instance, one couple reported that drilling blowouts on their land released chemicals into a creek, turning it white and igniting the water if lit. Health and safety is also a major concern. Randy Moyer, a worker for a hydraulic fracturing company who would climb into the vats and clean out the fracking fluid, was allegedly not told that the drilling mud is toxic and radioactive. He claimed he suffered for more than a year from inflammation, migraines, trouble breathing, as well as many trips to the emergency room. Another couple claims the animals on their farm, which were previously healthy, began dying after they allowed drilling on their land. The couple claims to suffer from headaches, nosebleeds, fatigue, and cirrhosis of the liver. Fracking has also lowered the values of homes; many people with fracking on their land have not been able to sell their houses. Unlike the *Exxon Valdez* and *Deepwater Horizon* disasters, fracking complaints are less on a massive scale and more from individuals living close to the drilling fields. Yet any type of major fracking disaster can have significant safety implications, since many fields are located close to highly populated areas.

Communities located near fracking operations are more susceptible to its risks, yet many also depend on fracking from an economic standpoint. This is why bans on fracking is such a hotly debated issue, especially in states like Colorado that extract a majority of the country's natural gas. When fracking was banned in Lafayette, Colorado in 2013, the city experienced economic consequences. XetaWave, a company specializing in wireless communication technology often used by oil and gas companies, decided to relocate to Louisville instead of moving from Boulder to Lafayette. The CEO of XetaWave claimed that the move out of Colorado was prompted by Lafayette's outright ban on fracking, including prohibiting companies from providing equipment or infrastructure to support fracking activities. Lafayette's outright ban on fracking is somewhat unique, and bans on fracking in other states are often met with resistance from the community and oil and gas industry. In 2014 the oil and gas industry filed lawsuits against the city of Denton, Texas, claiming that its ban on fracking was unconstitutional. Similar bans in Ohio and California were also met with resistance from the oil and gas industry.

Aside from full bans on fracking, efforts have been made to reduce the environmental impact of fracking through more strict industry regulation. For instance, a disproportionate number of hydraulic fracturing wells (up to 90 percent by some estimates) are located on federal and tribal land, despite these wells contributing only about 25 percent to the country's total fossil fuel output. Abundant fracking on federal and tribal lands prompted the interior department to implement a set of regulations in 2015 affecting current and future hydraulic fracturing operations. The new rules tighten the requirements of cement casings on wells to reduce leaks and protect the groundwater. Opponents to the legislation claim that the new cement casing standards are cost prohibitive, and some question whether more regulations will actually make the wells safer and less damaging to the environment.

Concerns also remain over the methane gas released from fracking activities. While methane's lifetime in the Earth's atmosphere is shorter than carbon emissions, its effects in trapping radiation are estimated to be 20 times greater. Many wells already have pollution-control equipment to catch methane and other volatile gases such as benzene, but pollution continues to be a formidable problem. In its quest to combat fracking pollution, the EPA mandated new measures to reduce methane emissions by 40 to 45 percent by 2025. The new rules will limit the amount of methane emissions from high-volume hydraulic fracturing (HVHF), a high-pressure fracking technique, and stipulate new requirements to capture methane and other volatile chemicals that flow to the surface as a result of fracking. There have also been promises from leaders of fracking organizations to increase the safety and sustainability of their activities. The CEO of Tamboran, for instance, committed to stop using chemicals in the firm's Irish fracking operations. While the benefits of fracking seem promising, natural gas companies must take the time to analyze the environmental and safety impacts of their operations to avoid the risks of environmental degradation.

CONCLUSION

Developing an ethical organizational culture requires an examination of the risks to various stakeholders. In the case of the oil and gas industry, several companies failed to put in the safeguards necessary to protect employees, local communities, suppliers, and the viability of many industries. After the *Exxon Valdez* disaster, there should have been a heightened awareness of the risks of offshore drilling and a mandate to implement every safeguard necessary to protect the environment. Yet BP appeared to assume that such a disaster would not happen to them, despite previous safety issues at the firm. Much like in the *Exxon Valdez* disaster, BP failed to implement certain safeguards that might have prevented or lessened the scope of the disaster.

This corporate culture of risk taking must stop in order for the oil and gas industry to restore its reputation. This requires ethical leadership and effective ethics and compliance programs that reach all employees. Employees need to be educated that they are responsible for displaying leadership to avoid misconduct that could create accidents. Although the nature of the industry makes certain risks inevitable, firms can develop improved safety measures and contingency plans to contain the disaster should things go wrong. Many actions occur when risks are present and there is a failure to observe existing ethical codes and policies. Companies involved in the lucrative field of hydraulic fracking can use the lessons from its predecessors to develop a culture that makes safety and environmental consideration top priorities during the drilling process. The industry has a new responsibility to provide leadership in safety and sustainability. The reputation of the oil and gas industry is dependent on its ability to commit to a socially responsible approach and stakeholder engagement.

QUESTIONS FOR DISCUSSION

1. How does managing ethical risk in the oil and gas industry relate to reducing accidents?
2. Compare the risks that BP, Exxon, and the fracking industry continue to face in providing an adequate supply of energy?
3. How can ethical leadership help the oil and gas industry to manage risk?

SOURCES

American Petroleum Institute, "Oil Spill Prevention and Response," http://www.api.org/environment-health-and-safety/clean-water/oil-spill-prevention-and-response (accessed April 1, 2015); Jeffrey Ball, "BP Spill's Next Major Phase: Wrangling over Toll on Gulf," *The Wall Street Journal*, April 13, 2011, http://online.wsj.com/article/SB1000 142405274870401360457624853153023442.html (accessed April 1, 2015); Jeffrey Ball, "Strong Evidence Emerges of BP Oil on Seafloor," *The Wall Street Journal*, December 9, 2010, A20; Kathy Barks Hoffman, "Oil Spill's Cleanup Costs Exceed $1.3B," *USA Today*, July 25, 1989, B1; Wayne Beissert, "In *Valdez*'s Wake,

Uncertainty," *USA Today*, July 28, 1989, A3; Joel K. Bourne, Jr., "The Deep Dilemma," *National Geographic*, October 2010, 40–53; Ellen Cantarow, "Fracking ourselves to death in Pennsylvania," *Grist*, http://grist.org/climate-energy/fracking-ourselves-to-death-in-pennsylvania/ (accessed April 1, 2015); Ben Casselman and Russell Gold, "BP Decisions Set Stage for Disaster," *The Wall Street Journal*, May 27, 2010, http://online.wsj.com/article/SB10001424052748704026204575266560930780190.html (accessed April 1, 2015); CBS News, "BP's Spill Contingency Plans Vastly Inadequate," June 9, 2010, http://www.cbsnews.com/stories/2010/06/09/national/main6563631.shtml (accessed April 1, 2015); Guy Chazan, "BP's Worsening Spill Crisis Undermines CEO's Reforms." *The Wall Street Journal*, May 3, 2010, A1; Ryan Dezember and Matt Day, "Oil-Drilling Boom Under Way," *The Wall Street Journal*, February 10, 2011, http://online.wsj.com/article/SB10001424052748704858404576134553990567750.html (accessed April 1, 2015); Carrie Dolan, "Exxon to Bolster Oil-Cleanup Effort after Criticism," *The Wall Street Journal*, May 11, 1989, A10; The Economist staff, "Shale of the century," *The Economist*, July 2, 2012, http://www.economist.com/node/21556242 (accessed April 1, 2015); Jim Efstathiou Jr. and Kim Chipman, "The Great Shale Gas Rush," *Bloomberg BusinessWeek*, March 7–13, 2011, 25–28; Peter Elkind, David Whitford, and Doris Burke, "'An Accident Waiting to Happen,'" *Fortune*, February 7, 2011, 107–132; Yousef Gamal El-Din, "US Energy Boom Is Great, unless You're the Saudis," *CNBC*, May 15, 2013, http://www.cnbc.com/id/100739228 (accessed April 1, 2015); Stuart Elliot, "Public Angry at Slow Action on Oil Spill," *USA Today*, April 21, 1989, B1; "Energy and our Future" *Colorado Biz*, March/April 2014, 5; Enerkol Research, "EPA Methane Rule Would Set Costly Bar for Oil and Gas Industry, Despite Current Reduction Efforts," *Breaking Energy*, January 22, 2015, http://breakingenergy.com/2015/01/22/epa-methane-rule-would-set-costly-bar-for-oil-and-gas-industry-despite-current-reduction-efforts/ (accessed April 1, 2015); Environmental Protection Agency, "Overview of Greenhouse Gases," http://epa.gov/climatechange/ghgemissions/gases/ch4.html (accessed April 1, 2015); "Exxon Valdez Disaster Haunts Alaska 14 Years On," *Sydney Morning Herald*, Jan. 16, 2003, http://www.smh.com.au/articles/2003/01/15/1042520672374.html (accessed April 1, 2015); "Exxon Will Pay $3.5 Million to Settle Claims in Phase Four of *Valdez* Case," *BNA State Environment Daily*, January 19, 1996; Tom Fowler, "BP Slapped with Record Fine," *The Wall Street Journal*, November 16, 2013, A1, A6; Tom Fowler and Russell Gold, "Engineers Deny Charges in BP Spill," *The Wall Street Journal*, November 19, 2012, A6; Daniel Gilbert and Justin Scheck, "Oil Prices to Play into BP Fine," *The Wall Street Journal*, January 18, 2015, http://www.wsj.com/articles/oil-prices-to-play-into-bp-fine-1421610065 (accessed April 1, 2015); William Glasgall and Vicky Cahan, "Questions that Keep Surfacing after the Spill," *Business Week*, April 17, 1989, 18; Russell Gold and Tom McGinty, "BP Relied on Cheaper Wells," *The Wall Street Journal*, June 19, 2010, http://www.wsj.com/articles/SB10001424052748704289504575313010283981200 (accessed April 1, 2015); Russell Gold, "BP Sues Maker of Blowout Preventer," *The Wall Street Journal*, April 21, 2011, B1; Angel Gonzalez and Brian Baskin, "'Static Kill' Begins, Raising New Hopes," *The Wall Street Journal*, August 4, 2010, http://online.wsj.com/article/SB10001424052748703545604575407251664344386.html (accessed April 1, 2015); Kate Good, "These 4 Countries Have Banned Fracking…Why Can't the U.S. Get On Board?" *One Green Planet*, Febuary 11, 2015, http://www.onegreenplanet.org/environment/countries-except-united-states-that-have-banned-fracking/ (accessed April 1, 2015); Dan Harris, Claudia Acosta, and Christina Ng, Lasting Effects of Exxon Valdez and the Future of the Gulf," ABC World News, July 18, 2010, http://abcnews.go.com/WN/exxon-valdez-lessons-bp-spill-gulf-mexico/story?id=11194132&page=1 (accessed April 1, 2015); Kevin A. Hassett and Aparna Mathur, "Benefits of hydraulic fracturing," *American Enterprise Institute*, April 4, 2013, http://www.aei.org/article/economics/benefits-of-hydraulic-fracking (accessed April 1, 2015); Siobhan Hughes, "BP Deposits $3 Billion in Spill Fund," *The Wall Street Journal*, August 9, 2010, http://online.wsj.com/article/SB10001424052748704388504575419281620436778.html (accessed April 1, 2015); *Institute for Crisis Management Newsletter*, 4 (March 1995), 3; Robert Jackson, "Expert answers your questions on fracking," *USA Today*, April 24, 2013, http://content.usatoday.com/communities/sciencefair/post/2012/04/expert-answers-your-questions-on-fracking/1#.UZP2gvUmx8E (accessed April 1, 2015); Rick Jervis, "New hurdles await survivors of drilling moratorium," *USA Today*, January 18, 2011, 3A; "Judge Cuts Exxon Valdez Punitive Damage Award," *Alaska Journal*, December 16, 2002, http://www.alaskajournal.com/Alaska-Journal-of-Commerce/December-2002/Judge-cuts-Exxon-Valdez-punitive-damage-award/ (accessed August 11, 2015); Neil King, Jr., "BP Claims Chief Faces Knotty Task," *The Wall Street Journal*, July 17–18, 2010,

A5; Monica Langley, "U.S. Drills Deep into BP as Spill Drama Drags on," *The Wall Street Journal*, July 21, 2010, A1, A14; Michelle Ye Hee Lee, "You can't trust the numbers on the new fracking regs," *The Washington Post*, March 30, 2015, http://www.washingtonpost.com/blogs/fact-checker/wp/2015/03/30/you-cant-trust-the-numbers-on-the-new-fracking-regs/ (accessed April 1, 2015); David Leonhardt, "Spillonomics: Underestimating Risk," *The New York Times*, May 31, 2010, http://www.nytimes.com/2010/06/06/magazine/06fob-wwln-t.html (accessed April 1, 2015); Jim Malewitz, "Denton Fracking Ban Tees up Local Control Fight," *Texas Tribune*, March 17, 2015, http://www.texastribune.org/2015/03/17/local-control-and-fracking-debate/ (accessed April 1, 2015); Charles McCoy and Ken Wells, "Alaska, U.S. Knew of Flaws in Oil-Spill Response Plans," *The Wall Street Journal*, April 7, 1989, A3; Peter Nulty, "The Future of Big Oil," *Fortune*, May 8, 1989, 46–49; Bruce Orwall, Monica Langley, and James Herron, "Embattled BP Chief to Exit," *The Wall Street Journal*, July 26, 2010, A1, A6; Tara Patel, "The French Say No to 'Le Fracking,'" *Bloomberg BusinessWeek*, April 4–10, 2011, 60–62; Natalie Phillips, "$3.5 Million Settles Exxon Spill Suit," *Anchorage Daily News*, January 18, 1996, 113; Byron Pitts, "Exxon Valdez Oil Spill: 20 Years Later," *CBS Evening News*, February 2, 2009, http://www.cbsnews.com/stories/2009/02/02/eveningnews/main4769329.shtml (accessed April 1, 2015); Jim Polson, "BP Oil Is Biodegrading, Easing Threat to East Coast," *BusinessWeek*, July 28, 2010, http://www.bloomberg.com/news/articles/2010-07-27/oil-from-bp-spill-is-biodegrading-quickly-in-gulf-of-mexico-agency-says (accessed April 1, 2015); Stephen Power and Ben Casselman, "White House Probe Blames BP, Industry in Gulf Blast," *The Wall Street Journal*, January 6, 2011, A2; Lawrence G. Rawl, letter to Exxon shareholders, April 14, 1989; "Recordings Reveal Exxon Captain Rocked Tanker to Free It from Reef," [Texas A&M University] *Battalion*, April 26, 1989, 1; Jim Roth, "The Shale Gas Revolution," *China Brief*, March 2012, 14–15; Dominic Rushe, "BP set to pay largest environmental fine in US history for Gulf oil spill," *The Guardian,* July 2, 2015, http://www.theguardian.com/environment/2015/jul/02/bp-will-pay-largest-environmental-fine-in-us-history-for-gulf-oil-spill (accessed August 11, 2015); Michael Satchell and Steve Lindbeck, "Tug of War over Oil Drilling," *U.S. News & World Report*, April 10, 1989, 47–48; Richard B. Schmitt, "Exxon, Alyeska May Be Exposed on Damages," *The Wall Street Journal*, April 10, 1989, A8; Stratford P. Sherman,"Smart Way to Handle the Press," *Fortune*, June 19, 1989, 69–75; Rich Smith, "Big Oil Isn't as Profitable as Everyone Thinks," *Daily Finance*, October 20, 2012, http://www.dailyfinance.com/2012/10/20/big-oil-isnt-as-profitable-as-everyone-thinks/ (accessed April 1, 2015); Jeff Short, Stanley Rice, and Mandy Lindeberg, 'The *Exxon Valdez* Oil Spill: How Much Oil Remains?" Alaska Fisheries Science Center, 2001, http://www.afsc.noaa.gov/Quarterly/jas2001/feature_jas01.htm (accessed April 1, 2015); "Status of Injured Resources & Services," *Exxon Valdez* Oil Spill Trustee Council, 2010, http://www.evostc.state.ak.us/recovery/status.cfm (accessed April 1, 2015); Allanna Sullivan and Amanda Bennett, "Critics Fault Chief Executive of Exxon on Handling of Recent Alaskan Oil Spill," *The Wall Street Journal*, March 31, 1989, B1; Cassandra Sweet, "BP Will Pay Fine in Spills," *The Wall Street Journal*, May 4, 2011, B3; Tennille Tracy, "Firms Given Time on Fracking," *The Wall Street Journal*, April 19, 2012, A3; Bryan Walsh, "The Gas Dilemma," *Time*, April 11, 2011, 40–48; Vivienne Walt, "Can BP Ever Rebuild Its Reputation?" *Time*, July 19, 2010, http://content.time.com/time/business/article/0,8599,2004701,00.html (accessed April 1, 2015); Harry R. Weber and Greg Bluestein, "Dudley: Time for 'Scaleback' in BP Cleanup." *Time*, July 30, 2010, http://content.usatoday.com/communities/greenhouse/post/2010/07/bp-hayward-gulf-oil-spill/1#.UZQAk_Umx8E (accessed April 1, 2015); Jonathon Weisman, "In Western Pennsylvania, an Energy Boom Not Visibly Stifled," *The New York Times*, June 20, 2012, http://www.nytimes.com/2012/06/21/us/an-energy-boom-in-western-pennsylvania.html?pagewanted=all&_r=0 (accessed April 1, 2015); Ken Wells, "Alaska Begins Criminal Inquiry of Valdez Spill," *The Wall Street Journal*, March 30, 1989, A4; Ken Wells, "Blood-Alcohol Level of Captain of Exxon Tanker Exceeded Limits," *The Wall Street Journal*, March 31, 1989, A4; Ken Wells, "For Exxon, Cleanup Costs May Be Just the Beginning," *The Wall Street Journal*, April 14, 1989, B1, B2; Ken Wells and Marilyn Chase, "Paradise Lost: Heartbreaking Scenes of Beauty Disfigured Follow Alaska Oil Spill," *The Wall Street Journal*, March 31, 1989, A1, A4; Ken Wells and Charles McCoy, "How Unpreparedness Turned the Alaska Spill into Ecological Debacle," *The Wall Street Journal*, April 3, 1989, A1, A4; Selina Williams, "For BP, the Cleanup Isn't Entirely Over," *The Wall Street Journal*, February 4, 2013, B2; Ben Wolfgang, "Methane study, EPA debunk claims of water pollution, climate change from fracking," *The Washington Times*, April 29, 2013, http://www.washingtontimes.com/news/2013/apr/29/pa-environment-agency-debunks-fracking-water-claim/?page=all (accessed April 1, 2015).

CASE 5

New Belgium Brewing: Engaging in Sustainable Social Responsibility[*]

Although most of the companies frequently cited as examples of ethical and socially responsible firms are large corporations, it is the social responsibility initiatives of small businesses that often have the greatest impact on local communities. These businesses create jobs and provide goods and services for customers in smaller markets that larger corporations are often not interested in serving. Moreover, they also contribute money, resources, and volunteer time to local causes. Their owners often serve as community leaders, and many choose to apply their skills and resources to tackling local problems and issues to benefit the whole community. Managers and employees become role models for ethical and socially responsible actions. One such small business is New Belgium Brewing Company, Inc., based in Fort Collins, Colorado.

HISTORY OF THE NEW BELGIUM BREWING COMPANY

The idea for the New Belgium Brewing Company (NBB) began with a bicycling trip through Belgium. Belgium is arguably the home of some of the world's finest ales, some of which have been brewed for centuries in that country's monasteries. As Jeff Lebesch, an American electrical engineer, cruised around that country on his mountain bike, he wondered whether he could produce such high-quality beers back home in Colorado. After acquiring the special strain of yeast used to brew Belgian-style ales, Lebesch returned home and began to experiment in his Colorado basement. When his beers earned thumbs up from friends, Lebesch decided to market them.

NBB opened for business in 1991 as a tiny basement operation in Lebesch's home in Fort Collins. Lebesch's wife at the time, Kim Jordan, became the firm's marketing director. They named their first brew Fat Tire Amber Ale in honor of Lebesch's bike ride through Belgium. Initially, getting New Belgium beer onto store shelves was not easy. Jordan often delivered the beer to stores in the back of her Toyota station wagon. However, New Belgium beers quickly developed a small but devoted customer base, first in Fort Collins and then throughout Colorado. The brewery soon outgrew the couple's basement and moved into an old railroad depot before settling into its present custom-built

[*]This case was prepared by Jennifer Sawayda and Jennifer Jackson for and under the direction of O.C. Ferrell and Linda Ferrell © 2015. We appreciate the input and assistance of Greg Owsley, New Belgium Brewing, in developing this case. It was prepared for classroom discussion rather than to illustrate either effective or ineffective handling of an administrative, ethical, or legal decision by management. All sources used for this case were obtained through publicly available material and the New Belgium Brewing website.

facility in 1995. The brewery includes two brew houses, four quality assurance labs, a wastewater treatment facility, a canning and bottling line, and numerous technological innovations for which New Belgium has become nationally recognized as a "paradigm of environmental efficiencies."

Under the leadership of Kim Jordan, who has since become CEO, NBB currently offers a variety of permanent and seasonal ales and pilsners. The company's standard line includes Sunshine Wheat, Blue Paddle, 1554, Ranger IPA, Abby, Shift, Trippel, Rampant, Slow Ride IPA, Snapshot, and the original Fat Tire Amber Ale, still the firm's bestseller. Some customers even refer to the company as the Fat Tire Brewery. The brewery's seasonal ales include Skinny Dip, Portage Porter, and Accumulation. The firm also started a Lips of Faith program, where small batch brews like La Folie, Gruit, and Salted Belgian Chocolate Stout are created for internal celebrations or landmark events. Additionally, New Belgium is working in collaboration with other craft brewers to come up with new products. Through this, they hope to create improved efficiency and experimentation, along with taking collaborative strides toward the future of American craft beer making. One product resulting from these collaborations is a beer brewed with Anaheim and Marash Chilies in collaboration with Cigar City Brewing.

NBB's most effective form of advertising has always been its customers' word of mouth, especially in the early days. Indeed, before New Belgium beers were widely distributed throughout Colorado, one liquor-store owner in Telluride is purported to have offered people gas money if they would stop by and pick up New Belgium beer on their way through Fort Collins. Although New Belgium has expanded distribution to a good portion of the U.S. market, the brewery receives numerous emails and phone calls every day inquiring when its beers will be available in other parts of the country.

Although still a small brewery when compared to many beer companies, like fellow Coloradan Coors, NBB has consistently experienced strong growth with estimated sales of more than $180 million (with NBB being a private firm, detailed sales and revenue numbers are not available). It now has its own blog, Twitter, and Facebook pages. The organization sells more than 800,000 barrels of beer per year and has many opportunities for continued growth. For instance, while total beer consumption has remained flat, the market share of the craft beer industry is now at 11 percent. Growth for craft beer is likely to continue as new generations of beer drinkers appear to favor beers that are locally brewed.

Currently, New Belgium's products are distributed in 38 states plus the District of Columbia, British Columbia, and Alberta. It plans to begin distribution in Hawaii in 2016. Beer connoisseurs that appreciate the high quality of NBB's products, as well as the company's environmental and ethical business practices, have driven this growth. For example, when the company began distribution in Minnesota, the beers were so popular that a liquor store had to open early and make other accommodations for the large amount of customers. The store sold 400 cases of Fat Tire in the first hour it was open.

With expanding distribution, however, the brewery recognized a need to increase its opportunities for reaching its far-flung customers. It consulted with Dr. Douglas Holt, an Oxford professor and cultural branding expert. After studying the company, Holt, together with former Marketing Director Greg Owsley, drafted a 70-page "manifesto" describing the brand's attributes, character, cultural relevancy, and promise. In particular, Holt identified in New Belgium an ethos of pursuing creative activities simply for the joy of doing them well and in harmony with the natural environment.

With the brand thus defined, NBB worked with New York advertising agency Amalgamated to create a $10 million advertising campaign. The campaign would target high-end beer drinkers, men aged 25 to 44, and highlight the brewery's down-to-earth image.

The grainy ads focused on a man, Charles the Tinkerer, rebuilding a cruiser bike out of used parts and then riding it along pastoral country roads. The product appeared in just five seconds of each ad between the tag lines, "Follow Your Folly … Ours Is Beer." With nostalgic music playing in the background, the ads helped position the growing brand as whimsical, thoughtful, and reflective. NBB later re-released its Tinkerer commercial during the U.S. Pro Challenge. The re-released commercial had an additional scene with the Tinkerer riding part way next to a professional cyclist contestant, with music from songwriter and Tour de Fat enthusiast Sean Hayes. The commercial was featured on NBC.

It would be eight more years before NBB would develop its next television advertising campaign. In 2013 NBB developed a campaign called "Pairs Well with People" that included a 30-second television advertisement. The television ad described the unique qualities of NBB as an organization, including its environmental consciousness and 100 percent employee ownership. The advertisement was launched on four major networks in large cities across the United States. Because the primary purpose of the campaign was to create awareness in areas not as familiar with the brand (such as Raleigh-Durham and Minneapolis), NBB did not air the commercial in Colorado and states where the brand is well-known. The campaign also featured four 15-second online videos of how its beer "pairs well with people." Bar patrons featured in the 15-second digital ads were NBB employees.

In addition to the ad campaigns, the company maintains its strategy of promotion through event sponsorships and digital media. To launch its Ranger IPA beer, New Belgium created a microsite and an online video of its NBB sales force dressed as rangers performing a hip-hop number to promote the beer. The only difference was that instead of horses, the NBB rangers rode bicycles. The purpose of the video was to create a hip, fun brand image for its new beer, with the campaign theme "To Protect. To Pour. To Partake." The company's Beer Mode mobile app gives users who download it access to exclusive content, preselects messages to post on the users' social media sites when they are spending time enjoying their beers, and provides users with the locations of retailers that sell NBB products. The company offers rewards to users for downloading the Beer Mode app, visiting the NBB website, sharing the website on social media networks, and attending NBB events.

NEW BELGIUM ETHICAL CULTURE

According to New Belgium, the company places great importance on the ethical culture of the brand. The company is aware that if it embraces citizenship in the communities it serves, it can forge enduring bonds with customers. More than ever before, what a brand says and what a company does must be synchronized. NBB believes that as the mandate for corporate social responsibility gains momentum, business managers must realize that business ethics is not so much about the installation of compliance codes and standards as it is about the spirit in which such codes and standards are integrated. The modern-day brand steward—usually the most externally focused of the business management team—must prepare to be the internal champion of the bottom-line necessity for ethical, values-driven company behavior.

At New Belgium, a synergy of brand and values occurred naturally because the firm's ethical culture (in the form of core values and beliefs) was in place long before NBB had a marketing department. Back in early 1991, when New Belgium was just a fledgling home-brewed business, Jeff Lebesch and Kim Jordan took a hike into Rocky Mountain National Park armed with a pen and a notebook. There they took their first stab at what the company's core purpose would be. If they were going forward with this venture, what were their aspirations beyond profitability? What was at the heart of their dream? What they wrote down that spring day, give or take a little editing, are the core values and beliefs you can read on the NBB website today.

Since its inception, NBB adopted a triple bottom-line (TBL) approach to business. Whereas the traditional bottom-line approach for measuring business success is economic, TBL incorporates economic, social, and environmental factors. In other words, rather than just looking at financial data to evaluate company success, NBB looks at its impact upon profits, people, and the planet. One way that it is advancing the TBL approach is through the creation of a high-involvement corporate culture. All employees at NBB are expected to contribute to the company vision, and accountability is spread throughout the organization. Just about any New Belgium worker can list many, if not all, of these shared values. For NBB, branding strategies are rooted in its company values.

New Belgium's Purpose and Core Beliefs

New Belgium's dedication to quality, the environment, its employees, and its customers is expressed in its mission statement: "To operate a profitable brewery which makes our love and talent manifest." The company's stated core values and beliefs about its role as an environmentally concerned and socially responsible brewer include the following:

1. Remembering that we are incredibly lucky to create something fine that enhances people's lives while surpassing our consumers' expectations.
2. Producing world-class beers.
3. Promoting beer culture and the responsible enjoyment of beer.
4. Kindling social, environmental, and cultural change as a business role model.
5. Environmental stewardship: minimizing resource consumption, maximizing energy efficiency, and recycling.
6. Cultivating potential through learning, participative management, and the pursuit of opportunities.
7. Balancing the myriad needs of the company, staff, and their families.
8. Trusting each other and committing ourselves to authentic relationships, communications, and promises.
9. Continuous, innovative quality and efficiency improvements.
10. Having Fun.

Employees believe that these statements help communicate to customers and other stakeholders what New Belgium, as a company, is about. These simple values—developed roughly 25 years ago—are just as meaningful to the company and its customers today, even though there has been much growth.

Employee Concerns

Recognizing employees' role in the company's success, New Belgium provides many generous benefits for its employees. In addition to the usual paid health and dental insurance and retirement plans, employees get a catered lunch every month to celebrate employees' birthdays as well as a free massage once a year, and they can bring their children and dogs to work. Employees who stay with the company for five years earn an all-expenses paid trip to Belgium to "study beer culture." Employees are also reimbursed for one hour of paid time off for every two hours of volunteer work that they perform. Perhaps most importantly, employees can also earn stock in the privately held corporation, which grants them a vote in company decisions. Employees currently own 100 percent of company stock. Open book management also allows employees to see the financial costs and performance of the company. Employees are provided with financial training so they can understand the books and ask questions about the numbers.

New Belgium also wishes to get its employees involved not only in the company but in its sustainability efforts as well. To help their own sustainability efforts, employees are given a fat-tired cruiser bike after one year's employment so they can ride to work instead of drive. An onsite recycling center is provided for employees. Additionally, each summer New Belgium hosts the Tour de Fat, where employees can dress in costumes and lead locals on a bike tour. Other company perks include inexpensive yoga classes, free beer at quitting time, and a climbing wall. To ensure that workers' voices are heard, NBB has a democratically elected group of coworkers called POSSE. POSSE acts as a liaison between the board, managers, and employees.

Sustainability Concerns

New Belgium's marketing strategy involves linking the quality of its products, as well as its brand, with the company's philosophy of environmental friendliness. As chair of the sustainability subcommittee for its trade group the Brewers Association, NBB is at the forefront in advancing eco-friendly business processes among companies in its industry. Co-workers and managers from all areas of the organization meet monthly to discuss sustainability ideas as part of NBB's natural resource management team. From leading-edge environmental gadgets and high-tech industry advancements to employee-ownership programs and a strong belief in giving back to the community, New Belgium demonstrates its desire to create a living, learning community.

NBB strives for cost-efficient energy-saving alternatives for conducting its business and reducing its impact on the environment. In staying true to the company's core values and beliefs, the brewery's employee–owners unanimously agreed to invest in a wind turbine, making New Belgium the first fully wind-powered brewery in the United States. NBB has also invested in the following energy-saving technologies:

- A smart grid installation that allows NBB to communicate with its electricity provider to conserve energy. For example, the smart grid alerts NBB to non-essential operational functions, allowing the company to turn them off and save power.

- The installation of a 20-kilowatt photovoltaic array on top of the packaging hall. The array produces 3 percent of the company's electricity.

- A brew kettle, the second of its kind installed in the nation, which heats wort sheets instead of the whole kettle at once. This kettle heating method conserves energy more than standard kettles do.

- Sun tubes, which provide natural daytime lighting throughout the brew house all year long.

- A system to capture its waste water and extract methane from it. This can contribute up to 15 percent of the brewery's power needs while reducing the strain on the local municipal water treatment facility.

- A steam condenser that captures and reuses the hot water that boils the barley and hops in the production process to start the next brew. The steam is redirected to heat the floor tiles and de-ice the loading docks in cold weather.

In April 2014, New Belgium was featured in a half-page advertisement supporting the EPA clean water rule that was introduced on March 26, 2014. Andrew Lemley, New Belgium's Government Relations Director, was quoted in an EPA news release championing continued support for the Clean Water Act while also associating quality water with quality beer.

In addition to voicing political support for environmental protections, New Belgium also takes pride in reducing waste through recycling and creative reuse strategies. The company strives to recycle as many supplies as possible, including cardboard boxes, keg caps, office materials, and the amber glass used in bottling. The brewery also stores spent barley and hop grains in an on-premise silo and invites local farmers to pick up the grains, free of charge, to feed their pigs. Beyond the normal products that are recycled back into the food chain, NBB is working with partners to take the same bacteria that create methane from NBB wastewater and convert it into a harvestable, high-protein fish food. NBB also buys recycled products when it can, and even encourages its employees to reduce air pollution by using alternative transportation. Reduce, Reuse, Recycle—the three R's of environmental stewardship—are taken seriously at NBB. The company has been a proud member of the environmental group Business for Innovative Climate & Energy Policy (BICEP), and it signed BICEP's Climate Declaration in 2013 which calls for American businesses, stakeholders, and regulators to address climate change.

Additionally, New Belgium has been a long-time participant in green building techniques. With each expansion of its facility, the company has incorporated new technologies and learned a few lessons along the way. In 2002 NBB agreed to participate in the United States Green Building Council's Leadership in Energy and Environment Design for Existing Buildings (LEED-EB) pilot program. From sun tubes and day lighting throughout the facility to reusing heat in the brew house, NBB continues to search for new ways to close loops and conserve resources.

New Belgium has made significant achievements in sustainability, particularly compared to other companies in the industry. For instance, New Belgium's goal is to use only 3.5 gallons of water to make 1 gallon of beer, which is more than 20 percent less than most other companies. The company is attempting to create a closed-loop wastewater system with its own Process Water Treatment Plant, in which microbes are used to clean the wastewater. NBB recycles over 99.9 percent of its waste, and today 100 percent of its electricity comes from renewable energy sources. Despite these achievements, it has no intention of halting its sustainability efforts. By 2015 the company hopes to reduce its carbon emissions by 25 percent per barrel. To encourage sustainability throughout the supply chain, NBB adopted Sustainable Purchasing Guidelines. The Guidelines allow them to pinpoint and work closely with eco-friendly suppliers to create sustainability throughout the entire value chain. For its part, NBB conducts life-cycle analysis on its packaging components while continually seeking more efficient refrigeration and transportation technology that can be incorporated into its supply chain.

Social Concerns

Beyond its use of environmentally friendly technologies and innovations, New Belgium also strives to improve communities and enhance people's lives through corporate giving, event sponsorship, and philanthropic involvement. Since its inception, NBB has donated more than $7 million to philanthropic causes. For every barrel of beer sold the prior year, NBB donates $1 to philanthropic causes within its distribution territories. The donations are divided between states in proportion to their percentage of overall sales. This is the company's way of staying local and giving back to the communities that support and purchase NBB products. NBB also participates in One Percent for the Planet, a philanthropic network to which the company donates 1 percent of its sales. In addition, NBB employees also partnered with Habitat for Humanity to build a house for a family who had lost their home to a fire.

Funding decisions are made by NBB's Philanthropy Committee, which is comprised of employees throughout the brewery, including owners, employee–owners, area leaders, and production workers. NBB looks for nonprofit organizations that demonstrate creativity, diversity, and an innovative approach to their mission and objectives. The Philanthropy Committee also looks for groups that incorporate community involvement in their operations.

Additionally, NBB maintains a community bulletin board in its facility and posts an array of community involvement activities and proposals. This community board allows tourists and employees to see the various opportunities to help out in the community, and it gives nonprofit organizations a chance to make their needs known. The NBB website also has a dedicated link where organizations can apply for grants. The company donates to causes with a particular emphasis on water conservation, sensible transportation and bike advocacy, sustainable agriculture, and youth environmental education, among other areas.

NBB also sponsors a number of events, with a special focus on those that involve "human-powered" sports that cause minimal damage to the natural environment. Through event sponsorships, such as the Tour de Fat, NBB supports various environmental, social, and cycling nonprofit organizations. In the Tour de Fat, one participant hands over his or her car keys and vehicle title in exchange for an NBB commuter bike and trailer. The participant is then filmed for the world to see as he or she promotes sustainable transportation over driving. In the course of one year, New Belgium can be found at anywhere from 150 to 200 festivals and events across the nation.

Organizational Success

New Belgium Brewing Company's efforts to embody a sustainability-oriented business has paid off with a very loyal following—in fact, the company expanded the number of tours it offers of its facilities due to such high demand. The company has also been the recipient of numerous awards. Past awards for NBB include the *Business Ethics Magazine's* Business Ethics Award for its "dedication to environmental excellence in every part of its innovative brewing process," its inclusion in *The Wall Street Journal's* 15 best small workplaces, and the award for "best mid-sized brewing company of the year" and best mid-sized brewmaster at the Great American Beer Festival. New Belgium has been awarded medals for three different brews: Abbey Belgian Style Ale, Blue Paddle Pilsner, and La Folie specialty ale.

Many applaud New Belgium Brewing Company's sustainability and philanthropic initiatives. According to David Edgar, former director of the Institute for Brewing Studies at the Brewers Association in Boulder, Colorado, "They've created a very positive image for their company in the beer-consuming public with smart decision-making." Although some members of society do not believe that a company whose major product is alcohol can be socially responsible, NBB has set out to prove that for those who make a choice to drink responsibly, the company can do everything possible to contribute to society. NBB also promotes the responsible appreciation of beer through its participation in and support of the culinary arts. For instance, it frequently hosts New Belgium Beer Dinners, in which every course of the meal is served with a complementary culinary treat.

Although NBB has made great strides in creating a socially responsible brand image, its work is not done. It must continually reexamine its ethical, social, and environmental responsibilities. In 2004 it received the Environmental Protection Agency's regional Environmental Achievement Award. It was both an honor and a motivator for the company to continue its socially responsible goals. After all, there are still many ways for NBB to improve as a corporate citizen. For example, although all electric power comes from renewable sources, the NBB plant is still heated in part by using natural gas. Furthermore, continued expansion requires longer travel distances to distribute its products, which increases the use of fossil fuels. Perhaps as a way to deal with these longer distances and expand production capacity, NBB opened a second brewery in Asheville, North Carolina, in 2015. In addition to addressing logistical challenges, NBB is part of an industry where there is always a need for more public dialogue on avoiding alcohol abuse. Practically speaking, the company has a never-ending to-do list.

NBB executives acknowledge that as its annual sales increase, the company will face increasing challenges to remain committed on a human level while also being culturally authentic. Indeed, how to boldly grow the brand while maintaining its perceptions of a humble feel has always been a challenge. Additionally, reducing waste to an even greater extent will require more effort on behalf of managers and employees, creating the need for a collaborative process that will require the dedication of both parties toward sustainability.

NBB also faces increased competition from other craft breweries. It remains behind D.G. Yuengling and Son, Boston Beer Co. (maker of Samuel Adams beer), and Sierra Nevada in market share. Like NBB, Boston Beer Co. and Sierra Nevada have plans to expand. Boston Beer allocated $35 million for capital investment projects at breweries in Massachusetts, Pennsylvania, and Ohio in 2012. NBB must also compete against craft beer alternatives released by traditional breweries, such as MillerCoor's New Moon Belgian White. It must constantly engage in environmental scanning and competitive analysis to compete in this increasingly competitive environment.

Every six-pack of New Belgium Beer displays the phrase "In this box is our labor of love. We feel incredibly lucky to be creating something fine that enhances people's lives." Although Jeff Lebesch and Kim Jordan are divorced and Lebesch has left the company to focus on other interests, the founders of New Belgium hope this statement captures the spirit of the company. NBB's most important asset is its image—a corporate brand that stands for quality, responsibility, and concern for society. Defining itself as more than a beer company, the brewer also sees itself as a caring organization that is concerned for all stakeholders.

QUESTIONS FOR DISCUSSION

1. What environmental issues does the New Belgium Brewing Company work to address? How has NBB taken a strategic approach to addressing these issues? Why do you think the company has taken such a strong stance toward sustainability?
2. Do you agree that New Belgium's focus on social responsibility provides a key competitive advantage for the company? Why or why not?
3. Some segments of society contend that companies that sell alcoholic beverages and tobacco products cannot be socially responsible organizations because of the nature of their primary products. Do you believe that New Belgium's actions and initiatives are indicative of a socially responsible corporation? Why or why not?

SOURCES

"The 2011 World's Most Ethical Companies," *Ethisphere*, Q1 2011, 37–43; The facts of this case are from Peter Asmus, "Goodbye Coal, Hello Wind," *Business Ethics* 13 (July/August 1999): 10–11; "A Tour of the New Belgium Brewery—Act One," LiveGreen Blog, April 9, 2007, http://www.livegreensd.com/2007/04/tour-of-new-belgium-brewery-act-one.html (accessed April 13, 2012); Robert Baun, "What's in a Name? Ask the Makers of Fat Tire," [Fort Collins] *Coloradoan.com*, October 8, 2000, E1, E3; Beerpulse.com, "New Belgium 2014 Update: Groundbreaking Hawaii, Kentucky, 3 Floyds Grätzer, FOCOIIab," March 25, 2014, http://beerpulse.com/2014/03/new-belgium-2014-update-hawaii-kentucky-2745/ (accessed August 18, 2014); The Brewer's Association, "Craft Brewer Volume Share of U.S. Beer Market Reaches Double Digits in 2014," March 16, 2015, http://www.brewersassociation.org/press-releases/craft-brewer-volume-share-of-u-s-beer-market-reaches-double-digits-in-2014/ (accessed April 7, 2015); Leigh Buchanan, "It's All about Ownership," *Inc.*, April 18, 2013, http://www.inc.com/audacious-companies/leigh-buchanan/new-belgium-brewing.html (accessed April 7, 2015); Karen Crofton, "How New Belgium Brewery Leads Colorado's Craft Brewers in Energy," *GreenBiz*, August 1, 2014, http://www.greenbiz.com/blog/2014/08/01/how-new-belgium-brewery-leads-colorados-craft-brewers-energy (accessed August 18, 2014); Robert F. Dwyer and John F. Tanner, Jr., *Business Marketing* (Burr Ridge, IL: McGraw-Hill/Irwin, 1999), 104; The Egotist Network, "New Belgium Pairs Well with People in New Campaign from Denver's Cultivator," *The Denver Egotist*, May 20, 2013, http://www.thedenveregotist.com/news/local/2013/may/20/new-belgium-pairs-well-people-new-campaign-denvers-cultivator (accessed May 6, 2015); Garrett Ellison, "New Belgium's Biere de Garde, a Collaboration with Brewery Vivant of Grand Rapids, Hits Shelves," *Michigan Live*, December 10, 2012, http://www.mlive.com/business/west-michigan/index.ssf/2012/12/new_belgiums_biere_de_garde_a.html (accessed August 18, 2014); Environmental Protection Agency, "Here's What They're Saying about the Clean Water Act Proposed Rule," March 26, 2014, http://yosemite.epa.gov/opa/admpress.nsf/docf6618525a9ef b85257359003fb69d/3f954c179cf0720985257ca7004920fa!OpenDocument (accessed August 18, 2014); Mike Esterl, "Craft Brewers Tap Big Expansion," *The Wall Street Journal*, December 28, 2011, http://online.wsj.com/article/SB10001424052970203686204577114291721661070.html (accessed August 18, 2014); "Four Businesses Honored with Prestigious International Award for Outstanding Marketplace Ethics," Better Business Bureau, press release, September 23, 2002, http://www.bbb.org/alerts/2002torchwinners.asp; Julie Gordon, "Lebesch Balances Interests in Business, Community," *Coloradoan.com*, February 26, 2003; Del I. Hawkins, Roger J. Best, and Kenneth A. Coney, *Consumer Behavior: Building Marketing Strategy*, 8th ed. (Burr Ridge, IL: McGraw-Hill/Irwin, 2001); "How New Belgium Brewing Is Positioning Itself to Remain Independent," *Denver Post*, January 15, 2013, http://blogs.denverpost.com/beer/2013/01/15/new-belgium-positio/7872/ (accessed April 16, 2013); "Industry Profile: Breweries," *First Research*, October 17, 2011, http://www.firstresearch.com (accessed February 17, 2012); David Kemp, Tour Connoisseur, New Belgium Brewing Company, personal interview by Nikole Haiar, November 21, 2000; Dick Kreck, "Strange Brewing Standing Out," *Denver Post*, June 2, 2010, http://www.denverpost.com/lifestyles/ci_15198853 (accessed August 18, 2014); Devin Leonard, "New Belgium and the Battle of the Microbrews," *Bloomberg Businessweek*, December 1, 2011, http://www.businessweek.com/magazine/new-belgium-and-the-battle-of-the-microbrews-12012011.html (accessed August 18, 2014); Karlene Lukovitz, "New Belgium Brewing Gets 'Hopped Up,'" *Media Post News*, February 3, 2010, http://www.mediapost.com/publications/article/121806/new-belgium-brewing-gets-hopped-up.html (accessed August 18, 2014); NBB Films, "NBBspotsonNBC," NBB Films, YouTube, http://www.youtube.com/watch?v=KCnzyX-x-WQ (accessed August 18, 2014); New Belgium Brewing website, http://www.newbelgium.com (accessed August 18, 2014); New Belgium Brewing, "Beer Mode," http://www.newbelgium.com/app.aspx (accessed May 6, 2015); New Belgium Brewing, "Beer Mode: A Brand (Spanking) New Mobile App! For Your Consideration…," April 23, 2013, http://www.newbelgium.com/community/Blog/13-04-23/Beer-Mode-a-brand-spanking-new-mobile-app-For-your-consideration.aspx (accessed May 6, 2015); "New Belgium Brewing Announces Asheville as Site for Second Brewery," *Denver Post*, April 5, 2012, http://marketwire.denverpost.com/client/denver_post/release.jsp?actionFor=1595119 (accessed April 19, 2012); "New Belgium Brewing Company, Inc.," *Businessweek*, http://investing.businessweek.com/research/stocks/private/snapshot.asp?privcapId=919332 (accessed August 18, 2014); New Belgium Brewing,

Corporate Sustainability Report, New Belgium Brewing website, http://www.newbelgium.com/culture/ alternatively_empowered/sustainable-business-story.aspx (accessed April 13, 2012); New Belgium Brewing, *New Belgium Brewing: Follow Your Folly*, May 9, 2007, http://www.newbelgium.com/Files/NBB_student-info-packet. pdf (accessed August 18, 2014); New Belgium Brewing, *New Belgium Brewing Packaging Reduction Goals*, 2014, http://www.newbelgium.com/files/sustainability/NBBPackagingReductionGoals2014.pdf (accessed April 7, 2015); New Belgium Brewing, *Our Sustainable Success Story*, http://www.newbelgium.com/files/sustainability/ New_Belgium_Sustainability_Brochure.pdf?pdf=sustainabilityreport (accessed April 7, 2015); New Belgium Brewing, "Philanthropy," http://www.newbelgium.com/sustainability/Community/Philanthropy.aspx (accessed August 18, 2014); "New Belgium Brewing Wins Ethics Award," *Denver Business Journal*, January 2, 2003, http:// www.bizjournals.com/denver/stories/2002/12/30/daily21.html (accessed August 18, 2014); One Percent for the Planet, "FAQ," http://onepercentfortheplanet.org/about/faq-about-1ftp/ (accessed August 18, 2014); Greg Owsley, "The Necessity for Aligning Brand with Corporate Ethics," in Sheb L. True, Linda Ferrell, O. C. Ferrell, *Fulfilling Our Obligation, Perspectives on Teaching Business Ethics* (Atlanta, GA: Kennesaw State University Press, 2005), 128–132; Steve Raabe, "New Belgium Brewing Turns to Cans," *Denver Post*, May 15, 2008, http://www.denverpost. com/breakingnews/ci_9262005 (accessed August 18, 2014); Steve Raabe, "Plans Brewing for New Belgium Facility on East Coast," *Denver Post*, December 22, 2011, http://www.denverpost.com/business/ci_19597528 (accessed August 18, 2014); Bryan Simpson, "New Belgium Brewing: Brand Building through Advertising and Public Relations," *Michaelcoronado.com*, http://www.michaelcoronado.com/michaelcoronado/images/pdf/NBB_ research/new_belgium_brewing.pdf (accessed August 18, 2014); Mike Snider, "Big Brewers Happy to Go Hoppy," *USA Today*, October 30, 2013, 4B; Mike Snider, "Sales of Craft beer Are Still Bubbling Up," *USA Today*, April 3, 2014, 3B; Jonathan Shikes, "New Belgium Airs TV Commercials for the First Time in Eight Years, but Not in Colorado," *Westword*, May 21, 2013, http://www.westword.com/restaurants/new-belgium-airs-tv-commercials- for-the-first-time-in-eight-years-but-not-in-colorado-5728121 (accessed May 6, 2015); Kelly K. Spors, "Top Small Workplaces 2008," *The Wall Street Journal*, February 22, 2009, http://online.wsj.com/article/SB122347733961315417. html (accessed August 18, 2014); "Tour de New Belgium," Brew Public, November 23, 2010, http://brewpublic. com/places-to-drink-beer/tour-de-new-belgium/ (accessed April 16, 2013).

CASE 6

National Collegiate Athletic Association Ethics and Compliance Program*

INTRODUCTION

Perhaps no sport at American colleges is as popular, or as lucrative, as college football. College football often has a significant impact on the school's culture. This is especially true for the more successful and prolific football programs, such as Texas A&M or Notre Dame. Football has increasingly become a big money maker for many colleges, with a significant amount of sports revenue coming from their football programs. Within the past two years, the sports channel *ESPN* made deals with certain teams to gain rights to air more games than usual. Because of this influx of revenue, the duties of coaches have evolved beyond just coaching. In many ways, they became the face of the team. Programs that show positive returns have coaches working hard to fill seats on game day and encourage college alumni to donate to the school. The more successful the football team, the more visibility it is given in the media. This visibility leads to greater awareness of the college or university among the public, and schools with the best football programs can see a greater influx of applications.

The collegiate football programs have an intangible influence within and outside their immediate surroundings. This is mainly seen in their fan base, composed of current students, alumni, staff, faculty, and local businesses. For example, when the University of Alabama won its 15th national championship, the victory was celebrated by an enormous crowd, fireworks, and a parade. Texas A&M University is one example of a football program that generates not only profits but also a sense of loyalty among its fans. Texas A&M is spending over $485 million to expand its Kyle Field stadium so that it will seat up to 102,500 spectators. Table 1 shows the value of some of the most successful college-football programs. These games also help local businesses generate more revenues.

Because of the financial support and widespread influence of the football program, the players, coaches, and football administrators have to deal with a lot of pressure to fundraise, sell tickets, and win games. These pressures open up opportunities for misconduct to occur, and it is increasingly important that university administrators and football program officials directly acknowledge opportunities for misconduct. While the university is ultimately responsible for the operation of each department and the behavior of its employees, it can be difficult for the administrators to have an objective view of incidents that occur, especially when it involves a successful football program that

*This case was prepared by Michelle Urban, Kathleen Dubyk, Ben Skaer, and Bethany Buchner for and under the direction of O.C. and Linda Ferrell. It was prepared for classroom discussion rather than to illustrate either effective or ineffective handling of an administrative, ethical, or legal decision by management. All sources used for this case were obtained through publicly available material © 2015.

benefits the entire university. The university administrators are often subject to the same pressures as those in the football program to increase the level of revenue and reputation. This led to the development of a more objective institution to set and enforce rules and standards: the National Collegiate Athletic Association (NCAA). The NCAA views ethical conduct as a crucial component to a college football program and works to promote leadership and excellence among student–athletes and the universities to which they belong. It also serves to protect the interests of student–athletes, ensure academic excellence, and encourage fair play.

TABLE 1 Value of Major-Conference College-Football Programs (in Millions)

Rank	School	Intrinsic Value
1	Ohio State	$1,127.6
2	Michigan	$999.1
3	Texas	$972.1
4	Notre Dame	$936.4
5	Florida	$815.4
6	Oklahoma	$776.5
7	Alabama	$760.6
8	Georgia	$710.9
9	LSU	$659.2
10	Nebraska	$536.0
11	Penn State	$520.6
12	Iowa	$491.3
13	Tennessee	$437.1
14	S. Carolina	$422.0
15	Washington	$418.6
16	Wisconsin	$415.9
17	Texas A&M	$382.1
18	Oregon	$358.7
19	Auburn	$340.4
20	Arkansas	$327.8
21	Florida State	$325.7
22	Oklahoma St.	$319.5
23	Virginia Tech	$308.5
24	S. California	$303.6
25	Texas Tech	$289.8
26	Kansas St.	$286.1
27	Arizona St.	$277.4
28	Michigan State	$260.8
29	Clemson	$255.1
30	California Berkley	$252.1
31	Stanford	$232.5
32	Mississippi	$226.9

TABLE 1 (*Continued*)

33	UCLA	$225.6
34	Oregon St.	$220.3
35	Kentucky	$217.5
36	Colorado	$208.3
37	Miami (Fla.)	$204.1
38	Minnesota	$202.4
39	Utah	$198.9
40	North Carolina St.	$182.6
41	Iowa St.	$182.3
42	Georgia Tech	$180.5
43	Arizona	$163.7
44	Virginia	$159.3
45	Northwestern	$156.5
46	Indiana	$149.4
47	Purdue	$140.1
48	Syracuse	$137.6
49	Washington St.	$135.3
50	North Carolina	$134.0

Source: Ryan Brewer, Indiana University-Purdue University Columbus, 2015.

In this case, we provide a brief history of the NCAA and examples of the rules they have regarding college football. We then view how these rules relate to ethics. The next section covers some of the major college football scandals within the past few years, how these scandals were handled by the schools and the NCAA, and the community impact resulting from the scandals. It is crucial to note, however, that these scandals are not common to college football as a whole. The majority of football teams receive no NCAA infractions during the year, and those reported are usually minor in nature. Universities have their own set of expectations for student–athletes, including showing up on time to practice and behaving responsibly, that go above and beyond NCAA rules. However, when NCAA violations occur, universities have a responsibility to report them in a timely manner. Therefore, the next section covers examples of ways universities address unethical behavior in their football programs through self-imposed sanctions, which signifies that they consider compliance to be an important component of their football programs. We conclude by analyzing how effective the NCAA appears to be in curbing misconduct and preventing future unethical behavior from occurring. This case demonstrates that ethics and compliance is just as important for nonprofit organizations and educational institutions as it is for businesses.

OVERVIEW OF NCAA

The NCAA was formed in 1906 under the premise of protecting student–athletes from being endangered and exploited. The Association was established with a constitution and a set of bylaws with the ability to be amended as issues arise. As the number of competitive college sports grew, the NCAA was divided into three Divisions, I, II, and III, to deal with the rising complexity of college athletic programs. Universities are given the freedom to decide which division they want to belong to based on their desired level of competitiveness in collegiate sports.

Each Division is equipped with the power to establish a group of presidents or other university officials with the authority to write and enact policies, rules, and regulations for their Divisions. Each Division is ultimately governed by the President of the NCAA and the Executive Committee. Under the Executive Committee are groups formed in each Division, such as the Legislative Committee, as well as Cabinets and Boards of Directors.

In the early 1980s, questions began to arise concerning the level of education student–athletes received. Some thought these students were held to lower academic standards so they could focus more on their sport, which could be detrimental to the students' education and negatively impact future career success. As a result, the NCAA strengthened the academic requirements of student–athletes to ensure academics were taken just as seriously as athletics. It also established the Presidents Commission, composed of presidents of universities in each Division that collaboratively set agendas with the NCAA. Table 2 provides a list of six of the Principles for Conduct of Intercollegiate Athletics that can be found in Article 2 of the Constitution.

Throughout the Constitution, the NCAA emphasizes the responsibility each university has in overseeing its athletics department and being compliant with the terms established by its conferences. The NCAA establishes principles, rules, and enforcement guidelines to both guide the universities in its oversight of the athletics department as well

TABLE 2 Principles for Conduct of Intercollegiate Athletics

The Principle of Institutional Control and Responsibility
- Puts the responsibility for the operations and behaviors of staff on the president of the university.

The Principle of Student–Athlete Well-Being
- Requires integration of athletics and education, maintaining a culturally diverse and gender equitable environment, protection of student–athlete's health and safety, creating an environment that is conducive to positive coach/student–athlete relationships, coaches and administrative staff show honesty, fairness, and openness in their relationships with student–athletes, and student–athlete involvement in decisions that will affect them.

The Principle of Sportsmanship and Ethical Conduct
- Maintains that respect, fairness, civility, honesty, and responsibility are values that need to be adhered to through the establishment of policies for sportsmanship and ethical conduct in the athletics program which must be consistent with the mission and goals of the university. Everyone must be continuously educated about the policies.

The Principle of Sound Academic Standards
- Maintains that student–athletes need to be held to the same academic standards as all other students.

The Principle of Rules Compliance
- Requires compliance with NCAA rules. Notes that the NCAA will help institutions develop their compliance program and explains the penalty for noncompliance.

The Principle Governing Recruiting
- Promotes equity among prospective students and protects them from exorbitant pressures.

Source: Adapted from National Collegiate Athletic Association, *2014–2015 NCAA® Division II Manual* (Indianapolis, IN: National Collegiate Athletics Association, 2014).

as penalize those schools that fail to regulate and address misconduct. In article 10 of the bylaws, a description of ethical and unethical conduct among student–athletes is provided, along with corresponding disciplinary consequences if any of the conditions are violated. Honesty and sportsmanship are emphasized as the basis of ethical conduct, while wagering, withholding information, and fraud are among the unethical behaviors listed. Article 11 describes the appropriate behavior for athletics personnel. Honesty and sportsmanship are again the basis for ethical behavior, but with an added emphasis on responsibility for NCAA regulations. Article 11 cites the Head Coach as responsible for creating an atmosphere of compliance and monitoring the behavior of his or her subordinates, including assistant coaches and players.

The NCAA takes the enforcement of rules seriously and tries to ensure the penalties fit the violation if misconduct does occur. The organization also makes sure the penalties are handed down in a timely manner, not only to indicate the seriousness of the infraction but also to maintain a credible and effective enforcement program. This method tries to correct or eliminate deviant behavior while maintaining fairness and objectivity toward those members of the Association not involved in violations. Employees (coaches and other administrative staff) are exhorted to have high ethical standards since they work among and influence students. The NCAA makes it a requirement that each employee engage in exemplary conduct so as not to cause harm to the student–athletes in any way. They are also given a responsibility to cooperate with the NCAA.

The NCAA lays out three types of violations and corresponding penalties, depending on the nature and scope of the violation. Secondary violations are the least severe and can result in fines, suspensions for games, and reduction in scholarships. For major violations, some of the penalties are the same as secondary violations, but the scope is far more severe. For example, suspensions will be longer and fines larger. However, some penalties are specific only to major violations, such as a public reprimand, a probationary period for up to five years, and limits on recruiting. The last type involves repeat violations that occur within a five-year period from the start date of the initial violation. The penalties for repeat violations are the most severe, including elimination of all financial aid and recruiting activities and resignation of institutional staff members who serve on boards, committees, or in cabinets. Table 3 lists some of the more prominent unethical practices the NCAA lists specifically concerning college football.

The NCAA incorporates a compliance approach to ethics by developing and enforcing rules to keep the games fair and respectful of student–athletes' rights. The NCAA Committee on Sportsmanship and Ethical Conduct identified respect and integrity as two critical elements in the NCAA 2013 and 2014 Football Rules and Interpretations. The NCAA strives to keep football games fun and entertaining without sacrificing the health and safety of the student–athletes participating. As previously mentioned, the NCAA places emphasis on the level of education student–athletes receive and encourages athletes to focus on their grades to ensure they have career opportunities post-athletics. The core of the NCAA concerns ethics. This organization takes not only key players into consideration, but also other stakeholders, such as the college community and the sports society as a whole.

Aside from its involvement with student–athlete academics, the NCAA is likewise involved with other off-the-field activities to protect the best interests of student–athletes. According to NCAA guidelines, college football coaches are not permitted to actively begin recruiting prospective players to their school until the prospective player is at least a junior in high school. These coaches have a limit on the number of phone calls and off-campus visits they are permitted to make to prospective students. These rules are in place to ensure student–athletes do not feel pressured by these colleges. Once the student–athletes are in

TABLE 3 Unethical Practices Prohibited by the NCAA

- Use of the helmet as a weapon.

- Targeting and initiating contact. Players, coaches, and officials should emphasize the elimination of targeting and initiating contact against a defenseless opponent and/or with the crown of the helmet.

- Using nontherapeutic drugs in the game of football.

- Unfair use of a starting signal, called "Beating the ball." This involves deliberately stealing an advantage from the opponent. An honest starting signal is needed, but a signal that has for its purpose starting the team a fraction of a second before the ball is put in play, in the hope that it will not be detected by the officials, is illegal.

- Feigning an injury. An injured player must be given full protection under the rules, but feigning injury is dishonest, unsportsmanlike, and contrary to the spirit of the rules.

- Talking to an opponent in any manner that is demeaning, vulgar, or abusive, intended to incite a physical response or verbally put an opponent down.

- For a coach to address, or permit anyone on his bench to address, uncomplimentary remarks to any official during the progress of a game, or to indulge in conduct that might incite players or spectators against the officials, is a violation of the rules of the game and must likewise be considered conduct unworthy of a member of the coaching profession.

Source: Adapted from National Collegiate Athletics Association, *Football 2013 and 2014 Rules and Interpretations* (Indianapolis, IN: National Collegiate Athletics Association, 2014).

college, a set of rules made between the NCAA and the individual college limit the types of gifts a student–athlete can accept. Parents of student–athletes, for example, are able to give any number and type of gifts to their own children, but must be wary when it comes to other members of the team. Student–athletes generally cannot accept gifts at reduced prices (for example, a free iPod) and other gifts, such as practice uniforms for the team, must be cleared by the school first.

Despite the NCAA's wide array of rules and regulations, there have been many criticisms of the organization's practices. One of these criticisms has to do with a former NCAA investigator, Ameen Najjar, who worked on investigating reports of rule violations from the University of Miami. Najjar was promptly dismissed from the NCAA when it was found he was going outside the NCAA's rules of investigation in order to collect more evidence for the case. Not only was this a major embarrassment for the NCAA, but critics state Najjar followed orders from others within the organization and was put up as a scapegoat when the rule-breaking investigative techniques came to light. The NCAA was also sued for allegedly allowing the video game company EA to use the likeness of NCAA basketball players in its video games without giving the players any compensation. EA later stopped producing college football video games altogether. The NCAA paid $20 million to settle these claims.

A major issue that has arisen for the NCAA is player safety. It is common for injuries to occur in sports, especially football. Over the past few years professional players have increasingly filed lawsuits as evidence has demonstrated that injuries such as concussions could lead to degenerative brain disease. College athletes have also gotten involved in the dispute, and former athletes filed a lawsuit against the NCAA seeking damages for injuries sustained during games. The fear is that concussion and other injuries could have long-term health impacts. The NCAA announced it would spend $30 million to track the impact of concussions on athletes and has changed its guidelines in how it manages concussion occurrences. This includes prohibiting players that suffered a concussion from playing again during the day and developing a medical monitoring program to assess whether self-reported symptoms might be indicative of a head injury.

Additionally, misconduct in college sports continues to be a challenge for the NCAA. Often other stakeholders are involved in the misconduct. For instance, college sports games that have been "rigged" (managed fraudulently) have often been traced to wealthy sports boosters with inside knowledge of the sports in which they heavily invest. A majority of the time, this rigging is done to benefit gambling outcomes among these boosters. Flopping—a tactic common in the NBA—is becoming more widespread in college basketball. Flopping occurs when a player exaggerates or fakes a blow so that the referee will call a foul. Despite anti-flopping measures adopted by the NCAA, this practice is hard to pinpoint exactly because it is hard to measure the intent of the player (that is, whether the player intentionally faked a blow).

When a college sports program is accused of misconduct that violates NCAA rules, the NCAA conducts an investigation to determine whether the allegations are true. If these schools are found to be in violation, the NCAA levies penalties against the team. However, the NCAA also receives criticism from those who disapprove of the severity and effectiveness of the sanctions meant to discourage misconduct. On the one hand, some stakeholders believe the NCAA sanctions are too tough. On the other hand, some feel they are not strict enough. They state some of the major college football programs hit by NCAA sanctions were able to recover from these penalties quickly and did not suffer much during the course of the sanctions. This argument implies that avoiding the risks of punishment is less costly to the team than the benefits of bending the rules. Whether NCAA sanctions are too harsh or not harsh enough, pressure to maintain the sports programs provides the opportunity for misconduct in the college sports community, as well as creates significant challenges for the NCAA.

CHALLENGES FOR ETHICS AND COMPLIANCE IN COLLEGE FOOTBALL

College football is far more than just a sport. For many universities, it is a business that brings millions of dollars to colleges all over the United States. Being a business, there are always ethical and compliance issues that take place. The question is whether schools ignore issues taking place because of the amount of money a football program generates for the school. If so, this creates a significant conflict of interest. In the past few years, a number of highly publicized scandals have rocked the college football industry and led to heavy criticism of the schools where the scandals occurred. The actions of the NCAA in response to these scandals received mixed reactions from stakeholders. However, a more serious concern for the NCAA is how to ensure college sports teams comply with ethical policies as well as combat the tendency for colleges to remain complacent because of the success of the sports team. The following examples describe two major college football scandals, how the schools reacted to the scandals, and the sanctions, if any, that the NCAA took against the team.

Penn State Scandal

In 2011 accusations arose alleging that a former assistant coach of the Penn State football team sexually assaulted at least eight young boys over the course of many years. It was not long before the school itself was implicated in suspecting or knowing about the crime but not taking adequate steps to stop it. Two university officials turned themselves in to authorities after being accused of covering up the crimes.

According to investigations, the first report of potential misconduct between the former assistant coach Jerry Sandusky and an underage boy came in 1998. The report came to University police and the Senior Vice President for Finance and Business, Gary Schultz. This matter was investigated internally and resulted in no criminal charges based on a lack of evidence. In 2001 a graduate assistant allegedly witnessed the perpetrator sexually assaulting a young boy in the Penn State football team's practice center. The graduate assistant reported the incident to Head Coach Joe Paterno, who staked his reputation on running a program known for ethics and integrity. While Paterno appeared to notify campus officials, the officials did not report the incident to police, allowing the crimes to continue. A later report conducted by former FBI director Louis Freeah indicated the coach and school officials covered up the crimes. This led to accusations that the school cared more about its reputation and the success of its football program than it did about the young victims. This case is even more serious as such misconduct does not just constitute an NCAA violation; it is a criminal act that harmed many people. Although Joe Paterno reported the crime to campus officials, some felt it was his responsibility to do more to ensure the crimes were reported to the proper authorities. The assistant coach continued to interact with young boys and be around the college campus after the reports were made.

The negligent behavior of Penn State officials, both within the administration and the football department, might be explained through the strength of the football program and the complacency of the university culture. Head Coach Joe Paterno had been at Penn State's football department for more than 60 years at the time of the scandal. The way he ran the department indicated a reliance on old football standards and an inability or unwillingness to adapt to new ones. Unfortunately, this culture had pitfalls that did not hold up to modern ethical standards. Some reports claim that on different occasions he advocated that football players should not be held to the same standards as regular students, implying football players should be treated differently than other students by the university. When football players got in trouble with the law, Paterno felt the university should not take action but rather let the police deal with it. Although he butted heads with many people when it came to these views, school directors were on his side of the argument. This is likely because of the large amount of revenue the program brought into the school. According to one accusation, Coach Paterno used this revenue as a threat to stop all fundraising if a certain director he disagreed with was not fired. If these allegations are true, then Paterno created a culture within the football department wherein members did not need to be held accountable according to school regulations. This in turn indicates a complacent university culture when it came to the football program.

The NCAA agreed the misconduct was partially the fault of the football program's and Penn State's complacency. In addition to the negative impact on the victims, Penn State suffered reputational damage and received a major blow to its football program. The NCAA imposed sanctions against Penn State costing $60 million in fines, a four-year post-season ban prohibiting the school from being eligible for any post games until 2016, and a four-year reduction in scholarships amounting to 10 scholarships per year for the football program. The football team's wins between 1998 and 2011 were vacated; however, in 2015 the NCAA reinstated the wins after a legal battle. The 2015 lawsuit settlement also included a repeal of the 2012 NCAA sanctions and agreement by Penn State to spend $60 million on programs intended to prevent child abuse. Indeed, the penalties imposed by the NCAA drastically hurt Penn State's football program's ability to compete against other teams. In total, there were seven penalties placed on the university and athletics program combined.

The NCAA's actions demonstrate its commitment to ensure the activities that took place at Penn State do not happen again. Although Joe Paterno died of lung cancer in 2012, close to two months after he was fired as head coach, the Paterno family filed a lawsuit against the NCAA and its President on behalf of Penn State, citing the investigation conducted by former director of the FBI Louis Freeah—a report the NCAA relied heavily upon in imposing sanctions against Penn State—was seriously flawed in its conclusions of blame.

The NCAA also put 10 corrective sanctions on Penn State formulated specifically for them. The main corrective measure was that the university must sign an Athletic Integrity Agreement. In doing so, this allowed the NCAA to require Penn State to take eight corrective steps. These steps include hiring a compliance officer for the athletics department, creating a compliance council and a full disclosure program, adding internal accountability and certifications for this accountability, implementing an external compliance review/certification process, drafting an athletics code of conduct, conducting training and education, and appointing an independent athletics integrity monitor. All of the steps will be continuously updated to ensure the internal and external controls stay relevant. The NCAA's goal for the corrective sanctions is to find and stop unethical behavior before it becomes a problem.

Ohio State

The Ohio State scandal was a result of rule violations from student–athletes and a subsequent cover-up of the violations by the coach. In December 2010, five players on Ohio State's football team were suspended for using the gear the football team supplied to barter for cash and tattoos. Under the NCAA rules, it is illegal for a Division I football player to receive any benefit, such as a discount or favor, that is not offered to the public. Head Coach Jim Tressel became aware of the violation and failed to report it to the school for a period of nine months. This enabled the team to continue to play in games they otherwise would have been ineligible to play. In addition to the suspensions, the NCAA also banned Ohio State from a bowl game for one year, took five scholarships away for the following three years, and put the team on a one-year probation. When it was discovered Tressel had prior knowledge of the violation, the NCAA issued a five-year show-cause order, forcing him to resign and virtually ending his career as a coach in collegiate athletics. A college can hire a coach who has an outstanding show-cause order, but it may also face penalties for doing so. In addition, if a coach with a show-cause order does in fact get hired and makes a subsequent violation, the consequences will be far more severe on both the coach and the university. Most colleges will not take the risk of hiring a coach with this kind of label.

This was not the only violation found among members of the Ohio State football team. After the bartering scandal, the NCAA suspended three other players for accepting money from a booster. A booster is a fan who has a significant amount of money and invests in the team to build better facilities, contribute to scholarships, and sometimes influence who the coaching staff will be. However, student–athletes are prohibited from accepting money or gifts from boosters directly and doing so is a direct violation of NCAA rules. Additionally, other players were suspended for being overpaid by the same booster for work completed during a summer job.

The NCAA placed these sanctions on Ohio State for failure to properly oversee its athletics program. Many of the administrators commented if they knew of the football players' conduct, they would have taken corrective action against it. Ohio State took responsibility for its actions and cooperated with the NCAA investigation. The university imposed its own penalties against the football program, including vacating the 2010 season. Yet the

NCAA made it a point to show the administrators it is their responsibility to know what is going on within their organization. Additionally, the NCAA also noted Tressel withheld information multiple times from NCAA investigators. In total, the sanctions cost Ohio State an estimated $8 million.

SELF-REPORTING AND MONITORING STUDENT–ATHLETES

Minor violations become scandals when the university, the football program authorities, or both cover them up for long periods of time. No matter where the cover-up begins or ends, the ultimate responsibility lies with the university to monitor the actions of the football program. If the culture of the university fosters misconduct, minor violations will inevitably become scandals. On the other hand, universities that monitor their athletics programs and swiftly address minor violations, including reporting the infractions to the NCAA, are less likely to be involved in major scandals. This act of self-reporting demonstrates a concern with ethical behavior and accountability for their actions. Furthermore, the NCAA takes these measures into account when deciding on the appropriate level of penalties to impose for violations.

In 2014 the NCAA penalized the University of Alaska Fairbanks for violations of eligibility requirements for college players. Most of the violations involved students who had not declared majors, did not have sufficient credits for their majors, or did not meet requirements for transferring from junior colleges. The University of Alaska Fairbanks discovered the violations had occurred over a five-year period. In 2011 and 2012, the university reported the violations to the NCAA and imposed penalties on the school for the infraction. The NCAA determined that the violations occurred not because of student misconduct but due to lapses in the school's compliance system. The NCAA imposed penalties against the university in the form of a $30,000 fine against the university, fewer scholarships for its hockey team, and the elimination of wins for games deemed to be ineligible.

A growing problem the NCAA is facing involves a rise in academic misconduct. Because sports bring a lot of money to the university, administrators and faculty are sometimes tempted to turn the other way when players engage in misconduct. It is not uncommon for coaches and professors to provide assistance to players that might violate NCAA rules or lower academic standards so they can continue to compete. In 2014 a massive fraud was uncovered at the University of North Carolina Chapel Hill when it was discovered that 3,000 students got credit for classes they did not attend, for which they did not do significant work, and/or were not supervised by a professor. The scandal took place over a 16-year period, and approximately half the students involved were athletes. Students were provided fake grades for fake classes. It is believed the misconduct largely occurred to keep athletes eligible to play and was exacerbated by a lack of institutional control. Ambiguous statements made to school personnel inexperienced with NCAA rules are also problematic. For instance, it is not uncommon for a coach to tell support staff to make sure a student is eligible to play without giving them directions on how to do so without violating the rules.

Many ethical issues involve providing college athletes with special favors. For decades a pressing issue has been one of paying college athletes. There are various rules that must be followed to avoid the appearance of paying college athletes or providing them with special treatment. At Ohio State University, student athletes disobeyed the rules by trading athletic equipment for tattoos. Assistant coach Tim Moser of Colorado State University was hit with sanctions—including suspension from three games and a letter of reprimand—for providing extra benefits to two athletes on the women's basketball team. Todd Gurley, who now plays with the National Football League, was suspended for four games as a student at the University of Georgia for accepting over $3,000 over a two-year period for signing autographs. Clearly compensation of players is a major issue. The main argument against athletes receiving compensation is that if the players were paid, then college sports would lose its appeal.

This issue gained even more traction in a 2014 antitrust lawsuit in which a federal judge ruled that the NCAA could not prohibit players from selling rights to their likeness and names. However, the judge did say that the NCAA could limit the amount paid to college athletes if the amount of compensation exceeded $5,000 annually. In other words, players could receive up to $20,000 over four years if they received the maximum $5,000 per year in deferred compensation. The money players earn is to be placed in a trust fund and distributed after the athletes graduate. Although deferred compensation is a major step away from only permitting academic scholarships to student–athletes, the major issue still remains over whether the athletes should be paid a salary or reimbursed for expenses caused by sports-related activities and medical care.

Not surprisingly, there is a lot of controversy surrounding the restrictions on providing student–athlete salaries when the coaches earn six or seven salary figures. Some think student–athletes should be classified as employees of the school (just like the coaches are classified), especially since the students' commitment of practicing and playing games equates to a full-time job. Furthermore, some find it unfair that only universities benefit from the immense revenue created through college sports. For the time being it appears that the NCAA will continue prohibiting schools from paying salaries to student–athletes, but the recent antitrust litigation ruling in favor of providing limited player compensation for the rights to use their likeness demonstrates that opinions are evolving. The next few years could bring even more changes to restrictions on student–athlete compensation.

The integrity of the NCAA and collegiate athletics depends on transparency and a level-playing field. The NCAA and universities are mindful that most collegiate athletes do not enter professional sports and will have to find a career outside of athletics. Therefore, any attempt to treat collegiate athletics like professional sports could be detrimental. The goal of all stakeholders should be to help young men and women develop the ability to have a career and contribute to society.

CONCLUSION

The NCAA strives to prevent unethical behavior in collegiate athletics by objectively setting and enforcing standards of conduct. It also encourages and helps universities establish their own system of compliance and control, since the ultimate responsibility lies with the universities and the cultures they create. Even when colleges impose sanctions on their football programs, the NCAA examines the sanctions objectively and either accepts the sanctions as sufficient or supplements them with more penalties that better match the misconduct. This should not discourage universities from self-reporting, however. While there is no guarantee a football program will not be penalized for reporting misconduct or adopting self-imposed sanctions, the more proactive a football program appears to be, the more consideration it may receive when the NCAA examines the situation. Additionally, a proactive ethical culture creates a reputation for ethics and compliance that may help the program bounce back quicker after a misconduct incident.

The NCAA stands as a compliance-oriented organization. At the same time, it promotes certain values the universities should adopt when developing sports programs. The NCAA rules should not be used as a sole source to build a complete ethics program, but instead used as a minimum benchmark for ethical conduct. NCAA guidelines serve as a framework for how collegiate sports programs should behave and offers consequences for noncompliance. Universities involved in both minor and major violations have come to realize the importance of emphasizing ethics and compliance in their sports programs.

QUESTIONS FOR DISCUSSION

1. How does the NCAA encourage collegiate football programs to develop a culture of ethics and compliance?
2. Is it a valid criticism that the NCAA is based more on compliance than ethical values?
3. How can student–athletes, coaches, and university administrators demonstrate a proactive response to ethics and compliance?

SOURCES

Zac Al-Khateeb, "Bama fans turn out en masse to celebrate the Tide's championship victory," *The Crimson White*, January 22, 2013, http://cw.ua.edu/2013/01/22/bama-fans-turn-out-en-masse-to-celebrate-the-tides-15th-bcs-national-championship/ (accessed May 4, 2015); Associated Press, "NCAA Settles with Former Athletes," *ESPN*, June 9, 2014, http://espn.go.com/college-sports/story/_/id/11055977/ncaa-reaches-20m-settlement-video-game-claims (accessed August 11, 2015); Associated Press, "Penn State lists 1st director of ethics and compliance," *WITF*, March 8, 2013, http://www.witf.org/news/2013/03/penn-state-names-1st-director-of-ethics-and-compliance.php (accessed May 4, 2015); Rachel Axon, "NCAA has settlement agreement in concussion lawsuit," *USA Today*, July 29, 2014, http://www.usatoday.com/story/sports/college/2014/07/29/ncaa-concussion-lawsuit-settlement-75-million/13309191/ (accessed May 5, 2015); Rachel Bachman and Matthew Futterman, "College Football's Big-Money, Big-Risk Business Model," *The Wall Street Journal*, http://online.wsj.com/article/SB100014241278873240240045781694726074078060.html (accessed May 4, 2015); Rachel Bachman, Kevin Helliker, and John Miller, "A Discipline Problem Paterno Fought Penn State Official over Punishment of Players," *The Wall Street Journal*, November 22, 2011, http://online.wsj.com/article/SB10001424052970204443404577052073672561402.html (accessed May 4, 2015); Thomas Bradley, "Breaking it down: 'Tattoo-Gate' scandal costs Ohio State almost $8M," *The Lantern*, June 16, 2012, http://thelantern.com/2012/06/breaking-it-down-tattoo-gate-scandal-costs-ohio-state-almost-8m/ (accessed May 4, 2015); Beth Bragg, "NCAA bans Nanooks from postseason, takes away victories," *Alaska Dispatch News*, November 5, 2014, http://www.adn.com/article/20141105/ncaa-bans-nanooks-postseason-takes-away-victories (accessed May 5, 2015); Chicago Tribune staff, "NCAA should punish the University of North Carolina for cheating scandal," *Chicago Tribune*, November 7, 2014, http://www.chicagotribune.com/news/opinion/editorials/ct-north-carolina-sports-scandal-edit-1108-20141107-story.html (accessed May 5, 2015); College Sports Scholarships, "NCAA and NAIA Sports Recruiting," http://www.collegesportsscholarships.com/ncaa-recruiting-rules-contact-visits.htm (accessed May 4, 2015); Brian Costa, "March's True Madness: Flopping," *The Wall Street Journal*, March 17, 2015, http://www.wsj.com/articles/marchs-true-madness-flopping-1426603260 (accessed May 5, 2015); Abby Davidson, "Why the N.C.A.A.'s Sanctions against Penn State Are Fair," *The New Yorker*, July 23, 2012, http://www.newyorker.com/online/blogs/closeread/2012/07/punishing-penn-state-sandusky-scandal.html (accessed May 4, 2015); Division III Commissioners Association, "Sportsmanship and Ethical Conduct Committee," http://www.diiicomm.org/

committees/sportsmanship/mission (accessed May 4, 2015); "Do college football or basketball teams cheat in recruiting? Does it really happen?" Recruiting-101.com, http://recruiting-101.com/do-college-football-or-basketball-teams-cheat-in-recruiting-%C2%A0does-it-really-happen/ (accessed May 4, 2015); Steve Esack and Peter Hall, "NCAA agrees to restore Joe Paterno's wins," *The Morning Call*, January 16, 2015, http://www.mcall.com/news/breaking/mc-ncaa-penn-state-corman-deal-20150116-story.html#page=1 (accessed March 25, 2015); ESPN.com News Services, "Judge rules against NCAA," *ESPN*, August 9, 2014, http://espn.go.com/college-sports/story/_/id/11328442/judge-rules-ncaa-ed-obannon-antitrust-case (accessed March 25, 2015); Mike Fish, "The Most Powerful Boosters," *ESPN*, January 12, 2006, http://sports.espn.go.com/ncf/news/story?id=2285986 (accessed May 4, 2015); Fox News, "NCAA: Georgia RB Gurley must sit four games for accepting money for autographs," *Fox News*, October 29, 2014, http://www.foxsports.com/college-football/story/ncaa-georgia-rb-todd-gurley-must-sit-four-games-for-accepting-money-for-autographs-102914 (accessed May 5, 2015); Marilee Gallagher, "Penn State Penalties: Did NCAA Give University the 'Death Penalty' in Disguise?" *Bleacher Report*, July 23, 2012, http://bleacherreport.com/articles/1268899-penn-state-penalties-did-ncaa-give-university-the-death-penalty-in-disguise (accessed May 4, 2015); The Ivy League, "NCAA Rules: A Guide for Parents of Student-Athletes," *Brown Bears*, www.brownbears.com/compliance/files/parentsrules.pdf?dec (accessed May 4, 2015); Jerry Hinnen, "Emails released in O'Bannon suit show 'real concern' at NCAA," *CBS Sports*, April 26, 2013, http://www.cbssports.com/collegefootball/blog/eye-on-college-football/22144772/emails-released-in-obannon-suit-show-real-concern-at-ncaa (accessed May 4, 2015); Vince Huth, "Column: NCAA sanctions maybe not severe enough," *The Daily Cardinal*, September 7, 2012, http://host.madison.com/daily-cardinal/sports/columnists/column-ncaa-sanctions-maybe-not-severe-enough/article_a7522bb0-f8b7-11e1-9517-001a4bcf887a.html (accessed May 4, 2015); Scott Jaschik, "The Football Dividend," Inside Higher Ed, October 29, 2012, http://www.insidehighered.com/news/2012/10/29/research-finds-financial-impact-colleges-win-football-games (accessed May 4, 2015); Armen Keteyian (correspondent) and Draggan Mihailovich (producer), "Has college football become a campus commodity?" *CBS News*, originally aired as part of "The College Game" on November 18, 2012, http://www.cbsnews.com/8301-18560_162-57551556/has-college-football-become-a-campus-commodity/ (accessed May 4, 2015); Bill Littlefield, "'Cheating The Spread': Scandals In College Sports," Only A Game, January 26, 2013, http://onlyagame.wbur.org/2013/01/26/cheating-the-spread (accessed May 4, 2015); Kelly Lyell, "CSU assistant sanctioned for NCAA violations at UAA," *Coloradoan*, May 2, 2014, http://www.coloradoan.com/story/sports/college/csu/basketball/2014/05/02/csu-assistant-sanctioned-ncaa-violations-uaa/8633695/ (accessed May 5, 2015); Jo Craven McGinty, "Short on Concussion Data, NCAA Sets Out to Get Some," *The Wall Street Journal*, April 17, 2015, http://www.wsj.com/articles/short-on-concussion-data-ncaa-sets-out-to-get-some-1429264981 (accessed May 5, 2015); National Collegiate Athletic Association Home Page, http://ncaa.org (accessed May 4, 2015); National Collegiate Athletic Association, *2011-2012 NCAA® Division I Manual* (Indianapolis, IN: National Collegiate Athletics Association, 2011); National Collegiate Athletic Association, "2012 AND 2013 NCAA Football Rules and Interpretations," NCAA Publications, http://www.ncaapublications.com/p-4292-2012-and-2013-ncaa-football-rules-and-interpretations.aspx (accessed May 4, 2015); "Ohio State gets one-year bowl ban," *ESPN*, December 22, 2011, http://espn.go.com/college-football/story/_/id/7372757/ohio-state-buckeyes-football-penalties-include-bowl-ban (accessed May 4, 2015); Chip Patterson, "Joe Paterno's family to sue NCAA on behalf of Penn State," *CBS Sports*, May 30, 2013, http://www.cbssports.com/collegefootball/blog/eye-on-college-football/22327207/joe-paterno-family-to-sue-ncaa (accessed May 4, 2015); Penn State, "Becker named as first director of University ethics and compliance," March 7, 2013, http://news.psu.edu/story/267725/2013/03/07/administration/becker-named-first-director-university-ethics-and-compliance (accessed May 4, 2015); Penn State, "Employee Ethics and Compliance Hotline," Office of Internal Audit, May 13, 2014, http://internalaudit.psu.edu/news/employee-ethics-and-compliance-hotline (accessed May 4, 2015); "Penn State Football Coach Sex Abuse Scandal: Officials Step Down," *YouTube*, November 7, 2011, http://www.youtube.com/watch?v=zkfcYHlvYpU (accessed May 4, 2015); "The Penn State Scandal, Piece by Piece," *Pittsburgh Post-Gazette*, http://blogs.post-gazette.com/scandal/timeline.php (accessed May 4, 2015); Darren Rovell, "EA Sports settles with ex-players," *ESPN*, September 26, 2013, http://espn.go.com/college-football/story/_/id/9728042/ea-sports-stop-producing-college-football-game (accessed March 25, 2015); Ralph D. Russo, "Head of NCAA enforcement:

Academic misconduct on rise," *Yahoo! Finance*, January 28, 2015, http://sports.yahoo.com/news/head-ncaa-enforcement-academic-misconduct-rise-225453967--spt.html (accessed May 5, 2015); Christopher P. Ryan, "Penn State NCAA Sanctions Go Too Far," *Policymic*, http://www.policymic.com/articles/11704/penn-state-ncaa-sanctions-go-too-far (accessed May 4, 2015); Mark Schlabach, "NCAA sends message to Ohio State," *ESPN*, December 20, 2011, http://espn.go.com/college-football/story/_/id/7373708/ncaa-sends-message-sanctions-ohio-state-buckeyes (accessed May 4, 2015); Trevor Stevens and Jennifer Keith, "Funding for Kyle Field Renovation Gains Clarity," *The Battalion Online*, January 17, 2013, http://www.thebatt.com/funding-for-kyle-field-renovation-gains-clarity-1.2972858#.UVdYZFeMBGM (accessed April 23, 2013); Mark Torrence, "Crimson Tide weight room gets $9 million makeover," *The Crimson White*, February 28, 2013, http://cw.ua.edu/2013/02/28/crimson-tide-weight-room-gets-9-million-makeover/ (accessed May 4, 2015); Dan Treadway, "Why Does the NCAA Exist?" *The Huffington Post*, August 6, 2013, http://www.huffingtonpost.com/daniel-treadway/johnny-manziel-ncaa-eligibility_b_3020985.html (accessed May 4, 2015).; USA Today Editorial Board, "NFL injuries bruise glitzy image: Our view," *USA Today*, April 30, 2015, http://www.usatoday.com/story/opinion/2015/04/30/nfl-draft-injuries-concussions-helmets-brain-disease-editorials-debates/26665097/ (accessed May 5, 2015); USCHO staff, "After NCAA violations, Alaska will lose scholarships, postseason play and must vacate past wins," *USCHO News*, November 5, 2014, http://www.uscho.com/2014/11/05/after-ncaa-violations-alaska-will-lose-scholarships-postseason-play-and-must-vacate-past-wins/ (accessed May 5, 2015); Steve Wieberg, "Sanctions against Ohio State Just the Latest NCAA Scandal," *USA Today*, December 21, 2011, http://usatoday30.usatoday.com/sports/college/football/bigten/story/2011-12-20/ohio-state-sanctions-ncaa-scandals/52132580/1 (accessed May 4, 2015); Dan Wolken, "NCAA enforcement staff's tasks won't get any easier," *USA Today*, February 18, 2012, http://www.usatoday.com/story/sports/college/2013/02/18/miami-ncaa-enforcement-ameen-najjar-julie-roe-lach-mark-emmert-ken-wainstein/1929011/ (accessed May 4, 2015); Charlie Zegers, "Show Cause," About.com, http://basketball.about.com/od/collegebasketballglossary/g/show-cause.htm (accessed May 4, 2015).

CASE 7

Google: The Quest to Balance Privacy with Profit*

INTRODUCTION

Google's ease of use and superior search results have propelled the search engine to its number one status, ousting the early dominance of competitors such as WebCrawler and Infoseek. Even later offerings by other large tech companies using comparable algorithms, such as Bing by Microsoft, have failed to make significant inroads, with Google retaining an impressive 65 percent global market share. As Google gained popularity, it began expanding into a number of different ventures, including multiple advertising platforms, a digital book publishing space, and social networking. It has spent billions to acquire hundreds of companies in a variety of industries, from robotics to smart home devices to intangibles such as voice recognition technologies. Approximately 3.5 billion searches a day are performed through Google's search engine.

As is common with most large companies, Google has experienced its share of ethical issues. Its mantra "Don't Be Evil" was called into question after it allowed the Chinese government to censor aspects of some of its sites in order to enter the market. Google has also been investigated and sued by multiple governments based on concerns that its widespread reach and market power violate antitrust laws.

The hot ethical topic on many Internet users' minds, however, is the company's approach to Internet privacy and collection of user information. To improve the effectiveness of its services, including customized search results, targeted ads, and more precise integration of its various offerings, Google tracks and leverages user information without explicit permission (although Google's privacy statement informs users about the record-keeping, and Google does allow users to opt out of some forms of tracking). Such tracking is common practice for Internet companies, but Google's deep access to so many different types of user information, as well as the seemingly dismissive attitude it has sometimes exhibited toward the public's concern, has led people to question whether Google violates its users' privacy. In light of the increasing amount of cyberattacks and the government's determination to crack down on these illegal attacks, consumers also worry their private information, tracked and stored by Google's algorithms, might be compromised.

This case analyzes Google's efforts to be a good corporate citizen and the privacy issues the company has faced. The analysis starts by providing background on Google,

*This material was developed by Jennifer Sawayda, Michelle Urban, and Isaac Emmanuel under the direction of O.C. Ferrell and Linda Ferrell, © 2015. This case is intended for classroom discussion rather than to illustrate effective or ineffective handling of administrative, ethical, or legal decisions by management. All sources for this case were obtained through publicly available material.

its technology, and its initiatives. Google's core principles will be discussed as well as its efforts to be a socially responsible company. We then discuss the criticisms levied against Google, including its initial attempts to break into the censored Chinese market, its tracking of users, and more recent changes to its privacy policies. We examine how Google has sometimes clashed with government authorities. Finally, we review some of the legal methods that have been proposed to regulate Internet data collection practices and Google's response to the proposals.

COMPANY CULTURE

Google adopted a decentralized approach to empower its employees. Its corporate headquarters in Mountain View, California, is known as the Googleplex and consists of a campus containing such amenities as on-site gymnasiums and swimming pools, an outdoor volleyball court, laundry services, and even high-tech "nap pods" for optimized downtime. When Sergey Brin and Larry Page founded the company, they recognized employees had to put in long hours to make the company not only successful but flexible enough to adapt to the changing environment. Thus, Google employees are provided with benefits to make the complex their second home. The company strives to make its corporate culture fun and innovative. In fact, two of its core principles, "You can be creative without a suit" and "You don't need to be at your desk to need an answer," demonstrate the company's divergence from a more formal office environment. The company's 10 core principles are outlined in Table 1.

At the same time, Google works to ensure it has top talent at the company. While it reinvents the office experience, it also takes different tactics in recruiting to ensure it hires the most creative, talented individuals. For instance, Google recruiters take a bottom-up approach when reading résumés. Recognizing that top items such as education and work experience do not always guarantee the applicant is innovative, some Google recruiters start at the bottom of the résumé where applicants put more creative information. This type of mentality—being more concerned with hiring creative people than those who

TABLE 1 Google's Ten Core Principles

Focus on the user and all else will follow.
It's best to do one thing really, really well.
Fast is better than slow.
Democracy on the web works.
You don't need to be at your desk to need an answer.
You can make money without doing evil.
There's always more information out there.
The need for information crosses all borders.
You can be serious without a suit.
Great just isn't good enough.

Source: Google, "Ten things we know to be true," http://www.google.com/about/company/philosophy/ (accessed May 22, 2015)

excelled in school—meshed well with Google's famous informal policy of allowing employees to spend up to 20 percent of the workweek pursuing their own unique projects. Not only did this policy make employees feel empowered, it led to some of Google's standout products including Gmail and key improvements to AdSense. However, in 2013 this "20% time" policy was largely discontinued after Google determined it was splitting its focus among too many projects. It decided to commit itself to putting "more wood behind fewer arrows." Nevertheless, Google's innovative company culture is one of the major reasons why it has become successful in so many different market niches.

PRODUCTS

Although Google started out as a search engine, it has since branched out into a variety of fields, including consumer electronics and productivity tools. While it would be too long to list all of Google's products, some of the more popular offerings are described below.

Search Engine

According to Larry Page, a good search engine "understands exactly what you mean and gives you back exactly what you want." This philosophy was the founding principle behind the creation of Google and is a top reason why the Google search engine surpassed its competitors.

Google could not have gained such prominence without an in-depth search index of the web's content. The company creates this index using programs called "Googlebots"—automated web crawlers that visit webpages, add their content to the index, and then follow the links on those pages to other parts of the Internet. This process is constantly ongoing, with every indexed page periodically revisited to ensure the index contains the most updated material. Google's index is one of the most extensive in the world, at well over 100 million gigabytes worth of information.

A good search engine's index must not only be comprehensive, but also easily accessible. Therefore, Google uses technology such as PageRank to organize search results according to their perceived relevancy. When a user types a search term into Google's search box, Google's index matches the term with what is deemed the most relevant materials and creates a list of these materials for the user. Each search result is followed by a few sentences describing the webpage (called a "snippet"). To maintain a competitive edge, Google responds quickly to its users' queries, with a response time on Google's side of approximately one-fourth of a second so users get information as quickly as possible.

Advertising

Google's main source of revenue is advertising. In 2014 the company earned over $59 billion in advertising revenue. Google's signature advertising platform is Google AdWords, first introduced in 2000. Google AdWords differs from traditional advertising in that advertisers do not pay Google anything upfront, but only pay when customers take action—either by viewing the ad (pay-per-impression), clicking on the ad (pay-per-click), or performing a certain predefined action such as making an online purchase (pay-per-conversion). This model is attractive to advertisers because they only pay when their ad is effective, as determined by the metric of their choice. The twist, however, is that Google does not set ad prices, but rather puts its limited advertising space up for auction; companies submit "bids" for how much they will pay per customer action, and higher bids generally get more ad time (other factors are also considered, such as how popular an ad has been so far). Google makes no money from even a very high bid if customers do not engage with the ad. Advertisers are therefore incentivized to bid high, which benefits Google's bottom line. Google promotes the model as a win-win; it makes a profit, and companies get more bang for their advertising buck.

Google leverages its various product offerings to provide a variety of attractive advertising options. Companies can choose to have their ads displayed as "sponsored links" alongside search results for certain keywords, or as banners on any of the more than two million websites that display Google ads in return for a cut of the profits (known as the Google Display Network). YouTube is another option, offering video ads before or during videos as well as traditional banner space on the site. Mobile is also becoming a critical advertising space, through both searches on mobile devices and apps that allow advertising. Google is even experimenting with bringing the AdSense model to traditional television advertising, testing its ability to serve targeted ads and track viewer response over its new cable-like Fiber TV service (currently only offered in Kansas City, Missouri). Improving the effectiveness of its AdWords service is a key driver of Google's collection of user information—the more it knows about its users, the more targeting options it can provide to advertisers and the more precisely it can serve targeted ads to the desired consumer segments.

Web Browser

Google Chrome is the second most popular web browser in the world with 25 percent market share. When Google Chrome was released, it was praised for its unparalleled speed, support, and security, forcing competitors to scramble to catch up. The Chrome browser is known for loading within seconds and maintaining a simplistic design to make it easier for users to navigate. Chrome is also updated more frequently than most of the other browsers, allowing Google to quickly push out new features and security improvements. The Chrome Web Apps Store contains a wide selection of apps and extensions, providing additional flexibility and functionality for users.

Email Account

Google's email account service, called Gmail, has over 500 million active users and is the world's largest email service provider. Gmail was initially revolutionary for the huge amount of space it offered—1 gigabyte per user when rivals were only offering 100 megabytes or less—and the integration of Google search, which gave users a robust way to search within their stored emails. Since then, Gmail has continued to offer popular features such as filters and labels for users to organize their mail, a variety of add-ons for special functionality from the former Google Labs, and deep integration with other Google products such as Google+, Hangouts, YouTube, Maps, Docs, and Calendar.

YouTube

In 2006 Google acquired video sharing site YouTube for $1.65 billion. YouTube allows users to upload and share original videos and has become the third most visited of all websites (Google.com is the most visited site in the world). Everyone from global corporations to the average consumer uses YouTube to share videos ranging from video blogs to parodies, to corporate messages to news events. By selling video advertising slots before and during videos, as well as placing banner ads in free space on the site, Google has made millions in advertising revenue. Additionally, YouTube content creators can share in advertising profits from their videos through YouTube's Partner Program, allowing popular "YouTubers" to make careers out of their channels.

Although YouTube opened up new opportunities in marketing and entertainment, it has not been without its share of controversy. YouTube has been sued by organizations such as Viacom for copyright infringement after finding copyrighted content on YouTube's site. YouTube's Community Guidelines specifically direct: "Only upload videos that you made or that you're authorized to use." However, not all users heed the warning. To detect and eliminate copyrighted material, YouTube enables users to "flag" videos for copyright infringement. If, upon review, the flag is found to be valid, the offending video is removed. YouTube also provides a more automated system called Content ID for certain situations, which automatically compares newly uploaded videos to a database of copyrighted material and notifies the copyright holder if a match is found. Google believes providing tools to enable self-interested copyright owners to protect their property is the best way to police YouTube, arguing it is simply not feasible for the company to screen the more than 300 hours of video uploaded to the site every minute.

Android

In 2005 Google acquired the startup firm Android Inc., which worked on mobile phone software technology. In 2008 the Android operating system was released by the Open Handset Alliance, a team of organizations led by Google whose mission is to promote development of open standards for mobile devices. The Android operating system is an open source platform, meaning the source code is available for outside users to view and use. However, Google has copyrighted the Android name and logo, as well as some proprietary features of Google's version of the software such as the Google App Store. Companies that wish to claim they make "Android" devices must enter into a licensing agreement with Google. The Android operating system is most often used in mobile devices and tablets but can also be found on other devices, including full computers, game consoles, and digital cameras.

Android has become the most popular mobile operating system in the world, making up nearly 80 percent of the market. Apple's iOS, while undeniably a strong competitor with a loyal customer base, trails far behind with 18 percent of the smartphone market. One reason for Android's larger market share is that, unlike Apple and its iPhone and iPad, Google is not the only company that makes Android phones and tablets; Samsung, HTC, Motorola, T-Mobile, Sony, and many other manufacturers develop Android devices. However, there are disadvantages to this approach as well. For example, Amazon built its mobile offerings, the Fire Phone and Kindle Fire tablets, off the Android open source code, and now competes directly with Google in the mobile sphere. Google is also a direct player in the mobile device market with its Nexus line of phones and tablets, placing it in the uncomfortable position of competing with its business partners. Still, Android has been a great success for Google, vastly increasing the company's reach into electronics. One top Google executive called the initial Android Inc. acquisition the company's "best deal ever."

Google+

In 2011 Google launched its social network Google+, positioning it as an alternative to Facebook that solved many of Facebook's glaring issues such as lack of privacy controls. Interest was initially strong. Within a month, Google+ had over 20 million unique visitors, and by 2013 Google claimed the social network had 300 million members that were active at least monthly. However, there were signs that these numbers were somewhat misleading because most "active" users spent very little time on the site, far less than average user time on Facebook. An independent analysis in 2015 concluded Google+ had only 111 million active profiles, and only 6.7 million with more than 50 total posts. By comparison, Facebook had an estimated 1.44 billion monthly active users. Many industry experts have called Google+ a "ghost town."

Even if Google+ has not ended up posing a significant threat to Facebook, it has been very successful in helping Google unify its products and better understand its users. Before Google+, all of Google's online products—Gmail, YouTube, Google Docs, Google Drive, etc.—required their own separate logins, meaning Google could not tell if the same user was using multiple services. Google used Google+ to create a single login system. Every Google user now has a Google+ profile, whether or not they ever access it, and uses the credentials of that profile to log in to nearly all the Google services they use. Coupled with Google's requirement that Google+ users provide their real names, this system allows Google to track individual user activity across all its sites, provides a more consistent feel across its services and better customizes them for individual user needs, and more.

Furthermore, some features of Google+ have become very popular. Google+ Hangouts, which unifies Google's online messaging, text messaging, audio and video call, conferencing, and other communications offerings into one service, is highly praised and has a strong base of loyal users. Similarly, Google+ Photos, an online photo management, backup, sharing, and basic editing service, is considered by fans to be the best service of its kind. Google has recently announced Google+ will be reorganized to break out these two services as separate products—named Hangouts and Photos, respectively—while Google+ itself will be renamed as Streams.

Expanding the Product Mix

Google offers a number of other popular products to businesses and consumers. Google Translate and Google Maps offer automated translation and mapping/directional services. Google Analytics tracks and freely reports website traffic statistics, giving businesses a market research tool to understand how customers are interacting with their websites. Google Drive allows users to store files in the cloud and share them with others. The service offers 15 gigabytes of free storage per user, and more can be purchased if desired.

Google is also known for its forays into exciting and cutting-edge technologies, especially through its secretive Google X department, whose mission is to develop "moonshots"—science fiction-like technologies that have a slim chance of succeeding but could change the world if they do. Research projects underway at Google X include self-driving car technology and a drone-based product delivery system. One of the only Google X initiatives that has resulted in an actual product so far is Project Glass, which looked into developing a real-time heads-up display for the average consumer. The end result was Google Glass, a wearable computer in the form of glasses worn on the face that can display information in front of the wearer's eyes, respond to verbal and movement commands, and more. Google Glass was publicly released in 2014, and although it has received only mixed feedback from the consumer market, it is already being applied to a wide variety of commercial applications, from providing doctors with hands-free information during surgery to helping autistic children interact with their environment. However, the device has also created privacy concerns, as the glasses are so unassuming that it is relatively easy to record others without their permission. There is concern that students could use Google Glass to cheat by wearing it during tests without anyone noticing. Cheating concerns are not limited to the classroom; many casinos have banned Google Glass from their floors. Google ended up pulling the prototype but plans to release a more developed version in the future.

GOOGLE'S INITIATIVES

Like all major corporations, Google is expected to act with integrity and give back to the communities where it does business. Google has therefore invested in a number of initiatives that support economic development, environmental awareness, and charitable endeavors.

Google Ventures

In 2009 Google formed Google Ventures as a separate entity to provide funding for startup firms. The venture capital fund began with $100 million in seed money, and now receives $300 million from Google each year as well as managing almost $2 billion in assets of its own. It invests this money in startup companies at the forefront of technological innovation. The money goes not only to firms that market Internet-based technologies or consumer electronics, but also to green technology firms, biotechnology and life-sciences companies, and more. One of its best-known investments is popular ride-sharing company Uber. Google Ventures goal is to invest in entrepreneurs that can change the world through technology by having "a healthy disregard for the impossible," mirroring what the Google X department is trying to do within Google itself.

Google Green

Google has recognized the business opportunities that come from adopting greener operations and technologies. Greener technology not only saves Google money in the long run with decreased energy costs, it also enables the company to create greener products for consumers. According to Google, running its servers for one month uses less energy than leaving a light on for three hours, and providing a user with one month of all of Google's online services uses less energy than driving a car 1 mile. Google also claims its data centers are 50 percent more energy efficient than the industry average and that 35 percent of its power comes from renewable energy sources. Google has purchased carbon offsets to reduce its effective emissions to zero since 2007. For employees, Google offers a shuttle system run on biodiesel, an on-campus car sharing program, company bicycles to commute between buildings and departments, and the largest electric vehicle charging station in the country. Other green successes for Google include a large solar installation on its campus and LEED-certified buildings.

Google.org

Google.org is the charitable arm of the organization. According to its website, the organization "develops technologies to help address global challenges and supports innovative partners through grants, investments and in-kind resources." Google.org contributes grant money, develops tools for nonprofits, and provides disaster relief. The tools Google.org offers include Google for Nonprofits and Google Dengue & Flu Trends. Google for

Nonprofits provides resources such as discounts on Google products and free AdWords advertising to nonprofit organizations. Google Dengue & Flu Trends is an innovative use of Google's existing data gathering; it attempts to predict outbreaks of the flu and dengue diseases by tracking where Google search requests related to the illnesses are coming from. Other organizations use the predictions to more effectively combat the diseases. Google.org has also partnered with nonprofits to offer them use of Google's considerable resources. For example, it provided tools to the National Center for Missing and Exploited Children to help the nonprofit in its fight against global child exploitation.

Google and Employee Charitable Initiatives

In addition to its work through Google.org, Google contributes hundreds of millions of dollars directly to various charities and socially responsible organizations. Just before the company's initial public offering in 2004, Google's cofounder Larry Page promised Google would continually contribute 1 percent of its profits, 1 percent of its equity, and a significant amount of employee time to philanthropic endeavors. In terms of giving employee time, Google encourages employees to get involved in giving back to their communities. For instance, Google matches up to $6,000 of each employee's contributions to nonprofits annually. Google also encourages employees to take time to volunteer in their communities, especially during its annual GoogleServe event, which sets aside one to two weeks each June for Google staff worldwide to get involved in their communities and donate time to good causes. Google also participates in the Dollars for Doers Initiative, in which companies agree to donate monetary amounts for every employee hour volunteered. For every five hours a Google employee volunteers at a nonprofit, Google will donate $50 to that organization.

PRIVACY

Being a large company, Google has many risks and ethical issues it must constantly address. In many ways Google helped advance ethical conduct in the web and technology industries. Google has been named among *Ethisphere*'s World's Most Ethical Companies for six years running due to its contributions to the community and the environment. The company also consistently ranks among *Fortune* magazine's "100 Best Companies to Work for" because of its fun and innovative work environment.

At the same time, Google has been accused of questionable activity, from antitrust issues to copyright infringement. For instance, Google's announcement that it would be digitizing the collections of several prominent libraries and making them available online through Google Books sparked outrage from publishers who still owned the copyrights. Google only made books out of copyright fully available—for books still within copyright, just small snippets could be viewed—but the Author's Guild sued Google over it, arguing the arrangement was without the permission of its members and violated their copyrights. Google eventually won that fight, with a judge ruling that Google's actions fell under fair use of copyrighted material.

Google has also faced intense antitrust scrutiny from the European community. Competitors in Europe claim Google uses its dominant market position to promote its own offerings and demote rival results in search listings. In 2010 the European Union (EU) began investigating Google's practices. Google proposed concessions and business changes it was willing to make to satisfy competitors and investigators, but none were accepted, and the EU announced formal charges against Google in 2015. Although the initial charges are very narrow—only that Google favors its comparison-shopping service over competitors—onlookers believe the accusations are likely to broaden, similar to the EU's investigation into Microsoft which eventually led to $2.3 billion in fines and significant changes in how Microsoft conducted business worldwide.

For the sake of brevity, this case will focus on one major ethical issue Google has continually wrestled with as it seeks to expand its reach: privacy. The advent of the Internet and mobile technology provides so many opportunities for stakeholders that many do not realize the cost for this information might be significant portions of their privacy. Many consumers are shocked to find that web companies such as Google and Facebook track their online activity and use this information to tailor advertisements or sell to marketers. Other consumers feel that Google's use of their personal information is a small price to pay in exchange for access to the company's superior services. For Google—which offers so much free content and gets most of its revenue from advertising—this information is extremely valuable to its continued business success. Google's privacy policy details what information it collects and how it uses that information. For instance, Google shares information with its partners but claims this information is non-identifiable to specific users. Google says it does not share any identifiable information with outside parties unless it has user consent.

Despite Google's attempts to be transparent, there are ethical gray areas regarding the collection and use of data. Because there is still little legislation regulating how Internet companies gather and employ user information, it is tempting for firms to push the limits on privacy. Going too far, however, creates reputational and legal problems. Google has sometimes appeared to take a cavalier attitude toward privacy. For instance, former CEO Eric Schmidt was quoted as saying, "If you have something that you don't want anyone to know, maybe you shouldn't be doing it in the first place." In 2007 Google was given a "hostile to privacy" rating by watchdog organization Privacy International. Although Google is the most popular search engine, one poll found that 52 percent of Google users have concerns about their privacy when using it. This could be a potential obstacle for Google since consumer trust plays a big role in how they interact with a company. The following sections discuss some of the major privacy issues Google has experienced.

Search Queries

One of the major privacy criticisms levied against Google is that the company keeps track of users' search terms. Consider all of the things you have ever searched for using Google's search engine. Now consider how comfortable you feel knowing the company has recorded and stored all those search terms…forever. This tracking cannot be turned off—users can disable their Google web history to remove any external record of searches and prevent the information from being used in certain ways, but Google will continue to record and store search terms for internal purposes. To be fair, this practice is not limited to Google—many other Internet firms do the same. However, because Google is the most popular search engine in the world, it is more heavily scrutinized.

The big question users ask is whether their search terms can be traced back to them personally. Google claims that although it stores users' search terms, after 18 months the data becomes "anonymized" and theoretically untraceable. However, critics debate this claim because supposedly anonymized data from other search engines had later been matched to specific users. Google claims it treats this information with respect, using it to refine its search engine. Yet under the Third Party Doctrine and the Patriot Act the U.S. government could subpoena the data if it is deemed necessary for national security. Needless to say, Google's storage of users' search terms is a controversial topic. In fact, several smaller search engines such as DuckDuckGo use the fact that they do not track user activity as a competitive differentiator from Google.

Tracking Users

Tracking users has become a major issue for Google. A storm of criticism was unleashed when government regulators and consumers learned the company's phones tracked users' locations. It was revealed that Android phones contained location-logging features enabling the firm to collect GPS coordinates of its users as well as the coordinates of nearby Wi-Fi networks. Similar tracking features were found on the Apple iPhone. The revelations spurred legislators to write letters to Google asking for clarification on how they track users and use this information.

Privacy advocates claimed these tracking features violated users' right to privacy, particularly since most users did not know about the feature. Google defended its phone tracking feature, stating the information it gathered was necessary to build Google's location-based network and allow it to effectively compete. It also claimed this data is often necessary for certain mobile applications and websites to work.

Google also tracks users on the Internet. For Google, offering advertisers the ability to specifically target their ads to desired users based on their interests is invaluable to remaining competitive in the advertising market. Google also uses this information to customize its services to individual users. For example, users will see different results for the same Google search terms based on what Google believes they most likely want, based on what it knows about them. Many privacy advocates do not like this pervasive use of tracking, and there is ongoing concern by regulators and others over how Google uses the information it collects. Google's privacy policy does allow users to opt out of many tracking functions, but users must actively do so—the default is to be tracked. This is especially problematic for the many users that do not realize they are being tracked and/or do not know how to use Google's settings to opt out. All of the popular web browsers, including Google Chrome, now include a "Do Not Track" option, which indicates to websites that the user does not wish to be tracked. However, the designation has no legal or regulatory authority and has so far remained mostly symbolic, with many websites simply ignoring it.

On the other hand, supporters of Google maintain that tracking is necessary to provide the best services to users. These services are often free because Google is able to generate revenue through advertising. Tracking also allows Google to customize its services to individual user needs. Consumers must therefore be proactive in deciding whether they place greater value on their privacy or Google's free services.

Although some people do not appear to mind having their web activity tracked in exchange for Google's free services, Google received heavy backlash for bypassing anti-tracking mechanisms. In 2012 security analysts revealed that Google was using loopholes in Apple's Safari browser to ignore its default privacy settings while simultaneously telling Safari users they were protected. The browser's default settings prevented installation of certain types of Internet "cookies"—streams of data placed on a user's computer when he or she visits certain sites. However, Google's cookies were still being installed. Google claimed the bypass was a mistake, meant only to help its Google+ "+1" button (similar to Facebook's "like") work properly on third-party websites, and removed it immediately after it was made public. Still, the Federal Trade Commission (FTC) launched an investigation to determine whether Google had violated a previous agreement to refrain from misrepresenting its privacy practices to the public. Google eventually paid $22.5 million to settle the FTC charges and an additional $17 million to settle similar charges brought by 37 states and the District of Columbia. Although Google might have legitimate reasons to track user activity, bypassing default mechanisms appeared deceptive.

Google has also been accused of failing to respect user privacy in the real world. In 2010 Google announced it had accidentally scanned data from some users' personal wireless networks in the U.K. Google uses vans with special detection equipment and cameras to drive around collecting data and photos for its location-based services. Unfortunately, because of software Google said had inadvertently been uploaded onto the company's equipment, its vans also scanned wireless networks of nearby residences and collected activity data from any networks that were unsecured and open, including URLs, emails, text messages, video and audio files, and more. Google promised the Information Commissioner's Office in the U.K. it would destroy the data it collected from U.K. users. However, a later investigation in 2012 revealed Google still retained some of this user data, placing the company in noncompliance with the agreement. Although Google apologized and called this retention of data another error, the violation likely exacerbated its image of being a firm that disregards privacy.

Soon after the U.K. incident, it was discovered Google had been collecting the same type of information from unsecured residential wireless networks in other countries as well. In the United States, Google was fined $25,000 by the Federal Communications Commission (FCC) for deliberately delaying and impeding its investigation. Evidence was uncovered suggesting that Google's collection of this information may not have been accidental but rather intentionally set up by Google engineers. Google asked the FCC to keep its findings confidential, but later pre-emptively released them itself after the FCC refused. The investigation led to a $7 million settlement among Google, the FCC, and 38 states and the District of Columbia. At least seven other countries also found Google guilty of similar activity in their jurisdictions.

Yet another privacy-related incident for Google involved the Google Play App Store. A developer who started selling a mobile application through Google's app store was shocked by the amount of information he was given about his customers, including their names, locations, and email addresses, even though nowhere in the app buying process were customers asked to give consent to release that information. The developer argued that this practice violated Google's privacy policy, which stated that identifiable information would never be given to third parties without user consent. Some privacy experts agreed with the developer; others did not, stating that the information shared was minimal and of the type commonly expected to be given out in making any purchase. Still, Google's approach to privacy continues to be a subject of controversy and debate.

Privacy Audits

Although Google has faced lawsuits from consumers claiming the company violated their privacy rights, a lack of Internet legislation enables Google to continue many of its practices. However, Google found itself in trouble with governmental authorities after allegedly violating its own privacy policies. In 2010 Google launched the failed social networking platform Google Buzz. Users with Gmail accounts received an email that gave them the option to join or decline joining the social network. However, most of those who chose to join were unaware that the identities of their frequent contacts on Gmail would be made publicly available on the Internet through Google Buzz. Although users could opt out of having this information released, they claimed the opt-out features were difficult to locate. Other accusations claimed that even those users who opted out of joining Google Buzz were still enrolled in certain features of the social network, and that those who requested to leave the network were not fully removed.

Although Google worked to fix these problems after many user complaints, the FTC launched an investigation. It found Google had acted deceptively and violated its own privacy policies. Google agreed to settle with the FTC by agreeing to never again misrepresent its privacy practices and allowing approved third-party firms to conduct privacy audits every other year regarding how the company uses information. These audits will take place for 20 years from the date of the settlement. That same year, Facebook agreed to a similar deal after allegedly violating its users' rights to privacy, and other companies have since become subject to privacy audits as well. If Google's audits reveal problems, the FTC may impose fines of $16,000 for each violation per day.

These audits are a blow to Google's operations. As one of the first Internet companies to have this kind of audit imposed on it, the company will have to tread carefully regarding how it collects and uses information. On the other hand, Google might choose to see this as an opportunity to improve its internal controls and privacy practices to ensure user information is respected. Doing so could gain more trust from users and prevent future legislative action against the company. So far, Google's record in honoring the settlement is mixed. Its 2012 privacy audit found no issues, but that same year the FTC found Google's bypassing of the Safari browser's default privacy controls to be a violation of the agreement and fined the company for it. As one of the world's largest Internet companies, the actions Google takes in this area will significantly impact the future activities of other companies.

From Many Privacy Policies to One

For the majority of its history, Google has had separate privacy policies for most of its products, each detailing how Google collects and uses information for that product. By 2012 Google's rapid growth and expansion from just search into an Internet behemoth had resulted in over 70 separate Google privacy policies across its offerings. This was beneficial in one sense, as consumers who took the time to read the policies could understand in great detail how Google was operating each product. On the other hand, the overwhelming amount of policies was confusing, tedious, and time-consuming to sift through, and the average consumer would have been hard-pressed to decipher them.

In 2012 Google announced it was unifying its myriad privacy policies into just one, which would govern Google's practices across its entire organization. At first glance, this seemed like an efficient change. However, it had many subtler implications that sparked widespread concern. Could consumers still opt out of specific information-sharing in individual products? Did the new policy adequately explain all the different ways Google gathered and shared information so consumers could be properly informed? Did the new policy expand Google's information-gathering power under the guise of making things simpler?

One especially concerning aspect of Google's new policy was that it allowed the company to take all the information it gathered on its users across all its products and combine them together. Coupled with the new unified login system based on Google+, the new privacy policy allowed Google to use information on a much larger and more encompassing scale. Users' Google searches might affect the ads they see on their Android phones, YouTube browsing histories could be combined with Gmail activity to better understand user interests, and more. Was this "all-seeing eye" approach acceptable, especially for such a large company with so many widely used services?

Understandably, the announcement of a unified privacy policy led to considerable backlash. Google received letters from Congress members and U.S. attorneys general asking questions and expressing concern about the new policy. Competitors such as Microsoft took advantage of the situation to run ads drawing consumer attention to Google's potentially unsettling approach to user privacy. The EU asked Google to delay implementation of the policy until it could study and better understand its implications. In defending itself, Google emphasized that it was not gathering any more information than before, nor was it making any changes to existing user ability to opt out of information-sharing or use product-specific privacy settings. It was merely making its existing practices simpler and clearer for customers to understand, as well as improving its own ability to serve users by unifying the information it gathered across offerings. It argued the new policy was in legal compliance and refused to delay the transition. On March 1, 2012, the unified policy took effect.

Google's new privacy policy was poorly received in Europe. The EU Justice Commissioner questioned the legality of Google's new policy according to EU law. French data regulators launched an investigation concerning the new policy, believing the policy might not adhere to EU Internet transparency and privacy laws. Google maintained its new policy met EU regulations. However, in 2013 six European countries banded together to take legal action against Google for not complying with the requests of the government. Google has since been fined by several European countries for breaking their privacy or data protection laws, including nearly $1 million by Spain and $204,000 by France. The Netherlands threatened a fine of up to $15 million if Google does not comply with its desired changes. The company narrowly avoided yet another fine in the U.K. by agreeing to change its privacy policy for U.K. users, and there are signs it may make such a change Europe-wide in an attempt to allay the concerns of the EU and its member nations. Google has learned that activities which are legal in one country might not be legal in another.

The public's reaction to Google's unified privacy policy once again brings to light the more general debate over the company's gathering and use of user information. Supporters argue that Google uses this information to create improved services for users. It helps the firm remain competitive with strong rivals such as Apple and Facebook. Critics are concerned that Google is constantly overreaching and seems to have little actual concern for user privacy, only slowing or backtracking when it is forced to by consumer backlash or governmental regulators. Critics are also worried by the ease with which Google appears to change its policies, which could spell trouble for users and their privacy rights. These concerns are especially serious because so many users depend on some aspect of Google, whether it be Gmail, Google+, Android phones, or other services.

"Right to Be Forgotten"

In 2014 the European Union's highest court ruled that EU citizens have a "right to be forgotten." In other words, consumers have the right to prevent certain types of content from showing up in online search results. Such content includes results that are inadequate, irrelevant, no longer relevant, or excessive. The court decision allows individuals to petition search engines to remove such content from search results, and if refused, to take the matter to a local data protection authority for adjudication.

The court decision sent shockwaves through the Internet search community. Was this censorship, or the beginning of an acknowledgment that search engines have a duty to at least somewhat curate their results? Was this a victory for privacy, or a defeat for freedom of speech? How will search companies be able to properly decide whether removal requests are legitimate or stretch beyond the boundaries of the court decision?

In response to the ruling, Google set up a process by which it processes "right to be forgotten" requests. The claimant fills out an online form, which is reviewed and processed by a team of Google lawyers, paralegals, and engineers. "Easy" cases, where the correct decision is relatively clear, are made by that team. Difficult cases are forwarded to a senior panel of Google experts and executives to decide. For instance, a published U.S. record of the name of a 16-year-old German individual convicted in the United States of a sex crime could be controversial because in Germany the record would not be published due to his minor status. Google also releases periodic "Transparency Reports" providing information on right to be forgotten requests. So far, Google has received over 250,000 requests, and has approved 41.3 percent of them.

Google and other Internet search companies continue to express their opposition to the "right to be forgotten" concept, and many others agree. Some are opposed to it out-right, citing freedom of speech concerns; others believe it may be a good idea but that private companies such as Google should not be the ones deciding which links to keep and which to take down. Simultaneously, EU regulators are dissatisfied with how Google has chosen to interpret the court decision. For example, Google is only removing links from its Europe-specific search engines such as Google.fr or Google.co.uk, meaning anyone can simply move to Google.com to find the hidden content. Simultaneously, other areas of the world are considering the right to be forgotten idea, with varying success. In Mexico courts have ruled for some individuals petitioning Google to remove content, but critics worry the right is being used largely by politically powerful individuals to remove unsightly aspects of their past. California has passed a law requiring websites to provide a mechanism by which minors can have content they post removed, believing children should not be pun-ished for online missteps. Hong Kong's top privacy regulator has embraced the concept wholeheartedly, suggesting Google should apply the EU ruling to its operations globally.

It is still too early to say what the long-term implications of the "right to be forgot-ten" will be. However, it adds another wrinkle in Google's privacy concerns. Now, at least in some parts of the world, Google must not only worry about the information it collects itself, but also about what information posted by third parties might be showing in its search results.

Google in China

Google has had a tough time in China. When Google decided to enter the world's most populous country, it faced an ethical dilemma. On the one hand, Google did not want to miss the opportunity to tap into a market consisting of more than one billion poten-tial consumers. On the other hand, Google could not enter China without censorship. If it created a Chinese version of Google and hosted it outside of China, it would be sub-ject to China's "Great Firewall," which the government uses to censor foreign sites. Google tried this method first, but its Chinese search engine was intermittently blocked and was otherwise slow and inconsistent for users, causing Google to steadily lose market share to domestic Chinese competitors such as Baidu. Google's other option, to host a search engine from within China, would require agreeing to self-censor its search results in accor-dance with Chinese law. Such an agreement went against the essence of what Google stood for—providing free and open access to information. Could Google agree to censor itself and still hold true to its "Don't Be Evil" mantra?

Despite criticism, Google applied the principles of utilitarianism to the situation and concluded that the benefits of setting up a search engine inside China outweighed the costs. It refused to offer localized email or blogging, finding the Chinese censorship and reporting requirements for these services to be too egregious. However, for search Google decided the greater good would be to provide Chinese citizens with "the greatest amount of information" possible, even if some of that information was censored. In 2006 Google opened its localized, self-censored, Chinese search engine. Whenever a search term led to censored results, Google added a message to the results page notifying the user that some entries were missing. It also left up its original, uncensored Chinese search engine hosted outside of China, so users could try to use it if they wanted.

Despite these precautions, Google's plan ran into problems almost from the outset. Google gained significant market share and became a serious competitor to Baidu, but the company's relationship with the Chinese government was continually tense, with Google accusing the government of interfering with the search engine beyond expectations. Google also faced intense backlash in the United States, including its leadership being called to testify at Congressional hearings about how they could justify self-censoring in China considering the principles they claimed to stand for everywhere else in the world. The breaking point was in 2010 when Google announced it had been targeted by a sophisticated cyberattack that appeared to originate from China and, among other things, had attempted to access the Gmail accounts of known Chinese human rights activists. Google stated that the implications of the cyberattack required it to reevaluate its approach toward the Chinese market, and it could no longer justify self-censorship. It shut down its China-hosted site and forwarded visitors to its external, uncensored but often-blocked Chinese search engine. As a result, Google saw its market share in China plunge and Baidu retaking its dominant position. The Chinese government was also not happy with Google's handling of the situation and immediately began blocking and/or censoring large portions of Google's services.

Although Google's approach to China has seen little substantial change since its withdrawal in 2010, it is not giving up on the largest market in the world. There are recent indications that the company might try to penetrate the market through another one of its signature products—Android. Android is actually the most popular mobile operating system in China, but it has been popularized and sold by third-party phone companies and device sellers with little direct involvement from Google. Google is rumored to be looking into creating a localized official app store to compete with the various unauthorized stores that have sprung up in Google's absence (Google's normal Play Store is blocked in China). The company will have to remember the lessons it learned in its first failed attempt and the sensitive ethical issues involved with censorship as it makes its next move into the Chinese market.

GOVERNMENT RESPONSE TO PRIVACY ISSUES

Consumer concerns over privacy issues prompted Congress to consider new legislation regulating what information Internet companies such as Google can collect and how they can use it. Internet companies, in turn, are attempting to make such legislation unnecessary by developing their own industry standards, such as the "Do Not Track" feature now found on all major web browsers. Such self-regulation is an attempt to ward off federal legislation that could seriously limit the tracking activities of companies like Google.

Some of the ideas that federal regulators have been discussing include a User's Bill of Rights and a mandatory Do Not Track mechanism. The Bill of Rights would, among other things, require companies to adhere to certain privacy practices. Its intent in this area would be to make Internet privacy policies easier for users to understand. A mandatory Do Not Track mechanism would be comparable to Do Not Call legislation, which makes it illegal for companies to sell to consumers over the telephone if those consumers are on the national Do Not Call registry. A similar law regulating Internet tracking could seriously impact how Internet companies collect information.

Many states are dissatisfied with the lack of federal action on this topic and have passed their own Internet privacy laws. California law, for example, provides special privacy protection to minors online and requires websites to disclose whether they are respecting the "Do Not Track" requests they receive from user browsers.

Because legislation could be a serious threat to Google, the company spends millions on lobbying and employs lobbyists on its staff. Google hopes to stave off regulation it feels restricts its ability to coordinate targeted advertising or offer customized services to users. However, with privacy issues and Internet breaches becoming a growing concern, the chance of increased regulation in the future is high. Although Google might not be able to prevent legislation restricting some of the activities of Internet firms, it can work with regulators to push for legislation with less of a negative effect on its operations. Google's lobbyists will have a profound impact on laws safeguarding Internet security.

CONCLUSION

Google's success story is unparalleled among search engine providers. The company started off as a small search engine and ranking system and has become one of the most profitable Internet companies in the world. Today the company is the owner and provider of products that go above and beyond simply a search engine. While there might be a risk of Google overextending itself, the company has a talent for making highly profitable acquisitions that increase its global reach.

As a way to manage its various businesses, in 2015 Google created a new publicly traded holding company called Alphabet run by Google founders Larry Page and Sergey Brin. Google was made a subsidiary of Alphabet with its own CEO. The founders believe that developing a holding company and "slimming down" Google to focus more on its Internet businesses will be beneficial for the firm in the long run.

Google has made itself into the epitome of a "best company to work for." The benefits Google offers employees are extensive, and Google empowers them to make decisions to improve the company's operations. The company has taken a strong stand on green initiatives and supports technologies to address global challenges. Google's 10 core principles provide a blueprint for how employees should conduct themselves within the company, and its "Don't Be Evil" mantra has become a popular yardstick to guide Google's actions.

On the other hand, Google has faced challenges in privacy, many of which continue to this day. Google is forced to draw a fine line between using user information to generate revenue and violating user privacy. Because Google is able to offer targeted advertising to advertisers through its collection of information, the company can provide quality Internet services to its users for free. At the same time, Google has committed questionable actions that seem to infringe on user rights and has encountered resistance from governmental authorities on many privacy-related initiatives.

With the threat of new regulation, Google takes measures such as lobbying to try and prevent legislation from being passed that proves unfavorable to the company. Because Google depends on tracking and similar activities to maintain profitability, it has a large stake in the privacy issue. However, rather than seeing this solely as a liability, Google might instead choose to improve its privacy practices and increase transparency in its operations. Google has the responsibility to ensure stakeholder rights are respected. Although Google has made great strides in social responsibility, both the company and society know there is room for improvement. Google's size, reputation, and history give it a unique opportunity to positively impact how companies interact on the Internet.

QUESTIONS FOR DISCUSSION

1. Has Google implemented a strategy that serves all stakeholders?
2. How can Google respect privacy and still maintain its profitability?
3. How will increasing global regulation of privacy affect Google's operations?

SOURCES

Doug Aamoth, "Google Turns 14, Was Initially Called 'BackRub,'" *Time*, September 27, 2012, http://techland.time.com/2012/09/27/google-turns-14-today-was-initially-called-backrub/ (accessed June 1, 2015); Elise Ackerman, "Google and Facebook Ignore 'Do Not Track' Requests, Claim They Confuse Consumers," *Forbes*, February 27, 2013, http://www.forbes.com/sites/eliseackerman/2013/02/27/big-internet-companies-struggle-over-proper-response-to-consumers-do-not-track-requests/ (accessed June 1, 2015); Byron Acohido, "Lawmakers request probe of tracking by Apple and Google," *USA Today*, April 25, 2011, 1B; Byron Acohido, "Most Google, Facebook users fret over privacy," *USA Today*, February 9, 2011, 1B; George Anders, "The Rare Find," *Bloomberg Businessweek*, October 17–October 23, 2011, 106–112; Julia Angwin, "Google, FTC Near Privacy Settlement," *The Wall Street Journal*, July 10, 2012, A1; Julia Angwin and Jennifer Valentino-Devries, "Google's iPhone Tracking," *The Wall Street Journal*, February 17, 2012, http://www.wsj.com/article_email/SB10001424052970204880404577225380456599176-lMyQjAxMTAyMDEwNjExNDYyWj.html (accessed August 11, 2015); Taylor Armerding, "Google Play shares too much personal info, app developer says," *CSO*, February 15, 2013, http://www.csoonline.com/article/2132939/privacy/google-play-shares-too-much-personal-info--app-developer-says.html (accessed June 1, 2015); Charles Arthur, "Google faces EC showdown over antitrust regulators," July 1, 2013, http://www.guardian.co.uk/technology/2013/jul/01/google-ec-antitrust-remedies (accessed June 1, 2015); Charles Arthur, "Google Facing Legal Threat from Six European Countries over Privacy," *The Guardian*, April 2, 2013, http://www.guardian.co.uk/technology/2013/apr/02/google-privacy-policy-legal-threat-europe (accessed June 1, 2015); Associated Press, "Developments Related to Google's Privacy Concerns," *The Huffington Post*, April 2, 2013, http://www.huffingtonpost.com/huff-wires/20130402/tec-google-privacy-history/?utm_hp_ref=travel&ir=travel (accessed June 1, 2015); Associated Press, "Google buys YouTube for $1.65 billion," *MSNBC*, October 10, 2006, http://www.msnbc.msn.com/id/15196982/ns/business-us_business/t/google-buys-youtube-billion/ (accessed June 1, 2015); Associated Press reporter, "Casinos ban gamblers from wearing Google Glass 'because the device could be used to cheat,'" *Daily Mail*, June 6, 2013, http://www.dailymail.co.uk/news/article-2337083/Casinos-ban-gamblers-wearing-Google-Glass-device-used-cheat.html (accessed June 1, 2015); Courtney Banks, "Top 10: The Quotable Eric Schmidt," *The Wall Street Journal*, January 21, 2011, http://blogs.wsj.com/digits/2011/01/21/top-10-the-quotable-eric-schmidt/ (accessed June 1, 2015); John Battelle, "The Birth of Google," *Wired*, August 2005, http://www.wired.com/wired/archive/13.08/battelle.html?pg=2&topic=battelle&topic_set= (accessed June 1, 2015); BBC, "Google agrees privacy policy changes with data watchdog," *BBC News*, January 30, 2015, http://www.bbc.com/news/technology-31059874 (accessed June 1,

2015); BBC, "Google privacy changes 'in breach of EU law," *BBC*, March 1, 2012, http://www.bbc.com/news/technology-17205754 (accessed June 1, 2015); BBC, "Google ranked 'worst' on privacy," *BBC News*, June 11, 2007, http://news.bbc.co.uk/2/hi/technology/6740075.stm (accessed June 1, 2015); Bryan Bishop, "Google responds to EU privacy policy questions, pausing rollout would have 'proved confusing," *The Verge*, April 5, 2012, http://www.theverge.com/2012/4/5/2928619/google-responds-eu-privacy-policy-questions-pausing-rollout-confusing-users/in/2527939 (accessed June 1, 2015); Jeff Blagdon, "Google's controversial new privacy policy now in effect," *The Verge*, March 1, 2012, http://www.theverge.com/2012/3/1/2835250/google-unified-privacy-policy-change-take-effect/in/2527939 (accessed June 1, 2015); Christina Bonnington, "Google's 10 Billion Android App Downloads: By the Numbers," *Wired*, December 8, 2011, http://www.wired.com/gadgetlab/2011/12/10-billion-apps-detailed/ (accessed June 1, 2015); Bianca Bosker, "Google Privacy Policy Changing for Everyone: So What's Really Going to Happen?" *The Huffington Post*, February 29, 2012, http://www.huffingtonpost.com/2012/02/29/google-privacy-policy-changes_n_1310506.html (accessed June 1, 2015); Katrina Brooker, "Google Ventures and the Search for Immortality," *Bloomberg*, March 8, 2015, http://www.bloomberg.com/news/articles/2015-03-09/google-ventures-bill-maris-investing-in-idea-of-living-to-500 (accessed June 1, 2015); Ian Chant, "Authors Guild Appeals Dismissal of Google Books Lawsuit," *Library Journal*, April 16, 2014, http://lj.libraryjournal.com/2014/04/litigation/authors-guild-appeals-dismissal-of-google-books-lawsuit/#_ (accessed August 11, 2015); Loretta Chao, "Google Tips Off Users in China," *The Wall Street Journal*, June 3, 2012, http://online.wsj.com/article/SB10001424052702303552104577439840152584930.html (accessed June 1, 2015); Costa Technologies, Inc., "Google Pay per Click Marketing," http://www.echicagoweb.com/internet-marketing/pay-per-click-marketing/google-adwords-ppc/ (accessed June 1, 2015); Jillian D'Onfro, "The truth about Google's famous '20% time' policy," *Business Insider*, April 17, 2015, http://www.businessinsider.com/google-20-percent-time-policy-2015-4 (accessed June 1, 2015); Morgan Downs (Producer), *Inside the Mind of Google* [DVD], United States: CNBC Originals, 2010; Josh Dreller, "A Brief History of Paid Search Advertising," *Search Engine Land*, January 21, 2010, http://searchengineland.com/a-brief-history-of-paid-search-advertising-33792 (accessed June 1, 2015); Dave Drummond, "A new approach to China: An update," *Google Official Blog*, March 22, 2010, http://googleblog.blogspot.com/2010/03/new-approach-to-china-update.html (accessed June 1, 2015); Jim Edwards, "Here's the Gaping Flaw in Microsoft's 'Do Not Track' System for IE10," *Business Insider*, August 29, 2012, http://www.businessinsider.com/heres-the-gaping-flaw-in-microsofts-do-not-track-system-for-ie10-2012-8 (accessed June 1, 2015); Amir Efrati, "Google Call Data 'Valuable," *The Wall Street Journal*, May 2, 2011, B3; Amir Efrati, "Google+ Pulls in 20 Million in 3 Weeks," *The Wall Street Journal*, July 22, 2011, http://www.wsj.com/news/articles/SB10001424053111904233404576460394032418286 (accessed June 1, 2015); Ben Elgin, "Google Buys Android for Its Mobile Arsenal," *Bloomberg Businessweek*, August 17, 2005, http://www.webcitation.org/5wk7sIvVb (accessed June 1, 2015); Ethisphere Institute, "Ehtisphere Announces the 2015 World's Most Ethical Companies®," *Ethisphere*, March 9, 2015, http://ethisphere.com/ethisphere-announces-the-2015-worlds-most-ethical-companies/ (accessed June 1, 2015); Tom Fairless, Rolfe Winkler, and Alistair Barr, "EU Files Formal Antitrust Charges against Google," *The Wall Street Journal*, April 15, 2015, http://www.wsj.com/articles/eu-files-formal-charges-against-google-1429092584 (accessed June 1, 2015); Federal Trade Commission, "FTC Charges Deceptive Privacy Practices in Google's Rollout of Its Buzz Social Network," March 30, 2011, http://www.ftc.gov/opa/2011/03/google.shtm (accessed June 1, 2015); Mia Feldman, "UK Orders Google to Delete Last of Street View Wi-Fi Data," *IEEE Spectrum*, June 24, 2013, http://spectrum.ieee.org/tech-talk/computing/networks/uk-orders-google-to-delete-last-of-street-view-wifi-data (accessed June 1, 2015); Klint Finley, "Thanks to Google, TV Ads Are about to Start Watching You," *Wired*, March 24, 2015, http://www.wired.com/2015/03/google-fiber-ads/ (accessed June 1, 2015); Kelly Fiveash, "Google bets biennial privacy audit after Buzz blunder," *The Register*, March 30, 2011, http://www.theregister.co.uk/2011/03/30/google_buzz_ftc_proposed_settlement/ (accessed June 1, 2015); Lisa Fleisher and Sam Schechner, "How Google's Top Minds Decide What to Forget," *The Wall Street Journal*, May 12, 2015, http://www.wsj.com/articles/how-googles-top-minds-decide-what-to-forget-1431462018 (accessed June 1, 2015); Sara Forden, Eric Engleman, Adam Satariano, and Stephanie Bodoni, "Can the U.S. Get Its Act Together on Privacy?" *Bloomberg Businessweek*, May 16–22, 2011, 27–28; Kent German, "A brief history of Android phones," *CNET*, August 2, 2011, http://reviews.cnet.com/8301-19736_7-20016542-251/a-brief-history-of-android-phones/ (accessed June 1, 2015); Jacob Gershman,

"California Gives Teens a Do-Over," *The Wall Street Journal*, September 25, 2013, http://blogs.wsj.com/law/2013/09/25/calif-gov-brown-signs-bill-giving-teens-online-eraser/ (accessed June 1, 2015); Jon Gertner, "The Truth about GoogleX: An Exclusive Look Behind the Secretive Lab's Closed Doors," *Fast Company*, May 2014, http://www.fastcompany.com/3028156/united-states-of-innovation/the-google-x-factor#1 (accessed August 11, 2015); Eric Goldman, "Top Ten Internet Law Developments of 2013," *Forbes*, January 9, 2014, http://www.forbes.com/sites/ericgoldman/2014/01/09/top-ten-internet-law-developments-of-2013/ (accessed June 1, 2015); Google, "Company," http://www.google.com/corporate/index.html (accessed June 1, 2015); Google, "Display Network," Google Ads, http://www.google.com/ads/displaynetwork/ (accessed June 1, 2015); Google, "European privacy requests for search removals," http://www.google.com/transparencyreport/removals/europeprivacy/?hl=en (accessed June 1, 2015); Google, "Explore the Chrome Browser," https://www.google.com/chrome/intl/en/more/index.html (accessed June 1, 2015); Google, "Frequently Asked Questions," Google Transparency Report, https://www.google.com/transparencyreport/removals/europeprivacy/faq/?hl=en (accessed June 1, 2015); Google, "Google Ads—Mobile Ads," Think with Google, http://www.google.com/ads/mobile/ (accessed June 1, 2015); Google, "Google AdWords," http://www.google.com/ads/adwords2/ (accessed June 1, 2015); Google, "Google Green," http://www.google.com/green/ (accessed June 1, 2015); Google, "Google Ventures," http://www.gv.com/ (accessed June 1, 2015); Google, "Google.org," http://www.google.org/index.html (accessed June 1, 2015); Google, "Human Rights Caucus Briefing," Google Blog, February 1, 2006, http://googleblog.blogspot.com/2006/02/human-rights-caucus-briefing.html#!/2006/02/human-rights-caucus-briefing.html (accessed June 1, 2015); Google, "Life at Google," http://www.google.com/about/careers/lifeatgoogle/ (accessed June 1, 2015); Google, "More about Content ID," YouTube, http://www.youtube.com/t/contentid_more (accessed June 1, 2015); Google, "Our Ad Platforms," Google Ads, http://www.google.com/ads/experienced/our-ad-platforms/ (accessed June 1, 2015); Google, "Understanding Bidding Basics," https://support.google.com/adwords/answer/2459326?hl=en (accessed June 1, 2015); Google, "Welcome to the Google Privacy Policy," Google Privacy & Terms, http://www.google.com/policies/privacy/ (accessed June 1, 2015); Richard Grey, "The Places Where Google Glass Is Banned," *The Telegraph*, December 4, 2013, http://www.telegraph.co.uk/technology/google/10494231/The-places-where-Google-Glass-is-banned.html (accessed August 11, 2015); Jessica Guynn, "Google creates company Alphabet, names new CEO," *USA Today*, August 11, 2015, http://www.usatoday.com/story/tech/2015/08/10/google-alphabet-sundar-pichai-larry-page-sergey-brin/31429423/ (accessed August 12, 2015); Josh Halliday, "Google's dropped anti-censorship warning marks quiet defeat in China," *The Guardian*, January 7, 2013, http://www.guardian.co.uk/technology/2013/jan/04/google-defeat-china-censorship-battle (accessed June 1, 2015); Kashmir Hill, "So, What Are These Privacy Audits That Google and Facebook Have to Do for The Next 20 Years?" *Forbes*, November 30, 2011, http://www.forbes.com/sites/kashmirhill/2011/11/30/so-what-are-these-privacy-audits-that-google-and-facebook-have-to-do-for-the-next-20-years/ (accessed June 1, 2015); IDC Corporate USA, "Smartphone OS Market Share, Q1 2015," *IDC*, 2015, http://www.idc.com/prodserv/smartphone-os-market-share.jsp (accessed June 1, 2015); Laurence Ilif, "Google Wages Free-Speech Fight in Mexico," *The Wall Street Journal*, May 27, 2015, http://www.wsj.com/articles/google-wages-free-speech-fight-in-mexico-1432723483 (accessed June 1, 2015); Independent.co.uk, "Rhodri Marsden: Why did my YouTube account get closed down?" *The Independent*, August 12, 2009, http://www.independent.co.uk/life-style/gadgets-and-tech/features/rhodri-marsden-why-did-my-youtube-account-get-closed-down-1770618.html (accessed June 1, 2015); InternetLiveStats.com, "Google Search Statistics," http://www.internetlivestats.com/google-search-statistics/ (accessed June 1, 2015); Betsy Isaacson, "Google Glass Captures Arrest On Camera, Sparks Controversy," *The Huffington Post*, July 10, 2013, http://www.huffingtonpost.com/2013/07/08/google-glass-arrest_n_3562095.html (accessed June 1, 2015); Don Jeffrey, "Google Argues for Dismissal of Author's Book-Scan Lawsuit," *Bloomberg*, May 3, 2012, http://www.bloomberg.com/news/2012-05-03/google-argues-for-dismissal-of-authors-book-scan-lawsuit.html (accessed June 1, 2015); Instant Joseph, "Google's new data-sharing privacy policy comes under scrutiny," *The Verge*, January 26, 2012, http://www.theverge.com/2012/1/26/2744683/google-privacy-policy-under-scrutiny/in/2527939 (accessed June 1, 2015); Jordan Kahn, "Google: We do not charge licensing fees for Android's Google Mobile Services," *9to5Google*, January 23, 2014, http://9to5google.com/2014/01/23/google-we-do-not-charge-licensing-fees-for-androids-google-mobile-services/ (accessed June 1, 2015); Don Karp, "Google

AdWords: A Brief History of Online Advertising Innovation," *Publishing 2.0*, May 27, 2008, http://publishing2. com/2008/05/27/google-adwords-a-brief-history-of-online-advertising-innovation/ (accessed June 1, 2015); Jamie Keene, "Google clarifies that its new privacy policy won't change users' privacy settings," *The Verge*, January 31, 2012, http://www.theverge.com/2012/1/31/2761089/google-clarifies-privacy-policy-leaves-privacy-controls-unchanged/in/2527939 (accessed June 1, 2015); Jemima Kiss, "Google admits collecting Wi-Fi data through Street View cars," *The Guardian*, May 14, 2010, http://www.theguardian.com/technology/2010/may/15/ google-admits-storing-private-data (accessed June 1, 2015); David Kravets, "A dissection of Google's Wi-Fi sniffing debacle," *Wired.co.uk*, May 3, 2012, http://www.wired.co.uk/news/archive/2012-05/03/googles-wi-fi-sniffing-debacle (accessed June 1, 2015); Tom Krazit, "Google's Chrome browser gets do-not-track feature," *Cnet*, January 14, 2011, http://news.cnet.com/8301-30684_3-20029348-265.html (accessed June 1, 2015); Heather Leonard, "The Google Investor: Mobile Advertising Is Google's Next Frontier," *Business Insider*, January 26, 2012, http://articles.businessinsider.com/2012-01-26/tech/30665888_1_iad-platform-mobile-advertising-google-wallet (accessed June 1, 2015); John Letzing, "Google Acknowledges Still Having Contested User Data," *The Wall Street Journal*, July 27, 2012, http://online.wsj.com/article/SB10000872396390443343704577553142360965420.html (accessed June 1, 2015); Natasha Lomas, "Google's Unified Privacy Policy Draws Threat of $15M Fine in the Netherlands," *TechCrunch*, December 17, 2014, http://techcrunch.com/2014/12/17/google-dutch-dpa-privacy-penalty/ (accessed June 1, 2015); Sean Ludwig, "Gmail finally blows past Hotmail to become the world's largest email service," *Venture Beat*, June 28, 2012, http://venturebeat.com/2012/06/28/gmail-hotmail-yahoo-email-users/ (accessed June 1, 2015); Douglas MacMillan, "Google's Display Ad Sales Should Top $1 Billion," *Bloomberg Businessweek*, February 8, 2010, http://www.businessweek.com/technology/content/feb2010/tc2010027_356976. htm (accessed June 1, 2015); Seth Marbin, "GoogleServe 2014: More opportunities to give back globally," Google Official Blog, July 10, 2014, http://googleblog.blogspot.com/2014/07/googleserve-2014-more-opportunities-to. html (accessed June 1, 2015); Matt McGee, "Google+ Hits 300 Million Active Monthly 'In-Stream' Users, 540 Million across Google," *Marketing Land*, October 29, 2013, http://marketingland.com/google-hits-300-million-active-monthly-in-stream-users-540-million-across-google-63354 (accessed June 1, 2015); Cade Metz, "8 Years Later, Google's Book Scanning Crusade Ruled 'Fair Use'," *Wired*, November 14, 2013, http://www.wired. com/2013/11/google-2/ (accessed August 11, 2015); Christopher Mims, "Google's '20% time,' which brought you Gmail and AdSense, is now as good as dead," *Quartz*, August 16, 2013, http://qz.com/115831/googles-20-time-which-brought-you-gmail-and-adsense-is-now-as-good-as-dead/ (accessed June 1, 2015).; Adam Minter, "Is Google Going Back into China?" *Bloomberg View*, November 24, 2014, http://www.bloombergview.com/ articles/2014-11-24/is-google-going-back-into-china (accessed June 1, 2015); Florian Mueller, "Google's once-secret, restrictive Android license agreements with Samsung and HTC published," *Foss Patents*, February 13, 2014, http://www.fosspatents.com/2014/02/googles-once-secret-restrictive-android.html (accessed June 1, 2015); Net Applications.com, "Desktop Search Engine Market Share," NetMarketShare, May 2015, https://www. netmarketshare.com/search-engine-market-share.aspx?qprid=4&qpcustomd=0 (accessed June 1, 2015); Dennis O'Reilly, "How to prevent Google from tracking you," *Cnet*, January 30, 2012, http://howto.cnet.com/8301-11310_39-57368016-285/how-to-prevent-google-from-tracking-you/ (accessed June 1, 2015); Doug Osborne, "Google uses high-tech nap pods to keep employees energized," *Geek.com*, June 18, 2010, http://www.geek.com/ news/google-uses-high-tech-nap-pods-to-keep-employees-energized-1264430/ (accessed June 1, 2015); Alexei Oreskovic and Michael Sin, "Google app store policy raises privacy concerns," *Reuters*, February 14, 2013, http:// www.reuters.com/article/2013/02/14/us-google-privacy-idUSBRE91D1LL20130214 (accessed June 1, 2015); Nicole Perloth, "Under Scrutiny, Google Spends Record Amount on Lobbying," *The New York Times*, April 23, 2012, http://bits.blogs.nytimes.com/2012/04/23/under-scrutiny-google-spends-record-amount-on-lobbying/ (accessed June 1, 2015); Paul, "FTC Releases Google Privacy Report—Minus the Juicy Details," *The Security Ledger*, October 4, 2012, https://securityledger.com/2012/10/ftc-releases-google-privacy-report-minus-the-juicy-details/ (accessed June 1, 2015); "Philosophy and Goals," Open Source Project, http://www.webcitation.org/5wiy036ap (accessed June 1, 2015); Emil Protalinski, "Chrome passes 25% market share, IE and Firefox Slip," *Venture Beat*, May 1, 2015, http://venturebeat.com/2015/05/01/chrome-passes-25-market-share-ie-and-firefox-slip/ (accessed June 1, 2015); Emil Protalinksi, "Google says it's 'thinking carefully' about Glass design as concerns arise from casinos, regulators over cheating," The Next Web, June 5, 2013, http://thenextweb.com/google/2013/06/05/casinos-in-two-states-have-now-banned-google-glass-over-fear-of-users-cheating-at-card-games/ (accessed June 1, 2015); Austin Ramzy, "Google Ends Policy of Self-Censorship in China," *TIME*, January 13, 2010, http://content.time.com/time/world/article/0,8599,1953248,00.html (accessed June 1, 2015); Don Reisinger, "Google responds to Congress over policy privacy inquiries," *Cnet*, January 1, 2012, http://news.cnet.com/8301-13506_3-57368788-17/google-responds-to-congress-over-privacy-policy-inquiries/ (accessed June 1, 2015); Reuters, "Google forms $100 million venture fund," March 31, 2009, http://uk.reuters.com/article/2009/03/31/google-fund-idUKN3135783620090331 (accessed June 1, 2015); Shane Richmond, "Google responds to European antitrust investigators," *The Telegraph*, July 2, 2013, http://www.telegraph.co.uk/technology/google/9371092/Google-responds-to-Europe-antitrust-investigators.html (accessed June 1, 2015); Adi Robertson, "Google France forced to notify visitors of €150,000 privacy policy fine," *The Verge*, February 8, 2014, http://www.theverge.com/2014/2/8/5393418/google-france-forced-to-notify-visitors-of-150000-privacy-policy-fine/in/2527939 (accessed June 1, 2015); Francis Robinson, "Sam Schechner, and Amir Mizroch, "EU Orders Google to Let Users Erase Past," *The Wall Street Journal*, May 13, 2014, http://www.wsj.com/news/articles/SB10001424052702303851804579559280623224964 (accessed June 1, 2015); Ryan Singel, "Google Busted with Hand in Safari-Browser Cookie Jar," *Wired*, February 17, 2012, http://www.wired.com/threatlevel/2012/02/google-safari-browser-cookie/ (accessed June 1, 2015); Megan Smith, "An update on Google.org and philanthropy @ Google," The Official Google.org Blog, March 8, 2010, http://blog.google.org/2010/03/update-on-googleorg-and-philanthropy.html (accessed June 1, 2015); Statista, "Google's advertising revenue from 2001 to 2014 (in billions U.S. companies)," http://www.statista.com/statistics/266249/advertising-revenue-of-google/ (accessed June 1, 2015); David Streitfeld, "Google Is Faulted for Impeding U.S. Inquiry on Data Collection," *New York Times*, April 15, 2012, http://www.nytimes.com/2012/04/15/technology/google-is-fined-for-impeding-us-inquiry-on-data-collection.html?pagewanted=1&ref=davidstreitfeld (accessed June 1, 2015); David Streitfeld and Kevin J. O'Brien, "Google Privacy Inquiries Get Little Cooperation," *New York Times*, May 23, 2012, http://www.nytimes.com/2012/05/23/technology/google-privacy-inquiries-get-little-cooperation.html?pagewanted=all&_r=0 (accessed June 1, 2015); Stephanie Strom and Miguel Helft, "Google Finds It Hard to Reinvent Philanthropy," *The New York Times*, January 29, 2011, http://www.nytimes.com/2011/01/30/business/30charity.html (accessed June 1, 2015); Victoria Stunt, "Why Google is buying a seemingly crazy collection of companies," *CBC News*, February 19, 2014, http://www.cbc.ca/news/technology/why-google-is-buying-a-seemingly-crazy-collection-of-companies-1.2537110 (accessed June 1, 2015); James Temperton, "Google changes UK privacy policy, but avoids hefty fine," *Wired.co.uk*, January 30, 2015, http://www.wired.co.uk/news/archive/2015-01/30/google-ico-privacy-policy (accessed June 1, 2015); Clive Thompson, "Google's China Problem (and China's Google Problem)," *The New York Times*, April 23, 2006, http://www.nytimes.com/2006/04/23/magazine/23google.html?pagewanted=all (accessed June 1, 2015); Owen Thomas, "Google exec: Android was 'best deal ever,'" *Venture Beat*, October 27, 2010, http://venturebeat.com/2010/10/27/google-exec-android-was-best-deal-ever/ (accessed June 1, 2015); Time Inc., "100 Best Companies to Work for," *Fortune*, http://fortune.com/best-companies/ (accessed June 1, 2015); Jennifer Valentino-DeVries, "What Do Google's Privacy Changes Mean for You?" *The Wall Street Journal*, January 25, 2012, http://blogs.wsj.com/digits/2012/01/25/what-do-googles-privacy-changes-mean-for-you/ (accessed June 1, 2015); Matt Warman, "Eric Schmidt's 'Gang of Four' tech giants: past, present and future," *The Telegraph*, June 2, 2011, http://www.telegraph.co.uk/technology/news/8550882/Eric-Schmidts-Gang-of-Four-tech-giants-past-present-and-future.html (accessed June 1, 2015); Graham Warwick, "Google Details 'Project Wing' Unmanned Package-Delivery R&D," *Aviation Week Network*, November 3, 2014, http://aviationweek.com/technology/google-details-project-wing-unmanned-package-delivery-rd (accessed August 11, 2015); Todd Wasserman, "Google Plus users spent just 3.3 minutes there last month," *CNN*, February 28, 2012, http://www.cnn.com/2012/02/28/tech/social-media/google-plus-comscore/index.html (accessed June 1, 2015); Todd Wasserman, "Report: Google+ Users Visitors Spent an Average of about 7 Minutes on the Site in March," *Mashable*, May 10, 2013, http://mashable.com/2013/05/10/google-has-20-million-u-s-monthly-mobile-users-report-says/ (accessed June 1, 2015); Ryan Whitwam, "Fire OS vs. Android: Can Amazon's new Fire Phone justify its ostentatious price tag?" *Extreme Tech*, June 19, 2014, http://www.extremetech.com/mobile/184791-fire-os-vs-android-can-amazon-fire-phone-justify-its-price-tag (accessed June 1,

2015); Brandon Widder, "Battle of the Best Browsers: IE vs. Chrome vs. Firefox vs. Safari vs. Opera vs. Project Spartan," *Digital Trends*, April 19, 2015, http://www.digitaltrends.com/computing/the-best-browser-internet-explorer-vs-chrome-vs-firefox-vs-safari-vs-project-spartan/ (accessed June 1, 2015); Christopher Williams, "Google Faces Privacy Investigation over Merging Search, Gmail, and YouTube Data," *The Telegraph*, April 2, 2013. http://www.telegraph.co.uk/technology/google/9966704/Google-faces-privacy-investigation-over-merging-search-Gmail-and-YouTube-data.html (accessed June 1, 2015); Rolfe Winkler, Alistair Barr, and Wayne Ma, "Google Looks to Get Back into China," *The Wall Street Journal*, November 20, 2014, http://www.wsj.com/articles/google-looks-to-get-back-into-china-1416527873 (accessed June 1, 2015); Molly Wood, "Sweeping Away a Search History," *The New York Times*, April 2, 2014, http://www.nytimes.com/2014/04/03/technology/personaltech/sweeping-away-a-search-history.html (accessed June 1, 2015); YouTube, "Community Guidelines," http://www.youtube.com/yt/policyandsafety/communityguidelines.html (accessed June 1, 2015); YouTube, "Copyright on YouTube," https://www.youtube.com/yt/copyright/ (accessed June 1, 2015); YouTube, "Statistics," https://www.youtube.com/yt/press/statistics.html (accessed June 1, 2015).

CASE 8

Zappos: Stepping Forward in Stakeholder Satisfaction*

INTRODUCTION

Can a company focused on happiness be successful? Zappos, an online retailer, is proving it can. Tony Hsieh, CEO of Zappos says, "It's a brand about happiness, whether to customers or employees or even vendors." Its zany corporate culture and focus on customer satisfaction has made Zappos both successful and a model for other companies. Zappos has built a culture of integrity in all of its activities. The company provides an incredible example of managing ethics and social responsibility by addressing challenges and responding to stakeholder issues.

This case examines how the company's focus on stakeholder happiness contributed to its success. First, we examine the history of Zappos, its core values, and unique business model. Next, we analyze its corporate culture and how it influences its relationships with employees, customers, the environment, and communities. We then look at some of the challenges the company faced and how it plans to move into the future.

HISTORY

Nick Swinmurn founded Zappos in 1999 after a fruitless day spent shopping for shoes in San Francisco. After looking online, Swinmurn decided to quit his job and start a shoe website that offered the best selection and best service. Originally called ShoeSite.com, the company started as a middleman, transferring orders between customers and suppliers but not holding any inventory (a "drop ship" strategy). The website was soon renamed Zappos, after the Spanish word for shoes (zapatos).

In 2000 entrepreneur Tony Hsieh became the company's CEO. Hsieh, 26 at the time, was an early investor in Zappos, having made $265 million selling his startup company to Microsoft in 1998. Hsieh was not initially sold on the idea of an Internet shoe store, but he could not help but become involved. After becoming CEO, Hsieh made an unconventional

*This case was developed by Harper Baird, Bernadette Gallegos, Beau Shelton, and Jennifer Sawayda under the direction of O.C. Ferrell and Linda Ferrell. It is intended for classroom discussion rather than to illustrate effective or ineffective handling of administrative, ethical, or legal decisions by management. All sources used for this case were obtained through publicly available materials. © O.C. Ferrell and Linda Ferrell, 2015

decision to keep Zappos going, even selling his San Francisco loft to pay for a new warehouse and once setting his salary at just $24.

Zappos struggled for its first few years, making sales but not generating a profit. The dot-com crash forced Zappos to lay off half its staff, but the company recovered. By the end of 2002, Zappos had sales of $32 million but was still not profitable. In 2003 the company decided in order to offer the best customer service, it had to control the whole value chain—from order to fulfillment to delivery—and began holding its entire inventory. Zappos moved to Las Vegas in 2004 to take advantage of a larger pool of experienced call center employees. The company generated its first profit in 2007 after reaching $840 million in annual sales. Zappos started to be recognized for its unique work environment and responsible business practices, as well as its approach to customer service.

In 2009 Amazon bought the company for $1.2 billion. Although Hsieh rejected an offer from Amazon in 2005, he believed this buyout would be better for the company than management from the current board of directors or an outside investor. Amazon agreed to let Zappos operate independently and keep Hsieh as CEO (at his current $36,000 annual salary). Hsieh made $214 million from the acquisition, and Amazon set aside $40 million for distribution to Zappos employees. After the acquisition, the company restructured into 10 separate companies organized under the Zappos Family. Zappos was able to keep its unique culture and core values.

CORE VALUES

Zappos has 10 core values that guide every activity at the company and form the heart of the company's business model and culture.

- Deliver WOW through service.
- Embrace and drive change.
- Create fun and a little weirdness.
- Be adventurous, creative, and open-minded.
- Pursue growth and learning.
- Build open and honest relationships with communication.
- Build a positive team and family spirit.
- Do more with less.
- Be passionate and determined.
- Be humble.[1]

These core values differ from those of other companies in several ways. In addition to being untraditional, the core values create a framework for the company's actions. This is exemplified in the company's commitment to its customers' and employees' well-being and satisfaction.

---

[1]Zappos, "Zappos Family Core Values," http://about.zappos.com/our-unique-culture/zappos-core-values (accessed May 18, 2015).

ZAPPOS'S CUSTOMER-FOCUSED BUSINESS MODEL

The Zappos business model is built around developing long-term customer relationships. Zappos does not compete on price because it believes customers want to buy from the business with the best service and selection. The company strives to create a unique and addicting shopping experience, offering a wide selection of shoes, apparel, accessories, and home products, free shipping to the customer, free shipping and full refunds on returns, and great customer service.

Shopping and Shipping

Zappos strives to make the shopping experience enjoyable. The website is streamlined for an easy shopping experience. Products are grouped in specialized segments, with some (like outdoor products) on their own mini-sites. Customers view each product from multiple angles thanks to photographs taken at the company's studio, and Zappos employees make short videos highlighting the product's features. Zappos analyzes how customers navigate the site to improve features, adapt search results, and plan inventory.

The spirit of simplicity, innovation, and great service extends to Zappos's inventory and distribution systems as well. Zappos has one of the few live inventory systems on the Web. If the Zappos website displays an item, it is in stock. Once the company sells out of an item, the listing is removed from the website. This reduces customer frustration. Its inventory and shipping systems are linked directly to the website via a central database, and all its information systems are developed in-house and customized to the company's needs. Its warehouses operate around the clock, which allows it to get a product to the customer faster. Fast shipping creates an instant gratification similar to shopping in a physical store.

Most companies have a negative view toward returns, but Zappos has the opposite mentality. It sees returns as the ability to maintain customer relationships and to increase its profits. Zappos offers a 100% Satisfaction Guaranteed Return Policy. If customers are not satisfied with a purchase, they can return it within 365 days for a full refund. The customer prints a prepaid shipping label that allows all domestic customers to return the product for free. This return policy encourages customers to order several styles or different sizes and return the items that do not work out.

While this strategy seems expensive, it actually works to Zappos's advantage. The average industry merchandise return rate is 35 percent, but the company's most profitable customers tend to return 50 percent of what they purchase. The customers who have the higher return percentages are the most profitable because they experienced Zappos's customer service and return policy, which create loyalty to the company. These customers are likely to make purchases more often and to spend more on each purchase. This is what helps makes Zappos so successful.

Customer Service

What makes the Zappos business model unique is the company's focus on customer service. The company established a method of serving customers and handling their issues distinctive from the rest of the industry. Zappos believes great customer service is an opportunity to make the customer happy.

Customers are encouraged to call Zappos with any questions. The number is displayed on every page of the website. According to Hsieh, Zappos encourages people to call the company because more interaction with customers increases their personal connections with the organization. Customer service representatives actively use social media sites such as Facebook and Twitter to respond to customer issues.

Another key aspect of its customer service model is that nothing is scripted. Zappos employees have free reign in their decision making and are expected to spend as much time as they need to "wow" customers. They help customers shop, even on their competitors' websites, encourage them to buy multiple sizes or colors to try (since return shipping is free), and do anything it takes to make the shopping experience memorable.

Zappos's customer service representatives develop relationships with customers and make them happy. Stories about great customer service include customer support calls that last for hours, sending flowers to customers on their birthdays, and surprise upgrades to faster shipping. Some extreme cases included Zappos hand-delivering shoes to customers who lost luggage and to a groom who forgot the shoes for his wedding. Zappos has even sent pizzas to the homes of customers who tweeted to the company about being hungry.

Zappos believes great customer experiences encourage customers to use the store again. In addition, its long-term strategy is based on the idea that great customer service will help it expand into other categories. While around 80 percent of company orders come from shoes, the markets for housewares and apparel are much larger. The company says it will expand into any area it is passionate about and meets customers' needs.

The company considers word-of-mouth marketing to be the best way to reach new customers. With over 75 percent of purchases made by repeat customers, it is evident that the Zappos mission to "provide the best customer service possible" works well for the company.

TRANSPARENCY

Transparency is a critical part of the Zappos model. Transparency is an ethical principle that involves maintaining open and truthful communication. Employees receive detailed information about the company's performance and are encouraged to share information about the company. Zappos believes employees should develop open and honest relationships with all stakeholders in the hope this will assist in maintaining the company's reputation. Hsieh uses Facebook and Twitter to share information with employees and customers (he has 2.78 million followers on Twitter). When Zappos laid off 124 employees in 2008, Hsieh announced the decision via Twitter and later blogged about it. Although some companies hesitate to open themselves to public criticism, Zappos feels it has nothing to hide. In fact, most of the public posts on its social media sites are praise from customers.

ZAPPOS INSIGHTS

The Zappos business model is so successful the company offers tours and workshops. Its three-day culture camp costs $6,000 and teaches participants about the Zappos culture and how to develop their own successful corporate cultures. The company also created Zappos Insights, an online service that allows subscribers to learn more about Zappos's business practices through blogs and videos. These programs have high profit potential for the company because they are built on what Zappos already does best.

CORPORATE CULTURE

The corporate culture at Zappos sets it apart from nearly every other company. It even caught the attention of Amazon CEO Jeff Bezos, who described the company's corporate culture as one-of-a-kind. Zappos's unorthodox culture is the work of CEO Tony Hsieh, an innovative and successful entrepreneur. Hsieh built the culture on the idea that if you can attract talented people and employees enjoy their work, great service and brand power naturally develops. This culture is built on an ethical foundation that respects all stakeholders. All aspects of Zappos's operations are built on integrity.

WORK ENVIRONMENT

Zappos is famous for its relaxed and wacky atmosphere. Employee antics include nerf ball wars, office parades, ugly sweater days, and donut-eating contests. The headquarters feature an employee nap room, a wellness center, and an open mic in the cafeteria. Other quirky activities include forcing employees to wear a "reply-all" hat when they accidentally send a company-wide email. This environment isn't just fun; it's also strategic. According to Zappos, "When you combine a little weirdness with making sure everyone is also having fun at work, it ends up being a win-win for everyone: Employees are more engaged in the work that they do, and the company as a whole becomes more innovative."

Hiring and Training

The key to creating a zany work environment lies in hiring the right people. The job application features a crossword puzzle about Zappos and asks potential employees questions about which superhero they'd like to be and how lucky they are. They may also check how potential employees treat people like their shuttle driver. Zappos is looking for people with a sense of humor who can work hard and play hard. Potential employees go through both cultural and technical interviews to make sure their character fits with a high-integrity company. However, even Hsieh admits finding great employees is tough. He believes pursuing too much growth at once harms the company if the organization starts caring more about the quantity of new employees rather than the quality.

All new employees attend a five-week training program that includes two weeks on the phones providing customer service and a week filling orders in a warehouse. To make sure new employees feel committed to a future with the company, Zappos offers $2,000 to leave the company after the training (called the "The Offer"). Amazon has adopted a similar practice.

Even after the initial training is over, employees take 200 hours of classes with the company—covering everything from the basics of business to advanced Twitter use—and read at least nine business books a year.

Benefits

Another aspect of Zappos that is unique is the benefits it provides to its employees. The company has an extensive health plan that pays 100 percent of employee medical benefits and on average 85 percent of medical expenses for employees' dependents. The company provides employees with dental, vision, and life insurance. Other benefits include a flexible spending account, prepaid legal services, a 40 percent employee discount, free lunches and snacks, paid volunteer time, life coaching, and a car pool program.

Along with the extensive benefits package, Zappos developed a compensation model for its "Customer Loyalty Team" (call center representatives) that incentivizes employee development. At Zappos the goal is to answer 80 percent of customer inquiries within 20 seconds, although employees are encouraged to take the time needed to ensure quality service. Initially, employees were paid $11 per hour for the first 90 days. After 90 days, the employee moved to $13 per hour. To move beyond $13 an hour, employees had to demonstrate growth and learning by completing specific skill set courses that allow employees to specialize in certain areas of the call center. Employees were given freedom to choose the shifts they wanted based on seniority. Although the reasoning for Zappos's compensation model is to motivate employees and promote personal growth, the base pay was less than the national hourly average of $15.92 earned by call center representatives.

Zappos determined that the pay structure and the process for employee shift sign-ups were inefficient for the company's needs. With Hsieh's encouragement the company adopted scheduling software called Open Market. Under this new system, call-center employees would be given 10 percent time flexibility to pursue their own projects. Employees could decide when to work, but the compensation system was revamped to mimic the surge-time pricing of popular ride-sharing service Uber. With this compensation system, call-center employees working during periods of high demand would receive higher pay. In other words, Zappos's hourly compensation for its call-center employees would be based on demand. Zappos hopes to expand this system to all departments eventually. For seniority-based jobs, this system holds risks. For instance, seniority-based incentives also take into account company loyalty, camaraderie with coworkers, and dedication that are also important to work productivity. However, Zappos believes the system works well for its call-center employees because many employees are employed for shorter periods.

Work-Life Integration

One of Zappos's core values is "Build a positive team and family spirit," so the company expects employees to socialize with each other both in and out of the office. In fact, managers spend 10 to 20 percent of their time bonding with team members outside of work. Zappos outings include hiking trips, going to the movies, and hanging out at bars. Hsieh says this increases efficiency by improving communication, building trust, and creating friendships.

Along with creating friendships, employees are encouraged to support each other. Any employee can give another employee a $50 reward for great work. Zappos employees compile an annual "culture book" comprised of essays on the Zappos culture and reviews of the company. The culture book helps employees think about the meaning of their work and is available unedited to the public. This is based on the principle of transparency.

As with its customers, the foundation of Zappos's relationships with its employees is trust and transparency. The company wants its employees, like its customers, to actively discuss any issues or concerns that come up. Hsieh does not have an office; he sits in an open cubicle among the rest of the employees. He believes "the best way to have an open-door policy is not to have a door in the first place." Zappos's management is open with employees by regularly discussing issues on the company blog.

However, this positive work environment comes with the expectation employees will work hard. Employees are evaluated on how well they embody the core values and inspire others; Zappos fires people who do great work if they do not fit with the culture of the company. This helps maintain a culture of integrity. The organization wants employees to be dedicated to the firm and believes appropriate conduct will not occur unless employees share the same visions and values of the organization.

Zappos's New Structure

In 2015 Tony Hsieh made a controversial decision to completely change the structure of the organization. For the past year the company had been transitioning toward an organizational structure that abandons the top-down managerial hierarchy in favor of a redistribution of power. Called a Holacracy, this organizational structure places empowerment at the core of the organization. Employees become their own leaders with their own roles. To be effective, a Holacracy requires periodic governance meetings where each employee understands his or her roles and responsibilities. Teams hold tactical meetings to discuss key issues. While governance meetings focus on clarity and role structure, tactical meetings are used to "sync and triage next actions." It is believed that this distributed authority increases clarity and transparency and decreases cognitive dissonance by recognizing tensions before they become a problem.

As Zappos continues to grow, there is a risk its expansion will make it harder to manage employees and control productivity. Hsieh cites statistics that demonstrate how growth often causes innovation and productivity per employee to go down. However, he also claims that when cities double in size, productivity and innovation per resident increases by 15 percent. Hsieh believes the key to sustainable growth at Zappos is to operate more like a city than a business. This is why he decided to restructure the organization. He feels the best way to handle growth is to become a Teal organization, starting out by using the Holacracy structure and evolving from there. In his book *Reinventing Organizations*, Frédéric Laloux uses a color scheme to describe the development of human organizations, with Teal being the highest. The concept of a Teal organization is based on three premises: self-management developed through peer relationships, involving the whole person in the work, and allowing the organization to grow and adapt instead of being driven. A Teal organization is structured under the premise that all units will work "together to support the whole." For Zappos this involves adopting a new structure promoting self-organization and self-management.

The transformation of Zappos's organizational structure started off slowly. However, Hsieh believed this slow transition hindered the company's transformation toward self-organization and self-management. He therefore sent an email to all 1,500 employees to inform them the organization was going to take immediate action to transform Zappos into a Teal organization. This involved eliminating bosses and the traditional functions of finance, technology, marketing, and merchandising to create task-oriented circles structured around specific businesses. Managers became employees and no longer engaged in traditional management functions, although their salaries stayed the same throughout 2015.

Hsieh handled the email carefully, making sure to praise traditional managers for their past contributions but stating they are no longer required for a Teal organization. He realized there would likely be much resistance from managers and other employees who did not agree with the new system. To address these concerns, Hsieh extended "The Offer." Zappos agreed to provide employees who wanted to leave severance pay for three months. Approximately 14 percent of employees chose to take the package.

This will have strong implications for Zappos, but Hsieh believes employees must be committed to the changes and acknowledges that some will not feel that the new structure is right for them. It is clear that this new organizational approach has divided up the company, but Hsieh believes this approach is necessary to handle the company's growth and maintain the same quality service and zany culture that has made it so successful.

CORPORATE SOCIAL RESPONSIBILITY

Zappos takes an unconventional approach to corporate social responsibility (CSR) and philanthropy. Many companies have CSR programs dedicated to a certain area or cause such as education, but Zappos prefers to support a variety of programs based on the needs of communities and the interests of employees.

Philanthropy

Zappos is involved in a variety of philanthropic efforts. Programs include donating shoes and gifts as well as giving gift cards to elementary school students. Zappos donates money to organizations such as the Shade Tree, a nonprofit that provides shelter to women and children, and the Nevada Childhood Cancer Foundation. The company even partnered with Britney Spears to hold an event at the zoo to raise money for the foundation. Zappos also has a donation request application available on its website.

Sustainability

Zappos started a campaign to improve the company's impact on the environment. A group of employees created the initiative, known as Zappos Leading Environmental Awareness for the Future (L.E.A.F.). The campaign focuses on several environmental efforts, including a new recycling program, community gardens, and getting LEED certification for the company. For instance, Zappos created an annual children's art contest that awards prizes for the best drawing involving a recycling-based theme. The winner was awarded a $50 Zappos.com Gift Card. Like the rest of the company, L.E.A.F. is open, with its progress posted on its Twitter account and blog.

Another area on the company's blog is a section on "Eco-friendly Products." Here, the company highlights new products that are organic or manufactured using environmentally friendly procedures. The postings also list ways customers can live more sustainable lifestyles, including tips on how to throw an eco-friendly party and green product recommendations.

Recognition

In addition to being the number one online shoe retailer, Zappos has been recognized for its innovative business practices. The company appeared on several prestigious lists including *Fortune*'s "Best Companies to Work For," *Fast Company*'s "50 Most Innovative Companies," *BusinessWeek*'s "Top 25 Customer Service Champs," and *Ethisphere*'s "World's Most Ethical Companies." The company continues to get recognized for its efforts in creating an environment and business model that encourages transparency and strong relationships among all stakeholders.

ETHICAL CHALLENGES FOR ZAPPOS

Like any company, Zappos faced some challenging business and ethical issues in the past. When these issues occur, Zappos handles situations in a professional and efficient manner. However, the transparency at Zappos makes some business and ethical issues more complex as the company strives to solve problems while keeping its stakeholders informed.

Laying Off Employees

Zappos is known for its commitment to its employees, but the company faced hard economic times that demanded tough decisions. In October 2008, Sequoia Capital, a venture capital firm that was a controlling investor in Zappos, met to discuss the problems presented by the economic downturn and its effect on their portfolio companies. Sequoia Capital instructed Zappos to cut expenses and make the cash flow positive. As a result, Hsieh made the difficult decision to lay off 8 percent of employees. This was not a desired event, but was required by Sequoia Capital.

Zappos strived to handle the layoffs in a respectful and kind manner. Hsieh sent an email notifying employees of the layoff and was honest and upfront about the reasons behind the decisions, even discussing the move on Twitter. Employees who were laid off received generous severance packages, including six months of paid COBRA health insurance coverage. Because of the company's honesty and transparency, employees and customers were more understanding of the tough decision Hsieh and Zappos had to make.

Acquisition by Amazon

In 2009 Zappos was acquired by e-commerce giant Amazon.com. Many Zappos customers were confused by the unexpected move and expressed concerns about the future of the company's culture and customer service. Most CEOs would not feel any obligation to address customer concerns over the acquisition, but Tony Hsieh values the support of Zappos's employees and customers.

Shortly after the acquisition, Hsieh issued a statement about why he sold Zappos to Amazon. In the statement, Hsieh discussed the disagreement between Zappos and Sequoia Capital over management styles and company focus. Specifically, Hsieh said, "The board's attitude was that my 'social experiments' might make for good PR but that they didn't move the overall business forward. The board wanted me, or whoever was CEO, to spend less time on worrying about employee happiness and more time selling shoes." Hsieh and Alfred Lin, Zappos's CFO and COO, were the only two members on the board committed to preserving the company's culture. The board could fire Hsieh and hire a new CEO who focused more on profits.

Hsieh decided the best way to resolve these issues was to buy out the board, but he could not do this on his own. After meeting with Amazon CEO Jeff Bezos, Hsieh committed to a full acquisition, as long as Zappos could operate independently and continue to focus on building its culture and customer service. Many customers were concerned Amazon was not a good fit for Zappos, but Hsieh addressed those concerns, stating Amazon and Zappos have the same goals of creating value for the customer but different ways of how to do it. He also assured customers Zappos would continue to maintain its unique corporate culture. Although consumers were not pleased with the acquisition, they at least understood why it occurred. Moreover, Hsieh's commitment to his beliefs and management style resonated with consumers.

More than Shoes Campaign

To bring awareness to the fact Zappos sells more than just shoes, Zappos created a marketing campaign in 2011 designed to catch people's attention. The company released several advertisements that featured people who appeared to be naked doing daily activities such as running, hailing a cab, and driving a scooter. The creative advertisements had certain parts of models' bodies blocked off with a box that said "more than shoes."

The campaign received criticism from several groups because of their "sexual nature." However, the catch with these ads was that the subjects of the ads were not actually nude; they wore bathing suits or small shorts that were later covered by the box. Because of the negative attention, Zappos pulled the ads and released an apology that explained the production process.

Technical Difficulties

Also in 2011 Zappos experienced some technical difficulties that resulted in delays and problems in customers' orders and shipments. Zappos upgraded one of its processing systems, and in the process many orders were deleted or delayed. Some orders had the incorrect shipping information, and products were shipped to the wrong location. Although this upset several customers, Zappos handled the problems and reassured customers that it would get them their merchandise as soon as possible. The company also offered different perks, depending on the circumstances of each customer experience.

Another problem Zappos encountered was that every item from 6pm.com, one of its websites, was priced at $49.95 for six hours in 2010. The company shut down the website for a few hours to solve the problem. Zappos honored all the orders from the pricing mistake, which resulted in a $1.6 million loss.

Theft of Customer Information

In 2012 hackers broke into Zappos's computer system, and the company had to respond to the theft of 24 million customers' critical personal information. The stolen data included customers' names, email addresses, shipping and billing addresses, phone numbers, and the last four digits of their credit cards. Zappos immediately addressed the situation by sending an email to customers notifying them of the security breach. Zappos assured customers the servers containing their full credit card information were not hacked. Its next move was to disconnect its call center, reasoning that the expected amount of calls would overload the system.

While Zappos has a reputation for delivering customer service that is unmatched by any competitor, some customers were unhappy with how Zappos handled the hacking. Many customers were upset by their information being hacked, but the situation was made worse by the company's action of disconnecting its call center. Although this situation caused problems for Zappos and blemished its customer service record, the company has worked to restore its reputation.

THE FUTURE OF ZAPPOS

Zappos remains committed to serving its customers and employees. So far, the company has retained its unique culture and continues to expand into new product categories. In one interview, Hsieh talked about the growth of Zappos and how he believes expanding into the clothing and merchandise market will help the company to grow. Hsieh says "the sky is the limit" for Zappos, and growing and expanding into many different types of businesses is Zappos's future. Hsieh continues to look for talented and creative individuals. He has pledged $1 million in partnership with Venture for America to bring at least 100 graduates to the Las Vegas area over a five-year period. As Zappos expands, it will have to work harder to hire the right people, avoid ethical issues, and maintain its quirky culture. The company's new organizational structure and compensation system for its call-center employees are major steps to expand without compromising Zappos's unique culture. Although many employees ended up leaving the company, Zappos believes these moves are the right ones to make and will enable the firm to continue growing both in employees and productivity.

Ethical leadership is a key factor in the success of any company, and for Zappos having Tony Hsieh as a leader is a strong indicator for future success. Hsieh expressed that he will do whatever it takes to make his employees, customers, and vendors happy. The future for any company looks bright when its leadership is committed to such strong values. However, Zappos needs to make sure it continues to focus on its stakeholders and its long-term vision with or without Hsieh.

Ultimately, Zappos intends to continue to deliver happiness to its stakeholders. Hsieh says, "At Zappos, our higher purpose is delivering happiness. Whether it's the happiness our customers receive when they get a new pair of shoes or the perfect piece of clothing, or the happiness they get when dealing with a friendly customer rep over the phone, or the happiness our employees feel about being a part of a culture that celebrates their individuality, these are all ways we bring happiness to people's lives."

QUESTIONS FOR DISCUSSION

1. Does Zappos effectively focus on stakeholder happiness, and how does this approach affect the ethical culture?
2. Has Zappos developed long-term relationships with customers and employees that provide a competitive advantage in the purchase of shoes and other products?
3. Has Zappos effectively managed ethical risk, and what are potential ethical risks in the future?

SOURCES

Scott Adams, "Refreshing Honesty on Why Zappos Sold to Amazon," *Tech Dirt*, 2010, http://www.techdirt.com/articles/20100607/0014299706.shtml (accessed May 18, 2015); Yinka Adegoke, "24 million customer accounts hacked at Zappos," *Reuters*, January 17, 2012, http://www.reuters.com/article/2012/01/17/us-zappos-hacking-idUSTRE80F1BD20120117 (accessed May 18, 2015); Peter Bernard, "Zappos Hacking Could Cause Consumer Problems Later," *The Tampa Tribune*, January 16, 2012, http://tbo.com/news/business/zappos-hacking-could-cause-consumer-problems-later-348177 (accessed May 18, 2015); Diane Brady, "Tony Hsieh: Redefining the Zappos' Business Model," *Bloomberg Business*, May 27, 2005, http://www.businessweek.com/magazine/content/10_23/b4181088591033.htm (accessed May 18, 2015); David Burkus, "The Tale of Two Cultures: Why Culture Trumps Core Values in Building Ethical Organizations," *The Journal of Values Based Leadership*, Winter/Spring 2011, http://www.valuesbasedleadershipjournal.com/issues/vol4issue1/tale_2culture.php (accessed May 18, 2015); Brian Cantor, "How Zappos Escaped Outrage over Customer Service Problems," *Customer Management*, October 11, 2011, http://www.customermanagementiq.com/operations/articles/how-zappos-escaped-outrage-over-customer-service-p (accessed May 18, 2015); Max Chafkin, "How I Did It: Tony Hsieh, CEO, Zappos.com," *Inc.*, September 1, 2006, http://www.inc.com/magazine/20060901/hidi-hsieh.html (accessed May 18, 2015); Max Chafkin, "The Zappos Way of Managing," *Inc.*, May 1, 2009, http://www.inc.com/magazine/20090501/the-zappos-way-of-managing.html (accessed May 18, 2015); Andria Cheng, "Zappos, under Amazon, keeps its independent streak," MarketWatch, June 11, 2010, http://www.marketwatch.com/story/zappos-under-amazon-keeps-its-independent-streak-2010-06-11 (accessed May 18, 2015); Michael Dart and Robin Lewis, "Break the Rules the Way Zappos and Amazon Do," *BusinessWeek.com*, May 2, 2011, 2; Eric Engleman. "Q&A: Zappos CEO Tony Hsieh on Life under Amazon, Future Plan," *Tech Flash: Seattle's Technology News Source*, 2010, http://www.techflash.com/seattle/2010/09/qa_zappos_ceo_tony_hsieh_on_life_under_amazon_and_moving_beyond_shoes.html (accessed May 18, 2015); Ethicsphere Institute, 2011 World's Most Ethical Companies," *Ethisphere*, http://ethisphere.com/worlds-most-ethical/wme-honorees/ (accessed May 18, 2015); Richard Feloni, "Inside Zappos CEO Tony Hsieh's radical management experiment that prompted 14% of employees to quit," *Business Insider*, May 16, 2015, http://www.businessinsider.com/tony-hsieh-zappos-holacracy-management-experiment-2015-5 (accessed May 18, 2015); Cheryl Fernandez, "Zappos Customer loyalty Team-Pay, Benefits, and Growth Opportunities," October 26, 2010, http://www.youtube.com/watch?v=OB3Qog5Jhq4 (accessed May 18, 2015); Fortune, "100 Best Companies to Work for," 2013, http://archive.fortune.com/magazines/fortune/best-companies/2013/snapshots/31.html (accessed May 18, 2015); Fortune, "Whitewater Rafting? 12 Unusual Perks. Best Companies Rank," 2012, http://archive.fortune.com/galleries/2012/pf/jobs/1201/gallery.best-companies-unusual-perks.fortune/3.html (accessed May 18, 2015); Ed Frauenheim, "Jungle survival," *Workforce Management*, September 14, 2009, Vol. 88, Issue 1018–1023; Carmine Gallo, "Delivering Happiness the Zappos Way," *BusinessWeek*, May 13, 2009, http://www.businessweek.com/smallbiz/content/may2009/sb20090512_831040.htm (accessed May 18, 2015); Rebecca Greenfield, "Zappos CEO Tony Hsieh: Adopt Holacracy or Leave," *Fast Company*, March 30, 2015, http://www.fastcompany.com/3044417/zappos-ceo-tony-hsieh-adopt-holacracy-or-leave (accessed May 18, 2015); "Holacracy," *Zappos Insights*, http://www.zapposinsights.com/about/holacracy (accessed May 18, 2015); HolacracyOne, LLC, "How It Works," http://holacracy.org/how-it-work; http://www.zapposinsights.com/about/holacracy (accessed May 18, 2015); Tony Hsieh and Max Chafkin, "Why I Sold Zappos," *Inc.*, June 2010, 100–104; Tony Hsieh, "Zappos: Where Company Culture is 1," Presentation, May 26, 2010, http://www.youtube.com/watch?v=bsLTh9Gity4 (accessed May 18, 2015); Harold Jarche,"Reinventing Organizations—Review," May 19, 2014, http://jarche.com/2014/05/reinventing-organizations-review/ (accessed May 26, 2015); John R. Karman III, "Zappos Plans to Add 5, 000 Full-Time Jobs in Bullitt County," *Business First*, October 28, 2011, http://www.bizjournals.com/louisville/print-edition/2011/10/28/zappos-plans-to-add-5000-full-time.html (accessed May 18, 2015); Aneel Karnani, "The Case against Corporate Social Responsibility," *MIT Sloan Management Review*, August 23, 2010, http://www.wsj.com/articles/SB10001424052748703338004575230112664504890 (accessed May 18, 2015); Sara Lacy, "Amazon-Zappos: Not the Usual Silicon Valley M&A," *BusinessWeek*, July 31, 2009, http://www.bloomberg.com/bw/technology/content/jul2009/tc20090730_169311.htm (accessed May 18, 2015); Greg Lamm, "Zappos Up-Front with Challenges of New Ordering System," *Tech Flash: Seattle's Technology News Source*, October 8, 2011, http://www.techflash.com/seattle/2011/10/zappos-up-front-with-challenges.html (accessed May 18, 2015); Nevada Childhood Cancer Foundation, "Wild Night at the Zoo presented by Britney Spears & Zappos.com," http://www.nvccf.org/news.cfm?id=303 (accessed May 18, 2015).; Jeffrey M. O'Brien, "Zappos Knows How to Kick It," *Fortune*, February 2, 2009, Vol. 159 Issue 2, 54–60; Joyce Routson. "Hsieh of Zappos Takes Happiness Seriously," *Stanford Center for Social Innovation*, November 4, 2010, http://csi.gsb.stanford.edu/hsieh-zappos-takes-happiness-seriously (accessed May 18, 2015); Rachel Emma Silverman, "At Zappos, Some Employees Find Offer to Leave Too Good to Refuse," The Wall Street Journal, May 7, 2014, http://www.wsj.com/articles/at-zappos-some-employees-find-offer-to-leave-too-good-to-refuse-1431047917 (accessed May 18, 2015); Aman Singh, "At Zappos, Getting Fired for not Contributing to Company Culture," *Forbes*, 2010, http://www.forbes.com/sites/csr/2010/11/23/at-zappos-getting-fired-for-not-contributing-to-company-culture (accessed May 18, 2015); Sun staff, "Henderson-Based Zappos Earns Honors for Ethics," *Las Vegas Sun*, 2009, http://www.lasvegassun.com/news/2009/apr/13/henderson-based-zappos-earns-honors-ethics/ (accessed May 18, 2015); Brad T. "2014

Children's Recycling Art Contest Winner Announced," *Zappos Blog*, December 1, 2014, http://blogs.zappos.com/taxonomy/term/786 (accessed May 18, 2015); Bill Taylor, "Why Amazon Is Copying Zappos and Paying Employees to Quit," *Harvard Business Review*, April 14, 2014, https://hbr.org/2014/04/why-amazon-is-copying-zappos-and-paying-employees-to-quit/ (accessed May 18, 2015); William Wei, "The Future of Zappos: From Shoes to Clothing to a Zappos Airline," *Business Insider*, October 22, 2010, http://www.businessinsider.com/zappos-shoes-clothing-airline-2010-10 (accessed May 18, 2015); Samantha Whitehorne, "Cultural Lessons from the Leaders at Zappos.com," *ASAE*, August 2009, http://www.asaecenter.org/Resources/ANowDetail.cfm?ItemNumber=43360 (accessed May 18, 2015); Marcie Young and Erin E. Clack, "Zappos Milestone: Focus on Apparel," *Footwear News*, May 4, 2009, http://about.zappos.com/press-center/media-coverage/zappos-milestone-focus-apparel (accessed May 18, 2015); "Zappos CEO Gives $1M to Lure Grads to Las Vegas," *8 News Now KLAS-TV Las Vegas*, December 4, 2012, http://www.8newsnow.com/story/20260504/zappos-ceo-gives-1m-to-lure-grads-to-vegas (accessed May 18, 2015); "Zappos gives up lunch to Give Back to the Community," *Blogs.Zappos.Com*, 2008, http://blogs.zappos.com/blogs/inside-zappos/2008/09/09/zappos-gives-up-lunch-to-give-back-to-community (accessed May 18, 2015); Masha Zager, "Zappos Delivers Service…With Shoes on the Side," *Apparel Magazine*, January 2009, Vol. 50 Issue 5, 10–13; Claire Zillman, "Zappos is bringing Uber-like surge pay to the workplace," *Fortune*, January 28, 2015, http://fortune.com/2015/01/28/zappos-employee-pay/ (accessed May 18, 2015).

CASE 9

Enron: Questionable Accounting Leads to Collapse

INTRODUCTION

Once upon a time, there was a gleaming office tower in Houston, Texas. In front of that gleaming tower was a giant "E," slowly revolving, flashing in the hot Texas sun. But in 2001, the Enron Corporation, which once ranked among the top Fortune 500 companies, would collapse under a mountain of debt that had been concealed through a complex scheme of off-balance-sheet partnerships. Forced to declare bankruptcy, the energy firm laid off 4,000 employees; thousands more lost their retirement savings, which had been invested in Enron stock. The company's shareholders lost tens of billions of dollars after the stock price plummeted. The scandal surrounding Enron's demise engendered a global loss of confidence in corporate integrity that continues to plague markets today, and eventually it triggered tough new scrutiny of financial reporting practices. In an attempt to understand what went wrong, this case will examine the history, culture, and major players in the Enron scandal.

ENRON'S HISTORY

The Enron Corporation was created out of the merger of two major gas pipeline companies in 1985. Through its subsidiaries and numerous affiliates, the company provided goods and services related to natural gas, electricity, and communications for its wholesale and retail customers. Enron transported natural gas through pipelines to customers all over the United States. It generated, transmitted, and distributed electricity to the northwestern United States, and marketed natural gas, electricity, and other commodities globally. It was also involved in the development, construction, and operation of power plants, pipelines, and other energy-related projects all over the world, including the delivery and management of energy to retail customers in both the industrial and commercial business sectors.

*This case was developed by Jennifer Sawayda, Harper Baird, Jennifer Jackson, Michelle Urban and Neil Herndon for and under the direction of O. C. and Linda Ferrell © 2015. The authors conducted personal interviews with Ken Lay in 2006 in the development of this case. In 2014 they invited Andy Fastow to speak and had the opportunity to assess his current perspective on Enron and how to prevent financial misconduct. It was prepared for classroom discussion rather than to illustrate either effective or ineffective handling of an administrative, ethical, or legal decision by management. All sources used for this case were obtained through publicly available material.

Throughout the 1990s, Chairman Ken Lay, CEO Jeffrey Skilling, and CFO Andrew Fastow transformed Enron from an old-style electricity and gas company into a $150 billion energy company and Wall Street favorite that traded power contracts in the investment markets. From 1998 to 2000 alone, Enron's revenues grew from about $31 billion to more than $100 billion, making it the seventh-largest company in the Fortune 500. Enron's wholesale energy income represented about 93 percent of 2000 revenues, with another 4 percent derived from natural gas and electricity. The remaining 3 percent came from broadband services and exploration. However, a bankruptcy examiner later reported that although Enron had claimed a net income of $979 million in that year, it had really earned just $42 million. Moreover, the examiner found that despite Enron's claim of $3 billion in cash flow in 2000, the company actually had a cash flow of negative $154 million.

ENRON'S CORPORATE CULTURE

When describing the corporate culture of Enron, people like to use the word "arrogant," perhaps justifiably. A large banner in the lobby at corporate headquarters proclaimed Enron "The World's Leading Company," and Enron executives believed that competitors had no chance against it. Jeffrey Skilling even went so far as to tell utility executives at a conference that he was going to "eat their lunch." This overwhelming aura of pride was based on a deep-seated belief that Enron's employees could handle increased risk without danger. Enron's corporate culture reportedly encouraged flouting the rules in pursuit of profit. And Enron's executive compensation plans seemed less concerned with generating profits for shareholders than with enriching officer wealth.

Skilling appears to be the executive who created the system whereby Enron's employees were rated every six months, with those ranked in the bottom 20 percent forced out. This "rank and yank" system helped create a fierce environment in which employees competed against rivals not only outside the company but also at the next desk. The "rank and yank" system is still used at other companies. Delivering bad news could result in the "death" of the messenger, so problems in the trading operation, for example, were covered up rather than being communicated to management.

Ken Lay once said that he felt that one of the great successes at Enron was the creation of a corporate culture in which people could reach their full potential. He said that he wanted it to be a highly moral and ethical culture and that he tried to ensure that people honored the values of respect, integrity, and excellence. On his desk was an Enron paperweight with the slogan "Vision and Values." Despite such good intentions, however, ethical behavior was not put into practice. Instead, integrity was pushed aside at Enron, particularly by top managers. Some employees at the company believed that nearly anything could be turned into a financial product and, with the aid of complex statistical modeling, traded for profit. Short on assets and heavily reliant on intellectual capital, Enron's corporate culture rewarded innovation and punished employees deemed weak.

ENRON'S ACCOUNTING PROBLEMS

Enron's bankruptcy in 2001 was the largest in U.S. corporate history at the time. The bankruptcy filing came after a series of revelations that the giant energy trader had been using partnerships, called "special-purpose entities" or SPEs, to conceal losses. In a meeting with

Enron's lawyers in August 2001, the company's then-CFO Fastow stated that Enron had established the SPEs to move assets and debt off its balance sheet and to increase cash flow by showing that funds were flowing through its books when it sold assets. Although these practices produced a very favorable financial picture, outside observers believed they constituted fraudulent financial reporting because they did not accurately represent the company's true financial condition. Most of the SPEs were entities in name only, and Enron funded them with its own stock and maintained control over them. When one of these partnerships was unable to meet its obligations, Enron covered the debt with its own stock. This arrangement worked as long as Enron's stock price was high, but when the stock price fell, cash was needed to meet the shortfall.

After Enron restated its financial statements for fiscal year 2000 and the first nine months of 2001, its cash flow from operations went from a positive $127 million in 2000 to a negative $753 million in 2001. With its stock price falling, Enron faced a critical cash shortage. In October 2001, after it was forced to cover some large shortfalls for its partnerships, Enron's stockholder equity fell by $1.2 billion. Already shaken by questions about lack of disclosure in Enron's financial statements and by reports that executives had profited personally from the partnership deals, investor confidence collapsed, taking Enron's stock price with it.

For a time, it appeared that Dynegy might save the day by providing $1.5 billion in cash, secured by Enron's premier pipeline Northern Natural Gas, and then purchasing Enron for about $10 billion. However, when Standard & Poor's downgraded Enron's debt to below investment grade on November 28, 2001, some $4 billion in off-balance-sheet debt came due, and Enron did not have the resources to pay. Dynegy terminated the deal. On December 2, 2001, Enron filed for bankruptcy. Enron now faced 22,000 claims totaling about $400 billion.

The Whistle-Blower

Assigned to work directly with Andrew Fastow in June 2001, Enron vice president Sherron Watkins, an eight-year Enron veteran, was given the task of finding some assets to sell off. With the high-tech bubble bursting and Enron's stock price slipping, Watkins was troubled to find unclear, off-the-books arrangements backed only by Enron's deflating stock. No one seemed to be able to explain to her what was going on. Knowing she faced difficult consequences if she confronted then-CEO Jeffrey Skilling, she began looking for another job, planning to confront Skilling just as she left for a new position. Skilling, however, suddenly quit on August 14, saying he wanted to spend more time with his family. Chair Ken Lay stepped back in as CEO and began inviting employees to express their concerns and put them into a box for later collection. Watkins prepared an anonymous memo and placed it into the box. When Lay held a companywide meeting shortly thereafter and did not mention her memo, however, she arranged a personal meeting with him.

On August 22, 2001, Watkins handed Lay a seven-page letter she had prepared outlining her concerns. She told him that Enron would "implode in a wave of accounting scandals" if nothing was done. Lay arranged to have Enron's law firm, Vinson & Elkins, and accounting firm Arthur Andersen look into the questionable deals, although Watkins advised against having a third party investigate that might be compromised by its own involvement in Enron's conduct. Lay maintained that both the law firm and accounting firm did not find merit in Watkins's accusations. Near the end of September, Lay sold some $1.5 million of personal stock options, while telling Enron employees that the company had never been stronger. By the middle of October, Enron was reporting a third-quarter loss of $618 million and a $1.2 billion write-off tied to the partnerships about which Watkins had warned Lay.

For her trouble, Watkins had her computer hard drive confiscated and was moved from her plush executive office suite on the top floor of the Houston headquarters tower to a sparse office on a lower level. Her new metal desk was no longer filled with the high-level projects that had once taken her all over the world on Enron business. Instead, now a vice president in name only, she faced meaningless "make work" projects. It is important to note that Watkins stayed in the company after warning Lay about the risks and did not become a public whistle-blower during this time. In February 2002, she testified before Congress about Enron's partnerships and resigned from Enron in November of that year.

The Chief Financial Officer

In 2002, the U.S. Justice Department indicted CFO Andrew Fastow—who had won the "CFO of the Year" award two years earlier from *CFO Magazine*—on 98 counts for his alleged efforts to inflate Enron's profits. The charges included fraud, money laundering, conspiracy, and one count of obstruction of justice. Fastow faced up to 140 years in jail and millions of dollars in fines if convicted on all counts. Federal officials attempted to recover all of the money Fastow had earned illegally, and seized some $37 million.

Federal prosecutors argued that Enron's case was not about exotic accounting practices but about fraud and theft. They contended that Fastow was the brain behind the partnerships used to conceal some $1 billion in Enron debt and that this debt led directly to Enron's bankruptcy. The federal complaints alleged that Fastow had defrauded Enron and its shareholders through off-balance-sheet partnerships that made Enron appear to be more profitable than it actually was. They also alleged that Fastow made about $30 million both by using these partnerships to get kickbacks that were disguised as gifts from family members, and by taking income himself that should have gone to other entities.

Fastow initially denied any wrongdoing and maintained that he was hired to arrange the off-balance-sheet financing and that Enron's board of directors, chair, and CEO had directed and praised his work. He also claimed that both lawyers and accountants had reviewed his work and approved what was being done, and that "at no time did he do anything he believed was a crime." Skilling, COO from 1997 to 2000 before becoming CEO, had reportedly championed Fastow's rise at Enron and supported his efforts to keep up Enron's stock prices.

Fastow eventually pleaded guilty to two counts of conspiracy, admitting to orchestrating myriad schemes to hide Enron debt and inflate profits while enriching himself with millions. He surrendered nearly $30 million in cash and property, and agreed to serve up to 10 years in prison once prosecutors no longer needed his cooperation. He was a key government witness against Lay and Skilling. His wife Lea Fastow, former assistant treasurer, quit Enron in 1997 and pleaded guilty to a felony tax crime, admitting to helping hide ill-gotten gains from her husband's schemes from the government. She later withdrew her plea, and then pleaded guilty to a newly filed misdemeanor tax crime. In 2005, she was released from a year-long prison sentence, and then had a year of supervised release.

In the end, Fastow received a lighter sentence than he otherwise might have because of his willingness to cooperate with investigators. In 2006, Fastow gave an eight-and-a-half-day deposition in his role as government witness. He helped to illuminate how Enron had managed to get away with what it did, including detailing how many major banks were complicit in helping Enron manipulate its financials to help it look better to investors. In exchange for his deposition, Fastow's sentence was lowered to six years from ten.

Fastow has also stated that Enron did not have to go out of business if there had been better financial decisions made at the end.

The case against Fastow had been largely based on information provided by Michael Kopper, the company's managing director and a key player in the establishment and operation of several of the off-balance-sheet partnerships and the first Enron executive to plead guilty to a crime. Kopper, a chief aide to Fastow, pleaded guilty to money laundering and wire fraud. He faced up to 15 years in prison and agreed to surrender $12 million earned from illegal dealings with the partnerships. However, Kopper only had to serve three years and one month of jail time because of the crucial role he played in providing prosecutors with information. After his high-powered days at Enron, Kopper's next job was as a salaried grant writer for Legacy, a Houston-based clinic that provides services to HIV-positive and other chronically ill patients.

Today Andy Fastow has been released from prison and works as a document-review clerk at a law firm. He also speaks about business ethics at many different forums, including Leeds Business School at the University of Colorado, the University of New Mexico, the University of Texas at Austin, and the Association of Certified Fraud Examiners global conference. During his speaking engagements, Fastow has emphasized that a major problem companies encounter in business ethics is not using principles and overly relying on rules. He claims that laws and regulations technically allowed the risky transactions he made at Enron. He also cited General Motors, IBM, and the nation of Greece as more recent examples of companies (or nations) that faced hardship and/or bankruptcy because they took actions that were highly risky but technically allowable by law.

The main idea that Fastow tries to communicate in his lectures is that it is not enough to simply obey rules and regulations. It is also easy to rationalize questionable behaviors. Fastow claims that ethical decisions are rarely black-and-white, and sometimes unethical decisions seem more or less unethical depending upon the situation. For instance, he used Apple's tax evasion as an example of an action that seemed less unethical because it was less pronounced than what often occurs in other cases. There are always murky areas where regulations can be exploited. Instead, businesspeople must be able to recognize when issues are going too far and stop them before they snowball into an Enron-esque crisis. Fastow recommends that the best way to deal with questionable situations is to construct and examine a worst-case scenario analysis and look at the risks of questionable deals with more scrutiny.

The Chief Executive Officer

Former CEO Jeffrey Skilling, generally perceived as Enron's mastermind, was the most difficult to prosecute. At the time of the trial, he was so confident that he waived his right to avoid self-incrimination and testified before Congress, saying, "I was not aware of any inappropriate financial arrangements." However, Jeffrey McMahon, who took over as Enron's president and COO in February 2002, told a congressional subcommittee that he had informed Skilling about the company's off-balance-sheet partnerships in 2000, when he was Enron's treasurer. McMahon said that Skilling had told him that "he would remedy the situation."

Calling the Enron collapse a "run on the bank" and a "liquidity crisis," Skilling said that he did not understand how Enron had gone bankrupt so quickly. He also said that the off-balance-sheet partnerships were Fastow's creation. However, the judge dealt a blow to Lay and Skilling when he instructed the jury that it could find the defendants guilty of consciously avoiding knowing about wrongdoing at the company.

Many former Enron employees refused to testify because they were not guaranteed that their testimony would not be used against them in future trials, and therefore questions about the company's accounting fraud remain. Skilling was found guilty of honest services fraud and sentenced to 24 years in prison, which he has been serving in Colorado. He maintains his innocence and has appealed his conviction. After his release from prison, Andy Fastow was quoted as saying that the bankruptcy of Enron was not Skilling's fault. In 2008, a panel of judges from the Fifth Circuit Court of Appeals in New Orleans rejected his request to overturn the convictions of fraud, conspiracy, misrepresentation, and insider trading. However, the judges did grant Skilling one concession. The three-judge panel determined that the original judge had applied flawed sentencing guidelines in determining Skilling's sentence. The Court ordered that Skilling be resentenced. The matter was taken to the Supreme Court.

In June 2010, the U.S. Supreme Court ruled that the honest services law could not be used to convict Skilling because the honest services law applies to bribes and kickbacks, not to conduct that is ambiguous or vague. The Supreme Court's decision did not suggest that there had been no misconduct, only that Skilling's conduct was not in violation of a criminal fraud law. The court's decision did not overturn the conviction and sent the case back to a lower court for evaluation.

The Chair

Ken Lay became chair and CEO of the company that was to become Enron in 1986. A decade later, Lay promoted Jeffrey Skilling to president and chief operating officer, and then, as expected, Lay stepped down as CEO in 2001 to make way for Skilling. Lay remained as chair of the board. When Skilling resigned later that year, Lay resumed the role of CEO.

Lay, who held a doctorate in economics from the University of Houston, contended that he knew little of what was going on, even though he had participated in the board meetings that allowed the off-balance-sheet partnerships to be created. Lay said he believed the transactions were legal because attorneys and accountants had approved them. Only months before the bankruptcy in 2001, he reassured employees and investors that all was well at Enron, based on strong wholesale sales and physical volume delivered through the marketing channel. He had already been informed that there were problems with some of the investments that could eventually cost Enron hundreds of millions of dollars. In 2002, on the advice of his attorney, Lay invoked his Fifth Amendment right not to answer questions that could be incriminating.

Lay was expected to be charged with insider trading, and prosecutors investigated why he had begun selling about $80 million of his own stock beginning in late 2000, even as he encouraged employees to buy more shares of the company. It appears that Lay drew down his $4 million Enron credit line repeatedly and then repaid the company with Enron shares. These transactions, unlike usual stock sales, do not have to be reported to investors. Lay says that he sold the stock because of margin calls on loans he had secured with Enron stock and that he had no other source of liquidity. According to Lay, he was largely unaware of the ethical situation within the firm. He had relied on lawyers, accountants, and senior executives to inform him of issues such as misconduct. He felt that he had been protected from certain knowledge that would have been beneficial and would have enabled him to engage in early correction of the misconduct. Lay claims that all decisions he made related to financial transactions were approved by the company's lawyers and the Enron board of directors. Lynn Brewer, a former Enron executive, states that Lay was not informed about alleged misconduct in her division. Additionally, Mike Ramsey, the lead attorney for Lay's defense, claimed that he was not aware of most of the items in the indictment. In the end

Lay was convicted on 19 counts of fraud, conspiracy, and insider trading. However, the verdict was thrown out after he died of heart failure at his home in Colorado in 2006. The ruling protected some $43.5 million of Lay's estate that the prosecution had claimed Lay stole from Enron.

The Lawyers

Enron was Houston law firm Vinson & Elkins's top client, accounting for about 7 percent of its $450 million in revenue. Enron's general counsel and a number of members of Enron's legal department came from Vinson & Elkins. Vinson & Elkins seems to have dismissed Sherron Watkins's allegations of accounting fraud after making some inquiries, but this does not appear to leave the firm open to civil or criminal liability. Of greater concern are allegations that Vinson & Elkins helped structure some of Enron's special-purpose partnerships. In her letter to Lay, Watkins had indicated that the firm had written opinion letters supporting the legality of the deals. In fact, Enron could not have done many of the transactions without such opinion letters. The firm did not admit liability, but agreed to pay $30 million to Enron to settle claims that Vinson & Elkins had contributed to the firm's collapse.

Merrill Lynch

The brokerage and investment-banking firm Merrill Lynch also faced scrutiny by federal prosecutors and the SEC for its role in Enron's 1999 sale of Nigerian barges. The sale allowed Enron to improperly record about $12 million in earnings and thereby meet its earnings' goals at the end of 1999. Merrill Lynch allegedly bought the barges for $28 million, of which Enron financed $21 million. Fastow gave his word that Enron would buy Merrill Lynch's investment out in six months with a 15 percent guaranteed rate of return. Merrill Lynch went ahead with the deal despite an internal document that suggested that the transaction might be construed as aiding and abetting Enron's fraudulent manipulation of its income statement. Merrill Lynch denies that the transaction was a sham and said that it never knowingly helped Enron to falsify its financial reports.

There are also allegations that Merrill Lynch replaced a research analyst after his coverage of Enron displeased Enron executives. Enron reportedly threatened to exclude Merrill Lynch from an upcoming $750 million stock offering in retaliation. The replacement analyst is reported to have then upgraded his report on Enron's stock rating. Merrill Lynch maintains that it did nothing improper in its dealings with Enron. However, the firm agreed to pay $80 million to settle SEC charges related to the questionable Nigerian barge deal.

Merrill Lynch continued to use risky investment practices, which contributed to severe financial losses for the company as the economy entered a recession in 2008. In 2008, Bank of America agreed to purchase the company for $50 billion, possibly after pressure from the federal government.

ARTHUR ANDERSEN LLP

In its role as Enron's auditor, Arthur Andersen was responsible for ensuring the accuracy of Enron's financial statements and internal bookkeeping. Investors used Andersen's reports to judge Enron's financial soundness and future potential, and expected that Andersen's certifications of accuracy and application of proper accounting procedures would be independent and free of any conflict of interest.

However, Andersen's independence was called into question. The accounting firm was one of Enron's major business partners, with more than 100 employees dedicated to its account, and it sold about $50 million a year in consulting services to Enron. Some Andersen executives even accepted jobs with the energy trader. In March 2002, Andersen was found guilty of obstruction of justice for destroying relevant auditing documents during an SEC investigation of Enron. As a result, Andersen was barred from performing audits. The damage to the firm was such that the company no longer operates, although it has not been dissolved formally.

It is still not clear why Andersen auditors failed to ask Enron to better explain its complex partnerships before certifying Enron's financial statements. Some observers believe that the large consulting fees Enron paid Andersen unduly influenced the company's decisions. An Andersen spokesperson said that the firm looked hard at all available information from Enron at the time. However, shortly after speaking to Lay Vice President Sherron Watkins took her concerns to an Andersen audit partner who reportedly conveyed her questions to senior Andersen management responsible for the Enron account. It is not clear what action, if any, Andersen took.

THE FALLOUT

Although Enron executives obviously engaged in misconduct, some people have questioned the tactics that federal investigators used against Enron. Many former Enron employees feel that it was almost impossible to obtain a fair trial for Lay and Skilling. The defense was informed that 130 of Enron's top managers, who could have served as witnesses for the defense, were considered unindicted co-conspirators with Lay and Skilling. Therefore, the defense could not obtain witnesses from Enron's top management teams under fear that the prosecution would indict the witnesses.

Enron's demise caused tens of billions of dollars of investor losses, triggered a collapse of electricity-trading markets, and ushered in an era of accounting scandals that precipitated a global loss of confidence in corporate integrity. Today companies must defend legitimate but complicated financing arrangements. Legislation like Sarbanes–Oxley, passed in the wake of Enron, has placed more restrictions on companies. Four thousand former Enron employees struggled to find jobs, and many retirees lost their entire retirement portfolios. One senior Enron executive committed suicide.

In 2003, Enron announced its intention to restructure and pay off its creditors. It was estimated that most creditors would receive between 14.4 and 18.3 cents for each dollar they were owed—more than most had expected. Under the plan, creditors would receive about two-thirds of the amount in cash and the rest in equity in three new companies, none of which would carry the tainted Enron name. The three companies were CrossCountry Energy Corporation, Prisma Energy International, Inc., and Portland General Electric.

CrossCountry Energy Corporation would retain Enron's interests in three North American natural gas pipelines. In 2004, Enron announced an agreement to sell Cross-Country Energy to CCE Holdings LLC for $2.45 billion. The money was to be used for debt repayment, and represented a substantial increase over a previous offer. Similarly, Prisma Energy International, Inc., which took over Enron's 19 international power and pipeline holdings, was sold to Ashmore Energy International Ltd. The proceeds from the sale were given out to creditors through cash distributions. The third company, Portland

General Electric (PGE), Oregon's largest utility, emerged from bankruptcy as an independent company through a private stock offering to Enron creditors.

All remaining assets not related to CrossCountry, Prisma, or Portland General were liquidated. Although Enron emerged from Chapter 11 bankruptcy protection in 2004, the company was wound down once the recovery plan had been carried out. That year, all of Enron's outstanding common stock and preferred stock were cancelled. Each record holder of Enron Corporation stock on the day it was cancelled was allocated an uncertified, non-transferable interest in one of two trusts that held new shares of the Enron Corporation.

The Enron Creditors Recovery Corporation was formed to help Enron creditors. It stated that its mission was "to reorganize and liquidate the remaining operations and assets of Enron following one of the largest and most complex bankruptcies in U.S. history." In the very unlikely event that the value of Enron's assets would exceed the amount of its allowed claims, distributions were to be made to the holders of these trust interests in the same order of priority of the stock they previously held.

In addition to trying to repay its shareholders, Enron also had to pay California for fraudulent activities it committed against the state's citizens. The company was investigated in California for allegedly colluding with at least two other power sellers in 2000 to obtain excess profits by submitting false information to the manager of California's electricity grid. In 2005, Enron agreed to pay California $47 million for taking advantage of California consumers during an energy shortage.

LEARNING FROM ENRON

Enron was the biggest business scandal of its time, and legislation like the Sarbanes–Oxley Act was passed to prevent future business fraud. But did the business world truly learn its lesson from Enron's collapse? Greed and corporate misconduct continued to be a problem throughout the first decade of the twenty-first century, culminating in the 2008–2009 global recession. Corporations praised high performance at any cost, even when employees cut ethical corners. In the mortgage market, companies like Countrywide rewarded their sales force for making risky subprime loans, even going so far as to turn their back on loans that they knew contained falsified information in order to make a quick profit. Other companies traded in risky financial instruments like credit default swaps (CDSs) when they knew that buyers did not have a clear understanding of the risks of such instruments. Although they promised to insure against default of these instruments, the companies did not have enough funds to cover the losses after the housing bubble burst. The resulting recession affected the entire world, bankrupting such established companies as Lehman Brothers and requiring government intervention in the amount of nearly $1 trillion in Troubled Asset Referendum Program (TARP) funds to salvage numerous financial firms. The economic meltdown inspired a new wave of legislation designed to prevent corporate misconduct, including the Dodd–Frank Wall Street Reform and Consumer Protection Act.

It is unfortunate that the Enron scandal did not hinder corporate misconduct. However, Enron still has lessons to teach us. Along with the business scandals of the financial crisis, Enron demonstrates that, first, regulatory agencies must be improved so as to better detect corporate misconduct. Second, companies and regulatory authorities should pay attention to the warnings of concerned employees and "whistle-blowers." Third, executives should understand the risks and rewards of the financial instruments their companies use and maintain a thorough knowledge of the inner workings of their companies (something that Ken Lay claimed he did not have). These conditions are crucial to preventing similar business frauds in the future.

CONCLUSION

The example of Enron shows how an aggressive corporate culture that rewards high performance and gets rid of the "weak links" can backfire. Enron's culture encouraged intense competition, not only among employees from rival firms but also among Enron employees themselves. Such behavior creates a culture where loyalty and ethics are cast aside in favor of high performance. The arrogant tactics of Jeffrey Skilling and the apparent ignorance of Ken Lay further contributed to an unhealthy corporate culture that encouraged cutting corners and falsifying information to inflate earnings.

The allegations surrounding Merrill Lynch's and Arthur Andersen's involvement in the debacle demonstrate that rarely does any scandal of such magnitude involve only one company. Whether a company or regulatory body participates directly in a scandal or whether it refuses to act by looking the other way, the result can be further perpetuation of fraud. This fact was emphasized during the 2008–2009 financial crisis, in which the misconduct of several major companies and the failure of monitoring efforts by regulatory bodies contributed to the worst financial crisis since the Great Depression. With the country recovering from widespread corporate corruption, the story of Enron is once again at the forefront of people's minds. Andy Fastow has stated that businesspeople are falling into the same trap as he fell into at Enron and believes fraud is "ten times worse" today than it was during Enron's time.

The Enron scandal has become legendary. In 2005, four years after the scandal, a movie was made about the collapse of Enron called *Enron: The Smartest Guys in the Room*. To this day, Jeffrey Skilling continues to maintain his innocence and appeal his case. In April of 2012, the Supreme Court denied his appeal, claiming that any errors made in the trial were negligible. However, the following year a federal judge reduced Skilling's sentence to 14 years. Enron's auditor, Arthur Andersen, faced over 40 shareholder lawsuits claiming damages of more than $32 billion. In 2009, the defunct company agreed to pay $16 million to Enron creditors. Enron itself faced many civil actions, and a number of Enron executives faced federal investigations, criminal actions, and civil lawsuits. As for the giant tilted "E" logo so proudly displayed outside of corporate headquarters, it was auctioned off for $44,000.

QUESTIONS FOR DISCUSSION

1. How did the corporate culture of Enron contribute to its bankruptcy?
2. Did Enron's bankers, auditors, and attorneys contribute to Enron's demise? If so, how?
3. What role did the company's chief financial officer play in creating the problems that led to Enron's financial problems?

SOURCES

Associated Press, "Ex-Enron CFO Fastow Indicted on 78 Counts," *The Los Angeles Times*, November 1, 2002, http://articles.latimes.com/2002/nov/01/business/fi-fastow1 (accessed May 26, 2015); Associated Press, "Merrill Lynch Settles an Enron Lawsuit," *The New York Times*, July 7, 2006, http://www.nytimes.com/2006/07/07/business/07enron.html?scp=3&sq=%22merrill%20lynch%22%20enron&st=cse (accessed May 26,

2015); Associated Press, "Two Enron Traders Avoid Prison Sentences," *The New York Times*, February 15, 2007, http://www.nytimes.com/2007/02/15/business/15enron.html?ex=1329195600&en=0f87e8ca83a557ed&ei=5090&partner=rssuserland&emc=rss (accessed May 26, 2015); Alexei Barrionuevo, "Fastow Gets His Moment in the Sun," *The New York Times*, November 10, 2006, http://www.nytimes.com/2006/11/10/business/10fastow.html (accessed May 26, 2015); Alexei Barrionuevo, Jonathan Weil, and John R. Wilke, "Enron's Fastow Charged with Fraud," *The Wall Street Journal*, October 3, 2002, A3–A4; Eric Berger, "Report Details Enron's Deception," *The Houston Chronicle*, March 6, 2003, 1B, 11B; Associated Press, "Enron Settles California Price-Gouging Claim," *USA Today*, July 15, 2005, http://usatoday30.usatoday.com/money/industries/energy/2005-07-15-enron-sate-settlement_x.htm (accessed May 26, 2015); John Carney, "The Truth about Why Jeff Skilling's Sentence Got Downsized," *CNBC*, June 21, 2013, http://www.cnbc.com/id/100835443# (accessed January 26, 2015); Christine Y. Chen, "When Good Firms Get Bad Chi," *Fortune*, November 11, 2002, 56; Scott Cohn, "Fastow: Enron Didn't Have to Go Bankrupt," *CNBC*, June 26, 2013, http://www.cnbc.com/id/100847519 (accessed May 26, 2015); Francesca Di Meglio, "Enron's Andrew Fastow: The Mistakes I Made," *Bloomberg Businessweek*, March 22, 2012, http://www.bloomberg.com/bw/articles/2012-03-22/enrons-andrew-fastow-the-mistakes-i-made (accessed May 26, 2015); Kurt Eichenwald, "Enron Founder, Awaiting Prison, Dies in Colorado," *The New York Times*, July 6, 2006, http://www.nytimes.com/2006/07/06/business/06enron.html (accessed May 26, 2015); Peter Elkind and Bethany McLean, "Feds Move up Enron Food Chain," *Fortune*, December 30, 2002, 43–44; Enron Creditors Recovery Co., "Enron Announces Completed Sale of Prisma Energy International, Inc.," September 7, 2006, http://www.enron.com/index_option_com_content_task_view_id_94_Itemid_34.htm (accessed August 8, 2014); Enron Creditors Recovery Corp. website, http://www.enron.com/ (accessed August 8, 2014); Greg Farrell, "Former Enron CFO Charged," *USA Today*, October 3, 2002, B1; Greg Farrell, Edward Iwata, and Thor Valdmanis, "Prosecutors Are Far from Finished," *USA Today*, October 3, 2002, 1–2B; Mark Felsenthal and Lillia Zuill, "AIG Gets $150 Billion Government Bailout; Posts Huge Losses," *Reuters*, November 10, 2008, http://www.reuters.com/article/topNews/idUSTRE4A92FM20081110?feedType=RSS&feedName=topNews (accessed May 26, 2015); O. C. Ferrell, "Ethics," *BizEd*, May/June 2002, 43–45; O. C. Ferrell and Linda Ferrell, "The Responsibility and Accountability of CEOs: The Last Interview with Ken Lay," *Journal of Business Ethics* 100 (2011): 209–219; O. C. Ferrell and Linda Ferrell, *Examining Systemic Issues That Created Enron and the Latest Global Financial Industry Crisis* (2009), White paper; O. C. Ferrell and Linda Ferrell, "Understanding the Importance of *Business Ethics* in the 2008–2009 Financial Crisis," in eds. Ferrell, Fraedrich, and Ferrell, *Business Ethics*, 7th ed. (Boston, MA: Houghton Mifflin, 2009); Jeffrey Fick, "Report: Merrill Replaced Enron Analyst," *USA Today*, July 30, 2002, B1; IBD's Washington Bureau, "Finger-Pointing Starts as Congress Examines Enron's Fast Collapse," *Investor's Business Daily*, February 8, 2002, A1; Daren Fonda, "Enron: Picking over the Carcass," *Fortune*, December 30, 2002–January 6, 2003, 56; Mike France, "One Big Client, One Big Hassle," *BusinessWeek*, January 28, 2002, 38–39; Bryan Gruley and Rebecca Smith, "Keys to Success Left Kenneth Lay Open to Disaster," *The Wall Street Journal*, April 26, 2002, A1, A5; Tom Hamburger, "Enron CEO Declines to Testify at Hearing," *The Wall Street Journal*, December 12, 2001, B2; Daniel Kadlec, "Power Failure," *Time*, December 2, 2001, http://content.time.com/time/magazine/article/0,9171,1001395,00.html (accessed May 26, 2015); Daniel Kadlec, "Enron: Who's Accountable?" *Time*, January 13, 2002, http://content.time.com/time/magazine/article/0,9171,1001636,00.html (accessed May 26, 2015); Jeremy Kahn, "The Chief Freaked Out Officer," *Fortune*, December 9, 2002, 197–198, 202; Matthew Karnitschnig, Carrick Mollenkamp, and Dan Fitzpatrick, "Bank of America to Buy Merrill," The Wall Street Journal, September 15, 2008, http://online.wsj.com/article/SB122142278543033525.html?mod=special_coverage (accessed May 26, 2015); Kathryn Kranhold and Rebecca Smith, "Two Other Firms in Enron Scheme, Documents Say," *The Wall Street Journal*, May 9, 2002, C1, C12; Scott Lanman and Craig Torres, "Republican Staff Says Fed Overstepped on Merrill Deal (Update 1)," *Bloomberg*, June 10, 2009, http://www.bloomberg.com/apps/news?pid=newsarchive&sid=a5A4F5W_PygQ (accessed May 26, 2015); Juan A. Lozano, "U.S. Court Orders Skilling Resentenced," *The Washington Post*, January 7, 2009, http://www.washingtonpost.com/wp-dyn/content/article/2009/01/06/AR2009010603214.html (accessed May 26, 2015); Bethany McLean, "Why Enron Went Bust," *Fortune*, December 24, 2001, 58, 60–62, 66, 68; Jodie Morse and Amanda Bower, "The Party Crasher," *Fortune*, December 30, 2002–January 6, 2003, 53–56; Belverd E. Needles, Jr. and Marian Powers, "Accounting for Enron," Houghton Mifflin's Guide to the Enron

Crisis (Boston, MA: Houghton Mifflin, 2003), 3–6; Floyd Norris, "Ruling Could Open Door to New Trial in Enron Case," *The New York Times*, January 6, 2009, http://www.nytimes.com/2009/01/07/business/07enron.html?scp=3&sq=skilling&st=nyt (accessed May 26, 2015); "Playing the Blame Game," *Time*, January 20, 2002, http://content.time.com/time/interactive/0,31813,2013797,00.html (accessed May 26, 2015); Brian Ross and Alice Gomstyn, "Lehman Brothers Boss Defends $484 Million in Salary, Bonus," *ABC News*, October 6, 2008, http://www.abcnews.go.com/Blotter/Story?id=5965360&page=1 (accessed May 26, 2015); Miriam Schulman, "Enron: Whatever Happened to Going down with the Ship?" Markkula Center for Applied Ethics, www.scu.edu/ethics/publications/ethicalperspectives/schulman0302.html (accessed August 8, 2014); William Sigismond, "The Enron Case from a Legal Perspective," in *Houghton Mifflin's Guide to Enron*, an uncorrected proof (Boston, MA: Houghton Mifflin, 2003), 11–13; Rebecca Smith and Kathryn Kranhold, "Enron Knew Portfolio's Value," *The Wall Street Journal*, May 6, 2002, C1, C20; Rebecca Smith and Mitchell Pacelle, "Enron Plans Return to Its Roots," *The Wall Street Journal*, May 2, 2002, A1; Andrew Ross Sorkin, "Ex-Enron Chief Skilling Appeals to Supreme Court," DealBook Blog, *The New York Times*, March 12, 2009, http://dealbook.blogs.nytimes.com/2009/05/12/former-enron-chiefskilling-appeals-to-supreme-court/?scp=1-b&sq=skilling&st=nyt (accessed September 7, 2009); "Times Topics: Enron Creditors Recovery Corporation (Formerly Enron Corporation)," *The New York Times*, http://topics.nytimes.com/top/news/business/companies/enron/index.html?scp=1-spot&sq=Enron&st=cse (accessed May 26, 2015); Jake Ulick, "Enron: A Year Later," *CNN Money*, December 2, 2002, http://money.cnn.com/2002/11/26/news/companies/enron_anniversary/index.htm (accessed May 26, 2015); "The Other Side of the Enron Story," Ungagged.net, http://ungagged.net (accessed May 26, 2015); Joseph Weber, "Can Andersen Survive?" *BusinessWeek*, January 28, 2002, 39–40; James Vicini, "Supreme Court Rejects Jeffrey Skilling's Appeal In Enron Case," *The Huffington Post*, April 16, 2012, http://www.huffingtonpost.com/2012/04/16/supreme-court-jeffrey-skilling_n_1428432.html (accessed May 26, 2015); Thomas Weidlich, "Arthur Andersen Settles Enron Suit for $16 Million," Bloomberg.com, April 28, 2009, http://www.bloomberg.com/apps/news?pid=20601072&sid=avopmnT7eWjs (accessed May 26, 2015); Winthrop Corporation, "Epigraph," *Houghton Mifflin's Guide to Enron*, 1; Wendy Zellner, "A Hero—and a Smoking-Gun Letter," *Business Week*, January 28, 2002, 34–35; Selah Maya Zighelboim, "Former Enron CFO Andrew Fastow Reflects on Business Ethics," *McCombs Today*, February 18, 2015, http://www.today.mccombs.utexas.edu/2015/02/former-enron-cfo-andrew-fastow-ethics (accessed May 26, 2015).

CASE 10

Lululemon: Encouraging a Healthier Lifestyle*

INTRODUCTION

Lululemon Athletica is an athletic apparel company intended for individuals with active lifestyles. The organization has deep roots in the yoga community and is one of the few businesses to offer apparel for this specific market. Lululemon is based in Vancouver, British Columbia, Canada, and operates its clothing stores in numerous countries throughout the world. The apparel store offers product lines that include fitness pants, shorts, tops, and jackets for activities such as yoga, running, and other fitness programs. It operates in three segments. These segments consist of corporate-owned and operated retail stores, a direct to consumer e-commerce website, and wholesale avenues. As of 2015, the company operates 302 stores predominantly in the United States, Canada, Australia, New Zealand, and Singapore. With more than 8,600 worldwide employees, Lululemon has grown rapidly in the last 20 years and is expected to continue its growth strategy well into the foreseeable future. It has also established a subsidiary geared toward youth called Ivivva Athletica.

Store growth and expansion into other countries has allowed Lululemon to achieve financial success. The organization has seen continuous increases in revenue, with its 2014 annual revenue nearing $1.8 billion. While financially stable, the organizational structure has seen changes with the hiring of a new CEO. Lululemon hired Laurent Potdevin in early 2014 hoping to appoint a worthy and experienced industry professional. The company also hopes to distance itself from negative headlines circling former CEO Denis "Chip" Wilson. Potdevin was once the CEO at Toms and has worked in the industry for over 20 years.

There is no question that Lululemon has seen great success in recent years. From its conception in 1998, the organization has grown tremendously in markets across the globe. However, Lululemon's success has also been tainted by controversy, negative publicity, and questionable ethical decisions. This case will detail the issues and controversies circling this organization and identify how Lululemon has managed these issues. In addition, we provide information regarding the positive ethical decisions that have been made throughout Lululemon's history.

*This case was prepared by Justus Adams, Kristen Bruner, Ivan Mora Juarez, and Jennifer Sawayda for and under the direction of O.C. Ferrell and Linda Ferrell ©2015. It was prepared for classroom discussion rather than to illustrate either effective or ineffective handling of an administrative, ethical, or legal decision by management. All sources used for this case were obtained through publicly available material.

BACKGROUND

Lululemon was founded by Denis "Chip" Wilson in 1998 in British Colombia, Canada. Prior to Lululemon, Wilson had spent two decades in the surf, skate, and snowboard business. He was looking for a change. After attending the first commercial yoga class offered in Vancouver, Wilson fell in love with the activity and felt incredible during and after the exercises. With a passion for technical athletic fabrics, Wilson realized that the current cotton clothing being used for power yoga was inappropriate and unpractical. Movements required breathability, flexibility, and a stretchiness that an individual could pour sweat into during exercise. With this in mind, Wilson created a design studio for his new clothing. Struggling to pay rent, the design studio became a yoga studio during the night hours. Yoga instructors who taught at the studio were asked to wear the new products and provided Wilson with useful insight and feedback on the clothing. In order to name the new company, Wilson surveyed 100 people and offered a list of 20 brand names as well as 20 logos. Lululemon is a created word that has neither roots nor meaning. It is believed that Wilson selected this name because he enjoys the sound of the 3 L's when the word is spoken. The logo, which is actually a stylized letter A, was a logo intended for the brand name Athletically Hip, which was not selected as the company's name.

The first store opened in November 2000, in the beach area of Vancouver, British Columbia. The store was intended to be a community-gathering place for individuals to discuss health topics like dieting, exercise, and cycling. However, the store was so popular and busy that satisfying the customer became nearly impossible. The business grew quickly as products were popular among customers and the staff was eager to learn, expand, and challenge themselves.

From the beginning, Lululemon had a strong mission that embraced a healthy and active lifestyle. Inspired by author and philosopher Ayn Rand, Chip Wilson modeled Lululemon with the intent that involves "elevating the world from mediocrity to greatness." The company adopted the following mission statement: "Creating components for people to live longer, healthier, fun lives." Lululemon tries to reflect this in its corporate culture. Store managers, for instance, are provided with much control over the operations of their stores, and Lululemon operates with a decentralized corporate culture. Lululemon employees are recruited and hired based on their level of commitment and how well they fit into the corporate culture. To bring its mission statement to fruition, Lululemon refers to its employees as "educators" to acknowledge the crucial role they play in helping customers to obtain a healthy and active lifestyle.

Lululemon stores today are focused heavily on community involvement and interaction with local enthusiasts. Nearly all stores host in-house events on a nightly or weekly basis, with classes ranging from beginner and advanced yoga to goal setting and self-defense workshops. Events and workshops generally occur after store hours on the sale-room floor after racks and products have been moved.

Unlike many stores, Lululemon does not offer discounts, but sells approximately 95 percent of its products at full price. It also sells its products at higher prices than its competitors, reflecting the value of Lululemon's products. Lululemon operates on the concept of scarcity to encourage customers to buy immediately. Its store shelves often have fewer products than the shelves can hold, and many products have quick life cycle times such as six-week life cycles. Customers are therefore encouraged to purchase the product before it is gone, which is thought to be a major influence in Lululemon's continued popularity and success with customers. In fact, even secondhand clothes for Lululemon sell for large amounts of money. Fans are willing to pay hundreds of dollars over the original store price to acquire limited-edition Lululemon products on sites like eBay.

In order to anchor its mission statement, Lululemon has adopted seven core values: quality, product, integrity, balance, entrepreneurship, fun, and greatness. These values serve to motivate employees and guide their decisions.

ETHICAL RISKS AND CHALLENGES

Despite Lululemon's strong mission statement and core values, Lululemon has faced much controversy over its history. Founder and former CEO Chip Wilson has also been criticized for controversial statements he has made, which eventually helped lead to his ouster as CEO. There have also been questions regarding whether Lululemon's corporate culture—with its strong emphasis on greatness and competitiveness—is necessarily healthy for employees.

Founder Chip Wilson

Lululemon founder Chip Wilson is thought of by many as a man with unorthodox opinions. Although Wilson has not been CEO since 2005, he has been known to do things without informing top management, such as printing out Lululemon tote bags with the phrase "Who Is John Galt?" from Ayn Rand's *Atlas Shrugged*. A former CEO at Lululemon felt pressured by Wilson to attend the Landmark Forum, a leadership-development training program which Wilson highly supports. Wilson has done other controversial actions that have generated concern from Lululemon's board.

Much of the controversy around Chip Wilson centers on his statements. For instance, in a 2009 interview with Canada's *National Post Business Magazine*, he admitted to having chosen the company name because "it's funny to watch [Japanese] say it." Wilson also stated on a blog his opinion that the rise in divorce rates and breast cancer among "Power Women" was due to a combination of smoking, taking birth control pills, and the additional stress which came from taking on the career responsibilities once held mostly by men. He attributed Lululemon's growth as stemming from the coming together of "female education levels, breast cancer, yoga/athletics, and the desire to dress feminine."

Another highly controversial statement of Chip Wilson's involves his opinions regarding child labor laws. Wilson argued that "third-world children should be allowed to work in factories because it provides them with much-needed wages." He claimed this can help lead citizens of these countries out of poverty. The practice of child labor is a hot-button issue in the Western world because of the poor working conditions and rampant abuse worldwide. This support of child labor has angered critics, who believe Lululemon might be exploiting children in developing countries. They argue that providing children with more education is much more likely to lift them out of poverty than having them earn low wages at a dangerous job. Lululemon founder Chip Wilson would continue to make controversial statements, eventually leading to his resignation as Chairman of the Board.

Chip Wilson later challenged the board, claiming that the current board was not aligned with Lululemon's core values. He released this statement at the June 2014 shareholders meeting and voted against the board's chairman and another director. Both men were reelected. A few months later, Wilson sold half of his 27 percent stake to private equity organization Advent International, who in turn received two board seats on Lululemon's board. With less of a stake in the firm, Wilson's impact on decision making at the organization may be reduced.

MISLEADING ADVERTISING

In 2007 the *New York Times* cast doubt on the authenticity of Lululemon's VitaSea line of products. Lululemon claimed that its VitaSea products were infused with seaweed, which had medicinal properties including stress relief. In November 2007, the *New York Times* released an article claiming that it had tested VitaSea products and could not find seaweed fiber in the product. This claim unleashed a storm of criticism.

Lululemon responded by refuting the claims of the *New York Times*. It cited independent tests performed the previous year. It also responded to the accusations by stating that a lab in Hong Kong had performed different tests on the product throughout the year, all of which confirmed that the products contained everything that it advertised.

However, Canada's Competition Bureau challenged Lululemon, not due to the content of the VitaSea product, but rather the company's claims about the product's health benefits. The bureau believed that these claims of health benefits from seaweed were unsubstantiated and ordered Lululemon to remove all such labeling.

Corporate Culture

As mentioned earlier, Wilson founded his company based upon the values of Ayn Rand. The notion of striving for greatness resonated with Wilson after having read Rand's book *Atlas Shrugged* at the age of 18. Since then, he has utilized the concept as a way to market his brand. This idea of "greatness" contributes to a competitive organizational culture. Wilson admits that the firm tries to hire employees with Type A personalities, or those with more competitive personalities who are concerned with achievement and personal improvement. New hires read books selected by Chip Wilson that he feels is critical to personal development. Employees are also required to write out their goals for the next 10 years, which are then posted in Lululemon stores. Employees are encouraged to exercise regularly and remain close-knit.

Some have questioned how this competitive culture obsessed with greatness fits in with the yoga tradition based on Buddhist and Hindu philosophies. Both ideologies promote the notion of ridding one's self of the Ego. The Ego is seen as a source of suffering, and Buddhism is based on the absolution of suffering. Enlightenment is achieved when the Ego has been successfully removed. There are specific postures used to accomplish this, and it can take years of practice. On the other hand, one of the criticisms of Lululemon goes back to Ayn Rand's teachings and their promotion of "rugged individualism," the elevation of mediocrity to greatness, and the relentless pursuit of happiness. Despite it being a business, some believe that these "individual" teachings do not belong in the yoga clothing industry, because they directly contradict the Vedic philosophy that underlies yoga. Others have claimed that Lululemon's corporate culture is almost "cultish" in its style. When Lululemon donated $750,000 to the Dalai Lama Center for Peace and Education, it received both praise and criticism. While the Dalai Lama Center's chairman cited the company's generosity, critics believed the Dalai Lama should not be associated with a profit-making organization. However, the company claims that the donation fits well with its vision of mind-body-heart.

In March 2011, an employee of a Lululemon store located in Bethesda, Maryland, was brutally murdered by her coworker after hours. It is believed the employee had observed the coworker trying to steal clothing from Lululemon. After the store closed, the coworker lured the employee back into the store and brutally murdered her. She then attempted to make the scene look as if two masked men had broken in and harmed them. After the truth was revealed, the coworker was sentenced to life in prison without parole.

Lululemon and many others attribute this brutality as a random act of violence. However, those who describe the corporate culture as "cultish" and "competitive" argue that the culture creates an environment where employees are pressured to live up to company standards. Although this in itself is certainly not the reason for the murder, critics have sometimes charged Lululemon with having an unethical corporate culture promoting competition over collaboration.

Too-Sheer Yoga Pants

A more recent ethical problem for Lululemon occurred in March 2013, when it released black Luon yoga pants that become sheer when the wearer would bend over. The company instituted a massive recall which comprised 17 percent of all the women's pants sold in their stores. Even more damaging, the *New York Post* released a statement from a customer who claimed that she had to demonstrate the sheerness of her yoga pants by bending over in the store so the associate could check. Lululemon immediately released a statement saying that such conduct was not company policy and that they would accept returns from customers with no questions asked.

The recall resulted in large shortages, which impacted financial results and drove the stock price down. The company lost $2 billion in market value. Certain styles of Lululemon pants have also been accused of pilling, which occurs when fiber in the pants balls up. After the recall of the too-sheer yoga pants, investors attempted to sue Lululemon, claiming that they purposefully hid defects in the pants. However, the lawsuit was dismissed the next year.

The scandal resulted in the resignation of CEO Christine Day. A few months later, in November 2013, Chip Wilson defended his product by suggesting that women's bodies are to blame for the fabric's sheerness and their tendency for pilling. He also claims that many women buy pants that are too small for them, which wears them out. When questioned about whether Lululemon is truly a clothing retailer for everybody, Wilson stated that the product is appropriate for all sizes but that some people simply misuse the product. Critics viewed this as a sexist comment, exacerbating the issue at hand. Perhaps in an attempt to make a joke, a store in Bethesda, Maryland, featured a poem on its window: "Cups of Chai, Apple Pie, Rubbing Thighs." A photo of the poem was shared on Twitter. The company apologized and the poem was removed. In the midst of consumer outrage, Wilson stepped down as Chairman of the Board.

Customer Privacy

Lululemon is known for wanting to avoid collecting large amounts of customer information through big data techniques. Instead, it desires to have a close and open relationship with customers. One of the ways it does this is by listening to customers as they shop in the store. Lululemon takes customer complaints or concerns seriously and will attempt to make decisions based on this information.

Although this emphasis on listening to the customer is an important part of Lululemon's customer relations, some people believe Lululemon takes it too far. A less well-known ethical risk that the company practices is the training of retail employees to eavesdrop on their customers. Lululemon prefers this to spending money on marketing software that tracks purchases, or sending out survey requests. Christine Day, the former CEO, used to spend much of her time in retail stores, pretending to be a customer, in order to listen to complaints and observe shopping habits. When she was with the company, she had stores set up their clothes-folding tables next to the fitting rooms so employees could better over-hear any complaints. Whether these practices are smart marketing techniques or infringe-ments on privacy is ambiguous.

POSITIVE ETHICAL PRACTICES

Despite the criticisms launched against Lululemon, the mission to help customers live a better life continues. Lululemon defines having a better life as living healthier, leading to a longer and more adequate life. Its mission to elevate humanity from mediocrity to greatness demonstrates that it wants consumers and employees to achieve their maximum potential. This is not too different from Abraham Maslow's concept of self-actualization. Lululemon has developed a manifesto to describe its way of business: "We are passionate about sweating every day and we want the world to know it. Breathing deeply, drinking water, and getting outside also top the list of things we can't live without. Get to know our manifesto and learn a little more about what lights our fire."

This manifesto clearly shows the backbone of Lululemon and the way it does business. The manifesto strives toward providing greatness to the people that use Lululemon prod-ucts. The higher prices Lululemon charges are a sign of excellence and the belief that it is selling more than just clothing to the customers. It is a belief that the customer is buying a lifestyle that comes with the Lululemon brand and the set of values that Lululemon is con-veying in the manifesto. As a result, Lululemon has gained a large following and clientele that believe in its products.

Contributions to Communities

Lululemon takes its responsibilities to communities seriously. It recognizes that commu-nity involvement will not only help gain new customers, but will also promote its mis-sion of creating a healthier lifestyle. For these reasons, Lululemon holds free weekly yoga classes taught by fitness professionals. Lululemon shoppers who have attended the free yoga classes can get a 15 percent discount on their purchases.

Additionally, while the practice of secretly observing customers might be controver-sial in some ways, it also demonstrates Lululemon's commitment toward meeting customer needs. Lululemon believes that customer relationships are not based on technology, but rather on more basic marketing techniques like simply talking with the customer. The Lululemon culture encourages employees to establish strong connections with their cus-tomers, which is why the company emphasizes that its employees are "educators." By lis-tening carefully to customer concerns as they shop, Lululemon gets an immediate picture of problems that the company can address. For instance, one time when the CEO was in a Lululemon store she overheard many complaints that a certain type of knit sweater had sleeves that were too tight. Based on this information, she canceled future orders. It is clear that Lululemon is willing to make quick product changes in response to customer feedback.

Lululemon also contributes to local charities throughout its communities. In many communities, Lululemon empowers customers by offering the clientele the opportunity to suggest organizations and charities to receive donations. Lululemon's program allows for up to eight local charities to receive donations. This shows its commitment to its local communities and willingness to give back as much as possible, while still maintaining a healthy bottom line. Lululemon's efforts display a stakeholder mindset as it makes decisions that benefit its shareholders, clients, local neighborhoods, and nearby businesses.

RELATIONSHIPS WITH EMPLOYEES

Lululemon recognizes that customer satisfaction is only as good as the employees that provide it. Lululemon therefore strives to make its employees into ambassadors for the brand. This can only happen if employees are passionate and committed to company products and values. The hiring process at Lululemon is extensive as the firm only wants to hire those who it believes will be the right fit with its company culture. It is also costly. Applicants may go through more than one interview, and those that get farther in the process are often asked to attend yoga classes where the recruiters can see how they interact with others. When an applicant is chosen as an employee, he or she will undergo 30 hours of training. They also spend three weeks working on the floor.

As mentioned before, Lululemon strives to get its employees inspired. Employees must develop their personal goals, which are then hung in the stores. To encourage healthy living and incentivize employees, the company offers staff free fitness classes. It also tries to help employees find the right balance between family and work. Lululemon frequently sends merchandising tips to sales employees and encourages them to take responsibility and ownership of the store.

Lululemon believes in hiring managers internally, which motivates lower-level employees because they know they have a good chance of becoming a leader. Approximately 70 percent of Lululemon managers are internal hires. Employee satisfaction at Lululemon appears to be high; in exit interviews, 90 percent of employees claim they would recommend for their friends to work at Lululemon.

Lululemon also offers its employees unique perks. It frequently sanctions events such as group hikes or exercise sessions to help its employees bond with one another. After a year of employment, Lululemon sends employees to the Landmark Forum, a three-day self-improvement program at a cost of approximately $500 per employee. (Some have criticized the Landmark Forum and Chip Wilson's endorsement of it, while others claim the experience transformed their lives.) Lululemon has also created the "Fund a Goal" program for high-performing employees. This incentive pays for these employees to achieve one of the goals on their list.

CONCLUSION

Lululemon focuses much of its efforts on the legacy that it will leave behind (the legacy it is creating now for future generations). Throughout the years, Lululemon has created a culture of promoting a healthy lifestyle, which can be achieved through healthy eating, yogi tradition, and in-store fitness classes. The company stresses a culture in which employees, customers, and other stakeholders can achieve greatness. As a result, the organization has seen rapid success and growth during the last decade. However, the company has been hit by a number of scandals, requiring it to rebuild its reputation and adopt new leadership.

The changes that Lululemon has implemented demonstrate that the organization is willing to make difficult decisions to do the right thing. If Lululemon continues to put stakeholders first and refuses to deviate from its values, it is likely to avoid similar ethical issues in the future. A strong values-based corporate culture will help Lululemon remain a successful company with a reputation for both ethical behavior and quality products. In addition, most companies the size of Lululemon have an effective ethics and compliance program to help build an ethical culture. Based on past issues that the company has faced, it appears that it is time to embrace a more proactive approach to managing ethics and social responsibility.

QUESTIONS FOR DISCUSSION

1. How has Lululemon handled various ethical issues that it has faced over the last few years?
2. How has the ethical culture of Lululemon impacted its relationship with customers and employees?
3. To avoid negative publicity and ethical challenges, what steps should Lululemon take to improve its stakeholder relationships?

SOURCES

Mae Anderson, "Lululemon: No demo needed to return yoga pants," *USA Today*, March 27, 2013, http://www.usatoday.com/story/money/business/2013/03/27/lululemon-pants-returns/2025041/ (accessed May 7, 2015); Kim Bhasin, "Lululemon Partners with Dalai Lama, Enrages Critics," *The Huffington Post*, October 25, 2014, http://www.huffingtonpost.com/2014/10/25/lululemon-dalai-lama_n_6044832.html (accessed May 7, 2015); Bloomberg L.P., "Lululemon Athletica Inc (LULU:Consolidated Issue Listed on NASDAQ Global Select)," *Bloomberg Businessweek*, May 7, 2015, http://www.bloomberg.com/research/stocks/snapshot/snapshot.asp?ticker=LULU (accessed May 7, 2015); David Creelman, "Embracing the Unorthodox: Welcome to the High Commitment Workplace," *HR Voice*, January 26, 2012, http://www.hrvoice.org/embracing-the-unorthodox-welcome-to-the-high-commitment-workplace/ (accessed May 16, 2014); Jim Edwards, "12 Utterly Bizarre Facts about the Rise Of Lululemon, the Cult-Like Yoga Brand," *Business Insider*, April 24, 2012, http://www.businessinsider.com/12-utterly-bizarre-facts-about-the-rise-of-lululemon-2012-4?op=1 (accessed May 16, 2014); Amelia Hill, "I Thought I'd Be Brainwashed. But How Wrong Could I Be…" *The Guardian*, December 13, 2003, http://www.theguardian.com/uk/2003/dec/14/ameliahill.theobserver (accessed May 16, 2014); "Hiring for Culture Fit at Lululemon Athletica," *Canadian HR Reporter*, http://www.hrreporter.com/videodisplay/190-hiring-for-culture-fit-at-lululemon-athletica (accessed May 16, 2014); Chris Isidore, "See-through pants problem causes Lululemon recall," *CNN Money*, March 19, 2013, http://money.cnn.com/2013/03/19/news/companies/lululemon-pants/index.html?iid=EL (accessed May 16, 2014); Suzanne Kapner and Joann S. Lublin, "Lululemon Founder Shrinks Role, Clears Way for New CEO," *The Wall Street Journal*, December 10, 2013, B1–B2; Sally Kempton, "Sophisticated Ego," *Ego*, http://www.yogajournal.com/wisdom/2502 (accessed May 16, 2014); Stewart J. Lawrence, "Murder at Lululemon: Yoga's 'Heart of Darkness'?" *The Huffington Post*, November 9, 2011, http://www.huffingtonpost.com/stewart-j-lawrence/when-yogis-kill-the-grisl_b_1077457.html (accessed May 16, 2014); Colleen Leahy and Christine Day, "Lululemon CEO: How to Build Trust Inside Your Company," *CNN Money*, May 16, 2012, http://management.fortune.cnn.com/2012/03/16/lululemon-christine-day/ (accessed May 16, 2014); Joann S. Lublin and Suzanne Kapner, "Lululemon Founder Sparks a Fight with Board," *The Wall Street Journal*, June 11, 2014, http://online.wsj.com/articles/lululemon-founder-votes-against-chairman-1402483176 (accessed

August 8, 2014); "Lululemon Athletica Inc (LULU) Snapshot," *Businessweek*, http://investing.businessweek. com/research/stocks/snapshot/snapshot.asp?ticker=LULU (accessed May 16, 2014); Lululemon Athletica website, http://www.lululemon.com/ (accessed May 16, 2014); Lululemon Athletica, "Lululemon Athletica Inc. Announces Fourth Quarter and Full Year Fiscal 2014 Results," March 26, 2015, http://files.shareholder.com/ downloads/LULU/150541151x0x817944/0356DF58-C65B-4617-96C2-CF0B6335E544/LULU_News_2015_3_26_ General_Releases.pdf (accessed May 7, 2015); "Lululemon to Remove Claims from Seaweed Product Line," *CBC News*, November 16, 2007, http://www.cbc.ca/news/business/lululemon-to-remove-claims-from-seaweed-clothing-line-1.655660 (accessed May 16, 2014); Lululemon, *Workplace Code of Conduct*, June 2007, http:// www.lululemon.com/about/lululemon_code_of_conduct.pdf (accessed May 16, 2014); Melissa Lustrin and Felicia Patinkin, "Lululemon Founder Chip Wilson Blames Women's Bodies for Yoga Pant Problems," *ABC News*, November 7, 2013, http://abcnews.go.com/US/lululemon-founder-chip-wilson-blames-womens-bodies-yoga/story?id=20815278 (accessed May 16, 2014); Ashley Lutz, "Lululemon Spends $500 for Workers to Attend a Controversial Retreat Endorsed by Founder Chip Wilson," *Business Insider*, January 9, 2014, http://www. businessinsider.com/lululemons-landmark-retreat-for-workers-2014-1 (accessed May 16, 2014); Ashley Lutz, "You Really Have to 'Drink the Kool-Aid' at Lululemon to Succeed at Lululemon," *Business Insider*, February 19, 2013, http://www.businessinsider.com/what-its-like-to-work-at-lululemon-2013-2# (accessed May 16, 2014); Mary Mann, "Yoga, Spinning and a Murder: My strange Months at Lululemon," *Salon*, December 31, 2013, http://www. salon.com/2013/12/31/yoga_spinning_and_a_murder_my_strange_months_at_lululemon/ (accessed May 16, 2014); Dana Mattioli, "Lululemon's Secret Sauce," *The Wall Street Journal*, March 22, 2012, http://online.wsj.com/ news/articles/SB10001424052702303812904577295882632723066 (accessed May 16, 2014); Laura McClure, "The Landmark Forum: 42 Hours, $500, 65 Breakdowns," *Mother Jones*, July/August 2009, http://www.motherjones. com/media/2009/07/landmark-42-hours-500-65-breakdowns (accessed May 16, 2014); Reuters, "Lululemon deals with new round of complaints about yoga pants," http://www.cnbc.com/id/101166793 (accessed May 7, 2015); Rheana Murray, "Lululemon rhymes 'apple pies' with 'rubbing thighs' on store window, enraging shoppers," *New York Daily News*, December 3, 2013, http://www.nydailynews.com/life-style/timeline-lululemon-controversy-article-1.1536169 (accessed May 7, 2015); Samantha Sharf, "Lululemon and Billionaire Founder Chip Wilson Call a Truce," *Forbes*, August 7, 2014, http://www.forbes.com/sites/samanthasharf/2014/08/07/lululemon-calls-a-truce-with-billionaire-founder-chip-wilson/(accessed August 8, 2014); Daniel Stashower, "The Yoga Store Murder: The Shocking True Account of the Lululemon Athletica Killing," *The Wall Street Journal*, November 29, 2013, http:// www.washingtonpost.com/opinions/the-yoga-store-murder-the-shocking-true-account-of-the-lululemon-athletica-killing-by-dan-morse/2013/11/29/36493e46-51fc-11e3-a7f0-b790929232e1_story.html (accessed May 16, 2014); Jonathan Stempel and Joseph Ax, "Lululemon Prevails in Lawsuit over Yoga Pants Recall," *Chicago Tribune*, April 4, 2014, http://articles.chicagotribune.com/2014-04-04/business/sns-rt-us-lululemon-lawsuit-yogapants-20140404_1_yoga-pants-dennis-chip-wilson-quality-control (accessed May 16, 2014); Mark Walker, "Lululemon Athletica—Driving a Culture of Individual and Organizational Development, Accountability and Innovation," *HRM Today*, September 29, 2011, http://www.hrmtoday.com/featured-stories/lululemon-athletica-driving-a-culture-of-individual-and-organizational-development-accountability-and-innovation/ (accessed May 16, 2014); "Yoga and Buddhism: Similarities and Differences," June 13, 2012, http://www.vedanet.com/2012/06/ yoga-and-buddhism-similarities-and-differences/ (accessed May 16, 2014).

CASE 11

Frauds of the Century*

Before Bernard Madoff, the average consumer had likely never heard of a Ponzi scheme. This little-known crime became a front-page headline in December 2008 when highly respected securities trader Bernard Madoff admitted to having operated a Ponzi scheme for more than a decade, leading to an investor loss of over $17 billion. Tom Petters, former CEO and chairman of Petters Worldwide, had already been arrested for an alleged $4 billion Ponzi scheme in October of that year. A few months later, respected financier R. Allen Stanford was arrested for a Ponzi scheme that cost investors $7 billion. Since then, over 500 additional Ponzi schemes have been uncovered; however, these three remain the largest in history.

A Ponzi scheme is a type of white-collar crime that occurs when a criminal—often of high repute—offers an apparent investment opportunity but never actually invests the money. Instead, the schemer spends the money for personal gain and keeps the façade going by using money from new investors to pay "earnings" for existing investors. The fraud therefore requires a constant influx of either new investors or reinvestment from current investors. When the scheme finally collapses, the most recent investors usually lose their entire investments.

Ponzi schemes are often confused with pyramid schemes, another form of fraud. Both types of criminal activity have the same basic structure. Pyramid schemes look like legitimate businesses, but actually lack genuine products or sustainable investment opportunities. A pyramid scheme offers individuals the opportunity to make money through selling a product, investing, or similar efforts. The key aspect of a pyramid scheme, however, is that an upfront fee is required to join. Participants are then encouraged and financially incentivized to bring in more recruits. Each new person pays to join in what is believed to be a legitimate opportunity to make a return, which is how the fraudster gets money. However, unlike a legitimate organization, pyramid schemes either do not sell a product, or the product or investment is almost worthless. All income comes from new people enrolling. Much like a Ponzi scheme, when enrollment dries up, the pyramid scheme dissolves; those few at the top of the "pyramid" profit, and those at the bottom of the "pyramid," such as newer enrollees, lose their investments.

The primary difference between a pyramid and a Ponzi scheme is that the perpetrator of the Ponzi scheme simply asks individuals to invest their money, promising an above-average return. No other action is required. The fraudster behind the pyramid scheme, on the other hand, leads individuals to believe they will be taking an active role in the venture such as selling a product, and in addition incentivizes them to recruit others. Also, pyramid schemes typically collapse much more quickly because they require exponential increases in participants to be sustained. In contrast, Ponzi schemes can survive simply by

*This case was prepared by Linda Ferrell, Jennifer Sawayda, and Isaac Emmanuel. It was prepared for classroom discussion rather than to illustrate either effective or ineffective handling of an administrative, ethical, or legal decision by management. All sources used for this case were obtained through publicly available material © 2015.

persuading most existing participants to reinvest their money, with a relatively small number of new recruits.

Both Ponzi schemes and pyramid schemes are highly damaging to consumers and the financial industry at large. They destroy lives when large investments or lifetime savings disappear overnight, often lead to years of costly and complicated litigation as investors try to recoup what they can, and sharply erode trust in the system, making it more difficult for legitimate businesspeople to find willing investors and participants. Pyramid schemes in particular look very similar to certain legitimate business models, sometimes making it difficult for interested individuals to determine if a new business opportunity is actually a pyramid scheme.

This case analyzes the detrimental impact of Ponzi and pyramid schemes on society. The first part of this analysis examines the harmful effects of Ponzi schemes as well as this century's most infamous Ponzi schemers. We then examine pyramid schemes, their negative impacts, and the confusion that can arise between them and legitimate business models. We conclude this analysis by reemphasizing the unique nature of white-collar criminals and reiterating the need for transparency, internal controls, and compliance standards within an organization.

THE IMPACT OF PONZI SCHEMES ON SOCIETY

Ponzi schemes are highly detrimental to society, not only because of the financial losses they incur but also due to the lack of trust they cause consumers to feel toward business in general. The financial industry in particular experienced a widespread loss of trust because of financial misconduct such as Ponzi schemes. One or two schemers can have an immense impact on an entire industry. Furthermore, Ponzi schemes do not seem to be decreasing in number: since 2008, over 500 Ponzi schemes have been uncovered, including over 100 actions taken by the SEC against 200 individual Ponzi schemers and 250 companies.

Victims of Ponzi schemes often lose major investments in the fraud. Victims range from low- to high-income individuals as well as companies and nonprofits. Organizations often lose the most money because of the significant investments they are able to make. For instance, in the Madoff scandal, many nonprofit organizations lost millions after the fraud was revealed. While participants that invest early enough may make money through fictional profits taken from newer investors, others may lose their entire lifesavings.

Additionally, while Ponzi schemes appear to thrive in the financial industry, they can exist in any industry where investments are made. In India, for instance, starting in 2005 farmers were made to believe that there was a significant market for emu meat, feathers, and oil. Farmers who purchased emu chicks received a promise from the con artist that the adult emus would be purchased at double the price originally paid for them. The farmers were also promised monthly payments. However, when the scheme collapsed in 2012 and the payments stopped, approximately 10,000 farmers were left with about 100,000 emus without any use for them. The total investor loss was estimated at between $50 and $100 million, not to mention the thousands of abandoned, starving birds. Albania was also the victim of several Ponzi schemes. In 1996 companies engaging in Ponzi schemes started promising Albanian investors more than 30 percent returns per month. Three million people whose average income was $8,000 per year invested more than $1.2 billion in the schemes. After they lost their investments, the Albanian economy collapsed and a massive uprising resulted in the deaths of 2,000 people.

It is also not uncommon for the victims of Ponzi schemes to unknowingly propagate the scheme through the recruitment of others. Investors with Bernard Madoff often convinced their friends and family members to invest and get in on the deal. The community of Lexington, North Carolina, was duped by a $600 million Ponzi scheme from online company ZeekRewards. Many investors were recruited by others in the community, resulting in a massive loss for the town when the scheme collapsed.

Fortunately, there are red flags for Ponzi schemes. These warning signs include high and/or consistent returns with little to no risk, unlicensed sellers, secret methodologies or strategies not divulged to investors, and paperwork problems. The biggest red flag is high and consistent returns. The reason is because the market itself is not consistent, so although an investor may have long-term profitability, short-term profits should vary yearly. Also, most Ponzi schemers are unlicensed sellers and use what they label "secretive" strategies to confuse investors. Lack of paperwork is another warning signal because Ponzi schemers want to avoid releasing information that could arouse suspicion. Unfortunately, Ponzi schemers are usually white-collar personas who, rather than fitting a stereotypical criminal profile, are often seen as successful people who inspire trust. The following examples bear this out.

The Original Ponzi Schemer

The Ponzi scheme was named after Charles Ponzi, who in the early twentieth century saw a way to profit from international reply coupons. An international reply coupon is a guarantee of return postage which can be included in an international letter and thus allow the recipient to reply without paying for postage. Ponzi determined he could make money by buying international reply coupons in countries where postage was cheaper and then redeeming these coupons for more expensive postage stamps in countries where the stamps were of higher value (an arbitrage transaction). Ponzi convinced investors to provide him with capital to trade coupons for higher-priced postage stamps. His promise to investors who joined in his scheme was a 50 percent profit in 45 days.

Ponzi's investment proposal quickly exploded in popularity and earned him a reputation as a financial wizard. He began living an opulent life just outside of Boston and would often bring in as much as $250,000 a day. Part of Ponzi's success came from his personal charisma and ability to con even savvy investors. People trusted Ponzi because he created an image of power, trust, and responsibility—much as Bernard Madoff did a century later. The problem with Ponzi's operation, however, was that in order to keep giving earlier investors their promised returns, Ponzi had to continually draw new people into the scam. In July of 1920 the *Boston Post* ran an article exposing the scheme, and soon after regulators raided Ponzi's offices and charged him with mail fraud, knowing his fabricated investment reports were mailed to his backers. Mr. Ponzi's scheme self-destructed after only about one year. In comparison, recent cases are unusual because the fraudsters were able to perpetuate their Ponzi schemes for many years.

Tom Petters

It is easy to overlook the case of Tom Petters's Ponzi scheme for those outside his home state of Minnesota. His arrest was eclipsed by that of the more infamous Bernard Madoff a few months later. However, Tom Petters operated the third largest Ponzi scheme in history at $3.65 billion in investor losses. Petters was a highly successful entrepreneur and CEO of Petters Group Worldwide (PGW). The company was involved in a number of different industries including airlines, direct marketing, Internet auction sites, and retailing, and acquired more than 150 companies including the Polaroid brand and Sun Country Airlines.

However, all was not well at PGW. The company's wholesale brokerage firm Petters Company Inc. (PCI) was operating a massive Ponzi scheme. PCI issued promissory notes to investors, who invested money they believed would be used to purchase merchandise for retail stores. The company promised consistent returns of 15 to 20 percent. Rather than being used to purchase merchandise, the money was used to pay returns to earlier investors and, according to prosecutors, fund Petters's lavish lifestyle and company acquisition spree. Investors were provided with falsified purchase orders to make them believe the purchases took place. The scheme is believed to have gone on for more than a decade.

Things changed when a business executive involved in the fraud confessed to authorities and agreed to help investigators gather evidence against Petters in exchange for leniency. Others involved in the fraud also agreed to cooperate. Authorities wiretapped conversations between Petters and his associates that implicated his knowledge of and participation in the fraud. Victims of the Ponzi scheme included pastors, hedge funds, missionaries, and more. Petters was arrested in October 2008 and eventually sentenced to 50 years in prison.

For years after his conviction, Petters continued to maintain his innocence, stating he did not find out about the fraud until shortly before his arrest. He said he trusted his associates, including the woman who blew the whistle on him, to handle the wholesale brokerage firm and had not been involved in the management of PCI since the 1990s. He claimed he was provided with the same falsified documents as everyone else and his biggest mistake was trusting the wrong people. Although Petters appealed his conviction to the U.S. Court of Appeals for the Eighth Circuit, they upheld his sentence, and the Supreme Court declined to hear his case.

In 2013 Petters tried to appeal again on the basis of new information, claiming his lawyer never told him about a deal prosecutors were willing to make that would have lessened his sentence in exchange for a guilty plea. At the court hearing on the matter, he admitted guilt for the first time, stating he had made a "horrible mistake." However, his claim was denied. Petters then moved to have his arguments re-heard by a different judge due to an alleged conflict of interest; this was also denied. It is likely that he will serve the remainder of his original sentence.

Bernard L. Madoff

No man has received as much notoriety for conducting a Ponzi scheme as Bernard Madoff. Until Madoff's time, pulling off a Ponzi scheme of such magnitude was not considered feasible. Much of the reason why Madoff's fraud went unchecked for so long likely had to do with his respectability and reputation for being a market genius. For instance, he served as chair of the NASDAQ in 1990, 1991, and 1993. Bernard Madoff was a highly successful, legitimate businessperson. He started a legal investment business in 1960 buying and selling over-the-counter stocks not listed on the New York Stock Exchange (NYSE). Eventually, Madoff began using his legitimate success and high visibility to start a second business managing money. He seemed trustworthy and promised consistent returns of 10 to 12 percent, attracting billions of dollars from hundreds of investors. Part of the appeal of investing with Madoff was the climate of exclusivity created by his inaccessibility and "invitation only" approach to new investors.

Many of Madoff's clients were already wealthy and looking for a stable and consistent rate of return. To these people, reliable constant returns managed by one of their own seemed like the perfect way to invest. Madoff's stated strategy was to buy stocks while also trading options on those stocks as a way to limit potential losses. His market timing strategy was called "split-strike conversion." To continuously draw in new clients, Madoff developed relationships with intermediaries, known as "feeders." Many of the feeders also invested money with Madoff. These feeders profited by receiving fees and ensured Madoff had a constant stream of money flowing into his operation.

Madoff later admitted he never invested any of his clients' funds. All of the money was deposited in banks, and Madoff simply moved money between Chase Manhattan Bank in New York and Madoff Securities International Ltd., a U.K. corporation. When the economy collapsed in late 2008, too many clients requested their deposits back. Because he knew the game was up, he turned himself in to his sons. Madoff was arrested on December 11, 2008. The official charge was criminal securities fraud. Madoff declared to his sons that he had roughly $200 to $300 million left in the company. The SEC records showed the firm should have had $17 billion in assets at the beginning of 2008. Total investor loss was eventually estimated at over $17 billion. After his trial, Madoff was sentenced to 150 years in prison for his crime.

Thousands of people submitted claims for restitution in the Madoff case. However, paying back all these investors is a difficult task. Although Madoff's fraud is billed as a $65 billion Ponzi scheme in total investments supposedly managed, Madoff never had anywhere near that amount of money. The figure of $65 billion is the total amount Madoff told people they had invested and earned with him. A New York lawyer, Irving Picard, was appointed as the trustee to manage Madoff's remaining funds and try to recover as much for victims as possible. He has sued financial institutions and other organizations he claims knew about the fraud and profited from it, as well as some of Madoff's "feeder" intermediaries. He has also brought so-called "clawback" lawsuits against many legitimate, innocent investors who were lucky enough to have made a profit from the scheme; the rationale for this kind of lawsuit is that because such profits were fictional, it best serves public policy for these false profits to be returned and instead given to defrauded investors. So far, Picard has managed to recover over 50 percent of lost investor funds, a significant achievement. However, billions remain unaccounted for, and waiting victims must hope that Picard's remaining lawsuits continue to be as successful.

The Securities and Exchange Commission was sharply criticized for not detecting Madoff's fraud earlier. Christopher Cox, SEC chair at the start of the fraud investigation, indicated the SEC examiners missed "red flags" in reviewing the Madoff firm. Allegations of wrongdoing started in the early 1990s, and Madoff confirms fraud dating back to that time. Repeated investigations and examinations by the SEC showed no investment fraud. In 2001 Harry Markopolos, a securities industry executive, raised concerns about Madoff's activities. Once again the SEC did not find evidence of improper practices. Because many SEC employees later ended up working in the investment industry on Wall Street, there has been speculation that an overall lack of objectivity clouded these investigations.

R. Allen Stanford

R. Allen Stanford was a highly successful financier who received knighthood from the islands of Antigua and Barbuda. Stanford was the founder and CEO of Stanford Financial Group, a group of financial services firms with its main operations on the island of Antigua. Stanford offered investors certificates of deposit (CDs) with consistent returns of 9.87 percent compounded annual interest. One red flag for investors was that this percentage was six percentage points higher than the U.S. average CD rates at the time. While higher returns are not necessarily indicative of fraud, consistently higher returns with few fluctuations should have acted as a warning signal. Another red flag was that employees at Stanford Financial did not appear to know how the company was able to generate such high returns. When investors inquired, they were told the information was proprietary.

In fact, Stanford allegedly operated a $7 billion Ponzi scheme for two decades. As early as 2003, people began accusing Stanford of a Ponzi scheme. Five years before the scheme was revealed, a former employee alerted the SEC and the National Association of Securities Dealers of activity she believed was fraudulent, yet nothing came of her claims. In 2006 the SEC opened an investigation into Stanford Financial, but closed it soon after. One year later, the firm paid a fine of $20,000 for violating net capital agreements.

Possibly due to the Madoff scandal shaking the financial world, in 2009 authorities began investigating Stanford Financial's consistently higher returns on its CDs. They found evidence that Stanford had misused funds and misrepresented and falsified documents to hide the fraud, including providing false information about the bank's investment portfolio. According to SEC allegations, although Stanford Financial told investors their money was in safe, liquid securities, in reality it was invested in real estate and private equity. Approximately 30,000 people are estimated to have been victims of the Ponzi scheme, more than 10 times the number of victims of Madoff's fraud (although Madoff's investors lost much more money overall).

Stanford was arrested and eventually found guilty on 13 of 14 counts including fraud, conspiracy, and obstructing investigators. His trial was delayed nearly a year from its original date due to a violent prison beating, which he claimed left him with amnesia and unable to stand trial. Stanford was sentenced to 110 years in prison, but continues to maintain his innocence. He is in the process of appealing the ruling, although he has fired his lawyers and is handling the appeal himself.

Because Stanford Financial had been accused of operating a Ponzi scheme years before Stanford's arrest, many stakeholders criticized the SEC for not detecting the fraud earlier. Victims of Stanford's fraud are also unhappy; after more than five years, the court-appointed receiver has recouped almost nothing of their losses, and many of the main sources of potential recovery have remained frozen during Stanford's lengthy and delayed trial and appeal. Many say they feel abandoned and have given up waiting for restitution.

PYRAMID SCHEMES

As mentioned earlier, pyramid schemes occur when an investment or product of minimal value is offered, new participants must pay to get involved, and the instigator makes money through these fees rather than legitimate sales. Pyramid schemes are illegal because of their intent to defraud. Once recruited, participants will be unable to recoup their investments, or will only be able to do so by recruiting others, as pyramid schemes usually offer financial incentives for bringing in more people. Therefore, a pyramid scheme is an unsustainable business model that involves defrauding investors and customers. Pyramid schemes can be hard to detect, but according to the FTC, the two main warning signs that a pyramid scheme might be taking place are inventory loading and a lack of retail sales. Inventory loading occurs when new investors are required to purchase large amounts of inventory upfront, with continuing automatic purchases at regular intervals. The fraudster makes money, but the purchased inventory then usually does not sell because its value is less than its price. A lack of retail sales is a red flag if the business claims its products are selling quickly, as it indicates the only people buying are those caught up in the scheme.

The FTC began to take action against pyramid schemes in the 1970s, and one of its first targets was Koscot Interplanetary, Inc., which recruited people for a fee, charged them for purchasing makeup supplies, and then compensated them for recruiting others without encouraging them to sell any product. The judgment against the company led to the "Koscot Test," which is still used today to determine whether a business is in fact a pyramid scheme. According to the Koscot Test, a pyramid scheme has four elements: (1) people pay the company to participate; (2) in return, they gain the right to sell a good or service; (3) they are also compensated for recruiting others; and (4) this compensation is unrelated to whether any of the good or service is actually sold.

The Koscot Test helps investors and investigators differentiate between pyramid schemes and legitimate business models that may look similar, such as direct selling and multilevel marketing. The multilevel marketing compensation model, for example, also provides participants with commissions for growing the network of sellers, but the key difference from a pyramid scheme is that commissions are based on whether the new members are actually selling products, not simply on whether they have joined the network. Thus, true multilevel marketing companies do not fit the fourth part of the Koscot Test, as recruitment compensation is directly linked to actual sales. Another important difference is that multilevel marketing companies provide products with actual value, and therefore their sellers can make an income without having to sign up new recruits. Furthermore, new members can advance beyond the people who recruited them, unlike a pyramid scheme where the "bottom" of the pyramid is generally always comprised of the newest participants. Finally, while a lack of retail sales is a clear warning sign of a pyramid scheme, it is not necessarily problematic if a significant portion of product sales are to the members themselves; many people join multilevel marketing networks simply to buy the products at a discount, which is known as internal consumption. Others join to earn money for only a short period of time and later leave.

As the above explanation implies, the line between a pyramid scheme and a legitimate business model is often less than clear. Amway, a company that sells a variety of health, beauty, and home care products, was accused in the 1970s of operating a pyramid scheme, but the FTC determined Amway was actually engaged in legitimate multilevel or network marketing. Similarly, Belgian courts could not agree as to whether nutritional products company Herbalife, the world's third largest global direct seller, was a pyramid scheme; the lower court's ruling against the company was overturned by the appeals court, which decided it was a legitimate business.

Herbalife: Ackman's Accusations

In 2012 Herbalife was again accused of being an elaborate pyramid scheme, this time by U.S. hedge fund manager William Ackman. His accusations against Herbalife included the following: (1) the majority of distributors for Herbalife lose money, (2) Herbalife pays more for recruiting new distributors than selling actual products, and (3) only the top 1 percent of distributors earn most of the money. However, Herbalife sells highly respected nutritional products. Its products are used in Los Angeles by firefighters and LAPD officers, and have even been adopted by some Chinese Olympic teams. This is quite different from the traditional pyramid scheme where the product has little or no value. Furthermore, Herbalife distributors are only compensated for recruiting others when the new participants actually sell products, which does not meet the definition of a pyramid scheme under the Koscot Test.

Herbalife has vehemently denied Ackman's allegations. Many others support Herbalife's model, arguing that if it was a pyramid scheme, it could not have managed to be so successful and avoid collapsing for over 30 years since its founding in 1980.

Another prominent hedge fund manager, Carl Ichan, responded by defending Herbalife and investing significantly in the firm. Ackman's critics also note that before making the accusations, Ackman heavily shorted Herbalife stock (an investment strategy that allows him to earn money if the stock price falls). Although criticizing a company while shorting its stock is neither uncommon nor illegal, it calls Ackman's motives and objectivity into question. Ackman has attempted to defuse this criticism by promising to donate any profit he makes from the short sale, consistent with his image as an "activist investor."

On the other hand, the FTC received 192 consumer complaints against Herbalife between 2006 and 2013, some of which accused Herbalife of being a pyramid scheme that deceptively creates unrealistic expectations of how much distributors can expect to earn by joining. A video also surfaced from a private management and distributor meeting showing a top Herbalife earner stating they "sell people on a dream business" when "the reality is that most of them aren't going to make it." At least one shareholder has sued the company to recover losses, claiming they were the result of fraud and misrepresentation by Herbalife in representing itself as a legitimate business (however, the lawsuit was dismissed). In 2014, in response to the allegations and pressure from legislators, the FTC began a civil investigation into Herbalife. There are also rumors that the FBI and the U.S. Department of Justice have begun a preliminary criminal inquiry.

If nothing else, Herbalife's story exhibits that the difference between a fraudulent pyramid scheme and a legitimate business model is sometimes an uncomfortably grey area. Companies considering a multilevel marketing or direct selling compensation model should attempt to distinguish themselves from pyramid scheme practices as much as possible to minimize any potentially damaging uncertainty.

NexGen3000.com: The Internet's Effect

The Internet has made pyramid schemes even easier to execute due to the ease of networking and recruiting others. In 2003 the FTC charged Arizona Internet company NexGen3000.com and its principals with operating an illegal pyramid scheme involving what the company called Internet "shopping malls." The firm marketed these "malls" to investors as a way to earn substantial income. Investors purchased a "Basic WebSuite" for $185 and a "Power Pack WebSuite" for $555. Investors were told they could earn commissions on each "WebSuite" they sold. In actuality most investors lost money. The FTC found deceptive marketing claims were used to mislead investors as well as convince them to unknowingly deceive others into investing.

This is a complex issue, and investors, distributors, and other stakeholders must exert caution when deciding what companies to get involved with. Perhaps the best advice in guarding against pyramid schemes is the same as in guarding against Ponzi schemes: do not put all your eggs in one basket, at least until you thoroughly research the company. In terms of pyramid schemes, investors should carefully examine the business model and determine if a legitimate product is being sold before investing large sums of money to join the network or buy products.

CONCLUSION

White-collar criminals dupe their victims by establishing themselves as trustworthy and respectable figures. For instance, Bernard Madoff was an educated and experienced individual in a position of power, trust, respectability, and responsibility who abused his trust for personal gain. Victims of white-collar crime are trusting clients who believe there are sufficient checks and balances to certify that an operation is legitimate. Fraudsters of both Ponzi and pyramid schemes use promises and elaborate deception to carry out their scams. While many times these types of schemes collapse fairly quickly due to their unsustainable nature, the examples in this case show that adept white-collar criminals are able to carry on the fraud for many years.

White-collar crime is unique because it is often perpetrated by a rogue individual who knowingly steals, cheats, or manipulates in order to damage others. Often the only way to prevent white-collar crime is to establish internal controls and compliance standards that detect misconduct. For Ponzi and pyramid schemes, any lapse in effective auditing, transparency, or understanding of the true nature of the operation gives fraudsters the opportunity to deceive others for long periods of time. As a result of these recent high-profile scams, individual investors, institutions, and regulators will hopefully exert more diligence in demanding transparency and honesty from those who manage and/or solicit investments.

QUESTIONS FOR DISCUSSION

1. How do Ponzi schemes and pyramid schemes differ? How are they similar?
2. Why are successful white-collar criminals such as Madoff able to carry out their schemes for so long when similar types of fraud often collapse at an early stage?
3. What should be done to ensure large-scale scams such as Ponzi schemes and pyramid schemes do not occur in the future?

SOURCES

"American Greed: Generous with Other People's Money," http://www.cnbc.com/id/100000111 (accessed March 25, 2015); Jake Anderson, "Tom Petters' Last Attempt to Remove a Judge Denied," *Twin Cities Business*, March 12, 2014, http://tcbmag.com/News/Recent-News/2014/March/Tom-Petters-Latest-Attempt-To-Remove-A-Judge-Is-De (accessed March 25, 2015); The Associated Press, "A look at some of the biggest Ponzi schemes," *Bloomberg Businessweek*, July 14, 2012, http://www.businessweek.com/ap/2012-06/D9VD1OU82.htm (accessed March 25, 2015); James Bandler and Nicholas Varchaver with Doris Burke, "How Bernie Did It," *Fortune*, May 11, 2009, 50–71; "Bernard L. Madoff," *The New York Times*, December 18, 2010, http://topics.nytimes.com/top/reference/timestopics/people/m/bernard_l_madoff/index.html (accessed March 25, 2015); Dan Browning, "Petters' cronies plead guilty in fraud scam," *Star Tribune*, October 9, 2008, http://www.startribune.com/business/30631384.html?page=1&c=y (accessed March 25, 2015); Cassel Bryan-Low, "Inside a Swiss Bank, Madoff Warnings," *The Wall Street Journal*, January 14, 2009, 1A; Business Wire via The Motley Fool, "Herbalife Continues to Foster Good Health and Fitness among Peace Officers in Los Angeles," May 30, 2013, http://www.dailyfinance.com/2013/05/30/herbalife-continues-to-foster-good-health-and-fitn/ (accessed March 25, 2015); CBS News, "Madoff: Pressure from big clients led to scam," April 9, 2011, http://www.cbsnews.com/stories/2011/04/09/earlyshow/saturday/main20052422.shtml (accessed March 25, 2015); Michelle Celarier, "Salve for Shorts," *New York Post*, February 4, 2013, http://nypost.com/2013/02/04/salve-for-shorts/ (accessed March 2, 2015); Michelle Celarier, "Top Herbalife salesman admitted 'deception,' high failure rate," *New York Post*, December 17, 2014, http://nypost.com/2014/12/17/top-herbalife-salesman-admits-deception-high-failure-rate/ (accessed March 2, 2015); Scott Cohn, "Could Allen Stanford go free? Convicted fraudster appeals," *CNBC*, October 22, 2014, http://www.cnbc.com/id/102111579# (accessed March 2, 2015); Robert Cookson and Michael Peel, "Whistleblower alleged Stanford 'Ponzi' scheme five years ago," *Financial Times*, February 27, 2009, http://www.ft.com/intl/cms/

s/0/2cafa90c-0471-11de-845b-000077b07658.html#axzz2THKO4SNe (accessed March 25, 2015); Julie Creswell, "U.S. Agents Scrutinize Texas Firm," *The New York Times*, February 12, 2009, http://www.nytimes.com/2009/02/13/business/13stanford.html?_r=1&ref=business (accessed March 25, 2015); Javier E. David, "Herbalife CEO Casts Doubt on Ackman's motives in selling stock," *CNBC*, January 10, 2013, http://www.cnbc.com/id/100369698 (accessed March 25, 2015); Jean Eaglesham and Jessica Holzer, "Schapiro Defends against GOP Fire," *The Wall Street Journal*, March 10, 2011, C1; Amir Efrati, "Q&A on the Madoff Case," *The Wall Street Journal*, March 12, 2009, http://online.wsj.com/article/SB123005811322430633.html (accessed March 25, 2015); Amir Efrati and Chad Bray, "U.S.: Madoff Had $173 Million in Checks," *The Wall Street Journal*, January 9, 2009, http://online.wsj.com/article/SB123143634250464871.html (accessed March 25, 2015); Tim Elfrink, "The Rise and Fall of the Stanford Financial Group," *Houston Press*, April 8, 2009, http://www.houstonpress.com/2009-04-09/news/the-rise-fall-of-the-stanford-financial-group/full/ (accessed March 25, 2015); Francis Elliott, "Thousands of farmers ruined as emu pyramid scheme collapses," *The Times (United Kingdom)*, August 15, 2012, 28; Robert Frank and Amir Efrati, "Madoff Tried to Stave off Firm's Crash before Arrest," *The Wall Street Journal*, January 7, 2009, http://online.wsj.com/article/SB123129835145559987.html (accessed March 25, 2015); Robert Frank and Tom Lauricella, "Madoff Created Air of Mystery," *The Wall Street Journal*, December 20, 2008, http://online.wsj.com/article/SB122973208705022949.html (accessed March 25, 2015); Federal Trade Commission, "FTC Charges Internet Mall Is a Pyramid Scam," July 7, 2003, https://www.ftc.gov/news-events/press-releases/2003/07/ftc-charges-internet-mall-pyramid-scam (accessed March 25, 2015); Daniel Gilbert and Jean Eaglesham, "Stanford Hit with 110 Years," *The Wall Street Journal*, June 14, 2014, http://www.wsj.com/articles/SB10001424052702303734204577466663406841
7466 (accessed March 2, 2015); Jamie Heller and Joanna Chung, "Life after Madoff's 'Big Lie,'" *The Wall Street Journal*, December 11, 2010, http://online.wsj.com/article/SB10001424052748703727804576011451297639480.html (accessed March 25, 2015); Diana B. Henriques, "Madoff Victims Have Their Day in Appeals Court," *The New York Times*, March 3, 2011, http://www.nytimes.com/2011/03/04/business/04madoff.html (accessed March 25, 2015); "How Pyramid Schemes and Ponzi Schemes are Prosecuted in the US: Do You Know Koscot Test and Howey Test?" *HubPages*, http://kschang.hubpages.com/hub/How-Pyramid-Schemes-and-Ponzi-Schemes-are-Prosecuted-in-the-US (accessed March 2, 2015); "Irving H. Picard," BakerHostetler, http://www.bakerlaw.com/irvinghpicard/ (accessed March 2, 2015); Chris Isidore, "Stanford found guilty in Ponzi scheme," *CNNMoney*, March 6, 2012, http://money.cnn.com/2012/03/06/news/companies/stanford_guilty/index.htm (accessed March 25, 2015); Clifford Krauss, Julie Cresswell, and Charlie Savage, "Fraud Case Shakes a Billionaire's Caribbean Realm," *The New York Times*, February 20, 2009, http://www.nytimes.com/2009/02/21/business/21stanford.html?pagewanted=1&ref=robertallenstanford (accessed March 25, 2015); Dale Kurschner, "Tom Petters Interview: Plausible Deniability?" *Twin Cities Business*, May 1, 2012, http://tcbmag.com/News/In-Depth/Tom-Petters-Interview-Plausible-Deniability (accessed March 25, 2015); Dale Kurschner, "Q & A with Tom Petters," *Twin Cities Business*, May 1, 2012, http://tcbmag.com/News/In-Depth/Tom-Petters-Interview-Plausible-Deniability/Q-and-A-with-Tom-Petters-I-believed-it?page=1 (accessed March 25, 2015); Michael A. Lindenberger and Murray Waas, "Allen Stanford files 299-page appeal of his 110-year sentence," *The Dallas Morning News*, October 4, 2014, http://www.dallasnews.com/business/headlines/20141004-allen-stanford-files-299-page-appeal-of-his-110-year-sentence.ece (accessed March 2, 2015); Michael Lindenberger, "Stanford appeal delayed 60 days as court grants DOJ more time to respond," *The Dallas Morning News*, December 4, 2014, http://bizbeatblog.dallasnews.com/2014/12/stanford-appeal-delayed-60-days-as-court-grants-doj-more-time-to-respond.html/ (accessed March 2, 2015); Aaron Lucchetti, "Victims Welcome Madoff Imprisonment," *The Wall Street Journal*, March 13, 2009, http://online.wsj.com/article/SB123687992688609801.html (accessed March 25, 2015); Bernard Madoff, "Plea Allocution of Bernard L. Madoff," *The Wall Street Journal*, March 12, 2009, http://online.wsj.com/public/resources/documents/20090315madoffall.pdf (accessed March 25, 2015); Calum MacLeod, "China's new rules open door to Amway, Avon, others,' *USA Today*, November 30, 2005, http://usatoday30.usatoday.com/money/world/2005-11-30-amway-china-usat_x.htm (accessed March 25, 2015); The Madoff Recovery Initiative website, http://www.madofftrustee.com/ (accessed March 2, 2015); Jordan D. Maglich, "$50 Million Avian Ponzi Scheme Busted in India; 100,000 Emus Looking for New Home," Ponzitracker, October 1, 2012, http://www.ponzitracker.com/main/2012/10/1/50-million-avian-ponzi-scheme-busted-in-india-100000-emus-lo.html (accessed March 2, 2015); Jordan Maglich, "A Ponzi Pandemic: 500+ Ponzi Schemes Totaling $50+ Billion in 'Madoff Era,'" *Forbes*,

February 12, 2014, http://www.forbes.com/sites/jordanmaglich/2014/02/12/a-ponzi-pandemic-500-ponzi-schemes-totaling-50-billion-in-madoff-era/ (accessed March 2, 2015); Jordan Maglich, "Top Ponzi Schemes," Ponzitracker, May 20, 2012, http://www.ponzitracker.com/top-ponzi-schemes/ (accessed March 2, 2015); Jordan Maglich, "Top Ponzi Scheme Recoveries," Ponzitracker, 2014, http://www.ponzitracker.com/top-ponzi-recoveries (accessed March 2, 2015); Mark Magnier, "In India, emu scheme leaves behind distraught investors, birds," *Los Angeles Time*, September 9, 2012, http://articles.latimes.com/2012/sep/29/world/la-fg-india-ponzi-schemes-20120930 (accessed March 2, 2015); Dan McCrum and Kara Scannell, "Criminal probe launched into Herbalife," *Financial Times*, April 11, 2014, http://www.ft.com/intl/cms/s/0/a9833e96-c198-11e3-b95f-00144feabdc0. html (accessed March 2, 2015); Rupert Neate, "Herbalife CEO accused of running 'Ponzi scheme,'" *The Guardian*, December 21, 2012, http://www.theguardian.com/world/2012/dec/21/herbalife-ceo-ponzi-scheme (accessed March 2, 2015); Liz O'Connell, "Petters Makes Tearful Plea for Shorter Prison Sentence," *Twin Cities Business*, October 23, 2013, http://tcbmag.com/News/Recent-News/Petters-makes-tearful-plea-for-shorter-prison-sent (accessed March 25, 2015); Sophia Pearson, Edvard Pettersson, and Duane Stanford, "Herbalife Wins Dismissal of Investor Suit Tied to Ackman Claims," *Bloomberg Businessweek*, March 18, 2015, http://www.bloomberg.com/ news/articles/2015-03-18/herbalife-wins-dismissal-of-investor-suit-based-on-ackman-claims (accessed April 23, 2015); Pershing Square Capital Management, L.P. *An Executive Summary of Pershing Square Capital Management, L.P.'s Presentation of "Who Wants to be a Millionaire?" A Short Thesis on Herbalife, Ltd (NYSE: HLF)*, December 2012, http://factsaboutherbalife.com/wp-content/uploads/2012/12/Final-Exec-Summary-1.pdf (accessed March 25, 2015); "Petters Wants Sentence Tossed Out," *KNSI*, May 12, 2013, http://knsiradio.com/news/local/petters-wants-sentence-tossed-out/ (accessed March 25, 2015); Stuart Pfeifer, "Herbalife says Belgian appeals court reversed pyramid scheme finding," *Los Angeles Times*, December 3, 2013, http://www.latimes.com/business/la-fi-mo-herbalife-pyramid-scheme-20131203-story.html#axzz2mRoscRbq (accessed March 2, 2015); David Phelps, "Petters aid: Everything was fake," *Star Tribune*, December 11, 2011, http://www.startribune.com/ business/134826203.html?refer=y (accessed March 25, 2015); David Phelps, "Petters' Associate Deanna Coleman freed after 11 months in prison," *Star Tribune*, August 25, 2011, http://www.startribune.com/business/128421168. html?refer=y (accessed March 25, 2015); David Phelps, "Tom Petters tries once again for a shorter prison sentence," *Star Tribune*, January 8, 2014, http://www.startribune.com/business/239165631.html (accessed March 25, 2015); Matthias Rieker, "Victims of Scandal Reflect on Shocking Turnabout," *The Wall Street Journal*, December 23, 2008, http://online.wsj.com/article/SB122972955226822819.html (accessed March 25, 2015); Steven Russolillo, "Herbalife Fights Back against Hedge-Fund Claims," *The Wall Street Journal*, January 10, 2013, http://online.wsj. com/article/SB10001424127887324581504578233811199427712.html (accessed March 25, 2015); Securities and Exchange Commission, "SEC Enforcement Actions," April 2, 2013, http://www.sec.gov/spotlight/enf-actions-ponzi.shtml (accessed March 25, 2015); Erin Skarda, "Albanian Ponzi Schemes," *Time*, March 7, 2002, http://www. time.com/time/specials/packages/article/0,28804,2104982_2104983_2104998,00.html (accessed March 25, 2015); Duane Stanford and David McLaughlin, "Herbalife Discloses Civil Investigation by FTC," *Bloomberg*, March 12, 2014, http://www.bloomberg.com/news/articles/2014-03-12/herbalife-discloses-civil-investigation-by-ftc (accessed March 2, 2015); Stanford International Victims Group, Stanford's Forgotten Victims website, February 18, 2015, http://stanfordsforgottenvictims.blogspot.com/2015/02/five-years-after-stanford-scandal-many.html (accessed March 2, 2015); Jenny Strasburg, "Madoff 'Feeders' under Focus," *The Wall Street Journal*, December 27–28, 2008, A1, A8; Ethan Trex, "Who Was Ponzi—What the Heck Was His Scheme?" *CNN.com*, December 23, 2008, http://www.cnn.com/2008/LIVING/wayoflife/12/23/mf.ponzi.scheme/index.html (accessed March 25, 2015); Debra A. Valentine, "Pyramid Schemes," Federal Trade Commission, May 13, 1998, https://www. ftc.gov/public-statements/1998/05/pyramid-schemes (accessed March 25, 2015); "Violent Protests of Pyramid Schemes Spread in Albania," *The New York Times*, January 27, 1997, http://www.nytimes.com/1997/01/27/world/ violent-protests-of-pyramid-schemes-spread-in-albania.html (accessed March 25, 2015); Mitch Weiss, "ZeekRewards scam leaves N.C. town millions poorer," *USA Today*, March 30, 2013, http://www.usatoday.com/ story/money/business/2013/03/30/authorities-600m-scheme-incubated-nc-town/2037975/ (accessed March 25, 2015); Kaja Whitehouse, "Bill Ackman takes shot at Herbalife with new video," *USA Today*, December 17, 2014, http://americasmarkets.usatoday.com/2014/12/17/bill-ackman-releases-internal-herbalife-video/ (accessed March 2, 2015).

CASE 12

Insider Trading at the Galleon Group[*]

The Galleon Group was a privately owned hedge fund firm that provided services and information about investments such as stocks, bonds, and other financial instruments. Galleon made money for itself and others by picking stocks and managing portfolios and hedge funds for investors. At its peak, Galleon was responsible for more than $7 billion in investor income. The company's philosophy was that it was possible to deliver superior returns to investors without employing common high-risk tactics such as leverage or market timing. Founded in 1997, Galleon attracted employees from prestigious investment firms such as Goldman Sachs, Needham & Co., and ING Barings. Every month the company held meetings where executives explained the status and strategy of each fund to investors. In addition, Galleon told investors that no employee would be personally trading in any stock or fund the investors held.

In 2009 Raj Rajaratnam, the head of Galleon, was indicted on 14 counts of securities fraud and conspiracy, as well as sued by the Securities and Exchange Commission (SEC) for insider trading. He and five others were accused of using nonpublic information from company insiders and consultants to make millions in personal profits. Rajaratnam's trial began in 2011, and although he pleaded not guilty, he was convicted on all 14 counts, fined over $158 million in civil and criminal penalties, and is currently serving an 11-year sentence.

RAJ RAJARATNAM

Rajaratnam, born in Sri Lanka to a middle-class family, received his bachelor's degree in engineering from the University of Sussex in England. In 1983 he earned his MBA from the University of Pennsylvania's Wharton School of Business. With a focus on the computer chip industry, he meticulously developed contacts. He went to manufacturing plants, talked to employees, and connected with executives who would later work with Galleon on their companies' IPOs.

In 1985 the investment banking boutique Needham & Co. hired Rajaratnam as an analyst. The corporate culture at Needham & Co. profoundly influenced Rajaratnam and his business philosophy. George Needham was obsessive about minimizing expenses, making employees stay in budget hotel rooms and take midnight flights to and from meetings. The company also urged analysts to gather as much information as possible. They were encouraged to sift through garbage, question disgruntled employees, and even place people in jobs in target industries. Analysts went to professional meetings, questioned academics doing research and consulting, and set up clandestine agencies that collected

*This case was prepared by John Fraedrich, Harper Baird, and Michelle Urban. Isaac Emmanuel provided editorial assistance. It was prepared for classroom discussion rather than to illustrate either effective or ineffective handling of an administrative, ethical, or legal decision by management. All sources used for this case were obtained through publicly available material.

information. At Needham & Co., Rajaratnam developed an aggressive networking and note-taking research strategy that enabled him to make accurate predictions about companies' financial situations.

Rajaratnam rose rapidly through the ranks at Needham to become president of the company by 1991. Rajaratnam's personality also began to impact the company's culture. Rajaratnam once told a new analyst that Needham's name was on the company, but he was the real center of power, the one who "makes things happen." He began to push ethical limits when gathering information about companies. For example, concerns about Rajaratnam's activities ended stock brokerage Paine, Webber and Co.'s interest in buying Needham. Soon, similar worries spurred complaints from some inside Needham. By 1996, at least five Needham executives were concerned about Rajaratnam's conduct. Additionally, many of Needham's clients complained. Rajaratnam's multiple company roles as president, fund manager, and sometimes stock analyst were a potential conflict of interest situation; investment banks usually separate those roles to prevent clashes between the interests of clients and bank-run funds. In 1996, after 11 years at Needham, Rajaratnam left the company and started the Galleon Group, taking several Needham employees with him.

ACCUSATIONS OF INSIDER TRADING AT GALLEON

At Galleon, Rajaratnam developed a flamboyant leadership style. During one meeting, Rajaratnam hired a dwarf to act as an analyst assigned to cover "small-cap" stocks. At another meeting, when Taser International, Inc. executives came to make an investment pitch, Rajaratnam offered $5,000 to anyone who would agree to be shocked. One trader, Keryn Limmer, volunteered to be tased and was rendered unconscious. Rajaratnam also used his personal fortune to grow Galleon's business. For the 2007 Super Bowl, he threw a lavish party for wealthy investors and executives at a $250,000-a-week mansion on a man-made island in Biscayne Bay off the Florida coast.

At the same time, Rajaratnam contributed to various causes promoting development in the Indian subcontinent, as well as programs benefiting lower-income South Asian youths in the New York area. He joined the board of the Harlem Children's Zone, an educational nonprofit. He also raised nearly $7.5 million for victims of the 2004 South Asian tsunami. For his philanthropy, he was later honored with a symphony performance at the Lincoln Center in New York.

However, Rajaratnam was already in trouble with the government. In 2005 he paid over $20 million to settle a federal investigation into a fake tax shelter used to hide $52 million from taxation. Rajaratnam and his business partner then sued their lawyers, claiming they had no idea the shelter was illegal; the pair was awarded $10 million in damages. Galleon also paid $2 million in 2005 to settle an SEC investigation into its stock trading practices. In addition, Intel discovered in 2001 that Roomy Khan, an Intel employee, had leaked information about sales and production to Rajaratnam. When Khan left Intel, she took a job with Galleon. Although Intel reported the incidents to the authorities, and Khan served six months of house arrest after pleading guilty to wire fraud and agreeing to cooperate in the investigation against Rajaratnam, the prosecutors could not prove that Rajaratnam actually made trades based on the inside information. As a result, the investigation was abandoned.

Analysts live or die by the information they acquire on publicly traded firms. As such, there is a constant struggle to gather key information that can predict changes in stock prices, quarterly reports, and revenue. Rajaratnam had a deep network of acquaintances, including employees at Goldman Sachs Group, Intel Corp., McKinsey & Co., and Applied Materials, Inc. However, federal investigators were suspicious that the networking and research at Galleon involved methods more illicit than simply maintaining a good contact list. In 2007 SEC lawyers discovered a new text message from Roomy Khan advising Rajaratnam to "wait for guidance" before buying a stock. The SEC convinced Khan to again cooperate in their investigation and allow them to record her conversations with Rajaratnam. This single wiretap eventually led to the discovery of several insider trading rings as investigators persuaded more people to participate in the operation over the course of two years. Table 1 describes the central players.

TABLE 1 Central Players in the Galleon Information Network

Player and employer	Shared insider information about	Charges/Convictions
Raj Rajaratnam Galleon		At the center of the insider trading network; pled not guilty to 14 charges of insider trading and fraud; convicted on all 14 counts, sentenced to 11 years in prison, and ordered to pay over $158 million in criminal and civil penalties
Danielle Chiesi New Castle/ Bear Stearns	IBM, Sun Microsystems, and AMD	Pled guilty to charges of securities fraud; sentenced to 30 months in prison, two years of supervised release, and 250 hours of community service
Roomy Khan Intel, Galleon	Intel, Hilton, Google, Kronos	Pled guilty to charges of securities fraud, conspiracy to commit securities fraud, obstruction of justice, and agreed to the government's request to use wiretaps; sentenced to one year in prison and ordered to forfeit $1.5 million
Anil Kumar McKinsey & Co.	AMD	Pled guilty to passing inside information to Rajaratnam in exchange for $1.75 million; sentenced to two years of probation
Rajiv Goel Intel	Intel	Pled guilty to passing inside information; sentenced to two years of probation
Rajat K. Gupta Goldman Sachs	Goldman Sachs, Procter & Gamble, McKinsey	Pled not guilty to passing insider tips to Rajaratnam; convicted and sentenced to two years in prison and a $5 million fine
Adam Smith Galleon	Galleon, ATI, AMD	Pled guilty to giving inside information directly to Rajaratnam over a six-year period; sentenced to two years of probation
Michael Cardillo Galleon	Axcan Pharma, Procter & Gamble	Pled guilty to receiving tips indirectly from Rajaratnam; allegedly possessed evidence about Rajaratnam's trades based on insider information; sentenced to three years of probation
Zvi Goffer, a.k.a. the "Octopussy" Schottenfeld Group, Galleon	Hilton, several others	Had a reputation for having multiple sources of inside information; allegedly paid others for tips and gave them prepaid mobile phones to avoid detection; pled not guilty to 14 counts of conspiracy and securities fraud; convicted on all 14 counts and sentenced to 10 years in prison

ARREST AND TRIAL

In October 2009, Raj Rajaratnam was arrested on 14 charges of securities and wire fraud. At the same time, the SEC filed civil insider trading charges against him. Rajaratnam was released on a $100 million bond and immediately hired several top defense attorneys and public relations specialists. His criminal trial began in March 2011.

The laws on insider trading are vague and often make it difficult to convict white-collar criminals. Prosecutors had to prove Rajaratnam not only traded on information he knew was confidential but also that the information was important enough to affect the price of a company's stock. The government's main evidence consisted of 45 recorded phone calls between individuals suspected of insider trading, including six witnesses who had already pled guilty and were aiding federal investigators. In many of these phone calls, Raj Rajaratnam discussed confidential information with investors and insiders before the information was released to the public. In one recording, Rajaratnam told employees to cover up evidence of insider trading. Another recording suggests Rajaratnam received a tip from someone on Goldman Sachs' board that the company's stock price was going to decrease. That information had been presented at a confidential Goldman Sachs board meeting only a day earlier.

The challenge for the prosecution was to prove Rajaratnam used these tips to make illicit trades. Wiretaps of conversations between Goldman Sachs's board member Rajat Gupta and Rajaratnam, along with Rajaratnam's subsequent actions, imply this occurred. For instance, during a board meeting on September 23, 2008, Goldman Sachs's board members discussed a $5 billion preferred stock investment in Goldman Sachs by Berkshire Hathaway along with a public equity offering. According to the prosecution, a few minutes after the meeting, Gupta called Rajaratnam. That same day, just before the market closed, Galleon bought 175,000 shares in Goldman Sachs stock. The news about Berkshire Hathaway was publicly announced after the market closed, and the next morning the stock went from $125.05 to $128.44. Galleon liquidated the stock and generated a profit of $900,000.

The government had several key witnesses from the insider trading rings who cooperated with investigators. Before the start of Rajaratnam's trial, 19 members of the Galleon network pled guilty to charges of insider trading, and some agreed to testify against Rajaratnam. Anil Kumar, who pleaded guilty to providing insider information in exchange for over $1.75 million wired to a secret offshore account, told the jury that Rajaratnam offered to hire him as a consultant but told him that he did not want traditional industry research. Rajaratnam also told Kumar his ideas were worth a lot of money.

The prosecution argued that Rajaratnam corrupted his friends and employees in order to make profits for himself and Galleon. In the closing argument, Assistant U.S. Attorney Reed Brodsky highlighted that Rajaratnam used his contacts to gain certainty in areas where everyone else had none.

In order to convict Rajaratnam of insider trading, the government had to prove the information he received could only have been acquired via inside sources. Rajaratnam's defense maintained that some of the information Rajaratnam used was publicly available and he was not aware other information had not been publicly disclosed. The defense argued Galleon's public announcements, press releases, investor meetings, government filings, and additional sources showed that the information had appeared days and weeks before Rajaratnam and others used that information. Good investment advisors are in the business of acquiring, analyzing, and making calculated predictions so their clients' investments increase. The defense attorneys argued that Rajaratnam's access to corporate executives was the reason his investors hired him. The defense also claimed these same executives were aware of the law and of their own duties to their employers and shareholders, and they should have known what they could and could not say about their businesses, whereas Rajaratnam's obligations were to his investors.

Rajaratnam lost money on some of the trades the government said were based on inside information. The defense argued that if he had insider information, the opposite should be true. The defense maintained that Galleon's analysts were right only about half of the time, and if they were cheating, they should have been right all of the time. The defense also questioned the validity of some of the prosecution's witnesses. For example, one witness confessed to the fabrication of a false affidavit, doctor's letter, tax forms, and bank letters, allegedly to protect his original statements to the prosecution. The defense argued that many of the prosecution's witnesses lied to save themselves from heavier prison terms for unrelated misdeeds. Anil Kumar testified that between 2004 and 2009, he gave material nonpublic information about several companies to Rajaratnam. However, although Galleon's records show that it paid Kumar consulting fees, he never shared these consulting fees with his McKinsey partners, instead hiding them in shell companies in overseas bank accounts and failing to report them on his tax returns. Then there is Rajiv Goel, who allegedly gave Rajaratnam material nonpublic information obtained from his employer, Intel. The defense brought out that Goel filed false tax returns unrelated to Rajaratnam and was therefore facing prison time (he was later sentenced to two years of probation). The only way out for these criminals caught red-handed, the defense argued, was to testify against Rajaratnam.

THE VERDICT

After 12 days of deliberation, the jury found Raj Rajaratnam guilty of all 14 counts of securities fraud and conspiracy. The jurors later explained the length of their deliberation was because some of them could not comprehend how such an intelligent person could do something so destructive. Jurors cited the recorded conversations between Rajaratnam and his trading network as some of the most convincing evidence.

In total, the counts carried a potential maximum sentence of 205 years in prison, although Rajaratnam was actually only sentenced to 11 years. In addition to his prison sentence, his criminal penalties amounted to $63.8 million. Rajaratnam also lost the SEC's parallel civil lawsuit for insider trading, and was ordered to pay a record $92.8 million in damages, the largest judgment ever imposed against one person in an SEC insider trading case. He later agreed to pay an additional $1.45 million to settle yet more civil charges. These various judgments added up to over $158 million in total penalties.

Rajaratnam and his defense team swiftly appealed the criminal conviction. Their argument centered on the aggressive wiretapping the federal investigators had employed to gather their evidence, a tactic never before used in an insider trading case. The appeal stated that judicial permission to place these wiretaps had been obtained deceptively in violation of Rajaratnam's constitutional rights, and thus the incriminating recorded conversations should not have been usable by the prosecution at trial. The federal court of appeals, however, found Rajaratnam's arguments "unpersuasive" and upheld his conviction. The U.S. Supreme Court then declined to hear the case, making Rajaratnam's sentence final.

Rajaratnam has also recently appealed the $92.8 million civil fine, claiming it is unfairly excessive and cumulative with the $63.8 million criminal penalty. The appeal is ongoing.

RAJAT GUPTA

Rajat Gupta was a man of high profile and influence with an illustrious career, including a nine-year term as managing director (CEO) of McKinsey & Co., a prestigious global management consulting firm, and serving on the boards of Goldman Sachs, Procter & Gamble, American Airlines, the Rockefeller, and the Bill and Melinda Gates Foundation. Well-known, well-respected, and considered a man of integrity, he was esteemed throughout the financial services sector, as well as in India for being the first Indian-born CEO of a multinational corporation. This golden reputation came to an abrupt end when he was charged and convicted of insider trading activities in 2012.

The charges were based on the phone call he made to Rajaratnam on September 23, 2008, regarding Berkshire Hathaway's purchase of Goldman Sachs stock. Immediately after this phone call, Galleon made a significant purchase of Goldman Sachs stock, turned a sizeable profit, and quickly liquidated the stock. Because of this sequence of events, and other similar incidents where Gupta contacted Rajaratnam just prior to especially profitable trading decisions by Rajaratnam and Galleon, Gupta was implicated in insider trading activity. After less than a day of deliberation, the jury convicted him of three counts of securities fraud and one count of criminal conspiracy.

Rajat Gupta faced a maximum of 20 years for each fraud charge, and five years for the conspiracy charge, but was only sentenced to two years in prison, as well as fined a total of $24.9 million in civil and criminal penalties.

Gupta's appeal rested on the use of wiretap evidence that his defense argued was hearsay and thus inadmissible at trial under evidentiary rules. His lawyers also maintained there was no evidence Gupta benefited in any way from giving the alleged insider tips, and that the conviction was based entirely on circumstantial evidence. The appeal furthermore claimed the defense team was prevented from presenting several pieces of critical evidence, including that of Gupta's nonculpable state of mind, of the possibility that an alternative person had actually provided the insider tips, and of Gupta's integrity. Because the court allowed the wiretap recordings but did not allow this evidence, Gupta's defense argued that he deserved a new trial.

Despite these arguments, the federal court of appeals upheld Gupta's conviction, and subsequently denied his petition for a rehearing. Gupta is in the process of appealing again to the U.S. Supreme Court, but his request to remain free on bail during this appeal was denied, and he reported to prison on June 17, 2014.

Many consider Gupta's conviction—considering his prominence and influence—to be a powerful symbolic victory for federal prosecutors and the SEC, sending a message to the financial sector that no wrongdoer, no matter how powerful, is safe from recrimination.

THE IMPACT OF THE GALLEON CASE

The Galleon case is the largest investigation in history into insider trading within hedge funds. Twenty-six people were charged with fraud and conspiracy. Galleon closed in 2009 after investors quickly withdrew over $4 billion in investments from the company. In addition, over a dozen companies' stocks were traded based on allegedly nonpublic information (see Table 2). These trades could have affected the financial status of the companies, their stock prices, and their shareholders.

TABLE 2 Companies Affected by Galleon's Alleged Insider Information Network

3Com Corp
Advanced Micro Devices
Akamai Technologies
Atheros
Axcan Pharma
Goldman Sachs
Google
Hilton Hotels
IBM
Intel
Kronos
Marvell Technology Group
Polycom
Procter & Gamble
Sun Microsystems

© Cengage Learning

The Galleon insider trading investigation was the first to use wiretaps, which are normally only used to convict people of involvement in terrorism, drugs, and organized crime. This set a precedent for insider trading cases, and many suspect this method may be used more frequently in the future. Because investment firms rely on email, phone calls, and other digital information, electronic surveillance will likely become the technique of choice for white-collar crime investigators. Federal authorities also hope the Galleon convictions will deter other powerful investment managers from engaging in insider trading. Manhattan U.S. Attorney Preet Bharara said, "Unlawful insider trading should be offensive to everyone who believes in, and relies on, the market. It cheats the ordinary investor.… We will continue to pursue and prosecute those who believe they are both above the law and too smart to get caught."

QUESTIONS FOR DISCUSSION

1. Are information-gathering techniques like Rajaratnam's common on Wall Street? If so, what could regulators, investors, and executives do to reduce the practice?
2. What are the implications of sharing confidential material information? Is it something that would affect your decision about how to trade a stock if you knew about it?
3. Do you think the secret investigation and conviction of Rajaratnam and other people in the Galleon network will deter other fund managers and investors from sharing non-public information?

SOURCES

William Alden, "Roomy Khan, Figure in Galleon Insider Case, Sentenced to One Year in Prison," *New York Times*, January 31, 2013, http://dealbook.nytimes.com/2013/01/31/roomy-khan-figure-in-galleon-insider-case-sentenced-to-one-year-in-prison/ (accessed February 20, 2015); Suzanna Andrews, "How Gupta Came Undone." *Bloomberg Businessweek*, May 23–29, 2011, 56–63; Alex Berenson, "For Galleon Executive, Swagger in the Spotlight," *The New York Times*, November 1, 2009, http://www.nytimes.com/2009/11/02/business/02insider.html (accessed February 20, 2015); Chad Bray, "Insider Witness Sentenced," *The Wall Street Journal*, February 1, 2013, C3; Chad Bray, "Rajaratnam, SEC Settle Gupta Suit," *The Wall Street Journal*, December 28, 2012, C3; Chad Bray, Michael Rothfeld, and Reed Albergotti, "Insider Case Lands Big Catch," *The Wall Street Journal*, June 15, 2012, http://www.wsj.com/articles/SB10001424052702303822204577468470878668722 (accessed February 20, 2015); Katherine Burton, "Danielle Chiesi's New Prison Home More Camp Cupcake Than 'Chained Heat,'" *Bloomberg*, October 17, 2011, http://www.bloomberg.com/news/2011-10-18/danielle-chiesi-s-new-prison-home-more-camp-cupcake-than-chained-heat-.html (accessed February 20, 2015); Dealbook, "Timeline of Key Events in the Galleon Case," *The New York Times Dealbook*, March 7, 2011, http://dealbook.nytimes.com/2011/03/07/timeline-of-key-events-in-the-galleon-case (accessed February 20, 2015); Economist staff, "An unlucky man," June 14, 2012, *The Economist*, http://www.economist.com/blogs/schumpeter/2012/06/rajat-gupta-trial (accessed February 20, 2015); Economist staff, "Who's Next?" *The Economist*, June 23, 2012, 74; "Former Goldman Sachs Director Rajat Gupta seeks re-hearing of insider trading conviction," *The Economic Times*, April 9, 2014, http://articles.economictimes.indiatimes.com/2014-04-09/news/48999807_1_rajat-gupta-geetanjali-gupta-gary-naftalis (accessed February 20, 2015); "Galleon's Web," *The Wall Street Journal*, March 10, 2011, http://online.wsj.com/public/resources/documents/Galleons-Web.html (accessed February 20, 2015); David Glovin, Patricia Hurtado, and Bob Van Voris, "Galleon's Rajaratnam Talked on Tape about Goldman Board Source," *Bloomberg Businessweek*, March 31, 2011, http://www.bloomberg.com/news/articles/2011-03-30/galleon-s-rajaratnam-taped-talking-about-source-on-goldman-sachs-board (accessed February 20, 2015); David Glovin, Patricia Hurtado, and Bob Van Voris, "Rajaratnam Sought to 'Conquer' Wall Street, U.S. Tells Jurors," *Bloomberg Businessweek*, April 21, 2011, http://www.bloomberg.com/news/articles/2011-04-20/raj-rajaratnam-corrupted-friends-u-s-says-as-defense-team-responds (accessed February 20, 2015); Robert A. Guth and Justin Scheck, "The Man Who Wired Silicon Valley," *The Wall Street Journal*, December 30, 2009, http://www.wsj.com/articles/SB126204917965408363 (accessed February 20, 2015); Patricia Hurtado, "Ex-Galleon Fund Manager Cardillo Gets 3 Years Probation," *Bloomberg*, October 25, 2012, http://www.bloomberg.com/news/2012-10-25/ex-galleon-fund-manager-cardillo-gets-3-years-probation.html (accessed February 20, 2015); Patricia Hurtado, "Galleon Ex-Trader Zvi Goffer, Brother Plead Not Guilty to New Indictment," *Bloomberg*, April 19, 2011, http://www.bloomberg.com/news/2011-04-19/former-galleon-trader-goffer-pleads-not-guilty-to-latest-insider-charges.html (accessed February 20, 2015); Patricia Hurtado and David Glovin, "Rajaratnam Appeal Judges Voice Concern Over U.S. Wiretaps," *Bloomberg*, October 25, 2013, http://www.bloomberg.com/news/2012-10-25/rajaratnam-appeal-judges-voice-concern-over-u-s-wiretaps.html (accessed February 20, 2015); Patricia Hurtado and Bob Van Voris, "Kumar Gets Probation for His Galleon Trial Cooperation," *Bloomberg*, July 19, 2012, http://www.bloomberg.com/news/2012-07-19/anil-kumar-gets-two-years-probation-in-insider-trading-case.html (accessed February 20, 2015); Katten Muchin Rosenman LLP, "Raj Rajaratnam Appeals $92 Million Civil Fine to Second Circuit Court of Appeals," *The National Law Review*, November 9, 2014, http://www.natlawreview.com/article/raj-rajaratnam-appeals-92-million-civil-fine-to-second-circuit-court-appeals (accessed February 20, 2015); Zachery Kouwe and Michael J. De la Merced, "Galleon Chief and Associate Indicted in Insider Case," *The New York Times*, December 15, 2009, http://www.nytimes.com/2009/12/16/business/16insider.html?_r=1 (accessed February 20, 2015); Peter Lattman, "2 Defendants Sentenced in Insider Trading Case," *The New York Times*, September 21, 2011, http://dealbook.nytimes.com/2011/09/21/2-defendants-sentenced-in-insider-trading-case/ (accessed February 20, 2015); Peter Lattman, "Galleon Official Is Spared Prison," *The New York Times*, June 26, 2012, http://dealbook.nytimes.com/2012/06/26/galleon-official-is-spared-prison/ (accessed February 20, 2015); Peter Lattman, "Rajaratnam

Conviction Upheld by Appeals Court," *The New York Times*, June 24, 2013, http://dealbook.nytimes.com/2013/06/24/rajaratnam-conviction-upheld-by-appeals-court/ (accessed February 20, 2015); Kevin McCoy, "Rajaratnam settles civil insider trading case," *USA Today*, December 27, 2012, http://www.usatoday.com/story/money/business/2012/12/27/insider-trading-settlement/1793855/ (accessed February 20, 2015); Duff McDonald, "The Humbling of Rajat Gupta: When Uncommon People Commit Common Crimes," *Observer*, October 30, 2012, http://observer.com/2012/10/the-humbling-of-rajat-gupta-when-uncommon-people-commit-common-crimes/ (accessed February 20, 2015); Walter Pavlo, "Danielle Chiesi—30 Months in Prison and a New Life," *Forbes*, July 21, 2011, http://www.forbes.com/sites/walterpavlo/2011/07/21/danielle-chiesi-30-months-and-a-new-life/ (accessed February 20, 2015); Walter Pavlo, "Government Witness Rajiv Goel Gets Probation in Galleon Case," *Forbes*, September 24, 2012, http://www.forbes.com/sites/walterpavlo/2012/09/24/government-witness-rajiv-goel-gets-probation-in-galleon-insider-case/ (accessed February 20, 2015); Securities & Exchange Commission, "SEC Obtains Record $92.8 Million Penalty against Raj Rajaratnam," November 8, 2011, http://www.sec.gov/news/press/2011/2011-233.htm (accessed February 20, 2015); Sakthi Prasad, "Rajaratnam agrees to pay $1.5 million disgorgement in SEC case," *Reuters*, December 27, 2012, http://www.reuters.com/article/2012/12/27/us-rajaratnam-seclawsuit-idUSBRE8BQ01B20121227 (accessed February 20, 2015); Dunstan Prial, "Rajaratnam's Appeal Denied by Supreme Court," *Fox Business*, June 16, 2014, http://www.foxbusiness.com/industries/2014/06/16/us-top-court-declines-to-hear-rajaratnam-appeal/ (accessed February 20, 2015); Susan Pulliam, "Fund Chief Snared by Taps, Turncoats," *The Wall Street Journal*, December 30, 2009, http://online.wsj.com/article/SB126213287690309579.html (accessed February 20, 2015); Susan Pulliam and Chad Bray, "Galleon Chief Seen Testifying at Trial," *The Wall Street Journal*, March 5, 2011, http://online.wsj.com/article/SB1000142405274870407680457618080341090355.html (accessed February 20, 2015); Susan Pulliam and Chad Bray, "Jury Hears Galleon Wiretaps," *The Wall Street Journal*, March 11, 2011, A1; Susan Pulliam and Chad Bray, "Seasoned Prosecutors Prep for 'War.'" *The Wall Street Journal*, March 9, 2011, http://online.wsj.com/article/SB100014240527487036628045761889606854 79264.html (accessed February 20, 2015); Susan Pulliam and Michael Rothfeld, "Trial Win Adds to Momentum," *The Wall Street Journal*, May 12, 2011, A7; Susan Pulliam and Michael Siconolfi, "Wiretapped Voice Spoke Volumes." *The Wall Street Journal*, May 12, 2011, A7; Nate Raymond, "Rajat Gupta Seeks Insider Trading Conviction Reversal," *Reuters*, January 23, 2013, http://in.reuters.com/article/2013/01/22/goldman-rajat-gupta-appeal-idINDEE90L0EN20130122 (accessed February 20, 2015); M. Rochan, "US Supreme Court Rejects Ex-Goldman Director Rajat Gupta's Plea to Stay Out of Prison," *International Business Times*, June 12, 2014, http://www.ibtimes.co.uk/us-supreme-court-rejects-ex-goldman-director-rajat-guptas-plea-stay-out-prison-1452311 (accessed February 20, 2015); Michael Rothfeld, Susan Pulliam, and Chad Bray, "Fund Titan Found Guilty," *The Wall Street Journal*, May 12, 2011, A1, A6; Cara Salvatore, "Raj Rajaratnam Takes Aim at $92M Fine in 2nd Circ. Appeal," *Law 360*, October 31, 2014, http://www.law360.com/articles/591968/raj-rajaratnam-takes-aim-at-92m-fine-in-2nd-circ-appeal (accessed February 20, 2015); Adam Shell, "Jury Finds Rajaratnam Guilty," *USA Today*, May 12, 2011, B1, B2; Yoshita Singh, "Appeals Court Denies Rajat Gupta's Petition to Rehear Case," *India West*, July 22, 2014, http://www.indiawest.com/news/global_indian/appeals-court-denies-rajat-gupta-s-petition-to-rehear-case/article_3a9e2066-11ef-11e4-aa4a-001a4bcf887a.html (accessed February 20, 2015); Yoshita Singh, "Rajat Gupta Seeks New Trial, Reversal of Conviction," *India West*, January 28, 2013, http://www.indiawest.com/news/global_indian/rajat-gupta-seeks-new-trial-reversal-of-conviction/article_2a7e12f9-1c67-5813-a5e1-2f1d581e9117.html?mode=jqm (accessed February 20, 2015); Jenny Strasburg, Jessica Silver-Greenberg, and Jeannette Neumann, "Inside the Galleon Jury Room," *The Wall Street Journal*, May 14, 2011, A1, A2; Bob Van Voris, "Former Galleon Trader Zvi Goffer Seeks Prison Term of Less Than 10 Years," *Bloomberg*, August 31, 2011, http://www.bloomberg.com/news/2011-08-31/former-galleon-trader-zvi-goffer-seeks-prison-term-of-less-than-10-years.html (accessed February 20, 2015); Bob Van Voris, "Galleon Scandal Scorecard: Hedge Funds, Lawyers and 'Octopussy,'" *Bloomberg*, November 7, 2009, http://www.bloomberg.com/apps/news?pid=newsarchive&sid=aRqWWXi06f4Y (accessed February 20, 2015); Katya Wachtel, "Meet John Dowd: The Lovable Curmudgeon, and Former Marine Whose Job Is to Save Rajaratnam," *Business Insider*, March 7, 2011, http://www.businessinsider.com/raj-rajaratnam-lawyer-john-dowd-2011-3 (accessed February 20, 2015).

CASE 13

Whole Foods Strives to Be an Ethical Corporate Citizen*

INTRODUCTION

In a period of time when green is on everyone's mind, it seems fitting that Whole Foods Markets are popping up with their distinctive green signs in neighborhoods across the country. Beginning with their first expansion in 1984, Whole Foods has consistently grown domestically. In 2007 Whole Foods began opening stores in the United Kingdom. While continually opening new stores, the company has fueled its expansion by acquiring other food chains as well. For instance, it acquired one of its largest competitors—Wild Oats—in 2007, and in 2014 purchased four New Frontiers Natural Marketplace stores. The company currently has more than 400 stores located throughout the United States, Canada, and the United Kingdom. Whole Foods consistently ranks as one of the World's Most Ethical companies because of its emphasis on organic food, healthy living, customer satisfaction, quality, and sustainability. The firm has also been elected as one of *Fortune's* top 100 companies to work for every year since the list was created in 1998. Although customers are considered to be the company's highest valued stakeholder, Whole Foods adopts a stakeholder orientation that focuses on the needs of all of its stakeholders, including its employees and the community.

Whole Foods spearheaded efforts in the grocery industry to source its food products responsibly and search for innovative solutions to improve its environmental footprint. The company emphasizes healthy living and seeks to contribute to the communities where it does business. However, despite Whole Foods's significant accomplishments in business ethics, it has not been free from criticism. In pursuit of growth, it has been accused of running local stores out of business and received mixed responses from some consumers. Other ethical issues include antitrust investigations and questionable activity by co-CEO John Mackey.

This case begins by providing brief historical background information on Whole Foods. Next, its mission and values are examined, followed by a look at how the company strives to live out its values to become a good corporate citizen. We also consider ethical issues Whole Foods has faced to demonstrate the complexity companies may experience when engaging in ethical decision making.

*This material was developed by Casey Caldwell, Erica Lee Turner, and Jennifer Sawayda under the direction of O.C. Ferrell and Linda Ferrell. Julian Mathias provided editorial assistance. This case is intended for classroom discussion rather than to illustrate effective or ineffective handling of administrative, ethical, or legal decisions by management. All sources for this case were obtained through publicly available material © 2015.

COMPANY BACKGROUND

In 1978 two entrepreneurs in their twenties used a $45,000 loan to open a small natural foods store in Austin, Texas. John Mackey and his then-girlfriend Rene Lawson Hardy wanted to help people live better. At the time, there were fewer than a dozen natural foods markets in the nation. The couple named their business SaferWay as a spoof on Safeway. The entrepreneurs had a rocky start. At one time they used the store as a residence after being kicked out of their apartment for storing food products. After two years Mackey and Hardy agreed to merge SaferWay with Clarksville Natural Grocery, owned by Craig Weller and Mark Skiles. The newly merged company called themselves Whole Foods Market.

The company continued to face challenges. Less than a year after opening, a devastating flood hit Austin, wiping out Whole Foods's inventory. With no insurance and $400,000 in damages, the company's future looked dire. Yet with the help of the community, the store reopened four weeks after the flood. In 1984 the company expanded into Houston and Dallas. Four years later they acquired a store in New Orleans, followed by one in Palo Alto, California, a year later. The company continued to grow during the 1990s as Whole Foods merged with over a dozen smaller natural groceries across the nation. Whole Foods continued to thrive in the early twenty-first century and today earns more than $14 billion in revenue, owns more than 400 stores, and employs more than 87,000 workers (compared to nineteen workers in 1980). John Mackey continues to lead Whole Foods as the company's co-CEO.

From the onset, Mackey desired to create a company that incorporated the values of healthy living and conscious capitalism. Conscious capitalists believe "that a new form of capitalism is emerging that holds the potential for enhancing corporate performance while simultaneously trying to advance the quality of life for billions of people."[1] For Mackey, businesses should seek to balance the needs of all stakeholders rather than simply try to earn a profit. As a result, Whole Foods places the customer as first priority. The company adopted criteria such as the Whole Foods Trade Guarantee and the Eco-Scale Rating system to ensure customers receive the highest quality organic products. Although Whole Foods sells a number of brands, it also sells its own private labels including its 365 Everyday Value and Whole Market. Its 365 Everyday Value private brand comprises 2,600 products that are targeted toward customers who desire high-quality organic food but who also wish to save money. Because organic food usually costs more, the 365 Everyday Value is meant to appeal to more budget-conscious consumers.

However, although Whole Foods recognizes the importance of customers, it also considers the health and well-being of its other stakeholders, including employees and communities. Its mission statement consists of three goals: (1) whole foods, (2) whole people (3) and whole planet. According to its mission statement, Whole Foods has adopted a stakeholder orientation to guide its activities. This approach, along with a strong adherence to its core values, has been crucial in establishing Whole Foods's reputation as a firm committed toward benefiting stakeholders.

---

[1]"What is Conscious Capitalism®?" http://consciouscapitalism.org/learnmore/ (accessed September 29, 2015).

MISSION STATEMENT AND CORE VALUES

Whole Foods's core values, described in Table 1, are an outreach of its mission statement. Whereas the mission statement provides a general direction, Whole Foods's values gives additional details about how it is turning its mission into a reality. The core values also provide an idea of how Whole Foods ranks certain stakeholders. Whole Foods calls the company values its Declaration of Interdependence to emphasize how interdependent the company is upon its stakeholders.

The first two values involve meeting customer needs. Whole Foods describes its commitment toward selling the highest quality natural and organic products available as attempts to be buying agents for customers and not selling agents for manufacturers. Next, Whole Foods turns its attention to the happiness of its employees. Whole Foods believes satisfying customers and employees creates wealth for shareholders. Communities, the environment, and suppliers are essential stakeholders for Whole Foods and are included in its value statements. It is clear from Whole Foods's core values that the company strives toward a stakeholder orientation as part of its core business practice.

TABLE 1 Whole Foods Market's Core Values

We Sell the Highest Quality Natural and Organic Products Available
We Satisfy, Delight, and Nourish Our Customers
We Support Team Member Excellence and Happiness
We Create Wealth through Profits and Growth
We Serve and Support Our Local and Global Communities
We Practice and Advance Environmental Stewardship
We Create Ongoing Win-Win Partnerships with Suppliers
We Promote the Health of Our Stakeholders through Healthy Eating Education

Source: Whole Foods, "Our Core Values," http://www.wholefoodsmarket.com/mission-values/core-values (accessed February 20, 2015).

LIVING ITS VALUES

The success of Whole Foods can be credited to the fact that it modeled its operations around its key stakeholders. Mackey's vision of a model company was one that earned a profit while also acting as a responsible corporate citizen by benefitting society. This vision turned Whole Foods into one of the most successful organic grocers in the world. The following section delves further into how Whole Foods meets the needs of its customers, employees, communities, and the environment.

Commitment to Customers

Because customers are the highest priority at Whole Foods, the company adopted a number of strategies to meet the needs of this stakeholder group. For instance, Whole Foods retail stores maintain an inviting environment, complete with eateries and tables both inside and outside the store for visitors to dine. Free sampling is common at Whole Foods locations to allow customers to try the products. Additionally, employees are instructed to treat customers like a valued part of the family. In 2014 the company introduced a customer reward program with the goal of becoming more competitive with retailers offering frequent sales and item discounts. For the first time since its inception, Whole Foods has also started running TV and print ads, which has significantly increased the firm's yearly advertising expenditure but is also helping the grocery store chain attract and retain more customers. The ads are focused on redefining Whole Foods as a company that cares about the entire life cycle of the products it sells. Whole Foods is hopeful that its new advertising and in-store discounting strategy will help it move beyond the satirical "whole paycheck" reputation that is still prominent in many consumers' minds because of Whole Foods's pricier products.

The company also builds customer relationships through the use of social media. Whole Foods actively uses Twitter and Facebook accounts to post information on sales, answering customer concerns, providing articles or tips about healthy eating, and even re-tweeting information from food experts. Each Whole Foods location has a social media presence, including dedicated social media pages for some store departments. This targeted approach allows Whole Foods to connect with customers and address concerns in real-time. Additionally, the company has worked on making its website more user friendly and adding features that encourage online purchases and in-store pickups. For instance, Whole Foods partnered with a grocery delivery service called Instacart, which offers home delivery of items purchased online. Implementing this delivery service is likely a move to offset the convenience that Amazon.com offers its "Prime" subscribers who get free two-day shipping (or same day delivery in select cities) on many grocery items.

Whole Foods's customer-centered focus has paid off. In the American Customer Satisfaction Survey, Whole Foods was voted second highest from 2010 to 2012 in the supermarket category after Publix. Whole Foods largely differentiates itself from its rivals by emphasizing quality over price. As consumers become more health-conscious and the trend toward organic food continues, Whole Foods has become well suited to attract this demographic. To reassure consumers its products are of the highest quality, Whole Foods offers a number of quality standards. Its Whole Trade Guarantee maintains that the company only purchases products that meet the following criteria:

- Meet its quality standards.
- Provide more money to producers.
- Ensure better wages and working conditions for workers.
- Utilize sound environmental practices.[2]

QUALITY STANDARDS Whole Foods compiled a list of standards to guarantee the highest quality for the organic food it sells. The company works to eliminate all genetically-modified products in stores whenever possible. It features foods free of artificial preservatives, colors, flavors, sweeteners, and hydrogenated fats. Its private labels are also free of high fructose corn syrup, thought to be a big ingredient contributor to obesity in America.

---

[2]Whole Foods Market IP, L.P., "Our Whole Trade Guarantee®," 2011, http://www.wholefoodsmarket.com/products/whole-trade.php (accessed July 16, 2012).

One way that Whole Foods differentiates itself from competitors is alerting customers to the presence of genetically-modified foods. If the company cannot find a product that is not genetically modified, then the product is labeled to inform customers they are buying something that is not completely "all natural." Unlike some countries in Europe that require GMO labeling or ban GMO products altogether, the United States requires no such labeling. However, Whole Foods voluntarily provides GMO labeling information to consumers even though there is no law in the United States requiring it. The company has also committed to labeling all GMO food products it sells by 2018, although many items are already labeled. This commitment demonstrates the company's intent to reduce or eliminate genetically-modified products from all parts of the supply chain. Although GMO labeling might dissuade customers from purchasing a particular product, it also gives Whole Foods a competitive advantage because customers can trust the company to be truthful. Customers tend to do more business with companies they trust, and Whole Foods' sixth place position on the American Customer Satisfaction Index for supermarkets indicates the firm has indeed reaped the rewards of high customer trust.

ECO-SCALE™ RATING SYSTEM   Another set of quality standards Whole Foods has adopted pertains to the cleaning supplies it sells. Whole Foods uses what it terms the Eco-Scale™ Rating System to inform users about the safety and the environmental impact of the cleaning products sold in its stores. According to Whole Foods, the Eco-Scale Rating System is the first such rating system for cleaning supplies sold in retail stores. To develop these standards, Whole Foods used a third-party audit system as a way to eliminate bias. The rating system separates products into red, orange, yellow, or green categories.

Products classified in the red category are not sold at Whole Foods because they do not meet the company's safety and environmental standards. Products in the orange category appear to be "safe" with no significant safety and environmental concerns and no animal testing. Those in the yellow category meet all the standards of the orange category and take further steps to be environmentally friendly. For instance, products in this category do not have synthetic, petroleum-based thickeners from nonrenewable resources. Products in the yellow category do not contain any ingredients with moderate environmental concerns, and those in the green category are considered to be the safest and most eco-friendly. These products do not have any petroleum-based ingredients but are made with plant- and mineral-based ingredients. Products in all of these categories have the ingredients labeled on the packaging and receive third-party verification, allowing consumers to make more informed decisions about which cleaning products to purchase. Because Whole Foods's reputation depends upon the organic and green claims of its products, this Eco-Scale Rating System and the company's Quality Standards ensure the truthfulness of its product quality claims.

Commitment to Employees

If customers are the highest priority stakeholder at Whole Foods, then employees come as a close second. Whole Foods consistently ranks as one of the "Best Companies to Work For" in *Fortune* magazine, and the company is committed to ensuring equality among its employees. At a time when executive pay has been highly criticized in proportion to employee salaries, Whole Foods capped the pay of its executives at 19 times the companies' average full-time employee salary. Co-CEO John Mackey takes $1 per year in compensation.

Employees receive 20 percent discounts on company products, and Whole Foods members that work at least 30 hours a week are eligible for health care coverage. Employees who work between 20 and 30 hours a week can also receive health coverage after working a certain number of service hours. When employees work 6,000 service hours, they are eligible for stock options, providing them with a stake in the company.

While Whole Foods desires for its customers to live healthy lives, it also desires the same for its employees. The company began the Team Member Healthy Discount Incentive Program to reward employees for living healthy lifestyles. Employees that meet certain benchmarks in cholesterol level, blood pressure, not smoking, and body mass index are eligible for an additional 10 percent discount on Whole Foods purchases.

Additionally, Whole Foods is known for its diversity. Forty-five percent of the Whole Foods workforce consists of minorities, with nearly the same percentage consisting of women. Whole Foods also offers domestic-partner benefits to same-sex couples. Whole Foods's treatment of its employees results in a low voluntary turnover rate of 9 percent, versus an average turnover rate of about 100 percent for the industry.

While Whole Foods cares for its employees, it also realizes happy employees translate into happier customers—and higher profits. Yet Whole Foods does not seek to empower employees simply through benefits. It also uses the talents of its employees to improve company operations. Self-directed work teams consisting of employees make many of the day-to-day operational decisions at the store level. For instance, teams can be part of the new employee hiring process, in addition to having some control over their own scheduling. New team members are elected onto the team by two-thirds of a vote. The company provides its team members with extensive training and resources including an online site called "Whole Foods University" that provides educational information on many aspects of the Whole Foods business. Courses provided through Whole Foods University range from information on the company's gain sharing program to the company's quality standards. By empowering its employees through teams, perks, and education, Whole Foods has been able to turn its workforce into significant contributors of value for the company.

Commitment to Other Stakeholders

As Whole Foods demonstrates with its values, consumers and employees are not the only stakeholders the firm recognizes as important. Its fourth value includes creating wealth through profits and growth, which is essential for any organization to survive. The more profit Whole Foods is able to generate, the better financial return for Whole Foods stockholders and investors. Whole Foods believes meeting the needs of consumers and employees translates into more wealth for its investors. Such a stakeholder orientation recognizes the interconnectedness of all the companies' stakeholders. Whole Foods has averaged 12 percent sales growth each year from 2011 to 2014, and its 2014 net income of $579 million jumped 235 percent from its 2010 net income. This growth is important since most grocery stores have experienced declining growth in recent years. Whole Foods's profitability demonstrates the company can succeed with a socially responsible focus on organic foods and quality standards.

Whole Foods strongly believes in giving back to the global community, and this is perhaps best emphasized through its Whole Planet Foundation established in October 2005. The Foundation was created with the mission to create economic partnerships with the poor in developing-world communities. Rather than simply providing immediate items such as food or clothing, Whole Foods creates strategic partnerships with microfinance institutions. Microfinance provides small loans, typically $200 or less, to entrepreneurs in developing countries wanting to start their own small businesses. The company's first grant in 2006 helped develop a microfinance program in Costa Rica. Consumers and employees interested in donating can do so on the Foundation's website. The foundation has raised $53.3 million since 2005, with Whole Foods suppliers contributing over $6 million.

On a more local level, Whole Foods also established the Whole Kids Foundation. The Whole Kids Foundation was founded with the mission to improve the nutrition of children. The company partners with schools and other organizations to increase children's access to healthier food. Company partnerships include the LunchBox Project, an online resource providing information for schools that want to increase their offerings of healthy food served in cafeterias, and the Let's Move Salad Bars to Schools Initiative that provided funds to increase the number of salad bars in schools across the United States. As a grocery store committed to selling healthy and organic foods, Whole Foods has been able to link its philanthropic endeavors to its value of supporting stakeholder health through healthy eating education.

In terms of supplier partnerships, Whole Foods partners with local farmers to offer a variety of produce. Whole Foods is committed to sourcing from local farmers that meet its quality standards, particularly from organic farmers who engage in sustainable agriculture. To qualify as local, food products must have traveled less than seven hours by car or truck to the store. Everyone of Whole Foods's 11 regions has guidelines about how to use the term "local" in their stores, and some stores have chosen to adopt stricter criteria for local products by lessening the travel time.

Whole Foods believes that sourcing locally grown produce embodies its values of giving back to the community, contributing to sustainability, and offering consumers a variety of high-quality product choices. For instance, because there is less of a need to package and transport products for long distances, local farmers can make more money, which they in turn can use to stimulate local economies. Additionally, Whole Foods states that support for local farmers encourages them to diversify, which increases Whole Foods's product selection and contributes to biodiversity in the environment. Transporting products shorter distances also reduces the greenhouse gas emissions released from vehicles. These win-win relationships with farmers help Whole Foods "give back" to its suppliers and to the environment.

Finally, although not specifically mentioned in its values statement, Whole Foods also considers the concerns of special interest groups. Whole Foods became the first large supermarket to adopt humane animal treatment standards for the meat products it sells. In developing these standards, Whole Foods discussed ideas with animal rights special interest groups to decide criteria for sourcing its meat products. Many companies pay little attention to special interest groups because they are considered secondary stakeholders. In other words, they are not necessarily required for the company's survival. However, Whole Foods realized that collaborating with special interest groups would not only secure their support but also provide an opportunity for input on how the company could improve its practices to become more socially responsible.

Whole Foods representatives met with members from special interest groups, farmers, and animal experts to determine humane animal-treatment standards species by species. The company eventually created a supplier certification program in partnership with the Global Animal Partnership to ensure its suppliers were adhering to company standards. The idea behind this program is not only to ensure compliance, but also to inform consumers about the meat they are purchasing. For this reason, Whole Foods adopted a ranking system consisting of five steps. Step 1 assures consumers that the animal lived outside of a crate or cage. Step 2 indicates that the farm provided some type of enrichment for the animal. Step 3 indicates that the animal had access to the outdoors, and Step 4 means the animal was free to roam or forage when outdoors. Step 5 means the animal lived its entire life with all the body parts it was born with. It is also possible to achieve a Step 5+ ranking, indicating the animal met all the five standards in addition to spending its entire life on one farm.

Whole Foods also introduced the similar "responsibly grown" rating system that ranks produce based on whether pesticides were used by the farmer. A "best" label indicates that a number of pesticides designated by Whole Foods were not used in the produce cultivation process. These ranking systems reiterate Whole Food's concern for the environment as well as consumer choice.

Commitment to Sustainability

Last but not least, Whole Foods is strongly committed to the environment. We have already seen how Whole Foods strives to reduce its environmental impact by selling organic food, sourcing from local farmers, selling eco-friendly products, and reducing transport times for its products. However, Whole Foods also strives to incorporate green practices at an operational level as well. The firm is invested significantly in renewable energy, such as solar, wind power, and biodiesel. On the other hand, this does not necessarily mean Whole Foods relies solely on renewable energy sources—the company continues to use conventional electricity as it is difficult for any large firm to use 100 percent renewable energy. Instead, in 2006 Whole Foods decided to purchase wind energy credits to offset its non-renewable energy use. This money goes to fund renewable energy projects associated with wind farms.

Some Whole Foods stores purchased solar energy installations to power their facilities. A solar energy installation can prevent 1,650 tons of carbon dioxide from being emitted into the atmosphere. The company also began using biodiesel fuel in its trucks and modified some of its truck designs to cut back on wind resistance, which in turn conserved fuel. The trucks are equipped with a fuel-saving system that allows the engines to turn off completely when products are being loaded or delivered, which saves fuel that would have been expended if the trucks were left idling. The firm began to obtain Leadership in Energy and Environmental Design (LEED) certification for some of its stores, meaning the stores adhere to strict environmental standards and are constructed with more eco-friendly building materials such as recycled wood.

Whole Foods embraces the concept of Reduce, Reuse, and Recycle in its stores. The company does not use plastic bags and encourages its customers to use renewable grocery bags when shopping. As an incentive to reduce shopping bag consumption, the stores provide a nickel refund to those who come with renewable shopping bags. The stores also use recycled paper when printing and have begun to use rechargeable batteries to cut down on the waste that results from the disposal of batteries. To reduce its energy use even further, Whole Foods began to replace its paper and plastic food containers and utensils with all-fiber packaging.

Finally, Whole Foods is continuing to work on selling products that are not only good for consumers but are more beneficial toward the environment. For instance, the company pledged to support more sustainable sourcing of palm oil, which has traditionally been a strong contributor to deforestation in some countries.

Perhaps one of its biggest landmark commitments, however, is a dedication to seafood sustainability. Whole Foods was the first grocery chain to adopt a sustainability program for wild-caught seafood. Because overfishing has become a substantial problem, Whole Foods implemented a three-color labeling system to help consumers make informed decisions. Red labels are a sign that the seafood should be avoided because it harms the environment or other marine life. Whole Foods has also developed standards for farmed seafood to make sure the fishes are being harvested responsibly.

ETHICAL ISSUES

It is obvious Whole Foods has made great strides in social responsibility. By adopting a stakeholder orientation, Whole Foods has received recognition for ethical business practices, environmental responsibility, and customer satisfaction. However, no company can avoid ethical issues completely, and even those that are the highest rated in social responsibility can make mistakes. The bigger the organization, the more ethical risks it assumes. As Whole Foods grew, it encountered several ethical issues that needed to be addressed. The following section describes some criticisms and legal issues that Whole Foods has faced, some of which represent risk areas for the company.

Reaction toward Competitors

In its more than 30 years in existence, Whole Foods grew significantly from its humble origins. Some of this growth came from acquiring other stores and caused criticism from those not wanting their smaller community grocery stores to shut down or be acquired. For instance, in the Jamaica Plain neighborhood of Boston, Whole Foods acquired a local Latin American store called Hi-Lo when it moved into the community. Many local residents objected, considering Whole Foods products to be too expensive. Most large retail chains must exert caution when moving into a new community since their arrival will almost inevitably have an impact on rival, and often smaller, retailers.

While not all its acquisitions went smoothly, Whole Foods had perhaps the most trouble when it wanted to acquire its competitor, organic grocery chain Wild Oats. Wild Oats was the second largest natural grocery chain in the country, and in 2007 Whole Foods announced it was acquiring its largest competitor for $565 million. This acquisition eliminated a key competitor and gave Whole Foods access into new markets. However, the proposed acquisition generated immediate controversy—this time from regulators. The Federal Trade Commission filed a lawsuit to block the acquisition, claiming it would reduce competition in the industry and thus violate antitrust laws. Cited in the complaint were emails from CEO John Mackey stating a merger between the two companies would help avoid "price wars." (Price wars often happen when two close competitors try to outdo one another and gain market share.) This was another sign that perhaps Whole Foods wanted to gain a strategic advantage from less competition.

The FTC also revealed that John Mackey wrote blog posts under a pseudonym between 1999 and 2006 that highly criticized Wild Oats. These postings included several negative comments about Wild Oats's stock prices and its future. While not illegal, many believed these postings were unethical and even manipulative. Whole Foods made sure to distance itself from John Mackey's postings by stating they were done outside of the company. However, as the voice of the company, Mackey's actions brought up serious questions about how Whole Foods approaches competing companies.

Eventually, the FTC and Whole Foods reached a deal. Whole Foods agreed to sell 31 Wild Oats stores and sell the Wild Oats brand. Mackey acknowledged the company would have been better off if it had not pursued the merger, particularly as drops in stock prices and the recession caused so much damage. In fact, both Mackey and co-CEO Walter

Robb admit that Whole Foods's rapid expansion and inability to anticipate and respond to changing retail trends nearly crippled the company. During the 2009 recession, Whole Foods's stock price dropped from $30 to $4 a share. Although the company recovered (with the stock price ranging from $30–$57 a share in 2015), it is important for Whole Foods to approach future acquisitions and relationships with rivals carefully with respect to laws and ethical considerations.

Veering Off-Course

In 2009 in the midst of a recession and a resolution with the FTC over the acquisition of Wild Oats, John Mackey admitted Whole Foods had strayed from one of its core values: healthy eating. In an interview, Mackey admitted, "We sell a bunch of junk." He said Whole Foods had "veered off-course" by selling junk food and unhealthy products to consumers. Part of the reason to stock shelves with less healthy alternatives was most likely to court consumers, particularly with the increase in competition. Competition from Trader Joe's and Costco had already led Whole Foods to modify some of its strategies, such as matching Trader Joe's prices on 365 Everyday Value items. However, companies begin to encounter problems when they stray from their corporate values, and Mackey appeared to think Whole Foods was not being a leader in promoting healthy eating habits.

After this admission, Whole Foods re-committed to its value of healthy eating education. The company hired Healthy Eating Specialists and began posting information on its website to educate consumers on healthy eating. The company created incentives for its employees to adopt healthier lifestyles, as described earlier. By proactively engaging in the fight against obesity, Whole Foods began to re-embrace its original core values.

In 2015 Whole Foods's stock dropped more than 30 percent after the New York City Department of Consumer Affairs found the company was overstating the price of pre-weighed packages. Whole Foods's CEOs admitted to overcharging and apologized. Nevertheless, there was much negative publicity across the country about the incident. The CEOs claimed that overcharging was a mistake that involved both overcharging and undercharging. If the priced item was not in the consumer's favor, they promised to give them the item for free.

Unions, Health Care, and Climate Change

It is no secret that Whole Foods prefers not to have unions. Mackey has cited unions as creating "an adversarial relationship in the workplace." However, he maintains that managers cannot stop employees from unionizing if they so desire. Some disagree and have accused Whole Foods of union-busting by threatening reprisals if employees join a union. For example, Whole Foods joined with Starbucks and Costco to oppose the proposed Employee Free Choice Act that gives employees the ability to form unions if a majority signs cards suggesting they desire to have a union. The three retailers instead advocated for a secret ballot process for unionization. While it is not necessarily unethical to be against unions, union busting—or purposefully trying to prevent unions by threats or other underhanded tactics—has ethical and legal implications. Whole Foods should remain vigilant to ensure store managers and other officials respect employee rights to organize.

Health care is another debate, but not because Whole Foods has a bad health care program for employees. Rather, the controversy stemmed from an op-ed article Mackey wrote against President Obama's universal health care plan. It might be argued that since Mackey wrote the article, Whole Foods should not be dragged into the controversy.

However, once again because founders and/or CEOs represent a company, society often associates their actions as speaking for the firm, even if an action was done outside of it. In this case, Mackey, a strong libertarian, wrote an op-ed article in *The Wall Street Journal* criticizing Obama's health care initiative and proposing alternatives for health care reform, using Whole Foods's health care plan as an example. For instance, Whole Foods provides up to $1,800 of funds per year for employees to use for medical care. Money not spent rolls over into the next year. Afterward, Whole Foods will not cover the insurance costs until the employee meets a $2,500 deductible. According to Mackey, this encourages employees to spend the first $1,800 carefully and provides them with the opportunity to determine what their health care needs are.

Mackey's letter led to anger from supporters of the nationalized health care initiative. Some unions and consumers began to boycott Whole Foods's stores because of Mackey's stance, claiming he sees health care as a privilege and not a right. Others, however, refused to boycott even though they disagreed with Mackey's views. They believed Mackey—and Whole Foods—had the right to express their opinions. Regardless, Whole Foods's sales did seem to be somewhat affected by Mackey's controversial remarks.

Mackey stirred more sentiment a few years later for allegedly downplaying the dangers of global warming. He mentioned that climate change is a normal process that should not be used as an excuse to curb economic growth. Mackey went on to say that society would learn to cope and adapt to rising temperatures and climate change is not as big of a deal as it has been made out to be. This is an interesting ethical issue, not because it had a drastic impact on Whole Foods's bottom line but because it brings up the issue of businesses' and business representatives' rights to express their viewpoints—particularly in the political limelight. These ethical issues are not always easy to settle and continue to be relevant for businesses that have major stakes in regulatory decisions.

CONCLUSION

Whole Foods strives to be a profitable company while also maintaining an ethical standpoint when making decisions related to its customers, employees, and all affected stakeholders. Consistently being ranked as one of the World's Most Ethical companies and best companies to work for, Whole Foods has demonstrated its commitment toward selling organic food, satisfying customers, and incorporating quality and sustainability into its products. Whole Foods evaluates all of the products it sells so it can more effectively educate customers about what they are buying and if it meets certain quality standards.

The company has continually demonstrated its commitment to the environment by implementing the Eco-Scale Rating System, aggressively promoting the use of renewable shopping bags, and beginning to obtain LEED certification for some of its stores. Whole Foods strives to make a beneficial impact within each community it operates in by adopting a stakeholder orientation. These actions contribute to Whole Foods's current status as one of the top natural grocers in the United States.

However, as Whole Foods expands, it faces many ethical challenges, some of which may extend into the future. For example, when opening new stores the company must anticipate the reactions from community members and attempt to alleviate any concerns. It also needs to continuously reexamine its expansion and acquisition strategy to ensure that pursuing the ventures will not run afoul with regulatory authorities, as it experienced with its unprofitable acquisition of Wild Oats. Finally, Whole Foods must continue to take a stakeholder orientation toward all stakeholders—even competitors. It is important for the firm to realize that just because an action might not be illegal does not mean that it is necessarily ethical.

Although Whole Foods has experienced some negative backlash, overall the company has developed a strong positive reputation among its stakeholders. As a desire for green product options and a concern for corporate social responsibility continually evolve among stakeholders, Whole Foods's careful attention to stakeholder needs and a strong commitment to core values provide it with a significant competitive advantage.

QUESTIONS FOR DISCUSSION

1. How has a commitment to corporate values contributed to Whole Foods's success?
2. Describe how Whole Foods's adoption of a stakeholder orientation has influenced the way it operates.
3. What are some ways that Whole Foods might have neglected certain stakeholders in the past?

SOURCES

"The 12 greatest entrepreneurs of our time," *NDTV Photos*, http://www.ndtv.com/photos/business/12-greatest-entrepreneurs-of-our-time-14280 (accessed February 23, 2015); Amanda Alix, "Whole Foods Market: A Steady Diet of Growth and Profit," The Motley Fool, February 21, 2012, http://www.fool.com/investing/general/2012/02/21/whole-foods-market-a-steady-diet-of-growth-and-pro.aspx (accessed February 23, 2015); American Customer Satisfaction Index, "Benchmarks by Industry: Supermarkets," http://www.theacsi.org/index.php?option=com_content&view=article&id=147&catid=&Itemid=212&i=Supermarkets (accessed February 20, 2015); Associated Press, "Whole Foods CEO's anonymous online life," *CNBC*, July 12, 2007, http://www.msnbc.msn.com/id/19718742/ns/business-us_business/t/whole-foods-ceos-anonymous-online-life/ (accessed February 23, 2015); George A. Bray, Samara Joy Nielsen, and Barry M. Popkin, "Consumption of high-fructose corn syrup in beverages may play a role in the epidemic of obesity," *American Journal of Clinical Nutrition* 79, no. 4 (2004): 537–543; Joseph Brownstein, "Is Whole Foods' Get Healthy Plan Fair?" *ABC News*, January 28, 2010, http://abcnews.go.com/Health/w_DietAndFitnessNews/foods-incentives-make-employees-healthier/story?id=9680047 (accessed February 23, 2015); Conscious Capitalism®, "What is Conscious Capitalism?" http://www.consciouscapitalism.org/learnmore/ (accessed February 23, 2015); Kerry A. Dolan "America's Greenest Companies 2011," *Forbes*, April 18, 2011, http://www.forbes.com/2011/04/18/americas-greenest-companies.html (accessed February 23, 2015); Catherine Dunn, "2014 Best Companies All Stars," *Fortune*, January 16, 2014, http://fortune.com/2014/01/16/2014-best-companies-all-stars-fortunes-best-companies-to-work-for/ (accessed February 20, 2015); Hadley Freeman, "Over the top and over here: 'Disney World' of food opens first UK store," *The Guardian*, June 6, 2007, http://www.guardian.co.uk/business/2007/jun/07/retail.supermarkets (accessed February 23, 2015); Katherine Goldstein, "Whole Foods Backlash: Bloggers Outraged over CEO's Anti 'Obamacare' Column," *Huffington Post*, May 25, 2011, http://www.huffingtonpost.com/2009/08/18/the-whole-foods-health-ca_n_262471.html (accessed February 23, 2015); Alison Griswold "Whole Foods Desperately Wants Customers to Feel Warm and Fuzzy again," *Slate*, October 20, 2014, http://www.slate.com/blogs/moneybox/2014/10/20/whole_foods_ad_campaign_can_values_matter_marketing_erase_the_whole_paycheck.html (accessed February 20, 2015); Maria Halkias, "Container Store, Whole Foods aim for conscious capitalism," *The Dallas Morning News*, August 8, 2010, http://www.dallasnews.com/business/headlines/20100808-Container-Store-Whole-Foods-aim-540.ece (accessed February 23, 2015); Josh Harkinson, "Are Starbucks and Whole Foods Union Busters?"

Mother Jones, April 6, 2009, http://www.motherjones.com/politics/2009/04/are-starbucks-and-whole-foods-union-busting (accessed February 23, 2015); Susanna Kim, "7 Companies Offering Health Care Benefits to Part-Time Workers," *ABC News*, October 25, 2011 http://abcnews.go.com/Business/companies-offering-health-care-benefits-perks-part-time/story?id=14805107#4 (accessed February 23, 2015); Paul R. La Monica, "Whole Foods Stock Cheaper Than 6 Bottles of Asparagus Water," *CNN Money,* August 11, 2015, http://money.cnn.com/2015/08/11/investing/whole-foods-lawsuit-john-oliver-asparagus-water/index.html (accessed August 11, 2015); Allison Linn, "Whole Foods up, Wal-Mart down in customer satisfaction survey," *MSN,* February 21, 2012, http://lifeinc.today.msnbc.msn.com/_news/2012/02/21/10437549-whole-foods-up-wal-mart-down-in-customer-satisfaction-survey?lite (accessed February 23, 2015); Donald Luskin, "Whole-Foods-Style Health Care," *SmartMoney*, August 21, 2009, http://www.smartmoney.com/invest/markets/whole-foods-health-care/ (accessed July 17, 2012); Jacqui MacKenzie, "Why I Follow Whole Foods," *Social Media Today*, May 7, 2012, http://socialmediatoday.com/jacqui-mackenzie/503334/why-i-follow-whole-foods (accessed February 23, 2015); John Mackey, "The Whole Foods Alternative to ObamaCare," *The Wall Street Journal*, August 11, 2009, http://online.wsj.com/article/SB10001424052970204251404574342170072865070.html (accessed February 23, 2015); John Mackey and *Grist* staff, "An interview with John Mackey, founder of Whole Foods," *Grist*, December 18, 2004, http://grist.org/article/little-mackey/ (accessed February 23, 2015); MarketWatch Inc., "Annual Financials for Whole Foods Market Inc.," *MarketWatch*, 2015, http://www.marketwatch.com/investing/stock/wfm/financials (accessed February 20, 2015); Katy McLaughlin and Timothy W. Martin, "As Sales Slip, Whole Foods Tries Health Push, *Wall Street Journal*, August 5, 2009, http://online.wsj.com/article/SB124941849645105559.html (accessed February 23, 2015); Melanie J. Martin, "Data on Employee Turnover in the Grocery Industry," *Chron.com*, http://smallbusiness.chron.com/data-employee-turnover-grocery-industry-18817.html (accessed February 23, 2015); Timothy W. Martin, "Whole Foods to Sell 31Stores in FTC Deal," *The Wall Street Journal*, March 7, 2009, http://online.wsj.com/article/SB123634938198152983.html?_nocache=1342806303055&user=welcome&mg=id-wsj (accessed February 23, 2015); "New Labelling Laws: What Has Changed?" *GMO Compass*, December 15, 2005, http://www.gmo-compass.org/eng/regulation/labelling/93.new_labelling_laws_gm_products_eu.html (accessed February 23, 2015); Non GMO Project, "GMO Facts," 2015, http://www.nongmoproject.org/learn-more/ (accessed February 23, 2015); Whole Foods Market, "GMO: Your Right to Know," http://www.wholefoodsmarket.com/gmo-your-right-know (accessed February 23, 2015); Hayley Peterson, "More Bad News for Whole Foods," *Business Insider,* August 10, 2015, http://www.businessinsider.com/more-bad-news-for-whole-foods-2015-7 (accessed August 11, 2015); Holly Rosenkrantz, "Whole Foods, Costco Offer Alternative to Union Bill," *Bloomberg*, March 22, 2009, http://www.bloomberg.com/apps/news?pid=newsarchive&sid=atnjqq9F6._c (accessed February 23, 2015); Christopher S. Rugaber, "Whole Foods attacks government case against Wild Oats acquisition," *Denver Post*, July 31, 2007, http://www.denverpost.com/business/ci_6508028 (accessed February 23, 2015); Brad Stone, "Whole Foods, Half Off," *Bloomberg*, January 29, 2015, http://www.bloomberg.com/news/articles/2015-01-29/in-shift-whole-foods-to-compete-with-price-cuts-loyalty-app (accessed February 20, 2015); Michael Theis, "Whole Foods plans customer reward program, report says," *Austin Business Journal*, September 17, 2014, http://www.bizjournals.com/austin/blog/retail/2014/09/whole-foods-plans-customer-reward-program-report.html (accessed February 20, 2015); Bruce Watson, "Whole Foods drama continues: Unions join in fight against CEO," *Daily Finance*, August 27, 2009, http://www.dailyfinance.com/2009/08/27/whole-foods-drama-continues-unions-join-in-fight-against-ceo/ (accessed February 23, 2015); "Whole Foods CEO On Climate Change: John Mackey Says Warming Is 'Not Necessarily Bad,'" *The Huffington Post*, January 24, 2013, http://www.huffingtonpost.com/2013/01/24/whole-foods-ceo-climate-change_n_2511482.html (accessed February 23, 2015); "Whole Foods' Controversy at Jamaica Plan," *Organic Guide*, January 21, 2011, http://www.organicguide.com/organic/news/whole-foods-controversy-at-jamaica-plain/ (accessed February 23, 2015); Whole Foods Market, "365 Everyday Value® products," 2015, http://www.wholefoodsmarket.com/about-our-products/product-lines/365-everyday-value (accessed July 23, 2015); Whole Foods Market,, "Animal Welfare," 2015, http://www.wholefoodsmarket.com/meat/welfare.php (accessed February 23, 2015); Whole Foods Market, "Declaration of Interdependence," 2015, http://www.wholefoodsmarket.com/company/declaration.php (accessed February 23, 2015); Whole Foods Market, "Green Mission," 2015, http://www.wholefoods.com/greenmission (accessed February 23, 2015); Whole

Foods Market, "Health Starts Here," 2015, http://www.wholefoodsmarket.com/healthstartshere/ (accessed February 23, 2015); Whole Foods Market, "How to Make the Best Seafood," 2015, http://www.wholefoodsmarket.com/seafood-ratings/ (accessed February 23, 2015); Whole Foods Market, "Locally Grown: The Whole Foods Promise," 2015, http://www.wholefoodsmarket.com/products/locally-grown/ (accessed February 23, 2015); Whole Foods Market, "Our Quality Standards," 2015, http://www.wholefoodsmarket.com/products/quality-standards.php (accessed February 23, 2015); Whole Foods Market, "Newsroom," 2015, http://media.wholefoodsmarket.com/fast-facts/ (accessed February 20, 2015); Whole Foods Market, "Seafood Sustainability," 2015, http://www.wholefoodsmarket.com/values/seafood.php (accessed February 23, 2015); Whole Foods Market, "Training & Development," 2012, http://www.wholefoodsmarket.com/careers/training.php (accessed July 17, 2012); Whole Foods Market, "Whole Foods Market Eco-Scale™ Rating System for Household Cleaning Products," http://www.wholefoodsmarket.com/eco-scale/ratingsystem.php (accessed February 23, 2015; Whole Foods Market, "Whole Foods Market's team members put company on FORTUNE Magazine's '100 Best Companies to Work For'," January 21, 2010, http://media.wholefoodsmarket.com/news/whole-foods-markets-team-members-put-company-on-fortune-magazines-100-best- (accessed February 20, 2015); Whole Foods Market, "Whole Trade," http://www.wholefoodsmarket.com/products/whole-trade.php (accessed February 23, 2015). "Whole Foods to acquire Wild Oats," *Austin Business Journal*, February 21, 2007, http://www.bizjournals.com/austin/stories/2007/02/19/daily28.html?surround=lfn (accessed February 23, 2015); Whole Kids Foundation website, http://www.wholekidsfoundation.org/index.php (accessed September 23, 2015); Whole Planet Foundation website, https://www.wholeplanetfoundation.org (accessed February 23, 2015); Whole Planet Foundation, "Our Impact," https://www.wholeplanetfoundation.org/about/our-impact/ (accessed February 23, 2015); Yahoo! Finance, "Whole Foods Market, Inc. (WFM)," http://finance.yahoo.com/q/is?s=WFM+Income+Statement&annual (accessed February 23, 2015).

CASE 14

Apple Inc.'s Ethical Success and Challenges*

Headquartered in Cupertino, California, Apple Inc. experienced many challenges throughout its business history. In 1997 Apple's share price was $3.30. Fifteen years later its share price rose to $705.07 (although its share price decreased to $425 the following year). In 2014 Apple split its stock 7-1, meaning each share was worth a seventh of its previous value, and stockholders were given seven extra shares of stock to make up the difference. Apple's stock price has become a key benchmark for the technology sector. For the past eight years, Apple earned first place among *Fortune* magazine's World's Most Admired Companies. To millions of consumers, the Apple brand embodies quality, prestige, and innovation.

Although companies tried to copy the Apple business model, none have been able to discover what it is that makes Apple so unique. Apple is ranked first in innovation by *Fortune* magazine and is a market leader in the development and sales of mobile devices. Many believe Apple's success stems from a combination of several factors, including the remarkable leadership skills of former CEO Steve Jobs, a corporate culture of enthusiasm and innovation, and the high-tech products for which Apple is known. These combining qualities allow Apple to revolutionize the technology and retail industries.

APPLE'S HISTORY

Apple's first product, the Apple I, was vastly different from the Apple products most are familiar with today. This first handmade computer kit was constructed by Apple cofounder Steve Wozniak. It lacked a graphic user interface (GUI), and buyers had to add their own keyboard and display. Cofounder Steve Jobs convinced Wozniak that it could be sold as a commercial product. In 1976 the Apple I was unveiled at the Home Brew Computer Club and put on sale for $666.66.

Jobs and Wozniak continued to create innovative products. Soon their new company, Apple Computer Inc., surpassed $1 million in sales. However, the mid-1980s brought difficult times for Apple. In 1983 the company introduced the Apple Lisa for $10,000. The product flopped. In 1985 Steve Jobs was ousted after internal conflicts with the Apple CEO. Its computer products the Mac I and the Newton were not successful, and the company underwent several CEO changes. With declining stock prices, the future of Apple was in jeopardy.

*This case was prepared by Jennifer Sawayda, Harper Baird, Danielle Jolley, and Julian Mathias for and under the direction of O.C. Ferrell and Linda Ferrell. It was prepared for classroom discussion rather than to illustrate either effective or ineffective handling of an administrative, ethical, or legal decision by management. All sources used for this case were obtained through publicly available material on the Apple website © 2015.

Steve Jobs returned to Apple in 1997 to try and save the struggling company. The return of Jobs introduced a new era for Apple. Jobs immediately began to change the company's corporate culture. Before Jobs's return, employees were more open about Apple projects. After he returned, Jobs instituted a "closed door" policy.

Aside from efforts to protect intellectual property internally, Jobs was also a proponent of using litigation against rival companies suspected of patent infringement. Apple sued Nokia, HTC, and Samsung in 2009, 2010, and 2011, respectively. Perhaps the most notable lawsuits were made against Samsung, where both companies filed suits against each other across nine countries over a three-year period. In total, Apple and Samsung filed over 40 patent infringement lawsuits and counter suits related to intellectual property rights. The companies decided to end litigation outside of the United States, choosing to focus instead on cases that are still active in the United States. Today Apple continues to remain vigilant in protecting its technology and ensuring information remains proprietary.

Jobs also created a flattened organizational structure; rather than go through layers of management to address employees, he addressed them directly. Perhaps one of the most noticeable changes, however, was Apple's expansion into new product lines within the electronics industry. In 2001 Apple launched the iPod—a portable music player that forever changed the music industry. The company also introduced iTunes, a type of "jukebox" software that allowed users to upload songs from CDs onto their Macs and then organize and manage their personalized song libraries. Two years later Apple introduced the iTunes Store, where users could download millions of their favorite songs for $0.99 each online.

The introduction of the iPhone in 2007 was a turning point for Apple and the beginning of a paradigm shift for the entire world. The iPhone was a revolutionary new smartphone with the music capabilities of an iPod. The success of the iPhone cannot be understated. In 2015 iPhone market share was nearly tied with Android smartphones in the United States. The new generation iPhone 6 accounted for close to half of all new smartphone sales.

The same year that Apple introduced the iPhone, Jobs announced Apple Computer, Inc. would be renamed Apple Inc. This signified that Apple was no longer just a computer manufacturer but also a driver in consumer electronics. Some saw this as a shift away from computers toward consumer electronics such as Apple TV, iPods, iTunes, iPhones, and iPads. However, it may be more accurate to say Apple is reinventing computers, or at least what they look like and how they are used. With the introduction of tablet computers such as the iPad, Apple began to take market share away from its top competitors in the computer industry, but in the process sales of its Mac computer line were also cannibalized by consumers opting for a tablet. Sales of desktops, laptops, and netbooks began to decline after tablet computers were introduced. Although analysts believed tablet sales would continue growing at a rapid rate, the tablet market became saturated with fewer than expected customers upgrading their current tablets to newer versions. Because nearly half of all U.S. households own at least one tablet, this has translated into stagnating industry growth and low sales. Consequently, just as Apple cannibalized its own line of Mac computers with the introduction of the iPad, it appears that its newest iPhone, which features a larger screen, is eroding the iPad market. The dynamic fluctuation in PC and Mac computer sales and the frequent introduction of new smartphones make it difficult to predict future sales of Apple products. Only time will tell if Apple's devices improve in market share or are overtaken by a rival platform.

APPLE'S CORPORATE CULTURE

Apple's transition from a computer to a consumer electronics company is unprecedented—and hard to replicate. Although many can only speculate about why Apple succeeded so well, they tend to credit Steve Jobs's remarkable leadership abilities, Apple's highly skilled employees, and its strong corporate culture.

The concept of evangelism is an important component of Apple's culture. Corporate evangelists refer to people who extensively promote a corporation's products. Apple even had a chief evangelist whose job was to spread the message about Apple and gain support for its products. However, as the name evangelism implies, the role of evangelist takes on greater meaning. Evangelists believe strongly in the company and will spread that belief to others, who in turn convince other people. Therefore, evangelists are not only employees but loyal customers as well. In this way, Apple was able to form what it refers to as a "Mac cult"—customers who are loyal to Apple's Mac computers and who spread a positive message about Macs to their friends and families.

Successful evangelism only occurs with dedicated, enthusiastic employees who are willing to spread the word about Apple. When Jobs returned to Apple, he instituted two cultural changes: he encouraged debate on ideas, and he created a vision employees could believe in. By implementing these two changes, employees felt their input was important and they were a part of something bigger than themselves. Such feelings created a sense of loyalty among many working at Apple.

Apple prides itself on its unique corporate culture. On its job site for corporate employees, it assures potential applicants that the organization has a flat structure, lacking the layers of bureaucracy of other corporations. Apple also emphasizes that it does not adhere to the average work day. Instead, Apple markets itself as a fast-paced, innovative, and collaborative environment committed toward doing things "the right way." By offering both challenges and benefits to applicants, Apple hopes to attract those who fit best with its corporate culture.

Apple also looks for retail employees that fit well in its culture. It wants to ensure that its retail employees make each consumer feel welcome. Inside Apple retailers are stations where customers can test and experiment with the latest Apple products. Employees are trained to speak with customers within two minutes of entering the store. To ensure its retail employees feel motivated, Apple provides extensive training, greater compensation than employees might receive at similar stores, and opportunities to move up to manager, genius (an employee trained to answer the more difficult customer questions), or creative (an employee who trains customers one-on-one or through workshops). Apple also offers young people the chance to intern with the firm, become student representatives at their schools, or work remotely during college as phone customer support representatives.

Another benefit Apple offers combines employee concerns with concerns of the environment. In an effort to reduce its overall environmental impact, Apple offers incentives such as transit subsidies for employees who opt to use public transportation. Additionally, as part of its long-term commitment to sustainability, Apple is spending $850 million for 25 years of solar power. Its Cupertino facility runs on 100 percent renewable energy and is equipped with shuttles for employees. Apple's free buses are powered by biodiesel. Apple also began construction on a new headquarters facility, named Apple Campus 2. With a budget of $5 billion, the new facilities will include a fitness center, underground auditorium, and 300 electric vehicle charging stations. The new buildings, expected to be completed in 2016, will be LEED certified and incorporate solar technology. The Campus is also conveniently located so that many employees can walk, ride, or carpool to work. These incentives reduce fuel costs for employees while simultaneously lowering emissions released into the environment.

APPLE'S ETHICS

Apple has tried to ensure its employees and those with whom they work display appropriate conduct in all situations. It bases its success on "creating innovative, high-quality products and services and on demonstrating integrity in every business interaction." According to Apple, four main principles contribute to integrity: honesty, respect, confidentiality, and compliance. To thoroughly detail these principles, Apple drafted a code of business conduct that applies to all its operations, including those overseas. It also provides specific policies regarding corporate governance, director conflict of interest, and guidelines on reporting questionable conduct on its website. Additionally, Apple provides employees with a Business Conduct Helpline they can use to report misconduct to Apple's Audit and Finance Committee.

Many of Apple's product components are manufactured in countries with low labor costs. The potential for misconduct is high because of differing labor standards and less direct oversight. As a result, Apple makes each of its suppliers sign a "Supplier Code of Conduct" and performs factory audits to ensure compliance. Apple may refuse to do additional business with suppliers who refuse to comply with its standards. To emphasize its commitment toward responsible supplier conduct, Apple releases an annual Apple Supplier Responsibility Report that explains its supplier expectations as well as audit conclusions and corrective actions the company takes against factories where violations occur.

ETHICAL ISSUES AT APPLE INC.

Although Apple has consistently won first place as the World's Most Admired Company, it experienced several ethical issues in recent years. These issues could have a profound effect on the company's future success. Apple's sterling reputation could easily be damaged by serious misconduct or a failure to address risks appropriately.

Privacy

Consumer tracking is a controversial issue. With the increase in social networking, mobile devices, and Internet use, the ability for companies to track customers is greater than ever before. For Apple, more customer information can help the company better understand consumer trends and subsequently market its products more effectively. However, the firm must still show respect for consumer privacy, and a perceived breach in privacy is likely to result in a backlash against the company.

In 2011 Apple experienced just such a backlash. Apple and Google disclosed that certain smartphone apps and software, often utilizing the phones' internal GPS devices, collected data on the phones' locations. Consumers and government officials saw this as an infringement on user privacy. The companies announced that users have the option to disable these features on their phones, yet this was not entirely true for Apple's iPhone. Some smartphones continued to collect location information even after users disabled the "location" feature. Apple attributed this to a glitch it remedied with new software. In future iPhone releases, Apple improved the privacy features of iOS, the mobile operating system found in the iPhone and iPad. The security feature upgrades include enhanced Wi-Fi security and a policy that location features are turned off by default on new iPhones. Once the smartphone is set up, users have the option of turning on the location feature if they desire. Both Google and Apple defend their data-collection mechanisms, but many government officials disagree that these tracking techniques are appropriate.

In 2015 the FCC investigated whether a major wireless carrier violated consumer privacy rules by tracking mobile Internet activity without users knowing. The wireless carrier claimed users can opt out of its tracking and advertising program. The FCC and other government agencies continually develop mobile privacy legislation that addresses the rapid technological advancements in mobile devices. While these actions should improve consumer privacy, they could also have profound effects on Apple, other electronics companies, and wireless carriers. Perhaps as a way to preempt legislation, some major mobile carriers have already decided to eliminate services that track user activity.

Another privacy controversy was related to Apple Pay, software that allows consumers to purchase items through their iPhones. The mobile payment system became a target for hackers, who exploited vulnerabilities in the verification process of adding a credit card to an Apple Pay account. Apple Pay was designed with simplicity at its core—users can complete transactions by waving their iPhone in front of a wireless reading machine. Apple also implemented a number of security features into Apple Pay so consumer information is safeguarded. The issue with hackers gaining access to payment information is at least partially the responsibility of the banking institutions, since they approve the addition of credit cards to Apple Pay accounts. Banks did not ask enough security verification questions, making it easier for consumers to add credit cards to their accounts but also leaving the door open for increased fraud.

Compromised information from Apple Pay was not the first time an Apple system was attacked by hackers. Just a few months before vulnerabilities in Apple Pay were exploited, hackers broke into 26 iCloud accounts belonging to celebrities. Many people use iCloud's remote cloud storage capabilities to store photos, videos, and music. When the hackers gained access to the cloud-based accounts, they leaked nude photos of the celebrities. These highly publicized scandals led many to criticize the security of iCloud, with some completely losing trust in Apple's ability to secure user information across the entire iOS ecosystem. These celebrity photo leaks came at a time when iCloud was also being targeted by cybercriminals trying to intercept and obtain usernames, passwords, and personal data from users in China. Apple responded to the attacks by enforcing more stringent password requirements and adding extra layers of encryption to its iPhone and iCloud infrastructure.

Price Fixing

Another major ethical issue for Apple includes allegations of price fixing. A judge ruled that Apple had conspired to fix prices on electronic books (e-books) in conjunction with five major book publishers. A federal judge ruled that Apple was part of a deal that required publishers to give Apple's iTunes store the best deals in the marketplace for e-books. According to allegations, Apple allowed publishers to set the e-book prices for the iPad, and Apple received 30 percent of the proceeds (known as the "agency model"). The agency model is thought to be less competitive than the wholesale model, in which retailers and publishers negotiate on the price. However, if a competitor was found to be selling the e-book for less, Apple was to be offered the same lower price. This scheme is more commonly referred to as a most-favored-nation clause and can be used by companies to dominate the market by keeping competitors out. After striking the deal with Apple, publishers then approached Amazon about participating in the contract. In court, Apple faced fines totaling $450 million as part of a settlement agreement. Apple denied any wrongdoing and acknowledged only passive association with the deal to set e-book prices.

Rioting

In early 2012 Apple halted sales of the iPhone 4S at retail stores in China. This result came after massive crowds waiting for 48 hours outside of the flagship store in Beijing began to riot. Tensions grew between prospective buyers waiting overnight who tried to edge themselves closer to the front of the line. The estimated crowd was upwards of 2,000 people, which alarmed police officials who asked Apple not to open the store as a safety precaution. Customers waiting for the iPhone retaliated by throwing eggs at the store and attacking a mall property manager mistaken for an Apple employee. To their dismay, customers were encouraged to purchase the iPhone online or through other authorized sellers. Other stores in Shanghai and one other in Beijing opened as scheduled and quickly sold out of the iPhone 4S. Many questioned Apple's ethics about how they handled this situation and the dangers to customer and employee safety.

Another instance of rioting associated with Apple occurred later in September when more than 2,000 Foxconn plant workers assembling the iPhone 5 broke out into a fight in the plant's dormitories. Authorities sent 5,000 police officials to restore order at the plant. Workers reportedly broke glass windows of guard shacks and destroyed railings throughout the property. Reasons given for the riot varied and included alleged beatings from factory guards, stress among workers required to produce products in a short period of time, and frustration with the work environment itself. This is not the first time Foxconn's environment has been questioned, and as a major Apple supplier, both companies have the responsibility to ensure workers at the plant are being treated fairly. More on Foxconn will be discussed later in this case.

Sustainability

Apple has taken steps to become a greener company and reduce the environmental impact of its facilities. It also has restrictions addressing the manufacturing, use, and recycling of its products. However, the company admits that the majority of its emissions come from its products. In 2013 Apple stated its operations contributed to 33.8 million metric tons of greenhouse gases released. While less than 2 percent came from its facilities, 98 percent came from the life cycle of its products, including manufacturing, product usage, transportation, and recycling. Since Apple's success hinges on constantly developing and launching new products, the environmental impact of its products is a serious issue.

One practice for which some consumers have criticized Apple is planned obsolescence—pushing people to replace or upgrade their technology whenever Apple comes out with an updated version. Since Apple constantly releases upgraded products, this could result in older technology being tossed aside. Apple undertook different approaches to combat this problem. For one, the company strives to build quality, long-lasting products with materials suitable for recycling. To encourage recycling, Apple implemented a program at its stores where old iPods, mobile phones, and Mac computers could be recycled.

Consumers that trade in their old iPods can receive a 10 percent discount on a newer version; those with old Mac computers that still have value can receive gift cards. Apple partners with hundreds of regional recyclers and has established recycling programs in 95 percent of the countries where its products are sold. Despite the recycling programs, many consumers still throw away their old products out of convenience, particularly if they have no value. E-waste remains a significant issue as consumers continue to improperly dispose of their old electronic devices.

Apple made a controversial move by temporarily removing 39 products from the Electronic Product Environmental Assessment Tool (EPEAT) rating system. The rating system provides green standards for computers and is used by many schools and governments when purchasing computer products. Apple stated it felt its products adhered to green standards not measured by EPEAT. Many consumers felt Apple might be embracing less eco-friendly products or was engaging in greenwashing. Many large buyers such as the city of San Francisco threatened to drop Apple computers as a result. Apple rejoined the EPEAT rating system after consumer feedback indicated that dropping the system was a mistake. With sustainability becoming a major concern for many buyers, Apple must carefully anticipate consumer reactions before implementing similar changes in the future.

Intellectual Property

Intellectual property theft is a key concern at Apple and is an issue the company aggressively pursues. Apple is serious about keeping its proprietary information a secret to prevent other companies from acquiring its ideas. This led to many lawsuits between Apple and other technology firms. In 1982 Apple filed a lawsuit against Franklin Computer Corporation that impacted intellectual property laws. Apple alleged Franklin was illegally formatting copies of Apple II's operating system and ROM so they would run on Franklin computers. Franklin's lawyers argued that portions of computer programs were not subject to copyright law. At first the courts sided with Franklin, but the verdict was later overturned. The courts eventually determined that codes and programs are protected under copyright law. This law provided technology companies with more extensive intellectual property protections.

Another notable case was Apple's lawsuit against Microsoft after Apple licensed technology to Microsoft. When Microsoft released Windows 2.0, Apple claimed the licensing agreement was only for Windows 1.0 and that Microsoft's Windows had the "look and feel" of Apple's Macintosh graphic interface system (GUI). The courts ruled in favor of Microsoft, deciding the license did not cover the "look and feel" of Apple's Macintosh GUI. Although there were similarities between the two, the courts ruled that Windows did not violate copyright law or the licensing agreement simply by resembling Macintosh systems.

Two other lawsuits involved more serious ethical issues on Apple's part. One involved Apple's use of the domain name iTunes.co.uk. The domain name had already been registered by Ben Cohen in 2000, who used the name to redirect users to other sites. Cohen eventually used the domain name to redirect users to the Napster site, a direct competitor of Apple. Apple attempted to purchase the domain name from Cohen, but when negotiations failed the company appealed to UK registry Nominet. Usually, whoever registers the domain name first gets the rights to that name. However, the mediator in the case determined that Cohen abused his registration rights and took unfair advantage of Apple. Apple won the right to use the domain name, which led to complaints that Apple was being favored at the expense of smaller companies.

Apple faced another trademark lawsuit from Cisco Systems in 2007. Cisco claimed Apple infringed on its iPhone trademark, a name Cisco had owned since 2000. Apple and Cisco negotiated to determine whether to allow Apple to use the trademark. However, Apple walked away from the discussions. According to Cisco, the company then opened up a front organization, Ocean Telecom Services, and filed for the iPhone trademark in the United States. Some stakeholders saw Apple's actions as a deceptive way to get around negotiation procedures. The lawsuit ended with both parties agreeing to use the iPhone name. However, Apple's actions in this situation remain controversial. In a twist of events, iOS, the name given to Apple's mobile software, was also a trademark owned by Cisco. This time, Apple avoided controversy by acquiring the iOS trademark from Cisco before publicly using the name.

As was mentioned in the introduction, a more recent case came in the form of a lawsuit between Samsung and Apple. Apple claimed Samsung infringed on multiple intellectual property rights, including patents, trademarks, user interface, style, false designation of origin, unfair competition, and trademark infringement. Specifically, Apple claimed Samsung used key features of its iPhone and iPad, including glass screens and rounded corners, along with many performance features and physical similarities. A jury found Samsung guilty of willfully infringing on Apple's design and utility patents. Apple was initially awarded $1.049 billion in damages, and Samsung's allegations of infringement against Apple were dismissed within the United States. After years of litigation Apple was ultimately awarded $119.6 million, only a fraction of the initial damages the company sought against Samsung.

Apple produces expensive and technologically competitive products, so it makes sense that the company takes great strides to protect its intellectual property from theft. Apple's aggressiveness regarding patent protection led it to file lawsuits against some powerful companies, including Microsoft and Samsung. It also filed a lawsuit against HTC Corporation, a Taiwanese smartphone manufacturer that makes phones for Google's Android products. Apple accused HTC of replicating a range of cellphone features protected under Apple's patents. Although the lawsuit is directed toward HTC, it also indirectly targeted Google since it is a major client of HTC. Eventually, HTC and Apple agreed to drop the lawsuits against one another and accepted a 10-year licensing agreement.

One overarching ethical issue is the question of the legitimacy of Apple's claims. Is Apple pursuing companies it honestly believes infringed on its patents, or is it simply trying to cast its competitors in a bad light to gain market share? Although it might seem Apple is too aggressive, companies that do not adequately protect their intellectual property can easily have it copied by the competition, which uses it to gain a competitive foothold. It is up to the courts to determine the validity of Apple's allegations.

Threats to Other Companies

A recently released document suggests that in 2007 former CEO Steve Jobs allegedly threatened former CEO of Palm, Edward Colligan, with patent litigation if Palm did not cease and desist poaching valuable Apple employees. Jobs suggested each company should respectively comply with the idea of not taking valuable employees away from competitors. This "unspoken agreement" seems to have also applied among companies such as Adobe, Google, Intel, Intuit, and Pixar. The document came to light because of lawsuits filed by former Apple employees. Jobs's firm stance on the matter was made clear to Colligan, who countered with a response that this type of collusion was highly unethical and Apple's employees had the right to work at other companies. In 2010 the U.S. Department of Justice filed an antitrust lawsuit against the aforementioned companies and required them to dissolve the agreement. Current CEO Tim Cook made it clear Steve Jobs was the only one with knowledge to this agreement and no other Apple employees were involved.

Supply Chain Management Issues

As mentioned earlier, Apple makes each supplier sign a supplier code of conduct and performs factory audits to ensure compliance. In addition, Apple says it has empowered over 6 million workers by teaching them about their rights, increased the number of suppliers it audits each year, and allows outside organizations to evaluate its labor practices. These audits appear to be an important component of controlling the supply chain. Apple discovered a correlation between improved compliance and the number of audits—facilities audited twice, instead of once, showed a 25 percent gain in compliance rating, while three audits resulted in an even greater 31 percent compliance score improvement. In the last few years serious supply chain issues have threatened to undermine Apple's status as a highly admired and ethical company. This threat is likely the catalyst to Apple's continuous supply chain improvements.

To meet the repeated demands of Apple consumers, products from the company must be readily available. Most of Apple's products are manufactured throughout Asia, with a majority produced within Foxconn and Pegatron factories in China. In the past, multiple accusations pertaining to improper working conditions, underage labor disputes, and worker abuse (that resulted in suicides) have come into question. Apple has been labeled as an unfair sweatshop, and critics launched multiple campaigns against the company. This resulted in negative publicity from protestors, who asked current Apple consumers not to support Apple's unlawful practices by purchasing its products.

Additionally, despite attempts to audit its factories and enforce strong supplier compliance standards, a large percentage of the suppliers audited by Apple violated at least one part of its supplier code of conduct every year since 2007. Suppliers claim Apple's manufacturing standards are hard to achieve because of the slim profit margins afforded to suppliers. In contrast, competitors like Hewlett-Packard allow suppliers to keep more profits if they improve worker conditions. According to suppliers, Apple's focus on the bottom line forces them to find other ways to cut costs, usually by requiring employees to work longer hours and using less expensive but more dangerous chemicals.

In this environment, mistakes and safety issues become more common. Thankfully, Apple appears to be making progress. According to the company's own audits, 92 percent of Apple's suppliers were in compliance of working-hour limits (60 hours per week). Additionally, audits discovered six facilities employing a total of 16 underage workers. Although Apple acknowledges that the problem of underage workers needs to be totally eliminated from the supply chain, each year the audits uncover fewer facilities out of compliance. In the past, problems with Apple's supply chain also included falsified records, overcrowded worker dormitories, and other labor violations. Apple claims suppliers who violate company policies are re-audited every 30, 60, and 90 days, or until the problem has been rectified. If a core violation is discovered, such as employing underage labor, employee retaliation, and falsified documents, the supplier is put on immediate probation while senior officials from both companies address the problem. Apple has dropped 18 suppliers for violations since 2007.

Several high-profile events at Apple factories generated criticism of its supply chain. In January 2010 over 135 workers fell ill after using a poisonous chemical to clean iPhone screens. In 2011 aluminum dust and improper ventilation caused two explosions that killed four people and injured 77. Additionally, over a dozen workers committed suicide at Apple supplier factories. Much of the media attention focused on the conditions at Foxconn, one of Apple's largest suppliers with a background of labor violations. Foxconn continues to assert it is in compliance with all regulations.

Some blame factory conditions on Apple's culture of innovation and the need to release new and improved products each year, requiring suppliers to work quickly at the expense of safety standards. However, the Foxconn and Pegatron factories are some of only a handful of facilities in the world with the capacity to build iPads and iPhones, making it difficult for Apple to change suppliers. Additionally, inconsistent international labor standards and fierce competition mean that virtually every major electronics producer faces similar manufacturing issues. As media and consumer scrutiny increase, Apple must continue to address its supply chain management issues. However, as one current Apple executive told *The New York Times*, customer expectations could also be a problem since customers seem to care more about the newest product than the labor conditions of those who made it.

Apple claims it is significantly improving supplier conditions and becoming more transparent about its labor processes. CEO Tim Cook visited Foxconn to personally see the labor conditions firsthand. Apple worked with Foxconn to improve worker safety, including testing more equipment and setting limits on workers' hours. The Fair Labor Association (FLA) states that Apple has dramatically improved the accountability of Foxconn and completed 280 of the FLA's recommendations. However, continual monitoring of its suppliers and enforcement of ethical standards are necessary to assure stakeholders that Apple takes the well-being of workers in its supply chain seriously.

THE FUTURE OF APPLE INC.

Apple appears optimistic about its future. The company has created a cult following of consumers who are intensely loyal to Apple products. Apple's products are meant to offer superior solutions to those of competitors. In one of Apple's newest offerings, the company is taking its forays in the music industry further. For instance, Apple acquired Beats Electronics for $3 billion. Beats Electronics is the company behind the popular Beats by Dre headphones and other co-branded electronics featuring Beats speaker systems, such as laptops. This purchase comes after Apple launched iCloud, a service enabling consumers to create and listen to their music collections without having to upload individual songs. While Google and Amazon offer similar music storage services, Apple has more songs at its disposal with iTunes and its record label agreements.

Also in 2015 Apple began selling the Apple Watch, a wearable computing device that functions as an extension of the iPhone. Wearable devices, often called "smartwatches," seem to be the new direction in innovation. Many of Apple's competitors, like Samsung and companies targeting fitness enthusiasts, have extensive lines of wearable devices that sync with various operating systems and mobile platforms. In an effort to combat investor speculation that it is no longer innovating, Apple introduced the iPhone 6 and iPhone 6 Plus after many consumers demanded an iPhone with a larger screen. Apple is designing products to continue expanding its customer base and remain relevant in the industry. The company is aiming to refine current products while continuing to develop new ones. Seizing on these opportunities can increase Apple's share of the smartphone, smartwatch, and tablet consumer electronics markets.

Apple has its share of threats. It constantly faces lawsuits from various competitors over alleged intellectual property violations. Additionally, although Apple's aggressive stance helped protect its intellectual property, its tight hold over its products and secrets could be disadvantageous as well. Google, for instance, has a more open-source approach. It has shown great support for the open-source movement, which advocates opening software and software codes in order to secure more input from outside sources. Although this openness increases the risks of intellectual property theft, it allows for innovation to occur more rapidly because of additional collaboration. This software strategy has helped Google compete with Apple; Android phones hold a nearly equal market share with Apple's iPhones. Apple may eventually need to re-examine whether its closed system is the best way to compete.

The most recognizable threat seen around the world was the death of Steve Jobs. In October 2011 Apple Inc. lost one of the most important aspects to its company. With the passing of the Apple founder and CEO, eyes are now turned to CEO Tim Cook. Tim Cook was Apple's corporate operations officer for many years before becoming CEO. Cook takes a more traditional approach in his management style by prioritizing project and supply chain management over creative engineering, attending investor meetings, being accessible to the media, and paying out dividends to stockholders, among other activities. He still maintains the secretive nature of the company but appears to be more approachable than Jobs.

Yet while Cook seems to possess the skills necessary for the CEO position, some fear he lacks the creative skills that made Jobs such a visionary. Jobs was considered to be a "creative builder," able to recognize consumer needs and develop revolutionary products to meet these needs in dynamic ways. A major concern is that Cook does not possess these skills. This prompted many to question whether Cook's leadership might change Apple's culture negatively. On the other hand, others feel Cook could make Apple more competitive with his strong strategic management skills. The change in tone of the company is the big difference between the leadership styles of Cook and Jobs and will likely have a profound impact on the firm.

In the last decade, Apple has excelled at keeping pace with the quickly evolving computer and consumer electronics industries. Although skeptics have raised questions on whether Apple is still the driving force behind innovation, many believe new products are on the horizon. Its diversification, collaborative corporate culture, and product evangelism propelled it to heights that could not have been envisioned when Jobs and Wozniak sold their first computer kit in 1976. Although Apple has experienced many challenges along the way, the company has clearly showcased its ability to understand consumers and create products that have been implemented and used in customers' everyday lives.

QUESTIONS FOR DISCUSSION

1. Explain how Apple's philosophy and organizational culture have impacted how it handles ethical decisions.
2. Why is Apple's industry so competitive and how could this affect the ethical risks in Apple's operations?
3. How do you think Apple has handled the various ethical issues that it has faced in the past?

SOURCES

Jim Aley, "The Beginning," *Bloomberg Businessweek*, Special Issue on Steve Jobs, October 2011, 20–26; Paul Andrews, "Apple-Microsoft Lawsuit Fizzles to a Close—'Nothing Left' to Fight about," *The Seattle Times*, June 2, 1993, http://community.seattletimes.nwsource.com/archive/?date=19930602&slug=1704430 (accessed May 4, 2015); Julia Angwin, "Apple, Google Take Heat," *The Wall Street Journal*, May 11, 2011, http://online.wsj.com/article/SB10001424052748703730804576315121174761088.html (accessed May 4, 2015); "Apple awarded $119.6m against Samsung in latest patent infringement case," *Daily Mail*, May 2, 2014, http://www.dailymail.co.uk/news/article-2619274/Apple-awarded-119-6-million-against-Samsung-latest-patent-infringement-case.html (accessed May 4, 2015); Apple History, http://www.apple-history.com/ (accessed May 4, 2015); Apple Inc., *Apple Regulated Substances Specification—Version H*, https://www.apple.com/environment/reports/docs/apple_regulated_substances_specification_sept2014.pdf (accessed May 4, 2015); Apple Inc., "Apple to Acquire Beats Music & Beats Electronics," *Apple Press Info*, May 28, 2014, http://www.apple.com/pr/library/2014/05/28Apple-to-Acquire-Beats-Music-Beats-Electronics.html (accessed May 4, 2015); Apple Inc. "Environmental Responsibility," http://www.apple.com/environment/#recycling (accessed May 4, 2015); Apple Inc., *Supplier Responsibility 2015 Progress Report*, 2015, https://www.apple.com/supplier-responsibility/pdf/Apple_Progress_Report_2015.pdf (accessed May 4, 2015); Apple Insider, "Apple begins counting down to 25 billion App Store downloads," February 17, 2012, http://www.appleinsider.com/articles/12/02/17/apple_begins_counting_down_to_25_billion_app_store_downloads.html (accessed May 4, 2015); Apple Inc., *Business Conduct: The way we do business worldwide*, October 2014, http://files.shareholder.com/downloads/AAPL/1283312876x0x443008/5f38b1e6-2f9c-4518-b691-13a29ac90501/business_conduct_policy.pdf (accessed May 4, 2015); Apple Inc., *Policy on Reporting Questionable Accounting or Auditing Matters*, November 16, 2010, http://files.shareholder.com/downloads/AAPL/1281913948x0x443017/68a6df9d-b0ef-4870-ba8e-accc695b39e2/reporting_accounting_auditing_matters.pdf (accessed May 4, 2015); Apple Inc., "Apple Recycling Program," Apple, http://www.apple.com/recycling/ (accessed May 4, 2015); Apple, Inc., *Apple Supplier Responsibility 2011 Progress Report*, February 2011; Apple Inc., "Apple Introduces iTunes—World's Best and Easiest to Use Jukebox Software," Apple, January 9, 2001, http://www.apple.com/pr/library/2001/jan/09itunes.html (accessed May 4, 2015); Apple Inc., *Environmental Responsibility Report*, 2014, https://www.apple.com/environment/reports/docs/Apple_Environmental_Responsibility_Report_2014.pdf (accessed May 4, 2015); Apple Inc., *Facilities Report: 2010 Environmental Update*, http://images.apple.com/environment/reports/docs/Apple_Facilities_Report_2010.pdf (accessed May 4, 2015); Apple Inc., "Jobs at Apple," https://www.apple.com/jobs/us/students.html (accessed May 4, 2015); Apple Inc. "Supplier Responsibility," https://www.apple.com/supplier-responsibility/ (accessed May 4, 2015); "Apple's iCloud Service Is under Attack in Mainland China," *The Wall Street Journal*, October 21, 2014, http://www.wsj.com/articles/apples-icloud-service-under-attack-in-mainland-china-1413895202 (accessed May 4, 2015); Jeffrey Ball and Lisa Jackson, "Lisa Jackson on Apple's Green Initiatives," *The Wall Street Journal*, March 30, 2015, http://www.wsj.com/articles/lisa-jackson-on-apples-green-initiatives-1427770864 (accessed May 4, 2015); *Bloomberg News*, "Apple's Tim Cook Visits Foxconn iPhone Plant in China," *Bloomberg News*, March 28, 2012, http://www.bloomberg.com/news/2012-03-29/apple-says-cook-visited-new-foxconn-plant-in-zhengzhou-china.html (accessed May 4, 2015); John Brownlee, "What It's Like to Work at Apple," Cult of Mac, July 7, 2010, http://www.cultofmac.com/what-its-like-to-work-at-apple (accessed May 4, 2015). "Building the Digital Age," BBC News, http://newsvote.bbc.co.uk/mpapps/pagetools/print/news.bbc.co.uk/2/hi/technology/7091190.stm (accessed May 4, 2015); Peter Burrows, "The Wilderness," *Bloomberg Businessweek*, Special Issue on Steve Jobs, October 2011, 28–34; Cable News Network, "Apple chronology," *CNNMoney*, January 6, 1998, http://money.cnn.com/1998/01/06/technology/apple_chrono/ (accessed May 4, 2015); Cable News Network, "Apple unveils two new iPhones, Apple Watch and Apple Pay," *CNN Money*, September 9, 2014, http://money.cnn.com/2014/09/09/technology/mobile/apple-iphone-iwatch-event/ (accessed May 4, 2015); Amanda Cantrell, "Apple's remarkable comeback Story," *CNNMoney*, March 29, 2006, http://money.cnn.com/2006/03/29/technology/apple_anniversary/?cnn=ye (accessed May 4, 2015); Amit Chowdhry, "Apple and Samsung Drop Patent Disputes against Each Other Outside of U.S.," *Forbes*, August 6, 2014, http://www.forbes.com/sites/amitchowdhry/2014/08/06/apple-and-samsung-drop-patent-disputes-against-each-other-outside-of-the-u-s/ (accessed May 4, 2015); Louis Columbus, "The 50 Most Innovative Companies of 2014: Strong Innovators Are Three Times More Likely to Rely on Big Data Analytics," *Forbes*, November 3, 2014, http://www.forbes.com/sites/louiscolumbus/2014/11/03/the-50-most-innovative-companies-of-2014-strong-innovators-are-three-times-more-likely-to-rely-on-big-data-analytics/ (accessed May 4, 2015); Alan Deutschman, "The once and future Steve Jobs," *Salon*, October 11, 2000, http://www.salon.com/technology/books/2000/10/11/jobs_excerpt/ (accessed May 4, 2015); Daniel Eran Dilger, "Why Apple, Inc. decided to split its stock 7-1," *Apple Insider*, April 29, 2015, http://appleinsider.com/articles/14/04/29/why-apple-inc-decided-to-split-its-stock-7-1- (accessed May 4, 2015); Eva Dou, "Apple Shifts Supply Chain Away from Foxconn to Pegatron," *The Wall Street Journal*, May 29, 2013, http://www.wsj.com/articles/SB10001424127887323855804578511122734340726 (accessed May 4, 2015); Charles Duhigg, "In China, Human Costs Are Built Into an iPad," *The New York Times*, January 25, 2012, http://www.nytimes.com/2012/01/26/business/ieconomy-apples-ipad-and-the-human-costs-for-workers-in-china.html?pagewanted=all (accessed May 4, 2015); Kit Eaton, "Steve Jobs vs. Tim Cook: Words of Wisdom," *Fast Company*, August 26, 2011, http://www.fastcompany.com/1776013/steve-jobs-vs-tim-cook-words-wisdom (accessed May 4, 2015); Paul Elias, "Samsung Ordered to Pay Apple $1.05B in Patent Case," *Yahoo! Finance*, August 25, 2012, http://finance.yahoo.com/news/samsung-ordered-pay-apple-1-004505800.html (accessed May 4, 2015); "The evangelist's evangelist," Academia.edu, http://www.academia.edu/4182207/The_Evangelist_s_Evangelist_Developing_a_Customer_Evangelism_Scale_using_Faith-Based_Volunteer_Tourism_Data (accessed May 4, 2015); Dan Farber, "When iPhone met world, 7 years ago today," *CNet*, January 9, 2014, http://www.cnet.com/news/when-iphone-met-world-7-years-ago-today/ (accessed May 4, 2015); Fortune, "Most Admired 2015: Apple," *Fortune*, http://fortune.com/worlds-most-admired-companies/apple-1/ (accessed May 4, 2015); Bryan Gardiner, "Learning from Failure: Apple's Most Notorious Flops," *Wired*, January 24, 2008, http://www.wired.com/gadgets/mac/multimedia/2008/01/gallery_apple_flops?slide=1&slideView=8 (accessed May 4, 2015); Phil Goldstein, "FCC is probing Verizon's 'super cookie' used to track mobile browsing," *FierceWireless*, April 10, 2015, http://www.fiercewireless.com/story/fcc-probing-verizons-super-cookie-used-track-mobile-browsing/2015-04-10 (accessed May 4, 2015); Matt Hamblen, "Tablet sales growth slows dramatically," *ComputerWorld*, October 15, 2014, http://www.computerworld.com/article/2834238/tablet-sales-growth-slows-dramatically.html (accessed May 4, 2015); Rob Hassett, IMPACT OF APPLE VS. FRANKLIN DECISION, 1983, http://www.internetlegal.com/impactof.htm (accessed May 4, 2015); Alex Heath, "How Steve Jobs Steamrolled Cisco on the Name 'iPhone,'" *Cult of Mac*, January 27, 2012, http://www.cultofmac.com/143006/how-steve-jobs-steamrolled-cisco-on-the-name-iphone/ (accessed May 4, 2015); Miguel Helft, "Will Apple's Culture Hurt the iPhone?," *The New York Times*, October 17, 2010, http://www.nytimes.com/2010/10/18/technology/18apple.html (accessed May 4, 2015); Inside the Minds of Most Hard-Charging CEOs," *Inc.* September 2012, 142–146; Yukari Iwatani Kane and Ethan Smith, "Apple Readies iCloud Service," *The Wall Street Journal*, June 1, 2011, B1; Yukari Iwatani Kane and Ian Sherr, "Apple: Samsung Copied Design," *The Wall Street Journal*, April 19, 2011, http://online.wsj.com/article/SB10001424052748703916004576271210109389154.html (accessed May 4, 2015); Apple Inc., "Jobs at Apple Inc.," Apple, https://www.apple.com/jobs/us/ (accessed May 4, 2015); Ashby Jones, "So What's up with this Apple/Google Lawsuit?" *The Wall Street Journal*, March 30, 2010, http://blogs.wsj.com/law/2010/03/03/so-whats-up-with-this-applegoogle-lawsuit/ (accessed May 4, 2015); Dawn Kawamoto, Ben Heskett, and Mike Ricciuti, "Microsoft to invest $150 million in Apple," *CNET*, August 6, 1997, http://news.cnet.com/MS-to-invest-150-million-in-Apple/2100-1001_3-202143.html (accessed May 4, 2015); J. Taylor Kirklin, "Second Circuit Hears Oral Argument in Apple E-Book Appeal," *Antitrust Update*, December 19, 2014, http://www.antitrustupdateblog.com/blog/second-circuit-hears-oral-argument-apple-e-book-appeal/?utm_source=Mondaq&utm_medium=syndication&utm_campaign=View-Original (accessed May 4, 2015); Adam Lashinsky, "How Tim Cook Is Changing Apple," *Fortune*, June 11, 2012; Adam Lashinsky, "The Secrets Apple Keeps," *Fortune*, February 6, 2012, 85–94; Robert Paul Leitao, "Apple's 25% Solution," *Seeking Alpha*, November 7, 2011, http://seekingalpha.com/article/305849-apple-s-25-solution (accessed May 4, 2015); Kif Leswing, "Android and iOS are nearly tied for

U.S. smartphone market share,' *Gigaom*, February 4, 2015, https://gigaom.com/2015/02/04/android-and-ios-are-nearly-tied-for-u-s-smartphone-market-share/ (accessed May 4, 2015); Ingrid Lunden, "Apple's iPhone Overtakes Android in US Sales for the First Time Since 2012," *Tech Crunch*, February 4, 2015, http://techcrunch.com/2015/02/04/apples-iphone-overtakes-android-in-us-sales-for-the-first-time-since-2012/ (accessed May 4, 2015); Kieren McCarthy "Apple threatens iTunes.co.uk owner," *The Register*, December 6, 2004, http://www.theregister.co.uk/2004/12/06/apple_itunescouk_domain_dispute/ (accessed May 4, 2015); Robert McMillan, "Apple Does About-Face on Green EPEAT Ratings," *Wired*, July 13, 2012, http://www.wired.com/wiredenterprise/2012/07/apple-epeat/ (accessed May 4, 2015); Scott Martin, "Apple invites review of labor practices in overseas factories," *USA Today*, January 16, 2012, 3B; Scott Martin, "Apple's Mac sales reported down again," *USA Today*, October 9, 2013, http://www.usatoday.com/story/tech/2013/10/09/apples-mac-sales-reported-down-again/2955735/ (accessed May 4, 2015); Scott Martin, "How Apple rewrote the rules of retailing," *USA Today*, May 19, 2011, 1B; Nilofer Merchant, "Apple's Startup Culture," *Bloomberg Businessweek*, June 24, 2010, http://www.businessweek.com/innovate/content/jun2010/id20100610_525759.htm (accessed May 4, 2015); Claire Milne, *Nominet UK Dispute Resolution Service Decision of Independent Expert*, March 10, 2005, http://www.nominet.org.uk/digitalAssets/766_itunes.pdf (accessed June 8, 2011); Amy Moore, "Complete guide to Apple's campus 2, everything we know about the new spaceship HQ, plus: 4k drone flyover video," *Mac World*, April 2, 2015, http://www.macworld.co.uk/feature/apple/apple-spaceship-campus-facts-pictures-video-info-3489704/ (accessed May 4, 2015); Chris Morrison, "Insanely Great Marketing," *CBS MoneyWatch*, August 10, 2009, http://www.cbsnews.com/8301-505125_162-51330244/insanely-great-marketing (accessed May 4, 2015); Steven Musil, "Apple reportedly tinkering with larger screens for iPhone, iPad," *CNet*, http://www.cnet.com/news/apple-reportedly-tinkering-with-larger-screens-for-iphone-ipad/ (accessed May 4, 2015); Joe Palazzolo, "Apple E-book ruling heaps new doubt on 'MFN' Clauses," *Wall Street Journal*, July 15, 2013, B1; Rocco Pendola, "Amazon vs. Apple: Jeff Bezos Just Squashed Tim Cook," *CNBC*, September 7, 2012, http://www.cnbc.com/id/48945231 (accessed May 4, 2015); Marguerite Reardon and Tom Krazit, "Cisco sues Apple over use of iPhone trademark," *CNET News*, January 10, 2007, http://news.cnet.com/Cisco-sues-Apple-over-use-of-iPhone-trademark/2100-1047_3-6149285.html (accessed May 4, 2015); Amanda Remling, "iCloud Nude Leaks: 26 Celebrities Affected in the Nude Photo Scandal," *International Business Times*, September 21, 2014, http://www.ibtimes.com/icloud-nude-leaks-26-celebrities-affected-nude-photo-scandal-1692540 (accessed May 4, 2015); Reuters, "Apple, Cisco agree both can use iPhone name," February 22, 2007, http://www.reuters.com/article/2007/02/22/us-apple-cisco-idUSWEN460920070222 (accessed May 4, 2015); John Ribeiro, "Apple, Samsung agree to settle patent disputes outside US," *PC World*, August 5, 2014, http://www.pcworld.com/article/2461940/apple-samsung-agree-to-settle-patent-disputes-outside-us.html (accessed May 4, 2015); Joel Rosenblatt, "Jobs Threatened Suit If Palm Didn't Agree to Hiring Terms," *Bloomberg*, January 22, 2013, http://www.bloomberg.com/news/2013-01-23/jobs-threatened-suit-if-palm-didn-t-agree-to-hiring-terms.html (accessed May 4, 2015); Greg Sandoval, "This is why DOJ accused Apple of fixing e-book prices," *CNET*, April 11, 2013, http://news.cnet.com/8301-13579_3-57412369-37/this-is-why-doj-accused-apple-of-fixing-e-book-prices/ (accessed May 4, 2015); Ashkan Soltani and Hayley Tsukayama, "Apple's new feature to curb phone tracking won't work if you're actually using your phone," *The Washington Post*, September 25, 2014, http://www.washingtonpost.com/blogs/the-switch/wp/2014/09/25/apples-new-feature-to-curb-phone-tracking-wont-work-if-youre-actually-using-your-phone/ (accessed May 4, 2015); Joanna Stern, "Apple and Foxconn Make Progress on Working Conditions at Factories," *ABC News*, August 21, 2012, http://abcnews.go.com/blogs/technology/2012/08/apple-and-foxconn-make-progress-on-working-conditions-at-factories/ (accessed May 4, 2015); Daisuke Wakabayashi, "Apple Seeks Japan iWatch Trademark," Wall Street Journal, July 2, 2013, B5; Daisuke Wakabayahsi and Robin Sidel, "Fraud Starts to Take a Bit out of Apple Pay," *The Wall Street Journal*, March 3, 2015, http://www.wsj.com/articles/fraud-starts-to-take-a-bite-out-of-apple-pay-1425430639 (accessed May 4, 2015); Martyn Williams, "Timeline: iTunes Store at 10 Billion," *ComputerWorld*, February 24, 2010, http://www.computerworld.com/s/article/9162018/Timeline_iTunes_Store_at_10_billion (accessed May 4, 2015); Nick Wingfield, "As Apple's Battle with HTC Ends, Smartphone Patent Fights Continue," *The New York Times*, November 11, 2012, http://www.nytimes.com/2012/11/12/technology/

as-apple-and-htc-end-lawsuits-smartphone-patent-battles-continue.html?_r=0 (accessed May 4, 2015); Yahoo Finance, "Apple Inc (AAPL)," http://finance.yahoo.com/q?s=AAPL (accessed May 4, 2015); Alberto Zanco, "Apple Inc: A success built on distribution & design," http://www.slideshare.net/Nanor/distribution-policy-apple-presentation (accessed May 4, 2015); ZDNet Staff, "Former Apple evangelist on company's history," *ZDNet*, March 29, 2006, http://www.zdnet.com/article/former-apple-evangelist-on-companys-history/ (accessed May 4, 2015).

CASE 15

PepsiCo's Journey Toward an Ethical and Socially Responsible Culture*

COMPANY OVERVIEW

PepsiCo is one of the largest food and beverage companies in the world. It manufactures and sells 22 brands of beverages and snack foods that generate over $1 billion in retail sales. PepsiCo encompasses the Pepsi Cola, Frito-Lay, Tropicana, Quaker, and Gatorade brands and products in over 200 countries. The company's headquarters are in New York and employs nearly 300,000 people. In 2006 Indra K. Nooyi became the CEO of PepsiCo. PepsiCo has received many awards and recognitions over the years, including being ranked in the top 25 of the best global brands and earning the Green Award by the Environmental Protection Agency.

COMPANY AND MARKETING HISTORY

The Pepsi recipe was developed by pharmacist Caleb Bradham in the 1890s. Originally marketed under the unassuming name "Brad's Drink," Bradham's creation was renamed Pepsi-Cola in 1898 because of the pepsin and kola nut ingredients used. Awareness of Bradham's new creation spread quickly, and in 1902 he decided to create the Pepsi-Cola Company so people everywhere could enjoy the drink. In 1903 the patent became official, and by 1910 Pepsi-Cola had franchises in 24 states and sold over 100,000 gallons of the syrup annually. However, the Pepsi brand encountered several rocky situations before becoming the success it is today. World War I proved to be an especially turbulent time for Pepsi-Cola. Severe fluctuations in sugar prices caused the company to lose money, and in 1923 Bradham sold the trademark to Craven's Holding Corp., who shortly after sold it to a New York stockbroker named Roy C. Megargel. Megargel fought to revitalize the company but failed. In 1931 the Pepsi-Cola Company underwent its second bankruptcy. Candy manufacturer Charles Guth, president of Loft, Inc., saw Pepsi-Cola as a great investment and decided to purchase the company. Within two years the company was earning over a million dollars and was on its way to making history.

*This material was developed by Danielle Jolley and Jennifer Sawayda under the direction of O.C. Ferrell and Linda Ferrell. It is based on a previous case developed by Kendra Berch and Kimberly Montoya. This case is intended for classroom discussion rather than to illustrate effective or ineffective handling of administrative, ethical, or legal decisions by management. All sources used for this case were obtained through publicly available material © 2015.

Building a Brand

Guth had many challenges to overcome in order to save the struggling brand. Through the Great Depression, Pepsi carefully positioned itself as a low-cost leader and made advertising history when it released the nation's first jingle "nickel, nickel." With financially strapped customers reluctant to pay a nickel for a drink, Guth began offering twice the amount of Pepsi for the same price, a tactic that met with resounding success. World War II continued to test Pepsi-Cola's strength with introduced sugar rationing, but Pepsi's marketing campaigns and brand design helped Pepsi make it through the difficult period. For instance, Pepsi changed the colors on the label to be red, white, and blue to show patriotism. Pepsi's success allowed it to begin marketing internationally in 1945.

As more people began earning more disposable income, Pepsi-Cola recognized the marketplace was changing. To maintain a strong brand, its marketing campaigns had to change too. Pepsi therefore said goodbye to the long-running "nickel, nickel" slogan and introduced a more lively "More Bounce to the Ounce" slogan to the after-war population. During the 1950s Pepsi evolved from the low-cost price leader to a more lifestyle drink approach. For example, as Americans became more health conscious, Pepsi introduced slogans such as "The Light Refreshment" and "Refreshing without Filling."

It was this younger target market and the post-war baby boom generation that set the stage for Pepsi's long-lasting brand image. It all started with Pepsi advertiser Alan Pottasch, who recognized the different nature of the newest generation of consumers. Whereas consumers before the war were more cautious and price-conscious, the post-war baby boomer generation was carefree and hopeful. Pepsi once again capitalized on the changing environment, and under Pottasch launched the "Pepsi Generation" campaign in 1963. The campaign was an advertising breakthrough as it helped set a new standard for advertising in America. The ads portrayed happy Americans living the American dream—with their Pepsis, of course. By associating its brand with youth and excitement, Pepsi-Cola became the forerunner of lifestyle marketing. Future campaigns continued to promote this brand image, with slogans such as "You've Got a Lot to Live. Pepsi's Got a Lot to Give" and "Come Alive. You're in the Pepsi Generation!"

Pepsi successfully adapted its practices and product positioning to the times through its marketing campaigns. The company also pursued a major acquisition strategy as well as an expansion of its product line. In 1964 Pepsi introduced Diet Pepsi in response to the nation's noticeable lifestyle change toward health, along with the Mountain Dew brand. PepsiCo broke into the bottled water industry with its rollout of Aquafina bottled water in 1997. However, the biggest milestone was Pepsi's monumental merger with Frito-Lay, Inc., to become PepsiCo, Inc., the company it is known as today. Pepsi also profited through corporate partnerships, such as a partnership with Starbucks in 1994 to develop coffee drinks.

Celebrity Endorsements

In more recent years, Pepsi used celebrity branding to build upon the Pepsi brand. The 1980s brought in celebrity endorsers like Tina Turner, Michael J. Fox, Gloria Estefan, and David Bowie. By far its biggest celebrity endorser in this time period was Michael Jackson. The singer and PepsiCo struck a $5 million partnership that linked the two together for the rest of the 1980s. With Jackson as its prime celebrity endorser, PepsiCo was able to set itself up as the hip, trendy drink for the new generation. Pepsi's celebrity partnerships enabled the company to gain market share even as Coca-Cola's market share was dropping. In 2012

PepsiCo celebrated its 25th anniversary of its Michael Jackson partnership by using Jackson's image on special-edition Pepsi cans and featuring his music in advertisements after reaching an agreement with Jackson's estate.

Another notable achievement in marketing history was the inroads Pepsi made into the Soviet market. Perhaps the biggest (indirect) Soviet endorser of the product was the Soviet Premier Nikita Kruschev, who was caught on camera drinking a Pepsi at the 1959 American National Exhibition in Moscow. A favorable relationship developed between the Soviet Union and the company, leading to a trade agreement in 1972 where Pepsi became the first foreign consumer product sold in the Soviet Union. In 1988 Pepsi became the first advertiser to buy time on Soviet television. A Pepsi advertisement aired later that year incorporated Soviet teenage actors to appeal to the younger generation. The Pepsi Generation remained popular in Russia after the Soviet Union's dissolution.

Recent Years

PepsiCo has continued to use celebrity marketing throughout the 1990s and early 2000s, including Ray Charles, Cindy Crawford, and Britney Spears. To appeal to sports fans, PepsiCo tapped into the celebrity status of Shaquille O'Neal and racecar driver Jeff Gordon. In 2006 PepsiCo got a new CEO, Indra Nooyi, who began reorganizing PepsiCo to focus on several initiatives. Under her leadership, PepsiCo's goals included focusing more on countries outside the United States, developing healthier snacks, having a net-zero impact on the environment, and creating a better working environment. PepsiCo began investing heavily in the countries where it does business. For example, PepsiCo created a strategic alliance with Chinese food and beverage company Tingyi Holding Corp. as a way of expanding into the Chinese market. In 2015 PepsiCo became an official marketing partner of the National Basketball Association (NBA), and Tingyi's leading beverage brand Master Kong became the lead brand of the partnership. As basketball is China's favorite sport, partnering with the NBA is a good way for PepsiCo to increase its credibility in China. The worldwide success of PepsiCo reflects the company's dynamic and adaptable strategy throughout the company's history, leading to its current revenues of over $66.6 billion.

PEPSICO DIVISIONS AND BRANDS

PepsiCo consists of six divisions: Frito-Lay North America; Quaker Foods North America; Latin America Foods; PepsiCo Americas Beverages; PepsiCo Europe; and PepsiCo Middle East, Asia, and Africa. These divisions are further split up into different businesses, including Tropicana and Gatorade. The following are some of PepsiCo's most well-known and profitable businesses.

Pepsi-Cola Brands

Over the years, Pepsi-Cola has gone above and beyond the original Pepsi beverage to incorporate a wide variety of brands. In the United States, some of the most well-known brands include Mountain Dew, Sierra Mist, SoBe, IZZE, and Aquafina. International brands include Mirinda, Walkers, and Kurkure.

However, in the last decade, the growth of soft drinks has lowered due to a new wave of health consciousness sweeping the nation. This is troublesome news for PepsiCo's most popular brand, the Pepsi soft drink. Sales have been declining, and some activist investors are calling on PepsiCo to split off its North America beverages business. It requires Pep-siCo to innovate in order to create or acquire healthier brands that appeal to the more health-conscious consumer. Some of these drinks include SoBe, Naked Juice, Quaker, and Tropicana. However, PepsiCo began a restructuring of its Beverages division to create better integration between its units. PepsiCo's Americas Beverages merged its two largest bottling companies, the Pepsi Bottling Group and Pepsi Americas, to give it control over 80 percent of its bottling network. PepsiCo's Americas Beverages includes the brands Pepsi-Cola, Gatorade, Mountain Dew, Naked Juice, and Tropicana. It also has partnerships with Starbucks and Lipton Tea to market and sell ready-to-drink coffee and ice tea drinks.

Frito-Lay

Even before the historic merger between Frito-Lay and Pepsi-Cola, Frito-Lay had a successful business history. It started in 1932 with entrepreneurs C.E. Doolin and Herman W. Lay. During that year, C.E. Doolin sampled corn chips in a Texas café and saw an opportunity for the small chip's future. He purchased the corn chip manufacturing company. Doolin then began selling bags of FRITO corn chips from his Model T Ford.

Also in 1932 a man named Herman W. Lay started selling potato chips. He purchased a manufacturing company and called it the H.W. Lay & Company. In 1961 the two companies joined together to form the Frito-Lay Company. Four years later, it merged with Pepsi-Cola to become the PepsiCo Company. Today, Frito-Lay owns over 50 percent of the snack food industry in America and includes such well-known brands as Lay's Potato Chips, Frito's Corn Chips, Doritos, Cheetos, Grandma's Cookies, SunChips, and Cracker Jack popcorn. It also partnered with the Strauss Group to manufacture and market Sabra refrigerated dips. The division contributes $14.5 billion to PepsiCo.

Frito-Lay has many accomplishments to be proud of that go beyond its products. One of its great prides is its Supplier Diversity Program, first launched in 1983. According to the company, PepsiCo spends about $1.3 billion annually in association with minority- and women-owned businesses. Additionally, Frito-Lay made strides in sustainability. Among its many initiatives, Frito-Lay converted its sales cars to hybrid vehicles and constructed a solar field and renewable energy generator at its plant in Arizona.

As with all big companies, Frito-Lay experienced its share of controversies. In 1967 Frito-Lay introduced a cartoon character named Frito Bandito, a Mexican bandit with a sombrero who stole other people's corn chips by gunpoint. The Mexican-American population launched a series of protests. They felt the cartoon character was a negative and highly offensive stereotype of Mexicans and Mexican-Americans. Due to the wide popularity of the character, Frito-Lay refused to pull Frito-Bandito, prompting the National Mexican-American Anti-Defamation Committee and other groups to file a $670 million lawsuit against the company. Finally, the cartoon character was removed from the scene in the early 1970s. The controversy emphasized the importance of cultural sensitivity and stakeholder analysis when launching any campaign that might alienate company stakeholders.

Gatorade

Gatorade, the official sports drink of the NBA and major league baseball, dates back to 1965. The formula was developed by a group of scientists after a study revealed players at the University of Florida were losing electrolytes and carbohydrates during games. Gatorade (named after the Florida Gators team) was meant as a solution to that problem by containing a balanced amount of electrolytes and carbohydrates to rejuvenate players.

Gatorade was a huge success among sports teams, leading to future innovation with products like the Gatorade Nutrition Shake and the Gatorade Bar. In 1983 Quaker Oats Co. acquired Gatorade, which in turn was acquired by PepsiCo in 2001 when PepsiCo bought the Quaker Oats Co. Gatorade is one of the most popular selling drinks under PepsiCo (after Pepsi and Mountain Dew).

Despite Gatorade's success, the brand has seen declining sales and added competition for the sports drink market. One of the problems Gatorade faces is the lack of appeal for the younger generation, who see the beverage as something their parents drank. As a result, PepsiCo created the Gatorade campaign and lineup called the "G Series." The G Series has two major purposes in revitalizing the Gatorade brand: demonstrate that Gatorade can be used for more than hydration and nutrient replacement and target a younger demographic. Consequently, the line has different types of Gatorade products meant to be used in a three-step process. The first step is called "Energy" and includes Prime Energy Chews and the Prime Sports Fuel Drink. These products are filled with carbohydrates and are meant to be used before a game. The second step, "Hydration," includes Thirst Quencher, Low-Calorie G2, Thirst Quencher Powder, and Low-Calorie G2 Powder. These products are meant to be used during the game. The final, "Recovery," involves protein-rich products for after the game and include Protein Shake, Post-Game Recovery Beverage, and Whey Protein Bar. With this new system of Gatorade drinks, PepsiCo targets every aspect of the athlete's game time. Gatorade also introduced G Endurance for endurance athletes that need extra energy.

CRITICISMS

PepsiCo's success has not come without major challenges or ethical dilemmas. One of the biggest difficulties for any multinational organization is how to successfully enter into other countries, particularly when laws vary from country to country. Although PepsiCo places high emphasis upon researching potential markets, the company encountered several problems that caused tensions with different cultures, in both the United States and abroad. Additionally, PepsiCo still faces heavy criticism for products viewed as largely unhealthy and whose packaging contributes to a large amount of waste. PepsiCo faces the same challenge as other major players in the soda industry: the decline of soda consumption in the United States. This problem is exacerbated by regulatory actions such as Mexico's tax on sugary drinks.

India

PepsiCo first entered the Indian market in 1989, and since then the company has become one of the largest food and beverage companies in the country. Unfortunately for the company, some of the largest and longest running allegations of PepsiCo's wrongdoing are also based in India. The company and other competitors in the industry have been heavily criticized about the quality and the quantity of the water used in their beverages. In 2003 the Centre for Science and Environment (CSE) claimed that the water which PepsiCo and other beverage companies in India were using contained toxins. These toxins included pesticides that contribute to cancer and the overall breakdown of the immune system. According to the CSE, Pepsi soft drinks had 36 times the level of pesticide residues permitted under European Union regulations. However, no such law bans the presence of pesticides in India.

Although there is not yet a law in place, PepsiCo found it could still face considerable repercussions for what its stakeholders perceive to be unethical activities. When pesticides were once again reported in the soft drinks a few years later, the Indian state of Kerala temporarily banned the sale of Pepsi and Coca-Cola. Five other Indian states also instituted partial bans. These extreme actions on the part of the local governments highlight the care multinational organizations must take to go above and beyond the national law in social responsibility.

Another major concern in India cited by farmers is that the Pepsi manufacturing plants are polluting the land, making it less fertile for growing crops. A study conducted in 1992 found that PepsiCo India and similar companies created 10,000 metric tons of plastic through their manufacturing and importation processes. About 60–70 percent of this plastic was recyclable, creating a large amount of unnecessary plastic waste. Similar allegations of waste and pollution arose again in 2006, concerning both farmers and government officials alike. The farmers complained that the PepsiCo plant takes the groundwater to run its operations, making it, once again, harder to effectively grow crops.

PepsiCo is attempting to repair its reputation in India. In 2009 it announced that it had replenished more water in India than it removed. PepsiCo also partnered with a number of organizations committed to water conservation, including the Safe Water Network, Water.org, and the Nature Conservancy. Additionally, PepsiCo made water a priority; it improved its water efficiency by 20 percent per unit of production by 2015, using 2006 as a baseline. Through partnerships with other organizations PepsiCo also helped provide three million people with access to clean water. A thorough stakeholder orientation is needed to discover ethical courses of action and avoid negative repercussions. In solving these ethical dilemmas, PepsiCo must continue to take different levels of government into account, as well as concerns of NGOs and individual Indians.

Health

The nature of the products manufactured and sold by PepsiCo caused problems for the company regarding health. Although PepsiCo now has numerous products geared toward health, its most popular product is still its signature Pepsi-Cola. At the same time, America is becoming more health conscious and desires low-calorie, low-fat, and natural items instead of processed sugary and salty foods. Some of the health concerns of drinking soda include the increased caloric intake as well as the possibility of tooth decay due to soda's acidity, caffeine dependence, and weaker bones. Pepsi fought back by creating sodas that have low calorie and sugar content. It recently substituted aspartame in its Diet Pepsi products with sucralose. Although sucralose is also an artificial sweetener, there is less controversy surrounding it than with aspartame. Diet Pepsi products can now be labeled "aspartame-free." Pepsi hopes this will renew interest in its Diet Pepsi products, but it is a risky move because it might change the taste of Diet Pepsi and alienate loyal customers.

Unfortunately, this only helps with the weight risk. The acidic nature of the product can still damage the teeth, and the artificial sweeteners used have their own set of health risks. However, PepsiCo has one advantage. Because it diversified into so many different product lines, PepsiCo can rely on sales in other categories to offset reduced sales in the soft drink area.

PepsiCo has also faced battles from the regulatory area. Some states adopted laws banning the sale of soda in schools. Former New York City Mayor Martin Bloomberg attempted to institute a tax in New York on sugary drinks in cup sizes of more than 16 ounces. Companies including PepsiCo fought back, and the proposed ban was defeated.

However, San Francisco and Berkeley, California, are seriously considering enforcing a soda tax in their cities. The fight is also continuing on a national scale. A U.S. panel has called for a tax to be placed on sugary foods and beverages to combat obesity and diabetes. One-third of adults and 17 percent of children in the United States suffer from obesity. Their recommendations will be considered by the Agriculture and Health and Human Services departments. Immediately after the report was released, stock from several food and beverage companies—including PepsiCo, Coca-Cola, and Hershey—fell. Whether the United States will eventually choose to institute a tax on sugary food products remains to be seen, but industry leaders like PepsiCo are prepared to push back.

On the other hand, PepsiCo has had to deal with backlash against its products in Mexico. Approximately three-fourths of consumers are obese in Mexico, prompting the Mexican government to institute a tax of one peso (eight U.S. cents) for every liter of sugary beverages. A tax was also placed on junk foods. The taxes have reduced snack food sales for PepsiCo in Mexico by 3 percent. The company will have to find ways to adapt to both the tax and the changing tastes of Mexican consumers.

PepsiCo's traditional snack items have met with similar criticism from health care professionals. Most of the products are processed and contain a high amount of sodium and sugar as well as being highly caloric and fatty. Frito-Lay Company tried to combat the issue by offering Baked Lays, Baked Cheetos, SunChips, and other healthier alternatives. These alternatives are claimed to be healthier all around. The health issue is going to be an ongoing battle for the company due to the nature of the industry it is in. Continual research and product development to offer healthier products is important for PepsiCo's future profitability.

Although the battle may be a long one, PepsiCo is making strides to address these concerns. For example, the Frito-Lay website has a special area devoted to health that describes the ingredients of Frito-Lay snacks and encourages consumers to practice moderation in snack food consumption. One of the goals of PepsiCo CEO Indra Nooyi is to invest more in healthier food. PepsiCo is a supporter of the Healthy Weight Commitment Foundation (HWCF) consisting of over 225 food and beverage manufacturers, retailers, sporting goods firms, insurance companies, and restaurants to fight against the obesity epidemic through awareness and other activities. One study found that the 16 food and beverage companies that support HWCF were together responsible for reducing 6.4 trillion calories from the marketplace.

In response to continuous customer concern, in early 2013 PepsiCo announced it would remove the controversial additive, brominated vegetable oil (BVO), used in citrus-flavored Gatorade. This comes after an online petition started by a Mississippi teenager brought attention to the chemical. The chemical possesses the ingredient bromine, which is used in some flame retardants. PepsiCo took customer complaints seriously and began formulating an alternative ingredient to replace BVO. The company settled upon sucrose acetate isobutyrate to take the place of BVO, which is aligned with countries outside of the United States, specifically within the European Union and Japan that have banned BVO. Over time Gatorade has aligned its brand with healthy activities such as athletic individuals and sports events and has evolved many "game day" product extensions. The need to keep this product as healthy as possible is essential for PepsiCo, which is ultimately why the company took necessary precautions by changing ingredients.

Interestingly, while PepsiCo's CEO Indra Nooyi is ready and willing to expand into healthier food products and make major changes when required, she has faced criticism in recent years from a major stakeholder: investors. In 2012 return on capital decreased to about 11.1 percent, the lowest in five years. Even new advertisements did not keep PepsiCo sales from slipping. It is not unusual for a company to suffer financially in the short-term in the midst of major changes. Yet investors are worried PepsiCo would continue to plunge, and some believe the firm should reduce its size by separating the underperforming beverage business from the snack food business (PepsiCo has so far refused).

While such a conflict seems to be more financial in nature, it has a strong ethical component. Ethical leaders must attempt to balance stakeholder interests, including those of society—who have concerns over the growing issue of obesity and diabetes—and investors who care about profitability and the financial viability of the company. In this case, it is easy to put blame on investors, who have more of a short-term perspective on this issue. While Indra Nooyi describes PepsiCo's changes as "the right thing" to do, investors at first appear to be placing profits over the good of society. However, business ethics is rarely so straightforward. A business's first role is to be economically viable; without succeeding financially, a business will fail, and not only drain society of precious resources but also lead to job losses. Hence, investors have a right, and even an ethical duty, to be concerned about the financial performance of a company. This requires PepsiCo to carefully balance the conflicting demands of multiple stakeholders.

Labeling and Packaging Issues

The public's attention was on Aquafina bottled water in 2007 when the watchdog group Corporate Accountability International claimed the company used tap water to fill the water bottles being sold. The water was not regular tap water but came from a public water supply before processing. Aquafina was accused of not being transparent in its business practices. It was not publicly known that the company's procedures included a rigorous seven-step process that removes unwanted substances and is then branded as purified drinking water. Additionally, the label on the Aquafina bottle had snow-capped mountains on it, which seemed to suggest that the water was purified spring water. PepsiCo is now required to put the words "Public Water Source" on the label.

This scenario brings up an ethical situation common in today's marketplace. Many corporations use idyllic scenes on their packages that do not reflect reality. A giant agribusiness, for example, might have a picture of a traditional farm on its package. Some consumers find this to be misleading. Additionally, many consumers do not realize that labeling laws are not as strict in the United States as in other countries. For example, U.S. manufacturers do not have to label when a food product contains genetically modified ingredients. In these cases, it is often the informed consumer or watchdog group that calls for action, as PepsiCo inevitably discovered.

On top of the tap water dilemma, water bottle companies are dealing with criticisms for the amount of plastic these bottles contribute to landfills. There are movements around the country like the "Think outside the Bottle" campaign to challenge people to go back to drinking tap water again in order to stop the amount of waste produced by the bottles. However, the increasing popularity of bottled water does not appear to be diminishing anytime soon. PepsiCo is in the process of developing bottles that use less amounts of plastic per bottle to help the waste issue. Today, the Aquafina bottle weighs 10.9 grams, compared with the 18.5 grams in 2001.This keeps millions of tons of plastic out of landfills.

PepsiCo also paid $9 million to settle a lawsuit alleging that claims about its Naked juices were not truthful. More specifically, Pepsi maintained that its Naked juices were all natural. However, according to the lawsuit, Naked juices contain synthetic vitamins developed by Archer Daniels Midland. This would seem to contradict Pepsi's claim that its Naked juices were all natural. On the other hand, because the term "natural" is ambiguous and not clearly defined, it is questionable whether Pepsi did anything misleading or unethical. The lawsuit also alleged that Naked juices contain genetically modified ingredients, which Pepsi vehemently denied. Pepsi agreed to lose the "natural" label and pay $9 million to settle the lawsuit.

SOCIAL RESPONSIBILITY AND SUSTAINABILITY

Despite the many criticisms it has encountered throughout its long history, PepsiCo has recognized the importance of social responsibility to its reputation. As such, PepsiCo continually emphasizes its commitment to sustainable growth and its focus on generating healthy financial returns, while giving back to those communities it serves.

PepsiCo's commitment to its community and toward sustainable growth is outlined in something it calls "Performance with Purpose." PepsiCo gives back to its communities and stakeholders while maintaining high standards, establishing and meeting goals, and producing attainable outcomes. CEO Indra Nooyi claims "Performance with Purpose" consists of three parts: products, the environment, and employees. These areas must be addressed for PepsiCo to be a socially responsible company.

Part of PepsiCo's commitment to this goal includes meeting consumer needs for a spectrum of convenient foods and beverages. PepsiCo has been scrutinized for its unhealthy products and criticized for contributing to obesity. Although PepsiCo made many changes to its product line, incorporating healthier options and reducing fat, sugars, and other unhealthy ingredients, it recognizes consumers' desires for easy and accessible snack foods and beverages. These food products may not be the healthiest option, but they meet the consumers' needs for easy access. The trick for PepsiCo is to balance the need for convenience with the need for healthier food offerings. Acting in the interests of the consumers, PepsiCo engages in research to develop healthier products and reduce unnecessary editions.

Some ways PepsiCo is trying to increase its responsibility to consumers is partnering with organizations to promote nutrition and avoid certain marketing practices. For instance, PepsiCo partnered with the International Food & Beverage Alliance to develop responsible marketing practices for children under the age of 12. PepsiCo made a commitment that by the end of 2013 it would no longer purchase advertising in programs with an audience consisting of more than 35 percent of children.

PepsiCo also demonstrates social responsibility and dedication to sustainability through several social responsibility efforts like the PepsiCo Guiding Principles, sustainability, commitment to employees, the PepsiCo Foundation, and the Dream Machine. These efforts are described in further detail below.

PepsiCo Guiding Principles

In order to maintain its commitment to its communities and assorted stakeholders, PepsiCo has high standards for quality. By adhering to processes and ensuring proper governance, the company tries to uphold its responsibilities and earn the confidence of stakeholders. To measure its progress and make certain it remains focused, PepsiCo developed the following six guiding principles used to sustain its commitment.

TABLE 1 PepsiCo Guiding Principles

We must always strive to:
Care for customers, consumers, and the world we live in.
Sell only products we can be proud of.
Speak with truth and candor.
Balance short term and long term.
Win with diversity and inclusion.
Respect others and succeed together.

Source: PepsiCo, "PepsiCo Values and Principles," http://www.pepsico.com/annual10/corporate/values-and-principles.html (accessed May 15, 2015).

These guiding principles encompass PepsiCo's overall commitment to its community. Like all companies, PepsiCo's success depends on its stakeholders, so PepsiCo strives to understand consumers' needs and wants. In order to meet stakeholder expectations, product quality, integrity, and honesty are essential to PepsiCo's goals. This requires that the company be transparent and foster communication. By having clear goals and focusing on attainable solutions, PepsiCo is able to grow in a relevant direction and analyze both short- and long-term consequences. Table 1 describes PepsiCo's Guiding Principles.

Sustainability

PepsiCo views its goal of decreasing its environmental impact not only as socially responsible but also in the best interest of its stakeholders. For PepsiCo, a large part of its sustainability efforts involves reducing the negative effects resulting from the production and consumption of its products. This includes "going green" (for example, through water conservation and the reduction of waste products) and reducing its carbon footprint. PepsiCo reduces its impact on the environment through various water, energy, and packaging initiatives. Because PepsiCo develops products using water, and actually sells bottled water, it is actively implementing programs to reduce waste and conserve resources. This involves water recycling and treatment efforts, where recycled water is treated thoroughly and reused within its products. PepsiCo also invests in clean energy sources, such as investing in alternatives to carbon-based fuel. In China PepsiCo developed a green plant in Chongqing that is LEED-certified, incorporates 35 water-and-energy-saving designs, and has the ability to reduce carbon emissions by 3,100 tons.

Water conservation has become important to PepsiCo. The company partnered with the Nature Conservancy to embark on a study for sustainable water use and water availability. This study helps PepsiCo understand how the company uses water, ways its use impacts the environment, and strategies for decreasing water usage. For example, in its report on water use, the company studied how several of its facilities throughout the world use water in their operations. It then brainstormed on ideas to restore the watershed. PepsiCo identified the fact that its facilities operate under different conditions in different parts of the world, so its water restoration strategies must be adapted to take advantage of each location's unique characteristics.

In addition to reducing the plastic in its Aquafina bottles, PepsiCo launched other environmental initiatives to reduce the harmful byproducts of its business. In 2010 the company conducted a study termed Abacus II that tracked its 2009 packaging footprint throughout the entire company to pinpoint areas of improvement. This was followed by a web-based tool PackTrackPlus to track its packaging footprint based on weight, carbon dioxide emissions, and materials. Understanding the environmental impact of these materials allows PepsiCo to identify ways it can make changes to increase its responsibility to its environmental stakeholders.

PepsiCo adopted a 5R system for improving its environmental impact—Reduce, Recycle, use Renewable resources, Remove environmentally sensitive materials, and promote the Reuse of packaging throughout its operations. PepsiCo has reduced its impact by adopting lighter-weight bottles for Aquafina, Propel, and Gatorade products and developing new lighter-weight package designs. The company sells its starch, a waste product from potatoes used in snack foods, for use in paper products, food manufacturing, and more. PepsiCo started using more post-consumer recycled materials in its products. In 2009 its Naked juice began using 100 percent post-consumer recycled plastic. The company is investigating ways to use more renewable materials and began to substitute less eco-friendly materials with renewable resources. Finally, PepsiCo is attempting to increase its reuse of materials. For instance, it began to reuse its shipping cartons, saving approximately 150,000 tons of paperboard each year.

Employee Commitment

Another aspect of PepsiCo's commitment to social responsibility is reflected in its support of and commitment to employees. It is PepsiCo's goal to encourage a diverse corporate culture along with employee engagement in the workplace and community. This is valuable to PepsiCo because the company sees this as an opportunity to benefit from new perspectives and encourage creativity within the workplace. The company understands employees are a key to success. According to the company's philosophy, it is important for PepsiCo to maintain mutual respect, integrity, and safety in the workplace. Because it inspires a collaborative culture, PepsiCo aims to recruit and retain world-class talent through employee satisfaction—what PepsiCo terms "Talent Sustainability." For instance, to encourage employees (associates) to speak out, PepsiCo provides them with a biennial Organizational Health Survey to get their opinions on the organization and the workplace. Additionally, PepsiCo values the talents of its employees and offers management courses at its institution Pepsi University to provide employees with the leadership skills necessary to take on managerial roles within the company.

PepsiCo has also developed a Code of Conduct that addresses various business ethics issues such as bribery and conflicts of interest. The company expects workers to be familiar with its Code of Conduct and employs a chief compliance officer to enforce the Code. PepsiCo provides annual ethics training programs for employees. Training sessions are available online or through workshops. PepsiCo's compliance programs are frequently reviewed by independent third parties to pinpoint key risks. More specific aspects of PepsiCo's compliance program, such as its environmental activities, are audited externally. Finally, the company has what it calls an "Internal Audit methodology" and maintains a 24-hour anonymous ethics hotline where employees can report concerns or ethical violations.

PepsiCo Foundation

The PepsiCo Foundation was established in 1962 and provides philanthropic contributions to a variety of nonprofits. Some of the ways the Foundation gives back to the community is through grants, employee programs, and disaster response and relief efforts. PepsiCo's focus is to improve the quality of life for those in the greatest need. Its approach consists of awarding grants to those programs and organizations with proven track records and strives to make an impact expanding beyond its own communities. Since 2006 the PepsiCo Foundation and its divisions have donated $600 million in cash, goods, and services to philanthropic organizations.

PepsiCo encourages employees to engage in its communities through its Matching Gifts Program, where the company matches employee contributions to nonprofit organizations considered eligible. By doing so, PepsiCo creates an ethical and philanthropic climate for its workers. PepsiCo supports the United Way Campaign as well as post-secondary education for employees' children through its ExCEL awards. Additionally, the PepsiCo Foundation contributes to disaster relief through financial assistance, product donations, and human resources. The PepsiCo Foundation contributed to disaster relief for the 2011 Japanese earthquake and tsunami with contributions of $1.5 million and for the China Sichuan province earthquake with a $1 million donation. PepsiCo also partners with water. org and the Safe Water Network to improve access to clean, affordable water in communities worldwide and committed $5 million to Save the Children for improving the lives of children in India and Bangladesh.

Dream Machine

On April 22, 2010 (Earth Day), PepsiCo announced its multiyear partnership with Waste Management, Inc., in support of the Dream Machine recycling initiative. The Dream Machine initiative recognizes that many plastic cans and bottles are needlessly thrown away each year, particularly by busy consumers on the go. The two partners want to see the U.S. beverage container recycling rate increase from a mere 34 percent to 50 percent by 2018. This is encouraged with PepsiCo's Dream Machine kiosks that act like reverse vending machines. The Dream Machine kiosks are computerized receptacles that give consumers points when they recycle their bottles. The process involves only a few steps. First, the consumer registers on the kiosk. Then he or she scans the can or bottle's barcode and puts it in the appropriate chute. The kiosk then issues the user a receipt that contains reward points redeemable for such things as movie tickets, coupons, or other goods. The Dream Machine kiosks have collected 15 million containers since their inception. In 2014 PepsiCo held a College Recycling Challenge to encourage recycling on campus. More than 65 colleges and universities have these kiosks on their campuses.

Consumers also have another incentive to recycle: the more recycling done, the more PepsiCo will help disabled veterans. PepsiCo has partnered with Entrepreneurship Bootcamp for Veterans with Disabilities (EBV) to offer training in business management to disabled veterans. Thanks to its work promoting careers for veterans, PepsiCo was nominated in 2013 as a Top 100 Military Friendly Employer. The Dream Machines are a way to meet the clear need for greater public access to recycling bins as well as to promote PepsiCo's sustainability efforts.

CONCLUSION

PepsiCo is the classic business success story, starting with one man's invention to becoming a multimillion dollar enterprise with operations across the globe. With success comes controversy, which ultimately the company could not avoid. PepsiCo is moving toward a more balanced stakeholder orientation by identifying stakeholders relevant to the firm and trying to understand and respond to their concerns and needs. The current leadership at PepsiCo understands the importance of stakeholders and the need to develop effective dialogues and other communication to help PepsiCo resolve conflicts. Issues such as nutritional concerns over soft drinks and snack foods create a serious dilemma in balancing the concerns of special interest groups and the desires of consumers for good tasting food.

While some of the company's past challenges were likely inevitable, some were caused by misunderstanding stakeholder needs or ethical lapses on the part of the company. From a lack of cultural sensitivity to health concerns to environmental degradation, PepsiCo faced its share of ethical dilemmas. However, it has also become a major leader in the sustainability and social responsibility movement. Although it has a long way to go before its snacks can be considered healthy or manufacturing processes truly sustainable, PepsiCo has demonstrated a willingness to invest in innovative solutions for these problems. If PepsiCo can continue to learn from its mistakes, it can make progress in solidifying a reputation as a socially responsible company. The future of PepsiCo depends on continuing to develop an ethical corporate culture built on values that help employees relate to the needs and desires of all stakeholders.

QUESTIONS FOR DISCUSSION

1. How does PepsiCo balance those stakeholders such as consumers and shareholders interested in good tasting products and financial performance with special interest groups and regulators that are more concerned about nutrition?
2. How effective do you think PepsiCo has been in responding to stakeholder concerns about nutrition and sustainability?
3. Do you think it is logical for PepsiCo to partner with nutrition and water conservation nonprofit groups since it received heavy criticism for unhealthy products and wasteful water practices?

SOURCES

Valerie Bauerlein, "Gatorade, before and after," *The Wall Street Journal*, April 23, 2010, B8; Valerie Bauerlein, "PepsiCo in Recycling Push," *The Wall Street Journal*, April 22, 2010, B5; Manjyot Bhan, "Environmental Management of Multinational Corporations in India: The Case of PepsiCo," *The Sustainability Review*, March 7, 2010, https://thesustainabilityreview.org/environmental-management-of-multinational-corporations-in-india-the-case-of-pepsico/ (accessed May 15, 2015); Alan Bjerga and Doni Bloomfield, "Tax on Sugary Foods Proposed by U.S. Panel to Fight Obesity," *Bloomberg Businessweek*, February 19, 2015, http://www.bloomberg.com/news/articles/2015-02-19/tax-on-sugary-foods-proposed-by-u-s-panel-to-help-fight-obesity (accessed May 15, 2015); Diane Brady, "Pepsi: Repairing a Poisoned Reputation in India," *Bloomberg*, June 10, 2007, http://www.bloomberg.com/bw/stories/2007-06-10/pepsi-repairing-a-poisoned-reputation-in-india (accessed May 15, 2015); Nanette Byrnes, "Pepsi Brings in the Health Police," *Bloomberg BusinessWeek*, January 14, 2010, http://www.businessweek.com/magazine/content/10_04/b4164050511214.htm (accessed May 15, 2015); Siddharth Cavale, "PepsiCo says won't spin off North America beverages," *Reuters*, February 13, 2014, http://www.reuters.com/article/2014/02/13/us-pepsico-results-idUSBREA1C0R520140213 (accessed May 15, 2015); Candice Choi, "Gatorade to Remove Brominated Vegetable Oil after Consumer Complaints," *The Huffington Post*, January 25, 2013, http://www.huffingtonpost.com/2013/01/25/gatorade-brominated-vegetable-oil_n_2551533.html (accessed May 15, 2015); Candice Choi, "Mexico's junk food taxes hitting Pepsi, Coke," *Washington Times*, October 9, 2014, http://

www.washingtontimes.com/news/2014/oct/9/mexicos-junk-food-taxes-hitting-pepsi-coke/?page=all (accessed May 15, 2015); Geoff Colvin, "Indra Nooyi's Challenge," *Fortune*, June 11, 2012, 148–156; Julie Deardorff, "Critics Pounce on Coke, Pepsi Health Initiatives," *Chicago Tribune*, February 5, 2012, http://articles.chicagotribune.com/2012-02-05/news/ct-met-coke-pepsi-health-20120205_1_coca-cola-north-america-health-groups-healthy-lifestyle-choices (accessed May 15, 2015); Ranjit Devraj, "Indian Coke, Pepsi Laced with Pesticide, Says NGO," *India Resource Center*, August, 5 2003, http://www.indiaresource.org/news/2003/4725.html (accessed May 15, 2015); Directors & Boards, "'Go There and Get the Business.' (interview with PepsiCo's Chairman of the Executive Committee Donald M. Kendall on business opp)," *The Free Library*, Winter 1991, http://www.thefreelibrary.com/%27Go+there+and+get+the+business.%27+%28interview+with+PepsiCo%27s+Chairman...-a010422697 (accessed May 15, 2015); Stuart Elliot, "For a New Brand, Pepsi Starts the Buzz Online," *The New York Times*, March 14, 2008, http://www.nytimes.com/2008/03/14/business/media/14adco.html (accessed May 15, 2015); Mike Esterl, "Is This the End of the Soft Drink Era?" *The Wall Street Journal*, January 19–20, 2013, B4; Mike Esterl, "PepsiCo Slips Despite New Ads," *The Wall Street Journal*, April 27, 2012, B5; Mike Esterl and Tripp Mickle, "PepsiCo to Drop Aspartame from Diet Pepsi," *The Wall Street Journal*, April 24, 2015, http://www.wsj.com/articles/pepsico-to-replace-aspartame-with-sucralose-in-diet-pepsi-in-u-s-1429885941 (accessed May 15, 2015); Mike Esterl and Suzanne Vranica, "Pepsi Brings Back the King of Pop," *The Wall Street Journal*, May 4, 2012, http://online.wsj.com/article/SB10001424052702304746604577381792902984470.html (accessed May 15, 2015); Frito-Lay "Company," http://www.fritolay.com/company (accessed May 15, 2015); Frito-Lay North America, Frito-Lay webpage, http://www.fritolay.com/ (accessed May 15, 2015); Frito-Lay, "Our Commitment to the Planet," http://www.fritolay.com/purpose/ (accessed May 15, 2015); Frito-Lay, "Our Commitment to You," http://www.fritolay.com/nutrition/ (accessed May 15, 2015); Frito-Lay, "Supplier Diversity," http://www.fritolay.com/company/supplier-diversity (accessed May 15, 2015); Gatorade, Inc., Gatorade webpage, http://www.pepsico.com/Company/Global-Brands (accessed May 15, 2015); Gatorade, Inc., "G-Series," http://www.gatorade.com/products/all-products (accessed May 15, 2015); Michael M. Grynbaum, "Judge Blocks New York City's Limits on Big Sugary Drinks," *The New York Times*, March 11, 2013, http://www.nytimes.com/2013/03/12/nyregion/judge-invalidates-bloombergs-soda-ban.html?pagewanted=all&_r=0 (accessed May 15, 2015); Amy Guthrie, "Survey Shows Mexicans Drinking Less Soda after Tax," *The Wall Street Journal*, October 13, 2014, http://www.wsj.com/articles/survey-shows-mexicans-drinking-less-soda-after-tax-1413226009 (accessed May 15, 2015); Monica Herrera, "How Michael Jackson, Pepsi Made Marketing History," *Ad Week*, July 6, 2009, http://www.adweek.com/news/advertising-branding/michael-jackson-pepsi-made-marketing-history-99789 (accessed May 15, 2015); Rahim Kanani, "Why PepsiCo Is a Global Leader in Water Stewardship and Sustainable Agriculture," *Forbes*, September 14, 2012, http://www.forbes.com/sites/rahimkanani/2012/09/14/why-pepsico-is-a-global-leader-in-water-stewardship-and-sustainable-agriculture/ (accessed May 15, 2015); Hercules Kataveli, "Pepsi announces $1B Russian investment," *Business 2.0 Press*, July 6, 2006, http://business2press.com/2009/07/06/pepsi-announces-1b-russian-investment/ (accessed May 15, 2015); Andrew Kaplan, "The Power of One," *Beverage World*, April 15, 2010, 20–24; Jason Kessler, "Groups: NYC soda ban unfair to small, minority-owned businesses," *CNN*, January 25, 2013, http://www.cnn.com/2013/01/23/health/new-york-large-drinks (accessed May 15, 2015); Flora Lewis, "FOREIGN AFFAIRS; Soviets Buy American," *The New York Times*, May 10, 1989, http://www.nytimes.com/1989/05/10/opinion/foreign-affairs-soviets-buy-american.html?pagewanted=1 (accessed May 15, 2015); N. Madison, "What Are the Health Effects of Drinking Soda," *WiseGEEK*, March 30, 2010, http://www.wisegeek.com/what-are-the-health-effects-of-drinking-soda.htm (accessed May 15, 2015); Sanjoy Majumder, "Indian State Bans Pepsi and Coke," *BBC News*, August 9, 2006, http://news.bbc.co.uk/2/hi/south_asia/4776623.stm (accessed May 15, 2015); Massachusetts Institute of Technology, "Robert Cade: Gatorade," Lemelson-MIT Program, http://lemelson.mit.edu/resources/robert-cade (accessed May 15, 2015); Betsey McKay, "Creative Father of the 'Pepsi Generation' Turned Lifestyle into a Selling Point," *The Wall Street Journal*, August 4, 2007, http://www.wsj.com/articles/SB118618836469587966 (accessed May 15, 2015); Betsey Morris, "The Pepsi challenge," *CNNMoney*, February 19, 2008, http://money.cnn.com/2008/02/18/news/companies/morris_nooyi.fortune/index.htm (accessed May 15, 2015); Chon A. Noriega, "There May Be a Frito Bandito in Your House," *San Diego Latina Film Festival 2005*, http://www.sdlatinofilm.com/trends12.html (accessed June 8, 2010); Anahad O'Connor, "Soda Bans in Schools Have Limited Impact," *The New York Times*, November 7, 2011, http://well.blogs.nytimes.com/2011/11/07/

soda-bans-in-schools-have-limited-benefit/ (accessed May 15, 2015); PepsiCo, *2009 Annual Report*, http://www. pepsico.com/annual09/talent_sustainability.html (accessed May 15, 2015); PepsiCo & the Nature Conservancy, *Striving for Positive Water Impact: Lessons from a Partnership Approach in Five Watersheds*, https://www.pepsico. com/docs/album/sustainability-reporting/water-agriculture-reports/pep_waterreport11_nar_mech13. pdf?sfvrsn=2 (accessed May 15, 2015); "PepsiCo and Waste Management Celebrate Earth Day with Announcement of Multi-year Partnership Designed to Improve On-the-Go Recycling," April 22, 2010, https://www.wm.com/ about/press-room/2010/20100422-wm-and-pepsico-multi-year-partnership.jsp (accessed May 15, 2015); PepsiCo, "Brand Family," PepsiCo, (accessed May 15, 2015); PepsiCo, "Disaster Relief and Humanitarian Support," http://www.pepsico.com/Purpose/Global-Citizenship/Disaster-Relief-and-Humanitarian-Support (accessed May 15, 2015); PepsiCo, "Encouraging Healthy Lifestyles," http://www.pepsico.com/Purpose/Human-Sustainability/Promoting-Healthy-Lifestyle (accessed May 15, 2015); PepsiCo, "Global Brands," http:// www.pepsico.com/Company/Global-Brands (accessed May 15, 2015); PepsiCo, "Global Citizenship," http://www. pepsico.com/Purpose/Global-Citizenship.html (accessed May 15, 2015); PepsiCo, "Global Divisions," http://www. pepsico.com/Company/Global-Divisions (accessed May 15, 2015); PepsiCo, "Our History," http://www.pepsico. com/Company/Our-History.html#block_1967 (accessed May 15, 2015); PepsiCo, "Packaging," http://www.pepsico. com/Purpose/Environmental-Sustainability/Packaging-and-Waste (accessed May 15, 2015); PepsiCo, *PepsiCo 50 Years and Growing: PepsiCo 2014 Annual Report*, http://www.pepsico.com/docs/album/default-document-library/ pepsico-2014-annual-report_final.pdf (accessed May 15, 2015); PepsiCo, "PepsiCo and NBA Announce Landmark Marketing Partnership; PepsiCo Partner Tingyi's Master Kong Becomes League Beverage Partner in China," April 13, 2015, https://www.pepsico.com/live/pressrelease/pepsico-and-nba-announce-landmark-marketing-partnership-pepsico-partner-tingyis-04132015 (accessed May 15, 2015); PepsiCo, "PepsiCo Dream Machine Recycling Initiative Donates \$500, 000 to the Entrepreneurship Bootcamp for Veterans with Disabilities for Third Consecutive Year," November 12, 2012, http://www.pepsico.com/PressRelease/PepsiCo-Dream-Machine-Recycling-Initiative-Donates-500000-to-the-Entrepreneurshi11122012.html (accessed May 15, 2015); PepsiCo, "PepsiCo Policy on Responsible Advertising to Children," https://www.pepsico.com/docs/album/responsible-marketing/pepsico_policy_responsible.pdf?sfvrsn=2 (accessed May 15, 2015); PepsiCo, "PepsiCo Recycling," https://www.pepsicorecycling.com/Programs/RecyclingOnCampus (accessed May 15, 2015); PepsiCo, "Performance with a Purpose," http://www.pepsico.com/Purpose/Performance-with-Purpose (accessed May 15, 2015); PepsiCo, *Performance with Purpose*, 2013, http://www.pepsico.com/docs/album/sustainability-reporting/ pep_2013_sustainability_report.pdf (accessed May 15, 2015); PepsiCo, "Responsible Marketing," http://www. pepsico.com/Purpose/Human-Sustainability/Responsible-Marketing (accessed May 15, 2015); PepsiCo, "Tingyi and PepsiCo Open New Beverage Plant in China," October 25, 2012, http://www.pepsico.com/PressRelease/ Tingyi-and-PepsiCo-Open-New-Beverage-Plant-in-China10252012.html (accessed May 15, 2015); PepsiCo, "Water," http://www.pepsico.com/Purpose/Environmental-Sustainability/Water (accessed May 15, 2015); PepsiCo India Region, "Company," http://www.pepsicoindia.co.in/company/about-pepsico.html (accessed May 15, 2015); The Pepsi Store, "History of the Birthplace," http://www.pepsistore.com/history.asp (accessed May 15, 2015); *The Pepsi-Cola Story*, 2005, http://pepsi.com/PepsiLegacy_Book.pdf (accessed May 15, 2015); Laura Petrecca, "Coke, Pepsi, others launch assault against NYC beverage ban," *USA Today*, July 18, 2012, http:// usatoday30.usatoday.com/money/industries/food/story/2012-07-09/Coke-Pepsi-fight-soda-ban/56279302/1 (accessed May 15, 2015); Reuters, "Aquafina Labels to Spell Out Source-Tap Water," *CNN*, 2007. http://www.cnn. com/2007/HEALTH/07/27/pepsico.aquafina.reut/ (accessed May 15, 2015); Duane Stanford, "Gatorade Goes Back to the Lab," *Businessweek*, November 23, 2011, http://www.bloomberg.com/bw/magazine/gatorade-goes-back-to-the-lab-11232011.html (accessed May 15, 2015); Rachel Tepper, "Naked Juice Class Action Lawsuit Settlement over Health Claims Means \$9 Million For Consumers," *The Huffington Post*, August 28, 2013, http://www. huffingtonpost.com/2013/08/28/naked-juice-class-action-lawsuit_n_3830437.html (accessed May 15, 2015); Suzanne Vranica, "Pepsi Benches Its Drinks—Beverages Will Snap Long Streak by Sitting Out Super Bowl," *The Wall Street Journal*, December 17, 2009, Eastern edition: Wall Street Journal, ProQuest, April 18, 2010; Yahoo! Finance, "PepsiCo, Inc. (PEP)," http://finance.yahoo.com/q/is?s=PEP+Income+Statement&annual (accessed May 15, 2015).

CASE 16

Ethical Leadership at Cardinal IG: The Foundation of a Culture of Diversity*

BACKGROUND

Cardinal Glass Industries, Inc., is a corporation that specializes in the design and manufacture of high technology insulating and solar glass. It is organized as a privately held S corporation with 70 shareholders, all of whom are employees. From the corporate offices in Eden Prairie, Minnesota, CEO Roger O'Shaughnessy oversees two research facilities and 29 manufacturing subsidiaries in 16 states. Cardinal Glass is the largest company of its kind in the world. Its 5,500 employees serve customers throughout the United States, Canada, Latin America, Europe, Asia, and the Middle East.

In any organization, ethical leadership is paramount to success, and by all accounts Cardinal Glass Industries is a successful corporation. Although the corporation as a whole has been profitable since its inception in 1962, one of its manufacturing plants, Cardinal Insulating Glass (Cardinal IG) in Fargo, North Dakota, consistently outperforms all others in production efficiency and financial performance. Its workforce is the most diverse of any Cardinal subsidiary. The company consists of over 50 percent New American employees (many who speak limited English and recently arrived from unfortunate circumstances in their home country).

This case study explores the main factors contributing to the Fargo plant's success through the stories of plant manager Dave Pinder, his leadership team, and the Cardinal IG employees.

THE CARDINAL IG STORY

It is an amazing story when you think about it. A diverse group of people, who knew very little about making glass, started up an insulating glass manufacturing plant in Fargo, North Dakota. In a very short period of time, they earned all of the business and the

*This case was developed by James Legler, Associate Professor, Offutt School of Business, Concordia College, Moorhead, Minnesota, and Mary Leff, Organizational Development Consultant, Sanford Health System, Fargo, North Dakota © 2012. This case was prepared for classroom discussion rather than to illustrate either effective or ineffective handling of an administrative, ethical, or legal decision by management. All sources used for this case were obtained through publicly available material and interviews with Cardinal IG management.

respect of one of the biggest window companies in the country and established their insulating glass plant as the very best in the world.

– Cardinal IG Fargo Leadership Handbook

When Dave Pinder, the newly hired plant manager of Cardinal IG, arrived in Fargo, North Dakota, in 1998, the future plant site was nothing but a flat grain field. He had been hired to start the plant from the ground up—build the new factory, hire and train new employees, and develop relationships with his customers. Along with these responsibilities, CEO Roger O'Shaughnessy gave him complete autonomy to establish the corporate vision of "designing and fabricating the most advanced residential glass products in the industry."

The 33-year-old Pinder brought an unlikely background to the position. A graduate of West Point, a commander in Desert Shield and Desert Storm, his last military assignment had been tactical officer in charge of 200 cadets at the United States Military Academy at West Point. While in the service, he completed a master's degree in leader development and counseling from Long Island University. He spent a brief time with International Paper before being approached by O'Shaughnessy to join the Cardinal leadership team.

Getting started was a daunting task, beginning with building the leadership team. Pinder did not hire glass experts. He couldn't find any. Instead he hired people with leadership potential, a positive attitude, and a passion for learning the business and teaching others. In his words,

We started with a group of 40 people in a 140,000 square foot building. We knew nothing about making glass. Our first employees jumped into a van and traveled to Iowa for training at another Cardinal IG plant to learn how it was done. We asked those first employees to trust us.

Today, Cardinal IG operates out of a state-of-the-art 500,000-square-foot facility in Fargo. The plant runs seven days a week, three shifts per day, supplying the majority of insulating glass found in Marvin Windows. Pella and Anderson Windows are also customers of the company. The Fargo plant became a leadership training center for other Cardinal plants, and Pinder's responsibilities expanded to include troubleshooting and leadership coaching at other manufacturing sites. Cardinal's workforce of 183 people is made up of 55 percent New Americans from 15 different countries, astonishing diversity in a region of the country where U.S.-born Caucasians make up 93 percent of the demographic mix.

Cardinal IG operates in a competitive business environment, and the economic recession and downturn in the building industry added volatility to its challenges. In spite of this, leaders have had to make only incremental changes in operations. The Fargo plant continues to be the best performing plant in the Cardinal manufacturing system.

MISSION AND VISION

Before hiring anyone, Pinder had a good idea of what he wanted to create.

I had a vision for what I wanted the organization and the culture to look like and a plan to get there to maintain the culture. I wanted a world-class facility—the best of its kind on the planet. The culture must enable you to get the vision. I wanted my employees to love to come to work every day because the work was challenging, meaningful and fun; the plant was clean and well lit; they felt like they had ownership and a say in the business; they were treated with dignity and respect; and they felt like they were part of a disciplined team … I wrote my leadership philosophy before I hired anyone. I use it to guide all that we do.

Cardinal IG's mission melds the business purpose with Pinder's vision of how that purpose will be achieved. The mission is a constant reference point for all Cardinal IG is working to achieve. It is simple and straightforward:

> *To make money, by thrilling our customers with our product and service, and by taking care of our people.*

The mission influences the hiring process, reward system, leadership, team culture, and work processes. Signs posted throughout the immaculately clean manufacturing floor and training rooms reinforce the mission, report team performance, and emphasize excellence. The company is intentional in keeping all three mission objectives (profitability, customers, and employees) paramount and visible.

VALUES, PRINCIPLES, AND BEHAVIOR

As defined in the *Cardinal IG Leadership Handbook*, company values include loyalty, duty, respect, selfless service, honor, integrity, and personal and moral courage. Values are the foundation of culture but remain abstract unless they are lived in day-to-day actions. Pinder's West Point background and beliefs are reflected in these values and made real in the behaviors he models and expects of his employees. The values are further translated into specific expectations in Cardinal's Guiding Principles, statements that serve as a code of conduct for the way employees do their work and treat one another:

- **Safety**
  Nothing we do is more important than safety. It is our #1 priority.

- **Quality**
  We ensure that every product we ship to our customer is flawless.

- **Service**
  We treat our customers like they are the most important people in the world.

- **Training**
  We develop, implement, and maintain a top-notch training program.

- **Leadership/Teamwork/Communication**
  This organization is led as a team to make Fargo IG the flagship of the company.

- **Cost Awareness**
  We will spend money wisely here—as if the money is our own.

- **Respect for Others**
  We treat others with dignity and fairness while encouraging others to do the same.

- **Care for Families**
  We encourage our people to spend time with their families and balance work accordingly.

- **Integrity**
  When in doubt, do the right thing. Trust is an important part of our relationship.

- **Attitude**
  Remember both positive and negative attitudes are contagious—keep a positive attitude.

- **Keep a Sense of Humor and Have Fun**
  We are serious about our business but have fun working, training, and growing together.

LEADERSHIP THROUGH A MULTILEVEL TEAM STRUCTURE

Structure is the process of aligning work through tasks, responsibilities, departments, and divisions. Cardinal IG has a hybrid-type structure that includes a traditional hierarchy—using basic centralized administrative functions that include accounting, sales, and marketing. Yet the heart of the company is an integrated team network embedded in this organizational framework. Teams operate both at the top level and within the many manufacturing divisions within the plant, assuring everyone is working toward the same purpose.

The six manufacturing divisions of the company are responsible for specialized components of production, such as glass cutting/tempering, spacer fabrication, insulating glass production, shipping, and receiving. Each division has a supervisor with broad management responsibility. Division supervisors are salaried workers that previously served as team leaders and are selected for their past performance and leadership potential within the organization. These supervisors meet as a team, and are responsible for upper-level decisions and the recognition program.

Within each of the six divisions, there are three teams, each with its own team leader. Team leaders serve at the front of production, managing the day-to-day operations and maintenance of the plant, and also take on a major part of the human resource functions of the employees. Cardinal IG does not have a human resource department, although it does maintain a centralized function for the technical administration of payroll and benefits to assure compliance with laws and regulations and internal consistency. Duties such as hiring, firing, personnel problems, scheduling, and training are done by the team leaders and department supervisors. "We do not send our problems to the HR department for them to solve. Our team leaders are empowered and taught to solve the problems. They are close to the situation," Pinder says.

This cuts down on bureaucracy, keeps decisions close to those that do the work, and creates ownership of results. The plant runs seven days a week with three weekday shifts and a maintenance team that works on weekends when the plant is not in production. Pinder comments that the team leaders are considered the most crucial part of the organization.

Pinder's philosophy of leadership extends beyond management. All Cardinal IG employees are considered leaders, accountable for their individual behavior and performance as team members. Developing the strong work culture at Cardinal IG Fargo starts when a team member is hired. Pinder meets with all new employees and makes sure it is understood that if they choose to work at Cardinal, they must meet four criteria: *First, be willing to work hard. Second, have a good attitude. Third, be a team player. Fourth, be willing to support the mission.*

The leadership training program established at Cardinal IG is extensive, continual, formal, and informal. It includes quarterly leadership training sessions reinforced by the *Cardinal IG Leadership Handbook*. Leadership development is a key part to building confident and competent leaders and ensures a ready bench of people prepared to lead.

Managers at all levels are trained and expected to serve as mentors and coaches for their employees. Division supervisors, team leaders, and Pinder himself are available to employees at all times. That accessibility is a critical component of teamwork, especially for a company that operates around the clock. Pinder and his entire management team continually reinforce and model teamwork, communication, and accessibility. The Employee Handbook states the following:

> My intention is to run this organization as a team. My role on the team will be like that of a coach. I will provide the vision and direction, while you will run the plant. Together, we will make Fargo IG the flagship plant in the corporation—a world-class performer. To do this, we also must communicate with each other. If you have an idea to make things work better, please let me know about it. Know that I am always available for you—anytime day or night. You are my top priority and you are the organization's most valuable resource.

A leader should always train his or her subordinates to be ready to take over their position at any time, a philosophy Pinder continually stresses in his leadership training. Recently, Pinder was promoted to president of Cardinal Glass Industries to manage nine IG plants (one of which is Cardinal IG Fargo). Mike Arntson, the production manager who has been with the company since it was started in Fargo, was promoted to plant manager. In a recent interview, Arntson was asked if it was difficult to transition into the new position. "It was not difficult at all. I have been trained for this position, and I have been part of developing the philosophy of the company since I started. It was a natural transition." Leadership is intentionally evolving at Cardinal IG.

A CULTURE OF DISCIPLINE AND RESPECT

In the book *Good to Great* (2001), Jim Collins describes companies that outperformed others as having a "culture of discipline." They have not settled on being just "good" but have characteristics that make them "great." They have a freedom (and responsibility) within a defined framework. They have a fanatical adherence to doing what they do best. These organizations as described by Collins are not autocratic, but caring.

Discipline in this sense is about having a consistent, orderly system of rules that govern conduct and activity. It is about making roles, responsibilities, and expectations clear, and fostering self-regulation. This view of a culture of discipline describes Cardinal IG well, and is influenced by the military background of Pinder. However, discipline is only half of the story. Love is the rest. Pinder describes the balance of love and discipline in an article:

> We hold subordinate leaders accountable and responsible—and the big thing is that you must love—truly love—your subordinates. People might think that sounds strange. "Love? What are you saying Love?" But every employee needs to know that their leaders and I love them and truly care about them, their families, and their futures. If you truly believe that I love you, you're not going to call in, show up late, because you don't want to let me down.
> (Bock, Open Magazine, Winter 2007)

Pinder models what it means to balance love and discipline. He has a unique ability to remember names, and he knows the names of all his team members, their family members, and the personal interests of all his employees. He is available 24/7 to all his employees. Pinder has an open-door policy and addresses problems immediately. He also emphasizes leadership continually through mentoring and formal training. As he walks around the plant, he stops to visit. Handshakes and hugs are characteristic. Through this constant interaction, he keeps a pulse on the organization, and knows what is happening with individual team members. He requires the same of his leadership team.

Stories are characteristics of Pinder's leadership style, and they contribute to Cardinal's strong culture and identity. He loves sports and brings in many interesting stories. Signs on the walls remind team members of their pursuit of excellence in all they do. The following quote from Vince Lombardi is posted in the plant and emphasized by team leaders:

> *Gentlemen, we are going to relentlessly chase perfection, knowing full well we will not catch it, because nothing is perfect. But we are going to relentlessly chase it because in the process we will catch excellence. I am not remotely interested in just being good.*

ETHICAL EXPECTATIONS

Employees are rarely terminated, but certain actions can result in dismissal. The non-negotiable aspects of behavior are clear, and they are backed by consequences. First, if employees are not living up to the four criteria (work hard, good attitude, team player, support the mission), they can be terminated. There are actually very few of those situations because the hiring and mentoring processes are so strong.

At the same time, Pinder has zero tolerance for racist or sexist comments and jokes, stealing, fighting, drugs, or alcohol in the plant. Pinder is a role model, and his actions match his words. If something is not right, he immediately talks to the team leaders and asks them why they handled the situation the way they did. If it was done incorrectly, he stresses the importance of doing it right. Generally, there is no mystery in knowing what should be done. The balance of discipline and respect/caring of the individual team members is discussed often by the management and the team members.

One story Pinder tells has to do with a Cardinal employee who reported a team leader made a racist joke. Another employee reported a similar incident with the same team leader. "It was honorable that these employees spoke up and alerted us to the situation. We called the team leader in and asked him if it was true. He admitted it and was terminated." Racism is unacceptable and dismissal, if it happens, is non-negotiable. All employees know this.

Although Cardinal's non-negotiable elements are clear, the more difficult part of leadership is dealing with consequences in situations where the solution is less defined. Another example that Pinder gives shows mentoring at a crucial moment.

> *Sometimes we just need to remind people of what is important. We had a team leader who I heard complaining about "all these people and how hard it was to work with them" (referring to New Americans). It was a leadership moment, and I asked him if he was just planted here or did his parents or grandparents come to this area from somewhere else? He said they had come from Norway, and I asked him if they spoke English when they came, and he replied "no." He realized that he was just being ignorant. After our talk he changed his attitude.*

ALIGNED INCENTIVES, REWARDS, AND RECOGNITION

There are positive consequences for meeting or exceeding performance expectations, too. All employees are part of Cardinal's profit-sharing plan. Cardinal IG pays their employees well but, in addition, they can receive anywhere up to 52 percent additional each month if they meet the target profit goal. The profit-sharing plan is aligned with the culture of performance and teamwork and serves another purpose as well—recruitment. Cardinal IG in general does not advertise or recruit outside of the company for new employees. According to Pinder, "...we have very low turnover. People leave mainly to return to school or to their family. When we want to hire someone new we ask our employees to recommend someone, and the candidates are brothers, sisters, husbands, wives, cousins, and friends. Nobody recommends anyone who would not work hard and contribute to the team."

An important part of the Cardinal IG culture is the award program for recognizing exceptional team members and exceptional teams. Since January 2000, the company has given 140 Employee of the Month awards. The New Americans received 80 of those awards, or 57 percent. Employee of the Month awardees are eligible to compete for the Employee of the Year Award. The Employee of the Year Award is presented at the company's annual employee banquet held at the Ramada Plaza & Suites in Fargo with all employees and spouses present. In the past 11 years, nine of the Employee of the Year awards have been received by New Americans.

SYNERGY THROUGH DIVERSITY

Pinder believes the success of "the Big Story" of Cardinal IG is largely a result of the numerous individual stories of the New Americans who found their way to Cardinal IG. While others viewed this segment of the population as too difficult to communicate and work with, Pinder applied his trademark formula of discipline and love and built an enormous strength for Cardinal IG.

> I believe—and many believe—that we've got the best workforce out of 29 factories in 16 states here in Fargo. Why is that? The only thing I can come up with is that we're different. We didn't grow up together and go to school together, go to church together—we don't know everything about each other so we're not all thinking alike. We're from 15 different countries, different cultures, different ways of doing things, and we bring different stuff to the table. And that, synergistic effect, I believe, has enabled us to get to a level that others have not gotten to.
> (Bock, Open Magazine, Winter 2007, p 38)

Pinder is often asked if language is a barrier as many of the New Americans come from poor and disrupted countries. He comments, "Heck, no. If someone comes to Cardinal and does not speak English, we put that individual with someone who does (they pair them with someone from their home country). Before long they are speaking English and getting along well. Many of the New Americans speak several languages, including their home country language and English."

The countries represented at Cardinal IG during the past few years include Albania, Algeria, Bosnia, Burundi, Central African Republic, Congo, Eritrea, Ethiopia, Haiti, Iraq, Iran, Kenya, Liberia, Macedonia, Nigeria, Romania, Russia, Rwanda, Somalia, Sudan, Thailand, Togo, Tunisia, Uganda, Vietnam, and the United States. Lutheran Social Services of North Dakota is the primary organization for bringing refugees into the area. It contracts with the U.S. government in relocating and supporting new refugees. Most of these New Americans came to the United States through a long journey consisting of war, violence, poverty, and persecution.

In a recent article for the Lutheran Social Services publication, *The Messenger*, Meg Luther Lindholm describes the New Americans at Cardinal IG. "The stories that people were telling me were so interesting and so strong. A lot of the people that I have met and interviewed for this project could have films made about their lives. They are dramatic. They have been through that kind of experience where they have just had to use their wits to survive from day-to-day. And they have lost so much." Some examples include the following:

> A young Cardinal IG worker from Somalia is a full-time student with a wife and children. He was orphaned at the age of 14 when thugs broke into his family's home. His father didn't have anything for them to steal because they had been robbed earlier in the week. This enraged the thugs, and they killed both of his parents. He fled and eventually made it to the United States and Fargo. Despite all the possible reasons for feeling down and sorry for himself, he has a very positive outlook.
>
> A husband and wife from Sudan fled their homes with only the clothes on their backs when northern Sudanese army troops came into their town and started killing villagers and looting homes. They were separated from their son who had to stay with his grandmother until being reunited with his parents several years later. The husband is now employed at Cardinal IG, and the son is a student at North Dakota State University.
>
> One of Cardinal IG's team leaders is from northwest Bosnia. In 1991, when he was 20 years old, civil war broke out. Serbs put him into slave labor for several years. He was caught in the fighting, was shot in the back, and spent 2½ months in a hospital. He was able to escape by crossing over to Croatia and lived in a refugee camp for several years. He later came to the United States and found his way to Fargo through the refugee program.

Pinder's leadership style breaks through communication and cultural barriers through the universal language of love, respect, and authenticity. By knowing his employees, their families, and their stories, he honors their dignity and makes it a powerful force in the culture and success of "the Big Story."

CONCLUSION

How effective is the Cardinal IG plant in Fargo? It excels at being a great company, not just a good company. From the research collected, success is evident in several areas. It accomplishes its mission well. The financial performance of the company as the top performer within the organization of 29 different plants is evidence of this along with the overall success of the corporation—Cardinal Glass Industries Inc. It is an exceptional plant in taking care of its employees. This is evident in its high retention rate, profit-sharing plan, recognition of excellence, exceptional team members, immaculately clean plant, and the shared values of a diverse workforce.

As we examine the company from a holistic and systems perspective, it is evident many of the elements of the organization are interrelated. They fit together to achieve a shared goal—a great example of an organization "designed" to accomplish its purpose. The elements that make this happen are the strength of its leadership, specific goals and objectives, a team-based structure, strong values and culture, and intentional and disciplined procedures throughout the organization. Cardinal's success cannot be attributed to any one factor but rather the alignment of all its parts in support of its mission.

The Cardinal IG plant also exemplifies ethical leadership. Under Pinder's direction, Cardinal employees are encouraged to pursue the company vision and participate in the firm's ethical corporate culture. The firm developed solid principles that are non-negotiable, such as respect for employees. The firm lives and breathes its values. For instance, 50 percent of the plant's employees are New Americans, demonstrating the firm's strong commitment toward its value of diversity. Additionally, all employees are treated with respect and dignity, reiterating the fact the company values their contributions. Cardinal's strong ethical leadership enables the company to thrive while providing it with the opportunity to become a positive force in its community.

QUESTIONS FOR DISCUSSION

1. How has David Pinder embraced ethical leadership to create an ethical culture at Cardinal IG?
2. How has Cardinal's principles and values shaped the ethical behavior of employees?
3. How has Cardinal empowered its employees to practice responsible and accountable leadership?

SOURCES

Jodee Bock, "From Westpoint to Fargo: A Leaders Journey," *Open Magazine*, no. 3 (Winter 2007), 34–40; Cardinal IG website, www.cardinalcorp.com (accessed May 6, 2015); Steven A. Cavaleri and Krzysztof Obloj, *Management Systems: A Global Perspective* (Belmont, CA: Wadsworth, 1993); Jim Collins, *Good To Great: Why Some Companies Make the Leap … and Others Don't* (New York, NY: Harper Collins, 2001); Interview with Mike Arntson, Cardinal IG Fargo, on April 11, 2012; Interviews with Yasmeen Frost and Darci Asche, Lutheran Social Services, New American employment, on May 2, 2011; Interviews with Dave Pinder, plant manager of Cardinal IG Fargo, on March 10, 2011, and April 7, 2011; Lutheran Social Services publication, "Finding common ground," *The Messenger*, Winter 2005; Presentation by Dave Pinder at the Center for Ethical Leadership, Concordia College, Moorhead, Minnesota, on November 1, 2002.

CASE 17

Belle Meade Plantation: The First Nonprofit Winery Engages in Social Entrepreneurship*

INTRODUCTION

Belle Mead Plantation, over 200 years old, is using social entrepreneurship to preserve the history of the nineteenth century. In 1807 John Harding founded the Belle Meade Plantation in Nashville, Tennessee. The plantation would become known for breeding some of the best-known thoroughbred horses in U.S. history. By the time of the U.S. Civil War, the Plantation had become famous as a 5,400-acre stud farm that was producing some of the best racehorses in the United States. Following the Civil War, much of the thoroughbred industry moved to the Lexington, Kentucky area. Kentucky remained in the Union and had the advantage during reconstruction. However, Belle Meade recovered, and various family members managed a successful thoroughbred breeding plantation that was among the best in the nation. After the plantation was sold early in the twentieth century, the grounds of Belle Meade Plantation were eventually converted into a museum focusing on its history. Today Belle Meade Plantation operates as a nonprofit to preserve its history and provide an opportunity to experience life in the nineteenth century. The plantation gives families the chance to have an educational experience. Guests can visit the plantation and tour the mansion, stables, and other buildings to experience "stepping back in time."

This case focuses on the challenges in 2004 when Alton Kelley, executive director of Belle Meade Plantation, and his wife, Sheree, were both facing the monumental task of securing adequate, long-term funding to maintain Belle Meade Plantation. At the time, the existing sources of funding for the operations of Belle Meade Plantation were (in descending revenue order): (1) ticket sales from visiting tourists, (2) hosting special events, (3) corporate and private donations, and (4) sales of items from the gift shop, including a line of private-labeled products, such as cheese, country ham, grits, and a variety of souvenirs. For the fifth consecutive year, donations from corporations and individuals had declined to the lowest levels in memory, and the couple believed they had little choice but to look for solutions that were well outside of the proverbial box. The organization and its board of

*Dr. Robert P. Lambert and Dr. Joe Alexander, Belmont University © 2014. Alton Kelley, Executive Director of Belle Meade Plantation, and Sheree Kelley, Belle Meade Winery Manager, participated in developing this case. Jennifer Sawayda assisted in editing a version of this case. It was prepared for classroom discussion rather than to illustrate either effective or ineffective handling of an administrative, ethical, or legal decision by management. All sources used for this case were obtained through personal interviews, publicly available material, and the Belle Meade website.

directors could no longer rely solely on corporate donations for the ongoing operations of the Belle Meade Plantation.

After evaluating and discarding a variety of other alternatives, the Kelleys set about pursuing an ambitious plan to use social entrepreneurship to generate revenue for maintaining the nonprofit. Their solution was to build and operate a nonprofit winery on the historic site to help sustain current and future long-term financing needs. The idea was bold, given that there were no other known nonprofit wineries in the United States. However, the Kelleys believed that if they could successfully navigate through the numerous legal and market-based challenges, this social enterprise would provide the necessary funding required for supporting the property's ongoing operations.

The first step was in 2009, when The Harding House Restaurant opened on the grounds, immediately adjacent to the mansion, to replace the popular "Martha's at the Plantation." The restaurant is an independent operation and pays rent to Belle Meade Plantation with all profits remaining in the restaurant.

This case will analyze the next step of Belle Meade's use of social entrepreneurship to create a sustainable organization. We begin by examining the history of Belle Meade Plantation. Next, background is provided on the challenges nonprofits encounter in trying to remain economically sustainable. Belle Meade recognized that the market for wine in Tennessee offered a major opportunity, leading them to adopt the nation's only nonprofit winery. We then discuss the different forms of promotion used to promote Belle Meade and its winery, including social media and events. We conclude with an examination of some of the challenges Belle Meade is likely to encounter as it continues to expand.

BRIEF HISTORY OF BELLE MEADE PLANTATION

The roots of Belle Meade extend back to its successful breeding of thoroughbreds. As early as 1816, founder John Harding was placing advertisements in Nashville newspapers to promote his horses. In 1820 he commissioned a brick home in the Federal style on his farm and officially named the estate "Belle Meade." By this time, he became interested in racing his horses locally. John registered his own racing silks with the Nashville Jockey Club in 1823 and was training horses on the track at another of his properties, McSpadden's Bend Farm. By the time John Harding's son, William Giles Harding, assumed management of the Belle Meade plantation, he already shared his father's interest in breeding and racing. Even though the Civil War interrupted both breeding and horse-racing in the southern United States, Belle Meade was large enough in acreage to elude Union troops by hiding the prized horses at various locations throughout the heavily wooded nearby hills.

After the Civil War, Harding became famous for winning more purses with his horses than any man living at that time in the United States—even though much of the thoroughbred industry had moved to Kentucky. He was also the first in Tennessee to use the auction system for selling thoroughbreds. With the auction system, he became the most successful thoroughbred breeding farm and distributor in the State of Tennessee. Belle Meade's breeding lineage has boasted some of the best-known thoroughbred horses in U.S. history, including *Bonnie Scotland, Secretariat, Seabiscuit, Barbaro,* and 2014 Kentucky Derby winner *California Chrome.* When General Harding died in 1886, *The Spirit of the Times* praised him as having done as much to promote breeding interests as any American in the nineteenth century.

After Harding's death, his son-in-law General William Hicks Jackson and oldest daughter assumed one-third ownership of the horse farm. General Jackson's flair for entertaining and his confident, outgoing nature helped the farm attract thousands of people to the yearling sales. He later modernized the mansion's interior. By the time the plantation was sold in the early twentieth century, it had hosted a number of American historical figures, including President Grover Cleveland, Robert Todd Lincoln, General Ulysses S. Grant, General William T. Sherman, General Winfield Scott Hancock, and Adlai E. Stevenson.

Today, the Greek revival-styled mansion is the centerpiece of the affluent Belle Meade region of Nashville, with the historic homestead surrounded by 30 acres of manicured lawns and shade trees. A long driveway leads uphill to the mansion, fronted by six columns and a wide veranda. Inside, the restored building is furnished with nineteenth-century antiques that illustrate the elegance and wealth that the Southern gentility enjoyed in the late 1800s. Tours are provided to the general public, with costumed guides following a theme that changes every three months with the seasons. These themed tours are intended to provide fascinating glimpses into the lives of the people who once lived at Belle Meade. During the tour, visitors are able to see the numerous historic facilities on the property, including a log cabin, smokehouse, and creamery. The tour makes the nineteenth century come alive and provides an opportunity to experience life in the nineteenth century. Belle Meade's park-like grounds has made it a popular site for festivals throughout the year.

NONPROFITS MOVE IN DIRECTION OF SOCIAL ENTREPRENEURSHIP

Recent decades have led to challenges for nonprofits like Belle Meade Plantation. Since the last economic downturn reduced household incomes and lowered investors' and consumers' confidence in the economy, nonprofit contributions plummeted. Most nonprofits' incomes dwindle during recessionary periods based on a variety of factors: (1) corporate and individual donations decrease, (2) federal, state, and local funding sources decline, and (3) earnings from endowments shrink with their capital market values. At the same time, economic downturns also put added demands on nonprofits' already dwindling resources, including (1) a typical increase in the frequency of client requests for financial or service needs, and (2) a decrease in the number of individuals who, based on concerns regarding their own household incomes, are either unable or unwilling to volunteer their time in support of the organizational mission. As a result, nonprofits tend to focus their dollars more directly into client services. Charitable contributions to nonprofits bottomed out in 2009. The average rate of growth in charitable giving during 2010 and 2011 was at its lowest in 40 years. Even as the economy began to improve, many nonprofits continued to report that their contributions had either decreased or remained stable.

Belle Meade was faced with exactly these problems. Like other nonprofits, its leaders needed to look for innovative solutions toward increasing the long-term sustainability of their organizations. As leaders of the nonprofit sector plan for the future, understanding the economic climate and the actions taken as a result of challenging economic times can assist executive directors and other leaders in determining strategically the operational needs of their organization and how to best serve their communities.

Nonprofit organizations, facing cuts in donations from individuals and organizations, have been experimenting with new ways to strengthen their bottom lines. In addition to cutting costs and eliminating waste, nonprofit leaders such as the Kelleys had to think more creatively about their fundraising strategies and consider the role of nontraditional philanthropic organizations or individuals. Even at significant levels of visitor traffic at Belle Meade, base admission ticket revenues were not nearly enough to fully support the site's operation. According to the Kelleys, "Every time there is a new charity in Nashville, the 'giving pie' gets thinner." The Kelleys therefore began to consider the idea of social entrepreneurship. Social entrepreneurship occurs when an entrepreneur founds a business with the purpose of creating social value. In this case, Belle Meade could sell a product and then use the proceeds to support the nonprofit. Generating their own revenue would reduce the dependence on outside contributions and make the nonprofit less susceptible to economic downturns.

The Kelleys knew that management clearly had no choice but to consider substantive changes in their revenue model in order to ensure long-term survival. The question involved deciding upon what product would be appropriate to sell to generate revenue and align with Belle Meade's strong historical roots. Management knew from historical research that Muscadine grapes were grown on the plantation back into the 1800s. The Hardings, Belle Meade's nineteenth-century founders, actually produced wine from the vineyards on their property. Curator John Lamb confirmed the story: "There are numerous invoices from the 1800s that show the Hardings purchased and served fine wines and also purchased empty wine bottles—presumably to fill with wines made on the property."

The Kelleys became convinced that resurrecting wine production and sales on the property would provide a major source of revenue and self-sufficiency for the property. The winery at Belle Meade Plantation would become the only winery registered in Nashville and the only nonprofit winery in the United States. Although it would operate as a nonprofit—reinserting profits into the maintenance and operation of the museum—the winery would effectively develop a strategic business approach and implement a successful revenue model.

MARKET FOR WINE IN TENNESSEE

The wine industry in Tennessee was dealt a blow with Prohibition during the 1920s, so until 1975 the state had no formal modern wineries. In the late 1970s, Judge William O. Beach championed legislation that enabled the state's wine industry to move forward more rapidly. Another industry leader was Fay Wheeler, who was instrumental in assuring passage of the Wine and Grape Act of 1977. In 1980 she started Tennessee's first licensed winery, and to many, Wheeler is considered the founder of Tennessee's contemporary wine industry. By 1995 Tennessee had 15 wineries, and in the next 10 years this number would double to 27. As of 2010, Tennessee boasted 45 registered wineries, with the likelihood of continued growth. Belle Meade recognized that these strong growth opportunities would be beneficial toward the decision to open a nonprofit winery.

There are, at present, between 500 and 750 acres of wine grapes grown in Tennessee—a number that is on the rise. Many vineyards are small (that is, less than five acres), which is a challenge to growers, since wineries juggle the decision to buy small quantities locally or purchase larger quantities from outside the state's borders.

Finally, it is worth noting that not all wines are produced from grapes. Several Tennessee fruit-bearing trees or bushes are commonly used to produce what are accordingly referred to as "fruit wines." The more common take advantage of fruits such as black raspberries, peaches, blackberries, strawberries, rhubarb, and apples—all of which grow well within a portion of the geographic areas included within the State. For example, one of the wines that Belle Meade offers is a blackberry wine.

BEGINNING OF THE WINERY

Belle Meade did understand the challenge of developing a successful winery. It was not enough just to sell wine with a Belle Meade label. To align with Belle Meade's mission, the product would have to fit with the organization's historical background. "There was a lot of brainstorming among staff to come up with new ideas," the Kelleys claim. "And as we continue to believe, it is important that everything we do is connected to the site's heritage. We just look for ways to modernize what the original owners did and make money to support the site."

With a desire to narrow viable possibilities to those that fit with the historical nature of the Plantation's roots, the seeds of a winery concept began to germinate. A decision was subsequently made to visit the Biltmore Estate's Winery in Ashville, North Carolina as it is the most visited winery in the United States. "We were looking for best practices," the Kelleys said. These practices would be used to establish their own winery to support its nonprofit mission.

While the Kelleys' initial concept for a winery in Nashville was relatively small compared to Biltmore's, they saw incredible potential for such an operation since there were currently no wineries in Nashville. They also learned that at Biltmore, one out of five guests to the Estate made a wine purchase before leaving the property. This further fueled their beliefs that a winery would generate the revenue needed to operate Belle Meade. Their next decision was to locate the winery *on* the Belle Meade property.

The Kelleys presented their proposal for a winery at the next meeting with the board of directors. Through their research, the Kelleys had determined that an existing building on the property built in 1998 as an education venue could be converted into the winery and a gift shop. However, this would not come without financial risk. In order to get the winery operational, an investment of $250,000 would be required. The Kelleys had determined that in the first year of operation, all of the bottling activities would be done by hand using employees of the historic plantation, the winery, and volunteers. If sales increased beyond $1,000,000, mobile bottling equipment would be used for the higher volume.

The Kelleys provided the board with projected revenues for the first five years, along with the planned operation's anticipated expenses. Two of the board members were presidents of local banks and were convinced that the proposed winery was a fairly low-risk investment. The remaining board members concurred, and ultimately a final vote yielded approval for the project.

The winery at Belle Meade first opened to visitors touring the mansion in November 2009. The building housing the winery made it a reasonably good fit for serving as the initial startup site. By 2009 the directors of the historic plantation renovated the building for use as a combination winery and tasting room, and Brian Hamm was appointed as the winemaker. The staff began to research which wines should be produced to meet plantation revenue objectives. Advice from the local wine-making community informed them that if their objective was 'status,' then dry wines should be the target. However, they advised Belle Meade to adopt sweeter wines if their objective was to make money. It is no secret that Belle Meade's current portfolio of wines leans heavily to the sweet end of the spectrum. This fits with its objectives to generate revenue for the plantation.

A major startup hurdle for Belle Meade turned out to be the issue of where to store the bottled wine. Ideally, the location needed to be secure and near the point-of-sale, as well as of sufficient size to accommodate growth in volume over time. It also needed to be "climate-friendly" to minimize significant variations in temperature to protect the product. The best solution turned out to be the historical dairy located right there on the property. It was a large building located relatively close to the mansion. Because it was made out of stone, it created an almost ideal environment for storing the cases of wine. This became Belle Meade's bonded storage facility.

When the idea of a winery was first conceived, the Kelleys immediately realized that the existing 250,000 annual visitors to the historic property were going to be the primary initial market for the wines produced at the winery. Property tours were redesigned to conclude with an opportunity for guests to be escorted to the tasting room for a complimentary tasting. Each wine would be presented to include the background on its composition and properties, along with any relevant historical facts that aligned with what had been presented on the earlier tour. Each bottle comes in Belle Meade-specific packaging with thoroughbred horse designer labels to connect it with the Plantation's past. Because of the unique vintages produced at the winery, tourists often purchase multiple bottles and sometimes cases to take back to their family and friends.

According to Sheree Kelley, Belle Meade Winery Manager, "We are different because people come to see the plantation and then discover the winery." As with all social entrepreneurships, the main purpose is to create social change. As the Belle Meade Plantation website explains, the site makes history real for visitors by educating them about their historical roots. The winery profits are used for historical preservation of the Plantation and educational initiatives on-site. One such educational initiative involves hosting summer camps for children. During the school year, the nonprofit also underwrites many school trips to the Plantation, enabling children to experience and learn about the history of the 1800s.

SUCCESS BEYOND EXPECTATIONS: TOURS, TASTINGS, AND SOCIAL MEDIA

An official tour of the Belle Meade Plantation begins as guests enter the front doors of the mansion. The mansion is maintained as closely as possible to how it is believed to have existed in the 1890s. Upon entering the mansion, visitors enter a dark, subdued foyer decorated with framed pictures of racing horses to emphasize the plantation's history in thoroughbred breeding and racing. Since the 1990s, every horse that has run the Kentucky Derby has been a blood descendent of Belle Meade Plantation. Many of these legendary horses grace the various Belle Meade labels on their wine bottles.

After touring the grounds, visitors are invited to wine tastings in Belle Meade's tasting room. The interior of the tasting room fits in with the historical roots of the plantation, from the medium dark wood supported by a stone base to a wood-burning fireplace to add ambience to the room. Glass windows allow visitors a direct view into the tank room where the wine is stored prior to bottling. To enhance its warmth and hospitality, the room also includes a dessert counter with Peanut Butter Pecans, artisanal chocolates, and other confectionaries. These desserts also serve as added revenue for the nonprofit. A wine garden is available outside the doorway for visitors who want to purchase a bottle of wine and enjoy it on the premises. Since opening in 2009, the winery has become an all-staff effort. The winery has been an overwhelming success, exceeding the first year's 10,000-bottle sales

TABLE 1 Pro Forma Income Statement—Belle Meade Winery

2010–2014	2010	2011	2012	2013	2014*
Revenue:					
Wine Sales	$456,485	$1,019,346	$1,536,865	$2,001,223	$3,050,000
Gift Shop Sales	31,500	42,478	45,650	53,275	60,100
Total Revenue	$487,985	$1,061,824	$1,582,515	$2,054,498	$3,110,100
Expenses:					
Cost of Sales	$165,212	$375,620	$566,552	$736,714	$915,000
Other Expenses	91,234	122,925	173,500	195,800	298,595
Total Expense	$256,446	$498,545	$730,052	$932,514	$1,213,595
Net Income	$231,539	$563,279	$852,463	$1,121,984	$1,896,505

*Projected based on data through August 2014.

goal with sales topping 54,000 bottles. Belle Meade ensures that everyone on staff is knowledgeable about the winery process. "Some of the grapes are grown and crushed in Middle Tennessee, and the juice is brought to our tanks on-site. Everyone on staff knows how to bottle wine—it's a great team-building exercise," the Kelleys explain.

The winery's annual revenues have grown to approximately $3.0 million, with an additional $200,000 in wine-related merchandise. Table 1 presents a pro forma income statement summarizing the winery's first four years of operations. However, despite their success, the Kelleys are careful to note that "starting a winery is a monumental decision. It's not for the faint of heart!"

Promoting the Social Enterprise

Belle Meade's staff does not rest on their laurels. Like any business, they recognize the need to engage in marketing. The winery sells all of its output each year at current prices, with the ability to sell more if storage and warehousing becomes available. The primary means of marketing the winery is through the organization's own website (www.bellemeadewinery.com), tourist visits, local press/media, social media, and word of mouth. Because of current demand for its products, the winery has not undertaken any traditional advertising. However, it does make extensive use of social media for no-cost promotions with a quick turnaround time.

"In 2011, we started a Groupon promotion in the third week of January," stated the Kelleys. "We offered two tours and two free wine tastings at half-price and sold 1,300 tickets. That is 2,600 people who have 60 days to redeem their voucher." Groupon's success prompted another discount voucher promotion through Living Social. A Valentine's Day special resulted in the sale of 1,000 tickets. Even more impressive, these incentives generated record sales in Belle Meade's slowest months. The winery also hosts several events for the local community, such as Jazz on the Lawn during the summer and Tennessee's largest Kentucky Derby Party.

The organization is also examining market trends to improve demand for its tours. "We were looking at travel trends, and we know that people want to be more involved than just taking a tour," said the Kelleys. As a result, Belle Meade is introducing a Southern culinary experience using graduate students from the University of Mississippi's *Southern Foodways* program to create the tour. The plan is to use the original kitchen to give visitors the chance to taste Southern biscuits, beaten biscuits, and cornbread. The experience includes a tour of the root cellar and smokehouse where visitors will learn why the South's heat and humidity created a need for food preservation techniques such as curing ham.

New tours are also being planned that further incorporate the winery. With help from Belmont University's MBA students, a marketing plan was developed suggesting an event called the Progressive Wine Tour. This event would provide guests with a tour of the historic Belle Meade Mansion and a personalized walking tour of historical points of interest on the plantation property. During the tour, guests would be treated to five of the Belle Meade premium wines paired with light appetizers at focal points throughout the property.

The winery has become exceedingly popular. Many local prominent restaurants in Nashville have requested that Belle Meade wines become the official wine of their restaurant. The winery has been forced to decline to sell to restaurants due to limited supply. The winery also sells its products online and is available in over 15 states.

APPROACHING CHALLENGES FACING BELLE MEADE PLANTATION

While the winery has experienced phenomenal success since opening, there are still significant risk factors that it must address. One of the major challenges involves managing future growth. The winery is constrained by liquor laws that require the production of wine be done on-site where the wine is sold. An off-site storage facility is not legal in the State of Tennessee. Because visitation to the Plantation has grown at a record pace and approached capacity limits, handling the growing crowds and staffing at Belle Meade has proven to be a challenge.

Currently, Belle Meade Winery is the only winery located in Nashville. However, like any entrepreneurial endeavor success tends to create more competition. Belle Meade must be on the lookout for rivals who might choose to establish themselves in Nashville. While the company has seen great success with social media, to date it has done little in the way of formal promotional spending. Its excellent sales staff, outstanding products, captive audience, social media marketing, and a lack of direct competition eliminate the need for formal spending on promotion, but this might change if competitors enter the same area. It is also possible that other historic properties in Nashville, such as The Hermitage or Belmont Mansion, might try to pursue similar social entrepreneurship opportunities. Belle Meade still faces competition from other historic sites that capture consumers' time and money. Finally, with Nashville as the epicenter of the food movement, Belle Meade is faced with more decisions regarding whether to pair local foods and wines within their operations. These challenges illustrate that Belle Meade must operate with the same business concepts as for-profit organizations. Social entrepreneurship rests on a sound business strategy.

QUESTIONS FOR DISCUSSION

1. Analyze the strengths and weaknesses of the Belle Meade strategy and implementation of its nonprofit winery.
2. Given the success of the current Belle Meade Winery, how can Belle Meade effectively address the challenges facing the winery for future growth?
3. Understanding the success of the Belle Meade Winery, what could other nonprofit organizations learn to create social entrepreneurship ventures to sustain their operations?

SOURCES

Robert Barro, *Crisis of governments: The ongoing global financial crisis and recession*, 2011, http://www.iea.org.uk/sites/default/files/publications/files/Crises%20of%20Government.pdfB (accessed August 27, 2014); Belle Meade, "The History of Belle Meade," bellemeadeplantation.com/history (accessed August 27, 2014); Belle Meade, "The Winery at Belle Meade Plantation," bellemeadewinery.com (accessed August 27, 2014); Woods Bowman, "Financial Capacity and Sustainability of Ordinary Nonprofits," *Nonprofit Management Leadership* 22, no. 1 (Fall 2011): 37–51; Julianne Gassman, Norma A Dolch, Ann Marie Kinnell, Regan Harwell Schaffer, Sue Ann Strom, and Amy Costliow, "A Three Year Study of the Nonprofit Sector's Response to the Economic Challenges in Six Cities Across the Nation," *Center for Nonprofit Strategy and Management*, Baruch College, The City University of New York, June 2012; GuideStar, "Late Fall 2011 Nonprofit Fundraising Study," 2014, http://www.guidestar.org/rxg/news/publications/nonprofits-and-economy-late-fall-2011.aspx (accessed August 27, 2014); Michelle Nichols, "Charities Still Struggling in Wake of Recession," *The Fiscal Times*, June 19, 2012, http://www.thefiscaltimes.com/Articles/2012/06/19/Charities-Still-Struggling-in-Wake-of-Recession (accessed August 27, 2014); Lisa M. Sontag-Padilla, Lynette Staplefoot, and Kristy Gonzalez Morganti, *Financial Sustainability for Nonprofit Organizations: A Review of the Literature* (Arlington, VA: Rand Corporation, 1200 South Hayes Street, 2012), 2; Terry and Kathy Sullivan, "Tennessee," *Wine Trail Traveler*, http://winetrailtraveler.com/tennessee/tennessee.php (accessed August 27, 2014); "Welcome to Tennessee Wine Country," *Tennessee Wines*, http://www.tennesseewines.com/ (accessed August 27, 2014).

CASE 18

Managing the Risks of Global Bribery in Business[*]

Bribery is one of the most pervasive forms of corruption in global business. In the United States, the United Kingdom, and many other countries, bribery in business is illegal, particularly when it involves the bribing of foreign officials. Unfortunately, bribery plagues even the most well-respected organizations. Corporations past and present have witnessed or participated in this illegal practice. Multinational organizations face the added challenge of having to monitor their subsidiaries in various countries, including some where bribes are expected as part of the normal course of business. IBM, for instance, paid fines of $10 million to settle claims it paid officials in China and Korea with gifts and other bribes to secure contracts. With fines often reaching into the millions, it is essential for companies to have systems in place to prevent this form of misconduct.

Bribery is defined as the offering of payments or other incentives to gain illicit advantages. In business, bribery can be used to influence an organization or individual to provide preferential treatment. Although bribery occurs on a widespread level, it is far from harmless; rather, it interrupts the competitive process between organizations. Many cultures, including the United States and the United Kingdom, consider bribery to be an unfair way of conducting business. For years corporations have adopted anti-bribery and anti-corruption policies in their organizations. However, these efforts mean little if they are not enforced.

The form and frequency of bribery vary depending on the culture. In some cultures, bribery is a common way of doing business. Many cultures, including the United States, allow companies to provide hospitality or small gifts to those with whom they wish to do business. In fact, in Japan it is often considered rude not to bring a gift. One challenge for many companies is how to determine what constitutes a gift or an act of hospitality and what can be construed as a bribe. Giving a potential client a mug with the company logo on it is likely to be seen as a form of hospitality because it is so small in value it will not likely influence the client's business decision. An all-expenses paid trip to the Bahamas is another question entirely. However, other items are not as easily defined. For instance, is a bottle of wine a gift or a bribe? What if the wine costs $20? How about if it costs $175? The distinction between gifts and bribes can be a gray area. It is the firm's responsibility to be aware of the bribery laws within each country it operates in and conduct business accordingly.

Even if the business has operations in a country where bribery is acceptable, anti-bribery laws sometimes reach across borders. For example, the U.S. Foreign Corrupt Practices Act and the United Kingdom Bribery Act prohibit companies with operations in the

*This case was prepared by Danielle Jolley, Julian Mathias, Michelle King, and Jennifer Sawayda for and under the direction of O. C. Ferrell and Linda Ferrell. Isaac Emmanuel provided editorial assistance. It was prepared for classroom discussion rather than to illustrate either effective or ineffective handling of an administrative, ethical, or legal decision by management. All sources used for this case were obtained through publicly available material © 2015.

United States or the United Kingdom, respectively, from bribing foreign officials anywhere. Another important measure for combating international bribery is the OECD Anti-Bribery Convention, meant to criminalize international bribery of foreign public officials. All 34 OECD member nations and 7 nonmember nations are subject to this convention, although some countries are more proactive in enforcement than others. Even countries where bribery is commonplace have passed bribery laws and are prosecuting individuals or companies for acts of bribery. For example, China recently amended its criminal code to allow prosecution of companies that offer bribes to foreign officials over $31,640 (RMB 200,000). Brazil also recently passed its own corporate bribery law, making companies civilly liable for bribing government or foreign officials. The new Brazilian law is actually much stricter in some ways than its U.S. and U.K. counterparts, although how effectively it will be enforced remains to be seen.

However, simply knowing the relevant bribery laws is only one step toward combating this practice. Unfortunately, the distinction between a gift and a bribe continues to remain ambiguous, and even the most wide-sweeping anti-bribery laws are not always clear on this issue. To eliminate this uncertainty for employees, generally accepted practices regarding bribery should be located in the company's code of conduct as well as communicated to all employees. By implementing a code of conduct with clear distinctions between bribery and gifts or entertainment, a company can set a proper precedent that bribery will not be tolerated.

This case analysis examines two of the major laws that impact the use of bribery on a global scale: the Federal Corrupt Practices Act of the United States and the Bribery Act of the United Kingdom. While there are many other global bribery laws, these are the most well-recognized anti-bribery laws in the world. We begin by examining the backgrounds of these two laws and then discuss the rules and regulations of each. The case explains why these laws were enacted and who is subject to their standards. The analysis also provides specific examples of bribery and its consequences. Finally, we offer an overview of how bribery negatively impacts national institutions, including political, social, and economic.

BACKGROUND OF THE UNITED STATES FOREIGN CORRUPT PRACTICES ACT

The Foreign Corrupt Practices Act of 1977 (FCPA) was developed after a number of scandals shook the nation. The Watergate scandal brought corruption under greater scrutiny. After Watergate, the U.S. Securities and Exchange Commission began investigating more than 400 U.S. companies, including long-term bribery at Lockheed Martin, and discovered many had made questionable and illegal payments to foreign officials in excess of $300 million. Their findings proved the necessity for regulation, which resulted in the creation of the FCPA.

The FCPA makes it illegal for individuals or entities to make payments to foreign government officials to assist in securing or retaining business. The FCPA does, however, allow for small payments to expedite routine transactions, known as facilitation payments, which are arguably necessary to conduct business in some countries. These facilitation payments are meant to speed up routine transactions and convince public officials to perform their functions, but are in no way intended to convince government officials to provide preferential treatment to a firm. While there is no set amount separating a bribe from a facilitation payment, gifts under $100 are generally deemed to be acceptable. However, as mentioned earlier, distinguishing between gifts and bribes can be difficult. Under the

FCPA, a bribe can be anything of significant value, including money, gifts, travel, or various types of entertainment. Forms of bribery vary from company to company; one organization may view anything less than $100 as acceptable, while another company may see anything more than $10 as a bribe. To avoid discrepancies, it is necessary for companies to include their standards on gifts and entertainment in their codes of conduct.

Any company with operations in the United States is subject to the FCPA over its entire business. The FCPA always applied to companies listed on the U.S. Stock Exchange, and in 1998 the law began applying to foreign companies as well. The FCPA was designed to encourage proper business transactions conducted by companies and individuals. Ultimately, Congress enacted the FCPA to bring a halt to the bribery of foreign officials and attempt to build and restore public confidence in the integrity of the American business system.

With the development of the FCPA, the implications and consequences for bribes changed. Punishment for violating the FCPA varies from case to case. However, penalties generally include up to five years in prison and fines of up to $250,000 for individuals. For business entities, fines can reach $2 million. Also, company executives who know about bribery but do not report it can face prison time.

Bribing government officials comes in many forms. In 2014 HP paid $108 million to settle allegations that it had bribed foreign officials in Mexico, Poland, and Russia. In 2012 Eli Lilly was charged with issuing improper payments to foreign government officials in order to conduct business in Poland, China, Russia, and Brazil. Additionally, in 2012 the Securities and Exchange Commission found Tyco International guilty of arranging improper payments to foreign officials in more than 12 countries. While most of these incidents involve gifts or money, other incidents of bribery under the FCPA have included improper travel, contributions to the public official's favorite charity, and even providing excessive tax breaks. The greatest considerations for whether a gift constitutes a bribe are whether it seeks to sway the public official's opinion to favor the bribing company and whether the bribe was willful and intentional. Intent is essential in establishing liability.

UNITED KINGDOM BRIBERY ACT

The first law dealing with bribery in the United Kingdom was passed in 1889. The law, called the Public Bodies Corrupt Practices Act, outlawed the bribery of any official working under the capacity of a public body. The act was followed by the Prevention of Corruption Acts in 1906 and 1916. However, as the United Kingdom became more globalized, these acts were regarded as unsuitable for complying with international anti-corruption agreements. Pressure increased to reform these laws. In 2008 a working party for the Organisation for Economic Co-operation and Development (OECD) insisted on new regulation. In 2009 a bribery bill was introduced, and eventually became the Bribery Act of 2010. It took effect in 2011. While many herald the Bribery Act as taking a strong stance against bribery and corruption, others believe the law may actually be too harsh. Concern that items traditionally seen as gifts could now be perceived as bribes have prompted many companies to update their anti-corruption policies and codes of conduct.

The Bribery Act includes provisions against all forms of bribery. The Act states the two general offenses as, first, the offering, promising, or giving of a bribe to any government official, and second, the acceptance or request for a bribe by any government official. The Bribery Act places liability on organizations for not detecting bribery in their operations and failing to adopt adequate procedures to detect bribes. This part of the Act is unusual because it is a "strict liability" offense, meaning the organization's intent is irrelevant; if it fails to adequately detect bribery for whatever reason, even if it acted in good faith, it is liable. The Bribery Act extends to companies within the United Kingdom operating abroad and to companies present in the United Kingdom. In other words, any company with operations in the United Kingdom is subject to this law. While penalties vary, violating the Bribery Act can carry a maximum of 10 years in prison, unlimited fines, and the possibility of the confiscation of property.

While the FCPA and the Bribery Act are similar in many ways, there are significant differences between the two. The Bribery Act is generally believed to be more encompassing than the FCPA. While the FCPA allows for facilitation payments, recognizing in some countries that it might be hard for businesses to get routine transactions done in a timely manner without them, the Bribery Act leaves no room for these payments. After facing pressure from small- and mid-sized businesses, the U.K. government has agreed to review and potentially lessen the restrictions against facilitation payments. For now facilitation payments remain illegal under the Act, but there have been very few investigations into facilitation payments, which suggests possible leniency in practice. Because of the new law, global organizations such as Hewlett-Packard began updating their codes of conduct to provide additional guidance on bribery.

Additionally, while the FCPA is specifically concerned with bribing foreign or government officials, the Bribery Act also makes it illegal to pay bribes to private and public officials or enterprises. This means a person who offers a bribe could be liable under the Bribery Act even if the bribe was not to a foreign official. Another difference is liability. Under the FCPA a company only has strict liability for bribery as it relates to accounting provisions for public companies. However, the Bribery Act applies strict liability to any commercial firm that does not have "adequate controls" for preventing bribery.

Some companies worry the Bribery Act will make it too hard to conduct business. The strict liability offense made firms particularly worried they could be held liable for bribery even if the majority of the company was not aware bribery was taking place. However, like the FCPA, penalties under the Bribery Act might be reduced if the company is found to have adequate controls against corruption and a proactive corporate culture supporting ethical conduct. Companies must also report bribery to the proper authorities the moment the bribery is discovered. While neither law states a firm will *not* be prosecuted because it reported bribery, active cooperation may significantly reduce the severity of penalties imposed, and officials can examine the firm to see if it adopted a proactive approach toward combating bribery. How a prosecution would impact the public interest is also considered when deciding on potential penalties for bribery violations. Finally, while there are no clear rules distinguishing gifts given as an act of hospitality from bribes, the Serious Fraud Office of the United Kingdom has stated it will not pursue reasonable gifts of hospitality.

PENALTIES UNDER THE FCPA AND THE U.K. BRIBERY ACT

The following section provides examples of companies or individuals found to be in violation of bribery laws. Table 1 provides a brief summary of additional companies fined under the FCPA. While many firms have been fined under the FCPA, the relative newness of the Bribery Act means that as yet there have been few prosecutions. However, the prosecutions that have occurred demonstrate the Serious Fraud Office in the United Kingdom takes the topic of bribery seriously.

TABLE 1 Companies Accused of Violating the FCPA

Firm	Accusation
Avon	Bribed foreign officials in Asia
Johnson & Johnson	Bribed doctors in Europe and offered kickbacks in Iraq
IBM	Bribed officials in South Korea with cash and gifts
Walmart	Bribed Mexican officials to win zoning permits
HP	Bribed officials in Mexico, Russia, and Poland

© Cengage Learning 2015

Pfizer

It is important for companies to carefully monitor their own practices and also those of their subsidiaries. In August 2012 the SEC charged Pfizer Inc. with violating the FCPA when its subsidiaries allegedly bribed doctors and other health care professionals employed by foreign governments to win business. The SEC charges stated that employees from Pfizer's subsidiaries in countries including Russia, China, the Czech Republic, and Italy made improper payments to foreign public officials in exchange for regulatory approvals and increased sales. Pfizer was charged with attempting to cover up these bribes through illegal accounting measures by recording these transactions as promotional activities, marketing, and other deceptive entries.

Ultimately, Pfizer was charged with two criminal counts: conspiracy to violate the FCPA, and a violation of the FCPA's anti-bribery provisions. However, the prosecutors agreed to defer prosecution and drop the charges if, after two years, Pfizer continued to take steps to correct and prevent such actions from reoccurring. Such remedial actions included proactively enforcing an anti-corruption program and appointing a senior executive to serve as chief compliance and risk officer. Furthermore, Pfizer was required to appoint compliance heads for each of its business units as well as develop an executive compliance committee. To settle the case, Pfizer and two subsidiaries agreed to pay $60.2 million. Ultimately, while Pfizer maintains that top leaders were unaware of the bribery, the action taken against the company shows it is still considered to be responsible.

Siemens: FCPA's Global Reach

In many cases the FCPA has resulted in significant penalties for foreign companies. An example of this is the company Siemens Aktiengesellschaft, a German company and global multinational in electronics and electrical engineering. Because Siemens's American Depositary Receipts (ADRs) are traded on the New York Stock Exchange, the company is subject to the FCPA even though it is a foreign firm.

In 2008 the U.S. Department of Justice alleged Siemens engaged in a global pattern of bribery and made thousands of payments to foreign government officials totaling more than $1.4 billion. The investigation suggested these practices were covered up and supported by inadequate internal controls. Several senior executives were involved in or had knowledge about the bribery. By the time of the ruling, these dishonest practices had resulted in a strong negative impact on the company's corporate culture, since many employees at different levels of the firm appeared to have knowledge of the bribery.

In 2008 Siemens pleaded guilty to violating both the Anti-Bribery and Company Records and Internal Control provisions of the FCPA. Siemens agreed to pay a fine of more than $800 million for violating the FCPA, as well as a fine in Munich, Germany for the board's failure to assume its proper supervisory responsibilities in the case. At the time of the judgment, this was an unprecedented case because of the geographic reach and scale of the bribery. Siemens is an example of the global reach of the FCPA. Currently there are several hundred non-U.S. companies with shares traded on the U.S. stock exchange that are subject to the FCPA.

Bribery is such a routine component of business transactions in some parts of the world that it is often overlooked as a practice capable of causing far-reaching damage. In reality, bribery has the potential to inflict social adversity on a variety of stakeholders. Transparent business transactions deter this deceitful behavior while encouraging fair and ethical market competition. The risks of global bribery are prevalent to everyone in the marketplace where it is used.

Ralph Lauren: Value of Cooperation with the FCPA

While corporations may take steps to avoid corruption and bribery, in a multinational and multicultural business environment, corrupt practices can still occur. As a result, how corporations respond to discovered problems has significant financial and reputational repercussions. This can best be seen in the case of Ralph Lauren Corporation, a designer and marketer of apparel, accessories, home furnishings, and fragrances. During an effort to improve its worldwide internal controls and compliance efforts in 2010, Ralph Lauren discovered its Argentine subsidiary paid bribes to government officials to improperly secure the importation of their products in Argentina. These bribes totaled $593,000 paid out over four years. Within two weeks of uncovering the illegal actions, Ralph Lauren reported these findings to the SEC and cooperated with the subsequent bribery probe.

In 2013 the SEC entered into a non-prosecution agreement (NPA) with Ralph Lauren, the first NPA the SEC had ever entered into for violations of the FCPA. The SEC stated it would not charge Ralph Lauren with violating the FCPA because of the company's prompt response, thoroughness of its investigation, and cooperation with authorities. In return, Ralph Lauren agreed to pay more than $700,000 in illicit profits and interest earned from the bribes that the subsidiary paid out over the four-year period. However, this amount was minimal in comparison to the financial, labor, and reputational costs Ralph Lauren would have incurred if it had been prosecuted for bribery.

Ralph Lauren is an exemplary case that will likely be used by the SEC as a model for companies to follow when discovering FCPA violations. George S. Canellos, former Acting Director of the SEC's Division of Enforcement, remarked that the SEC wanted to send a clear message that responding appropriately to such misconduct when discovered is beneficial to the company. Furthermore, the Ralph Lauren NPA demonstrates what the SEC views as corporate cooperation with the SEC. While violations of the FCPA may occur despite a corporation's best efforts, Ralph Lauren is an example of the benefits of prompt action and cooperation in light of any such discovery.

Prosecutions under the U.K. Bribery Act

Due to the recent passage of the U.K. Bribery Act in 2010, there have been few instances of prosecution. The first to be prosecuted under the Bribery Act was Clerk Munir Yakub Patel. Patel was convicted of accepting a bribe of £500 ($774) in exchange for not inputting details of a traffic summons into a court database. He was sentenced to four years in prison. The second conviction levied under the Bribery Act was for Mawia Mushtaq, who offered licensing officials £300 ($459) in exchange for passing him on a taxi driver test. A more recent conviction involves a student accused of attempting to bribe his tutor to change his dissertation grade. The student was sentenced to 12 months in prison.

Surprisingly, none of these initial prosecutions were actually carried out by the United Kingdom's Serious Fraud Office (SFO), which was expected to be the primary enforcer of the Bribery Act, but by other governmental agencies. The SFO's first action under the Bribery Act was not until 2013, when it charged three men with making and accepting bribes as part of a conspiracy to defraud U.K. biofuel investors using false sales invoices and misleading accounting. Two of the men were convicted of violating the Bribery Act and were sentenced to six and four years, respectively, in addition to sentences for other fraud-related charges.

These initial applications of the Bribery Act—prosecution of U.K. nationals in their individual capacities—differ significantly from the intent and history of the FCPA, which has frequently been used to prosecute foreign officials and corporations. While the United States government might prosecute individuals found guilty of bribing non-foreign officials under fraud charges, such bribery would not be considered a violation of the FCPA. These early prosecutions under the Bribery Act emphasize the British government's commitment to combating bribery in every sphere of life.

While these initial convictions under the Bribery Act dealt with individuals, the SFO has expressed its commitment to using it against offending companies as well, and has stated it has other investigations that are ongoing. Therefore, companies face increased pressure to carefully monitor the ethics and compliance of their operations. For example, Rolls-Royce is being investigated by the SFO for allegedly paying $20 million to the son of the former president of Indonesia, as well as for potential bribery in China and other countries. However, because the alleged bribery occurred before July 2011, when the Bribery Act took effect, it cannot be prosecuted under the Act. However, the firm could still be found culpable for bribery under another law, and a civil settlement is a possibility.

Despite the risks of penalties for bribery, an Ernst & Young survey revealed that only about half of British firms adequately check their suppliers to ensure compliance with the Bribery Act. As the actions of the SFO and the penalties under the Bribery Act attest, this ethical failure can result in significant costs to a firm.

Alstom: Bribery Leads to Convictions in both the United States and the United Kingdom

With multiple countries passing anti-bribery laws that have a global reach, there is a serious risk that an international company engaging in bribery could be prosecuted, and punished, multiple times by different countries for an offense. This is essentially what has happened to Alstom, a France-based power and transportation company. After an intensive, multi-year investigation, the company pled guilty in the United States to multiple violations of the FCPA, including paying tens of millions of dollars in bribes to secure business in many countries around the world, falsifying its accounting records to cover up its wrongdoing, refusing to cooperate with the FCPA investigation, and failing to implement proper internal controls. As part of its guilty plea, the company agreed to pay over $772 million in penalties. Several of its independent subsidiaries also pleaded guilty to similar offenses, each with their own penalties and punishments.

At the same time, the U.K. SFO brought charges against two of Alstom's British subsidiaries for similar offenses. These charges were not brought under the Bribery Act as they occurred prior to 2011, but they are punishable under other criminal bribery laws. If convicted, the company will face further fines and penalties in the United Kingdom.

Alstom's situation may be somewhat exceptional considering the extent and global reach of its acts of bribery; U.S. Deputy Attorney General James Cole called it "astounding in its breadth, its brazenness and its worldwide consequences." However, it highlights the potential for companies engaged in global wrongdoing to face multiplying charges as more countries pass wide-reaching anti-bribery laws. Such companies should pay even closer attention to establishing ethical internal cultures and strong compliance programs, as well as keeping close scrutiny on their operations to prevent any possibility of illegal bribery.

NATIONAL INSTITUTIONS AND THE IMPACT OF BRIBERY

To truly understand the impact of bribery on a country's society and economy, the influence of institutions and their tolerance of bribery must be examined. Organizations operate based on taken-for-granted institutional norms and rules. Institutions include political, social, and economic conventions. For example, in the political area, governments develop legislation to regulate business activities, including bribery. In Mexico bribery is not considered as major a concern as in the United States. While the U.S. Department of Justice views the FCPA as a top priority, in Mexico the authorities were unconcerned when Walmart allegedly paid government officials substantial sums to speed up zoning and licensing agreements. Social institutions also provide conventions of acceptable behavior. Again, in Mexico it is not unusual for individuals to pay bribes to law enforcement officers to avoid traffic violations. Economic systems have embedded conventions as well. Often bribery is more typical in communist countries such as China and is seen as an acceptable way of doing business. Nations with weaker institutions tend to have more incidences of bribery, which indicates corruption in the social, political, and economic sectors. Countries with high levels of corruption, such as Somalia and North Korea, therefore face political, social, and environmental costs.

The prominent political and social costs of bribery include the people's lack of trust in government. When politicians are corrupt, citizens have no incentive to follow rules and instead engage in the same type of corrupt behavior modeled in the political system. Transparency International reports that citizens who view their leaders as corrupt are more likely to act accordingly. Table 2 provides a list of the countries most likely to use bribery to conduct business. Civil unrest that can result from corruption carries the risk of inflicting extreme violence and harm. Thus, the political implications of bribery include a cognitive distancing and lack of trust in government as well as a culture permeated with corruption. Governments with a high amount of corruption are likely to be run by despots with little incentive to protect or acknowledge universal human rights.

The economic costs of corruption can be seen throughout the world. Mexico, rated at 103 for corruption in a ranking of 174 countries (174th being most corrupt) by Transparency International, received negative press when Walmex (Wal-Mart de Mexico) paid bribes to government officials in order to accelerate store expansions. Somalia, ranked as the most corrupt country in the world by Transparency International, is associated with piracy. It is important to realize the economic costs of bribery fall disproportionately on

TABLE 2 Ten Countries Most Likely to Use Bribery in Business

1. Russia	6. Argentina
2. China	7. Saudi Arabia
3. Mexico	8. Turkey
4. Indonesia	9. India
5. United Arab Emirates	10. Taiwan

Source: Associated Press, "The 10 Countries Most Likely to Use Bribery in Business," *Huffington Post*, November 2, 2011, http://www.huffingtonpost.com/2011/11/02/bribery-business-countries-most-likely_n_1071452.html#slide=449030 (accessed February 23, 2015).

the bottom half of the population living in poverty. A country perceived as lacking ethical integrity experiences reduced tourism and lowered regard from the rest of the world. There is an obvious relationship between the level of corruption in a country and its socioeconomic standing.

Countries with high levels of bribery and corruption are also more likely to have especially damaging environmental incidents. In other words, bribes constitute an ethical lapse that overshadows environmental interests. People engaging in bribery are looking to increase wealth and/or gain a competitive advantage in the marketplace. These are the same people that are unlikely to spend extra resources to protect the environment. Furthermore, places with high levels of corruption often have dictatorial and hierarchical types of government where there is little balance of power in government and few consequences for ignoring environmental initiatives.

Beyond the natural environment, bribery also hurts businesses and the individuals they deal with. When companies are disadvantaged by unfair competition from bribery, wealth distribution becomes more polarized in the marketplace and companies may be forced to lay off workers. The World Bank's conservative estimate of the annual worldwide cost of bribery is $1 trillion.

Combating bribery and corruption includes implementing and enforcing stiff anti-bribery regulations. Government, industry, and society must take a strong normative stand against the practice of bribery. Complacency toward bribery eventually leads to diffusion of responsibility, where the practice becomes prevalent and acceptable. Instilling descriptive values against bribery is only successful if a normative stance against the practice is followed. A world without bribery would mean a more competitive and ethical marketplace for companies and individuals.

Widespread corruption abroad imposes enormous costs on international business and causes damage to business as a whole. It undermines the integrity and effectiveness of governments, while simultaneously creating hardships for small- and medium-sized enterprises seeking to participate in the global economy. A culture of corruption raises the cost of penetrating foreign markets and undermines predictability and business confidence.

Overall, with the advent of the U.S. FCPA and U.K. Bribery Act, the potential implications for engaging in bribery have become stricter and more costly. However, there will always be some who attempt to find ways around the law. To support organizational compliance, top government officials must have strong market oversight by championing ethics training programs, enacting effective compliance and reporting mechanisms, and providing competitive structures that benefit the entities acting ethically. Unfair advantages in the marketplace that result from bribery inflict harm on a wide range of stakeholders. Reducing bribery strengthens political, economic, and social institutions, perpetuates a higher quality of life, and moves society toward a sustainable future.

CONCLUSION

It should be clear that bribery is a major ethical concern throughout the world. While many developed countries such as the United States and the United Kingdom have enacted laws to prevent bribery, in many other countries bribery is a part of the culture. This is because basic political, economic, and social institutions provide conventions for what is acceptable. If bribery is seen as an acceptable way to conduct business, then it will be more prevalent within a society. Bribery is considered to be unacceptable in many countries because it interferes with fairness in business relationships. It is also seen as stifling free competition and possibly resulting in inflated prices for consumers. Additionally, bribery creates conflicts of interest—for example, when an employee takes a bribe to gain a favorable position.

The companies given as examples in this case demonstrate that even highly respected businesses have difficulty fighting against bribery. This is because pressure is placed on many businesses to make payments in order to gain access to markets. An important takeaway is that many areas of bribery are gray areas because minor gifts or entertainment, while generally acceptable, can be questioned by stakeholders.

QUESTIONS FOR DISCUSSION

1. What are the differences between the provisions of the United States Foreign Corrupt Practices Act and the United Kingdom Bribery Act?
2. Check for more recent situations where companies have been accused of violating the Foreign Corrupt Practices Act. Why do you think these companies chose to engage in bribery?
3. Why is it so difficult to determine when a minor gift, entertainment, or incentive constitutes a bribe?

SOURCES

David Aaronberg and Nichola Higgins, "The Bribery Act 2010: all bark and no bite..?" *Archbold Review*, no. 5 (London: Sweet & Maxwell, 2010), ISSN 1756–7432; BBC News, "African corruption 'on the wane,'" July 10, 2007, http://news.bbc.co.uk/2/hi/business/6288400.stm (accessed February 23, 2015); Jeffrey Benzing, "Pfizer and Subsidiaries Settle FCPA Charges for $60.2 Million," *Main Justice*, August 7, 2012, http://www.mainjustice.com/justanticorruption/2012/08/07/pfizer-and-subsidiaries-settle-fcpa-charges-for-60-2-million/ (accessed February 23, 2015); Caroline Binham and Carola Hoyos, "SFO weighs deal to end Rolls-Royce probe," *Financial Times*, March 22, 2013, http://www.ft.com/intl/cms/s/0/ff136074-931e-11e2-b3be-00144feabdc0.html#axzz2SddrQtHr (accessed February 23, 2015); Caroline Binham and Elizabeth Rigby, "Relaxation of UK bribery law on government agenda," *Financial Times*, May 28, 2013, http://www.ft.com/intl/cms/s/0/cab2111c-c6c8-11e2-a861-00144feab7de.html#axzz2UcadHJe2 (accessed February 23, 2015); *Bloomberg Businessweek*, "I.B.M. to Settle Bribery Charges for $10 Million," *The New York Times*, March 18, 2011, http://www.nytimes.com/2011/03/19/business/global/19blue.html?_r=0 (accessed February 23, 2015); "Bribe conviction for court clerk Munir Patel UK-first," *BBC*, October 14, 2011, http://www.bbc.co.uk/news/uk-england-london-15310150 (accessed February 23, 2015); Siobhain Butterworth, "Government delays Bribery Act—again," *The Guardian*, July 23, 2010, http://www.guardian.co.uk/law/afua-hirsch-law-blog/2010/jul/23/bribery-act-law-bae (accessed February 23, 2015); Eric Carlson, "China's Overseas Bribery Law One Year On," *FCPA Blog*, May 29, 2012, http://www.fcpablog.com/blog/2012/5/29/chinasoverseas-bribery-law-one-year-on.html (accessed February 23, 2015); Richard L. Cassin, "SFO charges Alstom UK unit for bribes," *FCPA Blog*, July 24, 2014, http://www.fcpablog.com/blog/2014/7/24/sfo-charges-alstom-uk-unit-for-bribes.html (accessed February 23, 2015); Richard L. Cassin, "Alstom pays $772 million for FCPA settlement, SFO brings new charges," *The FCPA Blog*, December 22, 2014, http://www.fcpablog.com/blog/2014/12/22/alstom-pays-772-million-for-fcpa-settlement-sfo-brings-new-c.html (accessed February 23, 2015); Corpedia, "The Department of Justice and U.S. Securities and Exchange Commission Release Highly Anticipated Guidance on the Foreign Corrupt Practices Act: What does the Guidance Show and What does This Mean for Your Organization?," Aired on November 28, 2012; Criminal Division of the U.S. Department of Justice and the Enforcement Division of the U.S. Securities and Exchange Commission, A Resource Guide to the *U.S. Foreign Corrupt Practices Act*, November 14, 2012, http://www.justice.gov/criminal/fraud/fcpa/guide.pdf (accessed May 13, 2013); Stella Dawson, "Passage of Brazil anti-bribery bill key to OECD thumbs up," *Thomsen Reuters Foundation*, March 19, 2013, http://www.trust.org/item/?map=passage-of-brazil-anti-bribery-bill-key-to-oecd-thumbs-up/ (accessed February 23, 2015); Economist staff, "Hard to read," *The Economist*, January 29, 2014, http://www.economist.com/blogs/schumpeter/2014/01/brazil-s-new-anti-corruption-law (accessed February 23, 2015); David Gow, "Record US fine ends Siemens bribery scandal," *The Guardian*, December 15, 2008, http://www.guardian.co.uk/business/2008/dec/16/regulation-siemens-scandal-bribery (accessed February 23, 2015); Mary P. Hansen, "SEC Announces First Non-Prosecution Agreement Involving Foreign Corrupt Practices Act (FCPA) Violations," *The National Law Review*, April 27, 2013, http://www.natlawreview.com/article/sec-announces-first-non-prosecution-agreement-involving-foreign-corrupt-practices-ac (accessed February 23, 2015); Jaclyn Jaeger, "Brazil Passes Landmark Anti-Bribery Law," *Compliance Week*, July 9, 2013, http://www.complianceweek.com/blogs/enforcement-action/brazil-passes-landmark-anti-bribery-law#.VKH-hecB (accessed February 23, 2015); Daniel Kaufmann, "Six Questions on the Cost of Corruption with World Bank Institute Global Governance Director Daniel Kaufmann," *World Bank Group*, http://web.worldbank.org/WBSITE/EXTERNAL/NEWS/0, cont entMDK:20190295~menuPK:34457~pagePK:34370~piPK:34424~theSitePK:4607,00.html (accessed May 13, 2013); Roseanne Kay and Kimberley Davies, "A fiery dissertation—the third conviction under the UK Bribery Act of 2010," Association of Corporate Counsel, April 30, 2013, http://www.lexology.com/library/detail.aspx?g=6a6d9625-b9dd-4fd9-bc46-003f1fb13643 (accessed February 23, 2015); Ian King and Tom Schoenberg, "HP Pays $108 Million to Settle U.S. Bribery Investigation," *Bloomberg*, April 9, 2014, http://www.bloomberg.com/news/articles/2014-04-09/hp-pays-108-million-to-settle-justice-department-bribery-probe (accessed February 23, 2015); Eric Kraeutler, Iain Wright, Benjamin D. Klein, Nicholas Greenwood and David Waldron, "United States: Serious Fraud Office Gets Tough in UK Bribery Act Enforcement Guidelines," *Morgan Lewis*, http://www.morganlewis.com/index.cfm/bnodeID/4409d6fd-1d3d-486a-9485-7ae3082396ba/fuseaction/publication.detail/publicationID/aafc7908-eda0-4377-812b-1c0cf88fd926 (accessed February 23, 2015); Tony Lewis, "Corporate Crime & Corruption Informer: First SFO UK Bribery Act Convictions," *fieldfisher*, December 10, 2014, http://www.fieldfisher.com/publications/2014/12/corporate-crime-and-corruption-informer-first-sfo-uk-bribery-act-convictions#sthash.zvdszllH.dpbs (accessed February 23, 2015); Jonathon Marciano, "Only half of British businesses vet their suppliers for UK Bribery Act compliance, according to Ernst & Young," *Ernst & Young*, March 5, 2013, http://www.ey.com/UK/en/Newsroom/News-releases/13-03-05---Only-half-of-British-businesses-vet-their-suppliers-for-UK-Bribery-Act-compliance (accessed February 23, 2015); Daniel Margolis and James Wheaton, "Non-U.S. Companies May Also be Subject to the FCPA," Pillsbury, Winthrop, Shaw Pitman, LLC, August 30, 2009. http://www.pillsburylaw.com/sitefiles/publications/39ab4865beb55357dc2348ac196767cf.pdf (accessed February 23, 2015); Dan Milmo, "Rolls-Royce faces bribery claim inquiry," *The Guardian*, December 9, 2012, http://www.guardian.co.uk/business/2012/dec/09/rolls-royce-faces-bribery-inquiry (accessed February 23, 2015); Nixon Peabody LLP, "Foreign Corrupt Practices Act (FCPA), 2013, http://www.nixonpeabody.com/foreign_corrupt_practices_act_FCPA (accessed February 23, 2015); OECD, "OECD Convention on Combating Bribery of Foreign Public Officials in International Business Transactions," http://www.oecd.org/corruption/oecdantibriberyconvention.htm (accessed February 23, 2015); Andrew Parker, "SFO considers more arrests in Rolls-Royce bribery probe," *Financial Times*, September 2, 2014, http://www.ft.com/intl/cms/s/0/d31ffaf8-32c9-11e4-93c6-00144feabdc0.html#axzz3OaAvkYl4 (accessed February 23, 2015); Ben Protess, "Former Top S.E.C.

Enforcer Returns to Milbank," *The New York Times*, February 12, 2014, http://dealbook.nytimes.com/2014/02/12/former-top-s-e-c-enforcer-returns-to-milbank/ (accessed February 23, 2015); "Public Bodies Corrupt Practices Act 1889," *legislation.gov.uk*, http://www.legislation.gov.uk/ukpga/Vict/52-53/69 (accessed February 23, 2015); Reuters, "UK adds to Alstom's legal woes as power unit faces bribe charge," December 22, 2014, http://www.reuters.com/article/2014/12/22/alstom-bribery-uk-idUSL6N0U62C220141222 (accessed February 23, 2015); Kevin Roberts, Jarod G. Taylor, and Duncan Grieve, "UK Bribery Act Comes to Life?" *Morrison Foerster*, 2013, http://media.mofo.com/files/Uploads/Images/130815-UK-Bribery-Act.pdf (accessed February 23, 2015); Kevin Robinson, "Pressure Gauge: Facilitation Payments under the UK Bribery Act, *Fraud Intelligence*," *Morgan Lewis*, April 2, 2014, http://www.morganlewis.co.uk/index.cfm/fuseaction/publication.detail/publicationID/25136950-1d86-4cba-a4ba-58fcc9be88ce (accessed February 23, 2015); Jonathon D. Rockoff and Christopher M. Matthews, "Pfizer Settles Federal Bribery Investigation," *The Wall Street Journal*, August 7, 2012, http://online.wsj.com/article/SB10000872396390444246904577575110723150588.html (accessed February 23, 2015); Samuel Rubenfeld, "SFO Secures First Bribery Act Conviction,"*The Wall Street Journal*, December 5, 2015, http://blogs.wsj.com/riskandcompliance/2014/12/05/sfo-secures-its-first-bribery-act-conviction/ (accessed February 23, 2015); Securities and Exchange Commission, "SEC Announces Non-Prosecution Agreement with Ralph Lauren Corporation Involving FCPA Misconduct," April 22, 2013, http://www.sec.gov/news/press/2013/2013-65.htm (accessed February 23, 2015); Securities and Exchange Commission, "SEC Charges Pfizer with FCPA Violations," August 7, 2012, http://www.sec.gov/news/press/2012/2012-152.htm (accessed February 23, 2015); Siemens AG, *Siemens homepage*, http://www.siemens.com/entry/cc/en/ (accessed February 23, 2015); Florian Stamm, (Spring 2006). "The Foreign Corrupt Practices Act: Keeping All Hands on the Table," *Trust the Leaders*, Issue 15 (Spring 2006): 4–7; Valerie Surgenor and David Flint, "United Kingdom: The Bribery Act Strikes Again," *Mondaq*, http://www.mondaq.com/x/211498/White+Collar+Crime+Fraud/The+Bribery+Act+Strikes+Again (accessed February 23, 2015); Transparency International, "Corruptions Perceptions Index 2014: Results," http://www.transparency.org/cpi2014/results (accessed February 23, 2015); Transparency International UK, "The Bribery Act," http://www.transparency.org.uk/our-work/bribery-act (accessed February 23, 2015); Transparency USA, "U.S. FCPA vs. UK Bribery Act," http://www.transparency-usa.org/documents/FCPAvsBriberyAct.pdf (accessed February 23, 2015); The United States Department of Justice, "Alstom Pleads Guilty and Agrees to Pay $772 Million Criminal Penalty to Resolve Foreign Bribery Charges," December 22, 2014, http://www.justice.gov/opa/pr/alstom-pleads-guilty-and-agrees-pay-772-million-criminal-penalty-resolve-foreign-bribery (accessed February 23, 2015); The United States Department of Justice, "Foreign Corrupt Practices Act," http://www.justice.gov/criminal/fraud/fcpa/ (accessed February 23, 2015); Martin Walter, Michelle A. Luebke, and Dmitry Zhdankin, "The Impact of Corruption on the Environment," *SSRN*, November 26, 2012, http://papers.ssrn.com/sol3/papers.cfm?abstract_id=2181029 (accessed February 23, 2015); Graeme Wearden, "Queen's speech 2009: bribery bill," *The Guardian*, November 18, 2009, http://www.guardian.co.uk/politics/2009/nov/18/queens-speech-bribery-bill (accessed February 23, 2015); Michael Weinstein, Robert Meyer, and Jeffrey Clark, "The UK Bribery Act vs. the U.S. FCPA," *Ethisphere*, April 22, 2011, http://anticorruption.ethisphere.com/the-uk-bribery-act-vs-the-u-s-fcpa/ (accessed May 9, 2013); Alexandra Wrage and Ann Richardson, "Siemens AG—Violations of the Foreign Corrupt Practices Act," *International Legal Materials* 48 no. 2 (2009): 232–234. doi:10.2307/25691362.

CASE 19

Multilevel Marketing under Fire: Herbalife Defends Its Business Model*

INTRODUCTION

Herbalife International is the third largest direct selling, multilevel marketing company in the world. Its product line consists of weight management and nutrition products. These products are not sold in retail stores; rather, consumers interact with independent contractors, who are often everyday people like themselves, to order the products. Herbalife's headquarters are located in Los Angeles, California, and they operate in many countries throughout the world. Herbalife is a publicly traded company that is both loved and hated by investors and consumers.

This case first discusses the history of the company from its founding to its present status, followed by a description of the types of products Herbalife offers. Then we will get into a discussion of multilevel marketing and the role of independent contractors in the direct selling model. Next will be an analysis of pyramid schemes and why they are often confused with the multilevel marketing model. We then examine Herbalife to determine whether it is a pyramid scheme.

We will illuminate the role of hedge fund investor William Ackman, who has prominently accused Herbalife of being an elaborate pyramid scheme, in the backdrop of Herbalife's business model and describe his contentions with the company as well as some of the criticisms levied against him. The case shows that while Ackman's accusations may be the most widely known, Herbalife has had to face similar allegations (mostly referring to pyramid schemes) throughout the course of its existence. The case then briefly overviews Herbalife's social responsibility program, and finally ends with overall conclusions.

HISTORY

Herbalife is a company that focuses on nutrition, weight management, and personal care products with independent contractors selling in more than 90 countries. Mark Hughes founded the company in 1980 out of a desire to create a safe alternative to other weight

*This case was prepared by Michelle Urban, Katy Melloy, Carin Malm, Emily McGowan, and Isaac Emmanuel for and under the direction of O.C. Ferrell and Linda Ferrell ©2015. Jennifer Sawayda provided editorial assistance. It was prepared for classroom discussion rather than to illustrate either effective or ineffective handling of an administrative, ethical, or legal decision by management. All sources used for this case were obtained through publicly available material.

loss products. Herbalife's first sales were made from out of the trunk of Hughes's car in Los Angeles, California, and two years later the company reached $2 million in sales. Herbalife was taken public in 1986 on the NASDAQ stock exchange. Since then, Herbalife has become a multibillion dollar global company.

In 1999 Hughes planned to take the company back to the private sector by purchasing all of its remaining shares, but this attempt was stopped as investors sought legal action. The next year, Mark Hughes died unexpectedly at the age of 44. Christopher Pair, who was Herbalife's former Chief Operating Officer (COO), then became President and Chief Executive Officer (CEO) of the company. His reign at Herbalife was cut short when he stepped down one year later.

An Internet retailer, Rbid.com, made a bid of $173 million to acquire Herbalife, but the Mark Hughes Family Trust rejected the offer. In 2002 the investment firm J.H. Whitney & Co. purchased the company along with another investor and took it back to the private sector. However, in 2004 Herbalife went public once again and was traded on the New York stock exchange. Michael O. Johnson has been Herbalife's CEO since 2003. The company currently employs 7,800 people and has almost three million independent contractors throughout the world.

PRODUCTS

Herbalife sells weight management, targeted nutrition, energy and fitness, and personal care products, all intended to support a healthy lifestyle. Formula 1 Nutritional Shake Mix is a protein and fiber shake with minerals, vitamins, and nutrients offered in a variety of flavors. Formula 2 Multivitamin Complex is a multivitamin that contains over 20 vitamins, minerals, and herbs essential to healthy living. Formula 3 Cell Activator promotes absorption of minerals and vitamins while improving energy levels. These three core products are at the heart of the Herbalife product line and serve as the baseline for customer nutrition and weight management goals.

The weight management line consists of a variety of Formula 1 protein shakes, supplements, weight loss enhancers, protein bars, and snacks, all serving the purpose of helping customers attain their weight goals. There are three weight management program sets, each with a combination of shakes, supplements, and enhancers designed for different types of weight management needs. Each component of these sets can also be purchased separately. The Personalized Protein Powder and the Protein Drink Mix offerings provide an alternative to traditional meals while supplying energy and curbing hunger cravings, whether consumers want to lose or maintain their weight or build muscle mass. The enhancers and supplements offer a mix of vitamins, minerals, herbs, and nutrients. For example, Prolessa Duo and Snack Defense work to stave off hunger in order to control weight gain and help the body process sugars more efficiently. Other enhancers, such as Total Control, boost metabolism, energy, and alertness, while Thermo-Bond helps the digestive system. Cell-U-Loss helps the body eliminate unnecessary water and rejuvenate skin with its combination of herbal extracts. An assortment of healthy snacks and beverages are also offered in this line, such as protein bars, soups, teas, and soy nuts.

Targeted nutrition products include dietary and nutritional supplements that contain herbs, vitamins, minerals, and other natural ingredients to strengthen specific areas of the body that tend to be problematic for many people. For example, Tri-Shield helps the heart stay healthy by maintaining good cholesterol levels and providing antioxidants; Ocular

Defense Formula and Joint Support Advanced offer nutritional aid for the eyes and joints of aging adults; Active Fiber Complex and Herbal Aloe Powder help those with digestive issues; RoseGuard and Schizandra Plus strengthen the liver, immune system, and cells; and Relax Now and Sleep Now, which are part of the stress management line, serve to promote ease and rest. Herbalife also offers nutrition products specifically designed for women, men, and children.

In addition, Herbalife provides energy and hydration options for those engaged in sports and fitness activities. Customers can choose from drink mix-ins such as the H_3O Fitness Drink, which enhances clarity and rehydrates the body, or they can go with supplements such as N-R-G Nature's Raw Guarana Tablets, which also promote mental clarity. Herbalife24 is an athlete-focused program set, including drink mix-ins, shakes, and supplements, that includes formulas for hydration, prolonged endurance, restoration of strength, and recovery.

Herbalife's personal care products include skin cleansers, moisturizers, lotions, shampoos, and conditioners. In this product line, Herbalife again offers program sets called Herbalife SKIN, containing groups of cleansers, moisturizers, and creams customized for different types of skin from dry to oily. There are also a variety of individual Herbalife SKIN products, such as Energizing Herbal Toner and Firming Eye Gel. Another group of products, called Herbal Aloe, is comprehensive, including Strengthening Shampoo and Conditioner, Hand & Body Wash, Hand & Body Cream, Soothing Gel, Bath and Body Bar, and more, and is advertised to improve the look and feel of hair and skin. Other items include antiaging products and specialized skincare products such as Body Buffing Scrub and Contouring Crème.

MULTILEVEL MARKETING

Direct selling is the marketing of products to end consumers through person-to-person sales presentations at non-retail locations such as consumer homes, jobs, or online. This should not be confused with on-site salespeople such as at car dealerships; direct sellers go to the consumer, such as at their home or job, to sell the product. Also, direct sellers are generally not actually employees of the companies they represent but rather autonomous individuals who enter into independent contractor agreements with a company to sell its products.

People are attracted to becoming direct sellers for many reasons. Some are passionate about a product and want to promote the company. Others want to receive a discount on their personal orders, a common perk of being a direct seller. Many find working as a direct seller to be a flexible, part-time opportunity for extra income. Additionally, a lot of direct sellers simply enjoy the social aspect of the job.

Within the direct selling model are two compensation models: single-level marketing and multilevel marketing. Single-level marketing is when direct sellers only earn commissions for sales they make themselves. Multilevel marketing, sometimes called network marketing, means direct sellers earn income from their own sales of products as well as commissions from sales made by those they have recruited. The multilevel marketing model is permitted in nearly all countries, but is often strictly regulated and/or closely scrutinized due to its capacity to be abused and become a fraudulent pyramid scheme (discussed later in this case). In order for a multilevel marketing company to be legitimate, it cannot force sales or recruitment. It should also not be necessary for direct sellers to recruit others in order to earn a profit; this should merely be a choice available to sellers if they want to increase their earnings.

Nearly 75 percent of Herbalife members are single-level distributors, meaning they do not sponsor other Herbalife sellers. These single-level Herbalife members simply buy products from the company at a discount and resell to customers and/or consume the products themselves. Since many of these members simply want a discount on these products for their personal use, they may not be as interested in making profits but simply enjoy the opportunity to receive these discounts. See Table 1 for the top ten global direct selling companies.

This aspect of direct selling, where the seller purchases products at a discount from the firm for his or her own use, is known as internal consumption. Internal consumption is common in many industries; for example, most retailers provide internal consumption incentives by offering discounts to their employees. Department stores, automobile manufacturers, and airline companies provide incentives such as discounts that encourage internal consumption. Many direct selling customers become resellers to get discounts on the products for their own use. They believe in the brands, use them, and want to "spread the word" by creating a broader sales and communication network. Some do not even necessarily care about making a profit from their status as a reseller. This is a common and legal

TABLE 1 Top Ten Direct Selling Companies

	Company Name and Product Line	2014 Revenue (USD Billions)
1	Amway Nutrition, Beauty, Bath and Body, Home, Jewelry, Food and Beverage, Fragrances	$10.80
2	Avon Cosmetics, Skin Care, Fragrance, Personal Care, Hair Care, Jewelry, Gifts	$8.90
3	Herbalife Nutrition, Weight Loss Management, Personal Care	$5.00
4	Mary Kay Cosmetics, Skin Care, Body and Sun, Men's Products, Fragrance Gifts	$4.00
5	Vorwerk Household Appliances and Cosmetics	$3.90
6	Natura Cosmetics	$3.20
7	Infinitus Health Products	$2.64
8	Tupperware Food Storage and Preparation, Cookware, Serving Items, Cosmetics, Beauty Products	$2.60
9	Nu Skin Skin Care	$2.57
10	JoyMain Health and Personal Care Products	$2.00

Source: Direct Selling News, "2014 DSN Global 100 List," *Direct Selling News*, 2015, http://directsellingnews.com/index.php/view/2015_dsn_global_100_list#.VYBMFXn_FVI (accessed June 16, 2015).

approach for direct selling products around the world. In fact, most direct selling companies use multilevel marketing and permit or even encourage internal consumption.

Despite the general acceptance of multilevel marketing as a legitimate business model, a few countries have sharply restricted or even banned multilevel marketing, limiting direct selling to single-level marketing only. China, for example, only allows international direct selling companies to do business within its borders if they sign contracts saying they will not employ the multilevel marketing aspect of direct selling. It believes multilevel marketing is indistinguishable from or too closely linked to fraudulent activities such as pyramid schemes. There are key differences between pyramid schemes and multilevel marketing compensation models. For example, sellers caught up in pyramid schemes can generally only make a profit by recruiting others, as the product being sold has little value or is highly overpriced. Pyramid schemes also reward recruitment whether or not the new recruit sells anything, whereas multilevel marketing companies do not. The similarities and differences between the pyramid scheme and multilevel marketing are discussed in detail later in this case.

HERBALIFE'S DIRECT SELLERS

There are nearly three million independent contractor direct sellers of Herbalife products. Most, if not all, of them personally use these products as well. Many are attracted to the low startup cost of selling Herbalife, which begins at about $60 for a kit. For this price, new sellers will receive the Mini Herbalife Member Pack, which includes forms, applications, a tote bag, and samples of various Herbalife products. The pack includes informational and training materials which educate the contractor on using and retailing the products, business basics, and how to build a sales and marketing plan. The next step up for a new contractor is the Full Herbalife Member Pack for about $90, which includes everything in the mini pack as well as full-sized products (not just samples). Of course, once the new distributor starts selling, he or she will have to begin purchasing inventory to resell, but a member kit is the only purchase required to become a Herbalife network member, begin receiving discounts on Herbalife products, etc. There is no "fee" to join; the only money spent is for the value of the kit.

Sellers enjoy discounts on Herbalife products ranging from 25 to 50 percent depending on the level of contractorship (contractors move up levels by achieving certain sales and recruitment goals). Herbalife sellers usually purchase inventory themselves and then resell it to buyers; however, it is possible for the distributor to make the sale and then have Herbalife ship the product directly to the buyer. Contractors can sell the products at any price they want and can generally make most decisions on how they want to position and sell their Herbalife inventory, although they are subject to both legal and company rules and restrictions. The more successful an Herbalife seller, the higher up he or she moves on the contractorship ladder, gaining corresponding benefits at each step such as increased product discounts and networking and training opportunities. Seller success is measured by "Volume Points" and "Royalty Override Points." Volume Points are awarded when the seller purchases Herbalife products for resale or has Herbalife ship products directly to a buyer, and Royalty Override Points are accumulated based on the volume of products sold by the seller's personally sponsored recruits. Royalty Override Points, however, cannot be earned until the seller has already reached a certain contractorship level through his or her own sales.

To go from basic distributor to the Senior Consultant level, a Herbalife member must accumulate a minimum of 500 Volume Points in one month. To keep the Senior Consultant designation and perks, the member must maintain that minimum level of sales monthly. The second level of Senior Consultant requires 2,000 Volume Points in a month, or a seller can be named a Success Builder for the month by arranging a single sale valued at over 1,000 Volume Points. Levels after these include Qualified Producer (2,500 Volume Points accumulated within one to three months), Supervisor (either 4,000 Value Points in one month, 2,500 Value Points in each of two consecutive months, or 5,000 personally purchased Value Points within 12 months), and World Team (either 10,000 Volume Points in one month, 2,500 Value Points in each of four consecutive months, or 500 Royalty Override Points in one month). Once a contractor reaches the Supervisor level, he or she unlocks the maximum product discount of 50 percent as well as the ability to earn Royalty Override Points through sales of his or her recruits.

In the event that a contractor no longer wants to sell Herbalife products, the company will buy back any remaining inventory the contractor has on hand. Herbalife goes beyond the Direct Selling Association's ethical guidelines for buying back products by reimbursing the distributor for everything he or she initially paid for (100 percent buyback policy). The company also limits the amount of inventory a seller can initially buy in order to avoid association with inventory loading, defined by the Federal Trade Commission (FTC) as requiring a contractor to make a large upfront purchase of nonreturnable inventory (a fraud-inviting tactic often used by pyramid schemes). To renew their membership, contractors pay a $10 annual membership fee to Herbalife.

The Herbalife business model has succeeded due to the company's excellent products and customer support. Most of its distributors do not have a physical store location but practice direct selling from home. They are not employees but independent businesspeople who choose how they want to operate. However, there are strict company policies and legal requirements that contractors must abide by regulating product information, sales techniques, advertising, lead generation, social media, and related issues. For instance, members used to be able to sell online on their own websites, so long as they followed certain rules. In 2014, however, in response to regulatory scrutiny into its distributors' online marketing statements, Herbalife disallowed independent online selling. Instead, it created a centralized e-commerce section on its website which, when a customer places an order, randomly connects the customer to a suitable distributor to complete the sale and follow up with the classic person-to-person interaction of direct selling. This is now the only way Herbalife contractors can sell online. Contractors are also not permitted to resell products in retail stores (other than in China, where retail store sales are permitted).

Herbalife's selling policies are guided by the principles of the World Federation of Direct Selling Association (WFDSA) and the Direct Selling Association (DSA) in the United States. The WFDSA promotes ethical practices in direct selling globally through advocacy and strong relationships with government, consumers, and academia. The DSA also emphasizes ethical practices and requires that members such as Herbalife adhere to the DSA's code of ethics (See Table 2). This code of ethics recognizes the importance of a fair and responsible approach to direct selling, since direct selling requires sensitive and personal one-on-one interaction that can lead to undue pressure placed upon consumers. The code has no tolerance for deceptive or unlawful practices regarding recruits and customers; requires that direct sellers provide accurate and truthful information about the price, quality, promotion, etc. of the products; illuminates and enforces the need for a clear record of the sales made by contractors; necessitates that warranties and guarantees be fully acknowledged; requires sellers to clearly identify themselves to customers and maintain

TABLE 2 Direct Selling Association Code of Ethics (Summary Version)

As a consumer you should expect salespeople to:
Tell you who they are, why they're approaching you and what products they are selling.
Promptly end a demonstration or presentation at your request.
Provide a receipt with a clearly stated cooling off period permitting the consumer to withdraw from a purchase order within a minimum of three days from the date of the purchase transaction and receive a full refund of the purchase price.
Explain how to return a product or cancel an order.
Provide you with promotional materials that contain the address and telephone number of the direct selling company.
Provide a written receipt that identifies the company and salesperson, including contact information for either.
Respect your privacy by calling at a time that is convenient for you.
Safeguard your private information.
Provide accurate and truthful information regarding the price, quality, quantity, performance, and availability of their product or service.
Offer a written receipt in language you can understand.
Offer a complete description of any warranty or guarantee.

As a salesperson, you should expect a DSA member company to:
Provide you with accurate information about the company's compensation plan, products, and sales methods.
Describe the relationship between you and the company in writing.
Be accurate in any comparisons about products, services, or opportunities.
Refrain from any unlawful or unethical recruiting practice and exorbitant entrance or training fees.
Ensure that you are not just buying products solely to qualify for downline commissions.
Ensure that any materials marketed to you by others in the salesforce are consistent with the company's policies, are reasonably priced and have the same return policy as the company's.
Require you to abide by the requirements of the Code of Ethics.
Safeguard your private information.
Provide adequate training to help you operate ethically.
Base all actual and potential sales and earning claims on documented facts.
Encourage you to purchase only the inventory you can sell in a reasonable amount of time.
Repurchase marketable inventory and sales aids you have purchased within the past 12 months at 90 percent or more of your original cost if you decide to leave the business.
Explain the repurchase option in writing.
Have reasonable startup fees and costs.

Source: Direct Selling Association, "Summary Version of the DSA Code of Ethics," *Direct Selling Association*, http://www.dsa.org/code-of-ethics/code-of-ethics-(full-text) (accessed June 16, 2015).

the confidential information of their customers; prohibits signature pyramid scheme practices; and provides guidelines on inventory purchases, earnings reporting, inventory loading, fee payments, and training.

A 2013 independent survey conducted by Nielsen, a reputable global information and measurement company, showed the number of end consumers Herbalife serves in the United States. The study, which took place online over the course of two months, sampled

10,525 consumers and was balanced in terms of demographics, income, and geographic placement. The results indicated that 3.3 percent of the general U.S. population made a Herbalife purchase sometime within the last three months. This percentage of the population translates into 7.9 million customers. This number does include Herbalife's direct sellers as internal consumers, but the number of U.S. contractors at the time was only approximately 550,000, indicating that the number of end users was much higher than the number of independent contractors. This is a very good sign for the strength and legitimacy of the company's model, as pyramid schemes generally do not make significant sales outside of their own networks. Additionally, the study showed that those who had made a purchase in the last three months tended to make Herbalife purchases consistently (approximately every two months), and that the most popular products were those dealing with weight management (making up 95 percent of purchases recorded by the study).

One aspect of Herbalife's model that has raised concern is its approach to line commissions, or the way sellers can make money off the sales of their recruits. Currently, Herbalife contractors can earn commissions on what every recruit below them buys or sells, including not only the recruits they themselves sign up, but also those brought in by their recruits, and so on down the line. This structure, known as "unlimited down lines," means that those at the very top of the recruiting structure can make large amounts of money simply through recruiting, a classic warning sign of a pyramid scheme. Many other multilevel marketing companies limit commissions to, for example, three levels down line only, to avoid this issue.

PYRAMID SCHEMES

A pyramid scheme is a fraudulent business model that eventually inevitably collapses, with the vast majority of participants losing their investments while the few at the top of the "pyramid" profit. The four defining characteristics of a pyramid scheme are laid out by the Koscot Test, the foundational legal analysis used in the United States to determine whether a business is a pyramid scheme. These characteristics are: (1) people pay the company to participate; (2) in return, they gain the right to sell a product or service; (3) they also are compensated for recruiting others; and (4) this compensation is unrelated to whether or not any of the product or service is actually sold. In other words, participants have little or no incentive to sell products, but only to continually recruit others into the scheme. Each person recruited pays an up-front fee (usually expensive), and these fees trickle up the pyramid to be collected by the fraudsters at the top. Newcomers continue joining because, as explained by the FTC, they are promised large profits for buying in and continuing to recruit others. The Federal Bureau of Investigation (FBI) warns of pyramid schemes that come in the form of apparent marketing and investment opportunities where the individual is offered a contractorship or franchise to market a particular product. The key is where the real profit is earned; if it is not by actual product sales but by sales of new contractorships, it is likely a pyramid scheme.

Pyramid schemes and legitimate multilevel marketing businesses are both based on recruiting new participants in selling the product. The California Department of Justice explains the difference as the following: In a multilevel marketing model, money is primarily made through the eventual sale of the product to an end user, whereas in an illegal pyramid scheme, money is primarily or only made through recruiting new sellers. The participants at the top of the pyramid earn money when new members are recruited through the newcomers paying membership fees and/or buying initial product inventory. Each new member is then incentivized or required to recruit more new participants. As this cycle continues, the possible pool of untapped participants shrinks, making it hard for those at the bottom to gain a return on their investment (as the only money for them is in further recruitment). Because of this, a pyramid scheme will always ultimately collapse due to a lack of new recruits and is therefore unsustainable. Another important point is that the products offered by pyramid schemes are usually low quality or very overpriced, again making recruitment the only financially viable option for those involved. The recruits are being sold on an idea or model that, in reality, is unprofitable.

Pyramid schemes can be hard to identify clearly, but the FTC has warned consumers about two red flags. The first is inventory loading, a requirement that new participants purchase a large amount of nonrefundable inventory of the product. If the product is actually worthless, it is clear how this kind of practice invites fraud. Inventory loading can at first glance look similar to legitimate internal consumption, but it differs because internal consumption is voluntary and not a requirement of becoming a direct seller. Not only is inventory loading a red flag, but it is also illegal. The Direct Selling Association's Code of Ethics (see Table 2 above) requires member companies to have a refund policy and buy back excess inventory if a contractor no longer wants to sell. The second warning sign of a pyramid scheme is a lack of retail sales, or sales external to the selling network. If the only people buying the product are the ones supposedly selling it, there is likely a problem with the business. If such a business also requires inventory loading to get involved, it may well be a pyramid scheme.

Another way of detecting a pyramid scheme is by examining the intentions of the participants. If people are purchasing a product they really do not want just to participate, that is an indication they could be caught up in a pyramid scheme. It is for these reasons that some legitimate direct selling businesses using the multilevel marketing compensation method can appear to be pyramid schemes. The line between the two is not always clear, and when a direct selling business such as Herbalife is accused of being a pyramid scheme, the allegations can be difficult to shake.

IS HERBALIFE A PYRAMID SCHEME? ACKMAN'S ALLEGATIONS

Herbalife, like most other multilevel marketing companies, has been accused of being a pyramid scheme more than once. However, considering the firm's long and successful history, these claims were given little weight until 2012, when prominent hedge fund manager and billionaire investor William Ackman announced that he and his company, Pershing Square Capital Management, had spent a year studying Herbalife and concluded it was an elaborate pyramid scheme. Ackman is known as an "activist investor" and claimed it was his civic duty to expose Herbalife as fraudulent. Of course, his company also stood to profit heavily, having invested $1 billion in a short sale off Herbalife's stock (a complex investment strategy that earns money if the stock price falls, rather than rises). Ackman's target stock price for Herbalife was $0. In other words, he believed the company should and would fail. He has since continued to campaign and advocate against Herbalife, and has plunged the company into a never-before-faced level of controversy over its legitimacy as a business.

Ackman's accusations against Herbalife were initially laid out in a three hour, 342-slide presentation, the result of months of research and analysis by his team. The accusations included the following: (1) the majority of contractors for Herbalife lose money, (2) Herbalife pays out more for recruiting new contractors than selling actual products, and (3) only the top 1 percent of contractors earn most of the money. Ackman argues that Herbalife recruits contractors under false pretenses by unrealistically suggesting they can earn the income of those few at the top. Furthermore, he alleges that the real money in Herbalife comes not from selling products but from recruiting other contractors, as all the top earners make the vast majority of their income through down line commissions from the sales of those in their recruiting chain. Although Herbalife has published results apparently showing that the majority of its money is made through product sales, Ackman believes this information is false and/or misleading, instead estimating sales to be only 3 percent of Herbalife's revenue, with the rest made via recruiting.

Ackman also contends that when people go to purchase Herbalife products, the sellers usually try to convince them to become recruits rather than remain only customers. He claims that the only thing keeping the company running is new recruits and it will soon run out of available people to bring into the business, which is why it keeps entering new countries.

Supporters of Herbalife point out that many consumers and organizations buy and use Herbalife products and see them as high quality and credible. For example, Los Angeles fire and police departments offer Herbalife products in their fitness centers, and Herbalife products have even been adopted by some Chinese Olympic teams. Pyramid schemes, in contrast, do not offer high-quality, respected products. Additionally, because independent research such as the previously mentioned Nielsen study shows that the number of Herbalife end users is much larger than the number of Herbalife contractors, supporters of Herbalife claim it cannot possibly be operating a pyramid scheme. These viewpoints help validate Herbalife as a valid and successful business model that is producing profits directly related to product sales and is growing and expanding globally.

Ackman, however, says these arguments are invalid or based on faulty data. He claims the premium perception of Herbalife products is entirely a marketing scheme and that Herbalife conducts almost no unique research and development, indicating its products are no better than much cheaper competitor offerings. He also claims the survey measuring the number of contractors versus end consumers contradicts two others previously released by the company, that the survey sample was too small and thus made the results overly optimistic, and that there were not enough specifics in the survey (such as the actual prices consumers paid and an itemized breakdown of products purchased) to make it truly useful. He furthermore argues it is suspicious that Herbalife refuses to make the details of its recruiting process publicly available for scrutiny.

Herbalife has also been accused of issuing false accounting statements, although there has never been any official legal claim brought about how it records its sales. According to allegations, all products sold to contractors are shown as retail sales on the company's revenue numbers, without always tracking whether the product was consumed by the contractor (that is, internal consumption) or to whom the contractor sold the product. Critics believe the company should not be recording sales revenue off the contractors' consumption but only from sales made to end users. This argument falls into the larger backdrop of the legitimacy of internal consumption, which is sometimes contested in the context of direct selling. It should be noted that internal consumption is a common practice found in nearly every industry. For example, Coca-Cola has 100 percent internal consumption because all of its products are sold to resellers. Costco also has 100 percent internal consumption because all of its products are sold to Costco members. A high percentage of internal consumption has never been by itself enough to indicate a pyramid scheme, and there has never been major criticism of companies encouraging internal consumption except with the direct selling, multilevel marketing compensation model.

Furthermore, sometimes when new contractors are recruited, they need to buy products that they can consume themselves or sell to others. This practice has caused suspicion among Herbalife's critics, who draw similarities between it and inventory loading. On the other hand, contractors is only required to buy more products beyond the initial startup purchase if they want or need them for personal or business purposes, and generally the amount of products Herbalife contractors are required to purchase is lower than many other multilevel marketing businesses.

Ackman and other critics have emphasized that the majority of Herbalife contractors are not successful in selling their products. Herbalife's records show that only 1 percent of its registered contractors will make $100,000 or more from the business in their lifetime. One possible explanation is that the ease of entry and extremely low cost of becoming a Herbalife contractor makes it possible for those with little or no sales and business experience to give direct selling a try. Even if contractors are not successful at selling, the cost of entry is less than $100 and they still will have products that they can consume. Herbalife also points out that every kind of business requires a large amount of effort to make a good profit, and direct selling is no different. Even with businesses like Herbalife, if a contractor wants to make a living from distributing, he or she will have to develop marketing materials and a successful sales style, find unsaturated areas of the market, build relationships with customers, and more. If the contractor additionally wants to get into recruiting, he or she will also have to find new potential sellers, maintain relationships with recruits to encourage them to make sales and find new recruits of their own, and so on. Many who try direct selling are either not willing or lack the business knowledge to put in sufficient effort to make a living. Those who sign up for this opportunity as a side job only work part-time or less, depending on how much extra money they want to make. Ackman argues that Herbalife sugarcoats the truth behind promises of easy wealth, but Herbalife counters that it makes the heavy requirements of full-time selling clear in its promotional materials and advertisements. However, a video surfaced in 2014 from a private management and distributor meeting showing a top Herbalife earner stating they "sell people on a dream business" when "the reality is that most of them aren't going to make it."

Ackman's allegations—harsh, apparently well-researched, and made by a respected investor—launched an unprecedented storm of controversy for Herbalife. Four days after Ackman's initial presentation, the company's stock fell 43 percent, and has continued to fluctuate significantly in response to continuing developments. The debate over the company has become polarized, with prominent investors, analysts, public interest groups, and loyalists presenting heated arguments both for and against Herbalife's legitimacy. Recognizing the seriousness of the situation, Herbalife responded in force, including hiring an expensive lobbying team and launching one of the largest marketing campaigns in its history to bolster and reemphasize its brand. At this point, both Ackman and Herbalife have spent tens and possibly hundreds of millions of dollars supporting their positions and attacking each other.

CRITICISM AGAINST WILLIAM ACKMAN

As mentioned earlier, while Ackman accused Herbalife of operating a pyramid scheme, his investment company bet against its stock in the amount of $1 billion. Naturally, many people saw this coupling of a short sale and subsequent accusations as a serious conflict of interest that threw Ackman's motives and the validity of his claims into doubt. In an attempt to defuse this criticism, Ackman pledged to give any personal profit he makes from the short sale to charity, but his company still stands to benefit both financially and reputationally from Herbalife's setbacks. So far, Herbalife's stock has not yet fallen low enough for Ackman's short to be profitable, although it has come close a few times. Ackman continues to hold to his all-in $0 stock price prediction and claims he is committed to it over the long term, with no plans to cash out early even if the opportunity presents itself.

Ackman has also been criticized for the methods he has used in attempting to bring Herbalife down. For example, because one of Ackman's contentions is that Herbalife disproportionately targets vulnerable low-income and low-education minorities to pay into being part of its "pyramid," Ackman's company paid civil rights organizations $130,000 to collect names of people who were allegedly victims of Herbalife. However, the Nevada Attorney General found issues with some of the letters Ackman was supposed to have received from those organizations. Three of the letters from nonprofit groups signed by Hispanic community leaders were identical, and none of the leaders could identify any Herbalife victims by name. Other attorneys general had similar experiences. Some of the leaders who allegedly wrote the letters later denied they had written them. Such inconsistencies cast doubt over Ackman's claims and research as a whole.

Another example of potentially questionable methods came in 2015, when it was revealed that federal prosecutors and FBI agents were investigating Ackman and his company for evidence of illegal manipulation of Herbalife's stock. Ackman and his company have not yet been contacted or formally charged, but agents have reviewed documents and conducted interviews of lobbyists and consultants hired by Ackman. Proving illegal stock manipulation is not easy, requiring evidence that Ackman and his company knowingly made false or misleading statements in order to incite investigations against Herbalife and affect its market valuation. Still, that federal agents felt such an investigation was necessary is concerning.

Shortly after Ackman's accusations, another prominent billionaire investor, Carl Icahn, came to the defense of Herbalife and became a majority shareholder and board member. This helped boost investor confidence in Herbalife and led to a significant rise in stock value (although the stock later fell again and has continued to fluctuate). Icahn also publicly denounced Ackman and his claims, setting off a public feud between the two. Icahn's actions seemed to be a serious blow to Ackman at the time, providing a respected pro-Herbalife counterpart to Ackman. However, as Ackman continued to remind the public, pyramid schemes take time to reveal themselves, and he was prepared to go for the long haul and wait it out. Icahn and Ackman have since reconciled their personal disagreements, although they remain on opposite sides of the Herbalife issue.

An article in the March 15, 2014 issue of the *Economist* as well as a similar article in *The New York Times* provided a critical assessment of Ackman's attempts to use state-of-the-art lobbying in Washington to support his $1 billion short bet against Herbalife by attempting to convince legislators and regulators to investigate, speak out about, and otherwise stand against Herbalife. Ackman has been at the heart of well-executed lobbying, although he claims to have spent only $264,000 on his Herbalife lobbying campaign. On the other hand, Ackman's company's lobbying budget was seven times that much over the relevant period. According to the *Economist*, Ackman sees himself as a moral crusader against Herbalife, but his critics see him as simply a "greedy billionaire who is now exploiting America's newly laissez-faire attitude to political spending in pursuit of a big financial payday." Herbalife has responded in kind, spending millions on its own lobbying efforts to stave off regulators and call for investigations of Ackman instead.

THE CONTROVERSY CONTINUES

Herbalife has had to deal with significant issues and pressures since Ackman first went public with his allegations. It has spent millions on lobbying and marketing in an attempt to counteract Ackman's similar efforts and retain its hard-earned image of quality and legitimacy, and has watched its stock price fluctuate wildly from strong to weak and back again in response to various developments. It has also made internal changes, such as only permitting online sales through its own website and limiting the amount of products new members can initially order, hoping to more clearly show regulators and the public that it is a legitimate multilevel marketing company and not a pyramid scheme. Both Herbalife and Ackman have launched several websites as part of their respective campaigns. On Ackman's side, URLs such as factsaboutherbalife.com and herbalifepyramidscheme.com take users to a website outlining Ackman's allegations in detail and linking to anti-Herbalife news and developments. For Herbalife, the site iamherbalife.com features dozens of positive testimonials from users of Herbalife products. Herbalife also decided to go on the direct offensive with a website called therealbillackman.com, which compiles articles, videos, and other media exhibiting Ackman in a negative light. Herbalife even bought the rights to other inflammatory URLs such as billackmanlies.com, although it has not yet used them.

The threat of an official governmental probe was one of the most looming potential consequences of the controversy for Herbalife. In the wake of Ackman's claims, special interest groups such as the Hispanic Federation and the National Consumers League began urging the FTC to investigate Herbalife's operations. Not only did they stand behind the contention that Herbalife was operating a massive pyramid scheme, but they also claimed the company targeted vulnerable groups including low-income Hispanic immigrants and low-income African Americans. They alleged that Herbalife used aggressive recruiting techniques, promises of getting rich with minimal work, and other shady methods to take advantage of disadvantaged people with little or no business experience.

The claims arose from the proliferation of Herbalife "nutrition clubs" that had been established in Latino/Hispanic communities in Southern California. These nutrition clubs involved community members who paid a membership fee to discuss health issues and consume Herbalife products in a social setting. The popularity of these nutrition clubs originated in Mexico, which is where most of the Latino/Hispanic immigrants in Southern California immigrated from. Herbalife claimed the nutrition clubs started arising in California because Hispanics saw how successful they were in Mexico and wanted to import the idea to the United States. Others, however, claimed these clubs harmed the community because they usually turned out to be too costly for those who ran them and those involved ended up losing more than they bargained for. California Congresswoman Linda Sanchez wrote a letter to the FTC asking the agency to investigate Herbalife. She cited the intense media coverage and outreach from special interest groups and constituents as reasons for the FTC to investigate the company. Similar claims also abounded in New York, and New York City Councilwoman Julissa Ferreras wrote to the FTC advocating for an investigation as well. In 2014 Ackman profiled Herbalife's top distributors and continued his lobbying in Washington to have Herbalife investigated by the FTC, supporting the claims that the company sells a questionable product to vulnerable immigrants.

In response to these and other requests for an investigation, both the FTC and the SEC opened official inquiries into Herbalife in 2014. Herbalife is also being investigated by some state regulators. Herbalife has stated it is cooperating fully with investigators and invites the opportunity to prove the legitimacy of its business model. The agencies have reviewed documents, asked Herbalife for information about its policies and processes, and interviewed top Herbalife sellers on their business practices. Ackman has made much of these investigations, touting them as a major win for his position and the beginning of the end for Herbalife. He has also stated that top Herbalife executives are in the process of preemptively hiring criminal defense lawyers, a potentially concerning step. However, Ackman refused to reveal his source for this information, and it has not been corroborated.

The situation has also spawned several independent lawsuits claiming Herbalife defrauded investors by pretending to be a legitimate company. One, brought by two pension funds with investments in Herbalife, was dismissed by the U.S. District Court, which found the arguments that Herbalife was a pyramid scheme to be "unpersuasive." Another, however, led to a $17.5 million settlement after an 18-month legal battle. The suit was a class action complaint brought by a former Herbalife contractor on behalf of hundreds of thousands of distributors that claimed, among other serious allegations, the company was operating as a pyramid scheme. One of the key specific claims of the case was that a large majority of all Herbalife contractors (approximately 71 percent) make few, if any, external sales and are forced to self-consume the Herbalife products. As part of the settlement, Herbalife agreed to make a variety of changes to its business model for at least three years, including modifications to its corporate policies and the wording of its membership agreement, as well as paying for shipping of legitimately returned items by members. Herbalife will likely continue to face similar accusations in the future and must remain proactive in addressing them.

The concept of internal consumption—although in and of itself legitimate—also continues to be questioned by regulators. The belief prevails that a large amount of internal consumption in direct selling companies indicates a pyramid scheme. In 2012 a U.S. judge ordered an organization called BurnLounge to disband and reimburse customers $17 million after the FTC determined that the company was operating a pyramid scheme. BurnLounge marketed itself as a way for entrepreneurs to sell digital music and earn large incomes. Participants paid to enter the scheme. Very few sales were recorded, and 90 percent of participants did not act as independent distributors selling a product.

BurnLounge appealed. They stated that the FTC did not have enough evidence. The appeal was heard by the Ninth Circuit Court of Appeals in 2014. The implications of this case for the multilevel marketing direct selling industry were significant. In the initial judgment against BurnLounge, it was ruled that in determining the amount of product sales made by a multilevel marketing company to ultimate users, sales to participants should not be included—in other words, internal consumption did not count. It was feared that a legal decision could rule that the majority of products must be sold to people outside a direct selling company's network, with sales to distributors not counted. Such a ruling would have put significant limitations on the level of internal consumption considered to be legitimate, which would have led to troubling implications for companies like Herbalife that claim many of their members sign up just to get discounts for personal product use.

The federal appeals court upheld the FTC's decision that BurnLounge was operating an illegal pyramid scheme. However, the ruling was viewed favorably by the direct selling industry overall because it did not rely on an analysis of internal consumption; rather, BurnLounge was determined to be a pyramid scheme due to the fact that participants had to pay to join and were mainly motivated by recruiting others into the scheme (versus selling an actual product). The biggest relief for organizations like Herbalife was that the court did not rule that commissions generated from goods sold within the distribution network were illegal. Internal consumption was defined as purchases made by distributors for personal consumption or resale. The court distinguished this from buying products simply to qualify for bonuses or get a discount. Like any other reseller, direct sellers purchasing products for internal consumption have the option of consuming the products or selling them to others. It is unnecessary and likely impossible to measure the exact percentage of the product being consumed by independent contractors versus the exact percentage being sold to consumers.

Rather than singling out the amount of internal consumption as the key factor, the BurnLounge decision seemed to focus more on whether the emphasis of the business in question is sales of products or recruitment. Other important factors included how an organization calculates commissions and the importance of selling the product for the successful operation of the business. The intent for purchase is also a crucial component—if purchases are driven by the product's value, instead of by money-making ventures, then it is most likely a legitimate operation.

Additionally, the BurnLounge decision described some tests that could indicate a pyramid scheme. Specifically, red flags include focusing more on recruitment than merchandise; paying bonuses primarily based on recruitment activity; promoting the program instead of selling the product; having participants purchase the right to earn profits through the recruitment of other individuals; developing strong incentives for recruitment; motivating package purchases by the opportunity to earn money; and making it unlikely that meaningful retail sales will occur. Although each of these is not necessarily a red flag by itself, several of them taken together could indicate a pyramid scheme. For instance, the court found that 95 percent of BurnLounge distributors brought premium products but only 35 percent of non-distributors did so. BurnLounge products had little value, and distributors were required to buy premium packages if they wanted to be eligible to receive additional commissions.

Both Herbalife and Ackman claimed the BurnLounge decision validated their position. Herbalife argued that because Herbalife contractors sell products of value, participants do not have to pay simply to participate, and significant retail sales do occur, the decision lends credence to Herbalife's legitimacy. Ackman's company, on the other hand, issued a statement pointing to similarities between his allegations and several of the warning signs laid out by the court and argued that Herbalife's business model is dangerously similar to that of BurnLounge.

Beyond the possibility of another appeal to the Supreme Court, BurnLounge's story is over. Herbalife, however, continues. As the legal rules for determining the difference between a multilevel marketing company and a pyramid scheme continue to develop, and the federal agency investigations into both Herbalife and Ackman continue, stakeholders are watching closely to see how this threat to the 35-year-old company will play out. Many analysts have already labeled Ackman's campaign a failure, stating it has failed to seriously cast doubt on Herbalife's success and Ackman will eventually be forced to cut his losses and move on. Others still view his campaign as a serious threat to Herbalife's future and believe Ackman will keep pushing until he succeeds. Time, and how Herbalife decides to handle the situation moving forward, will tell who is correct.

HERBALIFE'S SOCIAL RESPONSIBILITY

The corporate social responsibility section of Herbalife's website makes it clear the company is proud of its corporate social responsibility program, which it believes summarizes its top values of doing "the right, honest and ethical thing." Herbalife's corporate governance helps to create increased accountability toward stakeholders and allows the firm to meet transparency requirements set forth by the New York Stock Exchange for publicly listed companies.

Herbalife's focus on business ethics helps it uphold high ethical standards in company operations. CEO Michael Johnson has said that the company's reputation is its greatest asset. According to Herbalife's Corporate Code of Business Conduct and Ethics, employees must engage in fair interaction with everyone associated with the company, including external stakeholders. The code has guidelines in place as to how contractors and employees of Herbalife should interact with suppliers, competitors, business partners, and regulatory authorities. Herbalife stresses legal compliance and sets boundaries on gifts and entertainment so that employees can tell the difference between small gifts for hospitality and bribes. It discourages conflict of interest situations and offers three methods of reporting unethical behavior: through its company hotline, its website, or by contacting the general counsel. Those who violate these standards are disciplined, suspended, or terminated. Herbalife holds annual ethics training for all employees worldwide.

Another aspect of Herbalife's social responsibility program is its philanthropic efforts. The Herbalife Family Foundation (HFF) and the Casa Herbalife program, founded in 1994 by Mark Hughes, provide funds and volunteerism to charities committed to supporting at-risk children. HFF also provides support to nutrition initiatives and disaster relief. Its partnership with the Global Alliance for Improved Nutrition (GAIN) and DSM Nutritional Products—a producer of vitamins and nutrition ingredients—focuses on providing essential nutrients to improve the health of women and children worldwide. In a similar vein, Herbalife in 2015 announced a one-year partnership with Global Health Strategies Institute (GHSI) to improve the nutritional intake of over 10,000 young children in India.

As part of Herbalife's corporate social responsibility program, it also focuses on its internal stakeholders. For instance, Herbalife proactively embraces employee wellness and eco-friendly initiatives. The company incentivizes employees to be healthy and participate in fitness activities. Such incentives include complimentary products and lower individual health insurance costs. The company has even been recognized by *Men's Fitness* magazine as "One of the 15 Fittest Companies in America." In terms of being environmentally conscious, Herbalife's headquarters have received accolades for its LEED certification and environmentally friendly design. It also encourages distributors to increase their own sustainability activities.

CONCLUSION

Herbalife continues to be a successful direct selling company despite various accusations of improper activity over the years—most recently Bill Ackman's campaign to prove it is a pyramid scheme. In 2014 the company reached worldwide net sales of $5 billion, up significantly from 2012 in spite of Ackman's efforts against the company. Herbalife's stock price has remained strong enough to retain the confidence of many investors, although it has fluctuated significantly over the past few years. However, the saga between Herbalife and Ackman is not over, with Ackman continuing to predict the company's imminent demise. Stakeholders are watching the FTC and SEC investigations into Herbalife closely.

The products of Herbalife are exclusively sold by nearly 3 million independent contractors in over 90 different countries. Herbalife sponsors several professional athletes, teams, and sporting events. Additionally, the company is proud of its corporate social responsibility initiatives. Herbalife is a successful company, but it will continue to face ethical issues as it moves forward, especially because multilevel marketing and direct selling firms often receive additional scrutiny due to their apparent similarities to fraudulent ventures such as pyramid schemes.

Certain aspects of Herbalife's business as a direct seller have come under special scrutiny. Internal consumption, for example, is often considered a red flag for pyramid scheme activity when it is found in multilevel marketing models. However, internal consumption exists in nearly all businesses, and U.S. Court decisions have made it clear that internal consumption itself is neither illegal nor problematic even in the multilevel marketing context; much more is required before a pyramid scheme can be suspected. Similarly, inventory loading is another common pyramid scheme warning sign. Herbalife has rarely been accused of inventory loading considering its low startup fee and generous inventory refund policies, but due to the nature of its business, it must always pay close attention to this part of its model to avoid suspicion and ambiguity.

Herbalife, like all companies, can fight against criticism of its operations by maintaining transparency concerning how its business works. Herbalife should also focus on due diligence in ensuring its contractors are not exploited in any way. Herbalife continues to have many loyal sellers and customers throughout out the world, showing that the firm has many supporters who believe the company is a legitimate and successful business operation.

QUESTIONS FOR DISCUSSION

1. Why has Herbalife's multilevel compensation model been accused of being a pyramid scheme?
2. Describe the differences between a legitimate business model and a pyramid scheme.
3. How has Herbalife demonstrated social responsibility?

SOURCES

David Benoit, "Herbalife Went Website Shopping, Bought BillAckmanLies.com," *The Wall Street Journal*, April 10, 2015, http://blogs.wsj.com/moneybeat/2015/04/10/herbalife-went-website-shopping-bought-billackmanlies-com/ (accessed June 16, 2015); Business Wire, "Pershing Square Responds to Recent Ruling in *FTC V. BurnLounge, Inc*," June 3, 2014, http://www.businesswire.com/news/home/20140603006090/en/Pershing-Square-Responds-Ruling-FTC-V.-BurnLounge#.VX8X7kYj-A (accessed June 16, 2015); Business Wire, "Herbalife Partners with Global Health Strategies Institute to Improve Children's Nutrition in India," April 7, 2015, http://finance.yahoo.com/news/herbalife-partners-global-health-strategies-120000177.html (accessed June 16, 2015); Michelle Celarier, "BurnLounge shutdown has implications for Herbalife," *New York Post*, June 2, 2014, http://nypost.com/2014/06/02/burnlounge-shutdown-has-implications-for-herbalife/ (accessed June 16, 2015); Michelle Celarier, "Little-known deal could be the downfall of Herbalife," *The New York Post*, February 6, 2015, http://nypost.com/2015/02/06/little-known-deal-could-be-the-downfall-of-herbalife/ (accessed June 16, 2015); Michelle Celarier, "NYC Pol: It's Herb-sploitation," *New York Post*, June 14, 2013, http://www.nypost.com/p/news/business/nyc_pol_it_herb_sploitation_zr63x783q4YqvSA3hReQEM (accessed June 17, 2013); Juliet Chung, "In Herbalife Fight, Both Sides Prevail," *The Wall Street Journal*, March 31, 2013, http://online.wsj.com/article/SB10001424127887323361804578388682197247250.html (accessed July 25, 2013); Anne T. Coughlan, "Assessing an MLM Business," Herbalife, July 2012, http://ir.herbalife.com/assessing-MLM.cfm (accessed July 10, 2013); Javier E. David, "Herbalife CEO Casts Doubt on Ackman's Motives in Shorting Stock," *CNBC*, January 10, 2013, http://www.cnbc.com/id/100369698 (accessed July 25, 2013); "Datamonitor the Home of Business Information," *Datamonitor the*

Home of Business Information, http://www.datamonitor.com/ (accessed April 21, 2013); "Direct Selling Methods: Single Level and Multilevel Marketing," More Business, March 26, 2007, http://www.morebusiness.com/running_ your_business/management/Direct-Sales.brc (accessed July 10, 2013); Economist staff, "The House of Cards Put," *The Economist*, March 15, 2014, http://www.economist.com/news/finance-and-economics/21599055-activist-investing-meets-activist-government-house-cards-put (accessed April 29, 2014); Facts about Herbalife website, http://www.factsaboutherbalife.com/ (accessed June 16, 2015); Federal Trade Commission, "FTC Action Leads to Court Order Shutting Down Pyramid Scam Thousands of Consumers Burned by BurnLounge," March 14, 2012, http://www.ftc.gov/news-events/press-releases/2012/03/ftc-action-leads-court-order-shutting-down-pyramid-scamthousands (accessed May 30, 2014); O. C. Ferrell and Linda Ferrell, "Defining a Pyramid Scheme," PowerPoint presentation, University of New Mexico, 2013; Agustino Fontevecchia, "The Anti-Ackman Effect: Herbalife Surges Then Plunges as Hedge Fund Billie Omits It from Ira Sohn Speech," *Forbes*, May 8, 2013, http:// www.forbes.com/sites/afontevecchia/2013/05/08/the-anti-ackman-effect-herbalife-surges-then-punges-as-hedge-fund-billie-omits-it-from-ira-sohn-speech/ (accessed June 11, 2013); Agustino Fontevecchia, "Investors Side with Carl Icahn: Herbalife Soars after Epic TV Battle with Ackman," *Forbes*, January 25, 2013, http://www.forbes.com/ sites/afontevecchia/2013/01/25/investors-side-with-carl-icahn-herbalife-soars-after-epic-tv-battle-with-ackman/ (accessed June 16, 2015); "Frauds of the Century," in O.C. Ferrell, John Fraedrich, and Linda Ferrell, *Business Ethics: Ethical Decision Making and Cases*, 10th ed. (Mason, OH: South-Western Cengage Learning, 2015); Karen Gullo, "BurnLounge Ruling in FTC Case Seen as Good for Herbalife," *Bloomberg*, June 2, 2014, http://www. bloomberg.com/news/2014-06-02/burnlounge-shutdown-by-ftc-upheld-by-federal-appeals-court-1-.html (accessed June 3, 2014); Herbalife, United States—Official Site, http://www.herbalife.com/ (accessed June 16, 2015); Herbalife, "Herbalife Ltd. Announces Record Fourth Quarter 2013 and Record Full Year Results, and Raises 2014 Earnings Guidance," February 18, 2014, http://ir.herbalife.com/releasedetail.cfm?ReleaseID=826429 (accessed June 16, 2015); Herbalife, "I Am Herbalife FAQs," http://iamherbalife.com/faq/ (accessed June 16, 2015); Herbalife, "International Business Pack (IBP)," http://www.beststarttoday.com/Herbalife_International_ Business_Pack_p/5000.htm (accessed June 17, 2013); Herbalife, "Mini International Business Pack (IBP)," http:// www.beststarttoday.com/Herbalife_Mini_International_Business_Pack_IBP_p/5043.htm (accessed June 17, 2013); Herbalife, "Product Catalogue," http://catalog.herbalife.com/Catalog/en-US (accessed June 16, 2015); Herbalife, The Real Bill Ackman website, http://www.therealbillackman.com/ (accessed June 16, 2015); Herbalife, *Sales & Marketing Plan and Business Rules*, 2012, http://factsaboutherbalife.com/media/2012/12/ Marketing-Plan-and-Business-Rules-2012.pdf (accessed June 16, 2015); Herbalife, "Social Responsibility," http:// company.herbalife.com/social-responsibilty (accessed June 16, 2015); Herbalife, "Statement of Average Gross Compensation Paid by Herbalife to United States Contractors in 2013," http://opportunity.herbalife.com/Content/ en-US/pdf/business-opportunity/statement_average_gross_usen.pdf (accessed June 16, 2015); "Herbalife Ltd.," Hoover's Company Records—In-depth Records, April 17, 2013; "Herbalife Review," *Vital Health Partners RSS*, Web, April 23, 2013; Svea Herbst-Bayliss, "Ackman outspent by Herbalife in lobbying," *Reuters*, March 9, 2014, http://www.reuters.com/article/2014/03/09/us-herbalife-idUSBREA280OH20140309 (accessed June 16, 2015); Svea Herbst-Bayliss, "Ackman says Herbalife execs are hiring their own lawyers," *Reuters*, April 13, 2015, http://www.reuters.com/article/2015/04/13/us-herbalife-ackman-idUSKBN0N428420150413 (accessed June 16, 2015); Tabinda Hussain, "Hispanic Federation Urges FTC To Investigate Herbalife," Value Walk, May 20, 2013, http://www.valuewalk.com/2013/05/hispanic-federation-urges-ftc-to-investigate-herbalife/ (accessed June 16, 2015); Investopedia staff, "Short Selling: What Is Short Selling?" Investopedia, http://www.investopedia.com/ university/shortselling/shortselling1.asp (accessed May 22, 2014); Devika Krishna Kumar, "This Is Not What Bill Ackman Needed for Herbalife," *Business Insider*, October 31, 2014, http://www.businessinsider.com/r-herbalife-to-pay-15-million-to-settle-class-action-lawsuit-2014-10 (accessed June 16, 2015); Paul R. La Monica, "Herbalife stock is having an INSANE month," *CNN Money*, March 24, 2015, http://money.cnn.com/2015/03/24/investing/ herbalife-stock-bill-ackman-carl-icahn/ (accessed June 16, 2015); Julia La Roche, "California Congresswoman Asks the FTC to Investigate Herbalife," *Business Insider*, June 13, 2013, http://www.businessinsider.com/sanchez-asks-ftc-to-probe-herbalife-2013-6 (accessed June 16, 2015); Richard Lee and Jason D. Schloetzer, "The Activism of Carl Icahn and Bill Ackman," Director Notes: The Conference Board, May 2014, No. DN-V6N10; Lehman, Lee, and Xu. "Direct Sale," Lehman Law, http://www.lehmanlaw.com/practices/direct-sale.html (accessed June 16, 2015); Linette Lopez, "REPORT: The FBI is interviewing people and asking for documents about Bill Ackman and Herbalife," *Business Insider*, March 12, 2015, http://www.businessinsider.com/the-fbi-is-investigating-bill-ackman-over-herbalife-2015-3 (accessed June 16, 2015); Rebecca McClay, "Herbalife Strikes Back at Ackman amid Reports of Federal Investigation," *TheStreet*, April 6, 2015, http://www.thestreet.com/story/13102435/1/herbalife-strikes-back-at-ackman-amid-at-reports-of-federal-investigation.html (accessed June 16, 2015); Dan McCrum, "Herbalife Faces Challenge of Greater Transparency over Sales," *Financial Times*, June 17, 2013, http://www.ft.com/intl/cms/s/0/9289508c-d2e6-11e2-aac2-00144feab7de.html#axzz2a59tMx00 (accessed June 16, 2015); Dan McCrum, "Keep an eye on the FTC vs Burnlounge," *Financial Times*, March 21, 2014, http://ftalphaville.ft.com/2014/03/21/1806772/keep-an-eye-on-the-ftc-vs-burnlounge/ (accessed May 30, 2014); "New Pyramid Scheme Allegations against Herbalife that Might Just Stick | Shortzilla LLC," Shortzilla LLC, April 11, 2013, http://www.shortzilla.com/new-pyramid-scheme-allegations-against-herbalife-that-might-just-stick/ (accessed July 25, 2013); Stuart Pfiefer, "Consumer Group Urges FTC to Investigate Herbalife," *Los Angeles Times*, March 12, 2013, http://articles.latimes.com/2013/mar/12/business/la-fi-mo-consumer-group-urges-ftc-to-investigate-herbalife-20130312 (accessed June 16, 2015); Stuart Pfeifer, "Herbalife now making its products available through company website," *Los Angeles Times*, April 6, 2015, http://www.latimes.com/business/la-fi-herbalife-online-20150407-story.html (accessed June 16, 2015); Stuart Pfeifer, "Herbalife Shares Surge Past Price When Ackman Made Allegations," *Los Angeles Times*, May 6, 2013, http://articles.latimes.com/2013/may/06/business/la-fi-mo-herbalife-stock-price-20130506 (accessed June 16, 2015); Steven Pfiefer, "Latinos Crucial to Herbalife's Financial Health," *Los Angeles Times*, February 15, 2013, http://articles.latimes.com/2013/feb/15/business/la-fi-herbalife-latino-20130216 (accessed June 16, 2015); Stuart Pfiefer, "Rep. Linda Sanchez Asks FTC to Investigate Herbalife," *Los Angeles Times*, June 14, 2013, http://articles.latimes.com/2013/jun/14/business/la-fi-herbalife-ftc-20130614 (accessed June 16, 2015); William Pride and O.C. Ferrell, *Foundations of Marketing*, 5th ed. (Mason, OH: South-Western Cengage, 2013), 444; Pyramid Scheme, "Funk & Wagnalls New World Encyclopedia," *EBSCOhost* (accessed April 20, 2013); Pyramid Scheme Alert, "China Leads the World in Fighting the Global Scourge of Pyramid Schemes," September 2009, http://pyramidschemealert.org/PSAMain/news/ChinaLeadsPyramidFight.html (accessed June 16, 2015); Reuters, "Group Says Herbalife Products Have Too Much Lead," *National Post*, http://www.nationalpost.com/life/health/story.html?id=c11516f7-6c38-4365-a1e7-049662727931 (accessed July 25, 2013); Reuters and Fortune Editors, "Ackman renews attacks on Herbalife, says it will be gone within a year," *Fortune*, January 13, 2015, http://fortune.com/2015/01/13/ackman-renews-attacks-on-herbalife-says-it-will-be-gone-within-a-year/ (accessed June 16, 2015); Martin Russell, "Herbalife Scam: Let's Review the Claims," Careful Cash RSS, March 4, 2011, http://www.carefulcash.com/herbalife-scam-lets-review-the-claims/ (accessed July 25, 2013); Steve Schaefer, "Ackman Takes Ax to Herbalife, Company Says It Is 'Not an Illegal Pyramid Scheme'," *Forbes*, 2012, 4; Steve Schaefer, "Herbalife Posts Record Results, Raises Guidance," *Forbes*, April 29, 2013, http://www.forbes.com/sites/steveschaefer/2013/04/29/herbalife-posts-record-results-raises-guidance/ (accessed June 16, 2015); Zachary Scheidt, "Capture Major Upside as Nu Skin Launches New Product," *Beta Fool*, June 14, 2013, http://beta.fool.com/traderzach/2013/06/14/capture-50-profits-as-nu-skin-launches-new-product/37167/?source=eogyholnk0000001 (accessed June 17, 2013); Michael S. Schmidt, Eric Lipton, and Alexandra Stevenson, "After Big Bet, Hedge Fund Pulls the Levers of Power," *The New York Times*, March 9, 2014, http://www.nytimes.com/2014/03/10/business/staking-1-billion-that-herbalife-will-fail-then-ackman-lobbying-to-bring-it-down.html?_r=0 (accessed May 30, 2014); Duane D. Stanford and Kelly Bit, "Herbalife Drops after Ackman Says He's Shorting Shares," *Bloomberg*, December 20, 2012, http://www.bloomberg.com/news/2012-12-19/herbalife-drops-after-cnbc-says-ackman-is-short-company.html (accessed June 16, 2015); Alexandra Stevenson and Ben Protess, "Bruised, Herbalife Swings Back at Accuser," *The New York Times*, June 2, 2015, http://www.nytimes.com/2015/06/03/business/dealbook/herbalife-steps-up-lobbying-to-counter-ackmans-attacks.html?_r=0 (accessed June 16, 2015); The Street Wire, "Herbalife, Ltd. Stock Buy Recommendation Reiterated," June 11, 2013, http://www.thestreet.mobi/story/11947125/1/herbalife-ltd-stock-buy-recommendation-reiterated-hlf.html?puc=yahoo&cm_ven=YAHOO (accessed June 16, 2015); Nathalie Tadena, "Ackman: Herbalife Should Come Clean on Surveys," *The Wall Street Journal*, June 18, 2013, http://blogs.wsj.com/moneybeat/2013/06/18/ackman-herbalife-should-come-clean-on-surveys/?mod=yahoo_hs (accessed June 16, 2015); Kevin Thompson, "The BurnLounge Court Decision Clears the Air on Many Issues," *Direct Selling News*, August 2014: 64–66; Kevin Thompson, "Inventory Loading: When Does a Company Cross the Line?" *Thompsonburton.com*, March 20, 2010. http://thompsonburton.com/mlmattorney/2010/03/20/inventory-loading-when-does-a-company-cross-the-line/ (accessed June 16, 2015); theflyonthewall.com, "Congresswoman asks FTC to Investigate Herbalife, NY Post Reports," June 13, 2013, http://finance.yahoo.com/news/congresswoman-asks-ftc-investigate-herbalife-101651927.html (accessed June 16, 2015); "Top Herbalife members contacted by law enforcement agencies: report," *The Globe and Mail*, April 6, 2015, http://www.theglobeandmail.com/report-on-business/top-herbalife-members-contacted-by-law-enforcement-agencies-report/article23804675/ (accessed June 16, 2015); Michelle Urban and Jennifer Sawayda, "The Network Marketing Controversy," Daniels Fund Ethics Initiative website, 2013, http://danielsethics.mgt.unm.edu/pdf/network-marketing-di.pdf (accessed June 16, 2015); Nathan Vardi, "Carl Icahn and Herbalife are Crushing Bill Ackman," *Forbes*, May 21, 2013, http://www.forbes.com/sites/nathanvardi/2013/05/21/carl-icahn-and-herbalife-are-crushing-bill-ackman/ (accessed June 16, 2015); "The Verge," *The Verge*, Web, April 21, 2013; Scott Warren, "MLM Laws in China," Wellman & Warren Attorneys at Law, February 3, 2014, http://w-wlaw.com/mlm-laws-in-china/ (accessed June 16, 2015); Miles Weiss, "Icahn Says No Respect for Bill Ackman after Herbalife Bet," *Bloomberg*, January 25, 2013, http://www.bloomberg.com/news/2013-01-24/icahn-says-no-respect-for-bill-ackman-after-herbalife-bet.html (accessed June 16, 2015); Kaja Whitehouse, "Bill Ackman's Herbalife short is backfiring—again," *USA Today*, March 23, 2015, http://americasmarkets.usatoday.com/2015/03/23/bill-ackmans-herbalife-short-is-backfiring-again/ (accessed June 16, 2015); World Federation of Direct Selling Association, "Objectives," http://www.wfdsa.org/about_wfdsa/?fa=objectives (accessed June 16, 2015); Yahoo! Finance, "Herbalife Announces Results of Study on Contractors and End Users in the U.S.," June 11, 2013, http://finance.yahoo.com/news/herbalife-announces-results-study-contractors-214500826.html (accessed June 12, 2013); Yahoo! Finance, "Herbalife Says Survey Indicates 7.9M Customers in the U.S.," June 12, 2013, http://finance.yahoo.com/news/herbalife-says-survey-indicates-7-103428808.html (accessed June 16, 2015); Daniel Yi and Tom Petruno, "Herbalife Investor Bids for Rest of Firm," *Los Angeles Times*, February 3, 2007, http://articles.latimes.com/2007/feb/03/business/fi-herbalife3 (accessed May 22, 2014).

CASE 20

The Mission of CVS: Corporate Social Responsibility and Pharmacy Innovation*

INTRODUCTION

In 1963 brothers Stanley and Sidney Goldstein founded the first Consumer Value Store (CVS) with partner Ralph Hoagland in Lowell, Massachusetts. The store originally sold health and beauty supplies. It was widely successful, and grew to include 17 stores in one year. By 1967 CVS began offering in-store pharmacy departments, and in less than a decade it was acquired by the retail holding corporation Melville Corporation. This marked the beginning of CVS's expansion across the east coast through new store openings or mergers and acquisitions. It soon reached the milestone of exceeding $100 million in sales in 1974.

As the company grew, it faced intense competition, which it responded to through a differentiation strategy. CVS focused on its core offerings of health and beauty products, placing stores in shopping malls to generate more foot traffic. This strategy worked well for the company, allowing it to hit $1 billion in sales by 1985. The company celebrated its 25th year in 1988 with 750 stores and $1.6 billion in sales. The acquisition of People's Drug stores enabled CVS to establish its presence more widely along the coast and spurred the launch of PharmaCare, a pharmacy benefit management (PBM) company providing services to employers and insurers. In 1996 the Melville Corporation restructured, and CVS became independent as a publicly traded company on the New York Stock Exchange.

This new surge of investment allowed the company to expand widely across the nation into the Midwest and Southeast. CVS's acquisition of 2,500 Revco stores became the largest acquisition in U.S. retail pharmacy history. With the rise of the Internet, CVS seized upon the opportunity to launch CVS.com in 1999 (and Caremark.com after the 2007 acquisition). This became the first fully integrated online pharmacy in the United States. In another first for the U.S. pharmacy retail industry, the company introduced the ExtraCare Card loyalty program in 2001. The company's 40th anniversary in 2003 was marked with increasing westward expansion, 44 million loyalty card holders, and more than 4,000 stores in approximately 30 states. In the following five years, the company's acquisitions allowed CVS to gain leadership in key markets, begin a mail order business, and open its 7,000th retail location. It would also undergo a name change to CVS/Caremark after acquiring Caremark Rx, a prescription benefits management organization.

*This case was prepared by Yixing Chen, Christine Shields, and Michelle Urban for and under the direction of O. C. Ferrell and Linda Ferrell © 2015. Julian Matthias provided editorial assistance. It was prepared for classroom discussion rather than to illustrate either effective or ineffective handling of an administrative, ethical, or legal decision by management. All sources used for this case were obtained through publicly available material.

The two most important acquisitions in the history of CVS include MinuteClinic walk-in health clinics (in 2005) and Caremark Rx, Inc. (in 2007), a pharmacy benefits management company. To date, MinuteClinic has facilitated over 18 million patient visits in 800 clinics across 27 states, putting the company in prime position to reach its 2017 goal of operating 1,500 clinics in 35 states. CVS/Caremark, as it was renamed after the acquisition, became the second largest pharmacy in the United States after Walgreen's, and began introducing new services such as online prescription refills. By 2014 the company had more than $139 billion in revenue, 7,800 retail pharmacies, 936 clinics, 26 retail specialty pharmacies, 11 specialty mail order pharmacies, 17 on-site pharmacies, and a pharmacy benefit management business.

CVS sells products that meet the highest quality standards as well as its own line of products whose specifications and performance are annually tested and reviewed to ensure compliance with applicable consumer safety laws. In addition, the company has instituted a Cosmetic Safety Policy that applies to all of the cosmetic products it sells. CVS employs 200,000 people in over 7,600 locations across 46 states, the District of Columbia, Puerto Rico, Brazil, and Northern Ireland. Corporate headquarters are located in Woonsocket, Rhode Island. In one year, CVS filled and managed 1.6 billion prescriptions, provided services to 63 million PBM clients, and surpassed $126 billion in net revenues. The company is proud to note its number 13 spot on the Fortune 100 list. It has also paid dividends to shareholders for 69 consecutive quarters, with dividend increases for 11 consecutive years. Today, CVS is one of the largest pharmacy health care providers and pharmacies in the United States and is comprised of four business functions: CVS/Caremark, MinuteClinic, PBM Services, and Retail Pharmacy.

The following case will explain some of the legal and ethical challenges CVS/Caremark has encountered, including a settlement with the Federal Trade Commission (FTC) and U.S. Department of Health & Human Services (HHS) regarding violations of the Health Insurance Portability and Accountability Act (HIPAA) Privacy Rule, deceptive business practices, and unseemly conduct by a manager resulting in a death. Our examination will also include how CVS/Caremark responded to such allegations, and how it has worked to redefine the company as a health care provider. We will analyze the company's ethical structure, including its recent decision to stop selling cigarettes, as well as provide an overview of some criticisms the company has received during its transition. The conclusion offers some insights into the future challenges CVS will likely experience.

ETHICAL CHALLENGES

Like most large companies, CVS must frequently address ethical risk areas and maintain socially responsible relationships with stakeholders. Although CVS has excelled in social responsibility, it has suffered from ethical lapses in the past. The next section addresses some of CVS's most notable ethical challenges, some of which resulted in legal repercussions.

HIPAA Privacy Case of 2009

As a company grows and achieves widespread influence, it also inherits a responsibility to act ethically and within the law. In 2009 CVS/Caremark was accused of improperly disposing of patients' health information. It was alleged that company employees threw prescription bottle labels and old prescriptions into the trash without destroying sensitive patient information, making it possible for the information to fall into public hands. This is a violation of the HIPAA Privacy Rule, which requires companies operating in the health industry to properly safeguard the information of their patients. The allegations initiated investigations by the Office of Civil Rights (OCR) and the FTC, marking the first such collaborative investigation into a company's practices. These investigations revealed other issues as well, including a failure of company policies and procedures to completely address the safe handling of sensitive patient information, lack of proper employee training on disposal of sensitive information, and negligence in establishing repercussions for violations of proper disposal methods. This was in spite of the fact that CVS materials reassure clients that their privacy is a top priority for the pharmacy. This claim, in addition to the investigative findings, prompted the FTC to allege that CVS was making deceptive claims and had unfair security practices, both of which are violations of the FTC Act.

CVS settled the case with the U.S. Department of HHS, which oversees the enforcement of the HIPAA Privacy Rule, for $2.25 million regarding improper disposal of patients' health information. The settlement also mandated that the company implement a Corrective Action Plan with the following seven guidelines: (1) revise and distribute policies regarding disposal of protected health information; (2) discipline employees who violate them; (3) train workforce on new requirements; (4) conduct internal monitoring; (5) involve a qualified, independent third party to assess company compliance with requirements and submit reports to HHS; (6) establish internal reporting procedures requiring employees to report all violations of these new privacy policies; and (7) submit compliance reports to HHS for three years. The company also settled with the FTC by signing a consent order, requiring the company to develop a comprehensive program that would ensure the security and confidentiality of information collected from customers. In so doing, the company agreed to a biennial audit from an independent third party. This audit is meant to ensure that CVS's program meets the FTC's standards for its security program. CVS is forbidden by law from misrepresenting its security practices.

Deceptive Business Practices

In addition to privacy challenges, CVS/Caremark has been accused of deceptive business practices. A 2008 civil lawsuit involving 28 states was filed against the personal benefits management division of CVS/Caremark, which acts as the prescription drug claim intermediary between employers and employees. It also maintains relationships with drugstores and manufacturers. The allegations of the lawsuit included urging doctors to switch patients to name brand prescriptions under the notion that it would save them money. Furthermore, these switches were encouraged without informing doctors of the financial burden it would impose on patients, and employer health care plans were not informed that this activity would benefit CVS/Caremark. This could be seen as a conflict of interest at the expense of customers. Due to these allegations, the suit called for a revision in how the division gives information to consumers. In the end, CVS/Caremark signed a consent decree without admitting fault and paid a settlement of $38.5 million to reimburse states for the legal costs and patients overcharged due to the switch in prescriptions. In a similar matter, a multi-year-long FTC investigation concluded in 2009 that the company had misled consumers regarding prices on certain prescriptions in one of its Medicare plans. The switch harmed elderly customers who were billed up to 10 times the amount they anticipated. CVS/Caremark settled with the FTC for $5 million to reimburse customers for the change in price.

Overdistribution of Oxycodone

In 2012 CVS faced challenges with another federal agency—the Drug Enforcement Administration (DEA). The DEA suspended the company's license to sell controlled substances at two Florida locations, only a few miles apart from one another. These locations were found to have ordered a total of three million oxycodone tablets in 2011. The average order for a U.S. pharmacy in the same year was 69,000 pills. Intensifying the matter, abuse of narcotics pain medications, especially oxycodone tablets, was prevalent in the area. In fact, some local clinics had become known as "pill mills" for their liberal distribution of prescriptions for pain pills. This prompted the state of Florida to implement legislation responding to and attempting to control the rampant misuse and diversion of pain medications.

CVS responded to the DEA's investigation by notifying some of the area doctors that it would not fill prescriptions written for oxycodone (Schedule II narcotics). However, it also requested a temporary restraining order against the DEA, which would disable the temporary suspension of selling oxycodone. The DEA suspension decreased the amount of such narcotics being distributed to the two CVS locations by 80 percent in a period of three months, limiting their ability to make a profit. When the matter came before a federal judge, he ruled that the company was at fault for lack of proper oversight in distributing oxycodone and other narcotics. The ruling further implied company negligence since such a large number of dispensed pills should have been noticed as a blatant abnormality.

Later that year, the DEA completely revoked the licenses of the two locations to sell controlled substances—the first time this has occurred with a national retail pharmacy chain. CVS claims that it has improved procedures regarding distribution of controlled substances; however, the DEA's claims explicitly assign negligence on the part of pharmacists in light of obvious "questionable circumstances." These circumstances included the fact that several customers were coming to Florida from out of state to fill prescriptions. Many lacked insurance and paid in cash, red flags that can suggest drug abuse. This was in addition to the heavy prescription drug abuse problem in the area that had already prompted state legislation.

Testimonies from employees indicated company negligence as many had knowledge of the top prescribing doctors in the area and awareness that daily oxycodone quotas were being depleted—sometimes within 30 minutes of the pharmacy opening. Pharmacists also indicated that they set aside pills for those patients they considered to have a real need for them because they had strong suspicions that most of the people purchasing the pills were abusers. They did not feel at liberty to refuse prescriptions to customers, however, because they are not trained to diagnose illnesses. In 2013 CVS announced a review of its database of health care providers to find abnormalities in narcotic prescriptions. It found and notified at least 36 providers to whom it would no longer fill orders due to high prescription rates.

In 2014 another incident involving the disappearance of 37,000 pain pills in four California stores brought the DEA and CVS together again. These stores have a history of not being able to account for several pain prescription drugs. This incident carries up to 2,973 violations of the Federal Controlled Substances Act and could cost the company up to $29 million in penalties. In 2012 the DEA investigated missing prescription drugs in a store wherein an employee admitted taking approximately 20,000 pills. This piqued the curiosity of investigators, who found three retail locations that each had thousands of pills missing.

Death of a Shoplifter

In 2010 a man accused of shoplifting toothpaste was chased out of a CVS store by a manager. Video surveillance footage showed an altercation between the two. Six bystanders came to the manager's assistance, one of whom was seen kicking and punching the perpetrator while the manager held him around the neck. Within seconds, the man was heard saying he could not breathe and died shortly thereafter. Police investigated the incident and did not file criminal charges. The medical examiner initially classified the death as a homicide, but later it was ruled an accident. The manager claimed that the shoplifter punched him, so he retaliated in self-defense. The victim's mother is filing a civil lawsuit against the manager and claiming CVS is liable for her son's death. Whether or not CVS is found culpable, the tragedy cast a shadow over CVS and how it handles shoplifters.

MOVING TOWARD A HEALTH CARE COMPANY

Despite the ethical challenges CVS has experienced, it is trying to reposition itself as a socially responsible organization that places priority on consumer health. Being a quality health care company not only offers reputational benefits, but financial advantages as well. Changes in both the economic and health care landscape are creating new opportunities for CVS to provide different programs and redefine itself. Trends including the declining number of primary care physicians, the 16 million baby boomers who are becoming eligible for Medicare benefits, and the more than 30 million newly insured Americans under the Affordable Care Act (ACA) offer CVS an attractive market in which to expand. For example, CVS has refocused its efforts on supplying the growing need for chronic disease management that consumes costly resources when patients do not adhere to physician recommended medications and monitoring methods to maintain health. PBM services are being successfully implemented, including mail order, specialty pharmacy, plan design and administration, formulary management, discounted drug purchase arrangements, and disease management services.

Innovative programs such as Pharmacy Advisor and Maintenance Choice, developed in collaboration with researchers from Harvard University and Brigham and Women's Hospital, help patients stay on their medications. Research shows that regular interaction between patient and pharmacist increases the likelihood that patients will adhere to their medication regimen. Many patients who take regular prescriptions often think that they are well enough to cease taking their medication. However, when the symptoms of their ailments reappear, the costs are great, both financially and medically. CVS's programs allow the company to inform patients about the benefits and risks of these effects through education and awareness. The entire industry also benefits from this knowledge by preventing more costly medical procedures due to medication non-adherence, which occurs when patients skip or incorrectly take their dosage requirements. This is estimated to cost between $5 and $10 for every $1 spent on adherence programs. These services are key components of CVS's competitive advantage, allowing it to provide the best possible patient care. It was also proactive in preparing patients for Health Care Reform. For instance, CVS/Caremark partnered with the Centers for Medicare and Medicaid Services to raise awareness about new services available to Medicare patients under the ACA.

To help people keep up with these and other changes in health care, CVS has established its presence on social media and mobile devices. The company introduced a mobile application allowing customers to conveniently refill prescriptions, while its Facebook and Twitter pages provide helpful health tips. Customers benefit from using CVS's digital tools through increased savings and easier access to many of CVS's services. For instance, CVS's iPad application allows individuals to have a 3D digital pharmacy experience reminiscent of shopping in-store. Customers that are unable to physically visit the store, or prefer the convenience of shopping from home, are able to partake in the CVS experience through the company's technology. With over 10 million registered users, many are saving money and time filling and refilling prescriptions as well as having instant access to essential drug information.

MinuteClinics are one of the major contributors to CVS's rebranding efforts. These clinics are the first in health care retail history to be accredited by the Joint Commission, the national evaluation and certifying agency for health care organizations and programs in the United States. This accreditation signifies the clinic's commitment to and execution in providing safe, quality health care that meets nationally set standards. In addition to health care services, MinuteClinics provide smoking cessation and weight loss programs that contribute positively to people's health. These clinics are also the first retail clinic provider to launch a partnership with the National Patient Safety Foundation for its health literacy program to help improve patient education and community health.

Under the ACA, health care organizations are eligible to become members of the Accountable Care Organizations (ACO) program. This program ensures that members are accountable in providing quality health care to the sick as well as meeting certain standards to provide health-conscious programs such as those related to smoking cessation and weight loss. Accountability is measured by positive outcomes, resulting in cost savings, which in turn is divided up among members to continue these effective programs and services. There are at least 123 ACOs in the United States, and more than 360 ACOs have been established as Medicare providers since the ACA went into effect—covering over 5.3 million patients.

REVEALING CVS'S NEW DIRECTION: TOBACCO-FREE CVS

In order to be consistent with its transition from pharmacy to health care company, CVS has made some landmark decisions aimed toward helping individuals lead healthier lives. In 2014 CVS announced that it would no longer sell tobacco products. The revenues generated from selling tobacco products are about $2 billion annually, so this bold decision sends a strong message to stakeholders regarding the values of the company. A company that is consistent in its actions will gain a good reputation, which will attract more customers and generate revenue. This decision also gives CVS an advantage in terms of the ACA. As the ACA changes the health care landscape, companies are racing to get a stronghold in the new system to be listed as a preferred pharmacy. CVS/Caremark's alignment in defining itself as a health care provider will likely result in stronger relationships with doctors and hospitals, creating an advantage of preference. The goal is that referrals for medication will be done through CVS and serve to boost reputation within all CVS segments. This, in conjunction with its status as an ACO, puts CVS in a competitive position to attract newly insured Americans.

This decision spurred 24 state attorneys general to send letters to other pharmacy retailers, including Walmart Stores, Inc., Walgreen Co., and Rite Aid Corp., highlighting the contradiction of selling deadly products and health care services simultaneously. The letter also noted that drug store sales make it easier for younger age groups to begin smoking and more difficult for those trying to quit smoking. Walmart and Walgreens acknowledged the letter, but made no indication that they would stop selling tobacco products. Rite Aid responded by saying it will continue to sell both tobacco products as well as smoking cessation services, as the practice is legal. While this letter does not seem to have much of an influence on retailers, some speculate that it increases the pressure on the $100 billion tobacco industry, which is already facing decreasing sales, rising taxes, and smoking bans. For CVS, the decision will affect its short-term profits and reduce each share by $0.06 to $0.09 each. Investors do not seem worried, however, as the long-term benefits will make up the difference.

CRITICISM AGAINST CVS

CVS's new programs are encroaching on the medical industry by providing services to patients. As customers increasingly choose to visit local pharmacy clinics for aches, pains, or common illnesses, primary physicians are feeling the losses, especially since this sectors' health care professionals are dwindling. Choosing a retail pharmacy clinic over a physician's office benefits the patient with lower costs and savings, which is a threat to traditional doctors' offices. Some groups are publicizing negative feedback on pharmacy care. For instance, the American Academy of Pediatrics issued a statement warning patients not to visit such clinics because they cannot offer the specialized care children need. Some groups argue that programs such as CVS's MinuteClinics do not offer the same caliber of service and care as a doctor. However, as stated above, CVS holds itself to a very high standard for care in trying to help patients be healthy. It continues to be accredited by the Joint Commission.

CVS MinuteClinics do recognize their limitations, however. Their website offers information to visitors regarding when they should and should not visit the clinics. For example, the website recommends that patients with severe symptoms such as chest pain, shortness of breath and difficulty breathing, poisoning, temperatures above 103 degrees Fahrenheit (for adults) and 104 (for children), and ailments requiring controlled substances should seek care elsewhere. MinuteClinics' staff nurse practitioners and physician assistants generally provide services for minor wounds, common illnesses, wellness tests, and physicals, etc. Other information regarding insurance and pricing are also available on the website.

STAKEHOLDER ORIENTATION

CVS's mission to be a pharmacy innovation company is guided by five values: innovation, collaboration, caring, integrity, and accountability. CVS uses these values to determine its actions and decisions, which offer a glimpse into its ethical culture. The company's goal is to use its assets to reinvent the pharmacy experience and offer innovative solutions that help people follow a better path toward health. This goal relays to stakeholders that the company cares about health care. CVS/Caremark's business is committed to fostering a culture that encourages creativity and innovation, recognizing that contributions from all members are a high priority. This commitment highlights the value placed on collaboration with partners and stakeholders, which also serves to hold the company accountable for its operating activities—thus strengthening its integrity. Another important factor in its ethical culture is to address enhanced access to care while also lowering its cost.

CEO Larry J. Merlo emphasizes the long-term perspective the company is committed to with each decision and how it will affect each stakeholder group. He states that CVS's priorities remain in customer health, the sustainability of health care systems, good stewardship, positive contributions to communities, and a meaningful workplace for employees. Such a statement from the top leader of the company sets the tone that fosters the ethical culture behind CVS. The company's Code of Conduct includes ethical behavior expectations—CVS is proud to have good relationships with employee unions who represent approximately 6 percent of its workforce. CVS employs a Chief Compliance Officer, offers regular compliance education and training, provides an ethics hotline for confidential reporting, and has developed a response and prevention guideline for addressing violations of CVS's policies or federal, state, or local laws. CVS's corporate governance includes a privacy program, information security, and a corporate framework that focuses on the company's values.

So far we have addressed how CVS meets the needs of its customer stakeholders. However, CVS tries to maintain a stakeholder orientation in which all stakeholder needs are addressed. The following sections will describe how the company meets the needs of other stakeholders.

Employees

CVS implemented the Values in Action program for employees, giving them a chance to recognize colleagues through online reward systems. Peers can nominate each other across the company for leadership traits and other commendable accomplishments. Each nomination grants points, which can be redeemed for merchandise, travel, and more. Programs like these let employees know they are valued and empower them in their commitment to CVS. The Values in Action Breakthrough Awards is an annual company-wide broadcast that honors specific individuals exemplifying the company's values in innovation, collaboration, caring, integrity, and accountability.

CVS focuses strongly on compliance and integrity training for employees. The compliance and integrity training for employees is led by a Compliance Officer. Regular compliance education and training programs, a confidential 24/7 ethics hotline, and an efficient audit, response, and prevention process are components that make this program comprehensive. The company also supports the development of employees through professional development training sessions. The purpose of such training is not only to keep employees current on new technologies and processes but also to help them advance in their careers within the company.

Shareholders

CVS seeks to protect shareholder interests while maintaining broad stakeholder engagement. As a result, CVS carefully designed a comprehensive corporate governance system ranging from board independence to executive compensation. Following a corporate governance framework, a variety of specialized committees have been established with different functions for shareholders. From an information governance standpoint, the oversight committee makes recommendations to enhance the ability of information security. On behalf of the board of directors, the audit committee is in charge of the risk oversight and is responsible for protecting the reputation and core interests of the company.

In order to balance the interests of different groups, senior management created a reformative executive compensation system. This system is based on financial performance as well as service quality and customer satisfaction. While a pay-for-performance compensation system is still utilized at CVS, a significant portion of annual executive compensation is delivered into long-term equity rather than short-term. In a move to further align the commitment of CVS to link pay with performance, total shareholder return is added on a three-year incentive plan. Each three-year period is known as a cycle that has a predetermined set of goals for the company/executive to accomplish. At the end of each term, performance is evaluated and the executive receives compensation based on these results. For example, if the results surpass the goal by 25 percent, the executive pay will increase by a certain predetermined amount. The details will vary for each cycle, but the purpose of the plan is to pay only when the company and its shareholders are benefited from the performance of the executive.

Communities

CVS has grown its ethical culture not only to include the company's functions but also the communities around it. Community engagement and philanthropic endeavors, for example, are long-standing commitments CVS has devoted time and resources in developing. Community partnerships have supported veteran hiring, scholarships to future pharmacists, and engaged high school, college, and post-graduate students' interest in science, technology, engineering, and math (STEM) careers. CVS believes that by helping to further advancements in providing the best health outcomes, it is investing in its current and future workforce.

CVS donated over $75 million to various organizations and built strategic partnerships with them to create an awareness of healthy behaviors and educate the community on ways to become insured under the ACA. The company also offers free health screenings and flu shots for the uninsured, prescription discount card programs, and other community programs to supply individuals with the medications they need to maintain health. The discount card program saves customers over 70 percent on medications, resulting in millions of dollars in savings every year. Volunteerism is also supported by CVS, as employees are encouraged to form groups and obtain sponsorship from the company to address needs within the community. The company reported 12 such national groups and 40 regional groups involving over 4,000 employees in 40 states who donated over 2,000 hours to community initiatives.

Suppliers

CVS has developed a commitment called Prescription for a Better World, which encompasses its Code of Conduct, Supplier Ethics Policy, Supplier Diversity, and Supplier Audit Program to promote integrity, accountability, and diversity. These programs work to ensure that human rights are respected throughout the entire supply chain. In developing these policies, CVS used principles initiated by the International Labor Organization and the United Nations' Universal Declaration of Human Rights. The human rights framework guides all suppliers of CVS to avoid unethical and illegal practices such as child labor, human trafficking, discrimination, and dangerous workplace conditions.

The Supplier Audit Program is a risk-based assessment conducted by multiple third parties to evaluate workplace conditions, including labor, wages and hours, health and safety, management system and environment, as well as operational, financial, and legal risks, to assure that employees' rights are not being invaded. This program was fully expanded to factories in countries considered to be at high risk for such violations, and it is in the process of implementing full social audits for subcontractors in these areas. In addition, CVS works with globally recognized organizations including Worldwide Responsible Accredited Production (WRAP) and Social Accountability International (SAI) to ensure its measurements are relevant and effective. Finally, partnerships with Intertek's GSV program maintains the company's certification status with the U.S. Customs-Trade Partnership Against Terrorism (C-TPAT) program to ensure quality of products made in countries such as China.

Environmental Impact

Environmental impact is also important to CVS. The company records its progress on this front in its annual Corporate Social Responsibility (CSR) Report. It has set a carbon intensity reduction goal of 15 percent by 2018, and through energy efficiency upgrades have been able to address 9 percent of that goal to date. CVS opened its first Leadership in Energy and Environmental Design (LEED) Platinum store, which will serve as a test site to determine the most effective and relevant environmental innovations for the company's environmental operations goals. This information will be used to set best practices before constructing other stores.

CVS expanded its Energy Management System (EMS), which is designed to ISO (International Organization for Standardization) specifications. This digital system tracks and manages energy use, so that each store can be continually monitored and adjusted according to each location's needs. It is also in the process of upgrading lighting in the stores by including more energy efficient bulbs. Increasing water use was identified as a significant inefficiency, and CVS has responded by eliminating irrigation at retail locations and opting for less water-intensive landscapes. Finally, CVS offers customers ways to recycle and properly dispose of expired, unused, or unwanted medications, which benefit both human and environmental well-being.

CONCLUSION

CVS is implementing strategies and allocating resources in the hope of achieving an ethical culture that benefits all stakeholder groups. This helps CVS to maximize ethical decision making and remain sustainable for years to come. It seems the company has learned from previous ethical lapses by being aware of addiction problems within its communities. In 2014 CVS voluntarily opted to stop selling some cold medications in West Virginia and surrounding areas as more methamphetamine labs and corresponding stimulant abuse became more prominent throughout the state. The company's impact on the environment is one of the next big challenges it will have to overcome. As one of the largest pharmacies in the United States, CVS has a long way to go to reduce its overall footprint. However, the company is on the right track, having set goals and implementing action steps to achieve these goals. With the mission of helping people live healthier lives and innovating the pharmacy industry, CVS has a great responsibility in developing a business model allowing the company to remain competitive while acting ethically at the same time.

QUESTIONS FOR DISCUSSION

1. How has CVS handled its ethical challenges?
2. Evaluate CVS's decision to no longer sell tobacco products.
3. What is the future of CVS in positioning itself as a health care company based on its decision to be socially responsible?

SOURCES

Reed Abelson and Natasha Singer, "CVS Settles Prescription Price Case," *The New York Times*, January 12, 2012, http://www.nytimes.com/2012/01/13/business/cvs-caremark-settles-charges-over-prescription-prices. html?pagewanted=all&_r=2& (accessed August 4, 2014); "Annual Report," CVS Caremark, 2013, http://ir2.flife. de/data/cvs1/igb_html/index.php?anzahl=1&bericht_id=1000001&lang=ENG (accessed August 5, 2014); Devlin Barrett, "Judge Rules against CVS in Oxycodone Fight," *The Wall Street Journal*, March 13, 2012, http://online.wsj. com/news/articles/SB10001424052702303717304577279871365405382 (accessed August 4, 2014); Rebecca Borison, "CVS/Pharmacy iPad App Mimics in-store Experience," *Mobile Commerce Daily*, August 14, 2013, http:// www.mobilecommercedaily.com/cvspharmacy-exec-offering-virtual-store-experience-via-ipad-app (accessed August 4, 2014); Hank Cardello, "CVS and the Rise of Corporate Profitable Morality," *Hudson Institute*, February 27, 2014, http://www.hudson.org/research/10138-cvs-and-the-rise-of-corporate-profitable-morality (accessed June 6, 2014); "Corporate Social Responsibility Report," CVS Caremark, 2012, http://investors.cvscaremark. com/~/media/Files/C/CVS-IR/reports/cvs-caremark-csr-report-2012.pdf (accessed August 5, 2014); "Corporate Social Responsibility Report," CVS Caremark, 2013, http://info.cvscaremark.com/CSR-Report/#1 (accessed August 5, 2014); "Company History," CVS Caremark, http://info.cvscaremark.com/about-us/our-purpose/ company-history (accessed June 6, 2014); "CVS Caremark Maintenance Choice Program Improves Medication Adherence for US Airways Employees and Dependents," CVS Press Release, September 15, 2010, http://info. cvscaremark.com/newsroom/press-releases/cvs-caremark-maintenance-choice-program-improves-medication-adherence-us (accessed August 4, 2014); "CVS Caremark Settles FTC Charges: Failed to Protect Medical and Financial Privacy of Customers and Employees; CVS Pharmacy Also Pays $2.25 Million to Settle Allegations of HIPAA Violations," The Federal Trade Commission, February 18, 2009, http://www.ftc.gov/news-events/press-releases/2009/02/cvs-caremark-settles-ftc-chargesfailed-protect-medical-financial (accessed August 2, 2014); "CVS Pays $2.25 Million & Toughens Disposal Practices to Settle HIPAA Privacy Case," U.S. Department of Health and Human Services, http://www.hhs.gov/ocr/privacy/hipaa/enforcement/examples/ cvsresolutionagreement.html (accessed August 2, 2014); Mike Estrel, "States Urge Retailers to Drop Tobacco," *The Wall Street Journal*, March 18, 2014, B3; "Everybody Loves a Quitter," CVS MinuteClinic, http://www.cvs.com/ minuteclinic/resources/smoking-cessation (accessed August 4, 2014); Joseph H. Harmison, "CVS Caremark Abuses Warrant through FTC Investigation and Remedies," *The Hill*, May 25, 2010, http://thehill.com/blogs/ congress-blog/healthcare/99759-cvs-caremark-abuses-warrant-through-ftc-investigation-and-remedies (accessed August 2, 2014); "Investor Fact Sheet," CVS Caremark, March 2014, http://investors.cvscaremark. com/~/media/Files/C/CVS-IR/reports/cvs-factsheet.pdf (accessed August 5, 2014); Chris Isidore, "Cigarette Sales: Walgreens, Rite-Aid, Wal-Mart, Kroger & Safeway Urged to Selling Tobacco," *CNN Money*, March 17, 2014, http://www.wptv.com/web/wptv/news/health/cigarette-sales-walgreens-rite-aid-wal-mart-kroger-safeway-urged-to-selling-tobacco (accessed August 6, 2014); Bruce Japsen, "How Obamacare Helps CVS Kick the Habit," *Forbes*, February 2, 2014, http://www.forbes.com/sites/brucejapsen/2014/02/15/how-obamacare-helps-cvs-kick-the-habit/ (accessed June 6, 2014); Elisabeth Leamy, "Drug Discount Cards Help You Save on Prescription Meds," *ABC News*, August 20, 2012, http://abcnews.go.com/Business/drug-discount-cards-save-money-prescription-meds/story?id=17029498 (accessed August 5, 2014); Donna Leinwand Leger, "DEA: Oxycodone Orders by

Pharmacies 20 Times Average," *USA Today*, February 7, 2012, http://usatoday30.usatoday.com/money/industries/health/story/2012-02-06/dea-cvs-oxycodone-raid/52994168/1 (accessed August 4, 2014); Natasha Leonard, "Homeless man Choked to Death after Shoplifting Toothpaste," *Salon*, January 18, 2013, http://www.salon.com/2013/01/18/homeless_man_choked_to_death_after_shoplifting_toothpaste/ (accessed August 4, 2014); "The Long-Term Incentive Plan," CVS Carenark, March 24, 2009, http://www.wikinvest.com/stock/CVS_Caremark_Corporation_(CVS)/Long-term_Incentive_Plan (accessed August 6, 2014); Kris Maher and Sara Germano, "CVS Takes Steps on Meth Abuse in West Virginia," *The Wall Street Journal*, July 8, 2014, A3; MarketWatch, "Annual Financial for CVS Health Corp.," http://www.marketwatch.com/investing/stock/cvs/financials (accessed March 16, 2015); Timothy W. Martin, "CVS to Kick Cigarette Habit," *The Wall Street Journal*, February 6, 2014, B1–B2; Erin Meyer, "Video Captures Death of CVS Toothpaste Shoplifter," DNA Info, January 17, 2013, http://www.dnainfo.com/chicago/20130117/chicago/video-captures-death-of-cvs-toothpaste-shoplifter (accessed March 16, 2015); James P. Miller, "CVS Caremark Settles Deceptive-practices Complaint for $38.5 Million," *Chicago Tribune*, February 15, 2008, http://articles.chicagotribune.com/2008-02-15/business/0802140788_1_cvs-caremark-caremark-rx-pharmacy-benefits (accessed August 2, 2014); Chris Morran, "CVS Being Investigated after 37,000 Pain Pills Go Missing," *The Consumerist*, March 11, 2014, http://consumerist.com/2014/03/11/cvs-being-investigated-after-37000-pain-pills-go-missing/ (accessed August 4, 2014); Mark Morelli, "Healthy First: CVS Will Stop Selling Cigarettes," *The Motley Fool*, February 7, 2014, http://www.fool.com/investing/general/2014/02/07/healthy-first-cvs-will-stop-selling-cigarettes.aspx (accessed August 6, 2014); "Our Pharmacy Advisor Program," *CVS Caremark*, http://info.cvscaremark.com/cvs-insights/our-pharmacy-advisor-program (accessed August 4, 2014); Paul Edward Parker, "Rite Aid Responds to CVS Decision to Stop Selling Tobacco," *Providence Journal*, February 6, 2014, http://www.providencejournal.com/breaking-news/content/20140206-rite-aid-responds-to-cvs-decision-to-stop-selling-tobacco.ece (accessed August 6, 2014); Amy Pavuk, "Rx for Danger: DEA Blasts CVS for Ignoring 'Red Flags' at Sanford Stores," *Orlando Sentinel*, October 28, 2012, http://articles.orlandosentinel.com/2012-10-28/news/os-cvs-dea-oxycodone-ban-20121028_1_sanford-cvs-sanford-pharmacies-sanford-stores (accessed August 4, 2014); Amy Pavuk, "Two Sanford Pharmacies Banned from Selling Oxycodone, Controlled Substances," *Orlando Sentinel*, September 12, 2012, http://articles.orlandosentinel.com/2012-09-12/news/os-sanford-cvs-caremark-revoke-drugs-20120912_1_revokes-prescription-drug-abuse-oxycodone-and-other-prescription (accessed August 4, 2014); PR Newswire, "CVS Health Reports Third Quarter Results," CVS Health, November 4, 2014, http://www.cvshealth.com/newsroom/press-releases/quarterly-earnings/cvs-health-reports-third-quarter-results (accessed March 16, 2015); "Press Release: More Partnerships between Doctors and Hospitals Strengthen Coordinated Care for Medicare Beneficiaries," Centers for Medicare and Medicaid Services Press Release, December 23, 2013, http://www.cms.gov/Newsroom/MediaReleaseDatabase/Press-Releases/2013-Press-Releases-Items/2013-12-23.html (accessed August 4, 2014); "Quality," CVS MinuteClinic, http://www.cvs.com/minuteclinic/visit/about-us/quality (accessed August 4, 2014); "Services," CVS MinuteClinics, http://www.cvs.com/minuteclinic/services (accessed August 4, 2014); Kyle Stock, "Pediatricians Seek Risk-to Kids and Themselves-in DrugStore Health Clinics," *Bloomberg Businessweek*, February 24, 2014, http://www.businessweek.com/articles/2014-02-24/pediatricians-see-risk-to-kids-and-themselves-in-drug-store-health-clinics (accessed June 6, 2014); "We're a Pharmacy Innovation Company and Every Day We're Working to Make Health Care Better," About CVS Caremark, http://info.cvscaremark.com/about-us/our-purpose-building-bridge-better-health (accessed August 5, 2014); Jessica Wohl, "CVS Cuts Off Docs Who Prescribe Too Many Narcotics," *NBC News*, August 22, 2013, http://www.nbcnews.com/health/health-news/cvs-cuts-docs-who-prescribe-too-many-narcotics-f6C10975693 (accessed August 4, 2014).

INDEX